Histories of Inter

In the pas
undergone
along with
has been ca
The older
new langua
sovereign
relations si
demands a
and legal t
the traditio
political hi
from class
philosoph
evolving i

Histories of International Law in China

All under Heaven?

Edited by
IGNACIO DE LA RASILLA
Han Depei Chair and One Thousand Talents Plan Professor, Wuhan University

JIANGYU WANG
Professor of Law, City University of Hong Kong School of Law

CONGYAN CAI
Professor of International Law, Fudan University School of Law

OXFORD
UNIVERSITY PRESS

OXFORD
UNIVERSITY PRESS

Great Clarendon Street, Oxford, OX2 6DP,
United Kingdom

Oxford University Press is a department of the University of Oxford.
It furthers the University's objective of excellence in research, scholarship,
and education by publishing worldwide. Oxford is a registered trade mark of
Oxford University Press in the UK and in certain other countries.

Published in the United States of America by Oxford University Press
198 Madison Avenue, New York, NY 10016, United States of America.

British Library Cataloguing in Publication Data
Data available

Library of Congress Control Number: 2025949647

ISBN 978-0-19-888834-5

DOI: 10.1093/oso/9780198888345.001.0001

Printed and bound by
CPI Group (UK) Ltd., Croydon, CR0 4YY

MIX
Paper | Supporting
responsible forestry
FSC® C013604

The manufacturer's authorised representative in the EU for product safety is
Oxford University Press España S.A. of El Parque Empresarial San Fernando de Henares, Avenida
de Castilla, 2 - 28830 Madrid (www.oup.es/en or
product.safety@oup.com). OUP España S.A. also acts as importer into Spain
of products made by the manufacturer.

Foreword

Randall Lesaffer

Among the great tectonic shifts in the economic and political order of the world since the end of the Cold War, China's rise to superpower status may safely be considered the most significant. Over this period, students and pundits of geopolitics have exercised themselves in questioning whether this change will occur in a peaceful and orderly fashion and the People's Republic of China will accommodate itself to the existing order and take its place at the helm next to the United States, or whether this will lead to disruption and confrontation. Since the early 2010s, many analysts have sharply veered from complacent optimism to stark pessimism, drowning out those voices that claim that there is a lot of middle ground between those two extremes, as myriads of agents prove in the daily business of diplomacy, business, and more generally any kind of human relations between China and the rest of the world.

Against this backdrop, the historiography of international law gains a high level of currency. The way Chinese students of international politics see the historic relationship of China with international law during the latter's emergence as a global system, and the way students from other countries and regions understand China's experiences, directly feed into the debate of the new superpower's world views and aspirations today.

In the dominant narratives of the history of China and international law, the forced opening of the Qing empire to the emerging order of modern international law, for which the First Opium War (1839–1842) is generally invoked as the key starting point, holds the central place. Many general histories of the Chinese experience with international law distinguish between a 'before' and an 'after' in relation to the First Opium War. On the one side stands the hierarchical, concentric Sino-centric system, with at its heart the emperor of China as the holder of the Mandate of Heaven; on the other side the forced encounter with Western international law in the context of the imperialist ambitions of Western and westernized great powers. In Western historiography of the late nineteenth and much of the twentieth century, the encounter was read as an 'opening' of China to the rules, benefits, and obligations of 'modern civilization'. In Chinese historiography, it is read as the start of a 'century of humiliation', with the foundation of the PRC in 1949 as the turn to a new era of development and rise. Although the narratives rest on solid factual foundations, here too they have been caught and threaten to remain caught between stark dichotomies that cloud the middle ground of constant dialogue, appropriation, adaptation, and mutual influencing. The 'reception and acculturation' by a great power such as China, with its deep-rooted and sophisticated culture, was sufficiently gradual to allow strong undercurrents of the old system to seep into its approach to modern international law, and start the process of remoulding international law in turn—something it has never stopped doing, first at a regional and recently at a global level. Moreover, while international law is surely an instrument of power in international relations, it is also one of management and restraint.

While broadly retaining the usual chronological frame, this book makes significant contributions to highlighting the middle ground between encounter as benefice and humiliation. It does so by 'thickening the story' in three significant manners. First, and most significantly, it broadens the lens from its traditional focus on the early decades of the encounter, to a more balanced purview over a period of almost two hundred years. The space granted to the twentieth century allows for viewing the different phases after 1911 more in their own terms rather than through the lens of the encounter. Second, this ambitious long-term history is told through highlighting a set of concrete episodes, which add new stories and new perspectives on familiar stories to the grand narrative of China's historic experiences with international law. Third, in its final part, the book singles out the contributions of leading Chinese international lawyers from the twentieth century, showing again how the encounter paradigm can never catch reality if this leads to thinking in terms of the meeting of two separate realities.

The editors of the book place the work within the tradition of national histories of international law. They are right to underscore the importance and potential of the national approach as a necessary building block, through spatial and/or diachronic comparison, to a global historiography of international law. Modern international law, as it emerged from the nineteenth century onwards, is just one particular approach to the normative ordering of inter- and trans-polity relations from human history. Its specificity lies in its claim to be the preserve of one form of political organization, the nation-state, and in its pretensions to regulate relations on the basis of formal equality and secularism. In that it is what the Dutch historian Jan Romein (1893–1962) called a 'diversion from the general human pattern'.[1] The Chinese imperial domestic and international system of the emperor as the holder of the 'Mandate of Heaven' and as the guardian of harmony between heaven and earth is altogether a far more common pattern for the ordering of human relations through global history, as Francis Oakley claims.[2] The fact that the Chinese tradition counts among the most sophisticated, enduring, and influential 'cosmic' orders, to adopt Oakley's term, in recorded history makes the stories of China and international law particularly relevant to construing a global historiography of international law.

[1] Jan Romein, with Annie Romein-Schoor, *Aera van Europa. De Europese geschiedenis als Afwijking van het Algemeen Menselijk Patroon* (Leiden: Brill 1954).

[2] Francis Oakley, *Empty Bottles of Gentilism. Kingship and the Divine in Late Antiquity and the Early Middle Ages (to 1050)* (New Haven and London: Yale University Press 2010) 18–20.

Series Editor's Preface

'International law' has sometimes been condemned as nothing more than a derivation of the older 'law of nations'—*ius gentium*—and since that indubitably had its origins in Roman imperial law, as a 'predatory system that legitimizes, reproduces and sustains the subordination of the Third World to the West'.[3] This genealogy mistakenly equates genesis with validity. It assumes that in its long history 'international law' has not substantially evolved from its Roman 'Western' 'imperialist' origins, and is thus doomed in perpetuity to reproduce is initial premises. Yet if history matters then it has to be *history*, not merely an insistence on the importance of one initial period of historical time—however long, however significant, however formative—and a stubborn disregard for all subsequent ones. It has to lead forward, not simply look back. As with all forms of knowledge, and in particular legal ones, what we now call 'international' law owes very little to its earliest historical origins, beyond, of course, its essential claim that it must, in principle, be applicable to all nations everywhere. And one of the most significant ways it has been changed in the more recent past is by continually expanding to include, and hence be modified by, other perceptions of what Jeremy Bentham when he coined the term in 1789 believed could only be not a 'law of peoples'—which is what the earlier *ius gentium* had been—but a law *between* peoples, based upon, 'the common and equal utility of all nations'. Until the late nineteenth century, however, it was certainly true that international law was still broadly assumed to be what was known as the law of the more 'civilized' nations on the planet, which meant, with very few exceptions, those of Europe and its overseas settler populations.

It is also frequently claimed that all the non-Western nations who now regulate their membership of the international order by means of a form of law have been humbled into doing so by the more powerful of the Western powers, that those peoples who belonged to what was once called the 'Third World', were merely passive recipients of Western legal norms. In some instance this may have been true. But by no means in all, and as the international community extended well beyond the West—by whatever means—international law came increasingly to include the laws of other non-Western nations, and to be modified by them in turn, in what Mingqian Li calls, a gradual process of 'reception and acculturation'.

Hence, as Ignacio de la Rasilla argues, the importance of understanding the *national* origins of the history of international law, as 'the necessary building

[3] Makau Mutua, 'What is TWAIL [Third World Approaches to International Law]?', *Proceedings of the Annual Meeting (American Society of International Law)* 94 (2000), 31–40.

block, through spatial and/or diachronic comparison, to a global historiography of the subject'. The national leads ineluctably to the inter-national and thence to the global. Nowhere, perhaps, has this been more true than in China, which has now become one of the political and economic great powers in the world, and whose presence in the 'Global South' expands even as that of the US—its closest geo-political rival—recedes. But it is not merely China's political and economic ascendancy that makes the Chinese understanding of 'international law' significantly transformative. For long before China was, on its own understanding at least, forcibly incorporated into the public law system of the 'civilized nations' of the world after the First Opium War in 1839–1842 it already possessed, a number of powerful legal idioms which, while they were not truly inter-*national* and served primarily to enhance a hierarchical, Sino-centric system, grounded on a concept of the emperor as the bearer of a 'Mandate of Heaven' were, nevertheless, intended to apply to a large number of disparate peoples, and in theory at least, and in some understanding of the term, to the entire world. It is also the case that the central distinction between those who were Chinese *Hua* and those who were 'outsiders' *Yi*—a term often rendered as 'barbarian' in the West—is at least commensurable with the Civilized/Barbarian distinction that emerged in the eighteenth century and was to have such a marked impact on the subsequent evolution of international law. It is in part at least from these, and from the attempted merger of the early 'Legalist' and Confucian perceptions of the legal order, that subsequent Chinese conception of what might constitute an international law begun to emerge. The editors of this volume are surely correct in their assumption that an understanding of what the Chinese themselves believe international law to be, is crucial to the form that all future debates 'on the global legal order in the twentieth-first century' (and indeed well beyond) will take. For it is evident that whatever may eventually be the outcome of those debates, however they may come to modify at least some of what the International Court of Justice still calls the 'general principles of law recognized by civilized nations', they will as they have always been in the past, the outcome of an ever-expanding conversation between all the nations of the globe. For this reason, the Editors are surely right to insist that it has become 'imperative to consider China's engagement with international law from a *longue durée* historical perspective'. In 1890, the Italian jurist, Pasquale Fiore, insisted, that, although what he called the 'civilized consciousness' of the world had indeed initially been European, the increasing contacts between peoples had already created a world in which: 'The unity of the human species conduces to the recognition that the empire of legal rules that are applicable to all forms of human activity... must be universal.' This wide ranging and ambitious book is a step toward making that recognition, finally possible.

Anthony Pagden
October 2025

Acknowledgements

Every book begins somewhere. This one began in Wuhan, where the Wuchang uprising against the Qin dynasty in 1911 paved the road for the establishment of the Republic of China. From central China, the book soon expanded in editorial terms to both Shanghai and Hong Kong, and from there it continued to reach, via its many contributing authors, many far-away locations at universities across the globe: Montreal and Philadelphia in North America; Leuven, Leiden, Tromsø, Tartu, London (and then Erlangen-Nuremberg), Lecce, and Florence in Europe; Singapore and Chiba (and then Fukuoka) in Asia, and Canberra in Australia. Many authors also joined this one-of-a-kind collective endeavour in research centres and universities across the vast lands of China, including in Beijing, Shenzhen, Shanghai, Macau, Hangzhou, Guangzhou, Hong Kong, and all the way back to Wuhan. As editors we are sincerely grateful to all of the book's contributing authors, who have remained faithful to its original intention and have generously contributed their research-based knowledge and intellectual creativity to this global multi-authored research project.

On different occasions since 2022, the authors have met virtually and in person to discuss a great variety of seminal research topics related to the exploration of the histories of international law in China from ancient times to the reform and opening-up process. We did so, first, during the monthly on-line lecture series hosted by the Centre for Comparative and Chinese Law (CCHL) at the Hong Kong City University with the title *Histories of International Law: Chinese and Global Perspectives from* December 2022 to June 2023. We are thankful to all the contributing authors who presented earlier versions of their chapters as speakers and also to all the scholars who took part in the series as discussants. Special thanks go to Martti Koskenniemi, David Armitage, Jose Maria Beneyto, and Randall Lesaffer for their supporting participation as distinguished speakers during this fruitful seven-month-long lecture series. We continued our vibrant academic conversation in person on the occasion of two workshops held in China. Also excellently organized by the Centre for Comparative and Chinese Law, the first of these was the hybrid workshop hosted by Hong Kong City University in November 2023. Similarly excellently organized and widely attended by the contributing authors, both in person and virtually, was our second author's workshop, generously organized by the Fudan University School of Law and held in Shanghai in mid-September 2024.

We are extremely appreciative of the institutional support of the City Univeristy of Hong Kong, Fudan University, and Wuhan University for providing opportunities for authors to engage with and contribute to each other's work. Our sincere thanks also go to the series editors of the Theory and History of International Law Series at Oxford University Press and to Dr Robert Cavooris and Lindsay Glick for their professional support. We also gratefully acknowledge the contribution of four anonymous reviewers appointed by OUP who favourably appraised the potential merits and opportunity of this collective volume and further contributed to its design by providing helpful suggestions. Except for Chapter 2, which builds on Ignacio de la Rasilla, 'Towards Comparative International Legal History?', *Journal of the History of International Law* 27 (2025): 197–236, and Chapter 12, which builds on Jie Liu and Congyan Cai, 'How Chinese International Lawyers Pursue Marxism: The Introduction of Soviet Theory of International Law to China (1950s–60s) and Afterwards', *Chinese Journal of Comparative Law* 13 (2025): 1–17, all chapters in the book were, to the best of our knowledge, unpublished at the moment of publication of the present multi-authored volume.

Ignacio de la Rasilla extends his gratitude to all his esteemed friends and colleagues at the Wuhan University Institute of International law, the Wuhan Academy of International Law and Global Governance, the Joint-Research Institute of International Organizations and the International Rule of Law, and the Wuhan University School of Law for their companionship, support and collegiality. He dedicates this book on the histories of international law in China to his wife, Dr Hao Yayezi, and to their daughter, Cristina Rya de la Rasilla Hao, a symbol of the limitless power of love whose great-grandfathers fought in the Spanish and Chinese Civil Wars.

Wang Jiangyu wishes to express his heartfelt thanks to his colleagues and friends at the City University of Hong Kong School of Law and the Centre for Chinese and Comparative Law. He especially appreciates the administrative staff and student research assistants for their meticulous organization of the numerous workshops and seminars related to this research project. Additionally, he is profoundly grateful to his family, who have been a constant source of support and inspiration.

Congyan Cai would like to extend his gratitude to his colleagues at Fudan Law School for their support since he arrived in Shanghai in 2021. He also especially wants to extend his gratitude to all his excellent student assistants from Fudan Law School who helped to organize the authors' workshop held in Shanghai in September 2024.

Ignacio de la Rasilla, Wuhan
Jiangyu Wang, Hong Kong
Congyan Cai, Shanghai
February 2025

Contents

Contributors

Congyan Cai, Professor of International Law, Fudan University

Maria Adele Carrai, Assistant Professor of Global China Studies, NYU Shanghai

Yifeng Chen, Associate Professor of International Law, Peking University

Wanshu Cong, Assistant Professor of Law, Australian National University

Ignacio de la Rasilla, Han Depei Chair in International Law and 'One Thousand Talents Plan' Professor, Wuhan University

Jacques deLisle, Stephen A. Cozen Professor of Law and Professor of Political Science, University of Pennsylvania

Yayezi Hao, Lecturer in International Law, Wuhan University

Hong Yu, PhD Candidate in International Law, Wuhan University

Pasha L. Hsieh, Professor of Law, Singapore Management University

Xinyu Huang, Assistant Professor of Law, Peking University School of Transnational Law

Jue Li, Associate Professor in International Law, Wuhan University

Feng Lin, Professor of Law, City University of Hong Kong

Jie Liu, Lecturer of International Law, Sun Yat-sen University

Guoqiang Luo, Professor of International Law, Zhejiang University

Randall Lesaffer, Professor of Legal History, KU Leuven & Tilburg University

Mingqian Li, Associate Professor of Foreign Studies and Legal History, East China University of Political Science and Law

Ryan Martinez Mitchell, Associate Professor of Law, Chinese University of Hong Kong

Lauri Mälksoo, Professor of International Law, Tartu University

Frédéric Mégret, Hans & Tamar Oppenheimer Chair in International Law, McGill University

Luigi Nuzzo, Professor of Legal History, University of Salento

Straton Papagianneas, PhD in Chinese Law & Governance, Leiden University

Eva Pils, Alexander von Humboldt Chair Professor of Human Rights Law, Friedrich-Alexander-Universität Erlangen-Nürnberg

Christopher R. Rossi, Professor of International Law and International Relations, Artic University of Norway

Inge Van Hulle, Associate Professor of Legal History, KU Leuven

Chao Wang, Professor of Law, University of Macau

Chao Wang, Post-doctoral Researcher in International Law, Wuhan University

Li Wan, Associate Professor of Foreign Studies and Legal History, East China University of Political Science and Law

Jiangyu Wang, Professor of Law, City University of Hong Kong

Qu Wensheng, Professor of Foreign Studies and Legal History, Zhejiang University

Yongping Xiao, Distinguished Professor of International Law, Wuhan University

Xiaobing Xu, Associate Professor of International Law, Shanghai Jiaotong University

Ken Yang, PhD in Law, European University Institute

Yang Liu, Lecturer in International Law, East China University of Political Science and Law

Masaharu Yanagihara, Professor Emeritus of International Law, Kyushu University

Zhuo Zenghua, Lecturer in Legal History, Chinese Academy of Social Sciences

Guoyong Zou, Associate Professor of International Law, Wuhan University

PART I

NATIONAL HISTORIES OF INTERNATIONAL LAW

1

Histories of International Law in China

An Introduction

Ignacio de la Rasilla, Jiangyu Wang, and Congyan Cai

1.1 Introduction

The rise of China has sparked renewed academic interest in China's relationship with international law.[1] As China continues to ascend as a highly influential international rule-shaper—and increasingly, a rule-maker and institution-builder—it becomes imperative to consider China's engagement with international law from a *longue durée* historical perspective. China's engagement with international law is a story of adaptation, resistance, and reinterpretation, deeply rooted in its historical experiences and civilizational identity. The historical trajectory of China's engagement with international law, which has significantly influenced the worldviews of Chinese elites and shaped China's relationship with the international legal order, reveals both remarkable historical patterns and significant discontinuities. China offers a unique case study of how a major nation's legal and political identity interacts with external normative frameworks.

In light of the interdisciplinary turn to the history of international law[2] and the accompanying blossoming of a mature historiography in international legal history on a global scale,[3] new studies on the histories of international law in China are poised to provide more well-informed perspectives on present trends in China's contemporary and foreseeable engagement with international law. In the fifty years since the seminal contribution of Jerome Alan Cohen and Hungdah Chiu's *People's China and International Law* in 1974,[4] international legal scholarship concerning

[1] See Ignacio de la Rasilla and Congyan Cai (eds) *The Cambridge Handbook of China and International Law* (CUP, 2024) and Congyan Cai, *International Law and the Rise of China. Taking Chinese Exceptionalism Seriously* (OUP, 2019).

[2] See Thomas Skouteris, 'The Turn to History in International Law', in Anthony Carty (ed.) *Oxford Bibliographies on International Law* (OUP, 2017) and Ignacio de la Rasilla, 'The Historical Turn in International Law', in John Linarelli (ed.) *Elgar Concise Encyclopaedia of Legal Theory and Philosophy* (Edward Elgar, 2025).

[3] See Randall Lesaffer and Anne Peters, eds, *The Cambridge History of International Law. Historiography of International Law, vol. 1* (CUP, 2024) and Ignacio de la Rasilla, *International Law and History. Modern Interfaces* (CUP, 2021).

[4] Jerome Alan Cohen and Hungdah Chiu, *People's China and International Law. A Documentary Study*, Vols 1 and 2 (Princeton University Press, 1974).

Ignacio de la Rasilla, Jiangyu Wang, and Congyan Cai, *Histories of International Law in China* In: *Histories of International Law in China*. Edited by: Ignacio de la Rasilla, Jiangyu Wang, and Congyan Cai, Oxford University Press.
 DOI: 10.1093/oso/9780198888345.003.0001

China has expanded exponentially—both in Mandarin and in English, with some growth in other languages as well.[5] However, compared to the existing scholarly work addressing various dimensions of China's engagement with contemporary international legal issues, the study of the history of international law in China remains relatively underdeveloped.[6]

Partly in the footsteps of the rejuvenation experienced by historical writing in international law in the past two decades, there has been a more regular scholarly tackling of different aspects of the Chinese history of international law in English, in the form of a limited number of books[7] and journal articles.[8] However, the turn to the history of international law has not spread evenly across all countries and languages, and the literature on China and the history of international law in Mandarin remains notably scarce and somewhat disconnected from the broader developments in international legal historiography comprehensively covering its evolution from ancient to modern times.[9] Moreover, with some exceptions, a

[5] See seminally in French, Jean Escarra (Publications de la Revue générale de Droit International public, Num. 4). Paris: A. Pedone, 1931.

[6] For a notable earlier work, see Immanuel C. Y. Hsü, *China's Entrance into the Family of Nations: The Diplomatic Phase, 1858–1880* (Harvard University Press, 1960).

[7] Rune Svarverud, *International Law as World Order in Late Imperial China: Translation, Reception and Discourse, 1847–1911* (Brill, 2007); Teemu Ruskola, *Legal Orientalism as well as China, the United States and Modern Law* (Harvard UP, 2013); Anthony Carty and Janne Nijman (eds) *Morality and Responsibility of Rulers: European and Chinese Origins of a Rule of Law as Justice for World Order* (Oxford University Press, 2018). See also more recently by contributors to the present volume, Marie Adele Carrai, *Sovereignty in China: A Genealogy of a Concept since 1840* (CUP, 2019) and Ryan Martinez Mitchell, *Recentering the World: China and the Transformation of International Law* (CUP, 2022). See also earlier Hague Academy Courses by Tieya Wang, *International Law in China: Historical and Contemporary Perspectives*, 221 Recueil des Cours 195 (1990); Hanqin Hue, *Chinese Contemporary Perspectives on International Law: History, Culture and International Law* (Nijhoff, 2012).

[8] See e.g. Yang Zewei, 'Western International Law and China's Confucianism in the 19th Century. Collision and Integration' Journal of the History of International Law 13 (2011) 285–306; Li Chen, 'Universalism and Equal Sovereignty as Contested Myths of International Law in the Sino-Western Encounter' Journal of the History of International Law 13 (2011) 75–116 See e.g. P. C. W. Chan, 'China's Approaches to International Law since the Opium War'. Leiden Journal of International Law 27 (2014) 859–892 See e.g. Zenghua Zhuo, 'China and the Unequal Treaties: Localization, Variation, and Response' Ius Gentium—Journal of International Legal History 6(2) (2021).

[9] 王铁崖：'中国与国际法：历史和当代'，《中国国际法年刊》(1991年) [Wang Tieya, 'China and International Law: Historical and Contemporary Perspectives, in Chinese Year Book of International Law (1991)]. 杨泽伟：《宏观国际法史》(武汉大学出版社 2001 年版), 第六章 [Yang Zewei, *A Macro History of International Law* (Wuhan University Press, 2001), Chapter 6]. 赖骏楠：《国际法与晚清中国：文本、事件与政治》，上海人民出版社2015年版(Junnan Lai, International Law and Late Qing Dynasty: Texts, Events and Politics (Shanghai People Press, 2015). 章永乐：《万国竞争：康有为与维也纳体系的衰弱》(Yongle Zhang, Struggles among Nations: Youwei Kang and the Decline of Vienna System (Business Press, 2017). 林学忠：《从万国公法到公法外交：晚清国际法的传入、诠释与应用》，上海古籍出版社2019年版 (Xuezhong Lin, From the Law of Nations to Public Law Diplomacy: The Introduction, Interpretation and Applicatin of Public International Law in Late Qing (Shanghai Guji Publishing House, 2019)；李育民：《晚清条约中外关系研究》Yulin Li, A Study on the China-Foreign Treaties of Late Qing Dynasty (Law Press, 2018). 屈文生：《不平等与不对等：晚清中外旧约章翻译史研究》，商务 印书馆2021年版 (Wensheng Qu, Inequality and Non-reciprocity: A Study on the History of Translation of China—Foreign Treaties of Late Qing Dynasty, Business Press, 2021).

persistent issue in Chinese scholarship in this area is that available works tend to closely align, to various degrees, with what their authors perceive as the 'official' position in China. As a result, they often overlook certain sensitive events and time periods, and fail to offer critical or alternative perspectives.

In this context, the primary aims of this book are, firstly, to uncover several illustrative—yet often little-known—historical episodes in the history of international law and China. These include, but are not limited to, China's efforts to protect its nationals abroad in the aftermath of the Rock Springs Massacre in 1885, as well as its international legal policies during the Cultural Revolution (1966–1976) and its immediate aftermath.

Second, the book aims to identify the historical origins and conceptual evolution of key concepts in Chinese international legal history, such as the Confucian vision of world order or Tianxia ('All under Heaven'), 'unequal treaties', 'the century of humiliation', and the 'Five Principles of Peaceful Coexistence'. Additionally, it explores historical patterns in China's international legal foreign policy, including the origins and evolution of its position as a champion of the 'Third World' or developing nations in international law. These and many other historical concepts and patterns form part of the living past of China's relationship with international law, and they find parallels or weigh heavily on China's still ambivalent relationship with the law, which, as Mirabeau once told us, 'one day will rule the world'.[10]

Third, this book aims to examine the role of the legacy of China's past experiences with—and deep-seated attitudes towards—international law, which has been viewed as a 'foreign construct' that the Western powers had 'unequally' imposed on China during the 'century of humiliation' (1842–1949). The book considers the effects this has had in shaping both Chinese foreign and domestic policies as well as China's own national identity at key turning points in its modern history. This was particularly conspicuous during the early days of the League of Nations.

Fourth, the book aims to present a series of historical 'portraits' featuring prominent Chinese scholars in international law who, in most instances, remain largely, if not completely, unknown beyond China. These scholars fundamentally contributed to shaping China's evolving stance on international law and academic developments in the field from the early twentieth century onward. Furthermore, this book also aims to illuminate an almost totally overlooked aspect of research: women's contributions to the study of international law in China.

[10] James Brown Scott, 'Preface, Richard Zouche, Iuris et iudicii fecialis, sive, iuris inter gentes, et quaestionum de eodem explicatio', in Thomas Erskine Holland (ed.) *The Classics of International Law* (Carnegie Institution, 1911) 2a.

1.2 General Structure

Set against this background, the book is divided into five parts. Part I begins with this introductory Chapter 1 by the editors, explaining the purpose, structure, main themes, and scope of the book. The editors' introduction is then followed by a historiographically oriented Chapter 2, written by one of the editors, which situates the study of the histories of international law in China within the broader modern revival of interest in the 'national' histories of international law across both the Western and non-Western worlds. Part II, which includes Chapters 3 to 9, covers the period from ancient times up to the First Opium War (1839–1842) and then from that point to the fall of the Qing Dynasty in 1911. In examining the evolution of the 'Celestial Empire'—from its Sino-centric isolation from the West and its *ius naturale et gentium* to its gradual adaptation and defensive acculturation into international law—this Part explores the profound impact of China's encounter with the West during the height of Western imperial expansion in Africa and Asia. The contributing authors analyse numerous historical events and processes, spanning from the ancient Spring and Autumn and Warring States periods through the First (1839–1842) and Second (1856–1860) Opium Wars, the subsequent Treaties of Nanjing (1842) and Tianjin (1858), and the first translations of international law textbooks in China in the 1860s. Additionally, this Part discusses China's participation in the Hague Peace Conferences of 1899 and 1907, along with some revealing yet less well-known episodes of China's interactions with Western powers and Japan through international law during this period.

Part III of the volume, comprising Chapters 10 to 13, focuses on the relationship between the Republic of China (1912–1949) and international law, as well as China's engagement with international organizations during the interwar period. This era is recognized as the foundational period of contemporary international law, during which the modern system of legal sources crystallized, and the first permanent international institutions were established. The contributing authors successively examine the Republic of China's (ROC) international legal strategy from the 1910s to the 1940s, with a particular focus on its participation in the League of Nations, which, in turn, reshaped the country's vision of the international order. This participation laid the groundwork for the ROC to play an active role in the founding of the United Nations. The Part also explores the ROC's official policies for training its foreign affairs staff, judicial officers, and law professors in international law, both in China and abroad, and how these efforts contributed to the professionalization of the academic discipline of international law in China. Equally explored in Part III are intriguing questions of how Marxist theory of international law was introduced to China in the 1920s and 1930s, as well as of China's relations with the United States—the rising great power that arguably had the most direct influence on China's engagement with international law during the interwar period.

Part IV of the book, spanning eight chapters (Chapters 14 to 21), explores the transformative effect that the establishment of the People's Republic of China (PRC) in 1949 and its subsequent political evolution had on China's approach to international law, extending to the early decades of the reform and opening-up period. Contributing to the growing interest of international legal historians in the evolution of international law during the Cold War, the authors provide new insights into China's governing principles in navigating this tumultuous and transformative era. Particular attention is given to China's engagement with the 'Third World', especially following the Afro-Asian Conference in Bandung in 1955 during the decolonization era; the role of international law in China's dealing with the geopolitical scenario of the Cold War; and the PRC's use of alternative vocabularies to conduct international relations during its period of exclusion from the United Nations. Additionally, this Part examines China's relationship with the USSR—the great power that arguably had the most direct influence on China's approach to international law and international legal education during the Revolutionary period (1949–1978). The authors who contribute to Part IV also shed light on the largely unexplored relationship between China and international law during the Cultural Revolution (1966–1976) and its aftermath, China's historical engagement with democracy and human rights, and the role of international law in the decolonization of Hong Kong. Furthermore, some authors analyse the domestic and foreign policy imperatives that shaped China's unprecedentedly deep and wide-ranging engagement with the international legal order from the beginning of the Reform and Opening Up period, which began in the late 1970s, up to the mid-2020s.

Last but not least, Part V, covering Chapters 22 to 33, shifts the focus from major historical events to the socio-professional level by examining the lives, careers, and contributions of some of the most influential Chinese international law scholars of the twentieth century. This part also introduces a representative sample of female Chinese scholars and educators in international law, emphasizing their significant contributions to the field.

Designed to appeal to both experts and those who are approaching the complex historical evolution of China's relationship with international law for the first time, this book provides a *longue durée* historical perspective woven together with a loosely shared analytical framework. This framework is shaped by the persistent tension that has defined China's ambivalent relationship with the international legal order for more than two centuries—balancing isolation from, acculturation to, strategic appropriation of, and outright rejection of Western international law. These historical tensions continue to shape the backdrop of China's contemporary new phase of offensive acculturation, leveraging international law in alignment with its great power status and actively seeking to reshape the international legal order from within. This, indeed, reaffirms the notion that, indeed, 'that's the thing about the past; it never quite belongs as much to the past as you think it does.".[11]

1.3 Navigating the Contents of the Book

This third part of the introductory chapter aims to provide a reader-friendly yet sufficiently detailed analytical guide to help readers navigate the contents of this book. It is divided into five sections, each corresponding to the five parts of this multi-authored book.

1.3.1 Part I: Historiographical Frameworks

After this introductory chapter, which places the present book in the context of existing research on the history of international law in China while providing an analytical survey of its research agenda and main contributions of its different chapters, the book proceeds to the complementary Chapter 2, which frames this book in terms of contemporary historiographical developments in the global history of international law. Written by Ignacio de la Rasilla, one of the editors, this chapter examines the rise of national histories of international law as the latest offspring of the great rejuvenation of research on the history of international law experienced over the past two decades, both quantitatively and qualitatively. After an initial survey of the historical and intellectual pedigree of the study of the national dimensions of the history of international law in the nineteenth and twentieth centuries, Sections II and III of Chapter 2 examine its recent twenty-first-century revival with reference to three main categories: national histories of international law of the great Western powers, national histories of international law of semi-peripheral Western countries, and national histories of international law of non-Western countries, paying particular attention to the new histories of international law in China's potential contributions to this research trend. Section IV goes on to analyse some of the normative, sociological, methodological, and historiographical arguments that favour the complementary use of the national lens in researching the history of international law from the perspective of its epistemological completeness, but also some of its possible dark sides. These include the risks of furthering 'nationalistic' and 'nativist' approaches to international law, a perpetuation of nationalistic myths, a fostering of 'hidden Eurocentrism', and a 'whitewashing' of the past. The conclusion highlights that existing scholarship already offers the building blocks for the materialization of comparative

[11] Philip Kerr, *The Other Side of Silence* (G.P. Putman's Son, 2016), 253.

international legal history as a field of studies and illustrates some features of its potential scope.

1.3.2 Part II: Before and Beyond the Encounter: from Sino-Centric Isolation to Adaptation to, and Forced Acculturation into, International Law during the Qing Dynasty

Part II opens with Chapter 3 by Xinyu Huang, who provides a bird's-eye view of the Chinese conception of world order from ancient times through the first half of the nineteenth century, when China began systematically encountering the West. This chapter explores China's indigenous concepts within the realm of international law and how these were practised by various dynasties throughout imperial history. Huang focuses on two key aspects: the ideological foundations of the Tianxia ('All under Heaven') system and the Hua-Yi distinction, as well as the institutions and practices built upon them, including the tribute system and foreign affairs institutions. According to Huang, these legacies have modern implications and provide insight into how the Chinese populace historically viewed the world. They also illuminate the foundations upon which modern international law was introduced into China in the early twentieth century. The chapter argues that while modern international law, rooted in the Westphalian system and European legal tradition, has profoundly influenced Chinese society since the nineteenth century, China—despite its distance from Europe—developed its own conception and practice of world order, reflecting the core essence of international law in its ancient context.

Chapter 4 by Inge Van Hulle tackles the profound impact of the Opium Wars on the evolution of international law and China's place in the global order through the little explored lens of the opium trade. It examines how the opium trade between Britain and China fuelled the creation of a system of unequal treaties and extraterritorial rights that infringed on Chinese sovereignty. These treaties, particularly the Treaty of Nanjing (1842) and the Treaty of Tianjin (1858), positioned China within a framework of Western-imposed legal obligations that privileged foreign interests and, particularly, legalized the opium trade despite China's domestic legislation. The chapter also traces the origins of the international narcotics regime which emerged in the early twentieth century partly in response to the opium crisis, while paradoxically upholding extraterritorial privileges. Beyond these immediate legal impacts, Van Hulle's chapter delves into the broader ramifications of its subject matter for legal theory, exploring how international lawyers justified extraterritoriality that flaunted the opium trade under a 'standard of civilization' masking economic motives with civilizational rhetoric. This selective application of international principles contributed to an early fragmentation within the field, where issues such as extraterritoriality and drug control were treated in isolation from each other and from broader concerns about sovereignty.

Chapter 5 by Frédéric Mégret and Wanshu Cong explores how China's position in relation to its nationals abroad in the late Qing period was in many ways not comparable to the position of Western states in relation to their nationals in China. China's early efforts in protecting its nationals abroad should be seen as a key part of its transformation into a modern sovereign state. They involved the development and exercise of external sovereignty, and represented a crucial aspect of the history of China's encounter with international law. Delving into the Sino–US negotiations after the Rock Springs Massacre in 1885, the chapter examines China's attempt at using international law 'mimetically', focusing on the idea of reciprocity and equity to demand equal treatment and protection of Chinese diasporas in the United States. The crucial claim made by Mégret and Cong is that China engaged in a form of 'rhetorical mimetism' against imperial powers such as the United States, which prefigured the ways in which international law might provide resources for 'subaltern' subversion: invoking arguments that the subject was never supposed to invoke against the 'master' but that in a sense begged to be used at counter-purpose. Even as China was itself on the receiving end of onerous obligations to protect foreign nationals on its territory, it drew on that very vulnerability to insist on its own sovereignty under international law.

Chapter 6 by Wensheng Qu and Li Wan examines how European international law became universalized in modern China through the unique lens of translation. Qu and Wan begin by reviewing the evolution of international law from a European-dominated framework to one of purported universal application, paying particular attention to its underlying methodologies. Focusing on the Chinese translations of key works by Vattel and Wheaton, they illustrate how Western theories of international law shaped Qing China's engagement with the world. The authors show how Chinese thinkers modernized their conception of world order by integrating elements of Chinese civilization with Western international legal theory. This chapter sheds light not only on how China—once the self-identified 'Middle Kingdom'—gradually abandoned its traditional worldview, but also on how international law itself evolved as a trans-civilizational enterprise.

Chapter 7 by Masaharu Yanagihara explores the transformation of East Asia's traditional Sino-centric world order into a system influenced by Western international law, focusing on the 1895 Treaty of Shimonoseki and extradition treaties. It begins by examining the historical Sino-centric tributary system, where China maintained hierarchical relationships with neighbouring states such as Korea, Vietnam, and Ryūkyū. This traditional order began to erode in the nineteenth century with the introduction of Western international law, particularly after China's defeat in the Sino-Japanese War (1894–1895). According to Yanagihara, the Treaty of Shimonoseki, signed in 1895, marked a pivotal moment in East Asian history. It symbolized the collapse of the Sino-centric order as China formally renounced its influence over Korea, recognized its independence under Western legal norms, and ceded Taiwan, the Pescadores Islands, and parts of the Liaodong Peninsula to

Japan. The chapter highlights differences in the treaty negotiation records kept by Japan and China, revealing discrepancies in their accounts of key issues, such as the cession of Taiwan and indemnities. Following the treaty, Japan adopted Western legal frameworks in its relations with East Asian countries but mirrored the unequal treatment it had experienced from Western powers. For instance, Japan resisted concluding extradition treaties with China, Korea, and Siam, viewing them as legally inferior, while it successfully negotiated an extradition treaty with the US in 1886. The chapter concludes by arguing that the 1895 Treaty ended the traditional East Asian order and established Japan as an imperial power. However, Japan's actions reflected a replication of Western-imposed hierarchies rather than the creation of an equitable regional legal system. This shift highlights the complex interplay between Western legal norms, Asian sovereignty, and imperialism in shaping modern East Asia.

Chapter 8 by Luigi Nuzzo explores the still relatively unknown history of the Italian presence in China, which led to the signature of the first Sino–Italian lease agreement in 1902. It allowed Italy to obtain 'in perpetuity, as a concession' (art. 1), and upon payment of an annual fee (art. 12), the territory it had materially occupied during the war against the Boxers. The Italian concession in Chinese territory was established at Tianjin alongside the already existing concessions of Great Britain, France, Russia, Belgium, Japan, Germany, Austria, and the United States. This chapter examines the different stages from the military occupation by Italian troops to the signature of a perpetual lease agreement by focusing on the politicians, diplomats, and businessmen who, in Italy and China, imagined transforming a forgotten corner of the Celestial Empire into a new social space. Nuzzo furthermore examines the legal ambiguity of the title concession, the legal category used by Italian jurists to give legal form to the occupation of the territory of Tianjin, and its effects on Chinese sovereignty. The chapter retraces the legal evolution of the Italian concession during the 1920s and 1930s, stressing the attempts of Italian legal scholars to transform the Italian concession in Tianjin into a proper Italian colonial domain in Chinese territory.

Chapter 9 by Mingqian Li examines China's participation in the 1899 and 1907 Hague Peace Conferences through the lens of the Western 'standard of civilization'. These conferences were significant platforms where Western powers employed civilization rhetoric to justify imperialism while non-Western states sought recognition as 'civilized' nations. As Li has observed, during the First Hague Conference (1899) China's delegation, led by Yang Ru, approached participation cautiously but strategically. While signing most conventions, including those related to the Red Cross, China refrained from signing the Convention on Laws of War, citing its army's incomplete Western-style training. Chinese officials interpreted Western concepts through traditional Chinese philosophical frameworks, as seen in their explanation of the Red Cross using Mozi's philosophy of universal love. At the Second Conference (1907), China took a more active stance under

Lu Zhengxiang's leadership. However, China faced discrimination in two key areas: the allocation of judges for the proposed Court of Arbitral Justice, where China was classified as a 'third-tier' nation despite its size and contributions, and the attempt to exclude extraterritoriality from obligatory arbitration. The chapter concludes that despite China's earnest efforts to meet the 'standard of civilization' through participating in international conferences and accepting international norms, these standards proved to be moving targets that ultimately served to maintain Western dominance. The author draws a parallel to Kafka's parable 'Before the Law', suggesting that for China, like the man in the story, the 'gate' of civilization was one that could never truly be entered.

1.3.3 Part III: International Law in China during the Republican Period

Part III of the book opens with Chapter 10 by Ryan Martinez Mitchell, which explores how during the First World War, several key figures in the Chinese international law and diplomatic communities influenced global discourse around postwar international legal order. Subsequently, Chinese representatives, although hardly negotiating from a position of strength, were active in the debates at the Treaty of Versailles that gave the League of Nations its definitive form. Alongside attempts to reassert territorial sovereignty and policy autonomy, Chinese participation during the League years was notable on a number of important legal topics, including advancing peaceful dispute resolution, codification of international law, and the articulation of prohibitions on interstate coercion. Moreover, Martinez Mitchell also shows how in the wake of the May Fourth Movement and society-wide ideological polarization in China, the Chinese public too became a newly important source of activism on issues of global governance. Yet, despite China's interwar emergence as a recognized full member of the society of nations, its ongoing vulnerability to the agendas of great powers ultimately exhibited the League's failure, disillusionment with its institutions, and the need for new visions of global legal order.

Chapter 11 by Pasha L. Hsieh reviews the development of the professionalization of international law during the Republic of China (ROC) era. Hsieh argues that the ROC's legal approach was shaped by a combination of statism, pragmatism, and idealism. He traces the evolution of international law through legal education, the Ministry of Foreign Affairs, and international law societies. The chapter demonstrates that the ROC's strategies in addressing unequal treaties, resisting Japanese aggression through legal means, and participating in international institutions and tribunals played a critical role in shaping postwar global governance.

Chapter 12 by Jie Liu and Congyan Cai examines a relatively underexplored issue: how Chinese international lawyers have turned to Marxism—a development that has drawn increasing interest from Western international lawyers over the past decade. Liu and Cai begin by reviewing the Soviet/Marxist approach to international law in China during the first half of the twentieth century, focusing on how Chinese international lawyers engaged with Western theories of international law. They then explore why the Soviet theory of international law was introduced to China and how it was received. This chapter illustrates how both international legal theories and the practice of international law adapt to fundamental political and ideological transformations. The core argument is that although the Soviet theory of international law significantly influenced the development of international legal thought in China during the 1950s and 1960s, Chinese international lawyers did not fully embrace it. Instead, driven by China's specific concerns and its ideological split with the USSR from the late 1960s onward, they gradually developed a Marxist approach to international law with distinct Chinese characteristics.

Chapter 13 by Christopher R. Rossi tackles the interesting subject of how Confucian moralism and Western legal rationalism crossed paths during the period that shaped US–Sino relations at the birth of Chinese republicanism in the early twentieth century. According to Rossi, the intersection did not remake the Chinese view of the legitimacy of the Western world so much as it refined China's view of Western power. Rossi interrogates this history, focusing on the attempted transmission of liberal internationalism to republican China. The formalistic and legalistic presumptions of Western international law, its notion of sovereignty, the exportation of the U.S.' common law courts and procedures to China, and the importation of Western pedagogical techniques and teachers influenced and stunted China's republican project, ultimately contributing to Chinese circumspection and the cautious embrace of legal gradualism in view of Western international law.

1.3.4 Part IV: International Law in China from the New China to the Opening-up and Reform Process

Part IV of the book opens with Chapter 14 by Ignacio de la Rasilla. Following the seminal periodization offered by Jerome A. Cohen and Hungdah Chiu's *People's China and International Law* in 1974, in his chapter de la Rasilla revisits a neglected part of the history of international law in the Cold War. The chapter pays special attention to China's international legal relationship with what is broadly known today as the developing world or Global South within the framework of the 'evolution of Chinese Communist foreign policy' and, by extension, international law, into five stages or 'basic periods' from 1949 to 1973–1978. The first of these stages (1949–1952), which included the People's Volunteers Army's participation in the Korea War and China's support for the 'Vyshinsky Doctrine', was, marked by China's embracement of the tenets of the Soviet Theory of International Law, upon which section I elaborates. The second stage (1953–1957) was, in turn, characterized by the rise of the five principles of 'peaceful coexistence', the passing of the first PRC Constitution in 1954, and the political emergence of the 'Third World', epitomized in the Bandung Conference. The third basic period (1958–1965) was largely marked by the Sino–Soviet Split and the formulation in its wake of a 'Sinocentric conception of socialist internationalism', positioning China as the self-appointed champion of post-colonial nations and revolutionary values during the decolonization era. The fourth period (1966–1969) saw the height of the Cultural Revolution, which fostered a further radicalization of China's approach to international law and international legal education. Last, but not least, the final section extends Cohen and Chiu's periodization (1969–1973) to 1978 in order to briefly revisit the effects of China's restoration to the UN in 1971 on its approach to international law during the stage of stabilization and decline of the Cultural Revolution and up to the beginning of the 'reform and opening-up' process in the late 1970s.

Chapter 15 by Jiangyu Wang explores the evolving and complex relationship between the People's Republic of China and international law during the Cold War (1949–1991). Set against the challenges of superpower rivalry, ideological strife, and the need for regime survival, alongside shifting alliances from the Soviet bloc to the West, China's engagement with the international legal framework was intricate. The chapter posits that even during times of revolutionary zeal and relative isolation, the PRC adopted a fairly consistent stance characterized by a mix of rigid Westphalian principles (highlighting sovereignty and non-interference), strategic instrumentalism (leveraging law for national interests), and revolutionary idealism (championing Third World anti-colonial efforts and disputing perceived imperialist legal systems).

Chapter 16 by Yifeng Chen studies the emergence of a principle-based vocabulary in China's international legal practice during the 1950s–1960s, tracing its roots to the rejection of Western treaties and customary norms—as a symbol of imperialist coercion—in the wake of the PRC's exclusion from the United Nations. He further revisits the adoption of the Five Principles of Peaceful Coexistence in 1954, arguing that these served not merely as diplomatic tools but as expressions of constitutional politics and ethical commitments rooted in China's political and cultural traditions, particularly Confucian legalism. His study further proposes that China's practice could signal an Asian emergent principle-based international order, offering an alternative to Western-centric, rule-based paradigms.

Chapter 17 by Lauri Malksoo examines the complex history of Sino–Soviet relations within the context of international law, highlighting the interplay of imperial legacies and Communist ideologies. It begins by contextualizing the Cold War dynamics between the Soviet Union and the People's Republic of China (PRC), marked initially by cooperation following the 1950 Treaty of Friendship, Alliance, and Mutual Assistance, and later by ideological and geopolitical conflicts. Drawing on the framework of international law, the chapter explores key moments of collaboration and discord, emphasizing the influence of earlier 'unequal treaties' and territorial disputes like those over Mongolia and the Sino–Soviet border. The chapter reveals how both powers, while claiming to be anti-imperialist, maintained imperialist legacies that shaped their policies. Soviet efforts to promote 'peaceful coexistence' and the PRC's radical opposition to perceived Soviet hegemonism often clashed. The Sino–Soviet split of the 1960s–1980s was reflected in legal scholarship, with divergent interpretations of socialist international law and debates over principles such as state sovereignty and *pacta sunt servanda*. While the PRC criticized the USSR's actions, such as its 1968 invasion of Czechoslovakia, as imperialist, the USSR accused China of nationalism and great power chauvinism. The chapter also discusses the eventual resolution of Sino–Soviet border disputes through treaties signed between 1991 and 2008, which reflected the waning ambitions of both states. Ultimately, the chapter argues that the Sino–Soviet legal and territorial conflicts were rooted in historical imperialism and power struggles, underscoring the persistent influence of 'great power' politics in shaping international law and relations.

Chapter 18 by Straton Papagianneas casts new light on the little explored engagement of China with international law during the Cultural Revolution (1966–1976), a period often characterized as one of legal nihilism. Papagianneas argues that despite the apparent upheaval, China maintained a limited yet significant involvement in international law, particularly through preliminary discussions leading to treaties such as the Sino–Japanese Peace and Friendship Treaty. The chapter goes on to examine two other pivotal events: the Third United Nations Conference on the Law of the Sea (1973–1982) and the 1972 Stockholm Conference on the Human Environment. It highlights how China's ideological stance shifted post-Cultural Revolution, resulting in a more pragmatic approach to international law, reflecting its national interests in sovereignty and development. The analysis emphasizes the enduring influence of historical contexts on China's contemporary legal perspectives and its growing role in shaping international law.

Chapter 19 by Eva Pils examines how China engages with human rights and democracy. Pils argues that China's long history of engagement with these concepts has been shaped by global debates. She calls for an analysis that juxtaposes the perspectives of powerholders with those of individuals and groups who confront, oppose, or compete with them. This approach suggests that while the possibility of peaceful power transition is a crucial test no genuine democracy can fail, democracies also rely on the successful institutionalization of legal accountability for rights violations. On this basis, the chapter attempts a comparison between the use of 'democracy' and 'human rights' in the official discourses and practices of the PRC—especially from the beginning of Deng Xiaoping's 'Reform and Opening' to Xi Jinping's notion of 'whole-process democracy'—and the historic struggles of nonstate actors advocating for democracy and human rights against the Chinese Party-State. This juxtaposition not only reveals that nonstate actors have consistently challenged the state, but also provides a basis for assessing the effectiveness of the state's attempts to reconceptualize the legitimating principles of democracy, human rights, and the rule of law.

Chapter 20 by Feng Lin examines Hong Kong's decolonization process through the lens of international law, focusing on the interplay between self-determination and territorial integrity. Hong Kong's unique colonial history stems from the three 'unequal treaties' through which Britain acquired the region. While China deems these treaties invalid under its revolutionary theory, they were considered legitimate under nineteenth-century international law. The chapter argues that Hong Kong's decolonization was distinct because China retained sovereignty over the 'New Territories' during British rule, creating a dual-sovereignty dynamic. The chapter explores in detail the principles of self-determination and territorial integrity, emphasizing their conflict in Hong Kong's case. Unlike most British colonies, Hong Kong's decolonization did not involve the exercise of self-determination by its people. Instead, the process was driven by territorial integrity claims, with China asserting its historical ties, geographical contiguity, and sovereignty over the 'New Territories'. These claims prevailed over self-determination, as supported by precedents such as the Goa, Aaland Islands, and West Irian cases. The chapter also examines the transitional period from the 1984 Sino–British Joint Declaration to the 1997 handover. It highlights China's commitment to internal self-determination through the 'one country, two systems' framework, reflected in the drafting of Hong Kong's Basic Law. While this granted Hong Kong a high degree of autonomy, it aligned more with internal self-determination than external sovereignty. In short, the chapter concludes that Hong Kong's decolonization prioritized territorial integrity over self-determination, with China's sovereignty claims dominating the process. However, Hong Kong's internal self-determination was acknowledged and institutionalized through the Basic Law.

Finally, Chapter 21 by Jacques DeLisle concludes, chronologically, the volume's long historical journey into China's engagement with international law from its *Tianxia* days and earlier by examining the PRC's evolving engagement with international law from the late 1970s, coinciding with the end of the revolutionary era and the opening up and reform period, to the present. DeLisle identifies three overlapping yet distinct phases: accession, participation, and influence. In the accession phase, China pursued integration into the international legal order by joining major institutions and treaties—particularly in economic and human rights law—often accepting prevailing norms and incurring significant legal commitments. The participation phase saw China implement obligations unevenly, using legal mechanisms to advance national interests while asserting interpretations that stretched or redefined existing norms, especially in trade, human rights, and maritime disputes. In the current influence-seeking phase, particularly under Xi Jinping, China has moved to reshape international law more proactively. Key strategies include building 'foreign-related rule of law', increasing discourse power, advocating for sovereign-centred interpretations, and establishing new institutions. While projecting support for multilateralism and existing rules, China's approach reflects pluralism, and developmental relativism, particularly favouring Global South states. The chapter concludes that although China has become a weighty international legal actor, it has not yet articulated or imposed a comprehensive alternative legal order, leaving the future of global legal norms in flux.

1.3.5 Part V: Chinese Historical Portraits in International Law

The last part of *Histories of International Law in China* contains twelve chapters, eleven of which are shorter chapters devoted to exploring the life, times, and work of eleven Chinese international law scholars, who despite being in many cases not so well-known by Western audiences, are, in most cases, famous and revered household names in the Chinese academia of international law. This is so because of their many academic achievements, and/or the positions they held in their lifetimes, including as judges of international courts and tribunals, but also due to their longstanding influence as teachers and mentors of subsequent generation of Chinese international lawyers across many different international legal specialized regimes.[12]

All of them were born in a period extending from the first two final decades of the nineteenth century to roughly the first two decades of the twentieth century and their lives and works traversed and reflected the myriads of vicissitudes and great transformations China experienced during the twentieth century. Furthermore, many of these scholars are representative of how China expressly trained its elites in international law during the interwar period, with many of them holding international law degrees from foreign universities in Britain, France, Canada, or the United States. The lives and careers of many of them are also symbolic of academic resilience in the face of political domestic adversity during the 'Cultural Revolution', after which several of them went on, furthermore, to become the founding architects of the restoration of international law in the early 'opening up and reform' process in China.

Ordered chronologically, with reference to their birth-date in each case, Chapters 22 to 32 include academic and professional portraits of: Wang Chung-hui (1881–1958), written by Liu Yang; Wellington Koo (1888–1985) written by Maria Adele Carrai; Zhou Gengshen (1889–1971), written by Luo Guoqiang and Wang Chao; Xiang Zhejun (1892–1987), written by Zhuo Zenghua; Li Haopei (1906–1997), written by Zou Guoyong and Li Jue; Ni Zhengyu (1906–2003), written by Hao Yayezi & Hong Yu; Han Depei (1911–2009), written by Yongping

[12] Nongji Zhang, *Legal Scholars and Scholarship in the People's Republic of China. The First Generation, 1949–1992* (Brill, 2022).

Xiao & Jue Li; Wang Tieya (1913–2003), written by Ken Yang; Shi Shaoheng (1913–2009), written by Chao Wang; Zhao Lihai (1916–1996), written, again, by Ken Yang; and Chen Tiqiang (1917–1983), written by Xu Xiaobin. All these historical portraits follow a loose common tripartite structure in which the chapter's authors first examine the 'biographical' dimension of the person, such as social environment, childhood, education, and general description of main events of his life. This is followed by discussion of the 'professional and academic' career of their international legal *dramatis personae*, with a special focus on his contributions to international law, whereas the final part is, generally, reserved for an analysis of the person's legacy in Chinese international law, including regarding his influence on the course of certain events, institutional developments, and/or academic careers of subsequent generations.

Last, but by all means not least, the last, and longer, chapter in Part V, written by Ken Yang, is devoted to casting light on the neglected contributions of generations of almost invisible Chinese women in the history of international law. Although, as was also largely the case in the Western world, women remained very much in the background of international legal studies until the mid–late 1990s in China, Chapter 33 provides a seminal collective portrait of Chinese women's engagement with, and contributions to, international law in China up to the early days of the opening-up and reform process in the late 1970s.

1.4 Conclusions

Much has happened since the following words, attributed to a French *chargé d'affaires* on hearing the news of William A.P. Martin's plan to translate Henry Wheaton's *Elements of International Law* to Mandarin in 1863, were uttered: 'Who is this man who is going to give the Chinese an insight into our European international law? Kill him—choke him off; he will make us endless trouble.'[13]

Understanding China's historical interaction with international law provides crucial insights into contemporary debates about the future of the global legal order in the twenty-first century. China's historical experiences raise fundamental questions about the universality of international law, the relationship between power and the shaping of international legal norms, and the potential for diverse civilizational perspectives to contribute to the development of international legal norms over time. The historical analysis this book provides—which we hope will spur further work on the histories of international law in China, but also about other 'national' histories of international law across the Global South—is particularly relevant today as China increasingly asserts itself on the global stage. In doing

[13] See Immanuel C. Y. Hsü, *China's Entrance into the Family of Nations: The Diplomatic Phase, 1858–1880* (Harvard University Press, 1960), 132–137.

so, China both challenges and embraces existing norms, while attempting to restyle the international legal order in accordance with its historical trajectory, its civilizational and political values, its national interests, and its own hopes for the future of humankind much as great powers[14] past and present have always done—moulding, in doing so, the course of human history.

[14] Wilhelm G. Grewe, *The Epochs of International Law*, translated and revised by Michael Byers (Walter de Gruyter, 2000).

2

China and the Turn to the National in the History of International Law

Ignacio de la Rasilla

2.1 Introduction

Recent historical writing about international law has increasingly paid attention to specific national histories of international law in the nineteenth and twentieth centuries. This research orientation towards the "local, the national and international together" springs from a realization, as Anthony Padgen notes, that "the national origin of all things international is undeniable and inescapable."[1] Increased study of the national dimension of histories of international law has accompanied the contemporary flourishing of the study of the history of international law and its historiography both in quantitative and qualitative terms in recent years. Enriched by contributions by international lawyers, and also legal historians, intellectual historians, historians of political thought, global historians, and those producing "historical IR work on international law,"[2] the new interdisciplinary character of the cultivation of international legal history has fostered the development of a great diversity of historical methodologies.[3] This development has prompted intense debates among different "scientific/intellectual trends"[4] in a field of study which, as recently noted by Randall Lesaffer did not "blossom into a significant sub-branch of legal history until the very end of the twentieth century."[5]

As part of these developments, historians of international law have recently been increasingly using a national lens and making strides in a new wave of nationally framed explorations of international legal history. Although the national research frame had, as we shall later see, earlier precedents in Western diplomatic

[1] Anthony Padgen, "Introduction," in *A History of International Law in Italy*, edited by Giulio Bartolini (Oxford: OUP, 2020): pp. 3–18.

[2] Randall Lesaffer and Anne Peters, eds, *The Cambridge History of International Law. Historiography of International Law Vol. 1* (Cambridge: CUP, 2024).

[3] See e.g. Ignacio de la Rasilla, *International Law and History: Modern Interfaces* (Cambridge: CUP, 2021).

[4] Anne Orford, *International Law and the Politics of History* (Cambridge: CUP, 2021).

[5] Randall Lesaffer, "Scope, Scale and Humility in the History of International Law," in *The Cambridge History of International Law: The Historiography of International Law Vol. I*, edited by Randall Lesaffer and Anne Peters (Cambridge: CUP, 2024), 1–46, p. 3.

Ignacio de la Rasilla, *China and the Turn to the National in the History of International Law* In: *Histories of International Law in China*. Edited by: Ignacio de la Rasilla, Jiangyu Wang, and Congyan Cai, Oxford University Press.
 DOI: 10.1093/oso/9780198888345.003.0002

history and in conventional intellectual history of international law centered on contributions to international legal thought by Western authors and the practice of Western European states, it only gained true global credentials in the decolonization decades. At that time, new contributions poured in from newly independent countries keen to assert that their peoples had not been merely passive recipients of a globalized European law of nations imposed on them in waves of Western colonization and informal imperialism; they had also been active contributors to it since time immemorial.

However, with the arrival of a globalizing post-Cold War institutional and normative liberal order, this national dimension of international legal history was pushed to the margins as a parallel revolution in new technologies and communication further contributed to fostering a new orientation in the writing of the history of international law in an ever-interconnected global age. This, although with its own particularities, finds parallels in what David Armitage has termed "the turn to the international," away from the national frame as the traditional container of history, and the rise of "global legal history," with its focus on connections and entanglements among legal historians.[6] It is only more recently, in the past decade or so, that a diverse set of new contributions have largely expanded the national dimensions of histories of, and contributions to, international law.

Studies that put the spotlight on the neglected national dimensions of international legal history include works that investigate the traditional themes or objects of historical investigation, those of "the history of events, the history of concepts and the history of individual people"[7] in different nations in the nineteenth and twentieth centuries. This enlargement of research orientation includes, first, great Western powers such as the United States[8] and the United Kingdom,[9] and also increasingly contributions on the history of international law in semi-peripheral Western nations such as Belgium,[10] Spain,[11] Italy,[12] and Russia,[13] to mention but a few. Moreover, the turn to the national in international legal history has been further apparent in arrays of new histories of international law written

[6] See e.g. Thomas Duve, "What Is Global Legal History," *Comparative Legal History* 8 (2020): p. 115, doi: 10.1080/2049677X.2020.1830488.

[7] Bardo Fassbender and Anne Peters, "Introduction: Towards a Global History of International Law," in *The Oxford Handbook of the History of International Law,* edited by Bardo Fassbender and Anne Peters (Oxford: OUP, 2012), p. 11.

[8] Mark Weston Janis, *America and the Law of Nations 1776–1939* (Oxford: OUP, 2010). Mark Weston Janis, *The American Tradition of International Law: Great Expectations 1789–1914* (Oxford: OUP, 2004).

[9] Barrett Jill and Jean-Pierre Gauci, eds, *British Contributions to International Law, 1915–2015: An Anthology Set,* 4 volumes (Leiden: Brill, 2020).

[10] Vincent Genin, *Le laboratoire belge du droit international: une communauté épistémique et internationale de juristes (1869–1914)* (Brussels: Académie royale de Belgique, 2018).

[11] Ignacio de la Rasilla, *In the Shadow of Vitoria. A History of International Law in Spain 1770–1953* (Leiden: Brill, 2017).

[12] Giulio Bartolini, ed., *A History of International Law in Italy* (Oxford: OUP, 2020).

[13] Lauri Mälksoo, *Russian Approaches to International Law* (Oxford: OUP, 2015).

after decolonization about hitherto semi-peripheral and peripheral nations such as China,[14] the Ottoman Empire,[15] Brazil,[16] and India.[17] To crown it all, both national and regional historical frames are tiptoeing into the historiographical domain as lenses through which to examine and organize past national contributions to the study of what Lassa Oppenheim once termed the "most neglected province of international law."[18]

A similar retrenching from a deeply ingrained form of "methodological internationalism" in the work of international legal historians also underlies a parallel contemporary move towards far greater attention to the national dimension in contemporary international legal scholarship. This focus on the national dimension of international law extends across other languages besides English[19] and across specific countries,[20] including middle and great powers such as Australia,[21] Russia,[22] China,[23] or India.[24] This search for elements of national, and occasionally also regional, singularity in the way different nations or even regional groups[25] approach international law has been further nurtured by a revitalization of "comparative international law" (CIL). Although its roots are in the Cold War, CIL has recently been defined as consisting in "identifying, analyzing and explaining similarities and differences in how actors in different legal systems understand, interpret, apply and approach international law."[26] A research emphasis on the national

[14] Maria Adele Carrai, *Sovereignty in China: A Genealogy of a Concept since 1840* (Cambridge: CUP, 2019).

[15] Umut Özsu and Thomas Skouteris, "International Legal Histories of the Ottoman Empire: An Introduction to the Symposium," *Journal of the History of International Law* 18 (2016): pp. 1–4, doi: 10.1163/15718050-12340049.

[16] George Bandeira Galindo, ed., *Direito Internacional no Brasil: Pensamento e tradição*, vol. 1 and 2 (Rio de Janeiro: Editora Lumen Juris, 2021).

[17] Amritha V. Shenoy, "The Centenary of the League of Nations: Colonial India and the Making of International Law," *Asian Yearbook of International Law* 24 (2018): 3–23, doi: 10.1163/9789004437784_002.

[18] David Armitage and Ignacio de la Rasilla, "The Most Neglected Province: British Historiography of International Law," in *The Cambridge History of International Law. The Historiography of International Law Vol I*, edited by Randall Lesaffer and Anne Peters (Cambridge: CUP, 2024).

[19] See e.g. Constantine Antonopoulos, "International Law in Greek," in *Oxford Bibliographies on* International Law, edited by Anthony Carty (Oxford: OUP, 2022).

[20] Pouria Askary, "Iran and International Law," in *Oxford Bibliographies on* International Law, edited by Anthony Carty (Oxford: OUP, 2021).

[21] Donald Rothwell and Emily Crawford, eds, *International Law in Australia* (3rd ed., Thompson Reuters 2017).

[22] Mälksoo, *Russian Approaches* (n 13).

[23] Congyan Cai, *International Law and the Rise of China: Taking Chinese Exceptionalism Seriously* (Oxford: OUP, 2019).

[24] Bimal Patel, ed., *India and International Law Vols I and II* (Leiden: Martinus Nijhoff, 2005 and 2008).

[25] See e.g. Simon Chesterman and others, eds, *The Oxford Handbook of Asia and the Pacific* (Oxford: OUP, 2019); Obregon Tarazona, Liliana and others, eds, *The Oxford Handbook of International Law and the Americas* (Oxford: OUP, 2023); Anne van Aaken and others, eds, *The Oxford Handbook of International Law in Europe* (Oxford: OUP, 2023); Babatunde Fagbayibo, "African Approaches to International Law," in *Oxford Bibliographies on* International Law, edited by Anthony Carty (Oxford: OUP, 2021).

[26] Anthea Roberts and others, "Conceptualizing Comparative International Law," in *Comparative International Law*, edited by Anthea Roberts and others (Oxford: OUP, 2018) 3, at p. 6.

as the unit of analysis among international lawyers engaged in analysis of contemporary developments in a transitional period from a Western-centric international law to a more inclusive and multipolar international legal order is revitalizing both comparative international law[27] and the comparative history of international law as intertwined fields of studies.[28]

After this introductory section, this chapter is divided into five further sections. Section 2.2 briefly surveys the historical and intellectual pedigree of the study of the national dimension of the history of international law. Sections 2.3 and 2.4 then examine its recent revival with reference to three main categories: national histories of great Western powers; national histories of semi-peripheral Western countries; and national histories of non-Western countries, paying particular attention to developments pertaining to the new histories of international law in China. Section 2.5 goes on to examine some of the normative, sociological, methodological, and historiographical arguments in favor of the complementary use of the national lens in researching the history of international law from the perspective of its epistemological completeness but also some of its possible dark sides. These include the risks of furthering "nationalistic" and "nativist" approaches to international law, a perpetuation of nationalistic myths, a fostering of "hidden Eurocentrism," and a "whitewashing" of the past. The conclusion recaps the main findings of the chapter and highlights that existing scholarship already offers the building blocks for the materialization of comparative international legal history as a field of study and illustrates some features of its potential scope.

2.2 The Rise, Fall, and Revival of National Histories of International Law

The national genre is not a new domain of international legal history. Histories of international law in particular European countries were written in the late nineteenth century[29] and the early twentieth century and there were also efforts to identify distinct historical regional particularities beyond Europe, notably in the Americas.[30] Moreover, in this period in some countries the foundations were laid for making the history of international law partly synonymous with a nationally framed and recurrently celebratory perspective on the intellectual contributions

[27] Anthea Roberts and others, eds, *Comparative International Law* (Oxford: OUP, 2018).

[28] This chapter is an abridged and revised version, with a more specific focus on Chinese history of international law, of Ignacio de la Rasilla, "Towards Comparative International Legal History," *Journal of the History of International Law* 27 (2025) 197–236, doi: https://doi.org/10.1163/15718050-bja10112.

[29] See e.g. Augusto Pierantoni, *Storia del diritto internazionale in Italia* (Modena: C. Vincenzi, 1869, reprinted Firenze, Libraria "Fratelli Cammelli," 1902).

[30] Alejandro Álvarez, *Le droit international américain: son fondement, sa nature: d'après l'histoire diplomatique des états du nouveau monde et leur vie politique et économique* (Paris: Pédone, 1910).

their own nationals made to international legal thought in different historical periods. The elevation of Francisco de Vitoria, Francisco Suarez, Alberico Gentili, Hugo Grotius, and Emer de Vattel to the status of Western classics of international law,[31] to mention just a few of those whose influence and contributions are still reiteratively debated, owes volumes to their early buttressing, spurred by what Peter Haggenmacher called the "contest of the putative fathers of the law of nations,"[32] by an often idealist and universalist historiography with Eurocentric, nationalistic, and also occasionally religious overtones.[33]

During the interwar period, the traditional reiterative intellectual focus among international lawyers on great Western international law thinkers and their followers became more specifically framed in "national" schools of international legal thought, including the Spanish school[34] and the Italian School,[35] or study of "contributions" to international law by "great" British authors,[36] and also with a distinct ultra-nationalistic "conception" of international law among fascist powers.[37] However, during the interwar years the national historical lens also began to be used to recover early contributions from territories still under colonial rule, such as India,[38] while regional lenses continued to be used widely by Latin American scholars who have often used a hybrid complementary category which takes regions as its main historical frame of analysis. Meanwhile, the regional frame was also incipiently employed to retrace the contributions and evolution of international law in geographically extended religious communities like the Islam by reference to the Arab world,[39] or Western semi-peripheral regions like Eastern Europe.[40]

Despite these precedents, and in contrast with the chief role of the nation as the traditional container of historical and legal historical studies, the national dimension, albeit often intermingled with or even substituted by the regional dimension

[31] Ernest Nys, *Les origines de droit international* (Brussels: A. Castaigne, 1894).

[32] Peter Haggenmacher, "La place de Francisco de Vitoria parmi les fondateurs du droit international," in *Actualité de la pensée juridique de Francisco de Vitoria*, edited by Antonio Truyol Serra and others (Brussels: Bruylant, 1988), pp. 27–80 at 29.

[33] See e.g. Martine J. Van Ittersum, "Hugo Grotius: The Making of a Founding Father of the History of International Law," in *The Oxford Handbook of the Theory of International Law*, edited by Anne Orford and Florian Hoffman (Oxford: OUP, 2016).

[34] See e.g. Camilo Barcia Trelles, "Fernando Vazquez de Menchaca (1512–1569): l'école espagnole du droit international du XVIe siècle," *Recueil des cours de l'Académie de droit international de La Haye* (*RCADI*) 69 (1939) 430.

[35] Enrico Catellani, "Les maîtres de l'école italienne du droit international au XIX siècle," *RCADI* 46 (1933).

[36] Pearce A. Higgins, "La contribution de quatre grands juristes britanniques au droit international (Lorimer, Westlake, Hall et Holland)," *RCADI* 40 (1932) 1.

[37] Detlev F. Vagts, "International Law in the Third Reich," *AJIL* 84 (1990) 661.

[38] See e.g. Pradipta Bandyopadhyay, *International Law and Custom in Ancient India* (Calcutta: Calcutta University Press, 1920); S. V. Viswanatha, *International Law in Ancient India* (London: Longmans, Green & Company, 1925).

[39] See e.g. Ahmed Rechid, "L'Islam et le droit des gens," *RCADI* 60 (1937) 385.

[40] See e.g. Michel Taube, "Études sur le développement historique du droit international dans l'Europe orientale," *RCADI* 11 (1926) 341.

as the lens through which to look at the history of international law, has not been the central unit of analysis in international legal history. Unlike historical legal studies, which had long been restricted by the corset of "methodological nationalism" and which have only recently embraced the notion that "a world history of law … is more than a collection of national legal histories,"[41] the opposite has been true to a significant degree among international lawyers. Long neglected by international lawyers, who have long disregarded most dimensions of international legal history in favor of legal-technical and theoretical analyses of international legal practice (which is often called "internal" international legal history), holistic study of the history of international law has also been restricted over time by the influence of a particular form of what one may call "methodological internationalism." This has been strengthened on the one hand by a universalist intellectual orientation upheld by a strong internationalist and cosmopolitan spirit, and on the other by the underlying structural reality of imperialism.

The large temporal and geographically extended grip of European imperialism, which had its apex in the first decade of the 20th century when it covered three fifths of the world's surface, largely accounts for why the national focus only gained truly global credentials in the wake of decolonization, as the regional focus had done before it in the wake of the birth of the new Latin American nations. Indeed, as new independent nations popped up in Africa and Asia, they sought to highlight the precedential character of their precolonial experiences and their contributions to the development of international law[42] in areas such as trade and diplomacy and on matters of war and peace, which had been displaced and largely obliterated by a colonial Eurocentric history of international law.[43] However, with the closing of formal processes of decolonization in Asia and Africa by the 1980s, with which no fewer than eighty former colonies had gained their independence since the establishment of the UN, and with the end of the Cold War, cultivation of this "contributionist" genre of national and regional histories of international law went on to be gradually diluted in favor of more ecumenical histories of the discipline in different languages which were more "universal" in orientation and global in their coverage.[44]

It is only more recently, as a coda of what is often termed the "turn to history in international law,"[45] diversely also known as the "historical turn" or, so as to

[41] Lauren Benton, "Law and World History," in *Architects of World History: Researching the Global Past*, edited by Kenneth R. Curtis and Jerry H. Bentley (Hoboken: John Wiley & Sons, 2014): pp. 134–135.

[42] Charles H. Alexandrowicz, *The Law of Nations in Global History* (Oxford: OUP, 2017).

[43] James Thuo Gathii, "Africa," in *The Oxford Handbook of the History of International Law*, edited by Bardo Fassbender and Anne Peters (Oxford: OUP, 2012): p. 407.

[44] See e.g. Martti Koskenniemi, "A History of the International Law Histories," in *The Oxford Handbook of the History of International Law*, edited by Bardo Fassbender and Anne Peters (Oxford: OUP, 2012): p. 943.

[45] Thomas Skouteris, "The Turn to History in International Law," in *Oxford Bibliographies on International Law*, edited by Anthony Carty (Oxford: OUP, 2017).

honor its characteristically interdisciplinary character, the "turn to the history of international law,"[46] that a new literature focusing on national histories of international law is opening new vistas of international legal historical knowledge. This new knowledge not only contributes to expanding the field of the history of international law but, crucially, has also the potential to bridge an important knowledge gap in both the fields of national legal histories and all national histories. Indeed, what is unearthed as a result is what may be described as an expanding network of national historical mosaics of international law, which gradually expands and intersects with other more or less developed national ones, creating a deeper and multi-layered global history of the discipline of international law. This growing knowledge has, in turn, the potential of addressing blind spots in the research areas of both legal historians and historians specialized in domestic contexts which they have either ignored or not been fully equipped to address in the past due to their otherwise understandable lack of sufficiently specialized knowledge of international law and or international legal history. Whether done, as we shall see, in a concerted manner to cover specific periods, or people following a prosopographical approach, or as the outcome of unconnected efforts on historical landmark events, the contemporary revival of the national histories of international law channels an effort to cast light on the margins of the dominant intellectual traditions and the epoch-making periodization of nineteenth and twentieth century Western great powers. In doing so, a focus on the national dimension of international legal history allows us to look beyond a totalizing so-called European tradition of international law which has been "constructed around the limited set of historical events, particular international law writers, and the specific experiences and circumstances of Western European great powers with an underestimation or mere exclusion of the rest."[47]

2.3 National Histories of International Law in Western Great Powers and Western Semi-Peripheral Countries

In recent academic literature, there are an unprecedented number of works that explore the national dimension of international law. Building on some of the earlier antecedents surveyed in Section 2, this is expanding, as Nehal Bhuta notes, through "accounts of the emergence of professional fields of 'international law' within distinct national contexts, and particular styles of thought characteristic of "national

[46] Ignacio de la Rasilla, "The Historical Turn in International Law," in *Elgar Concise Encyclopaedia of Legal Theory and Philosophy*, edited by John Linarelli (Cheltenham: Edward Elgar, 2025).
[47] Ignacio de la Rasilla, "Book Review: Le laboratoire belge du droit international. Une communauté épistémique et internationale de juristes," Leiden Journal of International Law 31 (2020) 257–260. See also a brief analysis of national histories of international law in De la Rasilla, *International Law and History* 257–259 (n 11).

traditions" in international law".[48] To provide a concise and reader-friendly analysis, this major development will be surveyed with attention to a selected number of historiographical features for what regards three main areas: national histories of great Western powers and national histories of semi-peripheral Western countries are examined in this section, while the next section addresses national histories of non-Western countries, in doing so paying special attention to China.

The first category in this sub-genre of national histories of international law comprises histories of international law in certain great modern Western powers such as the United States, the United Kingdom, France, and Germany. These, which may span shorter or longer periods of time,[49] explore in different scales and degrees the—political, economic, social, intellectual, religious, cultural, or legal—national context in great Western powers at particular times, with a particular focus on international legal professionals and their influence on the making and shaping of different areas of international law.[50] As is also the case among legal historians working on domestic settings, many of these shorter or longer works are "written in the style of legal biography" in order to show that "a subject's early life, background and experience had an impact on their legal ideas."[51] The extrapolation of this biographical approach to the history of international law has also been highlighted by Koskenniemi, who notes that some of these "newer histories seek to locate the jurists in their local environments as university professors, diplomats or counsels to governments, having institutional 'projects' of their own."[52]

While recent literature in international legal history shows that the reconstruction of the great historical mosaic of national histories of international law is gradually composed of uncoordinated contributions on disparate topics,[53] the focus on the life and works of international lawyers in historical context may also be the collective outcome of a specific programmatic intent to fill a historical lacuna, as can be observed in the case of the history of international law in Germany.[54] However,

[48] Nehal Bhuta, "A Thousand Flowers Blooming, or the Desert of the Real? International Law and Its Many Problems of History," in *The Cambridge History of International Law: The Historiograph of International Law Vol. 1*, edited by Randall Lesaffer and Anne Peters (Cambridge: CUP, 2024) 49–106, p. 101.

[49] see e.g. Benjamin Allen Coates, *Legalist Empire: International Law and American Foreign Relations in the Early Twentieth Century* (Oxford: OUP, 2016); Christopher Rossi, *Whiggish International Law Elihu Root, the Monroe Doctrine, and International Law in the Americas* (Leiden: Brill, 2019).

[50] See e.g. Weston Janis, *America* (n 8).

[51] Philip Bajon, Victoria Barnes, and Emily Whewell, "Global Legal Biography," *Comparative Legal History*, 9(2) (2021) 127.

[52] Koskenniemi, "A History" (n 43).

[53] Including, for instance, on the distinct main methodological approaches of French and German international legal scholarship over time. See e.g. Emmanuelle Jouannet, "A Century of French International Law Scholarship," *Maine Law Review* 61 (2009) 83; Felix Lange, "Between Systematization and Expertise for Foreign Policy: The Practice-Oriented Approach in Germany's International Legal Scholarship (1920–1980)," *EJIL* 28 (2017) 535.

[54] Like many of those included in the more than 40 volumes of the collection Studien zur Geschichte des Völkerrechts published since 2001, including many biographical historical works in context on many German international law scholars, starting with Florian Herrmann, *Das Standardwerk. Franz von Liszt und das Völkerrecht* (Baden-Baden: Nomos Verlag, 2001).

in other recent works, the research focus is not so much on the agency and historical influence of nationally situated international lawyers on international law-making and institution-building processes or on international judicial decisions[55] as on the collective impact of national individuals and institutions on the jurisprudential theoretical and historical international normative realm. In particular, such a legal–technical conceptually oriented approach is a feature of recent British historiography of international law. This is evidenced by the recent publication of an "anthology set" running to more than 3,000 pages of these so-called British contributions to international law[56] which aim to make apparent both British influences on international law and contributions to it through state practice, judicial decisions, the work of both domestic and international organizations, and individuals, whether through doctrinal works by legal scholars or by practitioners in public international law in multiple specialized regimes of international law.[57]

Although in-depth familiarity with language, history, and culture—including legal culture—may warrant that a national focus on some aspects of the history of international law requires a national author, this is not always the case. This is clearly illustrated by Koskenniemi's highly influential book-length works on the history of international law, which are ultimately nationally (or imperially depending on the epoch) framed intellectual histories in specific periods of Western great powers, including Spain, France, Britain, and Germany.[58] Koskenniemi's focus on the genre of international legal bibliography in the intellectual and historical context has had a great impact on the rise of biographically ridden investigations by other authors of the national histories of international law in Europe, both in great powers and in semi-peripheral nations. This having been noted, it is a particular—although not exclusive—feature of former great global imperial powers such as Britain and ones with global influence such as the US that their own national history of international law has also attracted authors coming from their former imperial colonies.[59] The national historiography of international law of such countries owes as much to such non-national authors as it does to the current or previous hegemonic positions of those nations in the history of international law.[60]

[55] See e.g. Philippe Sands, *East West Street: On the Origins of "Genocide" and "Crimes Against Humanity"* (New York: Alfred A. Knopf, Penguin Random House, 2016).
[56] Barrett and Gauci, eds, *British* (n 9).
[57] See Robert McCorquodale and Jean-Pierre Gauci, eds, *British Influences on International Law, 1915–2015* (Leiden: Brill, 2016); and also Barrett and Gauci, eds, *British* (n 9).
[58] Martti Koskenniemi, *The Gentle Civilizer of Nations: The Rise and Fall of International Law (1870–1960)* (Cambridge: CUP, 2001), and Martti Koskenniemi, *To the Uttermost Parts of the Earth* (Cambridge: CUP, 2021).
[59] Who are employed, or otherwise have studied, in their universities, See e.g. James Crawford, "Public International Law in Twentieth-century England," in *Jurists Uprooted: German Speaking Émigré Lawyers in Twentieth-century Britain*, edited by Jack Beatson and Reinhard Zimmermann (Oxford: OUP, 2004): p. 681.
[60] John Fabian Witt, "The View from The U.S. Leviathan: Histories of International Law in the Hegemon," in *The Cambridge History of International Law. The Historiography of International Law Vol I*, edited by Randall Lesaffer and Anne Peters (Cambridge: CUP, 2024).

A second category of new contributions to national histories of international law corresponds to Western European and increasingly also Eastern European semi-peripheral countries, including but not limited to Russia,[61] Spain,[62] Belgium,[63] Italy,[64] Greece,[65] the Netherlands,[66] the Nordic countries including Finland,[67] and Baltic countries such as Estonia.[68] On occasion, Europe[69] as a whole or sub-regionally and Eastern Europe[70] are taken as the geographical frame of reference, as reflected in a long series of intellectual portraits.[71] Although increasingly single- or multi-authored book-length scholarly treatments are devoted to their study, national histories of international law are, by definition, a work in progress in the sense that, as previously noted, it is in the nature of historical writing that they are progressively composed by the uncoordinated accretion of shorter contributions on specific peoples,[72] networks, events,[73] institutions, intellectual movements or periods,[74] and concepts, as well as on traditionally under-explored subjects. Included among the latter is the history of international law journals published in a country over time. Although traditional neglected in international legal history, these indeed "play a crucial role in framing research within a certain country"[75] and study of them in their historical context serves, furthermore, as a privileged gateway to delve deeper into specific "national" histories of international law.[76]

[61] Mälksoo, *Russian* (n 13).
[62] De la Rasilla, *In the Shadow* (n 11).
[63] Genin, *Le laboratoire belge* (n 10).
[64] Bartolini, A *History* (n 12) Eloisa Mura, *All'Ombra di Mancini. La disciplina internazionalistica in Italia ai suoi albori* (Pisa: ETS, 2017).
[65] Thomas Skouteris, *The Notion of Progress in International Law Discourse* (The Hague: T.M.C. Asser Press, 2010), 39–92.
[66] Henri de Waele, "A New League of Extraordinary Gentlemen? The Professionalization of International Law Scholarship in the Netherlands, 1919–1940," *EJIL* 31(2020) 1005, doi: 10.1093/ejil/chaa063.
[67] Martti Koskenniemi, "Diplomats, Professors, and Then Some: Notes for a History of International Law in 20th Century Finland Special Issue: A Nordic Approach to International Law?" *Nordic Journal of International Law* 85(2016) 322, doi: 10.1163/9789004343597_004.
[68] Lauri Mälksoo, "The Science of International Law and the Concept of Politics: The Arguments and Lives of the International Law Professors at the University of Dorpat/Iur"ev/Tartu 1855–1985," *British Yearbook of International Law* 76(2005) 383, doi: 10.1093/bybil/76.1.383.
[69] Peter Hilpold, ed., *European International Law Traditions* (New York: Springer, 2021).
[70] See e.g. Stefan Troebst, "Eastern Europe's Imprint on Modern International Law," in *History and International Law*, edited by Annalisa Ciampi (Cheltenham: Edward Elgar Publishing, 2019): p. 22.
[71] The EJIL series "European Tradition of International Law" expands more than two dozen symposia.
[72] Sometimes in unexpected ways, like in e.g. Leão Soares Pereira and Niccolo Ridi, "Mapping the 'Invisible College of International Lawyers' through Obituaries', *LJIL* 34 (2021) 67, doi: 10.2139/ssrn.3695028.
[73] See e.g. Carlos Fernandez Liesa, *La Guerra Civil española y el Derecho internacional* (Madrid: Civitas, 2014). Carlos Fernandez Liesa, "La guerra civil española y el derecho internacional," *Revista Española de Derecho Internacional* 61 (2009) 75.
[74] Vagts, "International Law in the Third Reich" (n 36).
[75] Giulio Bartolini, "What is a History of International Law in Italy For? International Law through the Prism of National Perspectives," in *A History of International Law in Italy*, edited by Giulio Bartolini (Oxford: OUP, 2020): p. 13.
[76] Otto Spijkers and others, eds, *Yearbooks in International Law: History, Function and Future 2019* (The Hague: T.M.C. Asser Press, 2021).

2.4 National Histories of International Law in Non-Western Countries including China

A third category of new contributions to national histories of international law concerns non-Western countries, and in particular histories of both historical and emerging great non-Western powers such as the Ottoman Empire,[77] Japan,[78] India,[79] or Brazil.[80] This rise of national histories of international law of non-Western countries was partly inspired and influenced by post-colonial/third world approaches to international law (also known as TWAIL) which, as Bhupinder S. Chimni notes, "proceed on the assumption that a reliable history of international law cannot be written without taking into account the narratives emanating from nations that were the objects of colonial oppression."[81] However, on occasion there is an overlap between the national frame and works which adopt a more "contributionist" approach, including, in particular, from Latin America[82] (where, as already noted, the regional "contributionist" genre has a long tradition both in general terms[83] and regarding specific historical events)[84] and Africa,[85] or which delve into the concept of regional traditions and increasingly also sub-regions such as East Asia.[86] Moreover, in other cases, following a tradition initiated, as previously noted, in the interwar periods, there is an overlap between the national frame and scholarship produced in a common language[87] with racial–cultural

[77] See e.g. Mustafa Serdar Palabiyik, "International Law for Survival: Teaching international law in the late Ottoman Empire (1859–1922)," *Bulletin of the School of Oriental and African Studies* 78 (2015) 271, doi: 10.1017/S0041977X14001037.

[78] See e.g. Yasuaki Onuma, "Japanese International Law in the Prewar Period: Perspectives on the Teaching and Research of International Law in Prewar Japan," *Japanese Annual of International Law* 29 (1986) 31; Yasuaki Onuma, "Japanese International Law in the Postwar Period-Perspectives on the Teaching and Research of International Law in Postwar Japan," *Japanese Annual of International Law* 33 (1990) 25.

[79] See e.g. Bhupinder S. Chimni, "International Law Scholarship in Post-Colonial India: Coping with Dualism," *LJIL* 23 (2010) 23. See also Carl Landauer, "Lather, Rinse, Repeat. The Historical Returns of International Law," *Jus Gentium: Journal of International Legal History* 9 (2024) 329–370.

[80] See e.g. George Bandeira Galindo, ed., *Direito Internacional no Brasil: Pensamento e tradição: Volume 1 and 2* (Rio de Janeiro: Lumen Juris, 2021).

[81] Chimni, "International Law" (n 12), p. 16.

[82] See e.g. Juan Pablo Scarfi, *The Hidden History of International Law in the Americas* (Oxford: OUP, 2017); also Arnulf Becker Lorca, *Mestizo International Law: A Global Intellectual History, 1850–1950* (Cambridge: CUP, 2015).

[83] See e.g. Jesus Maria Yepes, "La contribution de l'"Amérique latine au développement du droit international public et privé," *RCADI* 32 (1930), p. 691, doi: 10.2307/2190006

[84] Antônio Augusto Cançado Trindade, "Latin America and the II Hague Peace Conference of 1907," in *Latin America and the International Court of Justice: Contributions to International Law*, edited by P.W. Almeida and J. Sorel (London: Routledge, 2016), p. 28.

[85] See e.g. Jacob Zollmann, "African International Legal Histories–International Law in Africa: Perspectives and Possibilities," *LJIL* 31 (2018) 841, doi: 10.1017/S0922156518000468.

[86] Matsuhuo Yanagihara, "Significance of the History of the Law of Nations in Europe and East Asia," *RCADI* 371 (2014)

[87] See e.g. Société française pour le droit international, *Gallerie des internationalistes francophones*, available at https://www.sfdi.org/galerie_internationalistes/ (accessed 10 January 2024).

particularities[88] or with religion-based communities, such as Islam, spread over vast geographical areas[89] as the analytical parameters of international legal history.

In this context, China is increasingly close to entering a category of its own because of the fast pace of substantive additions in recent years, which is an indirectly presentist testimony to China's rising status in the international legal order.[90] Indeed, new studies related to the "encounter" between China and the West are particularly abundant in the wake of a recent emphasis on historicizing the role of international law in connection with Western imperialism and in relationship to its manifestations in China. As seen in the present book, contributions range from works on unequal treaties - with its regimes of extraterritoriality including foreignconcessions - to other works on the strategic appropriation of, and acculturation to, the language of international law by Chinese intellectual elite members as a reaction to them over time. However, although the present volume provides valuable additions to both these and other topics there are still few detailed studies on the relationship of China with international law during the Republican period[91] and even fewer studies devoted to the Cold War period, including during the Cultural Revolution, and no less decisively its aftermath.

The existing studies and, in particular, those included in the present volume, are net contributors to a clearer and distinct periodization in the relationship of China with international law. Indeed, a longue durée contextualist historical perspective on China's relationship with international law reveals that this relationship has traversed four distinct historical stages over roughly the past 200 years. First, a millennia-long prolonged period characterized by the traditional Confucian vision of world order known as 天下 (Tianxia or All under Heaven) of Sinocentric isolation from the West and its law of nations crowned by a loosely hierarchical tribute system premised on the cultural superiority of the "Central Realm" in East Asia which was presided by the Chinese emperor as the "Son of Heaven" was followed by a phase of defensive acculturation into international law during the height of Western formal imperialism in Asia. This phase, then, overlapped with a second period of strategic appropriation and adaptation to international law by Chinese foreign policy elites, as illustrated by the participation of Qing Dynasty officials in The Hague Peace Conferences (1899 and 1907) and, later, the involvement of the Republic of China in the League of Nations and its active participation in the foundation of the United Nations. However, the establishment of the PRC (1949) marked the beginning of a new third stage of ideological rejection influenced by

[88] See e.g. Liliana Obregón, "Between Civilisation and Barbarism: Creole Interventions in International Law," *Third World Quarterly* 27 (2006): p. 815, doi: 10.1080/01436590600780136.

[89] Khaled Ramadan Bashir, *Islamic International Law. Historical Foundations and Al-Shaybani's Siyar* (Cheltenham: Edward Elgar Publishing, 2018).

[90] Carrai, *Sovereignty* (n 15). Anthony Carty and Janne Nijman, eds, *Morality and Responsibility of Rulers: European and Chinese Origins of a Rule of Law as Justice for World Order* (Oxford: OUP, 2018).

[91] Ryan Mitchell, *Recentering the World: China and the Transformation of International Law* (Cambridge: CUP, 2022).

the Marxist tenets of the Soviet theory of international law of Western imperialism and "bourgeois" international law. Following the Sino-Soviet Split (1957), this orientation evolved into a Sinocentric conception of socialist international law, positioning China as the self-appointed champion of post- colonial nations and revolutionary values during the decolonization era. Yet, once again, the "reform and opening up" in the late 1970s prompted a fourth new phase of formally legalistic yet asymmetrical reintegration of China into international legal order, alongside a parallel Chinese move to international institutions. Since the onset of Xi's "New Era" in the 2010s, this on-going phase has been marked by renewed assertiveness and globalist undertones. Somewhat closing the historical circle in China's relationship with international law initiated by the first Opium War (1839–1842), this new tendency reveals the dawn of a process of reverse acculturation of international law to China as this, having risen to become a great power, seeks to partly reshape in its image, as all Western great powers have cyclically done before it, the international legal system *from within.*

Another area to which the development of new histories of international law in China contributes is that of intellectual biographical studies of individual Chinese characters in the history of international law, which had long been absent, notwithstanding some exceptions, including some with a particular focus on the educational experiences of some of them.[92] An example of such an endeavor which casts light on the twice invisible college of international lawyers in twentieth-century China is how the study of the national dimension of the history of international law in China enables light to be cast on the international legal biographies of highly influential Chinese international lawyers who constituted the first and second generations of "masters" of international law in China in the twentieth century. Included among them are prominent international law professors, scholars, and even international judges such as Wang Chung-hui (1881–1958), Wellington Koo (1888–1985), Zhou Gengshen (1889–1971), Xiang Zhejun (1892–1987), Li Haopei (1906–1997), Ni Zhengyu (1906–2003), Han Depei (1911–2009), Wang Tieya (1913–2003), Zhao Lihai (1916–1996), and Chen Tiqiang (1917–1983), to mention but a few of those who are included in this book yet rarely feature in the still predominantly Western-centric history of international law. This situation is further compounded in the case of the study of the contribution of Chinese women to international law, an area to which this volume offers, in fine, a seminal launchpad for further research. Last but not least, while there has also been disappointingly little in terms of a Chinese historiography of international law—until recent contributions began to bridge the existing knowledge gap in this domain[93]—it

[92] See e.g. Li Chen, "A Forgotten Proponent of a League of Nations and his Contributions to International Law," *Leiden Journal of International Law* 35 (2022) 245–263, doi: 10.1017/S0922156522000140.

[93] Maria Adele Carrai, "Historiographies of International Law from a Chinese Perspective," Clio@Themis [Online], 18 | 2020, Online since 01 June 2020, http:// journals.openedition.org/cliothemis/302; doi: 10.35562/cliothemis.302 (last accessed 1 January 2024).

is hoped that by reintegrating the study of the history of international law in China in a global historiographical context, this book would contribute to bolstering developments with the potential to open new vistas of knowledge in the new global historiography of international law.

2.5 The National Lens in the History of International Law: Promises and Perils

From the perspective of the epistemological completeness of the history of international law, there are multiple normative, sociological, methodological, and historiographical arguments in favor of using the national lens to research the history of international law. However, as this section examines, there also perils or pitfalls associated with the rise of a focus on the national in historical writing about international law, including but not limited, as we shall later see, to those of fostering nationalistic or nativist perspectives and promoting "hidden Eurocentrism."

From a normative perspective, research on national histories of international law provides historical granularity to the study of the normative evolution, regarding both general international law and more specifically the relationships of differently positioned nations with each of the specialized areas of international law in different moments in its history. Moreover, researching national dimensions of the history of international law allows for the deepening of existing knowledge of the conceptual and theoretical components of international law in a historical perspective while evidencing the relationship of mutual interpenetration between the national and the international in the making and shaping of the international legal order. More broadly, it also encourages attention to, and deeper investigations into, the international legal national history of countries that have been largely underrepresented in international legal scholarship (in particular, but not only, small states), thus enabling a more detailed study of the normative development of international law from multiple national perspectives.

From a sociological perspective, the use of national historical lenses in international legal history may be key to unearthing little-known yet nationally influential international law characters from semi-peripheral and peripheral locations who have remained hidden in the overgrown shadow of its over-familiar and predominant Western figures. Among these multiple hidden or invisible *dramatis personae* of the history of international law are also included women, whose contributions to international law have long remained undervalued.[94] Focusing on the national dimensions of international law not only contributes to developing

[94] Janne Nijman, "Marked Absences: Locating Gender and Race in International Legal History," *EJIL* 31(2020) 1025, doi: 10.1093/ejil/chaa072. See Immi Tallgren, ed., *Portraits of Women in International Law: New Names and Forgotten Faces?* (Oxford: OUP, 2023).

international legal biography across historically underrepresented national and regional areas but also helps to demythologize and provincialize the canonization of both classic and contemporary Western authors whose influence has largely benefited from conditions of political, economic, and military hegemony. Besides addressing the historical invisibility of many relevant individual actors, the focus on national histories enables the application of a prosopographical and network theory methodology which, in turn, can show the complicity of some international lawyers with imperial and totalitarian projects, including Nazism and fascism, but also with totalitarian regimes during the time of "real communism," and their influence in promoting different international legal doctrines over time.[95] However, nationally framed investigations do not need to be limited to the "dark sides" of the history of international law; they equally enable research on some of its "brighter" sides, including, for instance, on pioneering international lawyers or scholars working on such matters as international human rights law or international environmental law in their own national contexts, often at their own personal risk.

The complementary advantages of using a national lens in studying the history of international law from a historiographical and methodological perspective include that research on national histories of international law fosters the unearthing of archival resources and other materials which have broadly remained underresearched to date. In addition, national histories can make more apparent the existence of multiple national periodizations of international law based on events (e.g. civil wars, colonial encounters, regime changes, independence, etc.) that are often more relevant at the national level than the traditional periodizing landmarks often constructed around Western-associated events. Indeed, due to the analytical centrality of periodization in historical research, historians of international law have traditionally divided the historical evolution of their discipline "into historical periods built around conventional turning points, or stereotypical context-breaking events"[96] (e.g. the Discovery of America, the Treaty of Westphalia, the Congress of Vienna) of international character, which then serve as "temporal porticos through which" to "contemplate different historically and normatively intertwined international contexts."[97]

Against this background, the study of the historical national context allows the development of alternative national periodizations, as seen in Section 4 in the case of China, focused on specific national events as a launch pad for the "formation of new formerly unknown periods"—a task that can be considered "an essential

[95] Christian Joerges and Navraj Singh Ghaleigh, eds, *Darker Legacies of Law in Europe: The Shadow of National Socialism and Fascism Over Europe and Its Legal Traditions* (Oxford: Hart Publishing, 2003). See also Emmanuelle Tourme-Jouannet and Iulia Motoc, eds, *Les doctrines internationalistes durant les années du communisme réel en Europe* (Paris: Société de législation compare, 2012).

[96] Ignacio de la Rasilla, "The Problem of Periodization in the History of International Law," *Law and History Review* 37 (2019) 275, doi:10.1017/S0738248018000445.

[97] Ibid.

part of historiographical innovation."[98] Moreover, exploring national histories of international law can profitably be combined with new innovative methodologies in the history of international law. Cultivating them may, for instance, get us a bit closer to answering intriguing questions such as "what might we learn about international law if we began with objects, things and material culture,"[99] thus contributing to fulfilling the promise of bringing about new "expansions of international legal study," including through "an education of the senses,"[100] by revealing what "is marginalized or forgotten in our narrow focus on textual interpretation."[101] Indeed, while the study of texts has dominated the history of international law, the study of national histories also offers new opportunities to embrace the "material turn" in neighboring disciplines, thus allowing national histories of international law to engage, for instance, with the role "of objects and nonhuman infrastructures" in its development.[102]

However, as already noted, there are also perils or dark sides associated with the rise of a focus on the national in historical writing about international law. These include, first, that the fostering of nationalistic perspectives of international law through historical writing occurs when national histories do not clearly dissociate themselves from the nationalist, apologist, hagiographic, and racialized national histories of international law of the past and also from "contributionist" and "patriot-culturalist" ones, the main purposes of which are to highlight the contributions of the national legal culture, or of the nationals of one specific country, to the conceptual and/or technical knowledge-pool of international law. Needless to say, at a time of a global rise of the "radical right"[103] and its considerable implications for the shaping of international law,[104] a national history of international law can also nurture the wrong type of identitarian or nativist national tradition or national conception of international law, including by fostering the perpetuation of nationalistic myths in international law or enabling the "whitewashing" of the past, in particular in places where archival and/or other restrictions, including censorship, are still in place.[105] On the bright side, however, it is against the homogenizing and monolithic perspectives of older national "traditions" in

[98] Peter N. Stearns, "Periodization in World History Teaching: Identifying the Big Changes," *The History Teacher* 20 (1987) 561–562, doi: 10.2307/493757.

[99] Jessie Hohmann and Daniel Joyce, eds, *International Law's Objects* (Oxford: OUP, 2018), p. 1.

[100] Carl Landauer, "The Stuff of International Law" *EJIL* 32 (2021), p. 1076, doi: 10.1093/ejil/chab067.

[101] Hohmann and Joyce, *International Law's Objects* (n 99), p. 3.

[102] Daniel Ricardo Quiroga-Villamarin, "Beyond Texts? Towards a Material Turn in the Theory and History of International Law," *Journal of the History of International Law* 23 (2020), pp. 466–500.

[103] Jens Rydgren, *The Oxford Handbook of the Radical Right* (Oxford: OUP, 2018).

[104] See e.g. Martti Koskenniemi, *International Law and the Far Right: Reflections of Law and Cynicism* (The Hague: T.M.C. Asser Press, 2019).

[105] As Peter Hilpold cautions, this "might even call to mind long-overcome struggles and ambitions, politically incorrect ideas and ideologies." Peter Hilpold, "What Are and to What Avail Do We Study European International Law Traditions?" in *European International Law Traditions*, edited by Peter Hilpold (New York: Springer 2021): p. 1.

international law, which were composed with reference to the most commonplace identifiers of the national which have been largely romanticized and decontextualized over time, that the modern focus on the national dimensions of international law can break new ground by making far more apparent the political, ideological, and methodological dividing lines which existed—and have largely increased in contemporary times—within nationally situated epistemological communities of international law scholars. This greater modern diversity is the outcome, first, of specialization, which has led to a rise of transnational epistemological communities of international lawyers across different specialized international legal regimes. Second, diversity is also a result of the transnational impact on international law scholarship of a diverse array of "scientific/intellectual movements" understood, according to the characterization of Scott Frickel and Neil Gross, as "collective efforts to pursue research programs or projects for thought in the face of resistance from others in the scientific or intellectual community."[106]

It is also worth highlighting that even when histories of international law involving the colonial histories of great powers are approached through the application of global historical lenses to myriad "encounters" between Western and non-Western peoples and transnational networks across vast spaces, or even certain specific areas, this still risks fostering new variants of historiographical and epistemological "hidden Eurocentrism" and also, although this has been less remarked, "hidden US-centrism."[107] Indeed, one of the paradoxical outcomes of post-colonial historical narratives in international law is that deepening of the history of international law "of the rest" has also led to an even greater deepening of historiography of international law regarding the West and, in particular, great Western powers over recent years. For noted post-colonial international law scholars and self-styled representatives of TWAIL (Third World Approaches to International Law) such as Antony Anghie, this is however seen as almost a positive development, insofar as it unearths, in his view, a "global history of the world" which he defines as "one that is sensitive to the many connections between the First and Third Worlds and the constitutive significance of the non-European world to the creation of Europe itself."[108] However, there are some obvious difficulties with a post-colonial historiographical perspective of international law almost exclusively focused on the imperial West, including because, to begin with, such a strong focus on it occludes the hugely important constitutive role of relationships between non-Western peoples regarding their own national histories of international

[106] Scott Frickel and Neil Gross, "A General Theory of Scientific/Intellectual Movements," *American Sociological Review* 70 (2005) 205, doi: 10.1177/000312240507000202.

[107] As seen by the great extent to which recent research on the history of international law in Latin America has fostered a new focus on the history of international law in the United States: Scarfi, *Hidden History* (n 89).

[108] Antony Anghie, "EJIL Foreword: Rethinking International Law: A TWAIL Retrospective", *EJIL* 34 (2023) 54, doi: 10.1093/ejil/chad005.

law. By providing far greater attention to regional, sub-regional, and bilateral relationships among non-Western countries, national histories of international law are, thus, well positioned to correct a fundamental blind spot in the historiography of international law of many non-Western nations and regions in both the long and the short term. This noted, in doing so, attention should also be paid to avoid letting "methodological nationalism" in through the back door by, somewhat, forcing all histories of different polities that were not nations into Eurocentric categories. This propensity was already indicated by Dipesh Chakrabarti when he noted that the histories of post-colonial countries "tend to become variations on a master narrative that could be called the history of Europe."[109]

2.6 Conclusions

This chapter has surveyed a contemporary turn to the national in the history of international law with reference to three main categories: histories of great Western powers, of semi-peripheral Western countries, and of non-Western countries, paying particular attention to the contributions to the national turn to the new histories of international law in China. It has also highlighted that the national dimension of the history of international law can illuminate hitherto neglected aspects of the study of the history of international law in its normative, sociological, methodological, and historiographical dimensions, both for general public international law and also increasingly for substantive specialized areas of research and state practice. However, while there are many arguments favoring a renewed use of the national lens in researching the history of international law, these are also some risks, including, as noted in Section 5, furthering "nationalistic" and "nativist" approaches to international law, a perpetuation of nationalistic myths, and fostering of "hidden Eurocentrism" or a whitewashing of the past.

Moreover, the national turn in the history of international law, which has been illustrated by the renewed research focus on the national dimensions of international legal history in different countries and regions surveyed in Sections 2 and 3, suggests that this may provide a fulcrum for the emergence of comparative international legal history as an interdisciplinary field of study. Indeed, in the same manner that "legal history and comparative law ... are considered the building blocks of comparative legal history,"[110] comparative international legal history can be envisaged to build on, on the one hand, the great substantive and methodological enhancement international legal history has experienced in recent years,

[109] Dipesh Chakrabarty, *Provincializing Europe: Postcolonial Thought and Historical Difference* (Princeton: Princeton University Press 2000).

[110] Agustin Parise, "Comparative Legal History," in *Elgar Encyclopedia of Comparative Law*, edited by Jan M. Smits, Jaakko Husa, Catherine Valcke, and Madalena Narciso (Cheltenham: Edward Elgar Publishing, 2023): p. 357.

including its hitherto underexplored national dimensions, and on the other hand, the emerging development of "comparative international law" (CIL) as a field of study. In particular, advocates of CIL have highlighted its many potential positive contributions to the study of contemporary international legal affairs, including *inter alia* because it draws attention to scholarly work and international legal materials beyond the contemporary *lingua franca* and because its cultivation also fosters "multi-perspectivity" among international law scholars by enabling them to take "cognizance of which socializing factors and incentives influence their approaches to international law ... and how things might look different from other perspectives."[111]

The comparative history of international law (CHIL) is a particularly promising new research direction for international legal history because engaging with the comparative method alongside the axes of synchronicity and diachronicity in the history of international law would help to bring both comparative lawyers and comparative historians on board the interdisciplinary province of what has come to be known as the "turn to the history of international law." While the CHIL would not be cultivated by specialists in these areas alone, their engagement would surely further contribute, as has happened with representatives from other disciplines in the past, to the breadth and depth of the "historical turn" in international law.

Illustrations of the potential of the emerging field of comparative international legal history range from the macro-systemic global historical level down to some potential specific applications of CHIL, such as those involving the comparison of international legal phenomena in the same space but at different times or (but equally building on a detailed knowledge of national histories of international law) micro or macro comparative investigations with attention to the differences and commonalities among two (or more) spaces at the same time. Indeed, the broad scope of comparative history (or histories) of international law encompasses, as Lesaffer has pointed out, the global macro-international legal historical level, thus including "all systems and traditions of international law from various regions and periods."[112] However, Lesaffer's holistic approach to CHIL, while particularly helpful to diachronically dispel the "master narrative of the historiography of modern international law," can also more specifically include—but should not be limited to, following Parise—"research across the vertical and horizontal axes"[113] of time and space. An example of this would be a "study that compares" an aspect of international law "in a given space, yet in different time periods."[114] More

[111] Anthea Roberts, *Is International Law International?* (Oxford: OUP 2017), p. 22.

[112] The 13 volumes of The Cambridge History of International Law promise to lay deeper scholarly foundations for its always delayed fulfilment, as indeed Lesaffer points out when he pledges that "its concluding volume may take the comparative exercise a step further": Lesaffer, "Scale and Humility" (n 5) 35.

[113] Parise, "Comparative Legal History" (n 110).

[114] Parise, "Comparative Legal History" (n 110).

ambitiously, another illustration of this methodology would encompass comparative study of coetaneous national histories of international law of two (or several) countries over either the long or the short term and (or alternatively) in relation to specific historical events. Possibly, attention could also be paid in this context to how these engagements with international law and institutions shaped the course of mutual relations of these two (or several) nations and their domestic legal orders.

This basic framework could provide a point of departure for, *verbi gratia*, a comparative history of international law of China and the United States during the Cold War, or by the same token a comparative history of international law of Nicaragua and Turkey in the interwar period, since, as this latest and perhaps not so particularly far-fetched example attempts to illustrate, the possibilities for comparison in the history of international law extend across all regions and across all periods, from the dawn of any inter-polity recorded legal history to the most recent historical developments. These kinds of studies are bound to unearth new historical connections, entanglements, circulations, or interactions through the adaptation of the international legal historical realm to what Richard Drayton and David Motadel have called the "two key modes" of global history.[115] These are, first, the "connective approach," which would then seek to investigate "how" international legal "history is made through the interactions of geographically (or temporally) separate historical communities,"[116] and second, the "comparative approach," which would in turn seek "to understand" international legal historical "events in one place through examining their similarities with and differences from how things happened somewhere else."[117] These new explorations, including the writing of histories of international law in China as well as the study of histories of international law across many other unexplored national realms, are also bound to foster a greater engagement with the social dimensions of international legal history that a marked stress on "elite" intellectual history has often occluded in the construction of narratives about the historical evolution of international law across time and space.

[115] Richard Drayton and David Motadel, "Discussion: The Futures of Global History," *Journal of Global History* 13 (2018) 1–21, p. 3, doi: 10.1017/S1740022817000262.
[116] Ibid.
[117] Ibid.

PART II

BEFORE AND BEYOND THE ENCOUNTER: FROM SINO-CENTRIC ISOLATION TO DEFENSIVE ACCULTURATION TO INTERNATIONAL LAW

3
International Law in China
From Ancient Times to the Encounter

Xinyu Huang

'普天之下，莫非王土，率土之滨，莫非王臣'.
Where'er their arch the heavens expand,
The king can claim the land below.
Within the sea-bounds of the land,
All at his summons come or go.

The She King, 1046–771 BCE
James Legge trans. (London: Trübner & Co., 57 & 59, Ludgate Hill, 1876), p.247

3.1 Introduction

These famous lines from a poem in the *She King* (*Shijing*), or the *Book of Ancient Poetry*, offer a vivid reflection of how the ancient Chinese understood the world. The ancient Chinese comprehension of the world and the nation was fundamentally different to modern perspectives. In Chinese, *zhong* (中) refers to the centre, the heart of the world. The Chinese term for China, *zhongguo* (中国), signifies the central state, beyond which lie regions inhabited by barbarian tribes. In this framework, 'All under Heaven' (天下, *Tianxia*) and the 'Hua–Yi Distinction' (华夷之辨, *Huayizhibian*) persisted as core concepts in the mainstream Chinese worldview until the last imperial dynasty, the Qing (1644–1912).

Although the people of imperial China were not entirely ignorant of the world and other regions, a new understanding of the world based on the Westphalian system and sovereign states only began to form in the last few decades of Qing rule, that is, the late nineteenth and early twentieth centuries.[1] This abandoning of old notions and embrace of new ideas was directly related to external pressures faced by the Qing dynasty. The Opium War of 1840 was the first time that ancient

[1] Ge Zhaoguang, 'Seeing the World through Traditional Chinese Historiography'(传统中国史学中的世界认识)', (2021) 3(5) *Wen Shi Zhe* pp. 5–11.

Xinyu Huang, *International Law in China* In: *Histories of International Law in China*. Edited by: Ignacio de la Rasilla, Jiangyu Wang, and Congyan Cai, Oxford University Press.
DOI: 10.1093/oso/9780198888345.003.0003

Chinese civilization had faced challenges from a powerful foreign civilization in hundreds of years. Encounters with Western civilizations, forced the Chinese to awaken from the illusion of China being the central kingdom. Some enlightened Chinese individuals began to face reality and realized a need to understand the world beyond their borders, thereby initiating a wave of learning from the West. In the late nineteenth and early twentieth centuries, China's ruling class and intellectual elite began to adopt new perspectives on understanding the international community, marking a transition from the old traditional system to a new West-dominated international system. This process was termed 'opening eyes to the world' (开眼看世界, *kaiyan kan shijie*).

Due to the complexities and pressures of wars and international treaty negotiations in that era, the ruling class and intellectual elite in China were forced to ponder a fundamental question: what is international law, and how should it be understood? Today, matters of international law can be seen daily on television news channels and are naturally considered a means of governing international relations and resolving disputes in almost all international conflicts. However, 150 years ago in China, the situation was entirely different. When the societal elite members who had almost exclusively studied the Confucian classics encountered the 'international law' system which originated from a completely different social and political background, they initially chose to use the traditional Confucian classics to acquire new concepts and theories. It is not surprising that people sought to understand new things through familiar ones. For example, Chinese scholars coined a new term, 'Spring and Autumn International Law' (春秋公法, *Chunqiu gongfa*), attempting to connect wartime events in the Spring and Autumn period (770–481 BCE) with Western theories of international law. These new terms, derived from widely accepted Confucian classics, not only made it easier for the Chinese public of the time to accept modern international law but also provided a unique Chinese perspective on modern international law.

During the long imperial era, ancient China developed concepts and tools to interact with the world and nations. In fact, ancient China was quite sophisticated in handling 'foreign' affairs. Although these ideas and practices were not formally labelled 'international law' at the time, they should not be considered irrelevant to modern international law. Put another way, we should not take it for granted that the Chinese had no knowledge of handling 'foreign' affairs, which by their nature belonged to modern international law. However, if we further explore the extent to which China's understanding of modern international law was influenced by traditional knowledge, two questions arise. First: how did people in traditional Chinese society view the world and China? Second: how did this understanding affect China's diplomatic affairs?

This chapter explores these questions from multiple perspectives. Given international law's constitutive role in the contemporary global order—and its critical function in China's strategic and diplomatic calculus—re-examining its historical context and exploring how the concept of international law integrates with Chinese indigenous resources are of utmost significance. The academic community has already engaged in extensive discussions on this topic. This chapter, through a careful review of previous discussions, revisits the origins of international law in Chinese history. The first and second sections of this chapter analyse the core concepts in Chinese worldview and ideology, especially the 'All under Heaven' system. How the ancient Chinese and others understood the world differed. The 'All under Heaven' system guided diplomatic practices in ancient Chinese history. The remaining sections of this chapter focus on the institutions and practices related to the 'All under Heaven'-guided diplomacy of rulers, including the tribute system, wars and alliances, and the establishment of institutions to interact with other countries. Thus, a complete picture of ancient Chinese international law thoughts and practices is presented. These traditions contribute to modern Chinese society's understanding of international law.

3.2 'All under Heaven'

'All under Heaven', *tianxia* (天下) in Chinese, was central in the ancient Chinese worldview. In the earliest verifiable historical records, the *tianxia* concept initially represented a directional notion. Oracle bone inscriptions mention directions such as east, south, west, north, and centre—along with integrative descriptions of 'the four directions' (四方, *sifang*) and 'the four territories' (四土, *situ*)—making the Shang dynasty (1600–1050 BCE), from which these inscriptions came, the most reliable starting point for contemporary studies of the concept of *tianxia*. These descriptions represent an attempt to grasp the entirety of the world from the perspective of that time.[2]

For the ancient Chinese, heaven, *tian* (天) in Chinese, tangibly existed. Heaven was like a round tent covering the square earth. The entire world and human society were beneath heaven and were enveloped by it. This understanding can be found in the sacrificial and divination activities of Chinese people two thousand years ago.[3]

During the Spring and Autumn (770–476 BCE) and the Warring States periods (475 BCE–221 BCE), use of the term 'All under Heaven' became more frequent

[2] See Chen Mengjia, *Review of Yin Ruins Oracle Inscriptions* (殷虚（墟）卜辞综述) (Beijing: Zhonghua Book Company, 1988), p. 319; Hsing I-tien, 'Tianxia Yijia—The Chinese Concept of All under the Heaven (天下一家——中国人的天下观), in *The Eternal Torrent: New Discourse on Chinese Culture, The Origins* (永恒的巨流——中国文化新论·根源篇) (Taipei: Linking Publishing Company, 1981), pp. 433–78.

[3] Wang Ke, *Nation and State: The Genealogy of China's Multi-Ethnic Unified State* (民族与国家：中国多民族统一国家的系谱) (Beijing: Chinese Social Sciences Academic Press, 2001), p. 10.

and its meaning was expanded. In the Confucian classic *Shang Shu* (Book of Documents, 772–476 BCE), the term *tianxia* evolved into a more complex and nuanced concept. For instance, in the chapter *Lv Xing*, it is written that if a punishment from heaven does not reach its extreme, then the common people will not have good political order in the world.[4] The term also appears in inscriptions on unearthed Chinese bronzes from this period.[5] In this time 'All under Heaven' had two meanings. One refers to the human world governed by heaven, and the other refers to the various vassal states that were subject to the Zhou King.[6] In addition to the two meanings mentioned above, the concept of 'All under Heaven' was also extended to a political and geographical scope influenced by the Zhou kings plus even broader areas not under their influence.[7] In accordance with Zou Yan during the Warring States period, the area under heaven was vast, and China was just a small part of it.[8]

In a broad geographical sense, 'All under Heaven' usually includes *Jiu Zhou* (九州) and *Si Hai* (四海). This originated in the geographical view of *Yu Gong* and also a chapter in *Shang Shu*. While different historical texts offer varying definitions of *Jiu Zhou* and *Si Hai*, generally speaking they refer to the areas in which the Chinese and the Barbarians respectively resided.[9] From a narrow perspective, *tianxia* only refers to *Jiu Zhou*, which is China. This is also shown in some historical materials from the Warring States period.[10] Therefore, at the geographical level 'All under Heaven' has two interpretations. In a broad sense, the scope of *tianxia* includes the entire world under the dominion of heaven, while in a narrow sense *tianxia* is equivalent to China.

It is worth noting that 'All under Heaven' is not an entirely geographical concept but rather a political–geographical one. The 'All under Heaven' system was also used to explain political power and legitimacy. In ancient China, rulers were believed to have received a mandate from heaven and they governed all areas as its representatives. In other words, the legitimacy of rulers stemmed from their alignment with the commands of heaven. So, what does it mean to align with the mandate of Heaven?

[4] The original phrase is '天罚不极，庶民罔有令政在于天下'. *Shang Shu*, trans. Wang Shisun and Wang Cuiye (Beijing: Zhonghua Shuju, 2012), p. 331.

[5] Li Xueqin, *Studies of Chinese Ancient Civilization* (中国古代文明研究) (Shanghai: East China Normal University Press, 2006), pp. 126–136.

[6] Zhang Qixian, 'The Formation of Two Key Concepts: "Zhongguo" and "Tianxia" ("中国"与"天下"概念探源)' (2009) 3 *Soochow Journal of Political Science* 169, pp. 169–243.

[7] Ibid.

[8] Zou's worldview is well recorded in Shiji by Sima Qian. See Sima Qian, *Shiji* (史记) (Beijing: Zhonghua Shuju, 2014), p. 2344.

[9] Zhou Zhenhe, *Sixteen Lectures on Chinese History and Politics* (中国历史政治地理十六讲) (Beijing: Zhonghua Shuju, 2013), p. 78; Yang Nianqun, 'A Comparative Analysis of Views on "China", "Grand Unity" and "Tianxia" ("大一统"与"中国""天下"观比较论纲)' (2021) 2 *Historiography Bimonthly* 73, pp.73–87.

[10] Zhang Qixian, 'The Formation of Two Key Concepts: "Zhongguo" and "Tianxia"'.

In orthodox Confucianism, which was the mainstream for thousands of years of the imperial period in China, Confucius, Mencius, and Xunzi all discussed how a king, as the son of Heaven (天子, *tianzi*), should govern all areas under heaven. Confucius believed that the core of complying with the mandate of Heaven lies in the virtue of the monarch.[11] According to him, the kings Wen and Wu and the Duke of Zhou of the Western Zhou dynasty were virtuous rulers, and people were willing to follow their leadership. Mencius, on the other hand, emphasized benevolent governance, believing that with benevolent governance unity and peace would be achieved under Heaven.[12] Xunzi, who came after Confucius and Mencius, emphasized the establishment of ritual order to create order and govern under Heaven. Conversely, if a king loses the mandate of Heaven, he will lose legitimacy to rule under Heaven.[13]

Therefore, All under Heaven is a complex political–geographical concept. Under Heaven there are the king as Son of Heaven, feudal lords, and the people. The Son of Heaven is mandated by Heaven to rule the central state of China, with vast regions surrounding it, and on the periphery are barbarians and exiles.[14] Unlike modern nation-states with clear boundaries and sovereignty, ancient states existed in uncertainty in terms of borders, ethnic composition, and historical lineage.[15] The political territories and cultural spaces of ancient China radiated from the centre to the periphery, forming a rather stable cultural community. After unification reforms of language, script, ethics, customs, and political systems during the Qin and Han dynasties, China, centred around Han ethnicity, had a relatively clear sense of identity and cultural recognition. In this time, nevertheless, the ethnic elements, spatial factors, and boundary factors of the nation were quite weak.[16] The All under Heaven system is a manifestation of this.

This worldview prevailed until the twentieth century, though during the Song dynasty (960–1279) the northern regions were occupied by other dynasties, with the Khitans, Western Xia, and the Song emperor all being called monarchs. This was quite different to the Tang dynasty (618–907), when only the Tang emperor was regarded as king and the surrounding nations were given autonomy. This shift

[11] *Lun Yu* (论语), ed. Yang Bojun (Beijing: Zhonghua Shuju, 1980), p. 174.

[12] ‘Liang Hui Wang,’ in *Meng Zi* (孟子), eds Yang Bojun and Yang Fengbin (Wuhan: Chongwen Shuju, 2023), p. 10.

[13] ‘Wang Zhi,’ in *Xun Zi* 荀子, ed. Zhang An (Changchun: Jilin University Press, 2021), p. 88.

[14] See Bai Tongdong, ‘Tianxia: A Confucian Model of State Identity and Global Governance’, in *Challenges of Globalization and Prospects for an Inter-civilizational World Order* (Cham: Springer, 2020), pp. 969–982. See also June T. Dreyer, ‘The “Tianxia Trope”: Will China Change the International System?’ in *The Making of China’s Foreign Policy in the 21st Century* (Routledge, 2018), pp. 67–83; Zhao Tingyang, *All under the Heaven: The Tianxia System for a Possible World Order* (天下的当代性：世界秩序的实践与想象) (Beijing: Zhongxin Press, 2016), pp. 18–48.

[15] For the difference between the modern nation-state and nations in the ancient period, see Benedict Anderson, *Imagined Communities: Reflections on the Origin and Spread of Nationalism* (London: Verso, 2016).

[16] See Ge Zhaoguang, *Zhai Zi Zhongguo: Rebuilding Narratives of China* (宅兹中国：重建有关“中国”的历史论述) (Beijing: Zhonghua Press, 2011), pp. 26–29.

was quite significant. From this point on, the 'All under Heaven' system, along with the parallel concepts of the Hua–Yi Distinction and the tribute system, transitioned from practical strategies to imagined orders.[17]

3.3 The Hua–Yi Distinction

The 'Hua–Yi Distinction', also known as the Sino-barbarian dichotomy, is a historical Chinese concept that differentiated a culturally defined 'China' from 'outsiders' in a cultural or ethnical sense. It was another important cultural and political concept in ancient China, reflecting the self-identity of the Chinese and their attitude to the outside world. This section explores the meaning of the Hua–Yi Distinction, its relationship with the 'All under Heaven' concept, and how both drove the formation of an international order in the ancient East Asian world.

The central issue here concerns the differentiation between 'Chinese' (also known as *Hua* 华, *Hua-xia* 华夏, or *Xia* 夏) and 'outsiders' (*Yi* 夷, conventionally barbarians). There is prevailing scholarly agreement on the criteria used to differentiate between the two. It is not based on ancestry but instead on cultural factors.[18] Some scholars equate the notion of valuing *Hua* over *Yi* with a sense of superiority inherent in Sinocentrism. For example, Wang Gengwu considers that the Hua–Yi concept was gradually formed over a long period, with cultivation of a sense of cultural pride that then transformed into a practical moral constraint.[19] Hsing I-tien suggests that regardless of whether terms such as 'barbarians' inherently carry a derogatory meaning, in their long-term usage they have been gradually endowed with a cultural derogation, which started with the Zhou people.[20] Nevertheless, the distinction between *Hua* and *Yi* is not clear-cut and static. It is not based on territory or bloodlines but more on cultural identity.

The possibility of mutual transformation within the Hua–Yi distinction is especially noteworthy. In the 'All under Heaven' system, the capital city where the king resided was considered the centre of the world and the hub of civilization. The further away from this centre in geographical space, the more desolate the area becomes and the more barbaric the inhabitants are perceived to be, with a lower level of civilization. Through a process of cultural exchange and influence, however, 'barbarians' with lower levels of civilization could gradually learn Chinese culture, integrate into China, and become '*Hua*'.

[17] Ibid, pp. 44–47.

[18] Qian Mu, *Introduction to the History of Chinese Culture* (中国文化史导论) (Beijing: Jiuzhou Press, 2011), p. 39.

[19] Wang Gungwu, 'Early Ming Relations with Southeast Asia: A Background Essay', in *The Chinese World Order: Traditional China's Foreign Relations*, ed. John Fairbank (Cambridge, Massachusetts: Havard University Press, 1968), pp. 34–62.

[20] Hsing, 'Tianxia Yijia', p. 447; Luo Zhitian, *Nationalism and Modern Chinese Thought* (民族主义与近代中国思想) (Taipei: The Grand East Book Company, 1998), p. 2.

There was a focus on transforming *Yi* into *Hua*, although the transition itself was largely influenced by the situation of the state. As Hsing says:

> Those who emphasise the Hua–Yi distinction often focus on transforming *Yi* into *Hua*. If it is about transforming *Yi* into *Hua*, it aligns with those advocating the world as one family. When China's strength was abundant and full of confidence, such as during the prosperous periods of the Han, Tang, Ming and Qing dynasties, the ideal of considering the world as one family often emerged, leading to an expansionist tendency in Chinese culture and political power. When China's national strength was weak or threatened by outsiders … a more insular stance emphasising the separation of Hua and Yi would prevail.[21]

Xu Jilin echoes this and suggests that a rising great empire is usually very confident and pays little attention to the separation between *Yi* and *Hua*.[22]

Throughout the Chinese dynasties, people regarded the surrounding ethnic groups as an indispensable part of 'All under Heaven'. Almost all dynasties welcomed political, economic, and cultural exchanges with surrounding ethnic groups and the process of 'Sinicization'. Examples of this are abundant in the 2,000-year-long history of China. It is noteworthy that even during the powerful periods of the Han and Tang dynasties, Imperial China never used its overwhelming power to force the barbarian regions to accept Chinese civilization. However, with severe external crises and the constant threat of dynastic collapse, when the 'All under Heaven' system temporarily became impractical, the Hua–Yi distinction would be highlighted, emphasizing the incompatibility between *Yi* and *Hua* and the subjectivity of Chinese culture.[23]

Furthermore, the Hua–Yi distinction connected foreign affairs with domestic power dynamics. It acted as an ancient type of international relations system centred on the Chinese empire, where the core was the extension of Confucianism from domestic affairs to foreign relations. This system required neighbouring and distant regions to establish peaceful and stable relationships with the Chinese empire under the framework principles of Confucian doctrines such as 'ruler and subject, father and son'. The tribute system was the fundamental guarantee of these relationships.[24]

In short, the Hua–Yi distinction was a crucial cultural and political concept in ancient China encapsulating the self-identity of the Chinese nation and its stance

[21] Hsing, 'Tianxia Yijia', p. 465.

[22] Xu Jilin, *Jiaguo Tianxia: Individual, National, and Global Identities in Modern China* (家国天下:现代中国的个人、国家与世界认同) (Shanghai: Shanghai Renmin Press, 2011), pp. 56–58.

[23] See Xu, 'Cosmopolitanism, the Debate of the Civilized and the Uncivilized, and Their Variations in Modern Times' (2012) 6 *Journal of East China Normal University (Philosophy and Social Sciences)* 66, pp. 66–75.

[24] See He Fangchuan, 'An Essay on Huayi Zhixu ('华夷秩序'论)' (1998) 6 *Journal of Peking University (Philosophy and Social Sciences)* 30, pp. 30–45.

towards 'foreigners'. It underscored the shift from a mere bloodline distinction to a cultural one, suggesting that cultural assimilation could transform barbarians into a part of Chinese civilization. This idea was intertwined with the broader notion of 'All under Heaven' and it influenced the formation of the ancient East Asian international order. The possibility of mutual transformation in this distinction highlights a dynamic process of cultural integration and separation, which depended on China's strength and external relations.

3.4 The Tribute System

The 'All under Heaven' system and the Hua–Yi distinction allowed ancient Chinese to distinguish between China and peripheral regions, and between the Chinese and others. In the ancient Chinese worldview, China was considered the centre, with other nations and polities being peripheral. These peripheral others were expected to express respect and loyalty to the centre. The tribute system was established in response to this. With this system, other nations and polities would pay tribute to the Chinese imperial court in exchange for political recognition, trading rights and cultural exchanges. The tribute system had a long-standing presence in Chinese history, influenced the international relations landscape of East Asia and Southeast Asia, and formed an international order based on rituals and cultural exchange. With the development of modern international relations and the intervention of Western powers, however, the traditional tribute system gradually encountered challenges, and eventually declined in the eighteenth century.

The prototype of the tribute system was the ancient Chinese system of *jifu* (畿服), or the enfeoffment system. The monarch of the Central Plains was regarded as the king of 'All under Heaven' areas. He directly administered the central regions and enfeoffed local rulers in the peripheral areas beyond his direct jurisdiction. This structure echoed the All under Heaven system. With historical evolution and cultural diffusion, the central dominion expanded continually. After embracing the social organization and ideological cultural concepts of the central regions, many peripheral regions gradually became integrated in the core. This continual transformation is part of what is known as the Hua–Yi distinction. It reflected the dynamic process of cultural assimilation and expansion of the civilized sphere.[25]

The Qin dynasty (221–206 BCE) saw the unification of China under a single centralized rule. This empire introduced a structured administrative system known as the '*junxianzhi*' (郡县制), which divided the country into prefectures and counties. The Qin also standardized the tax system throughout the territory. Later imperial dynasties largely adhered to the Qin administrative framework and

[25] Gu Jiegang, 'Jifu, 畿服', in *Studies on History* (Beijing: Zhonghua Shuju, 1963), pp. 1–19.

maintained direct control over their territories.[26] Although peripheral regions inhabited by ethnic minorities maintained a great degree of autonomy, they participated in tributary and investiture rituals with the central government as a symbol of the supremacy of the central authority over these territories. However, the relationship was complex and extended beyond a simple vassalage arrangement.

As the dynasties in the Central Plains fell in the third century, the existing enfeoffment system collapsed with it. In this era, several competing regimes frequently asserted their legitimacy as rulers of the central realm and sought tributes from neighbouring countries. Some states paid tributes to multiple major powers at the same time. In this time, the Central Plains regime developed a *jimi* (羁縻) system to replace the original enfeoffment system. The most significant characteristic of this was that enfeoffment was no longer just a royal title but an official position identical to that of a direct subordinate. After the Song dynasty (960–1279), in addition to tribal chiefs, the central government appointed supervisory officials. This gradually evolved into the *tusi* (土司) system in the subsequent Yuan dynasty (1206–1368), effectively incorporating peripheral areas in the scope of governance.

Starting with the fourteenth century, under the rule of the Ming dynasty (1368–1644), when the tribute and enfeoffment system was at its most developed, the Ming dynasty's list of tributary states in Southeast Asia included Siam, Champa, Java, Malacca, Cambodia, Sulu, and Sumatra. In 1371 Ming Emperor Zhu Yuanzhang clearly stipulated that the Korean Peninsula, Japan, and fifteen other countries were to be considered neighbouring countries not to be conquered. This was known as the 'non-conquest of the barbarians' (*bu zheng zhi yi* 不征之夷).[27] In this system, the Chinese Central Plains regime became the central focus, with each tributary state acknowledging this central position and becoming a vassal to the central regime. In this period, in addition to countries with direct contact with the Ming Dynasty, such as Korea, Vietnam, and Burma, under the policy of generous gifts and meagre returns, other countries paying tributes to the Ming dynasty gradually evolved into a form of trade exchange. Especially under the mid-to-late Ming's maritime prohibition policy, tributes almost became the only means for these countries to conduct trade with China.[28]

However, the peak was followed by a swift descent. A sign of the decline of the tribute system came at the end of the sixteenth century, under the reign of the Ming. In 1592, no longer acknowledging the supremacy of the Ming, Japan dispatched troops to Korea. The Japanese began to strengthen their self-awareness

[26] Edgar Kiser and Yong Cai, 'War and Bureaucratization in Qin China: Exploring an Anomalous Case' (2003) 68 *American Sociological Review* 511, pp. 511–539.
[27] *Ming History* 明史 (Beijing: Zhonghua Shuju, 1974), p. 8407.
[28] See Wang Gungwu, 'Early Ming Relations with Southeast Asia: A Background Essay', in J. K. Fairbank (ed.), *The Chinese World Order*(Cambridge, Massachusetts: Harvard University Press, 1968), pp. 34–62; Zhang Feng, 'Rethinking the "Tribute System": Broadening the Conceptual Horizon of Historical East Asian Politics' (Spring 2009) 2 *Chinese Journal of International Politics* pp. 545–574.

and considered Japan a nation on an equal footing with China. A similar process also took place in Korea in the later period. Under the Ming, Korea largely recognized the superiority of China. When the Qing state replaced the Ming administration, Korea refused to acknowledge the supremacy of the Qing court since it believed conquerors were barbarians.[29] In the southeast regions, the Ming court practised a policy of political non-action towards neighbouring countries, as Western powers gradually conquered China's Southeast Asian neighbours.

In 1644, the Qing dynasty established its rule over mainland China and retained the Ming's tribute system. The Qing clearly divided its interactions with neighbouring tribes and countries between two different institutions: the Court of Colonial Affairs (理藩院, *lifanyuan*) and the Ministry of Rites (礼部, *libu*). Relations with regions such as Mongolia and Tibet, considered domestic affairs, were managed by the Court of Colonial Affairs, while relations with countries such as Korea, Japan, and Russia, regarded as foreign states, were handled by the Ministry of Rites.[30]

This unique international order based on the tribute system has been interpreted very differently by scholars. Fairbank's core assumption of Sinocentrism of the Chinese tribute system highlights the perceived centrality and superiority of the Chinese empire, which viewed the world as China-centred, with foreign trade considered a favour by the emperor done to other rulers.[31] Takeshi Hamashita focuses on the economic aspect of the tribute system, and employs the theory of international economic circles to analyse China-centric tribute trade and its connection to modern Asia's economic landscape. He contends that tribute trade constituted the system's fundamental essence, and that the East Asian tribute trade system of the sixteenth to eighteenth centuries served as a mediator for regional and global trade. Hamashita combined the Hua–Yi distinction with the Sinocentric view and the tribute system, and argued that China's foreign relations were essentially an ongoing expansion of domestic governance outward.[32] The classical English school of international relations defines a mechanism as 'a set of customs and practices formed to achieve common goals'. From this perspective, the tribute system organized the relationships between China and other countries, and constituted the fundamental mechanism of their cooperation. From the pre-Qin period, the East Asian international system led by ancient Chinese dynasties

[29] Ge, *Zhai Zi Zhongguo*, pp. 11≠–13.

[30] Charles O. Hucker, *A Dictionary of Official Titles in Imperial China* (Beijing: Peking University Press, 1989 repr.): p. 86; Peter C. Perdue, 'A Frontier View of Chineseness', in Giovanni Arrighi et al., eds, *The Resurgence of East Asia: 500, 150 and 50 Year Perspective* (London: Routledge, 2003), pp. 51–77.

[31] See J. K. Fairbank and S. Y. Teng, 'On The Ch'ing Tributary System' (1941) 6 *Harvard Journal of Asiatic Studies* 135, pp. 135–246; J. K. Fairbank, 'Tributary Trade and China's Relations with the West' (1942) 1 *The Far Eastern Quarterly* 129, pp. 129–149.

[32] Takeshi Hamashita, *International Opportunities in Modern China: the Tribute Trade System and the Modern Asian Economic Circle* (近代中国的国际契机：朝贡贸易体系与近代亚洲经济圈) (Beijing: Zhongguo Shehui Kexue chubanshe, 1999), p. 38.

was based on the tribute system. It involved a China-centred power structure, diplomatic norms with vassals adopting Chinese law, and a cultural identity shaped by Confucian values.[33]

This system, which was deeply embedded in the historical and cultural evolution of imperial China, functioned as a comprehensive solution to the challenges of conflicts, coexistence, and cooperation, thus setting the Chinese order apart from other global regions. Central to ancient Chinese foreign relations, the tribute system operated on hierarchical principles that positioned China as the cultural and political centre with the surrounding nations in a subordinate role. Over time it evolved to encompass various forms of interaction in which peripheral states paid tributes in exchange for political recognition and trading privileges. Notable for its flexibility and ability to adapt to shifting international dynamics, the system, grounded in notions of cultural superiority and Sino-centrism, acted as both a diplomatic and economic mechanism. It played a key role in promoting regional peace and stability, and shaped international relations in East and Southeast Asian until its decline in the eighteenth century.

3.5 Meng

The 'All under Heaven' system defined the international structure in ancient China and further extended its significance beyond the tribute system to include the formation of *meng* (盟), which served purposes akin to treaties and alliances in modern international society. Unlike a Western-originated alliance and treaty, a product of modern international law, the ancient Chinese concept of *meng* emphasized religious and moral obligations and put importance on ethical bonds and ritual ceremonies. Breaking a *meng* would lead to loss of honour and fear of divine punishment rather than formal legal consequences. While the concept of international treaties as we understand it today was not explicitly mentioned in historical Chinese records, the establishment of *meng* to regulate relations between states was a consistent aspect of Chinese history.

The *meng* concept in Chinese indicates that parties unite around common interests or to achieve certain common goals. It originates from the blood oath customs in earlier tribal times, which later evolved into a ceremony of swearing oaths with deities as witnesses. Establishing a *meng* involved using religious and divine beliefs as the highest authority to guarantee fulfilment of political and military agreements made between two or more parties. Initially, *meng* were mostly

[33] See Zhou Fangyin, 'Equilibrium Analysis of the Tributary System', (2011) 2 *Chinese Journal of International Politics* 147, pp. 147–178; Martin Wight, *Systems of States* (Leicester: Leicester University Press, 1977), p. 143.

used in marriages, serving as a means for clans to form stable marital unions; only later were they applied to public affairs.[34]

Meng were widely adopted in imperial China, in both peaceful and warring periods. In Chinese history, periods with a central authority ruling over the entire country were much longer than those of chaos and division. After Qin Shi Huang, the first emperor in the Qin dynasty, who unified the six states in 221 BCE and established a centralized government,[35] the Han Dynasty (202 BCE–220 AD), the Tang Dynasty (618–907), the Song Dynasty (960–1279), the Ming Dynasty (1368–1644) and the last imperial dynasty, the Qing Dynasty (1644–1912), were all periods of unified rule. The centralized monarch resided in the capital and acted as the head of a vast central government ruling over vast territories with the help of a bureaucracy. During these unified periods, wars mainly consisted of threats from border regions and domestic rebellions. The periods of chaos and division were primarily the Warring States period (476–221 BCE), the Three Kingdoms period (220–280), the Northern and Southern Dynasties (304–439), the Five Dynasties and Ten Kingdoms period (907–979) and the Ming–Qing transitional period (mid-seventeenth century). In these times, China had two or more regimes confronting each other, and therefore wars were frequent. Whether in periods of unified rule or division, *meng* were quite common, such as those formed between Chinese emperors and tribal leaders or foreign monarchs during unified times, and between rival rulers in times of division.

During the Warring States period, *meng* gradually developed into a formal means for feudal states to enter into agreements, and even alliances with each other. In this time, the feudal lords were only nominally under the control of the Emperor of the Zhou dynasty, but they had great autonomy. *Meng* can be roughly divided in four types: treaties between the emperor, as the 'son of heaven' (*tianzi*) and feudal lords (诸候, *zhuhou*); treaties among feudal lords; treaties between feudal lords and district grand masters (卿大夫, *qindafu*); and treaties among the district grand masters. *Meng* can be bilateral, such as the Jinchu Alliance (晋楚之盟, *jinchu zhi meng*) between Jin and Chu feudal lords in 546 BCE. Signed at the site of the Stone Tablet, it confirmed the spheres of influence and balance of power between the two dominant forces, and symbolized their standoff and peaceful co-existence. In addition, *Meng* can also be multilateral as is exemplified by the Kuiqiu Alliance (葵丘会盟, *kuiqiu huimeng*) in 632 BCE, which Duke Wen of Jin (晋文公, *jinwengong*) invited several feudal lords to participate in. With this alliance Jin established his supremacy. This was a pivotal event in which Duke Wen of Jin, one of the Five Hegemons of the Spring and Autumn Period (春秋五霸, *chunqiuwuba*,

[34] See Yan Liyuan, 'International Concept of Rites and Law: Tribute and Treaty in Qing Dynasty China 国际礼法观：清代中国的朝贡与条约', (2021) 1 *Nanjing University Law Journal* 85, pp. 85–100.

[35] The warring times in Chinese imperial history. See generally John K. Fairbank, *The Chinese World Order: Traditional China's Foreign Relations* (Massachusetts: Harvard University Press, 1968).

Duke Huan of Qi, 齐桓公, Duke Xiang of Song, 宋襄公, Duke Wen of Jin, 晋文公, Duke Mu of Qin, 秦穆公and King Zhuang of Chu, 楚庄王), established hegemony through diplomatic means. To establish a *meng*, certain procedures were followed. These usually included setting a date, choosing a location, ordering, drafting the alliance document, performing a blood oath, proclaiming to the deities, preserving the alliance document, and hosting a banquet.[36]

China entered a prolonged era of unified rule after the Spring and Autumn and Warring States periods. The focus of international relations therefore shifted from internal power struggles among feudal lords under the Zhou dynasty to external relations involving the unified dynasties, and interactions between coexisting dynasties in periods of division. In the period of great unification (大一统, *dayitong*), the forms of foreign interactions were diverse. For instance, in the Tang Dynasty there were multiple conflicts and resolutions between the Tang Dynasty and Tibet. After prolonged warfare between these two parties, the two sides signed several peace treaties by means of *meng*, among which the most famous was the '*Qingshui huimeng*' (清水会盟), which was signed in 783. After the treaty, peace was sustained between the Tang Dynasty and Tibet for several years. Moreover, the Tang actively pursued a policy of marital alliances in which they used royal marriages with neighbouring ethnic groups and states as a means to secure peace and stability. The marriage of Princess Wencheng of the Tang Dynasty to Tibetan King Songtsen Gampo was one of the most famous examples of this policy. It helped solidify a peaceful relationship between the Tang Dynasty and Tibet.[37]

Unlike many treaties in the unified period, the 'Chanyuan Treaty' (澶渊之盟, *chanyuanzhimeng*, 1004), which was signed between the Song and the Liao dynasties during a period of division suggests a sophisticated practical facet of the ancient Chinese All under Heaven system. In the twelfth century, the territorial extent of China's dynasties was dynamic. The southern region was ruled by the unified Song dynasty, the northwestern area was ruled by the Western Xia (西夏, *xixia*), while the Sixteen Prefectures of Yan and Yun in the northern part were occupied by the Liao. Both the Liao and Western Xia claimed the title of Emperor on equal terms with the Song.

In December 1004, the Liao and the Song exchanged oaths and signed the 'Chanyuan Treaty', in which they referred to each other as the Southern and Northern dynasties and agreed to a 'brotherly alliance' (兄弟之盟, *xiongdizhimeng*), which ended a prolonged twenty-five-year military conflict. The Chanyuan Treaty maintained peaceful relations between the Song and the Liao established on a basis of equality and friendship. In this treaty, apart from the Song's unilateral tribute

[36] Tian Zhaoyuan, *A History of Meng* (盟誓史) (Nanning: Guangxi People's Press, 2000), pp. 8–10, 76–80.

[37] Lin Guanqun, *Jade and War: A Study of the History of Tang–Tibetan Relations* (玉帛干戈: 唐蕃關係史研究) (Taipei: Linking Publishing Company, 2016), pp. 149–153, 446–449.

payments, all the other terms were mutually effective. In addition, the monarchs of the two states recognized each other as brothers, and diplomatic envoys were sent between them with equal and cautious details of etiquette.[38]

After the Chanyuan Treaty, the Song and the Liao established a relationship unlike the traditional tribute system which particularly emphasized political equality, although it highlighted the Song's economic and military weaknesses. However, the tribute trade and mutual respect for the border boundary maintained peace, and the Chinese dynasties lost their superior honour, receding to become the 'Southern Dynasty' (南朝, *nanchao*).[39] During the negotiations on the Chanyuan Treaty, a letter from the Song indicated that while the Song and the Liao had not previously been allies, the Song court hoped they could become such, and the term 'two countries' (两国, *liangguo*), indicating two equal nations, often appeared in subsequent state letters. This led to an emphasis on national boundaries. The Chanyuan Treaty explicitly stipulated 'no crossing of borders', reflecting the importance the Song gave to national boundaries.[40]

The Chanyuan Treaty constituted a great challenge to the 'All under Heaven' system and the tribute system. The original respect for the Central Plains and the Song's need for recognition by the less civilized could not explain the situation. Nevertheless, the openness of the 'All under Heaven' system allowed the Song to enhance their legitimacy in another way.[41] A sense of ethnic and national boundaries began to form during the Song dynasty. This period of the Song Southern dynasty and the Liao Northern dynasty was the first time that imperial courts in China had a consciousness of equal diplomacy, with the delineation of borders, the amount of tributes, the equivalence of trade, and the etiquette of envoys all signalling the existence of 'others' and bringing a sense of crisis. This led the Song dynasty to start restricting border crossings and to increase its vigilance over the activities of people from other regions. It began to resist the entry of foreign religions, customs, and other civilizations, while promoting and exaggerating its own civilization.[42]

In ancient China, *meng* played a critical role in shaping the country's international order in the 'All under Heaven' system. Throughout the history of imperial China, states frequently adjusted their inter-state relations with *meng*, a practice persistent in periods of both unity and division. From unification under

[38] Huang Renyu, *Conversation on Chinese History by the Hudson River* (赫逊河畔谈中国历史) (Beijing: Jiuzhou Press, 2007), p. 125. See also, Paul Jakov Smith, 'The Fragility of Peace: Song China's Northwestern Frontier and Erosion of the Chanyuan Paradigm in the Mid-Eleventh Century' (2023) 1 *Journal of Chinese History* 1: pp. 1–29; Huang Chunyan, 'China's Tributary System and National Security in the Song Dynasty' (2020) 2 *Journal of Chinese* Humanities 149: pp. 149–170.

[39] Tao Jinsheng, *A Study of the History of Song–Liao Relations* (宋辽关系史研究) (Beijing: Zhonghua Shuju, 2008), pp. 16–29.

[40] Ibid, pp. 84–86.

[41] Zhao Tingyang, *The Tianxia System: An Introduction to the Philosophy of World Institutions* (天下体系：世界制度哲学讨论) (Beijing: China Remin University Press, 2011): p. 55.

[42] Tao Jinsheng, *A Study of the History of Song–Liao Relations*, pp. 8–10.

Qin Shi Huang in 221 BCE to the fall of the Qing Dynasty in 1912, China experienced longer periods of centralized governance than chaos. Grounded on strict ceremonies and rituals, *meng* varied from bilateral agreements, such as the Jinchu Alliance between Jin and Chu, to multilateral ones such as the Kuiqiu Alliance, according to the diplomatic strategies of the time. Notably, the Chanyuan Treaty between the Song and Liao dynasties in 1004 marked a shift in the 'All under Heaven' system, moving towards a state of recognizing mutual sovereignties, emphasizing national boundaries and acknowledging the presence of 'others'. This indicated a nuanced understanding of China, the world, and international relations.

3.6 Foreign Affairs Institutions

Although the 'All under Heaven' system may appear distinct from today's international community, the imperial Chinese courts acquired experience in managing interactions with external affairs and *huawai* people (*huawairen*, 化外人), a cultural concept denoting non-Han people from alien or barbarian polities. For instance, in the Tang Code, there is an article entitled '*huawai ren xiang fan*' and legal principles governed how the Tang legal system dealt with crimes that took place between foreign individuals without directly involving Chinese citizens.[43]

Institutions specialized in diplomatic affairs were founded in the central state of imperial China. The etiquette of ancient Chinese diplomatic activities was characterized by strict ceremonies and rituals, covering things such as the reception of foreign envoys, banquets, exchanges of gifts, and cultural exchanges. These activities not only highlighted the central role of ritual in Chinese society but also embodied a diplomatic philosophy centred on mutual respect and peaceful coexistence between states (国, *guo*).

3.6.1 The Diplomatic Department

Officials specifically responsible for diplomatic affairs appeared as early as the Qin dynasty. The Chamberlain for Dependencies (大鸿胪, *dahonglu*), a senior officer in the central government of the Han dynasty, was responsible for overseeing the reception of princes (王, *wang*) and marquises (候, *hou*) in the capital, maintaining genealogical records of non-imperial nobles, managing diplomatic relations with foreign leaders and regulating the conduct of officials and visitors during imperial audiences.[44] In the reign of the later North Bei Wei (386–534) dynasty, a

[43] Victor K. Fong, 'Law, Subjecthood, and State Control in Early Tang (618–755)' (Australian National University PhD Thesis, 2022), pp. 36–41.

[44] Charles O. Hucker, *A Dictionary of Official Titles in Imperial China*, p. 466.

specialized office in the central government with responsibility for diplomatic relations, the Court of Dependencies (鸿胪寺, *honglusi*), was founded.[45]

Starting with the Tang dynasty, foreign affairs offices underwent gradual improvements and could be broadly categorized in four main divisions: the department responsible for foreign relations, the reception office, the foreign trade management office, and the immigration office.[46] Beyond these specialized agencies, diplomatic affairs were also managed and coordinated by various government offices and departments within the Tang administration. In the Tang central state, the Secretariat (中书省, *zhongshusheng*) and Chancellery (门下省, *menxiasheng*) were responsible for drafting and reviewing diplomatic edicts. They also participated in the Emperor's meetings with foreign monarchs and ambassadors. The Department of State Affairs (尚书省, *shangshusheng*) was responsible for foreign affairs activities involving government orders.[47]

The Court of Dependencies (*honglusi*) was the main diplomatic office in the Tang and subsequent dynasties. It dealt with all diplomatic and minor ethnic affairs. The most important duty of this office was organizing foreign affairs rituals, since strict and complicated rules were established and developed in accordance with the tribute system and Confucianism.[48] In addition, the office had to help foreigners solve practical difficulties and try to meet reasonable requests they might make. For example, the Court of Dependencies had a special pavilion, the *Sifangguang* (四方馆), to host emissaries and important guests. The Court of Dependencies was equipped with a number of translators. A certain amount of money and gifts were given to guests who stayed in the pavilion.Also, foreign guests had privileges in marriages, funerals, inheritances, competitions, and so on. These affairs would be organized by the officers of the Court of Dependencies.[49] The duty of the Court of Dependencies also extended to collecting information on foreign countries, including on culture, geography, politics, customs and so on. These findings were regularly reported to the central government.

The Court of Dependencies continued to be the main diplomatic office until it was replaced with the Ministry of Ritual (礼部, *libu*) in the Ming and Qing Dynasties. In addition, in the Qing reign a new agency, the Court of Colonial Affairs (*lifanyuan*), was established. Unlike the Court of Dependencies and the Ministry of Ritual, the Court of Colonial Affairs focused on relations with the Mongols, Tibet, Kokonor, and tribal chiefs in Xinjiang region.[50]

[45] Ibid, p. 264.

[46] See Fang Yaguang, 'A Study of Foreign Affairs Institutions in the Tang Dynasty' (唐代外事机构论考), 1996 (2) *Journal of Chinese Historical Studies* 65 (1996), pp. 65–73.

[47] Fang Yaguang, 'Tangdai waishi jigou lunkao', pp. 65–66.

[48] Li Yunquan李云泉, *A Historical Discussion on the Tribute System: A Study of the External Relations System in Ancient China* (朝贡制度史论:中国古代对外关系体制研究) (Beijing: Xinhua chubanshe, 2004), p. 110.

[49] See Ma Guorong, 'On the Tang Honglu Temple' (唐鸿胪寺述论), (1999) 2 *The Western Regions Studies* 20, pp. 20–28.

[50] Charles O. Hucker, *A Dictionary of Official Titles in Imperial China*, p. 304.

3.6.2 Trade Commissioners

Foreign trade emerged at a very early stage in Chinese history, with significant developments such as the Silk Road dating back to the second century.[51] However, starting in the Tang Dynasty, foreign trade became heavily regulated, with trade commissioners being established to address concerns over national security and economic interests. The law only permitted trade in government-regulated mutual markets, with designated supervisors being stationed at specific border points. Under their oversight, Chinese and foreign merchants could engage in barter-based trade. The Tang administration prohibited Chinese and foreign merchants from trading in any other way, and violators were sentenced to imprisonment. The Director of Tribute Trade (互市监,*hushijian*), an office that supervised the mutual market, was created to take charge of mutual trade in northwestern fringe areas between ethnic minorities and foreign merchants.[52]

Regarding maritime trade with overseas regions, after a gradual increase of prosperity in the Tang dynasty, specialized supervisors and supervisory agents were also established. In 661 the Tang Dynasty court nominated a Maritime Trade Commissioner (市舶使, *shiboshi*) in Guangzhou, who was responsible for collecting tariffs from incoming trade ships, purchasing a certain amount of imported goods on behalf of the imperial court, managing tribute gifts and supervising trading. In 971, the Song administration set up an office called the Maritime Trade Commission (市舶司, *shibosi*) for maritime trade in Guangzhou. With the development of overseas trade, similar offices were set up in Hangzhou, Ningbo, Quanzhou, and Jiaozhou. In the Song dynasty the power of Maritime Trade Commissions was increased. They were authorized to issue certificates to merchant ships according to the goods they declared, the people on board, and the places they went to. In addition, the Commissions sent officials on board to check if there was contraband. They also presided over the sea festival. In 1080, an act ruled that tribute goods would not be shipped to the capital but would be sold where they were. The act enabled the Court to profit from tribute goods and further elevated the significance and status of the Maritime Trade Commission.[53] Government supervision of maritime trade was continued by the Ming and Qing courts, although maritime trade was largely limited due to concerns over smuggling and pirates.[54]

[51] Valerie Hansen, 'The Time Capsule of Silk Road History: The Dunhuang Caves', in *The Silk Road: A New History* (Oxford and New York: Oxford University Press, 2012), pp. 167–198.

[52] Charles O. Hucker, *A Dictionary of Official Titles in Imperial China*, p. 259.

[53] See Zhang Shen, 'Reconsidering the Function of the Song Maritime Trade Commission' (重评宋代市舶司的主要功能) (1998) 4 *Guangdong Social Science* 75 (1998), pp. 75–81.

[54] See Chen Xuewen, 'The Restriction on Maritime Affairs and Pirates' (明代的海禁与倭寇) (1983) 1 *Journal of China Social and Economic History* 30 (1983), pp. 30–38.

The establishment of foreign affairs institutions in ancient China suggests that there existed a well-established system of dealing with 'others' based on the 'All under Heaven' system, the Hua–Yi distinction, and the tribute system. In short, a view of the world and interaction with foreigners were in fact never missing in the eyes and lives of the ancient Chinese.

3.7 Modern Interpretations

The 'All under Heaven' system faded away along with the fall of imperial dynasties. However, discussions of the 'All under Heaven' system and modern interpretation of it never ceased. In the nineteenth century, a tumultuous period marked by Western colonial expansion and intense cultural clashes between China and the West, it became increasingly evident that the traditional Chinese perspective, built on the tribute system, was no longer sustainable to navigate the complexities of global interactions. After enduring a series of diplomatic humiliations, Chinese intellectuals were compelled to shift from their traditional worldview and turn to modern international law, which represented a new and evolving world order.

From the late Qing Dynasty and in the early Republic of China (ROC) era, a trend emerged that sought to establish a connection between international law and ancient Chinese pre-Qin history. This endeavour resulted in numerous research works exploring the concepts of 'Ancient Chinese Public Law' (中国古世公法) and 'Pre-Qin International Law'(先秦国际法). Although the Spring and Autumn and Warring States periods in China differed significantly from the early nineteenth century, when Qing rulers for the first time encountered Western powers and international society, in the era of intense capitalist colonial competition among great powers, they were intriguing analogies. The international landscape featured interactions between great and smaller powers and phenomena such as conflicts, hegemony, alliances, negotiations, and fragmentation that bore some resemblance to the dynamics of the Spring and Autumn and Warring States periods. Chinese intellectuals then naturally drew parallels based on these similarities. They tried to combine the profound legacy of Chinese ideologies and knowledge of international law.[55] This significantly shaped the country's perspective on international law, which also influenced the way China viewed itself in the world, its interactions with foreign states, and the development of its own international legal principles.

[55] See Xu Guoqi, *China and the Great War: China's Pursuit of a New National Identity and Internationalization* (Cambridge: Cambridge University Press, 2005), pp. 19–24; Lai Junnang, *International Law and China in the Late Qing Dynasty Period: Texts, Events and Politics* (国际法与晚清中国：文本、事件与政治) (Shanghai: Shanghai People's Publishing House, 2015), pp. 220–230.

Scholars in the subsequent period continued to explore the legacies from ancient China and developed various ways of defining the scope of 'All under Heaven'. One of the early attempts began in the 1920s. Discourse on the concept was primarily qualitative, based on interpretations of archaeological materials and classic texts from the pre-Qin era. In 1926 Japanese scholar Masayoshi Tazaki was the first to explore issues related to the Chinese view of 'All under Heaven'. He grounded his analysis on Confucian classical texts such as *Shangshu* (尚书), *Liji* (礼记), and *Zhouli* (周礼), arguing that 'All under Heaven' signified the world and infinite lands, implying the idea of limitless territory and the concept of unified rule under heaven.[56] Subsequently, Takeo Yamada defined 'All under Heaven' as China, bounded by the Four Seas,[57] while Toru Hiraoka in his analysis proposed a worldview of 'All under Heaven', suggesting that the concept of 'Heaven' formed during the Zhou dynasty embodied a consciousness transcending clans.[58]

Chinese scholars offered differing perspectives. Gan Huaizhen saw 'All under Heaven' as a political system constructed by China and other countries related to tributes and investiture.[59] Xu Jilin pointed out that 'All under Heaven' consisted of three concentric circles. The first two circles were areas directly administered by the Chinese emperor through the county system, and vassal states controlled through the tribute and investiture system, without considering the barbarian lands beyond the reach of Chinese civilization. Xu's view essentially represents a middle ground between the broad and narrow concepts of 'All under Heaven'.[60] Scholarly discussions on the concept of 'All under Heaven' also expanded from the political order in China to its impact on international order. Gao Mingshi summarized the principles of political order under 'All under Heaven' as a concentric circle, extending outward from the centre, the capital of China, and being roughly divided into three layers: inner subjects, outer subjects, and regions not yet subjected. He also proposed integration, governance, kinship, and moral transformation as four principles under the 'All under Heaven' system.[61] Wang Ke proposed a triple-layer 'All under Heaven' system, suggesting a universal worldview which

[56] See Tazaki Masayoshi, *'Ou-Dou' and 'Ten-Ka': Traditional Chinese Political Thoughts and Institutions* (Tokyo: Naigai Publishing, 1932), pp. 7–8.

[57] See Yamada Sumeru, '"All under Heaven" and the Formation of the Nation' (天下という觀念と國家の形成), in *Yamada Sumeru Chosakushū* vol. 1 (Tokyo: Meiji Shoin, 1981).

[58] See Hiraoka Takeo(平岡武夫), *The Conception of the Confucian Canon: A Philosophical and Historical Study of the Formation of the Confucian Canon* (経書の成立：天下的世界観) (Tokyo: Sōbunsha, 1983),155–216.

[59] Gan, Huaizhen, 'Rethinking East Asian Kingship and Worldview—With "Tianxia" and "China" as Keywords' (重新思考东亚王权与世界观——以'天下'与'中国'为关键词, in *The Concept of Tianxia and China in East Asian History*, ed. Gan Huaizhen (Taipei: National Taiwan University Press, 2007), pp. 26–27.

[60] Xu Jilin, 'Cosmopolitanism, the Debate of the Civilized and the Uncivilized, and Their Variations in Modern Times', pp. 55–56.

[61] Mingshi Gao, 高明士, *Exploration of World Order and Cultural Spheres: Focusing on the Politics and Education of Ancient East Asia* (天下秩序与文化圈的探索——以东亚古代的政治与教育为中心) (Shanghai: Shanghai Chinese Classics Publishing House, 2008), pp. 3–17.

transcended geography and clan ties. His analysis illustrates the historical reasons for China maintaining a multi-ethnic state structure.[62] Li Yangfan differentiated between the subjectivity and objectivity of the order of 'All under Heaven' since the former came from the imagination of the literati and the latter can be seen in institutions such as the tribute system.[63]

American scholars showed similar interest in how the All under Heaven system influenced the world order centred on ancient China, viewing it as a political structure opposing modern nation-states. Schwartz saw China's world order as characterized by 'universal kingship' and 'All under Heaven' embodying Sinocentrism.[64] Fairbank attempted to assess Chinese foreign relations theory and practice with modern Western language and contrasted 'All under Heaven' with Western nationalism. He observed that the loyalty and reverence of the Chinese people were directed to the Son of Heaven (*tianzi*) and his formalistic rule, instead of the state or nation. The Son of Heaven's influence transcended borders, encompassing all humanity but diminishing with distance from the centre of his power.[65] Following Fairbank's reasoning, Levenson focused on the cultural attributes of 'All under Heaven', arguing that monarchs, by receiving the Mandate of Heaven (天命, *tianming*), became terrestrial agents of 'All under Heaven'. Therefore 'All under Heaven' represented a universal authority. Confucians equated this monarch with the monarch of the entire world, justifying monopolization of this right with understanding of the Mandate of Heaven as reflected in ritual interactions with other ethnic groups.[66]

These studies underscore the academic discourse surrounding 'All under Heaven' in relation to the emergence of modern Chinese statehood. By contrasting it with modern China, these discussions explore how ancient Chinese conceptions of the state, world order, and ethnicity differ from those of contemporary China and even Western nations. Nevertheless, some discussions further extended to its possible contribution to current international law and political order.

Recently, reflecting on the negative impacts of globalization and the failure of current international conflict resolution mechanisms, and even rethinking

[62] Wang Ke, *Nation and State: The Genealogy of China's Multi-Ethnic Unified Nation*, p. 1.

[63] Li Yangfan, 'The Concept of the "Chinese Empire" and Its World Order: The Misunderstood Tianxia Order' (中华帝国'的概念及其世界秩序：被误读的天下秩序), 2015(2) *The Journal of International Studies* 28 (2015), pp. 28–48.

[64] Benjamin I. Schwartz, 'The Chinese Perception of World Order, Past and Present', in *The Chinese World Order: Traditional China's Foreign Relations*, ed. John Fairbank (Cambridge, Massachusetts: Harvard University Press, 1968), pp. 276–290.

[65] John King Fairbank, 'A Preliminary Framework', in *The Chinese World Order: Traditional China's Foreign Relations*, ed. John Fairbank (Cambridge, Massachusetts: Havard University Press, 1968), pp. 276–290.

[66] Joseph Richmond Levenson, *Confucian China and Its Modern Fate, Volume 1: The Problem of Intellectual Continuity* (CA: University of California Press, 1958), p. 104.

nationalism—a foundation of modern Western politics—scholars have attempted to seek theoretical support from 'All under Heaven'. Zhao Tingyang attempts to construct an 'All under Heaven' system to counter international conflicts which transcends the theoretical limitations of the nation-state and expands the primary political analytical units to the world and 'All under Heaven', to establish a universal order above the state system.[67] Gan Chunsong comes up with a 'family ethics-based national sentiment' and 'compassion-based order of all under heaven', and argues that the hallmark of the order of 'All under Heaven' is not the size of the governed territory but that it is based on a moral foundation and kingly politics, ultimately proposing eight kingly political ideas to resolve the dilemmas of globalization.[68] Xu Jilin puts forward a 'New Tianxiaism' doctrine founded on the basis of the 'All under Heaven' system, and believes that the root of mutual suspicion and doubts among countries today is the supremacy of nation-state consciousness. Therefore, the real solution lies in a mindset that counters nation-state consciousness, namely adhering to a decentralized de-hierarchical 'New Tianxiaism'.[69] Neo-Confucian scholars also enrich the implications of the 'All under Heaven' system from a philosophical perspective. For example, Huang Lisheng believes that 'All under Heaven' signifies that the world comprises multiple different levels of interconnected units, but also transcends the boundaries of these units, representing the highest level of personal relational situations and the broadest scope of action and thought. He calls for modern individuals to follow the fundamental principle of 'All under Heaven' since all things grow together without harming each other, achieving a balance between modern technological civilization and the natural ecological order.[70]

Scholars in modern period have further expanded the meaning of 'All under Heaven', viewing it as a symbol of international order and discussing its impact on and shaping of international relations and political frameworks in the context of globalization. The term 'All under Heaven' reflects the unique perspective of ancient and modern China in understanding the world and constructing international relations.

[67] Zhao Tingyang, *The Tianxia System: An Introduction to the Philosophy of World Institutions*, p. 264.

[68] See Gan Chunsong, *The Politics of Kingly Way and Universalism: The Academic Anthology of Gan Chunsong* (王道政治与天下主义：干春松学术论集) (Guiyang: Kong Xuetang Shuji Press Company, 2017).

[69] Xu Jilin, *Jiaguo Tianxia*, pp. 411, 437.

[70] Huang Lisheng, 'The Connotations and Contemporary Significance of Confucian "Tianxia" Thought' (儒家'天下'思想的内涵及其当代意义), in *The Collision of Traditional Chinese Culture and Modern Values*, ed. Junjie Huang (Beijing: Chinese Social Sciences Academic Press, 2003), pp. 230–262.

3.8 Conclusion

In September 1793, envoys representing King George III of the British Empire arrived in Beijing to negotiate diplomatic issues such as expanding trade and exchanging envoys with the Qing Empire. However, the Qing officials with whom they interacted were more concerned with titles than with trade or envoys. The Qianlong Emperor and his ministers put great emphasis on the rituals of the audience, the titles, and the language used in state letters. To them, the British envoys' visit was perceived as a tribute mission to celebrate the emperor's birthday.[71]

On the day of the audience, Macartney and Staunton in the British Embassy performed the agreed-upon ceremony of kneeling on one knee. However, later Chinese accounts falsely claimed that Macartney, overwhelmed by the emperor's presence, involuntarily knelt on both knees. This small disagreement over whether to kneel on one knee or both reflected the fundamental difference in perceptions between the British and the Qing: the British saw the visit as a matter of modern international diplomacy, while the Qing viewed it within the framework of the tribute system. At the time, the British embassy's understanding of the world order was based on modern international law, while the Qing Emperor and his ministers' view was rooted in the traditional Sinocentric world order, the international law in ancient China.

International law in ancient China was deeply rooted in the philosophical and cultural traditions of the time. In ancient China, the term 'China' was often more a perception regarding civilization rather than a strict geopolitical entity with clearly defined borders. As a result, Chinese people believed that neighbouring countries and neighbouring nations were less civilized and should pay tribute to and venerate China.[72] This understanding came from the 'All under Heaven' system. From this worldview, areas 'All under Heaven' consisted of the Han Chinese territory, vassal states in China's realm where ethnic groups practised self-governance, and foreign states located beyond China's borders.[73]

The term 'All under Heaven' in China has a rich connotation, evolved from an initial concept of geography to a multi-layered concept with political, cultural, and moral dimensions. Initially, 'All under Heaven' was understood as a concept of direction, encompassing the comprehensive space of east, south, west, north, and the centre. Subsequently, the concept expanded into the political realm during the Zhou dynasty and Qin–Han period, and became a way to describe territories or nations under the control of a unified authority, reflecting a spatial order and political authority from the centre to the periphery. At the same time, 'All under Heaven'

[71] See Earl H. Pritchard, 'The Kotow in the Macartney Embassy to China in 1793' (1943) 2 *The Journal of Asian Studies* 2, pp. 163–203. James L. Hevia, 'A Multitude of Lords: Qing Court Ritual and the Macartney Embassy of 1793' (1989) 2 *Late Imperial China* 72, pp. 72–105.

[72] Ge Zhaoguang, *Zhai Zi Zhongguo*, p. 45.

[73] Wang Ke, *Nation and State: The Genealogy of China's Multi-Ethnic Unified Nation*, p. 77.

was also seen as a moral and cultural space, thus emphasizing the widespread dissemination of moral governance and cultural influence.

In short, the 'All under Heaven' system shaped China's diplomatic and legal practices in history. It embodied a worldview that saw China as the centre of the world with a moral and hierarchical order under a celestial mandate. The Hua–Yi distinction further emphasized cultural superiority, categorizing others as either part of Chinese civilization (*Hua*) or barbarians (*Yi*). These principles underpinned the tribute system and the practice of *meng*, through which China distinguished itself from others and managed its international relations. This framework, while not labelled 'international law' in modern terms, contributed to the conduct of foreign affairs, treaties, and the establishment of a unique international order that influenced China's interactions with neighbouring states and beyond for thousands of years.

4

The Opium Wars, Extraterritoriality, and International Drug Control

Inge Van Hulle

4.1 Introduction

The Opium Wars (1839–1842 and 1856–1860) represent pivotal moments in the history of international relations between China and the West, particularly in the context of informal imperialism and the spread of Western notions of international law. Also, for contemporaries who analyzed the conflict, the armed conflicts raised a number of important legal questions. From the viewpoint of use of force law, the First Opium War brought to light questions concerning the legitimacy of the British resort to force and whether or not the outbreak of violence should be qualified as a reprisal or as an actual war. Furthermore, questions and doubts circulated about the proportionality of the British response. Perhaps most famously, the "Opium question" and the conflicts that ensued eventually led to a series of treaties that drastically altered the political and economic landscape of China, positioning the country within a framework of Western-imposed legal and trade obligations. The resulting treaties, particularly the Treaty of Nanjing (1842) and the Treaty of Tianjin (1858), laid the foundation of what Chinese nationalists in the twentieth century would term as "unequal treaties."[1] While the treaties themselves contained a myriad of stringent obligations imposed on China in the area of trade and domestic law, the most harmful clauses of the treaties introduced extraterritorial rights for British and other Western nationals, which signified a severe infringement of Chinese sovereignty. They are remembered for the deep resentment they inspired in China, contributing to what would later be known as the "Century of Humiliation."[2]

The story of the imposition of extraterritoriality on China has, by now, become a famous one.[3] While extraterritoriality or so-called consular jurisdiction was a

[1] Matthew Craven, "What Happened to Unequal Treaties. The Continuities of Informal Empire" (2005) 74 *Nordic Journal of International Law* 335.

[2] William C. Kirby, "The Internationalization of China: Foreign Relations at Home and Abroad in the Republican Era" (1997) 150 *The China Quarterly* 440.

[3] The literature on this topic is vast. See, for example, Par Kristoffer Cassel, *Grounds of Judgment: Extraterritoriality and Imperial Power* (OUP 2012); Turan Kayaoglu, *Legal Imperialism: Sovereignty and Extraterritoriality in Japan, the Ottoman Empire, and China* (CUP

Inge Van Hulle, *The Opium Wars, Extraterritoriality, and International Drug Control* In: *Histories of International Law in China*. Edited by: Ignacio de la Rasilla, Jiangyu Wang, and Congyan Cai, Oxford University Press.
 DOI: 10.1093/oso/9780198888345.003.0004

tried method of Western—and particularly—British imperialism in virtually all regions of the world that felt the brunt of Western encroachments, it has become almost synonymous with China.[4] Much scholarly attention has been dedicated to these unequal treaties and their long-term consequences, but surprisingly little has been written about the international legal ramifications of what triggered the breakdown of peaceful relations between China and the West in the first place, namely the trade in opium. The history of opium as a commodity has attracted the attention of historians for decades, but has escaped that of international lawyers or historians of international law almost entirely.[5] This trade, which was the *casus belli* for the Opium Wars, had already framed Sino–British interactions decades prior to the war and, in fact, much like other commodities such as sugar and cotton, helped to shape the global commercial and legal order of the nineteenth century. The opium trade was not merely a backdrop but a central element of contention that influenced diplomatic relations, economic policies, and legal frameworks. It served as both a commodity of immense profit for the British Empire and a source of social and economic destabilization for China. Despite the growing concern and awareness related to the social and health consequences of addiction to opiates, the British government and its other Western counterparts, through both diplomatic and military means, fought to maintain and even expand the opium trade in China. By the end of the nineteenth- and the early twentieth centuries, the moral ambivalence concerning opium had generated the first international legal instruments that laid the foundation of a burgeoning international narcotics regime.

This chapter explores the centrality of the opium trade in the history of international law in the broader context of the Opium Wars, focusing on how this trade was intertwined with the unequal treaties, particularly extraterritoriality and morality. It therefore shifts the traditional scholarly focus of looking at extraterritoriality in China in isolation and investigates how extraterritoriality became intertwined with a new and upcoming field in international law, namely international drug control. In doing so, it investigates the paradox of Western powers advocating for legal reforms in China based on the "standard of civilization" backed by the

2010); Teema Ruskola, *Legal Orientalism: China, the United States, and Modern Law* (Harvard University Press 2013); Dong Wang, *China's Unequal Treaties: Narrating National History* (Lexington Books 2005).

[4] See for extraterritoriality as a tool of imperialism in (international) law: Gerrit Gong, *The Standard of "Civilization" in International Society* (Clarendon Press 1984); various contributions in: Daniel S. Margolies, Umut Özsu, Maïa Pal, and Ntina Tzouvala (eds), *The Extraterritoriality of Law. History Theory, Politics* (Routledge 2019); Inge Van Hulle, *Britain and International Law in West Africa: The Practice of Empire* (OUP 2020).

[5] The lone exception is Jessie Hohmann, "Opium" in Jessie Hohmann and Daniel Joyce (eds), *International Law"s Objects* (OUP 2018) 319–329. Concise historical introductions can also be found in Richard Lines, *Drug Control and Human Rights in International Law* (CUP 2017). See also John Collins, *Legalising the Drug Wars: A Regulatory History of UN Drug Control* (CUP 2022) whose primary focus lies on the UN.

use of force, while simultaneously engaging in and defending a trade that was increasingly condemned at home and in China for its moral deficiencies. While the unequal treaties and the extraterritorial regime that was implemented had a significant impact on China's freedom to develop its own opium policy, this went largely unnoticed by contemporary international lawyers, even when extraterritoriality became increasingly scrutinized during the first half of the twentieth century. This chapter argues that this blind spot stemmed, during the nineteenth century, from the so-called "standard of civilization", but also from the early onset of what today is described as the fragmentation and compartmentalization of international law. The international narcotics regime that took shape at the start of the twentieth century as a result of efforts to suppress opium was a highly specialized and technical topic, that was discussed separately from extraterritoriality and by only a handful of lawyers and political scientists. It was thereby epistemologically divorced from larger concerns about the role that Western countries had played in the tide of opium addiction that had flooded China and other countries.

While the history of the internal legal suppression and prohibition of opium in China is a long and interesting one, my analysis is limited to developments in the field of international law and will only marginally touch upon the Chinese domestic legal context.[6] I will also limit myself to a discussion of the state practice between China and Britain. The chapter first discusses the relationship between the Opium Wars and the principal unequal treaties concluded between China and Britain up until the end of the nineteenth century. It then looks at the manner in which international lawyers perceived or failed to perceive the impact of extraterritoriality on the trade in opium. Next, it discusses the early multilateral international instruments targeting the trade and consumption of opium from the start of the twentieth century until the 1930s, also in light of the limits that the unequal treaties placed on Chinese sovereignty. Finally, the chapter returns to how international legal theory of the early twentieth century received the new international narcotics regime in light of existing extraterritorial rights in China.

4.2 The (Il)legal Structure of the Opium Trade and the Treaty System (1729–1900)

Initially introduced as a medicinal substance, opium was prized for its analgesic and sedative properties. It was commonly used to treat pain, diarrhea, fever, and other ailments, particularly in tropical regions where diseases such as malaria were prevalent. However, beyond its medicinal applications, opium became a popular recreational drug, much like alcohol—especially in China, where smoking opium

[6] See for literature on this particular topic: Alan Baumler, *The Chinese and Opium under the Republic: Worse than Floods and Wild Beasts* (State University of New York Press 2007)

became a widespread practice.[7] The social profile of opium users was incredibly diverse. In China, opium was first adopted by the elite classes, including scholars, officials, and wealthy merchants, who smoked it as a luxury good in the early nineteenth century. Opium smoking soon spread to the lower classes as increased availability made the drug more affordable. Coolies, laborers, and even farmers began consuming opium, often using it as an escape from the hardships of their lives or as a way to temporarily relieve hunger, physical pain, and fatigue. While in many cases the use of opium was relatively benign and unproblematic, by the mid-nineteenth century the lower classes' real or perceived addiction to opium had become a widespread societal issue in China, contributing to the drug's notorious reputation as a destroyer of lives and families.

Despite its harmful effects, opium's allure as a source of profit and recreation made it a commodity of great significance in the global economy of the nineteenth century. The opium trade between Britain and China was not merely an informal exchange of goods, but was deeply embedded within a series of legal frameworks that evolved over time to legitimize and protect British commercial interests and those of other Western states. The legal and illegal structures of the trade can be understood in three stages: the early smuggling phase, the imposition of treaties following the First Opium War and the Arrow War, and the development of extraterritoriality as a legal safeguard for British traders. As is well known, the British East India Company (EIC) played a central role in initiating and maintaining the opium trade with China in the late eighteenth and early nineteenth centuries. Before the First Opium War, the opium trade operated largely in the shadows of official commerce. The first edicts against opium stem from the early eighteenth century and were modeled after those on tobacco. In 1729, Emperor Yongzheng prohibited the sale and distribution of opium. In 1780, the import of opium for non-medicinal purposes was prohibited and finally, in 1799, the Qing government banned the import of opium.[8] Yet, the latter ban remained ineffective due to the corruption of local officials or their inability to stem the tide of illegal smuggling and the British traders' dexterity in circumventing Chinese authorities.

The illegal opium trade itself was structured through a network of smugglers or so-called country traders who worked in conjunction with British merchants, particularly those connected to the EIC, to illegally transport the drug into China.[9] Opium itself was grown in India, primarily in Bengal and Bihar, and exported to China in exchange for tea, silk, and porcelain. While the EIC maintained a monopoly over the opium trade in India, the company sold opium to private traders, who then smuggled it into China from off-shore trading posts, hereby

[7] Joyce A. Madancy, *The Troublesome Legacy of Commissioner Lin: The Opium Trade and Opium Suppression in Fujian Province, 1820s–1920s* (Harvard University Press 2004) 29-31.

[8] Hong Lu and Bin Liang, "Legal Responses to Trafficking in Narcotics and Other Narcotics Offenses in China" (2008) 18 *International Criminal Justice Review* 214.

[9] Madancy, *The Troublesome Legacy of Commissioner Lin* 48.

circumventing and openly flaunting the Chinese laws that prohibited the import of the drug.[10] The final breakdown of peaceful relations between China and Britain was about more than opium, but was also—and fundamentally so—caused by a difference in world view and normative orders that were, nevertheless, both premised on universalistic and imperialistic tendencies and civilizing missions: the West having instrumentalized a secular discourse of equal sovereignty that did not recognize any superior moral authority; and China with its hierarchical vision of the world centered on *tian*.[11]

By the second half of the 1830s, opium imports into China had reached staggering levels. Historians estimate that as much as 40,000 chests of opium were being smuggled into China annually by 1838, a dramatic increase on earlier decades.[12] As the demand for opium grew, Qing authorities increasingly began to view the illegal trade in opium as a danger—not so much in terms of addiction, but rather as a problem of statecraft. The most important problem was that trade transactions were typically conducted in silver, contributing to a massive outflow of wealth from China, further destabilizing the Qing economy through a trade deficit. This drain on China's silver reserves contributed to internal financial crises. In 1839, the Qing government, under the leadership of Commissioner Lin Zexu (1785–1850), took a strong stance against the British opium traders in Canton. He demanded the surrender of all opium held by the British in their Guangzhou settlement and initiated a naval blockade to cut off their supplies.[13] In response, Charles Elliot (1801–1875), the British superintendent, chose to comply and promised—without the knowledge of the British government—that 20,000 chests of opium would be handed over, while also assuring British merchants that they would be compensated for their losses incurred. Since there were not enough chests in Guangzhou at the time, British merchants rushed to bring in additional opium, anticipating a secure and substantial profit. However, Lin eventually seized and destroyed more than 20,000 chests of opium. Lin's actions, though justified in the eyes of the Chinese government in view of the illegality of the opium trade, were considered by Britain as an affront to its nationals, and saw its trade and maritime interests under threat.

In response to Lin's crackdown, Britain launched a military expedition which was legitimated by reference to the supposed affront and harassment suffered by its nationals, hereby initiating the First Opium War, which dramatically altered the legal structure of the opium trade. Britain's superior naval and military power quickly overwhelmed Chinese forces, and by 1842 the Qing government was

[10] David Anthony Bello, *Opium and the Limits of Empire: Drug Prohibition in the Chinese Interior, 1729–1850* (CUP 2005) 33–43.

[11] Maria Adele Carrai, *Sovereignty in China: A Genealogy of a Concept since 1840* (CUP 2019).

[12] Zheng Yangwen, *The Social Life of Opium in China* (CUP 2005) 107.

[13] Randall Lesaffer, "Nanjing (1842): Unequal Treaties and the Right to War" in Randall Lesaffer (ed) *Oxford Historical Treaties* (OUP 2018).

forced to sue for peace. The Treaty of Nanjing, which concluded the war, compelled China to cede Hong Kong to Britain in perpetuity and to open five ports (Canton, Xiamen (Amoy), Fuzhou, Ningbo, and Shanghai) to British merchants. British nationals were allowed to reside in these ports, now under the supervision of a foreign consul, instead of the merchant guild of Hong Co. Importantly, the treaty explicitly mentioned the principle of "absolute equality" between the Chinese emperor and the British head of state.

The treaty provided for an indemnity for losses sustained during the war and, importantly, also a sum of 6 million dollars "as the value of Opium which was delivered up at Canton in the month of March 1839, as a Ransom for the lives of Her Britannic Majesty's Superintendent and Subjects, who had been imprisoned and threatened with death by the Chinese High Officers."[14] The treaty did not, in fact, mention the organization of the opium trade, but can nevertheless be viewed as an implicit, yet coerced, acceptance of British demands to continue the trade in opium, in spite of Chinese domestic laws that dictated otherwise. It was supplemented by the Treaty of the Bogue in 1843, signed between Henry Pottinger and Qi-ying, which granted British subjects extraterritorial rights and which set tariff rates for trade between the two nations.[15] It included a most-favored-nation clause which ensured that any privileges and immunities that China granted to other foreign powers would automatically apply to Britain.

The introduction of extraterritorial rights marked the beginning of a series of legal impositions on China by Western powers, as the Treaty of Nanjing was rapidly followed by the Treaty of Wangxia with the United States and the Treaty of Huangpu with France, which further developed the details of consular jurisdiction.[16] Unlike the Treaty of Nanjing, the Treaty of Wangxia did contain in its Article 13 an obligation on the part of the United States to prevent its citizens from trading in opium or in any other contraband article of merchandise.[17] By the start of the twentieth century a treaty system of extraterritoriality had been imposed that spanned eighteen states: Russia, the United States, Great Britain, France, Norway and Sweden (as two powers with one treaty), Germany, Portugal, Denmark, Holland, Spain, Belgium, Austria-Hungary, Japan, Peru, Mexico, and Brazil.[18] Exterritoriality importantly also had its impact on the opium trade: it meant that British citizens in China were subject to British law rather than Chinese law, a legal mechanism that protected opium traders from Chinese prosecution for violating China's ban on opium.

[14] Article 4, The Peace Treaty of Nanjing, August 29, 1842, 93 CTS 465.

[15] Supplementary Treaty between China and Great Britain, October 8, 1843, 95 CTS 323.

[16] Treaty of Peace, Amity, and Commerce, between the United States of America and the Chinese Empire, July 3, 1844, 97 CTS 105.

[17] Article 13, Ibid.

[18] F.E. Hinckley, "Extraterritoriality in China" (1912) 39 *The Annals of the American Academy of Political and Social Science* 97–108.

The tensions stemming from the First Opium War and the Treaty of Nanjing did not dissipate, as the Chinese authorities maintained the ban against opium, although enforcement along the lines of Lin Zexu's actions did not reappear until the early twentieth century. Meanwhile Britain sought the official legalization of the opium trade. The eventual legalization of the trade by the Qing government stemmed from an effort to turn opium into a source of revenue for the state, through the imposition of *likin*, a tax on goods moving through districts, and in fact happened two years prior to the formal legalization stipulated by the Treaty of Tianjin.[19] In reality, the trade remained in the hands of local officials and the central government never succeeded in exerting complete control over tax revenue. The Arrow War, termed by Karl Marx the Second Opium War, was triggered by a relatively minor diplomatic incident—the Arrow incident—in which Chinese officials boarded a Chinese-owned ship registered under a British flag, arresting its crew on suspicion of piracy and smuggling. Britain seized on this incident as a pretext for launching another war to secure broader commercial and diplomatic advantages in China. Alongside Britain, France joined the conflict, citing the murder of a French missionary in China as justification. This escalation of military conflict placed even greater pressure on the already weakening Qing dynasty, which was simultaneously grappling with internal uprisings, such as the Taiping Rebellion. The war culminated in the Treaty of Tianjin (1858) and the subsequent Beijing Convention (1860), which further expanded Western powers' legal and territorial rights in China.[20] The Treaty of Tianjin enshrined Britain's goal to bring the opium trade outside of the confines of illegality and stipulated the legalization of the opium trade, formally ending any pretense that Britain would cease its involvement in the opium trade.[21] The Rules of Trade appended to the treaty stipulated that opium was only to be carried into the interior by the Chinese and only as Chinese property, while "the foreign trader will not be allowed to accompany it." It also provided for the establishment of permanent foreign embassies in Beijing and the opening of additional ports to Western powers.

The "Additional Article" to the Chefoo Agreement between Britain and China of 1876 undermined the *likin* transit duties that China had created and provided that after a 30-taels duty had been paid on opium, transit certificates were extended to owners, which freed them from the imposition of any further tax in the interior.[22]

[19] Steffen Rimmer, *Opium's Long Shadow: From Asian Revolt to Global Drug Control* (Harvard University Press 2018) 44.

[20] Treaty of Peace, Friendship and Commerce between Great Britain and China, June 26, 1858, 119 CTS 163.

[21] J. Y. Wong, *Deadly Dreams: Opium and the Arrow War (1856–1860) in China* (CUP 1998) 413–415.

[22] Article 3, An Agreement between the Minister Plenipotentiary of the Government of Great Britain and China, September 13, 1876, in "Treaties and Documents Concerning Opium" (1909) 3 *The American Journal of International Law*. Hamilton Wright, "The International Opium Commission, Part 1" (1909) 3 *The American Journal of International Law* 657.

By the end of the nineteenth century government opinion towards opium had shifted again toward efforts at suppression.[23] Popular resentment against opium was on a steady rise and fit within a larger reform movement towards "self-strengthening," following the defeat of China by Japan in 1894, and which styled opium as a tool of particularly British imperialistic oppression. At the start of the twentieth century, China had become the world's principal source of opium production, supported by a large domestic consumer population. This once again led to a stricter Chinese control of opium, exemplified by the 1906 Imperial Edict that sought the suppression of opium production, trade, and consumption. This was followed by the Provisional Criminal Code of 1912, exacting heavy penalties for importation and opium-smoking.

4.3 Extraterritoriality and the Opium Trade in the Nineteenth Century

The unequal treaties and extraterritoriality had a significant impact on China's sovereign freedom to act against the opium trade. First, this manifested itself at the level of China's external sovereign ability to formulate an independent policy with regard to the opium trade. While after the First Opium War the ban against the opium trade remained in force, the Treaty of Nanjing provided protection to smugglers, as opium poured in via the newly opened treaty-ports. Nor was China's legalization of the opium trade following the Arrow War an entirely voluntary decision: it was pushed for by Britain and the United States. Meanwhile, the Qing government "felt compelled to lift official prohibitions on opium cultivation" in order to prop up its dire financial situation through tax revenues from the sale and transport of opium.[24] While domestic political factors also contributed to the financial crisis of the Qing government, it was certainly not helped by the stringent trade clauses of the unequal treaties.

Second, through extraterritoriality, British consuls had jurisdiction over their nationals in civil and criminal cases, effectively creating separate legal enclaves within China, in which opium traders were able to thrive in spite of China's initial prohibition of the opium trade. Since the Treaty of Nanking had not legalized the opium trade, the legal position of British subjects smuggling opium was that they *could* not be tried in Chinese courts and *would* not be tried in British courts, as the early consular ordinances entirely ignored the opium traffic, assuming that the smuggling of opium was not an offence against the Nanjing Treaty.[25] In fact, the

[23] Helena Barop, "Building the "Opium Evil" Consensus—The International Opium Commission of Shanghai" (2015) 13 *Journal of Modern European History* 119.

[24] Madancy, *The Troublesome Legacy of Commissioner Lin* 2–4.

[25] George W. Keeton, *The Development of Extraterritoriality in China*, vol 2 (Howard Fertig 1969) 134–135.

Imperial High Commissioner at Canton was informed by HM Government that he did have to expect "the British authorities to enforce against British subjects and British ships the requirements of the Chinese laws against any prohibited trade" and that "the persons of British subjects must not be molested for any act of smuggling."[26] However, it was accepted that Chinese officials confiscated suspected ships and their cargo. Opium smuggling did lead to some cooperation between the Chinese government and the British consuls in Shanghai when, for example, in 1843 three cases, *Amelia*, *Maingay*, and *William IV* resulted in fines and the confiscation of opium. The ships *Amelia* and *Maingay* had illegally transported opium to the Indiaman, *William IV*, after which both the captains of *Amelia* and *Maingay* were caught with a fraudulent manifesto and presented with fines. Interestingly, however, the captain of the *William IV* escaped the same fate, an illustration of how such occasional fines operated as window-dressing for the protection of the East India Company's trade.[27]

Following the Treaty of Tjianjin, which had legalized opium, it seemed that consular courts enforced the evasion of the Chinese taxes on opium.[28] However, problems remained with the traffic of opium itself. The passing of the Imperial Edict of 1906 and the Provisional Criminal Code of 1912 implied that while domestic Chinese law had made importation and opium-smoking illegal, the Treaty of Tianjin had legalized opium traffic, which effectively placed the opium trade itself in a legal grey zone. Also, following extraterritoriality, the assertion of foreign ownership of captured opium could lead to acquittal of opium smugglers. For example, in 1921, the case of Sung Ah-nyi was brought before the Mixed Court of Shanghai for possession of 117 lbs. of smuggled opium.[29] However, L.E. Jovino, an Italian national, appeared during the case, claiming that the opium belonged to him, upon which the case was dismissed as the Mixed Court did not have jurisdiction over Italians. Jovino was later charged before the Italian Consular Court and sentenced to two years for the illegal possession of 649lbs of opium. That consular courts were quite lenient in some cases of opium smuggling is illustrated by the fact that Jovino's sentence was postponed for two years, provided that he would refrain from further criminal activity, on the basis that it was his first offence and given "the necessity of his supporting of a large family." Similar problems occurred because Chinese subjects registered with foreign consulates. In 1923, the municipal police at Shanghai searched the premises of Kwan Chang, a Chinese, who was nevertheless in possession of a certificate identifying him as a Portuguese

[26] A.M. Kotenev, *Shanghai: Its Municipality and the Chinese* (North China Daly News & Herald, Limited, 1927) 268.

[27] George Lanning and Samuel Couling, *The History of Shanghai*, vol 1 (For the Shanghai Municipal Council by Kelly & Walsh 1921) 329.

[28] Kotenev, *Shanghai: Its Municipality and the Chinese* 269–271.

[29] Keeton, *The Development of Extraterritoriality in China*, vol 2, 137.

subject. Pending an application to the Portuguese Consulate, the search needed to be suspended.[30]

4.4 Moral Ambiguities and International Legal Theory

The eventual creation of an international regime that attempted to control the trade in opium cannot be viewed separately from changing Western ideas concerning the harmful effects of opium, which were anything but clear-cut. Improper opium use—during the nineteenth century in the West increasingly lumped under the term of "addiction"—was either medicalized, whereby the opium user was considered as the victim of a disease, or criminalized, whereby the user was rather typecast as a seditious criminal.[31] While opium was consumed by all social layers of society, it became particularly associated with drunkards, vagrants, and foreigners. Among these foreigners, members of the Chinese overseas community were stigmatized as harbingers of opium addiction, a stereotype popularized by the seemingly omnipresent opium den, which snared innocent Westerners into a Chinese trap of sin and depravity. In all cases, the user was viewed as weak-willed, easily corruptible, and deviant.

The narrative of addiction and corruption was spread particularly by missionary societies, who advocated that in order to solve the opium problem, China needed to be turned into a modern, Western-style country—which, in the eyes of missionaries, involved the embrace of Christian values, such as the creation of bourgeois family life.[32] Similar to what had been the case for the abolition of the slave trade, humanitarian societies were born that intended to lobby European governments to limit and, finally, suppress the slave trade. In 1874, for example, the British Society for the Suppression of the Opium Trade was founded.[33]

Most European international lawyers formed part of exactly the same bourgeois societies in which moral panic concerning opium abuse reigned supreme. Yet, nineteenth-century international lawyers remained largely silent on the morality of the opium trade and failed to recognize how the system of extraterritoriality imposed on China aided in sustaining the trade and use of opium, not merely in China, but also in the rest of the world. This blind spot is connected with the broader acceptance in nineteenth-century international legal theory of the necessity of consular jurisdiction as a means of normalizing particularly economic relations with China and as a tool to mold Chinese society to a Western image. The manner in which international relations ought to be conducted with China were

30 Ibid.

31 Alan Baumler, *The Chinese and Opium* 42.

32 Yangwen, *The Social Life of Opium in China* 98–99.

33 J. B. Brown, "Politics of the Poppy: The Society for the Suppression of the Opium Trade, 1874–1916" (1973) 8 *Journal of Contemporary History* 97-111.

subsumed under the larger dilemma of whether and how Western international law could be applied to so-called Oriental nations. This discussion was famously triggered by David Dudley Field, who presented a memorandum in 1874 to the *Institut de Droit International* in which he highlighted the seemingly stark contrast between the international legal traditions of "Oriental nations"—by which he seemed to have meant all non-Western countries—and those of "Christian" nations and in which he called for further discussion.[34] In the late nineteenth-century scholarly contributions concerning China, that followed Dudley Field's call, legal scholars were primarily preoccupied with questions of extraterritoriality, sovereignty, and the so-called standard of civilization.

It was generally recognized that China needed be accepted into the fold of Western international law, but that this could not happen until China had abided by the "standard of civilization"—a term that was never clearly defined, but which comprised a vaguely outlined set of political, cultural, and legal norms that mirrored Western Christian values. Such discussions functioned as much as a tool to define the Other as they did as a lens through which a version of international law premised on free trade, gunboat diplomacy, and the Western concept of sovereignty was enforced onto the Global South.[35] In light of the "standard of civilization," China was defined as a backward nation, comprising legal and diplomatic institutions that were not tailored to the modern needs of international law.[36] This was true not merely for public international law but also for private international law—or as A. Kraul (1848–1918), German consul in China, wrote in 1877: "all rules concerning personal relationships with individuals of other nations, such as marriage, divorce, tutelage and inheritance remain within any base in the Chinese Empire."[37] As a result, the system of extraterritoriality, which created separate legal spheres for foreigners, was thus framed as a necessary mechanism to protect Western merchants operating in China, despite the fact that many of these traders were deeply involved in the opium trade. Before the system of extraterritoriality could be lifted—or so it was argued—China needed to undergo comprehensive legal and administrative change.

Nevertheless, critical voices could be heard, notably in the form of the writings of Russian international lawyer, Fyodor Fyodorovich Martens (1845–1909). In an 1880 article, Martens discussed the conflict between Russia and China

[34] David Dudley Field, "De la possibilité d'appliquer le droit international Européen aux nations Orientales" (1875) 7 *Revue de droit international et de legislation comparée* 659–668.

[35] Luigi Nuzzo, "Territory, Sovereignty, and the Construction of the Colonial Space" in Martti Koskenniemi, Walter Rech, and Manuel Jiménez Fonseca (eds), *International Law and Empire: Historical Explorations* (CUP 2017) 266–267.

[36] Gustave Moynier, "La Chine et le droit international" (1885) 17*Revue de droit international et de législation comparée* 506; Thomas E. Holland, "International Law in the War between Japan and China" (1895) *American Lawyer* 387.

[37] A. Krauel, "Applicabilité du droit des gens européen à la Chine" (1877) 9 *Revue de droit international et de législation comparée* 397.

surrounding the Treaty of Livadia (1879).[38] The latter treaty was similar to other unequal treaties concluded between Western powers and China, in that it disproportionately disadvantaged Chinese trade and border interests. As a result, the Qing government had refused to ratify the treaty.[39] In his article, Martens favorably compared the manner in which Russia had historically conducted its international relations with China to that of the West, emphasizing how Russia had never let itself be guided by mundane commercial interests, but rather focused on respect for territorial integrity. The Treaty of Livadia could therefore not find fault with Martens.

This stood—according to him—in stark contrast to the pattern of British encroachments on Chinese sovereignty, which started with the signature of the Treaty of Nanking in 1842. According to Martens, the system of foreign privileges that existed in China was untenable and would eventually lead to violent conflict between China and the Western treaty powers. These tensions revolved around, on the one hand, the presence and arrogance of Christian missionaries, and on the other hand, the sustained British support of the opium trade.[40] Martens decried the immorality of Britain's position: "Everyone knows that the unlucky ones who take the habit of smoking opium are no longer capable of stopping, even though they themselves register the inevitable ruin of their fortune and the progressive extinction of their physical and moral capacities."[41] Confronted with the devastating effects of opium, China had, "according to the principles of international law," the right, if not the duty, to prevent the "systematic poisoning" of its population.[42]

A less elaborate argument can be found in an article by the Swiss lawyer Joseph Hornung (1792–1870), who is portrayed in the history of international legal theory as a rare voice of criticism against European colonialism.[43] While he did not call into question the legitimate duties of paternalistic protection that stronger, civilized nations had toward weaker, backward ones, he decried the manner in which Western powers conducted themselves in the context of the civilizing mission. This also extended to Britain, which had by its "entry by force of opium into China" damaged not only its international influence, but "that of our civilization in general."[44] He did not hesitate to describe opium as a poison, detrimental to Chinese society and inherently linked to British oppression.[45]

[38] Fyodor de Martens, "Le conflit entre la Russie et la Chine, son développement et sa portée universelle" (1880) 12 *Revue de droit international et de législation comparée* 602.
[39] This treaty would later be replaced by the Treaty of St. Petersburg (1881).
[40] de Martens (n 38) , 603.
[41] Ibid, 603.
[42] Ibid, 604.
[43] Andrew Fitzmaurice, "Scepticism of the Civilizing Mission in International Law" in *International Law and Empire* 359–384.
[44] Joseph Hornung, "Civilisés et barbares" (1886) *Revue de droit international et de législation comparée* 288.
[45] Ibid, 290.

Instead of linking extraterritoriality with opium, most international lawyers discussed the substance of treaties such as the Treaty of Nanjing and Treaty of Tianjin, which formalized the opium trade and entrenched Western control over Chinese commerce. In their writings, legal scholars did not acknowledge the paradox that while China was critiqued for being "uncivilized," the West itself was perpetuating and defending a trade that had at its outset been considered as illegal in China and which was increasingly viewed as repulsive by the majority of Western society. This silence on the opium trade reflects a broader moral ambiguity that pervaded nineteenth-century international legal theory connected with Western imperialism.[46]

4.5 The Origins of Multilateral Opium Suppression and Extraterritoriality

In the early twentieth century, these advocacy efforts culminated in the first multilateral initiatives to regulate and eventually prohibit the opium trade, which, in turn, provided the foundation for the current international narcotics regime. Domestic moral panic about the vices of opium were, in other words, now successfully elevated to the international plane. By the turn of the century, the control of opium was no longer viewed as merely a national problem but was, similar to the suppression of the slave trade and the restriction of alcohol consumption, considered to be of global interest. These developments coincided with the general embrace of liberal internationalism in the West, premised on the creation of intergovernmental institutions and of increased international legal cooperation.[47] The leading role in the international suppression of opium was reserved for the United States, which supported the total prohibition of the opium trade. A possible ban on opium had attracted the attention of the US government, which saw it align with the desires of the majority of its constituency and also considered it as a foreign policy instrument to isolate its commercial rival, Britain, from the Chinese market.[48] This became all the more urgent when it acquired, in 1898, control over the Philippines, and with it an opium-smoking Philippine population.[49] However, while the United States was thus a leading "moral entrepreneur" in global prohibition,[50] the idea of prohibition as such was not an American one but has a much

[46] Antony Anghie, *Imperialism, Sovereignty and the Making of International Law* (CUP 2012); Martti Koskenniemi, *The Gentle Civilizer of Nations: The Rise and Fall of International Law, 1870–1960* (CUP 2009).

[47] Glenda Sluga and Patricia Clavin, "Rethinking the History of Internationalism" in Glenda Sluga and Patricica Clavin (eds), *Internationalism: A Twentieth-Century History* (CUP 2017) 3–16.

[48] James Windle, "How the East Influenced Drug Prohibition" (2013) 35 *The International History Review* 1185–1199.

[49] Collins, *Legalising the Drug Wars* 15.

[50] Peter Andreas and Ethan Nadelmann, *Policing the Globe: Criminalization and Crime Control in International Relations* (OUP 2008).

longer and Eastern pedigree, as evidenced by the early Chinese laws prohibiting opium.[51] Also, the American push toward international drug control was equally influenced by xenophobic concerns about the so-called pollution of the American race by the intermingling of young women and men with foreigners.[52]

The triumph of internationalism in tackling the opium trade should nevertheless not be overstated. On the one hand, the early multilateral instruments illustrate that early twentieth-century internationalism still allowed for the existence of semi-sovereignty outside of the confines of the West. The continued existence of extraterritoriality in China meant that it could not exercise complete, sovereign control over its economy. On the other hand, Britain and other colonizing nations remained ambivalent about suppressing the opium trade. Colonial extractive economies depended on Chinese laborers or "coolies," who were made dependent on opium for recreation. Plans to suppress opium awakened fears that a lack of opium availability would lead to a shortage of Chinese laborers. Also, Britain's tentative membership of the ensuing international opium regime was not entirely inspired by humanitarian fervor, but coincided with declining profits from the Indian opium trade, due to the growing competition from Chinese domestic opium production. In the same context should the conclusion in 1907 and 1911 of the Ten-Year Agreement between China, India and the United Kingdom be viewed, which envisioned the gradual reduction and eventual total prohibition by 1917 of the opium trade and which, at first sight, seemed a complete *volte face* from previous policy attitudes. The agreement, however, was entirely prejudicial to Britain and presented it with the opportunity to gradually extract itself from a waning trade.[53] It also illustrated that ultimately, sovereign control over China's economy did not reside in Chinese, but rather in foreign, hands.

The issue of China's lack of sovereign control as a result of the unequal treaty system was placed high on the agenda of Chinese officials who were delegated to join the first multilateral initiatives for the suppression of the opium trade.[54] This first initiative materialized in the form of the International Opium Commission, convened in Shanghai in 1909, and which brought together the governments of China, Great Britain, the United States, France, the Netherlands, Germany, Japan, Austria-Hungary, Portugal, Italy, Russia, Siam and Persia. In his opening statement, Tuan Fuang, the Vice-Roy of the Liangkiang provinces, addressed the assembled representatives by pointing out how the creation of an international instrument targeting opium could not be viewed separately from the system of existing treaties which significantly constrained China's freedom to act, including the Ten Year Agreement:

[51] Windle, "How the East Influenced Drug Prohibition" 1185.
[52] H. Wayne Morgan, *Drugs in America. A Social History, 1800-1980* (Syracuse University Press 1982) 99–102.
[53] Agreement between the United Kingdom and China relating to Opium, TNA, FO 93/23/27/0.
[54] Barop, "Building the "Opium Evil" Consensus" 128–129.

> the attempts by this Government to suppress opium are hampered by existing treaties. Should a way be found by which such clauses in the treaties that restrict the freedom of my Government in its work of abolishing the consumption of the drug in the Empire may be got over, so that we may succeed in accomplishing our great and important task—fortunate indeed will it be for our Government and the people of this Empire.[55]

The eventual non-binding recommendations that were made by the Commission did not contain any references to the unequal treaties. References to the lack of territorial sovereignty of China could, however, be traced in the final document, as the eighth recommendation, for example, stated that "each delegation move its government to enter into negotiations with the Chinese government with a view to effective and prompt measures being taken in the various foreign concessions and settlements in China for the prohibition of the trade" of opium.[56] The difficult situation in which the Chinese government found itself was, in the years following the first meeting of the International Opium Commission, voiced by Charles D. Tenney, Chinese Secretary of the American Legation at Peking, who remarked that "it would seem probably that if China enjoyed full sovereign rights as to the control of the importation of foreign and Indian opium, the opium evil might be thoroughly stamped out of the empire in a very short time."[57]

In 1911, again following the initiative of the United States, the recommendations of the commission were turned into the first multilateral instrument on international drug control, the International Opium Convention, following the second International Opium Commission convened in The Hague.[58] The Convention drew a line between different types of addictive substances, such as raw opium, manufactured opium, medicinal opium, morphine, heroin, and cocaine, in order to establish a difference between opium abuse for leisure purposes and its use for medicinal and scientific purposes, still one of the cornerstones of international drug control. Article 3 of the Convention in particular was hailed as putting a stop to the decades-long practice of producing opium states to turn a blind eye to smuggling in China, as it prescribed that the contracting parties needed to take measures to prevent or to control the exportation of raw opium to countries which have or may prohibit its entry.[59] More specifically, the entire fourth chapter of the treaty dealt with relations between the "treaty powers" (i.e. those countries that had unequal treaties with China) and the Chinese government, stipulating that the treaty

[55] Report of the International Opium Commission, Shanghai, China, February 1 to February 26, 1909, 10.

[56] "Final Resolutions. International Opium Commission" (1909) 3 *American Journal of International Law* 275–276.

[57] Hamilton Wright, "The International Opium Conference" (1912) 6 *American Journal of International Law* 875.

[58] Collins, *Legalising the Drug Wars* 13–16.

[59] International Opium Convention, January 23, 1912, League of Nations, *Treaty Series*, Vol. 8, 187.

powers were obliged to prevent smuggling (Article 15) and to restrict and control the habit of smoking opium in their leased territories, concessions, and settlements (Article 17). However, while the treaty obliged China to adopt pharmacy laws regulating the use of morphine and other substances for medicinal purposes, the system of extraterritoriality entailed that these laws could not be enacted before "the contracting parties having treaties with China shall examine these laws and, if they find them acceptable, shall take the necessary measures to apply them to their nationals residing in China" (Article 16).

Ratification of the 1912 Convention proved slow and all but ground to a halt following the outbreak of the First World War.[60] The Peace Treaty of Versailles and the other accompanying peace treaties nevertheless all contained a specific article referring to the Opium Convention that obliged all signatories of the peace treaty to ratify the Convention within a year and that considered the signature of the peace as equivalent of the ratification of the Convention."[61] The foundation of the League of Nations also provided new impetus to international drug control and its Covenant made it one of its principal policy objectives by its inclusion of Article 23 (c), which entrusted the League "with general supervision over the execution of agreements with regard to traffic ... in opium."[62]

Meanwhile, the domestic political situation in China had changed dramatically, as in 1911 the Qing Dynasty collapsed and the country transitioned to the Republic under the Nationalist Party or Kuomintang. This heralded a period of instability which also affected China's willingness and ability to comply with the new Conventions that were about to be concluded under the auspices of the League. The Nationalist government, while in principle aligned with the anti-opium stance of the League, saw its authority challenged by powerful regional warlords, who wrested territorial control from the government and who benefited financially from the opium trade. It also needed to contend with the burgeoning Communist movements, which were gaining influence particularly among the rural population of China. These Communist movements considered opium as a tool of foreign oppression and supported its eradication also as a way to launch a campaign of national renewal and to reclaim full sovereignty.

As the League adopted its second major international instrument, namely the 1925 International Opium Convention, China's participation in these initiatives grew increasingly complex: on the one hand, the government supported international regulation as a means of advancing its anti-opium agenda; on the other, the fractured state of Chinese governance hindered effective implementation of League policies. Prior to the acceptance of the Convention, China had complained in the League's Advisory Committee on Traffic in Opium that it required

[60] Collins, *Legalising the Drug Wars* 21.
[61] See, for example, Article 195, Treaty of Versailles.
[62] Article 23(c), Covenant of the League of Nations.

full sovereignty in order to enforce its opium laws over foreigners.[63] As a response, the British representative had argued that extraterritoriality did not fall within the scope of the Advisory Committee, further highlighting Western powers' reluctance to recognize the connection with extraterritoriality, which bound China's hands in the traffic of opium. The result of this discussion was a non-binding recommendation which called for those powers who had extraterritorial rights in China to make and enact regulations applicable to their nationals that would tackle "any trade in drugs."

The main importance of the 1925 Convention lay in the fact that it addressed one of the major shortcomings of the 1912 Convention, which had materialized as soon as it was drafted: the lack of international oversight. The 1925 Convention, therefore, established a number of control instruments. The first one was aimed at facilitating governmental supervision through imposing mandatory import and export authorization certificates for all international transactions that involved the substances mentioned in the Convention. Also, the Health Committee of the League of Nations could use the Convention as a kind of "moving target" by—after scientific and medical review—including or excluding substances from the scope of the Convention. Most importantly, the Convention created the Permanent Central Opium Board (PCOB), composed of eight independent experts, to which the signatories of the Convention were required each year to submit statistics and estimates on the quantities of the substances imported within their territory and on the domestic production of raw materials, their manufacture, and their consumption, including a report on available stocks. The PCOB had a number of enforcement tools at its disposal. If one of the signatories was producing or consuming more than its estimated legitimate portion, it could request more information, raise concerns to the Council of the League, or, in the worst case, recommend an international embargo.

It is precisely the possible lack of enforcement that drew the attention of commentators to China's role in implementing the Convention, already during the phase of negotiation. As Dr J. Paulus remarked, "presently the Chinese government does not exercise any authority in a large part of its territory," as "different provincial chefs and army chefs, rebels and independents push towards cultivation, in order to assured themselves of financial advantages."[64] As a result, opium production in China was increasing at an "alarming rate" and was also threatening neighboring countries' efforts to stem the inflow and consumption of the drug.

Subsequently, the League of Nations next focused on limiting drug manufacturing strictly to levels needed for medical and scientific purposes, hereby preventing surplus production from fueling illicit markets. To enforce this, the

[63] Keeton, *The Development of Extraterritoriality in China*, vol 2, 139.

[64] Dr. J. Paulus, "La lutte contre l"opium et des dérivés et contre la cocaïne" (1925) 6 *Revue de droit international et de legislation comparée* 632.

Convention for Limiting the Manufacture and Regulating the Distribution of Narcotic Drugs of 1931 now required binding national estimates for total medical and scientific drug use. It also introduced a second regulatory body, the Supervisory Body, under Article 5, to oversee compliance. Considered a major advancement in the 1931 Convention was the insistence that effective drug limitation required universal application, as areas without the estimates system risked undermining control efforts. To ensure this global approach, Article 2 directed the Permanent Central Board to request consumption estimates from all countries, meaning also the ones that had not signed the Convention, hereby making drug control efforts truly international.

4.6 Early Twentieth-Century International Legal Theory: Between Extraterritoriality and the Opium Scourge

By the turn of the twentieth century, as the international consensus—albeit sometimes reluctantly—concerning the desirability of multilateral cooperation on the containment and prohibition of opium consumption grew, international lawyers also directed renewed attention to the opium question, though the topic remained at the margins of scholarship.[65] International lawyers who did study the burgeoning system of international drug control copied the humanitarian and by now also diplomatic discourse that depicted opium as a "contagious evil" that needed to be—if possible—eradicated, and, certainly, controlled.[66] This duty of curtailment now formed part of the narrative of civilization: it was the task of the civilized nations of the world to take upon themselves, on behalf of the rest of the world, the total disappearance of drug addiction. The 1920s also increasingly witnessed critical scholarly contributions on the system of extraterritoriality, following the promise of Western states to relinquish their extraterritorial rights. In the Commercial Treaty of 1902 made with China, Britain promised—wholly in line with the nineteenth-century spirit of the standard of civilization—that it was prepared to abandon extraterritoriality "when she is satisfied that the state of Chinese laws, the arrangement of their administration, and other considerations warrant her so doing."[67] These theoretical analyses were coterminous with Chinese international activism laboring toward the revision and eventual abolition of the unequal treaties. In spite of the clear historical link between the existence of the

[65] Apart from the studies by Hamilton Wright and Quincy Wright on international drug control discussed here, there are, for example, also the following principal studies: André-Jean Chanut, *Le régime de l'Opium en Droit international* (Caen Imprimerie 1933); Hoijer Olof, *Le trafic de l'opium et d'autres stupéfiants. Étude de droit international et d'histoire diplomatique* (Éditions Spes 1925); Westel W. Willoughby, *Foreign Rights and Interests in China* (The John Hopkins Press 1927) and a number of very short articles in medical journals.

[66] Ibid, 624.

[67] Article XII.

treaties and Chinese difficulties in creating a consistent governmental policy and enforcement of its opium legislation, extraterritoriality and international opium control were mostly discussed separately from each other.

For example, the *American Journal of International Law* (AJIL)—unsurprisingly, in light of the pivotal role of the United States in the international suppression process—devoted a series of articles to the International Opium Commission and the International Opium Convention, all by the hand of Dr Hamilton Wright (1867–1917). Wright, a health expert, was, together with the Right Reverend Charles Brent and Dr Charles C. Tenney, one of the moral crusaders lobbying the US government for greater drug control, both through domestic legislation and through international law.[68] He, too, was as much inspired by lofty principles of internationalism as by racist assumptions about the dangers and degenerate effects of Chinese opium-smoking men on the American populace. His contributions in AJIL and elsewhere painted a picture of the "heroic" efforts of the US government in tackling the international scourge of opium addiction. China is presented as a desperate nation, its population having fallen victim on a massive scale to the vices of opium abuse, and as mostly unable—in spite of its best efforts—to stem the tide of addiction independently of the West.

Wright devoted most of his attention to a detailed chronological outline of the various international and domestic legal instruments concluded since the mid-nineteenth-century until the era of multilateral cooperation, discussing in turn the relationship between various Western countries and China. Rarely can a glimpse of critique of the contributions that Western countries, through their unequal treaties, have played in ignoring Chinese prohibition laws and of, subsequently, depriving China of the revenues of the opium trade. One such lone remark, in covert terms, can be found in the concluding section of his article on the International Opium Convention, where he decried "the great wrong" committed against China "in permitting the influx of opium to her shores, at a time when it was known that her best men had set their faces steadily against it." The Convention—to Wright—had the effect "that an old wrong will be atoned" and the "difficult relations" between China and the West "will soon be obliterated."[69] As a US delegate at The Hague in the negotiations of the Convention, it was likely not opportune for Wright to highlight anything other than the spirit of international cooperation.

American International Relations scholar Quincy Wright (1890–1970), president of the American Society of International Law from 1955 to 1956, also devoted an article in 1924 in AJIL to the system of international drug control from the start of the Opium Wars until the League's 1925 Convention.[70] This is not surprising,

[68] H. Wayne Morgan, *Drugs in America* 100–102; Shane Blackman, *Chilling Out. The Cultural Politics of Substance Consumption, Youth and Drug Policy* (Open Press 2004).

[69] Hamilton Wright, "The International Opium Conference" (1913) 7 *The American Journal of International Law* 139.

[70] Quincy Wright, "The Opium Question" 18 (1924) *The American Journal of International Law* 281–295.

because Wright had a particular affinity with and interest in China as he taught international relations courses at Tsinghua University.[71] After having provided a chronological overview of each existing treaty describing its main achievement, Wright ended his article by pointing to—what he perceived as—the general agreement that now existed between nations of a number of principles.[72] The first was that the use of opium for other than medicinal or scientific purposes constituted an "evil" that needed to be abolished. The second was that the non-medical use of opium and narcotic drugs could only be suppressed by curtailing its production, as efforts at controlling their consumption or their international trade had proved impossible, adding that "if opium and narcotic drugs exist in large quantities, they will get to the addict even through prison walls." He admitted that while there was now principled agreement, its practical enforcement provided difficult, as nations still continued to profit from production and governments were reluctant to delegate enforcement to international agencies. Indeed, they "suffered greatly" from the drugs, but that this suffering was partly caused historically by the treaty system starting in the nineteenth century remained a blind spot in Wright's narrative.

The same Quincy Wright wrote a number of articles in the 1930s on the impending abolition of extraterritoriality in China. In "Some Legal Consequences if Extraterritoriality is Abolished in China" (1930), for example, Wright analyzed the bases on which extraterritoriality existed (e.g. on specific treaties, private law agreements, or a general international basis) and their legal consequences, but without a specific reference to the opium trade.[73] In a later article, "The End of Extraterritoriality in China" (1943), Wright does discuss the early nineteenth-century treaties that either wrested open the Chinese economy to foreigners or established extraterritoriality.[74] These included the British Treaty of Nanjing, the American Treaty of Wangxia, and the French Treaty of Wampoa, which all "gave unequal advantages to the Western Powers." Wright adds, though—almost as an excuse—that "China at the time considered these Powers inferior," citing the Chinese Emperor's letter to Caleb Cushing, which through its specific wording placed the Emperor above the American President in rank.[75] Here, also, was made no further mention of the opium trade, nor of a possible connection between the system of international drug control and extraterritoriality.

This epistemological separation can be considered indicative of, on the one hand, the inheritance of the nineteenth-century "standard of civilization" and the

[71] Yongjin Zhang and Teng-Chi Chang, "Introduction: The Making of Chinese International Theory" in Yongjin Zhang and Teng-Chi Chang (eds), *Constructing a Chinese School of International Relations. Ongoing Debates and Sociological Realities* (Routledge 2016) 8.

[72] Wright, "The Opium Question" 294–295.

[73] Quincy Wright, "Some Legal Consequences if Extraterritoriality is Abolished in China" 24 (1930) *The American Journal of International Law* 217–227.

[74] Quincy Wright, "The End of Extraterritoriality in China" (1943) 37 *The American Journal of International Law* 286–289.

[75] Ibid 287.

reluctance of early twentieth-century scholars to accept China as a full sovereign member of the "family of nations." On the other hand, it can also be viewed as the early onset of what today is often referred to as the fragmentation or compartmentalization of international law.[76] The new regime of international drug control was, after all, a highly specialized field that was discussed in detail by only a handful of international lawyers. It remains interesting that these very same scholars, such as Quincy Wright, had a specific interest in and were knowledgeable about China and its extraterritorial past. The result, however, of the epistemological disconnection between drug control and extraterritoriality was that any sense of moral condemnation of extraterritoriality on the basis of its relationship with global drug addiction was entirely absent from legal theory. This is similar to contemporary "compartmentalized" theoretical analyses of highly technical fields such as international investment law, and often its isolation from more fundamental environmental or human rights concerns.[77]

4.7 Conclusion

The legacy of the Opium Wars, the ensuing unequal treaties, and the system of extraterritoriality established a complex framework that shaped China's modern legal identity. The trade in opium played a defining role in China and the West's historical engagement with each other and with international law. Through extraterritoriality, foreign powers effectively carved out areas within China where Chinese laws held little or no authority over foreign nationals, a situation that not only fractured China's internal legal system but also stifled its ability to control the rampant opium trade. The entrenchment of trade rights and extraterritoriality in the unequal treaties also enabled British traders to continue the opium trade in defiance of Chinese legal norms, embedding an economic model where Chinese authorities lacked power over foreign-controlled commerce within their own borders. This arrangement institutionalized foreign influence in a way that prefigured later debates on China's sovereignty, setting a precedent for the approval but also the challenges of extraterritorial jurisdiction in international legal discourse.

By the early twentieth century, the legacy of opium had spurred international concern and, eventually, the first multilateral legal frameworks for drug control. However, while the emerging international narcotics regime marked a step toward cooperation, it fell short of addressing the international roots of China's crisis: the continued existence of unequal treaties and extraterritoriality. These

[76] Martti Koskenniemi and Päivi Leino, "Fragmentation of International Law? Postmodern Anxieties" (2002) 15 *Leiden Journal of International Law* 553–579; Peer Zumbansen, "Die vergangene Zukunft des Völkerrechts" (2001) 34 *Kritische Justiz* 46–68.

[77] Muthucumaraswamy Sornarajah, *Resistance and Change in the International Law on Foreign Investment* (CUP 2015) 58–59.

new multilateral conventions, primarily spearheaded by Western powers, sought to address a global drug problem without dismantling the extraterritorial privileges that exacerbated it.

In the realm of international legal thought, the separation of drug control efforts from discussions on sovereignty and extraterritoriality underscored a fragmented approach to law that would only come under scrutiny in the past few decades. Leading scholars of the period, while championing drug control on humanitarian grounds, largely avoided direct confrontation with the system that enabled the opium trade's endurance: the extraterritorial privileges of foreign nationals. This detachment, perhaps an unintentional byproduct of the era's legal compartmentalization, weakened the broader humanitarian goals of the international community by failing to address the systemic inequities that sustained China's drug crisis. The emergence of this specialized drug control regime was thus a double-edged sword, advancing certain humanitarian aims while allowing the unequal treaty system to continue under a veneer of legal legitimacy.

5

China's Early Insertion in International Law through the Protection of its Nationals Abroad

The Rock Springs Massacre, Mimetism, and External State Building

Frédéric Mégret and Wanshu Cong

5.1 Introduction

When and how did China become inscribed in international law and part of the society of nations? The traditional narrative emphasizes China's transition from an imperial conception of self to a modern state as the key to that inscription.[1] In this progressive transformation, China successfully challenged the unequal treaties and the legacy of encroachments on its territory, thus ensuring that its status and relationship to the rest of the world was 'normalized'.[2] That story, then, is a primarily territorial one, emphasizing a familiar narrative about sovereignty as unfolding within defined borders and on the basis of claims of uncontested jurisdiction.

In this chapter, by contrast, we emphasize the role of caring for one's nationals abroad, including the broader diaspora, as a foundational moment in China's transformation into a sovereign actor in international law. In doing so, moreover, we suggest that China was not claiming of others anything that others had not claimed of it. The demand for the protection of nationals was a classic imperial demand on the receiving end of which China had constantly found itself in the nineteenth century. By turning that argument on its head or at least refracting it onto the West, China managed to sustain powerful early claims about its equal standing in the 'Concert of Nations'. This was a powerful move because it put Western imperial

[1] E.g., Tieya Wang, 'International Law in China: Historical and Contemporary Perspectives' (1990) 221 Collected Courses of the Hague Academy of International Law 195, 226ff; Maria Adele Carrai, *Sovereignty in China: A Genealogy of a Concept since 1840* (Cambridge University Press 2019); Ryan Martínez Mitchell, *Recentering the World: China and the Transformation of International Law* (Cambridge University Press 2022).

[2] Congyan Cai, *The Rise of China and International Law: Taking Chinese Exceptionalism Seriously* (Oxford University Press 2019).

Frédéric Mégret and Wanshu Cong, *China's Early Insertion in International Law through the Protection of its Nationals Abroad* In: *Histories of International Law in China*. Edited by: Ignacio de la Rasilla, Jiangyu Wang, and Congyan Cai, Oxford University Press. DOI: 10.1093/oso/9780198888345.003.0005

powers in front of their contradictions: namely, that they could ultimately not offer less protection to Chinese nationals on their territories than they expected China to provide for their nationals in China.

The question of China's role towards its diaspora has of late attracted much negative attention, against the background of accusations of transnational repression and interference in the affairs of other states.[3] Whatever the validity of these accusations, they often exhibit a certain historical shallowness about the significance in international law of how states maintain ongoing relations with their nationals abroad. We argue that such relations are much older and not merely a late mutation of well-established states; rather, they are often constitutive, early on, of the state itself and its imagining as an entity which may well be primarily territorial but is also engaged in a quasi-pastoral relation of care to its broader population beyond territory. Specifically, the argument is that China was engaged in a form of *external* state building at a time when it did not exercise full sovereignty on its territory but could, paradoxically, contemplate claiming full protection for its nationals abroad.

Traditionally, concern with the fate of nationals abroad has been associated in the historiography of international law with the movement of Western subjects to the West's imagined 'periphery'.[4] The focus has thus been principally on the personal integrity of Western so-called aliens in these far-flung lands, as well as the protection of their property.[5] In some cases protection of nationals extended all the way to intrusive extraterritoriality regimes, as in the Ottoman Empire's capitulations regime, but also in the Far East, notably China.[6] As such, the international law of the protection of aliens is often rightly associated with imperialism and was understandably claimed by national independence and state-building movements as something to be abandoned. This imperial characteristic of the international law of the protection of aliens has also generated enduring critique about the law of state responsibility and international human rights law, which, especially from the perspectives of Third World Approaches to International Law, emerged to a large extent from it.[7]

[3] E.g., Marcus Michaelsen and Johannes Thumfart, 'Drawing a Line: Digital Transnational Repression against Political Exiles and Host State Sovereignty' (2023) 8 European Journal of International Security 151; Joshua Kurlantzick, *Beijing's Global Media Offensive: China's Uneven Campaign to Influence Asia and the World* (Oxford University Press 2022).

[4] Some recent historiographic works about the protection of aliens include Kathryn Greenman, *State Responsibility and Rebels: The History and Legacy of Protecting Investment against Revolution* (Cambridge University Press 2021); James Thuo Gathii, *War, Commerce, and International Law* (Oxford University Press 2010).

[5] The issue had been a major focus of various codification projects in the post-First World War and post-Second World War eras. See e.g., Alexander P Fachiri, 'International Law and the Property of Aliens' (1929) 10 British Yearbook of International Law 32.

[6] Skinner Turner, 'Extraterritoriality in China' (1929) 10 British Yearbook of International Law 56; George W Keeton, *The Development of Extraterritoriality in China* (H Fertig 1969).

[7] E.g., Antony Anghie, 'Rethinking International Law: A TWAIL Retrospective' 34 European Journal of International Law 7, 82–93.

Notwithstanding, the legacy of extra-territorial protection of a state's nationals abroad is, as this chapter will suggest, richer and more complex than this simplified account suggests, notably as a result of the status of early diasporas of Asian migrants in the West. China (and to some extent Japan) had to face the challenge of emigration early as Chinese labourers migrated to and built their lives in places such as the Americas, Australia, south Asia, and South Africa. This movement of people and the ability to maintain it became a stake in itself, evidencing China's growing concern about the ability of its citizens to emigrate to those other countries. This in turn led to an emphasis on the importance of Chinese nationals not being treated in a discriminatory fashion, very much in the way Western states had earlier insisted on the same vis-à-vis China. Moreover, past the point of initial immigration, the emergence of sizeable Chinese communities abroad, notably of vulnerable workers, put Chinese nationals at risk of ethnic and racial violence which at the time spread contagiously in various settler colonial countries.[8]

China's position in relation to its nationals abroad in the late Qing period was in many ways not comparable to the position of Western states in relation to their nationals in China. Throughout the nineteenth century, China had repeatedly suffered from Western military encroachments (some wars were launched precisely in the name of protecting Western nationals), and the protection of the citizens of Western countries was deeply woven into unequal treaties. These not only required China to defend foreign nationals' personal safety and property and to punish wrongdoers, but gradually created a complex system of extraterritoriality, subjecting Western nationals to their own laws and specialized courts.[9] By contrast, Chinese nationals abroad were often extremely vulnerable to rampant discrimination, harassment, and even pogroms, and felt the full force of prejudice in the application of local laws. They could certainly not claim any special extra-territorial treatment as such and were often in a particularly awkward situation: discriminated against by their country of immigration, but also often neglected by their country of emigration. Caught in a series of wars with imperial powers and domestic unrests in the second half of the nineteenth century, the Qing government was never able to create an extensive or effective mechanism of protection for its diaspora.

Nonetheless, as this chapter will argue, and although proceeding from a place that was quite different in terms of its structuring dynamics, China did develop an early sensitivity for how it might exercise its power to intervene on behalf of its

[8] E.g., Ching-hwang Yen, *Coolies and Mandarins: China's Protection of Overseas Chinese During the Late Ch'ing Period (1851–1911)* (Singapore University Press 1985); Zhu Shijia, *Historical Materials on the Persecution of Chinese Labourers in the United States [美国迫害华工史料]* (Zhong Hua Shu Ju [中华书局] 1958); Beth Lew-Williams, *The Chinese Must Go: Violence, Exclusion, and the Making of the Alien in America* (Harvard University Press 2018).

[9] Keeton (n 6); Jean Escarra, *Droits et intérêts étrangers en Chine* (Librairie du Recueil Sirey 1928); Chan Chung Sing, *Les Concessions en Chine* (Les Presses Universitaires de France 1925); Westel Woodbury Willoughby, *Foreign Rights and Interests in China* (Johns Hopkins Press 1927).

nationals abroad and, specifically, how it might use the language of international law to that effect. Thus, even as China was not considered a full member of the 'family of nations' and its sovereignty at home, on its own territory, was compromised, the Qing dynasty engaged in some quite remarkable diplomatic forays vis-à-vis Western imperial powers to protect Chinese nationals on their territories. In that respect, one could say that China 'anticipated' its eventual status as a full-fledged member of the family of nations, insisting that even as its internal sovereignty (e.g., law and order, taxation, effective control over its own territory) was compromised, its *external* sovereignty, that is, the capacity to deal with overseas affairs by projecting itself and engaging with others as equal, was to be treated with increasing respect.

In this chapter we thus revisit these efforts, often written out of the history of international law as well as Chinese history, as they manifested themselves in the late Qing dynasty. We contend that the role of governments in protecting their nationals abroad should be seen as a key part of processes of state formation which involve the development and exercise of external sovereignty: the ability to demand a certain standard or at least equality in the treatment of one's nationals. China thus put the cart before the horse, as it were, projecting its external sovereignty before its transformation into a modern sovereign state, but in the process also beginning to counter the dynamics of imperialism with some degree of success. In doing so, it quite deftly used the language of international law—a language that had been frequently deployed against it—to the advantage of its nationals abroad and, most importantly, for the benefit of its emerging sovereignty.

The crucial claim is that China engaged in a form of rhetorical mimetism against imperial powers such as the United States ('US'), which prefigured the ways in which international law might provide resources for 'subaltern' subversion: invoking arguments that the subject was never supposed to invoke against the 'master' but that in a sense begged to be used at counter-purpose. At the same time, as we will see, China was hardly always successful in its newfound consular adventures and its claims to equality in the Concert of Nations were often met with resistance from Western powers. The point, however, may lie less in the immediate success of such claims than in the way in which they foreshadowed the possibilities of 'dismantling the master's house with the master's tools'[10]—or at least symbolically going at the foundations of one's own oppression by challenging the oppressor to abide by the norms that it imposed on others.

The chapter starts, in Section 5.2, with a brief discussion of the issue of state liability for alien injuries in the imperial context and how Western interventions to protect their nationals in China effectively rendered China a lesser sovereign.

[10] For a recent exploration, see Ralph Wilde, 'Using the Master's Tools to Dismantle the Master's House: International Law and Palestinian Liberation' (2021) 22 The Palestine Yearbook of International Law 1.

In Section 5.3, we then consider how this imperial domination through the protection of Western nationals abroad was eventually turned against the West when China, appropriating that very discourse, demanded equality for its nationals as well and therefore implicitly for itself. In particular, we focus on the largely forgotten and neglected Rock Springs Massacre as a crucial moment in the development of China's relationship to international law. In the ensuing negotiations between China and the US, we examine China's rhetorical mimetism which centred especially on the idea of reciprocity to put pressure on and shame the US, with some success. Zooming out from this specific case, Section 5.4 discusses the episode's aftermath as an example of China asserting external sovereignty and part of the process of state building against the reality of Western imperialism through claims about the Chinese abroad. The chapter concludes with some general lessons offered by this historical episode.[11]

5.2 China's Obligations to Protect Foreign Nationals as a Form of Subjection

5.2.1 The International Law of 'Aliens' and Mob Violence in an Imperial Context

A growing body of international legal historiography considers the international law of the protection of aliens as a crucial tool which enabled Western nationals to travel to and trade in places which were abundant in economic opportunities but politically unstable. Broadly speaking, the nineteenth-century international law of the protection of aliens consisted of early bilaterial treaties of friendship, commerce, and navigation, which set out a number of rights enjoyed by Western nationals and corresponding obligations of the local governments to guarantee those rights. It led to a large body of jurisprudence and cases on diplomatic protection and state responsibility, especially regarding compensation. These were developed by European jurists and various mixed claims commissions, and gave rise to doctrines on military intervention to enforce alien rights (such as the collection of contract debt).[12]

This set of treaties, doctrines, and principles, in the words of Dunne, was 'ultimately concerned with the possibility of maintaining a unified economic and social order for the conduct of international trade and intercourse among independent political units of diverse cultures and stages of civilization, different legal and

[11] Lianlian Liu and Jessica Gammon, 'The Unique Role of the Chinese Government in the Protection of Overseas Citizens' (2022) 88 International Review of Administrative Sciences 793.

[12] Frédéric Mégret, 'Mixed Claims Commissions and the Once Centrality of the "Protection of Aliens"' in Ignacio de la Rassilla del Moral and Jorge Vinuales (eds), *Experiments in International Justice* (Cambridge University Press 2018).

economic systems, and varying degrees of physical power and prestige'.[13] Notably, it served as a critical legal vehicle for the expansion of global capitalism and its considerable needs for the rule of law as a tool for the security of both persons and property.

One particularly thorny issue in the protection of aliens concerned state responsibility for aliens injured by mobs. There was little doubt that a state could be liable under international law for harm inflicted on foreign nationals by its agents. What was more complicated was whether harm caused by private individuals would incur the responsibility of the state. International lawyers in this period, invoking Grotius, Pufendorf, Vattel, and the intra-European practice of previous centuries, often arrived at diametrically opposite conclusions.[14] The argument in favour of state responsibility relied on the claim that mob violence targeting aliens caused a distinct injury to the home state of the alien. The responsibility of the state, therefore, did not hinge on its fault but rather on the nature of the injury.[15] The argument for non-responsibility was, by contrast, that no states could possibly have absolute control over their subjects, that an alien travelling to another country for commerce should accept certain risks, and that foreigners should enjoy the same level of protection as the state's own nationals.[16]

The question was made more complex by the fact that states were likely to be quite demanding of other countries when the interests of their nationals were at stake, and much more forgiving of their own authorities when the rights of foreign nationals on their territory were involved. This led some states (the US being an example) to adopt a somewhat inconsistent position, demanding that other countries pay indemnities for harms suffered by their nationals as a result of mob violence as a matter of legal obligation, while claiming the indemnities which they, as they sometimes did, paid for mob injuries on their own territory as at most ex gratia payments.

Without delving in too much detail into this debate, the position in international law which emerged in the late nineteenth and early twentieth centuries was broadly that the state was not responsible for any harm to aliens caused by private individuals. There was therefore no absolute guarantee to foreigners that no harm could befall them. As we will see, this posed a problem, as much of the mob violence against Chinese communities in the West was effectively the product of spontaneous (if predictable) actions of loose groupings. The one

13 Frederick Sherwood Dunn, *The Protection of Nationals: A Study in the Application of International Law* (The Johns Hopkins Press 1932) 1.

14 Yun-Tan Tu, 'State Responsibility for Injuries to Foreigners on Account of Mob Violence, Murder, and Brigandage' (PhD, University of Illinois at Urbana-Champaign 1927).

15 Julius Goebel, 'The International Responsibility of States for Injuries Sustained by Aliens on Account of Mob Violence, Insurrections and Civil Wars' (1914) 8 American Journal of International Law 802, 812.

16 Calvo was a main proponent of this position. See Tu (n 14) 4.

counterpart for absence of international liability for purely private actions, however, was that the state might be liable if it had contributed to that harm or, more importantly, failed to put an end to it once it emerged.[17] Liability was therefore predicated on fault and depended on whether the state had fulfilled its due diligence to prevent a mob from assembling and committing violence and, subsequently, to suppress the mob. The state also had the responsibility to provide legal remedies to foreigners who suffered mob violence. This in turn required the injured foreigner to exhaust local remedies before a diplomatic claim for indemnity could be made on his behalf.[18]

Assessing a state's due diligence was often fraught. As Philip Jessup observed in 1946,

> statesmen, writers and judges on international tribunals have all too often set up in their minds an ideal condition which rarely exists and have tended to assert a perfect international standard which does not reflect actual conditions in the most orderly states. Municipal graft and corruption, packed juries, and delays in law administration have existed in the US while it has sought to hold others to a non-existent perfection.[19]

Whether a state had used due diligence was therefore largely a question of perception, which unsurprisingly was infused with deep racial biases and civilizational thinking. Ernest Wilson Huffcut wrote in the 1890s, for example, that the principle of exhaustion of local remedies 'carries with it the corollary that a State is bound to supply a judicial remedy or to be held at once responsible through its executive department. It is therefore the practice to submit claims for indemnity in such States as China directly to the executive department, while in European States they must first be adjudicated by the courts.'[20] The suggestion seems to have been that the courts of China were simply not worth deferring to. Yun-Tan Tu observed in the 1920s that the theories on international liability for mob violence, as briefly set out above, were observed by 'Great Powers in dealing with cases arising among themselves' and 'subject to various modifications and sometimes ignored when the Great Powers deal with weak states'.[21]

[17] Francis JR Mitchell, 'International Liability for Mob Injuries' (1900) 34 Am. L. Rev. 709; Ernest Wilson Huffcut, 'International Liability for Mob Injuries' (1891) 2 The ANNALS of the American Academy of Political and Social Science 69; Goebel (n 15); Kenneth Smith Carlston, *The International Responsibility of a State for Injuries to Aliens Arising from Mob Violence* (American University 1928); Philip C Jessup, 'Responsibility of States for Injuries to Individuals' (1946) 46 Colum. L. Rev. 903.

[18] Tu (n 14) 5.

[19] Jessup (n 17) 914.

[20] Huffcut (n 17) 74.

[21] Tu (n 14) 5, 9.

5.2.2 Mob Violence and the 'Rank' of Qing

China in the second half of the nineteenth century was relatively weak, and its status in the Concert of Nations ambiguous. The Qing dynasty was plagued by governmental corruption and waves of peasants' revolts (the most significant one being the Taiping Rebellion in 1851–1864). It was also the object of constant imperial interventions by Western powers. A series of wars forced the Qing government to cede territories, sign 'unequal treaties', allow foreigners to lease territories and establish concessions and settlements, and grant them privileges through extraterritoriality.

In the course of this process, the protection of aliens from mob violence was often both a cause and result of Western domination of China. As Western merchants and missionaries were allowed to reside and travel more broadly in inland China, they increasingly became targets of local mobs, and such incidents sometimes provided a direct *casus belli* for Western powers to launch further imperial wars against the Qing dynasty. One early example was the killing of French Christian missionary Auguste Chapdelaine, which triggered the Second Opium War.[22] About four decades later, xenophobic violence peaked with the Boxer Rebellion in 1899–1990, resulting in an alliance of eight powers storming Beijing, leading to the signing of the Boxer Protocol of 1901.[23] Systematically, imperial wars triggered by mob violence, or at least for which it provided an excuse, ended with the defeated Qing paying huge amounts of indemnity, pledging to protect the personal safety and property of Western nationals, and sometimes even granting the right to foreign powers to establish garrisons outside leased territories for such purposes.[24]

Whatever efforts the Qing government would engage in to defend their nationals abroad, therefore, would arise against the background of formidable Western as well as Japanese and Russian incursions into China itself, which evidently constrained what China could do. This was also a time of rising xenophobic violence in China, which further undermined China's claim to fit within the Concert of Nations. The denial of China's status as a member of the 'civilized nations' extended, quite literally, to efforts to limit the introduction of (Western) international laws to China. As remarked by American traveller Joseph Goodrich, 'When an American teacher undertook to translate a work on International Law, a French diplomat protested vehemently against this effort "to let the Chinese into our secrets!"'.[25]

[22] John F Cady, *The Roots of French Imperialism in Eastern Asia* (Cornell University Press 1954) 165ff.

[23] E.g., Paul H Clements, *The Boxer Rebellion: A Political and Diplomatic Review* (Columbia University Press 2019); Geoffrey Pen, *The Fists of Righteous Harmony: A History of the Boxer Uprising in China in the Year 1900* (Pen and Sword 1991).

[24] On foreign garrisons, see, Dashou Kang and Jiade Pan, *Extraterritoriality of Foreigners in China in Modern Times [近代外国人在华治外法权研究]* (Sichuan Remin Publisher 2002) 178–180.

[25] Joseph King Goodrich, *The Coming China* (AC McClurg & Company 1911) 239.

However, despite major Western spheres of influence in China, China remained nominally independent, if only to sign the treaties that further subjected it. China trade was highly prized by Western nations.[26] Furthermore, the country underwent gradual transformation under the pressure of Western encroachments. Rationalization of government, the emergence of a lively press, the modernization of the army, and the improvement of education coincided with a deeply wounded sense of pride, especially after loss of territory to both Russia and Japan.[27] Importantly, foreign affairs gradually shifted from the margins of the government's concern to become a focal issue, with the establishment of Waiwubu replacing the low-ranking governmental body of Zongli Yamen in 1901 after the Boxer Rebellion.[28] Also in this period, the Qing government began to dispatch diplomatic missions to Europe and the Americas, appoint ministers, and establish consulates and legations overseas. This growing system of Qing diplomacy, which channelled enormous amounts of information from overseas to the empire, proved crucial for the country's state building and modernization.

5.2.3 The Gradual Embrace by China of Its Diaspora

This also reinforced contact between the Qing court and Chinese diaspora communities, making the government more aware of the plight of its nationals abroad.[29] Indeed, due to the huge increase in the Chinese diaspora population since the second half of the nineteenth century and their strengthened economic status in foreign countries, remittances from these communities had become a tremendously important financial resource for the Qing government to compensate for the trade deficit, balance finances, and pay for its various self-strengthening programmes.[30] This provided the Qing government with practical reasons to protect its nationals abroad.[31] All these factors pushed China, a country significantly weakened but painstakingly transforming itself, to gradually demand equal treatment for itself and its nationals. As remarked by Sir Robert Hart (head of the Chinese Imperial Maritime Customs Service) after the Boxer Rebellion, the Chinese claims were essentially about this fundamental question: 'Why can you

[26] Foster Rhea Dulles, *The Old China Trade* (Houghton Mifflin Company 1930).

[27] John K Fairbank (ed), *The Cambridge History of China, Volume 10, Late Ch'ing 1800–1911* (Cambridge University Press 1978) 497ff.

[28] Cai Zhenfeng, *A Study on Waiwubu in the Late Qing Dynasty [晚清外務部之研究]* (Zhizhi Xueshu Publisher 2014).

[29] Jenny Huangfu Day, *Qing Travelers to the Far West: Diplomacy and the Information Order in Late Imperial China* (First paperback edition, University Press 2018); Yen (n 8); Shih-shan Henry Tsai, *China and the Overseas Chinese in the United States, 1868–1911* (University of Arkansas Press 1983).

[30] Fubin Wang, 'An Estimation of the Remittances of Overseas Chinese in Qing Dynasty and Their Social Impact [清代侨汇之数额估计及社会影响]' [2008] World Ethno-National Studies [世界民族] 48.

[31] Yen (n 8) 154–155.

not treat us as you treat others? Were you to do so you would find us friendly enough and there would be an end to this everlasting bickering and these constantly recurring wars.'[32]

Having said that, it was doubtful that Western powers were willing to extend to China the privileges that they demanded of it. Indeed, that willingness had been tested through a series of incidents targeting Chinese immigrants particularly in the US, a power that was otherwise not the most imperious in relation to China, but that was prone to interpret its international law obligations narrowly when it suited it. Those incidents arose against the background of increased Chinese immigration to the US and some of the social tensions this created, particularly in the mining sector. In 1880, a mob targeted its fury against the local Chinese population in Denver, with the result that one Chinese man was killed. This gave occasion to, as far as we could tell, the earliest recorded instance of the Chinese government exercising diplomatic protection over its nationals on the basis of international law. Chinese Minister to the US Cheng Lanbin (Chen Lan Pin, spelt in Wade–Giles system) (1816–1895) requested the US government to 'extend its protection to the Chinese in Denver', to arrest and punish the perpetrators, and to pay compensation to the owners whose property was wantonly destroyed by the mob.[33]

In itself this was a striking move as it inverted the pattern of recrimination, for the first time suggesting that China might have an interest of its own in addressing such cases. In that situation, however, the US could apparently point to the fact that the authorities had suppressed the riot and promptly arrested the ringleaders. As Secretary of State William Evarts put it:

> Under circumstances of this nature, when the government has put forth every legitimate effort to supress a mob that threatens or attacks alike the safety or security of its own citizens and the foreign residents within its borders, I know of no principle of national obligation, and there is certainly none arising from treaty stipulations, which renders it incumbent on the government of the United States to make indemnity to the Chinese residents of Denver.[34]

Those harmed were therefore expected to turn to the authorities of Colorado, just as any US citizen might have, even though the US itself in its dealings with foreign states was often happy to encourage its nationals to bypass local remedies.

[32] Robert Hart, '*These from the Land of Sinim*': *Essays on the Chinese Question* (London: Chapman & Hall, Ltd 1901) 122.

[33] 'Correspondence with the Legation of China at Washington Correspondence No. 187, Chen Lan Pin to Mr. Evarts' (1882) 1881 (1882) Foreign Relations of the United States 318, 318.

[34] 'Correspondence with the Legation of China at Washington Correspondence No. 188, Mr. Evarts to Chen Lan Pin' (1882) 1881 (1882) Foreign Relations of the United States 318, 320.

5.3 The Rock Springs Massacre Case

Quite different were the circumstances, a few years later, of the infamous Rock Springs Massacre. This can, in fact, help to illustrate the complex dynamics of China's attempts to vindicate the interests of its nationals abroad and specifically in the US. On 2 September 1885, a mob killed twenty-eight Chinese and wounded fifteen in Rock Springs, Wyoming, in addition to burning seventy-eight Chinese homes. The massacre of Chinese miners by white immigrant miners had clear racial dimensions in a context where the Chinese were accused of taking jobs away from whites (this was, as it happens, not entirely untrue, given the Union Pacific's tendency to hire Chinese workers at lower wages in ways that depressed the wages of white miners) and of being strike breakers.[35] It followed years of racial tensions and anti-Chinese sentiment marked by efforts to limit Chinese immigration (notably, the 1882 Exclusion Act). The Knights of Labor, a white supremacist group, had previously organized a chapter in Rock Springs and advocated openly against Chinese labour.[36]

The US Army did deploy to protect the surviving Chinese miners, at the request of Wyoming's territorial governor, but more violence ensued; sixteen men were subsequently arrested, but the local county grand jury refused to bring indictments, finding that no criminal act had been committed. Arrested suspects were thus promptly released and given a heroes' return by white crowds.[37] No one was prosecuted or convicted. In other words, not only was the violence far more significant and extensive in its effects than was the case in Denver several years prior, but the government's response (including that of the state of Wyoming) was also far less compelling than it had been in the previous case.

5.3.1 Zheng Zaoru's Investigation

China moved diligently in the aftermath of this and more aggressively pursued its cause, perhaps made wiser by the fact that the resolution of the earlier Denver incident had dragged on with no prospect of resolution. The Chinese Minister in Washington, Zheng Zaoru (Cheng Tsao Ju, spelt in Wade–Giles system) (1827–1894), dispatched to the scene an investigative team consisting of the consuls in San Francisco and New York and an interpreter, something that the US government facilitated by providing federal protection. While waiting for them to report back, on 22 September 1885, Zheng Zaoru telegraphed the Zongli Yamen in

[35] Dong Wang, *The United States and China: A History from the Eighteenth Century to the Present* (Rowman & Littlefield 2021) 63.

[36] Tsai (n 29) 73–74.

[37] 'Correspondence with the Legation of China at Washington Correspondence No. 64, Cheng Tsao Ju to Mr. Bayard' (1887) 1886 (1887) Foreign Relations of the United States 101, 103.

Beijing, asking for information about indemnities that China had previously paid to the US for injuries of US citizens in China. He also wrote to Zhang Zhidong, asking how mob violence against the foreigners in Shamian (in Guangdong) in 1883 had been handled.[38]

After receiving the report from the consuls, on 30 November 1885 Zheng wrote to the US Secretary of State, Thomas Bayard, to officially protest the violence and demand an indemnity. This was a striking move because, as far as we can document, China had never asserted its diplomatic protection over its nationals to such a full extent. The letter is remarkable for its deftness in invoking international legal arguments, some of the very arguments in fact long, and routinely, invoked by Western powers in China. It was later described by American historian Mary Roberts Coolidge as 'one of the most dignified, discriminating and logical documents ever presented by a Chinese diplomat before the time of the brilliant Minister Wu'.[39]

The letter emphasized, first, that Chinese labourers in Rock Springs had 'entered the territory of the United States in accordance with treaty stipulates' and 'for a number of years past had been engaged in the lawful pursuits of peaceful industry' before the massacre.[40] Furthermore, 'the attack upon the Chinese was unprovoked on their part' and the consuls had found no grievance had been made against them. They were described, in fact, as 'law-abiding, quiet, and peaceable, promptly complying with all exactions in the payment of taxes, never in any way becoming a tax upon the authorities'.[41] Not only the massacres themselves but, crucially, also the authorities' reaction to them was at issue, especially given that the massacre continued for twelve hours both in broad daylight and through the night. As Zheng Zaoru put it, '[i]t does not appear that any civil or other authorities made any attempt to prevent or suppress the riot' and '[t]he judicial proceedings which followed the sad event are described as "a burlesque"'.[42]

As a consequence, Zheng Zaoru solemnly continued:

> It therefore remains for me to ask, in the name of the Emperor and Government of China, that the persons who have been guilty of this murder, robbery, and arson, be brought to punishment; that the Chinese subjects be fully indemnified for all the losses and injuries they have sustained by this lawlessness; and that suitable measures be adopted to protect the Chinese residents of Wyoming Territory and elsewhere in the United States from similar attacks.[43]

[38] Wang Yuanchong, *The Sino-US Encounter: Great Power Diplomacy and the Rise and Fall of the Late Qing (1784–1911) [中美相遇: 大国外交与晚清兴衰(1784-1911)]* (Wen Hui Press [文汇出版社] 2021) 333–334.

[39] Mary Roberts Coolidge, *Chinese Immigration* (Henry Holt and Company 1909) 271–272.

[40] 'Correspondence with the Legation of China at Washington Correspondence No. 64, Cheng Tsao Ju to Mr. Bayard' (n 37) 101.

[41] ibid 102.

[42] ibid.

[43] ibid.

5.3.2 The Chinese Case for Reciprocity

Anticipating the line of argument which had already been used by the US following the Denver incident, Zheng Zaoru carefully insisted that the question was not one of US law, on which he professed to have no expertise (although he pointed out candidly that 'the administration of justice and the protection of life and property belong exclusively to the Government and authorities of the Federal Union').[44] Instead, he emphasized the question of *reciprocity* as central to the whole dispute:

> There is a principle of reciprocal justice and comity so fair and so true that it is incorporated as a cardinal doctrine, in common, in the system of religion and ethics of the people of America and of China. And in proof of the fact that this principle is equally applicable to Governments in their international relations as to persons in their individual duties, it has been inserted in one of the earliest treaties between China and the United States, and the maxim 'to do to others as they would have others do to them' remains in a treaty which is to-day the international law of the two nations (Article XXIX, treaty of 1858).[45]

If the US government were to insist upon and adhere to the view of Mr Evarts previously expressed in the Denver case, Zheng Zaro pointed out somewhat slyly, 'China should, in due reciprocity and international comity, accept and practice the same principle'.[46] Pointing to the fact that the US had, in fact, been a pioneer in renegotiating unequal treaties, Zheng Zaoru insisted that, despite the specifics of US citizens' extraterritorial rights in China:

> I think it is also clear that so far as the questions involved in this note are concerned, to wit, the full protection of the laws, punishment for acts of riot, murder, robbery, and arson, and pecuniary indemnity for losses occasioned thereby, American citizens in China have no other and no greater treaty guarantees and rights than Chinese subjects in the United States. They are placed on a common footing with the people of the country.[47]

This was based on the Sino–American treaties of 1868 and 1880, both of which anticipated the applicability of the most-favoured-nation treatment to Chinese subjects in the US. It is necessary to note, however, that in fact paying indemnities was never explicitly included in the Sino–American treaties of 1858, 1868, and 1880. This is why Zheng's argument did not dwell much on the treaty provisions

[44] ibid 104.
[45] ibid.
[46] ibid 103.
[47] ibid 105.

but put emphasis on the 'high principles of equity and national comity'.[48] These principles were reflected in the treaties' stipulation of most-favoured-nation treatment for the Chinese. But for Zheng, reciprocity meant that, since China valued its friendship with the US and paid almost every indemnity claim made by American nationals, the US government should reciprocate by not restricting itself to the black-letter treaty provisions.

In fact, for its part, the Imperial Court of Qing had been habitually particularly gracious and non-litigious:

> In making that payment my Government did not consider the strict obligations of international law or treaty, but was influenced by a desire to show its appreciation of the friendly conduct of the United States in a time of great trial. It neither examined the evidence upon which the claims were based, nor did it insist upon having a representative on the board which disbursed this large sum. The diplomatic representative of the United States, under instructions from his Government, had declared that the claims were equitable and just to that amount, and ought to be paid by China, and upon the faith of his representation the payment was made.[49]

Zheng Zaoru further pointed out the fact that US

> diplomatic and consular representatives, under direct and specific instructions or subsequent approval of the Department of State, [had] intervene[d] with the Chinese imperial and local authorities in all cases which came to their notice of injuries or losses suffered by American citizens from mob violence, and [had] asked these authorities not only to punish the offenders but to indemnify the citizens for all their losses.[50]

Zheng presented a string of evidence both in the letter and in Enclosures No. 3 and No. 4 attached to his claim relating to China's own compensation of US citizens in China for ill-treatment. In particular, a lump sum of $735,258.97 had been paid in 1858, in addition to isolated cases of reparation, 'in full liquidation of all claims of American citizens', including as they emerged from mob violence.[51] China,

[48] ibid 108.

[49] ibid 105.

[50] ibid 106.

[51] Inclosure no. 3 (accompanying Zheng's letter to Bayard) examined these claims and found that 41 of 48 claims were related to American losses during China's war with the British and French, and according to the US's own practice such war damages would not be repaired. For the rest of the claims, mainly pertaining to robbery and mob violence, the memo argued that if the indemnity commission followed the position as the one adopted in the 1880 Denver case, none of these claims would be accepted. It found that out of the $643,994.42 totally received by the American claimants, 'at least $600,000 was not warranted under a strict application of international law, as interpreted by the Government of the United States, but was conceded by China, as a mark of appreciation of the friendly attitude of the United States during the hostilities with Great Britain and France'. Ibid 145–147.

evidently, could do no less than demand similar reparations when confronted with essentially similar violence against its own nationals. Under such circumstances:

> It cannot be believed that in doing this the United States has required of China that which it would not, in the language of Secretary Fish, expect of a 'European or American state under the rules of the equitable code which regulated the intercourse of civilized nations'. Neither can it be believed that the United States would so far violate the spirit of the 'golden rule', incorporated by it in one of its treaties, or 'the usages of national comity', referred to by Mr. Evarts, as to require of China that which under similar circumstances it would not concede to China in reciprocity.[52]

5.3.3 The US Response

There was certainly hesitation within the US government about how to deal with the incident. It confronted Washington with a type of demand that was not entirely novel (e.g., Spain had made a similar claim in the aftermath of the 1851 riots at New Orleans) but that emanated for the first time from a nation otherwise under imperial yoke. One concern was that failing to provide an indemnity might infuriate China and compromise trade relations, especially in a context where rival imperial powers such as the British might seek to exploit the situation in China itself. At the same time, the government was keen not to set a precedent. Part of the bad will may also have been traceable to the fact that those responsible for the massacres were apparently not US citizens but unnaturalized miners of European stock.[53]

Eventually the State Department insisted, through Bayard, that the US was not liable under international law. The reason was partly that the massacre occurred in Wyoming, which was presented as a self-governing state of the Union.[54] As a result, it was if anything before the courts of Wyoming that an indemnity should be sought—an argument dubious at the time and obviously unreceivable nowadays, and that would have condemned the Chinese claim. Moreover, as in the Denver case, the acts in question were presented as private acts for which the US could not incur liability. In truth, this was part of a consistent line of arguments that was also invoked in relation to the citizens of Spain or the UK who had been victims of comparable violence in the US,[55] and so China was not particularly singled out.

[52] ibid 107.
[53] 'Correspondence with the Legation of China at Washington Correspondence No. 67, Mr. Bayard to Mr. Cheng Tsao Ju' (1887) 1886 (1887) Foreign Relations of the United States 101, 160.
[54] ibid 159.
[55] An example of mob violence against the British was the 1880 Texas mob. Tu (n 14) 48.

Moreover, and more significantly, the US constructed an entire response alleging that its reciprocity did not quite apply given the asymmetry of relations between the US and China. Bayard claimed that 'under the respective system and nature of the two Governments they could not have been made reciprocal, nor were they intended to be so'.[56] He argued that, in fact, the Chinese in the US enjoyed greater privileges than those enjoyed by Americans in China: whereas the Americans were only allowed to travel and sojourn in limited places in China, the Chinese were allowed to go anywhere and take up whichever occupation in the US.[57] He therefore insisted that:

> There was ... in all these years no reciprocity of treatment of the citizens or subjects of the one country within the jurisdiction of the other. There could not be, for the Chinese Government so restricted and hedged about its conceded and carefully limited privileges as to make reciprocity impossible on the part of the United States, unless taking the form of retaliation, which our system of laws makes impracticable.[58]

Interestingly, this argument was countered by the American Minister in Beijing, Charles Denby, who discussed extraterritoriality in one of his correspondences to Bayard informing the latter about the anti-American riots in China. Denby acknowledged that extraterritoriality gave foreigners in China far-reaching advantages, but because obviously it could not be extended to everywhere in the country, the compromise was that foreigners were restricted to specific places where extraterritoriality applied.[59] In other words, limitations on US mobility in China were also a consequence of the far-reaching rights which its nationals enjoyed.

At any rate, Bayard's argument reflected a very different understanding of what reciprocity entailed. For Zheng, reciprocity referred to the kind of remedies that each state (and particularly China) had been willing to provide, based on their specific circumstances. And since China always indemnified the American victims in China, the US should do the same; for Bayard, by contrast, reciprocity meant that the nationals of the two countries had to have substantively the same rights and treatment in each other's territory, and since Qing was not an open country like the US, there was no reciprocity to begin with.

The US government did offer eventually, ex gratia, an indemnity for the loss of damaged property, although not for the killings, while emphasizing the non-legal character of such payment. In the words of the US president Cleveland:

[56] 'Correspondence with the Legation of China at Washington Correspondence No. 67, Mr. Bayard to Mr. Cheng Tsao Ju' (n 53) 161.

[57] ibid 163.

[58] ibid 163.

[59] 'China Correspondence No. 62, Mr. Denby to Mr. Bayard' (1887) 1886 (1887) Foreign Relations of the United States 66, 97.

> whilst the United States Government is under no obligation, whether by the express terms of its treaties with China or the principles of international law, to indemnify these Chinese subjects for losses caused by such means and under the admitted circumstances, yet that in view of the palpable and discreditable failure of the authorities of Wyoming Territory to bring to justice the guilty parties or to assure to the sufferers an impartial forum in which to seek and obtain compensation for the losses which those subjects have incurred by lack of police protection, and considering further the entire absence of provocation or contribution on the part of the victims, the Executive may be induced to bring the matter to the benevolent consideration of the Congress, in order that that body, in its high discretion, may direct the bounty of the Government in aid of innocent and peaceful strangers whose maltreatment has brought discredit upon the country, with the distinct understanding that such action is in no wise to be held as a precedent, is wholly gratuitous, and is resorted to in a spirit of pure generosity toward those who are otherwise helpless.[60]

In early 1887, the US Congress finally approved the payment of indemnities totalling $147,748.74, which was disbursed through the new Chinese Minister Zhang Yinhuan (Chung Yen Hoon, spelt in Wade–Giles system) (1837–1900) in February that year.

5.4 The Assertion of Protection and Sovereignty Building Through Expatriate Nationals: An Assessment

China's intervention on behalf of its nationals in the Rock Springs case, while ultimately successful, did not fundamentally change the legal tenor of the conversation with the US along more egalitarian lines. A few factors which contributed to the indemnity payment also limited the impact of the case. For one thing, the position of the US was legally quite tenuous given the effective acquiescence of the authorities in the non-prosecution of those involved, irrespective of the fact that the US federal government might constitutionally not have had the powers to prosecute them in lieu of Wyoming. Indeed, President Cleveland himself later acknowledged that the proceedings following the massacre 'were a ghastly mockery of justice'.[61] This patent denial of justice, commented Huffcut, 'comes dangerously near the line at which governmental responsibility begins'.[62]

[60] United States, President (1885–1889: Cleveland), *The Public Papers of Grover Cleveland, Twenty-Second President of the United States. March 4, L885, to March 4, L889.* (Govt print-off 1889) 70.

[61] ibid 69.

[62] Huffcut (n 17) 81.

Another factor that weakened the US case in the circumstances was that, as Zheng Zaoru was prompt to point out, following the destruction of Spanish citizens' property by a mob in New Orleans in 1851 and after the Queen of Spain expressed displeasure at being opposed by the federal structure of the US, the US Congress had in fact authorized the Secretary of State to indemnify Spanish subjects. This led Zheng Zaoru to insist:

> If, therefore, in the past the equity and wisdom of the Secretary of State, of his excellency the President, and of the Congress of the United States have found a way whereby the obstructions [nota: flowing from the US's federal structure] have been overcome as to the subjects of other nations, I do not doubt that an equally efficacious method will be devised for the relief of the subjects of China, especially in view of the fact that the Government of the latter has uniformly and for a long series of years granted, at the request of the Government of the United States, similar relief to its citizens, and that, too, in the face of strong local prejudice and at the cost of many hundreds of thousands of dollars.[63]

Finally, perhaps wisely, China had sought to pursue its case more 'in the spirit' than 'in the letter' of international law and was itself keen to emphasize that it did not seek to create a precedent. This may have facilitated an award in that case, but also limited any precedential value such an award might then have. Indeed, the 'unfortunate Chinese ... more interested in compensation for wrongs done to them than in the principles of international law and ethics, accepted the generosity of Congress with gratitude'.[64]

However, the result of that particular dispute may ultimately matter less than the singular opportunity the incident afforded China to, as it were, take international law's vaunted reciprocity at its word. Although ornately polite, there was no doubt that Zheng Zaoru was remarkably aware of the usages of nations and international law. And in a sense, this was not that surprising: China had after all by then been on the receiving end of international law arguments deployed by imperial powers for decades, and was only too ready to turn these arguments to its own benefit.

Moreover, the Chinese intervention did arguably contribute to highlighting the fraught interracial subtext of the relation to imperial powers. The clear racist dimension of the massacre had led to divisions within the US government. Bayard went as far as to volunteer in correspondence with China's legation in Washington the 'personal' view that the violence was due to the fact that 'Chinese immigrants ... segregate themselves from the rest of the residents and citizens of the

[63] 'Correspondence with the Legation of China at Washington Correspondence No. 64, Cheng Tsao Ju to Mr. Bayard' (n 37) 108.

[64] HF MacNair, 'The Protection of Alien Chinese through Chinese Authorities' (1924) 8 Chinese Social and Political Science Review 48, 68.

United States and ... refuse to mingle with the mass of population'.[65] By contrast, President Cleveland in his State of the Union report to Congress in 1885 acknowledged that 'race prejudice is the chief factor to originating these disturbances'[66] and that it was a problem in US–Chinese relations. Although he affirmed 'the admitted right of a government to prevent the influx of elements hostile to its internal peace and security'[67] (as per exclusionary practices then also prevalent in Canada and Australia[68]), he nonetheless pleaded for 'the harmony of relations with China' and insisted that '[a]ll of the power of this government should be exhorted to maintain the amplest good faith towards China in the treatment of these men, and the inflexible sternness of the law ... must be insisted upon'.[69]

If China was only moderately successful with the US following the Rock Springs tragedy, the episode arguably paved the way for other instances that were marginally more decisive. For example, more than twenty years later, in September 1907, anti-Asian violence erupted in Vancouver, British Columbia, extensively damaging Chinese property. Rather than simply deny any obligation under international law, the Canadian government promptly appointed a Royal Commission in early 1908 to investigate. Although China had no consular office in Canada, it was represented by its diplomats from London, Portland, and San Francisco, who attended the inquiry.[70] The inquiry was largely productive and recommended a lump payment for all the damage suffered. Particularly notable was the fact that the final report to the Governor-General in Council noted that the presence of Chinese officials had been 'not only gratifying as an evidence of the appreciation by the Chinese government of the action of the Canadian Government in instituting the investigation, but was also salutary as affording to the several claimants an assurance, if any such were needed, that their interests would be fully protected before the Commission'.[71]

Indeed, even in the US one legacy of the Rock Springs episode may have been a heightened alertness by the federal government of the inherent risks of not intervening quickly to quell mob violence, at the risk of a diplomatic and legal headache in the aftermath. When in 1890 the population of Aberdeen (Washington State) ordered the Chinese to leave the town by a certain date, the Secretary of State

[65] 'Correspondence with the Legation of China at Washington Correspondence No. 67, Mr. Bayard to Mr. Cheng Tsao Ju' (n 53) 167.

[66] United States, President (1885–1889: Cleveland) (n 60) 19.

[67] ibid.

[68] David C Atkinson, 'The White Australia Policy, the British Empire, and the World' (2015) 8 Britain and the World 204; Constance Backhouse, 'The White Women's Labor Laws: Anti-Chinese Racism in Early Twentieth-Century Canada' (1996) 14 Law and History Review 315.

[69] United States, President (1885–1889: Cleveland) (n 60) 18.

[70] Government of Canada, 'Report by W.L. Mackenzie King, C.M.G. Deputy Minister of Labour, Commissioner Appointed to Investigate into the Losses Sustained by the Chinese Population of Vancouver, B.C. on the Occasion of the Riots in That City in September 1907' (Privy Council Office of Canada 1908) 9.

[71] ibid 14.

intervened with the Governor of Washington to ask him to use all necessary means to stop the disturbance: 'thus the principle was demonstrated that where there is a strong will there is a practicable way for protecting the persons and property of aliens within the United States.'[72]

Paradoxically, on the Chinese side, the Qing government agreed to limiting Chinese immigration to the US in exchange of more treaty assurances of protection of those Chinese who were already there. Following the Rock Springs massacre, Zheng Zaoru proposed to the Chinese government a policy of self-prohibition of emigration to the US, and Zheng's successor, Zhang Yinhuan, negotiated a new immigration treaty to the effect of restricting Chinese emigration to the US in 1888. The treaty did not enter into force due to internal opposition from both the Chinese and the American governments.[73] However, this still demonstrated that the Chinese were eager to create special treaty rights for Chinese immigrants in the US, above and beyond the application of 'the most favored nation clause', amounting to an expectation that 'some positive, affirmative, active, interposition of the executive department of the United States would be exercised when it received notice that Chinese subjects in its territory were receiving ill treatment at the hands of the local authorities'.[74]

This was not always sufficient to trigger the US into action, however, and more often than not the fault lines of state and federal powers, or executive and judicial competence prevented meaningful action, as in the case of the boycott of Chinese trade in Butte, Montana.[75] Moreover, there were complications involved that would soon suggest the deep connection between the situation in the US and the situation in China. Demands made on behalf of Chinese nationals abroad were subsequently tied to a renewed push in favour of the status of Westerners in China, leading to sometimes tense arguments about reciprocity and which was the worst treatment. In a sense, China could only claim reparations for harm suffered by the Chinese if it doubled down on the recognition that the Americans and the Europeans were entitled to demand the same; but it could also implicitly hold hostage the treatment of US nationals to improved treatment of Chinese ones. If reciprocity did not operate on its own, it could at least be encouraged through veiled threats and grievances.

In March 1886, agitation against Americans rose in the Canton region on receipt of news about anti-Chinese riots in the US and the ensuing unwillingness of the US government to provide redress. Mirroring Zheng Zaoru's actions in the US, the American Minister in Beijing, Denby demanded that the Zongli Yamen take

[72] MacNair (n 64) 69.
[73] Tsai (n 29) 89–93.
[74] 'Correspondence with the Legation of China at Washington Correspondence, Mr. Pung to Mr. Blaine' (1891) 1890 (1891) Foreign Relations of the United States 210, 222.
[75] 'China Correspondence, No. 207, Mr. Wu to Mr. Hill' (1902) 1901 (1902) Foreign Relations of the United States 39, 100–128; Tu (n 14) 267.

necessary measures to prevent any trouble in Canton, noting 'a repetition of the same thing on the part of the Chinese would neither be a justification nor lead to a solution of the difficulty'.[76] He even ordered the USS Monocacy to proceed from Tianjin to Canton, where another foreign gunboat was stationed.[77] At about the same time, the US consul at Canton, Charles Seymour, brought the riots to the attention of the Zhang Zhidong, Viceroy of Liangguang. Later, in September of the same year, more anti-American missionary riots broke out in Chongqing. Denby also handed a strong protest note to the Chinese government demanding compensation for American losses, punishment of the Chinese involved, and a guarantee against a recurrence of such incidents.[78]

In both cases, the Chinese authorities pushed back. For example, when Denby complained to the Zongli Yamen that the local Chinese authorities in Sichuan did not exert all their power to prevent the anti-American riot, he was told: 'This state of affairs [happens] rather too often in western countries'.[79] Similarly, Zhang Zhidong bluntly replied that the Chinese suffering in America was 'inhuman oppression to the extreme', which, compared to the American suffering in China, 'must be one hundred times as severe'.[80] Viceroy Zhang urged the US consul to 'personally telegraph and petition to his excellency the American minister at Peking to write to your honorable country's Secretary of State (within this day) to consider satisfactorily and pay the indemnities'.[81] It was even rumoured that agitation in Guangdong had the official sanction of Zhang Zhidong, which Zhang denied.[82]

At any rate, anti-American sentiment rose noticeably in China. In the 1920s, Harold MacNair pointed out that 'retaliation' in the form of attacks on foreigners in China and the boycotting of foreigners and their goods was one 'indirect form of protection of Chinese and their interests abroad'.[83] Such retaliation had culminated in the Boxer Rebellion, which coincided with anti-Asiatic legislation in America and Australia, where the latter could be deemed as a contributing factor to the former.[84] Certainly, a sense of grievous harm to Chinese communities abroad

[76] 'China Correspondence No. 50, Mr. Denby to Mr. Bayard' (1887) 1886 (1887) Foreign Relations of the United States 66, 77.

[77] ibid 78.

[78] 'China Correspondence, Inclosure 1 in No. 210, Mr. Denby to Foreign Office' (1888) 1887 (1888) Foreign Relations of the United States 159, 162–163; 'China Correspondence, Inclosure 2 in No. 212, Mr. Denby to the Tsung-Li Yamen' (1888) 1887 (1888) Foreign Relations of the United States 159, 164–165.

[79] 'China Correspondence Inclosure 1 in No. 212, The Tsung-Li Yamen to Mr. Denby' (1888) 1887 (1888) Foreign Relations of the United States 159, 164.

[80] 'China Correspondence Inclosure in No. 274, The Viceroy of Canton to Mr. Seymour' (1888) 1887 (1888) Foreign Relations of the United States 159, 177.

[81] ibid 178.

[82] 'China Correspondence, Inclosure 1 in No. 117, An Official Communication from His Excellency Chang, Governor-General of the Two Quangs, to Hon. Charles Seymour, United States Consul, Canton, Relative to Anti-Chinese Riots in San Francisco' (1887) 1886 (1887) Foreign Relations of the United States 66, 82.

[83] MacNair (n 64) 80.

[84] ibid 81.

further contributed to a sense of the unsustainability of China's position within its own territory given the presence of various Western powers. As a result, 'a groping and elementary patriotism'[85] among the Chinese within and outside China developed and would soon reach its climax with the 1905 anti-American boycott, where Chinese diasporas in the US were joined by Chinese merchants in China and diaspora communities elsewhere.[86]

Increasingly, then, the statuses of the Chinese in the US and of Americans in China came to be tied together, in ways that may certainly have driven home to both sides how they were increasingly linked by reciprocal relations. Ultimately, however, the reluctance to provide compensation to Chinese immigrants and the difficulties of even a rising China in championing its nationals reflected power differentials and the continuing reality of imperialism. As MacNair put it, 'the subjects of a military power [cannot be] ill-treated with impunity',[87] and clearly China was not in a position to exercise gunboat diplomacy vis-à-vis Western powers. Indeed, the treatment of China by the US differed from the treatment it reserved to relatively stronger states with significant diasporas in the US. Notably, in a series of cases of mob violence targeting Italians in 1891–1910, the US government systematically paid compensation.[88]

China's indignation about the inequality seen, and perhaps to some extent its disillusionment about international law, was vividly expressed by then Chinese Minister, Zhang Yinhuan, in his correspondence to Bayard on 16 August 1887. At that time the two countries were negotiating to revise the Sino–American treaty concerning Chinese immigration, and the position of the Qing government was that restriction of Chinese emigration should go in tandem with the guarantee of protection of Chinese in the US. After Bayard rejected much of Zhang's proposal, Zhang replied in a much less 'diplomatic' tone:

> In China, so far as is known, not a single American has lost his life by mob violence; while in every case where injury has been done to the property and rights of American citizens by conspiracy and mobs, punishment has been promptly inflicted upon the guilty, and full pecuniary indemnity has been made by the authorities.
>
> On the other hand … more than thirty Chinese have been murdered through mobs in the United States, and … so far as known not a single punishment has been inflicted on the murders; tens of thousands of peaceable and law-observing Chinese have been forcibly and in great fight driven out of their abodes and compelled to abandon their employment in the State of California and in the Western

[85] ibid 86.
[86] Tsai (n 29) 104ff.
[87] MacNair (n 64) 57.
[88] Tu (n 14) 51–58.

Territories, and the authorities have administer no punishment on the wicked men who have done these unlawful deeds ...

China is not now asking to be released from the treaty stipulations of 1844 and 1858, but it does feel that when the United States for a second time asks that the immigration stipulations of the treaty of 1868 be amended and restricted some degree of reciprocity in treaty guaranties as to protection should be enacted and enforced, and it appeals to the experience of Chinese laborers in the United States as its warrants for such a claim ...

It cannot be believed that you would insist that China is bound to grant a greater measure of protection to Americans in its territory than your Government is willing and able to grant to Chinese in the United States. Neither would you claim that protection to life and property is more certain and ample in China than it is or can be made in the United States, or that this difference would release your Government from its treaty obligations to enforce protection ...

If this is impossible under its system, then it must be inferred that the Government of the United States is impotent to discharge its international obligations, and I am unwilling to be understood as brining such an insinuation against this great and powerful nation. I understand that its first teacher of international law has laid down the doctrine that 'the whole international code is founded on reciprocity' ... And the Supreme Court of the United States ... declared that 'if the United States can require this (protection of its coinage and currency of another (nation)), that others may require it of them, *because international obligations are of necessity reciprocal in their nature*. This right, if it exists at all, is given by the law of nations, and what is law for one is, under the same circumstances, law for the other'.[89]

5.5 Conclusion: Legacies of Qing Protection of Chinese Abroad

Several stories can be told about this early effort at protection of the Chinese abroad. The most conventional one is that in asserting protective prerogatives over its nationals abroad, China was not so much doing the right, vaguely sentimental thing for those nationals as it was, first and foremost, constituting itself as a state. Early concern by China for its nationals abroad was very much part of a process of state building and self-strengthening in reaction to dissatisfaction with its status in the world as manifested, inter alia, in its inability to pursue a policy of protection of its diaspora. To protect one's nationals abroad, then, was to demand a modicum of

[89] 'Correspondence with the Legation of China at Washington Correspondence No. 246, Mr. Chang Yen Hoon to Mr. Bayard' (1889) 1888 Part I (1889) Foreign Relations of the United States 360, 376–377.

respect for their dignity but also, evidently, for one's national dignity. To the extent that Western powers enforced extraterritoriality in China, demanding respect for a minimum standard of treatment of Chinese immigrant populations was in a sense the least that Qing could do.

The invocation of diplomatic protection by China in the nineteenth century, then, also tells us something about some of the fundamental dilemmas of international law. It is a cliché that 'the master's house will not be dismantled by the master's tools'.[90] This is undoubtedly partly true in this case: relatively bold as China's early invocation of the law of the protection of aliens may have been, it certainly did not significantly shift the boundaries of Western imperialism in China proper. Its success abroad was, moreover, highly relative. Epistemologically, it involved a kind of mimesis, investing heavily in the already existing form of international law rather than challenging it, by for example invoking the general principles of reciprocity and equity or by securing more protection for Chinese diasporas through treaty negotiations.

At the same time, Chinese concern with its diaspora was not so much a by-product of modern national ideas as it was prepared by a slow realization of the potential of the diaspora and a reappraisal of its continued links to China. This realization, however, needed international law in order to convey a point that could potentially be understood by Western interlocutors. This was one element that led China on the path to sovereign modernization, as illustrated for example by the development of Qing's consular and diplomatic network. By in a sense turning the weapons of Western imperial powers against them, it was an early hint that the protection of aliens would have to work both ways. As such, the Chinese move, while not radical, certainly made the most of the fact that international law, for all its imperial origins, was also a universal vehicle on its face, whose benefits would be difficult to persistently deny to newcomers, especially when they were keen—and showed early adeptness—at using its tools. If anything, that gamble has proved prescient in the long term.

Interestingly, however, Qing's assertion of diplomatic protection over its diaspora also implicitly reproduced the imperialist character of the international law of alien protection. In this sense, Rock Springs can be seen as the precursor to far later incidents in which China would flex its diplomatic muscle much more, especially in relation to comparatively junior international partners. This was the case in 1911 following the Torreón massacre in Mexico, where approximately 300 Asian Americans (both Chinese and Japanese) were killed by a mob in the course of the Mexican Revolution. More than fifty years after Rock Springs, China was in a stronger position and more inclined to ask for an apology from the Mexican

[90] This comes from an influential essay by Audre Lorde. Audre Lorde, 'The Master's Tool Will Never Dismantle The Master's House' in Cherríe Moraga and Gloria Anzaldúa (eds), *This Bridge Called My Back: Writing by Radical Women of Color* (Kitchen Table: Women of Color Press 1983).

government as well as compensation, which it did, to the tune of 30 million pesos (or 100,000 pesos per Chinese killed). It also commissioned an extensive investigation and report.[91] Rumour had it that China had actually dispatched a warship in Mexican waters, an incident which would have been evidently striking in light of China's own historical vulnerability to gunboat diplomacy had it not turned out to be probably apocryphal.[92] The Qing dynasty did not get US support in pressing its claims and eventually settled for a lower indemnity (6 million pesos), but the Chinese Republic that took over after 1912 eventually came to an agreement with Mexico, although reparations were never actually paid.[93] It was only in 2021 that then-president of Mexico López Obrador apologized for the massacre.[94]

[91] Wilfley & Bassett Firm, *Memorandum on the Law and the Facts in the Matter of the Claim of China Against Mexico for Losses of Life and Property Suffered by Chinese Subjects at Torreón on May 13, 14, and 15, 1911* (American Book & Printing Company 1911).

[92] Leo M Dambourges Jacques, 'The Chinese Massacre in Torreon (Coahuila) in 1911' (1974) 16 Arizona and the West 233, 243–244.

[93] ibid 244.

[94] David Agren, 'Mexico Faces Up to Uneasy Anniversary of Chinese Massacre' *The Guardian* (16 May 2021) <https://www.theguardian.com/world/2021/may/16/mexico-chinese-massacre-centenary-torreon> accessed 25 October 2023.

6

Lost and Found in Translation

How European International Law Became Universalized in Modern China

*Wensheng Qu and Li Wan**

6.1 Introduction

International legal doctrine prior to the 18th century exhibited a more universal or cosmopolitan character in both theory and methodology than it did in the 19th and 20th centuries. From the 1890s onward, Europe and the United States emerged as leaders in international legal scholarship. Prevailing opinion held that the law originated in Europe, therefore the world should be governed by the European legal system, mirroring the traditional Chinese idea of a single normative order that governs "All under Heaven" (*tianxia,* 天下). Nonetheless, a critical question has yet to be thoroughly examined: How did European international law become universalized in the context of modern China? The Chinese translations of Emer de Vattel's *Le droit de gens (Law of Nations),* commissioned by Lin Zexu (林则徐) (1785–1850), and Henry Wheaton's *Elements of International Law,* overseen by W. A. P. Martin (in Chinese 丁韪良, 1827–1916), may provide valuable insight into this dual process.

This chapter examines the transformation of international law from a Eurocentric construct to its purported universal application, with particular emphasis on its implications for China in the 19th century. The analysis centers on the paradox inherent in the simultaneous Europeanization and universalization of international law, as reflected in China's interactions with the international community. The chapter considers developments in international law from the 18th to the 20th century, highlighting pivotal philosophical shifts and their consequences for non-European states, notably China. It further addresses the dissemination and translation of key international legal texts in China, including the works of

* This chapter has been adapted and expanded from the article "From the Law of Nations to International Law—Historicism and Translation in the Late Qing Dynasty" (从万国法到国际法—清季国际法翻译与国际法历史主义转向) (2024) 39(1) Journal of Tsinghua University (Philosophy and Social Sciences) 45, 45–64.

Wensheng Qu and Li Wan, *Lost and Found in Translation* In: *Histories of International Law in China.*
Edited by: Ignacio de la Rasilla, Jiangyu Wang, and Congyan Cai, Oxford University Press.
 DOI: 10.1093/oso/9780198888345.003.0006

Emer de Vattel and Henry Wheaton, and the resulting impact on Chinese theories on international order.

Excluding the Introduction and Conclusion, this chapter is organized into five substantive sections. Section 2 provides a historical overview of the development of international law, examining the early modern cosmopolitan tradition and its subsequent Europeanization. Section 3 addresses the introduction of international law into China, with particular attention to the translation of Vattel's *Law of Nations* and its impact on China during conflicts with British imperialists. Section 4 assesses the extent to which the transition from a cosmopolitan to a Eurocentric framework in international law can be linked to the First Opium War (1839–1842), analyzing how British imperialists deliberately promoted a Eurocentric model to circumvent Vattel's theories and justify the Opium War. Section 5 investigates the doctrinal shift from Vattel's voluntarism to Wheaton's historicism, focusing on the construction of European civilization as the normative foundation of international law to the exclusion and subordination of non-European states. Section 6 illustrates how the translation of Wheaton's *Elements of International Law* reframed the European law of nations within a cosmopolitan context, thereby shaping Chinese perceptions of global legal order. The Conclusion reflects on the enduring significance of these intellectual transformations for contemporary approaches to international law in China.

6.2 Imagined Universal Community and *jus gentium universale* (the Extension of Natural Law)

In the early modern era, jurists of international law articulated the concept of a universal community that would encompass all nations and individuals under a single law of nations, presupposing a shared consensus as its foundation. Although this cosmopolitan vision ostensibly extends equal standing to non-European states, in reality it neglects the distinctive normative frameworks of non-European societies, such as the *Tianxia* system in East Asia. As a result, what has been described as a universal law of nations was *jus publicum Europaeum*, grounded in European civilization and political experience. This European cosmopolitanism parochially excludes non-European perspectives, though without overt impoliteness. This methodological limitation is significant, as it underlies the presumption among European international legal scholars that there exists a universally applicable law binding even non-European regions.

After the 1750s, the ideal of a universal community gave way to the "family of nations," a construct that began to operate both as a theoretical and practical framework for international relations. Membership in this system was restricted to so-called civilized nations, with the result that many non-European polities were effectively excluded. This development replaced the *jus gentium universale* with *jus publicum Europaeum*, a body of law that applied chiefly to these so-called civilized nations. Nevertheless, this transition was not a fundamental change; rather, it perpetuated the limited and exclusionary cosmopolitanism characteristic of the early modern era.

Prior to the 18th century, the concept of international law was primarily grounded in natural law. Originating in pre-modern European philosophy, natural law encompassed principles of morality and reason that were initially applied within domestic legal systems. Over time, scholars such as Hugo Grotius (1583–1645) and Samuel von Pufendorf (1632–1694) adapted and extended these principles to the conduct of nations in the international context during the 17th century.[1] The German jurist Georg Stephan Wiesand (1736–1821) noted in 1759: "Natural law has come to be applied to peoples. For what is lawful among private individuals is also lawful among entire peoples."[2] Early treatises on natural law took the approach of *domestic analogy* to analyze legal relations between nations. Nevertheless, the concept of the law of nations remained ill-defined, and its formation was at times deductive, emerging either from natural law principles or from a presumed universal consensus among nations.[3] The international legal norms articulated by thinkers such as Christian Wolff (1679–1754) thus tended to be highly general, abstract, and at times lacking in practical credibility. This criticism applies equally to most pre-modern legal and quasi-legal writings that attempted to expound the law of nations in a similar manner.[4]

In sum, much of the law of nations was undeniably general in character. Leading international jurists constructed a normative order with universal aspirations. However, this law of nations, developed within the European context, often lacked practical relevance for international relations beyond Europe. Its universality was essentially theoretical, failing to account for the histories and circumstances of non-European societies.[5] Nevertheless, this normative framework was advanced as a governing order for the entire world. As Dietrich Heinrich Ludwig von Ompteda (1746–1803) observed in 1785: "The purely natural law of nations extends its rule over every and all peoples of this earth, be they civilized or uncivilized."[6] This

[1] Hugo Grotius, Rights of War and Peace, ed. Richard Tuck (Indianapolis: Liberty Fund, 2005) 162–163, 545–546. Peter Schröder, "The Constitution of the Holy Roman Empire after 1648: Samuel Pufendorf's Assessment in his Monzambano" (1999) 42 The Historical Journal 961, 961–983.

[2] Georg Stephan Wiesand, Kurzer Entwurf einer Historie des Natur-und Völker-Rechts, nebst einigen Anmerkungen über die Unvollkommenheiten der natürlichen Rechtsgelehrsamkeit (Leipzig: Iversen, 1759), 84.

[3] Christian Wolff, The Law of Nations Treated According to the Scientific Method (Indianapolis: Liberty Fund, 2017) 24.

[4] Miloš Vec, "Universalization, Particularization, and Discrimination: European Perspectives on a Cultural History of 19th Century International Law" (2012) 3(2) InterDisciplines 79, 82.

[5] ibid.

[6] Dietrich Heinrich Ludwig von Ompteda, Literatur des gesammten sowohl natürlichen als positiven Völkerrechts. Erster Theil (Regensburg: Montag, 1785) 18. Alain Wijffels, "Ompteda Revisited: The Metamorphoses of Scholarship on International Law" (2003) 38 The Irish Jurist 312, 312–330.

terminology implied that the authors did not necessarily treat inter-state relations and instead the intracommunity.. The sources, subjects, and applications of the law of nations were often obscured, presenting an artificial universality. In this context, *jus gentium naturale* and *jus gentium universale* were treated as equivalent concepts.[7] The system presumed the equality of all nations[8] and accordingly extended principles such as fundamental rights and obligations, originally developed for domestic governance, to nations in the international context.

Francisco de Vitoria (1483–1546), Hugo Grotius, and Alberico Gentili (1552–1608) regarded the common consensus of nations as the foundation of international law.[9] However, their approach is marked by a structural methodological flaw. Specifically, they did not account for why the normative systems of non-European nations could not constitute elements of the universal law of nations, while the so-called common consensus was derived predominantly from Christian doctrines, customs, or moral principles. In this sense, their cosmopolitanism was partial rather than universal. Voluntarism emerged as an attempt to address these methodological shortcomings, but it ultimately did not resolve them at a fundamental level.

6.3 From Cosmopolitanism to Voluntarism: Vattel

According to Georges Scelle (1878–1961), Vattel stood as the leading figure among positivists, as he was the one who introduced voluntarism into international law by establishing the dual principles that govern international relations, natural law, and positive law.[10] O'Connell observes that, for Vattel, the authority of international law does not stand above sovereign nations but serves as a tool for regulating relations among them.[11] Vattel's conception of international law is founded on voluntarism. Consequently, his framework excludes the imposition of Christian morality or utopian ideals, although it remains informed by the principles of natural law.[12]

Vattel's enduring significance lies in his depiction of the international order as a universal system composed of equally sovereign and autonomous nations. His voluntarist approach marked a turning point in the evolution of international law,

[7] Johann Heinrich Abicht, Kurze Darstellung des Natur- und Völkerrechts zum Gebrauch bey Vorlesungen (Bayreuth: Johan Andreas Lubers Erben, 1795) 143.

[8] Christian Wolff, The Law of Nations Treated According to the Scientific Method, trans. Joseph H. Drake (Indianapolis: Liberty Fund, 2017) 22. Emer de Vattel, The Law of Nations (London: G. G. and J. Robinson, 1797) lxiii, 149.

[9] See Nan Goodman, The Puritan Cosmopolis: The Law of Nations and the Early American Imagination (New York: Oxford University Press, 2018) 25, 28.

[10] Georges Scelle, Manuel de Droit International Public (Paris: Domat-Montchrestlien, 1948) 40.

[11] Mary Ellen O'Connell, "Peace and War," The Oxford Handbook of the History of International Law, edited by Bardo Fassbender and Anne Peters (Oxford: Oxford University Press, 2012) 278.

[12] Jean D'Aspremont, Formalism and the Sources of International Law: A Theory of the Ascertainment of Legal Rules (New York: Oxford University Press, 2011) 64–65.

inaugurating processes of secularization, universalization, professionalization, and the application of rational methodologies to the discipline.[13] Nonetheless, Vattel grounded the rights of nations in natural law principles and never fully adopted the strict voluntarism later advanced by 19th-century positivist international jurists.[14] Foundational notions such as national independence and equality, the principle of non-intervention, and the concept of a general society of nations, each formative to modern international law, feature prominently in Vattel's theory, which carefully integrates natural law traditions with emergent voluntarist tenets.[15] Vattel articulated a comprehensive metaphysical framework for natural law in which nations pursue their well-being through engagement in commerce, diplomacy, and other forms of interaction. He described self-preservation as the highest duty of each nation, justifying the orientation of foreign policy around national interest.

Historical evidence from across the globe demonstrates the wide dissemination and adaptation of Vattel's work in diverse and distant cultural contexts.[16] An illustrative case is the Chinese translation of his seminal treatise, *Le droit des gens*. In 1839, at the behest of Qing dynasty Imperial Commissioner Lin Zexu, American missionary Peter Parker produced a Chinese version of the text under the title *Huada'er Geguo Luli* (滑达尔各国律例). A second translation was carried out by Yuan Dehui (袁德辉) and subsequently incorporated into the *Haiguo Tuzhi* (海国图志), published in 1847.[17] Both Parker and Yuan selectively translated those portions of Vattel's work dealing with international legal doctrines relevant to trade and conflict, key issues in Chinese-British relations during the 19th century. Notably, they included Sections 100 (Entering the Territory) and 101 (Foreigners Are Subject to the Laws) from Chapter VIII, Book II, which articulate the principle of voluntarism. These sections provide a direct exposition of the doctrine of territorial jurisdiction:

> There are states, such as China, and Japan, into which all foreigners are forbid[den] to penetrate without an express permission: but in Europe the access is every where free to every person who is not an enemy of the state, except, in some countries, to vagabonds and outcasts. [Section 100]
>
> But even in those countries which every foreigner may freely enter, the sovereign is supposed to allow him access only upon this tacit condition, that he be

[13] Fernando Pérez Godoy, "Más Allá del voluntarismo: Derecho natural en el pensamiento de Emer de Vattel" (2019) 41 Revista de Estudios Histórico-Jurídicos 417, 419.

[14] Jason Ralph, Defending the Society of States: Why America Opposes the International Criminal Court and its Vision of World Society (Oxford: Oxford University Press, 2007) 36.

[15] See Ron Harris, "Is It Time for Non-Euro-American Legal History?" (2016) 56 American Journal of Legal History 60, 64.

[16] Elisabetta Fiocchi, L'eterno ritorno del Droit des gens di Emer de Vattel (secc. XVIII–XIX) (Frankfurt am Main: Max Planck Institute for European Legal History, 2017) 6–8.

[17] Sebastian Roll, Normgenese durch Re-Interpretation China und das europäische Völkerrecht im 19. und 20. Jahrhundert (Baden-Baden: Nomos, 2012) 15, 87.

> subject to the laws,—I mean the general laws made to maintain good order, and which have no relation to the title of citizen, or of subject of the state … The sovereignty is the right to command in the whole country; and the laws are not simply confined to regulating the conduct of the citizens towards each other, but also determine what is to be observed by all orders of people throughout the whole extent of the state. [Section 101][18]

According to Vattel's voluntarist doctrine, every sovereign nation, including China, possesses full authority over its own territory, and consequently, all foreigners must comply with the laws of the host nation. On this basis, British imperialists could not legitimately invoke a right to free trade or communication as a means of evading Qing law. Vattel's conception of sovereignty thereby afforded Qing China a principled legal rationale for defending its territorial authority. Although Chinese translations of Vattel's treatise were imperfect, Commissioner Lin nonetheless found Vattel's ideas to be an effective instrument in his contest with British imperialism during the Opium War.

Vattel's voluntarism expressly opposes both unrestricted free trade and coercive communication. While Vattel acknowledges that natural law is universally applicable and ideally suited to regulate society in all circumstances, he maintains that it requires the support of political laws in practice.[19] Vattel contends that natural law, by itself, is inadequate to realize a fully ordered society in the present human condition and must therefore be supplemented by voluntary law.[20] For Vattel, the proper application of natural law presupposes a genuine understanding of human nature and the inherent properties of things.[21] He is critical of attempts to derive obligations from natural law without considering whether the conduct at issue is consonant with human nature or the nature of things.[22] Fundamentally, Vattel rejects the notion that natural law is grounded in the arbitrary will of God.

We should bear in mind an important point in Vattel's theory: Human reason discerns the laws of nature and formulates the general principles that underpin the body of natural law.[23] According to Vattel, the law of nations is fundamentally voluntary, rooted in the consent of nations and manifested in pacts, treaties, and agreements, as well as through customary practices established by tacit consent. For Vattel, each nation constitutes a collective entity whose members pursue their collective perfection and happiness, possessing a will independent of any divine legislator or superior regulatory authority. The nation's will is directed toward

[18] Emer de Vattel, The Law of Nations, ed. Béla Kapossy and Richard Whatmore (Indianapolis: Liberty Fund, 2008) 312.
[19] ibid 776–777.
[20] ibid 779–780.
[21] ibid 748.
[22] ibid 749.
[23] ibid 747.

self-perfection and the attainment of collective well-being, necessitating a political system capable of executing this purpose.[24] Consequently, Vattel maintains that a nation's primary obligation to itself is to adopt the constitution best suited to the character of its people and their circumstances.[25] Additional responsibilities include practicing and advancing commerce, agriculture, diplomacy, and international economic relations.[26]

Consequently, European nations lack the authority to compel other nations to accept their diplomats, merchants, or religious missions. While Vattel articulates a vision of a universal republic predicated on the duty of nations to assist one another,[27] a duty that encourages commercial cooperation among nations,[28] he does not regard this obligation as absolute. According to Vattel, each nation retains the discretion to determine what is fair and may restrict trade if doing so serves its own interests. Moreover, Vattel recognizes that exceptional circumstances may justify intervention in the affairs of other nations under the principle of the balance of power,[29] and the determination of such circumstances rests with either a single nation or an alliance. This principle, therefore, provides a potential rationale for the expansionist policies of European powers.

In Vattel's theory, international law was conceived as universally applicable but did not possess the absolute binding authority of natural law. Vattel did not advocate a cosmopolitan approach that placed European nations in a dominant position. Rather, he maintained that European nations could not assert their imperfect rights, such as claims to free trade, against non-European nations. While Vattel envisioned a universal community of nations, he characterized it as a voluntary international society, meaning that national interests frequently outweighed the collective interests of the international order.[30] Accordingly, the law of nations did not equate to natural law, although it remained subordinated to it in certain respects. Had Vattel's principles been fully introduced in China, it is likely that the intellectual reception and doctrinal understanding of international law among 19th-century Chinese officials and scholars would have been markedly different.

Voluntarism is fundamentally compromised by its inherent egoism. Under this approach, a nation may unilaterally determine both the substance and implementation of universal rights, such as whether resorting to war is justified or whether a treaty that contravenes domestic law is enforceable. In the absence of a uniform

[24] Emer de Vattel, The Law of Nations, ed. Joseph Chitty (London: S. Sweet, 1834) 27.

[25] Tim Hochstrasser, "Introduction," Emer de Vattel, The Law of Nations, ed. Béla Kapossy and Richard Whatmore (Indianapolis: Liberty Fund, 2008) xvi.

[26] Emer de Vattel, The Law of Nations, ed. Béla Kapossy and Richard Whatmore (Indianapolis: Liberty Fund, 2008) 134–135.

[27] ibid xiv–xv.

[28] ibid 261.

[29] Emer de Vattel, The Law of Nations, ed. Joseph Chitty (London: S. Sweet, 1834) 23.

[30] See Ian Hunter, "Vattel's Law of Nations: Diplomatic Casuistry for the Protestant Nation" (2010) 31(1) Grotiana 108, 123.

standard or an authoritative international forum, the codification and application of the law of nations remains effectively stalled. This limitation helps explain why Immanuel Kant (1724–1804) famously referred to Grotius, Pufendorf, and Vattel as "sorry comforters" of international law.[31] In the 1830s, British imperialists faced the challenges posed by the voluntary law of nations, which signaled a broader theoretical shift from voluntarism to historicism as the foundation of international legal doctrine.

6.4 Fall of Voluntarism: British Imperialists' Conception of International Law in the Sino–Anglo Opium War and the Repositioning of Celestial China in the International Legal System

Vattel's conception of the law of nations as a system comprising equal and sovereign nations bore little relation to the realities of international relations and diplomacy in the late 18th and, especially, the 19th century.[32] Vattel's theories failed to prevent the evolution of a voluntary international community into a hierarchical "family of nations."[33] The rise of a distinctly European form of positivism supplanted the previously universalist tradition of natural law.[34] This shift became particularly evident during the Opium War, which marked a watershed moment.[35] Following this conflict, China found itself effectively excluded from international law. More precisely, it was not treated as a nation with international rights, but rather as a nation upon which international legal obligations were imposed without corresponding entitlements.

Vattel's theory of non-intervention in domestic jurisdiction, including the characterization of free trade as an imperfect right, posed a significant obstacle for advocates of free trade seeking access to the vast Chinese market. This theory provided a legal rationale for China to determine unilaterally whether to engage in trade with foreign nations, based on its own national interests. Opponents of the opium trade and the British war against China, including certain British legal

[31] Immanuel Kant, Political Writings, ed. Hans Reiss, trans. H. B. Nisbet (Cambridge: Cambridge University Press, 1991) 103.

[32] Jennifer Pitts, Boundaries of the International Law and Empires (Cambridge, Mass.: Harvard University Press, 2018) 69–71.

[33] The professionalization of international law is told as the emancipation from religion or politics, however, "international law continues to inhabit the pastoral mould". Quiroga-Villamarín, Daniel Ricardo, "Vicarius Christi: Extraterritoriality, Pastoral Power, and the Critique of Secular International Law" (2021) 34(3) Leiden Journal of International Law 629, 651.

[34] Miloš Vec, "Universalization, Particularization, and Discrimination: European Perspectives on a Cultural History of 19th Century International Law" (2012) 3(2) InterDisciplines 79, 86.

[35] With regard to Britsh argumentation for showing force or waging war, see also Li Chen, Chinese Law in Imperial Eyes: Sovereignty, Justice, and Transcultural Politics (New York: Columbia University Press, 2016) 226–230.

commentators, invoked Vattel's theories to support China's position. For instance, the British lawyer Sydney Bell maintained that, consistent with Vattel's theories, China was entitled to restrict commerce with British merchants. Bell asserted that each sovereign nation had the right to determine whether to enter into or abstain from trade with another nation. Moreover, if a nation consented to trade, it retained full authority to define the terms, limits, and conditions of such trade as it deemed necessary or expedient, without any obligation to justify the necessity or reasonableness of those restrictions.[36] Similarly, the British official T. H. Bullock argued that, under the law of nations, the principle of self-preservation, rooted in natural law, afforded China legitimate grounds to exclude British nationals. He maintained that all foreigners entering Chinese territory were subject to the Chinese law.[37]

As early as June 24, 1834, divergent opinions had already emerged in Britain. An article titled "International Law: If Applicable to China & c.," published in *The Canton Register*, explicitly excluded China from the community of nations and denied the applicability of international law to China. It contended that "asking the China *Hwang—te* to join in and be bound by the common *league of nations* will be received with the same ready and cordial feeling as we imagine a proposition to Bonaparte to resign his title of conservator of the confederation of the Rhine and join the band of mediatized princes would have been." (emphasis added) Thus, if the *jus gentium* were invoked as universally binding on all societies that claim the status of civilization, regardless of how civilization might be defined or interpreted, such an assertion would have been entirely incomprehensible to China.[38]

British advocates of shows of force who nonetheless rejected outright war recognized that Vattel's theories posed an obstacle to British policy in China.[39] Consequently, they adopted a different line of argument, contending that China should not enjoy the protections of international law. They maintained that sovereign independence, in terms of governance, ought to apply only to commercial nations that acknowledge the fundamental norms of international law. According to this view, if a nation endowed with extensive and valuable resources adopts isolationist policies that prevent those resources from benefiting others and pursues actions manifestly contrary to the interests of other nations, it may be legitimate to compel that nation to conform its policies to the broader welfare of humanity.

[36] Sydney S. Bell, Answer to the Opium Question by Samuel Warren (London: Smith, Elder, and Co., 1840) 5–6.

[37] T. H. Bullock, The Chinese Vindicated, or Another View of the Opium Question (London: Wm. H. Allen & Co., 1840) 23, 56.

[38] "International Law; If Applicable to China & c.," Canton Register (24 June 1834) 98.

[39] Hao Gao, "Prelude to the Opium War? British Reactions to the 'Napier Fizzle' and Attitudes towards China in the Mid Eighteen-Thirties" (2014) 87(237) Historical Research 491, 499–505. See also Wu Yixiong, "The Formation of a General Sentiment among Westerners in China for Waging War against China before the Opium War," (鸦片战争前在华西人与对华战争舆论的形成) (2009) 2 Modern Chinese History Studies (近代史研究) 23, 23–43.

To bolster their position, most proponents of force emphasized the characterization of the Chinese government as akin to a "village dog." In their rhetoric, the Chinese government's hallmark traits were timidity and arrogance, similar to the behaviors typically seen (to compare it to something more modest) in a stray dog.[40] This derogatory comparison reflected the dominant sentiment in Britain, where public opinion cast the Chinese as "barbarians." Such a position fundamentally precluded recognition of China as an equal under the law of nations and was used to rationalize British resort to military force.[41] Lord Palmerston (1784–1865), then British Foreign Secretary, further advanced this logic in defending the exclusion of China from the community of nations. He asserted that the opium trade had effectively received the government's acquiescence, especially following the Qing government's failure to curb its officials' overt violations of the opium prohibition, and even, at times, its tacit approval of official opium imports. Thus, by this reasoning, the Qing no longer retained legitimate grounds to prohibit the opium trade.[42] British imperial authorities went so far as to argue that the general law of nations could not apply to China, given what they described as its "imperfect civilization." They contended that China had neither recognized the necessity of nor acceded to the international law, "which must be looked upon as the universally acknowledged law of mankind."[43]

Some proponents of war and leading merchants in Canton, such as James Matheson (1796–1878), did not seek to exclude China from the scope of international law. Instead, they explicitly invoked concepts of "natural partnership and communication" and of "free trade" under the law of nations, maintaining that the Qing government was not "at liberty to disregard the law of nations, on the ground of her having never deigned to recognize it."[44] As they argued, because the law of nations is "the just and rational application of the law of nature to the affairs and conduct of nations," China, as a member of the international community, could not be "exempt from the obligations of that law which God himself has prescribed for the conduct of his creatures."[45] On this basis, even if "there is no formal treaty solemnly and in so many words agreed upon between the two nations," the principle of prescription recognized in municipal law could be invoked to obligate the Qing government to permit trade with British merchants. They asserted that the longstanding commercial relations authorized by Chinese emperors for nearly two

[40] "Treaty with the Chinese, a Great Desideratum" (1836) 4(10) Chinese Repository 441, 448.

[41] "Untitled," Canton Register (September 29, 1835) 156.

[42] "Palmerston to Elliot, 4 November 1839," The National Archives (Kew, UK), FO 881/75A. See "War with China," Hansard, HL Deb, May 12, 1840, vol. 54, c. 12.

[43] "Supply—China," Hansard, HC Deb, July 27, 1840, vol. 55, cc. 1035–1036. When dealing with the Canton administration concerning judicial proceedings in the 1830s, Matheson referred to Vattlian doctrine. James Matheson et al., "Free Intercourse between China and Christendom" (1836) 5(6) The Chinese Repository 244, 245.

[44] James Matheson, The Present Position and Prospects of the British Trade with China (London: Smith, Elder, and Co., 1836) 42–43.

[45] ibid 49–50.

centuries could reasonably be presumed to have rested on an original agreement tantamount to a formal treaty.[46]

British public opinion regularly invoked the principles of natural sociability and providential international commerce, both foundational to the law of nations,[47] to argue that the Qing government's restrictions on free trade amounted to a violation of the law of humanity. G. J. Gordon, a British merchant residing in Canton, asserted that "it is only by the interchange of commodities that the inhabitants of each portion can severally have their due share of the bounty prepared for all who, by their industry, are entitled to participate in the common stock."[48] In Gordon's analysis, the Qing government's policies constituted an "anti-commercial" and "anti-social" system regarding foreign nations. He consequently argued that "the contrary doctrine, which would exclude the Chinese from the society of nations, would divest them of all claim to the protection of international law," though, according to Gordon, the Chinese would still remain bound by the corresponding international legal obligations.[49]

China, whose laws "are all more or less hostile to a free and amicable intercourse with foreigners," was certainly "in a position of open violation of the law—thou shalt love thy neighbor as thyself [sic]."[50] Under the law of nations and in accordance with "the interest of all civilized nations," China, committing the common wrong of mankind, should be "compelled to abandon a position so hostile to the general interests of the human race."[51] In other words, "Common sense, reason, and the law of nations all exclaim against such an unnatural procedure," that is, "enforce their system of excluding foreigners from their country," and "interdict all friendly intercourse between itself and the inhabitants of other countries." Otherwise, it is a violation of the law of nature.[52] The war-supporters avowed solemnly that with regard to the use of force, "recent injuries demand this. Humanity demands it. And justice will approve of it."[53]

At the conference of the Massachusetts Historical Society in December 1841, John Quincy Adams (1767–1848), the sixth President of the United States, notoriously rejected "China's anti-commercial policy," stating that the Qing

[46] ibid 43.

[47] See Andrew Fitzmaurice, Sovereignty, Property and Empire, 1500–2000 (Cambridge: Cambridge University Press, 2014) 147–148; Ileana Porras, "Appropriating Nature: Commerce, Property, and the Commodification of Nature in the Law of Nations" (2014) 27 Leiden Journal of International Law 641, 648.

[48] G. J. Gordon, Address to the People of Great Britain, Explanatory of our Commercial Relations with the Empire of China (London: Smith, Elder and Co., 1836) 16.

[49] ibid.

[50] "British Authorities in China" (1834) 3(8) Chinese Repository 345, 363. "Negotiation with China" (1835) 3(9) Chinese Repository 417, 422.

[51] G. J. Gordon, Address to the People of Great Britain, Explanatory of our Commercial Relations with the Empire of China (London: Smith, Elder and Co., 1836) 16.

[52] "Treaty with the Chinese, a Great Desideratum" (1836) 4(10) Chinese Repository 441, 448.

[53] "Negotiation with China" (1835) 3(9) Chinese Repository 417, 421.

administration was obliged to develop commercial relations with other nations. Adams declared that

> There is also a Law of Nations between Christian communities, which prevails between the Europeans and their descendants throughout the globe. This is the Law recognized by the Constitution and Laws of the United States, as obligatory upon them in their intercourse with the European States and Colonies. But we have a separate and different Law of Nations for the regulation of our intercourse with the Indian tribes of our own Continent; another Law of Nations between us, and the woolly headed natives of Africa; another with the Barbary Powers and the Sultan of the Ottoman Empire; a Law of Nations with the Inhabitants of the Isles of the Sea wherever human industry and enterprize have explored the Geography of the Globe; and lastly a Law of Nations with the flowery Land, the celestial Empire, the Mantchoo Tartar Dynasty of Despotism, where the Patriarchal system of Sir Robert Filmer, flourishes in all its glory.[54]

As we can see, British imperialists thoroughly Europeanized international law because of the necessity of waging war or showing force against China.[55] They did elevate European powers to the universal monarch of the family of nations by using the "standard of civilization." Since then, the European framework of international order is best served by the non-universality of international law rather than by its universality. In the 1855 version of his work, Henry Wheaton (1785–1848) insisted that international law, "with slight exceptions, has always been, and still is, limited to the civilized and Christian people of Europe or to those of European origin,"[56] nevertheless also admitting that European international law can be extended beyond Europe.

In summary, the issue of legitimizing colonial expansion came to the forefront during the 1840s as tensions between China and Britain intensified. The voluntary law of nations, which claims universal applicability, was no longer deemed sufficient for these new geopolitical realities. There arose an urgent need to delineate the narrow scope of rights recognized under international law while asserting the universality of its obligations. Within this legal framework, the asserted superiority of European civilization became central, fortified by the application of historicism. According to the doctrine of historicism, international legal norms should derive from the historical evolution of European civilization, especially its political, legal,

[54] John Q. Adams, "J. Q. Adams on the Opium War" (Oct. 1909–Jun. 1910) 43 Proceedings of the Massachusetts Historical Society 282, 307.

[55] The majority of the British public opinion opposed open hostilities in favor of "show of force" even though a war with China became gradually unavoidable after the "Napier Fizzle." Hao Gao, "Prelude to the Opium War? British Reactions to the "Napier Fizzle" and Attitudes towards China in the Mid Eighteen-Thirties" (2014) 87(237) Historical Research 491, 509.

[56] Henry Wheaton, Elements of International Law, ed. William Beach Lawrence (Boston: Little, Brown and Company, 1855) 16.

and cultural traditions. This approach casts European civilization as the culmination of historical progress and implies that non-European nations, including China, are expected to emulate this developmental path.

It is unsurprising that 19th-century Britain, as the era's preeminent power, played a leading role in reshaping international law to advance its own interests and move beyond the voluntarist paradigm articulated by Vattel. This transformation became a tool for justifying British claims to free trade, culminating in the initiation of the Opium War against the Qing State. British officials, policymakers, and commercial interests in China classified the Qing State as "semi-civilized," thereby denying it the legal status and privileges accorded to "civilized" European nations under international law. Wheaton's articulation of international law, grounded in European historical experience, supplied the conceptual foundation for British legal arguments and effectively marginalized non-European legal traditions. In this context, the Opium War constituted a proving ground for the shift from voluntarism to historicism within the development of international law.

6.5 Wheaton's International Law and Historicism

Although Jeremy Bentham (1742–1832) introduced the term "international law" in the 1780s, the concept of international law continued to be shaped by Vattel's voluntarism until the 1830s. It was at this time that positivism, as articulated by Wheaton and informed by historical determinism, began to recast natural law from an abstract, metaphysical doctrine into a concrete and metaphysical system. A comparison of international legal theories before and after the Opium War reveals a fundamental divergence between Vattel's and Wheaton's theories of international law, a divergence reflected in the two translated works during the Qing Dynasty.

The ideological distinction between these two publicists centers on the sources of international law. Vattel contended that a national consensus could give rise to universally binding norms applicable to all nations. By contrast, Wheaton rejected the existence of such universal agreement, instead positing that the principles, customs, and practices that emerged from Western historical experience were distilled into the operative law governing international affairs. Wheaton's historicist view of international law affirmed the legitimacy of history and maintained that European international law was a product of "civilized" historical development. As a result, he effectively excluded non-European nations from full participation, relegating them to the status of mere adherents on the basis of presumed inferiority.

As previously discussed, Vattel's theory of the law of nations, or so-called Vattel voluntarism, remained the dominant theory in Europe through the early 19th century, thereby diminishing the legitimacy of British legal arguments concerning trade with China. As a result, the British increasingly relied on Wheaton's treatise.

Wheaton's book, first published in 1836, is recognized as the earliest comprehensive work on international law within English jurisprudence. Vattel's writings were translated into Chinese around the same time. These developments signaled a fundamental shift in international legal theory as well as in the way Britain and other nations engaged with international law in China.

Wheaton dismissed Vattel's abridgment of Christian Wolff's extensive works as a superficial and unsatisfactory treatise upon a science. Consequently, Wheaton argued that international law "calls for the skill of a new builder."[57] In particular, Wheaton emphatically rejected Vattel's universalism. He contended that there is no universal law of nations, as envisioned by Cicero in *De Republica*, that binds all of humanity in theory or practice, or that has been recognized or observed by people across time, whether ancient or modern, savage or civilized, Christian or pagan.

Wheaton maintained that "the international law of the civilized, Christian nations of Europe and America, is one thing; and that which governs the intercourse of the Mohammedan nations of the East with each other, and with Christians, is another and a very different thing."[58] In Wheaton's view, there existed "only a particular law of nations, applicable to a distinct set or family of nations," which developed in line with shifts in religion, customs, government, and other societal institutions.[59] The international legal system that Wheaton undertook to analyze was that pertaining to "the civilized and Christian people of Europe or to those of European origin."[60] For Wheaton, the distinct character of the European law of nations was self-evident, as the law of nations was constituted by the positive acts, conventions, and usages of nations; these could only be consistent "among nations of the same class or family, united by the ties of similar origin, manners, and religion."[61] It is apparent that Wheaton believed international law could arise only from a circumscribed set of nations, rather than the community of nations as a whole. Such reasoning necessarily challenges the universality of international law.

However, the 1855 edition of *Elements of International Law*, edited by William Beach Lawrence (1800–1881), advanced the view that European international law was universally applicable. This perspective, grounded in the conviction that European nations bore a historical duty to instruct non-European nations, perceived as "less developed" civilizations, in the norms of international law, persisted even though European civilization was in several respects no more advanced,

[57] Henry Wheaton, An Anniversary Discourse: Delivered before the New York Historical Society, on Thursday, December 28, 1820 (New York: E. Bliss, 1821) 42.

[58] Henry Wheaton, Elements of International Law (Philadelphia: Carey, Lea & Blanchard, 1836) 44–45.

[59] ibid 44–45.

[60] Henry Wheaton, Elements of International Law, ed. William Beach Lawrence (Boston: Little, Brown and Company, 1855) 16.

[61] Henry Wheaton, Elements of International Law (Philadelphia: Carey, Lea & Blanchard, 1836) 44.

and in some instances less developed, than its non-European counterparts.[62] This belief found expression in the extension of diplomatic recognition and treaty relations to nations such as Turkey, Persia, Egypt, and the Barbary States, signifying their formal inclusion under the regime of international law. The Ottoman Empire's recognized sovereignty and internal stability were said to situate it firmly within this legal order. Similarly, diplomatic pressures at the time compelled the Qing State to relinquish its longstanding "anti-commercial" and "isolationist" policies and to acknowledge the independence and equality of foreign nations in the conduct of war and peace.[63] In essence, the expectation was that non-European nations would conform to an international legal system grounded in European legal and political traditions.

In his *History of the Law of Nations in Europe and America*, Wheaton reinforced the universality of the European international legal order through a historicist perspective. He contended that, over centuries, rules of international law grounded in reason and custom had become widely accepted among so-called civilized nations and had been continuously adapted to the conditions prevailing in the international system.[64] For example, Wheaton noted that Roman law had influenced the development of canon law and that the clergy, possessing significant moral authority and expertise, established a system of justice oriented toward lasting principles inherited from ancient Greece and Rome. He praised Grotius for engaging deeply with Christian doctrines, which, in his view, furthered the cause of justice and generated new norms through interactions among European nations.[65] Consequently, nations deemed less civilized were expected to enter the community of European civilization by accepting its international legal standards. Nevertheless, Wheaton departed from Grotius's universalist approach by maintaining that international law applied only to nations sharing similar cultural or religious backgrounds.[66]

Accordingly, Vattel's principles of sovereign independence, equality among nations, freedom to determine domestic commercial practices, and the exclusion of missionaries are largely absent from Wheaton's treatise. Instead, Wheaton recognizes distinctions among nations based on their degree of "civilization," and thus accepts differential treatment in international law. For example, Western powers "legitimately" obtained extraterritorial jurisdiction in China and the Ottoman Empire through unequal treaties. With respect to Japan, its status under

[62] Henry Wheaton, Elements of International Law, ed. William Beach Lawrence (Boston: Little, Brown and Company, 1855) 105–106.

[63] ibid 21–22.

[64] Henry Wheaton, History of the Law of Nations in Europe and America, from the Earliest Times to the Treaty of Washington, 1842 (New York: Gould, Banks & Co., 1845) 29–30.

[65] ibid 54–56, 59.

[66] Henry Wheaton, Elements of International Law (Philadelphia: Carey, Lea & Blanchard, 1836) 45–46.

international law was formally recognized in the 1904 edition of Wheaton's work,[67] whereas Japan was not explicitly regarded as a civilized nation in the 1855 edition.

The emergence of the historical school of jurisprudence contributed significantly to developing rules of international law. British jurist and historian Henry Maine (1822–1888) advocated for a historical approach to international law. Maine regarded international law as a specific product of history rather than a universal system, characterizing it as "a body of rules which alone protects the European commonwealth from permanent anarchy,"[68] though he acknowledged its potential for expansion. This historical perspective ultimately informed a disenchantment methodology that rejects metaphysical notions or providential origins for international law, framing it instead as a concrete, human-constructed norm shaped by historical evolution.[69]

In short, historicism, with Wheaton as a central figure, had become the prevailing paradigm in international law at the time of China's interactions with the West in the 19th century. European history, incorporating elements of theology, natural law, and the development of international norms, formed the primary basis for international law. European jurists on international law focused almost exclusively on the European experience, creating an essentialized conception of European civilization through the lens of historicism. Within this framework, positivist scholars routinely limited their analysis to Europe. While historicism, codified through the "standard of civilization," functioned to exclude non-European nations from participation in the making of international law and denied them corresponding legal rights, its overarching purpose was to subject these nations to the authority of European international law. Yet, following the 1860s, Martin advanced a universalist interpretation of European international law through a flawed analogical reasoning, giving rise to the appearance that China could enter the community of nations by uncovering Chinese history of international law.

Following the 1830s, certain international jurists sought to recast the world order on a universal scale, not by envisioning a global community of nations, but by establishing a hierarchical system privileging European over non-European nations. Grounded in a historicist outlook, this approach treated the spread of European norms as the culmination of world history and, in doing so, disregarded the normative histories and interests of nations outside Europe. Consequently, so-called civilized nations were recognized in international law as universal monarchies, effectively constituting themselves as the gatekeepers to the family of nations. In this way, these international law jurists deliberately universalized

[67] Henry Wheaton, Elements of International Law, ed. J. B. Atlay (London: Stevens and Sons, 1904) 24.

[68] Henry Maine, "Roman Law and Legal Education (1856)," Village-Communities in the East and West (London: John Murray, 1881) 352.

[69] Henry Maine, International Law (London: John Murray, 1888) 21–22.

the Eurocentric structure of international society, asserting Europe's supremacy within the framework of international law.

6.6 A Conception of Universalist Public Law Accepted through the Translation in Modern China

Martin first considered translating Vattel's law of nations but judged that, despite Vattel's clarity and distinction as a writer, his treatise had become somewhat obsolete as a practical reference. Martin likened introducing Vattel's work to China to "teaching them the Ptolemaic system of the heavens." In contrast, Wheaton's treatise appeared current and was widely recognized as a comprehensive and impartial distillation of international law. It had been adopted by government ministries throughout Europe and, notably, served as the standard textbook in England for evaluating diplomatic candidates.[70] Martin therefore concluded that Wheaton's work was "more modern and equally authoritative."[71]

More significantly, in his translation of Wheaton's *Elements of International Law*, Martin frequently drew upon early Chinese history, particularly the normative systems of the Spring and Autumn Period (770–476 BCE).[72] By integrating historical Chinese sources and traditional cultural concepts into his translation and interpretation of European international law, Martin profoundly shaped Chinese understandings and applications of international law during the late Qing Dynasty, regardless of whether his engagement with theoretically reconstituted international law was deliberate. Martin used culturally resonant Chinese terminology, underscoring the parallels he perceived between the interstate norms of the Spring and Autumn Period and European international legal principles. This interpretive strategy represented a marked departure from Wheaton's original text. Through historical comparison, Martin ultimately set forth a vision of international law that he believed could be applied universally to all nations. This approach, which sought to amend the methodologies of 17th- and 18th-century international law, amounted in many respects to the invention, or even fabrication, of new legal constructs. Despite the impossibility of wholly reconstructing or appropriating European international law, a significant contingent of intellectuals in the late Qing and early Republican eras nonetheless aspired to synthesize China's historical legacy with European legal frameworks in their quest for admission into the "family of nations."

[70] Henry Wheaton, Elements of International Law (万国公法) trans. W. A. P. Martin (Peking: Chongshiguan, 1864), translator's preface 3.

[71] W. A. P. Martin, Cycle of Cathay (New York: Fleming H. Revell Company, 1896) 222.

[72] See Lydia H. Liu, The Clash of Empires: The Invention of China in Modern World Making (Massachusetts: Harvard University Press, 2004) 114–116.

The Chinese version of Wheaton's Elements of International Law, 万国公法, is divided into four separate volumes: *yuan* (元), *zhen* (贞), *li* (利), and *heng* (亨) correspond to the hexagram *qian* (乾卦) in the Book of Changes (易经).[73] From this, one may infer that *wanguo* (万国) signifies both heaven and all nations, and *gongfa* (公法) should be understood not as the opposite of private law in the modern sense but rather jus inter gentes. The concept *gong* (公) does not carry the positivist implications or reflect the collective will of nations. Fukuzawa Yukichi (1835–1901), the Japanese educator, philosopher, writer, and entrepreneur, observed that "the term *wanguo* does not refer to all nations in the world, and law of nations only applies to Christian countries."[74] Thus, international law in its historical form represented the law of European nations, rather than constituting a universally applicable law.

Compared to *quanli* (权利), *mingfen* (名分), *yiwu* (义务), and other concepts that have received significant scholarly attention, Martin's translation of *shuguo* (属国, lit. subordinate states) remains largely overlooked. Martin rendered *shuguo* (属国) as "colony," "vassal," or "dependent state," a choice that facilitated the Japanese government's removal of the Ryukyu Kingdom from the *Fanshu System*, often termed the Tributary System, by conflating deeply distinct political constructs.[75] Under international law, a colony is completely administered by its metropolitan power or suzerain, but *fanshu* were only nominally subordinated to China, and exercised substantial independence. The complexity is heightened by the involvement of the Japanese term zokkoku (属国, ぞっこく). While *shuguo* and zokkoku are morphologically equivalent, they are false friends and thus conceptually divergent and untranslatable in any meaningful sense. In international law (guojifa 国际法), zokkoku is accurately rendered as "colony," "vassal," or "dependent state." By contrast, under the Qing regime, *shuguo* denoted a polity that often enjoyed *de facto* independence, notwithstanding its ostensible submission to Chinese authority, yet this distinction was obscured in the context of *wanguo gongfa*, where *shuguo* was misrepresented as equivalent to "colony" or "vassal state."[76] In summary, while the Japanese concept of zokkoku justifiably corresponds to "colony," the same equivalence between *shuguo* and "colony" is spurious, amounting to a pseudo-translation.

[73] Prince gong reported in his memorial that "Wanguo gonfa has been translated into to four statutes." The Complete Account of the Management of Barbarian Affairs (Xianfan Period) (筹办夷务始末(咸丰朝)), edited by Zhonghuashuju editorial office & Li Shuyuan, vol. 3, Tongzhi Period (Beijing: Zhonghua shuju, 2008) 1185.

[74] Fukuzawa Yukichi zenshū (Collected Works of Fukuzawa), ed. Keio Gijuku, vol. 5 (Tokyo: Kokumintosho, 1925) 350.

[75] ibid 19b, 28a.

[76] So Yeon Kim, "Making International Law Truly 'International'? Reflecting on Colonial Approaches to the China–Vietnam Dispute in the South China Sea and the Tribute System" (2022) 24(2) Journal of the History of International Law 227, 237.

Through the use of these morphologically equivalent terms during the Ryukyu (1877–1882) and Korean (1876) issues, Japanese diplomats deliberately advanced the notion that a *shuguo* and a colony, vassal, or dependent state were interchangeable concepts. They constructed a surface-level equivalence between *shuguo* and "colony" based on the actual equivalence between "colony" and *zokkoku*, which deeply perplexed Qing officials. Chinese statesmen were unable to clarify that it was, in fact, the *fanshu* system, rather than the frameworks of international law, that determined whether the Ryukyu Kingdom formed part of the *Tianxia*,[77] as the translation of *fanshu* into "colony" obscured substantial differences between the two concepts. This rhetorical maneuver allowed Japanese negotiators to claim that if Ryukyu qualified as a *shuguo* under the *Fanshu system*, it must also be a colony (*shuguo*) under international law; ultimately this set the standard for recognizing a *shuguo* as dependent on its status as a colony. In this way, Japan undermined China's claim to its *shuguo*, which facilitated Japan's subsequent encroachment on Chinese *shugo* and contributed to the collapse of the *Tianxia* system. Consequently, the Japanese forcibly supplanted the *shuguo* system, which resembled but was not equivalent to a suzerain-vassal structure, with the framework of international law, thereby reclassifying Ryukyu and Korea from Chinese *shuguo* into Japanese territorial holdings and colonies, respectively.[78]

The complexities of translation between "sovereign state" (主权国家) and *zizhu zhiguo* (自主之国) are illustrative. Martin translated *zizhu zhiguo* as "sovereign state" or "independent state." However, *zizhu zhi guo* is another name for *shuguo* under the *Fanshu system*. A *zizhu zhi guo* submits to the Qing rulers, with its ruler acquiring legitimacy through imperial investiture in exchange for favorable trading terms and Qing protection during crises, such as attempted coups. At the same time, the Qing court functioned as the nominal suzerain, and the *zizhu zhi guo* exercised broad autonomy over its domestic administration and, in most cases, foreign relations.[79] Importantly, however, the *zizhu zhi guo* did not possess equal status with the Qing dynasty itself. In contrast, a "sovereign state" in the sense recognized by international law submits to no other authority and retains plenary power over both its internal and external affairs. The Japanese, however, sought to differentiate sharply between the concepts of "sovereign state" and *zizhu zhi guo*, contending that the Ryukyu Kingdom could not simultaneously be both. They covered up the fact that *fanshu* and *zizhu zhi guo* were essentially equivalent under the *Tianxia system*.[80] This rhetorical strategy placed Qing envoys at a disadvantage

[77] See Wan Li, "Fanshu System vs. International Law System: A Study on the Ryukyu Question, 1878–1881" (藩属体系对国际法体系—以清季中日琉球交涉为中心) (2024) 2 Open Times (开放时代) 141, 144–145.

[78] ibid 145.

[79] See Li Yumin, "The Main Difference between Late Qing Sino-Foreign Treaty Relationships and Tributary Relationships" (晚清中外条约关系与朝贡关系的主要区别) (2018) 5 Historical Research (历史研究) 53, 61–64.

[80] ibid 148.

in diplomatic negotiations, leaving them unable to defend effectively the claim that the Ryukyu Kingdom could be recognized as both a *zizhu zhi guo* and a *fanshu* within the Qing world order.

Through the manipulation of translation, the terms *shuguo* and *zizhu zhi guo* have been assigned the meanings of "*colony*" and "*sovereign state*," respectively, effectively detaching them from their original semantic meaning, which now survives only in dictionaries and historical records. In this sense, these Chinese terms have become English constructs through the process of translation, an effect that often goes unrecognized. Lydia Liu's compelling concept of "夷/i/barbarian" as a trinitarian supersign exemplifies a similar dynamic;[81] through translation, the Chinese character 夷 ceases to function as a Chinese term, operating instead within the epistemological framework of English.

Martin's translations drew upon a lexicon deeply embedded in Chinese classical texts, such as the Book of Changes and the Spring and Autumn Annals, thereby creating a "contact zone" through the use of terms that merely approximated Western legal concepts.[82] This practice fostered the illusion that European international law operated as a genuinely universal system, one in which China might participate as an equal member. As a result, Martin's translations obscured the Eurocentric foundations of international law established by Wheaton through historical analysis. Through historical interpretation, Martin reframed Chinese historical sources to advance cosmopolitan ideals. Paradoxically, the use of culturally resonant terms from the Chinese tradition served to construct a form of universal international law consistent with Wheaton's overarching vision. Martin's translations consequently reshaped Chinese perceptions of European international law and encouraged Chinese officials and scholars to pursue integration into the European international community by claiming that ancient China possessed its own distinctive tradition of international law.

Martin's principal methodology is historical comparison, through which he identifies corresponding terms within Chinese traditional political thought and culture. By this means, Martin prioritizes universal norms over national particularities, recasting international law as a universal law of the world analogous to *jus gentium*. The map of the Eastern and Western hemispheres included in the book's preface makes this objective clear: "There are tens of thousands of countries in the world, but the people actually belong to one faction; only the great ruler, starts its life, sustains its living, and manages its affairs."[83] Dong Xun (1810–1892), a high official in the Zongli Yamen (总理衙门), the Qing dynasty's Foreign Office, posed

[81] SeeLydia H. Liu, "The Battleground of Translation: Making Equal in a Global Structure of Inequality" (2018) 38 Alif: Journal of Comparative Poetics 368, 377.

[82] See Li Chen, Chinese Law in Imperial Eyes: Sovereignty, Justice, and Transcultural Politics (New York: Columbia University Press, 2016) 10.

[83] Henry Wheaton, Elements of International Law (万国公法), trans. W. A. P. Martin (Peking: Chongshiguan, 1864), frontmatter.

the following question: "There are currently numerous nations out of the pale of China. How can it be a nation if she is against the law [of nations]?"[84] Dong's inquiry suggests that, as nations now exist in competition with one another, they are necessarily subject to the law of nations.

In a similar manner, Martin took a historicist approach in his translation. Theodore D. Woolsey's *Introduction to the Study of International Law* (1860) was translated as *gongfa bainlian* (公法便览) and Johann Caspar Bluntschli's *Das moderne Völkerrecht der civilisirten Staten als Rechtsbuch dargestellt* (1872) as *gongfa huitong* (公法会通). Additionally, in his paper *International Law in Ancient China*, presented at the Berlin Congress of Orientalists in September 1881, Martin asserted that China had developed its own form of international law as early as the Spring and Autumn Period, thereby arguing for China's rightful place within the international society of nations. Martin challenged prevailing conceptions regarding the fundamental differences between ancient China and the ancient Greece and Rome. He maintained that, in contrast to the Greek states, which are described as "a cluster of detached tribes who had together emerged from barbarism, without any well-defined political connection," the Chinese states "were the fragmented empire, inheriting its laws and civilization, as the States of modern Europe inherited those of Rome."[85]

Martin asserted the existence of a "family of States" in ancient China, drawing an analogy to the European family of nations, both of which, he argued, were "united by the ties of race, literature and religion, carrying on an active intercourse, commercial and political."[86] Martin maintained that the law of nations was essential for governing inter-state relations in ancient China.[87] He further contended that a sophisticated international system had emerged in China, regulated by a "common code, originating in the will of a common suzerain, contributing to maintain for nearly a thousand years among the States of China."[88] Martin viewed this legacy as laying the groundwork for China's later adoption of European international law and its entry into the European family of nations. By the 1880s, however, China could no longer occupy its former central position and instead found itself relegated to a subordinate status. Nevertheless, Martin's strategic invocation of traditional Chinese legal concepts contributed to the further universalization of European international law.

Martin sought to integrate Chinese history into the European-centered development of international law, but his work consistently prioritized Eurocentric

[84] ibid, preface 1a.

[85] W. A. P. Martin, "Traces of International Law in Ancient China," The Chinese Recorder and Missionary Journal (September 1, 1883) 383.

[86] ibid 382.

[87] See Xin Fan, "'International Law in Ancient China': Eurocentrism and the Rethinking of Case Studies in Chinese Intellectual History" (2022) 7(2) Global Intellectual History 265, 271.

[88] W. A. P. Martin, "Traces of International Law in Ancient China," The Chinese Recorder and Missionary Journal (1 September 1883) 386.

perspectives. He not only emphasized the supposed civility of European nations and the superiority of European international law, but also marginalized the legal traditions of non-European nations, denying them equal consideration. Nevertheless, this approach reflects the substantive character of the international legal order shaped by Wheaton's historical methodology and advances the notion of a "universal international law." The exclusions of universality in international law and the implicit civilizational standards underlying this framework are thus often concealed or distorted.

Nevertheless, Martin's historical reconstruction of international law in ancient China gave rise to the idea of a universal law of nations ostensibly free from Eurocentric bias, thereby partially echoing Wheaton's thesis. This interpretation significantly influenced contemporary intellectuals, as Martin's translation framed international law as universal. Chinese scholars began to draw analogies between the late Qing and early Republican periods and the Spring and Autumn Period, employing Confucianism to interpret European doctrines of international law. This approach represented an effort to reconcile China's historic cosmopolitanism with European international legal norms, creating the impression that a genuinely universal legal order was attainable. However, such aspirations were ultimately unattainable, as these academics failed to recognize the presumption of European superiority.

Kang Youwei (康有为, 1858–1927), a central figure in the 1898 Reform Movement and a leading force in the modernization of Chinese intellectuals, uses the concept of *shi* (实), or "substantiality," in a manner akin to the Western concept of logos. For Kang, *shi* serves as the underlying principle governing both the laws of nature, articulated as geometric axioms, and human law. He distinguishes between *shili* (实理), or "substantial truth," dividing it into "eternal substantiality" (永远之实), which corresponds to the immutable laws of nature, and "voluntaristic substantiality" (两可之实), which characterizes the changeable nature of human law.[89] Although human law lacks the permanence of natural law, Kang contends it nonetheless possesses binding force within the international community, which retains the capacity to alter such laws by collective will. In Kang's analysis, the degree of substantiality determines the extent to which international law is subject to change: if its foundational values are immutable, it exercises universal authority; if not, it remains open to redefinition.[90] In short, the principle of *shili* embedded in *gongfa* provides a framework for evaluating the foundational principles and normative rules necessary to realize an ideal society.

[89] See Yin Zhiguang, "Heavenly Principles? The Translation of International Law in 19th-century China and the Constitution of Universality" (2016) 27 The European Journal of International Law 1005, 1021.

[90] Writings of Kang Youwei (康有为全集), vol. 1, edited by Jiang Yihua, Zhang Ronghua (Beijing: The Renmin University of China Press, 2017) 148.

Martin maintained that both ancient China and modern Europe developed comparable legal philosophies, as evidenced by historical sources. Although early modern European international jurists failed to acknowledge this parallel, Martin sought to legitimize European international law by drawing upon Chinese legal traditions. Yet he conceded that China was unlikely to achieve full equality within the international community.[91] Martin's intellectual successors aspired to construct a genuinely universal international order by synthesizing Confucian cosmopolitanism with the framework of international law. However, they underestimated the historicism and structural biases embedded in the European international law tradition. In reality, international law came to be both universalized and Eurocentric, thereby excluding non-European legal sources from meaningful recognition and precluding non-European nations from equal participation in the international order. In the aftermath of the Sino–Japanese War of 1894–1895, the approach of interpreting international law through a Confucian lens and integrating Chinese legal culture fell into disuse, gradually replaced by a Westernized legal discourse. Achieving a truly universal international law thus requires a reconceptualization, either through comparative international law or by adopting more equitable approaches advanced by nations on the periphery.[92]

In reality, the version of international law introduced to China was a distinctly Eurocentric construct shaped by the historicist tradition. This framework created the illusion of a universal legal order with legitimate authority over China. Martin translated European international legal concepts into concepts applicable to the Chinese notion of *Tianxia*.[93] He drew on Chinese cosmopolitan theories to translate international legal vocabulary that lacked true equivalence in Chinese. Through selective engagement with Chinese legal culture and terminology, Martin mitigated some of the methodological dilemmas that had confounded 17th and 18th-century European international lawyers, but he made no effort to dislodge the underlying Eurocentric premise of international law. As a result, a Eurocentric vision of international law was presented to China as if it were universal, or even cosmopolitan. This perception prompted Chinese elites to argue that ancient China possessed its own system of international law, with the aim of establishing China's credentials as an equal participant in the international order. Yet this aspiration proved unattainable, given the fundamental methodological shortcomings.

[91] See Xin Fan, ""International Law in Ancient China": Eurocentrism and the Rethinking of Case Studies in Chinese Intellectual History" (2022) 7 Global Intellectual History 265, 276.

[92] Anthea Roberts et al., "Conceptualizing Comparative International Law," in Comparative International Law, edited by Anthea Roberts et al. (New York: Oxford University Press, 2018) 6.

[93] Junnan Lai, Sovereignty and Civilization: International Law and East Asia in the Nineteenth Century (2014) 40 Modern China 282, 292.

6.7 Conclusion

Shortly after Martin passed away on December 17, 1916, American Board of Commissioners for Foreign Missions missionary Arthur H. Smith (1845–1922) published his eulogy in the *Peking Gazette*: “Dr. Martin is dead, but he still lives and may we not truly any [say] that by his words, his writings, and the lives he has touched he will live in China forever and forever?”[94] For Martin, someone who had lived in China for sixty years, translating international law into Chinese definitely is one of his key accomplishments, but he might not have been aware of the significance of his translation and historical interpretations to China at that time.

The trajectory of international law’s theoretical development in late Qing China was fundamentally shaped by two key translations, each representing divergent legal traditions. Lin Zexu’s translation of Vattel’s book proved more advantageous for China than that of Wheaton’s book, which was chosen by Martin. Vattel’s work underscored the principle of sovereign equality, privileging the practices of nations over reliance on European historical precedent. This framework allowed non-European nations such as China to claim equal standing within the system of international law. Under Vattel’s theory of imperfect rights, China and other nations were not obliged to observe the voluntary law of nations established by European nations, except insofar as the necessary law of nations applied. Had Lin produced a comprehensive translation of Vattel’s international law, it could have fundamentally transformed China’s reception and understanding of international law in the modern era. By contrast, Wheaton’s approach accentuated the specifically European origins of international law and maintained that non-European nations were “uncivilized” and lacked equal entitlement to its protections. Accordingly, a systematic and complete translation of Vattel’s work into Chinese might have exerted far greater influence on the development of international law in China than Martin’s translation of Wheaton’s work.[95]

In an effort to downplay its positivist origins, Martin translated *jus publicum Europaeum* as a universal law, seeking to construct a shared international order bridging China and the West through historical narrative. Drawing on language steeped in Chinese tradition, Martin sought to situate international law within the context of Chinese history and thereby shape elite Chinese perceptions. He drew comparisons between contemporary European law and the legal traditions of China’s Spring and Autumn Period, promoting the integration of China’s historical practices into the creation of a genuinely universal international legal

[94] Arthur H. Smith, “Dr. W.A.P. Martin: The Passing of a Prominent Pioneer,” Peking Gazette (December 19, 1916) 6.

[95] See Jennifer Pitts, Boundaries of the International Law and Empire (Mass.: Harvard University Press, 2018) 148–149.

system. Nonetheless, the European powers continued to dictate the contours of this legal order.

Although the translation process eroded the original Eurocentric framework, the adaptation of international law into *wanguo gongfa* reframed it within a more cosmopolitan tradition. In doing so, legal translators managed to integrate the European model of international law into the Chinese context, producing a reinterpreted and ostensibly universalized body of law, even as it retained a foundation shaped by European experience. Rather than passively adopting a Eurocentric paradigm, late Qing literati sought to reform and even reconstruct international law by drawing on Chinese historical traditions. In the aftermath of the Sino–French War in 1885, the Qing government recognized that existing doctrines of international law were inadequate for protecting China's sovereign interests. As Martin observed with characteristic irony: "[N]ow they are complaining that the right of people is nothing other than the reason of the strongest, for the moment, they doubt its effectiveness, but they have already gone too far to be able to retreat."[96] Following the 1911 Revolution, the majority of Chinese statesmen and intellectuals focused on judicial reforms aimed at abolishing extraterritoriality and securing China's place among the family of nations by upholding European standards of international law, thereby preserving national sovereignty.

Historicism, which largely faded from domestic legal discourse by the early 20th century, continues to exert significant influence within international law, where it is frequently invoked to justify prevailing doctrines and practices. Critics challenge historicism for perpetuating antiquated concepts of civilization, emphasizing their historical pedigree, and extending these constructs to non-European contexts in an effort to universalize global value systems. Nonetheless, historicism retains a constructive dimension. By adopting an evolutionary perspective, historical interpretation seeks to integrate diverse historical experiences into a shared framework, employing systematic methodologies that transcend mere comparability in order to facilitate the construction of a collective future.

[96] W. A. P. Martin, "La Chine et le Droit International" (1881) 17 Revue de Droit International et de Legislation Comparee 504, 505.

7

'Unequal' Relations between China, Korea, and Japan

The 1895 Treaty of Shimonoseki and Extradition Treaties

Masaharu Yanagihara

7.1 Introduction

7.1.1 Japan and the Traditional East Asian World Order

The traditional world order in East Asia was Sino-centric, founded on the concept of China as a central empire.[1] This order is plausibly claimed to have dominated East Asia, including Southeast Asia, for more than 2000 years, from 221 BC during the Qin dynasty until the end of the Qing dynasty in 1912.[2] "Vassal countries" such as Korea, Vietnam, Tibet, Ryūkyū, Siam (Thailand), Laos, and Burma acknowledged the virtue of the Chinese emperor and paid him tribute. The rulers of these countries were granted the title of king; and despite lacking an "equal" relationship with China, these countries were not "subordinate" to China. However, recent studies have cast considerable doubts about the traditional world order in East Asia.[3] Current academic specialists still discuss whether the idea was a Chinese tradition or existed only during the Qing dynasty. Moreover, even if only the Qing dynasty is considered, it is doubtful whether the actual operation of the relationships between Qing and other countries could

[1] The details of this sub-section are explained in Yanagihara Masaharu, "Significance of the History of the Law of Nations in Europe and East Asia," *Recueil des cours* 371 (2015): pp. 273–435; Yanagihara Masaharu, "Japan," in *The Oxford Handbook of the History of International Law*, edited by Bardo Fassbender and Anne Peters (Oxford: Oxford University Press, 2012), pp. 475–499.

[2] See, inter alia, John King Fairbank, "Preliminary Framework," in *The Chinese World Order: Traditional China's Foreign Relations*, edited by John King Fairbank (Cambridge, Mass.: Harvard University Press, 1968), pp. 1–19.

[3] See, e.g., Paul A. Cohen, *Discovering History in China: American Historical Writing on the Recent Chinese Past* (New York: Columbia University Press, 1984); Lydia H. Liu, *The Clash of Empires: The Invention of China in Modern World Making* (Cambridge, Mass.: Harvard University Press, 2004); "Tokushū: Sakuhō, chōkō taisei saikō" [Special Issue: Reconsidering the "Investiture-Tributary" System], *Higashi ajia kindaishi* 20 (2016): pp. 1–130. See also Toyoda Tetsuya, "Universality and Peculiarity of the Concept of Exclusive Territoriality," *Japanese Yearbook of International Law* 66 (2023): pp. 349–351.

Masaharu Yanagihara, *'Unequal' Relations between China, Korea, and Japan* In: *Histories of International Law in China*.
Edited by: Ignacio de la Rasilla, Jiangyu Wang, and Congyan Cai, Oxford University Press.
 DOI: 10.1093/oso/9780198888345.003.0007

be explained by the concepts of "tribute" and "bestowing peerage by Imperial edict." A notable example is illustrated by insights from a Japanese expert who observed that, while it was commonly accepted that gifts from China far surpassed the tributes offered by vassal states, this was not the case for the dynamics between Korea and the Qing dynasty during the seventeenth, eighteenth, and nineteenth centuries.[4]

Japan existed within its own world order for the majority of its history, distinct from both Chinese and European orders. While the Chinese world order was fairly well known to Japan, Japan was a complete stranger to modern Western international law at the time. In the Tokugawa era (1603–1867), Japan received substantial information about Western culture and civilization, especially through Dejima, an artificial islet in Nagasaki; however, almost all of this was limited to science and technology. No information on international law was officially provided to Dejima. The fact that the Tokugawa Shogunate had no knowledge of international law is plainly shown by the anecdote that Townsend Harris, the US general consul (1856–1861), was both a negotiator of an amity and commerce treaty with Japan and a teacher of international law.[5]

It is common knowledge that Japan maintained a policy of "seclusion" or "isolation" ("*sakoku*")[6] for almost 250 years in the Tokugawa era, from 1639 to 1854. However, it is wrong to argue that Japan was completely isolated from outside regions during this period, especially considering its relations with other East Asian countries and regions, including mainly China, Korea, Ryūkyū, and Ezo. Japan's door was never closed to East Asia.[7] The theory of "four gates"[8] and ideas of "*tsūshō no kuni*" (countries of trade) and "*tsūshin no kuni*" (countries of diplomacy) are indispensable in developing an accurate understanding of Japan's real relations with "foreign" countries, including China, in the so-called seclusion period.

[4] Korea actually paid much more, more than twice, in tribute than what was returned as gifts from China. Harada Tamaki, *Chōsen no kaikoku to kindaika [The Opening and Modernization of Korea]* (Hiroshima: Keisuisha, 1997), pp. 38–39. Harada worked out the number based purely on research undertaken by a Korean specialist, Chun Hea-jong. However, it would be extremely difficult to accurately compare the price of exchanged goods at the time.

[5] The Treaty was concluded in July 1858. See the dialog between Harris and Hotta Masayoshi, Senior Councilor of the Tokugawa Shogunate on December 12, 1857. Gaimushō [MOFA, Japan], ed., *Nihon gaikō nempyō narabini shuyō bunsho [Chronological Table and Major Documents of Japanese Diplomacy]*, vol. 1 (Tokyo: Hara shobō, 1965), pp. 10–16.

[6] The term "*sakoku*" was used for the first time when Shizuki Tadao published a Japanese translation of Engelbert Kaempfer's *The History of Japan* in 1801. The Tokugawa Shogunate never officially used this term even after 1801.

[7] Ronald Paul Toby, *State and Diplomacy in Early Modern Japan: Asia in the Development of the Tokugawa Bakufu* (Stanford, CA: Stanford University Press, 1991), p. 5.

[8] The four gates are as follows: "Matsumae Gate," open to the Ainu (indigenous people) in Ezo; "Tsushima Gate," open to Korea; "Nagasaki Gate," open to the Dutch and Chinese merchants; and "Satsuma Gate," open to the Kingdom of Ryūkyū.

Within the framework of the seclusion policy of the Tokugawa Shogunate, official "diplomatic" relations with China were not allowed; however, Chinese merchants alone were able to sojourn near Dejima to conduct trade with the Japanese. China, together with the Netherlands, was considered "*tsūshō no kuni*" rather than "*tsūshin no kuni*," which was strictly limited to two countries: Korea and the Kingdom of Ryūkyū. From a Chinese perspective, Japan was considered not a "vassal country," but a "place of trade."

The next question regarding Japan's relations with East Asian countries is whether Japan merely occupied a peripheral status in the history of the East Asian world order, as China was by far more powerful than other East Asian countries for most of its history in the realms of culture, economics, and politics in East Asia.[9] Undeniably, China's cultural dominance was central to the East Asian intellectual world, even in the Tokugawa era. This might have eventually led to the Tokugawa Government's pursuit of ensuring that Japan made every endeavor to be regarded not as a part of the Chinese world order but as having a unique relationship with the overseas world, including China.[10]

7.1.2 Structure of This Chapter

This chapter first examines the Shimonoseki Peace Treaty of 1895 and analyzes how the traditional East Asian world order was significantly disrupted, focusing on the peace treaty negotiation process. The 1895 Treaty marked the end of the traditional Chinese world order. However, this change of order in East Asia was not realized instantly after the Treaty, but ushered in as a gradual process. Further, after 1895, Japan did not regard East Asian countries, including China, as equals in the sense of modern Western international law.[11] To determine whether modern Western international law, based on sovereign equality as a fundamental principle, became relevant to the East Asian world, this author analyzes the negotiations for the conclusion of extradition treaties between China, Korea, the United States, and Japan, as extradition treaties within the framework of modern Western international law are usually based on equal relations between contracting States. No study has focused on extradition treaties from such a perspective. It is particularly

[9] For economic development in 18th-century China and two crises in China in the middle of the 19th century and in the period from the 1880s to 1911, see Murakami Ei, "Chūgoku keizai no hatten to jūkyū seiki shinchō no futatsu no kiki" [An Economic Development in China and Two Crises in the Qing Dynasty in the 19th Century], in *Ajia kara mita gurōbaru hisutorī [Creating Global History from Asian Perspectives]*, edited by Akita Shigeru (Kyoto: Minerva shobō, 2013), pp. 172–193.

[10] Arano Yasunori, "Bakuhan taisei kokka to gaikō" [The Shogunate State and Diplomacy], *Rekishigaku kenkyū, Bessatsu tokushū* (1978): p. 105; Watanabe Hiroshi, *Nihon seiji shisōshi [A History of Political Thoughts of Japan]* (Tokyo: University of Tokyo Press, 2010), p. 64.

[11] See, e.g., Benedict Kingbury, "Sovereignty and Inequality," *European Journal of International Law* 9 (1998): pp. 599–625.

valuable to find an in-depth connection between the treaty revision movement and the conclusion of extradition treaties and reconsider the equality between Asian and Western States.

This chapter's analysis is based on numerous primary sources stored in Japanese and foreign archives. In particular, regarding the 1895 Treaty, this author compares and contrasts four types of primary historical sources that exist as records of the peace treaty negotiations. Previous works have not carried out such an analysis.

7.2 The 1895 Treaty of Shimonoseki between China and Japan

7.2.1 Treaty Negotiations between Li and Itō: Four Different Minutes

With the Opium War starting in 1840 and the Arrow War (Second Opium War) in 1856, Western countries successively acquired concessions from China. However, undoubtedly, even in the latter half of the nineteenth century, the Qing dynasty was still the only major power in East Asia. Even in the 1880s, the presence of Qing in Korea was overwhelming, as symbolized, for example, by the China–Korea Treaty of Merchants' Trade on Land and Sea in October 1882, which stipulated that "Korea has long been in the ranks of the feudal states of China."[12] This situation was symbolically changed by the Sino-Japanese War in 1894–1895.[13]

The peace treaty ending the War was the Treaty of Shimonoseki, which was concluded on April 17, 1895. The Sino-Japanese War consisted of three wars: the first between Japan and Korea from July 23, 1894 to April 17, 1895; the second between Japan and China; and the third between Japan and the people of Formosa (Taiwan) from the end of May 1895 to April 1, 1896. The second war, the Sino-Japanese War, in a narrower sense, started with the battle of Pungdo on July 25, 1894, followed by formal declarations of war by both Japan and China on August 1.

The United Kingdom and the US made proposals to mediate in October and November 1894, respectively, but both were rejected by Japan.[14] Gustav Detring, a German commissioner at Tientsin Maritime Customs, was dispatched to Kobe,

[12] The Russian Minister to Japan told the Japanese Foreign Minister on December 22, 1894, in secret, that Russia would not intervene in the peace treaty unless the independence of Korea would not be injured, and added as his personal opinion that Russia would not make an objection to the occupation of Formosa. *Nihon gaikō bunsho [Collection of the Documents on Japanese Foreign Policy]*, vol. 27, no. 2 (1894), p. 519. See Okamoto Takashi, *Zokkoku to jishu no aida [Between a Vassal Country and an Autonomous Country]* (Nagoya: Nagoya daigaku shuppankai, 2004), pp. 133 and 368–374.

[13] See Yanagihara Masaharu, "The Treaty of Shimonoseki," in *The Encyclopedia of Diplomacy*, edited by Gordon Martel, vol. 4 (Chichester: Wiley Blackwell, 2018), pp. 1862–1864.

[14] *Nihon gaikō bunsho*, vol. 27, no. 2, pp. 467–470, 474–477, 483–486, 489–494, and 497–509; *Itō Hirobumi monjo [Itō Hirobumi Papers]*, vol. 17 (Tokyo: Yumani shobō, 2008), pp. 191–207.

Japan, on November 26 as a messenger of Li Hongzhang, a military strongman and a leading figure in Chinese economic development and diplomacy for 25 years from 1870 to 1895. However, Japan did not accept the messenger. The Japanese Government believed it could win the war and decided to continue the battle.

At the end of November, Port Arthur and Dairen were occupied by the Japanese army. Itō Hirobumi, the Japanese prime minister, submitted a report to the Imperial headquarters of Japan on December 4, warning that if the Japanese army advanced deeply into mainland China and threatened to bring about the collapse of the Qing dynasty, it might lead to an intervention by the Western powers, which would be extremely disadvantageous for Japan. Itō proposed an alternative plan: to capture the port of Weihaiwei on the Shandong Peninsula, where the base of the Chinese Beiyang fleet, sponsored by Li Hongzhang, was located, as well as to occupy Formosa in order to annex the island eventually via a peace treaty.[15]

The Chinese Beiyang fleet ceased to be an effective fighting force after the battle of Weihaiwei on February 17, 1895, whereas the Japanese military's operations in Formosa were delayed because of bitter fighting on the Liaodong Peninsula. However, on March 23, the Japanese troops landed on the Pescadores Islands and succeeded in occupying them three days later.[16]

Peace negotiations between China and Japan began officially on March 20 at the Shunpanrō, a Japanese-style inn located in the city of Shimonoseki. Japan's main representatives were Itō Hirobumi and Mutsu Munemitsu, the Foreign Minister, while China was represented by Li Hongzhang and Li Jingfang, Hongzhang's adopted son and the Chinese Minister to Japan. Emperor Guangxudi gave Li Hongzhang the authority to conclude a treaty of peace providing for the payment of an indemnity and the cession of some territory before he came to Shimonoseki.[17]

There are two types of minutes of the peace treaty negotiations written up by the Japanese side. The first in Japanese are the detailed minutes of seven meetings titled "kaiken yōroku" [Conference Memorandum] in the Diplomatic Archives of the Japanese Ministry of Foreign Affairs,[18] published in the *Nihon gaikō bunsho* [Collection of the Documents on Japanese Foreign Policy].[19]

[15] *Itō Hirobumi monjo [Itō Hirobumi Papers]*, vol. 17, pp. 237–245.

[16] As for the battles in the Sino–Japanese War, see, e.g., S.C.M. Paine, *The Sino–Japanese War of 1894–1895: Perception, Power, and Primacy* (Cambridge: Cambridge University Press, 2003); Hiyama Yukio, *Nisshin sensō no kenkyū [Research on the Sino–Japanese War]*, 3 vols (Tokyo: Yumani shobō, 2022–2023).

[17] A classic on the Peace Conference is Tabohashi Kiyoshi, *Nisshin sen-eki gaikō shi no kenkyū [Research on the Diplomatic History of the Sino–Japanese War]* (Tokyo: Tōyōbunko, 1951), pp. 449–632. Mutsu Munemitsu himself wrote a record of the Shimoneki meetings. Mutsu Munemitsu, *Kenken roku [Record of Kenken]* (Written in 1895), chs. 17 and 18.

[18] JACAR (Japan Center for Asian Historical Records): Ref. B06150073000. "Kaiken yōroku" is found also in *Itō Hirobumi monjo*, vol. 28 (2009), pp. 177–336; *Mutsu Munemitsu kankei monjo [Documents Relating to Mutsu Munemitsu]*, vol. 80–38 housed in the National Diet Library, Japan.

[19] *Nihon gaikō bunsho*, vol. 28, no. 2 (1895), pp. 380–436.

An English version of the minutes titled "The Proceedings of the Peace Conferences Held at Hiroshima and Shimonoseki in 1895" was created by Mutsu Hirokichi, the son of Mutsu Munemitsu, who entered the Ministry of Foreign Affairs of Japan as a translator in August 1894. The minutes inspected by Itō Hirobumi contain the seven Shimonoseki meetings in March and April 1895 and the Hiroshima Conference on February 1 and 2, 1895. In the Introduction, Mutsu Hirokichi wrote the following:

> I was instructed by the Count [Itō] to attend the meetings to take down the minutes of the proceedings which were conducted in the English language. Each day when the meeting had terminated it was my duty to transcribe the notes I had made at the Conference and submit them to the inspection of our Plenipotentiaries…
>
> In taking down the negotiations the time allowed for the revision of notes being so extremely limited together with my lack of ability prevented the work from being more worthy of such an important occasion. However, the faithful reproduction of what occurred was my essential aim and I have endeavored to place on record all such words and phrases as were actually employed by the respective negotiators without paraphrasing them into a more literary form.
>
> In view, however, of the fact that the present work is the only authentic record in existence of these memorable negotiations I venture to hope that it will not fail to attach to itself some historical value and will also serve as a book of future reference for the Department.
>
> Hirokichi Mutsu,
> Translator to the Department of Foreign Affairs.
> April, 1895.[20]

Mutsu's minutes contain not only the minutes of the peace conference but also a description of the movements of the two countries during the meetings and the draft treaties of each country.[21] Specifically, despite quite a few discrepancies in the details between Mutsu's minutes and the minutes in Japanese, they are almost identical with respect to the major points. It was suspected that the Japanese minutes were based on Mutsu's minutes and polished by the members of the Ministry of Foreign Affairs, as a great number of hand-written corrections were added to the text in Japanese.

The Chinese also compiled records of these meetings. An original text of China's records in Chinese, titled 中日議和紀略 *[History of the Peace Meetings between China and Japan]* or 五次問答節略 *[Summary of Five Verbal Discussions]*, is

[20] JACAR: Ref. B06150073400 (102nd picture). They are not included in *Collection of the Documents on Japanese Foreign Policy*.
[21] JACAR: Ref. B06150073400 (from the first picture).

stored in the National Archives of Japan.[22] The text is also housed in the French Diplomatic Archives. This document is attached to a letter dated July 2, 1895, sent by Auguste Gérard, French Minister to China, to Foreign Minister Gabriel Hanotaux. In his letter, Gérard referred to the English translation published in the *Peking & Tientsin Times* and noted that it was an "official translation" [*officiellement révisé*] (as the letter's date is July 2, it refers only to minutes published between June 8 and 29). He also wrote that, to his honor, he was able to obtain the Chinese version of the minutes [un examplaire chinois de ce compte-rendu], adding that the transcript of the meeting shows how Li Hongzhang felt about Japan and that Li's political style was well manifested.[23] It is unclear from whom Gérard obtained the Chinese text.

The records were prepared by Li Hongzhang, who reported them to the Emperor in Beijing in a letter dated April 21, 1895, which was received two days later.[24] It is uncertain whether the records were official. Although Mutsu Hirokichi explained that his minutes were "the only authentic record in existence," this does not mean that they were checked and approved by the Chinese side.

As written in Gérard's letter, an English translation of China's records was published in a newspaper of the time, *Peking & Tientsin Times*, first published in Tientsin in March 1894. The title of the article is "Report of the Verbal Discussions during Peace Negotiations, between the Chinese Plenipotentiary, Viceroy Li Hung-chang and the Japanese Plenipotentiaries, Count Ito and Viscount Mutsu, at Shimonoseki, Japan, March and April 1895. Translated from the Original Chinese Records. Officially Revised." As shown in the title, it is certainly an English translation checked by some public institution of the Chinese Government, even though the name of the institution that checked it is not specified. For this reason, it is considered an "official translation." It was published in newspapers six times: on June 8, 15, 22, and 29 and July 6 and 13, 1895, respectively.[25]

22 National Archives of Japan, Classification no. 289-0019. See also *Mutsu Munemitsu kankei monjo*, vol. 80-37. Hereinafter, this document is quoted as *Five Verbal Discussions*. The National Archives of Japan houses two more "Histories of the Peace Meetings between China and Japan": a collection of basic documents such as Truce Treaty (Classification no. 289-0008) and a collection of Itō Hirobumi's letters (Classification no. 289-0035).

23 Archives diplomatiques, La Courneuve, France: Correspondance politique, Chine, tome 91, 1895, juillet-sept, ff. 15–17.

24 清光緒朝中日交涉史料 *[Qing guang xu chao zhong ri jiao she shi liao]*, vol. 38 (Peking: Gu gonb bo wu yuan, 1932), no. 2993 (the text of the records is lacking). See also Takemura Noriyuki, "Shinmatsu shōsetsu "Setsuwa den" ni zenbun tensai sareta Li Hongzhang (hen) Chūnichi giwa kiryaku wo megutte" [Li Hongzhang (ed.) Concerning the Peace Negotiations between China and Japan, the Whole Text of Which Was Produced in "On the Japanese" Published at the End of the Qing Dynasty], *Bungaku kenkyū* 96 (1999): p. 16.

25 This newspaper is, for example, housed in Politisches Archiv des Auswärtigen Amtes, Berlin, Botschaft Peking (Peking II), Chinesisch-japanischer Krieg, vom Fehlschlagen der Friedensvermittlung und der Verlegung des Kriegsschauplatzes auf chinesisches Gebiet an (Oktober 1894–Juli 1896), Nr. 106 & 107. This English translation is reproduced in *History of the Peace Negotiations, Documentary and Verbal between China and Japan, March–April 1895. With Text of the Treaty of Peace and Portrait of the Viceroy Li Hung-chang. Officially Revised* (Tientsin, 1895).

This author closely compared China's records in Chinese with the English translation published in the *Peking & Tientsin Times* and found that the English translation is quite accurate and faithful.

In contrast, the comparison of Japan's records, in Japanese and English, with those of the Chinese side, in Chinese and English, shows substantially different descriptions of important issues, as explained later.[26]

The seven meetings featured in the Japanese records are outlined as follows.

The Japanese delegation was determined to have reached an early peace settlement to prevent Western intervention. However, when the negotiations began, Li Hongzhang insisted on the early conclusion of an armistice agreement, whereas the Japanese delegation proposed severe conditions for an armistice. At the third meeting, on March 24, Li Hongzhang chose to abandon the proposed armistice, but shortly after the meeting, he was shot on the street by a Japanese nationalist. Li was only slightly injured in the face, but the Japanese Government decided that it would be prudent to conclude an armistice agreement covering the next 21 days. The agreement was signed on March 30 and became effective immediately.

After the meeting resumed on April 1, in the absence of Li Hongzhang and Itō, the Japanese delegation sent a draft peace treaty comprising 11 articles. The main points were the recognition of the independence of Korea; the cession of the Island of Formosa, its attached islands, the Pescadores Group (known now as the Penghu islands), and the southern part of Mukden Province; and the payment of a war indemnity of 300 million taels.

At the next meeting, on April 10, with Li Hongzhang present, heated discussions took place, especially over the cession of Formosa and the indemnity. According to Japan's records, the April 15 meeting began at 2:30pm and ended at 7:30pm; thus, it was a five-hour meeting.[27] According to China's records, it started at 2:30pm and ended at 7pm. In either case, it was a long meeting. The main issues were the determination of the amount of reparations and the interest. However, the cession of Formosa was also discussed. It was finally agreed that China would pay an indemnity of 200 million taels over seven years and would pay no interest if the total amount of indemnity was paid within three years.

The peace treaty was signed on April 17, 1895, was ratified on April 20, and became effective on May 8. The main points were the following: to recognize "the full and complete independence and autonomy of Korea" (Art. 1); to cede to Japan the southern portion of the Liaodong Peninsula, "the Island of Formosa together

[26] One more interesting fact is the number of meetings. According to Japan's records, seven meetings were held, on March 20, 21, and 24 and April 1, 10, 15, and 17. However, according to China's records, there were only five meetings: on March 20, 21, and 24 and April 10 and 15. There were no Chinese original records of the meetings on April 1 and 17. Tabohashi, a Japanese specialist in Korea and China, wrote as well that the April 10 meeting was the fourth, although it is not clear about his idea of the April 17 meeting. Tabohashi, *Nisshin*, p. 526.

[27] *Nihon gaikō bunsho*, vol. 28, no. 2, pp. 415 and 432.

with all islands appertaining or belonging to the said Island of Formosa," and the Pescadores Islands (Art. 2); to pay "a war indemnity of 200 million taels" (Art. 4); to conclude a treaty of commerce and navigation, the basis for which the treaties now subsisting between China and European powers shall serve (Art. 6); and to allow Japanese forces to temporarily occupy Weihaiwei "as a guarantee of the faithful performance of the treaty" (Art. 8).

In the following sub-sections, to explore the implications for the validity and continuity of the East Asian world order, two topics are thoroughly analyzed based on the minutes of Japan and China: the cession of Formosa and the status of Korea in modern Western international law.

7.2.2 The Cession of Formosa

The "draft of peace conditions" sent by Japan to Li Hongzhang on April 1 included the cession of "the southern portion of the Province of Sheng-king [Mukden Province]," "Island of Formosa together with all Islands adjacent or belonging to the said Island of Formosa," and the Pescadores Group.[28] According to the amendment of the Chinese Delegation on April 9, the cession should be limited to some areas of Mukden Province and the Pescadores group of islands. Formosa and its attached islands should not be subject to the cession. The scope of the Pescadores group of islands was clearly written in this amendment: lying within the 23rd and 24th parallels of latitude and the 119th and 120th degrees of longitude east.[29]

At the meeting on April 10, Itō identified three lands to be ceded: "the southern portion of Mukden Province," "all the islands of Formosa and its attached islands," and "the Pescadores Islands of the British 'Greenwich' 119° to 120° east longitude and 23° to 24° north latitude."[30] Compared with the original draft prepared by Japan on April 1, this identification was more specific regarding a part of the Liaodong Peninsula and a part of the Pescadores Islands, without any change to Formosa and its attached islands.

Li offered stubborn resistance to the cession of Formosa and its attached islands at a meeting on April 10, arguing that those areas were not occupied by Japanese forces. Itō replied that Japan could promptly send soldiers to occupy Formosa if necessary.[31]

Itō also referred to the cession of Eastern Siberia from China to Russia as an example of the ceding of land that was not occupied by Russia. However, Li argued that "the cession of Eastern Siberia was not the result of the war ... Heilong Jiang

[28] JACAR: Ref. B06150072900 (from the 18th picture).

[29] JACAR: Ref. B06150072900 (from the 24th picture and the 129th picture).

[30] *Nihon gaikō bunsho,* vol. 28, no. 2, p. 408.

[31] Ibid., p. 414. In Mutsu's minutes we find the remark of Itō: "A victor is of course entitled to claim any place he likes whether occupied or not." JACAR: Ref. B06150073400 (43rd picture).

is almost barren land beyond the civilized areas, and a few people are living there, and no governance is found. On the other hand, Formosa is fertilized land, producing many crops. People there are subordinate to the cultivation by the Emperor, and the local Government is set up with officials. It is almost the mainland." Itō, however, opined that "I agree with you on the point that a territory where the sovereignty of Qing was exercised was ceded, while it is needless to discuss whether that land is fertilized or barren."[32]

According to Japan's records, the above statements arose in an exchange between Li and Itō. In contrast, according to Chinese records, passages on Siberia and Formosa are markedly different. Specifically, Li stated, "The territory given to Russia was a mere sop. It was a wilderness, cold and sparsely populated. Formosa which has already been constituted a province, with its dense population, is a totally different matter." Itō responded that "Every foot of land belongs to the Sovereign, be it a howling wilderness or a land of plenty."[33] It is noteworthy that the phrase "People there are subordinate to the cultivation by the Emperor" is contained in Japan's records but absent in China's records. This point will be discussed later.

Another important difference between Japan's and China's records is the following exchange, which is found only in China's records.

LI: Such precipitation is not fitting in a neighboring nation. Friendly relations are necessary for both of us.

ITŌ: The indemnity and the cession of territory constitute a debt. When the debt is paid friendship will be the natural result.

LI: With such extortionate demands, if peace is made, it will be insincere. The proposals I submitted were made in perfect good faith. Your Excellency is surprised at my not consenting to your conditions and I must speak without reserve. You will find Formosa difficult to take. France tried it but failed. The coast is stormy and the people are defiant.

ITŌ: Our naval and land forces can bear any hardship. Last year, it was cold in the North, and everybody thought that Japanese soldiers would not be able to endure. But they suffered no disadvantage throughout the winter and were successful everywhere.

LI: Formosa is very malarious. You have lost many lives there before. Most of the Formosans smoke opium to counteract the effects of malaria.

ITŌ: When we take Formosa, we shall forbid opium-smoking.

[32] *Nihon gaikō bunsho*, vol. 28, no. 2, p. 414. Mutsu's minutes are fairly different. Li said: "But Formosa should not be compared with the portion of Siberia which we ceded to Russia. The latter was a kind of neutral and waste land while the former is a regular Province." Itō replied: "The value of the two lands may differ certainly but their relations to Sovereign rights are just the same." JACAR: Ref. B06150073400 (42nd picture).

[33] *Five Verbal Discussions*, f. 25; *Peking & Tientsin Times*, June 29, 1895. Li wrote in the letter dated April 12 addressed to Itō of "the cession of a rich, populous and important part of the Empire (Formosa)." *Nihon gaikō bunsho*, vol. 28, no. 2, p. 359. See also Tabohashi, *Nisshin*, p. 520.

LI: It is an old habit with the Formosans.

ITŌ: Yet Formosa was populated before opium was produced. We have kept opium out of Japanese ports by the most stringent prohibitions and have consequently no opium smokers.

LI: I admire that.

ITŌ: I discussed the question of the prohibition of opium with Minister Yen and he heartily agreed with me.

LI: The United Kingdom insists on bringing opium into our ports. We have increased the duties but what more can we do?

ITŌ: The duty is much too low. Treble the amount would be none too much.

LI: We have spoken of it frequently, but the United Kingdom will not consent.

ITŌ: Opium-smokers are all indolent; you cannot make good soldiers of them.

LI: The United Kingdom had forced opium on us and we cannot stop it.[34]

Li, trying to prevent the cession of Formosa, cited various "facts" here. He was in an extremely difficult position during the treaty negotiations in Shimonoseki. As Liang Qichao wrote in an essay about Li Hongzhang in 1901: "He is the target of all the arrows with his body, was knocked down completely in his body and all people want to kill him [*sic*]."[35] This passage from the peace meeting is a good example of Li's desperate resistance to the severe proposal of Japan, an enemy country. It is not entirely clear why this passage is missing in Japan's records. One possibility is that Li intentionally added this to the minutes although there was no such exchange during the actual meeting. Another possibility is that the Japanese deemed the recording unnecessary because this was a kind of casual chat between the two sides.[36]

Regarding the April 10 meeting, despite crucial differences in several points between Japan's and China's records, an intense exchange undoubtedly occurred regarding the cession of Formosa, which had not yet been occupied. Understandably, the Pescadores Islands were not discussed, as they had been occupied by Japanese forces on March 26.

According to Japan's records, at the April 15 meeting Li first demanded that Chinese nationals, even if they did not have Japanese nationality, be recognized as owners of real estate before the cession. However, Itō brought up the

[34] *Five Verbal Discussions*, ff. 27–28; *Peking & Tientsin Times*, June 29, 1895.

[35] Liang Qichao, *Li Hongzhang zhuan* (Beijing: Dongfang Publishing, 2009) (Originally published in 1901), pp. 76–77.

[36] An interesting conversation between Li and Itō was held at the beginning of the April 10 meeting. Li said that "An-hui [a birthplace of Li] is inferior to Nagato [a birthplace of Itō], because you see I am beaten by you." Itō replied that "It was not An-hui but China itself that was defeated." JACAR: Ref. B06150073400 (47th picture); *Nihon gaikō bunsho*, vol. 28, no. 2, p. 406. China's records are roughly similar to Japan's records: Li said that "An Hui resembles this province [Nagato] but has produced too many unsuccessful officials." Itō replied that "China's defeat cannot be attributed to An Hui." *Five Verbal Discussions*, ff. 18–19; *Peking & Tientsin Times*, June 29, 1895.

most-favored-nation clause and argued that if foreigners were to own land in Formosa, they would have no choice but to recognize land ownership for other foreigners in all regions of Japan; thus, it would be unacceptable.

Li further provided information indicating that, according to a telegram from the Governor-General of Formosa, rumors of the cession of Formosa had spread locally, stating that "the residents are furious and they will not allow the landing of Japanese soldiers in Formosa." Itō dismissed this, arguing that he had an idea about Formosa and that China would not be troubled by the situation there.[37]

Further, at this meeting, there was a fierce debate on the timing of Formosa's transfer after the peace treaty's ratification exchange. As a result, it was agreed that the commissioners of the two countries would be sent to Formosa immediately upon the ratification exchange, and the final transfer of the islands would be completed within two months from the date of the exchange.[38] According to Japan's records, Li smiled and told Itō, "You are too hungry," to which Itō replied with a loud laugh. "You might think so. I feel I have a big appetite myself."[39]

At the end of the meeting on April 17, Li Hongzhang said, "As soon as the ratifications are exchanged, Japan will send a Commissioner Plenipotentiary to Formosa. It is my sincere wish that a temperate and broad-minded person would be appointed." Itō did not say anything about this request at this meeting.[40]

Despite a rather intense exchange on the Formosa issue at the meeting on this day, the scope of "entire islands and attached islands of Formosa" to be ceded does not appear in any of the records of Japan and China.

There are two possible interpretations for the lack of a clearly defined scope here. First, there was no need to discuss what the notion of "its attached islands" refers to because it was obvious for both countries. This is an acceptable interpretation when compared with the treatment of the Pescadores Islands. The draft peace conditions sent by Japan to Li Hongzhang on April 1 referred only to the Pescadores Islands. In contrast, the draft presented on April 10 clarified the extent of the Pescadores Islands in terms of latitude and longitude. It was adopted as in the

[37] *Nihon gaikō bunsho*, vol. 28, no. 2, p. 422; JACAR: Ref. B06150073400 (35th–36th pictures); *Five Verbal Discussions*, ff. 35–36; *Peking & Tientsin Times*, July 13, 1895.

[38] *Nihon gaikō bunsho*, vol. 28, no. 2, p. 424; JACAR: Ref. B06150073400 (34th picture); *Five Verbal Discussions*, ff. 47–48; *Peking & Tientsin Times*, July 13, 1895.

[39] *Nihon gaikō bunsho*, vol. 28, no. 2, p. 424. In Mutsu's minutes the contents of the conversation about this topic were fairly different. Li said: "(Then Smiling added) You need not be afraid of losing Formosa after all. You have got the food in your mouth already and we will not extract it again!" Itō replied, smiling, "But I am so hungry." Li said: "I am afraid you are too hungry." JACAR: Ref. B06150073400 (34th picture). No description of this anecdote is found in China's records. One more interesting talk was recorded only in Japan"s records in Japanese: Li said "I didn't think you were such a terribly strict and persistent person." Itō replied with a smile, "Such an attitude is indeed unavoidable in the affairs of state to be managed." *Nihon gaikō bunsho*, vol. 28, no. 2, p. 432.

[40] Ibid., p. 436. In Mutsu's minutes Li said: "As soon as the ratifications will be exchanged the High Commissioners of our respective Governments will be appointed to conduct the final transfer of Formosa in an amicable manner." JACAR: Ref. B06150073400 (24th picture). There is no description on this matter in China"s records.

peace treaty. In contrast, the expression "all Islands adjacent or belonging to the said Island of Formosa" was indicated in the draft peace conditions of April 1 and maintained roughly as it is in the April 10 draft and the peace treaty.

Another interpretation is that both sides possibly considered the scope of "all Islands adjacent or belonging to the said Island of Formosa" essentially a trivial issue. As evident from the conference minutes, the only thing discussed about Formosa was whether the island was occupied. Itō threatened to occupy Formosa as soon as it became necessary. It is presumed that Itō envisioned only the island of Formosa as a target of the occupation, not of the conquest.[41] However, this interpretation is not necessarily supported by evidence given that it clearly states the scope of the Pescadores Islands.

In the discussion between Li and Itō about the cession of Formosa, found only in Japan's records, it is noteworthy that Li argued that, in contrast to Siberia, "People there are subordinate to the cultivation by the Emperor." Li's talk about Formosa was still within the framework of the traditional Chinese idea of "territory." Here we may observe a notion that whether the people recognize the virtue of the Chinese Emperor is a crucial factor for deeming the region of the people as being within the "territory" of China. In contrast, Itō argued that both Siberia and Formosa were under the sovereignty of China and it was common for a cession of territory to be made as a result of war, understanding the territory under the concept of modern Western international law.[42]

7.2.3 The Status of Korea in Modern Western International Law

Even in the 1870s, China insisted on its traditional idea of world order, claiming, for example, in the dealings with Japan regarding Formosa in 1874 that "international law was quite recently invented in Western countries, but without China's involvement." Therefore, talking about international law in cases related to Formosa and China was futile.[43]

The situation changed gradually in the 1880s, although China still insisted on its traditional world order concerning its relations with East Asian countries, especially Korea, as typically shown by the 1882 China–Korea Treaty. The 1895 Treaty

[41] According to the prevailing international law of the time, cession and conquest (subjugation) were different territorial titles. Conquest was usually said to be a system in which regions that were militarily occupied and endorsed by peace treaty were considered as the territory of the conquering country. Cession differs from this conquest in that the defeated country cedes part of its territory to the victorious country, regardless of occupation. See, e.g., Lassa Oppenheim, *International Law: A Treatise*, vol. 1: Peace (New York and Bombay: Longmans, Green, and Co., 1905), pp. 268–274 and 287–292.

[42] *Nihon gaikō bunsho*, vol. 28, no. 2, p. 414; JACAR: Ref. B06150073400 (42nd and 43th pictures).

[43] *Nihon gaikō bunsho*, vol. 7 (1874), p. 230. As for the Formosa Incident, see, e.g., John Peter Stern, *The Japanese Interpretation of the "Law of Nations," 1854–1874* (Princeton, NJ: Princeton University Press, 1979), pp. 101–132.

of Shimonoseki with Japan was a highly symbolic turning point. China officially recognized that Korea was no longer a vassal country in the traditional East Asian world order but rather an independent country according to modern Western international law.[44]

Article 1 of the draft peace treaty presented by Japan on April 1 provides that "it is confirmed by China that Korea is a completely independent country."[45] On the other hand, Article 1 of China's counter-draft presented on April 9 provides that "China and Japan recognize definitely the full and complete independence and autonomy and guarantee the complete neutrality of Korea, and it is agreed that the interference by either in the internal affairs of Korea in derogation of such autonomy, or the performance of ceremonies and formalities by Korea inconsistent with such independence, shall wholly cease for the future."[46]

In the memorandum submitted to Li at the meeting on April 10, it was written that no word in the Japanese draft of Article 1 could be changed.[47] Article 1 of the final treaty provides that "China recognizes definitively the full and complete independence and autonomy of Korea, and in consequence, the payment of tribute and the performance of ceremonies and formalities by Korea to China in derogation of such independence and autonomy, shall wholly cease for the future." That means that phrases related to Korea's neutrality in China's counter-draft were omitted. Another important difference between China's draft and the final treaty was that the only country guaranteeing the independence and autonomy of Korea was China, and the equivalent status of both countries[48] concerning this point was not recognized.[49] This does mean, from a purely legal point of view regarding this Treaty, that the independence and neutrality of Korea were not guaranteed by Japan. Moreover, it is highly doubtful to find "Japan's unjustified greed"[50] to bring Korea under the control of Japan, by not admitting the status of Korea as an independent country, in the near future, or argue that the route to the annexation

[44] See, e.g., Banno Masataka, *Kindai chūgoku seiji gaikō shi [History of the Politics and Diplomacy in Modern China]* (Tokyo: University of Tokyo Press, 1973), especially pp. 371–539; Okamoto, *Zokkoku*, pp. 3–14. See also Cai Congyan, "Civilization, China and International Law (1840s–1940s): From Seeking Recognition to Making Contribution," in *Cambridge History of International Law*, vol. 2 (forthcoming).

[45] *Nihon gaikō bunsho*, vol. 28, no. 2, p. 331.

[46] Ibid., pp. 350 and 352. See the peace treaty condition shown by the United Kingdom on October 8, 1894 providing that "The Government of Japan recognizes that each country guarantee the independence of Korea." *Nihon gaikō bunsho*, vol. 27, no. 2, p. 474.

[47] *Nihon gaikō bunsho*, vol. 28, no. 2, p. 408.

[48] Ibid., p. 339. In a draft planned to reply to the United Kingdom's peace proposal on October 8, 1874, which suggested that the independence of Korea should be guaranteed by the Powers, there were two options for Korea: 1. China should recognize the independence of Korea, giving Port Arthur and Jalien Bay to Japan as a permanent guarantee of non-intervention in the affairs of Korea; 2. The independence of Korea should be guaranteed by the Powers. Japan adopted the first option in the first treaty draft on April 1, which became the final treaty provision. *Itō Hirobumi monjo*, vol. 17, pp. 191–203.

[49] JACAR: Ref. B06150073400 (16th picture).

[50] Mitchell A. Silk, "Imperial China and International Law: A Case Study of the 1895 Treaty of Shimonoseki," *Chinese (Taiwan) Yearbook of International Law* 2 (1982): p. 135.

of Korea by Japan in 1910 was worked out here. Japan had continuously insisted on the "*Jishu*" [autonomy] of Korea since the 1876 Treaty of Peace and Friendship between Japan and Korea (Ganghwa Island Treaty), although the meaning of "autonomy" differed considerably between China, Korea, and Japan.[51]

No substantial discussion was found on the status of Korea in either Japan's or China's records of the peace treaty negotiations. The Chinese side did not mount any strong resistance to Japan's draft on the status of Korea, as China had already proposed conditions for peace on November 22, 1894, long before the Shimonoseki negotiation, through the commissioning of the American Ministers to China and Japan: the independence of Korea and some amount of indemnity.[52] China focused on the issues of an amount of indemnity and the cession of Formosa at the peace conference.

The Treaty of Shimonoseki marked the end of the traditional East Asian world order. Symbolically, this was the end of the payment of tribute and the performance of ceremonies and formalities by Korea to China. The fact that Korea was no longer regarded as a "vassal country" of China but rather as an "independent and autonomous country" in modern Western international law was finally confirmed by a bilateral treaty between China and Korea. The Treaty of Commerce between China and Korea (Treaty of Seoul) was concluded on September 11, 1899, four years after the 1895 Treaty. Article 1 of the 1899 Treaty stipulates, "There shall be perpetual peace and friendship between the Empire of Korea and the Empire of China, and between their respective subjects, who shall enjoy equally in the respective countries of the High Contracting Parties full protection and the advantage of favorable treatment." China recognized Korea as an equal partner, gave equal rights to Korean subjects, and agreed to exchange diplomatic and consular representatives with Korea (Article 2).

The Treaty of Shimonoseki also marked the establishment of Japan as an imperial power and the creation of its colonial empire in East Asia. An indemnity totaling approximately 230 million taels, including compensation for abandoning the cession of the Liaodong Peninsula, equivalent to approximately four times the Japanese government's annual revenue, was used as a fund for industrial investment in Japan.

With China's defeat as a "sleeping lion" in the Sino–Japanese War, European powers and Japan advanced into China swiftly and earnestly. In 1898, the so-called partition of China occurred. The imperialist powers of the United Kingdom, France, Russia, Germany, and Japan divided and ruled China's land in the form of concessions such as leased land, railroad construction rights, and mining rights. Japan played a critical role in this movement.[53] Mounting anger among the

[51] Okamoto, *Zokkoku*, especially pp. 42–44 and 373–375.

[52] *Itō Hirobumi monjo*, vol. 28, p. 53. See also Tabohashi, *Nisshin*, pp. 404 and 435.

[53] See, e.g., Gilbert Reid, "The Powers and the Partition of China," *The North American Review* 170/522 (1900): pp. 634–641.

Chinese people manifested in the Boxer Rebellion in June 1900, and the conflict of interests among the great powers after the partition of China led to the Russo–Japanese War of 1904 over Manchuria.

7.3 Equality among East Asian Countries from the Perspective of an Extradition Treaty

7.3.1 Regulations of Handling a Japanese Fisherman Who Committed a Crime on the Korean Coast Agreed Upon between Korea and Japan in 1883

This section elaborates on the issue of extraterritoriality, particularly the extradition treaty system. The issue here is whether, after 1895, Japan regarded East Asian countries, including China, as equals in the sense of modern Western international law, whose fundamental principle is sovereign equality. The present extradition treaty system was supposed to be based on this fundamental principle.

In a letter dated July 1, 1896, to Japanese Foreign Minister Saionji Kinmochi Hayashi Tadasu, the Japanese Minister to China wrote that Wu Tingfang, Li Hongzhang's staff member from 1882, who attended the peace conference in Shimonoseki and was appointed in 1897 as the Minister to the US, proposed to Hayashi to conclude a treaty between China and Japan. This would stipulate extraditing a Formosan who commits crimes and flees to mainland China and a Chinese who commits crimes on the mainland and flees to Formosa, as Formosa became a possession of Japan. In the letter, Hayashi wrote that in his reply to Wu he had said that the proposal might be better made by Yugeng, the Chinese Minister in Tokyo, adding that it was Hayashi's idea that it was desirable to conclude a treaty, although he did not express to Wu his final consent to the treaty conclusion.[54]

Article 5 of the Shimonoseki Treaty granted the inhabitants of Formosa a period of two years from the date of the ratification exchange to choose their nationality. Those who chose Chinese nationality were required to relocate to mainland China. Hence, the people residing in Formosa in 1897 were considered to have chosen Japan as their home country.

The issue of the extradition treaty for Japan was probably first raised in 1873, in Meiji 6, when a proposal to conclude a Japan–Great Britain criminal treaty was proposed in a letter from Hayashi Michisaburō, the Vice Consul in Hong Kong.[55] The extradition issue was subsequently also taken up with Korea, the US, Russia, Mexico, Belgium, the Netherlands, France, Germany, Denmark, and so on. In this

[54] JACAR: Ref. B07080222300 (from the first picture).

[55] Diplomatic Archives of the Ministry of Foreign Affairs of Japan, Pre-war Period, Classification no. 4.1.8.1-1.

sub-section I will introduce the case of Korea, and in the next sub-section the case of the US.

On July 25, 1883, Japan and Korea concluded the "Regulations under which Japanese Trade is to be conducted in Korea," "Stipulations for the Treaty Limits in Korea," and "Regulations of Handling a Japanese Fisherman Who Committed a Crime on the Korean Coast agreed upon between Korea and Japan." The Regulations of Handling concluded after consultation between Takezoe Shin-ichirō, the Minister of Japan, and Min Young-ho, the Minister Plenipotentiary of Korea, were promulgated on October 15 of the same year. Article 1 stipulates that a Japanese person who violates the legal prohibition of Korea on the contracted coast of Korea shall be treated per the articles in the treaty, both on land and in water. Article 2 stipulates that when a Korean official seizes a Japanese fisherman who violates the law, that person should be handed over to the Japanese consular officer at the nearest port to demand appropriate punishment. According to Subsection 41 of the Regulations of Trade, fishing vessels belonging to Japan and Korea shall be permitted to frequent the coasts of Zenra-do, Keisho-do, Kogen-do, and Kankio-do in Korea, and the coasts of Hizen, Chikuzen, Nagato (opposite the coast of Korea), Iwami, Izumo, and Tsushima in Japan, to catch fish. The rules for Japanese fishermen who violate these trade rules are listed in Article 2 of the Regulations of Handling. However, the same rules are not found in the Regulations of Handling for Korean Fishermen. Korean fishermen who violate trade rules in Japan will be tried in the courts of Japan.[56]

Article 2 of the Regulations of Handling may be considered a provision within the framework of consular jurisdiction. However, it is not impossible to regard this article as one that provides for extradition. More specifically, in the extradition treaty section of the index by item of the *Handbook of Treaties (Bilateral Treaties)* compiled by the Treaty Bureau of the Ministry of Foreign Affairs, Japan, in 1958, the Regulations of Handling are listed in addition to the 1886 Extradition Treaty between Japan and the US and the 1911 Extradition Treaty between Japan and Russia.[57] However, there were no cases where a Japanese fisherman was handed over based on the Regulations of Handling.[58]

The extradition between Korea and Japan was again discussed 17 years later. In a letter dated November 6, 1900, from Hayashi Gonsuke, the Minister to Korea, to

[56] Related materials are housed in National Archives of Japan, *Kōbunroku [Records of Official Documents]*; Diplomatic Archives of the Ministry of Foreign Affairs of Japan, Pre-war Period, Classification no. 3.5.8.10; National Institute for Defense Studies, Ministry of Defense, *Rikugunshō dainikki [Records of Official Documents of the Ministry of Army]*.

[57] See Yanagihara Masaharu, *Kokusaihō senrei shiryōshū 3: Hanzai-nin hikiwatashi jyōyaku jyōrei [A Collection of Documents of International Law (3): Extradition Treaties and Ordinances]* (Tokyo: Shinzansha, 2023), no. 365. See also the provisions of Article 24 of the Sino–Japanese Treaty of Commerce and Navigation.

[58] Treaty Bureau, Ministry of Foreign Affairs, ed., *Handbook of Treaties (Bilateral Treaties)* (Treaty Bureau, Ministry of Foreign Affairs, 1958), p. 424.

Katō Takaaki, the Foreign Minister, Hayashi wrote that His Majesty the Emperor of the Korean Empire was eager to conclude an extradition treaty between Korea and Japan. However, Hayashi thought that concluding a treaty was unnecessary because there was extraterritoriality, police power, and rights at the open ports of Korea, and the nationality of all ships arriving and departing was Japanese. Korea was considered the same as inland Japan, and Japanese criminals who flee could be found at once and ordered to leave immediately. In addition, he wrote that "Korea is far inferior in civilization than Japan and that is perfectly true, especially in the field of judiciary. Therefore, it is needless to conclude an extradition treaty with Korea." Hayashi added that the benefits brought to Japan would be significant if extradition were restricted to ordinary criminals, excluding political offenders, and if the Korean mainland were liberated, allowing Japanese nationals to possess rights of residence, business, and ownership land.[59]

In a letter to Hayashi on the 27th of the same month, Katō stated that there was no need to conclude an extradition treaty with Korea, as "A judicial system in Korea is far inferior to that in normal civilized countries and its criminal procedure is still not reliable." He instructed that it was undesirable to present the terms of exchange for the conclusion of an extradition treaty.[60]

Furthermore, in a letter from Hayashi to Katō on December 6, Hayashi reiterated that the terms of exchange should be a different type of treaty, and that although various troubles may arise after the conclusion of an extradition treaty, there would be more than enough compensation for gains and losses if benefits such as opening up the inland land can be obtained.[61] However, an extradition treaty between Japan and Korea was never concluded.

The notion that Korea possesses an inferior civilization and judicial system brings to mind the unilaterality of the Regulations for Handling Japanese Fishermen from July 1883. By 1900, even five years after the conclusion of the Treaty of Shimonoseki, the underlying situation regarding the unequal relationship between Korea and Japan had not been altered.

7.3.2 US–Japan Extradition Treaty in 1886

The US–Japan Extradition Treaty, signed on April 29, 1886, was the first extradition treaty signed by Japan. The unequal treaties, especially the 1858 Ansei Five Treaties, which the Tokugawa Shogunate had concluded with the US, the Netherlands, Russia, the United Kingdom, and France, could not be amended until eight years later in 1894 (the treaties entered into force in 1899). The major

[59] JACAR: Ref. B07080229900 (from the first picture).
[60] JACAR: Ref. B07080229900 (from the fourth picture).
[61] JACAR: Ref. B07080229900 (seventh picture).

question of a relation between the unequal treaties and extradition treaties was how the arrest and extradition of criminals could be consistent with the extraterritoriality granted to the foreign nationals by the unequal treaties. In fact, regarding Hayashi Michisaburō's statement of June 1873, Ueno Kagenori, the Deputy Vice Minister of Foreign Affairs at the time, indicated in a letter to Hayashi dated July 10 that Japan would want to consult an extradition treaty conclusion when the unequal treaties would be revised.[62] Why, then, did Japan and the US agree to conclude an extradition treaty in 1886 when the unequal treaties had not yet been amended? Did Japan and the US conclude an extradition treaty as "equal" countries?

The motive for the extradition treaty between Japan and the US was derived from Calvin Pratt's case in November 1885.[63] In a letter dated December 10, 1885, to Inoue Kaoru, the Foreign Minister, Kuki Ryūichi, the Minister Plenipotentiary to the US, wrote that it would be desirable to conclude an extradition treaty between Japan and the US and have the US Secretary of State present a draft of the treaty and discuss it.[64] The draft treaty (in both Japanese and English), dated January 19, was drawn up, and a letter from Inoue to Kuki on January 20 initiated negotiations based on Japan's draft.[65]

Although Inoue was active in concluding an extradition treaty between Japan and the US, he recognized a major problem from an early stage. The argument of the US was clearly stated in a letter, the estimated date of which was in January 1886, from Inoue to Richard Bennett Hubbard, the US Minister to Japan: "The Government of Japan had given to the Treaties Parties full authority to arrest, interrogate, and punish a person of the Treaties Parties when the person has committed a crime at the open ports and within the areas of the ambulatory regulation."[66] The issue was whether Japan has the power to arrest an American who commits a crime at the open ports and within the ambulatory regulations areas of Japan. Inoue clearly stated his opinion that he was not in a position to abandon the right of arrest in Japan apart from its jurisdiction, also adding that this point should be

[62] Diplomatic Archives of the Ministry of Foreign Affairs of Japan, Pre-war Period, Classification no. 4.1.8.1-1.

[63] The Pratt case is as follows. On November 18, 1885, Thomas Francis Bayard, US Secretary of State, conveyed a request to Kuki that Pratt be arrested upon arrival in Yokohama, Japan and handed over to the US Consul in Yokohama, as he had stolen $12,000 from the Pacific Bank in San Francisco. As no extradition treaty had been concluded between Japan and the US, the request was based on international comity. In response to this request, Inoue sent a telegram to Kuki on November 20 to inform the Secretary of State that a formal request from the Secretary of State was necessary for Pratt to be handed over and that the Government of Japan wished to conclude a bilateral extradition treaty immediately. Pratt landed in Yokohama on December 1 and was handed over to a California agent at the Yokohama Settlement Police Station on January 7 of the following year, and set sail for the port of San Francisco on the same day. The primary source of the Pratt case is housed in Diplomatic Archives of the Ministry of Foreign Affairs of Japan, Pre-war Period, Classification no. 4.1.5.1-3-2.

[64] Yanagihara, *Kokusaihō*, no. 4.

[65] Ibid., nos 6, 7-1, 7-2, and 8.

[66] Ibid., no. 5.

fully deliberated upon at the treaty revision conference (the first meeting was held in May 1886).

The US State Department produced several drafts of the treaty. The first draft was attached to a letter from Bayard to Hubbard on March 24, 1886 (received on April 24). Of particular note in this letter is the following: The conclusion of an extradition treaty serves the friendly purpose of the U.S. to treat Japan on "the broadest basis of national equality" in all aspects of the powers and functions of justice in Japan, and it is up to the amendment of the treaty to determine in which court Americans who committed crimes in Japan are tried. The "phraselogy my draft scrupulously respects the fullest judicial autonomy of Japan."[67]

On the 27th, three copies of the draft treaty were mailed from Bayard to Kuki. In this letter, Bayard clarified that the US draft of the extradition treaty scrupulously respected Japan's fullest judicial autonomy.[68]

The draft treaty was immediately translated into Japanese and attached to a letter from Kuki to Inoue on April 1. In the letter, Kuki wrote:

> This treaty draft proves adequately that an autonomy of jurisdiction of Japan is truly acknowledged and respected by the U.S. Government, as shown in the letter of Secretary of State. A major amendment was added to the draft in comparison with equal extradition treaties between the U.S. and European countries ... If the draft is concluded and ratified, it would be shown to the public to prove that the statutes of Japan are quite sufficient for protecting life and property and that the jurisdiction laws of Japan deserve to be abided by the civilized people. I am sure that a conclusion of the extradition treaty is urgently necessary for Japan.[69]

Hubbard informed Inoue that he wanted to discuss the draft before convening the Convention Revision Conference.[70] Inoue and Hubbard signed the final draft on April 29, 1886. With some amendments at the US Senate, the extradition treaty between Japan and the US entered into force on November 27 of the same year.[71]

The *New York Tribune*, a US newspaper, stated on August 6 that this was the first extradition treaty between a civilized country and a "semi-barbarian" Asian country.[72] The journalist in the *New York Tribune* regarded Japan not as completely equal to the US, but as a semi-barbarian country. What was then the opinion of the

[67] Ibid., no. 11.

[68] Ibid., no. 13. In a reply from Kuki on April 8, he expressed his gratitude for the utmost consideration for judicial autonomy. General Records of the Department of State (R. G. 59): Diplomatic Despatches from Diplomatic Officers, 1789–1906: Despatches from the US Ministers to Japan, 1855–1906. M 163.

[69] Yanagihara, *Kokusaihō*, no. 15.

[70] Ibid., nos 19 and 20. The first meeting of the Convention Revision Conference was held on May 1, only two days later.

[71] Ibid., nos 60-1, 60-2, 61, 62, and 63.

[72] Ibid., no. 50.

US government? In certain US documents, some statements acknowledge the autonomy of Japan's jurisdiction, as shown above. Moreover, in a letter by Kuki addressed to Inoue dated June 14, 1886, Kuki argues that it is Bayard's fundamental stance to regard Japan as having a full right of jurisdiction and administration and an equal right to conclude treaties with Western countries. Moreover, he adds that Bayard desires the treaty revision of Japan, as Japan has an independent and self-deciding right, although it should be within the limits of not damaging the interests of the American people.[73]

7.3.3 The 1896 Treaty of Commerce and Navigation between China and Japan

Before the 1898 partition of China, the issues between Japan and China were the return of the Liaodong Peninsula based on the Triple Intervention, Formosa's governance, and Article 6 of the Shimonoseki Peace Treaty. Based on this Article, the Treaty of Commerce and Navigation was to be concluded between Japan and China. For Japan, the main purpose of the Treaty of Commerce and Navigation was to obtain rights in trade with China which were equal to those of the Western countries. The Treaty, concluded on July 21, 1896, established new additional rights for Japan in residence, trade, and court. Article 1 of the Annex Protocol, concluded in October of the same year, allowed Japan to establish exclusive concessions in newly opened ports. Those exclusive concessions were established between 1897 and 1899.

As mentioned earlier, an extradition treaty between China and Japan proposed by China around June 1896 was never concluded. The 1896 Sino–Japanese Treaty of Commerce and Navigation contained Articles 22 and 24, which might be interpreted as including extraditions.

Article 22 of the 1896 Treaty provides that

> Japanese subjects charged with the commission of any crimes or offenses in China shall be tried, and, if found guilty, punished by the Japanese Authorities according to the laws of Japan. In like manner, Chinese subjects charged with the commission of any crimes or offences against Japanese subjects in China shall be tried and, if found guilty, punished by the Chinese Authorities according to the laws of China.

Article 24 of the 1896 Treaty stipulates that

[73] *Nihon gaikō bunsho: Jyōyaku kaisei [Treaty Revision]*, vol. 2, p. 1356.

> If Japanese subjects in China, who have committed offenses or have failed to discharge debts and fraudulently abscond, should flee to the interior of China or take refuge in houses occupied by Chinese subjects or on-board of Chinese ships, the Chinese Authorities shall, at the request of the Japanese Consul, deliver them to the Japanese Authorities. In like manner, if Chinese subjects in China, who have committed offenses or have failed to discharge debts and fraudulently abscond, should take refuge in houses occupied by Japanese subjects in China or on-board Japanese ships in Chinese waters, they shall be delivered up, at the request of the Chinese Authorities to the Japanese Authorities.

These provisions were inserted out of necessity to ensure Japan's consular jurisdiction in China and protect the interests of Japanese citizens residing in China rather than to establish an equal extradition system between China and Japan.

The treaty did not include the extradition of a Formosan who commits crimes in Formosa and flees to mainland China, or the extradition of a Chinese who flees to Formosa after committing crimes on the mainland, as requested by the Chinese side around June 1896.

Article 11 of the Supplementary Treaty of Commerce and Navigation signed on October 8, 1903 stipulates that "The Government of China having expressed a strong desire to reform its judicial system and to bring it into accord with that of Japan and Western nations, Japan agrees to give every assistance to such reform, and will also be prepared to relinquish its extraterritorial rights when Japan expresses that the state of the Chinese laws, the arrangements for their administration and other considerations satisfies Japan."

Undoubtedly, as a result of the Sino–Japanese War, the people of Japan regarded China as a country inferior to Japan and Western countries, completely reversing the honorable status of China as a "teacher" of the Japanese people that had prevailed for almost 2000 years.[74] This was demonstrated in the negotiations of the extradition treaty and the conclusion of the commercial treaty with China.[75]

7.4 Concluding Remarks

Japan applied the same policy not only to China but also to other Asian countries. This is strongly reminiscent of Protocol I, annexed to the Japan–Siamese Treaty of Amity and Commerce of February 25, 1898. It is a provision that, until the completion of the judicial reform of Siam (implementation of the criminal, criminal prosecution, civil, civil prosecution, and court constitution codes), Japanese

[74] See Takemura, *Setsuwa den*, p. 269.

[75] See Yamamuro Shin-ichi, *Shisō kadai toshiteno ajia: Kijiku, rensa, tōki [Asia as an Intellectual Problem: A Foundation, a Chain, and a Project]* (Tokyo: Iwanami shoten, 2001), pp. 605–606.

consular officers shall exercise jurisdiction over Japanese subjects residing in Siam. From 1902 to 1913, Masao Tōkichi, a Japanese lawyer who studied law at West Virginia University and Yale University in the US, was a legal adviser to the Siamese Ministry of Justice and was involved in the country's domestic legislation. This consular jurisdiction lasted until the 1924 Japan–Siam Treaty of Commerce and Navigation, when the main domestic statutes were enacted in Siam.[76]

From the beginning of the Meiji era, Japan worked hard to revise unequal treaties concluded at the end of the Tokugawa Shogunate. For the sake of treaty revision, Japan enacted domestic statutes modeled after modern Western law, relying heavily on "*Oyatoi gaikokujin*" [employed foreigners] such as Hermann Roesler, Gustave Boissonade de Fontarabie, and Hermann Techow. In the face of stubborn resistance from conservative and nationalistic forces in the country, the Criminal and Criminal Procedure Codes were enacted in 1880 and implemented in 1882, the Constitution was enacted in 1889 and implemented in 1890, and the Civil and Commercial Codes were enacted in 1890. This means that around 1890 almost all the basic codes were enacted and implemented, except the Civil and Commercial Codes.[77] Considering these facts, four years before the enactment of basic codes in 1890 and eight years before the treaty revision in 1894, Japan succeeded in concluding the 1886 Extradition Treaty with the US, as an "equal" partner. One reason for this success may be that the Criminal and Criminal Procedure Codes in Japan had already been implemented in 1882. However, taking into consideration its failures to conclude an extradition treaty with other Western countries, especially the United Kingdom,[78] the real reason for its success with the US might be its extremely active attitude toward concluding a treaty with Japan, ahead of other Western countries. A cogent reason for this active attitude is a specific case that required extradition: the case of Calvin Pratt, as explained in subsection 3.2.

As was written in the letter from Kuki dated April 1, 1886, the conclusion of the extradition treaty with the US showed "the public that the statutes of Japan are quite sufficient for protecting life and property and the jurisdiction laws of Japan deserve to be abided by civilized people."[79]

[76] See, e.g., Tamara Loos, *Subject Siam: Family, Law, and Colonial Modernity in Thailand* (Chiang Mai: Silkworm Books, 2002), pp. 29–71. The Criminal Code was enacted in 1908 and the Civil and Commercial Code in 1925.

[77] The Civil Code sent to the throne in July 1889 and enacted in April 1890 was to be implemented in January 1893. However, in 1889, the University of Tokyo Law Bachelor's Association announced its opposition to the Civil Code, arguing that it destroys the human morals of society based on the theory of natural human rights, and a controversy arose over whether to postpone or implement the Civil Code. At the same time, the Commercial Code debate was also held. The controversy stemmed from the ideological confrontation between liberalism and nationalism, and the conflict between the French and British legal schools was also involved. In 1892, the Third Parliament passed a bill to postpone the implementation of the Commercial and Civil Codes, which was postponed until 1896. The new Civil Code was enacted in 1897.

[78] A considerable number of treaty drafts were drawn up and exchanged between the United Kingdom and Japan from 1892 to 1934, but no extradition treaty was concluded. See Yanagihara, *Kokusaihō*, pp. 35–37.

[79] Ibid., no. 15.

In contrast, Japan did not desire to conclude an extradition treaty with China and Korea, nor with Siam, as it regarded those countries as unequal partners. With the 1895 Treaty of Shimonoseki, Japan ended the traditional order in East Asia and laid the foundation for modern Western international law to start to play a role in the region, at least indirectly. However, Japan imposed the same policy on Asian countries that Western countries had adopted against Japan from the end of the Tokugawa Shogunate to the early Meiji era. The essence of the policy was that unless the legal system of each country, which should not be a traditional Asian-style but a Western-style one, was improved, equal relations could not be established between Japan and the Asian countries, and extradition treaties could not be concluded between them.

Japan certainly had the possibility to assert its own international order as an Asian country. However, instead of taking such a position, it sought to slavishly adhere to the framework of traditional, modern Western international law. From the end of the 1930s to the 1940s Japan developed a unique theory of international law, called the "Greater East Asia International Law Order," but whether it aimed to form an international order unique to Asia as per its philosophy or was based solely on Japan's national interests, colonialism, or militarism is still a matter of debate.

8
A History of Italian Colonialism in China at the Turn of the 20th Century

*Luigi Nuzzo**

8.1 Introduction

This is what medical lieutenant Messerotti Benvenuti wrote to his mother on September 13, 1900, at the end of the long journey that had taken him from Naples to Tianjin, "a beautiful city" on the mouth of the Hai River, by then ravaged by clashes with Chinese troops and militias belonging to the nationalist and anti-Western Boxer movement:

> The city of Tien-Tsin was a beautiful city and still is where it is. The European concessions vast enough to form by themselves a big city of ours, are made of beautiful wide tree-lined streets, all palaces, villas and cottages surrounded by gardens. The climate is milder than in Peking, it must have been a splendid residence. Now many houses are still standing, but a great many have been burned down, many torn down completely… The Chinese city which is immense, containing before the war about a million inhabitants, is also reduced to a deplorable state. Entire neighborhoods are reduced to a heap of rubble. Around the concession for a radius of almost a kilometer there is nothing but rubble.[1]

Only two months earlier, Tianjin had been liberated by international coalition forces, but on the ground, there was still much to be done to locate and set up the Italian expeditionary force's quarters and, politically, to define the objectives of Italian participation in an international police operation in a country about which, in Italy, very little was known, and with which there were few trade relations.[2]

* The topic of this contribution is currently undergoing further research as part of the study activities related to the PRIN PNRR 2022 "HiLArI. Histories, Laws & Architectures for Inclusion," funded by the European Union—Next Generation EU, under the M4C2 component, investment 1.1.

[1] Giuseppe Messerotti Benvenuti, "Tien-Tsin 13 settembre 1900," in Un italiano nella Cina dei Boxer. Lettere e fotografie (1900–1901), edited by Paolo Battaglia and Nicola Labanca (Modena: Associazione Giuseppe Panini archivi modenesi, 2000), p. 17..

[2] Diplomatic relations between the Kingdom of Italy and China formally began with the trade treaty of October 26, 1866, s. Andrea Francioni, Il "banchetto cinese." L'Italia fra le treaty powers (Siena: Nuova immagine editrice, 2004).

Luigi Nuzzo, *A History of Italian Colonialism in China at the Turn of the 20th Century* In: *Histories of International Law in China*. Edited by: Ignacio de la Rasilla, Jiangyu Wang, and Congyan Cai, Oxford University Press.
 DOI: 10.1093/oso/9780198888345.003.0008

Lacking a clear strategic line and divided by personalistic conflicts, the action of the Italian government was driven by the aspiration to open an eastern market to the interests and investments of Italian capitalism. It was also animated and by a revanchist attitude aimed at reclaiming a central role for Italy in European colonial policy, erasing the dishonor arising from the defeat at Adwa and the embarrassment caused by the Chinese refusal of the request for a concession in Sanmen Bay.[3] Humbled militarily in Africa and diplomatically in China, the Italian monarchy saw, therefore, in the Boxer revolt the long-awaited opportunity to rebuild its cracked colonial respectability and to satisfy its aspiration to establish a new trading space.

The following pages tell the history of the beginning of an Italian presence in China. It is still a relatively unknown history that, starting from a military occupation, led in 1902 to the signing of the first Sino–Italian lease agreement. It allowed Italy to obtain "in perpetuity, as a concession" (art. 1) and upon payment of an annual fee (art. 12), the territory it had materially occupied during the war against the Boxer. Finally, an Italian concession was established at Tianjin alongside those already existing for Great Britain, France, Russia, Belgium, Japan, Germany, Austria, and the United States.[4]

This chapter intends to reconstruct, in the second section, the path that led from the military occupation by Italian troops to the signing of a perpetual lease agreement, focusing on the politicians, diplomats, and businessmen who, in Italy and China, imagined transforming a forgotten corner of the Celestial Empire into a new social space. In the third section I examine the ambiguity of the concession, the legal category used by Italian jurists to give legal form to the occupation of the territory of Tianjin, and the transformation it produced for Chinese sovereignty. Finally, in the last section I reconstruct the legal evolution of the concession during the 1920s and 1930s, pointing out in particular the attempts of Italian jurisprudence to transform the concession into a proper colonial domain.

[3] On the Sanmen affair from an Italian perspective Rosaria Quartararo, "L'affare di San-Mun. Un episodio dell'imperialismo coloniale italiano alla fine del XIX secolo," Clio, 33, 3 (1997): pp. 453–498; more recently Orazio Coco, Colonialismo europeo in Estremo Oriente. L'esperienza delle concessioni territoriali in Cina (Roma: edizioni nuova cultura, 2017), pp. 39–58.

[4] The agreement was signed by the Italian minister plenipotentiary in China Giovanni Gallina, and by Tang Shaoyi, Daotai of Maritime Customs, Archivio storico del Ministero degli Esteri (henceforward ASMAE), ASMAE, Affari Politici 1891–1916, Serie P, b. 426. On the Italian concession in Tianjin, Luigi Nuzzo, "Italiani in Cina: la concessione di Tien Tsin," in Diritto, istituzioni e economia nell'Italia fascista, ed. Aldo Mazzacane (Baden Baden: Nomos, 2002), pp. 255–281. More recently Maurizio Marinelli, "The genesis of the Italian concession in Tianjin: a combination of wishful thinking and realpolitik" and Aglaia De Angeli, "Italian Auctions in Tianjn: Italian Colonialism in early twentieth Century China," both in Journal of Modern Italian Studies, 15(4) (2010), respectively pp. 536–566 and pp. 557–572. For a history of Tianjin Provisional Governement of Tianjin see Pierre Singaravélou, Tianjin Cosmopolis. Une autre histoire de la mondialisation (Paris: Seuil, 2017).

8.2 From the Occupation to the Lease Agreement: The Origin of an Italian Concession

Tianjin had entered the Western colonial discourse in 1858 as the site where China, Great Britain, and France signed a peace treaty at the end of the second opium war (1856–1860) and two years later as a treaty port, thanks to the Beijing Convention (1860), by which it was opened to Western trade under the same conditions observed for other Chinese treaty ports.[5]

However, to look for a normative reference to concessions in the treaties that China was forced to sign between the 1840s and the early years of the next century would be a futile exercise. The Treaty of Nanjing (1842) provided only that British subjects could reside "without molestation or restraint" in the ports specified in the treaty (art. 2), while the so-called supplementary treaty (art. 7), as well as the Treaties of Wanghia (art. 17) and Whampoa (art. 23) respectively signed in 1844 with the United States and France, added that they could rent land, houses, or places for business.[6] On the basis of those general provisions, China and Great Britain signed the first organic body of legislation, the Land Regulations of 1845, by which foreign merchants were allowed to lease land permanently and the British consuls were entrusted with a territorial jurisdiction regardless of the citizenship of the parties.[7]

The Tianjin Treaties and the Beijing Convention, while identifying new ports and expanding Western prerogatives, did not introduce significant changes, and it was not until the Anglo-Chinese Chefoo Convention of 1876 that there came about not only the recognition of an individual right to reside in open ports, but also the collective right to a settlement.[8] Nevertheless, between the end of 1860 and the beginning of 1861, on the assumption that the Tianjin Treaty provided for the

[5] Convention of Peace and Friendship between Great Britain and China, Peking, 24.10.1860, art. 4, in Treaties between Great Britain and China; and between China and Foreign Powers; and Orders in Council, Rules, Regulations, Acts of Parliament, Decrees affecting British Interests in Cina, ed. Godfrey E.P. Hertslet, with the assistance of Edward Parkes, vol. 1, part. 1, London, 3. Ed., Harrison and Sons, 1908, p. 50 .

[6] Treaty of Nanking 29.8.1842, Wilhelm Grewe, ed., Fontes iuris gentium, Bd. 3,1 (Berlin: de Gruyter, 1988), pp. 258–262; The Supplementary Treaty, 8.10.1843, edited by William L. Tung, ed., China and the Foreign Powers: The Impact of and the Reaction to Unequal Treaties (New York: Oceana Publications, 1970), p. 436; Treaty of Peace, Amity and Commerce between the United States of America and Chinese Empire (3.7.1844), and Traité d'amitié de commerce et de navigation conclu le 24 septembre, 1844, entre la France et la Chine both edited in China Imperial Maritime Customs, III Miscellaneous Series: n. 30, Treaties Conventions, etc., China and Foreign States, vol. 1 (Shanghai: Statistical Department of the Inspectorate of Customs, 1908), respectively, pp. 76–83, 49–58.

[7] Anatol M. Kotenev, Shanghai: Its Mixed Court and Council (North China: Daily-News & Herald, 1925). The French concession was established on April 6, 1849; see Wanshu Cong and Frédéric Mégret, "International Shanghai (1863-1931): Imperialism and Private Authority in the Global City," Leiden Journal of International Law, 34 (2021): pp. 915–933.

[8] Agreement between Great Britain and China for the Settlement of the Yunnan Case, Official Intercourse, and Trade between the two Countries. Signed at Chefoo, 13 September, 1876, section III, edited by Hertslet, n. 5, pp. 77-78.

possibility of renting land and buildings to be used for homes, hospitals, churches, or commercial activities, and that the Beijing Convention included also Tianjin among the treaty ports, France and Great Britain obtained a concession for the areas they had already occupied militarily and claimed them in perpetuity.

In the volume of the Treaties series dedicated to the treaties concluded between Great Britain and China, the agreement relating to Tianjin is officially stipulated on September 3, 1861, and it is the latest in a series of leases that allowed the European power to have its own concessions in Zhenjiang (February 23, 1861), Hankou (March 21, 1861), and Jujiang (March 25, 1861) and to expand the existing one in Guangzhou. However, in the English archives there is no trace of the agreement.[9] All that remains in the Foreign Office papers is, in fact, only the request presented by James Bruce, VIII Earl of Elgin, to Prince Gong for the perpetual lease of an area south of Tianjin, a memorandum indicating the boundaries of the future grant, and a receipt issued in 1865 by the Chinese district officer to the English consul Mongan for the annual payment of the land lease.[10]

The lack of a lease also characterizes the French concession, the legal basis of which must be sought in the official proclamation of the superintendent of the three northern ports, Chonghou, in an administrative regulation affirming the perpetuity of the territories included in the space ceded to France and especially in article 10 of the Franco-Chinese Treaty of Tianjin, to which both documents refer.[11]

Even more uncertain, then, were the origins of the American concession. Through the most-favored-nation clause, in fact, even the United States had obtained a perpetual concession of its tract of land along the Hai River, despite not taking part in the second opium war and remaining neutral even in the two years separating the Treaty of Tianjin from the Beijing Convention.[12] Even in this case, however, no official document emerged from the archival investigations relating to a possible territorial acquisition, nor was it possible to obtain any information about the methods by which the land plots were distributed among the American citizens residing there.[13]

When Germany and Japan also succeeded in imposing the opening of their own concession on China 34 years later, only the British were able to profit from the space obtained, subletting all the land of the settlement with a long-term lease lasting 99 years. The American concession, on the other hand, was in a state of

[9] Annex 7, Tien-Tsin, British Concession, in Lease Treaty Series, n. 34 (London: His Majesty"s Office London, 1925), p. 26.

[10] Luigi Nuzzo, "The Birth of an Imperial Location. Comparative Perspectives on Western Colonialism in China," Leiden Journal of International Law, 31(3) (2021): pp. 4–5.

[11] Nuzzo, n. 10, pp. 12–14.

[12] Nicolas Vaicbourdt, "De la "me too policy" aux ambitions contradictoires: la brève histoire de la concession américaine de Tianjin, 1860–1902," Outre-Mers. Revue d'histoire, 382/383 (2014): pp. 27–46.

[13] Nuzzo, n. 10, p. 21.

complete abandonment, while the French one, penalized by a less favorable geographical location requiring major urbanization interventions and by the concentration of ownership of almost all the land in the hands of Jesuits and Lazarists, had not yet aroused the interest of investors.[14]

At the end of the century, the fragile political balance in Tianjin was definitively compromised. Following the defeat of the Celestial Empire in the first Sino–Japanese war, the signing of five new lease agreements in 1898, and the establishment of German and Japanese concessions in Tianjin, the resentment and anger of the Chinese towards the Western invasive presence had greatly increased, and coalesced in the nationalistic Boxer movement.[15] On 20 June 1900, when the first contingents of the allied powers had already arrived in China, the killing of the German plenipotentiary minister von Ketteler became, in the representations of European international lawyers, the ultimate proof of China's inability to grasp the values and spirit of international law, and was used by jurists to justify the violence of the repression.[16] Tianjin was occupied, entrusted to a provisional government composed of representatives of the allied powers, and divided into four sectors, each controlled by a different power: France, Great Britain, the United States, and Japan.[17]

In early September 1901, before the Tianjin Provisional Government experience ended, the Chinese government was forced to sign the so-called Beijing Protocol, formally recognizing the winners the right to occupy "certain points" which they had already taken physical possession of during military operations, "in order to maintain free communications between the capital and the sea."[18] Russia, Austria, Italy, and Belgium thus managed to conquer their portion of China along the Hai River, while France, England, Germany, and Japan obtained an expansion of their concessions.[19]

Time was running out at Tianjin and there were not many available slots along the Hai River. This prompted, on 1 December 1900, the Italian minister plenipotentiary in China, Giuseppe Salvago Raggi, to inform the dean of the international diplomatic corps that he wished to reserve the right to establish an Italian consulate in Tianjin, announcing the submission of a formal request to the Chinese government to grant the necessary land for the establishment of a settlement. Three months later the minister of foreign affairs Giulio Prinetti received a letter

[14] Singaravélou, n. 4, pp. 261–281.

[15] Wen-Tsing Tao, Leased Territories in China (Masters dissertation: University of Illinois, 1915).

[16] Dominik Nowak, "Der Tod des deutschen Gesandten Clemens von Ketteler," in Kolonial Krieg in China. Die Niederschlagung der Boxerbewegung 1900–1901, hrsg. von Mechtild Leutner and Klaus Mühlhahn, Ch. Link (Berlin: Verlag, 2007), pp. 111–117.

[17] S. Procès Verbaux des Sciénces du Conseil du Government Provisoire du Tientsin (Tientsin: The China Times Ltd, 1911); Singaravélou, n. 4.

[18] Boxer Protocoll, Beijing, 7.9.1901, art. 9, Trattati e convenzioni fra il Regno d'Italia e altri Stati raccolti per cura del Ministero degli Affari Esteri (Roma: Ministero degli affari esteri, 1903), p. 266.

[19] Singaravélou, n. 4, pp. 270–276.

from Beijing announcing that the Italian army had peacefully occupied a small portion of China.[20]

Being the last to arrive, however, had consequences. Stretched along the left bank of the Hai River, between the Russian and Austrian concession and the railway line connecting Tianjin to Beijing, the "Italian concession" was nothing but five hundred thousand square meters of "swampy land and with almost perennial ponds," including an old cemetery, salt deposits, and "a filthy Chinese village" with about 17,000 inhabitants.[21]

A month later, Valli, commander of the Italian military force, published in the *Tien-Tsin Express* a notice in Italian and English detailing the boundaries of the Italian concession and inviting Italian or foreign subjects with property rights to land or buildings within those boundaries to present their titles to the Beijing Legation or the military command at Tianjin.[22]

Italy had finally secured its portion of China, but the problems facing Salvago Raggi were not trivial. First, he needed to give legal form to the occupation by entering into a contract with the Chinese government, similar to those already signed by the other powers, and then proceed with expropriations and reclamation work. By the end of 1901, this process appeared far from being concluded. Despite the Peace Protocol, signed on 7 September 1901 between China and the Allied Powers, stating the possibility of new or further occupations in Tianjin, Italy—due to a lack of preparedness, weak diplomatic influence, hostility from powers already in the territory, resistance from the Provisional Government, and a series of unfortunate coincidences—had not yet been able to obtain China's verbal commitment. It was only some months later, on June 7, 1902, that the Italian plenipotentiary minister Gallina and the director of maritime customs Tang Shaoyi signed the agreement that finally recognized the Italian concession of Tianjin. The contract, prepared by *chargé d'affaires* in Beijing Romano Avezzana and drafted on the model of the lease agreements signed by the other occupying powers, provided for the cession, "in perpetuity, as a concession" (art. 1) and against the payment of an annual fee, of the territory materially occupied by the Italian troops.[23]

According to article 3, Italy would become the owner of all land within the concession without any payment. However, formally, Italy would not have acquired new territory but just leased land that it had already occupied. Italy committed

[20] The request of occupation had been sent by Giuseppe Salvago Raggi to Emilio Visconti Venosta on January 19, 1901 in a telegram, followed two days later by the authorization: see Ministero degli affari esteri, ed., I Documenti diplomatici italiani, Terza serie, 1896-1907, vol. IV (Roma: Istituto poligrafico dello Stato e della Zecca di Stato, 1972), pp. 431, 438. Giuseppe Salvago Raggi to Giulio Prinetti, Pechino, 11.03.1901, ivi.

[21] S. the report of Salvatore Denti Amari di Pirayno, "Breve studio sulla Concessione Italiana di Tientsin," in ASMAE, Affari Politici, 1891–1916, Serie P., b. 426.

[22] The advice was published by Mario Valli on 1.4.1901, ASMAE, Affari Politici, 1891–1916, Serie P., b. 426.

[23] ASMAE, Affari Politici, 1891–1916, Serie P., b. 426.

to paying the Chinese government an annual fee of "one tiao of sapeche to be delivered for each mu of land in the area of the present concession" (art. 12).[24] The lack of a formal acquisition, along with the payment of an annual fee, indicated that China retained sovereignty over the territory within the concession, making unnecessary a legislative ratification and excluding any claim that it could be classified as a colony.[25]

Nevertheless, Italy, like the other powers, was granted full jurisdiction and a perpetual possession right of the territory. Perpetuity, in particular, was a key aspect of the arrangement, eroding China's formal sovereignty. This, departing from the typical temporary nature of the lease agreement, complicated the categorization of Western concessions in China. At the same time, Italy's full jurisdiction over the concession tied the retention of Chinese properties within the concession to Italy's superior interests. While acknowledging that the Chinese had "the possession of their properties" and their free management, if evidenced by valid titles, the Italian government secured the right of expropriation if there were requirements of public utility or hygiene, or if the "turnout of Italian merchants and the development of the concession" necessitated it.[26] This was a clarification that showed the Italian commercial aspirations and shaped the legal discourse according to the needs of entrepreneurs willing to face the unknowns of the Chinese market.

To exclusively reserve the Italian space for national entrepreneurial activities and prevent speculation by stronger foreign investors and companies, the Italian government implemented a system requiring "prior permission of the Italian municipality" for any sale, lease, or mortgage involving foreign citizens (art. 5). However, still in 1902, Gallina did not know whether foreigners owned parts of the Italian concession lands. He recognized that if their ownership pre-dated the Italian occupation, their titles had to be acknowledged. Most importantly, he excluded the possibility that the rules established for the expropriation of Chinese owners could be applied to them, even if they had acquired land after Valli's proclamation had been sent to the consuls in Tianjin (art. 6).[27] The doubts regarding the legal validity of the proclamation, which had been unprecedented in the history of the Tianjin settlements, pushed the Italian embassy to consider that foreign owners, particularly Chinese, could have had valid titles but failed to present

[24] The tael was equivalent at the time of the convention to 3.75 liras, and the mu (or mow) was a measurement fee equivalent "more or less" to 0.06 hectares: v. Coco, n. 3., p. 201-206.

[25] Enrico Catellani, La penetrazione straniera in Estremo Oriente. Sue forme giuridiche ed economiche (Firenze: Barbera, 1912), with reference to the Italian concession, pp. 218–238.

[26] About the price for expropriation, art. 8 stated: "Il prezzo dei terreni e delle case dovrà essere uguale al prezzo corrisposto nella concessione giapponese, meno il dieci per cento, secondo la classificazione che sarà fatta dalla municipalità del *settlement*."

[27] Giovanni Gallina to Giulio Prinetti, Pechino, 8.6.1902, in ASMAE, Affari Politici, 1891–1916, Serie P, b. 426.

their requests by the deadline, increasing to as much as 12 months the period after which confiscation could take place if no well-founded claim was made.[28]

However, the management of the populous Chinese village was not the only problem that the administrators and consuls had to face. They also had to deal with the difficulties posed by the marshy nature of the terrain, the presence of a large cemetery, and salt deposits along the banks of the Hai River, owned by the Chinese Salt Merchants Company. The Italian area, although crossed by two important communication routes, the river and the railway, was therefore in a situation that was anything but favorable, since it would have required long and costly land reclamation as well as leveling works, the expropriation of the village, the removal of the cemetery, and finally the purchase of the salt docks, for it to be transformed into a buildable and commercial area.[29]

For the Italian government, this was an excessive commitment that it could not take on, and that prevented it, at least temporarily, from transforming it into an autonomous municipality, following the model of other European settlements.[30] Instead, the lack of residents and the disastrous conditions made it more convenient to entrust it to the administration of a company of Italian investors for it to take care of its valorization. In December 1901, in Shanghai, several Italian businessmen entered into a compromise for the establishment of a joint-stock company for the development of Tianjin, and in October of the following year, foreign minister Prinetti and the company's managing director, engineer Rizzardi, agreed on a contract outline that placed extremely onerous conditions on the company, the acceptance of which can only be explained by a limited knowledge of the real conditions of the concession and the actual possibilities of its exploitation.[31]

The hope of easy money seemed to animate the company's initiative. Gallina, however, was well aware of their insubstantiality. He drew the minister's attention with a detailed report in which he suggested to "take due account of the true state of affairs." Gallina was certain that the conditions of the Italian concession would discourage investors and exclude a great demand for land. Therefore, the company should not be forced to abide by the contractual stipulations, which imposed too tight a time frame for resolving the dispute with the salt merchants, moving the graves, and reclaiming the area; above all, the expropriation of the Chinese village should not be demanded immediately.

[28] In 1905 Consul Giuseppe Chiostri re-issued the advice, ASMAE, Affari Politici, 1891–1916, Serie P, b. 427.

[29] Ministero degli Affari Esteri. Direzione generale degli Affari Commerciali. Concessione italiana in Tien Tsin, "Promemoria," in ASMAE, Affari Politici, 1891–1916, Serie P, b. 429; S. De Angeli, n. 4, pp. 557–572.

[30] Denti Amari di Pirayno, n. 21.

[31] S. the "Compromesso per la costituzione di una società per la messa in valore della concessione italiana di Tientsin and the "Schema di convenzione" between the Italian government and the company, in ASMAE, Affari Politici, 1891–1916, Serie P, b. 426.

However, it was the underlying assumption of the entire convention that required further clarification. Italy, having received the land in perpetuity, was obligated under the convention to transfer it to the concessionaires likewise without any time limitation. While parliamentary authorization had not been necessary to conclude the agreement with China—since the payment of rent formally allowed for the exclusion of both a transfer of sovereignty and an expansion of national territory—what would happen once the government decided to sell the acquired "property"?

The question, echoing between Tianjin and Rome, illustrates the paradoxes inherent in legal discourse and the confusion wrought by a legal concept that blurred the boundary between public and private law—projecting the medieval categories of *dominium directum* and *dominium utile* on to the Far East. Indeed, the recognition of Chinese sovereignty and ownership of the leased territory were reduced to a mere name, undermined by the perpetual nature of the concession. This superimposed on the faculty of enjoyment implied in the lease a right whose *ius in rem* nature seemed rather reminiscent of that of a perpetual tenant or a leaseholder. The possibility that a private subject might take over ownership of the concession made the picture even more uncertain and prompted the government to ask the legal office of the Treasury Department (*Avvocatura erariale)* and the Council of State whether a special law authorizing the government to enter into the contract was needed.[32] By the end of May no decision had been taken, and an anxious Gallina wrote to the foreign minister, urging a prompt resolution. The company's members were considering withdrawing, the settlement was in a precarious state, and no other opportunities were on the horizon. In any case, however, regardless of the actions of the company led by the engineer Rizzardi, it seemed clear that a prior law would be crucial for the development of the concession, preventing even the interest of new investors from being hindered while awaiting subsequent parliamentary approval.[33] Finally, on January 30, 1903, the Council of State, tasked with dispelling doubts raised by the foreign ministry, ruled on the matter. While the government had the freedom to set the most suitable conditions, since it involved property belonging to the State's assets, the convention had to be submitted to the parliament for approval.[34]

The ruling is interesting and deserves our attention. The Council of State argued that the 1902 Italo-Chinese agreement did not require parliamentary approval since it did not produce an increase of national territory as Tianjin was considered

[32] ASMAE, Affari Politici, 1891–1916, Serie P, b. 426. The need to establish a special procedure or jurisdiction for the resolution of any disputes was also emphasized by the Council of State (28.11.1902).

[33] Rizzardi himself remembered, writing to minister Tittoni on July 14, 1903, ASMAE, Affari Politici, 1891–1916, Serie P, b. 426 that "all'ultimo momento si sollevò il dubbio da parte del Ministero che fosse necessaria una legge per autorizzare la stipulazione del contratto, e quindi la pratica rimase temporaneamente sospesa per dar tempo al Ministero di interpellare in proposito il Consiglio di Stato."

[34] "Quel che si fa con legge—the Consiglio di Stato stated in its opinion of 30.1.1903, ASMAE, ivi,—con legge soltanto si può mutare, modificare, emendare."

to be under Chinese sovereignty. At the same time, however, it recalled that the law on the administration of State property required an authorizing legislative measure on the assumption that the contract with the *Società per la messa in valore di Tient Tsin* would have produced a transfer of "acquired" territory.[35] The result was a legal discourse of increasing complexity, in which public and private dimensions overlapped and blurred, while the laws of the Kingdom extended their normalizing force as far as the Far East—on to a territory that, nonetheless, continued to be formally regarded as Chinese.

8.3 The Italian Legal Debate on the Nature of the Chinese Concession

While back in China Rizzardi and his partners were entrusting the last hopes of establishing their company to the promulgation of the law required by the Council of State, in Italy the opening of a concession in China had begun to attract the interest of Italian jurists.[36] Between 1902 and 1903 Enrico Catellani (1856–1945), professor of international law at the University of Padua, reconstructed in two volumes the political and diplomatic history of settlements and privileges enjoyed by Western citizens in the Far East.[37] Over the following years Catellani returned to the subject several times, reworking the previous writings and following the developments of the Italian concession in China.[38] Convinced that only the study of political, economic, and socio-historical elements allowed international law to adapt to the transformations of international society, he glossed over the issues related to the relationship between sovereignty and territory, preferring instead to dwell on the aspects more directly related to the old theme of extraterritoriality and consular jurisprudence. Catellani argued that Italy, like the other powers, had not acquired territorial sovereignty over the area that had been granted as concession, but only a "partial delegation of sovereignty," the ownership of land, and the jurisdiction over the indigenous population, which remained subjects of the Chinese empire.[39] The study of the legal nature of settlements and the recognition

[35] In fact, R.D. 17.2.1884, n. 2016, art. 13, which approved the Testo Unico sull'Amministrazione e Contabilità generale dello Stato, stated "le alienazioni dei beni immobili dello Stato devono essere autorizzate per legge speciale."

[36] Ibid.

[37] Enrico Catellani, I "settlement" europei e i privilegi degli stranieri nell'Estremo Oriente, voll. 2 (Venezia: Ferrari 1902). In 1902 he published in the *Rivista italiana di sociologia* an article on the "Formazione di gruppi municipali nell'Estremo Oriente contemporaneo" (Roma: Tipografia degli Olmi, 1902: pp. 1–38.

[38] Enrico Catellani, "Organizzazione e funzionamento del settlement italiano in Tientsin," in Secondo congresso degli italiani all"estero (Roma: Tipografice nazionale, 1911): pp. 1–19; Enrico Catellani, "I privilegi degli stranieri in Oriente e nell'Estremo Oriente: condizione attuale e tentativi di riforma," Rivista di diritto internazionale, 9 (1915): pp. 3–22.

[39] Catellani, n. 25, p. 456. On this point the doctrine was almost unanimous. Santi Romano in his *Corso* ruled out that such concessions could qualify as "larval alienations of territory" because of the

of the relevance of the concept of autonomy in international law made inevitable the comparison with the category of *fragments of State* put forward by the Austrian jurist Georg Jellinek (1851–1911).

Sovereignty, territory, and subjects, Jellinek had written a few years earlier, were still necessary elements of statehood, but the absence of one of them—even the most important, sovereignty—did not necessarily condemn the political formation which was missing it within the administrative bodies. This meant that sovereignty was not an essential category of the State, but just a historical category useful to understand the process of formation of the Western State.[40] Outside the realm of Western States, sovereignty could lose exclusivity and indivisibility, coexisting with the recognition of broad spheres of autonomy. For the Austrian lawyer, therefore, only an approach free from "doctrinal preconceptions" could recognize the existence of ambiguous political subjects. Provided with territory, population, and varying decrees of legislative, administrative, and jurisdictional autonomy, they could be defined as *fragments of State*, "Staatsfragmente." It was an extremely flexible category able to include the Danuban principalities or other territories of the Ottoman Empire, explaining the particular legal nature of Finland, or being applied to foreign concessions in China as well as to the German colonial possessions in Africa.[41]

Building on Jellinek's analysis, Catellani argued that settlements could also be considered "fragments of the State" and placed in an intermediate position between the State and administrative bodies. This would make the Italian concession in China fall, according to the classification envisioned by the famous Austrian jurist, within the subcategory of "organized territories entitled, within certain limits, to some autonomous competence in regard to changes in their own order."[42]

At the beginning of the 20th century it was not easy to free oneself from Jellinek's overwhelming presence, not only because his theory made it possible to give institutional existence to political subjectivities that, although lacking sovereign powers, insofar as they were subject to a higher power, could not be reduced to mere administrative entities, but because he had consciously addressed the problem of the limits of the concept of sovereignty and the concept State and had been the first public law scholar to study with great attention the legal nature of the lease by which China ceded Jiaozhou Bay to Germany.[43]

temporary nature of the concession, the permanence of sovereignty in favor of the lessor State, and the absence, on the other hand, for the lessee State of a *ius in rem* right over the territory. Cfr. Santi Romano, Corso di diritto internazionale (Padova: Cedam, 1926), pp. 175 ff. See also Cajo Enrico Balossini, Concessioni in Cina (Firenze: Sansoni, 1934), pp. 74–76.

[40] Georg Jellinek, Ueber Staatsfragmente (Heidelberg: Koester 1896), p. 11; Georg Jellinek, Die Lehre von der Staatenverbindungen (Wien: Hölder 1882), pp. 63–68. The *Staatsfragmente* became part of the main work of Jellinek, the "Allgemeine Staatslehre," 3rd ed (Aleen: Scientia, 1966), pp. 647–660.

[41] Nuzzo, n. 10.

[42] Catellani, n. 25, p. 415.

[43] Nuzzo, n. 10.

Also, one of Catellani's students, Arrigo Cavaglieri (1880–1935) who was engaged in a research project on fundamental State rights, could not avoid using the Chinese perspective to observe the relationship between State and territory, and to confront, between 1903 and 1906, both the Austrian jurist's interpretation of the German occupation in Shandong and the different readings on the nature of that relationship advanced in Germany by Fricker, Jellinek, and Listz and in Italy by Romano and Forti.[44]

Cavaglieri recognized the merits of Santi Romano (1875–1947) in freeing public law reflection from any analogy with private law, claiming the personal nature of the State–territory relationship and, consequently, qualifying State law as a manifestation of its personality.[45] However, Cavaglieri complained that international lawyers were still unable to overcome the organicist metaphors that had been used to define State subjectivity and to critically rethink the consequences that followed from that identification. They continued, therefore, to confuse, unlike the scholars of public law, property and sovereignty, and to use the abused category of *iura in rem*. At the same time, delays in adopting a positivist approach led those same jurists to overlap political evaluation and legal reflections, failing to understand not only that the observation of political and social reality had to be a continuous stimulus to think up new legal categories when those in use no longer seemed to correspond to it, but also that politics and law always remained on completely different planes and that therefore the formal solutions imagined by legal scholars could conceal a different political situation.[46]

International servitudes, concessions in administration, or lease agreements were good examples. What had happened in China between 1898 and 1901 and even earlier in Bosnia and Cyprus clearly demonstrated that there was no need for private law and its categories. In fact, the 1878 Treaty of Berlin with which the Russian–Ottoman war had ended, had offered, according to Cavaglieri, new opportunities to reflect on the limits of the concept of sovereignty in reading the relationship between State and territory.[47] As is well known, in Berlin, Bulgaria had become an autonomous and tributary principality subject to the suzerainty of the Porte, while Bosnia and Herzegovina had been ceded *in administration* to the Austro-Hungarian Empire.[48] In the same years of the Berlin Conference,

[44] Arrigo Cavaglieri, "Il diritto internazionale e alcune recenti concessioni di territori" (Verona: Manunzio), 1903; Arrigo Cavaglieri, "Il diritto internazionale e il rapporto tra Stato e territorio," Archivio giuridico Filippo Serafini, 73 (1904): pp. 77–127; Arrigo Cavaglieri, "Contributo alla definizione di alcune figure del diritto pubblico contemporaneo" (Roma: Tipografia dell'unione cooperativa editrice 1906), pp. 1–34; s. Luigi Nuzzo, "Pluralismo giuridico e ordine coloniale in Santi Romano," Quaderni Fiorentini, 50 (2021): pp. 207–249

[45] Cavaglieri, n. 44 ("Il diritto internazionale e il rapporto tra Stato e territorio"), p. 94.

[46] Cavaglieri, n. 44 ("Il diritto internazionale e alcune recenti concessioni di territori"), p. 29; ("Contributo"), pp. 1–5.

[47] Cavaglieri, n. 44 ("Contributo"), pp. 20–25.

[48] Traité de Berlin, 13.07.1878, art. 25, edited by Benoit Brunswik, "Le Traité de Berlin annoté et commenté" (Paris: Plon, 1878), p. 101. The Convention of 21.4.1879—"Nouveau Recueil général de Traités," edited by Georg Friederich von Martens, Charles Samwer, Jules Hopf, deuxième série, t. 4

the Ottoman sultan had allowed Britain to "occupy and administer" the island of Cyprus until Russia returned Batoum, Ardhan, and Kars to him.[49]

In both cases, from the legal point of view there was no real annexation but a provisional transfer, due to the existence of certain conditions or political necessities, of the mere exercise of the Ottoman sovereignty, which formally remained the legitimate holder.[50] In the presence of an absolute cession of that exercise and without any temporal limit, however, Turkish sovereignty over Cyprus, Bosnia and Herzegovina became a blurred memory, revealing a now unbridgeable gap between the world of facts and the world of law and leaving jurists with the task of rethinking the old categories of international law and reinterpreting, in new forms, the relationship between space and law.

Even in China, in Jiaozhou and Tianjin, according to Cavaglieri, there had not been a limitation of the proprietary sphere, but a clear compression of the Celestial Empire's sovereign power over its territory. Through an international convention, legal form had been given to an entirely new situation in which one State delegated to another the exercise of its sovereignty, without ever, however, going so far as to completely relinquish it. At least formally, in fact, tracing the rights of the occupiers back to the willingness of self-obligation manifested by China in the various treaties left a glimmer of Chinese sovereignty in view.

The long duration of the leases (or their perpetuity in Tianjin), coupled with the forced expropriation of Chinese property, the expulsion of the natives, and the recognition of the full jurisdiction of the consular judiciary, appeared to sever definitively the relationship between State and territory, completing the cession and establishing *iura in rem* in favor of the occupying powers. Yet, the defining element remained the provisional nature or revocability of the concessions.[51]

The problem posed by these strange concessions of territories, then, was a different one and forced jurists, as Georg Jellinek had seen at the end of the 19th century, to a reflection on the concept of sovereignty and statehood that had to be free of dogma and pre-conditioning. Squeezed between the improper use of the categories of private law and the simplistic responses of politics and diplomacy considering the permanence of Chinese sovereignty as a legal fiction, jurists had to chase social reality in its transformations and give it legal form, "modifying legal

(Gottingue: Dieterich, 1879), p. 422—specified that the occupation would not affect the Sultan's right to sovereignty. V. Lothar Classen, "Der völkerrechtliche Status von Bosnien-Herzegovina dem Berliner Vertrag vom 13.7.1878" (Frankfurt am Main: Peter Lang, 2004), p. 64 ff.

[49] "Convention d'alliance défensive entre la Grande-Bretagne et la Turquie, Constantinople, 4,6.1878," art. 1, Archives Diplomatiques, Recueil international de diplomatie et de histoire, deuxième series, 23, VI (1882–1883), p. 315. Cfr. Brunswik, n. 48, pp. 122–124.

[50] Jellinek, n. 40 ("Die Lehre"), pp. 115–119. In this sense also Cavaglieri, n. 44 ("Il diritto internazionale e alcune recenti concessioni di territori"), pp. 16–22.

[51] Cavaglieri, n. 44 ("Il diritto internazionale e alcune recenti concessioni di territori"), p. 29; Cavaglieri, n. 44 ("Contributo"), p. 11.

concepts and types when they no longer correspond to the new constructions of politics." The jurist, Cavaglieri continued, always following Jellinek's teaching, "would make a grave mistake if he were content to note the strange and irregular character of those forms and phenomena, denying them legal value because they are incompatible with current concepts of public law or have nothing in common with established political figures."[52]

Cavaglieri, however, did not go so far as to share the conclusions reached by Jellinek. He ruled out, in fact, that the 1898 *Pachtvertrag* between Germany and China could be brought under the category of lease, or that international servitudes could be configured as constituting a *ius in rem* in favor of one State over a portion of the territory of another, or even that Bosnia-Herzegovina, Cyprus, and Jiaozhou were "fragments of State."[53] Even if there was no shortage of similarities and points of contact, concessions in administration and lease agreements presupposed international relationships that had their source in an international treaty. In the above cases, the final transfer of sovereignty to Austria-Hungary, Great Britain, and Germany would have been possible only, then, through a new international convention in which the Ottoman Empire and China would have had to participate respectively. According to Cavaglieri, therefore, the correct approach was to bring together all the territories "where a State, reserving to itself the bare right of sovereignty, cedes to other States the effective exercise of it" within the category of the internationalized territories. "Like condominium, so too do international territories represent a generally transient political form, which may last even a long period of years, but to which political events sooner or later necessarily mark an end, reuniting in one way or another sovereignty with its actual exercise."[54]

Santi Romano, arguably the most relevant Italian public lawyer of the 20th century, also dealt, albeit briefly, with the issue of concessions in his *Course on Colonial Law* (1918) and *Course on International Law* (1926). Following Cavaglieri, for Romano too, politics and law offered two different representations: in the first case, the Western and Japanese settlements in China appeared as larval colonies in which the sovereign power of the Celestial Empire was now emptied of all content; in the second, they were instead territorial spaces over which the lessors only temporarily enjoyed a territorial right; not a *ius in rem* though *propter territorium*, but a personal one that could invest, depending on the interpretation, the entire governmental power or its exercise alone. The territory, therefore, continued to be Chinese and Chinese remained the people living within the concessions

52 Cavaglieri, n. 44 ("Contributo"), p. 4.

53 Cavaglieri, n. 44 ("Il diritto internazionale e il rapporto tra Stato e territorio"), p. 120, 109.

54 Cavaglieri, n. 44 ("Contributo"), pp. 33–34. Later also Arrigo Cavaglieri, "Corso di diritto internazionale," 3rd ed. (Napoli: Rondinelli, 1934) qualified the right of the State on its territory as a *ius in rem*, "un vero potere di natura reale, sia nello stretto significato di *jus in re*, sia in quello più assoluto di un diritto esclusivo di attività statuale esercitato *erga omnes*" (p. 259), thinking that the *concessioni in affitto* allowed to transfer public *iura in re aliena* through "la scissione della sovranità come diritto astratto, *nudum ius*, dal suo materiale ed effettivo esercizio" (p. 368).

themselves. This seemed confirmed, for Romano, precisely by the legal analysis of the Italian settlement in Tianjin. With the Italo–Chinese agreement of 1902, as we have seen, an attempt had been made to give legal form to the occupation, proceeding to the identification of the territory as Italian, outwardly, through the indication of the boundary lines, and inwardly, recognizing full jurisdiction to the Italian government and introducing a series of limitations on the maintenance of Chinese or foreign property. The legal figure resorted to, a concession free from any temporal expiration and economic burden except the payment of an annual rent, should not have resulted, even in the absence of a temporal expiration, in the transfer of the original Chinese territorial power, but only in its temporary delegation. There had been, therefore, no increase in the national territory, nor had any additional financial burden on the State resulted from the agreement, and for this reason the government had not asked the parliament for its approval.[55]

However, the personal character that marked the rights transferred from China to the concessionary States did not exclude the possibility, according to Romano, that a State could grant *iura in rem* over a part of it. If, in fact, in the case where the territory was considered as a whole, it was not possible to recognize any *iura in rem* in favor of the lessee, Romano admitted the possibility of configuring whole (dominion and condominium) or partial (eminent domain, servitudes, and a right of lien) *iura in rem* over parts "distinct and isolated from the rest."[56] Romano reiterated that the old categories of *domium utile* and *dominium directum* could not apply to Chinese concessions because each concessionary State exercised an own power not supported by a *ius in rem*, but he was forced to admit that they were in "a state of transition" toward the establishment of full colonial dominion and with it, therefore, it became possible to recognize a *ius in rem* nature to the right exercised over the territory.[57]

8.4 Toward Fascism: The Legal Evolution of the Italian Concession

Earlier, we left Rizzardi and his partners waiting for the Italian Parliament, in compliance with the opinion of the Council of State, to authorize the government to divest the lands of the concession. Rekindled by foreign minister Tittoni's drafting of an authorizing bill, their last hopes were, however, dashed by the Council of Ministers' decision to suspend its publication process, forcing Rizzardi to dissolve the Company.[58]

[55] Nuzzo, n. 4, p. 274 ss.
[56] Romano, n. 39, p. 160.
[57] Santi Romano, "Corso di diritto coloniale" (Roma: Athenaeum 1918), p. 99.
[58] The text of the bill is in ASMAE Affari Politici, 1891–1916, Serie P, b. 426. On 9.9.1903 the Italian consul in Shanghai Nerazzini informed Minister Tittoni (ASMAE, Affari Politici, 1891–1916,

Two years later, after other initiatives—including the application of the *Associazione nazionale per il soccorso dei missionari* and that of a group of businesspeople headed by Count Pallavicino—failed to obtain the administration of the settlement, Guido Fusinato (1860–1914), a leading Italian international lawyer and at that time undersecretary of State, was called upon, at the request of the consul in Tianjin, to express an opinion on the need for legislative authorization.[59]

In fact, by 1905 the picture had changed. Indeed, the Italian government had decided to administer the settlement directly and to alienate to private parties only individual separate tracts of land. With, therefore, the hypothesis of a complete transfer of ownership having disappeared and the transfer of the entire administrative management to a company of investors having been discarded, the issue for Fusinato had lost its relevance.

The undersecretary's opinion, however, is particularly interesting because it attributes the government's withdrawal of the bill to "reasons of political expediency." This is an ambiguous formula, behind which we can discern not only the new course of Giolitti's foreign policy, aimed at a gradual strengthening of the State's presence in the conduct of political and economic activities, but also the lively protests and uproar aroused in parliament and public opinion by journalistic inquiries such as those carried out by *Il Sole* or *Il Secolo* on the failed experience of the trading companies in Benadir, which had led in 1905 to the termination of the agreement between the government and the Benadir Company and the State's assumption of direct administration of the concession.[60]

Fusinato, however, not only returned to the decision of the Council of State, highlighting its limits, but also noted the novelty introduced by the Italo-Chinese agreement in the definition of relations between parliament and government. On the one hand, in fact, it was evident that the formal provision for the payment of an annual rent, however much it might be considered a "diplomatic combination expedient," prevented the recognition of Italian ownership over the concession lands and their qualification as patrimonial property. Appropriately, therefore, Italian diplomacy in China, in the wake of the practice followed by the other powers in Tianjin, no longer suggested ceding those lands in absolute ownership to a concessionaire, but more simply resorting to a contract of emphyteusis for 99 years. No prior or subsequent parliamentary intervention would then have been necessary, but only a simple ministerial authorization. The Italo-Chinese agreement was the

Serie P, b. 426) of the dissolution of Rizzardi's Company and suggested continuing the search for a concessionaire.

[59] Guido Fusinato, "Osservazioni sul quesito posto dal R. Console in Tientsin nel suo rapporto del 20.11.1904, sulla necessità o meno, di una legge speciale per dar facoltà al Governo di alienare tratti di terreno nel 'settlement' italiano di Tientsin," Roma, 18.1.1905, in ASMAE Serie P, b. 428.

[60] Ibid.

product of a new and changing world that required the identification of equally new legal forms and categories. "It is a matter, Fusinato continued, of a new law being constituted, and of new relations with an ill-defined and variable nature, for which fluency and speed of action must be left to the government. More than by the domestic laws of individual States, this matter is regulated by international law in that form which it is taking under the pressure of legal political necessity and convenience."[61]

In Tianjin, too, by late 1903 and early 1904 the picture was changing. The "fever of building speculation" had risen and the hopes, this time governmental, of making quick, easy profits were accompanied by the knowledge that with the taxes paid by the Chinese not only was the settlement surviving, despite the total absence of government aid, but it had also managed to expropriate "a good half of the land and to carry out most of the work to make it buildable."[62] Under the impetus of the favorable economic situation, the government was not content simply to raise the asking price for the settlement, but opted for its direct administration, entrusting a royal administrator with the management and development of the settlement and reiterating the need for direct intervention in the construction and recognition of an Italian space.[63] The Chinese village and its 17,000 inhabitants, however, were still there. They were an inexhaustible source of cheap labor and the main financial resource of the royal administration, but at the same time a real and symbolic obstacle to the definition of the *italianness* of the territory and to the landing of the Italian capitalism that had been regularly announced, but had never really happened.

A few years later the housing bubble burst and a serious economic crisis hit Tianjin between 1907 and 1908. The excessive prices that were not proportionate to the real conditions of the concession; the delays in the reclamation operations, which were moreover paralyzed by the scarcity of funds; and the continuing uncertainty about the necessity of a parliamentary law authorizing the government to alienate even individual lots soon led the government's illusions to fade and once again forced the postponement of the expropriation of the village.[64] Still in 1910 the Italian concession was experiencing difficult times. In that year, Consul Da Vella asked the foreign minister, after several auctions had been unsuccessful, to benevolently accept the applications of the first Italian investors, despite the fact that the offers were lower than the conditions initially set by the royal administration.[65]

[61] Fusinato, n. 59.

[62] Vincenzo Fileti, "Direttiva generale per la sistemazione definitiva del Settlement," ASMAE, Affari Politici, 1891–1916, Serie P, b. 429.

[63] Vincenzo Fileti, "Proposte che riterrei opportuno fare," ivi; Ministero degli Affari Esteri. Direzione generale degli Affari Commerciali. Concessione italiana in Tien Tsin, "Promemoria," ASMAE, Affari Politici, 1891–1916, Serie P, b. 429.

[64] Fileti, n. 63.

[65] See il Regolamento d'asta written by Da Vella nel 1907, in ASMAE, Affari Politici, 1891–1916, Serie P, b. 427.

Consideration had to be given not only to the "present and truly unbeautiful conditions" but also to the fact "that so far no offers either from foreigners or from countrymen have ever been made for our lands; that the said royal subjects are the first to invest, and at truly unpropitious times, in our settlement; that they in such investment rely, with patriotic élan, entirely on the unknowns of the future."[66]

It was not until 1912, however, that the "sum of some importance" so long awaited by the Italian administrators was finally allocated, and now made the survival of the village superfluous.[67] Indeed, the four hundred thousand liras disbursed by the *Cassa Depositi e Prestiti* made the taxes paid by the Chinese, and with them the Chinese themselves and their village, no longer necessary.[68] The demands of new buyers who "no longer made a question of price" led to demolition of the "Chinese hovels."[69] By a significant coincidence, then, the enactment of the first and unique legislative text that finally recognized the Italian presence in China was followed by the destruction of the village, gutted by the new arteries and concealed by the elegant European cottages and the cheap but "decent" semi-foreign style buildings designed for wealthy Chinese ready to be Westernized.[70]

Architecture and urban planning put a new and stronger State power into circulation and served as a backdrop for the representation of a renewed image of government and its sovereignty. A single disciplining logic ran through and led urban planning interventions in the city, now equipped at last with electric lighting and a tramway connection, to interact with the debate over the nature of the concession and the existence of Italian sovereignty, preparing for the implementation of those long vague institutional and regulatory projects that found fulfillment only with the advent of the fascist regime.

In fact, in September 1922 the concession became an autonomous Italian municipality whose life was governed by a statute and an implementing regulation, by which the concession was entrusted to a municipal administration, chaired by the consul, composed of an elective council of five members—one of whom was not an Italian citizen—and flanked by a Chinese advisory committee of three members, elected by the Chinese owners and residents of the concession.[71] This

[66] Da Vella, Rapporto n. 31/8 M al Ministro degli Affari Esteri, Tientsin 21.2.1910, ASMAE, Affari Politici, 1891–1916, Serie P, b. 428.

[67] Ministero Affari Esteri, n. 63; see also the report of Carlo Sforza, Italian plenipotentiary minister in Beijing 11.5.1912, ivi, Rapporto 382/91, "Concessione di Tientsin."

[68] L. 30.6.1912 n. 707 authorized the allocation of *lire* 400,000 in advance from the Cassa Depositi e Prestiti.

[69] The two statements are both from Fileti. The first is taken from "Direttiva," n. 62; the second is from "La concessione italiana" (Genova: Barabino e Graeve, 1921), p. 31.

[70] On the urban transformation s. Sforza, ASMAE, Affari Politici, 1891–1916, Serie P, b. 429 and the report of Fileti, n. 69; Id., n. 62.

[71] Lo Statuto municipale e il Regolamento d'attuazione were approved by a dispatch from the Ministry of Foreign Affairs, directed to the Italian embassy in Bejing on January 31, 1923, No. 200345/1. They are published in Municipio della Concessione italiana, Tientsin. Regolamenti. Regulations (Tientsin: 1924). The following year the municipal council was abolished and the administration of the concession entrusted to a *podestà*.

committee exhausted the problem of Chinese representation in the administrative management of the settlement, although it performed only advisory functions and had limited competence to preventive control over the taxes and expenses of the concession.[72] The municipal council, on the other hand, composed of councilors elected for a two-year term by the resident Italians and foreigners who had been owners and residents for at least one year had much broader powers.[73] All matters of a fiscal nature, those of a patrimonial nature, the approval and execution of public projects and works, expropriations for public utility, the drafting of the cadaster and road plan, and the promulgation of hygiene, building, and police regulations were within its mandate.[74]

Within China, whose sovereignty over Tianjin was never formally denied, an Italian space was being constructed. It pretended to be a modern and metropolitan space, subordinated to the authoritarian and centralizing vocation of the State and inspired by its rationalizing and centripetal will that, through careful building regulation, set its coordinates and through pervasive police regulation projected its disciplining force on the subjects who lived and worked within the concession.

The 1924 building regulation took up the discourse introduced by the 1902 lease agreement, which subjected all acts of sale, lease, and mortgage to the prior consent of the municipality. Considering the major land reclamation works, the creation of a road network, and the gutting of the indigenous village that had begun in 1912, the same regulation entrusted planners "qualified under Italian law" or in possession of a special permit issued by the municipality[75] with the task of rethinking according to the canons of *italianness*, and in such a meticulous manner as to fix even the number of toilets required for each apartment, the geographic and urbanistic space of Tianjin[76]—a spatial representation that could no longer be denied or violated by the construction of Chinese and semi-foreign houses, allowed only in the industrial part of the concession and for those who worked there (Reg. ed., art. 13). The laws of the kingdom and the jurisprudence of the Consular Court were then entrusted with the task of settling disputes arising between owners, of whatever nationality, concerning the properties in the concession (Reg. ed., art. 57).

This new spatiality enclosed and denied Chinese diversity within the disciplinary plots of hygiene and police regulations and in the prohibitions that Western progress and modernity imposed. Thus, in 1924 the municipal legislature subjected all Chinese personnel working within the municipality to a medical examination to ascertain their physical fitness,[77] allowed the deceased to be "kept in the

[72] "Statuto municipale," art. 25.
[73] "Statuto municipale," art. 10.
[74] "Regolamento per l'applicazione dello Statuto municipale," art. 1.
[75] "Regolamento edilizio," 23-25.7.1904, art. 26.
[76] Ivi, art. 48: "ogni casa deve avere almeno un cesso per appartamento o per serie di tre camere affittate separatamente."
[77] "Regolamento sanitario," 25.7.1924, art. 4.

dwellings" for no more than two days (Reg. san., art. 7), and stated that the houses must be a "healthy and hygienic shelter" by prohibiting "crowding" (Reg. san., art. 16, c. 12). In the same year, the police regulation imposed prior authorization for religious and funeral processions, for the celebration, even in private homes, of ritual ceremonies accompanied by musical events (art. 6) and for the explosion of firecrackers and fireworks (art. 7), and went so far as to deny the innocent flight of kites by peremptorily establishing a ban on "throwing flying kites in public streets" (art. 10).

In the mid-1930s, while in Tianjin Fascism was imparting a more authoritarian bent to the strategies of governance of the concession with the implementation of minor measures of local scope and with modest conceptual adjustments, and was jointly initiating a program of profound transformation of the urban district layout culminating in the rationalism of the *Casa degli Italiani* and *Il Forum*, in Italy a young administrative lawyer, Enrico Balossini, devoted a small volume to the problem of the Chinese concessions.[78] It is a text of considerable usefulness for jurists and historians, not only because of Balossini's comparatist sensibility and his attempt to study the case through the application of the general figure of administrative concession but also because, written in 1934, it presents a synthesis of the legal debate of the preceding 30 years and sets out to recompose, through a careful dogmatic-legal analysis, the implied diversities and inevitable antinomies present in the political language of international treaties. Law and its rhetoric and its sociolinguistic system of justification of existing reality was entrusted with the task of reconstructing events, establishing the boundaries within which to carry out its textual practices, and fixing, even in the indeterminacy of the political moment, the lines of development of concessions. However, the construction of a "legal field" presupposed the solution of a semantic problem. Indeed, in order to answer the basic question about the nature of the cession, jurists had to reconstruct the meanings of concession and settlement, and before that to identify the distinctive features distinguishing the term concession and the English term settlement. In the few pages devoted to the legal nature of the Italian presence in China, Santi Romano had not detected a rift between concession and settlement, identifying the origin and nature of these institutions "in the unique position in which foreigners found themselves in China: on the one hand, they were subject to an extensive set of limitations, on the other hand, they enjoyed a variety of privileges and immunities."[79] Balossini on the contrary, lamenting the terminological confusion that reigned in the doctrine, recalled that the concession involved a transfer of land rights between two public law entities, the Chinese government and the

[78] Balossini, n. 39.

[79] Romano, n. 57, pp. 94–95; in this sense also Umberto Borsi, "Principii di diritto coloniale" (Padova: Cedam, 1938), p. 221; Fileti, n. 69, pp. 10–11; and Arnaldo Chicchiti, "Se la concessione italiana di Tien Tsin sia un possedimemento coloniale," Rivista di diritto pubblico e della pubblica amministrazione in Italia, 1(1) (1929): pp. 141–157.

concessionary State, which in turn could transfer them to private entities. The settlement indicated, rather, only an establishment of foreign citizens on Chinese soil, that is, in an enclosed territorial space, separate from the rest of the local population and subject to the legislative, executive, and jurisdictional control of the consul. It was therefore a *de facto* entity, endowed with legal personality, in which members of Western communities could acquire directly from Chinese authorities and private individuals, without the mediation of a public subject, land and real estate within its borders.[80]

Despite the differences identified on the theoretical level by Balossini between the concession and settlement, we can sense in the doctrine, in the official acts, in the confidential reports, and even in the bill for the financing of the concession a widespread vagueness, a continuous overlapping of signifiers that highlights the influence exerted by the English private and economistic model in the construction of a colonial space in China that would guarantee residents the free exercise of commercial activities under the protection of the laws of their own nationality.[81] There is, in other words, a semantic insecurity that translated, at least in the initial phase of the Italian occupation, also a difficulty and profound indecision in choosing between two different discursive strategies for the control: a French one dominated in the construction of the relations between politics, law, and economics by the idea of State preeminence; and a more flexible one, structured on the Anglo-Saxon model, open to private individuals and their interests and tending to separate control of the territory and management of productive activities.

The Tianjin concession was imagined as a mere tool to foster the development of Italian commercial activities in northern China. Legally, its act of birth was a lease agreement that did not require legislative ratification and by which no new territories were acquired. The Italian government simply leased land that was already materially occupied. Thus, there was no increase in national territory, nor any additional financial burden on the State. The absence of approval by the parliament and the payment of an annual fee thus led the doctrine, almost unanimously, to recognize the permanence of Chinese sovereignty over the concession and to exclude any qualification as a colony.[82]

On the contrary, jurisprudence, perhaps incorporating the fascist government's interest in a strengthening of the Italian position in the Far East and in the ultimate transformation of the concession into a full-fledged colonial possession, began to legally substantiate Italian sovereignty. In 1923, the Tianjin Consular Court, called

[80] Ivi, p. 21; Alessandro Ausiello, "La 'concessione italiana' in Cina," Rivista giuridica del medio e estremo oriente e giustizia coloniale, 2 (1938), pp. 61–72.

[81] The title of the 1902 agreement reads "Accordo con la Cina per il settlement di Tien Tsin," while the word concession is used in the articles of the text. See the Tittoni"s bill (1903), ASMAE, Affari Politici, 1891–1916, Serie P, b. 426.

[82] Romano, n. 58, pp. 40–41. See A. Cavaglieri's note to the sentence of the Italian Consular Court at Tien Tsin (23.4.1923), Foro italiano, 1924, I, col. 434–36.

to rule on a violation of the concession's building regulation regarding compliance with distances between buildings, ruled out the plea of lack of jurisdiction raised by the Chinese defendant. In fact, it denied the application of the procedural principle *actor sequitur forum rei*, also transposed by the Italian–Chinese Treaty of 1866, on the assumption of the full jurisdiction granted to Italy by virtue of the 1902 agreement, confirmed with the 1913 building regulation, and the obligation of Chinese subjects to comply with regulations that would be issued in the future, contained in the same agreement and then specified in the *Regolamento Fondamentale* issued also in 1913.[83]

The final confirmation of Italian jurisdiction and a strong signal for a reconsideration of the nature of the concession itself came, however, from the reference to procedural law. In fact, the Consular Court, bringing the public law dimension back to procedural law and private law, affirmed its jurisdiction over citizens of different nationalities on the basis of the rules governing "actions on immovable property existing in the Kingdom": "Actions, that is, of a patrimonial nature which by their nature have a closer relationship with public order than matters of a personal nature and for which it is necessary that respect for the law has to be ensured by its application by national Courts."[84]

The application of procedural law norms to the present case transcended the narrow legal boundaries of the trial and expressed a new discursive strategy aimed at bringing the concession back within an Italian spatial dimension: the trial concerned real estate existing in the kingdom, which could not escape Italian law for those same reasons that prevented a foreign citizen, owner of real estate, and defendant before an Italian court from resorting to his own court. The Code of Civil Procedure thus projected the categories and principles of Italian legal culture onto distant Tianjin buildings as well and openly revealed ambiguities, contradictions and limits of the public law discourse contained in the 1902 agreement and confirmed by majority doctrine. The already "abstract" sovereignty of the Chinese State, further "attenuated and suspended by the personal and local privileges" enjoyed by foreigners, had become intangible, denied by an article of the Code of Civil Procedure.[85]

This continuous erosion of Chinese sovereignty from within found confirmation in the decision of the Ancona Court of Appeal, which had jurisdiction on cases decided by the Tianjin Consular Court. As a matter of fact, the Court confirmed the sentence issued by the Italian consul at Tianjin proclaiming the

83 On 4.7.1913, based on the regulations issued in 1907 by consul Da Vella, plenipotentiary minister Sforza, promulgated a Fundamental Regulation, a Police Regulation and a Building Regulation. These regulations were later replaced by the Final Regulations in 1924; see ASMAE, Affari Politici, 1891–1916, Serie P, b. 427.

84 Trib. Cons. It. Tien Tsin, Foro italiano, 1924, I., col. 439.

85 The words quoted are from Cavaglieri, n. 82, who, while agreeing with the decision (23.4.1923) strongly criticized the sentence's reference to art. 105 c.p.c.

universal character of Italian law and the impossibility for the State to "abdicate the jurisdictional function with respect to things, acts and persons, whether citizens or foreigners, as long as they live in the territory itself."[86]

Once again it reiterated the special nature of the settlement, "a public law entity living in a foreign territory, that neither has nor can therefore have all the attributes of sovereignty." At the same time, however, it thwarted the limitation by recalling full jurisdiction over all residents without regard to their nationalities, and above all, it rhetorically introduced the doubt that the recognition of the exercise of the jurisdictional function, contained in the first article of the agreement and specified by all the regulations that governed the life of Tianjin from 1907 to 1924, could express, "if not a transmission of territorial sovereignty, its tacit delegation." It was a rhetorical doubt, precisely, that vanished in the face of the recognition of the concession as a municipal body, endowed with its own charter, exercising a true sovereign power and unequivocally manifesting "the obvious tendency toward the transformation [of the concession] into a definitive colonial possession."[87]

The construction of the legal and political discourse of Italian sovereignty and the inevitable transformation of the nature of the concession could not yet get rid of private law argumentations. They concealed the exceptional nature of the institution and allowed the inevitable uncertainties of regulations and statutes, albeit fundamental ones, which were too conditioned by the mutability of the political datum. They thus brought the Italian concession at Tianjin back within traditional textual categories, within the fabric of a known and legitimized language.

In upholding the appealed judgment, the Ancona Court not only applied the 1902 convention and the 1913 building regulation, but reinforced the Consular Court's reasoning by recalling Article 7 of the preliminary provisions of the Civil Code, according to which "the law governing iura in rem for immovable property is the lex rei sitae." It was a principle arising from the intimate connection of the regime of real estate with "the general interest of the State, which, consequently, since it cannot confer enjoyment of rights without assuming the corresponding jurisdictional protection, is more than authorized, compelled to exercise it even in comparison with the foreigner, to whom it attributes the quality of private subject under the same conditions recognized to the citizen."[88]

The public dimension dissolved itself into private law, but this in turn transcended its boundaries and colored itself with publicist hues, allowing the jurists to overcome the last doubts preventing them from considering the "all special institution" of the concession as the territory of the Italian kingdom. Jurisprudence thus participated, with the definition of a renewed image of Italian sovereignty and its projection onto Chinese space and bodies, in the refinement of the normative and

[86] See artt. 105 and 139 Consular Law 28.1.1866, n. 2804 (modified by L. 14.5.1894).
[87] Corte di Appello di Ancona, 1.7.1925, Foro italiano, 1926, I, col. 195.
[88] Ivi, col. 196.

regulatory system and in the rethinking of the strategies of governance, giving legal form to the Italian aspirations for a colonial possession also in the Far East.

8.5 Conclusion

The story of the Italian concession in China ended a few years later in the same way it had begun. Occupied by Japanese troops after September 8, 1943, the concession and its memories were returned to their rightful owners by the 1947 Treaty of Paris, which sanctioned the cancellation of the lease agreement, resorting in this way to a current remedy provided by civil law in cases of invalidity of contracts.[89] This is not only, however, an Italian story. On the contrary, it goes beyond the simple national dimension by becoming a tool for understanding the legal debate on the exceptionalism of non-Western spaces.

Taking as an object of study the strange lease that enabled the foundation of the Italian settlement in China has allowed us, first of all, to return to the categories of private law and to verify how they were used to transform a "piece" of the Chinese empire into a new social space, breaking the relationship between governmental power, territory, and subjects and making possible a profound transformation of the concept of sovereignty. The perpetual lease by which Italy gave legal form to its occupation, in fact, raises questions about the limits of the concept of sovereignty outside the West.

At the same time, the appropriative acts that are the premise of the contract signed by Italy, as well as by all the other foreign powers involved in the scramble for Tianjin, make it possible to look more consciously at the history of international law and the relationship between law and violence, identifying occupation as the founding act of a new legal order. In China, too, it all begins with the seizure of large tracts of land along the Hai River. Its measurement, its division, and finally its economic exploitation constitute the stages of constitutional process that can redefine the relationship between space and law, make visible a new political and social order, and guarantee to each occupier an original title that could be validly opposed to all those who should claim the same tract of land.

[89] Art. 15 d.lgs. C.P.S. 28.11.1947, n. 1430, "Esecuzione del trattato di pace fra Italia e le Potenze Alleate e Associate" (Parigi, 10.2.1947).

9

China, the Western Standard of Civilization, and The Hague Peace Conferences of 1899 and 1907

Mingqian Li

9.1 Introduction

The Hague Peace Conferences, held in 1899 and 1907, were significant in the development of international law and the regulation of warfare.[1] The legacy and heritage of the Hague Conferences has been well recorded and received wide attention in contemporary political and academic discussions.[2] William Isaac Hull (1908) explored the significant role of the two Hague Peace Conferences in shaping the modern framework of international law.[3] W. F. Dodd (1908) explored the achievements of the Hague Peace Conferences, especially the specific content of the thirteen conventions reached at the second conference.[4] In 1912, the journal of Andrew White, the head of American delegation to the First Hague Peace Conference, was reprinted as *The First Hague Peace Conference*. The journal offered valuable 'inside views' on the conference from its convening to its closing, and offered it high praise.[5] James Brown Scott's *The Proceedings of the Hague Peace Conferences* serves as a foundational source, carefully documenting the chronological developments, legal debates, and institutional outcomes of the Hague Peace Conferences.[6] Calvin DeArmond Davis (1964, 1986) explored US involvement in the two Hague Peace Conferences. The two books focused largely on the United

[1] Arthur Eyffinger, 'A Highly Critical Moment: Role and Record of the 1907 Hague Peace Conference' (2007), 14 Netherlands International Law Review 197–228.

[2] William Isaac Hull, *The Two Hague Conferences and Their Contributions to International Law* (Boston: Grinn 1908); Calvin DeArmond Davis, *The United States and the First Hague Peace Conference* (Ithaca, NY: Cornell University Press 1962); Calvin DeArmond Davis, *The United States and the Second Hague Peace Conference* (Durham, NC: Duke University Press 1975); Arthur Eyffinger, *The 1907 Hague Peace Conference* (The Hague: JudiCap, 2007).

[3] Hull (n 2).

[4] W. F. Dodd, 'The Work of the Second Hague Conferences' (1908), 6(4) Michigan Law Review 294–303.

[5] Andrew. D. White, *The First Hague Peace Conference* (Boston: World Peace Foundation, 1912).

[6] James Brown Scott ed., *The Proceedings of the Hague Peace Conferences: Translation of the Original Texts* (New York: Oxford University Press, 1920, 1921).

Mingqian Li, *China, the Western Standard of Civilization, and The Hague Peace Conferences of 1899 and 1907*
In: *Histories of International Law in China*. Edited by: Ignacio de la Rasilla, Jiangyu Wang, and Congyan Cai,
Oxford University Press. © Mingqian Li 2026. DOI: 10.1093/oso/9780198888345.003.0009

States' strong advocacy for international arbitration as a means for peaceful resolution of international disputers.[7]

Recent literature, such as the writing of Geoffrey Best (1999), has reflected on the legacy of the 1899 Hague Conference in shaping modern approaches to war and peace. He argued that while it did not prevent future hostilities, it did initiate important dialogues about international cooperation and legal norms that would influence subsequent generations.[8] Arthur Eyffinger (1999) explored how the first Hague Peace Conference became a precursor to later institutions such as the League of Nations and the United Nations. He has also considered the differing motivations and perspectives of major powers, including Germany, Russia, and Great Britain, showcasing why certain treaties and agreements were or weren't reached.[9] Maartje Abbenhuis (2019) offered a fresh perspective on the Hague Peace Conferences by examining the international media frenzy surrounding them.[10]

The above literature has provided a thorough explanation of the backgrounds and historical details of the two Hague Peace Conferences. Beyond that, scholarly attention has been increasingly paid to the relationships between the Hague Peace Conferences and the participants. Michael Jonas (2021) studied the perspectives and actions of Hjalmar Hammarskjöld (1862–1953), a particularly vocal and influential delegate, using his role as a lens through which to view international legal diplomacy and the unique contributions of northern neutral countries.[11] The 'small states', and especially the periphery states, at the Hague Peace Conferences shared this effort to address an imbalance in the historical focus on major powers.

While the two Hague conferences were convened to promote peaceful settlement of conflicts and establish legal frameworks for regulating warfare among the civilized family of nations, they were also platforms for the non-major powers to pursue their respective agendas. Thus, increasing research has been on the relationship between the standard of civilization and participants at the Hague. For example, Carsten-Andreas Schulz (2017) explained Latin American representatives' diplomatic posturing at the 1907 Hague Conference, arguing that it was due to Latin American foreign policy elites' ambitions to elevate their national stature.[12] Japan's role at the Hague Conferences has also been examined as a case

[7] Davis (n 2).

[8] Geoffrey Best, 'Peace Conferences and the Century of Total War: The 1899 Hague Conference and What Came After' (1999), 75 International Affairs 619–634.

[9] Arthur Eyffinger, *The 1899 Hague Peace Conference: 'The Parliament of Man, the Federation of the World'* (Hague: Kluwer Law International, 1999).

[10] Maartje Abbenhuis, *The Hague Conferences and International Politics, 1898-1915* (London: Bloomsbury, 2019).

[11] Michael Jonas, 'Hammarskjöld at The Hague: Sweden and the Peace Conference of 1907', in Marcus M. Payk and Kim Christian Priemel eds, *Crafting the International Order: Practitioners and Practices of International Law since c.1800* (Oxford: Oxford University Press 2021).

[12] Carsten-Andreas Schulz, 'Accidental Activists: Latin American Status-Seeking at The Hague' (2017), 61(3) International Studies Quarterly 612–622.

study of a non-Western nation successfully navigating the 'standard of civilization'. Klaus Schlichtmann (2003) delved into the historical context and significance of the Hague Peace Conferences, particularly focusing on the parts played by Japan and Germany in shaping international relations during a transformative period, highlighting Japan's contribution to international arbitration.[13] Arnulf Becker Lorca (2015) explored how non-European states like Japan and Latin American countries actively engaged with and modified the standard of civilization rather than passively accepting it, as well as analysed the agency of non-European states in transforming international law.[14]

China, of the twenty-six participants at the first Hague Peace conference, was also highly sensitive with respect to the doctrine of the standard of civilization that was emerging as a criterion used by Western nations to evaluate the legitimacy and modernity of non-Western states. Clémence Lizé (2020) reflected upon China's involvement in the 1907 Hague Peace Conference, considering it as the country's volition to interact with a non-Chinese universal system, as opposed to their more passive participation at the 1899 Hague Conference.[15] Ryan Mitchell (2021) argued that Qing diplomats for the first time, played a role in multilateral negotiations at the 1907 Hague Conference. There, they discovered a budding solidarity with other 'weak' states, particularly from Latin America and Asia. This joint resistance against great power initiatives fostered discussions on state equality.[16]

Within Chinese-speaking academia, China's participation in the Hague Peace Conferences of 1899 and 1907 represents important steps toward interacting with the Western-dominated international legal order. Discussions on the Hague Peace Conferences are mostly found in treatises on diplomatic history and the history of international relations, among other fields.[17] Li Shunmin (1995) systematically discussed the Qing government's participation in the two Hague Peace Conferences using firsthand historical materials such as the *Diplomatic Archives* and *Historical*

[13] Klaus Schlichtmann, 'Japan, Germany and the Idea of the Hague Peace Conferences' (2003), 40(4) Journal of Peace Research 377–394.

[14] Arnulf Becker Lorca, *Mestizo International Law: A Global Intellectual History 1842–1933* (Cambridge, Cambridge University Press, 2015).

[15] Clémence Lizé, 'The 1907 Hague Peace Conference: Understanding China's Initial Steps towards the "International Society"' (2020), 1 China and World Review 147–166.

[16] Ryan Mitchell, 'China's Participation in the Second Hague Conference and the Concept of Equal Sovereignty in International Law' (2021), 11(2) Asian Journal of International Law 351–371; Also see Ryan Mitchell, 'Towards an "Asian Faction" in International Law? On Third Worldism and Contingent Eurocentrism Since the Second Hague Conference of 1907,' https://journals.law.harvard.edu/ilj/2021/12/towards-an-asian-faction-in-international-law-on-third-worldism-and-contingent-eurocentrism-since-the-second-hague-conference-of-1907, 2021, accessed 7 September 2024.

[17] For example, Wang Shengzu ed., *History of International Relations (国际关系史) (Volume 3, 1871–1918)* (Beijing: World Knowledge Press, 1995); Fang Lianqing, *History of International Relations in Modern Times* (国际关系史-近代卷) *(Volume 1 and 2)* (Beijing: Peking University Press, 2006).

Materials on Qing Dynasty Diplomacy preserved in Taipei. He argued that the selection of diplomatic professionals and active involvement in international affairs were key aspects of the Qing government's efforts to modernize its diplomacy.[18] Tang Chi-Hua (2005) interpreted the Qing government's participation in international organizations as a strategic move to gain recognition as a civilized nation, thereby facilitating its integration into the international legal and political order.[19] In his comprehensive investigation into the late Qing's interaction with international law, Lin Xuezhong (2009) observed that the efforts made during the two Hague Conferences were Qing's commitment to internationalization.[20] These analyses reveal that the focus of Qing's participation in the Hague Conferences was on China's pursuit of modernization and civilization.[21] Through the lens of civilization, scholars describe how a non-Western country could be accepted as a 'civilized' nation and gain entry into European international society. Nevertheless, the 'standard of civilization' is not fixed nor closed, but a fluid and changing discourse, subject to the dominant powers' priorities and necessities. There is so far sparse analysis of how Chinese intellectuals and officials interpreted, internalized, and responded to the 'changing' standard of civilization during the two Hague Peace Conferences. Furthermore, China's contributions to international law during these engagements were undervalued.

This chapter is composed of five parts, including an introduction and conclusion. After providing a literature review and setting the stage for the research topic in the Introduction, Section 2 examines how the concept of the 'standard of civilization' is reflected in the Hague Peace Conferences. Sections 3 and 4 explore how China engaged with the Hague Peace Conferences and the standard of civilization during the two conferences. It is proposed that the standard of civilization served both as an obstacle and a pathway for China's integration into the 'family of nations'. The Conclusion presents a pessimistic view, suggesting that despite Qing China's contributions to international law, the standard of 'being civilized' is one that can never truly be met—much like the man in Franz Kafka's parable who can never succeed in passing through the 'gate' of the law.

[18] Li Shunmin, 'The Efforts in Modernizing Late Qing Diplomacy through Participation in the Hague Conferences' (从保和会的参与看清末外交现代化的努力) (1995), 1 Shiyun 141–162.

[19] Tang Chi-Hua, 'A Study on China's Participation of the Hague Peace Conferences, 1899–1917' (清末民初中国对海牙保和会之参与) (2005), 23 Journal of History, National Chengchi University 45–90.

[20] Lin Xuezhong, *From International Law to Public Law Diplomacy: The Introduction, Interpretation, and Application of International Law in Late Qing* (从万国公法到公法外交：晚清国际法的传入、诠释与应用) (Shanghai: Shanghai Ancient Books Publishing House, 2009).

[21] Zhang Yongjin, *China in the International System 1918–1920* (New York: St. Martin's Press, 1991) 15.

9.2 Hague: Under the Banner of Civilization

The term 'civilization' held profound significance in the international society of the late 19th century, functioning as both a rhetorical tool and a normative framework to structure international relations.[22] In this section I will delve into how the standard of civilization is reflected in the Hague Conferences, after examining its implication.

Initially introduced during the era of the Holy Alliance, the concept of 'Civilized Nations' gradually attained an unquestionable, self-evident status, supplanting prior references to the Christian Commonwealth.[23] According to Gerrit W. Gong, 'civilized nations' were those who are capable of protecting the lives, rights, and property of foreigners; possessing 'a bureaucratic system that enables effective national administration and the ability to defend themselves; adhering to international law and providing avenues for democracy; and following the civilized norms of international society, acting in a civilized manner'.[24] From this definition, we can see three features of standard of civilization in the nineteenth century.

First of all, a progressive hierarchical system that privileged European states while marginalizing others was established. The progress and prosperity brought about by the European Industrial Revolution reinforced the European nations' belief that the white race was leading humanity's progress, while other places were imagined as 'naive children, incapable of achieving growth on their own'.[25] European states cast themselves as agents of progress and modernity, while depicting non-Western societies as inherently backward. This worldview rested on the belief that 'the more we progress, the more civilized we become individually and collectively; the more civilized we become, the further we are removed from the vestiges of savagery and barbarism'.[26] Not appealing to war was considered as civilizational 'progress'. The Alabama case of 1872 was thought of highly for its success in peaceful settlement of interstate disputes.[27]

Second, the concept of civilization became a central factor in establishing a sense of European superiority over other communities—in particular, legally. A collection of legal norms and customs, shaped within the cultural and religious framework of European traditions, gradually evolved into legal 'standard(s)'. With the support of many international lawyers at that time, the differentiation of states

[22] Prasenjit Duara, 'The Discourse of Civilization and Pan-Asianism' (Spring 2001) 12(1) Journal of World History 99–130; Gerritt W. Gong, *The Standard of 'Civilization' in International Society* (Oxford: Clarendon Press, 1984).

[23] Eyffinger (n 2) 9.

[24] Gong (n 22) 14–15.

[25] John M. Hobson, *The Eastern Origins of Western Civilization* (Cambridge: Cambridge University Press, 2009) 228.

[26] Brett Bowden, 'Civilization and Its Consequences', in Oxford Handbooks Editorial Board ed., *Oxford Handbook Topics in Politics* (Oxford: Oxford University Press, 2015).

[27] William W. Park, 'Swords into Plowshares: A Pilgrimage for the CSS Alabama' (2021), 37 Arbitration International 515–532.

according to the standard of civilization became indeed far more than a descriptive exercise. By determining which states could be recognized as civilized, this standard has become a legal criterion that directly determines a nation's entry into the international community as a subject of international law. Nations that adhered to these standards were regarded as 'civilized', while those that did not were often labelled as 'barbaric' or 'uncivilized'.[28] For example, James Lorimer categorized the world into three groups: *humanité civilisée* (civilized humanity); *humanité à demi barbare* (semi-barbaric humanity); and *humanité sauvage* (savage humanity).[29] Only the civilized can participate as full members of the international community and enjoy legal personality. William E. Hall also stated that nations outside European civilization must undergo reforms to align with European ideals, and act with the implicit consent of all or part of these European states.[30] The standard of civilization, in this sense, 'provided a theoretical basis in international law for limiting the eligibility of some states for recognition'.[31]

Furthermore, at that time, prominent in the discourse of civilization were the significant roles played by pacifists and peace advocates,[32] who contributed to the discourse around what it meant to be a 'civilized nation' through the lens of international cooperation, diplomacy, and peaceful conflict resolution. The emergence of peace societies and organizations, particularly in Europe and the United States, played an important role in influencing the international climate towards resolving conflicts peacefully.[33] A series of international peace conferences and activities were organized to advocate for the peaceful settlement of interstate disputes through arbitration and renouncing wars.[34] The word 'pacifism' closely connected with the civilized world where peace groups actively championed ideals such as disarmament and arbitration.[35] The efforts of peace activists significantly contributed to fostering a culture that prioritized dialogue over warfare, making diplomatic conferences on peace not only possible but increasingly desirable. International law and arbitration thus became essential components of the

[28] Liliana Obregón, 'The Civilized and the Uncivilized', in Bardo Fassbender and Anne Peters eds, *The Oxford Handbook of the History of International Law* (Oxford: Oxford University Press, 2012) 929–931.

[29] Eyffinger (n 2) 10.

[30] W. E. Hall, *A Treatise on International Law* (Clarendon Press, 2nd edn, 1884) 51–52.

[31] Gong (n 22) 24.

[32] James D. Fry, 'The Role of Peace Movements in the 1899 Creation of the Permanent Court of Arbitration', Swiss National Science Foundation Workshop 'New Directions in the Theory & History of International Law', Graduate Institute of International and Development Studies, Geneva, Switzerland, https://hub.hku.hk/handle/10722/323024, accessed 7 June 2024.

[33] Cecilie Reid, 'Peace and Law—Peace Activism and International Arbitration, 1895–1907' (2004), 29(3–4) Peace & Change 527–548.

[34] Stephen C. Neff, 'The Hague Peace Conferences and a Century of Further Struggles,' in Thomas Giegerich and Ursula E. Heinz eds, *A Wiser Century? Judicial Dispute Settlement, Disarmament and the Laws of War 100 Years after the Second Hague Peace Conference* (Berlin: Duncker & Humblot GmbH, 2009) 59–88.

[35] Eyffinger (n 9) 53.

'standard of civilization', which pacifists framed as part of the moral and legal progress of humanity.

The pursuit of peace and humanity, and the efforts towards regulating warfare, peaked with the 1899 and 1907 Hague Peace Conferences. In fact, civilized nations and civilization are repeatedly referred to throughout and even before the Hague Peace Conference.

As the arms race in Europe reached an unprecedented level of intensity, comments calling for peace appeared in journals and newspapers corresponding with the 'innermost feelings of all nations and their dearest wishes'.[36] As mentioned above, at this time peace was seen as a hallmark of civilization, with the expectation that civilized nations would resolve disputes through diplomatic means rather than warfare. Under the prevailing sentiment, Tsar Nicholas II of Russia proposed to other countries on 24 August 1898, and again on 11 January of the following year, calling for the convening of a peace conference and the conclusion of a disarmament agreement.[37] In the proposal for the convocation of the conference the Tsar emphasized that 'in the course of the last twenty years, the longings for a general appeasement have become especially pronounced in the consciences of civilized nations'.[38] This moral appeal to the collective conscience of 'civilized nations' laid the ideological groundwork for the conference, and reinforced the idea that civilized nations had a moral duty to uphold higher standards of conduct in their international relations.[39] Being 'civilized' in this context was intrinsically tied to adherence to a discourse of peace and moral progress, embedding humanitarian sentiment into international law. It is reflected throughout both Hague Peace Conferences.

This idea is especially revealing in American politicians' words and actions towards the second Hague Peace Conference. After the first Hague Peace Conference, advocates in the United States had been promoting arbitration as a civilized enterprise. In a letter from Andrew D. White to Oscar S. Straus, White called to 'create a public opinion throughout the world which will make the great mass of mankind in every civilized country a unit in favor of demanding from their respective governments arbitration rather than war'.[40] He strongly advocated preventing nations

[36] Frederick W. Holls, *The Peace Conference at The Hague and Its Bearings on International Law and Policy* (New York: The Macmillan Company, 1900) 13.

[37] Eyffinger (n 9) 15–22.

[38] On 24 August 1898, Count Mouravieff, then Russian Foreign Minister, presented a formal note to the diplomatic corps at a weekly reception in the St Petersburg Foreign Office. In this communiqué-now known as the Mouravieff Circular-Russia proposed convening an international conference to address the dangers of unchecked armaments and to promote lasting peace among nations. See Yale Law School Lillian Goldman Law Library, 'Peace Conference at the Hague 1899: Rescript of the Russian Emperor(1) August 24 (12, Old Style), 1898', http://avalon.law.yale.edu/19th_century/hag99-01.asp, accessed 7 September 2024.

[39] Andrew Linklater, 'The Classical European "Standard of Civilization"', in *The Idea of Civilization and the Making of the Global Order* (Bristol: Bristol University Press, 2020) 125–250.

[40] Andrew D. White, 'Compulsory Arbitration and the Hague Court' (December 1904), 66(12) The Advocate of Peace 233–234.

from resorting to war before fully exploring arbitration and diplomacy embodied the humanitarian ideals championed by the Hague Conferences.[41] Unlike the first Hague Peace Conference, which was held under Russian invitation, the second Hague Peace Conference was marked by prominent American influence where the US played a crucial role in the organization and proceedings of the conference. The discourse of civilization dominates the language of the politicians and scholars at that time. In 1907, former Secretary of State Richard Olney, speaking at the annual meeting of the American Society of International Law, emphasized the critical role of arbitration as the main means for resolving international disputes at the annual meeting of the American Society of International Law.[42] He argued that the 'interests of civilization' brought civilized nations closer together and made it more necessary to reach agreements, through which 'war, universally recognized as the greatest violation of common sense and morality, would be deemed a crime under international law, and organized civilization would employ all its power to prevent and punish it'.[43] The world which Richard Olney envisioned, where organized civilization would replace war, reflects a recurring theme in early twentieth-century international law—the belief that 'civilized' nations had a duty to exemplify peaceful conduct.

Immersing itself in the rhetoric of civilization, Qing China was preparing to be part of the civilized family of nations through following the 'standard of civilization' at Hague Peace Conferences. The following sections of this chapter will examine Qing China's participation in the 1899 and 1907 Conferences, arguing that its experience reveals how international law in this period functioned as an instrument of imperial hierarchy. Through this lens, China's attempts to gain recognition demonstrate how the civilization discourse legitimized structural inequalities in what was then the international order.

9.3 China's Participation in the First Hague Peace Conference

Its invitation to the peace conference of great powers was of great significance to the then Qing China, although the 1899 Hague Peace Conference was essentially an old-world conference, with most of the participants being European states, and primarily reflected the power dynamics and geopolitical interests of European states.[44]

Peace movements, initially prominent in Europe and America, eventually influenced intellectual discourse in China, particularly through the work of

[41] ibid.

[42] Richard Olney, 'Address of Hon. Richard Olney, of Boston, Mass.' (1907), 1 (19 and 20 April) Proceedings of the American Society of International Law at Its Annual Meeting 221–231.

[43] ibid.

[44] Eyffinger (n 2) 2–4.

missionaries. Missionaries such as Timothy Richard and Young John Allen played an important role in introducing the then prevailing peace movements to China. Through their writings in *The Globe Magazine* (万国公报), they translated the idea of convening a peace conference for a Chinese audience, framing it as 'The MibingHui' (Disarmament Conferences, 弭兵会), one of the earliest recorded attempts in Chinese history to resolve conflicts through multilateral diplomacy rather than military force during China's Spring and Autumn Period (770–476 BCE).[45] For Chinese reformers and intellectuals, who were exposed to the idea of peacefully solving international conflicts, accepting the invitation to the Hague Peace Conference meant aligning with the great powers in the emerging trends of diplomacy and international law while having traditional resources as intellectual support.[46] More importantly, the Qing court hoped to be recognized as civilized through participation in the Hague Conferences to prevent further imperialist encroachment.[47]

The rhetoric of civilization central to the 1899 Hague Peace Conference positioned the event as a gathering of civilized nations. Beyond codifying norms of state conduct, the conference also functioned as a gatekeeper of international legitimacy, defining both the standards of civilized behaviour and the criteria for membership within this privileged group. As Joseph Choate remarked, any country participating in the Hague conference had 'been recognized as an equal power vested with complete and perfect nationality and equal sovereignty, and entitled to be treated as a civilized nation, and not to be classed with African aborigines as a fair prey for the spoiler'.[48] Choate's remarks foreshadowed China's fraught relationship with Western-dominated international law, but there were not a lot of options left for China.

The Qing court sent a delegation represented by Yang Ru (杨儒), the Envoy to Russia, He Yansheng (何彦升), the Second-Class Counselor to Russia, Hu Weide (胡惟德), the Third-Class Counselor to Russia to attend the conference and Lu Zhengxiang (陆征祥) was appointed as the Second-Class Translator.[49] The Qing court issued a decree to Yang Ru, the head of delegation, to investigate whether

[45] The Globe Magazine (万国公报), as a key medium for introducing Western political, social, and scientific ideas to China, played a pivotal role in informing the Chinese intellectual elite about: global peace movements; the idea of war prevention as an organized, moral and political objective; broader international trends, such as the rise of arbitration and diplomacy as alternatives to military confrontation. Tian Tao, 'The Influences of the Hague Conferences in China' (海牙和会在中国的反响) (2015), 3 Journal of Tianjin Normal University 11.

[46] Li (n 18) 145.

[47] Tian (n 45).

[48] Joseph H. Choate, The Two Hague Conferences (Princeton, NJ: Princeton University Press, 1913) 26.

[49] 'Memorial from Envoy Yang Ru to Russia on Attending the Hague Peace Conference and Returning to Russia' (使俄杨儒奏遵赴和都保和公会蒇事返俄情形折), in Wang Yanwei and Wang Liang eds, *Documents on Qing Dynasty Diplomacy* (清季外交史料), Book 6, Vol 140 (Changsha: Hunan Normal University Press, 2015) 2709.

there would be any obstacles or impediments before making a decision on whether to access the Conventions.[50]

At the end of the first Hague Peace Conference, three Conventions, namely the Convention for the Pacific Settlement of International Disputes, Convention with respect to the Laws and Customs of War on Land, Convention for the Adaptation to Maritime Warfare of the Principles of the Geneva Convention of 22 August 1864, and a series of declarations on the Prohibition of the Use of Forceful Arms were concluded. Representatives from Germany, Austria-Hungary, Britain, Japan, Switzerland, Serbia, and Luxembourg expressed their intention to postpone signing the convention. Seeing this, the Chinese delegation also stated that it would need to obtain instructions from the home country before signing any documents. After returning to Russia, Yang Ru submitted a memorial to the Qing court, stating the purpose and general situation of the first Hague Peace Conference, explaining the main achievement of the Conference and offering his suggestions whether to sign the Conventions adopted in the Conference.[51] From his memorials, we can see Qing elites' interpretation of 'standard of civilization'.

In the memorial, Yang Ru reported that the Convention for the Pacific Settlement of International Disputes created a permanent body to mediate disputes among States. All disputes among States could be referred to it, but it was still up to each State to decide whether or not to accept its mediation. The Declarations on the Prohibition of the Use of Forceful Arms provided that no projectiles or explosives would be launched from balloons, and no deleterious gases and dum-dums would be used in any war. Given that these weapons were not yet produced in China, Yang Ru believed that these declarations would not be detrimental to China and could be signed on to. According to Yang Ru, the Convention on the Laws and Customs of War on Land would not have a significant impact on Western countries. In contrast, although the Chinese army had recently begun implementing Western-style training in a few regions, this programme was still in its early stages. 'There will be hurdles and obstacles on the battlefield if this Convention is ratified.'[52] Yang thus recommended that the Convention on the Laws and Customs of War on Land should not be signed.

Yang Ru focused especially on the relevance of China's accession to the Geneva Conventions. At the Hague Peace Conference, the phrase 'civilized nations' was repeatedly cited to legitimize constraints on warfare and to advocate for the pursuit of peace. As noted earlier, peace was portrayed as a defining trait of civilization, standing in stark opposition to the perceived 'barbarism' of unregulated conflict. Profoundly shaped by this perspective, the aspiration to gain recognition

[50] 'Telegram Instructing Yang Ru to Submit a Report on Reducing Troops for the Hague Peace Conference and to Attend the Conference at the Scheduled Time' (旨寄杨儒着奏减兵保和会并届时赴会电), in Wang (n 49) 2654.
[51] Wang (n 49) 2709.
[52] ibid.

as a 'civilized' and equal participant within the international community emerged as the dominant theme in correspondence between the delegation and the Qing court.

By framing the Red Cross as 'the most civilized act of benevolence', Yang highlighted how humanitarian concerns was of importance as a marker of civilization in the so-called family of nations. He noted that if the Convention for the Adaptation to Maritime Warfare of the Principles of the Geneva Convention of 22 August 1864 was ratified, 'in the event that China is one of belligerents, or a neutral state, China would be required to treat all wounded soldiers according to the standard specified in the Convention, which would seem to be unfavorable to China, because there are no government-run Western-style hospitals, physicians, or hospital ships in China's ports'.[53] However, he remarked that 'all countries already have Red Cross Societies, and this time it is merely an extension from land warfare to maritime warfare', thereby broadening the scope of the Geneva Conventions. Furthermore, Yang Ru reminded the Qing Court that since the Red Cross has been regarded by various countries as the most civilized act of benevolence, not signing the Convention would make foreign powers regard China as an uncivilized country.[54]

Yang Ru remarked that participation in the Hague Peace Conference held significant symbolic value for Qing China's international standing. Through attending the Conference and signing the agreements reached in the Hague, China could demonstrate its willingness to engage with the international community and thus assert its position as a legitimate and equal member.[55] Conversely, Yang Ru cautioned that abstaining from such multilateral forums risked perpetuating perceptions of China as isolationist, further marginalizing it within the prevailing world order. 'In the event that China declines to sign or ratify the convention, then foreign powers may conclude that China is intentionally isolating itself from other states and might be unwilling to engage with us in future pertinent international congresses.'[56] Thus, signing the Conventions was seen as the Qing government's effort to align itself with the western standards of civilization from the perspective of Qing China's politicians. It was part of an enterprise to maintain and improve China's international standing.

Yang's recommendation led the Zongli Yamen, the de facto minister of foreign affairs, to request on September 28 that 'all the treaties should be signed'. Reviewing the report of Zongli Yamen, the Grand Council[57] however, out of caution, replied,

[53] ibid.

[54] ibid.

[55] 'The Zongli Yamen Submits a Memorial in Accordance with the Deliberation on the Circumstances of Yang Ru's Participation in the Peace Conference for Consideration and Signing' (总署奏遵议杨儒赴保和会参酌情形以便画押折, in Wang (n 49) 2711.

[56] Wang (n 49) 2709.

[57] The Grand Council (军机处Jun Ji Chu) was a central institution in the Qing Dynasty, functioning as the emperor's top advisory body, especially prominent during the later period of the dynasty. See

'Zongli Yamen should review the documents in detail to see if there is any hindrance, and to find out what the Red Cross good will actually is'.[58]

In the corresponding memorial, the Zongli Yamen made a detailed analysis of the treaty drafts reached at the Conference. 'According to Yang Ru's statement, signing the *Convention for the Pacific Settlement of International Disputes* does not mean the arbitration is obligatory. Whether or not to submit the dispute to arbitration remains at one's own discretion, thus our country is not in the risk in this respect.'

Zongli Yamen also explained the origins and implications of the Red Cross in its memorial. It noted that the Red Cross referred by the Westerners was established in Geneva, the capital of Switzerland, originating in the third year of the Tongzhi era (circa 1864). At that time, ten articles were established by a general agreement among various nations, outlining the principle that in times of war, hospitals would be set up on the battlefield to treat wounded and sick soldiers. Both warring sides were to regard these personnel as neutral parties, providing them with mutual protection.[59]

Notably, in clarifying the nature of the Red Cross to the Grand Council, the Zongli Yamen invoked Mozi's philosophy of jian'ai (兼爱, 'universal love'), highlighting its emphasis on benevolence and altruism that transcend national boundaries.[60] By drawing parallels between Western political norms and Mohist principles, the Zongli Yamen asserted that 'Western customs closely align with Mozi's doctrine of universal love'.[61] This conceptual linkage positioned the Red Cross's humanitarian mission as a modern embodiment of jian'ai. Consequently, the Zongli Yamen concluded that China's accession to this particular Convention would affirm its moral commitment to global good, rather than pose any risk to its interests.[62] The Zongli Yamen's framing of the Red Cross through Mozi's jian'ai was more than a cultural translation. Locating the Red Cross's humanitarianism within Mozi's ethics could be taken as a contribution of Qing China to international law, for it demonstrated that the international legal norms could be articulated through a non-European epistemology.

The deliberate effort to situate international law within China's pre-Qin historical tradition was particularly evident in the diplomatic correspondence between Qing delegates and the Qing court. Following the publication of W. A. P. Martin's

Linsun Cheng, 'Qing Grand Council,' https://www.oxfordreference.com/display/10.1093/acref/9780190622671.001.0001/acref-9780190622671-e-532, accessed 20 March 2023.

[58] 'The Zongli Yamen Submits a Memorial Reporting the Review of the Provisions of the Peace Conference and the Statutes of the Red Cross, Finding No Obstacles' (总署奏遵查保和会各款并红十字会章程尚无窒碍折), in Wang (n 49) 2714.

[59] ibid 2715.

[60] ibid.

[61] ibid.

[62] ibid.

Traces of International Law in Ancient China (1864), late-Qing scholars and officials increasingly drew parallels between Western international law and classical Chinese historical practices, a tendency notably reflected in Yang Ru's memorial on singing up the Hague Conventions.[63] By strategically aligning these pre-Qin conceptual frameworks and practices with modern Western legal discourse, late-Qing elites hence created the possibility for dialogue between China and the West, effectively mobilizing China's classical tradition as an interpretive lens through which to engage with-and legitimate-European norms of international order.

Zongli Yamen further stated that all nations around the world regarded signing the Convention for the Adaptation to Maritime Warfare of the Principles of the Geneva Convention of 22 August 1864 as a most commendable act, and that China ought to sign this convention to demonstrate its spirit of benevolence.[64] Ultimately, Zongli Yamen persuaded the Empress Dowager and appointed Yang Ru to go back[65] to Hague to sign the Conventions and Declarations other than the *Convention on the Laws and Customs of War on Land*.[66] Upon arriving at The Hague, Yang Ru informed the other powers that although China had not yet signed the Convention Respecting the Laws and Customs of War on Land, it was fully prepared to observe the convention in practice. He clarified that China's abstention from signing stemmed from the incomplete Western-style modernization of its military, which had not yet fully assimilated the relevant laws and customs. However, he assured them that once the military reforms were sufficiently advanced, China would promptly accede to this Convention.[67]

FollowingZongli Yamen's practice of interpreting the world situations in line with traditional Chinese legal thought, when seeking permission to sign up the original Geneva Convention of 1864, Yang Ru also appealed to the Confucian and classical frameworks. He commented: 'the Red Cross Society is universally valued by nations, seen as an indispensable duty of benevolence and justice in civilized society.'[68] This statement illustrates how Qing China associated civilization with adopting institutions like the Red Cross, seeing them as manifestations of universal humanitarianism. Through ratifying the Hague Conventions and embracing the Red Cross-justified via Confucian principles of benevolence and justice-the Qing positioned itself as a participant in peace efforts, aligning with the era's standards of civilized statehood.

[63] 'Memorial by Envoy Yang Ru to Russia, on Signing the Hague Convention in the Netherlands, Petitioning for Accession to the Geneva Conventions, and Plans to Organize a Relief Society (Red Cross Society)' (使俄杨儒奏遵赴和兰画押请补签日来弗原议并筹办救生善会折), in Wang (n 49) 2725–2726.

[64] Wang (n 49) 2716.

[65] As noted above, Yang Ru, the Envoy to Russia, went back to Russia immediately after the first Hague Conference and submitted his memorials to the Qing Court from Russia. With the decree to sign up to the Convention, Yang Ru was going to The Hague again.

[66] Wang (n 49) 2724.

[67] ibid.

[68] ibid 2725–2726.

Furthermore, discussions among Chinese officials indicated a strong emphasis on Japan's model. The Qing elites recognized that Japan's strategic embrace of international law had facilitated its acceptance as a 'civilized' nation, which might have influenced China's gradual adoption of similar approaches to diplomacy and law. This is reflected in Yang Ru's suggestion of drawing on the practices of Japan. 'Japan has effectively adopted an approach that combines private and government fundraising to gather the necessary financial support for the Red Cross ... China could follow Japan's example by organizing a similar Red Cross society.'[69] The First Sino–Japanese War of 1894–1895 significantly altered the political dynamics in East Asia. During this conflict, Japan, once a devoted follower of traditional Chinese culture, defeated China, delivering a tremendous blow to the late-Qing government. Japan also framed this war as a struggle between civilization and barbarism.[70] The success of Japan led Chinese intellectuals to believe that its embrace of Western institutions and involvement in international organizations had elevated Japan to a status equal to that of European powers. Yang Ru's proposal to mirror Japan's approach by forming a Red Cross society reflects the admiration and aspirations of late-Qing intellectuals and politicians who sought to transform China into a civilized nation like Japan, which actively engaged in the Red Cross Conventions and emphasized the importance of codifying humanitarian law. Consequently, signing up to the original Geneva Convention and establishing similar societies such as the Red Cross was seen as a way to demonstrate adherence to international law and gain entry into the ranks of civilized nations.

9.4 China's Participation in the Second Hague Peace Conference

Around the time of the second Hague Peace Conference, the desire to use peaceful methods to resolve conflicts among the civilized nations, if not stronger, remained equally evident. While the US sought to assert its influence on the international stage through proposing holding another peace conference and promoting the idea of replacing the sword with judicial means, Qing China, anxious about the 1905 Russo–Japanese War, considered the conference an opportunity to fight for international status and protect its national interests.

Enthusiasm for multilateral diplomacy among Qing officials had grown markedly. The decision to send its envoy resident in the Netherlands and a special envoy, along with hiring American expert Foster as an advisor, reflects Qing

[69] ibid 2724–2725.

[70] Arthur Eyffinger, 'Caught Between Tradition and Modernity: East Asia at The Hague Peace Conferences' (2008), 1 Journal of East Asia and International Law 7–46, 20.

China's increasing recognition of the importance of active participation in foreign affairs, and indicates Qing China's preparation for more active participation in the 1907 Hague Peace conference.[71] In fact, participation in such forums was increasingly viewed by Qing's elites as a means to assert sovereignty, mitigate foreign domination, and project China's commitment to 'civilized' norms seeking recognition within the Western-dominated international order.[72]

In all, 256 representatives from 44 nations attended the conference, which opened on 15 June 1907 and ran until 18 October 1907.[73] The Chinese delegation was led by plenipotentiary representative Lu Zhengxiang and included American advisor John Foster and Envoy to the Netherlands Qian Xun. They were accompanied by military representative Ding Shiyuan (丁士源), deputy representatives Zhang Qingtong (张庆桐) and Zhao Yishu (赵诒璹), and counselors Shi Shaochang (施绍常), Chen Lu (陈箓), and Wang Guangqi (王广圻), who joined the mission to gain training and practical experience.[74] When reporting to the Qing court, Lu Zhengxiang noted the number of representatives dispatched by Qing China was roughly the same as that of Britain, Russia, Germany, France, and Japan.[75] The comparison to these powers reflects Qing China's growing awareness of inclusion on an equal footing with the other civilized nations, reinforcing the idea that full participation in international institutions such as the Hague Peace Conference was reserved for those who met the European-defined criteria of civilization. However, it is observed that while the seats were arranged in alphabetical order according to the French names of the countries, and the grouping of the seats was different in several of the plenary sessions, 'each time the alphabet favored the large powers by bringing their delegates to the front'.[76] This subtle hierarchy embedded in the procedural arrangements might foreshadow a different ending from that which Qing anticipated. Rather than achieving recognition as an equal sovereign state, the Chinese delegation, led by Lu Zhengxiang, was exposed to the structural barriers maintaining its subordinate position. They would soon encounter a very different interpretation of what it meant to be a 'civilized nation', particularly in the disputes over the selection of judges for the Court of Arbitral Justice and the scope of compulsory arbitration.

71 Lizé (n 15).
72 Tang (n 19).
73 Eyffinger (n 2) 83.
74 First Historical Archives of China, 'Memorial from Lu Zhengxiang to the Qing Emperor Guangxu Regarding Attending Hague Peace Conference, 12 December 1907' (陆征祥出席海牙保和会奏折两件) (2000), 2 Archives of Republic of China (民国档案) 37–42, 37.
75 ibid.
76 Hull (n 2).

(1) Allocation of justices

The primary contention involved the apportionment of arbitral seats among member states in the proposed Court of Arbitral Justice. The First Hague Peace Conference stipulated the establishment of the Permanent Court of Arbitration (PCA) in the Hague, allowing each contracting power to nominate members of the court. When a dispute arose between the countries, the states involved would select arbitrators from this list of members to resolve the issue. Each nominee served a six-year term.[77] However, as the American delegation noted, the PCA was not a true 'court' in the sense of having permanently sitting judges; its members did not reside in the Hague and were convened only on an ad hoc basis. This made it difficult to respond promptly to pressing international disputes. To remedy this, the United States proposed the creation of a new body-the Court of Arbitral Justice-that would consist of a limited number of judges with permanent residence in The Hague and with evenly apportioned representation among nations.[78]

The US delegation at the Second Hague Peace Conference, under Root's instructions, made their efforts to make a definite plan for the constitution of the court to turn their expectation of promoting international justice by the establishment of an international court into the agenda of the 1907 Hague Conference.[79] However, its arbitration court proposal was intertwined with the 'standard of civilization' as it sought to promote legal norms and peaceful dispute resolution while simultaneously reflecting and reinforcing the existing power dynamics and hierarchies of the time. According to the US delegation, a new arbitral court shall be organized, 'to consist of fifteen judges of the highest moral standing and of recognized competency in questions of international law',[80] because 'it is obvious at the outstart that a court, to be truly international, should represent not only one or many but all nations. It is equally obvious that a court composed of a single representative from each independent and sovereign nation would be unwieldy. Forty-five judges, sitting together, might compose a judicial assembly; they would not constitute a court. And our purpose is to establish a court, not to call into existence a judicial assembly.'[81]

In this context, while the court was envisioned as a mechanism for civilized nations to resolve their conflicts, the participating powers faced challenges in reaching a consensus on the precise method of appointing judges to this proposed

[77] Holls (n 36) 260.
[78] ibid 261–262.
[79] Martti Koskenniemi, 'The Ideology of International Adjudication and the 1907 Hague Conference', in Yves Daudet, *Topicality of the 1907 Hague Conference, the Second Peace Conference* (Leiden/London: Martinus Nijhoff Publishers, 2008) 127–152, 129.
[80] Denys P. Myers, 'The Origin of the Hague Arbitral Courts' (April 1916), 10(2) The American Journal of International Law 270–311, 278.
[81] ibid 286.

court of justice. The proposal raised complex questions about seat distribution and national equality, which remained unresolved.

In the US proposal, out of the total members, eight would be designated as permanent judges representing the great powers. The remaining members of the panel would rotate based on different time frames: ten years, four years, or two years, with the lowest-ranked group serving for just a single year.[82] Despite being recognized as having the largest population in the world, China was placed in the third class of this proposed system.[83] This meant that it could only appoint judges for four years out of a twelve-year rotation, significantly limiting its influence and representation in the judicial panel compared to the great powers. The very language of the discussions of the proposed arbitral court implied a distinction between 'civilized' nations and others, and the underlying tone positioned Western states as the standard-bearers of civilization and progress.

On this issue, Lu Zhengxiang and other delegation members expressed their opposition and emphasized that China had consistently been classified as a first-class nation. In the memorial regarding the 1907 Hague Peace Conference to the Qing court, Lu Zhengxiang's attitude and response to the composition of justice was detailed. He firmly maintained that Qing China had been a member of the first-class nations, and 'in terms of population and territorial extent, China is in no way inferior to other nations'.[84] Furthermore, Lu argued that 'in the previous court, China's annual financial contribution was equal to that of Russia, France, and Germany, each bearing 25 shares of the expenses, which serves as a well-established precedent'.[85] Lu and his colleagues insisted that the allocation of representation should continue to be based on the number of financial shares contributed. 'With the purpose of removing all inequality in the distribution of the judges in question and to facilitate its constitution, the delegation of China has the honor to suggest the committee ... to take the table of the distribution of the expenses of the International Bureau among the participating countries as a basis ... thus fixing the classification of the State. Any deviation from this principle would be exceedingly difficult to accept and advocated adherence to the established rules.'[86] This proposal reveals more than a technical suggestion for institutional design. It reflects a deeper political aspiration for equal standing within the international legal order. By linking judicial representation to financial contributions, Lu positioned Qing China as a rule-abiding participant in the international community. This move signalled a strategic effort to recast Qing China's international identity.

[82] First Historical Archives of China (n 74) 37.
[83] ibid 38.
[84] ibid.
[85] ibid.
[86] ibid 39.

Interestingly, in his memorial, Lu particularly mentioned Turkey, which was granted a ten-year term for the appointment of justices, while China was only allocated a four-year term and categorized as a 'third-tier' nation. As the Ottoman Empire was often labelled the 'sick man' of Europe, its ability to secure a better position than China, from Lu Zhengxiang's perspective, demonstrates the importance and urgency of following the 'standard of civilization'. He noted that the 'excuse' for the classification of Qing China as a third-tier nation was 'incomplete legal system'.[87] His tone reflects a strong sense of indignation and frustration over this arrangement. Still, it seems that Lu Zhengxiang implicitly suggests a need for domestic reforms to meet the externally imposed standards. In other words, Lu was ready to accept this seemingly objective justification for excluding or marginalizing nations such as China, out of a deep anxiety over China's declining status. At that point, to be a civilized nation, more criteria must be met than simply embracing humanitarian principles and peace causes. For Lu Zhengxiang, the top priority was to reform China's outdated institutions and promote legal modernization—which would be reflected in his later activities.

(2) Obligatory arbitration

Lu Zhengxiang's commitment to institutional reform and legal modernization shaped not only his domestic vision but also his diplomatic stance in international forums. Lu's efforts to position China as a sovereign and equal participant in the international legal system were closely tied to his broader project of strengthening China's juridical capacity and national dignity. Within this context, his strong opposition to exempting issues related to extraterritoriality from arbitration should not be overlooked.

The 1899 Hague Peace Conference stimulated notable public optimism about institutionalizing arms control mechanisms, measures widely regarded within contemporary discourse as hallmarks of civilized international conduct.[88] While those expectations were ultimately unmet due to political disagreements and the reluctance of major powers to impose binding restrictions on their military capabilities, the 1899 Hague Peace Conference paved the way for the second Hague Conference in 1907 and offered hope for extended application of arbitration. A key development at the 1907 Hague Conference emerged in the First Commission's extensive debates on compulsory arbitration, specifically addressing the jurisdictional parameters for mandatory cases. It marked a significant evolution from the

[87] ibid 38.
[88] Reid (n 33).

1899 Conference's non-binding approach to dispute resolution.[89] On this occasion, the United States proposed that all participating states formally commit to submitting their legal disputes to the newly envisioned Court of Arbitral Justice.[90]

Influenced by the notion that obligatory arbitration could institutionalize peaceful conflict resolution by requiring states to submit specific disputes to arbitration instead of resorting to war, Chinese delegates expected arbitration mechanisms to be a platform to solve legal disputes arising from unequal treaties or imperial interventions imposed on China. Although the arbitral court was envisioned as providing legal redress against the exploitation of powerful nations, Chinese delegates such as Lu Zhengxiang also warned that arbitration is not always in the favour of the weaker nations.[91] Lu Zhengxiang's worry was soon proven to be not without reason. In fact, it is recorded that representatives from seventeen nations voiced their governments' positions on a general treaty for obligatory arbitration. Among them, thirteen were smaller states. The larger powers, on the other hand, were often reluctant to commit to such obligations.[92] At this point, nations such as Qing China, despite their large populations and historical significance, were grouped into the 'small powers'. But these small powers aligns the practice of arbitration with the 'standard of civilization'. According to Lu Zhengxiang, the broad application of arbitration is a marker of 'progress of civilization'.[93] There was at this time an idealistic vision of international law, where arbitration is seen as a universal and impartial tool for maintaining peace, among Chinese intellectuals and elites.

Still, intense debates arose over what kind of cases could be subject to obligatory arbitration.[94] The British delegation proposed a case list covering a wide range of disputes from international working men's protection to patents, trade marks, and commercial names,[95] but it also included an article that would exempt consular jurisdictional matters from a proposed agreement on obligatory arbitration, aiming to preserve its legal advantages and control over its nationals abroad, which faced strong opposition from Lu Zhengxiang.[96]

In the memorial to Qing, Lu Zhengxiang reported this issue and expressed his position. He identifies extraterritorial rights as a significant hindrance to China's sovereignty, emphasizing the extensive damage already inflicted. Accepting the British proposal would lead to the absence of avenues for arbitration regarding

[89] David D. Caron, 'War and International Adjudication: Reflections on the 1899 Peace Conference' (2000), 94(1) The American Journal of International Law 4–30.

[90] Heinrich Lammasch, 'Compulsory Arbitration at the Second Hague Conference' (Jan. 1910), 4(1) The American Journal of International Law 83–94.

[91] Eyffinger (n 70) 38.

[92] Hull (n 2) 311.

[93] First Historical Archives of China (n 74) 39.

[94] Lammasch (n 90).

[95] Hull (n 2) 332.

[96] Scott (n 6) 83–84; Li Shunmin, Li (n 18) 152.

disputes tied to extraterritorial rights, further complicate the issue, and leave China with no recourse to resolve conflicts.[97] In addition to expressing deep dissatisfaction, Lu also mentioned his strong objection to the clause: 'this conference was convened in the name of fairness and equality, inviting nations to participate ... if this paragraph is not removed, I will oppose the entire clause.'[98] Lu stated the collective resistance by various nations, including Persia and Siam, alongside China, to this clause. Ultimately, the resolution to delete this paragraph was supported by a majority of nations, including major powers such as Germany, the United States, Russia, Austria, Italy, and the Netherlands, although Britain and France stood in opposition.[99] Lu Zhengxiang's comprehensive report does not only reveal personal satisfaction with this diplomatic resistance, but more significantly documents a strategic triumph in challenging institutionalized discrimination within the structures of international law.

While the proposal concerning the composition of the Court of Arbitral Justice faced strong opposition primarily from Latin American countries led by Brazil, it was Lu Zhengxiang's determined intervention that eventually thwarted the British initiative to exclude issues of extraterritoriality from the scope of compulsory arbitration. In this sense, during the Hague Peace Conferences, Qing China's response involved more than passive observation but also active opposition to proposals that were perceived as harmful to its national interests. In another memorial to the Qing Emperor, Lu Zhengxiang critiques the discriminatory practices of classifying nations into different tiers and excluding issues such as extraterritoriality from arbitration,[100] and alerts the Qing court that the so-called civilized powers are unwilling to address injustices against China. Instead, these civilized powers will likely continue to pursue their interests at China's expense. Lu's observation suggests a deeply cautious and sceptical perspective regarding China's position in the international arena during the Hague Peace Conferences.

While frustrated, their exposure to international legal frameworks and the discourse of the standard of civilization continuously prompted Chinese diplomats and government officials to advance domestic legal reforms aimed at modernizing their legal system and actively preparing for their participation in the Hague Peace Conferences to come.

At the end of the second Hague Peace Conference, a resolution was voted unanimously that in the summer of 1915 a third International Peace Conference would assemble at the Hague and convert some of the attempts made at the second conference into accomplished fact.[101] This determination to institutionalize peace through international law and diplomacy, alongside the anxiety and awareness

[97] First Historical Archives of China (n 74) 39.
[98] ibid.
[99] ibid.
[100] ibid 41.
[101] Hull (n 2) 502.

of its precarious position in the international, leads to Lu's conclusion in the memorial that it is necessary to externally safeguard the rights of equality while internally promoting constitutional reform.[102] In order to secure equal footing in international relations with other civilized nations, Lu strongly advocated speeding up the legal reform—since an 'incomplete legal system' was the excuse for lowering China's international status—and leverage reform as a means of resisting foreign domination. 'The Third Hague Peace Conference is about to convene soon; if we can implement legal reforms ahead of schedule, it would serve to silence the criticism of other nations and curb their ambitions against us.'[103] Furthermore, since his return from the Hague, Lu Zhengxiang had actively emphasized the importance of cultivating international law scholars, and he believed international jurists representing their countries at international conference symbolized the progress of civilization.[104] At this point, for the elites of late-Qing China, the essence of what constituted a 'civilized nation' was understood to encompass more than merely possessing a complete and codified legal system. Being civilized also required an active commitment to the study, development, and application of international law. By aligning legal reform at home with active participation abroad, these elites sought not only to modernize China's institutions but also to demonstrate that China was fully capable of meeting-and would soon meet-the formal criteria of being civilized, and thus should be conferred sovereign statehood.

9.5 Conclusion: The 'Gate' of Civilization

The nineteenth century witnessed the central place of international law in the 'civilizing mission'. The language of 'civilization' was frequently invoked to reinforce the idea that peace and adherence to international law were hallmarks of civilized nations. After numerous humiliating, unequal treaties, Qing China decided to embrace European international law, engage international institutions, and reform its domestic law.[105] All of these efforts were aimed at one purpose: to be recognized by

[102] First Historical Archives of China (n 74) 42.

[103] 'Memorial Reporting on the Actual Situations Before and After the Peace Conference, Submitted for Transmission' (具奏保和会前后实在情形等折片请代递由) (17 February 1908, Guangxu Year 34, First Month, Sixteenth Day), held at the Archives of the Institute of Modern History, Academia Sinica, Archives of the Ministry of Foreign Affairs, 02-21-004-01-003, https://archivesonline.mh.sinica.edu.tw/detail/351a802a33eb6ab55de0819d894279da/, accessed 15 March 2023.

[104] John Hsien-Hsiang Feng, 'A Preliminary Study of The International Law Association and Its History (1912–1916)' (2019), 51 Journal of History, National Chengchi University 55–82.

[105] On 16 July 1905 (Year 31 of the Guangxu era), the Grand Secretariat, acting on imperial orders, issued a decree titled 'An Imperial Edict Sending Zai Ze and Others Eastward and Westward on a Mission to Study Foreign Politics'. Prominent officials, including Zaize (载泽), Dai Hongci (戴鸿慈), Xu Shichang (徐世昌), and Duan Fang (端方), were dispatched abroad to observe and study the political systems and administrative practices of foreign nations. The mission aimed to 'examine

the civilized world. However, in its high expectations of attending such 'grand occasions' as the Hague Peace Conference to endeavour to prove its 'civilized' status, it ultimately returned disappointed.

Does China's plight not sound similar to that of the 'country man' in Franz Kafka's parable *Before the Law*?[106] China's experiences with the Hague Peace Conferences mirror the willingness of the man to do anything to be permitted into the 'Gate of the Law'. China's participation in the conferences did not translate into its recognition as a fully civilized member of the Family of Nations. While the conferences provided a platform for China to voice its concerns and engage diplomatically with other states, they failed to enable China to effectively challenge the unequal treaties and foreign interventions it faced, nor did they satisfy the prevailing standard of 'being civilized'. The standard of civilization is not a cure for national humiliation, but an obstacle preventing it from realizing its aspirations for equality with other 'civilized nations'.

Qing China was disappointed to find its term for justices of the Permanent Court of Arbitration associated with its classification as 'a third-tier country'. For Qing China, civilization was a condition that can never be met. Outside the 'gate of the law' stood Chinese intellectuals and reformers who were in desperate search of the aid of international law for China to be recognized as a civilized state, and a full member of international society.

China's participation in the Hague Peace Conferences was a critical moment in its interaction with international law. Unfortunately, Qing China was not able to assert itself as a 'civilized' state, as it had planned, by adhering to international practice and laws, participating in international activities, acceding to conventions, and assuming international responsibilities. Instead, the Hague Peace Conferences institutionalized the 'standard of civilization' and solidified the civilization rhetoric that inherently excluded China and other non-Western states or required their compliance with decisions of great powers.

China's response to the standard of civilization at the Hague Peace Conferences reflected its desire and efforts to be recognized by the Western-dominated international legal system. It is, indeed, the same standard of civilization that obstructs China from acting as an equal within this system. These failed efforts highlight the hierarchical structure and imperial nature of international law during the late nineteenth and early twentieth centuries. While the formal use of distinctions of civilized and uncivilized has been dismantled in contemporary international law,

various forms of governance and adopt the most beneficial aspects for China's reform efforts'. See Pan Chong, *The Late Qing Dynasty Five Ministers Went Overseas Study Tour* (清末五大臣出洋考察研究) (Beijing: China Social Sciences Press, 2014)..

[106] Franz Kafka, *Selected Stories* (ed. and trans. by Mark Harman, Cambridge: Harvard University Press, 2024).

the historical legacy of these ideas continues to influence global power structures, as reflected in ongoing debates around economic justice, sovereignty, and equality among nations. The formerly 'civilized' countries firmly maintain their discourse power and influence, while the voices of Global South countries remain severely marginalized. To cite Kafka's *Before the Law* again, as the guard told the country man: 'even if you pass me, there are more gates, and there are more guards who are stronger than me.'[107]

[107] ibid 188.

PART III

INTERNATIONAL LAW IN CHINA DURING THE REPUBLICAN PERIOD

10
The Republic of China and the League of Nations

Ryan Martínez Mitchell

10.1 Introduction

The years comprising the late stage of the First World War and their immediate aftermath have been aptly described, in terms of domestic politics, as "the most disorderly period in the history of modern China."[1] This was an era in which "formal institutions decay[ed] and informal alignments and tactics [came] to the fore."[2] The initially promising project of a constitutionalization of Chinese governance proved, amidst factional struggles, emerging ideological divisions, and the machinations of foreign powers, to be illusory. The following years of recurring civil war and external intervention would bring the Chinese polity into a state of division that, indeed, would only be resolved after immense conflicts.

And yet, by contrast, on the plane of foreign policy and China's role in global affairs, this period inaugurated new forms of active assertion and contestation, involving a high degree of coordination (amidst continued rivalry) across regimes and factions.[3] Despite its internal divisions, the China that "entered 'international society'" during the 1918–1920 dealings bringing an end to the Great War was one exhibiting the potential to, at least at times, speak with a single voice—most notably in rejecting the Treaty of Versailles and its provisions for Japanese succession to the German leased territory in Shandong.[4] The developing substantial unity as to the basic premises of China's aspirations in connection with international legal norms and structures led to parallel initiatives to realize these national aims, many occurring through the medium of the newly founded League of Nations.

The League was the site for some of China's most important interwar diplomatic and legal initiatives, at the same time as being the embodiment of an explicitly

[1] Andrew James Nathan, *Peking Politics, 1918–1923: Factionalism and the Failure of Constitutionalism* (Berkeley, CA: University of California Press, 1976) 2.

[2] ibid.

[3] Julia C. Strauss, *Strong Institutions in Weak Polities: State Building in Republican China, 1927–1940* (OUP 1998) 169–170.

[4] Yongjin Zhang, *China in the International System, 1918–20: The Middle Kingdom at the Periphery* (Springer 1991).

Ryan Martínez Mitchell, *The Republic of China and the League of Nations* In: *Histories of International Law in China.* Edited by: Ignacio de la Rasilla, Jiangyu Wang, and Congyan Cai, Oxford University Press.
 DOI: 10.1093/oso/9780198888345.003.0010

hierarchical global order that continued to facilitate various forms of inequality and marginalization. From the beginning, in the eyes of some Chinese observers, the League could be associated with traditional Confucian aspiration for a time of universal harmony (*da tong*), even as for others it was the manifestation of a "path of collective invasion" by exploitative imperial powers.[5] The outcome of China's tumultuous two decades with the League would suggest that both assessments of the organization might be justifiable; they would also often show the necessity of extra-League action in order to realize both official and subaltern goals.[6] Rather than proclaiming one or the other view of the League—noble experiment in "peace through law" or thinly disguised imperialist club—today's historians might strive for a multi-perspectival position actively acknowledging epistemic pluralism.[7]

If the League years began with China's overcoming of the imperialist diplomatic formulae that had been the basis for Japanese claims to legitimized hegemony, they would conclude with China's rise to great power status as a co-founder and permanent Security Council member of the League's successor, the United Nations. It is hard to dispute the assessment that "the story of Chinese diplomacy in the Republican era is one of stunning accomplishments from a position of unenviable weakness."[8] These accomplishments, moreover, went considerably beyond the realm of diplomatic maneuvering in defense of the national interest.

One often under-emphasized aspect of League-era success-amidst-crisis comprised Chinese advocacy for revised international legal norms entailing protections of territorial integrity, national autonomy, and the restriction of unilateral coercion by powerful states. From the perspective of the history of international law, in particular, the story of China and the League is one of striking progress in asserting positions with an impact out of scale with the country's geopolitical stature at the time, even if corresponding to its widely recognized, and since realized, vast potential as a central player in the international system.

10.2 China and the Formation of the League

10.2.1 The Great War and the Remaking of Chinese Statehood

The Republic of China's entry into the First World War entailed a major process of internal political contestation with implications for the country's external relations

[5] Ryan Martínez Mitchell, *Recentering the World: China and the Transformation of International Law* (CUP 2022) 133, 140.

[6] ibid 132.

[7] Allan Megill, *Historical Knowledge, Historical Error: A Contemporary Guide to Practice* (University of Chicago Press 2007) 181–187.

[8] William C. Kirby, "The Internationalization of China: Foreign Relations at Home and Abroad in the Republican Era" (1997) 150 The China Quarterly 433, 436.

and, ultimately, the transformation of its position in global affairs.[9] This process also entailed a newfound activism of Chinese diplomats in international settings and of the Chinese international law profession as an emerging source of normative critique and reform proposals for the international legal order. Crucial to these transformations, and particularly to the emergence of a professionalized diplomatic corps whose mandate included the development and deployment of international legal expertise on behalf of the nation, was the increasing self-awareness and influence of China's "foreign policy public."[10] By the early postwar years, Chinese positions on core questions of international law would often be defined as direct expressions of the popular will, transcending political factions.

Even before the advent of the First World War, some of the key members of China's foreign policy community were intensively discussing the stances their country should take at a future international conference deciding fundamental norms of international law. One significant official forum for such internal debates was the "Preparation Committee for the Third Hague Conference," which met between November 1912 and October 1914.[11] These meetings featured exchanges between both seasoned Chinese diplomats and state-sponsored students who had accumulated expertise on international law. The former group included Lou Tseng-tsiang (Lu Zhengxiang), foreign minister of the "Beiyang" government of Yuan Shikai and veteran of the First and Second Hague Conferences,[12] while the latter included Wellington Koo (Gu Weijun), then a recent PhD graduate of Columbia University, who had studied with the prominent US international lawyer John Bassett Moore.[13]

During these meetings, some delegates, including Koo, argued that China should strive to recapture its jurisdiction over judicial proceedings involving foreigners—one of the key rights that had been surrendered to foreign imperial powers in the "unequal treaties" that the Qing Dynasty had signed since the mid-19th century.[14] Others were less convinced that China could lay claim to a right of national sovereignty implying any ability to override such treaty arrangements.[15] In part, these differences of opinion reflected the general lack of clarity in legal doctrine of the era regarding the nature of state sovereignty and its relationship with international law.[16] However, this kind of dispute also had to do with the fact that

[9] Zhang n 4, *China in the International System*, 187, 195–196.

[10] Xu Guoqi, *China and the Great War: China's Pursuit of a New National Identity and Internationalization* (CUP 2005) 68–72.

[11] Mitchell n 5, *Recentering the World*, 125.

[12] ibid; see also Ryan Martínez Mitchell, "China's Participation in the Second Hague Conference and the Concept of Equal Sovereignty in International Law" (2021) 11 Asian Journal of International Law 351.

[13] Stephen G. Craft, *V.K. Wellington Koo and the Emergence of Modern China* (The University Press of Kentucky 2004), 19–20.

[14] Mitchell n 5, *Recentering the World*, 125–127.

[15] ibid.

[16] As Hans Kelsen remarked after the war, there had for years been a "a very uncertain and contradictory vacillating back and forth of the theory [of sovereignty and its relationship to international

perceptions of the state as a legally defined political unit with enumerated powers were, in China, very much a recent intellectual import from the West and Japan.[17]

Of course, the planned Third Hague Conference was ultimately not to occur, given the outbreak of the world war. Instead, any new proposals for the modification of China's constrained national autonomy, compromised territorial integrity, or international legal status would have to wait until the war's conclusion. This, in turn, would be greatly influenced by the question as to whether China joined as a party to the conflict. Views on this question differed among China's leading officials, ultimately with dramatic implications for the viability of the Beiyang regime.[18]

The post-Qing government was dominated by the former military governor Yuan Shikai, whose own dictatorial policies and then imperial aspirations would do much to provoke years of civil strife and regime collapse.[19] In May 1915, Yuan signed the so-called Twenty-One Demands, essentially a wartime ultimatum presented by the Ōkuma Shigenobu government of Japan.[20] These demands reflected both Japanese policymakers' longstanding aims to exert hegemony over the East Asian region, especially China, and the major acceleration of plans in this direction during the first years of the war.[21] Several articles of the "Demands" reflected Japan's recent occupation of the German leased territory of Kiaochou Bay (Jiaozhou Wan), and its aim to use this as the springboard for general extension of authority, on a permanent basis, across northeast China.[22]

Though they would still be colloquially referred to as the "Twenty-One Demands," the Yuan government actually signed only fourteen of the articles.[23] When the originally secret protocols were leaked, a wave of protests, particularly from overseas Chinese students and merchants engaged in letter campaigns and anti-Japanese boycotts, sought to compel Yuan to abandon these capitulations.[24]

law]" while "neither of the two basic approaches" (i.e., a sovereignty-first or an international law-first interpretation) "has really been consistently implemented so far." Hans Kelsen, *Das Problem Der Souveränität und Die Theorie des Völkerrechts: Beitrag Zu Einer Reinen Rechtslehre* (J.C.B. Moore 1928) 120–121.

[17] Mitchell n 5, *Recentering the World*, 126–127.

[18] Hu Sheng, *Imperialism and Chinese Politics* (Foreign Languages Press 1955) 227.

[19] Nathan n 1, *Peking Politics*, 1–10.

[20] Thomas W. Burkman, *Japan and the League of Nations: Empire and World Order, 1914–1938* (University of Hawaii Press 2007) 19–20.

[21] ibid.

[22] Article 1 of the Twenty-One Demands entailed: "The Chinese Government engages to give full assent to all matters that the Japanese Government may hereafter agree with the German Government respecting the disposition of all the rights, interests and concessions, which, in virtue of treaties or otherwise, Germany possesses vis-à-vis China in relation to the province of Shantung."

[23] See Thomas F. Millard, *The A B C's of the Twenty-One Demands* (The Weekly Review of the Far East 1921) 1–10.

[24] Luo Zhitian, "National Humiliation and National Assertion: The Chinese Response to the Twenty-One Demands" (1993) 27 Modern Asian Studies 297. The leaking of the documents and the subsequent pressure campaigns were, in fact, in large part the result of a deliberate policy of "publicity" taken by the Yuan regime in the hopes of dissuading Japan's encroachments. Ibid, 299.

At the same time, this popular outrage as well as diplomatic pressure from Western powers anxious over Japan's ambitions, and misgivings among its own policy elite as to the ensuing reputational harms, led to the retraction of several particularly egregious clauses which would arguably have made China a true "semicolony" of Japan.[25] However, even with these parts removed, the remaining articles sufficed to grant Japanese economic, political, and military authority in northeast China to an extent beyond that of any other power—even in the context of a Chinese state that had already lost many of its territorial, judicial, and fiscal rights to foreign empires.[26] Meanwhile, a series of additional secret agreements between Japan and various powers, particularly Britain and France (which sought to keep Japan in the war), included acknowledgments of its assumption of extensive rights over Shandong.[27]

Yuan's own political position was weakened by these transactions. His subsequent late 1915 attempt to restore the imperial Chinese system, with himself as Emperor, was a fateful and disastrous decision that ended in ignominious defeat.[28] Yuan's rule was opposed by a rebellion to "defend the constitution" that was centered in Yunnan and soon spread, including to Guangdong, where a regime was established with Sun Yat-sen, the leader of the oppositional Nationalist Party (Guomindang), then living in Japanese exile, returning for a brief stint to build a rebel coalition.[29] While Sun soon departed after perceiving that the insurgents had little interest in more democratic governance, the rebellion successfully pressured the Beiyang regime.

Following the collapse of Yuan's plan and his death from illness in 1916, a new administration was instituted with former Vice-President Li Yuanhong as the head of state and Yuan's former military deputy Duan Qirui, as both Premier and Minister of War, holding practical authority. Li and Duan disagreed over the question as to whether China should join the war against the Central Powers.[30] Duan, who had broad military support as well as deep connections with Japan, effectively "had the Peking government under his thumb until July 1920" following his maneuvering to remove Li from office by mid-1917.[31] China's entry into World War I on 14 August 1917 formally relied upon a course of protests concerning

[25] Burkman n 20, *Japan and the League of Nations*, 19–20. The relevant group of stricken provisions included vaguely defined domestic police authorities as well as provisions for an expanded Japanese military presence in the Chinese heartland. Millard, *The A B C's*, 7–9.

[26] Among the signed articles, for example, were provisions giving Japan exclusive rights in Shandong and China's northeast provinces (aka Manchuria) regarding rail construction, the opening of commercial ports, and the management of public finances. Millard n 23, *The A B C's*, 2–6.

[27] Ge-Zay Wood, *The Shantung Question: A Study in Diplomacy and World Politics* (Fleming H. Revell Company 1922) 66–81.

[28] See Paul Samuel Reinsch, *An American Diplomat in China* (Doubleday 1922) 171–192.

[29] Hu n 18, *Imperialism and Chinese Politics*, 232–233.

[30] ibid 226–227.

[31] ibid.

German neutrality-violating blockades and unrestricted submarine warfare.[32] After a series of complaints reiterating that China was "animated by the desire to respect the peace of the world and uphold international law," the declaration of war noted the additional objectives to "develop the national existence of the Chung Hua Republic, so that we may establish ourselves amidst the family of nations and share with all mankind the prosperity and blessings drawn from our common association."[33]

The declaration of war reflected both these aspirations and Duan's own policy preference, but was also in part a manifestation of continued Japanese influence.[34] The Terauchi Masatake cabinet which in 1916 replaced that of Ōkuma had adopted a more subtle approach to pursuing hegemony, including by providing extensive loan payments under the guise of wartime cooperation, procuring monopoly rights in key industries, expanding Japan's military presence in Chinese territory, and procuring recognition of its "special interests" in Shandong and Manchuria.[35] The latter point was also the subject of additional diplomacy between Japan and other powers, including the United States, with the November 1917 exchange of notes by Secretary of State Robert Lansing and Japanese special envoy Viscount Ishii Kikujirō serving as a quasi-formal recognition of this status by the Wilson administration.[36]

These sorts of Japanese aspirations were at times explicitly modeled on the US Monroe Doctrine over Latin America, and upon recent US administration applications of that doctrine, including those of the Wilson administration.[37] They nonetheless sat uncomfortably with the principle of national self-determination at the core of Woodrow Wilson's January 1918 Fourteen Points platform on the postwar order, which inspired many Chinese intellectuals.[38] Also emerging as a surprising new source of normative challenge to great power imperialism was the radical revolution unfolding in Russia throughout 1917. Like some other Chinese intellectuals, Li Dazhao, a future co-founder of the Chinese Communist Party, saw these events as forecasting "that the dictatorship cannot be revived, that the sovereignty of the people cannot again be repressed, that the republic cannot once more be destroyed," both in Russia itself and in China.[39]

[32] Ministry of Foreign Affairs, *Official Documents Relating to the War (For the Year 1917)* (Peking Leader Press 1918) 1–13.

[33] ibid.

[34] Burkman n 20, *Japan and the League of Nations*, 20.

[35] Hu n 18, *Imperialism and Chinese Politics*, 230–231.

[36] "Mutual Interests in China (Lansing–Ishii Agreement)" (*Library of Congress*) <https://maint.loc.gov/law/help/us-treaties/bevans/b-jp-ust000009-0425.pdf> accessed 12 July 2025.

[37] Foreign Minister Gotō Shinpei, for example, argued that "The Wilson policy of helping the Mexicans to help themselves by picking out the strongest men in that country and supporting them liberally is now amply vindicated ... Japan must pursue the same tactics with China." Burkman n 20, *Japan and the League of Nations*, 19.

[38] Zhang n 4, *China in the International System*, 49–41.

[39] Maurice Meisner, *Li Ta-chao and the Origins of Chinese Marxism* (Harvard University Press 1967) 58.

Following the October Revolution, more Chinese intellectuals developed great interest in the emerging post-Tsarist Russian state. Sun Yat-sen sent a message of congratulations to the Bolsheviks in January 1918, and over the course of that year both Leninist and Wilsonian doctrines of self-determination became fixtures of political discourse. The end of the war in late 1918 was hailed by Li as a "victory of the masses."[40] As with a growing number of contemporaries, the wartime years and in particular the experience of intensified imperialist encroachments led Li toward a conviction of the need for "social revolution and a strong internationalism."[41]

10.2.2 Forming Unified Stances

China's diplomats and its emerging corps of international lawyers had a tumultuous experience of the war years. Wellington Koo, for example, had been dispatched as an envoy to the United States in 1915 as part of the effort to secure support for Yuan's monarchist initiative.[42] Under Duan, he was made minister to the United States. Shortly after the armistice, Koo met briefly with Woodrow Wilson to discuss the arrangements for the peace conference that would be held the next year. Though Koo, like many educated Chinese, held great hopes for the Wilson administration to take action to preserve China's sovereignty in line with the Fourteen Points, he received only non-committal statements from the man himself.[43]

A major problem, which Wilson now personally revealed to Koo, was the existence of various "secret agreements" with regard to China.[44] Meanwhile, on a more fundamental level, Wilson stated that the Fourteen Points would be "probably more difficult to apply to the Far East" than to the peoples of Europe.[45] This phrasing, along with Wilson's promise to "do his best to support China at the peace conference", was apparently a tactful way to indicate his limited motivation in seeking to implement principles of self-determination in the non-Western world.[46]

Chinese diplomats elsewhere, including in the major European capitals, were experiencing similar, indeed even more stark, reminders of their subordinated status.[47] Altogether, the prospects of either overturning the assignation of Jiaozhou to Japan or making meaningful headway regarding other concerns over tariff autonomy and extraterritorial jurisdiction seemed quite limited. A major

[40] ibid, 70 FN37.

[41] Michael H. Hunt, *The Genesis of Chinese Communist Foreign Policy* (Columbia University Press 1996) 66–67.

[42] Reinsch n 28, *An American Diplomat*, 171–172.

[43] Zhang n 4, *China in the International System*, 47.

[44] ibid.

[45] ibid.

[46] ibid; see also Erez Manela, *The Wilsonian Moment: Self-Determination and the International Origins of Anticolonial Nationalism* (Oxford University Press 2007) 25.

[47] Zhang n 4, *China in the International System*, 47–48.

obstacle was that these objectives were at cross purposes. Indeed, Duan explicitly instructed his delegation to the peace conference that it should not focus on recovering the former German leasehold and should instead "limit itself to revising the unequal treaties."[48] While not sharing Duan's faith (or personal investment) in Sino-Japanese cooperation, members of the delegation were themselves unsure what would be the best way to pursue their multiple, ambitious aims. One possible route was to defer the "Shandong Question" to a separate future conference, rather than attempt to resolve it at Paris in 1919. Yet, as Koo objected, this could also raise the risks of presenting an opportunity for *de jure* legitimation of Japanese hegemony.[49]

Lu Zhengxiang was the senior representative for the officially recognized Beiyang government. Among the most important other delegates were Guomindang representative C. T. Wang (Wang Zhengting), Beiyang Minister to the United Kingdom Alfred Sze (Shi Zhaoji), Minister to Belgium Wei Chentsu (Wei Chenzu), and Koo. This "joint delegation" thus bridged the Beiyang and Guomindang regimes in the name of pursuing shared national goals on the international plane.[50] Along with the phenomenon of the developing foreign policy public and its influence over government policymaking, these forms of unity and cooperation across factions in the realm of diplomacy would recur later during the interwar and wartime years.[51]

Beyond the delegation, meanwhile, recent years had also seen the development of a growing body of Chinese experts in diplomacy and international law that provided regular commentary on ongoing affairs of state. Writing from Tsing Hua College in mid-1918, for example, lecturer on international law Tyao Min-chien (Diao Minqian) had listed a set of doctrines that could be invoked at the coming peace conference in pursuit of the aim of treaty revision.[52] One was to emphasize the inherent "illegality of force," even though existing doctrine attached little jurisprudential (as opposed to moral) relevance to a treaty provision having been imposed by force or coercion.[53] A potentially more promising point to pursue was the doctrine of *rebus sic stantibus*, or the vital change of circumstances, which was recognized as a potential ground for the termination of treaty terms.[54]

Other international law experts included Tchéou Wei (Zhou Wei), a former student of the Swiss jurist and politician Émile Bise who published in 1917 a

[48] Craft n 13, *V.K. Wellington Koo*, 49–50.
[49] ibid.
[50] At the time of the Paris Peace Conference, Sun Yat-sen had left Guangzhou after multiple attempts at forming a stable government with backing of warlords aligned with the "constitutional protection" movement. Yet another attempt would occur in 1920–1921.
[51] Cf. Mitchell n 5, *Recentering the World*, 190.
[52] Min-chien Tyau, *China's New Constitution and International Problems* (Commercial Press 1918) 282–286.
[53] ibid 282.
[54] ibid 282–284.

well-received monograph with the title *Essai sur l'organisation juridique de la Société international* (*Essay on the Juridical Organization of International Society*), in which he argued for the creation of an international organization with judicial, legislative, and executive powers and the capacity to enforce norms against violating states.[55] As an entry into ongoing wartime discussions over postwar order, Zhou Wei's contribution was considered a valuable, if ambitious, articulation of one potential route.[56] Also beginning to publish significant works during this period was Zhou Gengsheng, who took a critical position deconstructing ways in which Western legal concepts such as "suzerainty" had been applied to China in a manner that devalued its sovereignty.[57]

Before the conference, Lu Zhengxiang had convened meetings in Beijing to solicit and review preparatory materials in order to formulate China's stances. These included detailed contributions from Zhou Wei, among others, noting that it would be a major challenge to seek to revise the Boxer Protocol and other unequal treaties.[58] This would indeed prove to be the case, with the Shandong Question posing similar difficulties. Major developments on this issue began to unfold soon after arrival of the Chinese delegation in Paris on 11 January 1919. It was on the 28th that Wellington Koo made his speech before the so-called Council of Ten, comprising the leaders and foreign ministers of the US, the UK, France, Italy, and Japan.[59] He argued, on the one hand, in moralistic terms, emphasizing the importance of Shandong as the "birthplace of Confucius and Mencius," the "cradle of [Chinese] civilization," and "a Holy Land for the Chinese" as a justification for its return to Chinese administration.[60] At the same time, he presented a legal argument based on the doctrine of *rebus sic stantibus*.[61] With the speech generally acclaimed as a remarkable performance by Koo, word of the argument and its apparent success in rousing sympathies of the great powers led to an atmosphere of celebratory hope among the conference's many observers in China.[62]

These hopes, however, were soon to be dashed, as the ensuing months of diplomatic confrontation proved a direct restitution of Shandong to China effectively impossible. The chief obstacle was the network of secret agreements that Japan had made, both with Chinese leaders and with its wartime allies. By April, the

[55] Tchéou Wei [Zhou Wei], *Essai sur l'organisation juridique de la Société international* (Libraire Atar 1917).

[56] Otfried Nippold, *The Development of International Law after the World War* (The Lawbook Exchange, Ltd. 2004) (original publication 1923) (translated by Amos S. Hershey) 44; Paul Fauchille, *Traité de droit international public* (Rousseau & Cie 1923) 183; H. Lepert, *Projet de constitution pour la Société des nations: projet soumis à la Ligue* (Ligue por une Société des Nations Basée sur une Constitution Internationale 1917) 24.

[57] Gengsheng, "Zongzhuquan Lun [The Theory of Suzerainty]" [1918] 1 Taipingyang 10.

[58] Tang Qi-hua, *Chinese Diplomacy and the Paris Peace Conference* (Springer Nature 2020) 73–79.

[59] Zhang n 4, *China in the International System*, 54–55.

[60] ibid.

[61] ibid.

[62] ibid.

Shandong question would be effectively concluded in Japan's favor, with the resulting Articles 156–158 in the Treaty of Versailles constituting German's direct renunciation to it of Jiaozhou and all related rights.[63] Meanwhile, the Chinese delegates' other objectives—to restore tariff autonomy, secure the withdrawal of foreign troops, and pursue the revision of extraterritorial jurisdiction—were also rejected by the Council as being outside the scope of the peace conference.[64]

These failures on the ground were matched by a major new wave of patriotic popular activism back at home. The emergence of what has come to be remembered as the "May Fourth Movement" was most directly sparked by a telegram from the statesman Liang Qichao, who was in Paris as a quasi-official "observer" from the so-called Research Clique (Yanjiu Xi) faction in Beiyang politics.[65] Liang's account, which was published in Beijing by the Research Clique-aligned Association of Public Diplomacy, helped to influence the view that failures by the Chinese delegates, as well as complicity of the pro-Japanese faction within the Beiyang government, had led to the failure to secure Jiaozhou's return.[66] Soon after, there erupted a tumultuous wave of student activism that sought to force the government to reject the terms being decided in Paris.[67] Based in large part on these ongoing protests and their impacts upon the Beiyang government, which was forced to undergo a wave of high-profile resignations, the delegates in Paris indeed ultimately chose to refuse to sign the treaty—although up until the very day of signing, they sought instead to attempt to introduce reservations on the Shandong-related articles, which were rebuffed by the Allies.[68]

Despite this refusal to sign, the Chinese delegates were able to secure membership for their country in the prospective League of Nations via signature of the Treaty of St Germain, which concluded the war with Austria-Hungary. The League itself had been crafted through the meetings of the Commission on the League of Nations, on which China had secured participation as a "small nation."[69] With Koo acting as China's main representative during the Commission's March–April meetings, he had focused on supporting Wilson's overall vision for the organization while seeking, carefully, to modify one of the US demands: for a carve-out clause in the League Covenant entailing "explicit recognition of the Monroe Doctrine."[70] Koo's concern—which would turn out to be quite justified—was that official recognition of the Monroe Doctrine, especially in terms that could be used

[63] "The Versailles Treaty, June 28, 1919" (*Avalon Project*) <https://avalon.law.yale.edu/subject_menus/versailles_menu.asp> accessed July 12, 2025.
[64] Zhang n 4, *China in the International System*, 44–48.
[65] Tang n 58, *Chinese Diplomacy*, 238; Nathan n 1, *Peking Politics*, 239–244.
[66] Tang n 58, *Chinese Diplomacy*, 298–310.
[67] ibid; see also Craft n 13, *V.K. Wellington Koo*, 66.
[68] Zhang n 4, *China in the International System*, 90–95.
[69] Tang n 58, Qihua, *Chinese Diplomacy*, 187–191; Tang Qihua, *Beijing Zhengfu Yu Guoji Lianmeng (1919–1928)* [The Beijing Government and the League of Nations (1919–1928)] (Dongda Tushu Gongsi, 1998).
[70] David Hunter Miller, *The Drafting of the Covenant* (G.P. Putnam's Sons, 1928), 30, 441–450.

to generalize it as a model for other major powers, would be invoked by Japan to justify its pursuit of hegemony in China and the broader Asian region.[71] Despite his efforts, the eventual Covenant did include, as Article 21, a recognition for "regional understandings like the Monroe doctrine," although the exact meaning of this provision was debatable.[72] Koo also contributed to discussion of other issues, such as the representation on the League Council of smaller powers alongside the (permanent) great power seats.[73]

10.3 China within the League

10.3.1 Achieving Integration

China was in an anomalous position as a state that had attended the peace conference as an Allied power, had actively participated in the drafting of the Covenant of the League of Nations, yet had such profound reservations about aspects of the agreement that it had refused to sign the Treaty of Versailles.[74] Signing the Treaty of St Germain had, in practice, meant the deferral of the issues of Shandong and unequal treaty revision to a later date, via a specialized conference. In that sense, China's situation actually somewhat resembled that of the defeated powers, which had major unresolved territorial issues. For China, a (provisional) resolution of its concerns would occur via the Washington Naval Conference of 1921–1922, held under the auspices of the US Republican Harding administration.[75]

The immense public pressure generated during the peace conference had not only resulted in a firm stance against Japan's efforts to retain Jiaozhou but also led to a transformation of China's domestic politics away from the Japanese-affiliated "Anhui Clique" of Duan Qirui and towards the "Zhili Clique," associated with General Wu Peifu, which was relatively more Anglo-American in its leanings.[76] From 1920 to 1924 the Zhili government would pursue policies that entailed closer collaboration with the United States and the United Kingdom, including in League of Nations affairs (and despite ongoing dramatic factional struggles). Meanwhile, throughout this period of tumult, China's representatives in the League at Geneva continued to pursue diplomatic initiatives aimed at embodying and extending

[71] Tang n 58, *Chinese Diplomacy*, 187–191.
[72] Miller n 70, *The Drafting of the Covenant*, 140–148.
[73] ibid.
[74] The United States signed the Treaty of Versailles, but the Senate would refuse ratification in 1920.
[75] Robert H. Van Meter, "The Washington Conference of 1921–1922: A New Look" [1977] 46 Pacific Historical Review 603.
[76] Cf. Anthony B. Chan, *Arming the Chinese: The Western Armaments Trade in Warlord China, 1920–28* (UBC Press 2010) 132.

their country's hard-won recognition as a recognized member of international society.[77]

The question of China's status within the international community was only effectively resolved in the aftermath of the League's founding. Up until that point, even leading international law treatises published in the West were not unanimous in the belief that China should be considered as a "civilized" country that was part of the "Family of Nations."[78] The League Covenant itself had included, in the Mandate system, an explicit hierarchical organization of peoples that ranged from the great powers of Europe to "[o]ther peoples, especially those of Central Africa, [who] are at such a stage that the Mandatory must be responsible for the administration of the[ir] territory."[79] For decades, some Western international lawyers, statesmen, and diplomats had also contemplated an explicit internationalized management of China, often portraying this as a progressive proposal in China's own interest.[80]

In general, notions of hierarchy remained extremely pronounced in international law and diplomacy well into the League years, and even from the perspective of the relatively egalitarian-presenting US foreign policy community. Former US President Theodore Roosevelt, for example, had expressed in a January 1919 editorial his incredulity that Wilson could "really intend[] that ... we shall admit Russia, Germany ... Turkey, China and Mexico into the League on a full equality with ourselves."[81] Domestic Republican opposition to the League, which had resulted in an American refusal to join, was also mobilized by the charge that the organization would disrupt US hemispheric hegemony via the Monroe Doctrine, despite Wilson's successful effort to ensure its mention in the Covenant.[82]

It was thus a remarkable achievement for China's delegates at Geneva to become active, even leading, figures within the newly founded League. Particularly striking milestones included Wellington Koo's role as acting Council President in late 1921 and his position as a commissioner reporting upon and helping to decide Germany's territorial and populations disputes with respect to Upper Silesia and the British–French occupied Saar Basin.[83] In connection with the latter developments, Cecil Hurst of the UK Foreign Office remarked that there was something "almost grotesque in letting a Chinaman preside over a body which is to decide

[77] Alison Adcock Kaufman, "In Pursuit of Equality and Respect: China"s Diplomacy and the League of Nations" (2014) 40 *Modern China* 605.

[78] Franz Lizst, *Das Völkerrecht Systematisch Dargestellt*, 10th ed. (Berlin: Springer, 1915), 5–6; Henry Wheaton, Wheaton, *Wheaton's Elements of International Law*, 5th ed. (London: Stevens and Sons, 1916) (Coleman Phillipson, ed.), 20.

[79] Covenant, Article 22.

[80] Mitchell n 5, *Recentering the World*, 117–118.

[81] Theodore Roosevelt, "The League of Nations," in *World Peace Foundation Pamphlet Series*, Vol. 1917–1919, pp. 466–[iv].

[82] James Wilford Garner, "The Recrudescence of the Monroe Doctrine" (1930) 45 Political Science Quarterly 231.

[83] Mitchell n 5, *Recentering the World*, 136.

an issue of importance between France and Great Britain."[84] The actual content of Koo's recommendations regarding these disputes was, however, generally seen as judicious (and quite pragmatic in declining to challenge Western great power interventionism).[85]

Chinese diplomats and policymakers hoped that the League would both help to consolidate China's international status and act as a vehicle for practical resolutions of outstanding problems such as the return of Jiaozhou, tariff autonomy, foreign troop presence, and extraterritorial jurisdiction.[86] However, despite some initial efforts to present these issues to the Assembly via Covenant Article 19 (permitting the Assembly to "advise the reconsideration by members of the League of treaties which have become inapplicable"), it was eventually decided that this forum would not prove amenable to a satisfactory resolution, at least in the near term. Instead, China's delegates concentrated their intra-League proposals on issues that were connected with regional order. On the one hand, they continued to seek to modify the language of Article 21 in order to deter Japanese efforts to claim a Monroe Doctrine for Asia.[87] These arguments, raised throughout the 1920s by China and some Latin American states, did not succeed in revising or clearly defining the scope of Article 21 to reduce possible ambiguities over its endorsement of regional hegemons, but did help make visible opposition to such uses.[88]

Considerably more successful was another Chinese intra-League venture during the early 1920s. This entailed the issue of election of non-permanent members of the League Council. At each of the annual sessions of the League Assembly, China's delegates raised the proposal for a "geographical principle" regarding the allocation of seats.[89] Although China's ultimate aspiration was, of course, to attain a permanent seat alongside the great powers, this was not realistic in the early League years and was first raised as a proposal for immediate implementation in 1926.[90] That proposal would prove unsuccessful. However, the inclusion of geographical factors in the allocation of non-permanent seats was considerably more fruitful. The premise of interventions on this point, more literally referred to by China's delegates as the "continental principle" (*fenzhouzhuyi*), was that the Council's non-permanent seats should embody equal representation of world regions.[91]

[84] Memorandum by Sir C. Hurst on Upper Silesia, C 16545/92/18, 326–328, in *Documents on British Foreign Policy 1919–1939*, (eds Medlicott, W.N., Douglas Dakin, and M.E. Lambert, eds.) (Her Majesty's Stationery Office 1968), 236–238, 238.

[85] Wellington Koo, "Presence of French Troops and Exercise of Jurisdiction by French Courts-Martial" (1921) 2 *League of Nations Official Journal* 683.

[86] Kaufman n 77, "In Pursuit of Equality and Respect," 616–617.

[87] ibid 620–621; Henry Wilson Harris, *An Account of the Second Assembly of the League of Nations* (Daily News 1921) 10.

[88] Ryan Martínez Mitchell, "Monroe's Shadow: League of Nations Covenant Article 21 and the Space of Asia in International Legal Order" (2021) 2 TWAIL Review 200; Green Haywood Hackworth, *Digest of International Law* (U.S. Government Printing Office 1940) 443–445.

[89] Kaufman n 77, "In Pursuit of Equality and Respect," 623–624.

[90] ibid.

[91] Mitchell n 88, *Monroe's Shadow*, 217, 226.

In practice, of course, this constituted an argument for China's continuous presence on the Council as a small power representative of Asia. Though this principle was never adopted as an official League rule, it has lasted to the present day as a norm characterizing the election of members to most leading international organizations, especially those within the UN system.[92] The connection between these current practices and Chinese advocacy during the League years is generally overlooked in modern accounts of this norm.[93]

For China's core foreign policy issues, nonetheless, action outside of the League was necessary. The most important early official venue for such action was to be the Washington Naval Conference. The US proposal for a "conference on limitation of armaments" in July 1921 was motivated by many factors of both domestic and foreign policy.[94] In terms of its geopolitical context, the initiative carried the weighty goals of both resolving China's outstanding demands and settling the major points of contention between the US, UK, and Japan, especially in the realm of the ongoing naval arms race. Issues of disarmament had been postponed at the Paris Peace Conference, and were only now to be dealt with.[95]

The Washington Naval Conference was convened between November 12, 1921 and February 6, 1922. The invitation sent by US Secretary of State Charles Evans Hughes to eight states (the UK, Japan, France, Italy, China, Belgium, the Netherlands, and Portugal) would lead to discussion of naval reductions as well as the situation in the Far East.[96] With respect to the crucial Shandong matters, negotiations at Washington proceeded via the "good offices" of Hughes as well as the British lead representative, and former Prime Minister, Arthur Balfour.[97] As had been the case at Versailles, the Chinese main delegates—Alfred Sze, Wellington Koo, and Wang Chung-Hui (Wang Chonghui)—were under great pressure to secure the return of Jiaozhou, which they managed with US/UK assistance.[98] Aside from this issue, the results of the Conference were widely viewed as at least incrementally accomplishing most of China's specific demands—for example, the arrangement for future conferences to evaluate the revision of the longstanding unequal treaty obligations.[99]

The sole agreement to which China was a member, the so-called Nine-Power Treaty, also required all parties to "respect the sovereignty, the independence, and the territorial and administrative integrity of China," though it simultaneously

92 ibid.

93 See, for example, Ingo Winkelmann, "Regional Groups in the UN" in Helmut Volger (ed.) *A Concise Encyclopedia of the United Nations*, 2nd ed. (Martinus Nijhoff Publishers 2010) 592–596.

94 Akira Iriye, *After Imperialism; the Search for a New Order in the Far East 1921-1931* (Atheneum 1969) 13–22; W. W. Willoughby, "China, Our Chief Far East Problem" (1922) 101 The Annals of the American Academy of Political and Social Science 237.

95 Burkman n 20, *Japan and the League of Nations*, 160.

96 Elihu Root, "Conference on the Limitation of Armament" (1922) 16 AJIL 159.

97 ibid 197.

98 Craft n 13, *V.K. Wellington Koo*, 69–71.

99 ibid.

legalized China's own obligations to provide free access to "the commerce and industry of all nations."[100] Essentially a multilateral quasi-constitutional agreement on China's international status, the agreement was hailed by Hughes as a "Magna Charta for China."[101] It could hardly escape the notice of more radical critics of imperialism and hierarchy, however, that an agreement of this nature still placed China in a subordinated, legislated-for position rather than treating it as an equal.[102] Nonetheless, with the conclusion of the agreements at Washington, China's status in international society, and the principle of its inherent right to maintain territorial integrity, were accorded recognition on a more universal basis than ever before.

10.3.2 Resistance and Future-oriented Initiatives

In China itself, the period of high activism and intensified political discourse brought about under the auspices of the May Fourth Movement was still underway.[103] Particularly significant in this regard was the founding of the Chinese Communist Party in Shanghai in mid-1921.[104] Among the earliest publications of leading party members on foreign issues would be those criticizing the Washington Conference as a forum for "collective invasion and joint-sharing of profits" by foreign commercial empires.[105] This darker view of the agreement was supported by the postponement of issues such as the envisioned conferences on tariffs and extraterritoriality to an unspecified later date, as well as by the ongoing practices of foreign military reprisals in China in response to alleged interstate wrongs.[106]

A very different approach to that of the Western great powers and Japan was then being taken by the emerging Soviet regime. Still unrecognized by the powers (as well as by China), the Soviet state's foreign policy in the early 1920s made a shift from emphasizing world revolution by oppressed proletarians to pursuing state recognition and the stabilization of its foreign relations and geopolitical situation.[107] With regard to Soviet–Chinese relations, one of the most important

[100] "Foreign Relations of the United States: Treaty Between the United of States of America, Belgium, the British Empire, China, France, Italy, Japan, the Netherlands, and Portugal. Signed at Washington February 6, 1922" (*Avalon Project*) <https://avalon.law.yale.edu/20th_century/tr22-01.asp> accessed July 12, 2025.

[101] Charles Evans Hughes, "Conference on the Limitation of Armament" (1922) 16 American Journal of International Law 159–233, 200.

[102] Cf. Mitchell n 5, *Recentering the World*, 136–142.

[103] Ya-pei Kuo, "The Making of the New Culture Movement: A Discursive History" (2017) 42 Twentieth-Century China 52.

[104] Ishikawa Yoshihiro, *The Formation of the Chinese Communist Party* (Columbia University Press 2013) (Joshua Fogel, trans.) 139, 221, 275.

[105] Zhou Enlai, "Huafu Huiyi Hou de Meiguo Diguozhuyizhe [American Imperialists After the Washington Conference]" *Chiguang* (Paris, February 15, 1924).

[106] William C. Dennis, "The Settlement of the Nanking Incident" (1928) 22 AJIL 593.

[107] Hu n 18, *Imperialism and Chinese Politics*, 255–257.

ventures in this respect was the proactive abandonment of former Russian rights to extraterritoriality under the unequal treaties.[108] As relations with the Soviet Union were rebuffed by the Beiyang government leaders under successive regimes, Soviet backing for the Chinese Communist Party as well as the development of Soviet co-operation with the Guomindang would hugely influence China's political future.[109]

Throughout the mid-1920s, both the Nationalist and Communist parties were excluded from League affairs, but exerted an increasingly important role in China's external affairs. This was in part due to the increasing strength of the Guomindang government based in Guangzhou as compared with the embattled Beiyang "warlord" regime (in which Duan had again returned to power), and in part due to the waves of activism, protests, strikes, and boycotts against imperial powers and the unequal treaties that were sponsored by both insurgent parties.[110] Continuing the legacy of an activist foreign policy public that had formed by the early post-Boxer Protocol years, intensified during the opposition to Yuan's regime during World War I, and reached a watershed point in the May Fourth Movement, these outpourings of pressure were met with reprisals from Beijing and, at times, from foreign powers.[111]

The situation during much of the 1920s was, thus, that at the same time as the Guomindang regime in the South was exerting pressure for a radical assertion of China's sovereignty and equal status with foreign empires, the Northern Beiyang government's representatives sought to achieve much the same goals within official diplomatic and legal settings. For these purposes they relied primarily on the same corps of diplomatic and international legal experts that had been in formation since the last years of the Qing Dynasty.[112] Figures such as Wellington Koo and Wang Chonghui, who would also continue to serve in key roles even after the Nationalist government's success in overturning the Beiyang government in 1928, represented a striking continuity of the foreign policy and international legal profession over the course of decades.[113]

Wang Chonghui played a key role in many of China's key interwar engagements with international law. On September 1, 1921, he had become China's first international judge as a deputy on the new Permanent Court of International Justice (PCIJ).[114] He was, however, extremely occupied during most of the 1920s with both diplomatic affairs and domestic politics, where he was a recurring figure in

[108] ibid.

[109] Hunt n 41, *The Genesis*, 102–104.

[110] Cf. Ming K. Chan, "Hong Kong in Sino-British conflict: Mass Mobilization and the Crisis of Legitimacy, 1912–26," in *Precarious Balance: Hong Kong Between China and Britain, 1842–1992* (Chan Ming K., ed.) (Routledge 2015) 27–57.

[111] Goto-Shibata Harumi, *Japan and Britain in Shanghai, 1925–31* (Springer 1995) 13–41.

[112] Cf. Strauss n 3, *Strong Institutions*, 169–170 ("Below the level of minister and vice-minister . . . both the consular and the diplomatic service remained remarkably constant").

[113] ibid.

[114] "Composition of the Court" (1921) 2 League of Nations Official Journal 929.

(often short-lived) caretaker governments with warlord backing.[115] In terms of his activities within the League, one significant role was Wang's participation as China's representative on the League of Nations Codification Commission beginning in 1924. As part of this initiative, Wang collaborated with the El Salvadoran jurist José Gustavo Guerrero, later President of the PCIJ and of its successor the International Court of Justice (ICJ), on a report calling for an end to special rights of foreigners abroad and a restrictive theory of state responsibility, as against the then prevalent permissive doctrines of intervention.[116] This report, with Guerrero as the drafter and Wang's endorsement of the initial text, would ultimately help to form the basis for later drafting efforts on state responsibility that departed from the subjective and interventionist practices established in the 19th century.[117]

Wang was also at the head of the Beiyang government's efforts at treaty revision, in the setting of the Special Tariff Conference held in October 1925 where, finally, the Chinese side had the opportunity to directly pursue national tariff autonomy (*guanshui zizhu quan*).[118] This would not be achieved via the conference; nor would the parallel issue of extraterritorial jurisdiction be effectively resolved.[119] Nonetheless, the interstate meetings and public engagement on these issues provided the setting for a dramatic assertion of principles of national sovereignty and self-determination. In the course of these dealings the PCIJ judge Wang even remarked that China was "no longer interested in treaty technicalities."[120]

This newly strident position was also on display in the 1926 Sino–Belgian dispute before the PCIJ concerning China's April 1926 denunciation of the Sino–Belgian Treaty of 1865. Prompted by Belgium's invocation of the Optional Clause of the PCIJ Statute, these would be China's only adversarial proceedings before a permanent international tribunal, as well as the closest that China's many complaints over unequal treaties ever came to actual legal adjudication.[121] Several leading international lawyers advised the Beiyang government to invoke the principle of *rebus sic stantibus* in denouncing the sixty-year-old treaty terms—the same move that China's own legal experts had contemplated as early as 1912.[122] China

[115] Nathan n 1, *Peking Politics*, 193–200, 238–239.

[116] League of Committee of Experts for the Progressive Codification of International Law, "Questionnaire No. 4 adopted by the Committee at its Second Session, held in January 1926: Responsibility of States for Damage Done in Their Territories to the Person or Property of Foreigners, Report of the Sub-Committee" [1926] 20(Special) AJIL.

[117] Shabtai Rosenne, ed. *The International Law Commission's Draft Articles on State Responsibility: Part 1, Articles 1–35* (Martinus Nijhoff Publishers 1991) 3–6.

[118] "Wang Chung-hui Scores Austen Chamberlain For Restricting China Tariff Asserts If Peking Agrees To Sign Tariff Treaty Under Such Restrictive Lines, Confab Would Sell Sovereignty Cheaply" *The China Press* (Shanghai, 26 September 1925).

[119] Ching-Chun Wang, "How China Recovered Tariff Autonomy" (1930) 152 The Annals of the American Academy of Political and Social Science 266–277, 269.

[120] "China Is Not Willing to Be Led by Hand: Is No Longer Interested In Treaty Technicalities, Says Dr. Wang," *The China Press* (Shanghai, November 19, 1925) *The China Press*, November 19, 1925.

[121] Wang n 119, "How China Recovered Tariff Autonomy," 274.

[122] Mitchell n 5, *Recentering the World*, 154, 160, 172.

objected to PCIJ jurisdiction on the basis that the dispute was political in nature, arguing that "no nation can consent to the basic principle of equality between States being made the subject of a judicial inquiry."[123] And, indeed, the ultimate outcome would be Belgium's withdrawal of its case amidst a diplomatic settlement of the dispute. As Hersch Lauterpacht would write afterwards, this result could be understood as a precedent for the idea that "political" disputes are presumed to be excluded from compulsory adjudication; though he nonetheless believed that, had the case gone forward, the PCIJ would have reached the opposite conclusion on this jurisdictional question.[124]

Chinese positions on international law's political limitations regarding impediments to state sovereignty did not, however, mean the abandonment of codification efforts. Wang's support for the League's Codification Commission was matched by important initiatives in other settings. At the Hague Codification Conference of 1930, for example, China's delegate Wu Chaoshu argued for the principle that states had duties to treat foreign nationals on an equivalent basis to their own (i.e., what has come to be accepted in various contexts as the "national treatment" norm), rather than to accord exceptional legal protections to foreign citizens.[125] In the context of international law societies such as the Institut de Droit International (IDI), Chinese members also made important proposals. Zhou Wei, who was still one of China's most active diplomats at Geneva throughout the 1920s, argued at the IDI's 1926 annual meeting for an official condemnation of the use of armed reprisals.[126]

This proposed norm, entailing the position that that "measures of coercion or reprisal ... should be excluded forever from modern international law," would have gone considerably further than the subsequent Kellogg–Briand Pact of 1928 "outlawing war as an instrument of national policy."[127] Zhou's proposal helped to push the IDI towards a position "tending to exclude as much as possible" war as a sanction under international law.[128] Along with other Chinese advocacy during the 1920s, and in connection with the increasingly vocal protest and resistance against foreign empires' uses of force on Chinese territory (often in the guise of reprisals), the advocacy of China's diplomats helped to embody aspirations for a new and less violent international legal system. This was, of course, a vision shared with many global reformist voices on international law during the interwar years.[129]

[123] Hersch Lauterpacht, *The Function of Law in the International Community* (Oxford University Press 2011), 207–209.

[124] ibid.

[125] *Acts of the Conference for the Codification of International Law, No. 14-17* (League of Nations, 1930).

[126] *Annuaire de l'institut de Droit International*, vol. 33/1, 1927 (1927) 515.

[127] Axel Moller, "The Briand–Kellogg Pact" (1932) 3 Nordisk Tidsskrift Intl Ret 3, 94–71.

[128] W. van. Hille, "Étude sur la Responsabilité Internationale de l'État" (1929) 56 Revue de Droit International et de Législation Comparée 531.

[129] Quincy Wright, "The Outlawry of War" (1925) 19 AJIL 76; Rafael Altamira, *Cuestiones internacionales y de pacifismo* (C. Bermejo 1932) 74–75.

10.4 China in the League's Collapse and Reconstruction

10.4.1 International Law during a Time of Crisis

The Nationalist quasi-unification of China in 1928 prompted a new era of rapprochement between the Chinese government and many global partners but also the radical worsening of relations with Japan, which soon turned to a policy of outright conquest as its prospects to solidify an informal ("Monroe-like") hegemony dwindled.[130] Initially, however, this longstanding threat was overshadowed by the outbreak of a major conflict with the Soviet Union, in which the Nationalist ambition for restoring territorial integrity manifested in the seizure of the Russian-built and controlled China Eastern Railway, leading to a *de facto* state of war.[131] The success of the USSR's military intervention as a means of recovering its "rights" over the rail infrastructure on Chinese soil was an early sign of the limits of the Kellogg–Briand Pact, which both parties had joined even as guns were blazing across the Northeast.

The overthrow of the Zhang Xueliang regime in Northeast China and the establishment of the "Manchukuo" puppet state in 1931 as a form of disguised Japanese annexation prompted Chinese attempts to bring the matter before the Council for a resolution.[132] These developments were, of course, occurring in the midst of a dramatic economic collapse whose effects were felt severely throughout the West, and which affected the willingness of states, particularly the great powers, to respond to the crisis.[133]

Chinese appeals to the League Council in 1931 were very limited in their efficacy. Although Article 10 of the League Covenant referred to the prohibition of "external aggression" and preservation of "territorial integrity," it did not establish automatic enforcement mechanisms for violations of these norms, holding only that "the Council shall advise upon the means by which this obligation shall be fulfilled."[134] Soon after the outbreak of the conflict on September 18, 1931, the Council passed a resolution for interim measures calling for a drawdown of hostilities.[135] However, it neither identified Japan as the aggressor nor applied sanctions. Chinese delegates argued in vain at Geneva, in bilateral diplomacy, and in the public sphere for action in this direction, but it was not forthcoming. Ultimately, advocacy efforts did result in a December 10 resolution creating a commission of inquiry "to study

[130] Mitchell n 88, Monroe's Shadow, 223–224.
[131] Michael Walker, *The 1929 Sino-Soviet War: The War Nobody Knew* (University Press of Kansas 2021).
[132] Arthur K. Kuhn, "The Lytton Report on the Manchurian Crisis" (1933) 27 AJIL 96, 97.
[133] Henry L. Stimson, *The Far Eastern Crisis* (Harper 1936) 5.
[134] "Covenant of the League of Nations" (*Avalon Project*) <https://avalon.law.yale.edu/20th_century/leagcov.asp> accessed 12 July 2025.
[135] Kuhn, "The Lytton Report," 96.

on the spot and to report to the Council on any circumstances which, affecting international relations, threaten to disturb the peace between China and Japan, or the good understanding between them upon which peace depends."[136] The non-committal description and limited mandate of this purely advisory committee (the "Lytton Commission") stood in stark contrast to the reality of Japanese annexation on the ground in "Manchukuo."[137] Meanwhile, the much stronger actions contemplated under Article 16, involving comprehensive economic and diplomatic sanctions for states committing wars of aggression, were never applied.[138] The Commission itself produced a set of recommendations that, in the eyes of most Chinese observers, were woefully inadequate to any resolution of the dispute.[139]

The question of possible sanctions was an important one, and indeed the Chinese advocacy on this point was very likely a major factor in bringing about a new significance for this tool of enforcing international legal norms. US Secretary of State Henry L. Stimson pioneered a "non-recognition doctrine" regarding the Japanese initiative, which was embraced by China and has become an important precedent for other situations of illegal aggression (and similar violations of fundamental norms of international law). Still, although this policy was appreciated in China, it was actually framed by the US as an *alternative* to economic sanctions or other strong forms of enforcement.[140] Throughout the troubled 1930s, public opinion in the United States was heavily in favor of maintaining strict neutrality and avoiding foreign entanglements. Successive rounds of neutrality legislation were seen by some as preventing the application of sanctions to Japan (or to other aggressors).[141] The other great powers, as well, were reluctant to pursue enforcement via the League machinery, instead affirming non-recognition as the organization's sole sanction.[142] This situation would only change by the early 1940s, as total war loomed in both Asia and Europe.

Despite these challenges, Chinese representatives during the years of progressive Japanese invasion argued at length for the need to radically revise international relations in the direction of the rule of law and the recognition of the rights of small and weak states. As the global situation decayed, opportunities to work towards such developments were increasingly limited. Nonetheless, diplomats in Geneva

[136] ibid.
[137] Ryan Mitchell, "Manchukuo"s Contested Sovereignty: Legal Activism, Rights Consciousness, and Civil Resistance in a "Puppet State"" (2016) 3 Asian Journal of Law and Society 351.
[138] ibid.
[139] Notably, the Commission's recommendations included recognition of the "rights and interests of Japan in Manchuria," significant "autonomy" for the region then governed by a Japanese puppet regime, and "[s]ome form of temporary international cooperation" that was left extremely ill-defined. Kuhn, "The Lytton Report," 99; see also Chen Tiqiang. "Wei Shenme Bixu Queding Qinlüe Dingyi? [Why Is It Necessary to Define Aggression?]" [1953] 2 Shijie Zhishi 9, 9–10.
[140] Foreign Relations of the United States, 1931, vol. 5 (1931), 496-497.
[141] See Edwin Borchard, "Dragging America into War" [1934] 40 Current History 392.
[142] Extraordinary Assembly of the League of Nations, March 11, 1932; February 19, 1933.

were able to significantly mobilize international opinion in favor of China's stances, even if the League itself was largely ineffectual.[143]

The former Shanghai judge Liang Yuen-li (Liang Yunli), for example, spent much of the 1930s in the United States, advocating for new rules limiting the use of force, non-recognition of annexations, and sanctions against Japan after its invasion of Manchuria. He argued in numerous settings that "whatever runs counter to the settlement of disputes by pacific means is war, and as such must be considered as in violation of the Kellogg pact."[144] In his postwar role as a key figure within the UN Secretariat, as well, Liang would continue this advocacy in prominent international law settings, including in coordinating work with the International Law Commission.[145] Another of China's contributions to the early development of the norm on non-recognition of annexation came with its support for Ethiopia in the face of Italy's invasion, where it stuck to the stance of non-recognition even as most states shifted their positions by 1938.[146]

Despite the intense focus of China's foreign policy and international law community on the crisis of Japan's invasion, the country's other longstanding concerns were not forgotten. As the international law student Wang Tieya would say to Hersch Lauterpacht when meeting him in London in 1937, "the joint aspiration of the whole people is to overcome these [unequal] treaties."[147] In practice, the abandonment of the extraterritorial rights for the UK and the US would only finally be effected in 1942, as a result of wartime coordination. The same would be the case for many other critical issues regarding China's international legal status and its (and other non-Western peoples') equality within the international system.

10.4.2 Envisioning Postwar Legal Architecture

The Atlantic Charter signed by Franklin Roosevelt and Winston Churchill in 1941 rejected in principle "territorial changes that do not accord with the freely expressed wishes of the peoples concerned."[148] It also stood, once again, for the principle of national self-determination as a fundamental norm of international

[143] Stephen G. Craft, "Saving the League: VK Wellington Koo, the League of Nations and Sino-Japanese Conflict, 1931–39" (2000) 11 Diplomacy and Statecraft 91.

[144] "Stimson View Held Aid to Peace Pact" *The New York Times* (New York, August 14, 1932).

[145] Yuen-Li Liang, "Le développement et la codification du droit international" (1948) 73 Recueil des Cours 407.

[146] Chang Li, "China's Response to the Ethiopian Crisis (1935-1938)", in *East Asians in the League of Nations: Actors, Empires and Regions in Early Global Politics* (eds Christopher R. Hughes and Hatsue Shinhara) (Singapore: Palgrave Macmillan, 2023) 171-193, 181-189.

[147] Lin Hai, "Wang Tieya: Guojifa Shengya Qi Shi Er Zai [Wang Tieya: A 72-Year-Long International Law Career]" (*China Law Society*, May 19, 2015) <https://www.chinalaw.org.cn/portal/article/index/id/16096/cid/71.html> accessed July 12, 2025.

[148] "Atlantic Charter" (Avalon Project) <https://avalon.law.yale.edu/wwii/atlantic.asp> accessed July 12, 2025.

organization. Yet these commitments were relatively vague and their practical relevance to states outside of Europe was in doubt. Indeed, Churchill himself informed Parliament the same year that these principles would not affect Britain's colonial empire and would be restricted in application to European peoples.[149]

Chinese foreign policy officials and experts, notably Wang Chonghui, responded to the Atlantic Charter by calling for direct application of its protections to non-Western peoples as well as greater specification of the envisioned norms.[150] This should involve, for example, much clearer and more definite understandings of what would constitute illegal uses of force and acts of aggression. Similar views were expressed by China's other representatives, including Foreign Minister T. V. Soong (Song Ziwen), who in many wartime speeches and meetings advocated for greater international legal protections for weak states, as well as the "freedom of all Asiatic nations" and even "economic justice for Asia."[151] These ambitious goals went beyond what the United States or United Kingdom were willing to contemplate in their initial discussions regarding postwar order.

The question of globalism versus regionalism was a major topic of debate during the wartime years, amidst uncertainty over the war's outcome as well as a sense that China's interests (and those of other non-Western peoples) might not be adequately dealt with by another global organization. The example of the League's inefficacy in response to the Japanese invasion was, of course, the most pertinent example in this respect. Yet other criticisms, such as that of the League's lack of progress in promoting decolonization even before the eruption of the crises of the 1930s, and its general weakness in terms of norm enforcement, also motivated new proposals. Some of these took the form of proposed regional organizations, such as a "United Nations of the Pacific" (Taipingyang Lianheguo) proposed by Zhou Gengsheng in 1943.[152] Wang, Soong, and others called for new forms of regional solidarity as well as a strengthened "executive" power at the international level for the enforcement of norms and the application of measures against states committing acts of aggression.

Between the Cairo Conference of 1943 and the San Francisco Conference of 1945, Chinese officials were closely involved with planning for what would become

[149] Hansard, HC Deb September 9, 1941 vol 374 cc67-156.

[150] Wang Chonghui, "Zhan Hou Shijie zhi Jiti Anquan: Zuori Zai Zhongguo Zhengzhixue Hui Nian Hui Jiangyan [Postwar Collective Security: Yesterday"s Address at the Annual Meeting of the China Political Science Association]" *Da Gong Bao* (Chongqing, July 7, 1942).

[151] "Soong Says China Wants Asia Freed," *The New York Times* (New York), June 10, 1942.

[152] Zhou Gengsheng, "Zhanhou de Nanyang [The South Sea after the War]" [1943] 11 *Nanyang Yanjiu* 1; "Zhou Gengsheng Zhu Wenlun: Taipingyang Yongjiu Zhixu [Zhou Gengsheng"s Essay: A Permanent Order for the Pacific]" *Yishibao* (Chongqing, January 8, 1943); "Zhou Gengsheng Lun Taipingyang Yongjiu Zhixu; Bixu Wanquan Jiechu Riben Wuzhuang; Zhuzhang Chengli Taipingyang Lianheguo [Zhou Gengsheng Writes on a Permanent Order for the Pacific; Japan Must be Permanently Disarmed; Advocates Setting Up a United Nations of the Pacific]" *Zhongyang Ribao Saodang Bao Lianhe Ban* (Nanjing, January 8, 1943).

the United Nations system. At Dumbarton Oaks in 1944, China's proposals emphasized the progressive codification of international law as an important activity of the organization, as well as the need for an empowered international tribunal.[153] As China's lead delegate, Wellington Koo once again represented his country in the setting of negotiations for the creation of a new international organization and the dramatic reorganization of interstate legal relations.[154] While he and China's other representatives would be a consistent presence arguing for the establishment of robust norms of legal constraint on the unilateral power of individual states, there were many issues on which they could not hope to exercise a decisive influence. In terms of major technical questions, one key example was the voting procedure and institution of the veto within the UN Security Council, which was decided between the US and the Soviet Union in the context of the early 1945 Yalta Conference.[155]

At the San Francisco Conference, China's delegation supported compulsory jurisdiction of the ICJ over disputes, as well as related principles such as the view that international law itself should be the standard for what was a "purely domestic" matter and that the Security Council could take action to enforce ICJ judgments.[156] The Soviet Union, China, and several other states also shared the view that in the Charter provisions regarding Trusteeship and Non-Self-Governing Territories, the goal of "independence" should be explicitly included in both sections.[157] Another Chinese suggestion was for the Council to be able to take provisional measures in addressing ongoing threats to international peace and security, in advance of a final resolution. This was, of course, a suggestion based in significant part on the memory of the League's delays and failure in resolving China's own invasion by Japan.[158]

10.5 Conclusion

China's entry into and activities within the League of Nations marked a major transformation in its international status and in the ability of Chinese diplomats, statesmen, and experts to bring forward their own proposals about global affairs. The promises of the conferences of Versailles and Washington, and of China's ongoing interactions at Geneva, proved difficult to realize in practice. Although China's territorial integrity was "guaranteed" on a multilateral basis, and its role as a participant in global governance became an accepted aspect of international

[153] Robert C. Hilderbrand, *Dumbarton Oaks: The Origins of the United Nations and the Search for Postwar Security* (UNC Press Books 2001) 229.
[154] ibid.
[155] Clark M. Eichelberger, *Proposals for the United Nations Charter: What Was Done at Dumbarton Oaks* (Commission to Study the Organization of Peace 1944) 6–7.
[156] Evans Luard, *A History of the United Nations* (St. Martin's Press 1982) 64–67.
[157] ibid 60–62.
[158] ibid.

society, it continued to be marginalized in terms of major decisions regarding decades-old imperialist arrangements on its territory, and also subjected to unilateral coercion. Despite these challenges, Chinese officials argued with substantial success for key principles including non-Western representation in international organizations, the inability of regional hegemonic arrangements to invalidate rights of (recognized) states, and even the applicability of *rebus sic stantibus* to unequal treaty clauses.

The Japanese invasion of first the Northeast and then all of China led to a period of crisis throughout the 1930s and early 1940s in which Chinese representatives abroad and intellectuals at home argued for the principles of non-recognition and sanctions against violators of the norms prohibiting aggression. This advocacy, along with related activism, protests, and other forms of national resistance, helped to bring about global consensus that, in the post-World War II order, the use of force would have to be tightly constrained by international law. Other now globally accepted principles, including self-determination, national sovereignty over financial and economic affairs, and rejection of secret treaties, among others, were also greatly bolstered by Chinese advocacy and activism. Simultaneously, Chinese representatives expressed consistent commitment to both peaceful resolution of international disputes and codification of international law.

It may be the case that China's activities and influence during the League years have not yet been fully appreciated from the perspective of general histories of international law. Although it was never a leading player in the strictly hierarchical interwar geopolitics, China's unique status within it as a "newly arrived" middle power that was intimately embedded in legal and diplomatic relations with every major state facilitated forms of engagement that left major lasting impacts. Cross-factional agreements on China's semi-colonial predicament and the basic aims of any legitimate foreign policy agenda helped to facilitate considerable continuity between the international law platforms of the interwar years and those of the People's Republic of China after 1949. The League era thus served as an important foundation for China's later rise as a core power within the UN system, for its pursuit of institutionalized and (largely, but not exclusively) legalistic interstate relations, and for its advocacy on behalf of marginalized states within international society, especially when this advocacy reinforces its own global prestige.

11
Professionalizing International Law in China during the Republican Period

Pasha L. Hsieh

11.1 Introduction

Professionalizing the discipline of international law in Republican China had salient implications for the modern international legal order. The founding of the Republic of China (ROC) or Republican China in 1912, and its legal strategies during two World Wars, raised the status of the fragile country to that of a recognized "civilized nation."[1] Using declassified diplomatic archives and extensive interviews, this chapter fills a gap in the existing literature on the history of international law.

Once known as the "public law of Europe," international law study has inevitably focused on the state practice of the Global North.[2] The dissemination and universalization of international law in other regions has been marginalized in pertinent research. China's approach to international law has recently been underscored due to geopolitical issues such as the US–China trade war and conflicts in Ukraine and the Taiwan Strait. Yet, existing research largely ignores the normative and political contributions of Republican China. International law scholars have conventionally focused much more on the developments in the Qing Dynasty and the People's Republic of China (PRC) than on the 'Grotian moment' in the ROC.[3] This approach overlooks the legal strategies utilized by China's first-generation international lawyers to argue for and defend their country, which remained disadvantaged in international society. These jurists and diplomats played a critical

[1] The preamble to the 1907 Hague Convention, to which China was a signatory, first mentioned the term, "civilized nations": see Gustavo Gozzi, "History of International Law and Western Civilization" (2007) 9 International Community Law Review 353, 354, 365.

[2] See generally, Alexander Orakhelashvili, "The Idea of European International Law" (2006) 17(2) European Journal of International Law 315, 336–338.

[3] See, for example, Bing Bing Jia, "A Synthesis of the Notion of Sovereignty and the Ideal of the Rule of Law: Reflections on the Contemporary Chinese Approach to International Law" (2010) 53 German Yearbook of International Law 11; Xue Hanqin, *Chinese Perspectives on International Law: History, Culture and International Law* (Martinus Nijhoff Publishers 2012).

Pasha L. Hsieh, *Professionalizing International Law in China during the Republican Period* In: *Histories of International Law in China*. Edited by: Ignacio de la Rasilla, Jiangyu Wang, and Congyan Cai, Oxford University Press.
 DOI: 10.1093/oso/9780198888345.003.0011

role in shaping Asian diplomacy and creating both the League of Nations and the United Nations (UN).[4]

Most ROC international lawyers relocated to Taiwan in 1949 as the result of civil war. Authentic, key diplomatic instruments, such as the Treaty of Nanking (1842) and the Treaty of Shimonoseki (1895), also moved to Taipei's National Palace Museum. However, the derecognition of the ROC government after the loss of the China seat in the UN and the tendency for Taiwan-focused studies made research on international law in Republican China less popular.[5] Regardless of political differences, the legacy of international law in the Republican China has a profound impact on the legal and academic capacity across the Taiwan Strait. Consequently, this research is of significance not only to Greater China but also to global governance.

The chapter argues that statism, pragmatism, and idealism underpin the major features of the international law approach of Republican China.[6] These characteristics propelled the law of nations to universally valid normative claims and enabled modern China's intellectual shift to the civilized nation concept. Following this Introduction, the chapter proceeds as follows. Section 11.2 sheds light on the introduction and development of international law as an academic discipline in late Qing and Republican China. It also explores the cultivation of Chinese jurists and diplomats in the government, international law societies, and practice in the Shanghai Mixed Court. Section 11.3 examines international lawyers' utilization of international law in advancing Chinese diplomacy. In particular, it provides a systematic analysis of the ROC's legal strategies for dealing with unequal treaties and Japanese aggression, as well as participating in the UN and international tribunals. Section 11.4 concludes the chapter by highlighting the findings of the research. The findings of the chapter underscore the key characteristics of Republican China's approach to international law and demonstrate Asia's significant role in shaping international law, which is critical to global governance.

[4] International court judges nominated by the Republic of China (ROC) include Wang Chung-hui (1921–1939) and Cheng Tien-hsi (1939–1946) of the Permanent Court of International Justice (PCIJ), Hsu Mo (1946–1957) and Wellington Koo (1957–1967) of the International Court of Justice (ICJ), and Mei Ju-ao (1946–1948) of the International Military Tribunal for the Far East (Tokyo War Crimes Tribunal).

[5] United Nations General Assembly Resolution 2758 (25 October 1971) transferred the China seat from Taipei to Beijing.

[6] The Republican Chinese characteristics are distinct from well-known "Chinese characteristics," which refer to the PRC's neo-Confucian approach that focuses on the Westphalian concept of absolute sovereignty.

11.2 Transforming International Law in the Qing Dynasty and Republican China

In conventional understanding, China's first treaty was the 1689 Treaty of Nerchinsk (尼布楚條約) concerning Sino–Russia border disputes.[7] It is relatively little known that the 1662 peace treaty concluded between Koxinga (郑成功 1624–1662) of the defunct Ming Dynasty and the Dutch governor constituted the prelude to international agreements in Chinese history.[8] The treaty facilitated the withdrawal of Dutch troops, ending almost 40 years of Dutch rule over Taiwan.[9] Because these treaties were largely reciprocal, they did not stimulate intellectual interest in international law in China. Understanding the law of nations only became a national necessity when the Qing Court was exposed to unequal treaties that were tremendously harmful to China, beginning with the 1842 Treaty of Nanking with Britain. Against this background, the ROC expedited the professionalization of international law through the statist approach to legal education and government reforms.

11.2.1 International Law as an Academic Discipline

W. A. P. Martin (丁韪良 1827–1916), an American Presbyterian missionary, first systematically introduced international law into China by translating Henry Wheaton's *Elements of International Law* in 1864.[10] The Chinese translation, known as *Public Law of All Nations* (万國公法), had a profound impact on the discipline in the East Asia.[11] In 1873, Martin began his teaching of "Law of Nations" at the Interpreters College (同文馆).[12] He became China's first professor of international law. The Interpreters College was also the first national institution that offered an international law course. Nonetheless, the fact that only 9 of 102 students enrolled in the elective course suggests that international law was viewed as a fringe discipline.[13] The Imperial University of Peking (京师大学堂), the predecessor to

[7] Wang Tieya, "International Law in China: Historical and Contemporary Perspectives" (1990) 221(II) Recueil des Cours de l'Académie de Droit International 195, 227.

[8] Hungdah Chiu, "The Reception of Modern International Law in China" (1973) 9 Chengchi Law Review 189, 189, 192. The peace treaty consists of Dutch and Chinese versions, which include 18 and 16 provisions respectively.

[9] Taiwan was under Dutch rule from 1624 to 1662.

[10] Lydia Liu, *The Clash of Empires: The Invention of China in Modern World Making* (Harvard University Press 2004), 113–115.

[11] ibid; Han San-hee, "The Circulation of International Legal Terms in East Asia" (2010) 14 Asian Law Institute Working Paper 14, 3–25.

[12] Lin Xuezhong, *From Law of Nations to Public Law Diplomacy: The Introduction, Interpretation and Application of International Law in Late Qing* (从万国公法到公法外交—晚清国际法的传入诠释与应用) (Shanghai: Shanghai Ancient Books Publishing House 2009) 126–127, 153.

[13] ibid 130.

today's Peking University, subsequently replaced the Interpreters College. Martin was appointed as the president of the new university. In the Department of Law, public international law and private international law were collectively taught as "Law of Negotiation" (交涉法).[14]

There were several key features of the reception of international law in the late Qing era. First, the Western notion of sovereignty came as an intellectual shock. According to *Public Law of All Nations*, "sovereignty is the supreme power by which any State is governed" and a state should function "independently of foreign powers."[15] That book, in some sense, enabled Chinese officials to understand that the privilege of extraterritoriality and the right of foreign warships to navigate in internal waters actually encroached upon Chinese sovereignty.[16]

Second, the university course entitled "Law of Negotiation" illustrated that international law was commonly regarded as a tool of negotiation rather than as a universal value. For instance, before the First Opium War, Lin Zexu's (林则徐) ban on the opium trade was based on passages from Emerich Vattel's 1758 *Law of Nations* on embargos and blockades.[17] His letter to Queen Victoria challenged Britain's double standards on opium and urged the British to obey Chinese law in the same way that foreigners follow British law in the United Kingdom.[18] Instead of believing the normative truth of international law, Lin's intention was simply to use "Western" arguments to persuade the British.[19] With respect to the reception of international law, it is premature to conclude that 19th-century Chinese scholars were positivists.[20]

Finally, the difference between Vattel's universalism and Wheaton's parochial understanding of international law, which was limited to Christian civilization, did not influence Chinese reception of international law.[21] The discipline of international law in the Chinese context rarely considered the diverse schools of thought on the application of international law. As pragmatism dictated, the concept of natural law as the basis of international law was de-emphasized.

[14] ibid 153; Sun Huei-min, "From Tokyo, Beijing to Shanghai: Japanese Legal Education and the Development of Chinese Lawyers (1902–1914) (从东京、北京到上海:日系法学教育与中国律师的养成 [1902-1914])" (2002) 3 Journal of Legal History Studies 157, 176.

[15] Peter Zarrow, *After Empire: The Conceptual Transformation of the Chinese State, 1885–1924* (Standford: Stanford University Press 2012) 91 (discussing Wheaton's explanation of sovereignty).

[16] See, for example, Arnulf Becker Lorca, *Mestizo International Law: A Global Intellectual History 1842–1933* (Cambridge: Cambridge University Press 2014) 116–117.

[17] Liu (n 10) 119; Chi-Hua Tang, "China–Europe" in Bardo Fassbender and Anne Peters (eds), *The Oxford Handbook of the History of International Law* (Oxford: Oxford University Press 2012) 704–705.

[18] See, for example, Appendix: Lin Zexu's Communication to Queen Victoria, reprinted in Liu (n 10) 235–237.

[19] Liu (n 10) 119.

[20] Arnulf Becker Lorca, "Universal International Law: Nineteenth-Century Histories of Imposition and Appropriation" (2010) 51 Harvard Journal of International Law 475, 486–490, 534–535.

[21] Odd Arne Westad, *Restless Empire: China and the World Since 1750* (New York: Basic Books 2012) 81–82.

During the first wave of the reception of international law, translations from Europe and the United States were critical to China's efforts to enter the family of nations. One example of an important treatise is Charles de Martens' *Le Guide Diplomatique*.[22] This book helped early Chinese diplomats, starting from those posted to the London-based Chinese Legation in 1877, understand diplomatic customs and rules.[23] In addition, the translation of Robert Joseph Phillimore's *Commentaries upon International Law* became China's first book on private international law.[24]

The second wave of international law learning shifted to Japan. Although Japan's exposure to the law of nations began with *Public Law of All Nations*, the Meiji Restoration led to Japan outpacing China in legal reform and legal material translations. Japan's complete abolition of extraterritoriality in 1899 and its military victory over Russia in 1905 transformed the state into Asia's first "civilized nation."[25] Thus, the Qing government "looked East" for international law instructors. From 1905 to 1908, Iwai Takafumi served as an invited international law professor at the Peking College of Law (京师法律学堂).[26] These significant events, along with language proximity and lax immigration requirements, encouraged Chinese students to pursue legal studies in Japan. Chinese graduates from Japanese schools subsequently influenced the ROC's discipline of international law.

Until the 1920s, the majority of China's international textbooks were translated from Japanese either by Japanese professors in China or by Chinese students in Japan.[27] These translations fortified the Chinese understanding of statehood and sovereignty under international law.[28] Another conspicuous influence was Japan's international law terminology. The most notable example is the term "international law," which Jeremy Bentham first coined in 1789.[29] Mitsukuri Rinsho's translation

[22] The Chinese translation, entitled Xingyao Zhizhang, is based on Le Guide Diplomatique, Précis des Droits Et des Fonctions des Agents Diplomatiques Et Consulaires; Suivi d'un Traité des Actes Et Offices Divers Qui Sont du Ressort de la Diplomatie, Accompa De Pièces Et Documents Proposés Comme Exemples (5th edn, Leipzig, Paris: F. A. Brockhaus, A. Durand 1866).

[23] See Immanuel Hsü, *China's Entrance into the Family of Nations, 1858–1880* (Massachusetts: Harvard University Press 1960) 167–184 (discussing the posting of Qing envoys to European nations).

[24] The Chinese translation, entitled Geguo Jiaoshe Bianfalun, is based on Robert Phillimore, "Commentaries upon International Law, Private International Law or Comity" (3rd edn, London: Butterworth 1889).

[25] The Paquete Habana, The Lola, 175 US 677 (1900) 700.

[26] Yuan-Sheng Huang, "The Reception of Law and Modern Chinese Law (法律继受与现代中国法)" (Taipei: Angle Publishing 2007) 64.

[27] For the list of texts translated from Japanese, see Rune Svarverud, *International Law as World Order in Late Imperial China: Translation, Reception and Discourse, 1847–1911* (Leiden: Brill 2007) 269–302.

[28] Zarrow (n 15) 98–100.

[29] Jeremy Bentham created the English term "international law" in his book wherein "international law" replaced the older term "law of nations": see Jeremy Bentham, *An Introduction to the Principles of Morals and Legislation* (Oxford: Clarendon Press 1876); Mark Weston Janis, *America and the Law of Nations 1776–1939* (Oxford: Oxford University Press 2010) 12–13.

of "international law" (国际法) mostly replaced the Chinese indigenous translation, "Public Law of All Nations" or "Public Law" (公法), in the 1920s.[30]

Moreover, as many Japanese-trained students joined the revolutionist camp and served as ROC bureaucrats, their international law understanding influenced the early Republic's foreign policy. Honoring the principle of *pacta sunct servanda* (treaties must be observed) by confirming the validity of Qing treaties that they deemed unfair indicated their commitment to international law. Given the failure of the Taiping Rebellion (1850–1864) and the short-lived Republic of Formosa (1895), the ROC's founding fathers understood that only the "civilized" approach could gain the West's diplomatic recognition.[31] In addition to the new government's legitimacy, the pragmatic need behind the search for recognition was to attain the legal capacity for the purposes of securing foreign loans to finance ammunition and infrastructure.

Although Wheaton introduced the civilized nation concept to China, the concept only received attention when Qing officials participated in the two Hague Peace Conferences.[32] Foreign-trained ROC elites drove the standard of civilized nations in international law to be the nation's highest guiding principle.[33] In the words of Sun Yat-sen (孙中山 1866–1925), the first provisional president of the ROC, upholding this principle would help China "obtain the rights of a civilized state."[34] To demonstrate the centrality of statism and pragmatism in its international law approach, the ROC government made international law a mandatory subject in both judicial and diplomat examinations in the 1910s.[35] The subject also became compulsory in the college curriculum. For instance, Beiyang University had the longest teaching hours of international and comparative law courses, including public international law (10 credit hours) and English law (12 credit hours).[36]

[30] Hungdah Chiu, "The Development of Chinese International Law Terms and the Problem of Their Translation into English" (1968) 27(3) The Journal of Asian Studies 485, 490.

[31] The Taiping Rebellion was a significant political and religious upheaval against the Qing Court. The Republic of Formosa in Taiwan declared independence following the Treaty of Shimonoseki and existed for about six months before being taken over by Japan.

[32] Liu (n 10) 135; Lin (n 12) 306–340.

[33] For discussions on the standard of civilized nation in international law, see James Sloan, "Civilized Nations" (*Oxford Public International Law*, 2011) <https://opil.ouplaw.com/display/10.1093/law:epil/9780199231690/law-9780199231690-e1748> accessed June 10, 2024.

[34] Proclamation of President Sun Yat-sen on the Establishment of the Republic of China on 1 January 1912.

[35] Li Qicheng, "The 1900 Judicial Examination (宣统二年的法官考试)" (2002) Journal of Legal History Studies 197, 198–207; Li Zhaoxiang, "New Changes to Early Diplomacy of the ROC: Focusing on Diplomatic Legislation (中华民国早期外交的新变化)" in Jin Guangyao and Wang Jianlang (eds), *Chinese Diplomacy in the Beiyang Era* (北洋时期的中国外交) (Shanghai: Fudan University Press 2006) 91, 107–108.

[36] Beiyang University is the predecessor to Tianjing University: see Pan Maoyuan and Liu Haifeng (eds), *Compilation of Reference Materials related to China's History in Modern Education* (中国近代教育史资料汇编) (Shanghai: Shanghai Education Press 2007) 419. International law courses offered by Peking University's Department of Law were divided into "International Law in Peace Time" and "International Law of War": see Pan (n 36) 395.

After the 1920s, America became the most important country for China's third wave of international law learning. US influences on Chinese diplomacy and universities shaped the ROC's new-generation international lawyers. Located in Shanghai, Soochow University Law School offered the first English-taught international law course.[37] John Wu (吴经熊 1899–1986), who received his Juris Doctor (JD) from the University of Michigan in 1921, served as the Dean of Soochow University Law School in the 1920s. Moreover, many graduates from Tsinghua School, which was founded with the American remission of the Boxer Indemnity, pursued college and legal education in America.[38] Starting in the 1920s, overseas-trained lawyers started returning to China to augment the quality of China's legal scholarship in international law.

Prominent examples were Zhou Gengsheng (周鲠生 1889–1971) of Peking University and Wang Huacheng (王化成 1903–1965) of Tsinghua University, who studied at Paris and Chicago universities, respectively. Zhou's 1929 *Outline of International Law* (国际法大纲) became the first international law textbook authored by a Chinese national.[39] Hsu Mo (徐谟 1893–1956), who later became a judge of the International Court of Justice (ICJ), established the Department of Diplomacy and served as a department chair at the Central Political Institute in Nanjing in the 1930s.[40] During the Sino–Japanese war (1937–1945), international law professors fled to the temporary capital of Chongqing and continued teaching at the Central Political School and the National Southwestern Associated University, composed of Peking, Tsinghua, and Nankai universities.[41] The Central Political Institute became the National Chengchi University after the war and was subsequently reestablished in Taipei.

[37] As the 1930–1931 curricula demonstrate, a four-credit-hour international law course was offered in both English and Chinese at Soochow, also known as the Comparative Law School of China: see generally, Alison Conner, "Training China"s Early Modern Lawyers: Soochow University Law School" (1994) 8(1) Journal of Chinese Law 1.

[38] In 1901, the Qing Court agreed to pay indemnities to the foreign powers, including the United States, for their losses in the Boxer Rebellion. Funded by the American remission of the Boxer Indemnity, Tsinghua Xuetang served as a preparatory school for Chinese students to pursue college education in the United States. It was renamed Tsinghua School in 1912 and became National Tsinghua University in 1928.

[39] Chen Tiqiang, "The People"s Republic of China and Public International Law" (1984) 8 Dalhousie Law Journal 3, 11.

[40] The Department of Diplomacy continues to exist as part of National Chengchi University in Taipei and remains a major source for Taiwanese diplomats.

[41] National Southwestern Associated University (Lianda) was set up in 1938. The international law professors included Tsui Shu-chin in the Department of Political Science and Yan Shutang in the Department of Law. John Israel, *Lianda: A Chinese University in War and Revolution* (Standard: Stanford University Press 1998) 178–183.

11.2.2 Professional Jurists and Diplomats

The role of the Ministry of Foreign Affairs (MOFA) in promoting international law and cultivating first-generation international lawyers was equally vital. The MOFA was built upon Zongli Yamen (總理衙門 Office of Foreign Affairs), the first centralized agency of international affairs, which the Qing Court set up in 1861.[42] The Boxer Protocol of 1901 mandated that the agency become "a Ministry of Foreign Affairs (外務部), which takes precedence over the six other Ministries of State."[43] The movement to reform the MOFA's bureaucratic status was carried out by meeting foreign expectations of an efficient "single window" channel for diplomatic communication.

As none of the Qing officials selected from the imperial examination formally studied law, their successful assertion of international law was confined to isolated incidents. To illustrate, during the Prussian–Danish war, a Prussian battleship captured three Danish merchant ships in China's Bo Hai Gulf in 1864.[44] Based on the Chinese translation of Wheaton's book *Public Law of All Nations*, Zongli Yamen protested against this capture because of its violation of Chinese sovereignty over territorial seas.[45] Prussia's subsequent release and compensation for detaining the ships surprised the Qing government with the "usefulness" of international law. Notably, the often criticized notion of extraterritoriality exemplifies the problem.[46] The consular jurisdiction granted to Western powers was "not [initially] construed as a derogation of sovereignty."[47] Instead, it was provided under a convenient assumption that foreigners should settle their own disputes without disturbing Chinese courts.

China's first-generation international lawyers also emerged on the world stage. These jurists dominated the diplomatic circles of various regimes, including the Provisional Government (Nanjing, 1912), the Beiyang Government (Beijing, 1912–1928), the Nationalist Government (Nanjing and Chongqing, 1927–1949), and the ROC government that relocated to Taipei in 1949.[48] Their positions as

[42] Imperial Decree to Establish the Tsung-li Ya-men (Office of Foreign Affairs): see Feng Mingzhu and Shen Luxun, *A Century of Resilient Tradition: Exhibition of the Republic of China's Diplomatic Archives* (百年传承 走出活跃：中华民国外交史料特藏) (2011) 260.

[43] Boxer Protocol (1901), art. XII.

[44] Chen (n 39) 7; Tang (n 17) 705.

[45] The Qing government's assertion on the territorial sea was influenced by the Chinese translations of Henry Wheaton"s Elements of International Law. James Li Zhaojie, "The Impact of International Law on the Transformation of China's Perception of the World: A Lesson from History" (2012) 128 Maryland Journal of International Law 128, 135-138.

[46] E.g., Menno T Kamminga, "Extraterritoriality (2020)" (*Oxford Public International Law*, 1 January 2020) <https://opil.ouplaw.com/display/10.1093/law:epil/9780199231690/law-9780199231690-e1040> accessed June 11, 2024.

[47] Milton J. Helmick, "United States Court for China" (1945) 14(18) Far Eastern Survey 252, 252–253.

[48] The Guangzhou Military Government coexisted with the Beiyang Government from 1917 to 1927.

heads of state or foreign ministers enabled them to apply international law to negotiations without bureaucratic interference.

The impact of international lawyers on Chinese diplomacy and international tribunals was significant. For instance, many Americanized diplomats, due to their substantial American education, fortified the ROC–US alliance during the Republican period.[49] Wu Tingfang (伍廷芳 1842–1922), a Hong Kong lawyer trained in Lincoln's Inn, was China's first international lawyer. He was involved in the Treaty of Shimonoseki, which ceded Taiwan to Japan, and subsequently sided with the ROC government.[50] Chen Tien-his (郑开锡 1884–1970) and Wang Chung-hui (王宠惠 1881–1958), graduates of Yale University and University College London respectively, served as Permanent Court of International Justice (PCIJ) judges.[51] Wang was also the first international lawyer serving as the Chief Justice of the ROC Supreme Court.

Hsu Mo and Wellington Koo (顾维钧 1888–1985), Columbia University and George Washington University-trained lawyers, became ICJ judges. Mei Ju-ao (梅汝璈 1904–1973) received his JD from the University of Chicago and served as the judge of the International Military Tribunal for the Far East (Tokyo War Crimes Tribunal). US-educated John Wu (吴经熊 1899–1986) was the principal drafter of the first ROC Constitution (1946), in which a provision honoring "treaties and the Charter of the United Nations" was included in modern China's constitution.[52]

These international lawyers galvanized MOFA reforms. The first legal document that delineated the MOFA's authority was the 1911 Organizational Outline for the ROC Provisional Government (中华民国临时政府组织大纲).[53] Provisional President Sun Yat-sen appointed Wang Chung-hui as the first foreign minister of the new Republic. The Nanjing regime lasted only four months. The venue of foreign affairs power transferred to Beijing, where the Beiyang government led by Yuan Shikai (袁世凯 1859–1916) sat. Paradoxically, due to the Beiyang warlords' lack of interest and ability in diplomacy, the MOFA became highly professionalized. Yuan's promise not to intervene with the MOFA allowed foreign minister Lu Zhengxiang (陸征祥 1871–1949) to lay the groundwork for the ROC's diplomatic system.[54]

[49] Stacey Bieler, *Patriots or Traitors: A History of American Educated Chinese Students* (London: Routledge 2003) 167–168. The ROC–US alliance continued after the ROC government moved to Taiwan in 1949.

[50] Wu Tingfang became acquainted with Guo Songtao, China's first minister to the United Kingdom, and subsequently served as the legal advisor to Li Hongzhang, one of Qing's most respected politicians.

[51] Ole Spiermann, "Judge Wang Chung-hui at the Permanent Court of International Justice" (2006) 5(1) Chinese Journal of International Law 115, 117.

[52] Li Xiuqing, "John C. H. Wu at the University of Michigan School of Law" (2008) 58(4) Journal of Legal Education 545, 545 (Nicholas Howson tr); ROC Constitution (1946), art. 141.

[53] Li (n 35) 99–100.

[54] Shiyuan Hua, "Lue Lun Yuan Shikai Yu Beijing Zheng Fu Wani Jiao [Brief Discussion on Yuan Shikai and the Diplomacy of the Beijing Government]" in Jin Guangyao and Wang Jianlang (eds), *China's Diplomacy during the Beiyang Period* (北洋时期的中国外交) (Publishing House 2006) 157, 165–166.

Based on the Qing legacy and Lu's reform, the Beiyang MOFA became the top governmental ministry, and the foreign minister ascended to a critical position in the political hierarchy.[55] In 1912 the Beijing Congress passed China's first Organization Act of the Ministry of Foreign Affairs (外交部官制), which detailed its constitutional mandate.[56] Because managing treaty affairs was China's priority task, the ad hoc Treaty Study Commission (条约研究会) was set up in 1912 and later evolved into the Department of Treaty (条约司).[57] The Department, which was in charge of treaties related to the League of Nations, remained the Ministry's most important division.

Lu's reform also expedited the professionalization of Chinese diplomats. To avoid the nepotism that had affected the Qing envoys' capacity in language skills and international law, Lu selected overseas Chinese students to join the government and introduced a diplomat examination in 1916.[58] Wellington Koo, who was then studying under John Bassett Moore of Columbia University, was invited to be Yuan's English language secretary.[59] Hsu Mo also joined the Beiyang Government after passing the diplomatic service examination in 1919.

From 1928 onwards, Chiang Kai-shek's Nationalist Government re-unified China following the Northern Expedition (1926–1928) and continued to enlist university professors to serve in government positions. For instance, according to the official records published in 1935, 25.6 percent and 30 percent of 86 prominent diplomats were PhD holders and lawyers, respectively.[60] During World War II, the ROC's highest decision-making power was vested in the Supreme National Defense Council. Both the Council and the MOFA were dominated by international lawyers, such as Wang Chung-hui and Wang Shijie (王世杰 1891–1981). Despite the lack of a Chinese equivalent to the United States Office of the Legal Advisers, the international lawyers serving as professional diplomats enhanced the legalist approach to diplomacy.

[55] The Foreign Minister, who was nominated by the Prime Minister and was appointed by the President, would be the acting Prime Minister should the incumbent Prime Minister resign.

[56] Li Zhaoxiang (n 35) 99–100.

[57] ibid 101. The Department of Treaty was later renamed as the Department of Treaty and Legal Affairs under Article 3 of the 1984 Organization Act of the Ministry of Foreign Affairs.

[58] The ROC's diplomat examination was based on the 1913 Provisional Rules on the Diplomat and Consular Examination, 1915 Diplomat and Consular Examination Ordinance, and the 1919 Diplomat and Consular Examination Law.

[59] John Bassett Moore was Columbia"s first full professor of international law: see Jonathan Clements, *Wellington Koo: China* (London: Haus Publishing 2008) 31, 174.

[60] Yue Qianhou, *Study on the Human Resources Development Mechanism of ROC Diplomats* (民国外交关系史研究) (Beijing: Orient Publishing 2004) 159–166.

11.2.3 International Law Societies

International law education and MOFA reforms prompted the involvement of ROC jurists and diplomats in international law societies in China and abroad. The participation of Qing officials in the London-based International Law Association (ILA) was China's first encounter with the Western concept of international law societies. Founded as the Association for the Reform and Codification of the Law of Nations in 1873, the ILA remains one of the world's most esteemed international law societies.[61] Guo Songtao (郭嵩焘 1818–1891), the Qing's first minister appointed to the United Kingdom, and Japanese minister Ueno Kagenori (上野景范 1845–1888) were both invited to attend the ILA meeting in 1878.[62] Both Guo and his successor Marquis Zeng Jize (曾纪泽 1839–1890) were subsequently elected to be ILA honorary secretaries.[63] Their ILA experiences introduced them to the vast scope of international law and fortified their belief in "importing" additional international law knowledge to China. Later, in Changsha of Hunan Province, the Public Law Association (公法学会) and the Law Association (法律学会) emerged as China's nascent international law societies.[64] They were both established in 1894, with the primary goal of increasing the international law understanding that is pivotal for the purposes of revising treaties.[65] The aforementioned societies preceded the Japanese Society of International Law, the American Society of International Law, and the Netherlands Society of International Law which were founded in 1897, 1906, and 1910, respectively.[66] Nonetheless, the two Chinese societies soon ceased operation because of the failure of the Guangxu Emperor's short-lived reform.

Similarly, the top-down approach influenced the formation of international law societies in the ROC. Lu Zhengxiang (陸徵祥), the key Beiyang reformer of the MOFA, initiated the Society of International Law (国际法学会) in 1912.[67] This was China's first full-fledged, nationwide international law society with strong government support, representing pragmatism in merging academic research with governmental needs. As a Qing envoy to the first two Hague Peace Conferences,

[61] Cecil Olmstead, "The International Law Association: A World-wide Organization for Development and Promotion of International Law" (1973) 43 Nordic Journal of International Law 18, 18.

[62] Hsü (n 23) 206–207.

[63] ibid 207.

[64] Lin (n 12) 70–71.

[65] ibid.

[66] Toshiya Ueki, "Greeting from the President (2022)" (Insitute of International Law, 2022) <https://jsil.jp/home/about-jsil> accessed June 11, 2024; Janis (n 29) 149; Nico Schrijver, "A Missionary Burden or Enlightened Self-interest? International Law in Dutch Foreign Policy" (2010) 57(2) Netherlands International Law Review 209, 210. The Japanese Society of International Law was founded in 1897: see Yoshiro Matsui, "The Social Science of International Law: Its Evolution in Japan" (2002) 45(25) The Japanese Annual of International Law 47, 47.

[67] Chi-hua Tang, "A Study on China's Participation of the Hague Peace Conferences, 1899-1917 (清末民初中国对海牙保和会之参与)" (2005) 23 NCCU Journal of History 45, 72–73.

Lu understood the strategic importance of implementing the treaties on the resolution of international disputes and the laws of war.[68] British and American proposals to exclude extraterritorial disputes from the jurisdiction of the Permanent Court of Arbitration (PCA), which was established in 1899, prompted him to urge the Qing Court to expedite legal reform.[69] To increase Chinese influence on the Court, the Qing government nominated several PCA members, including Wu Tingfang and former Belgium Minister of State Jules Van den Heuvel.[70] With Wang Chung-hui's support, Lu founded the Society of International Law. This initiative aimed to prepare the ROC to actively participate in the Third Peace Conference and to strengthen the country's standing as a civilized nation.[71] Although the conference never took place due to World War I, the attempt to enter the family of nations as a civilized nation garnered official support for building China's international law capacity.

Based on a proposal by the US Minister to China, Paul S. Reinsch, Lu Zhengxiang and Wellington Koo established the Chinese Social and Political Science Association (中国社会及政治学会) in Beijing in 1915.[72] The Association, modeled on the American Political Science Association, became China's first academic society of political science.[73] While the Association was not an international law society, the majority of its work concerned "international law and diplomacy."[74] The waning of the Society of International Law was attributed to the failure of the Third Peace Conference to take place, and its overlapping membership with the Association made the latter the most prominent academic society for promoting international law in China.

Interestingly, ROC President Li Yuan Hong (黎元洪) supported the Association by making a $1,000 private donation.[75] The direct involvement of Reinsch, together with Professor W. F. Willoughby of Princeton University and Professor Henry C. Adams of the University of Michigan, also enhanced American influence in the elite circle of Chinese diplomats.[76] The Association's English publication, *The Chinese Social and Political Science Review* (中国社会及政治学报), published 24 volumes from 1916 to 1941. The majority of authors were Chinese,

[68] These conventions, which represented China's first participation in multilateral treaties, include the Convention for the Pacific Settlement of International Disputes and the Convention with respect to the Laws and Customs of War on Land.

[69] Tang (n 67) 62, 67.

[70] ibid 66–69.

[71] ibid 73. With President Yuan Shikai's support, Lu also organized the Preparatory Society for the Third Hague Conference (Bao He Hui Zhun Bei Hui), which convened in the Ministry of Foreign Affairs from 1912 to 1917: see Tang (n 70) 73–74.

[72] "Editorial Note: The Origin of the Association" (1916) 1 The Chinese Social and Political Science Review 1, 2.

[73] ibid 1.

[74] ibid; James Brown Scott, "The Chinese Social and Political Science Association" (1916) 10(2) The American Journal of International Law 375, 376.

[75] Editorial Note (n 72).

[76] Scott (n 74) 375, 377.

and the topics covered critical issues on international law and diplomacy that the Chinese government faced. In terms of its content, the Review can be regarded as China's first international law journal.

11.2.4 International Mixed Court

In Southern China, the growth of the legal profession and the International Mixed Court, also known as the Shanghai Mixed Court (上海公共租界会审公廨), enabled ROC legal talents to familiarize themselves with Western adjudication mechanisms. The Court existed in the Shanghai International Settlement and continued from the 1860s to the 1920s.[77] Modeled after Japan's Barristers Law, the 1912 Provisional Regulations on Lawyers governed the qualification and disciplinary procedures for the legal profession.[78] By the 1930s, the Shanghai Bar Association became the nation's largest bar association.[79] The law schools of the English-speaking Soochow University and the French-speaking Aurora University also made the city an intellectual centre of comparative law.[80]

The Mixed Court system made Shanghai's legal landscape increasingly complex.[81] The *in personam* jurisdiction under the multiplicity of courts was the most challenging legal experiment on Chinese soil. The Shanghai International Settlement, which co-existed with the French Concession, constituted large exclaves of the extraterritorial zone.[82] The treaty right of consular jurisdiction granted to foreigners gave them immunity from Chinese jurisdiction. For example, the United States Court for China and the British Supreme Court for China and Japan were conferred jurisdiction over American and British citizens, respectively.[83] Legally speaking, unlike colonies, China did not lose its sovereignty over the Shanghai International Settlement. Rather, the Chinese government continued to exercise jurisdiction over Chinese and non-treaty foreigners (i.e. nationals domiciled in countries that were not accorded extraterritorial rights). Consequently, to

[77] Pär Cassel, "Mixed Court of the Shanghai International Settlement" Max Planck Encyclopedias of International Law (*Oxford Public International Law*, 2020), <https://opil.ouplaw.com/display/10.1093/law-mpeipro/e3151.013.3151/law-mpeipro-e3151> accessed June 11, 2024.

[78] Xiaoqun Xu, *Chinese Professionals and the Republican State: The Rise of Professional Associations in Shanghai 1912–1937* (Cambridge: Cambridge University Press 2001) 108.

[79] Alison Conner, "Lawyers and the Legal Profession during the Republican Period" in Kathryn Bernhardt and Philip Huang (eds), *Civil Law in Qing and Republican China* (Standford: Stanford University Press 1994) 215, 229, 237.

[80] Aurora University was known as Zhendan Daxue: see Alison Conner, "The Comparative Law School of China" in Stephen Hsu (ed), *Understanding China's Legal System: Essays in Honor of Jerome A. Cohen* (New York: New York University Press 2003) 210, 222–225.

[81] Xu (n 78) 229; Thomas Stephens, *Order and Discipline in China: The Shanghai Mixed Court 1911–1927* (Washington: University of Washington Press 1992) vii–xi.

[82] Stephens (n 81) xi; Manley Hudson, "The Rendition of the International Mixed Court at Shanghai" (1927) 21(3) American Journal of International Law 451.

[83] Hudson (n 82) 454.

deal with cases involving Chinese and non-treaty foreign defendants, the Mixed Court was set up.[84] The "mixed" nature of the Court meant that Chinese magistrates and foreign consular representatives, known as foreign assessors, jointly tried the cases.[85] Eventually, the presence of foreign judges and lawyers with diverse nationalities presiding over a single case became the norm.

The Mixed Court's establishment was based on convenience rather than on treaty rights. None of the treaties gave foreign consulates the power to appoint judges to the Court. As the British government acknowledged, the sole "legal" basis for the Court's foundation was President Yuan Shikai's 1913 declaration to permit the continuity of existing foreign "privileges and immunities" based on "established usages."[86] Arguably, while privileges and immunities granted under previous treaties may have provided Western powers with extraterritorial jurisdiction, they did not establish a legal basis for setting up a "court." Therefore, Western-educated ROC judges opposed the authority of the court. The ROC Supreme Court eventually found that due to the absence of a legal foundation, the cases decided by the *de facto* Mixed Court lacked legal effect and thus "a plea of *res judicata* [could not] be entertained" in the Chinese courts.[87]

Notwithstanding the legal challenges to the Mixed Court's legal authority and its non-recognition of *stare decisis*, its jurisprudence demonstrated the salient impact of legal cases on the nation.[88] In 1925, the Beiyang government sought an injunction to avoid the destruction of certain ammunition that the Mixed Court had ordered.[89] In the following year, the Mixed Court dealt with the Netherlands' request to extradite a German national who had committed crimes in Dutch Java.[90] The Court declined the request on the ground that the Netherlands–China treaties confined extradition to Dutch citizens.[91] These complex cases made Shanghai a training ground for China's first-generation international lawyers. Ni Zhengyu (倪征日奥 1906–2003), a graduate of Soochow and Stanford Universities, was a prominent example. Before Ni was appointed as the Chief Advisor to the ROC Prosecutor Group in the Tokyo War Crimes Trial, he had gained substantial experience as a commercial lawyer and judge in Shanghai.[92]

[84] The French Mixed Court was also established in the French Concession and had jurisdiction over French nationals.

[85] Hudson (n 82) 460.

[86] Stephens (n 81) 69–70.

[87] ibid 70–71 citing Case Brought on Appeal from Kiangsi 16th Day 3rd Month, 6th Year of the Chinese Republic.

[88] ibid 93–94.

[89] Hudson (n 82) 454.

[90] Stephens (n 81) 96 citing Consul-General for the Netherlands v. Weidemann, Shanghai Mixed Court (May 1, 1926).

[91] ibid.

[92] Ni Zhengyu was elected as the first People's Republic of China (PRC) judge of the ICJ: see Ling Yan, "In Memoriam: Ni Zhengyu" (2004) 3(2) Chinese Journal of International Law 693, 693–695.

11.3 International Law in Chinese Foreign Policy

With the guiding "civilized nation" concept, China's first-generation international lawyers took a positivist stance on international law and adopted a legalist approach to tackle diplomatic obstacles.[93] The ROC's assertive international legalism approach was evidenced in the revision of unequal treaties and in its participation in international organizations and courts. These case studies refute the claims that the ROC succumbed to imperialism.[94] The efforts of the ROC's international lawyers also influenced the global order in the post-World War II era.

11.3.1 Dealing with "Unequal Treaties"

Revising unequal treaties, as noted earlier, was a major catalyst for professionalizing international law in Republican China.[95] None of the early translations of Western books alluded to such a concept.[96] The term "unequal treaties" first appeared in the 1923 Kuomintang (Chinese Nationalist Party) declaration that condemned the Qing Dynasty's conclusion of such treaties and pledged to "restore China's free and equal status."[97] Thereafter, the term became popular and buttressed Chinese nationalism, enabling the Chinese Communist Party (CCP) to use the "century of humiliation" slogan as a powerful weapon against the West and the Kuomintang from the 1920s on.[98]

The concept of unequal treaties began with the 1842 Treaty of Nanjing. The common features of unequal treaties included the rights of extraterritoriality, leased territories, the stationing of troops, and navigation on inland waters.[99] These privileges were "unequal" because they lacked reciprocity and encroached upon Chinese sovereignty. However, many scholars overlooked the fact that some of the rights requested by Western powers were aimed at remedying the unfair treatment encountered by Westerners in China. For example, the Treaty of Wangxia, the first unequal treaty with the United States, mandated the abolition of Chinese

[93] William C. Kirby, "The Internalization of China: Foreign Relations at Home and Abroad in the Republican Era" (1997) 150 The China Quarterly 433, 441.
[94] See, for example, Mao Tse-tung, "Report to the 2nd National Congress of Worker's and Peasant's Representatives" (January 23, 1934).
[95] See Anne Peters, "Treaties, Unequal" (*Oxford Public International Law*, 2018) <https://opil.ouplaw.com/display/10.1093/law:epil/9780199231690/law-9780199231690-e1495> accessed 11 June 2024.
[96] Hungdah Chiu, "Comparison of the Nationalist and Communist Chinese Views of Unequal Treaties" in Jerome A. Cohen (ed), *China's Practice of International Law: Some Case Studies* (Massachusetts: Harvard University Press 1972) 239, 241–246.
[97] ibid 245–246.
[98] Alison A. Kaufman, "Testimony before the U.S.-China Economic and Security Review Commission: Hearing on 'China's Narratives Regarding National Security Policy'" (March 10, 2011) 3.
[99] Wang (n 7) 252–253.

law banning foreigners from learning Chinese.[100] The Treaty of Tianjin prohibited Chinese official documents from referring to the British as "barbarians."[101]

Arguably, the treaty right of extraterritoriality that Chinese intellectuals often condemned was not (at least not fully) based on an imperialist design or purpose.[102] Rather, it protected foreigners from suffering the effects of Qing criminal proceedings that frequently forced confession by torture. On the "positive" side, foreign powers in the respective treaties promised to relinquish extraterritoriality should China revamp its legal system to be on par with Western standards.[103] This treaty obligation, along with the experiences in the two Hague Peace Conferences, prompted modern China to expedite its legal reform.

The attempt to end the unequal treaty system posed a complex legal challenge. The system, intertwined with the most-favored-nation (MFN) treatment, started China on a vicious cycle. Although the MFN clause was not conventionally understood as part of unequal treatment, this procedural requirement was more detrimental than other substantive treaty rights. Under Article 8 of the 1843 Treaty of the Bogue, the Chinese Emperor agreed that any "additional privileges or immunities" granted to other nations would be extended to British subjects.[104] It was the prelude to the unilateral, instead of reciprocal, MFN provision that subsequent treaties included.[105] The unequal treaties system became a locked-in regime.

On the basis of the MFN claim, the United Kingdom enlarged its consular jurisdiction in accordance with a subsequent US treaty; moreover, Mexico and Switzerland could gain extraterritoriality despite the absence of such a treaty arrangement.[106] The legal effect of unequal treaties has been controversial, as the unequal nature can stem from force or various types of coercion.[107] The positivist approach of the ROC's international lawyers was demonstrated by their non-denial of the unequal treaties' validity and by their search for legal justification to revise or abrogate such treaties.[108] Differing from ROC jurists, decision-makers in the early PRC simply considered unequal treaties *void ab initio*, which, in turn, led to them not developing a consistent legal approach to the treaty regime.[109] Importantly,

[100] US–China Treaty of Wangxia (signed on July 3, 1844), art. 18.

[101] UK–China Treaty of Tianjin (signed on June 26, 1858), art. 51.

[102] Matthew Craven, "What Happened to Unequal Treaties? The Continuities of Informal Empire" (2005) 74(3–4) Nordic Journal of International Law 335, 346.

[103] See, for example, UK–China Commercial Treaty (signed on September 5, 1902), art. 12; US–China Commercial Treaty (signed on July 28, 1903), art. 15.

[104] UK–China Treaty of the Bogue (signed on October 8, 1843), art. 8. The Treaty of the Bogue was the supplemental treaty to the 1842 Treaty of Nanjing.

[105] In the modern trade regime, the most-favoured-nation (MFN) requirement accords reciprocal treatment: see General Agreement on Tariffs and Trade (opened for signature 30 October 1947, entered into force 1 January 1948) 55 UNTS 187, art. 1.

[106] Albert Putney and Raymond Buell, "The Termination of Unequal Treaties" (1927) 21 Proceedings of the American Society of International Law at Its Annual Meeting (1921–1969) 87, 96.

[107] Ian Brownlie, *Principles of Public International Law* (7th edn, Oxford: Oxford University Press 2008) 619.

[108] Chiu (n 96) 267.

[109] ibid 259, 267.

upholding the civilized nation principle, the ROC did not directly challenge the normative value of the doctrine of *pacta sunct servanda*. To circumvent this doctrine, the ROC's international lawyers resorted to three legal approaches which illustrate the overarching characteristic of pragmatism in the international law approach.

First, based on the suggestion of foreign legal counsel to the Beiyang Government, the ROC declared war against Germany and Austria-Hungary during World War I.[110] The goal underlying this opportunistic declaration of war was to invalidate Chinese treaties with these powers.[111] In addition to declaring the bilateral treaties invalid, the ROC revoked the extraterritorial privileges of Germany and Austria-Hungary and took over German concessions in Tianjin and Hankou.[112] The ROC also disarmed enemy troops and accommodated them as prisoners of war in compliance with the 1899 Convention with respect to the Laws and Customs of War on Land.[113] These experiences constituted the ROC's first trial for abolishing foreign privileges and the first implementation of the laws of war in China.[114]

Second, the Chinese Senate claimed the absence of congressional ratification as a justification to invalidate the Sino–Japanese Treaties of 1915, which were commonly known as the Twenty-One Demands. Such demands compelled the Beiyang Government to confirm Japan's "succession" to German rights over Shandong at the end of World War I.[115] Since Japan insisted on the validity of the treaties, the ROC's attempt to abolish the 1915 treaties at the Paris Peace Conference was futile.[116] The Chinese delegation refused to sign the Treaty of Versailles because Article 156 of the Treaty mandated the transfer of German rights in Shandong to Japan.[117] In 1923, the ROC Senate passed a resolution invalidating the 1915 treaties.[118] In the Senate's view, such treaties should be *void ab initio* because they lacked congressional ratification.[119] The weakness of such a claim lies in the fact

[110] China declared war against Germany and Austria-Hungary on 14 August 1917.

[111] Arnold Pronto, "The Effect of War on Law—What Happens to Their Treaties When States Go to War?" (2013) 2(2) Cambridge Journal of International and Comparative Law 227, 230.

[112] Chen-Feng Tsai, "Zong Guo Show Guan De Ao Sh Guan Wei Dui Ji Jun Xie Zhi Yan Jiu (1917–1922) [The Research of China's Taking over German and Austro-Hungarian Embassy Guards and Weapons" (中国收管德奥使馆卫队及军械之研究) in Hui-Min Chou (ed.), *The Interpretation and Application of International Law in China* (国 际法在中国的的解释与运用) (Beijing: Office of Foreign Affairs 2012) 81, 97–101.

[113] ibid 86, 98.

[114] Germany relinquished rights and privileges under the 1921 peace treaty with the ROC.

[115] During World War I, Japan declared war against Germany and occupied the Shandong Peninsula. After the war, Japan requested that the German concessions in Shandong be transferred to Japan.

[116] See also, Stephen R. Mackinnon, "Review of Stephen Craft, *V. K. Wellington Koo and the Emergence of Modern China*" (2006) 28(1) The International History Review 192.

[117] Based on Washington's mediation, Japan agreed to return Shandong to China at the 1922 Washington Naval Conference.

[118] Lin-chun Wu, "Appealing to Legal Procedure: China's Endeavour to Abolish the Twenty-One Demands in 1923 (1923年北京政府廢除《中日民四條約》之法理訴求)" (2008) 3 New History 157, 170.

[119] ibid 171.

that Yuan's administration was considered China's sole legitimate government and that the country's internal political changes could not affect the validity of treaties.

Lastly, the most broad-ranging claim against unequal treaties was the reliance on *rebus sic stantibus* (a fundamental change of circumstances) that Zhou Gengsheng actively advocated.[120] He believed that *rebus sic stantibus* would have enabled China to assert a vital change of circumstances that warranted the denunciation of the treaties. Both the Beiyang Government and the National Government resorted to revision clauses in treaties and the principle of *rebus sic stantibus* as the basis for renegotiating the treaties. The ROC's invalidation of the 1865 Sino–Belgium Treaty was a landmark case.

After the ROC government unilaterally terminated the treaty, Belgium brought a complaint against China before the PCIJ.[121] Belgium argued that Article 46 of the treaty solely conferred on Belgium the right to revise the treaty and that China had no right to denunciate it.[122] In anticipation of the PCIJ proceedings, China intended to rely on *rebus sic stantibus* as its major defense.[123] As UK-led Western powers attempted to improve ties with Chiang's National Government, Belgium reluctantly agreed to the ROC's request for treaty revision and withdrew its complaint from the PCIJ.[124] The renegotiated 1928 Treaty of Amity and Commerce with Belgium became the precedent for China's treaty revisions. In the midst of World War II, characterized by the ROC's new treaties with the United States and Britain that abolished extraterritoriality, all unequal treaties ceased to exist in 1943.[125] Correspondingly, foreign concessions and the Mixed Court came to an end in Republican China.

11.3.2 Legal Battles against Japanese Aggression

The ROC's legalist approach to unequal treaties demonstrated Chinese international lawyers' positivist stance on international law.[126] Influenced by US President Woodrow Wilson's Fourteen Points, the idealism of the ROC's international law approach contributed to its Grotian moment.[127] The Republican

[120] Tang (n 17) 707; Chiu (n 96) 255, fn 64.

[121] Craven (n 102) 368–369.

[122] Tang (n 17) 708.

[123] ibid.

[124] *Denunciation of the Treaty of 2 November 1865 between China and Belgium (Belgium v. China)* (1929) P.C.I.J., Ser. A, No. 18 (Order of May 25).

[125] Putney and Buell (n 106) 97–98.

[126] In comparison, other "semi-peripheral jurists" also employed various strategic approaches to international law: see Lorca (n 20) 49–52, 221–251.

[127] At the Paris Peace Conference, the Chinese delegation intended to rely on Wilsonianism to resolve the Shandong Problem: see Stephen Craft, *V. K. Wellington Koo and the Emergence of Modern China* (Lexington: University Press of Kentucky 2004) 56–57. For additional discussions on the Grotian moment, see Tom Sparks and Mark Somos, "Grotian Moments: An Introduction" (2021) 42 Grotiana 179, 180–191.

Chinese characteristics also influenced the ROC's legal battles against Japanese invasion. The ROC was a founding member of the League of Nations, which was established as a result of the Paris Peace Conference. Wellington Koo served as the chairman of the League Council, in which China was a non-permanent member.

To respond to Japanese aggression in Manchuria and to the creation of Manchukuo (1932–1945), Koo advised the government to appeal to the League of Nations on the basis of Articles X, XI, and XV of the League Covenant. To garner support from the United States, a non-member of the League of Nations, the ROC asserted that the Japanese invasion violated the 1922 Nine-Power Treaty and the 1928 Kellogg–Briand Pact. These two agreements, to which Japan, the United States, and the ROC were signatories, respectively ensured China's territorial integrity and outlawed war as an instrument of foreign policy.[128] The League Covenant, along with the two treaties, constituted the ROC's legal basis for the complaint against Japan. The reliance on the League of Nations and international treaties, while arguably acknowledging their limited effect, demonstrates the ROC's idealism in international law.

These well-devised claims prompted Washington to adopt the Stimson Doctrine, which confirmed the principle of *ex injuria jus non oritur* (law does not arise from injustice) by declining to recognize territorial changes by force. Japan's British legal adviser, Thomas Baty (1869–1954), devised the justification of Japan's right of self-defense in Manchuria.[129] However, such a defense did not hold much water. It encountered fierce criticism from both foreign and Japanese scholars. A prominent scholar opposing the official argument was Kisabura Yokota (横田喜三郎 1896–1993), who became Japan's first international lawyer sitting on the postwar Supreme Court.[130] Arguably, the Stimson Doctrine and the League of Nations' adoption of the Lytton Report, which condemned Japanese military action, were futile.[131] Yet, their relevance cannot be underestimated. The ROC's legal strategy effectively isolated Japan and gained moral support from the allies proved to be crucial for China's final victory.

The ROC's declaration of war also exemplified statism and pragmatism. At the inception of the Japanese invasion in 1937, the National Government only issued the Proclamation of Self-Defense and War of Resistance. It did not declare war against the Axis powers until the US Congress declared war on Japan after the Pearl

[128] "Milestones: 1921–1936, The Washington Naval Conference, 1921–1922" (Office of the Historian) <https://history.state.gov/milestones/1921-1936/naval-conference> accessed August 1, 2023.

[129] Shinya Murase, "Thomas Baty in Japan: Seeing Through the Twilight" (2002) 73(1) British Yearbook of International Law 315, 327–332.

[130] ibid 330; Takeso Shimoda, "In Memoriam: Dr. Kisaburo Yokota (1896–1993)" (1993) 36 Japanese Annual of International Law 1, 2–3.

[131] China Institute of International Affairs, *China and the United Nations: Report of a Study Group Set up by the China Institute of International Affairs* (New York: Manhattan Publishing Company for the Carnegie Endowment for International Peace 1959) 8 [China and the United Nations].

Harbor attack in 1941. In the interim *de facto* war period, neither Japan nor the ROC declared war on each other or terminated diplomatic ties. Generalissimo Chiang made this heavily-criticized decision based on international lawyers' advice.[132]

These lawyers' greatest concern was that the legal effect of the declaration of war would enable Japan to exercise the belligerent's right of visit and search on the high seas.[133] The exercise of this right would effectively cut off the supply of arms and ammunition to China by ships of neutral states through ports in Vietnam and Myanmar.[134] This was a matter of survival because most Chinese harbors were already occupied by Japan. Also, due to the US Neutrality Acts, the Chinese military could not receive American arms should the ROC become a belligerent.[135] Given its fragile military power, the ROC's long-overdue declaration of war in tandem with Washington and London was a pragmatic approach to ensure the support of allies.

11.3.3 Founding the UN and Participating in International Tribunals

The ROC's international lawyers also profoundly influenced postwar multilateral institutions. A preliminary, yet fundamental, debate concerned China's own status as one of the Big Four on par with the United States, the United Kingdom, and Russia. While Wang Shijie opposed the position, Wang Chung-hui and Wellington Koo determined that the Big Four status would raise China's international standing.[136] Among the Allies, Britain and Russia objected to the ROC's Big Four status, since they deemed China a "secondary power and preferred to place priority on Europe."[137] Nevertheless, they reluctantly succumbed to Roosevelt's insistence on China's status. As enshrined in Article 23 of the UN Charter, the ROC, a founding member of the UN, became one of the five permanent members of the Security Council.[138]

The ROC's idealism culminated in the 1944 Dumbarton Oaks Conversations and the 1945 San Francisco Conference that created the UN and the ICJ. To a

[132] "Letter Orders of Zhang Zhongfu and Others on Japan"s Declaration of War on China (张忠紱等对于日本对华宣战问题等函令)" (2010) 5(2) The Second Historical Archives of China 76–83.

[133] ibid; Carl Jacob Kulsrud, *Maritime Neutrality to 1780: A History of the Main Principles Governing Neutrality and Belligerency to 1780* (New Jersey: Lawbook Exchange Ltd 2000) 256–257.

[134] Letter Orders of Zhang Zhongfu and Others on Japan's Declaration of War on China (n 132).

[135] Presumably also because of the US Neutrality Acts that would ban arms exports, Japan did not declare war against China.

[136] Tang (n 17) 721.

[137] Zi Zhongyun, "Big Power Assurance of Peace versus the Principle of Equality among All Nations" in Ernest May and Angeliki Laiou (eds), *The Dumbarton Oaks conversations and the United Nations, 1944–1994* (Dumbarton Oaks Research Library and Collection 1998) 47, 55.

[138] Note that Article 23 remains the same even after the ROC on Taiwan left the UN.

certain extent, even the US delegates claimed that the ROC "placed too much faith in international law."[139] Other powers disagreed with the ROC's proposals for creating a permanent international police force and conferring compulsory jurisdiction on the ICJ.[140]

The ROC's proposals made unique contributions to the UN Charter in certain regards. Article 13, which mandates the General Assembly to promote "the progressive development of international law and its codification," was based on the Chinese delegation's proposal.[141] Article 13 subsequently led to the creation of today's International Law Commission, which is composed of prominent jurists committed to the statutory mandate.[142] Moreover, the ROC's main effort was reflected in the trusteeship system. The United States, the United Kingdom, and France initially objected to the ROC's position that the trusteeship's basic objective should be independence rather than merely self-government.[143] With smaller states' support, Article 76 includes the "progressive development towards self-government or independence" as the primary goal of trust territories.

In addition to the ROC's wartime diplomacy, its assertive legalism in international tribunals was distinct from the hesitant approach of the Qing Dynasty and the earlier PRC. Although the Qing government took part in the two Hague Peace Conferences that created the first multilateral arbitral mechanism, the PCA and Qing officials were suspicious about the impartiality of the West-dominated court. In 1909, the Qing government declined Portugal's proposal to resort to the processes of the PCA to adjudicate territorial disputes between China and Portugal-ruled Macao.[144]

The ROC's participation in international tribunals was based on an aspiration to act as a civilized nation. Its first attempt to resort to the PCA related to the declaration of war against Germany as a means to revoke unequal treaties. During World War I, Germany sought the assistance of the Netherlands, a neutral state, to attend to German interests in China.[145] The Beiyang Government and the Netherlands disagreed as to whether German arms and ammunition should be taken over by China or the Dutch Embassy.[146] In 1917, the ROC requested that this issue be referred to the PCA on the basis of the 1915 Sino–Dutch treaty on dispute resolution.[147] This dispute never entered formal proceedings due to a delayed Dutch response.

[139] Craft (n 127) 175.
[140] ibid 174–176; China and the United Nations (n 131) 32–37.
[141] China and the United Nations (n 131) 46–47.
[142] Yuen-Li Liang, "Roscoe Pound and the Science of International Law" (1948) 22 Tulane Law Review 369, 374.
[143] Tang (n 17) 21; China and the United Nations (n 135) 58-60.
[144] Jerome Cohen and Hungdah Chiu, *People's China and International Law, Volume 1: A Documentary Study* (Princeton: Princeton University Press 1974) 11.
[145] Tsai (n 112) 81. With respect to German issues, Dutch Minister, Jonkheer Frans Beelaerts, became the key negotiators with the Chinese government: see Tsai (n 112) 82.
[146] ibid 97–110.
[147] ibid.

The first instance in which the ROC defended a case before the PCA was in a 1935 case involving a US corporation, Radio Corporation of America (RCA). The dispute arose from the ROC's conclusion of the Radio Traffic Agreement and a supplemental agreement with Mackay Radio and Telegraph Company.[148] RCA claimed that these agreements violated the Traffic Agreement that the ROC had concluded with RCA. According to the arbitrators, the texts of the Traffic Agreement were not "exclusive by nature," and such an agreement did not constitute "a relation of partnership or a joint venture" that inhibited potential competition.[149] Furthermore, they accepted the ROC's defense that a radio circuit was "a public service" and enabling nationals to use other facilities should be "the Chinese Government's duty."[150] The arbitrators, all of whom were Europeans, ruled in favor of the ROC. As a result, the RCA case became China's first successful state-to-state case.

The ROC's assertive legalism grew in tandem with the emergence of Chinese jurists serving on international court benches, including Wang Chung-hui and Chen Tien-his of the PCIJ and Hsu Mo and Wellington Koo of the ICJ. The ROC participated in the ICJ's first two advisory proceedings in 1948 and 1949.[151] The written submissions detailed its views on reparation for injuries suffered in the service of the UN. Koo was the last judge nominated by the ROC government, which relocated to Taiwan in 1949, and his term ended in 1967.

11.4 Conclusion

The chapter explored the professionalization of the discipline of international law in the ROC. It argued that the approach to international law in the Republican period was characterized by a blend of statism, pragmatism, and idealism. These characteristics also enabled the nation's intellectual shift toward being recognized as a "civilized nation" on the global stage.

Through top-down reforms spearheaded by international lawyers serving in government, the ROC made significant strides in developing legal education, the foreign ministry, law societies, and legal practice. The introduction of international

148 *Radio Corporation of America v China*, PCA Award 1934-01 (April 13, 1935) 1.

149 ibid 5–7.

150 ibid 4.

151 Hunghui Chang, Letter from the Chinese Ambassador at the Hague to the Registrar of the Court (19 January 1948), in Cour Internationale de Justice [International Court of Justice], 1948 Conditions de L'admission d'UN Etat Comme Membre des Nations Unies (Article 4 de la Charte) [Conditions of admission of a State to membership in the United Nations (article 4 of the Charter)] (Advisory Opinion of 28 May 1948) 14; Henry Kunghui Chang, Letter from the Chinese Ambassador at the Hague to the Registrar of the International Court of Justice (26 January 1949), in Cour Internationale de Justice [International Court of Justice], 1949 Reparation des Dommages Subis au Service des Nations Unies [1949 Reparation for Injuries Suffered in the Service of the United Nations] (Advisory Opinion of 11 April 1949) 13–14.

law into university curricula and the establishment of the first full-fledged national society for international law study reflected the state's commitment to professionalizing this discipline. The cultivation of skilled diplomats and jurists equipped to engage with Western legal concepts and institutions was critical for enabling China to revise the unequal treaty system and assert its sovereign rights against foreign aggression.

The ROC's utilization of international law in its diplomatic and legal struggles demonstrated an innovative yet pragmatic approach, blending both the positivist and idealist schools of international legal thought. While generally operating within established international norms such as *pacta sunt servanda*, Chinese diplomats adopted creative interpretations of principles including *rebus sic stantibus* to justify abrogating unequal treaties. Their participation in international tribunals marked an assertive turn from the Qing Court's hesitancy toward Western-dominated dispute resolution mechanisms.

At the same time, the ROC embraced Wilsonian ideals and placed its faith in newly established international institutions such as the League of Nations and the Kellogg–Briand Pact, even as these proved ineffective in restraining Japanese militarism. The ROC's proposals at the foundational meetings of the UN, reflecting both its aspiration for sovereign equality and its legalist worldview, left an enduring mark on the UN Charter. Articles on the development and codification of international law reflect these distinctly Republican Chinese contributions.

Overall, Republican China's approach to international law catalyzed the universalization of this once Euro-centric discipline and opened pathways for greater Asian representation in its interpretation and evolution. The ideals of sovereign equality and normative commitment to international order balanced against pragmatic flexibility in revising anachronistic arrangements laid the foundations for China's stance on global governance. While the PRC has reframed international law through the prism of its "socialist" identity, many continuities can be traced back to the pioneering efforts of Republican China's first generation of international lawyers.

Though marginalized in conventional international law narratives, Republican China played an underappreciated role in shaping key junctures of the 20th-century international order through its strategic embrace of international legalism. Recovering this history and examining the dialectical interplay between statism, pragmatism, and idealism at its core offers valuable insights into the universalization of international law. By documenting this overlooked history, the research enhances understanding of Asia's influence in the evolution of the international rules-based order, a legacy that remains highly germane to navigating the shifting dynamics of contemporary global governance.

12

The Introduction of Soviet International Law Theory in China

How Chinese International Lawyers Turned to Marxism

Jie Liu and Congyan Cai

12.1 Introduction

In the past decade, Marxism, which lost its prominence as it was abandoned in most socialist states in the late 1980s, has regained international currency.[1] Arguably, this trend is largely motivated by the financial crisis which initially erupted in the United States in 2008 and then worsened into global economic stagnation and social division in the following years. Unlike its prevalence in the Cold War era, during which Marxism was overwhelmingly debated between the Eastern/socialist bloc and the Western/capitalist bloc as an agenda of ideology and international power politics, its recent resurgence mainly stems from a recognition by many people, including people in Western countries, that it provides many insights explaining the systematic challenges that the world, and particularly global liberal capitalism, faces, and is helpful in exploring some potential solutions. In general terms, Marxism explains the crisis of Western liberalism in which the world has been deeply imbedded in recent centuries.[2] In concrete terms, while Karl Marx and Friedrich Engels never devised any systematic 'theory' of law or international law, in addition to expressing many specific views on law they provided useful thoughts and approaches related to law in their theories of philosophy, sociology, and economics which are still relevant to understandings of law in the contemporary world.[3]

In the current process of re-engaging with Marxism, it is interesting that Marxism seems to be gaining greater currency in the international legal sphere than the domestic one. A potential explanation may be that international law is

[1] See Sara R. Farris (ed.), *Returns of Marxism: Marxist Theory in a Time of Crisis* (Haymarket Books 2016).

[2] Igor Shoikhedbrod, *Revisiting Marx's Critique of Liberalism*: Rethinking Justice, *Legality and Rights* (Palgrave 2019).

[3] See, for example, Anna Piekarska, 'Challenging the Rule of Law Universalism: Why Marxist Legal Thought Still Matters' (2023) 34 Law and Critique 269.

Jie Liu and Congyan Cai, *The Introduction of Soviet International Law Theory in China* In: *Histories of International Law in China*. Edited by: Ignacio de la Rasilla, Jiangyu Wang, and Congyan Cai, Oxford University Press.
 DOI: 10.1093/oso/9780198888345.003.0012

more 'primitive' than domestic law and is therefore more susceptible to being unduly misused and abused, thus leading to greater global injustice, a crucial concern for generations of Marxists. This is perhaps why Marxism is considered a 'new agenda' for international law instead of domestic law.[4] A debate which appeared in the *Leiden Journal of International Law* in 2004[5] signaled a turn in international scholarship to Marxism, albeit with several such attempts having previously been made.[6] Since then, referring to Marxist thought on materialism,[7] ideology,[8] class,[9] capitalism, exploitation,[10] race, colonization, and imperialism,[11] more international lawyers have engaged in critiques of the history of international law and contemporary international law, and debated a more desirable international legal order.[12]

Although it is desirable to understand the Marxist approach to international law by heavily relying on Marx and Engels' own writings, we should bear in mind that it was the Union of Soviet Socialist Republics (USSR), the first socialist country, that developed an overall international law theory based on Marxism distinct from its Western counterparts. Soviet international lawyers not only used what Marx and Engels themselves said to develop their theories but also referred to the writings of USSR leaders, especially Lenin and Stalin, and USSR foreign policy. For instance, based on Marx and Engels' insights into colonization, Lenin developed his theory

[4] Akbar Rasulov, 'A Marxism for International Law: A New Agenda' (2018) 29 European Journal of International Law 631.

[5] B. S. Chimni, 'An Outline of a Marxist Course on Public International Law' (2004) 17 Leiden Journal of International Law 1; Brad R. Roth, 'Retrieving Marx for the Human Rights Project' (2004) 17 Leiden Journal of International Law 31; Martti Koskenniemi, 'What Should International Lawyers Learn from Karl Marx?' (2004) 17 Leiden Journal of International Law 229; Anthony Carty, 'Marxism and International Law: Perspectives for the American (Twenty-First) Century?' (2004) 17 Leiden Journal of International Law 247; China Mieville, 'The Commodity-Form Theory of International Law: An Introduction' (2004) 17 Leiden Journal of International Law 271.

[6] See particularly Susan Marks, *The Riddle of All Constitutions: International Law, Democracy and the Critique of Ideology* (Oxford University Press 2000).

[7] See for, example, Daniel Ricardo Quiroga-Villamarín, 'Beyond Texts? Towards a Material Turn in the Theory and History of International Law' (2021) 23 International Law 466.

[8] See, for example, Tor Krever, 'International Criminal Law: An Ideology Critique' (2013) 26 Leiden Journal of International Law 701.

[9] See, for example, B. S. Chimni, 'Prolegomena to a Class Approach to International Law' (2010) 21 European Journal of International Law 57.

[10] See, for example, Mark Neocleous, 'International Law as Primitive Accumulation; Or, the Secret of Systematic Colonization' (2012) 23 European Journal of International Law 941; George Forji Amin, 'Marxism, International Law and the Enduring Question of Exploitation: A History' (2021) 7 Athens Journal of Law 359.

[11] See, for example, Robert Knox, 'Valuing Race? Stretched Marxism and the Logic of Imperialism' (2016) 4 London Review of International Law 81; B.S. Chimni, 'International Institutions Today: An Imperial Global State in the Making' (2004) 15 European Journal of International Law 1.

[12] China Miéville, *Between Equal Rights: A Marxist Theory of International Law* (Brill 2005); Susan Marks (ed.), *International Law on the Left: Re-examining Marxist Legacies* (Cambridge University Press 2008); Ntina Tzouvala, *Capitalism as Civilisation* (Cambridge University Press 2020); B. S. Chimni, *International Law and World Order: A Critique of Contemporary Approaches* (Cambridge University Press 2017).

of imperialism,[13] which characterized Soviet international law theory. Therefore, an examination of Soviet international law theory is helpful for understanding how Soviet jurists understood Marxism in order to develop new international legal theories distinct from their Western counterparts, regardless of whether they accurately reflected or misunderstood Marx and Engels' own thoughts and whether they were helpful or detrimental in building an international legal order desirable for mankind. At least in other socialist countries, including China, Soviet international law theory was considered to represent the 'real' Marxist approach to international law.[14] Therefore, while Soviet international law theory is no longer on the Western research agenda,[15] it remains relevant in exploring the role of Marxism in the changed landscape of international law theories.

Along these lines, this chapter reviews how Soviet international law theory was introduced in China and shows how Chinese international lawyers turned to Marxism. After briefly considering how Chinese international lawyers treated Marxism before the 1940s, it focuses on the 1950s and 1960s. The reason is simple. After the USSR established a diplomatic relationship with the People's Republic of China (PRC), which was founded in 1949, the two socialist countries experienced a honeymoon period until the late 1950s, during which they undertook cooperation in a wide range of fields including education. Afterwards, however, their mutual relations began to worsen, culminating in military conflicts in border areas in the late 1960s.[16] As a result, mutual cooperation, including in legal education, largely reduced or stopped. China began to pursue Marxism in its own way. By revisiting how Soviet international law theory was introduced in socialist China, this study (1) reveals how theories of international law and international lawyers adapted to fundamental political and ideological transformations, and (2) examines how China adopted Marxism. The core argument is that while Soviet international law theory significantly changed the contours of international law theory in China during the 1950s and 1960s, Chinese international lawyers did not totally embrace Soviet theory. Instead, due to Chinese concerns and China's division from the USSR after the late 1960s, Chinese international lawyers began to develop a Marxist approach to international law with Chinese characteristics.

[13] Vladimir Lenin, *Imperialism, the Highest Stage of Capitalism* (帝国主义是资本主义的最高阶段) (Foreign Language Press 1949).

[14] See William E. Butter, 'Anglo-American Research on Soviet Approaches to Public International Law', in William E. Butter (ed.), *International Law in Comparative Perspective* (Sijthoff & Noordhoff 1980) 169–190.

[15] For a long time, only the writings of Grigory Tunkin were known in the West. See Andrea Bianchi, *International Law Theories: An Inquiry into Different Ways of Thinking* (Oxford University Press 2016) 73.

[16] See Shen Zhihua (ed.), *Revisiting Several Issues in the History of Sino-Soviet Relations 1917–1991* (中苏关系史纲：1917–1991 年中苏关系若干问题再探讨) (3nd edn, Social Sciences Academic Press 2016) 151–529.

12.2 China and Western International Law Theory before the PRC Era: A Short Story

Until the mid-1900s, China, the once Middle Kingdom with an 'All under Heaven' worldview, had little idea of the international law developed in the seventeenth century in Europe with the nation-state worldview. However, several European states repeatedly attacked and defeated Qing China (1616–1912), and the once Middle Kingdom was forced to sign the Treaty of Nanking (1842) with Britain after the First Opium War (1840–1841). This was followed by dozens of 'unequal treaties' with Western powers.[17] China came to recognize that its 'All under Heaven' worldview could no longer be sustained, and that it could not avoid accepting a new set of rules developed by European nations, namely (Western) international law.

Our research aim does not require us to review how China abandoned its traditional worldview while accepting international law in the nineteenth century, which has already been much studied by others.[18] Instead, it suffices to look into how leading international lawyers who were prominent in international law teaching, researching and legal service in the PRC era engaged with international law in the Republic of China (ROC) era (1912–1949). These leading figures include Zhou Gengsheng (1889–1971), Ni Zhengyu (1906–2003), Li Haopei (1906–1997), Han Depei (1911–2009), Wang Tieya (1913–2003), Zhao Lihai (1916–2000) and Chen Tiqiang (1917–1983), none of whom were Marxists before 1949. Given that these figures are portrayed elsewhere, from their lives to their teachings, their scholarship, and their legal service,[19] it is not necessary to exhaustively cover their engagement with international law here. Instead, we focus on two issues: what international law they engaged with before 1949, and how they did it. All seven of these scholars studied international law in Western countries: Zhou studied at the University of Edinburgh and then the University of Paris (1916–1918; 1918–1921); Ni studied at Stanford Law School (1928–1929); Li and Wang studied at the London School of Economics and Political Science (1936–1939 and 1937–1939 respectively); Han studied at the University of Toronto (1940–1942)

[17] Wang Dong, *China's Unequal Treaties: Narrating National History* (中国的不平等条约：国耻与民族历史叙述) (Lexington Books 2005) 9–34.

[18] See, for example, Immanuel C. Y. Hsü, *China's Entrance into the Family of Nations: The Diplomatic Phase 1858–1800* (Harvard University Press 1960); Lydia H. Liu, *The Clash of Empires: The Invention of China in Modern World Making* (Harvard University Press 2004); Rune Svarverud, *International Law as World Order in Late Imperial China: Translation, Reception and Discourse 1847–1911* (Brill 2007); Maria Adele Carrai, *Sovereignty in China: A Genealogy of a Concept since 1840* (Cambridge University Press 2019); Lai Junnan, *International Law and China in the Period of Late Qing Dynasty: Texts, Events and Politics* (国际法与晚清中国：文本、事件与政治) (Shanghai People's Publishing House 2015); Lin Xuezhong, *From the Law of Nations to Diplomacy based on the Law of Nations: Introduction, Understanding and Application of International Law in the Late Qing Dynasty* (从万国公法到公法外交：晚清国际法的传入、诠释与应用) (Shanghai Classics Publishing House 2009).

[19] See Ni Zhengyu, Chapter 27; Li Haopei, Chapter 26; Han Depei, Chapter 28; Wang Tieya, Chapter 29; Zhao Lihao, Chapter 31; Chen Titiang, Chapter 32.

and Harvard University (1942–1945), Zhao studied at Chicago University (1940–1941) and Harvard University (1941–1944); and Chen was educated at Oxford University (1945–1948).

Due to their Western education, these Chinese lawyers were well acquainted with Western theories of international law. However, we focus on Zhou for a simple reason. Unlike the other six persons, who were in the early stages of their careers before the PRC was founded, Zhou, who returned to China with a PhD in international law in 1921, had already been recognized as a senior lawyer because of the dozens of books and journal articles he had published, especially *Outline of International Law* (国际法大纲) in 1929,[20] the first international law textbook written by a Chinese lawyer.

Largely speaking, Zhou appreciated Western international law theories. This can be seen in the definition of international law he provides in his 1929 textbook. Referring to Oppenheim's *International Law*,[21] Zhou defined international law as a legal system governing the relations between 'civilized nations'.[22] Western international lawyers, largely like their governments, generally relied on the theory of 'civilized nations' to humiliate non-Western nations to different degrees by denying them the capacity to have rights and interests under international law.[23] For instance, Oppenheim was of the view that the position of China in international society was 'doubtful'.[24] While Oppenheim recognized China as a civilized nation, he contended that Chinese civilization had 'not yet reached that condition which is necessary to enable [its government] and [its] people in every respect to understand and carry out the command of the rules of international law'.[25] Therefore, until it raised its civilization to the Western level, China was 'not yet able to be received as [a] full member of [the] family of nations.'[26] Interestingly, in his textbook Zhou was critical of neither the Western theory of 'civilized nations' nor Oppenheim's view of China's international status. It should be stressed, however, that in addressing Western colonization Marx had categorically opposed the 'civilized nations' theory, and particularly criticized Western colonialism in China in the nineteenth century.[27]

For all early Chinese international lawyers, 'unequal treaties', which caused tremendous harm to China in terms of tariffs, leased territories, concessions,

[20] Zhou Gengsheng, *Outline of International Law* (国际法大纲) (The Commercial Press 1929, reprinted in 1934, 1935, 1947, and 2013).

[21] Oppenheim, *International Law (Vol. 1)* (Longmans, Green, and Co. 1905) 1.

[22] Zhou Gengsheng (n 20) 1–2.

[23] See Gerrit W. Gong, *The Standard of "Civilization" in International Society* (Clarendon Press 1984); Wilhelm G. Grewe, *The Epochs of International Law, translated and revised by Michael Byers* (Walter de Gruyter 2000) 445–496.

[24] Oppenheim (n 21) 33.

[25] Ibid 33.

[26] Ibid 33.

[27] *Collection of Marx and Engels* (马克思恩格斯全集) (Vol.12) (The People's Press 1962) 177, 584–585.

extraterritoriality, and non-reciprocal most-favoured nation treatment,[28] were a major, bitter concern. Zhou was no exception. In 1928 he published *Ten Lectures on Unequal Treaties*,[29] the first systematic study of this topic. Zhou suggested that unequal treaties 'not only formally damaged China's sovereignty but also by their nature impeded the free development of the Chinese economy … therefore the termination of unequal treaties was a prerequisite for the emancipation of the Chinese people'.[30] How Zhou addressed the Western theory of 'civilized nations' to terminate unequal treaties is interesting, however. In Zhou's view, China should not accept improvement of the Chinese judiciary as a precondition for terminating extraterritoriality,[31] which the Western powers claimed was due to poor administration of justice in Qing China. Zhou was not critical of the precondition itself. His concern was that the Western powers would enjoy great discretion to identify when the Chinese judiciary reached the Western level. In Zhou's view, in order to maintain extraterritoriality the Western powers would be highly likely to abuse this discretion by downplaying Chinese efforts to improve the judiciary. Therefore, Zhou proposed that China should seek individual negotiations with Western powers to set a definite timetable for extraterritoriality to be terminated. Meanwhile, China should make more effort to modernize its judiciary.[32] Clearly, Zhou's thinking coincided with Oppenheim's view. According to Oppenheim, nations such as China must succeed in being admitted as full members of the family of nations on condition that they made enough efforts to educate their people, modernize their institutions, and raise their civilizations.[33]

Indeed, Zhou had some knowledge of the political transformation in the wake of the October Revolution.[34] It is therefore likely that Zhou knew the USSR's policy of 'unequal treaties' with China. On 8 November 1917, immediately after the October Revolution, the USSR issued a 'Decree of Peace'. The decree announced the 'unconditional and immediate annulment of everything contained in the secret treaties' concluded by the former Russian empire. In July 1919 Lev Karakhan,

[28] See, for example, Wang Dong (n 17) 9–18. For recent Chinese literature on Chinese unequal treaties, see, for example, Li Yumin, *A Study of Sion-Foreign Treaty Relations in the Late China* (晚清中外条约关系研究) (Law Press 2018); Cao Ying, *The Collapse of Traditional System and the Establishment of Treaty Relations, 1689–1860* (传统体制的打破与条约关系的建立 1689–1860) (Zhonghua Book Company 2022).

[29] Zhou Gengsheng, *Ten Lectures on Unequal Treaties* (不平等条约十讲) (Shanghai Taipin Book Company 1928), reprinted in Wang Tieya and Zhou Zhonghai (eds), Zhou Gengsheng, *Selected Articles of International Law* (周鲠生国际法论文选) (Haitian Press 1999).

[30] Zhou Gengsheng, *Steps of Termination of Unequal Treaties* (废止不平等条约的步骤), in Wang Tieya and Zhou Zhonghai (n 29) 370.

[31] Zhou Gengsheng, 'The Conference of Extraterritoriality and the Termination of Extraterritoriality' (法权会议与收回法权), in Wuhan International Law Institute (eds), *The Selection of Zhou Gengsheng* (周鲠生文集) (Wuhan University Press 1993) 49.

[32] Ibid 49.

[33] Oppenheim (n 21) 34.

[34] Zhou Gengsheng, 'Political Transformation in Russia' (俄罗斯的政治改造), in Wuhan International Law Institute (ed.), *The Selection of Zhou Gengsheng* (n 31) 174–192.

the USSR deputy commissioner for foreign affairs, issued a statement called the Karakhan Manifesto. In the manifesto, the USSR offered China the relinquishment of privileges that the Russian empire had seized, including extraterritoriality. In May 1924, the two states signed a treaty declaring that all treaties between the former Russian government and any third state harming Chinese sovereignty were null and void.[35] However, the Soviet revolutionary approach to Chinese 'unequal treaties' was resisted by the Western powers, which wanted to maintain their privileges in China. Mindful of the Western opposition, the ROC government did not take the Soviet approach to repudiate the 'unequal treaties' with Western powers but instead adopted a pragmatic approach and sought renegotiations with them.

Interestingly, however, Zhou never discussed the USSR policy on China's 'unequal treaties'. Instead he supported the pragmatic stance of the ROC government. In his view, while China at that time would be justified in unilaterally announcing the termination of 'unequal treaties', it should not take a revolutionary approach that would incur strong resistance from the Western powers and therefore have tremendous political and economic impacts.[36] Besides his pragmatic approach, Zhou's reluctance to embrace the revolutionary approach to 'unequal treaties' arguably resulted, at least partly, from his general thinking about the USSR. In fact, as a non-communist Zhou was critical of Marxist ideology.[37] Before 1949 he had never written anything about Marxist thought on law or Soviet international law theory.

The early Chinese communists embraced Lenin's theory of imperialism as an instrument to win political support against the ROC government.[38] However, they had limited knowledge of Marxist thoughts on law.[39] In short, until 1949 Chinese lawyers knew little about Soviet international law theory, even though they had some knowledge of USSR foreign policy.

12.3 The Turn to Marxism: The Introduction of Soviet International Law Theory in China during the 1950s and 1960s

In the early 1950s, Soviet international law theory was intensively introduced in China. This process was not only intellectual but also political. It significantly transformed international law theory in China.

[35] Li Bing, *Challenges and Transformation of Unequal Treaties, 1912–1927* (不平等条约的动摇与转折 1912–1927) (Zhonghua Book Company 2022) 97–114.

[36] Zhou Gengsheng, 'Steps to Terminate Unequal Treaties' (废止不平等条约的步骤), in Wang Tieya and Zhou Zhonghai (n 29) 371.

[37] Ibid 191–192.

[38] Wang Dong (n 17) 71–76, 88–91.

[39] See, for example, Li Dazhao, *Selection of Legal Works of Li Dazhao* (李大钊法学文集) (Law Press 2014).

12.3.1 Background

China's turn to Soviet international law theory in the 1950s was the result of the PRC 'Leaning to One Side' policy on the USSR during the Cold War.

Under the Common Programme adopted on 29 September 1949, the provisional constitution of the PRC. There would be a transitional period of New Democracy or People's Democratism towards socialist countries.[40] This meant that the political, economic, social, and legal ideology in the ROC era would, to some degree, be maintained. However, as the Cold War worsened, on the eve of the founding of the PRC, the CCP leaders recognized that China could only maintain the 'Leaning to One Side' policy by joining the USSR-led socialist camp.[41] Nevertheless, there existed different views within the PRC leadership on how to engage with the USSR.[42]

Due to the 'Leaning to One Side' policy, in February 1950 China and the USSR signed a Treaty of Friendship, Alliance and Mutual Assistance (China–USSR Alliance Treaty). Article 5 of the Alliance Treaty (1950) provided that the two states would develop economic and cultural relations. Chairman Mao suggested that with the Alliance Treaty (1950) China would 'have a reliable ally, which facilitates our unreserved engagement in domestic construction work and joint defence against potential imperialist aggression, striving for world peace'.[43]

Nevertheless, due to an attitude of Chinese nationalism after the humiliation of the nineteenth century, from the very beginning the PRC leaders did not support USSR socialist internationalism. Under socialist internationalism, it was not the principle of equality of sovereignty but the so-called international socialist course that applied to relations between socialist countries.[44] The USSR sought to use this to justify interference in the internal affairs of other socialist countries. Perhaps mindful of the potential threat of USSR socialist internationalism, in explaining the 'Leaning to One Side' policy Chairman Mao stressed that the policy put China on an equal footing with the Soviet Union, believing in Marxism–Leninism and combining its universal truths with the actual situation in China, not the experience of the Soviet Union.[45] In other words, the PRC leadership never had any intention of totally embracing the Soviet conception of Marxism, but instead sought to introduce Marxism with Chinese characteristics. Therefore,

[40] Common Programme, Art. 1.

[41] Mao Zedong, 'On the People's Democratic Dictatorship: Commemorating the 28th Anniversary of the Chinese Communist Party' (论人民民主专政：纪念中国共产党成立二十八周年), in *Selected Works of Mao Zedong* (毛泽东选集) (People's Publishing House 1991) 1468–1482.

[42] Mao Zedong, 'Is "Leaning to One Side" Right? (December 8, 1956)' ('一边倒'是否正确？), in *Selected Diplomatic Works of Mao Zedong* (毛泽东外交文选) (Central Literature Publishing House 1994) 278.

[43] Mao Zedong, 'The Great Significance of Concluding the Sino–Soviet Treaty and Agreements' (缔结中苏条约和协定的重大意义), People's Daily, 13 April 1950.

[44] G. I. Tunkin, *Theory of International Law*, trans. W. E. Butler (Massachusetts Harvard University Press 1974) 3–4.

[45] Mao Zedong (n 42) 278.

it came as no surprise that during the negotiations on the Alliance Treaty (1950) China unequivocally rejected the USSR's proposal that the treaty should not refer to the principle of equality of sovereignty. Finally, the principle was included in the treaty.[46] China was also against the USSR interventions in Hungary and Poland in 1956.[47] More importantly, in 1954 China proposed Five Principles of Peaceful Coexistence: (a) mutual respect for each other's territorial integrity and sovereignty; (b) mutual non-aggression; (c) mutual non-interference in each other's internal affairs; (d) equality and mutual benefit; and (e) peaceful coexistence.[48] The Five Principles were later included in the 1975 Constitution[49] and were reaffirmed in the 1982 Constitution.[50]

In short, in the 1950s the PRC's 'Leaning to One Side' policy provided a strong political impetus to introduce Soviet international law theory in China. On the other hand, China's stance on the USSR's aggressive foreign policy discouraged a complete embrace of Soviet international law theory. As a result, while Western international law theory began to be marginalized after the founding of the PRC, it did not totally lose its relevance in China, as is shown below.

12.3.2 How Soviet International Law Theory Was Introduced in China

As a result of the 'Leaning to One Side' policy, China made efforts to learn from the USSR in various fields. Among these was the introduction of Soviet international law theory.

In 1952, China's Ministry of Education called for 'a planned and systematic' translation of Soviet textbooks so as to 'learn from Soviet advanced scientific and technological expertise, reform teaching content and enhance teaching quality'.[51] As far as international law teaching was concerned, China first reset its institutional teaching framework. In 1952, an International Law Teaching and Research Division was established at the Renmin University of China (RUC) School of Law,[52] a major hub to disseminate Soviet international law theory in China. Several leading Soviet jurists were invited there to teach international law (Table 12.1).

[46] China–USSR Alliance Treaty (1950), art. 5.

[47] John W. Garver, *China's Quest: The History of the Foreign Relations of the People's Republic of China* (Oxford University Press 2016) 117–120.

[48] The preamble stated that the two countries would resolve their relations on the basis of '(a) mutual respect for each other's territorial affairs and sovereignty; mutual non-aggression; mutual non-interference in each other's internal affairs; equality and mutual benefit; peaceful coexistence.'

[49] Constitution (1975), Preamble.

[50] Constitution (1982, as amended in 1988, 1993, 1999, 2004, 2018), Preamble.

[51] Directives on Matters to Be Noted When Formulating Plans for Translating Soviet Textbooks by Various Higher Education Institutions under the Ministry of Education (教育部《关于各高等学校组织翻译苏联教材制订计划时应注意的事项的指示》), November 27, 1952, No. 200030.

[52] Preliminary Draft of the Work Summary for the Second Year of the Law Department, the Archives of Renmin University of China, file number 1952-XZ16-02-1.0001.

Table 12.1 USSR experts teaching international law in China

Name	Period	Host institution
Л.И.Савинский	1950–1951	RUC
В.И.Менжинский	1950–1951	RUC
	1954–1956	University of Foreign Affairs
Колостолев	1951–1953	RUC
К.А.Аджаров	1953–1954	RUC
С.Л.Тихвинский	1950–1951	RUC

Second, as will be seen in Section 12.3.3, many Soviet textbooks and monographs by international lawyers were translated into Chinese. In 1954 the Ministry of Higher Education directed the RUC to review the Soviet legal textbooks already translated and recommended them to other Chinese universities and institutions.[53]

Third, a number of Soviet international lawyers were invited to work as legal advisors in China. From 1950 to 1957 at least ten Soviet lawyers worked for China's government each year, including in the Ministry of Foreign Affairs (MFA).[54] Although the work of these Soviet experts was not released, it is safe to say that they played some role in introducing Soviet international law theory in China.

Finally, Chinese students received international law education in the USSR. In the 1950s, dozens of Chinese students were selected to study law in the USSR. It should be noted, however, that most Chinese students did not study international law.[55] Nevertheless, several of them later became leading international lawyers in China. One was Liu Nanlai. Liu studied at Lomonosov Moscow State University from 1956 to 1961 and focused on state and legal studies. He later worked for the Chinese Academy of Social Sciences. He was also vice-president of the Chinese Society for International Law and editor-in-chief of the Chinese Yearbook of International Law. Another one was Wei Min. From 1951 to 1957 Wei first studied at Kazan University and subsequently moved to the Faculty of Law at Lomonosov Moscow State University. After he came back to China, Wei taught at Peking University for decades.

[53] China Education Yearbook Editorial Board, *China Education Yearbook 1949–1981* (中国教育年鉴·1949–1981) (Educational Science Publishing House 1984) 267.

[54] Tang Shichun, 'A Collective Examination of Soviet Legal Experts in China in the Early Years of the Founding of the Nation' (建国初期来华苏联法学专家的群体考察) (2010) 5 Global Law Review 137.

[55] See He Qinhua, 'On the Initial Steps of Law and Legal Studies in New China—Following the Clues of the Abolition of the KMT's Six Guidebook and the Judicial Reform Movement' (论新中国法和法学的起步—以"废除国民党六法全书"和"司法改革运动"为线索) (2009) 4 China Legal Science 140.

12.3.3 What Was Introduced in China: Translations

As was noted above, some Soviet international lawyers were invited to teach in China. Unfortunately, we do not know what they taught. Nevertheless, we have attempted to find out what was introduced by investigating translations. After the founding of the PRC, some books by Marx, Lenin, and Stalin were translated, including the *Collected Works of Marx and Engels*,[56] *Collected Works of Lenin*,[57] and *Collected Works of J. V. Stalin*;[58] some of this work is relevant to international law, for instance *Socialism and War*,[59] *Imperialism, the Highest Stage of Capitalism*,[60] and *Marxism and the National and Colonial Question*.[61] As was noted above, while Marx, Engels, Lenin, and Stalin were not legal theorists, in their publications there are many insights on law, including international law. Therefore, these translations helped disseminate Soviet international law theory in China.

As Table 12.2 shows, in the 1950s and 1960s at least nineteen books on Soviet international law theory and practice were translated into Chinese. These books can be roughly grouped into three categories. The first category relates to the thinking of Soviet leaders on international law. For instance, Qian Kexin translated Koshchyunikov's *Stalin on the Basic Principles of Modern International Law*. The second category is international law textbooks. For instance, the University of International Relations and Peking University School of Law co-translated the textbook *International Law* edited by the Soviet Academy of Sciences Institute of Law. The third category is publications with a more theoretical bent. For example, Liu Huishang et al. translated Tunkin's renowned *Issues of Theory of International Law*.

The translation project was obviously government-driven. Table 12.2 shows that the University of Foreign Affairs affiliated with the MFA and RUC, the two major institutions sponsoring Soviet international law theory in China, organized seven of the nineteen translations. Eight of the nineteen were published by the World Affairs Press affiliated with the MFA.

[56] Compilation and Translation Bureau of the CPC Central Committee, *Collected Works of Marx and Engels* (马克思恩格斯选集) (People's Publishing House 1956).

[57] Compilation and Translation Bureau of the CPC Central Committee, *Collected Works of Lenin* (列宁选集) (People's Publishing House 1955–1963).

[58] Compilation and Translation Bureau of the CPC Central Committee, *Collected Works of J.V. Stalin* (斯大林选集) (People's Publishing House 1953–1956).

[59] Vladimir Lenin, *Socialism and War* (社会主义与战争), translated by Yang Song, Yuan Wei, Xu Zhizhen, and Lin Zhong (Renmin University of China 1952).

[60] Vladimir Lenin, *Imperialism, the Highest Stage of Capitalism* (帝国主义是资本主义的最高阶段), translated by Xu Bing (Time Press 1950).

[61] Joseph Stalin, *Marxism and the National and Colonial Question* (马克思主义与民族、殖民地问题), translated by Zhang Zhongshi (People's Publishing House 1953).

Table 12.2 Chinese translations of Soviet international law theory

Year	Title	Author/Editor	Translator	Publishing House
1950	*Stalin on the Basic Principles of Modern International Law*	Koshchyunikov	Qian Kexin	World Affairs Press
1951	*Basic Characteristics of Cooperation between the USSR and People's Democracies on International Law*	Gnieralov	You Li	World Affairs Press
1951	*Soviet International Private Law*	Lunts	Lu Feng	Dadong Bookstore
1952	*The State Sovereignty Principle as the Most Important Principle in International Law*	Zuyev	International Law Division, RUC School of Law	RUC
1953	*The System of International Private Law*	Beletsky	International Law Division, RUC School of Law	RUC
1953	*Stalin on International Cooperation and International Treaties*	Gaïdoukhov	International Law Division, RUC School of Law	RUC
1954	*Soviet State and International Law* (the first four chapters)	Kozhevnikov	International Law Division, RUC School of Law	RUC
1955	*Soviet State and International Law* (the last four chapters)	Kozhevnikov	International Law Division, RUC School of Law	RUC
1954	*International Law and International Organisations*	Vyshinsky	Shao Jin	RUC
1955	*Selected Translations of the Encyclopaedia of the USSR: International Law and Private International Law*	Korovin	Wang Shu	Law Press
1955	*International Law of the Navy (Vol. 1): Common Principles of International Law Relating to Warships in Times of Peace and War*	V. A. Beryulin	People's Liberation Army Navy Command	People's Liberation Army Navy Headquarters

(continued)

Table 12.2 Continued

Year	Title	Author/Editor	Translator	Publishing House
1956	*USSR Trade Treaties and Agreements*	Korolyenko	China Council for the Promotion of International Trade and Beijing Foreign Trade College	Law Press
1956	*Basic Principles and Problems of Modern International Law*	Kozhevnikov, Zuyev, Kholostarenko	Not available	Law Press
1956	*Issues of Territorial Waters in International Law*	Nikolayev	Xu Junren, Yu Daxin	Law Press
1958	*Selected Essays on Soviet International Law*	Turkin, Volchikov, Portolak, Peletsky, et al.	Not available	World Affairs Press
1956 1958	*Basic Issues of Modern International Law*	Tunkin	Zhang Ruixiang et al.	World Affairs Press
1958 1959	*Lenin on International Politics and International Law*	Vladimir Lenin	University of International Relations	World Affairs Press
1959	*International Law*	The Soviet Academy of Sciences Institute of Law	University of International Relations Translation Group and International Law Division, Peking University School of Law	World Affairs Press
1961	*International Court of Justice*	Krylov	University of International Relations Translation Group	World Affairs Press
1965	*Issues in International Law Theory*	Tunkin	Liu Huishan, Liu Wenzong, Wang Keju, Ma Xiangcong, Huang Jiahua	World Affairs Press

12.4 The Impacts of Soviet International Law Theory on China

12.4.1 General Observation

As was indicated above, the introduction of Soviet international law theory in China was not merely an intellectual process but also part of China's political alignment with the USSR, and more generally China's ideological turn to Marxism.

The impacts of Soviet international law theory and Marxism on Chinese international law can be examined from the perspective of how Chinese international lawyers conceived Western international law theory, which was considered 'bourgeois' international law until the late 1970s. As Soviet law theory, including international law theory, was introduced in China, Western international law theory encountered more and more criticism. From April 1959 to July 1960, *International Studies*, a journal affiliated with the MFA, successively published eight articles fiercely criticizing 'bourgeois' international law theory. For instance, in the view of Tiao Yue, who wrote the opening article, China recognized that '[O]nly if we have a clear understanding of bourgeois international law, can we understand our country's international law practice with Marxism-Leninism and learn and draw on the international law research in the USSR and other friendly countries too.'[62] Tiao was of the view that Oppenheim, List, Hyde, Kelsen, and Jessup studied international law precisely to defend the interests of the bourgeoisie and of imperialism.[63] As a result, almost all the international lawyers who had been previously educated in Western countries and had then taught in Chinese universities in the pre-PRC era were not allowed to teach international law in Chinese universities and had to teach foreign languages and history instead.[64]

These pre-PRC international lawyers were supportive of the introduction of Soviet international law theory.[65] However, they disapproved of the nihilistic approach to Western international law theory. According to Chen Tiqiang, the Soviet and Western international law perspectives should not be exclusively compared with each other: '[T]hose who study the old system should learn from the Soviet Union, while those who study the new system should learn from the West. This is because the Soviet Union has only been researching international law for three to

[62] Tiao Yue, 'A Preliminary Critique of Bourgeois International Law' (对于资产阶级国际法的初步批判) (1959) 3 International Studies 9.

[63] Ibid 4.

[64] Wang Tieya, '"Three Evils" in Political and Legal Education Circles Are Very Serious' (政法教育界的"三害"很严重), in Literature Division of China Political and Law Society (ed.), *Collection of the Fallacy of the Rightists in Political and Legal Circles* (政法界右派分子谬论汇集) (Law Press 1957) 45.

[65] However, Wu Wenhan was highly critical of Soviet legal theory. He suggested that '[A]fter 1938, the Soviet social sciences, especially legal research, did not make important progress. Soviet jurists' publications were largely analogous. China now followed them.' Wu Wenhan, 'Conjuring the Old Law' (为旧法'招魂'), in Literature Division of China Political and Law Society (ed.) (n 64) 25.

four decades, whereas the West has over four centuries of research.'[66] Implicit in Chen's view is that Western international law theory was intellectually more advanced than Soviet international law theory. According to Wang Tieya, pre-PRC international lawyers should be allowed to continue teaching international law. He suggested that, while some younger lawyers offered international law courses at the RUC and the University of Foreign Affairs, they were still in their early careers and were not fully qualified to teach well. According to Wang, this was not good for the development of international law in China. Wang was of the view that the Chinese international law teaching of the time did not match the Chinese international status or meet Chinese diplomatic needs. Interestingly, Wang suggested that the exclusion of pre-PRC lawyers from teaching international law was not totally the result of China's turn to Marxism but was caused by sectarianism in pro-Soviet legal theory.[67]

However, it should be noted that while Western international law theory was largely demonized after the founding of the PRC, pre-PRC international lawyers still played significant roles in Chinese international law practice. While they could no longer teach international law in universities, some of them (for instance, Ni Zhengyu and Li Haopei) worked for the MFA as legal advisors.[68] It should also be noted that Western international law publications continued to arrive in China. In 1954, on an invitation by the Chinese People's Institute of Foreign Affairs—a quasi-governmental institution established in December 1949 as the second track for Chinese diplomacy—Wang Tieya and Chen Tiqiang translated Oppenheim's *International Law* (seventh edition, 1948 and 1952) into Chinese. Although the names of Wang and Chen did not appear on the book and the translation was not accessible to the public, the project was obviously approved by China's government. After Lauterpacht revised the first volume of Oppenheim's *International Law* (seventh edition) in 1955, Wang and Chen updated their translation, which was published in 1971 and 1972.[69] To explain the reason for the 1954 translation, the Chinese People's Institute of Foreign Affairs noted that 'Oppenheim and Lauterpacht are famous bourgeois public law scholars, and their book is one of the most authoritative works recognised by the bourgeois legal community ... To expose the nonsense of imperialist aggressors and their apologists, and to uphold the principles of just, peaceful and democratic international law, it is necessary to understand the reactionary rhetoric of bourgeois international law and the

66 Chen Tiqiang, 'Opinions on the System of People's Congresses and the System of Law' (对人民代表大会制度和法制的意见), in Literature Division of China Political and Law Society (ed.) (n 64) 37–38.

67 Wang Tieya (n 64) 45.

68 Ibid.

69 He Qinhua (ed.), *Selection of Western Classics of Law* (西方法学名著精萃) (China University of Political Science and Law Press 2002) 144.

materials it is based on.'[70] This note may be readily explained as reiterating the critique of Western international law theory. However, it may also suggest that the attitude of the PRC government to Western international law theory was actually not as radical as that of some lawyers, such as Tiao.

In short, in the 1950s and 1960s Western international law theory lost prominence in China but at least partly still mattered in Chinese international law practice. The reasons may be twofold. First, in the early years of the PRC era, those educated with Soviet international law theory were still junior and not qualified to address the international legal issues that the government encountered. Second, as was noted above, from the beginning the PRC did not fully support USSR foreign policy. Furthermore, from the mid-1950s there appeared to be a reduction in disagreement between Soviet international law theory and Western international law theory. For instance, in October 1956 the Khrushchev-led USSR adopted a new foreign policy on other socialist countries. In this new policy, while still insisting on socialist internationalism, the USSR recognized that the principle of sovereign equality applied between socialist countries.[71] These developments arguably helped pre-PRC international lawyers and Western international law theory to remain somewhat relevant in the PRC era.

12.4.2 A Case Study: Zhou Gengsheng's *International Law* (1976)

The *International Law* textbook by Zhou Gengsheng is a good example to illustrate the impacts of Soviet international law theory on China. In 1964, Zhou wrote his second textbook on international law—the first in the PRC era to feature contributions by international lawyers. Understandably, this book was not allowed to be published in the 1960s and it finally came out in 1976.[72]

As was noted above, in his 1929 textbook Zhou was largely in sympathy with Western international law theory. In contrast, however, the 1976 textbook showed the impact on Zhou of Soviet international law theory. In the new textbook, Zhou referred to the textbook *International Law* edited by the Soviet Academy of Sciences (Chinese edition, 1959) more than thirty times. In addition, he referred to 'imperialism' more than 290 times, 'the bourgeoisie' more than 100 times and 'the Soviet Union' more than 260 times.

[70] Lauterpacht (ed.), *Oppenheim's International Law* (奥本海国际法), Compilation Committee of the Chinese People's Institute of Foreign Affairs (Xinhua Bookstore 1954), Note on Translation.

[71] Declaration by the Soviet Government on Principles of Development and Further Strengthening Friendship and Cooperation between the Soviet Union and Other Socialist States, Moscow, 30 October 1956.

[72] Zhou Gengsheng, *International Law* (国际法) (Wuhan University Press 1976, reprinted 2007) (hereinafter referred to as Zhou (2007)).

In contrast with the 1929 textbook, which fully agreed with Oppenheim's definition of international law, the 1976 textbook argued that Oppenheim's definition of international law 'represents the perspective of the Western bourgeoisie on international law and disguises its class nature', and Zhou unequivocally argued that the term 'civilized nations' represented colonialism.[73] In his new textbook, Zhou turned to the Soviet conception of international law. Referring to the definition given in the Soviet international law textbook,[74] Zhou suggested that international law 'is the totality of behavioural norms, including principles, rules and institutions, which arise in the course of international interactions and are recognised by all states, expressing *the will of the ruling classes of those countries* (emphasis added) and having legal binding force on states in international relations'.[75] Wang Tieya later observed that Zhou's definition of international law, especially his reference to the will of ruling classes of states, was obviously influenced by Soviet scholars.[76]

Zhou's new textbook agreed on Soviet lawyers' understanding of the nature and dynamics underlying international law. The international law textbook edited by the Soviet Academy of Sciences Institute of Law (1957) stated: '[A]s the social development in a particular period brings to international law new principles that are consistent with the social-economic structure in that period, it is demonstrated that international law, like any other law, is characterised by class and superstructure.'[77] Zhou suggested that such understanding 'captured the essence and class nature of law'.[78]

As for the structure of international law, Zhou did not agree with Oppenheim that 'there is a special international law that is binding only on two or a few countries, in addition to general international law'.[79] Zhou instead argued for universal international law. In his view, the argument for regional international law (for instance, American international law) risked legalizing 'some of the unlawful means by which Western imperialism and colonialism have seized privileges and plundered colonies in Asia and Africa'.[80] Nevertheless, Zhou recognized that

[73] Ibid 1–8.

[74] Ibid 2–3. 'International Law', edited by The Soviet Academy of Sciences Institute of Law, defined international law as follows: 'International law is the aggregate of norms that regulate the relations among nations in their struggles and cooperation, aiming at ensuring peaceful coexistence among states, reflecting the will of the ruling classes of these nations and maintaining with enforcement measures implemented by states individually or collectively when necessary.' The Soviet Academy of Sciences Institute of Law, *International Law* (国际法), Translation Group of the International Institute and the International Law Teaching and Research Section of Peking University trans. (World Affairs Press 1959) 2.

[75] Zhou Gengsheng (n 72) 3.

[76] Wang Tieya, *Introduction to International Law* (国际法引论) (Peking University Press 1998) 24.

[77] The Soviet Academy of Sciences Institute of Law (ed.), *International Law* (国际法), Translation Group of the International Institute and International Law Teaching and Research Section of Peking University trans. (World Affairs Press 1959) 4.

[78] Zhou Gengsheng (n 72) 7–8.

[79] Zhou Gengsheng (n 72) 6.

[80] Zhou Gengsheng (n 72) 6–7.

contemporary international law was structurally divided. On the one hand, the contemporary international legal order, which embodied progressive socialism and aligned with the desires and interests of most people around the world, was gradually developing. On the other hand, international law, representing imperialism, was striving to resist this progressive trend.[81] Zhou suggested that the USSR resisted the imperialism that capitalist states consistently pursued by taking advantage of international law.[82] In other words, Zhou agreed with Soviet jurists that there existed two distinct international legal orders: socialist international law and capitalist international law.

In fact, anti-imperialism, which was created by Lenin and featured in Soviet international law theory, was omnipresent in Zhou's new textbook. For instance, Zhou suggested that international organizations 'are indeed important forms of international cooperation, but they also become arenas for sharp international struggles. Especially because imperialism and reactionary forces in various countries exploit their positions in the organs of international organisations to interfere with the internal affairs of other nations and infringe upon national sovereignty.'[83] Since some Western countries denied the PRC government the capacity to represent China in the UN and replace the ROC government, Zhou criticized some Western states for maliciously attempting to create 'two Chinas' in the UN, represented by the PRC and the ROC.[84] Fortunately, due to resistance by the USSR, which had jointly created the UN, the attempt failed.[85]

In short, compared with the 1929 textbook, the 1976 textbook is more critical of the Western-dominated international legal order. In fact, in his 1976 textbook Zhou referred to the inequality of international law more than seventy times on a wide range of principles: state equality, unequal treaties, the legal status of foreigners, consular jurisdiction, extraterritoriality, monopolization of transportation by riparian states along international waterways, borders, international servitude, the laying of submarine cables, passive legation rights, dispatch and acceptance of diplomatic representatives, and the scope of legal disputes under Article 36 of the Statute of the International Court of Justice.[86]

Nevertheless, Zhou had an approach to international law that transcended the capitalist–socialist ideological division, indicating that he did not fully accept Soviet international law theory. This can be clearly seen in his discussion of the famous Five Principles of Peaceful Coexistence that China began to advocate in the 1950s. He suggested that, in accordance with the Five Principles, all states

[81] Zhou Gengsheng (n 72) 33–48.
[82] Zhou Gengsheng (n 72) 45.
[83] Zhou Gengsheng (n 72) 588.
[84] Zhou Gengsheng (n 72) 588.
[85] Zhou Gengsheng (n 72) 47–48.
[86] See Zhou Gengsheng (n 72) 182–185, 202, 236–252, 260, 269, 290, 331, 368, 376, 395, 412, 448, 455 and 680.

'should undertake intercourses equally, regardless of their social systems, power and positions, and should not impose their will on others. No states should politically force others to do things and neither should they economically exploit others or do what benefits themselves while harming others.'[87]

12.5 The Legacy of Soviet International Law Theory in China

As was noted above, while turning to Marxism and politically aligning with the USSR, China did not totally agree with the USSR in terms of foreign affairs. Their mutual relations worsened in the late 1950s. China's leader, Mao, increased his critique of the détente policy regarding the West that the Khrushchev-led USSR adopted after Stalin died. This irritated Khrushchev and so the USSR suspended or reduced much of the previously agreed assistance to and cooperation with China.[88] The worsening mutual relations culminated in border military conflict in 1969.[89] In 1974, Mao proposed a 'Three Worlds Theory'. In this theory, the USSR and the US were grouped in 'the First World' of 'superpowers' while China and many other developing states belonged to 'the Third World'.[90] In this theory China called the USSR a 'socialist imperialist' country.[91] As a result, the 1950 Alliance Treaty, which officially terminated on 14 February 1980, actually ceased to apply in the late 1960s. More importantly, in the late 1970s China embarked on the Reform and Opening-up Policy, and looked to integrate itself into the West-led international order by, among other things, seeking resumption of its membership of the General Agreement on Tariffs and Trade (GATT). As a result, the relevance of ideology reduced in China, especially in the field of foreign affairs.[92] Turning to the West-led international order and departing from the Soviet conception of Marxism was considered a new phase of China's practice of Marxism with Chinese characteristics in new national and international landscapes.

Against these new backgrounds, Soviet international law theory lost its importance in China. In the 1970s, the Chinese government stopped inviting Soviet international lawyers to teach in China and selecting students to study international law in the USSR. In addition, few Soviet international law publications were translated into Chinese. Meanwhile, pre-PRC international lawyers such as Wang Tieya and

[87] Zhou Gengsheng (n 72) 183–185.
[88] Zhou Gengsheng (n 72) 124–130.
[89] Zhou Gengsheng (n 72) 275–283.
[90] China's Ministry of Foreign Affairs and Literature Office of the Central Committee of the CPC (eds), *Selected Works of Mao Zedong on Diplomacy* (毛泽东外交文选) (The Central Committee of CPC Press/World Affairs Press 1973) 600.
[91] Speech by Chairman of the Delegation of the People's Republic of China, Deng Xiaoping, at the Special Session of the UN General Assembly, April 10, 1974.
[92] Deng Xiaoping suggested that China should not waste time on 'ideological debates' any longer. Literature Office of the Central Committee of the CCP (ed.), *Selected Works of Deng Xiaoping* (邓小平文选) (Vol. 3) (People's Publishing House 1993) 353.

Chen Tiqiang came to the fore again in international law teaching and studying in China.

In this respect, it suffices to examine how textbooks of international law edited by Wang Tieya and published in 1981 and 1995,[93] which were two major texts used nationwide in China, treated Soviet international law theory and Marxism. On the one hand, the 1981textbook still largely takes the Marxist approach to international law. This textbook refers to the *Selected Works of Marx and Engels* once, to the *Collected Works of Marx and Engels* twice, to the *Complete Works of Lenin* five times, and to the *Selected Works of Lenin* once. The word 'socialism' appears nineteen times, 'Lenin' twenty-six times, 'Soviet Union' seventy-seven times, 'bourgeoisie' thirty-three times, and 'imperialism' eighty-six times. In introducing the principle of self-determination of people, it repeatedly refers to Lenin's *On the Right of Nations to Self-Determination*[94] and praises Lenin for providing 'a comprehensive theoretical and policy discussion on the principle of national self-determination and the peaceful coexistence of states with different social systems after the victory of the first socialist state'.[95] It still insists on the 'class nature' of international law in explaining the source of the legal effect of international law.[96] While contending that the will of a state belongs to the will of the ruling class, it stresses that the legal effect of international law derives from 'agreement' between states.[97] Obviously, the nature of class is understood in a limited sense in the 1981 textbook. In fact, it does not refer to the ruling classes in defining international law, as Zhou's 1976 textbook does. International law is defined as a technically normative system, namely a totality of principles, rules, and regimes mainly regulating state–state relations with legal binding force.[98] Furthermore, unlike Zhou's 1976 textbook, the 1981 textbook does not suggest that there exist socialist and capitalist international legal orders. Noticeably, it does not refer to any Soviet international law literature, including the international law textbook edited by the Soviet Academy of Sciences, which was cited several times in Zhou's 1976 textbook.

The 1995 textbook further distances itself from Soviet international law theory. Noticeably, it includes a critical comment on Zhou's definition of international law. Wang suggests that Zhou's definition 'including the will of the ruling class of a country with an aim to illustrate the class nature of international law is clearly influenced by the predominant definitions among Soviet international lawyers at the time'.[99] The 1995 textbook went further to suggest that it is theoretically and

[93] Wang Tieya (ed.), *International Law* (国际法) (Law Press 1981); *International Law* (国际法) (Law Press 1995).

[94] Vladimir Lenin, 'On the Right of Nations to Self-Determination' (论民族自决权), in *The Collected Works of Lenin* (Vol. 20) (列宁全集) (People's Publishing House 1979) 397–400.

[95] Wang Tieya (ed.), *International Law* (国际法) (Law Press 1981) 66.

[96] Ibid 9.

[97] Ibid 9.

[98] Ibid 1.

[99] Wang Tieya (ed.), *International Law* (国际法) (Law Press 1995) 2.

in practice hard to identify the 'class nature' of international law on state–state relations.[100] Furthermore, it includes a critique of socialist international law. It observes that the socialist international law regulating relations between socialist countries around the world, which the USSR once advocated, 'has gradually faded away' as the USSR-led socialist camp disappeared.[101]

12.6 Conclusion

From the mid-nineteenth century onwards, China came to abandon its traditional 'All under Heaven' worldview and embraced the national state-based Western international law developed by European countries. China struggled for international membership and defended its national interests by taking advantage of international law. For this purpose, it tried to grasp Western international law theory by various means, including studying in Western states.

However, this process of embracing Western international law theory was interrupted by the founding of the socialist PRC and its alignment with the USSR. The new China introduced Soviet international law theory by translating Soviet publications into Chinese, inviting Soviet international lawyers to teach in China, and sending Chinese students to study international law in the USSR. This was part of China's overall process of turning to Marxism. In this fundamental moment of political and ideological transformation, Western international law theory was inevitably denounced while Chinese international lawyers educated in Western countries in the pre-PRC era turned to Marxism and especially Soviet international law theory, whether they wished to or not. Nevertheless, Western international law theory did not totally lose relevance in China. Instead, pre-PRC era Chinese international lawyers still played a considerable role in Chinese international legal practice.

The introduction of Soviet international law theory in China during the 1950s and 1960s and its legacy reveal how theories of international law and international lawyers adapt to political and ideological transformations. In other words, the introduction of Soviet international law theory in China was not merely an intellectual process of resetting the contours of international law teaching and researching in China. It was also part of an ideological process of building China into a socialist country with Marxism and a political process of aligning with the USSR. While the PRC embraced Marxism, it did not totally agree with the USSR's conception of Marxism and especially the USSR's international affairs policy. As ideological and political disagreements between the two countries emerged and

100 Ibid.
101 Ibid 5.

enlarged in the late 1950s and China turned to the West-led international order in the late 1970s, China started the process of de-Sovietization, reorienting Chinese international legal theory based on Marxism with Chinese characteristics. As a result, while Chinese international lawyers insist on the importance of Marxism, since the 1980s Soviet international law theory has lost its prominence in China.

13

In the Garden of Gethsemane

US–Sino Relations in the History of International Law during the Republican (ROC) Period (1912–1949)

Christopher R. Rossi

13.1 Introduction

A double-pull of Confucian virtuous moralism (*li*, 礼) and Western legal rationalism (*fǎ*, 法) crossed paths following the collapse of the Qing Dynasty in China.[1] This intersection shaped US–Sino relations at the birth of Chinese republicanism in the early 20th century. It facilitated the developing lingua franca of international law, with its spreading emphases on liberal idealism, sovereignty, non-intervention, self-governance, and peaceful dispute settlement. And yet, turbulent crosscurrents created by this double-pull exposed the tensions connected to exporting liberal internationalism. These tensions did not remake the Chinese view of the legitimacy of the Western world as much as they refined China's view of Western power.[2] They reverberate in discussions about the history of US–Sino relations between 1912 and 1949 (the Republic of China (ROC) period).

The Qing Dynasty's late engagement with multilateral Western diplomacy began with representations at the Hague Conferences of 1899 and 1907.[3] It bequeathed to Chinese republican internationalists a cautious regard for international law, which had a deep 19th-century association with imperialism. The outcome of the Versailles Peace Conference (1919–1920) also reinforced this cautious regard when the Allied powers overlooked China's war efforts[4] and rejected on three

[1] The concept of *li* derived from the classic Confucian text *The Book of Rites*, which linked the ideal of government to the demeanor of the ruler, the majesty and gravity of the ruler"s office and "regulated composure" of administrators, and the "alertness," "simplicity," and "humility" of the commoners. The Western legal notion of *fa* elevated a rule of law dependent on method, punishments (*xing*, 刑) and reward and moved away from personal status relationships between the ruler and ruled toward rational, rule-based relations. *See* Michell Chan, "Rule of Law and China's Unequal Treaties: Conceptions of the Rule of Law and its Role in Chinese International Law and Diplomatic Relation in the Early Twentieth Century" (2019) 25 Penn History Review 13–15.

[2] John King Fairbank, *The Chinese World Order: Traditional China's Foreign Relations* (Harvard UP 1973) 262.

[3] For more on Mingqian Li, see the accompanying chapter on his life's work in this collection.

[4] China had joined the Triple Entente, first secretly offering to the British 50,000 troops to retake Qingdao in eastern Shandong province. See Lorraine Boissoneault, "The Surprisingly Important Role China Played in WWI," Smithsonian, August 17, 2017 <https://www.smithsonianmag.com/hist

Christopher R. Rossi, *In the Garden of Gethsemane* In: *Histories of International Law in China*.
Edited by: Ignacio de la Rasilla, Jiangyu Wang, and Congyan Cai, Oxford University Press.
 DOI: 10.1093/oso/9780198888345.003.0013

occasions a proposal to include a "racial equality" provision in the Covenant of the League of Nations.[5] Suspicions solidified when the Allied powers handed over to Japan defeated Germany's concession in the North-Eastern province of Shandong (oft called the "cradle of Chinese civilization"[6]), rather than return it to China.[7] China's inability to prevent this transfer, or to attach reservations to the treaty, resulted in its refusal to sign the Versailles Treaty.[8]

This inauspicious start to the US–Sino relationship during the ROC period marked a "Garden of Gethsemane moment," where pragmatic international diplomacy, in conflict with fledgling Chinese republican ideals, ended in a sense of betrayal.[9] Here, major power interests and subaltern objectives attempted to balance moral imperatives against collective security. The load teetered decidedly toward collective security.

Notwithstanding lingering suspicions about the multilateral process, the ROC's engagement with multilateralism marked a radical departure from the Qing Dynasty's longstanding Sino-centrism. This new movement incorporated the rhetoric of international law, with its emphases on sovereign equality, respect for territorial integrity, the protection of minorities, and self-determination.[10] China's republicans "self-consciously" attempted to adapt these principles into a

ory/surprisingly-important-role-china-played-world-war-i-180964532/> accessed July 2, 2025, and then by contributing 140,000 laborers to the allied war effort in Britain, France, and Russia. *See* Vasilis Trigkas, "Sino–US Relations at a Crossroads: Shandon"s Importance at the Centenary of World War I" (2018) 73 Journal of International Affairs <https://jia.sipa.columbia.edu/online-articles/sino-us-relations-crossroads-shandongs-importance-centenary-world-war-i> accessed July 2, 2025.

[5] China supported in spirit Japan's proposed amendment to the Covenant (where it was suspicious of Japanese intentions at Versailles "in every other respect"), although it privately feared that Japan intended to wreck the Covenant based on a belief that the US Congress would never support such a racial equality provision given hyper-restrictive US immigration policy at the time excluding Japanese and Chinese immigrants. Jo-Anne Pemberton, *The Story of International Relations, Part One: Cold-Blooded Idealists* (Palgrave Macmillan 2020) 157 and 165.

[6] The expression is attributed to Wellington Koo. See Stephen G. Craft, "V.K. Wellington Koo and the Emergence of Modern China" (2004) 5 Asian History 51.

[7] See generally, Yongjin Zhang, *China in the International System, 1918–20: The Middle Kingdom at the Periphery* (Palgrave Macmillan 1991); Wunsz King, *Woodrow Wilson, Wellington Koo and The China Question at the Paris Peace Conference* (AW Sythoff 1959).

[8] See Charlotte Ku, "Abolition of China's Unequal Treaties and the Search for Regional Stability in Asia, 1919–1943" (1994) 12 Chinese (Taiwan) Year Book of International Law and Affairs 73 (noting China was not allowed to make reservations to articles 156–58, which confirmed Japanese rights in Shandong).

[9] The Garden of Gethsemane is the site on the western slope of Mount of Olives next to the Old City of Jerusalem. Gethsemane is derived from the Aramaic word meaning "to press" or "extract," as in an oil press. It is the site where Judas Iscariot betrayed Jesus. Judas was one of Jesus's original disciples, or Twelve Apostles. In the Garden of Gethsemane, Judas identified Jesus to the Romans and received 30 pieces of silver for his deed, which led to Jesus's arrest (Matthew 26: 36–56, Mark 14:43–52, Luke 22:39-46, John 18:1–14), making the Garden of Gethsemane deeply symbolic in Western history and iconography as a metaphor for deceit, betrayal, and agony. For a discussion of another Garden of Gethsemane moment, see Jianbiao Ma, "'At Gethsemane': The Shandong Decision at the Paris Peace Conference and Wilson's Identity Crisis" (2021) 54 Chinese Studies in History 45.

[10] See generally Lassa Oppenheim, *International Law: A Treatise, 2 Vols.* (1st edn, Longmans Green, and Company 1905 and 1906).

'constitutionally defined order',[11] which would support the transition from the collapsing universality of China's dynastic "Middle Kingdom thesis" to the modern nation-state. These antecedents reverberate today in the form of the Five Principles of Peaceful Coexistence, which have guided Chinese foreign policy since the 1950s.[12]

13.2 International Law as a Useful Tool with an Inherent Tension: Unequal Treaties

International law presented a useful tool for Chinese and American jurists alike. It allowed China to defend suzerainty against foreign encroachments by quoting Western governments in their own doctrinal tongue. This double-play bolstered China's defense of its territorial borders and political independence while demonstrating its sophisticated acceptance of the fundamental building-blocks of the post-First World War order. The keystone building block of this new order (and indeed of any legal order) centered on the principle of *pacta sunt servanda* (the good faith performance of obligations). It, too, had a complement, which Chinese republicans cited as the basis for negating unequal treaties: *rebus sic stantibus* (negating good faith performance because of a fundamental change of circumstance).[13]

International law usefully served the double interests of US policymakers, as well. They attempted to spread the commercial and ideological precepts of liberal internationalism into Southeast Asia. China presented a *tabula rasa* for progressive American reforms to the international system,[14] while simultaneously spreading the competitive advantage of an "Open Door Policy" that promised greater commercial gains for America.[15]

[11] Teemu Ruskola, *Legal Orientalism: China, the United States, and Modern Law* (Harvard UP 2013) 200.

[12] The Five Principles include mutual respect for sovereignty and territorial integrity, mutual non-aggression, non-interference in each other's internal affairs, equality and mutual benefit, and peaceful coexistence. For more on China's international law vocabulary, see Chapter 16 "Towards a Principle-based International Order? The Origin of China"s International Law Vocabulary in the 1950s–1960s" by Chen Yifeng in this collection.

[13] See Phil C.W. Chan, *China, State Sovereignty and International Legal Order* (Brill 2015) 82–84 (noting instances of invocation to negate unequal treaties).

[14] Jerry Israel, *Progressivism and the Open Door: America and China, 1905–1921* (University of Pittsburgh Press 1971) xi.

[15] ibid 13. US Secretary of State John Hay developed the US policy towards China and the Far East in a series of notes sent to European powers and Japan between 1899 and1900. The so-called Open Door Policy attempted to secure equal trading relations for all nations engaging in commercial trade with China. The idea of open markets and equal access extended the emphasis on most favored nation status initiated by the Treaties of Wangxia (1844) and Tianjin (1858) notwithstanding restrictions on Chinese commercial activities in the US beginning in the 850s and extended federally in 1882 with the passage of the Chinese Exclusion Act. For more, see generally John Soennichsen, *Chinese Exclusion Act of 1882* (Bloomsbury Publishing 2011); Delber L. McKee, *Chinese Exclusion versus the Open Door Policy 1900–1906: Clashes over China Policy in the Roosevelt Era* (Wayne State University Press 1977).

A point never reconciled, however, and evident at the start of US–Sino Republican-era relations, related to the Western emphasis on the sanctity of treaties. Treaties signed between 1842 and 1917 had provided the pathway for foreign power entry into China. They led to spheres of influence that ultimately established 92 coastal and riverine entrepôts,[16] penetrated non-riparian interiors, controlled trade, and began to carve up China in ways reminiscent of the Scramble for Africa. Treaties retained important significance for both countries throughout the republican period, and yet they portaged expectations and experiences that facilitated and undermined the interests of those for whom they were made.

The 1899 annexations of Hawai'i, Guam, and Western Samoa,[17] the introduction of 1,200 US marines to help quell the Boxer Rebellion in 1900,[18] and the US establishment of a protectorate over the Philippines in 1902[19] presaged growing American involvement in Asia. US entry into China came after enclaves had been established by the other six Western powers and Japan. This involvement carried forth America's own ideological agenda, which emphasized the written agreement and sought "assurances that recent extension of spheres of influence ... will not result in restricting [US] commercial freedom of action in China."[20] Failing a later attempt to persuade Japan "to hand over a portion of the [Shandong] territory to the five powers (including Japan)" as an intermediary step toward restoring the territory to China, US president Woodrow Wilson (1856–1924) openly confessed his support of legal formalism: "It would be better to live up to a bad treaty than to tear it [up]."[21]

This underlying support of the written agreement challenged US–China international legal relations throughout the republican era. It turned Wilson's ideologically pure interwar vision of liberal internationalism into a brackish admixture of intentions. Sometimes these intentions reflected cross-fertilizing influences in support of Chinese parliamentarianism. Sometimes they provoked suspicions about the use of international legal concepts as a pretext for further subjugation.[22] If liberal internationalism's selective application of its ethos fell short of the ideal, so

16 See Catherine Ladds, "China and Treaty-Port Imperialism" in John MacKenzie (ed), *Encyclopedia of Empire* (Wiley 2016) 1–2.

17 See Christophe R. Rossi, *Whiggish International Law: Elihu Root, the Monroe Doctrine, and International Law in the Americas* (Brill Nijhoff 2019) 3.

18 Trevor K. Plante, "US Marines in the Boxer Rebellion" (Winter 1999) 31(4) Prologue Magazine <https://www.archives.gov/publications/prologue/1999/winter/boxer-rebellion-1.html> accessed July 2, 2025.

19 See Philippine Organic Act of 1902, July 1, 1902, ch. 1369, 32 Stat. 691.

20 Confidential letter from John Hay to William Rockhill (24 August 1899), William Woodville Rockhill papers, 1826–1941. Ms Am 2121 (1047–84). Houghton Library, Harvard University <https://iiif.lib.harvard.edu/manifests/view/drs:23014971$16i> accessed July 2, 2025.

21 Ku 72 (quoting Wunsz King's account).

22 See Chan 3.

too did China's attempt to recast its political structure away from "age-old themes" of Sino-centrism and the tributary system.[23]

China's emerging distrust of Western treaty law developed from the 1870s.[24] By 1912, as Dong Wang noted, the first cohort of professional Chinese diplomats methodically took to the practice of re-examining treaty texts through a Treaty Studies Association formed under the Foreign Ministry of the First Republic.[25] At some times the textual analysis was used to "put pressure on foreign countries to carry out their treaty obligations" to repel excessive demands, and at other times to argue that imposed demands were invalid.[26] This practice did not depend on a wholesale adaptation of Western syllogistic reasoning or the universal ordering constructs assumed by Eurocentrism and its civilization standards, but developed from a genealogy that filtered the logic of Western legal reasoning through a normative sieve of Chinese politics, culture, and tributary history.[27]

An ambivalent shroud surrounded China's republican engagement with international law and its double-edged applications. Except for the case of Outer Mongolia, which eventually fell into the ambit of the Soviets, the "greatest accomplishment" of republican diplomacy may have been the defense of the multicultural and multinational expanse of borderlands that would evolve into China's national state.[28] Certainly, Wilson's New Diplomacy supported the inviolability of borders in Asia; less so in America's backyard of Latin America.

Two such admixtures came to dominate US–China international legal relations during the republican era: the interplay of liberalism and republicanism as set against the problem of extraterritoriality, and the "Open Door policy" itself. Both themes dominated republican China's relations with the United States. And both traced to the sanctity of the mid-nineteenth-century treaties of Wangxia (1844)[29] and Tianjin (1858).[30]

[23] See Jacques deLisle, "China's Approach to International Law: A Historical Perspective" (2000) 94 Proceedings of the American Society of International Law 271.

[24] Dong Wang, "The Discourse of Unequal Treaties in Modern China" (2003) 76 Pacific Affairs 402.

[25] ibid 403–04.

[26] ibid 404.

[27] See generally Maria Adele Carrai, *Sovereignty in China: A Genealogy of a Concept since 1840* (CUP 2019).

[28] William C. Kirby, "The Internationalization of China: Foreign Relations at Home and Abroad in the Republican Era" (1997) 150 China Quarterly 437.

[29] The Treaty of Wangxia was the first formal treaty signed between the United States and China in 1844. It was the American counterpart to the Anglo-Chinese Treaty of Nanjing that ended the First Opium War in 1842 and it established five open treaty ports at Guangzhou, Xiamen, Fuzhou, Ningbo, and Shanghai and the principle of extraterritoriality.

[30] The Treaty of Tianjin (1858) extended to the United States trading rights secured by the British following the Second Opium War. France and Russia also signed separate such treaties with China in 1858.

13.2.1 The US' Cautious Interplay with Chinese Republicanism and Its Reception in Chinese Circles

Wilson formulated his vision for liberal internationalism with his famous 14-Point plan for a restructured world order. His emphasis on open covenants of peace (Point 1) and political independence and territorial integrity (Point 14) galvanized China's first generation of international lawyers. Ironically, Chinese delegates at Versailles experienced first-hand the problem of secret agreements and self-betrayal when they were caught unaware of two such agreements previously signed by China and Japan. These secret treaties undercut the delegation's position on the return of Shandong,[31] and reinforced Wilson's international initiative, which specifically repudiated such practices and impliedly repudiated early 20th-century spheres of influence in China.

There was a double irony here. It testified to the twists and turns of the secret agreement. Wilson's Secretary of State, Robert Lansing (1864–1928), had secretly negotiated an agreement with Japan's special envoy to Washington, Kikujirō Ishii (1866–1945), in 1917. The Lansing–Ishii agreement sought to induce Japanese co-operation in the war effort. In exchange, the US recognized Japan's "special interests" in China, ambiguously suggesting an understanding on Shandong made to safeguard the US Open Door policy. Japan later exploited this ambiguity, as Chinese interlocutors had predicted, and the US effectively annulled the agreement in the Nine-Power Treaty (1922), a point of which the "Japanese publicly approved ... but privately held reservations as to the future."[32]

Nevertheless, Wilsonian internationalism significantly impacted republican thinking in China. Guoqi Xu noted this impact drew from the underappreciated influence that the Great War had on China's perception of itself and of the world.[33] The conventional supposition was that China had been "too passive in its diplomacy" and too "politically confused" during the warlord era to shape its

[31] See Bruce A. Elleman, *Wilson and China: A Revised History of the Shandong Question* (Routledge 2002) 36 (noting two 1918 secret agreements between China and Japan conferring on Japan political and economic rights to Shandong province in exchange for various infrastructure improvements, both not known to the Chinese delegates at Versailles). Britain and France had also concluded secret agreements with Japan, which acknowledged Japan's special interests in China. See David Wen-wei Chang, "The Western Powers and Japan's Aggression in China: The League of Nations and The Lytton Report" (2003) 10 American Journal of Chinese Studies 45.

[32] J. Chal Vinson, "The Annulment of the Lansing–Ishii Agreement" (1958) 27 Pacific Historical Review 69 ("Japanese publicly approved"), and 59 (Chinese prediction). See also "Treaty Between the United of States [sic] of America, Belgium, the British Empire, China, France, Italy, Japan, the Netherlands, and Portugal, Feb. 6, 1922 [the Nine-Power Treaty]", art. 1 (4), reprinted in Avalon Project, Yale Law School <https://avalon.law.yale.edu/20th_century/tr22-01.asp> accessed July 2, 2025 ("The Contracting Powers, other than China, agree ... To refrain from taking advantage of conditions in China in order to seek special rights or privileges which would abridge the rights of subjects or citizens of friendly States, and from countenancing action inimical to the security of such States").

[33] Guoqi Xu, *China and the Great War: China's Pursuit of a New National Identity and Internationalization* (CUP 2011) 3.

status during the emerging interwar era.[34] This view interpreted China as an internally reactive rather than externally active member of the international system. Only later would it shed its sense of victimization by being drawn into the world by forces beyond its control. Although the country was weak and marginalized within the international system, Xu argued that early figures in the ROC adeptly applied diplomatic means cultivated during the war to engage the world in ways that would ultimately help shape and support the Chinese national state;[35] China emerged from the war "fundamentally different" in social, intellectual, cultural and ideological terms.[36]

According to Pasha Hsieh, a Wilsonian roadmap, with dual emphases on idealism and legalism, created another kind of moment in Republic of China thinking, a "Grotian moment" of sorts.[37] Wilsonian idealism sprang from his 14-Point plan for a liberal world order. Wilson's legalism drew from the emphasis on a multilateral rulemaking process. These pathways animated a new breed of Chinese jurists who turned out to be "more Wilsonian than their Western counterparts."[38] This coterie of jurists included Wang Chung-hui (1881–1958)[39] and Cheng Tien-his (1884–1970),[40] who would serve as judges on the Permanent Court of International Justice during the interwar period, and Wellington Koo (1888–1985),[41] who would later sit on the International Court of Justice. These intellectuals bore an abiding attachment to liberal ideals.

Koo had attempted to enlist his advisor at Columbia University—one of the leading international legal authorities, John Bassett Moore (1860–1947)—as the Chinese legation's "technical delegate" at Versailles.[42] This attempt followed in the footsteps of Moore's father-in-law, the former US Secretary of State, John W. Foster (1836–1917: office term: 1892–1893), who had extensive ties in China and had advised China since the 1895 Shimonoseki treaty ending the First Sino–Japanese war (1894–1895).[43] Wilson, however, rejected the request as improper, although

[34] ibid 4–5.
[35] ibid 5.
[36] ibid 16.
[37] The phrase "Grotian Moment" was coined by Richard Falk in 1980 to signify the unusual rapid acceptance of a transformative system of rules that ushered in the state system after the Treaty of Westphalia in 1648. See Richard Falk, "Some Thoughts on the Decline of International Law and Future Prospects" (1980) 9 Hofstra Law Review 408. It has become something of an "irresistible catchphrase" in international legal circles. SeeJohn T. Parry, "What is the Grotian Tradition in International Law?" (2014) 35 University of Pennsylvania International Law Review 300–01. See also (2023) 44 (1) Grotiana, which is entirely devoted to analyses of the Grotian Moment.
[38] See Pasha L. Hsieh, "The Discipline of International Law in Republican China and Contemporary Taiwan" (2015), 14 Washington University Global Studies Law Review 113.
[39] For more on Wang Chung-hui, see the accompanying chapter on his life's work in this collection.
[40] For more on Cheng Tien-his, see the accompanying chapter on his life's work in this collection.
[41] For more on Wellington Koo, see the accompanying chapter on his life's work in this collection.
[42] Stephen G. Craft, "John Bassett Moore, Robert Lansing, and the Shandong Question" (1997) 66 Pacific Historical Review 233. Moore had also privately been in the employ of the Republic of China as a legal adviser. See ibid (n 4) 233.
[43] See S.C.M. Paine, *The Sino-Japanese War of 1894–1895: Perceptions, Power, and Primacy* (CUP 2003) 247. See also Michael J. Devine, *John W. Foster: Politics and Diplomacy in the Imperial Era,*

Moore did later assist China in crafting its legal claim to the return of Shandong province.[44]

The legal argument regarding Shandong's return placed much stock in Wilson's rhetoric condemning territorial aggrandizement by powerful states against weaker nations.[45] An imperfect agreement regarding Shandong was reached with the Nine-Power Treaty at the 1921–1922 Washington Conference,[46] where China was *allowed* to purchase the return of the province from money borrowed from Japan.[47] Counterbalancing political calculations again collided with precepts of liberalism, leading to the mortgaging of interest in promoting China's republicanism. The ultimate outcome nevertheless affirmed China's territorial integrity, and Koo invoked the principles of that treaty at the Far East Conference in Brussels in 1937 as the basis for reestablishing world order following the Japanese invasion of Manchuria (1931).[48]

Additional support for republicanism came from a new generation of Chinese intellectuals associated with the 1919 New Culture Movement.[49] Other Western-educated diplomats also secured key ambassadorships in London, Washington, Rome, Paris, and Berlin, and represented China at the Versailles Conference, the Washington Naval Conference, the 1924–1925 International Opium Conference, the 1944 Bretton Woods Conference reconstituting the international economic order, and the Dumbarton Oaks Conference (1944), which led to the creation of the UN Charter (1945).[50] Cosmopolitan jurists came to dominate the Republic of China's Foreign Ministry. They transformed the diplomatic practice of international law into an elite and relatively non-bureaucratic ministry that spanned the periods of the Provisional Government (Nanjing, 1912), the Beiyang Government (1912–1928), and the National Government (Nanjing and Chongqing,

1873–1917 (Ohio University Press 1981) (noting Foster's extensive ties with foreign governments doing business with his law firm).

44 Stephen G. Craft, "John Bassett Moore, Robert Lansing, and the Shandong Question" (1997) 66 Pacific Historical Review 234.

45 ibid 236.

46 The Washington Conference dealt with disarmament issues and with unresolved issues relating to the Pacific and East Asia. Participants included Belgium, China, France, Great Britain, Japan, Italy, The Netherlands, Portugal, and the United States. See Erik Goldstein and John Maurer (eds), *The Washington Conference 1921–22: Naval Rivalry, East Asian Stability and the Road to Pearl Harbor* (Routledge 1922).

47 See Craft 248–49.

48 Speech by Wellington Koo, Far East Conference in Brussels (1937), British Pathé <https://www.youtube.com/watch?v=20nn6fPunTw> accessed July 2, 2025 (time mark: 1:03).

49 See Elisabeth Forster, *1919—The Year That Changed China: A New History of the New Culture Movement* (De Gruyter Oldenbourg 2018) 9 (referencing the loose network of academics and students at Beijing University, including Hu Shi, Chen Duxiu, Fu Sinian, Luo Jialun, Qian Xuantong, and Li Dazhao).

50 Alison Adcock Kaufman, "In Pursuit of Equality and Respect: China's Diplomacy and the League of Nations" (2014) 40 Modern China 611–12 (citing V. K. Wellington Koo, Victor Chi-tsai Hoo, Alfred Sao-ke Sze, Chao-hsin Chu Cheng-ting Wang, C. C. Wang, C. C. Wu, and Wang Chung hui).

1927–1949).[51] The diplomatic and executive administration of republican-era governments remained, according to Julia C. Strauss, "remarkably consistent in terms of agendas and goals" despite considerable internecine political fighting.[52] In important ways, the cosmopolitan disposition of republican diplomacy contrasted with the traditionalist and rigid structures of the republican-era governments.

In line with its broader campaign to promote legal internationalism,[53] the Carnegie Endowment in Washington, DC also assisted at the start of China's republican era. In 1912, it facilitated the creation of a transnational network of elites by placing leading American scholars in Chinese academies. Carnegie Endowment trustees nominated the accomplished Columbia University political scientist Frank J. Goodnow to commence a three-year term to consult on the Chinese preparation of their own constitution.[54] According to historian Noel Pugach, Goodnow had his own idea of what to teach the Chinese, "whether or not they agreed or wanted to hear it."[55] Yale University sinologist Jonathan Spence dated the presumptive tutelage to 17th-century Jesuit fathers, commencing a 300-year Western tract more cautionary in terms of accomplishments than inspirational with an "idea of help meant to make China more like the West."[56] Goodnow's solution was to formulate a draft proposal in 1915 for a constitutional monarchy to usher China into "the modern age," an idea that fit his preconception of what China needed, and one which the Chinese largely ignored.[57]

However, a "standard package" of American legal thinking followed.[58] Harvard Law professor Warren Seavey (1880–1966) introduced the American casebook method to Tianjin's Peiyang University. William Blume (1893–1982), who later served for decades on the University of Michigan Law faculty, became dean of Soochow University (1921–1927).[59] Former Harvard University president

[51] See Hsieh 97. For a cultural anthropological perspective of the urgency with which the modern Chinese intelligentsia engaged with the Western notion of sovereignty, see Mayfair Mei-hui Yang, "Postcoloniality and Religiosity in Modern China: The Disenchantments of Sovereignty" (2011) 28 Theory, Culture and Society 3.

[52] Julia C. Strauss, "The Evolution of Republican Government" (1997) 150 China Quarterly 331.

[53] In 1909, the Carnegie Endowment committed, at the prompting of American jurist James Brown Scott, to the republication of so-called Classics of International Law. See "Editorial Comment" (1909) 3 American Journal of International Law 701 (announcing the republication initiative and reprinting Scott"s 1906 conceptual proposal). Between 1911 and 1950, the Carnegie Endowment published 22 titles containing 40 volumes assimilated mostly through Scott's general editorship. See Christopher R. Rossi, *Broken Chain of Being, James Brown Scott and the Origins of Modern International Law* (Kluwer Law International 1998) 40–42.

[54] See Noel Pugach, "Embarrassed Monarchist: Frank J. Goodnow and Constitutional Development in China, 1913–1915" (1973) 42 Historical Review 502.

[55] ibid 516.

[56] Jonathan D. Spence, *To Change China: Western Advisers in China* (Penguin Publishing Group 1980) 291.

[57] Pugach 516.

[58] See Jedidiah Joseph Kroncke, *The Futility of Law and Development: China and the Dangers of Exporting American Law* (OUP 2016) 123 (noting the "standard package of 'American law' that began to be exported to China at the birth of the republican era").

[59] See Robert H. Hu, "Arthur C.Y. Yao (1906-2004): A Pioneer Chinese professor at St. Mary's University School of Law" (2020) 51 St. Mary's Law Journal 131, 140.*h a focus on case method and case*

and Carnegie Endowment trustee Charles Eliot (1834–1926), along with Johns Hopkins-trained twin brothers William and Westel Willoughby (1867–1960/1945), were sent to advise the new Republic on domestic affairs and foreign policy.[60] This Carnegie project stimulated Chinese discussions of constitutionalism and debates about comparative forms of weak and strong executive administration.[61] It formed part of what Paul Carrington aptly described as America's "lawyer-missionaries."[62] Unquestionably the leading proponent of this export of the American legal project to China was Roscoe Pound (1870–1964), the longstanding Harvard Law School dean (1916–1936) and preeminent legal scholar. Pound accepted a position in 1946 as legal advisor to the Guomindang party.[63] Pound had been a paragon of comparative legal study and a believer in the capacity of law to socially engineer society.[64] His lectures in, and writings about, China emphasized curricular reform and statutory analysis, and he produced reports for the Ministry of Education on judicial and administrative reforms.[65]

Efforts to professionalize the practice of law contributed to the project. Charles Lobingier (1866–1956), who taught law at the universities of Nebraska, California, the Philippines, and Soochow, and also served on the US Court for China, helped to create a branch of the American Bar Association in Shanghai in 1914 (the Far Eastern American Bar Association). The aims of the association drew personal praise from US presidents Taft and Roosevelt and from the supreme US statesman, Elihu Root (1845–1937). Such was the enthusiasm which China's republican project drew from luminaries of the American legal establishment.[66]

Institutions of higher education in China had already begun to expand international language instruction (*Tongwenguan*, 同文館) in the 1860s, and through the introduction of international legal principles, starting with Lin Zexu's (1785–1850) commission of a partial translation of Emer de Vattel's (1714–1767) *Droit*

law (2013) 21–24 <http://blogs.colgate.edu/lampert/wp-content/blogs.dir/39/files/2013/09/XuNeal.pdf> accessed 2 July 2025. Michigan Law School's George Sellet replaced Blume in 1924, served as Soochow"s acting dean, and imported the case method of study to Soochow. See Neal Nianyi Xu, *Rise and Demise of the Comparative Law School of China: With a focus on case method and case law* (2013) 21–24 <https://perma.cc/4HHK-9M5E> accessed July 2, 2025.

60 See Teng Kaiwei, "Trans-Pacific Intellectual and Political Interactions: The Carnegie Endowment, Legal Internationalism, and Sino–US Relations, 1912–1925" (2021) 54 Chinese Studies in History 20.

61 See ibid 19.

62 See generally Paul D. Carrington, *Spreading America's Word: Stories of its Lawyer-Missionaries* (Twelve Tables Press 2005).

63 For a critical evaluation of Pound's "export-driven," formalistic, and largely "ineffectual" association with China's republican project, see generally Jedidiah J. Kroncke, "Roscoe Pound in China: A Lost Precedent for the Liabilities of American Exceptionalism" (2012) 38 Brooklyn Journal of International Law 77.

64 See ibid 86.

65 See ibid 96–97.

66 See ibid 123. Kroncke noted the important community connections facilitated by the association but concluded it was not clear that the association actually operated as anything more than a social club. See ibid 124.

des gens (1758; pertaining to the right to embargo trade).[67] Engagement accelerated after William A. P. Martin's (1827–1916) full translation of Wheaton's *Elements of International Law* (*Wanguo Gongfa*, 万国公法) in 1863. At the cusp of the republican era, international law became a mandatory examination subject for lawyers and diplomats, and it would become a compulsory component of the college curriculum around this time as well.[68] A total of 67 law schools arose during the republican period.[69] During this rich period of cross-fertilization, Zhou Gengsheng (1889–1971)[70]—educated at the Universities of Edinburgh and Paris, and later to be considered the father of modern international law in China—of Peking University and then Wuhan University, where he served as President, published his *Outline of International Law* (*Guo Ji Fa Da Gang*, 国际法大纲) in 1929, the first international law textbook authored by a Chinese national.[71]

These intellectual penetrations implicated presumptions about China's level of 'civilization' as measured by imperialism's late 19th-century standard of admission to the family of nations. This standard also reflected international law's turn to formalism before the advent of the republican era. Formalism implied that international law presented a fully formed set of substantive principles and judicial techniques that always led to the application of the one and only solution to a legal problem. Rather than embrace the self-contained inclusivity of this Western approach, Chinese internationalists proceeded with more circumspection, ultimately revealing China's cautious embrace of "legal gradualism." Writing in the early 1990s, Arthur Waldron concluded that this legacy 'has probably been more important and more fruitful than the revolutionary national assertion and treaty repudiation which have received the bulk of scholarly attention'.[72]

13.2.2 The Principle and Practice of Extraterritoriality in Sino–US Relations

Chinese circumspection about the influx of US-shaped Western international legal pedagogies and practices had root causes beyond the formalistic emphasis on treaties and the pejorative superintendency of the West's *mission civilisatrice* or civilizing mission. Extraterritoriality and the "Open Door policy" also affected

[67] See Ryan Mitchell, China"s Engagement with Public International Law in its Historical Context, CUHK Greater China Legal History Seminar (November 22, 2019), YouTube <https://www.youtube.com/watch?v=pJp2lZS7zy0> accessed July 2, 2025 (time mark: 19:24).

[68] See Hsieh 94–95.

[69] Qingjiang Kong, "International Law Teaching in China: Engaging in a Pedagogical Reform or Embracing Professionalism and Internationalization?" (2017) 12 Cambridge Journal of China Studies 13.

[70] For more on Zhou Gengshen, see the accompanying chapter on his life's work in this collection.

[71] See Hsieh 95.

[72] Arthur Waldron, "Book Review" (1992) 131 China Quarterly 797 (reviewing Yongjin Zhan's *China in the International System, 1918–20: The Middle Kingdom at the Periphery* (1991)).

Sino–US relations during the Chinese republican period. Extraterritoriality challenged Chinese republican idealism most directly, and the US Court for China, which had been established in 1906,[73] reflected this concern.[74] This court, secured by treaty exemptions, ultimately spread between China and 18 Western powers.[75] It granted foreign nationals, both defendants and plaintiffs, privileges to seek redress for injuries suffered in the courts of their nationality. Established in China's business hub of Shanghai, this court essentially acted as a US federal district court operating on Chinese soil.[76] Appeals were overseen by the Ninth Circuit Court of Appeals in San Francisco. Larger legations, such as Great Britain and the United States, allowed judges of these courts to ride circuit around China and hold sessions in other consular cities.[77]

The US Court of China represented a "unique extraterritorial judicial agency ... unprecedented in US diplomatic and legal history."[78] It was abolished in 1943 and yet during its operation it exercised a "kind of colonialism absent a colony" over all American citizens within the "District of China."[79] The extension of these courts and the practice of extraterritoriality stunted confidence in Chinese republicanism. More "inescapably disquieting" than an assessment of the court's jurisprudence was, as Teemu Ruskola has noted, the banality of its regard for extraterritoriality, as if the "court's jurisdiction were of no particular significance"[80] to its creators.

The jurisdiction attaching to this federal-like court in China posed problems for the US, as well. The court meant to apply US law—general acts of Congress—and not state law, which more often dealt with cases relating to embezzlement, petty crime, breach of contract, and wills and estates. And yet, these sundry cases filled the court's docket. The court's jurisdiction was "simply irrelevant to the disputes that were typically brought before it."[81] To remedy this deficiency, Congress allowed the court to apply an idiosyncratic common law.[82] This idiosyncrasy underscored the capriciousness of the Western idea of the rule of law, particularly its

[73] An Act Creating a United States Court for China and prescribing the jurisdiction thereof. Act of June 30, Pub. L. No. 59-403, 34 Stat. 814.

[74] See Kaiwei 22 ("most direct manifestation").

[75] In order of the dates of their first treaties, Russia, United States, Great Britain, France, Norway and Sweden, Germany, Portugal, Denmark, Holland, Spain, Belgium, Italy, Austria-Hungary, Japan, Peru, Mexico, and Brazil. See F.E. Hinckley, "Extraterritoriality in China" (1912) 39 Annals of the American Academy of Political and Social Science 97.

[76] On the international rise of Shanghai in relation to its extraterritorial status, see Wanshu Cong and Frédéric Mégret, "'International Shanghai' (1863–1931): Imperialism and Private Authority in the Global City" (2012) 34 Leiden Journal of International Law 915.

[77] Hinckley 98.

[78] Kaiwei 23.

[79] Teemu Ruskola, "Colonialism without Colonies: On the Extraterritorial Jurisprudence of the US Court for China" (2008) 71 Law and Contemporary Problems 217. See also Ruskola *Legal Orientalism* Ch. 5 (The District of China Is Not the District of Columbia) (Harvard UP 2013).

[80] Ruskola 241.

[81] ibid 222.

[82] ibid 219, 222–23.

transmuted application to China, and only further complicated China's republican project of embracing liberal international law.

The establishment of a multi-tiered system of justice in China, differentiating foreigners and their treatment from the treatment of nationals, began immediately following the conclusion of the First Opium War between China and Britain (1839–1842).[83] The concluding Treaty of Peace signed in Nanjing,[84] and the Supplementary Treaty of the Bogue (1843),[85] contained the first such concession and established the principle of extraterritoriality.[86] Thus, the practice of "living up to a bad treaty" would carry over into the twentieth century to persistently bedevil American relations with the Nationalist Government throughout the republican era.[87]

Article XXI of the Sino–American Treaty of 1844 encapsulated the method by which the US government exercised extraterritorial jurisdiction until the waning years of the republican era:

> Subjects of China, who may be guilty of any criminal act toward citizens of the United States, shall be arrested and punished by the Chinese authorities according to the laws of China; and citizens of the United States, who may commit any crime in China, shall be subject to be tried and punished only by the Consul, or other public functionary of the United States thereto authorized, according to the laws of the United States.[88]

Extraterritoriality fundamentally attacked the notion of China's republican sovereignty by carving out exceptions to self-rule. It undercut the rising tide of self-determination that had been a driving, although less than explicitly detailed, emphasis of American foreign policymakers at the Treaty of Versailles.[89] It

[83] For more on the First Opium War, see Chapter 4 "The Opium Wars, Extraterritoriality and International Drug Control" by Inge Van Hulle in this collection.

[84] See Treaty of Nanjing, 29 August 1842.

[85] See Supplementary Treaty Signed by their Excellencies Sir Henry Pottinger and Ki Yin Respectively, on the part of the Sovereigns of Great Britain and China, at the Bogue, 8th October, 1843 [Supplementary Treaty of the Bogue], Wikisource <https://en.wikisource.org/wiki/Treaty_of_the_Bogue> accessed 2 July 2025. For a discussion of noteworthy translation problems comparing the official Chinese and English-language versions of these first two "unequal" treaties, see Wensheng Qu, "Translations of Early Sino–British Treaties and the Masked Western Legal Concepts" (2017) 216 Semiotica 169.

[86] For more, see Luigi Nuzzo's chapter in this book.

[87] See Xiaohua Ma, "The Invisible War between the United States and Japan over China: A Study of the Abolition of Extraterritoriality in 1943" at 94 <https://dept.sophia.ac.jp/is/amecana/wp-content/uploads/2018/09/15-5_Xiaohua_Ma.pdf> accessed July 2, 2025 (noting the abolition of unequal treaties was one of the most important goals for the Chinese Nationalist Government since its establishment in 1911 by Sun Yat-sen).

[88] Frank B. Kellogg, "American Policy and Chinese Affairs" (1925) 11 American Bar Association Journal 576 (quoting art. xxi).

[89] Point 5 of Wilson's Fourteen Point Plan referred to colonialism, noting that "A free, open-minded and absolutely impartial adjustment of all colonial claims based upon a strict observance of the principle that in determining all such questions of sovereignty the interests of the populations concerned must have equal weight with the equitable claims of the Government whose title is to be determined."

hampered the development of endogenous reforms to the Chinese legal system that had progressively incorporated or modelled civil law and code-based practices elsewhere.[90] It complicated the mobilization of the constitutional reform movement in China, which since the 1890s had embraced the idea that a legitimate state apparatus was the *sine qua non* for China's entry into the state system as an equal member.[91] It forestalled the establishment of an independent judiciary by depriving Chinese judges of credibility to rule on important matters of jurisdiction (*compétence de la compétence*). Ironically, extraterritoriality also reinforced a condition of capricious indeterminacy that the legal formalists (led by Pound) purported to protect against. More than its placement among the unequal treaties (*bupingden tiaoyue*, 不平等条约) that served as the centerpiece of what has been retrospectively termed China's "Century of Humiliation,"[92] extraterritoriality allowed for a perplexing multiplicity of courts and judgments operating in the same locality;[93] it allowed Chinese persons claiming foreign citizenship the protection of foreign courts while doing business in China;[94] it facilitated tax evasion while insulating other foreign merchants from the laws of China in tariff schedule disputes;[95] and it solidified perceptions of endemic underdevelopment that colored the understanding of what it meant to open China to foreign trade and economic penetration. Intended as a "happy solution" to perceived irregular and arbitrary methods of port administration, it became evident to American policymakers that

As argued by Trygve Throntveit, however, this provision fell far short of what the call for self-determination meant to the Wilson Administration, to colonized peoples across the world, and in terms of the coming Mandates system established by the League of Nations. See generally Trygve Throntveit, "The Fable of the Fourteen Points: Woodrow Wilson and National Self-Determination" (2011) 35 Diplomatic History 445.

[90] For instance, the MacKay Treaty in 1902, art. XV of the 1903 China–US Treaty, and China's 1908 treaty with Sweden, held out the prospect that foreign powers would relinquish extraterritorial rights based on reforms to China's judicial system. By 1904, China had begun revisions to its civil code. Similar revisions began in 1912 on establishing a criminal code, with promulgated codes of civil procedure, criminal procedure, and a commercial code. See "Extraterritoriality in China", CQ Researcher <https://library.cqpress.com/cqresearcher/document.php?id=cqresrre1925121800> accessed 11 January 2024).

[91] See Steven Wang, "Indigenous Constitutionalism and Global Legitimacy: Excavating the Roots of Chinese Constitutionalism" (2021) 46 Yale Journal of International Law Online 100-01.

[92] China's "Century of Humiliation" (*bainian guochi*, 百年国耻) began with a series of unequal treaties imposed from 1842 onwards. These treaties resulted in the diminished status of China as a sovereign country and established foreign privileges in China that affected consular jurisdiction, leased territories, demilitarization, management of the Pai and Whampoo rivers, internal navigation, pilots, coastal trade, ports, customs, postal management, railway and mining rights, missionaries, and most-favored-nation status. *See* Shian Li, "The Extraterritoriality Negotiations of 1943 and the New Territories" (1996) 30 Modern Asia Studies 618–19. Referencing the work of Peking University's Wang Tieya, Xue Hanqin called the period between the first Opium War in 1840 and 1949 the most miserable period in modern Chinese history, indelibly conditioning an understanding of China"s position on international law today. Xue Hanqin, "Chinese Contemporary Perspectives on International Law: History, Culture and International Law" (2011) 355 *Recueil des cours* 14–15.

[93] See n 1 .

[94] ibid.

[95] See Joseph Gordon, "China Wins Tariff Independence" (1931) 34 Current History 547.

the "tariff schedules and various treaties" had from the Chinese perspective "become a sever[e] handicap."[96]

On relinquishment of extraterritorial rights in 1943, a supporting memorandum summarized the sentiment in State Department hallways that "China has grown up" and "should in all respects be treated as an equal."[97] The sentiment was by no means unanimous,[98] as extraterritoriality provided a bargaining chip in view of "a period of confusion and of unsettled conditions in China."[99] Relinquishing extraterritoriality had public support in America due to sympathy for China's defense against Japanese aggression. It formed the basis for a short-lived attempt to create a Pacific Charter analog to the Atlantic Charter,[100] which crafted common principles of Anglo-American cooperation in support of the postwar world. America's popular support against extraterritoriality and the advancing US role in Asia prompted the British "to follow the American lead" to avoid looking weak.[101]

13.3 The Open Door Policy: A Checkered Provenance

The establishment of sovereign equality during the Republican era also implicated commercial and trade relations, along with ideological complexities associated with the Open Door policy. US Secretary of State John Hay's 1899 diplomatic notes promoting the Open Door policy became the cornerstone of American foreign policy in East Asia[102] and a key part of the Nine-Power Treaty concluded at

[96] Kellogg 576.

[97] "Memorandum by Mr. Walter A. Adams of the Division of Far Eastern Affairs (Washington, March 19, 1942)," *Foreign Relations of the United States: Diplomatic Papers 1942, China* (United States Government Printing Office 1956) 268.

[98] For instance, Oppenheim's eighth volume on the law of peace, edited by Hersch Lauterpacht and published in 1955, placed China in the lowest, fourth tier of developmental barbarity formerly co-occupied by Korea and Persia. According to Xue, this "classification [not] only show[ed] the attitude of the [editors]," but carried with it "the position as to how to treat these states under international law." Xue (n 26) 27.

[99] "Memorandum by the Chief of the Division of Far Eastern Affairs ([Maxwell H.H.] Hamilton), (Washington, March 27, 1942)," *Foreign Relations of the United States: Diplomatic Papers 1942, China* (United States Government Printing Office 1942) 272–73.

[100] The United States Commander of the Pacific Fleet, Admiral Harry Yarnell, had addressed a message to the Chinese people in which he advocated a Pacific Charter, akin to the Atlantic Charter that articulated common principles to promote postwar economic prosperity, high seas freedoms, and post-war self-government. The Atlantic Charter provided that Britain and the United States would respect the right of peoples who "wish to see sovereign rights and self-government restored." Yarnell"s appeal was predicated in part on the abolition of extraterritoriality. It reappeared in 1954 as part of the Southeast Asia Collective Defense Treaty, 6 UST 91. The Atlantic Charter was a statement of common principles, not a treaty. See "Atlantic Charter," *Yearbook of the United Nations, 1946–47* (1947) 2 <https://www.unmultimedia.org/searchers/yearbook/page.jsp?volume=1946-47&bookpage=2> accessed 2 July 2025.

[101] Li 630.

[102] Attributing the maintenance of the policy, in large part, to the influence and longstanding tenure of Stanley Hornbeck at the Far Eastern desk of the US State Department. See Shizhang Hu, *Stanley K. Hornbeck and the Open Door Policy, 1919–1937* (1995) 13 (noting Hornbeck's "obsessive interest").

the Washington Naval Conference.[103] The concept itself had a checkered provenance. Hugo Grotius (1583–1645) had invoked the freedoms of commerce and navigation in his pamphlet, *Mare Liberum* (1609), to promote Dutch access rights in Portuguese-contested waters surrounding the Malay Peninsula. His motive was not to secure the freedom of the seas. It was to secure unimpeded Dutch access to Asian emporia through hegemonic command of trade routes.[104] Hay's announcement that other powers agreed with the policy turned out to be more wishful than "final and definitive,"[105] although it did secure for the US commercial privileges that otherwise would have been difficult to obtain.[106] Despite its purported significance, the Open Door policy never created the trade surplus anticipated by its US progenitors, nor did its purported emphases on transparency and openness impede or prevent Japan's shattering invasion of Manchuria in 1931.[107]

That invasion, however, did animate reconsideration of the "*ex injuria jus non oritur*" principle, which precludes the establishment of proper legal title for acts arising out of wrongdoing. Presented in identical notes to the Imperial Japanese and Republican Chinese governments in January 1932, the Stimson Doctrine upheld the principal of non-recognition of territory acquired by force. The doctrine applied *in extenso* to any treaty secured by illegal means and was adopted by the League Assembly that same year.[108] Stimson's attempted to establish an international "peer review" system to deny "the legality of any situation *de facto* … which may impair the treaty rights of the United States or … the territorial and administrative integrity of the Republic of China."[109] International law scholar Quincy Wright claimed that "[n]o diplomatic note of recent or even more distant years is

[103] See art. III, Nine-Power Treaty, ("With a view to applying more effectually the principles of the Open Door …").

[104] See Christopher R. Rossi, *Sovereignty and Territorial Temptation: The Grotian Tendency* (CUP 2017) 51.

[105] Howard Jones, *Crucible of Power: A History of American Foreign Relations from 1897* (Bloomsbury Academic 2008) 26 (quoting Hay).

[106] The policy also presented a proto-formulation of the most-favored-nation (normal trade relations) principle—a surviving pillar of the 1947 General Agreement on Tariffs and Trade. See United Nations Conference on Trade and Employment, held at Havana, Cuba, Final Act and Related Documents, April 1948 <https://www.wto.org/english/docs_e/legal_e/havana_e.pdf. It became a fundamental principle of the World Trade Organization. See art. 1, General Agreement on Tariffs and Trade (GATT); art. 2, General Agreement on Trade in Services (GATS); and art. 4, Agreement on Trade-Related Aspects of Intellectual Property Rights (TRIPS). For more, see Principles of the trading system, World Trade Organization <https://www.wto.org/english/thewto_e/whatis_e/tif_e/fact2_e.htm> accessed 2 July 2025.

[107] See Mark Atwood Lawrence, "Open Door Policy," American Foreign Relations <https://www.americanforeignrelations.com/O-W/Open-Door-Policy.html> accessed January 11, 2024).

[108] See Christopher R. Rossi, "*Ex Injuria Jus Non Oritur, Ex Factis Jus Oritur*, and the Elusive Search for Equilibrium after Ukraine" (2015) 24 Tulane Journal of International Law and Comparative Law 159.

[109] Foreign Relations of the United States Diplomatic Papers, 1932, The Far East, 793.94/3437b: Telegram 7 January 1932 (Telegram from Secretary of State Stimson to the Consul General at Nanking (Peck)) (the Stimson Doctrine), reprinted in Office of the Historian <https://history.state.gov/historicaldocuments/frus1932v03/d10> accessed July 2, 2025.

likely to go down in history as of greater significance."[110] The more circumspect Stimson later acknowledged that only "spears of straw and words of ice" supported the doctrine,[111] and yet the formalistic emphasis on enshrined treaty commitments served the purpose of isolating Japan as punishment for its aggression.[112]

When Japan attacked Shanghai in 1932, thus threatening the commercial center of China and its constellation of foreign concessions, the Four-, Five-, and Nine-Power treaties signed at the Washington Naval Conference (1921–1922) to preserve the balance of power in Asia began to break down. Stimson publicly signaled to the Senate Foreign Relations Committee that the hostilities in Manchuria, extended to Shanghai, could not alter the terms of the Nine-Power Treaty.[113] However, he did not conceal his impending concern given the complex interrelationship among the three treaties: "No one of these treaties can be disregarded without disturbing the general understanding ... effected by the group of agreements arrived at in their entirety."[114] The Five-Power Treaty had already prompted the US, UK, Japan, France, and Italy twice to return to the negotiating table (in 1927 and 1930) to stem naval competitions involving the unrestricted tonnage of cruiser warships. Japan's violation of the Nine-Power Treaty prompted Stimson to declare that the US would not consider itself bound by the naval limitations agreements.[115] The global depression and the protectionist trade contraction caused by

[110] Quincy Wright, "The Stimson Note of January 7, 1932" (1932) 26 American Journal of International Law 342.

[111] U.S. Department of State <https://2001-2009.state.gov/r/pa/ho/time/id/16326.htm> accessed July 2, 2025.

[112] The Tobar Doctrine was propounded by Ecuadorian Foreign Minister Carlos Tobar to deny recognition of de facto governments arising from revolutionary activity in Latin America. See Rossi, "*Ex Injuria Jus Non Oritur*" (n 108) 159. It was succeeded by the Hallstein Doctrine in 1955. The Hallstein Doctrine was propounded by Federal Republic of Germany Foreign Secretary Minister Walter Hallstein to punish by severance of diplomatic relations any country that recognized the German Democratic Republic (East Germany). The Republic of China (Taiwan) asserted the doctrine following the UN General Assembly's decision to seat the People's Republic of China. References to the doctrine arose in disputes between Greece and the Turkish Republic of Northern Cyprus, during the failed Biafran independence movement in Nigeria in 1967, in Morocco and Mauritania's dispute over Western Sahara, in Russia vis-à-vis putative independence claims of Chechnya, and in debates over the independence of Kosovo, Crimea, and elsewhere. For more, see generally Christopher R. Rossi, "Nagorno-Karabakh and the Minsk Group: The Imperfect Appeal of Soft Law in an Overlapping Neighborhood" (2017) 52 Texas International Law Journal 45. It was suggested, at least by implication, in discussions about the One China policy. The US recognized the People's Republic of China as "the sole legal Government of China" in 1979 and acknowledged that Taiwan was part of China. China attempted to change the Chinese text from the original "acknowledged" to "recognize," a substation that the US rejected. See Michael J. Green and Bonnie S. Glaser, "What Is the U.S. 'One China' Policy, and Why Does it Matter?", CSIS (January 13, 2017) <https://www.csis.org/analysis/what-us-one-china-policy-and-why-does-it-matter> accessed July 2, 2025.

[113] "Letter from Henry L. Stimson to William Borah (1932)," February 23, 1932, Teaching American History <https://teachingamericanhistory.org/document/letter-to-senator-borah-committee-on-foreign-relations/> accessed July 2, 2025.

[114] ibid.

[115] See "The Mukden Incident of 1931 and the Stimson Doctrine", Office of the Historian, Department of State <https://history.state.gov/milestones/1921-1936/mukden-incident> accessed July 2, 2025.

the Smoot–Hawley tariff (1930) limited public tolerance for extending economic sanctions against Japan and elevated reliance on the rhetoric of the rule of law. The Nine-Power Treaty, like the Four-Power Treaty, contained a *pactum de consultatio* provision but no method of enforcement other than this contingent pledge to consult with each other in the event of a violation. When the League's ineffectual investigation (the Lytton Report) failed to effectively deal with Japanese aggression,[116] the era's entire project of treaty-based peace agreements, non-aggression, non-recognition, and disarmament fell prey to the all-out Second Sino–Japanese War (1937–1945).

Furtive efforts to tend to China's fraying republicanism, complicated by the grand strategy to secure the Western theatre before turning to the Pacific region, included patchwork extensions of credit to the Nationalists. This allotment provided \$25 million in credit in 1938,[117] then \$100 million in 1940,[118] and then extended lend-lease support in 1942.[119]

Other efforts followed. The American Volunteer Group of P-40 Tomahawk aviators known as the Flying Tigers deployed in 1941–1942 to provide military defense against the Japanese.[120] Political hindrances associated with extraterritoriality and the six-decade-long Chinese Exclusion Acts (beginning in 1882) ended in 1943.[121] A series of Special Envoys, including generals Joseph

[116] According to a summary of the report:

On the night of September 18, 1931, anti-Japanese activists set off explosions on the Japanese-owned South Manchurian Railroad in Manchuria, northeastern China. The Japanese army used the incident as a pretext to invade Manchuria, and quickly occupied key Manchurian cities. China appealed to the world's powers for help. The Council of the League of Nations, supported by the United States, sought to negotiate a peaceful solution to the conflict. In early 1932, the Council dispatched an inquiry commission to China under the leadership of the British diplomat, the Earl of Lytton. By the time the so-called Lytton Commission arrived in China in April 1932, the Japanese army had already established the Manchurian puppet state of Manchukuo. The Lytton Commission issued its report in September 1932. On the advice of the report, the League of Nations refused to recognize Manchukuo as a legitimate state and proposed measures to reestablish the status quo. China accepted the League of Nations recommendations for restoring peace in the area; Japan did not and withdrew from the League in 1935. The report discusses recent events, issues between Japan and China, the situation in Shanghai and Manchukuo, economic interests, and the conditions for a settlement, and it offers recommendations to the Council. A number of maps illustrate the political organization of Manchuria, its railroads, the military situation at various dates from September 1931 to August 1932, and the routes taken in China by the Lytton Commission. The report is in the archives of the League, which were transferred to the United Nations in 1946 and are housed at the UN office in Geneva. They were inscribed on the UNESCO Memory of the World register in 2010."

See "Situation in Manchuria: Report of the Lytton Commission of Inquiry," Library of Congress <https://www.loc.gov/item/2021666890> accessed July 2, 2025. For more, see Chang 56.

[117] See "US–China Exchange," USC Annenberg <https://uschinaexchange.usc.edu/exchange/united-states-extended-credits-nationalists> accessed July 2, 2025.

[118] ibid.

[119] See Lend-Lease Agreement between the United States and China, signed June 2, 1942, Documents 457–62, Department of State <https://history.state.gov/historicaldocuments/frus1942China/comp5> accessed July 2, 2025.

[120] John T. Correll, "The Flying Tigers," Air Force Magazine December 1, 2006 <https://www.airforcemag.com/article/1206tigers/> accessed July 2, 2025.

[121] See Negotiations for relinquishment by the United States of extraterritorial rights in China, Foreign Relations of the United States: Diplomatic Papers, 1942, China, Documents 209-314, Department of State <https://history.state.gov/historicaldocuments/frus1942China/comp3?start=

Stilwell (1883–1946), Albert Wedemeyer (1896–1989), George Marshall (1880–1959), and Vice President Henry Wallace (1888–1965), attempted to shore up and advise the Nationalist government up to 1947. In 1948 Congress again sought financial solutions, passing the $400 million China Aid Act.[122] This money flowed to mollify China bloc supporters in Congress, who threatened to block European aid legislation to Europe unless accommodations to China's Nationalist government were also made.[123] Assessments from the Defense Department, the Secretary of State's Policy Planning staff, and the CIA informed that a political calculus had once again required restoration of the balance of power in Asia, which after the defeat of Japan inclined heavily toward Soviet Russia and its "position of unmatched power" among Far Eastern nations.[124] Recourse to the ethos of international law had little left to offer the late stages of the republican era, which already emitted a sense of doom.

The new political calculus, as opposed to the strategic calculus forming around the idea of containment, put the onus on China after the fall of the republican era to prove itself worthy of membership into other systems of Western international legal creation: the Bretton Woods system of liberal international economic reform and the United Nations. The litmus test for membership quickly devolved into the organization's first crisis—the Cold War deadlock over attempts to gain numerical supremacy in the General Assembly.

13.4 The End of the Beginning: Representation at the UN

Another representational issue also framed the end of the republican era. It would hamper the UN for more than two decades following. According to Eva Luard, the question of Chinese representation on the newly formed Security Council of the United Nations did not arise until the autumn of 1949, when Communist China's Foreign Minister Chou En-lai petitioned the UN Secretary-General to transfer the Nationalist China seat to the PRC. Prior to that time, the issue of the credentials of the Chinese Nationalist delegate had not been challenged, even by the Soviet Union.[125] Myres McDougal and Richard Goodman noted that "[c]redentials questions were all but ignored at the San Francisco Conference."[126] Both the Nationalist

91> accessed 2 July 2025; Act of 17 December 1943, Public Law 78-199, 57 STAT 600, to repeal the Chinese Exclusion Acts, and for other purposes (Magnuson Act) (permitting a quota of 105 Chinese immigrants annually).

[122] See John H. Feaver, "The China Aid Bill of 1948: Limited Assistance as a Cold War Strategy" (1981) 5 Diplomatic History 107–08.
[123] See ibid 108.
[124] ibid (n 24) 119.
[125] Evan Luard, "China and the United Nations" (1971) 47 International Affairs 729–30.
[126] Myres S. McDougal and Richard M. Goodman, "Chinese Participation in the United Nations: The Legal Imperatives of a Negotiated Solution" (1966) 60 American Journal of International Law 695.

Party and the Communist Party "had enthusiastically supported the formation of the UN," and a mixed team of Nationalist and Communist delegates represented China at the San Francisco Conference in April–June 1945.[127] The four representatives of the ruling Nationalist Party included T. V. Soong, Wellington Koo, Wang Chung-hui, and Wei Tao-ming; minority party representatives included Carson Chang (State Socialist Party) and Li Huang (Nationalist Youth Party). Tung Pi-wu represented the Communist Party, and Hu Shih, Wu Yi-fang, and Hu Lin represented the civil and education institutions.[128]

Certainly, China's resistance to Japanese aggression against its Northeastern Provinces from 1931 up to the attack on Pearl Harbor in 1941 generated much Western sympathy; "[i]t was by virtue of these losses that the ROC was given a permanent seat on the Security Council."[129] The acceptance of the idea of a Security Council had seemingly been decided at the Dumbarton Oaks Conference in Washington, DC from August to October 1944, but its composition remained in dispute.[130] As early as 1942, Roosevelt had broached the idea of a postwar United Nations centered on the concept of the "Four Policemen"—the US, UK, Soviet Union, and China.[131] Stalin balked at the idea during a meeting of the Big Three in Tehran in December 1943, arguing that "three policemen were all that were needed to keep the peace," and "China could not qualify."[132] The American position eventually won out as a means originally conceived to watch over Japan and Germany, a point that began in earnest when Allied Powers then included the ROC in the Far Eastern Commission in 1946 to deal with matters subsequent to the surrender of Japan. The Nationalist Constitution adopted by the ROC National Assembly in December 1946 expressly incorporated respect of the UN Charter (and treaties) and similar approving references to the UN Charter found expression in a number of bilateral friendship treaties concluded by Communist China beginning in 1950.[133]

In January 1950, Chou En-lai again cabled the Security Council to repudiate the legal status of the Nationalist delegation. Two days later, the Soviets lent support and formally proposed not to recognize the Nationalists. The US led a coalition of

[127] Winberg Chai, "China and the United Nations: Problems of Representation and Alternatives" (1970) 10 Asian Survey 397–98.

[128] ibid 398.

[129] S.H. Tan, "Representation of China in the United Nations" (1971) 65 American Journal of International Law 20.

[130] See Charles E. Bohlen, *Witness to History: 1929–1969* (Norton 1973) 159 ("Dumbarton Oaks settled all but two issues regarding the organization of the United Nations—the voting procedure in the Security Council and the Soviet pressure for the admission of all sixteen of the Soviet republics to the General Assembly. It took the conference at Yalta, plus further negotiations with Moscow, before these issues were resolved").

[131] Richard W. Van Alstyne, "The United States and Russia in World War II: Part I" (1950) 19 Current History 260.

[132] ibid.

[133] See Hungdah Chiu (assisted by R.R. Edwards), "Communist China's Attitude toward the United Nations: A Legal Analysis" (1968) 62 American Journal of International Law 21.

six countries against the proposal and with two abstentions, the proposal failed. The dispute led to a Soviet seven-month boycott of the UN and paved the way for the veto-free decision to engage the UN in the Korean conflict.

13.5 Conclusions

The transmission of liberal internationalism to republican China overestimated the internal contested restructuration needed to radically move away from the Manchu imperial bureaucratic state. International law's American-centric project of exporting international legal practices and policies to China underestimated the radical nature of its own presumed and inconsistently applied logic. It also underestimated the temporal consideration needed to dislodge an imperial system in place since 1644, when the Manchus succeeded the Han Chinese. Legal formalism's reliance on the written treaty, and the certainty with regard to its application and appropriateness to the Chinese context, created banal and unexamined presumptions that worked against the efforts to establish liberalism's roots in China. The practice of extraterritoriality hindered this process of international legal absorption most obviously. International law's long and contested construction of the idea of free trade also complicated this project. Its presentation in the terms of the metaphorical Open Door policy did not negate the cross-cutting strategic interests intended by the US to level the political playing-field in terms of European access to Chinese markets. It did, however, establish roots that have taken hold over decades involving tariff reductions, lower barriers to trade, banking reforms, privatization, and partial economic reforms sensitive to foreign investment.

Wilsonian internationalism's efforts to socialize China into a legalistically rule-based system had important and lasting consequences, none more important that the Chinese adaptation of the concept of sovereignty, non-intervention, and self-determination. Chinese cosmopolitan jurists during the republican era interpreted these principles as restraints to defend territorial integrity, thus paving China's entry into the state system in ways that functionally allowed it to benefit from and participate in the emerging normative international legal order while ultimately preserving the non-disruptive Communist Party model of compliance and Confucian piety.[134] The compliant adaptation of international law during the republican era conforms now to the argument of China as a status quo supporter of international law, a twist to the vine growing from the garden of the republican era.

[134] See deLisle 275.

PART IV

INTERNATIONAL LAW IN CHINA FROM THE NEW CHINA TO THE OPENING-UP AND REFORM PROCESS

14
China's International Law and the Third World during the Revolutionary Period (1949–1978)

Ignacio de la Rasilla

14.1 Introduction

After twenty-two years of civil war (1927–1949), which included the phase of formal, yet shaky, alliance known as the Second United Front between the Chinese Communist Party (CCP) and the Kuomintang during the Second Sino–Japanese War (1937–1945), the People's Republic of China (PRC) was established in October 1949. Then war-torn, deeply impoverished, plagued by widespread epidemics and diseases and minimally industrialized, with an estimated population of 540 million people, 85 per cent of whom lived in rural areas and with a literacy rate of less than 20 per cent,[1] much went on to change in the attitude of the 'New China' towards international law and international organizations.

Haunted by the excruciating memory of roughly a 'century of humiliation' at the hands of Western powers and Japan through 'unequal treaties'—which imposed extraterritorial and economic privileges, resulted in the loss of territory, and established foreign concessions that progressively reduced China to semi-colonial status after the First Opium War (1839–1842)—the PRC's main political priority was to embark on a radical economic and social makeover of the mainland. However, finding itself internationally excluded from the United Nations (UN), where Taiwan went to hold China's seat with the active support of the United States until 1971, and in line with Mao Zedong's 'leaning to one side' foreign policy directive in 1949, the PRC was also soon formally aligned with the Soviet Union through the thirty-year-long Sino–Soviet Treaty of Friendship, Alliance, and Mutual Assistance (1950), and adopted a radical anti-imperialist stance against bourgeois international law.

In the mid-2020s, seventy-five years after its foundation, the PRC has a population of approximately 1.426 billion people (or 1.450 billion including Taiwan),

[1] See e.g. Julia Strauss, ed., *The History of the People's Republic of China, 1949–1976* (CUP 2007).

Ignacio de la Rasilla, *China's International Law and the Third World during the Revolutionary Period (1949–1978)*
In: *Histories of International Law in China*. Edited by: Ignacio de la Rasilla, Jiangyu Wang, and Congyan Cai,
Oxford University Press. DOI: 10.1093/oso/9780198888345.003.0014

with more than 65 per cent residing in urban areas and a literacy rate of around 97.3 per cent. China is also 'the world's largest economy on a purchasing power parity basis (PPP) manufacturer, merchandise trader and holder of foreign exchange reserves'.[2] Additionally, it possesses the third most powerful military in the world.[3] The PRC's once straightforward and ideologically driven rejection of what it deemed the international law of Western imperialist and bourgeois-capitalist states began to shift at the onset of the 'opening-up and reform era' (改革开放) in 1978. During this period, the PRC became increasingly 'willing to address many of its most important external concerns in international legal terms and through international legal means'.[4] This initiated a forty-five-year process of pragmatic assimilation into, and influence over, the international legal order.

This process has culminated in the past decade of Xi Jinping's 'new era' characterized by an even more proactive and assertive engagement with international law, in accordance with the guidelines issued by the CCP's Central Committee in 2014. These guidelines called for China to 'strengthen foreign-related legal work' and 'vigorously participate in the formulation of international norms, promote the handling of foreign-related economic and social affairs according to the law, strengthen our country's discourse power and influence in international legal affairs, and use legal methods to safeguard our country's sovereignty, security and development interests'.

Once considered, at the height of its 'revolutionary period' from 1949 to 1978, 'from the legal standpoint of international law to function as "an anti-system regime"',[5] China now presents itself as a champion of the multilateralist embracement of international institutions, the international rule of law and an UN-centred international legal system. This 'legalist approach to international relations' is accompanied by a sophisticated, asymmetrical, and strategically based international legal regime-specific approach to the international legal order,[6] which is further characterized by a clearly defined globalist orientation.[7]

However, despite the nearly Copernican turn in China's approach to international law and the accompanying tectonic transformation in its relative position

[2] Wayne M. Morrison, 'China's Economic Rise: History, Trends, Challenges, and Implications for the United States', *US Congressional Research Service* (25 June 2019), http://fas.org/sgp/crs/row/RL33534.pdf. (accessed 25 February 2025).

[3] 2025 Military Strength Ranking, https://www.globalfirepower.com/countries-listing.php (accessed 8 June 2025).

[4] Jacques deLisle, 'China's Approach to International Law: A Historical Perspective', *Proceedings of the ASIL Annual Meeting*, Vol. 94 (5–8 April 2000): pp. 267–275, 267.

[5] Prof. Lipton, introduction to the panel. Jerome Alan Cohen, 'Chinese Attitudes toward International Law—and Our Own', *Proceedings of the American Society of International Law at Its Annual Meeting (1921–1969)*, Vol. 61 (27–29 April 1967): pp. 108–116, 108.

[6] See, generally, Ignacio de la Rasilla and Congyan Cai, eds, *The Cambridge Handbook of China and International Law* (CUP 2024).

[7] See Ignacio de la Rasilla and Yayezi Hao, 'The Community of Shared Future for Mankind and China's Legalist Turn in International Relations', *Chinese Journal of International Law* (2021).

within the international system between the Mao and post-Mao eras, many concepts that shaped the Chinese approach to international law during its 'revolutionary period' continue to influence China's international legal strategy and rhetorical apparatus. Paramount among the latter, and particularly consistent over time, is the centrality in China's international legal policies of what Alfred Sauvy described in 1952 as the 'Third World',[8] drawing an explicit parallel with Abbé Sieyès' *Qu'est-ce que le Tiers-État?* during the French Revolution.[9]

Following the periodization presented by Jerome Alan Cohen and Hungdah Chiu in their seminal *People's China and International Law* in 1974, this chapter revisits a neglected aspect of the history of international law during the Cold War,[10] paying special attention to China's international legal relationship with what is broadly known today as the developing world or Global South. This analysis is framed within the context of the 'evolution of Chinese Communist foreign policy' and, by extension, international law, which can be divided into five stages or 'basic periods' from 1949 to 1973–1978.[11]

The first stage (1949–1952), which included the participation of the People's Volunteer Army in the Korean War and China's support for the 'Vyshinsky Doctrine', was marked by China's adoption of the tenets of the Soviet Theory of International Law, as elaborated in Section 14.2. The second period (1953–1957), which is surveyed in Section 14.3, was characterized by the rise of the five principles of 'peaceful coexistence', the passing of the first PRC's Constitution in 1954, and the political rise of the 'Third World', epitomized in the Asian-African Conference held in Bandung, Indonesia, in April 1955. Section 14.4 of the chapter examines the basic period (1958-1965) in China's foreign policy and its approach to international law was largely marked by the Sino–Soviet Split and the formulation in its wake of a 'Sinocentric conception of socialist internationalism', positioning China as the self-appointed champion of post-colonial nations and revolutionary values during the decolonization era.

Section 14.4 examines the fourth stage in China's approach to international law (1966–1969), during the Mao era. This witnessed the height of the Cultural Revolution, which further radicalized China's 'revolutionary' approach to international law and led to the eradication of international legal education in the country. Section 14.5 extends the last stage of Cohen and Chiu's periodization (1969-1973) to 1978 and the early 1980s to briefly examine the effects of China's restoration to the United Nations in 1971 on its approach to international law

[8] Alfred Sauvy, Le Tiers Monde, L'Observateur (1952), http://www.homme-moderne.org/societe/demo/sauvy/3mondes.html (accessed 8 June 2025).

[9] Abbé Sieyès, 'Qu'est-ce que le Tiers-État?' (Jan. 1789).

[10] See e.g. more recently, Matthew Craven, Sundhya Pahuja, and Gerry Simpson, eds, *International Law and the Cold War* (CUP 2019).

[11] Jerome Alan Cohen and Hungdah Chiu, *People's China and International Law*, Vol.1 (Princeton University Press 1974): pp. 18–22.

during the stabilization and decline of the Cultural Revolution, leading up to the beginning of the 'reform and opening-up' process in the late 1970s. The concluding Section 14.6 briefly recaps the chapter's contents and connects China's major foreign policy initiatives since the 2010s to its special relationship with the 'Third World' during the revolutionary period.

14.2 A Revolutionary Spirit for the Wretched of the Earth (1949–1952)

Considered the paramount example of denial of representation to show disapproval of a revolutionary government at the United Nations,[12] the international institutional isolation resulting from the PRC's exclusion from the UN from 1949 to 1971 confronted it from its foundation with 'questions of government succession and international recognition'.[13] The impact on the PRC of this forced disassociation from the emerging global institutional order should be put in the context of China's earlier efforts to integrate into it.

As discussed in previous chapters of this book these efforts included earlier stages of defensive acculturation to international law following the first (1839–1842) and second (1856–1860) Opium Wars, as well as China's early active engagement with the Hague Conferences in 1899 and 1907 during the final days of the Qing Dynasty. During this period, China sought to climb the slippery ladder of the Western-biased and racialized 'standard of civilization' in international society.[14] This integrative pattern intensified during the Republican period (1912–1949), which witnessed a deepening of China's strategic appropriation of and adaptation to international law, alongside high expectations for the potential egalitarian opportunities brought about by the 'move to institutions'.[15] This blending of patriotic aspirations and a spirit of cosmopolitanism with which China joined the League of Nations and later the United Nations was somewhat encapsulated in Sun Yat-sen's slogan 'Tianxia wei gong' 天下为公—'All under Heaven is for the common good'.

Against this backdrop, China's period of exclusion from the UN (1949–1971) would largely condition, as we shall see, its approach to international law, prompting it to a heightened embrace of the fundamental tenets of the Soviet theory of international law (STIL) in the early years of the PRC and, later, a re-adaptation of these principles to align with China's unique position in the international legal order. The Soviet theory of international law was an offspring of the

[12] Kathryn Greenman, Anne Orford, Anna Sounders, and Ntina Tzouvala (eds), *Revolutions in International Law: The Legacies of 1917* (Cambridge: Cambridge University Press, 2021).

[13] DeLisle (n 4) 372.

[14] See e.g. Gerrit W. Gong, *The Standard of 'Civilization' in International Society* (New York: Clarendon Press; Oxford University Press 1984).

[15] David W. Kennedy, 'The Move to Institutions', 8 *Cardozo Law Review* 8 (1987): 841–988.

Marxist-Leninist political, economic, and ideological foundations, which assert that all law is a 'super-structure' derived from the prevailing modes of production in a society, or its economic base, as well as a reflection of the will of the ruling class. In capitalist societies, this results, according to Marxist theory, in the maintenance of exploitative and unequal class-based social relations.[16] This theoretical framework presented Soviet theorists of international law with 'an ever-recurring scholastic problem' which, in the 1950s, was seen 'as a nightmare to Soviet lawyers';[17] namely, what economic basis to assign to international law which is binding on both the capitalist and the socialist states. Additionally, they faced the complex theoretical question of reconciling international law with the 'Marxist tenet that each law reflects the will of the ruling class in a given society'.[18] Albeit sometimes at pains in its grappling with these theoretical difficulties in its squaring the circle of orthodox Marxism with international law, the overarching political aim of STIL was to position itself as a counterpoint to Western liberal approaches to international law. These approaches, often referred to at the time as 'bourgeois international law', were characterized as an international legal system applied among capitalist states, shaped and developed to serve capitalist interests and their imperialist social elites.[19]

By contrast, 'socialist international law' or, as it was also sometimes termed, 'proletarian international law' was defined as the international law governing a community of communist and socialist states bound together by a common class struggle and solidarity ties in pursuit of a range of collective interests that embodied the will of the proletariat and amounted to more than just the mere aggregation of the national interests of its member states. From this standpoint a limited conception of sovereignty emerged, along with a set of special international legal obligations among socialist states, all aimed at advancing socialist goals such as development, economic and social justice, and the democratization of international relations. This approach sought to purge the influence of 'bourgeois international law' in the historical shaping of a hegemonic and unequal international legal order. A related corollary of this conception was a staunch sovereigntist defence of the application of the principle of non-intervention and non-interference by Western liberal states in the internal affairs of other states. However, a nuanced interpretation of the principle of non-intervention and non-interference was adopted by socialist states, a position particularly espoused by the PRC during the 1960s. This flexible approach was employed in support of wars of national liberation and the decolonization of Western colonies, grounded in the principle of self-determination for

[16] See e.g. W. W. Kulski, 'The Soviet Interpretation of International Law', *The American Journal of International Law* 49, no. 4 (Oct. 1955): pp. 518–534, 518–521.

[17] ibid 518–521.

[18] ibid 518–521.

[19] See e.g. John N. Hazard, 'The Soviet Union and International Law', *Soviet Studies* 1, no. 3 (Jan. 1950): pp. 189–199.

peoples which subsequently evolved into a fundamental principle of international law during the decolonization era.

Soviet international legal doctrine and practice was 'a source of inspiration and emulation' for many socialist and developing countries during the decolonization decades.[20] Far from having been thrown into the dustbin of history, echoes of the 'ontological and epistemological ultimates of Marxism'[21] in their application to international law remain present in the international legal rhetorical policies of many states, including, notably, China.[22] Moreover, intellectual echoes of many of the main foci and *topoi* of the STIL are still foundational across the left political spectrum of contemporary international legal scholarship, particularly in particular among critically oriented international law scholars who emerged or were inspired by the Critical Legal Studies movement (CLS) and the interrelated Third World Approaches to International Law (TWAIL).

Such foci and *topoi*, occasionally blended with post-modernist theories addressed at questioning liberal progress narratives,[23] include, to mention but a few of its intellectual legacies: the stress on the historical structural continuity of imperialism in its contemporary forms of neo-imperialism and neo-colonialism;[24] the emphasis on the irreducibly political nature of international law;[25] the critique of international human rights as providing inter alia camouflage for hegemonic interventionist policies;[26] the critique of the civilized binary and its iterations, including that of authoritarian versus democratic states as well as related criticism of the hitherto emerging norm of democratic governance in international law;[27] the insistence on a developing countries/developed countries lens—more recently in the form of Global North–Global South—in the study of international law;[28] the celebration of the historical landmarks of the Global South as sites of resistance;[29]

[20] William E. Butler, 'American Research on Soviet Approaches to Public International Law', *Columbia Law Review* 70, no. 2 (Feb. 1970), 218–235, 218.

[21] Suzanne Ogden, 'China and International Law: Implications for Foreign Policy', *Pacific Affairs* 49, no. 1 (Spring 1976) 28–48, 29.

[22] See more recently Raluca Grosescu and Ned Richardson-Little, 'Socialism and International Law: Legacies of Innovation, Contradiction, and Failure', in *Socialism and International Law: The Cold War and Its Legacies, The History and Theory of International Law*, edited by Raluca Grosescu and Ned Richardson-Little (OUP 2024): pp. 1–16.

[23] Susan Marks, ed., *International Law on the Left: Re-Examining Marxist Legacies* (CUP 2008). For an intellectual retrospective see David Kennedy and Martti Koskenniemi, *Of Law and the World: Critical Conversations on Power, History and Political Economy* (Harvard University Press 2023).

[24] Antony Anghie, *Imperialism, Sovereignty and the Making of International Law* (CUP 2005).

[25] Martti Koskenniemi, *The Politics of International Law* (London: Bloomsbury Publishing 2011).

[26] David Kennedy, 'The International Human Rights Movement: Part of the Problem?', *Harvard Human Rights Journal* 15 (2002): p. 101.

[27] Susan Marks, *The Riddle of All Constitutions* (OUP 2000).

[28] See e.g. Dimitri Van Den Meerssche, 'Global South Perspectives on Methodology and Critique in International Law', *Leiden Journal of International Law* 37, Issue 4 (2024): pp. 763–772.

[29] Luis Eslava, Michael Fakhri, and Vasuki Nesiah, eds., *Bandung, the Global South, and International Law: Critical Pasts and Pending Futures* (CUP 2017).

a stress on the intertwining of political economy and international law;[30] a critique of the 'structural bias' of the international institutions;[31] a critique of the universalism of international law as a veiled form of Eurocentrism and as masking deep-seated geopolitical and geo-economic entrenched interests;[32] distrust of global law and global governance institutions as vehicles for hegemonism and the entrenched interests of elite capitalist transnational classes;[33] and strong ideological partisanship as well as an adversarial stance in international legal theory.

Like other countries at the time, the semi-insulated 'New China', which maintained diplomatic relations with only about twenty-six states, initially subscribed to the ideologically infused theoretical conception of Western international law as a 'class law serving the needs of the ruling capitalist class'.[34] This perspective was particularly evident in China's strong emphasis on sovereignty as a hard-won prize and its related state-centric vision of international law, in which individuals were entirely subordinated to the state and, therefore, not considered subjects of international law. This stance contrasted with Western notions of 'world law', which were anchored in an individualistic and universalist conception of human rights—seen by China as 'neo-colonialist subterfuges' designed to interfere in the domestic affairs of other states. Similarly, over time, China rejected what the leading Chinese international law scholar of the period, Zhou Gengsheng, viewed as the detrimental effects of 'the monist view' on national sovereignty. He was particularly wary of any proposal that might limit state sovereignty—whether it called 'for a "world state", collective intervention, compulsory jurisdiction, the expansion of the subjects of international law, or the development of transnational law for weak states and socialist and progressive states'.[35]

Following its founding, China soon undertook efforts to support the expansion of revolutionary politics in Asian states as evidence of its commitment to proletarian internationalism. It placed a strong emphasis on anti-imperialism and decolonization as the cornerstones of global revolution. In the highly politicized and strategic context of the early Cold War, China viewed international law as a malleable tool within its foreign policy arsenal—one to be utilized when advantageous and left aside when disadvantageous. Consequently, rather than being normatively

[30] David Kennedy, 'Law and the Political Economy of the World', *Leiden Journal of International Law* 26, Issue 1 (2013): pp. 7–48; John Haskell and Akbar Rasulov, 'International Law and the Turn to Political Economy', *Leiden Journal of International Law* 31, Issue 2 (2018): pp. 243–250.

[31] Martti Koskenniemi, 'The Politics of International Law—20 Years Later', *European Journal of International Law* 20, Issue 1 (Feb. 2009): pp. 7–19.

[32] Martti Koskenniemi, 'International Law in Europe: Between Tradition and Renewal', *European Journal of International Law* 16, Issue 1 (Feb. 2005): pp. 113–124.

[33] Bhupinder S. Chimni, 'International Institutions Today: An Imperial Global State in the Making', *European Journal of International Law* 14, no. 1 (2004): pp. 1–37.

[34] Ivy Leng-eng Chua, 'Communist China and International Law', *The Quarterly Journal of the Library of Congress* 24, no. 4 (Oct. 1967): pp. 319–334, 322.

[35] Cited by Ogden (n 21) 34.

seen as an autonomous constraint on state behaviour, international law was framed in strict Realpolitik terms as merely a 'political instrument'.[36]

In this context, the PRC heartily subscribed to what has sometimes been known as the 'Vyshinsky Doctrine', named after Soviet Minister of Foreign Affairs (1949–1953) Andrey Vyshinsky, who introduced it in the UN General Assembly in 1950. According to this 'neo-just-war thesis',[37] the prohibition of the threat and use of force under Article 2.4 of the UN Charter did not apply to wars of national liberation from Western colonialism. Similarly, allowing the US deployment of the Seventh Fleet in the Taiwan Strait in June 1950—later reinforced by a US–Taiwan mutual defence treaty in 1954—hostility between the PRC and the United States deepened. The US refused to recognize the PRC and sought to encourage other nations to adopt a similar stance. This antagonism characterized most of China's revolutionary period until a certain rapprochement with the West in the early 1970s. Against this backdrop, the PRC authorized the formation of a 'People's Volunteers Army' (rather than the 'People's Liberation Army') to intervene in the Korean War (1950–1953) at the request of the Democratic People's Republic of Korea (DPRK). This marked the first of the four major military interventions undertaken by the PRC since its founding.[38]

The radical shift in China's foreign policy and its approach to international law soon permeated legal education. During the first phase of the 'Establishment of the Legal Education System' (1949–1956) in the PRC, this transformation was carried out in line with what Han Depei and Stephen Kanter described as the 'broader guiding principle for the reform of legal education', as articulated by the Central People's Government: 'to learn from the successful experience of Soviet legal education and combine it with the actual conditions of China.'[39] Translations of Soviet international law textbooks, particularly those in 1950 by the prominent Soviet jurist and Director of the Institute of Law of the Academy of Sciences of the USSR Eugene A. Korovin (1892–1964), played a key role in this shift. Additionally, a monthly publication entitled *Collected Translations of International Problems* (Kuo-chi wen-t'i yi-ts'ung), which from 1953 to at least 1959 translated articles from Soviet sources, further reinforced Soviet influence. This trend contributed to what Suzanne Ogden has characterized as the general subservience of academic international law scholarship to the rationalization of foreign policy decision-making in China.[40] Meanwhile, as Maria Carrai notes, 'the new government,

[36] Hungdah Chiu, 'Communist China's Attitude toward International Law', *American Journal of International Law* 60, no. 2 (Apr. 1966): pp. 245–267 247.

[37] Stephen C. Neff, *Justice Among Nations: A History of International Law* (Harvard University Press 2014) 422.

[38] See further Zhixiong Huang and Yaohui Ying, 'The Chinese Approach to Jus ad Bellum in International Law and Cyberwarfare', in *The Cambridge Handbook of China and International Law*, edited by Ignacio de la Rasilla and Congyan Cai (CUP 2024): pp. 203–218 206–208.

[39] Han Depei and Stephen Kanter, Legal Education in China, *The American Journal of Comparative Law* 32, no. 3 (1984): pp. 543–582, 546.

[40] ibid 31.

lacking experts in the discipline', largely relied on some elite Chinese international law professors from the Republican period who had remained in their university positions on the mainland. Scholars such as Zhou Gengsheng (1889–1971), Wang Tieya (1913–2003), Chen Tiqiang (1917–1983), and Han Depei (1911–2009), all of whom are included in the portraits section of this book, continued to condemn the 'unequal treaties', the abolition of which had become a 'repository of techniques for achieving national salvation and national strength'.[41]

14.3 Peaceful Coexistence Takes Centre Stage (1953–1957)

In the 'second broad phase of its foreign policy', which, according to J. A. Cohen and H. Chiu, 'lasted until mid-1957', the PRC focused on the 'relaxation of international tensions to facilitate both China's development at home and its renewed quest for legitimacy abroad'. This shift involved toning down its support for wars of national liberation in neighbouring countries and advocating for 'peaceful coexistence between Communist and non-Communist states'.[42] It was as part of this broader diplomatic reorientation that the Five Principles of Peaceful Coexistence (Five Principles) emerged. These principles—mutual respect for sovereignty and territorial integrity, mutual nonaggression, mutual noninterference in internal affairs, equality and mutual benefit, and peaceful coexistence—were touted, alongside the doctrine of 'unequal treaties', as 'Chinese contributions to general doctrine' in international law.[43] The Five Principles are also known as the *Panchsheel* Agreement (or 'five virtues' in Sanskrit), as they were first formally enunciated in the Agreement on Trade and Intercourse between the Tibet region of China and India, signed on 29 April 1954 by Indian Prime Minister Jawaharlal Nehru and Chinese Premier Zhou Enlai to ease tensions in a Sino–Indian border conflict. Shortly thereafter, in June 1954, the Five Principles were included in China's joint declarations with India and Burma (now Myanmar) as a statement of the fundamental guidelines governing both their bilateral relations and their diplomatic engagements with other countries.

Often described as the cornerstone of China's approach to international law and international relations, the Five Principles have been the subject of extensive scholarly analysis by Chinese international law experts.[44] They were incorporated into the Preamble of China's 1954 Constitution, alongside the statement that 'the firm

[41] Maria Carrai, *Sovereignty in China: A Genealogy of a Concept since 1840* (CUP 2019): pp. 154–155.
[42] Cohen and Chiu (n 11) 19.
[43] DeLisle (n4) 372.
[44] See e.g. numerous references to it in Tieya Wang, *International Law in China: Historical and Contemporary Perspectives*, 221 Recueil des Cours 195 (Nijhoff 1990) 263–287; and also Hanqin Hue, *Chinese Contemporary Perspectives on International Law: History, Culture and International Law* (Nijhoff 2012).

and consistent policy of our country is to strive for the noble aims of world peace and the progress of mankind', serving as the principled foundation for 'establishing and extending diplomatic relations with all countries'.[45] The Five Principles have remained in the Preamble of all subsequent Chinese Constitutions, including those enacted in 1975, 1978, and, most recently, 1982. Although in terms of its legal status the Preamble to the Chinese Constitution is considered 'a symbolic preamble',[46] it plays a central political role by providing the substantive part of China's so-called mother of all laws with a legitimizing 'narrative of peoplehood'.[47] The 1982 Constitution is one of the world's most ideologically charged constitutions, as it is customary for each generation of CCP leadership to incorporate its main ideas, policies, and practices into it. Despite being one of the most frequently revised constitutions worldwide—with amendments in 1988, 1993, 1999, 2004, and 2018—the Five Principles of Peaceful Coexistence have remained a consistent element in its Preamble.[48]

The high point of China's shift towards peaceful coexistence was the Asian-African Conference held in Bandung, Indonesia, in April 1955, which was hailed as 'the first intercontinental conference of coloured peoples in the history of mankind'.[49] Under the leadership of Zhou Enlai (1898–1976), the inaugural Premier of the People's Republic of China (PRC) from 1949 until his death in 1976 and its first Minister of Foreign Affairs (1949–1958), China attended the conference with a clear programmatic intent: 'to foster bilateral relationships with other participating countries and to break down the Western isolation and containment policy.'[50]

China played a significant role in the conference's success. Officially termed the 'Declaration on the Promotion of World Peace and Cooperation', but widely known as the 'Ten Principles of the Bandung Conference', the final declaration adopted by the twenty-nine participating Asian and African countries incorporated the Five Principles of Peaceful Coexistence. However, as Yifeng Chen notes, the 'terminological similarities' between the UN Charter and the Ten Principles should not lead to an underestimation of the declaration's 'distinctive significance

[45] 1954 Constitution of the People's Republic of China, https://ecommons.cornell.edu/items/7ba1f815-e4c0-4bcf-9693-74cf0de56202?utm=. (accessed 25 February 2025).

[46] Liav Orgad, 'The Preamble in Constitutional Interpretation', 8 *International Journal of Constitutional Law* (2010) 714.

[47] Adeno Addis, 'Constitutional Preambles as Narratives of Peoplehood', 12 *Vienna Journal of International Constitutional Law* (2018): p. 125.

[48] 1982 Constitution of the People's Republic of China (Rev. 2018), https://www.constituteproject.org/constitution/China_2018 (accessed 8 June 2025).

[49] Speech by President Soekarno at the Opening of the Asian-African Conference (Apr. 18, 1955), reprinted in George McTurnan Kahin, Asian-African Conference: Bandung, Indonesia, (Apr. 1955) (Ithaca: Cornell University Press 1956), 39–51. Cited in Yifeng Chen, 'Bandung, China, and the Making of World Order in East Asia', in *The Global South and International Law: Critical Pasts and Pending Futures*, edited by Luis Eslava, Michael Fakhri, and Vasuki Nesiah (Cambridge University Press 2017): pp. 177–195, 187.

[50] Chen (n 49) 182.

and relevance to the development of a postcolonial world order'. This is because the 'UN Charter was drafted before most Asian and African countries gained national independence, and by the time of the conference, many of these countries were blocked from admission to the UN due to Cold War antagonism'.[51] Over time, the Five Principles were endorsed in subsequent UN General Assembly resolutions, particularly Resolution 1514 on Decolonization (1960). Moreover, the Conference of Non-Aligned Nations adopted the Five Principles as the core of the Non-Aligned Movement in 1961 and, a few years later, the Five Principles also inspired the Friendly Relations Declaration contained in Resolution 2625 (1970) of the UN General Assembly.

For the PRC, the Bandung Conference was a pivotal moment in establishing the foundation of its own independent diplomacy, planting the seeds for a Chinese 'third way' beyond the bipolarity of the Cold War. As Section 14.4 examines, this approach became further consolidated after the Sino–Soviet Split, which reached a point of no return in 1960 when the USSR abruptly withdrew technical aid, recalled around 1,400 Soviet experts, and cancelled more than 200 scientific collaborative projects. Bandung also served as a launching pad for China's longstanding close diplomatic relations with Asian and African states. This is corroborated by the fact that before Bandung, China had diplomatic relations with only six Asian and African countries, but this number grew to eighteen by 1959 and thirty-two by 1966.[52] These close connections would ultimately prove decisive, as Section 14.5 explores, in China's restoration to its seat in the United Nations in 1971. Although Bandung marked the beginning of China's diplomatic focus on African-Asian solidarity—emphasizing opposition to racial discrimination, anti-colonialism, and full sovereignty over natural resources—the influence of the Five Principles briefly extended beyond the newly developing countries. During this period, the PRC also sought to improve relations with major Western powers and non-Communist states on the basis of these principles.[53]

Although there was no specialized international law periodical published in China at the time, the mid-1950s saw the publication of several articles on international law, largely inspired by the Soviet Theory of International Law (STIL), in existing Chinese legal journals. This period also witnessed a 'structured debate over the nature of international law' which benefited from the 'Hundred Flowers' movement (1956–1957)—named after Mao's slogan, 'Let a hundred flowers bloom, let a hundred schools of thought contend'. However, this brief period, during which the CCP encouraged intellectuals and citizens to criticize the government in order to improve the socialist system, was soon followed by the Anti-Rightist Campaign or 'Rectification Campaign' (1957–1966). During this campaign, many

[51] ibid 188.
[52] ibid 192.
[53] Ivy Leng-eng Chua (n 34) 332.

prominent international law professors who had been trained abroad during the Republican period—including Wang Tieya, Chen Tiqiang, and Han Depei—were removed from their university positions and sent for re-education, in some cases through physical labour, to instil the socialist and proletarian values of the new regime. Writing years later as the Dean of Wuhan Law School in the mid-1980s, Han Depei reflected that the Anti-Rightist struggle of 1957 had 'led to the spread of legal nihilism—despising the law, negating the legal system, and ignoring legal education'.[54] This erosion would eventually pave the way for the even more radical effects of the Cultural Revolution, which profoundly impacted legal education and, by extension, the academic study of international law in China from the mid-1960s onward.

14.4 The Sino–Soviet Split and China's Quest for Leadership of the Third World (1958–1965)

Although the Sino–Soviet Treaty of Friendship, Alliance, and Mutual Assistance of 1950 remained in force, as originally planned by Mao and Stalin, until 1979, the so-called Sino–Soviet Split gradually crystallized and evolved from the late 1950s into a 'complex interplay of political, ideological, economic, and strategic differences'.[55] These tensions, initially triggered by Stalin's death in 1953 and further exacerbated by Khrushchev's 'secret speech' in 1956—along with subsequent policies of de-Stalinization and the Soviet approach of 'peaceful coexistence' with the capitalist world—fuelled China's renewed revolutionary orientation across the Third World in the 1960s. Indeed, while, as noted by Odgen, 'in the 1950s and early 1960s, it would not be unfair to say that almost all Chinese positions on international law were derived from the Soviet position',[56] China's international political stance gradually shifted 'from alliance with Moscow to a self-appointed champion of post-colonial nations' and, ultimately, 'to world wellspring of revolutionary values' during the remainder of the decade.[57] This transformation also led to an increasingly independent Chinese position in the international legal sphere and the emergence of 'different views toward international law in some aspects'.[58]

China, while still adhering to the general tenets of 'socialist international law', embraced the revolutionary-decolonization spirit of the late 1950s and 1960s 'on the basis of militant anti-imperialism rather than peaceful coexistence'[59] with the

[54] Han and Kanter (n 39) 555.
[55] See generally Shao-Chuan Leng, 'Legal Aspects of the Sino-Soviet Dispute', *Asian Survey* 12, no. 6 (Jun. 1972): pp. 493–509.
[56] Ogden (n 21) 30.
[57] DeLisle (n 4) 372.
[58] Chiu (n 36) 245.
[59] Cohen and Chiu (n 11) 19.

West. This stance positioned China in opposition to, and as an alternative to, both American and Soviet influence on the world stage and the Cold War's rigid dichotomy between two antagonistic blocs. As it had done in the aftermath of the founding of the PRC in 1949, China redoubled its support for the fight against imperialism by colonized and early post-colonial nations, promoting solidarity among independence movements and actively 'encouraging national liberation struggles'.[60] However, unlike its approach in the early 1950s, China now pursued this strategy as part of what Teemu Ruskola describes as the 'reconceptualization of the Cold War model of Three Worlds' in which Mao presented 'the two superpowers as de facto allies in world domination, seeking to divide the planet between them and standing in opposition to all the oppressed peoples of the world led by China'.[61]

The Sino–Soviet dispute had several significant international legal dimensions during the late 1950s and 1960s. As Shao-Chuan Leng explains, these included, but were not limited to, bilateral aspects such as 'controversy over the treatment of diplomats and nationals'; a 'border dispute' between China and the USSR inherited from the 'unequal treaties' imposed by Tzarist Russia upon the Qing Dynasty; and 'debates over the issues in the Indo-Pakistani war'.[62] However, beyond these specific disputes, the broader ideological and legal conflict between China and the USSR over 'the principles governing relations among Communist countries' had profound theoretical and practical implications. At the heart of this conflict were two opposing positions. On one side, the USSR asserted hegemonic control over the 'socialist camp', portraying itself as the self-appointed guarantor of its 'common interest'. This translated into the position that the national interest of any individual socialist country should be subordinated to the defence of 'proletarian internationalism' as defined by Moscow.[63] On the other side, China championed the hard-won sovereignty of socialist nations, arguing that 'the socialist camp is a social, economic, and political community of free and sovereign people united by Marxism-Leninism and proletarian internationalism and that every country in the socialist camp is ensured genuinely equal rights and independence' with no 'superiors and subordinates in relations among fraternal parties'.[64] This fundamental divergence reached its breaking point, as the next section will examine, with the USSR's invasion of Czechoslovakia in 1968.

Meanwhile, during the early 1960s, China continued to build diplomatically on the spirit of Afro-Asian unity and solidarity among new developing nations

[60] ibid.

[61] Teemu Ruskola, 'The Dao of Mao: Sinocentric Socialism and the Politics of International Legal Theory', *International Law and the Cold War*, edited by Matthew Craven, Sundhya Pahuja, and Gerry Simpson (CUP 2019): pp. 376–396 388.

[62] Shao-Chuan Leng (n 55) 493.

[63] ibid 495.

[64] ibid.

that had emerged in Bandung and was later reinforced through the recognition of the right to self-determination as a core principle of international law. This principle was affirmed by UN General Assembly Resolution 1514 on the 'Granting of Independence to Colonial Countries and Peoples' in 1960 and further developed through the formation of the Non-Aligned Movement. In particular, China invested in trade, economic aid, technical assistance, and cultural exchange while simultaneously conducting 'people-to-people' diplomacy with developing nations. At the same time, it actively 'encouraged wars of national liberation' in some countries and even advocated for the establishment of an 'international organization of the new emerging forces' to rival the United Nations from which it was still excluded.[65]

14.5 The Cultural Revolution Takes Centre Stage (1966–1969)

Broadly speaking, the Cultural Revolution (1966–1976), which was a sociopolitical movement aimed at 'renewing the spirit of the communist revolution and rooting out "bourgeois infiltrators" ',[66] was divided into three distinct phases, each characterized by different shifts in intensity and focus. The first stage of 'launching and mobilization', which was the period of greatest intensity, began in May 1966 and lasted until 1969. During this phase, millions of youths joined the Red Guards and zealously targeted the 'Four Olds'—old customs, old culture, old habits, and old ideas—across all sectors of society, including the legal system and international legal education. As Straton Papaginneas notes in this volume, by 1967, 'all branches of China's legal system (judiciary, procuratorate, legislature ...) and all their functions had been taken over by military and revolutionary committees', while all law schools and departments across the country were shut down. In many cases, their members faced persecution. This is how Han Depei, who personally experienced the persecutions of the Cultural Revolution, later described the events retrospectively in the mid-1980s: 'Many leading cadres of institutes and departments of political science and law were labeled "capitalist roaders", renegades, spies, or conspirators. Some law teachers were branded "reactionary academic authorities" or counterrevolutionaries ... and a number of law teachers were sent to "cowsheds" (places where so-called "class enemies" were kept in custody) or "isolation study classes"; were transferred to perform manual labour in May 7 cadre schools or sent to settle in the countryside as peasants.'[67]

[65] Byron S. Weng, 'Communist China's Changing Attitudes toward the United Nations', 20 *International Organization* 677 (1966).

[66] Britannica, The Editors of Encyclopaedia, 'A Brief Overview of China's Cultural Revolution', *Encyclopedia Britannica*, 20 Mar 2018, https://www.britannica.com/story/chinas-cultural-revolution (accessed 29 January 2025).

[67] Han and Kanter (n 39) 553.

In its foreign policy dimension, the radical phase of the Cultural Revolution saw the climax of a pattern that Jacques DeLisle has identified as a recurring feature throughout China's revolutionary period—namely, 'clinging to ideological rectitude, sometimes at the expense of apparent national interests'.[68] In this phase, this tendency manifested in how China 'stridently rejected the international legal order' (and the political and diplomatic orders as well), according to DeLisle.[69] With the USSR, its former paramount ally, combative rhetoric reached its pinnacle when China denounced the Soviet Union as a 'revisionist state and betrayer of the revolutionary cause' due to its application of the Brezhnev Doctrine, which asserted the 'limited sovereignty of a Communist nation' under the 'supreme sovereignty of the Communist bloc' during the USSR's intervention in Czechoslovakia in 1968.[70] Alongside other incidents involving diplomatic personnel, premises, and port authorities during the radical phase of the Cultural Revolution, the Czechoslovak crisis brought China and the USSR to the brink of severing diplomatic relations and even risked military conflict in 1969 over unrest in several areas along the Sino–Russian border that the PRC saw as the result of 'unequal treaties' that had enabled the annexation of 1.5 million square kilometres of Chinese territory by Czarist Russia.[71]

Diplomatic relations with Western countries also deteriorated during this period, with diplomatic missions in Beijing becoming the object of protests and harassment of foreign diplomats. Moreover, with the Ministry of Foreign Affairs having been taken over by extremist officials, China recalled almost all its ambassadors from abroad and gave instructions to its diplomats to behave in a strong activist manner, which in turn led to constant protests against its activities. China's policy support for wars of national liberation led to open calls for revolution in specific countries, offering the colonial and semi-colonial countries of Asia, Africa, and Latin America a 'strategy of waging revolutionary warfare known as "people's war" based on supposedly universal elements in the Chinese Communist Party's own experience in attaining power'[72] and providing them with military materials and supplies. It was also translated into the offering of political sanctuary in China to representatives of foreign revolutionary organizations, giving them semi-diplomatic status.[73] Open opposition against the US during this phase of the Cultural Revolution was further crystallized in China's strong support for anti-US communist fighters in the Vietnam War and its opposition to any possible negotiated settlement to the conflict.

[68] DeLisle (n 4) 372.
[69] ibid.
[70] Shao-Chuan Leng (n 55) 498.
[71] ibid 498–506.
[72] Jerome Alan Cohen, 'China and Intervention: Theory and Practice', *University of Pennsylvania Law Review* 121, no. 3 (Jan. 1973): pp. 471–505, 488.
[73] ibid 493.

Another of the fundamental crucibles of the Sino–Soviet Split that attained its climax during the Cultural Revolution was the denunciation by China of the USSR's efforts at 'peaceful coexistence' with the West and China's efforts to replace the USSR as leader of the 'world revolution'. Rather than seeing this denunciation in contradiction with the central role of the 'Five Principles of Peaceful Coexistence' in China's foreign policy, China argued in favour of an exception to the application of the principles of peaceful existence, which included non-intervention in the domestic affairs of other states, between socialist and non-socialist states, with regard to imperialist nations. China's strong support for carving out an exception to the principle of non-intervention in regard to wars of national liberation against imperialist states in the name of the principle of self-determination of peoples, epitomizes the Chinese stance that there was no 'inconsistency in a state striving for peaceful coexistence while simultaneously supporting revolution' against imperialist powers.[74] This international legal position against a continued violation of people's right to self-determination by colonial rule and foreign occupation remains a cornerstone of China's foreign policy up to the present day.[75]

14.6 China's Gradual Reintegration in the International Legal and Institutional Order (1969–1978)

The final stage of China's revolutionary period, which marked the beginning of its reintegration into the international legal order, coincided with the second and third phases of the Cultural Revolution and the gradual groundwork laid after Mao's death in 1976 for the 'opening and reform period' from 1978 onwards. In response to the growing sense of anarchy caused by its most radical phase, the second phase of the Cultural Revolution (1969–1971), during which the army was deployed to restore stability, also had immediate effects on China's foreign policy. The security of foreign embassies, diplomats, and nationals was guaranteed, and the Foreign Office initiated a campaign to restore credibility abroad. This included the return of Chinese ambassadors to their posts[76] and a proactive negotiating stance on unresolved conflicts, including the resumption of diplomatic talks regarding the Sino–Soviet border in October 1969. During this phase, which ended with the Lin Biao Incident—where Mao's designated successor mysteriously died in a plane crash over Mongolia in 1971—the PRC also renewed its campaign to join the United Nations.

[74] Cohen (n 72) 496.

[75] China's written statements in advisory opinion on Palestine in 2024, https://www.icj-cij.org/sites/default/files/case-related/186/186-20230725-wri-21-00-en.pdf. (accessed 20 February 2025).

[76] Cohen and Hungdah Chiu (n 11) 22.

The PRC's restoration to the UN was largely made possible by its significant material investment in Africa and South Asia, with African states making up more than one-third of the countries endorsing Resolution 2758 of the UN General Assembly in October 1971 that declared the PRC 'the only legitimate representative of China to the United Nations.' China's return to the UN led to 'China's participation in a multitude of UN meetings, adding a multilateral dimension to its legal concepts and practice, which had previously remained largely bilateral in nature and application'.[77] This re-engagement with international law remained limited in the early 1970s due, in good part, to a lack of international legal expertise in China following the upheaval of the Cultural Revolution. Initially, as S Papagianneas explains in this volume, this translated into the PRC's active participation in the UN Conference on the Law of the Sea and the 1972 Stockholm Conference on the Human Environment. Similarly high on the PRC's agenda during its first years in the UN was its strong support for the 'New International Economic Order' (NIEO), as part of its broader foreign policy objective of revising the structure of the international legal order in alignment with the Third World's struggle for 're-distributive justice'.[78]

The restoration of the PRC to the UN, which, with 'its sudden establishment of diplomatic relations with numerous states, virtually achieved its long-sought goal of securing international recognition of its legitimacy',[79] also had constructive effects on Sino–US relations, despite the US voting against Resolution 2758. This development coincided with the third phase of 'decline and consolidation' of the Cultural Revolution (1972–1976), which lasted until Mao's death in 1976 and the subsequent arrest of the 'Gang of Four'. The PRC's policy of people-to-people diplomacy towards US citizens culminated in Richard Nixon's historic visit to China and the signing of the Shanghai Communiqué in early 1972, in which both countries pledged to respect the 'Five Principles of Peaceful Coexistence'. This was followed by China's support for negotiations that led to the withdrawal of US troops from Vietnam in 1973, an event that represented 'a great leap for the Sino-American détente.'[80] On 1 January 1979 the US formally recognized the People's Republic of China, although the Taiwan Relations Act (1979) allowed it to maintain 'unofficial' relations with Taiwan, including in the fields of trade and defence.

Already weakened by the rectification and anti-rightist campaigns that began in the late 1950s, China's legal scholarship suffered even more during the Cultural Revolution. As Sompong Sucharitkul noted, 'no legal scholarship could

[77] Samuel S. Kim, 'The People's Republic of China and the Charter-Based International Legal Order', *The American Journal of International Law* 72, no. 2 (Apr.1978): pp. 317–349 317.

[78] Kim (n 80) 328.

[79] Cohen and Chiu (n 11) 22.

[80] ibid 22.

conceivably outlive the Cultural Revolution'[81]—a state of affairs which applied even more starkly to international legal studies. Published in 1965, Fu Zhu's article titled 'Rusk's "International Law" Cannot Cover Up the American Imperialists' Crime of Invading Vietnam' was reportedly the last work on international law published in the PRC until 1979. This prolonged gap in legal scholarship resulted in a significant lack of expertise in international law. This became particularly evident when China did not nominate any candidate for the International Law Commission until 1981, when Ni Zhengyu (born 1906) was elected. Likewise, no Chinese nominee was put forward for the International Court of Justice until the 1984 elections, a position that was ultimately filled, once again, by Ni Zhengyu.[82] While what was termed 'restoration of China's legal system' began after 1972, and the law department of Peking University resumed limited operations, including some international law teaching in 1973,[83] by 1976 none of China's legal periodicals that used to publish works on international law had reappeared.

The epistemological reorganization of teaching and research in international law had to wait until the end of the revolutionary period in 1979. The goals of reviving international legal education and research in China were outlined in the article 'The Study of International Law Must Be Strengthened', by Wang Tieya and Wei Min, published in the *People's Daily* in March 1979. These goals included: '(1) the restoration of research institutes on international law, (2) the establishment of a professional society of international law, (3) the strengthening of teaching and research of international law in institutions of higher learning, and (4) the formulation of short and long- range planning to develop international law studies.'[84] Immediately thereafter, the first research centre for international law in China was founded by Han Depei in 1980 at Wuhan University.[85] In the same year, the Chinese Society of International Law was established in Beijing. One year later, the most authoritative textbook of the period, written by Wang Tieya and Wei Min, was published[86] and soon thereafter China's first specialized international law periodical, the *Chinese Yearbook of International Law*, was launched, in 1982.[87]

Over the following years, in parallel with the PRC joining multiple multilateral conventions and actively participating in the work of international organizations, Chinese international legal scholarship became increasingly prolific and engaged

[81] Sompong Sucharitkul, 'Rebirth of Chinese Legal Scholarship, with Regard to International Law', *Leiden Journal of International Law* 3, no. 1 (1990) 5.
[82] Ibid 17.
[83] Ogden (n 21) 28–48; Chiu (n 36) 1159.
[84] Chiu (n 36) 1159.
[85] Han and Kanter (n 39) 558.
[86] Wang Tieya and Wei Min, Guo Ji Fa Gai Lun (International Law) 1 (Law Press 1981).
[87] See further, Hao Yayezi and Chen Mohan, 'The Chinese Yearbook of International Law 1982–2022', in *The Journals of International Law*, edited by Van Hulle and Carl Landauer (Brill-Nijhoff, forthcoming 2026).

in contemporary doctrinal debates.[88] This development coincided with a broader, all-encompassing effort toward the 'self-conscious development of its legal system, with important implications for underlying jurisprudential theory and values'.[89] At the core of this process was the official recognition—highlighted by Huan Xiang, the first President of the Chinese Society of International Law, during its establishment in February 1980—that international law was an essential instrument for realizing China's 'Four Modernizations'.[90] These modernizations, as articulated by Deng Xiaoping in 1978, served as the fundamental pillars of China's reform and opening-up process, focusing on agriculture, industry, defence, and science and technology. This transition, in which international law became an important vector, marked China's shift from a centrally planned economy to a more open and market-oriented socialist system with Chinese characteristics. As Han Depei summarized it in 1984: 'The days of the Cultural Revolution and the "gang of four", in which laws were defied, the legal system negated, legal education strangled and law teachers cruelly persecuted are gone forever. Guided by the correct line of the Communist party of China, the science of law is thriving and prospering throughout the country.'[91]

14.7 Conclusions: The Past Lives in the Present

This chapter has briefly surveyed the evolution of the PRC's approach to international law during its thirty-year revolutionary period, examining its five main stages or basic periods. As we have seen, this historically unique era lasted until the mid-to-late 1970s, when the gradual lifting of what US Secretary of State John Foster Dulles helped popularize in the 1950s as the 'Bamboo Curtain' between China and the West also marked a renewed Chinese approach to international law. Although many of the most negative attitudes toward 'bourgeois international law' that emerged during the revolutionary period and the Cold War stand in stark contrast to China's current proactive embrace of contemporary international law and global governance, the legacy of that period nonetheless lives on. Many of its core tenets continue to shape China's theoretical approach to international law and influence its policy-related orientations.

In a process that began, as we have seen, in the late 1970s, international law is now deeply embedded in contemporary China's legal education system and foreign policy, where it is regarded as an essential tool in the PRC's strategy for a 'peaceful rise and development' in the twenty-first century. Key components of

[88] Chiu (n 36) 1127.
[89] Han and Kanter (n 39) 543.
[90] Chiu (n 36) 1128–1129.
[91] Han and Kanter (n 39) 559

China's contemporary approach to international law and international relations are its two major—and deeply intertwined—policy initiatives: the Community of Shared Future for Mankind and the Belt and Road Initiative. Albeit global in scope and orientation, both of them are particularly addressed to developing countries.

The Community of Shared Future of Mankind (CSFM) is the soft power cornerstone of a new phase of greater Chinese assertiveness in international law and relations known as 'the strategy of *fenfayouwei* (striving for achievement)' (奋发有为)[92] led by Xi Jinping.[93] President Xi's multiple speeches on, and references to, the CSFM[94] have boosted its use in Chinese public diplomacy. Furthermore, as a core component of Xi Jinping's 'Thought on Socialism with Chinese Characteristics for a New Era', of which the CSFM is one of the 'fourteen points', the CSFM was included in the Chinese Communist Party's (CCP) Charter in November 2017 and soon afterwards in March 2018 the Preamble to the Chinese Constitution was amended to include, inter alia, a reference to it. More recently, the Law on Foreign Relations of the People's Republic of China, which was passed in June 2023, also includes among its six paramount goals to 'build a community with a shared future for mankind'.[95]

While Xi Jinping has characterized the CSFM as a 'new development paradigm and pursuing mutual benefit and win-win cooperation'[96] on a global scale, thus signifying that it encompasses all members of the international community, China has particularly addressed the CSFM, which, furthermore, presents reformist similarities in addressing 'global redistributive justice' to NIEO, to 'developing countries' in Africa, Asia, and Latin America. Particular addressees of the CSFM are countries in these regions that have become closely connected to the Belt and Road Initiative (BRI) which Xi Jinping has presented as his 'hallmark of the vision of a community of common destiny'[97] and which, since its Action Plan was launched in March 2015,[98] has become the 'centrepiece of China's foreign policy and international economic strategy'.[99] According to the latest available statistics,

[92] See early on, Xuetong Yan, 'From Keeping a Low Profile to Striving for Achievement', *Chinese Journal of International Politics* 7 (2014), pp. 153.

[93] For a detailed analysis of its different components in connection to international law, see Ignacio de la Rasilla and Yayezi Hao, 'The Community of Shared Future for Mankind and China's Legalist Turn in International Relations', *Chinese Journal of International* Law 20 (2021): pp. 341–379.

[94] Jinping Xi *The Belt and Road Initiative* (Foreign Languages Press, 2019)

[95] Huikang Huang, Milestone of China's Foreign-Related Legislation—A Review of the Law of the People's Republic of China on Foreign Relations', *Chinese Journal of Transnational Law* 2 (2024) 1

[96] Jinping Xi, 'Fostering a New Development Paradigm and Pursuing Mutual Benefit and Win-Win Cooperation, 19 November 2020, vn.china-embassy.org/eng/xwdt/t1833641.htm. (accessed 8 July 2025).

[97] Linggui Wang and Jiangli Zhao, eds, *China's Belt and Road Initiative and Building the Community of Common Destiny* (World Scientific 2019) pp. 47.

[98] The State Council of the People's Republic of China, Action plan on the Belt and Road Initiative outlines its principles, framework, cooperation priorities and cooperation mechanisms, english.www.gov.cn/archive/publications/2015/03/30/content_281475080249035.htm. (accessed 8 July 2025).

[99] Michael M. Du, 'China's "One Belt, One Road" Initiative: Context, Focus, Institutions, and Implications', *The Chinese Journal of Global Governance* 2 (2016): pp. 30.

as of August 2024, in the context of BRI, which is a mega-development programme focused on the construction of and infrastructure for a 'Silk Road Economic Belt' and a 'Maritime Silk Road', China has already signed agreements or memoranda of understanding (MOUs) with 146 to 151 countries across Sub-Saharan Africa (44), Europe & Central Asia (34) East Asia & Pacific (25) Latin America & Caribbean (22), the Middle East & North Africa (19) and South East Asia (6) .[100]

This contemporary focus on the developing world is consistent with China's traditional siding with 'developing countries as default political partners while fostering ties with developed countries as "economic partners"',[101] with whom China's partnership is often described as a 'community of common interests' (*liyi gongtongti* 利益共同体).[102] China's international legal emphasis on the developing world, along with many other features of Chinese contemporary international legal policies, is deeply rooted in an approach to international law that emerged and began to flourish during its revolutionary period.

[100] Christoph Nedopil, Countries of the Belt and Road Initiative (2023), Green Belt and Road Initiative Center FISF Fudan University, www.greenfdc.org. (accessed 8 July 2025).
[101] Denghua Zhang, 'The Concept of "Community of Common Destiny" in China's Diplomacy: Meaning, Motives and Implications', *Asia & the Pacific Policy Studies* 5 (2018): pp. 196.
[102] ibid.

15
China, the Cold War, and International Law

Jiangyu Wang

15.1 Introduction

The engagement of the People's Republic of China (PRC) with international law during the Cold War era remains significantly under-studied within the realm of international law and history scholarship. Nonetheless, this subject holds considerable importance not only in the field of legal historiography but also due to its profound implications for contemporary international relations, particularly concerning the dynamics characterizing the relationship between China and the United States, which has been described as existing in a state of a 'new Cold War'.[1]

To provide context, a brief introduction to the development of international law during the Cold War is helpful. The Cold War (1947–1991) was predominantly characterized by ideological and geopolitical confrontations between the United States (US) and the Soviet Union (USSR) along with the countries in their respective spheres of influence. The aftermath of the Second World War represented a significant turning point in the evolution of international law. Driven by the horrors of the Holocaust, the devastation of war, the rise of the US and USSR as the two superpowers, and the emergence of newly independent states, '[i]nternational law in the post-World War II era was, in short, off to a spectacular start', as noted by Stephen Neff.[2] Nonetheless, Neff believed that this 'spectacular moment' for international law 'was not sustained' because of the ascendance of the Cold War.[3] In his words, '[t]he immediate postwar decades, while vibrant ones in so many ways, were not, on the whole, a glorious period for international law'.[4]

It was indeed the few 'immediate postwar decades', most of which were during the Cold War, that transformed both the spirit and substance of international law. This transformation, under a new global legal climate, featured the expansion of traditional legal doctrines, the emergence of new legal regimes, the establishment

[1] See Todd F. Buchwald, 'International Law and the "New Cold War": An Opportunity for Reflection on International Law in the "Old" Cold War' (2023) 55 *Case Western Reserve Journal of International Law*, 175. See also Adam Segel, 'The Coming Tech Cold War with China' (2020) *Foreign Affairs*, 9 September 2020, available at www.foreignaffairs.com (visited 1 April 2025).

[2] Stephen C. Neff, *Justice among Nations: A History of International Law* (Harvard University Press, 2014) 395.

[3] Ibid, 395–396.

[4] Ibid, 396.

Jiangyu Wang, *China, the Cold War, and International Law* In: *Histories of International Law in China*.
Edited by: Ignacio de la Rasilla, Jiangyu Wang, and Congyan Cai, Oxford University Press.
 DOI: 10.1093/oso/9780198888345.003.0015

of new institutions, and the dominance of new philosophical ideas in international law, among others.[5] Specifically, the formation of the United Nations (UN) in 1945 represented a paradigm shift in both international relations and international law. As 'a new world parliament',[6] the UN was on the path to make significant contributions to the development of international law not only as an international institution but also by creating new institutional arrangements and legal doctrines. Remarkably, the collective security mechanism, centred on the UN Security Council (UNSC),[7] represents a foundational shift in international law, an attempt to institutionalize global cooperation to deter aggression and prevent arms conflict by obligating member states to act collectively against threats to peace. Most notably, what differentiates the UN from the League of Nations, its much less powerful predecessor, is the general binding prohibition against the use of force by states,[8] described as 'the corner-stone of the Charter system'.[9] The UN system introduced a more legalized and institutionalized approach to international law-making through the General Assembly, Security Council, and specialized agencies, rendering a phenomenon characterized by Jose Alvarez as 'international organizations as law-makers'.[10] The Cold War also witnessed the rise and expansion of human rights law, environmental law and common concerns, and international economic law (with the rise and demise of the New International Economic Order, or NIEO). In addition, the two superpowers often used international law as a tool for their ideological and geopolitical interests.[11] The emergence of the Third World and decolonization movements prompted scrutiny regarding the legitimacy of the traditional international legal discourse and the interpretation of rules long dominated by the West. However, it is crucial to emphasize that the foundational 'positivist' principles of international law, rooted in state-centric Westphalian concepts of state sovereignty and non-interference, largely stayed intact during the Cold War, though adherence to these principles was significantly influenced by the Cold War geopolitics.

China's complex relationship with international law throughout the Cold War was shaped, and functioned, within the international legal framework previously delineated. The PRC was a revolutionary nation created at the outset of the Cold War, and rose to the status of a great power during this period. The popular view of China's relationship with international law during this period was, as a

[5] See generally, Martti Koskenniemi, 'History of International Law, Since World War II', Max Planck Encyclopedia of Public International Law, June 2011. See also Neff, n 2, 400.

[6] Neff, n 2, 400.

[7] UN Charter, Chapter VII, Articles 39–51.

[8] In contrast, the League did not outlaw war but viewed it as a legitimate foreign policy instrument. See Neff, n 2, 400.

[9] Ian Brownlie, *Principles of Public International Law*, 7th ed (OUP, 2008) 732 (quoting J.L. Brierly, *The Law of Nations: An Introduction to the International Law of Peace* (6th ed., 1963) 414).

[10] See generally, Jose E. Alvarez, *International Organizations as Law-makers* (OUP, 2005).

[11] See Henry Kissinger, *Diplomacy* (Simon & Schuster, 1994), Chapters 21, 22.

commentator wrote in 1979, that 'the [PRC] remains in many respects an isolated and enigmatic society, remarkably closed and separate from an increasingly interdependent international legal order'.[12] Indeed, the PRC entered the realm of international law during the Cold War with an attitude characterized by a combination of contempt, scepticism, and pragmatism. To the extent that China was inclined to engage, international law functioned as both a protective shield and a strategic instrument for the nation: a shield to safeguard its sovereignty and territorial integrity, and a tool to assert its identity, endorse the Third World's anti-colonialism movement, and navigate the complex triangular diplomacy with the United States and the Soviet Union, then the two global superpowers.

This chapter argues that, despite varying degrees of self-isolation throughout different periods, the PRC has maintained a relatively stable approach to international law. This approach combines Westphalianism, which emphasizes traditional international law principles of sovereignty and non-interference; instrumentalism, where international law is used to fulfil national interests; and idealism, which promotes communist revolutionary ideas by supporting the Third World and advocating for the 'export of revolution'. The chapter is organized as follows: Section 15.2 provides a historical overview and explores the 'change of mindset' in China's approach to international law and its underlying rationale, focusing on the effects of the Common Programme and the Sino–Soviet Treaty; Section 15.3 analyses the evolution of academic thought and legal discourse on international law during the Cold War; Section 15.4 addresses the emergence of the Five Principles of Peaceful Co-existence, positioned within and extending beyond traditional Westphalian international law principles; Section 15.5 examines the implications of international law regarding China's handling of territorial disputes during the Cold War; Section 15.6 investigates the international law aspects of China's relations with the Third World; and Section 15.7 concludes.

15.2 Embrace of Communism with a Revised Approach to International Law

15.2.1 Lean to One Side: The Common Programme and International Law

The Republic of China (ROC, 1912–1949), recognized as Asia's first republic, dealt with a complicated relationship with international law, which was influenced by its historical background, internal politics, civil wars, Japanese invasions, and broader geopolitical factors.[13] Particularly, the legacy of the unequal treaties and foreign

[12] Daniel J. Hoffheimer, 'China and International Legal Order: An Historical Introduction', (1979) 11:2 *Case Western Reserve Journal of International Law*251.

[13] Authur Cotterell, *China: A History* (Pimlico, 1995) 245–289.

encroachments which the ROC inherited from the Qing Dynasty profoundly influenced the republic's approach to international legal norms, creating a pragmatic attitude blending selective adherence, strategic invocation, and occasional resistance. Nevertheless, as initially a prospective and subsequently an actual ally of the West and the United States during the better part of this period, the ROC generally endorsed and adopted the Western conception of international law. It actively participated in international legal processes, commencing with the 1919 Paris Peace Conference, and engaged with the then prevalent international institutions, ranging from the League of Nations to the United Nations, though the League's inability to halt Japanese invasion of Manchuria in 1931 aroused a significant degree of scepticism within the ROC regarding international law and justice.[14]

In 1949, the newly formed PRC confronted a global order marked by rival Cold War blocs. Yet it did not encounter a complex foreign policy dilemma, as Mao Zedong clearly stated that the 'lean to one side' policy was to align with the Soviet camp rather than forge an alliance with the US or adopt a neutral stance.[15] As a historian observed, this policy 'was prompted not only by ideological affinity but also by practical considerations: the infant People's Republic needed Soviet aid and protection to forestall Western intervention, such as that which occurred in Siberia after the Bolshevik Revolution'.[16] This foreign policy orientation was soon codified in the so-called Common Programme of the Chinese People's Political Consultative Conference, a constitutional framework agreement reached by the CCP and other political parties and organizations, known collectively as the 'Minzhu Dangpai' (democratic parties), to guide the establishment of the PRC.[17] Article 11 of the Common Programme, quoting almost entirely Mao's own words, provided for the paramount principle of the new People's Republic's foreign policy:[18]

> The People's Republic of China shall unite with all peace-loving and freedom-loving countries and peoples throughout the world, first of all, with the U.S.S.R., all People's Democracies and all oppressed nations. It shall take its stand in the camp of international peace and democracy, to oppose imperialist aggression to defend lasting world peace.

[14] David Scott, *China and the International System, 1940-1949: Power, Presence, and Perceptions in a Centuiry of Humiliation* (State University of New York Press, 2008) 244.

[15] Chen Jian, *Mao's China and the Cold War* (The University of North Carolina Press, 2001) 50. Mao Zedong unequivocally announced the 'lean to one side' policy in an article titled "On People's Democratic Dictatorship' on 30 June 1949.

[16] Immanuel C. Y. Hsu, *The Rise of Modern China* (6th ed) (OUP, 2000) 661.

[17] Jinfan Zhang, *The History of Legal Civilization: Modern and Contemporary China (From 1840–)* (Springer, 2020) 698–699.

[18] The Common Program of the Chinese People's Political Consultative Conference, adopted by the First Plenary Session of the Chinese People's PCC on 29 September 1949 in Peking (the 'Common Program').

The Common Programme served as a pivotal document of extreme significance, as it not only outlined the governance rules and structures for the People's Republic of China (PRC) but also articulated a normative framework that established the basis for China's socialist foreign policy approach throughout the PRC period. From the perspective of international law, this document amalgamates a variety of principles that either align with, incorporate, or diverge from the established norms of international law at the time, synthesizing traditional Westphalianism, instrumentalism, and communist idealism. These principles, collectively forming a durable policy framework largely reflecting China's current approach to international law, warrant further evaluation:

a. *Affirmation of sovereignty and territorial integrity*. Both the Preamble and Article 1 emphasized achieving the full unification of China. Article 54 asserted protection of 'the independence, freedom, integrity of territory and sovereignty of the country'. Clearly, the emphasis on sovereignty and territorial integrity demonstrated an alignment with the Westphalian concepts of state sovereignty and non-interference in a state's internal affairs, principles which are embodied in the UN Charter.[19]
b. *Rejection of unequal treaties and imperialist privileges*. The Common Programme declared the abolition of 'all the presogatives of imperialist countries in China' (Article 3), and provided for the review and possible abrogation or renegotiation of treaties concluded by the previous Kuomintang regime (Article 55). This indicated the adoption of a nationalist, instrumentalist approach of selective engagement with international legal obligations. While the conventional wisdom of international law generally upholds the continuity of treaty obligations as per the doctrine of *pacta sunt servanda*, the Common Programme's stance reflected a revolutionary regime's prerogative to reject agreements perceived as products of an illegitimate or progressive regime.
c. *International relations based on equality and mutual benefit among states and peoples*: The Common Programme stressed equality and mutual benefit in foreign relations. Article 56 stated that the PRC may negotiate with foreign governments on the basis of 'equality, mutual benefit and mutual respect for territory and sovereignty'. Article 57 extended this principle to commercial relations, emphasizing 'equality and mutual benefit with foreign governments and peoples'. These provisions reiterated the traditional principle of legal equality of states, which is a fundamental norm of international law

[19] UN Chater, Article 2(1) and Article 2(4).

codified in the UN Charter.[20] Additionally, they mentioned the concept of 'mutual benefit', which, though not coined and pioneered by China, was significantly popularized and formalized by China's state practice in international law, starting from the Common Programme.

d. *Peaceful co-existence and opposition to aggression.* The Common Programme advocated for 'lasting international peace and friendly co-operation between the peoples of all countries' and expressed 'opposition to the imperialist policy of aggression and war' (Article 54). Such an endorsement of peace and opposition to aggression mirrored the post-war international legal order's focus on preventing conflict through diplomacy and the prohibition of unilateral use of force. On the other hand, reflecting the 'leaning to one side' policy, the Common Programme also emphasized alliance with the USSR and members of the Soviet camp, prioritizing alignment with the socialist bloc and anti-colonial states and putting conditions on the previously expressed universalist principles of peace and cooperation.
e. *Rejection of Imperialism and Support of Post-Colonial Independence Movement.* Articles 1, 11, and 54 expressed opposition to 'imperialism' and called for national independence and non-intervention. The Common Programme's rejection of imperialism as a system of international relations can be seen as a precursor to the Bandung Conference (1955) principles of solidifying anti-imperialism, anti-colonialism, and national independence of Third World countries.

In conclusion, the implications of international law stemming from the Common Programme of 1949 should be recognized when analysing both the historical and present-day Chinese stance on international law. It integrated essential legal principles such as sovereignty, equality, non-interference, peace, and security, while categorically rejecting the remnants of imperialism, external interventions, and obligations perceived as imposed by foreign powers. It set the stage for China's ongoing approach to international law, characterized by strong defence of sovereignty, selective acceptance of traditional international legal norms, and a preference for a state-centric, non-interventionist global legal order based on peaceful coexistence and collaboration. From the early days of the PRC, the Common Programme represented an affirmation of China's entrance into the international legal system as a sovereign equal and a revolutionary manifesto aiming to resist and reform aspects of international law viewed as imperialistic, unjust, or harmful to China's national interests or the ruling party's regime interest. In summary, the fundamental components of the PRC perspective on international law, as articulated in its initial

[20] Article 2(1), UN Charter.

foreign policy framework of the Common Programme, remain predominantly evident in the contemporary Chinese approach to international law.

15.2.2 The Sino–Soviet Treaty and Its Impact on China's Approach to International Law

The Sino–Soviet Treaty of Friendship, Alliance and Mutual Assistance, signed on 14 February 1950, established a system of strategic alliance, collective security, aid, and cooperation between the PRC and the Soviet Union. This treaty held great importance for both China and the world, as its conclusion and subsequent implementation—or the lack thereof—significantly deepened the Cold War's global divide and profoundly shaped China's foreign policy for the next forty years.[21] Additionally, the treaty serves as a case study and testing ground for international law principles outlined in the Common Programme of 1949.

On its surface, the treaty appeared to be a typical Westphalian-style international agreement incorporating the traditional principles of international law. Most conspicuously, the text of the treaty reflected the principles of sovereign equality and non-intervention. Article 5 provided:

> Each contracting party undertakes, in the spirit of friendship and cooperation and in conformity with the principles of equality, mutual benefit and mutual respect for the national sovereignty and territorial integrity of and non-interference in the internal affairs of the other contracting party, to develop and consolidate economic and cultural ties between China and the Soviet Union, to render the other all possible economic cooperation.

It is evident that the international legal foundation of the Sino–Soviet Treaty was articulated to be predicated upon the fundamental Westphalian principles of state sovereignty, territorial integrity, and non-interference, alongside a strong emphasis on the aforementioned concept of 'mutual benefit'. Additionally, the treaty endorsed the binding character of international agreements, indicating presumptively the communist nations' acceptance of the traditional international law principle of *pacta sunt servanda*.

However, the treaty also departed from conventional international law norms and practices in various ways. Its mutual defence arrangement, which obliged each party to support the other militarily in case of an attack by Japan or its allies (Articles 1–2), complicated the UN's conception of collective security. This situation was quite common during the Cold War, as evidenced by the US-led North

[21] 牛军：《冷战时代的中国战略决策》(Niu Jun, *China's Strategic Decision-Making during the Cold War* (Shijie Zhishi Chubanshe, 2018) 90.

Atlantic Treaty Organization (NATO), the USSR-led Warsaw Pact (formally called the Treaty of Friendship, Cooperation, and Mutual Assistance), and the many military cooperation agreements between superpowers and their allies or protectorates. These entities all established their own collective security mechanisms, creating a tension between UN members' universal obligations and alliance commitments. Additionally, the treaty's brevity—consisting of only six articles—and vague language emphasized ideological solidarity over legal reciprocity and enforceable responsibilities. Most notably, the treaty failed to embody an adequately 'equal' relationship between China and the USSR, as the latter, through the supplementary agreements to the Sino–Soviet Treaty, secured strategic concessions such as control over Port Arthur (known as Port Lushun in China) and Changchun Railway (thus infringing upon China's territorial integrity) and exerted influence over China's military and economic policies.

For China, the Sino–Soviet Treaty represented its first major encounter with a chance to use an instrument of international law to govern the relationship with a superpower and a 'big brother' in its foreign relations. As Chinese historian Niu Jun pointed out, China's decision to conclude this treaty was fundamentally shaped by the Cold War-shaded international system at the time. The CCP leadership's determination to 'lean to one side' and form an exclusive alliance with the Soviet Union was formulated during the three-year civil war with the Kuomintang government, which took place at the outset of the Cold War. The Cold War provided two development models for newly created states. Mao Zedong came to the belief that the Soviet model was more suitable for China to achieve the status of a strong state, and ultimately decided to join the socialist camp.[22]

From an international law standpoint, the treaty's significance is twofold. First, it marked and announced China's entry into the international legal order as a sovereign state fully entitled to the rights of an independent state under, particularly, the Westphalian principles of international law. Second, the treaty exemplified the instrumental use of international law during the Cold War alliances, wherein the language of legal rights and obligations was harnessed to obscure strategic calculations and power imbalances. However, as previously mentioned, the tremendous power disparity between the USSR and China undermined the principle of 'equality' provided in the treaty, locking China into a junior partnership that generated domestic resentment in China and later fuelled the ideological rift between Beijing and Moscow.[23]

The Sino–Soviet split, formalized by China's denunciation of the treaty in 1969, underscored the fragility of alliances that are established on ideological alignment

[22] Ibid, 91.

[23] Odd Arne Westad, *Restless Empire: China and the World since 1750* (Basic Books, 2012) 293 (noting that, although Mao got security and assistance through the treaty, 'his nationalist pride had suffered sharply in the process, as his wish to be deal with as an equal by the Soviets had gone unfulfilled').

underpinned by power asymmetry rather than on shared long-term interests grounded in mutual respect. It also exposed the limitations of international legal instruments in reconciling socialist internationalism with state sovereignty. The principal lesson for China was, indeed, that it must consistently safeguard its independence in all dealings with other nations, which also shaped China's role as a leading global advocate for state sovereignty and equality.

15.3 Changing Chinese Discourse on International Law during the Cold War: From Revolutionary Radicalism to Legal Rationalism

In its initial establishment phase, the PRC maintained a fundamentally sceptical yet pragmatic stance towards the Western-dominated international legal framework. This perspective was influenced by two key factors: first, China's historical encounters with traditional international law were marred by humiliating memories of foreign invasions, 'unequal treaties', and legal imperialism;[24] second, the communist regime mandated the 'application' of the analytical tools of Marxism-Leninism in all respects of social life, including academic research and practice, and the Marxist-Leninist ideology casts international law as an instrument of bourgeois and imperialist states. The 'lean to one side' policy also determined that '[i]n the 1950s and 1960s it would not be unfair to say that almost all Chinese positions on international law were derived from the Soviet position'.[25] On the other hand, as Hungdah Chiu correctly observed, 'Communist China does accept many principles of international law proclaimed or applied by the Soviet Union or by Soviet jurists, but in view of the growing differences of views between the two countries in handling many international problems and in conducting the international communist movement, it is reasonable to infer that Communist China may have developed different views toward international law in some respects'.[26]

Debates within the PRC about the nature, universality, and scope of application of international law, among other related issues, emerged after 1957.[27] A major concern was whether the PRC should adopt a universal international law system. Initially, there was a perspective suggesting the coexistence of both bourgeois and socialist international law, but this view was soon rejected.[28] A second view

[24] See, generally, Teemu Ruskola, *Legal Orientalism: China, the United States, and Modern Law* (Harvard University Press, 2013).

[25] Suzanne Ogden, 'China and International Law: Implications for Foreign Policy', (1976) 49:1 *Pacific Affairs* 28 at 30.

[26] Hungdah Chiu, 'Communist China's Attitude toward International Law', (1966) 60:2 *American Journal of International Law*, 245.

[27] James C. Hsiung, 'Peking's Attitudes toward International Law', *Chinese* (1970) 3:1 *Law & Government* 3.

[28] Ibid. See also Chiu, n 26, 253–256.

proposed a unified international law system applicable to all states, irrespective of their social or political structures. This standpoint stemmed from a derivative of Marxist-Leninist theory asserting that, to the extent that law embodies the ruling class's will, there should be a distinction between domestic and international law. Therefore, international law should not simply be viewed as reflecting the will of the dominant (imperialist) powers. Instead, aligning with the Soviet theory of international law, some Chinese jurists contended that 'agreements' formed through 'struggle, cooperation, compromise, and consultation' among states demonstrated an element of equality, which formed the foundation for the universal validity of international law.[29] Nevertheless, China's breakup with the USSR dealt a significant blow to this perspective, leading to a decline in its support in the 1960s, indicating the influence of the rise and demise of the Sino–Soviet alliance.

What eventually prevailed was the third school, which, incorporating elements of the first two views, contended that 'there was a general international law over and above, as well as distinct from, the bourgeois body of law'.[30] Professor Zhou Gengsheng (Chou Keng-sheng), a Western-educated international law scholar who later became the founder of socialist international law studies in the early PRC period, offered an authoritative view about the definition and nature of international law in a textbook published in 1976. Considering that the book was published during the Cultural Revolution, when no academic voice differing from the government's official policy could be made public, it is reasonable to conclude that Zhou's relevant articulation represented China's official stance on international law during the Mao era. Zhou compared the Western and Soviet definitions of international law,[31] and pointed out that the Western definition, namely the definition articulated in Oppenheim's *International Law: A Treatise*, completely overlooked the 'class' nature of international law, whereas it demonstrated a colonial nature by emphasizing 'civilized' states.[32] Meanwhile, the Soviet definition overemphasized the promise of peaceful coexistence and the role of collective compulsory measures in international relations.[33] Instead, Zhou offered the following definition for international law from the perspective of the Chinese socialist revolutionary state:[34]

[29] Hsiung, n 27, 4.

[30] Ibid.

[31] 周鲠生：《国际法》（上册）(Zhou Gengsheng, *International Law*, Vol. 1) (Wuhan University Press, 2007) 2–3 (reprinting Zhou Gengsheng's *International Law*, Vol. 1, published by The Commerce Press in 1976).

[32] Oppenheim defined 'Law of Nations or International Law' as 'the name for the body of customary and conventional rules which are considered legally binding by civilised States in their intercourse with each other'. See L. Oppenheim, *International Law: A Treatise. Vol 1. Peace* (London: Longmans, Green and Co., 1912) 3.

[33] Zhou, n 31, 3.

[34] Ibid, 3.

> International law is the collection of behavioral norms, comprising an overall body of principles, rules and institutions, that have been formulated in the course of international interactions, are acknowledged by all countries, reflect the will of the ruling classes of these countries, and have legally binding force on states in international relations.

Under this definition, Zhou pointed out, international law should have four characteristics. The first aspect was that international law was 'international'; specifically, it was 'inter-state' law recognized by nations, not 'world law' of supernational nature. Second, international law was 'law', so its rules were legally binding upon states, even though it still lacked the enforcement power. Third, international law was universal, applicable to all states with a generally binding effect. Fourth, international law had a 'class character'. Law serves politics and the ruling class's interests, and international law is no exception. However, as no 'collective will' of the ruling classes of all nations existed in the international society, international law was supposed to represent the 'coordinated will of the ruling classes of states'.[35]

The above definition of international law, as articulated by Zhou Gengsheng and representing China's official perspective at that time, clearly signified the PRC's pragmatic approach to international law throughout much of the Mao era. While preserving the class nature, this definition accepted the universality and binding nature of international law, indicating the incorporation of a significant degree of legal rationalism. The adoption of rationalism in China's stance on international law was remarkable given the context of a revolutionary domestic political climate that had undergone several devastating political campaigns initiated by Chairman Mao to achieve his mysterious political agendas.

It is however important to note that the ultimate embrace of rationalism in international law by the pre-reform PRC was largely a result of China's rejoining the West-led international community in the 1970s, following the Sino–American détente after US President Richard Nixon's visit to China in 1972, the signing of the Shanghai Communiqué, the Sino–Japanese rapprochement (1972), and, most importantly, China's 'resumption' of its status as an UN member and permanent member of the UN Security Council in October 1971. To the extent that the PRC had sought to be recognized as the legitimate representative of China in the UN for many years since its establishment, Mao's words which follow, often used to illustrate the PRC's disregard of international law,[36] were more likely a rhetorical display of unhappiness rather than a formal rejection of international law:[37]

[35] Ibid, 3–8.

[36] Teemu Ruskola, 'The Dao of Mao: Sinocentric Socialism and Politics of International Legal Theory', in Matthew Craven et al, *International Law and the Cold War* (CUP, 2020) 376 at 381.

[37] Jerome Alan Cohen and Hungdah Chiu, *People's China and International Law: A Documentary Study* (Princeton University Press, 1974) vol. 2, 1295 (quoting Mao Zedong's words in a conversation with a Costa Rican Communist delegation).

> China has no legal status in the international arena. The Western countries consider China an outlaw state. And that is why we can act without regard for laws that restrict us. We act in whatever way we please. This is not why we are in no hurry to join the UN. We shall not poke our nose into this cesspool.

Zhou Gengsheng's restatement of China's international law perspective indicated a shift towards greater satisfaction and integration into the global system. This change in perception facilitated China's transition from Mao's 'war and revolution' ideology in the 1960s to Deng Xiaoping's 'peace and development' approach during the Reform and Opening-Up period starting in the late 1970s. Deng's policies emphasized economic growth, modernization, and opening up to foreign trade and investment, moving away from isolationism and conflict. This strategic shift helped China become a significant player in international affairs and laid the foundation for its rapid economic rise.[38]

The Reform era's new worldview also reshaped China's stance on international law toward universalism, as embodied in an officially sanctioned new textbook on international law edited by Wang Tieya and featuring a cohort of younger international law scholars committed to establishing a new school of international law aligned with the 'open door' policy in the post-Mao era.[39] In this textbook and its later editions, Wang provided a rudimentary definition of international law in the introductory chapter as 'the body of law comprising binding principles, rules, regulations and institutions'.[40] However, more importantly, as part of China's new interpretation of the international landscape and the shift away from revolutionary politics domestically,[41] Wang also transformed the essence of international law by eliminating its class-based nature. Referencing Zhou Gengsheng's earlier definition that included 'the will of the ruling class' in international law, Wang stated: 'Since international law governs relations among states, determining the class nature of international law remains an insurmountable challenge in both theory and practice.'[42]

Wang further unequivocally endorsed the universality of international law.[43] As interpreted by the late Canadian international law professor Ronald St. John Macdonald, a leading scholar in the field of international law of his time in both the US and Western Europe, Wang Tieya epitomized a liberal internationalist perspective, warranting classification within the school of H. Lauterpacht in terms of the understanding of the nature and value of international law.[44] Wang's perspective

[38] See John W. Garver, *China's Quest: The History of Foreign Relations of the People's Republic of China* (OUP, 2016) 377–382.

[39] 王铁崖 主编：《国际法》(Wang Tieya (ed), *International Law* (Law Press, 1981).

[40] See ibid, 1. See also 王铁崖 主编：《国际法》(Wang Tieya (ed), *International Law* (Law Press, 1995), 1.

[41] Garver, n 38, 378.

[42] Wang, n 40, 2.

[43] Ibid, 5.

[44] See Ken Yang, 'Wang Tieya (1913-2003)', Chapter 29 of this book.

on international law has emerged as the leading approach shaping both the academic study and state practice of international law in China since the early 1980s. In summary, during the last decade of the Cold War, China rapidly changed its stance on international law to mirror the prevailing Western perspective.

15.4 Creating the Five Principles during the Cold War and Its International Law Implications

The Five Principles of Peaceful Coexistence (referred to as 'the Five Principles', known as the *Panchsheel* or Panch Shila in India) continue to be a fundamental aspect of China's foreign policy, consistently reflecting the basis of China's approach to international law since the 1950s and influencing the international law discourse in the Global South. As Wang Tieya put it, the 'enunciation of the [Five Principles] is one of the major contributions made by the PRC since its establishment to the development of international law'.[45] The principles initially emerged in the discussions between Chinese Premier Zhou Enlai and Indian Prime Minister Jawaharlal Nehru on the status of Tibet (Xizang). Whether Zhou or Nehru first proposed the formula remains obscure, but both men certainly agreed to it. As a result, the Five Principles were written into the Preamble of the Agreement between the PRC and the Republic of India on Trade and Intercourse between the Tibet Region of China and India signed on 20 April 1954 (also known as the Panchsheel Agreement), with the following specific content: '(a) mutual respect for territorial integrity and sovereignty; (b) mutual non-aggression; (c) non-interference in each other's internal affairs; (d) equality and mutual benefit; and (e) peaceful coexistence.'[46] The two prime ministers announced in a Joint Statement on 28 June 1954 that these principles 'should be applied in their relations with countries in Asia, as well as in other parts of the world' and 'in international relations generally'.[47]

The Five Principles emerged in a specific historical context of post-Second World War decolonization, Cold War polarization, and China's search for diplomatic recognition and a united front against Western powers. As former Chinese Premier Wen Jiabao put it, for both China and the Third World countries, the 'Five Principles came about as a historical inevitability':[48]

[45] Wang Tieya, *International Law in China: Historical and Contemorary Perspective*. Recueil de cours, Vol. 221 (published by M. Nijhoff for the Hague Academy of International Law) 263.

[46] See 'The Five Principles of Peaceful Coexistence', *China Keywords* on the website of the PRC State Council Information Office (SCIO), at http://english.scio.gov.cn/featured/chinakeywords/2018-03/16/content_50715204.htm (visited 1 April 2025).

[47] Quoted in Wang Tieya, *International Law in China*, n 45, p. 263.

[48] See Wen Jiabao, 'Carrying Forward the Five Principles of Peaceful Coexistence in the Promotion of Peace and Development', speech at the ceremony celebrating the 50th anniversary of the Five Principles, available at https://www.gov.cn/gongbao/content/2004/content_62873.htm (visited 1 April 2025).

> Following the collapse of the world colonial system after World War II, there emerged a large number of newly independent nation-states in Asia and Africa. Their most pressing task was to safeguard independence and sovereignty, resist aggression and outside interference, cultivate equal relations with other countries, and secure an international environment for peace to develop their national economies … It was at this critical juncture that China, India and Myanmar, countries that gained independence fairly early in Asia, went along with the tide of history by jointly initiating the [Five Principles], which was enthusiastically echoed by many more countries.

As mentioned earlier, the historical context for the Five Principles originates from the 1953–1954 China–India discussions about Tibet. Using India as a base, Britain secured numerous special privileges in Tibet via a sequence of 'unequal treaties' forced upon the Qing dynasty which the PRC refused to accept. Viewing Tibet as an integral part of China's historical territory, Mao ordered the People's Liberation Army (PLA) to move into and control Tibet in October 1950. India, acquiring its independence from the British Empire in 1947, recognized Tibet as part of China de facto but believed it inherited the privileges and influence that Britain once enjoyed in Tibet. However, neither Britain nor India intervened when the PLA liberated Tibet in 1950.[49] China, while strongly rejecting India's requests for privileges, engaged in negotiations regarding India's relationships with Tibet, which took place in Beijing from December 1953 to April 1954. According to China's official narrative, Premier Zhou Enlai first proposed the Five Principles in his meeting with the Indian government delegation on 31 December 1953, which the Indian side agreed to accept as the guiding principles for the negotiations.[50] As noted above, eventually the Five Principles were officially outlined in the Panchsheel Agreement, which led India to relinquish its inherited British privileges in Tibet but facilitated trade and pilgrimage routes between India and Tibet. Thus, as a landmark diplomatic effort, the Panchsheel Agreement served not only to reduce tensions and stabilize relations between the two Asian powers, but also as a formula that advanced a set of principles which have had profound influences on international law and international relations.

China has considered the Five Principles as its major contribution to international law and justice. President Xi Jinping, in a ceremony celebrating the seventieth anniversary of the Five Principles, remarked that the principles 'have become open, inclusive, and universally applicable basic norms for international

[49] Jonathan D. Spence, *The Search for Modern China* (2nd ed) (London: W.W. Norton & Company, 1999) 500.

[50] 'China's Initiation of the Five Principles of Peaceful Co-Existence', the website of the PRC Ministry of Foreign Affairs, at https://www.mfa.gov.cn/eng/zy/wjls/3604_665547/202405/t20240531_11367542.html (visited 20 April 2025).

relations and fundamental principles of international law'.[51] Indeed, the Five Principles, since their birth in the 1950s, have been accepted by a large number of countries, including many Third World governments as well as the Soviet Union.[52] More significantly, the principles were arguably endorsed by the Asian-African Conference at Bandung in April 1955 (the Bandung Conference), though in a slightly varied form. A Declaration on the Promotion of World Peace and Co-Operation adopted at the Bandung Conference contained ten principles that incorporated most of the Five Principles but omitted reference to 'peaceful coexistence'. Instead, the phrase 'live together in peace', directly borrowed from the UN Charter, was used to express a similar concept.[53] Interestingly, it was Chinese Premier Zhou Enlai who proposed and persuaded the conference delegates to accept substituting 'live together in peace' for 'peaceful coexistence', in a diplomatic gesture to demonstrate the peaceful intentions of the PRC government and ensure the success of the Bandung Conference. Zhou later told the Standing Committee of the PRC National People's Congress on 13 May that 'in actual fact, for countries of different social systems to live together in peace is the same as peaceful co-existence'.[54] Therefore, it is reasonable to contend that the Chinese delegation headed by Zhou Enlai significantly influenced the inclusion of the Five Principles in the ten principles embraced by the Bandung Conference. From China's perspective at that time, these principles were essentially 'an extension and development of the Panch Shila'.[55] Furthermore, the impact of the Five Principles is also reflected in their endorsement by the Non-Aligned Movement in the 1960s, the Declaration on Principles of International Law adopted at the 25th Session of the UN General Assembly in the 1970s, and the Declaration on the Establishment of the New International Economic Order adopted at the Sixth Special Session of the UN General Assembly in 1974.[56]

From an international law perspective, the Five Principles were not non-Western legal innovations that significantly depart from the traditional Westphalian doctrines of international law. Wang Tieya pointed out that the principles had 'more direct inspiration' from the UN Charter than other sources.[57] For example, the following clauses of the UN Charter are concerned: the principle of mutual respect for sovereignty and territorial integrity reinforces the principle of state sovereignty

[51] Xi Jinping, 'Address at the Conference Marking 70th Anniversary of Five Principles of Peaceful Coexistence', 28 June 2024, at https://english.www.gov.cn/news/202406/28/content_WS667e6d1dc6d0868f4e8e8a82.html (visited 10 April 2025).

[52] Russell H. Fifield, 'The Five Principles of Peaceful Co-Existence', (1958) 52:3 *American Journal of Comparative Law* 504 at 505.

[53] Ibid, 506–507.

[54] Ibid, 507 (quoting George McTurnan, *The Asian-African Conference* 63 (Ithaca: Cornell University Press, 1956)).

[55] Ibid, 507 (quoting Li Kao, 'China and Panch Shila', *People's China*, No. 14, p. 10 (16 July 1957).

[56] Xi, note 51.

[57] Wang Tieya, *International Law in China*, note 45, 264.

enshrined in Article 2(1); the non-aggression principle reflects the prohibition on the use of force articulated in Article 2(4); non-interference in internal affairs echoes principles in customary international law and Article 2(7) protecting states from external intervention. The principles of mutual benefit and coexistence may not directly correspond to any existing provisions, but could still be inferred from the relevant rules concerning sovereignty, equality, and Article 2(3)'s obligations to settle disputes peacefully.

However, put together in a single structure advocated by China as the paramount framework of the fundamental principles of international law which places the strongest emphasis on the traditional Westphalian doctrines of sovereignty, equality, and non-interference, the Five Principles embody and protect the aspirations of postcolonial states for maintaining independence and resisting inventions from powerful states, significantly impacting international legal debates on issues such as international human rights protection, humanitarian intervention, the Responsibility to Protect (R2P), and global governance structures, among others.[58] As ICJ Judge Xue Hanqin put it,[59]

> Theoretically, one may argue that the Five Principles, to a large extent, resemble the basic principles of international law enshrined in the Charter of the United Nations. Given the Cold War background, however, it would be well argued that, ideally and practically, the Five Principles contain many elements that basically reflect the common inspirations of small and weak countries for equality and justice in international relations.

In short, as a cornerstone of the PRC's foreign policy and its engagement with international law, the Five Principles presented a universal framework for interstate relations, representing both a strategic assertion of sovereignty and a normative challenge to the Eurocentric view of international law. It is pretty remarkable that the PRC developed such a framework to guide its foreign policy and, as early as the beginning of the Cold War, signal its regulatory philosophy regarding how the international community should be governed, which has remained unchanged ever since.

[58] As Li Zhaojie, a Chinese international law scholar, put it: 'China's sovereignty-bound thinking is most persistent and resonant in the domain of international human rights. The most recurring theme in the Chinese human rights discourse is the primacy of state sovereignty—no state sovereignty no human rights.' See Li Zhaojie, 'Legacy of Modern Chinese History: Its Relevance to the Chinese Perspective of the Contemporary International Legal Order', (2001) 5 *Singapore Journal of International & Comparative Law* 314 at 324.

[59] Xue Hanqin, *Chinese Contemporary Perspectives on International Law: History, Culture and International Law* (The Hague Academy of International Law, 2012) 39.

15.5 Chinese State Practice on Territorial Disputes during the Cold War: A Case Study

15.5.1 PRC Practice in Addressing Territorial Disputes

Having discussed the origin and evolution of the PRC's philosophical and discursive approaches to international law, it is helpful to examine the country's actual practice in the international legal order. The selected area is the territorial disputes and the use of force. As can be seen, China's Cold War international legal practices demonstrated a complex pattern of continuity and change, ideological proclamation, and pragmatic adaptation. Rather than representing a consistent revolutionary challenge or gradual assimilation to international norms, China's approach, even during the Cold War, exhibited strategic selectivity and contextual adaptation to changing circumstances.

China's approach to territorial disputes during the Cold War was crucial to its international law practices. The country shares land borders with fourteen countries and has maritime boundaries in the East and South China Sea, leading to conflicts with multiple states. However, by 2005, China had established border agreements or treaties with twelve neighbouring countries, addressing land disputes along 90 per cent of its total borders. These agreements were reached in two phases: in the 1960s, with Myanmar, Nepal, Mongolia, Pakistan, and Afghanistan; and in the 1990s to 2000s, with Russia, Laos, Vietnam, and the newly independent Central Asian countries including Kazakhstan, Kyrgyzstan, and Tajikistan.[60]

Due to the revolutionary tones China often demonstrated through its rollercoaster-style domestic politics under Mao Zedong, '[l]eading theories of international relations would expect a state with China's characteristics to be uncompromising and prone to using force in territorial disputes, not conciliatory'.[61] However, as Taylor Fravel observed in a book published in 2008 that conducted a thorough empirical study of China's handling of border disputes:[62]

> In its territorial disputes, however, China has been less prone to violence and more cooperative than a singular view of an expansionist state suggests. Since 1949, China has participated in twenty-three unique territorial disputes with its neighbours on land and at sea. Yet it has pursued compromise and offered concessions in seventeen of these conflicts. China's compromises have often been

[60] '外交部条约法律司司长谈中国与邻国的划界工作' ('Interview of Liu Zhenmin, the Director-General of the Department of Treaty of Law of the Ministry of Foreign Affairs, on Border Demarcation between China and Its Neighbours'), the website of PRC Ministry of Foreign Affairs, at https://www.mfa.gov.cn/web/ziliao_674904/tytj_674911/tyfg_674913/200508/t20050831_7949576.shtml (visited 1 April 2025) (hereinafter 'Interview of Liu Zhenmin').

[61] M. Taylor Fravel, *Strong Borders, Secure Nation: Cooperation and Conflict in China's Territorial Disputes* (Princeton University Press, 2008) 1.

[62] Ibid, 1–2.

> substantial, as it has usually offered to accept less than half of the contested territory in any final settlement. In addition, these compromises have resulted in boundary agreements in which China has abandoned potential irredentist claims to more than 3.4 million square kilometres of land that had been part of the Qing empire at its height in the early nineteenth century. In total, the [PRC] has contested roughly 238,000 square kilometres or just 7 percent of the territory once part of the Qing.

In a nutshell, China's management of land border disputes during the Cold War demonstrated a pragmatic approach belied by revolutionary rhetoric. In the 1950s and 1960s, China concluded boundary agreements to settle borders with Burma (1960), Nepal (1961), Mongolia (1962), North Korea (1962), Afghanistan (1963), and Pakistan (1963).[63] In the negotiations with Burma (Myanmar), China proposed a two-phase model for resolving the border disputes.[64] Initially, China and Burma established a framework outlining general principles, including methods for dispute resolution and early proposals on major issues. As part of this, China proposed a comprehensive 'package deal' addressing all three disputed territories between the two nations. Both sides agreed to uphold the status quo in the three regions before progressing to the next step. Marking the accomplishment of the first phase, the Agreement between the Government of the People's Republic of China and the Government of the Union of Burma on the Question of the Boundary between the Two Countries was signed on 28 January 1960, in which the parties agreed to establish a Joint Committee to conduct negotiations. The second phase witnessed the discussions and agreements on specific arrangements, leading eventually to the conclusion of the Boundary Treaty between the People's Republic of China and the Union of Burma signed on 1 October 1960, which was the PRC's first border treaty with a neighbour, presenting a model for its future negotiations with other neighbouring countries.

Chinese discourse on its management of territorial disputes has framed the Sino–Burma Boundary Treaty as an example of applying the Five Principles analysed above. In preparation for the negotiations, Premier Zhou Enlai reported to the PRC National People's Congress on 9 June 1957 that:[65]

> In the process of discussing the China–Myanmar boundary issue, our government has always emphasised sincerity and friendly consultations based on the

[63] Xinjun Zhang and Xidi Chen, 'China and the Settlement of Territorial Disputes', in Ignacio de la Rasilla and Congyan Cai (eds), *The Cambridge Handbook of China and International Law* (CUP, 2024) 522, 523 (noting the settlement with the first five neighbours, except Pakistan, was final).

[64] See 周鲠生：《国际法》下册 (Zhou Gengsheng, *International Law*. Vol. 2) (Beijing: Commerce Press, 1976) 436–437. See also Zhang and Chen, n 63, 524.

[65] 中华人民共和国外交部，中共中央文献研究室 编：《周恩来外交文选》(PRC Ministry of Foreign Affairs and the Central Literature Research Office of the CPC (eds.), *Selected Works of Zhou Enlai on Diplomacy*) (Beijing: Zhongyang Wenxian Chubanshe, 1990) 236–237.

> Five Principles of Peaceful Coexistence to achieve a fair and reasonable solution. This resolution of the China–Myanmar boundary issue will not only further consolidate and develop the friendly relations between China and Myanmar but also contribute to the unity of Asian and African countries. Our government's stance on resolving the China–Myanmar boundary issue is based on safeguarding our national interests while also promoting the friendship between China and Myanmar and the unity of Asian and African countries.

The PRC broadly applied the same or a similar formula in dealing with border disputes with other countries in the 1960s, such as Nepal and the DPRK. However, not all disputes resulted in amicable outcomes through negotiations. For example, the negotiations between China and India were protracted and largely unsuccessful during the Cold War and continue to be so today. The Sino–Indian War of 1962 serves as a poignant example of the intricate relationship between legal claims and military actions in territorial disputes. The conflict was rooted in the differing interpretations of the boundary line between China and India. China vehemently rejected the McMahon Line, which British colonial authorities drew during the 1914 Simla Convention without the Qing government's consent. From China's perspective, the McMahon Line represented an illegitimate colonial imposition that disregarded historical and cultural ties to the region.[66] On the other hand, India staunchly defended the McMahon Line, viewing it as a legitimate and inviolable boundary established during the colonial era. India's position was grounded in the belief that colonial-era agreements should be respected and upheld, despite the changing political landscape. Thus, India's insistence on the sanctity of the McMahon Line clashed sharply with China's anti-colonial legal rhetoric, which sought to dismantle remnants of imperialist influence and assert sovereignty based on historical claims.[67]

The conflicting legal stances led to escalating tensions and ultimately armed conflict. The war saw significant military engagements along the disputed border, with both sides suffering casualties and territorial losses. Despite the intensity of the conflict, China unilaterally declared a ceasefire and withdrew its forces from the contested areas on 21 November 1962, shocking the world.[68] This move was indicative of China's preference for resolving disputes through diplomatic negotiation rather than prolonged military occupation. By declaring a ceasefire and withdrawing, China signalled its desire for territorial stabilization and peaceful resolution, emphasizing the importance of diplomacy over permanent control as embodied in its traditional approach discussed above. The aftermath of the

[66] Neville Maxwell, *India's China War* (Bombay: Jaico Publishing House, 1970) 23–26, 39–62. See also Zhang and Chen, n 63, 530.

[67] Maxwell, n 66, 67–83.

[68] Ibid, 417.

Sino–Indian War highlighted the complexities of boundary disputes influenced by colonial legacies and differing national narratives. For the purpose of this chapter, arguably, China's action in the Sino–India war illustrates China's inclination towards a peaceful resolution of territorial disputes while also showing its commitment to using force, but only in a limited way when deemed essential.

15.5.2 The Consistency of Considerations in the Chinese Approach to Territorial Disputes during the Cold War

China's approach to managing border disputes reveals consistent patterns, originating during the Cold War and continuing into today's territorial policy and practices. First, the resolution of territorial disputes was always placed in a broader strategic framework incorporating the totality of China's national development and foreign policy objectives.[69] That is, China prioritized settlements with neighbouring states where improved relations served strategic objectives, particularly during periods of heightened security concerns. Thus, compromises made often reflect strategic considerations rather than normative commitments to peaceful resolution. As Eric A. Hyer put it,[70]

> Beijing's approach to a [territorial] dispute is largely determined by the relationship or desired relationship with the country involved in the dispute ... The PRC has demonstrated great flexibility in order to reach a boundary settlement in an attempt to bolster amicable relations and maintain a favorable balance of power. The handling of boundary disputes with Burma, Nepal, Mongolia, Pakistan and Afghanistan illustrates this pattern.

In the early years of the PRC, the compromises contributed to securing diplomatic recognition from neighbouring states, maintaining harmonious relations with neighbours in order to create a favourable external environment for domestic state building, achieving a favourable geopolitical balance of power, and consolidating Third World solidarity, while consolidating control over strategically vital territories.[71] The timing of the settlements often coincided with periods of domestic vulnerability or international isolation, suggesting instrumental rather than principled motivations.[72] For example, in the boundary treaty with Nepal, Premier

[69] 张清敏："中国解决陆地边界经验对解决海洋边界的启示"，《外交评论》2013年第4期，第2页 [Zhang Qingmin, 'Chinese Experiences in Solving Land-based Border Disputes: Lessons for Its Maritime Disputes', (2013) 4 *Diplomacy Review* 2].

[70] Eric Ariel Hyer, *The Politics of China's Boundary Disputes and Settlements*, PhD thesis, Columbia University (Published by U.M.I with Order Number 9118590, 1990) 7–8.

[71] Eric Hyer, *The Pramatic Dragon: China's Grand Strategy and Boundary Settlements* (Vancouver: UBC Press) 53 and 91.

[72] Ibid, 80.

Zhou Enlai noted that regarding the location of Mount Everest, although the Chinese map and China's historical claims identified the mountain as being within Chinese territory, China still decided to offer concessions and accept Nepal's position that the mountain was on the border line between the two countries, leading to the division of the mountain equally between the two nations. China's adoption of this policy clearly aimed to 'promote "Sino-Nepalese friendship"' to demonstrate China's willingness to take a conciliatory and friendly approach in dealing with its neighbours, in order to further attract more countries to establish and develop relationships with the PRC.[73]

Second, the PRC consistently highlighted the importance of a peaceful resolution to territorial disputes, grounded in the Five Principles. In a discussion with U Nu, the Prime Minister of Burma, on 11 December 1954, Chairman Mao Zedong emphasized that the Five Principles reflected China's enduring policy towards international relations, including the border issue between China and Burma. He remarked: 'the Five Principles are suitable for our situations; we too need a long period of peaceful environment [for our development].'[74] In his speech during the Political Committee meeting of the Asian-African Conference (Bandung Conference) on 23 April 1955, Premier Zhou Enlai emphasized that the PRC was prepared to maintain the status quo in border disputes with neighbouring countries prior to initiating talks. He stated: 'as to how we eventually determine the border lines with our neighbours, there is only the peaceful means to resort to, and any other means are not allowed.'[75] As discussed above, China's actions during the Cold War largely conformed to this policy.

Third, China overwhelmingly preferred bilateral negotiations for territorial disputes, largely excluding multilateral or third-party mechanisms, although after the Cold War it has not entirely excluded regional frameworks in specific contexts. This approach is evident in China's approach to disputes with all its land-based neighbours and the East and South China Sea claimants. This preference is rooted in historical, ideological, and, arguably, legal factors, as well as strategic considerations. Dai Bingguo, former State Councillor in charge of China's foreign affairs, explained to American think tanks in Washington DC in June 2016, prior to the final award of the South China Sea Arbitration was issued:[76]

[73] '在四月二十八日离开尼泊尔前夕，周总理在加德满都答记者问' [Premier Zhou Answers Questions of a Reporter in Kathmandu before His Departure from Nepal on 28 April], *People's Daily*, 1 May 1960, quoted in Zhang and Chen, n 63, 524.

[74] 中华人民共和国外交部，中共中央文献研究室 编：《毛泽东外交文选》[PRC Ministry of Foreign Affairs and the Central Literature Research Office of the CPC (eds.), *Selected Works of Mao Zedong on Diplomacy* (Beijing: Zhongyang Wenxian Chubanshe; Shijie Zhishi Chubanshe, 1994), 186–187.

[75] *Selected Works of Zhou Enlai on Diplomacy*, n 63, 130.

[76] '戴秉国统治在中美智库南海问题对话会上的讲话' (Comrade Dai Bingguo's Speech at the Dialague between Chinese and American Think Tanks), 5 July 2016, Washington DC, available at the website of the PRC Ministry of Foreign Affairs: https://www.mfa.gov.cn/gjhdq_676201/gj_676203/bmz_679954/1206_680528/1209_680538/201607/t20160705_9361592.shtml (visited 5 April 2025).

> Since modern times, China has consistently been a victim of hegemonism and power politics, suffering humiliation from Western powers. For example, the Versailles Conference after World War I sold out China's Shandong, the League of Nations' Lytton Commission endorsed the Japanese invasion of China's northeastern provinces, and even the U.S.-led negotiations of the 'San Francisco Treaty' after World War II excluded China. These events remain vivid in the memory of the Chinese people. This is why China insists on firmly controlling its own destiny regarding territorial sovereignty issues and resolutely rejects any third-party solutions.

China legally argued that bilateral negotiation is the main solution outlined in international legal documents such as the UN Charter. It believed that this approach better reflected a country's sovereign will and upheld the sovereign equality of the involved nations. If other mechanisms for dispute resolution were to be utilized, the initiation must depend on the relevant countries' consent.[77]

Nevertheless, one could argue that China's inclination towards bilateral negotiations stems from strategic, pragmatic, and realist factors. Such negotiations give China greater control and influence over both processes and outcomes, thereby sidestepping the uncertainties associated with the potential internationalization of disputes. In individual discussions, China can leverage its economic and political clout more effectively than in regional or multilateral settings. Additionally, bilateral talks provide increased flexibility and the opportunity for practical solutions tailored to the specific nuances of each dispute. Importantly, confidentiality is easier to maintain in bilateral discussions, especially when China must offer concessions to its neighbours for strategic reasons, which the government prefers not to disclose to the Chinese public.

Last but not least, China pragmatically balanced its historical background with current realities in handling territorial disputes during the Cold War. Even today, the PRC frequently invokes historical narratives to legitimize its claims, portraying itself as a victim of colonial aggression seeking to restore its rightful territories. On the other hand, from the inception of the PRC's establishment, the ruling CPC leadership warned China's diplomatic team not to be overly ambitious. Zhou Enlai once told China's National People's Congress that 'if we base our territorial claims on the historical territory of the [Yuan Dynasty established by the Mongols], then the whole world will be shocked'.[78] In practice, although China firmly rejected 'unequal treaties' imposed on previous Chinese governments by imperial powers during the 'century of humiliation', it did not always explicitly demand the

[77] 周健：'新中国解决陆地边界问题的国际法实践' (Zhou Jian, 'New China's International Law Practice in Solving Land-based Border Disputes'), (2021) 6:3《边界与海洋研究》(*Journal of Boundary and Ocean Studies*) 5, 28.

[78] 廖心文：'20世纪五六十年代中国解决陆地边界问题的历史回顾与成功经验', (2019) 4:5《边界与海洋研究》(*Journal of Boundary and Ocean Studies*) (2019) 42, 49 (quoting Zhen Enlai's report to the PRC National People's Congress on 9 July 1957).

wholesale nullification of borders based on these treaties. Instead, it used the rejection as leverage and a justification for seeking renegotiations and adjustments. For instance, on Sino–Burma border negotiations, the Central Committee of the CPC provided the following guiding principle: 'The borders between our country and foreign countries, if they have been determined by old treaties [signed by the previous Chinese governments], shall be dealt with in accordance with the general principles of international law.'[79] The relevant 'general principles of international law' here was understood by the PRC as the following:[80]

> After a country undergoes a change in its political regime and establishes a new government, it may choose to inherit or not inherit political or other types of treaties signed by the previous government with foreign governments. However, treaties that delineate the boundaries between two countries must be inherited. If adjustments are needed, they must be made through negotiations with the foreign government concerned, acknowledging the existing treaties.

In summary, China, emerging as the PRC in 1949, faced unresolved territorial ambiguities stemming from historically vague treaties (often regarded as 'unequal'), colonial border setups, and competing national claims. The fledgling PRC adopted a strategic and practical approach to managing these disputes, emphasizing sovereignty, favouring peaceful resolutions, prioritizing bilateral negotiations, remaining flexible in considering historical factors, and pragmatically weighing costs and benefits in light of domestic political and geopolitical considerations. Additionally, it selectively applied international law. Notably, revolutionary rhetoric did not overshadow pragmatism in China's foreign policy and actions regarding territorial disputes.

15.6 China–Third World Relations: Implications in International Law

As Premier Zhou Enlai put it in 1975, '[t]he Third World is the main force in combating colonialism, imperialism, and hegemonism. China is a developing socialist country belonging to the Third World.'[81] During the Cold War, China aimed to establish itself as a leader in anti-imperialism, anti-colonialism, and economic justice. Throughout this period, the PRC's ties with the 'Third World'—a broad descriptor for newly independent, developing, and non-aligned countries primarily in Asia, Africa, and Latin America—became a pivotal element of its foreign

[79] Ibid, 48–49 (quoting the 'Instructions of the CPC Central Committee on the Question of Sino-Burma Borders', issued on 31 October 1956).

[80] Ibid, 49.

[81] SeeGeorge T. Yu, 'China and the Third World', (1977) 17:11 *Asian Survey* 1036.

policy. This relationship was intricate, dynamic, and influenced by a combination of ideology, pragmatism, geopolitical strategy, and national interests. From the perspective of international relations, it focused on forging alliances, countering the influence of superpowers (both the US and later the Soviet Union), and positioning China as a significant global actor. In terms of international law, it was about advocating for principles such as sovereignty, non-intervention, and self-determination, and seeking to revise existing international legal frameworks, especially economic ones, to benefit developing nations.

15.6.1 From the 'Intermediate Zone' to the 'Three Worlds': Mao Zedong's Conceptualization of Global Politics

The PRC, at its formation, proclaimed its version of socialist internationalism—the basic orientation of its foreign policy—as (a) uniting with the USSR, members of the Soviet camp, and 'all oppressed nations' and (b) opposing 'imperialist aggression to defend lasting world peace'.[82] To some extent, this served as the constitutional basis for the PRC's continuous and active engagement with Third World nations. In 1951, one year after the establishment of the PRC, Zhou Enlai attempted to direct the attention of China's diplomatic community to the uprising of the 'national liberation movement' (民族解放运动), namely the rapid growth of newly independent states after the Second World War. He pointed out:[83]

> The success of the Chinese revolution has added new strength to the national liberation movements of oppressed peoples around the world, providing them with immense encouragement and promoting the development of these movements. The national liberation movement has already become the main force of the current revolution. We cannot underestimate this force, nor can we consider it merely an auxiliary force. This force is developing and will inevitably achieve final victory. History will ultimately make this conclusion. Our task is to support and promote the development of the national liberation movement.

Not surprisingly, the PRC's foreign policy orientation, including its stance on Third World nations, was primarily shaped by Mao Zedong's conceptualization of world politics. In a nutshell, Mao Zedong constructed theoretical guidelines for the CPC's foreign policy by transcending a simplistic bipolar perspective even before the founding of the PRC. He developed frameworks—initially the 'intermediate zone' (中间地带) and later the 'three worlds theory' (三个世界理论—to

[82] Common Program, n 18.

[83] 周恩来：'民族解放运动的国际地位和作用' [Zhou Enlai, 'The International Status and Role of the National Liberation Movement'], in *Selected Works of Zhou Enlai*, n 65, 36–37.

analyse international contradictions, identify potential allies and adversaries, and strategically position China on the global geopolitical map. These doctrines were not mere academic concepts; they were dynamic tools that reflected China's changing national interests, ideological commitments, and perceptions of global power relations, especially regarding imperialism and hegemonism.

Mao first articulated the concept of the 'intermediate zone' in 1946, right after the Anti-Japanese War and before the Chinese Civil War, during an interview with American journalist Anna Louise Strong.[84] This concept referred to the vast area between the USA and the USSR, the two superpowers of the time. Mao identified this zone as comprising countries in Asia, Africa, and Latin America, which were neither aligned with the capitalist bloc nor the socialist bloc.[85] In 1963, Mao further developed this theory and stated that there were two intermediate zones: one comprising Asia, Africa, and Latin America and the other encompassing Europe, including both Western Europe and Soviet-controlled Eastern Europe. The evolution of the 'intermediate zone' concept, particularly its division into two distinct zones after the Sino–Soviet split, laid the direct conceptual groundwork for the 'Three Worlds Theory'. On 22 February 1974, during a meeting with Zambian President Kenneth Kaunda, Mao formally proposed the concept of dividing the world into three categories of countries: the USA and the USSR as the First World; the developed countries of Europe, Japan, Canada, and others, which were economically advanced but not as dominant as the superpowers, as the Second World; and the developing countries in Asia, Africa, and Latin America as the Third World, which Mao identified as the main force in the global struggle against imperialism.[86] On 10 April 1974, Deng Xiaoping, the then Vice Premier of the PRC, delivered a landmark speech at the Sixth Special Session of the UN General Assembly which outlined China's worldview and foreign policy, the most significant part of which was the formal presentation of Mao's 'Three Worlds Theory'.[87]

This theory, once professed, left immense and profound marks on international relations. This division provided the overarching strategic framework for China's foreign policy, guiding its diplomatic efforts, alliances, and actions within international organizations such as the UN. It aimed to build the broadest possible international united front against superpower dominance. By positioning itself firmly in the Third World, China signalled its strategic alignment and aspiration

[84] 牛军：'重建"中间地带"：中国亚洲政策的缘起 (1949–1955)' (Niu Jun, 'Rebuilding the "Intermediate Zone": The Birth of China's Asia Policy (1949–1955)), (2012), No. 2, 《国际政治研究》 (*Review of International Politics*) (61 at 63).

[85] Ibid, 64.

[86] 毛泽东：'关于三个世界划分问题' (Mao Zedong, 'On the Question of the Division of the Three Worlds'), in *Selected Works of Mao*, n 74, 600–601.

[87] '邓小平在联大第六届特别会议上的发言' ('Deng Xiaoping's Speech at the Six Session of the UN General Assembly'), 10 April 1974, available at the website of Communist Party Members: https://news.12371.cn/2015/09/28/ARTI1443384874163974.shtml (visited 1 April 2025).

to be a leader and champion of developing nations' interests, distinct from the superpowers.

15.6.2 Promoting the Five Principles in the Bandung Conference

The PRC's first major engagement with the Third World was at the Asian-African Conference, known as the Bandung Conference, held from 18 to 24 April 1955 in Bandung, Indonesia. China mainly used its newly formed 'Five Principles' to charm the twenty-nine Asian and African countries, 'practically the entire community of independent nations in Asia and Africa at that time', who participated in the conference.[88] Premier Zhou Enlai, recognized for his diplomatic brilliance that facilitated the success of the Bandung Conference, delivered a speech emphasizing peaceful coexistence.[89] In his speeches, Zhou proposed the principle of 'Seeking Common Ground, Reserving Differences' (求同存异), which became the defining theme of not only the Conference but also interstate relations in the Global South. More significantly, Zhou strongly advocated for the Five Principles of Peaceful Coexistence, and aligned China firmly with the anti-colonial struggle by committing to solidarity with nations still fighting for independence and condemning imperialism as a source of conflict.[90] As historians noted, '[a]t Bandung, Chou made use of his considerable personal charm and diplomatic adroitness to sap the hostility of leaders suspicious of China ... or of communism.'[91]

In summary, the Bandung Conference represented a pivotal moment in the evolution of international relations following the Second World War. It constituted the inaugural significant assembly of Asian and African nations convened to deliberate upon their collective interests without the participation and intervention of the great powers, thereby instituting foundational doctrines in international law such as respect for national sovereignty and territorial integrity, alongside a commitment to non-interference in the internal affairs of countries. In alignment with the Bandung Spirit, China has persistently stood together with developing nations by providing development assistance, fostering regional integration, and enhancing cooperation among South–South nations. The conference culminated in a joint communiqué that articulated ten fundamental principles of solidarity, friendship, and cooperation, which were rooted in China's Five Principles of Peaceful Coexistence.

[88] Roderick MacFarquhar and John K. Fairbank (eds), *The Cambridge History of China, Vol. 14. The People's Republic of China, Part I: The Emergence of Revolutionary China 1949–1965* (CUP, 1987) 283.
[89] Ibid.
[90] 周恩来：'在亚非会议全体会议上的发言 (含补充发言)' [Zhou Enlai, 'Speech at the Plenary Session of the Asia-African Conference (including the Supplementary Speech)'], 19 April 1955, in *Selected Works of Zhou Enlai*, n 65, 112–125.
[91] *The Cambridge History of China: PRC, Part I*, n 88, 284.

15.6.3 Anti-Imperialism, Anti-Colonialism, and China's Short-Lived 'Export of Revolution'

Any study of China's Third World Policy during the Cold War must consider the ideological foundation of this policy. Particularly during the peak of Maoist revolutionary diplomacy in the 1960s and early 1970s, China portrayed itself as a leader of global revolution, opposing both Western imperialism and Soviet 'social imperialism'. It vigorously supported national liberation movements across Third World nations, regarding their fights against imperialism and colonialism as essential to the worldwide socialist revolution. China provided political, material, and technical support to liberation efforts in countries such as Vietnam, Laos, Cambodia, Algeria, and Zimbabwe. For instance, during the Vietnam War, China delivered considerable military and economic assistance to Vietnam, which was crucial for the country's resistance against the US and its subsequent reunification.[92]

The earliest five years of the Cultural Revolution represent the most extreme phase of Chinese foreign policy, characterized by Chinese historians as 'diplomacy under the influence of extreme leftist ideology (极左思潮下的中国外交)'.[93] In a speech on 7 November 1967 marking the fiftieth anniversary of Russia's October Revolution, General Lin Biao, then Mao's Number 2 in the Chinese leadership, called for the following:[94]

> We must build our great motherland into an even stronger base for the world revolution. We must more vigorously support the revolutionary struggles of the world proletariat and the people of all countries. We must join the revolutionary people of the world in carrying the struggle against imperialism, led by the United States, and modern revisionism, centered on the Soviet revisionist traitor group, to the end. We must work harder to study and master Mao Zedong Thought and spread it more widely throughout the world. This is the glorious mission history has entrusted to the people of our country, and it is our internationalist duty.

In a series of other top leaders' speeches and editorials of state-owned flagship newspapers, China was positioned as 'the new centre for world revolution'.[95] Even though Mao displayed disagreement with this self-centred position,[96] the ideas of 'People's War' and 'World Revolution' inspired revolutionary movements in

[92] See generally, 杨公素:《当代中国外交理论与实践》[Yang Gongsu, *Contemporary China's Diplomacy: Theory and Practice*] (Lizhi Chubanshe, 2002), 96–101; 166–181.
[93] Ibid, 151.
[94] 林彪：'在首都人民纪念十月革命五十周年大会上 林彪同志的讲话' [Comrade Lin Biao's speech at the meeting of the people of the capital to commemorate the 50th anniversary of the October Revolution], *People's Daily*, 7 November 1967.
[95] Yang, *Contemporary China's Diplomacy*, n 92, 151–152.
[96] Ibid, 152.

the Third World, establishing China as an 'exporter of revolution' that supported liberation efforts throughout Africa and Asia. It provided ideological guidance, material resources, and training to groups opposing colonial or oppressive governments, as shown by its assistance to Algeria and backing for anti-apartheid factions in southern Africa.[97]

China characterized its support with legal norms in international law, asserting that national liberation movements were valid forms of resistance against colonial rule, not violations of sovereignty. This stance contested traditional views on non-interference. Overall, China's opposition to imperialism and hegemonism, along with its pushback against the unfair practices of Western nations in international law, questioned the Eurocentric dominance of the global legal system. It motivated Third World nations to assert their rights and engage in shaping international law actively. From China's perspective, this bolstered the unity and impact of Third World countries in the international legal sphere, advancing the democratization of international law.

15.6.4 The New International Economic Order

China's approach to economic relations with the Third World evolved significantly over time. Initially framed in terms of 'proletarian internationalism', China's economic aid programmes in the 1950s and 1960s emphasized solidarity over commercial benefit. The Tanzania—Zambia Railway (TAZARA) exemplified this approach—providing substantial assistance with minimal expectation of economic return.

By the 1970s, China had enthusiastically embraced the New International Economic Order (NIEO) movement, supporting Third World demands for restructured economic relations and resource sovereignty. During his 1974 address at the UN, Deng Xiaoping delivered a pointed critique of the current but 'outdated' international economic order:[98]

> In the past few centuries, colonialism and imperialism have ruthlessly enslaved and plundered the people of Asia, Africa, and Latin America. They exploited the cheap labor and abundant natural resources of the local people, implemented a deformed single economy, seized cheap agricultural and mineral products, dumped their industrial products, stifled national industries, engaged in unequal exchanges, and extracted excessive profits. The wealth of developed countries

[97] See generally, Steven F. Jackson, 'China's Third World Foreign Policy: The Case of Angola and Mozambique' (1995) *The China Quarterly* 142, 388–422.

[98] Deng's speech at the UN, n 87.

> and the poverty of developing countries are the results of the plundering policies of colonialism and imperialism.
>
> Even after many Asian, African, and Latin American countries achieved political independence, colonialism and imperialism still controlled the economic lifelines of these countries to varying degrees, and the old economic structures did not fundamentally change. Imperialism, especially the superpowers, adopted new forms of colonialism, intensifying their exploitation and plundering of developing countries. They exported capital to developing countries, established 'states within states' through international monopoly organizations like 'multinational corporations,' plundered economically, and interfered politically. They used their monopoly positions in the international market to raise the export prices of their products and lower the prices of raw materials from developing countries, reaping huge profits. As the political and economic crises of capitalism deepened and their competition intensified, they also exacerbated their plundering of developing countries by shifting economic and monetary crises onto them.

China's advocacy for NIEO principles at the UN reflected both genuine solidarity and strategic positioning against the superpowers. China's legal advocacy focused particularly on sovereignty principles. It supported expanded understandings of permanent sovereignty over natural resources and consistently opposed interventionist interpretations of international law. This position aligned with both China's own sovereignty concerns and the interests of many postcolonial states seeking to consolidate independence.

However, China's NIEO advocacy contained contradictions. While championing economic justice internationally, China's domestic development model did not necessarily align with NIEO principles of economic distributive justice. Furthermore, as China's Reform and Opening-Up progressed in the late 1970s and 1980s, its economic engagement with the Third World increasingly reflected commercial interests rather than pure solidarity.

To summarize, during the Cold War, the PRC implemented proactive strategies to connect with, support, and engage Third World nations. By participating in events such as the Bandung Conference and promoting anti-imperialism, anti-colonialism, and a New International Economic Order, China forged strong, collaborative ties with these countries. These initiatives not only safeguarded the sovereignty and interests of Third World nations but also contributed to the evolution of international law and the democratization of global relations, significantly influencing the international landscape throughout the Cold War.

15.7 Concluding Remarks

This chapter has traced the People's Republic of China's multifaceted engagement with international law throughout the Cold War. Challenging simplistic narratives of isolation or pure revolutionary defiance, the analysis reveals a relatively consistent strategic posture blending Westphalian insistence on sovereignty and non-interference, pragmatic instrumentalism in pursuit of national interests, and periods of revolutionary idealism, particularly in its support for Third World anti-colonialism. From leveraging foundational principles in the Common Programme and the Sino–Soviet Treaty to navigating the complex triangular diplomacy and championing the Five Principles of Peaceful Coexistence at Bandung and beyond, the PRC utilized international law as both a shield to protect its nascent statehood and a tool to advance its geopolitical agenda.

Key findings underscore China's selective adherence to international norms. While upholding sovereignty as paramount, it simultaneously engaged in revolutionary support for liberation movements, framing this within an anti-imperialist interpretation of self-determination. Its approach to territorial disputes often demonstrated surprising pragmatism and compromise, prioritizing strategic stability and bilateral negotiations over rigid historical claims or multilateral mechanisms. Furthermore, China's theoretical discourse evolved significantly, moving from Marxist-Leninist scepticism and Soviet alignment towards a more rationalist and ultimately universalist acceptance of international legal norms, a shift catalysed by its entry into the UN and the launch of the Reform and Opening-Up era. China's active promotion of the Five Principles and its leadership role in advocating for the New International Economic Order marked significant efforts to influence international legal discourse from a Third World perspective.

The legacy of China's Cold War engagement with international law endures. The deep-seated emphasis on sovereignty and non-interference enshrined in the Five Principles continues to anchor its foreign policy and shape its approach to contemporary issues ranging from human rights to maritime disputes and global governance reform. The blend of principled advocacy and strategic pragmatism observed during the Cold War offers valuable insights into China's current interactions within international institutions and its efforts to reshape aspects of the global legal order. Understanding this historical trajectory—from revolutionary outsider to pragmatic participant and now assertive stakeholder—is crucial for navigating the complexities of China's role in the twenty-first-century international system and appreciating the historical context informing present-day geopolitical dynamics, including the intensifying Sino–US rivalry often framed as a 'new Cold War'.

16
Towards a Principle-based International Order? The Origin of China's International Law Vocabulary in the 1950s–1960s

Chen Yifeng

16.1 Introduction

At the time the People's Republic of China (PRC) was founded in 1949, international law had yet to establish a legitimate vocabulary to be employed by the Chinese government in its international conduct. While international customs were seen as vague, uncertain, and incapable of offering protection for China's sovereignty and independence, international treaties were hardly any better. The bilateral treaties between China and foreign powers were largely unequal, exploitative, and excessively unjust. China was not in a position to invoke the Charter of the United Nations either, as the PRC government was excluded from representation in the United Nations system as a consequence of the non-recognition policy enforced by the United States and its allies. A positivistic image of international law did not lend much to the PRC government in its imposed isolation. It is against this perceived inappropriateness of positivistic international law that the PRC government resorted to principles of international law to proclaim its normative propositions about the world order.

The chapter foremost attempts a historical account of the PRC government's practice of principles in its early years. The most noticeable example of this has been the five principles of peaceful coexistence, introduced in 1955 and adhered to ever since. The five principles of peaceful coexistence have been widely seen as a trade mark of China's international law and foreign policy positions. An examination of the turn to principles offers a useful angle to explore the efforts made by China to engage with international society through constitutive languages rather than positivistic rights and obligations in searching for peace and in defending sovereignty.

The study further makes an intellectual attempt at political philosophy. Principles are political institutions. They align and affirm the virtues and moralities of a community, express and consolidate political ideals and commitment, and function as common denominators for political debates and contestation. The

Chen Yifeng, *Towards a Principle-based International Order? The Origin of China's International Law Vocabulary in the 1950s–1960s* In: *Histories of International Law in China*. Edited by: Ignacio de la Rasilla, Jiangyu Wang, and Congyan Cai, Oxford University Press. DOI: 10.1093/oso/9780198888345.003.0016

use of principles has been an important part of China's political tradition, and its application to the conduct of international relations has been an important development. On the occasion of celebrating the seventieth anniversary of the five principles of peaceful coexistence in 2024, President Xi Jinping applauded those principles for having become "open, inclusive, and universally applicable basic norms for international relations and fundamental principles of international law."[1] Principles may also be understood as a unique style of China's practice and development of international law, in opposition to the positivistic tradition of European international law. It is a valid question to explore, in the sphere of secondary rules of international law-making, whether there is a Chinese approach that stands out.

As such, the current study is also of contemporary relevance in interpreting China's international law positions and attitudes. The gradual integration of China into the international system after the reform and opening-up in the late 1970s has transformed China from a norm-taker to a norm-maker, and China has repeatedly voiced its support for the universalism of international law. Yet, China's support of international law as a universal legal system has to be interpreted against its reliance on principles in formulating its diplomatic and international law positions. The practice of China's resort to principles in international law assertions and diplomatic negotiations is extensive. Therefore, it would be practically relevant to examine whether China has engaged in the making of a principle-based international order, in opposition to a US-type, self-centred, rule-based international order. It is further intellectually relevant to examine whether the invocation and practice of principles may carry with it implications of Confucian legalism to international society.

16.2 Forms of International Normativity: Neither Treaty Nor Custom

By 1949, positive international law had yet to establish itself as a universal system of normativity for China. And in the view of China, the positivistic expressions of international law, namely treaties and customs, are flawed forms of normativity. Formidable difficulties existed for China to adopt these forms, partly due to its earlier encounter with Western colonialism practiced through the language of international law. The acceptance of international law as a form for international normativity, therefore, cannot be taken for granted and would have to be seen as a political choice.

[1] Xi Jinping, "Carrying Forward the Five Principles of Peaceful Coexistence and Jointly Building a Community with a Shared Future for Mankind," Speech at the Conference Marking the 70th Anniversary of the Five Principles of Peaceful Coexistence (June 28, 2024) <https://www.fmprc.gov.cn/eng/xw/zyjh/202406/t20240628_11443852.html> accessed July 20, 2025.

China's skepticism toward treaties was understandable from a historical perspective. Starting with the Treaty of Nanjing in 1842, a sophisticated system of unequal treaties was developed over decades between China and foreign powers, which effectively displaced the applicability of European international law to China. Treaties were coerced and enforced against China primarily as instruments to legalize and institutionalize the privileges and interests of Western powers at the expense of China's sovereignty and independence. Advocating for the abrogation of unequal treaties was a prominent political cause during the Republican era, consensually supported across different political parties and social factions. Having suffered a century of humiliation, new treaties were eventually signed in 1943 to terminate, at least nominally, unequal treaties respectively between China and the US, and China and the UK.

In 1949, the PRC government set as a high priority to eliminate and repel the remaining political, economic, and cultural influence of colonial powers in China.[2] The Common Program of the Chinese People's Political Consultative Conference, adopted on September 29, 1949—the de facto constitution of China then—affirms unequivocally the resolve of China to "abolish all the prerogatives of imperialist countries in China." Article 55 of the Common Program expressly mandates the Central People's Government to "examine the treaties and agreements concluded between the Kuomintang and foreign governments." And the Central Government shall "recognize, abrogate, revise, or re-negotiate them according to their respective contents."

An evaluation committee on Sino–British treaties was established accordingly within the Chinese Ministry of Foreign Affairs in the 1950s. The committee consisted of experts in international law, international relations, and diplomacy. From the 1842 Treaty of Nanjing until the 1948 Hong Kong Financial Agreement, a total of 213 treaties, agreements, and contracts were reviewed. It was found that 132 of the 213 pieces of documents had already expired, leaving 79 documents pending for further review. After further examinations, the committee concluded that none of those 79 agreements or treaties would be worth full recognition or application without revision, and as a consequence, all the existing bilateral agreements between China and the UK should be abrogated.[3] Similar evaluations were exercised against existing bilateral treaties between China and the US, and China and other Western powers. And the evaluation conclusions were very similar. Very few of those treaties were worthy of continuation.[4]

[2] See Zhou Enlai, "Guidelines and Tasks of Our Diplomacy (我们的外交方针和任务) (30 April 1952)," in *An Anthology of Zhou Enlai on Foreign Affairs* (周恩来外交文选) (Beijing: Central Party Literature Press 1990) 50. Mao Zedong referred to this as "cleaning up the house before hosting guests."

[3] Duan Jielong (ed), *China's International Law Cases and Practice* (Beijing: Law Press 2011) 222–223.

[4] It is noticed that the PRC Government has a broader definition of unequal treaties compared to the Nationalist Government. Huangdah Chiu, "Comparison of the Nationalist and Communist

When it comes to multilateral conventions and international organizations, the PRC government was excluded from participation in the West-dominated international system. The PRC government was not recognized by most Western countries. The United States insisted on its non-recognition policy on China,[5] and pressed its policy at the United Nations. While the PRC government had no difficulty in accepting the ideals and norms embodied in the Charter of the United Nations, it had serious concerns about the risk of the UN having fallen into an instrument of the imperialistic policies of the United States.[6] The representation of the PRC government at the United Nations was not restored until 1971, when Third World countries had gained numerical prominence in the UN General Assembly.

The quick conclusion was that by the early 1950s, the resort to treaties was not a viable option for China to develop its normative relationship with other sovereigns. This was a fundamental difference from the case of the former Soviet Union, known for its preference for the use of international treaties. For the Soviet Union, international treaties would be the primary sources of international law.[7] The Soviet Union relied heavily on the conclusion of international treaties to rewrite international law to promote socialist values.

Customary international law was not a viable form for China to elaborate its normative positions either. Customs are often vague and general, and seem difficult to grasp for the Chinese government. Customs are also slow to evolve, and do not necessarily reflect the changing reality of international life in a timely way. Therefore, the PRC government's attitude was ambiguous and it had refrained from passing a definite judgment on customs.[8] The Chinese Constitution has been silent on the matter of custom to date.

Like many other newly independent developing countries, China did not have a very strong formalistic legal tradition. To a certain extent, the formalism of international law is a Western or European construction, or a capitalist commodity

Chinese Views of Unequal Treaties," in Jerome Alan Cohen *et al* (eds), *China's Practice of International Law: Some Case Studies* (Massachusetts: Harvard University Press 1972) 267.

[5] For an exposition of the US considerations on the non-recognition policy, see State Department Memorandum, Circulated to Overseas Missions, on Question of Recognition of the PRC (August 12 1958), in Roderick MacFarquhar, *Sino-American Relations, 1949–1971* (New York: Praeger Publisher 1972) 144–153.

[6] See "Statement of Zhou Enlai on Approving the Convocation of the Foreign Ministers' Meeting of Five Powers (周恩来关于赞同召开五大国外长会议的声明) (8 October 1953)," in the Bureau of Archives of the Ministry of Foreign Affairs of the People's Republic of China (ed.), *Selective Collections of Diplomatic Archives of the People's Republic of China, Volume One: the 1954 Geneva Conference* (中华人民共和国外交档案选编[第一集]: 1954年日内瓦会议) (Beijing: World Affairs Press 2006) 3.

[7] G. I. Tunkin, *Theory of International Law*, translated with an introduction by William E. Butler, (Massachusetts: Harvard University Press 1974).

[8] Ahmed Sheikh, "The People's Republic of China and International Law," (1973) 7 *The International Lawyer* 770, 779.

product.[9] For developing countries, especially in Asia or Africa, legal formalism, which is associated with authoritative legal texts, judicial bodies, and legal professionals, only accounts for a very limited part of the sophisticated regime of social ordering. As in the case of China, while formal laws grew significantly since the legal reform undertaken as of the early 20th century, a considerable degree of inter-state relations is still run at the personal or relational level.[10]

16.3 The Turn to Principles

Upon inaugurating the new government, China pronounced two basic conditions to be met for the establishment of diplomatic relations with foreign governments.[11] The first requirement is that foreign governments shall "recognize the People's Republic of China as the only legitimate government." This is a firm stand in response to the problem of the "Two Chinas" policy that some Western countries advocated. This required foreign governments to sever official relationships with the Kuomintang government. The other condition pronounced by China was that mutual relationships had to be built on the basis of "the principles of equality, mutual benefits and mutual respect of territorial sovereignty." This requirement directly emanates from the colonial experience of China, where Chinese sovereignty was deeply encroached upon by imperial powers through political, military, and economic means. It was for this reason that China put special emphasis on the principle of political equality, and, when it comes to economic issues, the principle of mutual benefits. These principles laid the basis for the subsequent development of the five principles of peaceful coexistence.

The five principles of peaceful coexistence jointly advocated by Jawaharlal Nehru of India, U Nu of Burma, and Zhou Enlai of China represented a possible political alternative to hegemonic ordering. The five principles of peaceful coexistence—namely, mutual respect for each other's territorial integrity and sovereignty, mutual non-aggression, mutual non-interference in each other's internal affairs, equality and cooperation for mutual benefit, and peaceful coexistence—were codified in the preamble to the Agreement on Trade and Intercourse between Tibet Region of China and India, signed at Peking on April 29, 1954.[12]

[9] China Miéville, *Between Equal Rights: A Marxist Theory of International Law* (Leiden: Brill 2005).

[10] Emilian Kavalski, "Relational Theory in International Relations," in *Oxford Research Encyclopaedia of International Studies* (January 31, 2023).

[11] See Mao Zedong, "Principles concerning Establishing Diplomatic Relations between Chinese Government and Foreign Governments" (中国政府和外国政府建立外交关系的原则) (October 1, 1949), in *An Anthology of Mao Zedong on Foreign Affairs* (毛泽东外交文选) (Beijing: Central Party Literature Press 1994) 116; also Common Program of The Chinese People's Political Consultative Conference (September 29, 1949), art. 56.

[12] The text of the agreement in Hindi, Chinese, and English is available at 299 *United Nations Treaty Series* 57–81. The five principles, with slight terminological differences, first appeared in a talk given by

Subsequently, India and China, and then Burma and China, issued joint declarations respectively on June 28 and 29, 1954, in which the five principles were formally acknowledged as the basic principles governing their mutual relations and their relationships with other Asian countries or any other countries in the world. In his concluding remarks at the Geneva Conference, Zhou Enlai openly advocated the application of the five principles to the Asian countries in their mutual consultation and cooperation, with the aim to realize regional peace in Asia.[13] The five principles represent an endogenous vision of a new world order and an alternative Asian style of diplomacy. The idea of peace underlying the five principles is one based on legal principles instead of military alliance, on equality instead of submission, on sovereignty instead of hegemony. It is an expression of being tired of the diplomatic policies of military coercion, containment, and confrontation under the games played by superpowers in the Cold War.

Using the five principles of peaceful coexistence, China attempted to make a general commitment to the international legal system, which is otherwise not easily accessible to China. Zhou Enlai brought the five principles to the Bandung Conference in 1955, and the five principles helped build trust and mutual understanding between China and other Asian and African countries.[14] Indeed, after the Bandung Conference, China concluded a significant number of bilateral diplomatic and economic agreements with African and Asian countries. The five principles could be considered a starting point for China's independent foreign policy engagement.

The substance of the five principles resembles, to a great extent, the principles embodied in the Charter of the United Nations. "Apparently, the Five Principles of Peaceful Coexistence had its more direct inspiration from the Charter of the United Nations."[15] The five principles are, however, considered to be innovative in placing emphasis on mutuality.[16]

Zhou Enlai in Beijing to the Indian Government Delegation that came to negotiate issues concerning Indian interest in the Tibetan area on December 31, 1953. The terms used then were "mutual respect for each other's territorial sovereignty (相互尊重领土主权) " and "equality and reciprocity(平等互惠)." Zhou Enlai, "The Five Principles of Peaceful Coexistence (和平共处五项原则) (31 December 1953)," in *An Anthology of Zhou Enlai on Foreign Affairs* (周恩来外交文选) (Beijing: Central Party Literature Press 1990) 63.

[13] See the Bureau of Archives of the Ministry of Foreign Affairs of the People's Republic of China (ed.), *Selective Collections of Diplomatic Archives of the People's Republic of China, Volume One: the 1954 Geneva Conference* (中华人民共和国外交档案选编[第一集]: 1954年日内瓦会议) (Beijing: World Affairs Press 2006) 207.

[14] See Yifeng Chen, "Bandung, China and the Making of World Order in East Asia," in L. Eslava, V. Nesiah, and M. Fakhri (eds), *Bandung, Global History and International Law: Critical Pasts and Pending Futures* (Cambridge: Cambridge University Press 2017) 177–195.

[15] Wang Tieya, "International Law in China: Historical and Contemporary Perspectives (Volume 221)," in *The Hague Academy Collected Courses Online* (Leiden: Brill Nijhoff 1990) 264.

[16] Wei Min, "The Significance of the Five Principles of Peaceful Coexistence in Modern International Law (和平共处五项原则在现代国际法上的意义)," (1985) *Chinese Yearbook of International Law* 237.

In addition, the five principles are stipulated in the Chinese Constitution of 1975 as the foundation of China's international relations affairs. This constitution made clear that China shall fight against imperialism and hegemonic policies based on these five principles. The five principles have been widely recognized not only as a guiding principle for China's conduct concerning international relations, but also as a symbol of the continuity of China's international law positions.

The doctrine of basic principles is well established in Chinese international law scholarship. In the Chinese textbooks of international law, it has been standard practice to arrange the basic principles of international law as a separate chapter.[17] Wang Tieya's definition of the basic principles of international law is widely accepted. "The so-called basic principles of international law are not individual norms of international law, but rather those principles that are generally recognized by states, of universal significance, applicable to all spheres of international law, and forming the foundation of international law."[18] The role of principles is placed at the top level of international legal normativity.

16.4 Principles as Constitutional Politics

In China's political practice, principles are central to political discourse and are constantly resorted to for political actions. Principles are expressions of distilled political ideals. Principles are instruments of politics as well as spaces for politics. The emphatic use of principles in China's political discourse may constitute a distinct style of politics, where principles are invoked as an affirmation of previously voiced commitment, or as a contestation of political actions, or as a call for political change.

The proclamation of principles is not only central to the formulation of China's foreign policies, but also essential for the systematization of China's international law positions. Principles can be seen as a systematic expression of structured, stable, and profound positions of the Chinese government in its international relations. In the area of foreign aid, China has developed its doctrine of eight principles.[19] In the field of international law, the five principles of peaceful coexistence is the most prominent example. In addition to that, China supported the ten principles, adopted at the Final Communiqué of the Bandung Conference in 1955, which was seen as a further extension of the five principles of peaceful coexistence.

[17] Wang Tieya (ed.), *International Law* (国际法) (Beijing: Law Press 1995); Bai Guimei, *International Law* (国际法) (Beijing: Peking University Press 2006).

[18] Wang Tieya, *Introduction to International Law* (国际法引论) (Beijing: Peking University Press 1998) 214.

[19] Zhou Enlai, "The Eight Principles for Economic and Technical Aid(对外经济技术援助的八项原则)," in *An Anthology of Zhou Enlai on Foreign Affairs* (周恩来外交文选) (Beijing: Central Party Literature Press 1990) 388.

The 1970 Declaration on Principles of International Law adopted by the United Nations General Assembly has also served as an important reference of authority for China when invoking international law.

The functions of principles are not only legal but, most importantly, constitutional and political.[20] First of all, principles, when formulated in a set, are often constitutional in the sense that they aim to legislate an image of the world. They are more constitutive than administrative or regulatory. The five principles were born out of pursuing peaceful and cooperative relationships among states. It is a world ideal commonly espoused by states with colonial pasts. For this purpose, the five principles has reinforced a Westphalian notion in advocating the respect for territorial sovereignty, non-interference, and non-aggression. At the same time, the five principles is also progressive as it calls for sovereign equality irrespective of the size of nations, embraces economic cooperation, and emphasizes mutual benefit.

Second, principles are architectural of political debates, and structural for political framing, enabling, or exclusion. Claiming of principles is also community-making activities. They are deployed strategically to shape how international issues are epistemized, contested, and resolved. Principles may embrace a legal edifice and give reasons for the rules of international law. It is Lowe's opinion of the principles that "they are rather reasons for reaching a conclusion, factors weighing in favour of a particular decision."[21] Fitzmaurice also offers a useful definition of a principle along this line. "By a principle, or general principle, as opposed to a rule, even a general rule, of law is meant chiefly something which is not itself a rule, but which underlies a rule, and explains or provides the reason for it. A rule answers the question 'what': a principle in effect answers the question 'why'."[22]

Third, principles are aspirational for performative exercise and constructive politics. While legal rules are often stated in terms of rights, obligations, prohibitions, or authorizations, principles are more malleable in normativity. Quoting Dworkin, Lowe suggests the distinction between principles and rules applicable to international law. "Rules have an all-or-nothing character but principles do not."[23] Principles are often presented as an invitation for application under specific circumstances. The primary function of principles is not to enact concrete rights or principles, but rather to generate productive relationships among the interlocutors. The openness and mutuality of principles are also an invitation for political contestation and mutual checks.

Fourth, principles are more stable than rules and have a dynamic and evolutionary function. Unlike the rigidity of rules, principles allow for interpretive

[20] For a useful discussion on various constitutional functions of principles, see Robert Kolb, "Principles as Sources of International Law," (2006) 53 *Netherlands International Law Review* 1.

[21] Vaughan Lowe, *International Law* (Oxford: Oxford University Press 2007) 101.

[22] Gerald G. Fitzmaurice, "The General Principles of International Law," (1957) 92 *Recueil des cours* 1, 7.

[23] See Vaughan Lowe, *International Law* (Oxford: Oxford University Press 2007) 101.

growth. Principles establish a broad normative framework that leaves substantial room for implementation. "General principles of law play a prominent role in legal dynamics, in the development of the law, in the adaptation of the law, in the filling of lacunae, in the transformation of stained situations."[24] This evolutionary function ensures that principles stay relevant amid technological developments and political shifts.

16.5 Reading Principles from Confucian Legalism

Principles play an important and unique role in the functioning of a legal system. They lie in the middle ground between *lex lata* and *lex ferenda*, between legal and extra-legal, between law and policy. Referring to Dawkins, the distinction between rules and principles is relevant to our discussion. Rules prescribe specific and concrete rights and duties, while principles express more general values. Rules can be violated, but principles cannot. Principles are often in conflict with each other.[25] His theory emphasizes the importance of how principles have been used to structure the legal system.

In international law, principles function as a language of international politics, bridging international law on the one hand and politics and society on the other. Principles are inherently general, susceptible to change, and even fallible to manipulation. Yet at the same time, principles function as the underlying structure of the international legal system,[26] providing stability to the system. They permeate various sectors of international law and guide the operation of international law.

Moreover, principles invite participation of those actors who claim the principle and who apply the principles. Therefore, it is both possible and conducive to read the use of principles by situating it in the tradition of Confucian legalism. Quite different from liberal legalism, Confucian legalism is less formalistic and more principle-oriented. As attention is often given to particular situations and to individualistic circumstances, Confucian legalism might also allow more room for interactions between law, justice, reason, morality, and even emotions. In the understanding of Confucian legalism, the world order is constructed through participation rather than given by fixed rules.

It is well noticed that the Confucian legal tradition is a combination of Li and law, of rituals and punishments, of symbolism and administration. "The entire Confucian structure rests on a notion of underlying human good (not sin), which the relational structure is meant to facilitate and serve. It is self-cultivation which

[24] See Robert Kolb (n 20).

[25] See Ronald Dworkin, *Taking Rights Seriously* (Massachusetts: Harvard University Press 1977) 22–39, 60–64, 71–80.

[26] Armin von Bogdandy, "General Principles of International Public Authority: Sketching a Research Field," (2008) 9 *German Law Journal* 1909, 1910–1911.

is key to governance, collapsing the means-end distinction so that each person is both an end in themselves and a means for everyone else. Li is a means of registering one's importance, leaving a mark on the tradition, in the same way as each is creator of Talmudic tradition."[27]

The debate between the Confucians and legalists, which happened more than 2000 years ago, was about what kind of normativities and techniques should be used to govern the relationship between individuals. The legalists advocated for the application of those written laws and the enforcement of written laws through harsh punishment. This view assumes that human nature would be easy to corrupt and it encourages the centralization of power and authority in the hands of the prince. Legalists would also, in a way, create equalization among subjects.

For the Confucians, human nature is assumed to be good, and they emphasize the significance of education. For them, the law cannot be completely dissociated from ethical principles. The realization of Li or the ritual, which is by nature relational, would require a personal contribution and participation. It has its own dimension of aesthetics. The performance of law also brings important dimensions of inner satisfaction, so the idea of ritual is to make a world that would not need punishment. It is famously claimed that "a government based on virtue can truly win the hearts of men, one based on force can only gain their outward submission." To the contrary, "the Li are suasive and hence the instrument of a virtuous government; laws are compulsive and hence the instrument of a tyrannical government."[28] "Formal laws, in contrast, induce no higher form of behavior, leading only to manipulation of texts, litigation and over-regulation."[29]

Confucian legalism offers a useful lens to interpret and assess the use of principles in international law and international relations. Principles not only allow for the dynamics of the positive international legal system to keep up with the contemporary conditions of international society, but also encourage the cultivation of positive international politics through commitment, solidarity, and deliberation. In this sense, China's turn to principles may be appreciated and analysed in terms of its own legal and political tradition in ordering and in elaborating political ideals. This may provide a useful perspective to understand the international legal normativity beyond positivism.

[27] H. Patrick Glenn, *Legal Traditions of the World: Sustainable Diversity in Law* (4th edn, Oxford: Oxford University Press 2010), Chapter 9 "A Confucian Legal Tradition: Making it New (with Marx)" 338.

[28] Derk Bodde and Clarence Morris, *Law in Imperial China: Exemplified by 190 Ch'ing Dynasty Cases (Translated from the Hsing-an hui-lan), with Historical, Social, and Juridical Commentaries* (Massachusetts: Harvard University Press 1967) 20

[29] H. Patrick Glenn (n 27) 329.

16.6 Towards a Principle-based International Order?

In recent years, the Chinese government has advocated an international law-based international order. This is largely a response to accusations by the United States against Russia and China regarding violation of a rule-based international order. China's position was reiterated unambiguously in its Foreign Relations Law of 2023: "China upholds the international system with the United Nations at its core, the international order underpinned by international law, and the fundamental norms governing international relations based on the purposes and principles of the Charter of the United Nations."[30] Read in this way, the difference between China and the United States can be reduced to a discursive struggle about who has the final say about what the international rules eventually are. It may be further reduced to a formalistic question of whether the rules are in fact referring to rules of general international law or those of American law. Seen in this light, the debate is about the fight for the authority to give authentic meanings to the rules of international law to strengthen one's position of augmentation. But this chapter endeavors to present a different interpretation of China's international law engagement.

One may venture to suggest that it may be more appropriate to interpret China's engagement with international law as contributing to the emergence of a principle-based international order. The difference between China and the United States lies further in the sources of normative guidance, the normative shape of the international order, and the relationships among the interlocutors. For China, principles are the backbone of the international order, which not only benchmark the international conduct of states but also make the international order ethically meaningful. International agreements are meant to further implement those principles in the relationships among states in concrete settings. International order is a participatory process of constant making and remaking through relating and elucidating principles. Practicing principles is a performative exercise, and the interlocutors are seen as equal in their reciprocal application of the same principle. Principles function as positivistic normative guidance but also as an invitation for performance, connection, and contribution.

Such a principle-based international order necessarily involves, in the first place, the ascertainment of relevant principles. The five principles of peaceful coexistence may seem too narrow in scope and too Westphalian in value orientation. They would need to be contemporized with new principles to reflect the conditions and needs of modern international society.[31] For example, the principles of

[30] National People's Congress of the People's Republic of China, Foreign Relations Law of the People's Republic of China (entered into force 1 July 2023).

[31] See, for example, Boutros Boutros-Ghali, "The Five Principles," (2004) 3 *Chinese Journal of International Law* 373.

human rights and environmental protection are not yet included. There may also be a need to include principles that promote the common goods of international society.

Leaving aside the substantive discussion about the principles, the point is that China's practice of principles offers a distinct concept and institution of international legalism. It exhibits certain elements of Confucian (international) legalism. If principles largely bridge those traditional debates between Confucians and legalists, practicing principles may be seen as a path to virtue governance in the world. Principles are forward-looking, sites for the negotiation of a just world order.

A further question is whether this principle-based international order, arising from China's international law practice, would be generalizable. Having observed "this plethora of principles to emerge in the post-World War II era," with "its genesis in the UN Charter, the Five Principles, the Friendly Relations Declaration and so on," Under-Secretary-General Miguel de Serpa Soares rendered useful reflections on "the role of first-order principles in the formulation of answers to complex questions."[32] "For me, in my function as the Legal Counsel, I often find myself leaning heavily on principles, both as means to clarify issues, and as a way to remind myself of the broader objectives within which I operate."[33] The experience of de Serpa Soares could offer a useful case to think of virtue ethics in global governance based on sound principles and commitment to virtues.

Surely, a principle-based international order also has its shortcomings. In most cases, principles are practiced in bilateral settings in mutuality. More inclusive mechanisms for the deliberation and practice of principles at multilateral levels may foster broader acceptance of and greater confidence in principles. This brings the important question of whether the practice of principles may be meaningfully translated into open, inclusive, and transparent international institutions. Those principles and institutions should be sites for positive political transformation toward a world of sustainable peace, solidarity, and common prosperity.

[32] Miguel de Serpa Soares, "The Five Principles of Peaceful Coexistence and the Development of International Law," in Department of Treaty and Law, Ministry of Foreign Affairs of China & Chinese Society of International Law (eds), *Proceedings of the Colloquium on the Five Principles of Peaceful Coexistence and the Development of International Law* (Beijing: Law Press 2014) 30.

[33] Ibid.

17

Two Empires

China, Russia, and the Soviet Union in the History of International Law

*Lauri Mälksoo**

17.1 Introduction: The Ups and Downs of China–Russia Relations

In George Orwell's dystopian novel *1984*, three regional powers or empires—Oceania, Eurasia and Eastasia—are at constant war with each other but also change their alliances over time, while simultaneously trying to erase their peoples' memories of previous alliances and confrontations.[1]

Orwell's fantasy came to mind when reflecting on Chinese–Soviet relations during the Cold War in the context of international law. Before Russia's full-scale invasion of Ukraine started in February 2022, the leaders of the People's Republic of China (PRC) and the Russian Federation met in Beijing in connection with the Winter Olympic Games and proclaimed that their countries' friendship had 'no limits'.[2] In the 2020s, many view the current Chinese–Russian alliance as a geopolitical certainty, often overlooking the decades during the Cold War when the relationship between the Soviet Union and the PRC was adversarial. Furthermore, historically, China regarded Russia as one of the European imperialist powers.

During the Cold War, the world was by and large divided into the Western world, the Communist world, and non-aligned states.[3] Initially, the Soviet Union was a major example and influence for the PRC because its revolutionary ideas

* This research was funded by grant PRG969 from the Estonian Research Council and benefited from a research visit to Academia Sinica's Institutum Iurisprudentiae in Taipei in 2023, in the framework of academic exchange between Estonia and Taiwan. The author would like to acknowledge inspiration from his father Ürjo Mälksoo, who was an Estonian recruit in the Soviet army, stationed at the Soviet–Mongolian border in 1969, and has shared stories of how the conflict with the PRC was perceived on the Soviet side. The author would also like to acknowledge the influence of Jerome A. Cohen (1930-2025), whose course on China and international law he audited as a fellow at NYU School of Law in 2014.

[1] George Orwell, Nineteen Eighty-Four (Oxford University Press, 2021).

[2] Joint Statement of the Russian Federation and the People's Republic of China on International Relations Entering a New Era and the Global Sustainable Development, 4 February 2022, http://www.en.kremlin.ru/supplement/5770, part iv, passage 5 (last accessed on 10 July 2025).

[3] See Antonio Cassese, International Law in a Divided World (Oxford: Clarendon Press, 1986).

Lauri Mälksoo, *Two Empires* In: *Histories of International Law in China*. Edited by: Ignacio de la Rasilla, Jiangyu Wang, and Congyan Cai, Oxford University Press. © Lauri Mälksoo 2026.
DOI: 10.1093/oso/9780198888345.003.0017

had been implemented there several decades earlier. After the Soviets came to power in Russia in November 1917, Soviet Communists were trying to figure out whether they could accept and share one and the same international law with the capitalist world. In the early years of their revolutionary bravado and radicalism, the Soviet answer was 'rather not', or reached the extent of 'yes, but only in a quite limited way'.[4] But the geopolitical environment changed for the Soviet Union after the Allied victory in the Second World War and the creation of the United Nations. The Soviet Union achieved significant territorial gains in the Second World War and established its hegemony over most states in Central and Eastern Europe, which turned socialist with the help of military-political intervention by Moscow. As an isolated, revolutionary power of the 1920s and early 1930s, the Soviet leaders were acutely aware that they had had little choice but to give up some of the former Western territories of the Russian Empire. After 1945 the Soviet Union became a territorially saturated superpower, and its discourse of international law changed accordingly. Especially during the leadership of Nikita Khrushchev, Moscow started to propagate 'peaceful coexistence' with the capitalist West, and this was elevated to one of the main principles of international law in Soviet theory.[5]

This chapter deals with Soviet-Chinese relations during the Cold War and how these played out in the context of international law, treaties, and theoretical debates. When the Communists came to power in mainland China in 1949, it seemed that the two major socialist nations could look forward to a great historic friendship. Yet, from 1960 onwards, something quite different happened: instead of a 'special friendship' between the two biggest Communist nations and the smooth practice of 'socialist international law',[6] serious ideological and practical disputes and rivalries broke out between the two powers. Not only was the world divided; the state socialist camp was divided, too. The underlying question of this chapter is: 'why?' What, from the perspective of the history of international law, explains the fallout between the two powers and how they later reconciled most of their disagreements? The chapter also makes excursions to earlier events in Chinese-Russian history in the context of international law—because without those references the Sino-Soviet split cannot be understood.

The structure of this chapter is as follows. Section 17.2 discusses Sino-Soviet relations during the Cold War and how these played out from the perspective of international law and its literature. Section 17.3 discusses aspects of international

[4] See Evgeny Korovin, Mezhdunarodnoe pravo perekhodnogo vremeni (International Law of the Transition Period) (Moscow: Gosudarstvennoe izdatel'stvo, 1924).

[5] See, e.g., Bernard A. Ramundo, Peaceful Coexistence. International Law in the Building of Communism (Baltimore, MA: The Johns Hopkins Press, 1967); Edward McWhinney (ed.) Law, Foreign Policy, and the East-West Détente (University of Toronto Press, 1964); Edward McWhinney, '"Peaceful Coexistence" and Soviet-Western International Law', 56 American Journal of International Law 1962, pp 951–970.

[6] Theodor Schweisfurth, Sozialistiches Völkerrecht? Darstellung—Analyse—Wertung der sowjetmarxistischen Theorie vom Völkerrecht 'neuen Typs' (Berlin: Springer, 1979).

legal theory, especially the question of Soviet influence over PRC scholars' understanding of theoretical aspects of international law. Section 17.4 focuses on the legacy of earlier unequal treaties and the dispute over the Soviet–Chinese border during the Cold War. This section also narrates how, from the last year of the existence of the Soviet Union, 1991, China and Russia settled their border dispute in a series of treaties. The concluding part of the chapter tackles the underlying reasons for the ups and downs of Sino–Soviet relations in the history of international law.

This chapter is limited in that it mostly approaches Sino–Russian history of international law through Russian and Western sources. As far as the views of the PRC and its scholars on international law are concerned, linguistic limitations mean my research in this chapter is limited to secondary sources in Western literature.

17.2 International Legal Issues in Sino–Soviet Relations during the Cold War

The history of Sino–Soviet relations in international law involves complex facets and some surprising turns.[7] The weight of unequal relations in the nineteenth century continued to influence the relationship between the two powers. For example, during the interwar period it was already an issue (with the Nationalist Government of China) whether the Soviets had kept their initial promises to reshape relations with China based on equality, as they had proclaimed they would. In his declaration to the Congress of Soviets on 4 July 1919, the Soviet People's Commissar for Foreign Affairs, Georgy Chicherin, stated that Soviet Russia had withdrawn from all secret agreements directed against China and had reestablished Chinese rights in Manchuria, recognizing Chinese ownership of the Chinese Eastern Railway. Furthermore, he declared that the Soviet government was ready to abandon the extraterritorial rights of Russian citizens.[8] However, later in the 1920s Soviet instructions changed, stressing the need to protect the interests and the property of Russia in Chinese territories, and in particular to continue to control the Chinese Eastern Railway. At that time, Soviet policy vis-à-vis China was to rely on the binding force of the Russo–Chinese Treaty of 1896, namely, a treaty concluded under the old regime.[9] On 12 October 1929, Soviet troops invaded Manchuli and Hailar in China's Northeast Provinces during a dispute over

[7] See generally Philip Snow, China and Russia. Four Centuries of Conflict and Concord (New Haven: Yale University Press, 2023). From earlier literature, see Aitchen K. Wu, China and the Soviet Union. A Study of Sino-Soviet Relations (London: Methuen & Co, 1950) and O. Edmund Clubb, China and Russia: The 'Great Game' (New York: Columbia University Press, 1971).

[8] Kazimierz Grzybowski, Soviet Public International Law. Doctrines and Diplomatic Practice (Leyden: A.W. Sijthoff, 1970), pp. 445–446.

[9] Ibid., p. 281.

the Chinese Eastern Railway,[10] for which the Soviets argued that the nationalist Chinese had violated the terms of the agreement for common administration of the Chinese Eastern Railway.[11]

On 14 August 1945, the USSR concluded the Treaty of Friendship and Alliance with the Republic of China, which was then led by Chiang Kai-shek (the Nationalist Government). When the Communists came to power in mainland China on 1 October 1949, they owed a great deal to Soviet military, material, and other assistance during the preceding years. On 14 February 1950 Stalin and Mao concluded a new treaty between the USSR and the PRC, namely the Treaty of Friendship, Alliance, and Mutual Assistance.[12] Through an exchange of notes, the treaty with the Nationalist Chinese Government of 1945 was abrogated on the same day. In the Soviet Union, the treaty of 1950 was celebrated as historic;[13] in turn, the PRC issued several series of stamps celebrating the treaty.

With the Korean war (1950–1953), events related to Communist China were at the epicentre of world politics at the UN. Soviet international jurists rejected the view of the UN General Assembly at the time,[14] which held that the Korean war was, legally speaking, aggression by the PRC against Korea.[15] To the contrary, the Soviet government and and its international jurists argued that what was being witnessed in Korea was US aggression.[16] The Soviet government and international jurists also supported the PRC's interpretation, namely that the USA had committed 'aggression' in Taiwan by not allowing the island to be taken over by the PRC military.[17] Until 25 October 1971, the Republic of China continued to

[10] See further Chiang Kai-shek, Soviet Russia in China. A Summing Up at Seventy (Taipei: China Publishing Company, 1969), pp. 62–71.

[11] Evgeny B. Pashukanis, Ocherki po mezhdunarodnomy pravu (Essays on International Law) (Moscow: Sovetskoe zakonodatel'stvo, 1935), pp. 52–53.

[12] See further Austin Jersild, The Sino–Soviet Alliance. An International History (The University of North Carolina Press, 2014).

[13] See K.A. Baginian, M.I. Lazarev, 'Mezhunarodnyi dogovor istoricheskogo znachenia' (International treaty of historical significance), Sovetskoe gosudarstvo i pravo No 4, 1950, pp 68-78; M. K. Korostorenko, 'Velikii sojuz i druzhba narodov SSSR i Kitaia. (K chetvertoi godovoshchine zakliuchenia sovetsko-kitaiskogo dogovora o druzhbe, soiuze i vzaimnoi pomoshchi) (Great alliance and friendship of the peoples of the USSR and China. On the fourth anniversary of the conclusion of the Soviet-Chinese treaty on friendship, alliance and mutual assistance), Sovetskoe gosudarstvo i pravo 1954, No 1, pp. 46–64.

[14] The Uniting for Peace resolution of the UNGA (Resolution 377 (v)), 3 November 1950.

[15] N.A. Ushakov, 'K voprosu o prave 'veto' v organizatsii ob'edenennykh natsii' (On the Question of the Right to 'Veto' at the UN), Soviet Yearbook of International Law 1959, pp. 212–228 at 216.

[16] See, e.g., A.F. Volchkov, 'Amerikanskaia agressia v Koree' (American aggression in Korea), Sovetskoe gosudarstvo i pravo 1950, No 11, pp. 59–67; V.N. Durdenevski, A.M. Ladyzhenski, 'Agressia i interventsa na Dal'nem Vostoke v svete mezhdunarodnoga prava' (Aggression and intervention in the Far East from the perspective of international law), Sovetskoe gosudarstvo i pravo 1951, No 2, pp. 53–59; G. Tavrov, 'Bezzastenchivoe narushenie mezhdunarodnykh soglashenii i norm mezhdunarodnoga prava (Amerikano-angliiskaia interventsia v Koree)' (Shameless violation of international agreements and norms of international law. American-English intervention in Korea), Sovetskoe gosudarstvo i pravo 1951, No 9, pp. 49–61.

[17] B.A. Aleksandrov, 'Vooruzhennaia agressia SshA na Taivane' (Military aggression by the USA on Taiwan), Sovetskoe gosudarstvo i pravo 1951, No 3, pp. 44–51.

represent China at the UN Security Council (UNSC). The Soviet Union as well as Soviet international lawyers criticized this situation, claiming that the Chinese people were being deprived of genuine representation at the UNSC.[18] Thus, during the initial decades of the Cold War the Soviet Union in several ways vocally defended the PRC's international legal positions at the UN and in legal scholarship.

Both the Soviet Union and the PRC competed for the hearts and minds of 'third world' countries during the Cold War. In 1955, a PRC delegation led by Premier and Foreign Minister Zhou Enlai participated in the Bandung conference in Indonesia. The conference had an anti-colonial and anti-imperialist agenda, bringing together Asian and African nations who had only recently become full subjects of international law. The Soviet Union was not invited to this important international conference and the question whether the USSR should also be criticized through the anti-imperialist and anti-colonial lens remained an unresolved theme at Bandung.[19] So, in this regard, the outcome of the Bandung conference remained ambivalent. However, the question itself soon started to trouble relations between the PRC and the USSR.

On 23 April 1958, the Sino–Soviet Trade and Navigation Treaty was concluded.[20] Nevertheless, around 1960, disagreements between the Soviet and PRC leaderships became increasingly visible. The Soviets did not back the PRC strongly enough in the 1958 Taiwan Strait Crisis; then in 1959 they did not support China in the Indo–Chinese border conflict; and arguably they also supported the opposition against Mao Zedong within the Chinese Communist Party.[21] Tensions also started to play out in contexts relevant for international law and treaties. On 5 August 1963 in Moscow, the Soviet Union, the USA, and the UK signed the Partial Nuclear Test Ban Treaty, which was then opened for signature by other countries. The PRC refused to sign the treaty; its own first nuclear weapon test took place on 16 October 1964. Beijing strongly criticized the conclusion of the Moscow treaty, arguing that the treaty reflected the interests of Western 'imperialist' states more than those of socialist nations. The Soviet government felt forced to rebuke the position of Beijing publicly.[22] At the essence of this disagreement lay Beijing's conclusion that Moscow was willing to leave the PRC behind in terms of *Realpolitik*, considering only itself, along with the two leading Western powers, as a first-rate

[18] L.A. Modzhorian, 'K voprosu o vosstanovlenii zakonnykh prav Kitaia v OON' (On the Question of Restoring the Legal Rights of China at the UN), Soviet Yearbook of International Law 1959, pp. 202–211.

[19] Chen Yifeng, 'Bandung, China, and the Making of World Order in East Asia', in: Luis Eslava, Michael Fakhri, and Vasuki Nesiah (eds) Bandung, Global History, and International Law. Critical Pasts and Pending Futures (CUP, 2017), p. 186.

[20] See George Ginsburgs, The Legal Framework of Trade between the USSR and the People's Republic of China (The Hague: Martinus Nijhoff, 1976), p. 96.

[21] Gerd Kaminski, Chinesische Positionen zum Völkerrecht (Berlin: Duncker & Humblot, 1973), p. 179.

[22] See The Nuclear Test Ban Treaty and Beijing. Soviet Government Statement, *Soviet Weekly* (Supplement), 26 September 1963 and 3 October 1963.

(nuclear) superpower. The PRC soon acquired its own nuclear weapons anyway. It appears that the dispute about the Partial Nuclear Test Ban Treaty was also a proxy dispute about hierarchies in the Sino–Soviet relationship as well as about how the two leading Communist powers should relate to the outside world.

17.3 Sino–Soviet Split in Soviet Writings on International Law

Soon the Sino–Soviet split was also showing in the Soviet literature on international law. Writing in the *Soviet Yearbook of International Law*, Evgeny T. Usenko (1918–2010), one of the leading international lawyers in Moscow, criticized Chinese views on the Partial Nuclear Test Ban Treaty but also what the USSR saw as violations of international diplomatic law vis-à-vis its diplomats in Beijing.[23] Usenko concluded that the government of the PRC had embarked on a 'great power' and 'nationalist' course but also that one could no longer idealistically overlook that serious disagreements between some socialist states had indeed become part of the geopolitical reality.[24]

The Sino–Soviet split was a serious challenge for the construction of Soviet international legal theory because the Soviets would have greatly preferred to show harmonious relations in the socialist camp as an expression of a new type of progressive international law.[25] The main idea was that the root cause of international conflicts was the capitalist system and private property on which that system was based. As in their rhetoric, socialist states considered their camp incomparably more progressive than the 'imperialist world' of the capitalist states, Soviet international legal theoreticians had a hard time explaining the tensions and accusations of hegemonic attitudes between the USSR and the PRC.

Let us take a closer look at how the Sino–Soviet split was dealt with in Soviet writings on international law. From 1967 onwards, an authoritative Soviet treatise on international law in six volumes was published.[26] A collective work by leading Soviet international lawyers, it summed up Soviet theory and doctrine in terms of international law. The authors of the series emphasized continuous progressive contributions to the development of international law by, first, Soviet Russia, and

[23] E.T. Usenko, 'Mezhdunarodnoe pravo v vzaimootnosheniakh sotsialisticheskikh gosudarstv' (International Law in the Mutual Relations of Socialist States), Soviet Yearbook of International Law 1964/1965, pp. 30–50.

[24] Ibid., pp. 45–46.

[25] See also Bernard A. Ramundo, The (Soviet) Socialist Theory of International Law, Institute for Sino-Soviet Studies at the George Washington University, Series No 1, January 1964.

[26] V.M. Chikvadze, F.I. Kozhevnikov, V.M. Koretski, D.B. Levin, G.I. Tunkin, N.A. Ushakov, and V. M. Shurshalov (eds), Kurs mezhdunarodnoga prava v shesti tomakh, Vol I: Poniatie i sushtshnost sovremennogo mezhdunarodnoga prava (Course of International Law in Six Volumes. Vol I: The Definition and Nature of Contemporary International Law) (Moscow: Nauka, 1967).

then (from 30 December 1922) the Soviet Union. The first volume of the treatise highlighted that after 1917 Russia's Soviet government had formulated positive principles in its relations with 'Eastern' countries, including China.[27] The second volume acknowledged that in the nineteenth century, some 'imperialist' states—England, France, and the USA (Tsarist Russia was not mentioned) —had intervened in Chinese affairs, and their behaviour had caused uprisings in China. Then in 1842 and 1858 the imperialist states imposed unequal treaties on China.[28] In contrast, the Soviet treatise narrated that, in the Soviet–Chinese treaty of 31 May 1924, both sides had agreed to build their relations on the principles of equality, mutuality, and justice, exactly in the spirit of the earlier Soviet declarations of 1919 and 1920.[29] The authors of the treatise also noted approvingly that both Soviet Russia and the PRC rejected certain treaties agreed upon by previous governments of their countries which appeared unacceptable to them from a class perspective.[30]

In 1973, several years later than the other volumes, the sixth volume of this authoritative Soviet international law treatise was published. It dealt with international law between socialist states.[31] The Soviet-led military suppression of the Prague Spring in Czechoslovakia in 1968 was possibly one of the reasons why publication of the last volume in the series was delayed. In general, the series argued that relations between socialist countries were special in the context of international law—they were based on unique principles such as socialist proletarian internationalism and brotherly help. The first volume had merely indicated this in broad strokes, but stopped there.[32] The sixth volume further elaborated on these principles. However, by the time the sixth volume was published, a problem which had emerged in state practice could no longer be ignored by the authors of the treatise. That is, from the Soviet perspective, at least one major socialist state had an attitude and pattern of behaviour that did not fit the pattern of socialist internationalism—the PRC.

The authors of the sixth volume of the Soviet leading course on international law—led by E. T. Usenko, who had already authored the 1964 Soviet Yearbook article which was critical of the PRC—levelled the criticism that the 'gang' around Mao Zedong was pursuing' 'adventurist' policies, attempting to use force against other states, which was not reconcilable with Marxism.[33] The government of the PRC had accused the Soviet government of aggressive intentions, but this was all

[27] Ibid., Vol I, p. 257.

[28] Ibid., Vol II, Osnovnye printsipy sovremennogo mezhdunarodnogo prava (Main principles of contemporary international law) (Moscow: Nauka, 1967), p. 86.

[29] Ibid., Vol II, p. 108.

[30] Ibid., Vol II, p. 274. The same point was made in Vol III, p. 43, with reference to the Republic of China's treaties with the USA.

[31] Ibid., Vol VI, Mezhdunarodnoe pravo v otnosheniakh mezhdu sotsialisticheskimi gosudarstvami (International law in relations between socialist countries) (Moscow: Nauka, 1973).

[32] Ibid, vol I, p. 6.

[33] Ibid., vol VI, p. 12.

untrue, countered the authors of the Soviet treatise. The proof was that, in 1971, the Soviet government had proposed to Beijing a bilateral treaty pledging non-use of force but had not received a serious response to its proposal. The Soviet authors concluded that Beijing had thus been libellous towards the Soviet Union when claiming that *Moscow* had aggressive intentions.[34] In general, the Soviet authors found signs of 'nationalism and great power chauvinism' as well as 'ideological splitting activities' on display in the actions of the PRC government.[35] The 'imperialist' powers were of course also helping the PRC government in taking these anti-Soviet positions.[36] In particular, Maoist China's claims to Soviet territory were 'subjectivist' and rooted in 'great power chauvinism'.[37] In its hostility towards the Soviet Union, Maoism was in fact 'anti-communist', the authoritative Soviet treatise maintained.[38] The Soviet authors insisted that so-called Chinese Communism was nothing but 'Chinese nationalism and great power chauvinism'.[39] Yet the Soviet authors observed that the Maoist attempt to encourage other socialist countries to leave the regional organizations set up by Moscow had nevertheless been a failure—'only' Albania had left the Council for Mutual Economic Assistance (COMECON).[40] This was a considerable change in approach compared to 1954, when the Soviet government had proposed, in opposition to NATO, that both the USA and the PRC should participate, along with the Soviet Union, in creating a common 'indivisible' security architecture in Europe.[41]

In addition, Soviet political literature published since the late 1960s explained what had gone wrong in Soviet relations with Mao Zedong's China. According to these texts, the drastic worsening of relations had been Beijing's fault.[42] However, even so, Soviet jurists propagating peaceful coexistence, especially Grigory Tunkin (1906–1993), concluded even during the Sino–Soviet split that the PRC remained a socialist country and that therefore its core interests remained similar to those of other socialist countries.[43]

[34] Ibid., vol VI, p. 13.
[35] Ibid., vol VI, p. 14.
[36] Ibid., vol VI, p. 33.
[37] Ibid., vol. VI, p. 64.
[38] Ibid., vol VI, p. 69.
[39] Ibid., Vol VI, p. 70.
[40] Ibid., Vol VI, p. 235–236. On COMECON and other socialist international organizations, see, e.g., Kazimierz Grzybowski, Soviet International Law and the World Economic Order (Duke University Press, 1987), pp 143–184.
[41] A. S. Bakhov, 'Pravovye aspekty Varshavskogo dogovora' (Legal Aspects of the Warsaw Pact), Soviet Yearbook of International Law 1964/65, pp. 134–149 at 135.
[42] See, e.g., Fedor Burlatski, Maoizm—ugroza sotsializmu v Kitae (Maoism—a Danger to Socialism in China) (Moscow: Izdatel'stvo politicheskoi literatury, 1968), p. 185 (concluding pessimistically that in Chinese historical development there were 'objective preconditions for hegemonic, chauvinist moods'.)
[43] G. I. Tunkin, 'V. I. Lenin i printsipy otnoshenii mezhdu sotsialisticheskimi gosudarstvami' (V.I. Lenin and Principles of Relations between Socialist Countries), Soviet Yearbook of International Law 1969, pp. 16–32 at 28.

Chinese officials in Beijing saw the root causes of the split exactly in the opposite way—it was Soviet imperialism and pursuit of hegemony which was to blame for the worsening of relations between the two great socialist nations. After the Soviet military intervention to suppress the Hungarian uprising in 1956, the PRC had still lined up behind the Communist Party of the Soviet Union, which tended to portray itself as the 'elder brother' in the socialist camp.[44] In 1960, Sino–Soviet disagreements were made public and from then on, the PRC's leaders and state media began to heavily criticize the Soviet Union. The Soviet-led 1968 invasion of Czechoslovakia by the Warsaw Pact countries and the related 'Brezhnev doctrine'[45] seeking to justify it were the ultimate proofs of Soviet imperialism, hegemonism, and willingness to violate the sovereignty of other socialist nations.[46] The PRC's condemnation of Soviet policies within the socialist camp was colourful in style and language. For example, a *People's Daily* editorial of 20 September 1968, supporting the Albanian withdrawal from the Warsaw Pact, maintained: 'The Warsaw Treaty has long become an instrument for aggression in the hands of the Soviet revisionist renegade clique in pushing ahead with its social-imperialism ... The Warsaw Treaty controlled by the Soviet revisionist renegade clique is no different from NATO controlled by U.S. imperialism.'[47]

Similarly, articles published in China at the time argued that COMECON, the Soviet-led organization of economic cooperation between socialist states, was a tool of neocolonialism.[48]

The main criticism from the PRC at that time was that, as far as the Soviet Union was concerned, a previously progressive and revolutionary socialist country had degenerated into a 'social-imperialist' one.[49] On several occasions, PRC agencies even characterized the Soviet-led suppression of the Prague Spring in Czechoslovakia as 'fascism' or 'social fascism'.[50] After deadly clashes on the Sino–Soviet border, a popular slogan in China was 'down with the new Tsars'.[51] In the PRC constitution of 1975, the fight against 'social-imperialism' was mentioned as a state task of the PRC (Article 15).[52] When the Soviet leader, Leonid Brezhnev, said in a speech on 18 January 1977 that the Soviet Union would never raise a

[44] Theodor Schweisfurth, Sozialistiches Völkerrecht? Darstellung—Analyse—Wertung der sowjetmarxistischen Theorie vom Völkerrecht 'neuen Typs' (Berlin: Springer, 1979), p. 138.

[45] See John Norton Moore and Robert F. Turner, International Law and the Brezhnev Doctrine (Lanham, NY: University Press of America, 1987).

[46] Gerd Kaminski, Chinesische Positionen zum Völkerrecht (Berlin: Duncker & Humblot, 1973), p. 206.

[47] Cited in Hungdah Chiu, 'Comparison of the Nationalist and Communist Chinese Views of Unequal Treaties', in Jerome Alan Cohen (ed.) China's Practice of International Law: Some Case Studies (Harvard University Press, 1972), pp. 239–267 at 266.

[48] Kaminski (n 46), p. 207.

[49] Wei Chi, The Soviet Union under the New Tsars (Peking: Foreign Languages Press, 1978), p. 1.

[50] Schweisfurth (n 44), p. 157.

[51] Schweisfurth (n 44), p. 157.

[52] See O. Vladimirov, Sovetsko-kitaiskie otnoshenia v sorokovykh-vosmidesiatykh godakh (Soviet–Chinese Relations in the 1940s-1980s) (Moscow: Mezhdunarodnye otnoshenia, 1984), p. 249.

sword against other peoples, the PRC news agency New China commented sarcastically that the 1968 Soviet-led invasion of Czechoslovakia demonstrated that the USSR would raise 'not only swords but also airplanes, tanks, and rockets against other peoples'.[53] At that time, several foreign policy editorials in the PRC were interpreted as calling for popular uprisings in Soviet-dominated Central and Eastern Europe.[54] The PRC's strongly critical rhetoric towards the USSR lasted until the 1980s.

The PRC was not alone in warning of the perils of Russian imperialism on display in the Soviet Union. On the island of Taiwan, Chiang Kai-Shek, the President of the Republic of China, wrote in a book dedicated to Soviet–Chinese relations and containing the memoirs of his own three-month, disillusioning 1923 trip to the Soviet Union:

> And we should especially notice that Marxism by now has absorbed the brutal characteristics of Pan-Slavism and Czarism ... But just now, the danger of Soviet aggression masquerading in the garb of 'peaceful coexistence' cannot be overemphasized ... 'Peaceful coexistence', I repeat, is another name for ultimate Russian domination of the world and enslavement of humanity.[55]

This reflected the views expressed in Kuomintang-led China even before the Second World War. For example, T. Z. Koo (1887–1971)—the secretary of the Student Christian Movement of China and representative of China at the Opium Conference in Geneva in 1924–1925—wrote in 1930 that China was threatened in the north by the red imperialism of Soviet Russia and in the south by Japan's territorial ambitions.[56]

At the United Nations, where the government of the PRC had replaced the government of the ROC on 25 October 1971, the PRC accused both the USSR and the USA of 'hegemonism', 'the desire of some states to dominate over other states and peoples'. The PRC government emphasized the importance of sovereign equality at the UN and accordingly criticized the two superpowers for their policies.[57] Curiously, however, it was the Soviet delegation which formally seized the initiative at the UN on the question of 'hegemonism'[58] and on 14 December 1979, the UNGA adopted a resolution initiated by the USSR and titled 'Inadmissibility

[53] Schweisfurth (n 44) p. 4.
[54] Schweisfurth (n 44), p. 577.
[55] Chiang Kai-shek, Soviet Russia in China. A Summing Up at Seventy (Taipei: China Publishing Company, 1969), pp. 6, 9, 10.
[56] Cited in Gerd Kaminski, Chinesische Positionen zum Völkerrecht (Berlin: Duncker & Humblot, 1973).
[57] Schweisfurth (n 44), p. 168.
[58] See Guy de Laccharrière, La politique juridique exteriéure (Brussels: Bruylant, 2023), p. 20.

of the Policy of Hegemonism in International Relations'.[59] This resolution, among other things, condemned 'imperialism'.[60] In substance, this had been the PRC's accusation against both the USA and the USSR. However, as several times before in diplomatic history, such as the prohibition of aggression in the late 1920s–early 1930s,[61] Soviet diplomacy skilfully appropriated the popular trope initiated by other nation(s) and played it out as its own initiative, thus giving a different connotation to the whole initiative.

The Sino-Soviet dispute in the 1960s–1980s did not look good for the socialist camp as it made clear to everyone that the claim of genuinely special relations between socialist states, including in the context of international law, was nothing more than an ideological postulate, a theory which did not reflect the reality of international relations. Several developments in international relations and treaty-making—including even the conclusion of the Indo-Soviet treaty on 9 August 1971—were to an extent also interpreted against the backdrop of the Sino-Soviet split.[62] Especially after the invasion of Czechoslovakia in 1968, the PRC criticized Soviet 'hegemonism', which meant that voices in the West were not the only ones critical of Soviet policies in its claimed sphere of influence, particularly in Central and Eastern Europe.[63]

17.4 Contested Theories of International Law

In terms of the theory and doctrinal foundations of international law, a significant academic contribution in the West was made by Hungdah Chiu (1936–2011) and Jerome Alan Cohen (1930), the US pioneer of the study of the law of the PRC, who analysed the PRC's understandings of international law in detail, also in some aspects in comparison with Soviet approaches.[64] In Europe, notable scholarship was carried out by Gerd Kaminski (1942–2022), an Austrian jurist, who

[59] Inadmissibility of the policy of hegemonism in international relations, UN General Assembly resolution, 14 December 1979, https://www.refworld.org/docid/3b00f03424.html (last accessed on 10 July 2025).

[60] UNGA Resolution, p. 5.

[61] The story of the Briand-Kellogg Pact of 1928 is told in Oona A. Hathaway and Scott J. Shapiro, The Internationalists. How a Radical Plan to Outlaw War Remade the World (New York: Simon & Schuster, 2017). Starting with the Litvinov Pact in 1929 and especially the 1933 Convention for the Definition of Aggression, signed in London, at the Soviet initiative, the Soviets outperformed Western treaty initiatives and commitments on *jus ad bellum*—by violating the sovereignty of their six border states in the aftermath of the German-Soviet Non-Aggression Pact's secret protocols, concluded on 23 August 1939.

[62] A.P. Jain (ed.) Shadow of the Bear. The Indo-Soviet Treaty (Delhi: Shri P.K. Deo, M.P, 1971), p. 27.

[63] See also J.A.B. Gawenda, The Soviet Domination of Eastern Europe in the Light of International Law (Richmond, UK: Foreign Affairs Publishing Company, 1974).

[64] Hungdah Chiu, 'Communist China's Attitude toward International Law', 60 American Journal of International Law 1966, pp. 245–267; Jerome Alan Cohen and Hungdah Chiu, People's China and International Law. A Documentary Study, Vol I and II (Princeton: Princeton University Press, 1974).

also made insightful comparisons between Soviet and Chinese theories of international law and who had conversations about international law with people in power while travelling in the PRC.[65] As Austria had been a neutral country since 1955, Kaminski may occasionally have enjoyed better access to the PRC elites than some representatives of Western 'imperialist states', or members of NATO, might have had.

In both the Soviet Union and the PRC, the theory of international law was closely linked to general debates about proper interpretations of Marxism-Leninism, foreign policy, and the laws of history. In that sense, views and disagreements on international legal theory followed from general debates on questions such as what is the nature of the state and law, whether Communists in capitalist countries could come to power exclusively through peaceful means, and whether peaceful coexistence meant that socialist states had to avoid war and violence in their international relations.[66] In the 1960s, Maoist Chinese positions tended to be more radical and revolutionary than those in the USSR under Khruschev and Brezhnev. For example, in an open letter of 14 July 1963 from the Chinese Communist Party to its Soviet counterpart, Chinese Communists claimed that it was not possible to apply the principle of peaceful coexistence vis-à-vis 'imperialist' powers such as the USA.[67] In 1964, Wu De-feng, the President of the Chinese Society of Political Science and Law, criticized the Soviet policy of peaceful coexistence vis-a-vis the USA in the following way: modern revisionism propagates peaceful coexistence with the US imperialists.[68]

Chiu and Cohen observed that Communist Chinese criticism of bourgeois theories of international law owed a great debt to earlier Soviet publications—despite the Sino-Soviet split.[69] However, they also pointed out that when Communist Chinese jurists sought to construct an adequate theory of international law, they found 'Soviet scholarship a less certain, and apparently less persuasive, guide'.[70] Kaminski, too, concluded that the Soviets exerted a major influence on the PCR's international legal theory and debates—even though after the Sino-Soviet split the Soviet treatises of international law were quickly removed from Chinese academic libraries.[71] Thus, after the Sino-Soviet split, the PRC isolated itself not only from Western thought on international law but also from the most recent Soviet influences.[72] On the Soviet side, it was quite symbolic that in the late 1950s and early 1960s, the *Soviet Yearbook of International Law*—a Russian-language publication

[65] Gerd Kaminski, Chinesische Positionen zum Völkerrecht (Berlin: Duncker & Humblot, 1973).

[66] See further John Yin, Sino-Soviet Dialogue on the Problem of War (The Hague: Martinus Nijhoff, 1971).

[67] Kaminski (n 65), p. 181.

[68] Kaminski (n 65), p. 182.

[69] Cohen and Chiu (n 64)Vol I, p. 67.

[70] Cohen and Chiu (n 64) Vol I, p. 47.

[71] Kaminski (n 65), p. 180.

[72] Kaminski (n 65), p. 180.

in Moscow published by the Soviet Association of International Law under Grigory I. Tunkin—also had Chinese-language table of contents (besides English, French, and German), but in the mid-1960s this was unceremoniously dropped.

In both countries, the prevailing Communist view was that law always expressed the will of the ruling classes.[73] International law, too, was primarily a tool of foreign policy and therefore had relatively little autonomous value. Capitalist and Communist countries inevitably saw the world and international law differently; the question was what followed from this for the theory and practice of international law. In the PRC, during the years of the Cultural Revolution, the study and teaching of law fell more generally into disrepute and for a while international law was essentially not studied and discussed at universities and research institutions, along with other 'bourgeois' disciplines.[74] Teemu Ruskola observes that, at that time, the PRC held international law in low esteem, contesting not only specific interpretations or doctrines of international law, but even whether there was such a thing as international law, and, if so, whether it had anything to do with China.[75]

Several starting points in international legal theory in the PRC were identical to Soviet approaches, such as the principled value put on state sovereignty and the preference for the dualist concept of the interrelationship between international and municipal law.[76] In a study published in 1963 on new tendencies in Anglo-Saxon legal scholarship, Zhou Geng-sheng strongly criticized the theories of Hans Kelsen, Philip Jessup, James Brierly, and Hersch Lauterpacht on limitations to state sovereignty. The conclusion was that state sovereignty had remained the biggest legal obstacle for the 'imperialist' rule of the world, which was why Western legal theory had started to attack it.[77] At the level of principles, Soviet legal theory similarly defended state sovereignty from attempts to relativize or weaken it.[78] Both Communist nations were also sceptical of judicial settlement of international disputes and much preferred negotiations as a method for dispute resolution.[79] In the twenty-first century, both China and Russia, have maintained this preference for negotiations among the methods of international dispute settlement;[80]

[73] Kaminski (n 65), p. 167.

[74] Kaminski (n 65), p. 189.

[75] Teemu Ruskola, 'The Dao of Mao: Sinocentric Socialism and the Politics of International Legal Theory', in Matthew Craven, Sundhja Pahuja, and Gerry Simpson (eds) International Law and the Cold War (Cambridge: CUP, 2020), pp 376–396 at 377.

[76] Kaminski (n 65), pp. 200–202, 219.

[77] Kaminski (n 65) pp. 200–202.

[78] See e.g. Grigory I. Tunkin, Theory of International Law, translated with an introduction by William E. Butler (Cambridge, MA: Harvard University Press, 1974).

[79] Kaminski (n 65) pp. 220–223. For a similar Soviet view, see E.A. Korovin, Sovremennoe mezhdunarodnoe publichnoe pravo (Contemporary Public International Law) (Moscow/Leningrad: Gosudarstvennoe izdatel'stvo), 1926, p. 137.

[80] The Declaration of the Russian Federation and the People's Republic of China on the Promotion of International Law, 25 June 2016, https://archive.mid.ru/en/foreign_policy/news/-/asset_publisher/cKNonkJE02Bw/content/id/2331698, p. 5 (last accessed on 10 July 2025).

the main reason must be that negotiations are flexible and generally favour the stronger party.

In Communist Chinese scholarship, significant effort was devoted to addressing the same question that had long occupied Soviet scholars since the 1920s and 1930s: was a common international law with capitalist states even conceivable or desirable? One PRC text from 1963 railed against American 'universalism' and pursuit of one 'world order'.[81] Writing in 1958, Lin Hsin, when discussing the basic understanding of international law, created a colorful metaphor: 'At this moment capitalist and socialist countries are sleeping in the same bed, but dreaming different dreams.'[82] Just as in the Soviet Union of the 1930s certain international lawyers had been persecuted (Evgeny Pashukanis was even shot in 1937), in the PRC of Mao's era some international jurists, such as Wang Tieya (1913–2003) were also criticized and punished for being 'rightist elements'.[83] The desire to conceptually uphold the autonomy of law vis-à-vis revolutionary politics was apparently already a 'rightist' position. Nevertheless, Wang Tieya remained one of the most prominent PRC international lawyers even after Mao's era; for example, he was a judge at the ICTY in the period 1997–2000.[84]

Cohen and Chiu concluded on the Communist Chinese debate regarding the correct relationship between general and 'socialist' international law:

> Most Chinese writers who took part in the 1957–8 theoretical dispute argued in favor of the existence of general international law, and all agreed that there is such a thing as socialist international law. But these writers could not agree whether there are two systems of international law (general and socialist) or three systems (general, socialist, and bourgeois).[85]

Again, this PRC debate reflected directly what had happened in the USSR, where in the 1920s Evgeny Korovin (1892–1964) took a different position from that which Grigory Tunkin (1906–1993) and other international lawyers would represent after the Second World War. The Maoist search for ideological mistakes in communist interpretation of international law also recalled similar debates in the Soviet Union during the Stalinist period.[86] Moreover, both the Soviet Union and the PRC talked a great deal about 'peaceful coexistence'[87], although in practice it

[81] Cohen and Chiu (n 64) pp. 42–46.

[82] Ibid., vol I, p. 58.

[83] Ibid., p. 59.

[84] See also his Hague Academy course: Wang Tieya, 'International Law in China: Historical and Contemporary Perspectives', 221 RCADI 1990, pp. 199–369.

[85] Chiu and Cohen (n 64) Vol I, p. 63. Cf Kaminski (n 65), pp. 175–178.

[86] See O burzhuaznykh vlianiakh v sovetskoi mezhdunarodno-pravovoi literature. Diskussia na mezhdunarodnom otdelenii 1 MGU (On bourgeois influences in Soviet international legal literature. Discussion at International Department 1 of Moscow State University) (Moscow: Ranion, 1930). (Presentation by David Levin, inter alia criticizing the international legal views of Evgeny Korovin, and the ensuing discussion including Korovin himself.)

[87] Cohen and Chiu (n 64), p. 75.

turned out that they meant quite different things by it, as op-eds in state newspapers in the PRC also observed.[88]

Chi Hsiang-yang, a PRC author, condemned the 1968 Soviet-led intervention in Czechoslovakia as an 'atrocious act of aggression'. He criticized the Soviet 'revisionist renegade clique' and postulated:

> The relationship between Soviet revisionism and other member countries in this 'community' is one between plunderer and the plundered, between master and slave, a relationship between a suzerain state and its colonies and dependencies... This Soviet revisionist fallacy is entirely calculated to serve the purpose of collaborating with US imperialism in a vain effort to redivide the world. US imperialism invented the so-called 'free world community', and Soviet revisionism followed suit by concocting the so-called 'community of socialist countries'... To put it bluntly, the 'internationalism' of the Soviet revisionists is nothing but imperialist cosmopolitanism and big-power chauvinism aimed at conquering and enslaving other nations and establishing world hegemony.[89]

One of the most practically relevant Soviet influences on the PRC doctrine of international law concerned international treaties. Both states and their jurists argued that, for revolutionary states, the fundamental principle of *pacta sunt servanda* only had a limited meaning. When 'class interests' so required then the revolutionary state could opt for the exception, *clausula rebus sic stantibus* (the doctrine of fundamental change of circumstances), and legitimately refuse to fulfil previous treaty commitments.[90] However, the biggest disagreement between both governments regarded what this would mean in the historical context of unequal treaties which Tsarist Russia had concluded with China, and whether or to what extent they had been unequal in the first place. For the Chinese, the Soviets had condemned Tsarist Russia's unequal treaties mainly in words alone but did not follow up on their condemnation in deeds, at least regarding China. The Soviets were not ready to consider corrections of the border vis-à-vis the PRC. In terms of Soviet counter-arguments from the 1960s, perhaps the most compelling was the notion that China's own territorial expansion in the course of history—for example in Tibet and Xinjiang—had also been a result of unequal, hierarchical relationships, and agreements. If history contained many unequal and, in this sense, unfair expansions by empires, where should one start and where should one stop when

[88] Ibid., p. 143.
[89] Ibid., pp. 153–155.
[90] Ibid., Vol II, p. 1119, 1257. In the USSR, the representative academic work on this question was Natalia V. Zakharova, Vlianie sotsial'noi revoljutsii na silu mezhdunarodnogo dogovora (The Influence of the Social Revolution on the Power of International Treaty) (Moscow: Nauka, 1969). However, in Soviet scholarship, the argument in favour of *clausula rebus sic stantibus* was already elaborated in Evgeny B. Pashukanis, Ocherki po mezhdunarodnomy pravu (Essays on International Law) (Moscow: Sovetskoe zakonodatel'stvo, 1935), pp. 155, 161–162.

condemning them? Should one then examine the historical formation of China's borders with the same anti-imperialist dialectic as well?

17.5 Unequal Treaties and the Question of the Sino–Soviet Border

In the 1960s, the question of the Sino–Soviet border became one of the main symbols of the differences between the two countries.[91] Several border incidents and clashes involving fatalities occurred, the most significant of these being on 2 March 1969 on the island of Damanskiy (Zhenbao). More than 300 Chinese soldiers clashed with Soviet border guards, of whom 31 were killed.[92] The PRC began to assert that the *de facto* border between the USSR and the PRC was a result of unequal treaties concluded in the nineteenth century between Tsarist Russia and Imperial China.[93]

For several centuries, the border between the Russian and Chinese Empires had been fixed by the treaty of Nerchinsk (1689). In the Far East, near the Amur River, this border had been much less favourable to imperial Russia than the border fixed by the treaty of Aigun (1858). With the treaty of Beijing (1860), Russia made gains on the Ussuri river and reached the Pacific Ocean where nowadays the city of Vladivostok (in Russian: 'rule the East') is located. China lost further territories with the protocol of Chunguchak (Tarbagatai) in 1864, which dealt with the border in Central Asia. Overall, with these treaties the Russian Empire gained more than 1.7 million square kilometres.[94] However, from the Chinese perspective, the problem was that these treaties were concluded against the backdrop of English and French military intervention in China, of which the Russian Empire took advantage. Examples of military intervention in China during the period include an English army's burning and looting of the imperial palace in Beijing in 1860.

With the St Petersburg treaty (1881), the Russians further gained more than 40,000 square kilometres in Central Asia, in the Ili valley region.[95] Moreover, in 1895 England and Russia concluded a treaty in which they determined mutual spheres of interest in the Pamir region. In that way, the south-eastern border of today's Tajikistan was established without China's participation and the Chinese

[91] See further George Ginsburgs and Carl F. Pinkele, The Sino–Soviet Territorial Dispute, 1949-64 (New York: Praeger Publisher, 1978); Tsien-hua Tsui, The Sino–Soviet Border Dispute in the 1970s (Oakville, Ontario: Mosaic Press, 1983); Sören Urbansky, Beyond the Steppe Frontier. A History of the Sino-Russian Border (Princeton University Press, 2020).

[92] Vladimirov, Sovetsko-kitaiskie otnoshenia, ibid., p. 207.

[93] See See Horst Pommerening, Der chinesisch-sowjetische Grenzkonflikt. Das Erbe der ungleichen Verträge (The Chinese- Soviet Border Conflict. Legacy of Unequal Treaties) (Olten: Walter Verlag, 1968).

[94] Ibid., p. 137.

[95] Ibid., p. 144.

Empire lost control over the Pamir Mountains. In the treaty of Tsitsihar (1911), Russia pushed the border further, between Russia's Aigun and Mongolia (then part of China), compared to the earlier treaty of Kiakhta (1727).

It is revealing to see how, in the Soviet Union, evaluation of the earlier Russian–Chinese treaties diametrically differed over time, reflecting the changing 'moods' in Sino–Soviet relations. For example, a Soviet study in 1958 on the Treaty of Nerchinsk (1689) concluded that the treaty 'strengthened and broadened peaceful relations between both countries'.[96] The author of the study, P. T. Iakovleva, argued that the first Chinese–Russian treaty had been concluded on an equal footing, unlike the treaties which the West European empires later concluded with China, which of course were unequal treaties.[97] However, writing in 1980, another scholar from Moscow, V. S. Miasnikov, came to the opposite conclusion: the treaty of Nerchinsk had been concluded under threat of force by the Chinese at the time. Miasnikov argued that the Russian negotiator, Golovin, was forced to abandon to the Qing Empire part of the territory on the left bank of the Amur and the right bank of the Arun which had belonged to Russia in the 1640s–1680s. In the Treaty of Nerchinsk, the border was not even fixed based on the international legal norms of that time; territorial damage was inflicted on the Russian state.[98] In an post-Soviet publication, V. S. Miasnikov asserted that the treaty of Nerchinsk was perhaps not even a 'treaty' in the European sense at all but the mandate of a Chinese emperor who saw all other rulers under heaven[99] as his inferiors and vassals.[100]

Writing as early as 1880, Tsarist Russia's leading international lawyer, Fedor Martens, had argued that it was highly 'contested' whether the Amur region had historically been part of China.[101] Rather, with the Treaty of Nerchinsk (in which the Chinese were helped in negotiations by two Jesuit priests[102]), Russia was forced to yield territory.[103] Because the discourse of 'international law', borrowed from the West, was only starting to emerge in China at the time,[104] Imperial Chinese foreign policy representatives did not yet have access to Western academic outlets such as the *Revue de droit international et de législation comparée* to present their views and counter-arguments to other imperialist powers such as the Russian Empire.

[96] P. T. Iakovleva, Pervyi russko-kitaiskii dogovor 1689 goda (The first Russo–Chinese Treaty of 1689) (Moscow: Izdatel'stvo akademii nayk SSSR, 1958), p. 210.

[97] Ibid., pp. 211–212.

[98] V. S. Miasnikov, Imperia Tsin i russkoe gosudarstvo v XVII veke (The Empire of Xin and the Russian State in the 17th century) (Moscow: Nauka, 1980), p. 259.

[99] Tianxia; all under heaven.

[100] V. S. Miasnikov (ed.) Russko-kitaiskie dogovorno-pravovye akty (1689–1916) (Russian–Chinese treaty legal acts (1689–1916) (Moscow: Pamiatniki istoricheskoi mysli, 2004), p. 11.

[101] F. Martens, 'Le conflit entre la Russie et la Chine, ses origines, son développement, et sa portée universelle', RDILC 1880, 513 at 520.

[102] See Joseph Sebes, S.J., The Jesuits and the Sino–Russian Treaty of Nerchinsk (1689). The Diary of Thomas Pereira (S.J., Rome: Institutum historicum S.I., 1961).

[103] Martens (n 101), p. 523.

[104] See Arnulf Becker Lorca, Mestizo International Law. A Global Intellectual History 1842–1933 (Cambridge: CUP, 2014).

Historically, two territories in which Russia and China clashed were Manchuria and (Outer or Northern) Mongolia. Soviet authors of the interwar period were honest about the fact that, in its last years of existence, Tsarist Russia had colluded with Imperial Japan to grab Manchuria from China. Interestingly, these agreements were made quite soon after the 1904–1905 Russo-Japanese war, which the Russian Empire lost. Japan and Tsarist Russia concluded four predominantly secret treaties also affecting China: in 1907, 1910, 1912, and 1916.[105] The objectives of these secret treaties were later also discussed in Western scholarship.[106]

In the 1907 treaty, concluded by Russian foreign minister Izvolski and the Japanese ambassador to Russia, Motono, the secret part stipulated that Manchuria was divided into two spheres of influence—the North to Russia and the South to Japan. Russia recognized Japan's special interests in Korea and in turn Japan recognized Russia's interests in outer Mongolia.[107] The 1910 secret treaty went a step further and, building on previous spheres of interest, laid out what measures could be further taken in the respective spheres.[108] The 1912 secret treaty was concluded by Russian foreign minister Sazonov and Japanese ambassador Motono, even after the 1911 revolution in China. Again, Russian and Japanese special interests in Manchuria and Mongolia were reiterated. In addition, China's Inner Mongolia was also divided into two spheres of influence.[109] Finally, during the First World War, on 3 July 1916, Russia and Japan concluded two treaties in St Petersburg, one public and the other secret. The secret treaty laid down that neither of the two empires wanted to see any third foreign states intervening in China and that they would act together against them. In the words of Korovin, one of the foremost international law scholars in the Soviet Union during the interwar period, by then the whole of China had already become the object of an imperialist treaty.[110]

In the West too, during the Second World War, earlier Russian and Soviet designs in Manchuria and Mongolia gained the attention of scholars when evaluating the situation in the Far East.[111] On 2 September 1945, Japan was defeated in the Second World War. However, the Soviet Union initially maintained its special rights in Manchuria, especially regarding the Chinese Eastern Railway and certain ports where the Soviet navy enjoyed privileges. Only in the early 1950s did the Soviet Union give up its previous extraterritorial treaty rights in Manchuria and withdraw from Port Artur and the Chinese Eastern Railway. During the Cold

[105] Evgeny A. Korovin, *Iaponia i mezhdunarodnoe pravo* (Japan and International Law) (Moscow: Sotsekgiz, 1936), p. 48.

[106] Ernest Batson Price, The Russo-Japanese Treaties of 1907–1916 Concerning Manchuria and Mongolia (Baltimore: The Johns Hopkins Press, 1933).

[107] Korovin (n 105), p. 49.

[108] Ibid., p. 50.

[109] Ibid., p. 51.

[110] Ibid., p. 53.

[111] Quincy Wright, 'The Legal Background in the Far East', in: Legal Problems in the Far Eastern Conflict (New York: Institute of Pacific Relations, 1941), pp. 32–35, 59-61 etc.

War, the memory of the situation in Manchuria continued to play a role. On the one hand, Mao Zedong was arguably wondering: if the Soviets could be convinced to withdraw from Manchuria, from where else might they withdraw? On the other hand, the history of secret and unequal treaties played a big role in Chinese political and popular consciousness when dealing with the Soviet Union. The big question for the Chinese was whether the Soviet Union was as different from Tsarist Russia as it proclaimed. Of course, during the Cold War decades, Soviet writers on international law no longer emphasized or spoke candidly about Tsarist Russia's attempts to expand to Manchuria as well. What used to be Russian 'imperialism' in the past had now become Soviet 'brotherly help', which was not optional.

Besides Manchuria, another contested twentieth-century territorial situation between Russia (later the Soviet Union) and China concerned Mongolia. At the end of the Tsarist period, in 1915, the Russians had invaded part of the Chinese Empire called Outer (or Northern) Mongolia and established a protectorate there. In March 1921, Soviet Russian forces helped the Mongolians to establish the People's Republic of Mongolia, whose government did not recognize Chinese supremacy. On 5 November 1921, the Soviet government concluded a treaty with the government of the People's Republic of Mongolia. In Soviet international legal literature, the 1921 treaty with Mongolia was praised as a selfless treaty in which the stronger party (Soviet Russia) agreed to have fully equal relations with the much weaker party and even handed over the Russian-built infrastructure to the Mongolians.[112] Nevertheless, in the Soviet–Chinese Agreement on General Principles, signed on 31 May 1924, the Soviet government declared (Article 5) that it 'recognizes that Outer Mongolia is an integral part of the Republic of China and that it respects China's sovereignty therein' and promised that 'it will completely withdraw all Soviet troops from Outer Mongolia.'[113]

In short, Soviet treaty practice regarding Mongolia initially mirrored the changing balance of power and circumstances on the ground. On 12 March 1936, the Soviet Union concluded a Mutual Assistance Pact with the Mongolian People's Republic which was incompatible with the Soviet-Chinese Agreement on General Principles of 31 May 1924.[114] In the Sino–Soviet Treaty of Friendship and Alliance (1945), the Republic of China agreed that if, after the defeat of Japan, a plebiscite of the Outer Mongolian people should confirm their 'repeatedly expressed desire for independence', then the Chinese government would recognize the 'independence' of Outer Mongolia.[115] As in the Soviet-dominated countries of Central and Eastern Europe, no such genuine referendum took place. Nevertheless, on 1 February

[112] E.A. Korovin, Sovremennoe mezhdunarodnoe publichnoe pravo (Contemporary Public International Law) (Moscow/Leningrad: Gosudarstvennoe izdatel'stvo, 1926), p. 47.

[113] See Jan F. Triska and Robert M. Slusser, The Law, Theory, and Policy of Soviet Treaties (Stanford University Press, 1962), p. 204.

[114] Ibid., p. 235.

[115] Ibid., p. 238.

1952, during the Korean War, at the request of the Republic of China the UN General Assembly adopted a resolution stating that the USSR 'had failed to carry out' its 1945 treaty obligations 'ever since the surrender of Japan'.[116] Finally, in the 1950 treaty, the PRC recognized the sovereignty and independence of the People's Republic of Mongolia. Concerning this period, Grzybowski even refers to a short-lived Sino–Soviet 'condominium' in the People's Republic of Mongolia, which ended in 1962 when Mongolia became a member of COMECON.[117] Writing in 1969, Kuomintang leader Chiang Kai-shek in Taiwan was not content with how Russia had handled the situation in Mongolia and questioned whether Mongolia under Soviet hegemony was an independent state.[118] In some parts of the literature, Mongolia was even characterized as a Soviet 'colony' at the time.[119] The ROC has still not officially recognized the independence of Mongolia.

While recognizing the independence of the People's Republic of Mongolia, the Soviet Union also carved a territory out of it: Tannu-Tuva (the former Chinese province of Tangnu Urianghai), where a People's Republic (separate from Mongolia) was proclaimed in 1921, with the presence of the Red Army. During the interwar period, Moscow upheld the formal independence of Tannu-Tuva, probably to experiment with the model of the coexistence of separate socialist republics, not all included in the USSR. Nevertheless, in 1944, the Soviet Union still annexed Tannu-Tuva,[120] which nowadays forms part of the Russian Federation.

Nevertheless, the border issue between the PRC and the Soviet Union (and later the Russian Federation) was eventually resolved. The PRC and the Soviet Union reached an agreement on the first parts of their mutual border about six months before the Soviet Union was dissolved in December 1991. On 16 May 1991 in Moscow, Soviet foreign minister Alexander Bessmertnykh and PRC foreign minister Qian Qichen signed a border agreement on the eastern part of their countries' mutual border. The ratification documents were exchanged in Beijing on 16 March 1992, the day on which the treaty entered into force.[121] The last years of the Soviet Union raised existential uncertainties regarding the future of China's northern neighbour so the timing of concluding the first border treaty was probably not

[116] UNGA Resolution 505, 1.02.1952, Threats to the political independence and territorial integrity of China to the peace of the Far East, resulting from Soviet violations of the Sino-Soviet Treaty of Friendship and Alliance of August 14, 1945 and from Soviet violations of the Charter of the United Nations. See also Triska and Slusser (n 113), p. 238.

[117] Kazimierz Grzybowski, Soviet Public International Law. Doctrines and Diplomatic Practice (Leyden: A.W. Sijthoff, 1970), p. 102.

[118] Chiang Kai-shek (n 55), p. 154.

[119] Jeanne Nickell Knutson, Outer Mongolia: A Study in Soviet Colonialism (Kowloon, Hong Kong: Union Research Institute, 1959), p. 142.

[120] Grzybowski (n 117), p. 73; Chiang Kai-shek (n 55), p. 106.

[121] G.B. Karasin, L.P Moiseev, L.A. Skotnikov, V.V. Chikvadze, P.V. Stegnii, E. Yu, N. Tomikhin, and Yu Kuriatnikova (eds) Sbornik rossiisko-kitaiskikh dogovorov. 1949–1999 (A Collection of Russian–Chinese Treaties. 1949–1999) (Moscow: Terra-Sport, 1999), pp. 117–125.

accidental. The PRC wanted to have certainty, which was still available in these otherwise uncertain times.

This was followed by other border treaties including a tripartite treaty between Russia, China, and Mongolia, concluded on 27 January 1994 in Mongolia's capital city Ulan-Bator. The treaty fixed the border where the three nations met geographically. The ambassadors of Russia and China in Ulan-Bator signed for their respective countries.[122] The Russian–Chinese border treaty fixing the western part of the border was signed in Moscow on 3 September 1994 by Russia's foreign minister Andrei Kozyrev and the PRC's foreign minister Qian Qichen. The exchange of ratification documents took place in Beijing on 17 October 1995.[123] Furthermore, on 5 May 1999, Russia, China, and Kazakhstan agreed on their mutual borders in the area concerning the previous Soviet–Chinese border.[124] Nevertheless, writing in 2003, one Russian author still worried that the question of the PRC–Russian border had not been resolved with finality and that the Chinese apparently continued to think that unequal treaties had shaped the interstate border between the two countries.[125]

On 21 July 2008 in Beijing, Russia's foreign minister Sergei Lavrov and the PRC's foreign minister Yang Jieshi signed the final border agreement, reaching a consensus on demarcation of the border. The PRC claimed that it received back 174 square kilometres of its former territory—Yinlong island (Tarabarov island) and half of Heixiazi island (Bolshoi Ussuriysky Island).[126]

17.6 In Conclusion: Transformations of Two Empires

During the Cold War, the international legal relations and doctrines of the Soviet Union and the PRC were shaped by two factors: both were Communist countries, but, historically, both were also empires par excellence.[127] Vladimir Lenin's concept of 'imperialism' was that 'imperialism was the highest stage of capitalism' and, according to this Communist theory, Russia should have finished with imperialism in 1917 and China in 1949. However, Cold War-era relations between Beijing and Moscow demonstrate that the legacy of empires also lived on in the context of state socialism. In this sense, Lenin's theory of imperialism, although

[122] Ibid., pp. 206–208.

[123] Ibid., pp. 275–277.

[124] Ibid., pp. 492–493.

[125] Yu M. Galenovich, Rossiya-Kitai. Shest' dogovorov (Russia–China. Six Treaties) (Moscow: Muravei, 2003), p. 344.

[126] China Daily, 22.07.2008, 'China, Russia Sign Border Agreement', https://www.chinadaily.com.cn/china/2008-07/22/content_6865847.htm (last accessed on 10 July 2025).

[127] See also S.C,M. Paine, Imperial Rivals. Russia, China, and Their Disputed Frontier (Armonk, NY: M. E. Sharpe, 1996).

popular in some academic works on international law,[128] does not adequately reflect the imperial histories of the socialist 'great powers', the USSR and the PRC, during the Cold War.

A certain irony lay in the fact that both powers vehemently insisted that they were 'anti-imperialist' and therefore both had a hard time seeing imperialist patterns in their own country's legacies, including in the context of international law. These myopic views concerning their own imperial and imperialist legacies and patterns aggravated the Sino–Soviet split during the period of the 1960s–1980s. It seems that the question 'which of the two interprets Marxism properly?' was at least partly a proxy for the very *realpolitik* question: who would play first violin in their mutual relations and as leader of the communist world? The question of nuclear weapons—and the status that came with it—was in the end much more important than the 'right answer' to the theoretical question whether one, two, or even three 'systems' of international law stood between socialist and capitalist countries.

The conclusion of the Chinese–Russian border treaties was facilitated by the fact that the PRC saw that the historical Russian Empire in its Soviet incarnation was going through similar or worse turbulence than the Chinese Empire had experienced in the early twentieth century. During the first part of the twentieth century, China lost (Outer) Mongolia, whereas in December 1991 the Central Asian Soviet republics—Kazakhstan, Uzbekistan, Kyrgyzstan, Tajikistan, and Turkmenistan—became independent states, along with other Soviet republics in Europe. The self-determination of peoples became real; both historical empires had to pay a price and experienced shocks, but at different times. That the Russian Empire lost significant territory also made it easier for the PRC to (by and large, with some minor concessions on the Russian side) accept its northern border which, as the Chinese knew, was historically a result of Russian imperial activities during the nineteenth century. Both empires had got used to looking at their common border exclusively as a competition between two 'great powers' but now they had to see that there were several distinct peoples among the Han Chinese and the Russians who were eager to exercise their own sovereign statehood in international law. The creation of several independent 'buffer states' between the two 'great powers' eased the development of friendly relations between them.

Their shared belief in Marxism-Leninism did not prevent the Soviet Union and the PRC from experiencing hostile relations from 1960 until the end of the Cold War. Although both the PRC and the Soviet Union presented themselves as defenders of 'small and weak nations' in international relations during the Cold War and indeed competed in this regard,[129] they were nevertheless both maintaining

[128] Ntina Tzouvala, Capitalism as Civilization. A History of International Law (Cambridge: CUP, 2020), pp. 2, 219.

[129] Kaminski (n 65), p. 197.

continuity with their own historical empires. This reveals that ideologies such as Marxism, Leninism, and Maoism may come and go, but claims and problems related to imperial and 'great power' status usually remain. In this sense, Russia and China still exist in much the same shape as they were already in at Nerchinsk in 1689. Debates about the proper interpretation of Marxism-Leninism in the context of international law were partly genuine but partly also proxy debates reflecting claims for hegemony, dominance, and the mutual border of the two 'great powers'. Although Marxism-Leninism no longer unites the two nations, China and Russia are still united by their analysis of the big picture of international law and relations as two 'great powers' in Eurasia for whom 'imperialists' tend to be others.

18

China and International Law during the Cultural Revolution and Its Aftermath

Straton Papagianneas

18.1 Introduction

The influence of China's historical past on its interaction and relationship with international law has received extensive attention in academic literature.[1] Among these historical events, the Opium War has played a significant role in shaping and influencing China's perspective on the international legal order.[2] The People's Republic of China (PRC) has significantly increased its engagement with the international community since the initiation of the reform and opening-up period in the 1980s. This includes its accession to various multilateral treaties that encompass a broad range of areas, such as international trade, intellectual property, investment, and environmental protection. However, it is imperative not to disregard the preceding decades, as the rapid pace and extent of China's involvement in the international arena may overshadow the significance of earlier periods. In particular, the Cultural Revolution is often overlooked when attempting to comprehend China's historical context in relation to international law.

Nevertheless, the decade spanning from 1966 to 1976 stands as an unparalleled era of upheaval in the history of the PRC. This period witnessed an unprecedented surge of Marxist-socialist fervour, during which ideological interpretations of the world reached their zenith. In its most tumultuous phase, roughly between 1966 and 1970, this fervour led to a complete disintegration of society. The initial episodes of violence in 1966 and 1967, pitting various political factions against one another, brought the PRC close to the brink of civil war.[3]

[1] See, e.g., Phil CW Chan, 'China's Approaches to International Law since the Opium War' (2014) 27 Leiden J Int'l L 859. Simon Chesterman, 'Asia's Ambivalence about International Law and Institutions: Past, Present and Futures' (2017) 27 Eur J Int'l L 945.

[2] See, e.g., Julia Lovell, *The Opium War: Drugs, Dreams and the Making of China* (Pan Macmillan 2012). Li Chen, *Chinese Law in Imperial Eyes: Sovereignty, Justice, and Transcultural Politics* (Columbia University Press 2016). Stephen R. Platt, *Imperial Twilight: The Opium War and the End of China's Last Golden Age* (Penguin Random House 2019).

[3] Michel Oksenberg, 'Occupational Groups in Chinese Society and the Cultural Revolution' in Carl Riskin, Ezra F Vogel and Michel Oksenberg (eds), *The Cultural Revolution: 1967 in Review* (University of Michigan Press 1968) 24.

Straton Papagianneas, *China and International Law during the Cultural Revolution and Its Aftermath* In: *Histories of International Law in China*. Edited by: Ignacio de la Rasilla, Jiangyu Wang, and Congyan Cai, Oxford University Press.
 DOI: 10.1093/oso/9780198888345.003.0018

In regard to China's legal system, the functioning of judicial organs such as public security institutions, the procuratorate, the judiciary, and the legislative, was completely halted. Following 1967, the roles fulfilled by the judicial and procuratorial departments were taken over by military and revolutionary committees. Any form of due process or separation of investigative and adjudicative powers was absent. To put it simply, this decade witnessed a significant decline in China's legal system. All law departments in universities across the country were shut down during this time.[4] It was indeed a period characterized by extreme legal nihilism. The restoration of China's legal system only began to take place after 1972.[5]

Consistent with its historical context, a significant portion of the literature on the history of (international) law in the PRC devotes little to no attention to this particular decade. Sucharitkul even goes as far as to claim that 'legal scholarship was condemned to eternal death' during this period.[6] Han Depei, a renowned Chinese scholar of international law who himself fell victim to political persecution during this era, dismisses this period as a 'painful experience'.[7] Wang Tieya agrees that there was no study of international law during this time. He asserts that education and research on international law were only reinstated following the initiation of the reform and opening-up period in 1979.[8]

During the early 1980s, the production of knowledge in international law primarily focused on international trade, economic cooperation, and matters pertaining to the PRC's national sovereignty and territorial integrity.[9] Additionally, the PRC increased its participation in international law-making conferences. However, Chinese delegations mostly played a passive role, with delegates rarely actively engaging in discussions on international law.[10]

Contrary to the prevailing belief of a 'lost decade' in the literature regarding the Cultural Revolution, this chapter posits that the PRC did indeed exhibit some level of involvement with international law, albeit limited. Although the majority of bilateral agreements pertaining to friendship, trade, and economic cooperation were not finalized until after 1976, preliminary discussions had been under way well in advance. A case in point is the Sino–Japanese Peace and Friendship Treaty, which was ultimately concluded in 1978. However, it is worth noting that it took a span of

[4] Han Depei and Stephen Kanter, 'Legal Education in China' (1984) 32(3) Am J Comp L 552.

[5] Cao Shouliang, 'Overview of Rule of Law Work during the Cultural Revolution' (2015) 31(1) J Langfang Tchrs Univ 57 (in Chinese).

[6] Sompong Sucharitkul, 'Rebirth of Chinese Legal Scholarship, with Regard to International Law' (1990) 3 Leiden J Int'l L 3, 14.

[7] Han Depei, 'Legal Education in China' in Huang Jin and Liu Wen (eds), *Selected Works of Han Depei* (Wuhan University Publisher 1995) 383 (in Chinese). For a short biography on Han Depei, see, e.g., Nongji Zhang, 'Han Depei (韩德培) (1911–2009) Private International Law' in *Legal Scholars and Scholarship in the People's Republic of China* (Harvard University Asia Center 2022).

[8] Wang Tieya, 'Teaching and Research of International Law in Present Day China' (1983) 22 Colum J Transnat'l L 77.

[9] ibid 80.

[10] Hanqin Xue, 'China's Open Policy and International Law' (2005) 4 Chin J Int'l L 133.

six years following the normalization of Sino–Japanese relations in 1972 for China and Japan to reach a mutually acceptable resolution.[11] The failure to acknowledge China's engagement with international law during this period necessitates a re-evaluation of the relationship between China and international law amidst the Cultural Revolution.

Therefore, this chapter aims to examine the impact of China's stance on international law during the Cultural Revolution on its positions and attitudes towards events concerning international law-making. Moreover, it provides a brief discussion of Han Depei's legacy, who played a significant role in shaping China's renewed involvement with the international legal community.

To address this issue, the chapter delves into two specific cases, namely the Third United Nations (UN) Conference on the Law of the Sea ('Third LOS Convention') and the 1972 Stockholm Conference on the Human Environment (SCHE). By conducting these case studies, China's early involvement with international law is examined in terms of both continuities and changes. The findings highlight that China's engagement was primarily motivated by the pursuit of its own national interests, specifically those related to national sovereignty and territorial integrity, as well as a desire to be recognized as a leader of the Third World. Additionally, the chapter argues that, following the Cultural Revolution, China's ideological positions regarding international law became less rigid. Moreover, the chapter demonstrates that the pragmatism that had already begun to emerge in the early 1970s continued to evolve. Consequently, China's engagement with international law witnessed a reversal in its two defining characteristics, namely a decrease in pronounced ideological interpretations and an increase in opportunities for pragmatic involvement and compromise within the realm of both international law and international relations. These arguments are supported by a thorough analysis of Chinese and English language academic literature, as well as official reports and documents.

The second section of the chapter provides a comprehensive overview of the People's Republic of China's (PRC) overall approach to international law during the Cultural Revolution. By conducting two case studies, it analyses the impact of this approach on the PRC's behaviour and perspectives regarding specific aspects of international law at international conferences on rulemaking. These events are examined in the context of China's domestic situation and its international standing as a leader of the Third World. The third section explores the consequences of the Cultural Revolution and the influence exerted by Chinese legal scholars, such as Han Depei, who contributed to the reconstruction of China's legal system. The chapter concludes with a reflection on China's present position in the international

[11] For an account on the developments and negotiations of the treaty, see: Chae-Jin Lee, 'The Making of Sino–Japanese Peace and Friendship Treaty' (1979) 52 Pac Aff 420. Makoto Inoue, 'The Japan–China Treaty of Peace and Friendship as History' (2018) 25 Asia-Pac Rev 75.

community and how its experiences during the Cultural Revolution may still have relevance for understanding its current attitudes.

18.2 The PRC and International Law during the Cultural Revolution

Between 1966 and 1976, China's legal education was suspended, resulting in the absence of study of international law during this period.[12] Nevertheless, it is possible to gain insights into China's perspective on international law by examining scholarly publications pre-dating this era. Generally, Chinese scholars and official stances adhered to a dogmatic Soviet interpretation of domestic and international law, heavily influenced by Marxist-Leninist theory.

The PRC viewed international law, alongside international relations, as a normatively charged endeavour in an interpretive manner. Both municipal law and international law were perceived as tools of the state and inherently interconnected: the type of international law applied hinged upon a nation's internal system, whether it was communist or capitalist. Law signified the manifestation of the ruling class's intentions within a country. This recognition acknowledged the existence of both general, capitalist or bourgeois, and socialist international law.[13] In the decade prior to the Cultural Revolution, the PRC embraced socialist international law while condemning bourgeois international law. Similarly, PRC scholars regarded international law as an instrument of a state's foreign policy.[14] Furthermore, it reflected the aspirations of all ruling classes from various states that partook in its formulation. In this sense, international law was predominantly shaped by imperialist states, thus reflecting their will and serving their interests.[15]

The interpretation of the PRC is characterized by a strong emphasis on state sovereignty, a restrictive stance on the origins of international legal rules and obligations, and a comprehensive understanding of impermissible international actions.[16] These views are said to have been significantly shaped by China's initial

[12] Sompong Sucharitkul, 'Rebirth of Chinese Legal Scholarship, with Regard to International Law' (1990) 3 Leiden J Int'l L 3, 14. Han Depei, 'Legal Education in China' in Huang Jin and Liu Wen (eds), *Selected Works of Han Depei* (Wuhan University Publisher 1995) (in Chinese) 383.

[13] Jacques deLisle, 'China's Approach to International Law: Historical Perspective' (2000) 94 Am Soc Int'l L Proc 267, 272. Jerome A Cohen and Hungdah Chiu, *People's China and International Law, Volume 1: A Documentary Study* (Princeton University Press 1974) 47–64.

[14] Hungdah Chiu, 'Communist China's Attitude toward International Law' (1966) 60 Am J Int'l L 245. Jerome A Cohen and Hungdah Chiu, *People's China and International Law, Volume 1: A Documentary Study* (Princeton University Press 1974) 31.

[15] Chen Tiqiang, 'The People's Republic of China and Public International Law' (1984) 8 DLJ 3, 17–19.

[16] Jacques deLisle, 'China's Approach to International Law: Historical Perspective' (2000) 94 Am Soc Int'l L Proc 267, 272.

encounters with international law during the nineteenth century, which subsequently influenced its approach. Consequently, the PRC places particular importance on state sovereignty and equality, non-intervention, non-aggression, anti-hegemonism, and anti-colonialism.[17]

The Cultural Revolution can be understood as a phase characterized by the fervent manifestation of China's revolutionary and Marxist-Leninist ideology, thereby adopting an immensely radical approach to international law, rather than embracing a fundamentally distinct perspective from the previous period. Consequently, it led to a complete denial of the established international legal framework, as well as political and diplomatic protocols.[18] Similarly, China's subsequent understanding of international law and relations can be observed as an extension of the aforementioned ideology, albeit intermingled with pragmatism and calculated caution.[19]

As an extension of international law, the PRC faced significant challenges in maintaining coherence and rationality in its diplomatic relations during the early stages of the Cultural Revolution. The country's foreign policy was paralyzed and heavily influenced by Mao Zedong's personal authority. Consequently, Mao's personal views on international matters drove policy decisions. By 1965, radicalization had reached its peak, with Mao regarding US imperialism as a grave threat to China's interests and denouncing the Soviet Union as a revisionist state and a betrayer of the revolutionary cause. As a result, China's foreign policy was guided by revolutionary ideology rather than adherence to international law. This ideological shift resulted in incidents such as the burning of the British mission in Beijing in 1967.

Similarly, the relationship between the PRC and the United Nations (UN) was characterized by tension. While the PRC expressed unwavering support for the principles and objectives of the UN, it contended that the organization had failed in fulfilling its obligation to promote global justice. The PRC asserted that the United States, in its pursuit of imperialist interests, sought to manipulate the UN and transform it into a vehicle for aggressive policies.

[17] Chen Tiqiang, 'The People's Republic of China and Public International Law' (1984) 8 DLJ 3, 8. Phil CW Chan, 'China's Approaches to International Law since the Opium War' (2014) 27 Leiden J Int'l L 859.

[18] Jacques deLisle, 'China's Approach to International Law: Historical Perspective' (2000) 94 Am Soc Int'l L Proc 267, 272.

[19] A similar argument exists for China's international engagement under Xi Jinping. Rather than a significant departure from Xi's predecessors, it is, simply put, a different approach to the same strategy. See: Avery Goldstein, 'China's Grand Strategy under Xi Jinping: Reassurance, Reform, and Resistance' (2020) 45 Int'l Security 164. Going even further, Howard French argues that China's views of international law and international relations in general, as well as its difficulty to adjust to the new international order in the nineteenth and twentieth centuries, come from its own great traditional history of Chinese world order. His point is that this still bears on China's thinking today. See: Howard W. French, *Everything under the Heavens: How the Past Helps Shape China's Push for Global Power* (Penguin Random House 2018).

Furthermore, despite the PRC's persistent efforts during the 1950s and 1960s to secure membership, it was consistently denied recognition and a seat at the UN. The United States played a pivotal role in ensuring that the Republic of China continued to be represented. As a result, the PRC contended that it had been unfairly deprived of its rightful position within the global community.[20] China's stance towards the United Nations in the 1960s was characterized by a sense of frustration and resentment due to the denial of membership.

During the Cultural Revolution, the PRC displayed a notable lack of interest in becoming a member of the UN, as its domestic turmoil took precedence over matters of international politics. The radicalization and inward orientation of the Cultural Revolution resulted in significant neglect of the PRC's foreign policy agenda, thus constraining its engagement with the UN to a limited extent.

Nonetheless, the PRC was actively engaged with the Third World during this period. Influenced by radical revolutionary ideology, the PRC implemented a significant amount of foreign aid, which ultimately facilitated the establishment of diplomatic relations with numerous African countries.[21] This strategic move was part of the PRC's policy of proletarian internationalism, which aimed to combat the oppression of China by other nations and also oppose the oppression of any nation by another.[22] This approach can be seen as a manifestation of solidarity among Third World nations. During the Cultural Revolution, this commitment extended to supporting communist and liberation movements worldwide.

The PRC allocated substantial political, human, financial, and military resources to Indonesia, Indochina, and Africa.[23] The support garnered from African nations played a pivotal role in enabling the PRC to gain recognition as the legitimate representative of China within the UN. Thanks to this engagement, international support for its admission to the UN began to grow. By 1970, a shift in global sentiment was becoming evident, and the PRC became a member of the UN in 1971. Notably, African votes represented more than one-third of the countries endorsing Resolution 2758 of the UN General Assembly in 1971, which solidified the PRC's UN membership.[24] This contradicts the commonly held perception of Maoist China as an isolationist state and presents a markedly distinct perspective. It was around this time that the PRC also undertook steps for rapprochement with the US and stabilized its relations with other countries.[25]

[20] Jerome A Cohen and Hungdah Chiu, *People's China and International Law, Volume 2: A Documentary Study* (Princeton University Press 1974) 1289.

[21] Yun Shinn, 'Africa in China's Foreign Policy' (Brookings, 2014) <https://www.brookings.edu/research/africa-in-chinas-foreign-policy/> accessed 6 July 2025.

[22] Chen Tiqiang, 'The People's Republic of China and Public International Law' (1984) 8 DLJ 3, 20.

[23] Julia Lovell, *Maoism: A Global History* (Alfred A Knopf Inc 2019).

[24] UNGA Res 2758 (XXVI) (25 October 1971) UN Doc A/RES/2758 <https://digitallibrary.un.org/record/192054?ln=en> accessed 6 July 2025.

[25] Thomas D Curran, 'Chinese Foreign Policy during the Cultural Revolution (Book Review)' (2000) 34 J Asian Hist 86.

After its accession to the UN, the PRC began to actively engage in and contribute to the development of international law, despite its initially hostile attitude. The Chinese delegations, although lacking significant experience in international law and the processes involved in international rulemaking conferences, endeavoured to participate and safeguard their interests as a developing Third World country, even during the domestic turmoil of the later years of the Cultural Revolution. Two specific cases concerning China's involvement in UN Conferences warrant closer examination, as they demonstrate a heightened ideological interpretation of international law and a steadfast commitment to Third World solidarity. China regarded these moments as critical opportunities to advance its struggle as part of the Third World against the imperialism and colonialism propagated by dominant superpowers.[26]

The first event is the Third UN Conference on the Law of the Sea ('Third LOS Conference'). This event signifies the PRC's initial involvement in the development of a novel international treaty, specifically the UN Convention on the Law of the Sea (UNCLOS). Moving on to the second event, it took place during the 1972 Stockholm Conference on the Human Environment (SCHE), during which the Chinese delegation successfully exerted considerable influence on the formulation processes of the Declaration.

18.2.1 Third UN Conference on the Law of the Sea

The Third United Nations Conference on the Law of the Sea spanned eleven sessions from 1973 to 1982. In anticipation of this event, the United Nations General Assembly directed the Committee on the Peaceful Uses of the Seabed and the Ocean Floor beyond the Limits of National Jurisdiction to serve as a preparatory body in 1970. This committee convened six sessions and held additional meetings from 1971 to 1973.[27] Notably, these preparatory sessions coincided with the PRC's admission to the United Nations.

Before 1971, the PRC had only issued a Declaration on the Territorial Sea in 1959 in response to the Taiwan Strait crisis in the summer of 1958. This declaration was presented as a significant measure aimed at safeguarding China's national sovereignty and territorial integrity, while also reinforcing its national security and protecting its economic interests.[28] During the period between 1959 and 1970, the PRC did not clarify or modify its stance on the territorial sea. However, in 1970 its

[26] Jerome A Cohen and Hungdah Chiu, *People's China and International Law, Volume 2: A Documentary Study* (Princeton University Press 1974) 1298–1300.

[27] Third United Nations Conference on the Law of the Sea, Official Records <https://legal.un.org/diplconf_records/1973_los/> accessed 6 July 2025.

[28] Jerome A Cohen and Hungdah Chiu, *People's China and International Law, Volume 1: A Documentary Study* (Princeton University Press 1974) 469–487.

interests were rekindled as it began expressing strong support for the territorial waters claims of Latin American countries, advocating for a 200-nautical-mile limit.[29]

The issue of the territorial sea became an increasingly significant factor in the PRC's support of the Third World's fight against hegemonic superpowers.[30] The PRC's membership in the UN and its election to the UN Seabed Committee, in preparation for the Third LOS Conference, sparked a renewed interest in international legal matters pertaining to the sea.

This section will examine a consistent factor in China's stance throughout the preparations and the conference itself: the significant value of national sovereignty. It will be demonstrated that, similar to various other aspects of foreign policy and international law, this concept plays a critical role in comprehending and elucidating the perspectives of the PRC at the Seabed Committee and during the LOS Conference. It also served as a crucial tool in China's critique of what it perceived as the hegemony of superpowers, namely the US and the USSR. It is important to note that China's proposals often took the form of broad policy frameworks rather than specific regulations. Additionally, their position on the issue remained largely unchanged throughout the entirety of the Third LOS Conference.[31] Therefore, despite the conclusion of the Cultural Revolution in 1976, China's involvement in the Seabed Committee and Third LOS Conference remains within the context of its engagement with international law during that period.

This conference and its preparations held significant importance due to the growing discontent with the current legal framework governing the world's oceans. It was acknowledged that numerous countries were excluded from active participation in this development and therefore should not be forced to abide by the outcomes.[32] The PRC was a member of Subcommittee II, which was responsible for deliberating traditional law of the sea matters, such as territorial sea, straits, the high seas, fisheries, and the seabed within national jurisdiction.[33] Four points of discussion during the negotiations highlight the significance of national sovereignty as the underlying principle that substantiates and elucidates the perspectives of the Chinese delegation.

18.2.1.1 Four Points of Discussion

The first issue related to the determination of the extent of the territorial sea. The position put forth by the PRC, as articulated in its working paper to the Seabed

[29] ibid 487–488.

[30] Jerome A Cohen and Hungdah Chiu, *People's China and International Law, Volume 1: A Documentary Study* (Princeton University Press 1974) 497. Hungdah Chiu, 'China and the Law of the Sea Conference' (1981) 4 Md Series Contemp Asian Stud 1, 5–6.

[31] Zhiguo Gao, 'China and the LOS Convention' (1991) 15 Marine Policy 199, 203.

[32] ibid 200.

[33] John R Stevenson and Bernard H Oxman, 'The Preparations for the Law of the Sea Conference' (1974) 68 Am J Int'l L 1, 2–3.

Committee and during the ensuing deliberations, asserted that the territorial sea constitutes an integral part of the coastal state's territory, over which it exercises complete sovereignty.[34] The PRC's stance on this matter was by no means unique, as previous international conferences had failed to establish a universally recognized territorial boundary.[35] Consequently, the Chinese proposal to the Seabed Committee concerning this issue refrained from specifying a precise upper limit for the territorial sea.[36]

The second issue revolved around the determination of the contiguous zone. The PRC delegation argued that the 1958 Convention on the Territorial Sea and the Contiguous Zone, which sets the boundary of the contiguous zone at 12 nautical miles from the baseline used to measure the breadth of the territorial sea, infringed upon the national sovereignty of smaller coastal states. It restricted their ability to independently decide whether to extend their territorial sea or contiguous zone beyond the 12-nautical-mile limit.[37]

The third issue addressed in this context pertains to innocent passage. The PRC delegation argued that under the previous regime, innocent passage represented a clear violation of coastal states' sovereignty over their own territorial seas.[38] To address this concern, the delegation proposed a more restrictive interpretation to the Seabed Committee, advocating for the application of innocent passage throughout the entirety of the territorial sea, rather than solely in international straits that intersect with a 12-mile territorial sea.[39] Furthermore, during the negotiations, the Chinese delegation emphasized that this principle should also apply to transit through international straits that overlap with the 12-mile territorial seas. According to their perspective, a strait situated within a coastal state's territorial sea constitutes an indivisible component of that state's territorial sea. Consequently, the coastal state possesses the absolute right to exercise its sovereignty as it deems appropriate.[40]

The fourth and final issue pertained to the continental shelf. China argued that the continental shelf should be considered as the natural extension of the coastal state. In its submission to the Seabed Committee, China did not propose a specific outer limit. Instead, it maintained that the coastal state possessed the exclusive jurisdiction to determine the boundaries of the continental shelf based on its unique geographical conditions. Furthermore, China asserted that a coastal state

[34] Hungdah Chiu, 'China and the Law of the Sea Conference' (1981) 4 Md Series Contemp Asian Stud 1, 7.

[35] Tao Cheng, 'Communist China and the Law of the Sea' (1969) 63 Am J Int'l L 47, 54–57.

[36] John R Stevenson and Bernard H Oxman, 'The Preparations for the Law of the Sea Conference' (1974) 68 Am J Int'l L 1, 9.

[37] Hungdah Chiu, 'China and the Law of the Sea Conference' (1981) 4 Md Series Contemp Asian Stud 1, 7.

[38] Zhiguo Gao, 'China and the LOS Convention' (1991) 15 Marine Policy 199, 200–201.

[39] John R Stevenson and Bernard H Oxman, 'The Preparations for the Law of the Sea Conference' (1974) 68 Am J Int'l L 1, 11.

[40] Zhiguo Gao, 'China and the LOS Convention' (1991) 15 Marine Policy 199, 204–205.

could even extend the limits of its continental shelf beyond its territorial sea or economic zone.[41] The PRC's position on these matters was communicated to the Seabed Committee through its working paper and remained largely unchanged throughout the Conference.

18.2.1.2 The Persistence of National Sovereignty

The Third LOS Conference took place between 1973 and 1982.[42] The passing of Mao Zedong in 1976 marked the conclusion of the Cultural Revolution, yet China's stance and involvement remained unchanged throughout the sessions pre-1976 and post-1976. Owing to a dearth of legal experts, China was unable to make any significant contributions to the formulation of the convention. Consequently, China adopted a more passive approach, aligning itself with other developing nations in providing support.

What remained consistent, however, was the PRC's unwavering commitment to the principle of equality based on national sovereignty. During the inaugural session in December 1973, the Chinese delegation staunchly advocated for upholding the principle of 'one state, one seat' in order to counterbalance the privileged position of larger nations, particularly the US and the USSR, at the conference. These countries, owing to their status as permanent members of the United Nations Security Council, would be entitled to multiple seats across various working committees of the conference. As a fellow permanent member, China would have been afforded this same privilege. However, at that juncture, it was not yet adequately equipped to effectively participate in the majority of committees due to its lack of legal expertise. Consequently, its exclusion from certain committees would have had minimal repercussions. Hence, it was in China's best interest to exclude all major powers from serving on crucial committees by adopting the 'one state, one seat' principle. This principle clearly favoured smaller or mid-sized countries, the majority of which belonged to the Third World.[43]

In summary, the PRC displayed the utmost significance of the concept of national sovereignty in its standpoints and arguments presented at the Seabed Committee and the Third LOS Conference. A considerable portion of its positions originated from a limited interpretation of national sovereignty, paralleling its stance prior to the Cultural Revolution as outlined in the 1959 Declaration. Hence, it can be inferred that although the PRC did involve itself with international law during the Cultural Revolution, its position had predominantly remained

[41] Hungdah Chiu, 'China and the Law of the Sea Conference' (1981) 4 Md Series Contemp Asian Stud 1, 10.

[42] Third United Nations Conference on the Law of the Sea, Official Records <https://legal.un.org/diplconf_records/1973_los/> accessed 6 July 2025.

[43] Hungdah Chiu, 'China and the Law of the Sea Conference' (1981) 4 Md Series Contemp Asian Stud 1, 14–17.

unaltered throughout the decade leading up to its admission to the United Nations in 1970.

In a certain sense, it is not surprising that China's approach to international law was influenced by its radical communist ideology, which had remained unchanged since its establishment in 1949 and was further intensified during the Cultural Revolution. This was evident in China's rejection of the 1958 Geneva Convention in the run-up to the Third LOS Conference, as well as its open criticism and attacks on the US and USSR during the negotiations. The radical influences of the Cultural Revolution were clearly manifested in China's foreign policy objectives of supporting Third World countries and opposing hegemonic powers. Consequently, China often aligned its positions at the Seabed Committee and during the Third LOS Conference with those of small and medium-sized countries, in line with its foreign policy goals.

What is evident from the PRC's involvement in this conference is that its radical and revolutionary worldview hindered China's ability to fully comprehend the complexities of international lawmaking. Additionally, it prevented them from adopting a pragmatic and flexible approach to negotiations. The PRC perceived the conference as an ideological battleground, pitting the Third World and China against the hegemonic superpowers. However, they failed to acknowledge the emergence of overlapping interests that transcended the divisions between developed and developing nations. The PRC was hesitant to take sides in disputes between Third World countries, only willing to do so if it meant opposing one or both of the superpowers. This ideological rigidity persisted even after the Cultural Revolution ended in 1976, and it took at least another five years, until the introduction of more market-oriented policies in the 1980s, for significant changes to occur.

Nonetheless, the impact of the PRC on the UNCLOS negotiations was positive, particularly for developing nations. Despite its limitations, the PRC's ideological approach played a role in promoting a fairer international legal framework. Its participation in the negotiations was characterized by a strong emphasis on national sovereignty and support for Third World countries in opposition to what it viewed as the hegemony of the United States and the Soviet Union. For instance, its endorsement of the 200-nautical-mile limit corresponded to the interests of numerous developing countries, particularly those in Latin America. This stance posed a challenge to prevailing legal regimes that were dominated by more influential nations and advocated for a framework that acknowledged the rights and sovereignty of smaller and less powerful states.

18.2.2 The 1972 Stockholm Conference on Human Environment

The SCHE, which took place in Sweden in June 1972, marked a significant milestone in international efforts to address environmental issues. During this conference, participants reached a consensus on a set of principles for environmental management.[44] The SCHE was widely regarded as a successful event, as it led to the establishment of a central environmental agency, the enactment of the Declaration on the Human Environment, and the adoption of an action plan. Notably, the conference provided a platform for intense discussions and conflicts between developing countries and industrialized nations, highlighting the intersection of environmental protection and economic growth.[45]

It was a significant event in the PRC's growing global engagement, representing one of the initial UN Conferences attended by the PRC since its membership in 1971. China actively engaged in the conference, exerting influence on the formulation of the Declaration.[46] This marked one of its early engagements in international law-making as a UN member. Comparable to its approach at the Third LOS Conference, the PRC perceived this occasion as an opportunity to lend support to the Third World in opposition to the so-called imperialist major powers. It underscores the PRC's strategy of leveraging UN Conferences to establish itself as a leader among Third World nations.

In a statement delivered by the Chinese delegation at the SCHE, China firmly asserted that the primary culprits behind environmental pollution were the developed nations. According to China, these nations are responsible for the policies of exploitation, aggression, and warfare propagated by imperialism, colonialism, and neo-colonialism, especially those pursued by the superpowers.[47] The delegation condemned the US and other imperialist superpowers for their role in environmental degradation and demanded compensation on behalf of underdeveloped countries. Furthermore, the delegation grounded its arguments on the principles of national sovereignty, opposing the subjugation of underdeveloped nations to the control of developed nations under the guise of improving the human environment.[48]

[44] Stockholm Declaration on the Human Environment (adopted 16 June 1972) UN Doc A/CONF.48/14/Rev.1.

[45] Lars Emmelin, 'The Stockholm Conferences' (1972) 1 Ambio 135.

[46] For a detailed account on the drafting process of the Declaration, see: Louis B Sohn, 'Stockholm Declaration on the Human Environment' (1973) 14 Harv Int'l L J 423. For Chinese discussions, see: Wang Qing, 'The Prologue of China's Ecological Diplomacy Practice: Historical Review and Impact—From the Perspective of the United Nations Conference on the Human Environment in 1972' (in Chinese) (2012) 6 Party History and Teaching 12. Ding Jie, 'The Beginning of China's Environmental Diplomacy: Achievements and Issues' (in Chinese) (2007) 5 Gansu Social Sciences 168. Xu An, Xia Xu An, and Xia Zongguo, 'Stockholm Human Environment Conference and Sino–US Relations' (in Chinese) (2010) 1 History Research and Teaching 68.

[47] Jerome A Cohen and Hungdah Chiu, *People's China and International Law, Volume 2: A Documentary Study* (Princeton University Press 1974) 1379.

[48] Graham Hill, 'China Denounces U.S. on Pollution' The New York Times (11 June 1972) <https://www.nytimes.com/1972/06/11/archives/china-denounces-us-on-pollution-reparations-to-poor-nations.html> accessed 6 July 2025.

18.2.2.1 A Significant Impact

There were several factors contributing to China's enduring opposition to the initial draft declaration. The Chinese representative contended that the declaration failed to acknowledge capitalism and imperialist wars as the primary societal factors responsible for environmental pollution. Furthermore, the declaration remained silent on the issue of nuclear weapons, which the Chinese delegation sought to unequivocally prohibit.[49] China's resistance to the draft declaration, which had been formulated through pre-Conference deliberations, was so robust that it suggested a complete redrafting of the document.[50]

The Chinese delegation successfully proposed the establishment of a working group and advocated for a variety of its own amendments, right up until the final moments of the conference.[51] A report from Xinhua during that time outlines the ten main principles that the Chinese delegation wished to include in the redrafting. These principles emphasize the significance of national sovereignty in determining environmental policies based on each country's unique circumstances. They also reject the idea of a negative correlation between population growth and environmental degradation, cite 'imperialist wars of aggression' and capitalism as the primary social causes of environmental pollution, emphasize the right to self-determination in the utilization of natural resources and the fight against pollution, and call for international cooperation and the exchange of scientific and technical knowledge in addition to the preservation of the human environment.[52]

Although these principles were not fully incorporated during the drafting process, China exerted a noteworthy influence on the formulation of the Declaration. Notably, paragraph 2 of the preamble to the Declaration drew heavily from a Chinese proposal. This section establishes a connection between environmental improvement, the well-being of individuals, and the economic advancement of nations. It posits that safeguarding the environment is a precondition for economic development and places the responsibility for environmental protection squarely on the shoulders of all governments. Though it met with some controversy, the Chinese delegation managed to persuade other members to accept this proposal and position it prominently at the beginning of the document.

[49] 'Chinese Delegation Makes Statement on "Declaration on Human Environment"' (1972) 15 Peking Rev (23 June) 8, reprinted in Jerome A Cohen and Hungdah Chiu, *People's China and International Law, Volume 2: A Documentary Study* (Princeton University Press 1974) 1377–1380.

[50] Lars Emmelin, 'The Stockholm Conferences' (1972) 1 Ambio 135.

[51] Louis B Sohn, 'Stockholm Declaration on the Human Environment' (1973) 14 Harv Int'l L J 423, 430.

[52] 'China's Ten Cardinal Principles on Amending "Declaration on Human Environment"' (1972) 15 Peking Rev 9, reprinted in Jerome A Cohen and Hungdah Chiu, *People's China and International Law, Volume 2: A Documentary Study* (Princeton University Press 1974) 1381–1384.

Other examples of the drafting process demonstrate China's consistent emphasis on the recognition of state sovereignty and independence. This was particularly significant given China's aim to prevent the Declaration from being utilized as an instrument of 'anti-development' by developed nations. China sought to safeguard not only its own independence and development potential, but also that of Third World countries. Numerous proposed amendments by China underscored the necessity of prioritizing developing nations and highlighting the importance of national sovereignty and equality among states. While some of China's proposals were incorporated in the final version, a considerable portion of its revolutionary language was modified.

At the conclusion of the Conference, the Chinese representative highlighted that the Declaration exhibited enhancements compared to the initial draft and effectively embodied the justifiable aspirations of developing nations. However, reservations persisted with regard to certain principles.[53] In essence, the subject of national sovereignty emerged as a primary source of contention during the conference, with numerous less developed nations asserting that environmental considerations should not encroach upon their entitlement to pursue economic progress.[54]

While there were other conferences in the early 1970s in which China participated, these two conferences demonstrate the influence of China's revolutionary ideology on its positions at international law-making events. However, they do not indicate a complete rejection of the international legal order by the country. Instead, they highlight China's recognition of the significance of the international legal order for its own survival. Although China's primary objective was to acquire knowledge and expertise about international conferences, the proceedings reveal the emergence of a growing power already capable of influencing various aspects of international law-making. Following Mao's death and the end of the Cultural Revolution in 1976, China's participation and acknowledgment of the importance of international law as the lingua franca of the global community only continued to expand. While its ideological rigidity gradually declined, it never completely vanished. The fundamental principles of mutual respect for national sovereignty and non-interference in internal affairs remain crucial elements in China's approach to both international law and international relations to this day.

[53] Louis B Sohn, 'Stockholm Declaration on the Human Environment' (1973) 14 Harv Int'l L J 423, 432.

[54] William Kennet, 'The Stockholm Conference on the Human Environment' (1972) 48 Int'l Aff 33, 37–38.

18.3 International Law after the Cultural Revolution: Increased Engagement and Rebuilding Local Knowledge

After the conclusion of the Cultural Revolution in 1976, the process of reviving and rebuilding China's legal education commenced. This undertaking was a protracted and gradual one, spanning several years and even decades. While the PRC acknowledged the significance and relevance of the international legal order, active participation in events pertaining to international law-making only began in 1971. The revival of the study of international law itself, however, did not commence until after 1976, with full restoration occurring in 1979.[55] Deng Xiaoping played a pivotal role in initiating the rejuvenation of China's legal system and legal education by declaring it a national policy in 1978.[56] A year later, universities and colleges reinstated instruction and research in international law. Additionally, various other measures were set in motion, including the establishment of national associations dedicated to the study of international law, the publication of periodicals, and the development of new textbooks on the subject.[57]

China's recent reinvigorated interest in international law can be understood in the context of its ongoing modernization programme, which was initiated by Deng Xiaoping in 1978. This programme aimed to achieve the country's modernization objectives by fostering a peaceful international environment, cultivating friendly relations and collaboration with other nations, and expanding its international economic cooperation.[58] In this pursuit, international law emerged as an important instrument.

China's renewed emphasis on international cooperation marked a clear departure from the previous dominance of the class analysis of international law, which had prevailed before and during the Cultural Revolution. It was widely acknowledged that in order to maintain and enhance cooperation among states, recourse to international law was indispensable. International law served as a means to regulate and adjust relations among nations.[59] In this regard, China adopted an instrumentalist interpretation of international law, distancing itself from the Soviet perspective that viewed both domestic and international law as tools for

[55] Wang Tieya, 'Teaching and Research of International Law in Present Day China' (1983) 22 Colum J Transnat'l L 77.

[56] Han Depei and Stephen Kanter, 'Legal Education in China' (1984) 32(3) Am J Comp L 552, 555.

[57] Wang Tieya, 'Teaching and Research of International Law in Present Day China' (1983) 22 Colum J Transnat'l L 77.

[58] Chen Tiqiang, 'The People's Republic of China and Public International Law' (1984) 8 DLJ 3, 9. Hungdah Chiu, 'Chinese Attitudes Toward International Law in the Post-Mao Era, 1978–1987' (1987) 21 Int'l Law 1128.

[59] Wang Tiqian and Wei Min (eds), *International Law* (in Chinese) (Law Press 1981) 10.

oppressing enemy classes—a view that had become increasingly marginalized since the 1960s.[60]

Building expertise in international law would be of paramount importance in the coming decades. From 1971 to 1976, China exhibited a sluggishness in joining intergovernmental organizations. It was only after the conclusion of the Cultural Revolution that China began actively participating in various other organizations, such as the World Bank, the International Monetary Fund (IMF), and the International Labour Organization (ILO).[61] In the initial ten years following the Cultural Revolution, China intensified its involvement and became a party to a vast number of multilateral law-making conventions.[62] Subsequently, China embarked upon participation in the international legislative and judicial processes. In 1982, a Chinese representative was elected to the UN International Law Commission and later nominated as a judge to the International Court of Justice in 1984. Additionally, China joined the UN International Trade Law Commission in 1982. All these developments necessitated that China rapidly cultivated expertise and knowledge in international law.

Immediately following the Cultural Revolution, China experienced a dearth of international legal experts, as the majority of them fell victim to persecution during this tumultuous period. Consequently, China faced a severe scarcity of proficient Chinese international lawyers and educators, accompanied by a notable shortage of essential literature and instructional resources.[63] Nonetheless, a handful of international legal scholars persevered. Their instrumental contributions were pivotal in the reconstruction of legal education within China.

18.3.1 Han Depei: Architect of China's New Legal Education

One notable scholar in this regard is Professor Han Depei, who, despite enduring two decades of persecution, made a triumphant return to Wuhan University in 1979 with the objective of revitalizing its law department. Professor Han Depei is widely acknowledged as one of the pioneers of China's contemporary legal education and civil law. His unwavering commitment was to reinstate the credibility and meticulousness of legal education. He firmly believed that the nation's modernization and progress necessitated a proficient and well-educated legal workforce.

[60] Hungdah Chiu, 'Chinese Attitudes Toward International Law in the Post-Mao Era, 1978–1987' (1987) 21 Int'l Law 1128, 1132–1137.

[61] ibid 1151–1152.

[62] ibid 1154–1158.

[63] Wang Tieya, 'Teaching and Research of International Law in Present Day China' (1983) 22 Colum J Transnat'l L 77, 82.

Consequently, his primary emphasis was on cultivating legal professionals who would actively contribute to the reconstruction of the legal system in the PRC.[64]

Han Depei's vision for legal education played a crucial role in moulding the contemporary Chinese legal education system. His focus on proficiency, adherence to the rule of law, international integration, scholarly inquiry, ethical conduct, and a comprehensive curriculum laid the foundation for the advancement of a resilient legal profession in China. This profession has displayed constant growth and transformation in the years following the reform and opening-up era.

In 1980, Professor Han established the International Law Research Institute and the Environmental Law Research Institute at Wuhan University. He was reinstated as professor at its Law School and later became the dean. His mentorship contributed to the development of numerous students who later became influential legal scholars and practitioners. Han Depei's endeavours were instrumental in reinstating the scholarly rigour and credibility of legal studies in China post the disruptions caused by the Cultural Revolution. By 1984, Wuhan University's law department had a faculty of approximately 50 teachers and researchers, catering to around 200 law students.[65]

According to Han Depei, the primary objective of legal education during the post-Cultural Revolution era was to cultivate students' fundamental understanding of the Marxist-Leninist theory of law. It was crucial for them to be well versed in the party's political–legal initiatives and guiding principles, as well as to develop a socialist political consciousness. This indicates the enduring political and ideological implications of law during that time. However, Han Depei argued that legal education should not solely focus on theoretical knowledge but should also emphasize practical skills. This dual emphasis would enable students to effectively address real-life legal issues and actively participate in the legislative and judicial processes. As a result, legal education, encompassing both international and domestic law, aimed to equip a cohort of lawyers, bureaucrats, and officials with the essential legal knowledge necessary for managing the extensive political and legal responsibilities required to position China as an appealing investment destination and a capable member of the international community during the reform and opening-up period.[66]

During this period, Han Depei showed notable academic productivity and influence. He authored a total of fifty-eight papers, offering valuable insights into the development of China's legal framework and legal education, as well as delving into complex legal theories. As a pioneer in the field of environmental law, he

[64] For an account of the tribulations of Han Depei and some of his colleagues at Wuhan University between 1957 and 1976, see: Miao Min, 'The Violent Storm at Wuhan University in 1957' WeChat (12 October 2019) <https://freewechat.com/a/MzU5OTcwNjU2Mg==/2247484729/4> accessed 6 July 2025.

[65] Han Depei and Stephen Kanter, 'Legal Education in China' (1984) 32(3) Am J Comp L 552, 558.

[66] ibid 563.

formulated a comprehensive theoretical framework that advanced China's environmental legal studies. Furthermore, his research on the integration of legal principles with economic development provided important legal backing for China's economic reforms.[67]

Han Depei's instrumental view of both domestic and international law is in line with China's legal tradition and Chinese Marxist-Leninism. The Chinese party-state perceives law as a reflection of the will and self-discipline of the party and the people.[68] Hence, law is inherently flexible and instrumental. This flexibility also applies to China's approach to international law, allowing the PRC to engage in a process of 'selective adaptation', whereby its interpretation of international rule regimes is influenced by local norms.[69] This approach was particularly evident in the aftermath of the Cultural Revolution, as the PRC primarily prioritized international economic law as part of its reconstruction efforts. Domestically, law served economic development, while internationally, it safeguarded sovereignty and territorial integrity.[70] This pragmatic approach of endorsing international norms when they align with its interests and rejecting them when they do not has remained consistent in the decades following the Cultural Revolution.

18.4 Conclusion

International law, despite the upheaval of the Cultural Revolution and the halt in legal education, was never truly abandoned during this period. The notion that China completely lacked an international legal framework during this time, similar to earlier portrayals of Maoist China as isolationist, requires correction. As elucidated in this chapter, China did indeed interact with the process of international law-making, albeit to a limited extent. Its initial refusal to conform to the international legal order proved to be unsustainable, as evidenced by its cautious yet resolute participation in both the Third LOS Conference and the Stockholm conference. These instances demonstrate China's commitment to not only acquire knowledge and understanding, but also actively shape the evolution of international law.

No longer content to hide its strengths and bide its time, under Xi Jinping's leadership the PRC has become increasingly proactive in attempting to shape

[67] Guo Yong, Che Yan and Li Jun, 'Research on Han Depei's Legal Thought' (in Chinese) (2007) 60 Wuhan Univ J 309, 310.

[68] Ding Xiaodong, 'Law According to the Chinese Communist Party: Constitutionalism and Socialist Rule of Law' (2017) 43 Mod China 322.

[69] Pitman B Potter, *Law, Policy and Practice on China's Periphery: Selective Adaptation and Institutional Capacity* (Routledge 2011) 56–61.

[70] Phil CW Chan, 'China's Approaches to International Law since the Opium War' (2014) 27 Leiden J Int'l L 859, 871-875.

international law.[71] Although international law is formally impartial, it cannot be denied that it reflects the preferences of those who have influenced its development. China firmly believes that the majority of the international legal framework was established without its presence or when it lacked sufficient influence. While discussion of China's aspirations for a future international legal order is beyond the scope of this chapter, its experiences during the Cultural Revolution remain pertinent for comprehending China's current perspectives.[72] As highlighted at the outset of this chapter, China's fundamental outlook on international law and relations has remained consistent throughout its seventy-year history. This necessitates a serious consideration of the PRC's history, including the period of what was known as 'legal nihilism'.

First, the concept of national sovereignty is fundamental to China's notions of international law. This principle has been consistently upheld throughout China's contemporary history. Despite China's limited expertise in the field of international law of the sea, it has consistently emphasized the criticality of national sovereignty, enabling the country to adopt resolute and firm stances on several specific matters pertaining to the law of the sea, including the rights of nations to establish their own territorial waters.

Second, China perceives the domestic and international legal orders as closely interconnected.[73] Consequently, its understanding of law, both domestically and internationally, is influenced by an instrumentalist perspective. As mentioned earlier, this perspective is rooted in Marxist-Leninist ideology and traditional Chinese legal culture, which views law primarily as a political and administrative tool for maintaining social order.[74] Therefore, law is seen as a means to achieve certain goals, and these goals have remained consistent since the establishment of the PRC. These goals include restoring China to 'a position of material prosperity and political strength'.[75] During the Cultural Revolution, however, there was a radical interpretation of how to achieve these goals, which marginalized the role of law and institutions, leading to an initial rejection of the international legal order. This position was swiftly reversed, though, and the subsequent resurgence of law as a

[71] Charles Clover, 'Xi Jinping Signals Departure from Low-Profile Policy' Financial Times (20 October 2017) <https://www.ft.com/content/05cd86a6-b552-11e7-a398-73d59db9e399> accessed 6 July 2025.

[72] For an attempt at identifying elements that would reflect Chinese ideas for a future international legal framework, see: Björn Ahl, 'Chinese Positions on Global Constitutionalism, Community of Common Destiny for Mankind and the Future of International Law' (2021) 9 Chinese J Comp L 304.

[73] Björn Ahl, 'China's New Global Presence and Its Position towards Public International Law: Obeying, Using or Shaping?' in Lutz-Christian Wolff, Chao Xi, and Jenny Chan (eds), *Legal Dimensions of China's Belt and Road Initiative* (Wolters Kluwer 2016) 482–483.

[74] Jacques deLisle, 'China's Legal System' in William A Joseph (ed), *Politics in China: An Introduction* (Oxford University Press 2014). Donald Clarke, 'Order and Law in China' (2020) GW Law Faculty Publications & Other Works <https://scholarship.law.gwu.edu/faculty_publications/1506> accessed 6 July 2025.

[75] Rogier Creemers, 'Party Ideology and Chinese Law' in Rogier Creemers and Susan Trevaskes (eds), *Law and the Party in China: Ideology and Organisation* (Cambridge University Press 2020) 36.

crucial instrument for reform enabled China to adopt a pragmatic approach and demonstrate flexibility in its engagement with the international legal order.

As China assumes an expanding role as an influential global policymaker, it becomes imperative to delve into its historical background and explore how this shapes its perspectives on the world and the international legal framework. This chapter addresses a less explored facet of China's international legal history and demonstrates that ideological conceptions of law and the international legal order have exhibited noteworthy consistency throughout the PRC's past. The Cultural Revolution, however, marked a period of extreme and inflexible interpretation of these conceptions. While subsequent shifts have occurred, the fundamental ideas have endured. Ultimately, comprehending the significance and historical contexts of these ideas will enable a more nuanced understanding of contemporary trends and developments in China's engagement with international law.

19

Human Rights and Democracy for All under Heaven in China

Historical Engagements with Two Challenging Principles

Eva Pils[*]

19.1 Introduction

According to its Constitution,[1] the People's Republic of China ('China') is a democracy that 'respects and protects' human rights. As its leaders frequently assert, however, China is not—nor (in their view) should it be—a 'Western' constitutional democracy,[2] and the Chinese Communist Party ('the CCP' or 'the Party') rejects Western liberalism.[3] Since 2013 PRC leaders have claimed to be upholding 'human rights with Chinese characteristics',[4] and since 2019 the Party has propagated the notion that China is a 'whole-process democracy' and as such, superior to democracy's 'Western' forms.[5]

* The author notes her thanks to the Alexander von Humboldt Foundation for generous funding that contributed to work on this project, and to Nathalie Schneider for excellent research assistance.

1 Constitution of the People's Republic of China (1982, last amended in 2018), arts 1–3 and 33.

2 ChinaFile. 2013. 'Document 9: A ChinaFile Translation'. https://www.chinafile.com/document-9-chinafile-translation accessed 4 July 2025 (关于当前意识形态领域情况的通报), Zhongbanfa [2013] No.9, https://chinadigitaltimes.net/chinese/309756.html.

3 Wang, Fengqing, [Resolutely resisting and fighting liberalism (坚决防止和反对自由主义). *Theory*, 5 March 2018. http://theory.people.com.cn/n1/2018/0503/c40531-29961796.html, accessed 4 July 2025, Global Times, 2024. 'Chinese Whole-Process People's Democracy Fully Demonstrated by Two Sessions', March 2024. https://www.globaltimes.cn/page/202403/1308069.shtml, accessed 4 July 2025, Tang, Yalin, 'Whole-Process People's Democracy: A Manifestation of and Contribution to Democracy in the New Era (全过程人民民主：新时代中国民主的新形态与新贡献),' People's Daily, 6 March 2025, http://www.npc.gov.cn/npc/c2/c30834/202503/t20250306_443523.html#:~:text; accessed 4 July 2025, Holbig, Heike, 2022. 'Official Visions of Democracy in Xi Jinping's China', accessed 7 September 2024, https://www.giga-hamburg.de/en/publications/contributions/official-visions-of-democracy-in-china; Yeh, Ming-Deh, 'A Study of Xi's Anti-Western Thought and Policy' (习近平"反西方"思想与政策之研究), Prospect and Policy, https://www.mjib.gov.tw/FileUploads/eBooks/c350a6234069477c9cb3e02bf501c51d/Section_file/250d22c1f935481bb52cb57bc3a03751.pdf;

4 'Human Rights with Chinese Characteristics' is used in China's Country Report to the UN Human Rights Council in 2013 (A/HRC/WG.6/17/CHN/1, available at http://theory.people.com.cn/n1/2018/0503/c40531-29961796.html), accessed 4 July 2025.

5 Xinhua, 'Xi Jinping: China's Democracy Is a Whole-Process Democracy'. 习近平：中国的民主是一种全过程的民主-新华网 3 November 2019. http://www.xinhuanet.com/politics/leaders/2019-11/03/c_1125186412.htm; Chen, Stella, 'Whole-Process Democracy', China Media Project, 23 November 2021. https://chinamediaproject.org/the_ccp_dictionary/whole-process-democracy/., accessed 4 July 2025.

Eva Pils, *Human Rights and Democracy for All under Heaven in China*. In: *Histories of International Law in China*. Edited by: Ignacio de la Rasilla, Jiangyu Wang, and Congyan Cai, Oxford University Press.
DOI: 10.1093/oso/9780198888345.003.0019

'People's democratic dictatorship', 'human rights with Chinese characteristics', and 'whole-process democracy' mark inflection points in the history of the People's Republic: historic and momentous transitions in the evolution from the Mao era, to 'Reform and Opening-Up' with its limited liberalizations, to in more recent years the propagation, under President Xi Jinping, of a 'New Era'.

These terms also point to the role of competing interpretations of the concepts of democracy and human rights. They are manifestations not only of the Chinese Party-State's ongoing effort to justify its governing power by coming up with changing interpretations of related discourses and practices, but also of the emancipatory counter-discourses and practices of disobedience and resistance it keeps encountering. In light of China's increasingly global presence as a state actor in international fora, of current democratic systems' many dysfunctionalities and fragilities, and of globally rising support for autocratic governance, these tensions and contestations are all the more worth exploring.

This chapter comments on the PRC's engagement with these concepts as part of a longer history of democracy and human rights in China.[6] It begins by setting out historically competing conceptions of democracy and their relationship with human rights (Section 19.2), arguing that since a minimal requirement for genuine democracy is the facilitation of peaceful power transition, both concepts call for an analysis juxtaposing the perspectives of powerholders with those who confront, oppose, and/or compete with them, and that while the possibility of peaceful power transition is an important test that no genuine democracy can fail, democracies also depend on the successful institutionalization of legal accountability for rights violations. This conception of democracy tracks but also exceeds the—in the view of this author, not fully coherent—requirements of mainstream understandings of UN-based public international law.

On this basis, subsequent sections examine, first, the evolution of official discourses and practices related to both concepts in the PRC history, focusing on the developments since the beginning of 'Reform and Opening-Up' under Deng Xiaoping through to Xi Jinping's 'whole-process democracy' (Section 19.3).[7] Second, the chapter selectively assesses some nonstate actors' historic struggles for democracy and human rights against the Chinese Party-State (Section 19.4). The juxtaposition of uses of 'democracy' and 'human rights' emerging from this account not only shows that nonstate actors have continuously challenged the state, exposing its autocratic and repressive character; it also allows us to assess

[6] Béja, Jean-Philippe, *A la recherche d'une ombre chinoise: Le mouvement pour la démocratie en Chine (1919–2004)* (Paris: Éditions du Seuil 2004), chapter 1; Svensson, Marina, *Debating Human Rights in China: A Conceptual and Political History* (Oxford: Rowman & Littlefield 2002) p. 3 and *passim*.

[7] 'Whole-Process Democracy', China Media Project. 23 November 2021. https://chinamediaproject.org/the_ccp_dictionary/whole-process-democracy/, accessed 4 July 2025.

the success or otherwise of state attempts to reconceptualize the legitimating principles of democracy, human rights, and the law.[8]

19.2 Competing Conceptions of Democracy and Human Rights in Global Perspective

We may initially—and imprecisely—define democracy as government with consent of the governed, but this initial definition raises many further questions pointing to substantive disagreement about what, precisely, the core legitimating features of democracy are. Central among the questions identified by Dahl is the question of who constitutes the *demos*: who belongs, who should belong, who is excluded from those whose consent to being governed matters, and how the process of political participation must be designed for any consent to count as genuine.[9] In the wake of the rise of global governance norms driven by the United Nations, an apparent consensus on some key features has evolved, but as the examples of China and other countries show, consensus has always been challenged and fragile.

The constitutional model of democracy underpinning constitutionalism, liberally conceived (*xianzheng* 宪政), includes free and fair elections (majoritarianism and opportunities to achieve the peaceful transfer of governing power), representation (in most existing democracies), and the protection of constitutional principles such as constitutionally protected human rights and organizational principles safeguarding the separation of powers. On this understanding, majoritarianism is central to democracy functioning 'on the ground'; however, it is not the only principle that must be safeguarded for democratic systems to work. Rather, 'barriers to unrestrained majority rule, none of which would be clearly inconsistent with basic democratic principles', are key to limiting what legislative authorities may lawfully enact, and the protection of those whose views have lost out in the electoral competition, or who are members of other minorities, is understood as indispensable.[10]

Liberal and liberal–egalitarian conceptions of democracy demand respect for human rights as norms that protect everyone from abuses,[11] and require many rules to secure principles of non-discrimination and inclusiveness. They recognize

[8] Gerschewski, Johannes, 'The Three Pillars of Stability: Legitimation, Repression, and Co-Optation in Autocratic Regimes' 2013(1) *Democratization* 13–38. https://doi.org/10.1080/13510347.2013.738860.

[9] Dahl, Robert A., 'Theory of Democracy', *Encyclopaedia Britannica*, 18 November 2019, https://www.britannica.com/topic/democracy, accessed 4 July 2025.

[10] Ibid.

[11] Nickel, James, and Adam Etinson, 'Human Rights'. In *The Stanford Encyclopedia of Philosophy*, edited by Edward N. Zalta and Uri Nodelman, Summer 2024, Metaphysics Research Lab, Stanford University, 2024. https://plato.stanford.edu/archives/sum2024/entries/rights-human/, accessed 4 July 2025.

the rights associated with citizenship without reference to political class or affiliation, and they prohibit discrimination, including against noncitizens, that cannot be justified. Accordingly, these conceptions of democracy correspond to hybrid mechanisms of decision-making that separate the power of the state out into (three or more) different powers and ensure the counter-majoritarian protection of human rights.[12]

This basic approach is reflected in the position taken by the Office of the High Commissioner for Human Rights (OHCHR) of the United Nations,[13] as well as the human rights treaty norms by which the OHCHR is guided. However, the treaties, including the International Covenant on Civil and Political Rights (ICCPR), have stopped well short of articulating a human right to democracy.[14] On the contrary, mainstream conceptions of international (human rights) law have also articulated the need for this body of law to be 'ideologically neutral', suggesting that human rights must be compatible with nondemocratic forms of governance.[15] Historically, the UN and some other international treaty frameworks have been designed to include autocracies, and they continue to be formally inclusive in this way even today, as a glance at the ICCPR and the International Covenant on Economic, Social and Cultural Rights (ICESCR) ratification status of countries such as the Republic of Cuba, the Kingdom of Saudi Arabia, and the Islamic Republic of Iran illustrates.

Moreover, despite an appearance of consensus reflected in the domestic and international law frameworks that have enshrined principles of liberal democracy, there are competing accounts of 'rule with consent of the governed'. Accounts critical of the liberal constitutional account of democracy have always competed with liberal conceptions. They have, if anything, regained traction as the 'third wave' of global autocratization has spread, successfully undermining liberal democracies in numerous countries and thereby also challenging belief in the success of liberal democracy.[16]

Unitary and exclusionary theories of democratically legitimated rule in support of illiberalism have been proposed by political theorists from Jean-Jacques

[12] Sun Yat-Sen's (Sun Zhongshan's) theory of state powers has rightly been characterized as a variant of these theories. Ip, Eric, 'Building Constitutional Democracy on Oriental Foundations: An Anatomy of Sun Yat-Sen's Constitutionalism' 2008(9) *Historia Constitucional* 327–339. Tan, Sor-hoon, 'Is Chinese Democracy Democracy?' The Loop, 5 January 2022. https://theloop.ecpr.eu/is-chinese-democracy-democracy/, last accessed 4 July 2025.

[13] OHCHR. 'About Democracy and Human Rights', https://www.ohchr.org/en/about-democracy-and-human-rights, referencing Human Rights Commission's 2002 Resolution E/2002/23- E/CN.4/2002/200.

[14] Fox, Gregory H. 'International Protection of the Right to Democracy', in *Max Planck Encyclopaedia of Public International Law*, 2008 http://opil.ouplaw.com/view/10.1093/law:epil/9780199231690/law-9780199231690-e773?rskey=Yh0lQI&result=1&prd=EPIL; Bugarič, Bojan, 'The Right to Democracy in a Populist Era,' AJIL Unbound, 21 May 2018

[15] Marks, Susan, *The Riddle of All Constitutions: International Law, Democracy, and the Critique of Ideology* (New York: Oxford University Press, 2000), p. 1–5.

[16] Lührmann, A., and Lindberg, S.I., 'A Third Wave of Autocratization Is Here: What Is New about It?' 2019 26(7) Democratization 1095–1113.

Rousseau (1762)[17] to Lenin (1905)[18] and Carl Schmitt (1926).[19] They lend themselves to an understanding of the *demos* that relegates to the status of enemies those seen as disloyal to the government supposedly representing the People. To quote US President Trump's characteristically incoherent, yet poignant, version of this account during his first election campaign in 2016: '[T]he only important thing is the unification of the people—because the other people don't mean anything.'[20] This approach makes a deeply problematic, exclusionary claim of identity between the ruler and the ruled. It also associates those who do not belong as part of 'the People' with the People's enemies, and it reduces the function of the 'true' People to acclaiming masses content to be governed by the only person or organization truly representing them.

There is an internal consistency to Carl Schmitt's argument that democracy—the exclusionary 'democracy' that Schmitt envisages—and dictatorship do not conflict.[21] But this argument also reveals how malleable 'democracy' can be; it reveals that just because a system is called a democracy does not mean it cannot be autocratic. Unitary and exclusionary accounts of democracy do not only not envisage politically relevant, legitimate dissension among the People; they are illiberal. They also place no theoretical limits on the dismissal or even outright suppression of dissent, a position central to contemporary populism's anti-pluralism,[22] potentially undermining the basic notion of 'governing with consent'. This has implications for the relationship between democracy, conceived along these different lines, and human rights.

First, the state in systems based on unitary, exclusionary conceptions of democracy may still be subject to formal commitments to respect human rights, of course. However, expressed commitments tend to be rendered shallow by the state's opposition to accountability and willingness to suppress even mere criticism based on human rights. Some exclusionary conceptions of democracy claim to be in support of some but not other human rights, moreover, and even in systems designed as liberal democracies, authoritarian practices and discourses can arise.[23]

[17] Jean-Jacques Rousseau's *On the Social Contract (Du contrat social)* of 1762 argued that the individual finds their true being and freedom only in submission to the 'general will' of the community.

[18] Lenin, Vladimir Ilyich, *The Revolutionary-Democratic Dictatorship of the Proletariat and the Peasantry*. Vperyod No. 14, 12 April (30 March), 1905; available in translation by Bernard Isaacs and Isidor Lasker at Marxists Internet Archive, https://www.marxists.org/archive/lenin/works/1905/apr/12b.htm.

[19] Salzborn, Samuel, 'The Will of the People? Schmitt and Rousseau on a Key Question in Democratic Theory' 2017(4) *Democratic Theory* https://doi.org/10.3167/dt.2017.040102.

[20] Quoted by the scholar Jan-Werner Müller in Hotchkiss, Michael, Q&A with Müller: 'Populism in Today's World'. Princeton University, 2016 https://www.princeton.edu/news/2016/10/25/qa-muller-populism-todays-world

[21] Schmitt, Carl. *The Position of Today's Parliamentarianism in Intellectual History (Die geistesgeschichtliche Lage des heutigen Parlamentarismus)*, originally published in 1926, 8th edition (Berlin, 1996), 26.

[22] Müller, Jan-Werner, *What Is Populism?* (Philadelphia: University of Pennsylvania Press, 2016), chapter 1.

[23] Glasius, *Authoritarian Practices in a Global Age* (Oxford University Press, 2024).

For example, US President Trump's campaigns have generally claimed to be in in support of freedom of expression but against antidiscrimination rights, sometimes portraying the latter as dangerous manifestations of a leftist-identitarian denial of freedom,[24] and previous Philippines President Duterte at times explicitly instructed his police force to ignore human rights in his 'war on drugs'.[25]

Second, even theories sympathetic to human rights may be critical towards the institutions created to ensure respect for and protection of such rights, and/or specific aspects of how these institutions have been designed. Situated at one end of the spectrum of liberal conceptions of democracy are approaches such as the Dworkinian one, according to which the judicial protection of rights is not in conflict with free and fair elections and majoritarian decision making but rather complements these principles, as both support a general, underlying, political–legal principle of equal respect and concern.[26] According to this and similar liberal-democratic theories, representation achieved through free and fair elections is a necessary but by far not a sufficient condition of achieving democracy, understood as a principle informing not only the production of representative bodies legitimated by consent, but also the way such bodies operate and the outcomes their decisions produce.

Especially, formalistically democratic practices could result in violations of the rights of minorities and vulnerable or disenfranchised groups such as ethno-religious minority groups, disadvantaged genders, and migrants. They could also be delegitimized in settings without adequate protection of human rights, so as to prevent the emergence of electoral autocracy, in which elections have degenerated to a merely formal exercise without genuine competition for the power to govern.[27] Institutionalized protection of human rights therefore guards against potential breakdowns of *democratic* legitimacy regarding the processes and outcomes of democratic legislation, rendering judiciaries a necessary institutional feature of democracy.

At the other end of the liberal-democratic spectrum are views such as Waldron's greater scepticism towards the institutions meant to secure liberal legal principles, especially the courts. Waldron identifies a tension between democratic

[24] Alston, Philip, 'Populist Challenge to Human Rights | Journal of Human Rights Practice | Oxford Academic'. https://academic.oup.com/jhrp/article/9/1/1/3772736, last accessed 4 July 2025; American Civil Liberties Union, 'Trump on DEI and Anti-Discrimination Law', 2 July 2024. https://www.aclu.org/publications/trump-on-dei-and-anti-discrimination-law.

[25] Berlinger, Joshua, 'Philippines' Duterte Tells Police to Ignore UN Human Rights Investigators', *CNN*, 2 March 2018. https://www.cnn.com/2018/03/02/asia/duterte-philippines-un-probe-intl/index.html.

[26] Dworkin, Ronald. *Taking Rights Seriously* (Cambridge, MA: Harvard University Press, 1977) 223–248

[27] 'A phrase used by Lord Hailsham in a public lecture in 1976. Hogg, Quintin, 'Lord Hailsham', Oxford Reference. https://www.oxfordreference.com/display/10.1093/acref/9780191866692.001.0001/q-oro-ed6-00005117, last accessed 4 July 2025.

and rights-protective institutions, mechanisms, and practices,[28] which lawyers educated in the British constitutional tradition may be familiar with from Dicey's juxtaposition of parliamentary supremacy and the rule of law. Rather like Dicey, Waldron treats representative democracy and rights-based adjudication as two constitutional principles in tension. In the hierarchy of principles, these writers defend parliamentary supremacy as it is regarded as the only clearly democratically legitimated representation of the will of the people.[29] This kind of position lends itself to critiques of judicial counter-majoritarian decision-making as lacking democratic legitimation and potentially detrimental to, if not even undermining, 'the will of the people'.[30]

Of course, 'the will of the people' ascertained by means of free and fair elections may well be to support certain human rights concerns. In the constitutional experience of countries such as the United Kingdom, there are important instances of specific rights being fought for and won through legislative struggles for parliamentary majorities—for example, the long and ultimately successful struggle for legislation to support women's rights. Yet there is also no question that majoritarian support for human rights and rule of law principles is likely limited and contingent when it comes to inherently less 'popular' rights issues, such as the human rights of convicted criminals or socially disrespected groups.[31]

It is that very limitation of popular support for human rights that is central to proponents of populism and 'illiberal democracy', such as the Hungarian populist leader Viktor Orban.[32] The more illiberalism is propagated and practised in a democracy, the closer it takes us back to the exclusionary, unitary, and collectivist conception of democracy, in which dictatorship and democracy are no longer necessarily opposed. But once this is the case, any consent to being ruled is merely a claim made by the ruling power, which typically sees to it that it cannot be peacefully removed, be it by representing the will of the People without free and fair elections or be it by suppressing criticism.[33] 'Democracies' that do not rule out

[28] Waldron, Jeremy, 'Judicial Review and the Conditions of Democracy' 1998(6)4 *Journal of Political Philosophy* 335–55, https://doi.org/10.1111/1467-9760.00058; Waldron, Jeremy, 'The Crisis of Judicial Review'. *SSRN Scholarly Paper* (Rochester, NY, 2024), https://doi.org/10.2139/ssrn.4763558.

[29] In the UK, this concern has contributed to blocking the codification of the Constitution on the supposed grounds that codifying the Constitution would necessarily alter it, as it would reduce Parliament's legislative power to make or unmake any law whatsoever. Loveland, Ian. 'Parliamentary Sovereignty', in *Constitutional Law, Administrative Law, and Human Rights* (Oxford: Oxford University Press, 2021) 19–42. Accessed 19 January 2025. https://www.oxfordlawtrove.com/display/10.1093/he/9780198860129.001.0001/he-9780198860129-chapter-2.

[30] Salzborn, Samuel. 'The Will of the People? Schmitt and Rousseau on a Key Question in Democratic Theory' 1 January 2017(4) *Democratic Theory* 34–41. https://doi.org/10.3167/dt.2017.040102

[31] A famous example in recent years is the *Miller II* decision in the UK. Young, Alison, 'Lessons from the United Kingdom's "Enemies of the People" Case'. *Verfassungsblog*, 29 September 2022. https://doi.org/10.17176/20220929-110346-0.

[32] Orban, Victor (Hungarian President), speech at Băile Tuşnad (Tusnádfürdő), 26 July 2014, budapestbeacon.com/public-policy/full-text-of-viktor-orbans-speech-at-baile-tusnad-tusnadfurdo-of-26-july-2014/10592, last accessed 4 July 2025.

[33] Krennerich, Michael, *Free and Fair Elections? Standards, Curiosities, Manipulations* (Bonn: Dietz 2021), chapter 1.

dictatorship are not true democracies, because they inevitably violate democracy's most basic justifying moral principle.

In summary, competing conceptions of democracy correspond to historically grown and widely different understandings of the relationship between democracy and human rights in scholarship and legal–political practices. In the reality of contemporary autocracies claiming to be democracies, the way the government deals with internal criticism and competition for political power is a crucial indicator of the genuineness of democracy. Different conceptions of democracy and their relationship to human rights are important for the history of official discourses and practices also in China, and it is against this background that we should consider the role played by competing conceptions of democracy and human rights in China's history.

19.3 Official Perspectives: Collectivist and Exclusionary Conceptions of Democracy, Changing Approaches to Human Rights

The idea of democracy, as Tan notes in her aptly titled paper 'Is Chinese Democracy Democracy?', has always been indispensable to the Party's self-legitimation.[34] In official discourse and practice, collectivist-exclusionary, unitary conceptions of governing with consent of the People have generally dominated. Both 'Democratic Centralism' and 'People's Democratic Dictatorship', as principles enshrined in today's Constitution of the People's Republic of China, are Mao-era legacies whose conceptual history connects them to the collectivist-exclusionary strands of democratic theory set out in the previous section.

Mao Zedong's 1949 essay 'On People's Democratic Dictatorship' draws on Lenin's approach mentioned earlier.[35] This essay also nods to Marxism's vision that the final victory of the Communist revolution will make state power unnecessary, and it mainly postulates the existence of internal and external enemies of the People, justifying—indeed, necessitating—'dictatorship' towards these enemies, while also stipulating 'democracy' for the People, *renmin* (人民).[36] The very term

[34] Tan, Sor-hoon, 'Is Chinese Democracy Democracy?' *The Loop*, 5 January 2022. https://theloop.ecpr.eu/is-chinese-democracy-democracy/.

[35] Mao Zedong, 'On the People's Democratic Dictatorship—Commemorating the 28th anniversary of the founding of the Chinese Communist Party (论人民民主专政 --- 纪念中国共产党二十八周年), 30 June 1949, available at https://www.marxists.org/chinese/maozedong/marxist.org-chinese-mao-19490630.htm, last accessed 4 July 2025.

[36] Wong Yiu-Chung and Willy Lam, 'The Legacy of Mao Zedong', in Willy Lam (ed.), *Routledge Handbook of the Chinese Communist Party* (Abingdon: Routledge 2018), 33–36. The complex conceptual history of the 'People's Democratic Dictatorship' is explored in depth by Du Guang, 'The Paradox of People's Democratic Dictatorship—Myths of the Current Constitution Explained', (人民民主专政的悖论––现行宪法的迷思与解读)' May 2013, https://2newcenturynet.blogspot.com/2013/05/blog-post_8100.html.

renmin, 'the People', is collectivist and exclusionary. It stands in contrast to the concept of the citizen of a (liberal) democracy, where no one is to be treated as an enemy deprived of rights.[37] As often noted, the decision who does and does not count as belonging is inevitably the preserve of the Party in its role as uncontested representative of the People. The tools of dictatorship are available to control anyone on the Party's say-so.

The constitutional principle of People's Democratic Dictatorship is complemented by the principle that all state power belongs to the People and the principle of 'Democratic Centralism':[38] The People may criticize the authorities and make suggestions to them ('democracy'), but they must obey a decision once taken; the minority must obey the majority and the lower ranks must obey the higher ranks ('centralism').[39] Complementing 'Democratic Dictatorship', Democratic Centralism assumes a command structure as the fundamental mode of governance. It envisages no orderly competition for government power; its democratic content is reduced to allowing the People to submit views. Democratic Centralism is thus an important corollary to the principle of People's Democratic Dictatorship, whose very point, according to Mao Zedong, is 'to deprive the reactionaries (*fandongpai* 反动派) of the right to speak and let the People (*renmin* 人民) alone have that right'.[40]

Seen together, these principles point to an overarching, albeit not explicitly stated, further constitutional principle: a principle of unity of powers, or of undivided power, justified by a claim to represent the People on the one hand, and a claim to protect them against the People's enemies on the other.[41] As the Party traces this claim to be exclusively legitimated to represent and protect the People to its historical success in acquiring power, the very fact of its power exercise is treated as a justification of its power to 'motivate [others] to think or act in a certain way intended by the reason-giver'.[42]

This is not to say, however, that the vocabulary of liberal democracy, with its emphasis on law, legal rights, citizenship, and democratic elections, has been entirely

[37] Ignatieff, Michael, 'The Politics of Enemies' 2022(33) *Journal of Democracy* 5–19. *Loci classici* include Charles de Secondat, Baron de la Brède et de Montesquieu, *De L'Esprit des Lois*, Geneva, 1748, 111; Jefferson, Thomas, *Federalist Papers no 47*, 1788.

[38] Constitution of the People's Republic of China, arts 2 and 3.

[39] In practice, Zhang Qianfan has argued, the 'centrist inclination has always overwhelmed the democratic counterpart'. Zhang Qianfan, *The Constitution of China: A Contextual Analysis* (Portland, OR: Hart Publishing 2012) 51.

[40] Mao Zedong, *supra* note 35.

[41] These claims are reminiscent of populism, but in contrast to many populist movements, parties, and individuals with political rivals, the Party does not need to garner popular support to stay in power. On populism, *see* Müller, Jan-Werner, *What Is Populism?* (Philadelphia: University of Pennsylvania Press 2016), In this book, the author adopts an analytical distinction between what populists say and do that is congenial to the present chapter.

[42] 'To be a subject of power is to be moved by reasons that others have given me and that motivate me to think or act in a certain way intended by the reason-giver.' Rainer Forst, 'Noumenal Power' 2015(23)2 *The Journal of Political Philosophy* 111–127.

banned from the language of the Party-State. The Reform era, on the contrary, has been marked by expansive uses of liberal ideas partly already contained in, and partly added to, official terminologies of governance adapted to China's post-Mao legal construction (法制建设, *fazhi jianshe*) project. The phrase 'reliant on laws' (依法 *yi fa*), for example, becomes a central concept in the developments following the Constitution of 1982,[43] including the discourses and practices of 'socialist rule of law with Chinese characteristics',[44] and steps to integrate into the UN-based system of international human rights treaties[45] as the PRC signs and ratifies the ICESCR and other UN-based human rights treaties, signs the ICCPR, and establishes interaction with the institutions of the OHCHR, beginning with a 1998 visit by the UN High Commissioner on Human Rights to China.[46]

As a few selective examples discussed here show, these terminologies open up space for debate about liberal, pluralistic ideas within official and officially tolerated circles, even as illiberal, unitary, and collectivist conceptions of 'People's Democratic Dictatorship' and so on remain hardwired into the system.

First is the terminology of citizenship and practices of governance shaped by it. *Gongmin* (citizen, 公民) is not merely a concept that contrasts with that of *renmin* (the People, 人民) in contemporary usage. Its roots reach back into China's indigenous liberal and republican traditions. It is associated with intellectuals of the late imperial era, such as Kang Youwei, and with the political theory developed by Sun Yat-sen, drawing on a larger, much older concept of publicness, *gong* (public, 公), articulated in the Book of Rites: 'when the Great Way prevails, the Universe will belong to all.'[47] This phrase creates distance from received dynastic conceptions of good governance assigning responsibility for All under Heaven (*tianxia*, 天下) to the emperor, or Son of Heaven (天子),[48] thereby affirming social and political hierarchies supposed to ensure good order. As Barmé has pointed out, the notion of *tianxia wei gong* (天下为公) in this liberal interpretation holds a rebellious and revolutionary potential in any setting in which one organization

[43] 1982 Constitution of the People's Republic of China, last revised 2018, article 5.

[44] Xinhua, 'Xi Jinping: China's Democracy Is a Whole-Process Democracy' (习近平：中国的民主是一种全过程的民主-新华网) 3 November 2019. http://www.xinhuanet.com/politics/leaders/2019-11/03/c_1125186412.htm, last accessed 4 July 2025; China Media Project, 'Whole-Process Democracy,' 23 November 2021. https://chinamediaproject.org/the_ccp_dictionary/whole-process-democracy/ See also The State Council Information Office of the People's Republic of China, 'China: Democracy That Works,' December 2021, http://download.china.cn/en/doc/1204fulltext.docx.

[45] An overview with further links can be found on the website of the OHCHR: OHCHR, 'The Core International Human Rights Instruments and Their Monitoring Bodies', available at http://www.ohchr.org/EN/ProfessionalInterest/Pages/CoreInstruments.aspx, last accessed 4 July 2025.

[46] Macbean, Nicola, 'UN OHCHR', March 2022, draft chapter on file with author.

[47] This phrase is referenced and explained, for example, at https://www.chinesethought.cn/shuyu_show.aspx?shuyu_id=2161 and with different emphasis by Barmé, Geremie, '*Tian Xia Wei Gong*', *China Heritage*, available at http://www.chinaheritagequarterly.org/019/019_editorial.inc, last accessed 4 July 2025.

[48] Barmé, Geremie. 2009. '*Tian Xia Wei Gong*', *China Heritage*. http://www.chinaheritagequarterly.org/019/019_editorial.inc, last accessed 4 July 2025.

claims legitimacy as the only one truly entitled to rule, because it rejects dynastic legitimations of ruling power,[49] a connection aptly illustrated by the example of Chu Anping, whose 1957 essay titled 'The Party's All-under-Heaven' or, in Barmé's translation, 'The Party Empire' (党天下), uses a liberal *tianxia wei gong* approach to critique the Party's then tendency to 'treat the nation as its personal property'. As Barmé notes, Chu was disappeared in 1966 and never resurfaced.[50]

Second, the criminal justice process is the earliest area of legal governance to become infused with human rights, even paradoxically, but it remains a site of massive human rights infringements. From the late 1970s onwards, the Criminal Law and Criminal Procedure Law gradually codified rules and principles of liberal criminal justice, including some of the elements of the right to a fair trial, rights-based limits to the power of the state to deprive people of their liberty for the purposes of criminal investigation of punishment, and clear, albeit incomplete, rules to protect the absolute human right not to be tortured. These rules are complemented by institutional reforms to revive a professional criminal process based on the roles of criminal investigation, prosecution, and adjudication, as well as criminal defence. While the laws and institutions put in place fail to result in a decent criminal process measured by basic requirements, while torture has often occurred in the criminal process, and while criminal defence lawyers willing to stand up to the authorities in defence of their clients face enormous risks, the codifications and institutional reforms of the Reform and Opening-Up Era do greatly expand the range of tools available to advocates to challenge human rights violations, and over time lead to some positive changes in official practices.

Thirdly, the Reform and Opening-Up Era also sees some attempts to institutionalize elections approximating credible democratic processes. Efforts during the Reform era to enhance, for example, village democracy and render it meaningful as a mechanism for the peaceful change of government at least carry the promise of bringing governance closer to the principles of Article 25 ICCPR (in anticipation of ratification). Measures such as the suppression of independent candidates at local People's Congress elections remind us that the system remains in essence autocratic and repressive. But the struggles which such measures seek to control show that at their lowest level, elections can become sites for contestation, in which a liberal reading of 'democracy' challenges the deeply flawed illiberal conception propagated by the Party-State

The dynamics initiated by these and similar legal reforms is responsible, lastly, for the growth of a domestic, transnationally connected civil society and (embattled) human rights movement. The pattern of interaction with the international community and transnational civil society that evolves in the wake of the Reform

[49] Barmé, ibid. The author points out that this liberal conception has a 'sinister twin' in the form of an authoritarian Party appropriation of the concept.

[50] Barmé, ibid. Using Barmé's translation.

era is characterised by the dynamics of commitment to these liberal principles on the one hand, and their fundamental conflict with the Mao-era principles, mechanisms and institutions of governance that have by and large remained in place.

Despite the emergence and flourishing of liberal legal ideas, including in particular human rights ideas, in China's societal and public discourses, the system never once experiences the kind of shock that might have seen it change in terms of its basic power structures and institutions. The (from the perspective of the authorities) insurgent democracy movement of Spring 1989, which perhaps gets closest, fails, as do other movements and initiatives discussed below. Throughout the Reform era, the Party-State responds to challenges and opposition by domestic repression and international rejection dismissal. It also avails itself of the security- and sovereignty-based arguments against human rights-based constraints of state power developed elsewhere, for example, in the United States' and its allies' so-called 'war on terror' and in more recent populist attacks on (international) human rights law as detrimental to democracy and self-determination.[51] The threat likened to terrorism by the Chinese authorities is that of a 'colour revolution' of the kind experienced by the former Soviet Union and its satellite states.

It is no surprise that against this backdrop, the Party-State, especially under Xi Jinping, has doubled down on the autocratic principles that are legacies from the Mao era. For instance, 'People's Democratic Dictatorship' and the requirement that the Party 'lead on everything' (党领导一切) are re-emphasised in the language of the Constitution and of political rhetoric, especially since 2018.[52] The current iteration of a collectivist democracy conception in Xi Jinping's New Era draws on Mao era iterations, as it returns to greater concentration of power. However, it is launched in an in many ways radically different legal-political, economic and societal setting, not least due to the shifts and turns performed by the Party-State vis-à-vis human rights and their protection under international and domestic law. These need to be discussed before reverting to the history of official approaches to 'democracy.' As has been discussed elsewhere, the Party-State's attitude towards human rights undergoes a decisive shift, away from Mao-era reservations to what Chen Yu-Jie has termed a 'cautious embrace' from the 1980s onwards.[53]

These efforts' culmination up to now is the notion of 'whole-process People's democracy" (全过程人民民主), developed as an aspect of the 'New Era,' proclaimed in 2019 by Xi Jinping in a speech, and since widely propagated online and further elaborated into a set of arguments about the existing system. In a speech

[51] Pils, 'Autocratisation and international human rights,' forthcoming in Cora Chan, Madhav Khosla, Benjamin L. Liebman and Mark Tushnet (editors), *Oxford Handbook of Law and Authoritarianism*, 2026.

[52] Gruenhausen and Drinberg, 'The Party Leads on Everything', Merics, 2019. https://merics.org/en/report/party-leads-everything, last accessed 4 July 2025.

[53] Chen, Yu-Jie, 'China's Challenge To The International Human Rights Regime', 2019 (51) *NYU Journal of International Law and Politics* 1179–1222

expounding the virtues of whole-process in 2021, Xi Jinping characteristically places 'whole-process democracy' after 'party leadership,' describing it as a form of governance that 'realises the unity of process and outcome democracy, procedural and substantive democracy, direct and indirect democracy, and People's democracy and the will of the State.' and that he considers to be democracy's 'most comprehensive, most authentic and most effective' realisation.[54] The account of 'whole-process' democracy does not set out the conditions that must be met for a system to be democratic, however, and claiming to unite contradictions in dialectic fashion, it avoids committing to any specific process, practice or institution. Its purpose, according to Stella Chen, is 'to make the case before domestic audiences for the strength of China's political system, as well as to throw off criticism internationally of China on human rights grounds.'[55] It is against this background that we need to engage with societal challenges to official conceptions, discourses and practices of democracy in China and address the question of how these challenges interact with international law.

19.4 Societal Bottom-up Perspectives in Civil Society Advocacy for Democracy and Human Rights

Despite the Mao era's rejection of human rights and exclusionary conception of People's Democratic Dictatorship, scholars who formed oppositional groups, such as the China Democratic League whose founders included Luo Longji, Shen Junru, Shi Liang and Zhang Bojun, were never entirely ostracised. Rather, according to Tiffert, the CCP courted such intellectuals, 'appealing to their self-image as successors to China's imperial scholar-officials, their patriotism and their frustrated ambitions to undertake national salvation,' in an effort to create support for the new regime.[56]

Among the Republican-era intellectuals directly engaging with the concept of the rule of law was Luo Longji, who together with Hu Shih remains one of China's most important advocates for the idea of human rights. In his essays 'On the rule of law' and 'On human rights,' Luo contrasts 'the rule of law' (*fazhi*) with 'party rule'

[54] Xi Jinping, Speech delivered at the Central People's Congress Work Meeting on 10 March 2021 (在中央人大工作会议上的讲话), https://www.gov.cn/xinwen/2022-02/28/content_5676076.htm/ https://www.12371.cn/2022/09/19/ARTI1663566683274108.shtml, last accessed 4 July 2025.

[55] Chen, Stella, China Media Project, 'Whole-Process Democracy,' *China Media Project*, 23 November 2021. https://chinamediaproject.org/the_ccp_dictionary/whole-process-democracy, last accessed 4 July 2025. *See* also Cabestan, J.-P. (2025). Xi Jinping and China's whole-process democracy: A new form of consultative Leninism. *China Information*, 0(0). https://doi.org/10.1177/0920203X251361713.

[56] Who 'played significant roles in the drafting of the 1954 Constitution and the development of the early PRC legal system.' Tiffert, Glenn D., 'Epistrophy: Chinese Constitutionalism and the 1950s' in Balme, Stéphanie and Dowdle, Michael W. (eds), *Building Constitutionalism in China* 59–76 (New York: Palgrave Macmillan US, 2009).

(*dangzhi*), here of course referencing the rapid autocratic closure of the system under the Guomindang,[57] but coining phrases and articulating ideas that will be taken up decades later and that feed into periodic expressions of criticism towards the government in the following decades.

The very concept that is currently widely used to support theories of governance opposed to liberal democracy, *tianxia*, is also used in rebellious interpretations to critique the Party. Opposition expressed from the liberal margins of the intellectual elite includes Chu Anping's 1957 'Party Empire' (*dang tianxia* 党天下) essay. As Barmé notes, Chu was disappeared in 1966 and never resurfaced.[58]

Liberal ideas come to inspire bottom-up social action primarily in the post-Mao era, when China's opening, 'legal revival' and efforts to engage globally enable uses of the reforming, expanding legal institutions, of new communication technologies, and of transnational connections that allow for the rapid, albeit precarious, growth of civil society advocacy actors and organizations taking on the Party-State's human rights violations. The 1990s and early 2000s mark a period of expansion of a style of advocacy that fluctuates between insisting on adherence to the law and—precisely because of such insistence—calling for systemic changes that would allow greater democratic freedoms.

As noted, the Party-State begins to clamp down on such efforts almost at the moment they emerge. A stark early example of persecution and silencing of human rights advocates is the experience of (eventually disbarred) lawyer Gao Zhisheng, whose trajectory of being cast first as a hero of top-down reforms of the legal profession and then as a villain attempting to subvert the system within the span of five years creates a pattern seen to be repeated many times.[59]

Overall, the Party-State never achieves the level of control over UN and foreign government-based and civil society-driven criticisms of its human rights violations that it would need to achieve, following the logic of its basic governance principles. If we use the perspective of the People's Democratic Dictatorship, it never succeeds in silencing its critics, whom it must by virtue of the logic of this concept regard as its enemies, at least until the 2010s, when liberal constitutional democracies including the United States start showing unmistakable signs of weakening and decline.

[57] Luo, Longji, 'On Human Rights (论人权)' 1929(5)2 *Xin Yue*, , reprinted in Luo, Longji, *Reflections on my Arrest* (我被捕的经过与反感), edited by Xie, Yong (Beijing, China Youth Publishing House, Distributed by Xinhua Bookstore, 1999) at 59–78; Luo, Longji, 'What Is the Rule of Law? (什么是法治)' 1930(11)3 *Xin Yue*, reprinted in Luo, Longji, *Reflections on my Arrest* (我被捕的经过与反感), edited by Xie, Yong (Beijing, China Youth Publishing House, Distributed by Xinhua Bookstore, 1999) 139–153.

[58] Barmé, Geremie, 'Tian Xia Wei Gong' (China Heritage 2009). http://www.chinaheritagequarterly.org/019/019_editorial.inc.

[59] Pils, Eva, 'Asking the Tiger for His Skin: Rights Activism in China' [2007] Fordham International Law Journal 1209–1287; Pen America, 'China: Release Human Rights Lawyer Gao Zhisheng and End the Practice of Enforced Disappearances,' 14 August 2023, https://pen.org/china-release-human-rights-lawyer-gao-zhisheng-and-end-the-practice-of-enforced-disappearances/, last accessed 4 July 2025.

Advocacy for liberal democracy adapts to shifting official discourses and practices of the post-Mao era. The 'Democracy Wall' movement of 1979 and the protest movement leading up to 4 June 1989 bookend a decade of (in the PRC) unprecedented liberal opening that leads to experimental discussions on separating the power of the Party from that of the State—thus creating a requirement for Party control of the state to be justified and for curbing the power of the Party-State through law, even if 'success' of the 1989 movement would not, at least not from the perspective of the organizers, have entailed ousting the Party.[60]

Seen from this perspective, the protagonists of the 1989 movement driving the articulation of its specific requests towards the Party do not explicitly question the collectivist and exclusionary conception of democracy that underpins Party-State propaganda. With some over-simplification, one might conclude that the 1989 movement, coming as it does at the end of a mere decade of deepened engagement with the rules and mechanisms of the law, is a movement that calls for democracy without—as yet—clear articulations of human rights norms, as defined and interpreted by the international community, despite unquestionable enthusiasm for the general idea of human rights and clear demands for some specific rights such as that of freedom of expression.[61] The movement appears focused on creating pressure for political reforms that leave the legal prerequisites and further implications of such reforms rather unaddressed.

In the wake of June Fourth, on the other hand, not only official 'top-down' but also 'bottom-up' attention is narrowed and sharpened in focus, shifting towards the specificity of legal reforms that promise, and in some cases also fulfil the promise of, better (human) rights protections.

From the perspective of Party-State officials, as Nathan has noted, there are advantages to commitments to the UN-based international human rights treaty system, much of which China joined after 1989 (even though it merely signed but has not yet ratified the ICCPR).[62] Béja has critically analysed these reforms as part of an attempt to develop China without democratizing.[63] In this context, the

[60] Wang, Dan. 2018. '30 Years After Tiananmen: The Meaning of June 4th,' *Journal of Democracy* https://www.journalofdemocracy.org/articles/30-years-after-tiananmen-the-meaning-of-june-4th/ https://muse.jhu.edu/article/721642, last accessed 4 July 2025. Wang characterizes the movement as a 'popular democracy movement' to which calls for freedom of expression are central, but which does not go so far as to explicitly address the tension between a one-Party system that treats rivals for power as enemies, and a system that could afford to allow freedom of expression.

[61] ' Béja, Jean-Philippe. 'Human Rights, A Major Political Issue in Contemporary China [Les droits de l'homme, un enjeu politique de taille dans la Chine contemporaine]' 2019(104) *Communications*, Les droits humains au XXIe siècle51–61; https://doi.org/10.3917/commu.104.0051.

[62] Nathan, Andrew J., 'Human Rights in Chinese Foreign Policy' September 1994(139) *The China Quarterly* 622–643.

[63] Béja, Jean-Philippe. 2007. 'The Chinese Gamble: Developing without Democratising (Le pari chinois: se développer sans démocratiser),' 6 *Le Grand Dossier*, https://www.scienceshumaines.com/le-pari-chinois-se-developper-sans-democratiser_fr_15398.html.

concept of 'development' allows for a conveniently wide range of interpretations not necessarily informed by the UN conception of rights-based development.[64]

From the perspective of advocates opposed to power abuse and injustice, however, including human rights lawyers and other civil society-based human rights advocates, the langue, rules, and principles of human rights offer a platform on which to engage the authorities, admonishing them to adhere to rules to which they have themselves committed, without having to question their legitimate authority to govern.

In organizing human rights defence, these advocates not only give an activist and hopeful meaning to 'developing without democratizing', deliberately opting for case-by-case strategies of initiating change. They also realize, often through their work with transnational civil society organizations with offices and/or resident staff in mainland China or Hong Kong, that international human rights law can be drawn on to support their arguments insisting on adherence to domestic law, and that despite its many limitations, international human rights law mechanisms give them a platform that will not be entirely ignored by their government.

If 'bottom-up' human rights advocacy, at least initially, consists of calls for human rights without explicitly demanding democracy, this is in conformity with the international community and most transnational NGOs adherent to a mainstream conception of international human rights law as 'ideologically neutral'.[65] This conception can claim support from theorists as widely different as Rawls and Raz who, writing in the post-Cold War era, come up with accounts of international law that are less threatening to autocracies such as China than theories explicitly arguing that human rights and democracy are inseparable.[66]

It is their conformity with the mainstream-shaped expectations of sponsors and donors among state and other actors, in turn, that leads to great complexity in the relations between civil society advocacy groups on the one hand, and Party-State agencies on the other. In one sense, advocacy groups challenge Party-State practices and are therefore always at risk of persecution. In another, the Party-State has an interest in cultivating some groups and in maintaining an image of benevolent tolerance.

[64] United Nations, 'The Human Rights Based Approach to Development Cooperation: Towards a Common Understanding among UN Agencies,' http://www.unescobkk.org/fileadmin/user_upload/appeal/human_rights/UN_Common_understanding_RBA.pdf; Resolution adopted by the General Assembly on 17 December 2018 (A/73/589/Add.2), https://documents.un.org/doc/undoc/gen/n18/449/06/pdf/n1844906.pdf.

[65] Scanlon, Tom M., 'Human Rights as a Neutral Concern' in Scanlon, Tom M. (ed.), *The Difficulty of Tolerance: Essays in Political Philosophy* (Cambridge: Cambridge University Press 2003) 113–23 https://doi.org/10.1017/CBO9780511615153.007.

[66] Waldron, Jeremy, 'Human Rights: A Critique of the Raz/Rawls Approach' in Etinson, Adam (ed.), *Human Rights: Moral or Political?* (Oxford: Oxford University Press 2018) 117–138https://doi.org/10.1093/oso/9780198713258.003.0007.

As a result, a hierarchy of political sensitivity and corresponding graduated political control of these groups emerges.[67] Just like outright proposals of democracy, so too are advocacy efforts for the rights of 'sensitive' groups and, indeed, for 'sensitive' human rights themselves unacceptably risky. Civil society organizations staffed by people whose lives and likelihood depend on the continuity of these entities avoid taking such risks, just as the agencies of the Party-State tasked with keeping them under control avoid their total obliteration. The destruction of the fragile networks of domestic and transnational civil society organizations advocating adherence to international and domestic human rights standards would in different ways have burdened, or at least inconvenienced, both sides, and on both sides practices of accommodation evolve, even as the power to destroy human rights defenders remains firmly in the hands of the Party-State.

As a result of these complex relationships, the very mechanisms that enable rights advocacy also impose disabling constraints on advocates working, for example, as criminal defence lawyers, forced eviction advocates, and lawyers representing those informally persecuted, for example through the many systems for arbitrary detention. Human rights advocacy quickly comes to be regarded as attempts to subvert the system by the Party-State. Even if it is tolerated to a degree, the relationship between human rights advocates and their state 'minders' is also always a latently abusive one. Their experience often leads advocates to the conclusion that they must oppose the legal-political system in which they have tried to work if they ever want to succeed in their primary goal of winning human rights cases.

At a deeper conceptual level, moreover, advocacy is inevitably the exercise of human rights fundamental to democracy, liberally conceived. In this regard, some propagandists of 'whole-process democracy' seem to make a point echoed by serious and credible critics of electoral democracy: democracy does not merely require, nor is it achieved merely by, periodical voting in a mass participatory exercise. At the very least, it also builds on everyone's ability to express critical views and engage in meaningful deliberation.[68]

Against this backdrop, the symbiotic-abusive relationships between defenders and oppressors often fracture in the later years of the post-Mao Reform Era, and calls for deeper political–legal reforms come back to the fore. In a communication environment and socio-economic setting widely different from the situation of

[67] Wu, Fengshi and Kin-man Chan, 'Graduated Control and Beyond: The Evolving Government-NGO Relations' (2012) *China Perspectives* 9–17.

[68] Fishkin, James, 'Deliberative Democracy' in Scott, R. A. and Kosslyn, S. M. (eds), *Emerging Trends in the Social and Behavioral Sciences* (Stanford, CA: Stanford University Press 2015) 1–16 at p. 2; Habermas, Jürgen, 'Interview with Jürgen Habermas' in Bächtiger, Andre and others (eds), *The Oxford Handbook of Deliberative Democracy*, Oxford Handbooks (online edn, Oxford Academic 2018), https://doi.org/10.1093/oxfordhb/9780198747369.013.60, accessed 23 Nov. 2025.

the 1980s, these more recent democratic movements increasingly make use of the communication and organization technologies the internet affords them.

Prominent among these is the 2008 online appeal for radical political–legal reforms known as Charter 08, which consciously draws on a century-old liberal Chinese tradition of asserting this and other fundamental rights.[69] Charter 08 calls, *inter alia*, for 'freedom of speech, freedom of the press, and academic freedom'; a Press Law; the abolition of the crime of incitement to subvert state power; and more widely the practice of 'treating words as crimes';[70] and it states that to achieve a better protection of human rights, profound constitutional reform is necessary.

A mere four years after the suppression of Charter 08, the 'New Citizen Movement' co-initiated by constitutional law scholar and human rights advocate Xu Zhiyong extols conceptions of citizenship deliberately taking recourse to Sun Yat Sen's ideas, whereas the movement's specific advocacy campaigns draw on international human rights law rules and principles safeguarding antidiscrimination rights and substantive socioeconomic rights such as right to education.[71] It also makes use of decentralized, 'organizing without organization' digital communication technologies to try and mobilize much greater numbers of citizens. In its substantive work, the New Citizen Movement thus distils the human rights advocacy and organizing experience of the preceding decades of civil society work. It reflects the insight that those efforts by themselves had been limited, because the tools provided by China's limited legal institutions are insufficient, necessitating—from the perspective of the initiators—a wider mobilization of fellow citizens that very consciously goes well beyond case-by-case advocacy. When, having been imprisoned for his work in 2014, Xu Zhiyong makes a further appeal to his fellow citizens in 2020, he was characteristically direct in his call for the President to step down.[72]

Civic advocacy such as that co-initiated by Xu Zhiyong remains within the boundaries set by public international law. It draws on civil and political rights. Even though China has not ratified the ICCPR, it is nevertheless subject to some obligations to respect the provisions of the 1969 Vienna Convention on the Law of Treaties,[73] because it has signed the ICCPR. Even so, the substantive demands

[69] 'China's Charter 08', translated by Link, Perry, *New York Review of Books*, 15 January 2009, available at http://www.nybooks.com/articles/2009/01/15/chinas-charter-08/. See also 'Charter 08' (08 宪章), available at http://www.bannedbook.org/forum2/topic2716.html.

[70] Teng Biao, 'The Political Meaning of the Crime of "Subverting State Power"', in Jean-Philippe Béja, Fu Hualing, and Eva Pils (eds), *Liu Xiaobo, Charter 08, and Challenges of Political Reform in China* (Hong Kong: Hong Kong University Press 2012), chapter 11.

[71] Teng, Biao. 'Rights Defense and New Citizen's Movement' June 2019 Handbook on Human Rights in China, 605–30, https://www.elgaronline.com/view/edcoll/9781786433671/9781786433671.00040.xml; Pils, Eva, 'From Independent Lawyer Groups to Civic Opposition: The Case of China's New Citizen Movement' 2019(19)1 *Asian-Pacific Law & Policy Journal* 110–152.

[72] Xu, Zhiyong, 'Letter Calling on Xi Jinping to Resign' (许志永：致习近平《劝退书》), 2020, https://chinadigitaltimes.net/chinese/635691.html, last accessed 4 July 2025.

[73] Article 18 provides that a State which has signed or ratified a treaty has the obligation to refrain from acts which would defeat the object and purpose of that treaty prior to its entry into force. Palchetti, Paolo, 'Article 18 of the 1969 Vienna Convention: A Vague and Ineffective Obligation or a Useful Means for Strengthening Legal Cooperation?' in Cannizzaro, Enzo, *The Law of Treaties Beyond the Vienna*

of this and similar initiatives emphasize a close connection between human rights and democracy, liberally conceived, in ways that are patently unacceptable to the authorities and from which actors in the international community have been cautious to refrain except in the most abstract of terms.

A recent episode of protests in support of democratic and human rights principles, namely the Blank Paper or A4 Protests of 2022, is a continuation of this trend. The protests were triggered by an incident involving the deaths of residents who perished in a building fire they were unable to escape due to Covid-19-related public health restrictions. In the wake of the incident, university campus and street protest erupted in several cities across the entire country in November and December 2022.[74] While the protest *prima facie* addressed Covid restrictions, it also included chants of 'down with Xi Jinping', signalling the close relation of dissatisfaction with specific policies and broader political resentment.[75] Protesters characteristically held up blank paper to evade censorship. The protests were suppressed and some protesters were later charged with and convicted of crimes.[76] As the Party-State becomes more repressive, and at the same time propagates the superiority of its system over others with increasing confidence, the desire for more democratic participation and better protection of human rights can no longer be based on the incrementalist rhetoric that prevailed in the immediate post-Mao era.[77]

19.5 Conclusion

This chapter has attempted to frame the debate in the PRC regarding concepts of democracy and human rights as part of a longer conceptual history and to understand their significance for global governance. Different conceptions of democracy and their relationship to human rights are important for the history of official discourses and practices leading to 'whole-process democracy' in contemporary China. The history of contestation around democracy and human rights in the PRC seems almost to be coming full circle: contestation about the meaning of democracy in the Mao and early post-Mao eras is followed by a period of 'Reform

Convention (Oxford: Oxford University Press, 2011), https://doi.org/10.1093/acprof:oso/9780199588916.003.0002.

[74] Chan, Kin-Man. 'Unwritten Endings: Revolutionary Potential of China's A4 Protest' 2023(17) Sociologica https://doi.org/10.6092/issn.1971-8853/16877 58–59.

[75] Voice of America. '白纸革命"蔓延 习近平如何应对执政10年来最大危机 [As the "Blank Paper Revolution" Spreads, How Will Xi Jinping Deal with the Biggest Crisis in His 10 Years in Power?]', 2022, https://www.youtube.com/watch?v=3hEFvfnNtGY, last accessed 4 July 2025.

[76] Chan, Kin-Man. 'Unwritten Endings: Revolutionary Potential of China's A4 Protest' 2023(17) Sociologica https://doi.org/10.6092/issn.1971-8853/16877 59.

[77] Wang, Tiancheng, *The Great Transition: A Research Framework for Democratisation Strategy in China* (大转型 : 中国民主化战略研究框架) (Hong Kong: Chenzhong Publishing, 2012) chapter 1.

and Opening-Up' in which legal reform and human rights compliance move into focus, only to be replaced by a particularly anxious contestation in the present era. Once more, the Party-State assertively disseminates an anti-liberal conception of democracy while suppressing challenges domestically and abroad.

This tense and difficult, if often latent and suppressed, domestic contestation coincides with global crises of liberal democracies affected by populist politics and, arguably, a tendency to engage in authoritarian practices.[78] This means not only that competing and deeply conflicting conceptions of democracy are once more in play in these countries, but also that discourses and practices of autocratic governance increasingly take on transnational dimensions. Even though, in the view of this author, attempts to defend the present system as a 'whole-process'—or any other kind of—democracy must fail, an awareness of the history of contestation of both concepts in China alerts us to the potentials for further contestation, and perhaps change, in the future.

[78] Glasius, Marlies, *Authoritarian Practices in a Global Age* (Oxford: Oxford University Press, 2024) chapter 1.

20

The Decolonization of Hong Kong

From the Unequal Treaties to the Basic Law

Feng Lin

20.1 Introduction

Hong Kong (HK), a British colony from 1843 to 1997, comprises Hong Kong island, the Kowloon Peninsula, and the New Territories.[1] Discussions between the People's Republic of China (PRC) and the United Kingdom (UK) about HK's future began after Prime Minister Thatcher's visit to the PRC in 1982.[2] After two years of negotiation, the PRC and the UK reached an agreement in 1984,[3] stipulating that on July 1, 1997, the UK would return HK to the PRC, which would then resume full sovereignty over the region.[4] During the transitional period from 1984 to 1997, the PRC and the UK collaborated to ensure a smooth transfer of sovereignty on July 1, 1997. HK's decolonization was unique, unlike many other global decolonizations, which was notably demonstrated by the limited participation of the HK people.[5]

This chapter explores several controversial international law issues arising from HK's decolonization, viewed through the lenses of historical, Chinese, and comparative law perspectives. Section 20.2 examines the validity of the three unequal treaties through which the UK acquired HK, revealing that the PRC's approach differed significantly from Western norms. This divergence may explain why HK's decolonization differed from that of other colonies. Section 20.3 analyzes the roles

[1] George Beer Endacott, *A History of Hong Kong* (2nd edn, Oxford University Press 1973) 1–4.

[2] The abrogation of 'unequal treaties' was one of the major foreign policy objectives of Republic of China (ROC) since it came to power. But the PRC has been content to leave HK in the possession of the UK until the time is ripe. For details, see Hungdah Chiu, "China's Struggle Against the Unequal Treaties (1927–1946)" (1985) 5 Chinese Yearbook of International Law and Affairs 1, 1. Anthony Dicks, "Treaty, Grant, Usage or Sufferance? Some Legal Aspects of the Status of Hong Kong" (1983) 95 The China Quarterly 427, 427–428.

[3] The Governor-General of HK participated only as a representative of the British delegation. See Peter Wesley-Smith, *Unequal Treaty 1898–1997: China, Great Britain, and Hong Kong's New Territories* (Oxford University Press 1980) 117.

[4] See paras 1 and 2 of Joint Declaration of the Government of the United Kingdom of Great Britain and Northern Ireland and the Government of the People's Republic of China on the Question of Hong Kong 1984.

[5] See generally Wesley-Smith (n 3).

Feng Lin, *The Decolonization of Hong Kong* In: *Histories of International Law in China*. Edited by: Ignacio de la Rasilla, Jiangyu Wang, and Congyan Cai, Oxford University Press.
DOI: 10.1093/oso/9780198888345.003.0020

of self-determination and territorial integrity in HK's decolonization, highlighting that while self-determination was pivotal for most former British colonies, it played a minor role in HK's case. Instead, the PRC's territorial integrity claims, bolstered by historical ties, geographical proximity, and its undisputed sovereignty over the New Territories, prevailed. Section 20.4 discusses the transitional period from the Joint Declaration to the sovereignty transfer on July 1, 1997, demonstrating that internal self-determination, including participation in drafting HK's Basic Law, and ensuring a high degree of autonomy, was provided by the PRC and exercised by HK representatives. This chapter concludes by arguing that the strong historical and territorial link between HK and the PRC means that the PRC's territorial integrity should supersede HK's self-determination, although the PRC is obligated to promote internal self-determination post-sovereignty resumption.

20.2 Validity of the Three Unequal Treaties

20.2.1 Conclusion of the Three Unequal Treaties

Extensive literature exists on HK's colonial origins.[6] According to GB Endacott, China did not start direct trade contacts with Western countries until 1557, when the sea route to China was found first by the Portuguese, followed by the Dutch, British, and French. British merchants imported large quantities of silk, tea, and porcelain from China but exported little, leading to a significant trade deficit by the mid-19th century.[7] To address this problem, the British introduced opium into China, violating Imperial Edicts. The resultant silver drain, together with British merchants' dissatisfaction with the trade conditions in Canton, eventually led to the First Opium War in 1840. Following the defeat and under threat of an attack on Nanking, China signed the Treaty of Nanking, ceding Hong Kong island to Britain in perpetuity.[8]

Witold Rodzinski documented the period post-First Opium War,[9] noting that foreign trade in China remained restricted to some coastal cities. To force

[6] See generally Endacott (n 1); Chapter 2 of SD Ho, *A Hundred Years of Hong Kong* (University Microfilms 1964). Witold Rodzinski, *A History of China* (Pergamon Press 1979).

[7] See generally Endacott (n 1).

[8] Article 3 of the Treaty of Nanking reads: "[i]t being obviously necessary and desirable that British subjects should have some port whereat they may careen and refit their ships when required, and keep stores for that purpose, His Majesty the Emperor of China cedes to Her Majesty the Queen of Great Britain, &c., the island of Hong-Kong,.to be possessed in perpetuity by Her Britannic Majesty, Her Heirs and Successors, and to be governed by such laws and regulations as Her Majesty the Queen of Great Britain, &c., shall see fit to direct." The full context is reprinted in George Beer Endacott, *An Eastern Entrepot: A Collection of Documents Illustrating the History of Hong Kong* (Her Majesty's Stationery Office 1964) 25. For details of the First Opium War, see Chapter 2 of Ho (n 6).

[9] See Rodzinski (n 6).

China to open its capital city and the entire interior to foreign trade, British and French forces occupied Peking in 1858, compelling China to sign the First Convention of Peking in 1860 ceding the Kowloon Peninsula to Britain. Other colonial powers then joined the scramble for China, challenging Britain's dominant position. To protect its interests in China, Britain, backed by its navy power, secured a 99-year lease on the New Territories in 1898, establishing the modern HK colony.[10] All three treaties resulted from colonialism and its expansion,[11] imposed on China through force or threat, and are labelled as unequal treaties by China.[12]

20.2.2 Validity of the Three Unequal Treaties

20.2.2.1 The Concept of Unequal Treaties

The classification of treaties as either equal or unequal is based on the principle of equality of states, which emerged in the 16th century.[13] Dr. Chen, in his book *State Succession Relating to Unequal Treaties*, explores the concept of the "unequal treaty" in depth. He concludes that "two principles—equality among contracting parties and reciprocity for treaty rights and obligations—had been applied in defining whether a treaty is equal or unequal." He identifies four criteria for determining an "unequal treaty": (a) the power bases of the contracting parties, (b) the object of treaties, (c) the strategies employed, and (d) the outcome of treaty application. If any criterion is met, a treaty can be deemed unequal.[14]

China signed all three treaties either following a defeat in war or under the threat of force, clearly indicating that military coercion played a role in the formation of the treaties. That satisfies the third criterion. Historical evidence shows that the other three criteria were also met. Consequently, the three treaties are unequal treaties.

[10] The relevant Articles of the First and Second Conventions of Peking are reprinted in Endacott (n 8) 288–290. See also Rodzinski (n 6) 293, 357.

[11] For the analysis of the two Conventions, see Endacott (n 1) 287; Wesley-Smith (n 3) 149–161; LA Castle, "The Reversion of Hong Kong and China: Legal and Practical Questions" (1985) 21 Willamette Law Review 327, 329.

[12] This view is expressed in two Chinese textbooks (in Chinese) on modern history. See Chung-Kuo Tung Ch'uan-hsi and Chiang Kao Shik, *Lectures on General History of China* (Beijing University Press 1984) 46. Bai Shouyi, *Zhong Guo Tong Shi Gang Yao Outline of General History of China* (People's Publishing House 1980) 378–382.

[13] See generally Katherine A Greenberg, "Hong Kong's Future: Can the People's Republic of China Invalidate the Treaty of Nanking as an Unequal Treaty?" (1983) 7 Fordham International Law Journal 534, 539; JG Starke, *Introduction to International Law* (10th edn, Butterworths 1989) 108–112.

[14] The concept of "unequal treaty" had been discussed by many earlier scholars, such as Zouche, Gentili, Grotius, Vattel, and Oppenheim. For discussion of their views, see Lung-Fong Chen, *State Succession Relating to Unequal Treaties* (Archon Books 1974) 28–52. Dr Chen's view of the two principles in the definition of "unequal treaty" has been fully supported by Greenberg (n 13) 545.

20.2.2.2 The Principle of *Pacta Sunt Servanda* and Its Exceptions

The validity of these unequal treaties hinges on international law, particularly the law of treaties applicable at the time they were concluded. The Vienna Convention on the Law of Treaties (Vienna Convention), signed in 1969, and effective from 1980,[15] codified international law of treaties in accordance with Article 13 of the UN Charter.[16] The Vienna Convention upholds "*Pacta Sunt Servanda*" as a general principle,[17] a customary international law rule prior to its codification.[18] However, the Vienna Convention also recognizes exceptions such as "Fundamental Change of Circumstances"[19] and "Coercion by the Threat or Use of Force."[20] State succession is another exception acknowledged by the 1978 Vienna Convention on State Succession relating to Treaties.[21] Though the "unequal treaty" exception is not recognized by the Vienna Convention, it is frequently invoked by jurists from Communist and newly independent states.[22] Since the three unequal treaties were concluded properly, they would only be held invalid if one of these relevant exceptions applies.

2.2.1 "Unequal Treaty" Exception

There is a divergence of opinion on the validity of unequal treaties between Western and Communist jurists. In the 19th century, the prevailing international law position was that using armed force to resolve international disputes was legal,[23] and war was simply viewed as diplomacy continued by different means. According to Greenberg, most Western jurists believed that repudiation of any treaty was unlawful under international law. He noted that "under the traditional Western approach there existed no ambiguities in the law on this point. Unequal treaties were absolutely binding."[24]

While Communist jurists also recognize "*pacta sunt servanda*" as a customary international law rule, they argue that it does not apply to treaties involving aggression and slavery, as these are unequal. They assert that all

[15] The Convention was the product of 15 years of work by the ILC and two sessions of a 110 nations' conference. For a discussion of the Convention see P McDade, "The Effect of Article 4 of the Vienna Convention on the Law of Treaties 1969" (1986) 35 International and Comparative Law Quarterly 499.

[16] Article 13 stipulates: "The General Assembly shall initiate studies and make recommendations for the purpose of: a. promoting international co-operation in political field and encouraging the progressive development of international law and its codification." See Charter of the United Nations and Statute of the International Court of Justice 1945 5.

[17] Article 26, Vienna Convention on the Law of Treaties 1969 679.

[18] Hans Wehberg, "Pacta Sunt Servanda" (1959) 53 The American Journal of International Law, 775–786.

[19] Article 62, Vienna Convention on the Law of Treaties.

[20] Article 52, ibid.

[21] Article 73, ibid.

[22] See Ian Brownlie, *Principles of Public International Law* (4th edn, Clarendon Press 1990) 616.

[23] See "Yearbook of the International Law Commission Vol. 2: Documents of the Fifteenth Session Including the Report of the Commission to the General Assembly 1963" (United Nations 1964) 51.

[24] See Greenberg (n 13) 540.

unequal treaties violate international law and are legally invalid.[25] Beyond the objective condition of "unequal," Professor Detter identified another prerequisite for such treaties' invalidity: "the treaties should be forced upon one of the parties." He observed that some communist delegates to the International Law Commission (ILC) emphasized that "coercion [is] the cause of inequality."[26] He suggested: "perhaps we have to deal with the combination of two circumstances that produce, together, the voidance of treaties."[27] Despite differing opinions among Communist jurists as to whether the "inequality of treaty" should be an independent principle or not, they all agreed that unequal treaties are illegal and void.[28]

The PRC's stance on treaties concluded by its predecessor is explicitly stated in Article 55 of the "Common Program," its interim Constitution,[29] which reads, "The Central People's Government will examine agreements concluded between Kwomingtan and foreign governments, and shall recognize, abrogate, revise, or re-negotiate them according to their contents."[30] This position also applies to treaties concluded by Imperial China.[31] Professor Chen Tiqiang expressed the rationale underlying the "Common Program" as follows:[32]

> The Government of New China, as revolutionary government, has flatly declared that it would abrogate all the unequal treaties it deems at variance with international justice. This is a revolutionary action which absolutely does not need to rely on the theory of change of a state. Such a revolutionary action, which is just and understandable to the people of the world, has set a correct criterion for modern international law to distinguish between right and wrong.

Professor Chen believed that the revolutionary action undertaken by "New China" empowered it to annul all the "unequal treaties."[33] From his comments, we can infer that this revolutionary change represented a fundamental transformation in

[25] This view was expressed in a Chinese textbook on international treaties by Wang Yao-t'ien; see Jerome Alan Cohen and Hungdah Chiu, *People's China and International Law: A Documentary Study Volume 2* (Princeton University Press 1974) 1119 <https://legal.un.org/ilc/publications/yearbooks/english/ilc_1963_v2.pdf> accessed 17 February 2025.

[26] Some scholars suggested that inequality is a separate ground of voidance. See Ingrid Detter, "The Problem of Unequal Treaties" (1966) 15 1069, 1083.

[27] ibid.

[28] See Cohen and Chiu (n 25) 1119.

[29] It was adopted at the First Session of the Chinese People's Political Consultative Conference soon after Communist Party came into force. See Chinese Society of International Law, *Selected Articles from Chinese Yearbook of International Law* (China Translation and Publishing Corporation 1983) 246.

[30] See Cohen and Chiu (n 25) 1122.

[31] See "Peking MCC Requisitions Foreign Barracks in City (1950)" in Ronald Cohen (ed), *Justice: Views from the Social Sciences* (Plenum Press 1986) 1154–1155.

[32] See (n 29) 245–246.

[33] It is believed that the right to abrogate unequal treaties is the essence of the Chinese concept; see Greenberg (n 13) 546.

China sufficiently distinct from the imperial government of Qing Dynasty to justify the abrogation of these 'unequal treaties'.

Professor Chen's revolutionary theory was echoed by Mr. Tammes, the representative of Holland to the ILC. At a meeting in 1968, he commented on the contrast between evolutionary and revolutionary independence. His views can be summarized as follows:[34]

> In the case of evolutionary independence, the treaty-making capacity exists before independence. The territory and government remain the same throughout the whole process, and the independent state continues to enjoy the same international rights and to be under the same obligations as before; while in the case of revolutionary succession, the new state begins a new life of its own in international relations. It is therefore logical for a tendency in favour of the clean slate approach.

In practice, however, the PRC adopted a pragmatic attitude towards the unequal treaties concluded by its predecessor. It consistently maintained that HK was "a legacy from the past" that should be addressed when "the conditions are ripe and that, pending a settlement, the status quo should be maintained."[35]

On the other hand, the revolutionary theory is viewed as an attempt to circumvent the complexities and uncertainty involved in distinguishing between State succession and Government succession.[36] This theory has not garnered significant attention from the Western international community. Most Western jurists[37] recognize only two conditions under which a state can legitimately rescind a treaty: first, when a state claims that the treaty was concluded under force; second, on grounds of changed circumstances, applying the principle of *rebus sic stantibus*.[38]

2.2.2 "Coercion by Threat or Use of Force" Exception

In his second special report to the ILC on the Vienna Convention, Sir Humphrey Waldock noted that "with the Covenant and the General Treaty for the Renunciation of War ... there began to develop a strong body of opinion which

[34] See speech by Tammes in "Yearbook of the International Law Commission Summary Records of the Twentieth Session Volume 1 1968" (United Nations 1969) A/CN.4/SER.A/1968 137 <https://legal.un.org/ilc/publications/yearbooks/english/ilc_1968_v1.pdf> accessed February 18, 2025.

[35] See A Comment on the Statement of the Communist Party of the USA (1963) in Cohen and Chiu (n 25) 380.

[36] See above Chen (n 14) 13.

[37] Greenberg submits that this broad view of "unequal treaty" is not a customary rule of international law: see Greenberg (n 13) 545. For a discussion of how customary law is created, see Hans Kelsen, *Principles of International Law* (2nd edn, Holt, Rinehart and Winston, Inc 1967) 540–541; See also Hungdah Chiu, "Certain Legal Aspects of Communist China's Treaty Practice" [1967] American Society of International Law Proceedings 125–126.

[38] See above Cohen and Chiu (n 25) 1084; see Albert H Putney, "Termination of Unequal Treaties" (1927) 21 American Society of International Law Proceedings 87, 89.

advocated that validity of such treaties ought no longer to be admitted."[39] Article 2, Paragraph 4 of the UN Charter reinforced this view by stipulating: "[a]ll members shall refrain in their international relations from threat or use of force." The process of decolonization and efforts to codify the law of treaties compelled the international community to address this issue. This doctrine was incorporated into the 1969 Vienna Convention, with Article 52 stating: "A treaty is void if its conclusion has been procured by the threat or use of force in violation of the principles of international law embodied in the Charter of the United Nations." The Vienna Convention, however, is non-retroactive.[40]

All three unequal treaties were secured either through threat or use of force. Their validity depends on whether this exception was a principle of customary international law at the time these treaties were concluded. Lord McNair provides a clear perspective on its evolution:[41]

> The traditional opinion accepted by the majority of writers has ... been that a treaty becomes and remains binding upon a State in spite of the fact that that State was acting under coercion in concluding the treaty, and that the invalidating effect of coercion must be confined to cases where it is applied to the representative of a state engaged in the final act which concludes the treaty.
>
> The last half-century has, however, witnessed a change, if not a transformation, in the attitude of international law towards the use or threat of armed force for the purpose of attaining national objectives ... We cannot do more than mention certain landmarks in this progress: a). In 1919 the Covenant of the League, which placed certain limitation upon resort to, or threat of war.

He concurs with most scholars that *pacta sunt servanda* is the general principle, and the use or threat of armed force does not invalidate a treaty unless applied to a state's representative. Yet, he argues that international law's attitude towards coercion has evolved since 1919.

This view is shared by Mr. Elias, the Chief Justice of Nigeria, who observes:[42]

> Although it [invalidity of a treaty concluded by use or threat of force] is a principle generally agreed- by customary international law, it was not the position under customary international law before 1919 when the Covenant of League of Nations first prohibited the use of force as means of settling international disputes.

[39] See "Yearbook of the International Law Commission Vol. 2: Documents of the Fifteenth Session Including the Report of the Commission to the General Assembly 1963" (n 23) 51.

[40] See "Yearbook of the International Law Commission Vol. 2: Documents of the Fifteenth Session Including the Report of the Commission to the General Assembly 1963" (n 23) 52.

[41] See Arnold Duncan McNair, *The Law of Treaties* (Clarendon Press 1961) 207–210.

[42] See Taslim Olawale Elias, *The Modern Law of Treaties* (Oceana Publications Inc 1974) 170.

We can conclude from the above discussion that this principle was not consolidated into a widely accepted principle of customary international law before the League of Nations' establishment in 1919. The three unequal treaties were concluded in the 19th century, with no indication that coercion was applied to the Chinese representatives signing them. Therefore, this exception could not be relied upon to annul the three unequal treaties.

2.2.3 *The* "Rebus Sic Stantibus" *Exception*

"*Rebus sic stantibus*" is another exception to the *pacta sunt servanda* rule and has been frequently invoked by states in international practice.[43] After studying the international practice and traditional theories up to 1927, Professor Garner asserted that this is an exceptional case to general principles "where either party of a treaty has a moral, if not a legal, right to demand that the treaty be revised, replaced by another or even terminated." The rationale for this principle is that the change of circumstances "must be such as to make the continued performance of the obligations flagrantly inequitable, unjust, oppressive, difficult of performance, or derogatory to the dignity or sovereignty of one of the parties" and "of such a character as to alter in any essential manner the obligations of the parties to the treaties."[44] Regarding the right of the dissatisfied party under this principle, he posited that "the rule merely gives the dissatisfied party a right to demand a revision or termination of the treaty, or its replacement by another." If the request is denied, the dissatisfied party would have the right to abrogate the treaty.[45]

Forty years later at the ILC, Sir Humphrey Waldock's comments on the condition for this principle remained similar: "The change of the circumstances makes the treaty obligations today something essentially different from the obligations originally undertaken."[46] He further observed that it could not be invoked to terminate a treaty but only "as a level to induce a spirit of compromise in the other party."[47] In order to apply this principle, the change in circumstances must be "vital, essential or substantial."[48]

This principle has been well discussed and affirmed as a principle of customary international law by the Permanent International Court of Justice (PICJ) in some cases.[49] In the *Nationality case*,[50] the French government contended

[43] It has been invoked by a lot of countries, such as Austria-Hungary, France, Switzerland, China, etc. For an outline of those cases see James W Garner, "The Doctrine of Rebus Sic Stantibus and the Termination of Treaties" (1927) 21 American Journal of International Law 509, 509–510.

[44] See Garner (n 43) 513.

[45] See Garner (n 43) 514.

[46] See "Yearbook of the International Law Commission Vol. 2: Documents of the Fifteenth Session Including the Report of the Commission to the General Assembly 1963" (n 23) 84.

[47] See ibid 82.

[48] See Garner (n 43) 511.

[49] The "*Rebus Sic Stantibus*" rule was invoked in the "Nationality Decrees" case and the "Denunciation of the Sino-Belgian Treaty of 1865" case and affirmed by the PCIJ. For a summary of the cases, see ibid 509–510. See "Yearbook of the International Law Commission Vol. 2: Documents of the Fifteenth Session Including the Report of the Commission to the General Assembly 1963" (n 23) 81.

[50] See Garner (n 43) 510.

that "perpetual" treaties were always subject to termination under the "rebus sic stantibus clause and claimed that the establishment of the French protectorate over Morocco had for that reason had the effect of extinguishing certain Anglo-French Treaties."[51] In the *Denunciation case*,[52] China invoked a change of circumstances to justify its denunciation of a 60-year-old treaty, supporting the contention with a reference to Article 19 of the Covenant of the League of Nations.

International practice demonstrates that *rebus sic stantibus* applies to both perpetual and long-term treaties. It is widely accepted by scholars for perpetual treaties, but opinions differ on its applicability to long-term treaties. Based on these cases, Sir Humphrey Waldock asserted that the principle could extend to long-term treaties.[53]

In the *Free Zone case* before the PICJ, Switzerland raised three contentions, one of which was that "the doctrine does not apply to treaties creating territorial rights."[54] The PICJ did not comment on it. In his second report to ILC, Sir Humphrey Waldock suggested that this principle should not apply to the treaties establishing territorial rights, a view recognized by the Vienna Convention. However, according to Sir John Fischer Williams, this principle does not apply to "such parts of it (a treaty) as have been already executed."[55] It "relates solely to the engagements which are still executory, to whatever still remains to be done or is agreed to be left undone" because "the treaty, in so far as it has operated as an international conveyance, is intact; it is only its operation as a covenant for something still to be performed or not to be performed which is affected."[56]

Since the cession of Hong Kong island and the Kowloon Peninsula, along with the lease of the New Territories, involved territorial rights that were already executed following the ratification of the treaties, the doctrine of *rebus sic stantibus* could not be invoked by the PRC to demand renegotiation of these three unequal treaties.

2.2.4 "State Succession" Exception

The doctrine of state succession is another exception to the general principle of *pacta sunt servanda*. Professor Brownlie interprets it to mean that "[w]hen a new state emerges it is not bound by the treaties of the predecessor sovereign."[57] Some authors have invoked this doctrine to argue for the annulment of the three

[51] Ibid.
[52] Ibid.
[53] See "Yearbook of the International Law Commission Vol. 2: Documents of the Fifteenth Session Including the Report of the Commission to the General Assembly 1963" (n 23) 83.
[54] See ibid 85; the case is in PCIJ Series. A/B. No.46, p. 157.
[55] See n 56.
[56] According to Sir John, the doctrine of "*Rebus Sic Stantibus*" comes from the doctrine of frustration municipal law. For a discussion of the comparison, see John Fischer Williams, "The Permanence of Treaties" (1928) 22 American Journal of International Law 94.
[57] See Brownlie (n 22) 668.

unequal treaties.[58] However, the PRC has never relied on this doctrine on any occasion. As Professor Zhou Gengsheng, an authoritative Chinese scholar, commented: "The PRC, as a subject of international law, is the continuation of the pre-liberation China, not a new State."[59] This view is fully supported by professor Chen Tiqiang, who stated that "[t]here is only one China, both Old and New."[60] The PRC may recognize itself as a successor government, not a successor state.

2.3 Summary

The analysis above demonstrates that the revolutionary theory regarding the validity of treaties has not been widely accepted as a principle of international law. The coercion rule did not evolve into a principle of customary international law in the 19th century, and the PRC has not invoked state succession. The *rebus sic stantibus* rule, which underlies the "revolutionary theory," is not applicable to executed territorial rights. Consequently, the three unequal treaties should be regarded as valid at the time they were concluded. Therefore, HK was a legitimate colony of the UK. Though China lost its sovereignty over Hong Kong Island and the Kowloon Peninsula, it retained sovereignty over the New Territories. As a result, HK was a unique colony because it had two sovereigns simultaneously during its period of colonization by the UK. This dual sovereignty has fundamentally influenced HK's decolonization process, which will be discussed in more detail later in this chapter.

20.3 Self-determination versus Territorial Integrity: Their Roles in the Decolonization of HK

The decolonization process of a colony is typically begun either by the colony itself or by a sovereign state asserting territorial claim over the colony.[61] In the case of HK, the colonial sovereign initiated the process primarily because the lease term for the New Territories was nearing its end.[62] This section provides a detailed analysis of the roles played by the principles of self-determination and territorial integrity in the decolonization of HK, comparing with their roles in the decolonization of some other colonies.

[58] Greenberg suggested that the PRC might be able to invoke this rule to invalidate the Treaty of Nanking; see Greenberg (n 13) 558.

[59] See (n 29) 245.

[60] See ibid.

[61] Raymond F. Betts, *Decolonization* (2nd edn, Routledge, 2004) 30–37.

[62] Peter Wesley-Smith, "Settlement of the Question of Hong Kong" (1987) 17 California Western International Law Journal 116.

20.3.1 The Principle of Self-determination and Its Application

20.3.1.1 Establishment of the Principle of Self-determination

The evolution of the principle of self-determination has been well documented in scholarly writings.[63] Despite President Woodrow Wilson's advocacy for constructing a new world order based on self-determination, the principle remained in law, as Professor Pomerance describes it, "essentially what it had been before the First World War—a right of revolution, a matter of self-help."[64] This situation persisted until the end of World War II. The concept of self-determination gained much greater practical significance after World War II.[65] It appeared twice in the UN Charter, in Articles 1(2) and 55, bringing it into the sphere of international relations. One writer offered the following summary:[66]

> In the years following the founding of the UN, the world witnessed a period of historic decolonization between 1947 and 1970, over fifty former colonies joined the international order. This trend is striking evidence of state practice favouring self-determination. In addition, the new states added their voices and votes to the process of norm creation, and the new states overwhelmingly supported the right of self-determination.

During the same period, the UN passed a series of resolutions and other covenants supporting this right. The two resolutions adopted at the end of 1960, Resolution 1514 and Resolution 1541, are prime examples of the development of the principle. Resolution 1514, as one commentator noted, marked "another watershed in the emergence of a binding right of self-determination when it was adopted"[67] and has been hailed as "momentous and historic."[68] It has been frequently cited by the following General Assembly Resolutions.[69]

[63] See generally W Ofuatey-Kadjoe, *The Principle of Self-Determination in Lnternational Law* (Nellen Publishing Company Inc 1977) 21. Michla Pomerance, *Self-Determination in Law and Practice* (Martinus Nijhoff Publishers 1982). Andres Rigo Sureda, *The Evolution of the Right of Self-Determination* (AW Sijthoff 1973). Harold S Johnson, *Self-Determination within the Community of Nations* (AW Sijthoff 1967) 31–58; Hector Gros Espiell, 'The Right to Self-Determination: Implementation of United Nations Resolutions: Study/Prepared by Héctor Gros Espiell, Special Rapporteur of the Sub-Commission on Prevention of Discrimination and Protection of Minorities' (1980) UN Doc.E/CN.4/Sub.2/405/Rev.1 <https://digitallibrary.un.org/record/13664?ln=en&v=pdf> accessed February 18, 2025. Aureliu Cristecu, "The Right to Self-Determination: Historical and Current Development on the Basis of United Nations Instruments: Study/Prepared by Aureliu Cristescu, Special Rapporteur of the Sub-Commission on Prevention of Discrimination and Protection of Minorities" (1981) UN Doc.E/CN.4/Sub.2/404/Rev.1 <https://digitallibrary.un.org/record/25252?ln=en&v=pdf> accessed February 18, 2025. See Lea Brillmayer, "Secession and Selfdetermination: A Territorial Interpretation" (1991) 16 Yale Journal of International Law 177, 179–181; Johnson 31–58.

[64] See Pomerance (n 63) 7.

[65] See ibid 9–13.

[66] See Jon Hinck, "The Republic of Palau and the United States: Self-Determination Becomes the Price of Free Association" (1990) 78 California Law Review 915, 948.

[67] See ibid 949.

[68] See Espiell (n 63) 8.

[69] For a discussion of those resolutions see Cristecu (n 63) 17–21.

There exist two schools of thought regarding the status of the principle of self-determination under international law. One, represented by Professor Leo Gross, argues that the "principle of self-determination in Article 1(2) of the Charter has not been transformed into a right of self-determination."[70] Professor Gross notes that "nowhere in the Charter has the right to self-determination in the legal sense been established and subsequent practice as an element of interpretation does not support the proposition that the principle of self-determination is to be interpreted as a right." He further argues that "the practice of decolonization is a perfect illustration of a usage dictated by political expediency or necessity or sheer convenience, and moreover, it is neither constant nor uniform."[71] Professor Pomerance observes that the content of self-determination remained ambiguous because it had not been defined in the UN Charter or any other International Instruments. In her view, the principle of self-determination is merely new terminology which provides no substantive answer.[72] The effectiveness of the principle of self-determination depends more on the political strength of the claimant and its influence in the UN than on "its characterization as a right to self-determination"[73] or "whether a people is qualified for and deserves the right."[74]

Most scholars and jurists, however, hold a different view.[75] They generally accept that self-determination has developed into an international legal right, though its extent and scope remain open to some debate. Professor Rosalyn Higgins comments:[76]

> It seems academic to argue that as Assembly Resolutions are not binding nothing has changed, and that self-determination remains a mere principle and to insist upon this interpretation is to fail to give any weight either to doctrine of bona fides, or to the practice of states as revealed by unanimous and consistent behaviour.

Two UN Special Rapporteurs have taken a similar stance. Espiell concludes that this principle "has become one of the most important and dynamic concepts in contemporary international life."[77] Cristescu argues that the right of

[70] See Leo Gross, *Essays on International Law and Organization*, vol 1 (Transnational Publishers Inc 1984) 273.
[71] See Rupert Emerson, "Self Determination" (1971) 65 American Journal of International Law 459, 461.
[72] See Pomerance (n 63) 13.
[73] See Gross (n 70) 274.
[74] See Emerson (n 71) 475.
[75] Among them there are R Higgins, M N Shaw, I Brownlie, G Espiell, A Cristescu, YZ Blum, etc.
[76] See Rosaline Higgins, *The Development of International Law through the Political Organs of the United Nations* (Oxford University Press 1963) 101–102.
[77] See Espiell (n 63) 117.

self-determination is now both well defined and nearly universally accepted as a rule and fundamental principle of conventional and customary international law.[78]

Given the numerous UN Declarations passed and the wide acceptance of the principle by international community, Professor Shaw posits: "Without delving into the agonizing issue of precisely at which stage the principle became a legally right, it is safe to say that it has so become."[79] Today it is difficult to deny the right of self-determination a true legal status consistently with a realistic interpretation of the practices of the political organs of the UN. The principle has also been affirmed by the advisory opinions given by the ICJ in the *Western Sahara* and *Namibia* cases.[80]

20.3.1.2 The People's Approach towards the Principle of Self-determination

The objective of the people's approach is to establish a suitable definition or criteria to define "people" within the context of the right to self-determination, focusing on the subject entitled to this right. There is a substantial body of literature exploring the definition of "people." In a special report prepared for the UN, Cristescu proposes the following three elements:[81]

(a). The term "people" denotes a social entity possessing a clear identity and its own characteristics;
(b). It implies a relationship with a territory, even if the people in question have been wrongfully expelled from it and artificially replaced by another population; and
(c). A people should not be confused with ethnic, religious or linguistic minorities, whose existence and rights are recognized in Article 27 of the International Covenant on Civil and Political Rights.

Drawing on recent historical events and UN practices, Professor Pomerance argues that in defining "people," "[t]he territorial and ethnic criteria are not neatly separable; they are rather inextricably interwoven, and are bound up with yet a third factor, the factor of time."[82]

[78] See Cristecu (n 63) 21–24.
[79] See Malcolm N Shaw, *The Definition of Minorities in International Law*, vol 20 (Israel Yearbook of Human Rights 1990) 17 <https://brill.com/display/book/edcoll/9789004423046/BP000003.xml> accessed 18 February 2025.
[80] See *Legal Consequences for States of the Continued Presence of South Africa in Namibia (South West Africa) notwithstanding Security Council Resolution 276 (1970)* (International Court of Justice) 31. *Western Sahara* (International Court of Justice) 31.
[81] See Cristecu (n 63) 279.
[82] For the detail of her discussion of the definition of "self," see Pomerance (n 63) 14–23.

Both Cistescu and Pomerance acknowledge the importance of the territorial factor.[83] Professor Hurst Hannum goes further, asserting that "[t]erritory, not nationhood, is the determining factor." He believes that "[t]he primary, and often sole, definition of peoples [is] that of non-European inhabitants of former colonies."[84] While agreeing that "the territorial emphasis is significant," Professor Shaw contends that not all peoples in a sociological sense have the right of self-determination. That suggests that some peoples in a sociological sense have special characteristics: we might call them "peoples in a legal sense."[85] The criterion to distinguish one from the other is likely the territorial element, as it is not a requirement in the definition of people provided by UNESCO, which states:[86]

> [People] should comprise a group of individual human beings who enjoy certain common features, such as historical tradition, cultural homogeneity or linguistic unity. But, as well, there must be a will to be identified or consciousness as a people usually accompanied by institutional or other means for expressing common characteristics and the will for identity.

Compared to other definitions, this one emphasizes the subjective criterion—the will to belong to a people. Professor Hannum also acknowledges the importance of the subjective criterion. It is clear that neither objective criteria (such as ethnical, cultural, linguistic) nor subjective criterion can be overlooked in defining "people."

There is consensus that only a narrow definition of the concept of people for self-determination purposes can be accepted. At the international level, consensus has been reached only on people in colonies and other non-self-governing territories as those deprived of their right of self-determination, despite declarations that all peoples are entitled to self-determination.[87]

20.3.1.3 Application of the Principle of Self-determination

A review of the List of Former Trust and Non-Self-Governing Territories shows that most became independent sovereign states between the 1940s and 1980s.[88] Most

[83] Their view is also agreed by another commentator. See Richard Kiwanuka, "The Meaning of 'People' in the African Charter on Human and Peoples' Rights" (1988) 82 American Journal of International Law 80, 80.

[84] See Hurst Hannum, *Autonomy, Sovereignty, and Self-Determination* (University of Pennsylvania Press 1990) 36.

[85] According to Professor Shaw, "all groups may be entitled to domestic self-determination in the sense of participating fully within the internal constitutional structure of a particular State, but they will not thereby acquire a right under international law to self-determination in the sense of being able to decide freely their own political status up to and including secession from an already independent State." See Shaw (n 79) 19.

[86] See JG Starke, "International Legal Notes" Australian Law Journal 293–294.

[87] It is asserted that all people have the right to self-determination in the 1514 Resolution and two International Covenants on Human Rights.

[88] Emerson (n 71) 461.

achieved independence through the exercise of their right to self-determination, which was particularly true for many former British colonies.[89]

In the case of HK, as Professor Wesley-Smith has argued, the population of HK constituted a distinct people because both subjective and objective criteria were met. Subjectively, "the inhabitants have no desire to become subject to the political and economic systems currently prevailing in the People's Republic." Objectively, "the political, constitutional, legal and economic systems in HK are substantially different from its mainland" and "the inhabitants are in some ways culturally distinct from most mainlanders."[90] Therefore HK people should have been granted "the right to determine the future status of their territory."

Before the signing of the Sino–British Joint Declaration, the UK did discuss the possibility of allowing HK people to exercise their right to self-determination through radical democratic reform and even pushing for Hong Kong independence.[91] That proposal was initiated by the then Prime Minister Thatcher, but was not supported by the HK Governor Edward Youde and British Ministers and officials in charge of HK affairs.[92] According to Wanglai Gao, Prime Minister Thatcher did intend to raise the issue of whether HK people should be given the right of self-determination despite the existence of the lease over the New Territories in one of her meetings with Deng Xiaoping. She didn't do so and was disappointed because China took sovereignty so seriously and insisted that HK must return to China.[93]

In its actual decolonization process, HK people were given absolutely no say in determining the transfer of sovereignty. It's fair to say that the right to self-determination was not exercised by HK people during the decolonization process.

Historically, this is because HK was removed from the list of colonies upon the request of Chinese government in 1972.[94] That implies the UN's tacit acceptance of the PRC's position; that is, HK is "entirely within the PRC's sovereign right and does not at all fall under the ordinary category of colonial territories."[95] As discussed earlier in this chapter, China never lost its sovereignty over the New Territories, with the consequence of dual sovereigns over HK during its colonial period, as noted earlier in this chapter. Such nature of dual sovereignty might well be the reason the majority of countries of the United Nations didn't object to the PRC's proposal to remove HK from the list of colonies at the General Assembly

89 See "The United Nations and Decolonization" at: https://www.un.org/dppa/decolonization/en/history/former-trust-and-nsgts, last visited on February 23, 2025.

90 See Wesley-Smith (n 3) 118–119.

91 See Wanglai Gao, Sino–British Negotiations on the Handover of Hong Kong (1979–1997) (Palgrave Macmillan, 2024) 55.

92 Ibid 56.

93 Wanglai Gao, Negotiation Strategies of Big Countries—Inside Information of Negotiation on Hong Kong between China and the United Kindgom (Daguo Tanpan Moulue—Zhongying Xianggang Wenti Tanpan Neimu) (in Chinese) (Shishi Press 2012) 70–71)

94 The Chinese Ambassador to the UN objected to the topic of HK (and Macao) being on the agenda of the 24th Committee in 1972. For the text of the letter, see Wesley-Smith (n 3) 120.

95 See ibid.

meeting in 1972. It may also be one of the main reasons why the argument for HK people to exercise the right to external self-determination has never been taken seriously by the PRC, the UK, and the international community.

20.3.2 The Principle of Territorial Integrity and Its Application

20.3.2.1 The Principle of Territorial Integrity and Its Conflict with Self-determination

The fundamental dilemma in self-determination is encapsulated in the notion that "[t]he recognition of one self entails a denial of the rights of a competing self."[96] Claims of self-determination often clash with other principles, particularly the principle of territorial integrity. While the principle of territorial integrity is well established in international law,[97] balancing it with the right to self-determination has sparked considerable academic debate. Espiell notes that reconciling these principles raises "fairly awkward questions," while Pomerance considers it the "very heart of the self-determination conundrum."[98]

Examining a series of UN Resolutions can help elucidate the relationship between these two principles. The renowned Declaration on Colonialism asserts that "[a]ny attempt aimed at the partial or total disruption of the national unity and the territorial integrity of a country is incompatible with the purposes and principles of the Charter of the United Nations."[99] Subsequently, the Declaration on Friendly Relations affirms the right of the people of a colony and other Non-Self-Governing Territory to self-determination. Regarding non-colonial territories, it states:[100]

> Nothing ... shall be construed as authorizing or encouraging any action which would dismember or impair, totally or in part, the territorial integrity or political unity of sovereign and independent States conducting themselves in compliance with the principle of equal rights and self-determination of peoples ...
>
> Every State shall refrain from any action aimed at the partial or total disruption of the national unity and territorial integrity of any other State or country.

The Resolution on the importance of universal realization of the right of peoples to self-determination declares:[101] "Any attempt aimed at the partial or total

[96] See Pomerance (n 63) 2.
[97] James Summers, "The Principle of Territorial Integrity," in Jure Vidmar, Sarah McGibbon, and Lea Raible (ed), Research Handbook on Secession (Elgar 2022) chapter 4.
[98] See Pomerance (n 63) 43.
[99] See Declaration on the Granting of Independence to Colonial Countries and Peoples 1960.
[100] See Declaration on Principles of International Law concerning Friendly Relations and Cooperation among States in accordance with the Charter of the United Nations. 1971.
[101] See Resolution 2728 (2024) adopted by the Security Council at its 9586th meeting, on 25 March 2024 2024.

disruption of the national unity and territorial integrity of a State established in accordance with the right of self-determination of its people is incompatible with the purposes and principles of the Charter."

The Consensus Definition of Aggression reaffirms "the duty of States not to use armed force to deprive peoples of their right to self-determination, freedom and independence, or to disrupt territorial integrity."[102]

This overview reveals that principles of self-determination and territorial integrity are frequently mentioned together in those Resolutions, with their relationship articulated in various ways. Based on these Resolutions, Professor Pomerance suggests that "the General Assembly has in no way given any real guidance for the reconciliation of the conflicting principles. It has simply restated the problems."[103] She views the General Assembly resolutions as follows:[104]

> a package of principles, inherently conflicting, is presented without any indication of how a desirable balance might be struck between them ... self-determination is not viewed even by the "New UN Law of Self-determination" as an overriding right for all selves in all instances; it is a relative right, which may sometimes have to give way to the principles of territorial integrity, non-intervention, and sovereign equality.

Special rapporteur Espiell offers a different interpretation of those Resolutions in his study. His position is:[105]

> [w]ith regard to the preservation of the territorial integrity of the State in relation to implementation of the right of peoples to self-determination, both the Declaration on the Granting of Independence to Colonial Countries and Peoples and the Declaration on Principles of International Law concerning Friendly Relations and Co-operation among States assert in strong terms the need to respect and preserve that integrity. Where the territorial integrity of the State is involved, the right to self-determination does not in principle apply.

He continues:

> But even the Declaration on Principles of International Law concerning Friendly Relations and Co-operation among States provides that sovereign and independent States, in order to be entitled to respect for their territorial integrity,

[102] See Definition of Aggression General Assembly Resolution 3314 1974.
[103] See Pomerance (n 63) 43–47.
[104] See ibid 47.
[105] See Espiell (n 63) 13.

should conduct themselves in compliance with the principle of equal rights and self-determination.

The differing views on the relationship between territorial integrity and self-determination stem from varied approaches to the interplay among legal principles. In Dworkin's view,[106] legal principles can conflict with one another yet remain legally binding, requiring them to be weighed against each other. The principles themselves remain constant, and whether one principle prevails over another is determined by the merits of each particular case.[107] Based on his theory, both principles of self-determination and territorial integrity are legally binding. The question of which one takes precedence can only be resolved, in Blum's words, "by the nature of the intended beneficiaries"[108] in specific cases.

20.3.2.2 A Comparative Study of Application of Territorial Integrity in the Decolonization of Some Colonies

There are precedents where claims of historical territorial links made by existing sovereign states have been convincing and accepted by the international community.

2.2.1 The Goa Case

Dr Sureda thoroughly analyzed the case of Goa,[109] a colonial enclave occupied by Portugal for 450 years before India annexed it in December 1961. India's justification was that "Goa formed part of India and as such should share independence, which was prevented by the Portuguese presence in the territory."[110] India viewed the "colonial conquest st destructive of the integrity of India, as a vivisection of India," claiming that "the detached territory should be given back to India."

It is generally accepted that mere "territorial contiguity does not by itself confer title to territory" in international law.[111] Dr Sureda argued, however, that India could contend that Goa was "contiguous to the Indian Union and inhabited by people akin to those of the rest of that state."[112] The reason is that "geographical contiguity would operate, in the case of colonial enclaves, in favour of the nearby independent state." He further noted that the General Assembly "has in recent

[106] This is the view of legal positivism presented by Dworkin. For a discussion on this view, see NE Simmonds, *Central Issues in Jurisprudence* (Sweet and Maxwell 1986) 97–113.
[107] See ibid 98.
[108] YZ Blum, "Reflections on the Changing Concept of Self-determination", (1986) 18 International Law and Politics 441–472.
[109] This case is mainly drawn from Sureda (n 63) 172–177, 329–332; Quincy Wright, "The Goa Incident" (1962) 56 American Journal of International Law 617.
[110] This position was supported by the Soviet delegation in the Security Council debate.
[111] See Sureda (n 63) 173–174. CHM Waldock, "Disputed Sovereignty in the Falkland Islands Dependencies" (1948) 25 British Yearbook of International Law 311, 342. Robert Yewdall Jennings, *Acquisition of Territory in International Law* (Manchester University Press) 75.
[112] See Sureda (n 63) 172–173.

years given a fair amount of support to the ideas of contiguity and reversion to sovereignty on which India based its case."[113]

India's annexation of Goa has been implicitly accepted by the General Assembly.[114] Dr. Blay categorized this case as an enclave exception, viewing it as an acceptable case of retrocession of a colonial enclave. While the importance of territorial contiguity is acknowledged, India's annexation of Goa would likely not have been tolerated if Goa did not have a historical connection to India. It is the historical title, supported by the territorial contiguity, that influenced the opinion of international community. Although it could be argued that the population in Goa constituted a distinct people, India's historical grievance had persisted since Goa's separation. In this instance, territorial integrity took precedence, despite the historical title dating back a fairly long time.

2.2.2 The Aaland Islands Case

The Aaland Islands,[115] together with Finland, were ceded by Sweden to Russia by the Treaty of Fredriksham in 1809. When Finland declared itself independent in 1917, the Islanders, of whom 92.2 percent were of Swedish origin, expressed a desire to join Sweden and sought support from Sweden for their claim. Sweden attempted to assist, but Finland refused to conduct a plebiscite. The issue was brought before the Council of the League of Nations by Britain.[116] Despite Finland's objection,[117] the Council commissioned a group of jurists to assess the feasibility of separating a minority from the state of which it formed a part.[118] The Council determined that sovereignty over the Aaland Islands belonged to Finland. As Sureda noted, "so far as external self-determination was concerned, i.e. the international status of the islands, the criterion applied was a territorial one with the emphasis on territorial integrity. So far as internal self-determination was concerned, i.e. the question of what degree of constitutional autonomy should be enjoyed, the criterion applied was a personal one."[119]

The territorial and personal criteria can be seen as different expressions of historical title and people's rights, respectively. The Commission recognized the Islanders as a distinct entity, granting them the right to internal self-determination. Professor Shaw concurred, asserting that all people are entitled to internal self-determination.[120] However, Finland's historical connection and claim to territorial

113 See ibid 175–176.

114 See Wright (n 109) 631–632.

115 This case is mainly drawn from AR Sureda's book. See above Sureda (n 63) 29–35, 111–118, 233–238.

116 According to Article 11 of the Covenant of the League of Nations, such issues can be brought by a third country on the ground that it is a threat to the peace. See Sureda (n 63) 30–31.

117 Finland relied on Article 15 para. 8 of the Covenant. See Sureda (n 63) 30.

118 See Sureda (n 63) 34–35.

119 See Wright (n 109) 116–117.

120 See Shaw (n 79) 19.

integrity took precedence over the external self-determination of the Aaland people.[121]

2.2.3 *The West Irian Case*

When the Charter of Transfer of Sovereignty was signed by the Netherlands and Indonesia in 1949, the dispute over West Irian was left unresolved, leading to further negotiations that failed to yield any positive results.[122] Indonesia argued at the UN, emphasizing territorial integrity and maintaining that negotiation should focus solely on transfer of sovereignty over West Irian to Indonesia. Conversely, the Netherlands opposed this restricted view and supported West Irian's right to self-determination. In 1962, both parties reached an agreement to transfer administration to Indonesia through the UN, with Indonesia committing to take appropriate steps to ascertain the wishes of the people of West Irian. West Irian was incorporated into Indonesia through a plebiscite in 1969.[123]

Professor Pomerance argued that Indonesia's claim to territorial integrity took precedence over West Irain's right to self-determination.[124] Dr. Blay, however, contended that "this view fails to take account of the events leading to the decision in the West Irian plebiscite."[125] He argued that "despite Indonesia's claims of territorial integrity, its incorporation of West Irian had to be based on a legitimate act of self-determination by the people of West Irian. The General Assembly's approval of the 1962 Agreement and its involvement in the plebiscite would have been unnecessary if the territorial integrity principle categorically preempted the right to self-determination."[126] Dr Blay asserted that the initial intention of the New York Agreement and UN involvement was to promote both internal and external self-determination for the West Irian people. The UN's acceptance of the Musjavarah system for plebiscite indicated its tacit consent of Indonesia's sovereignty over West Irian, suggesting that the primary purpose of the UN was to promote internal determination.

2.2.4 *Summary*

In the three cases examined above, self-determination and territorial integrity were claimed by competing parties respectively. A common factor in all of them was the historical territorial links supported by convincing evidence, with claimants being former sovereigns of the territories. The reversion of these colonies to their former

[121] This case was settled through negotiation between Sweden and Finland. See Sureda (n 63) 234–237.
[122] See generally ibid 77–78, 143–151.
[123] See Sureda (n 63) 151.
[124] See Michla Pomerance, "Methods of Self-Determination and the Argument of Primitiveness" (1975) 12 Canadian Yearbook of International Law 38, 65.
[125] See SKN Blay, "Self-Determination versus Territorial Integrity in Decolonization" (1986) 18 New York Journal of International Law and Politics 441, 453.
[126] See ibid 454–455.

sovereigns has been recognized by the international community. Other factors, such as territorial contiguity and colonial enclave status, also influenced the outcomes. In the cases of the Aaland Islands and West Irian, claimants were required to promote internal self-determination to reclaim sovereignty.

2.3 Application of Territorial Integrity in the Decolonization of HK

The decolonization of HK was achieved through voluntary negotiation between the PRC and UK, culminating in the conclusion of the Joint Declaration, rather than through the exercise of the right to self-determination by the HK people. A Review of the Joint Declaration reveals the PRC's reliance on territorial integrity in several clauses.[127]

Similar to the three cases discussed above, there is substantial evidence supporting China's sovereignty over HK before its colonization by the UK in the 1840s. HK shares certain historical similarities with Goa, having been part of China 150 years ago whereas Goa was part of India 480 years ago. China's historical sovereignty over HK was underscored by the three unequal treaties, and its historical grievance has remained more recent and alive than India's. If India could annex Goa based on territorial integrity and historical title, the PRC is in an even stronger position to demand HK's return on the same grounds.

Geographically HK resembles Goa as a colonial enclave surrounded by its former sovereign, though HK is much larger in size. This geographical contiguity was a factor in the General Assembly's inaction regarding India's annexation of Goa. One commentator noted that "geographical contiguity would operate, in the case of colonial enclaves, in favour of the nearby independent state."[128] This idea gained support from the General Assembly in the 1960s,[129] further bolstering the PRC's claim of territorial integrity over HK.

Moreoever, there was no dispute over China's territorial rights to the New Territories even during HK's colonial period. Since China never lost sovereignty over the New Territories, external self-determination for HK would infringe upon China's sovereignty and violate the PRC's territorial integrity. Insisting on external self-determination would constitute an act of secession concerning the New Territories, which is clearly denied by the UN Charter and various General Assembly Resolutions and Declarations.

The New Territories constitute nine-tenths of HK's total area, meaning HK would lose its international status if divided between two sovereigns. Economic

[127] See Joint Declaration of the Government of the United Kingdom of Great Britain and Northern Ireland and the Government of the People's Republic of China on the Question of Hong Kong.

[128] This is because geographical separateness is one of the factors according to which a territory can be classified as being a colony and colonial title has been eroded and colonial possession made illegal under the present day international law of nations. See Sureda (n 63) 174–175.

[129] The Walvis case is another precedent which proves the importance of territorial contiguity. For a discussion of this case, see Blay (n 126) 467–468.

continuity considerations require treating HK as an inseparable unit, likely influencing the UK to restore sovereignty over HK entirely to the PRC.

The chief representative of the British team (of negotiators), Ambassador Percy Cradock, was fully aware that dual sovereignty over HK leaves the UK no cards in its effort to extend the lease over the New Territories beyond 1997. In his view, China "had only to wait until 1997, when under a treaty we (the UK) recognized, 92 percent of the territory would pass to them, the remaining 8 percent not being viable on its own."[130] This demonstrates that China's territorial sovereignty over the New Territories was the key factor which influenced the UK's willingness to negotiate transfer of its de facto sovereignty over HK back to the PRC.

The dual sovereignty over HK during its colonial occupation by the UK distinguished it from all other colonies. When the Chinese Communist Party took over China in 1949, it could easily have also taken over HK. However, it decided to maintain the status quo in HK, primarily because it was of the view that British governance of HK was to the benefit of the PRC at that time.[131] (The UK also realized that the PRC possessed overwhelming military force and HK was militarily indefensible.[132]) The PRC's intentional decision to let the UK maintain its colonial occupation of and governance in HK was the reason why HK continued to retain its dual sovereignty characteristic for the period from 1949 to 1997. In most other colonies the colonial people's claim to right to self-determination was against a territorial claim of the colonizing countries. Even in those three cases studied above, the former sovereigns had actually lost their respective sovereignty over those colonies. It can therefore be argued that such dual sovereignty characteristic created a sui generis legal status for HK in international law. This sui generis legal status demands a different approach towards its decolonization from the traditional approach of exercise of the right to self-determination.

In conclusion, the case of HK involves arguments for reversion to sovereignty based on the PRC's existing territorial title, historical title, geographical contiguity, pending territorial right, and economic continuity in a case of colonial enclave. The principle of territorial integrity, supported by substantial evidence, takes precedence over self-determination in this case.

[130] See Percy Cradock, Experiences of China (John Murray Ltd, 1994) 211. See also Wanglai Gao (n 91) 11.

[131] See Wang Yu, The Resumption of the Exercise of Sovereignty (Lun Huifu Xingshi Zhuquan) (People's Press 2016) 32–33.

[132] See Wanglai Gao (n 91) 11.

20.4 From Joint Declaration to the Basic Law: Phase Two of HK's Decolonization

20.4.1 The Joint Declaration, Its Binding Effect, and Enforceability

The Joint Declaration is recognized as a bilateral international treaty, registered with the United Nations, which underscores its legitimacy and binding nature.[133] It consists of the main text and three annexes detailing the arrangements for the transfer of sovereignty and the future governance of HK. It guarantees that HK will maintain a high degree of autonomy under the "one country, two systems" principle, preserving its existing legal, social, and economic systems for 50 years after the handover.[134] It is a pivotal international treaty that laid down the legal foundation for the transfer of sovereignty over HK from the UK to the PRC on July 1, 1997.

One controversial issue after the change of sovereignty is the continuing binding effect of the Joint Declaration. Under international law, treaties are binding on the parties that sign them, and the Joint Declaration was crafted to ensure that the commitments made by both the UK and the PRC were clear and enforceable. The UK has repeatedly emphasized that the Joint Declaration remains a legally binding treaty and urged the PRC to honor its commitments.[135] However, the PRC's stance is that the Joint Declaration is a historical document in that its key contents (such as transfer of sovereignty and transitional arrangements) had been implemented by July 1, 1997. As a result, the Joint Declaration no longer holds any practical significance and the governance of HK after its change of sovereignty is now solely a domestic matter for the PRC, which no foreign country should interfere with.[136] Actually, both the UK and the PRC agree that the Joint Declaration is a binding treaty. The difference in their opinion lies in whether there were still obligations thereunder which the PRC has not fulfilled or breached, which the UK has a treaty right to urge the PRC to honor. The different positions of the UK and the PRC reflect their divergent interpretations of the Joint Declaration.

Even if the Joint Declaration remains a binding treaty, its enforceability is another problem. This is because the Joint Declaration does not specify any international oversight body or arbitration mechanism to address disputes arising from

[133] See Registration Number 23391: Joint Declaration on the question of Hong Kong, at: https://treaties.un.org/Pages/showDetails.aspx?objid=08000002800d4d6e, accessed on 15 March 2025.

[134] Ibid.

[135] See Louisa Brooke-Holland, "Hong Kong: the Joint Declaration, Research Briefing, 5 July, 2019, at: https://commonslibrary.parliament.uk/research-briefings/cbp-8616/, accessed on March 15, 2025.

[136] China emphasised that the authority to govern HK derives from Chinese Constitution and the Basic Law, not authorization of the Joint Declaration. See "The Practice of the 'One Country, Two Systems" Policy in the Hong Kong Special Administrative Region, at: https://english.www.gov.cn/archive/white_paper/2014/08/23/content_281474982986578.htm, accessed on March 15, 2025.

its implementation. This lack of enforcement mechanism means that the adherence to its terms relies heavily on the goodwill and diplomatic relations between the UK and the PRC.

In practice, the enforceability of the Joint Declaration has been challenged by developments in Hong Kong post-1997. Critics argue that certain actions taken by the PRC towards Hong Kong (HK) have undermined the autonomy promised under the Joint Declaration, such as the introduction of the National Security Law in 2020, which many view as a direct infringement on HK's high degree of autonomy. These actions have led to international criticism and calls for the PRC to adhere to its commitments under the Joint Declaration. The ongoing situation in HK concerning enforcement of the National Security Law[137] serves as a poignant example of the difficulties in enforcing international treaties when geopolitical interests and interpretations diverge.

20.4.2 The Drafting of the Basic Law and Roles of the HK Representatives

Following the conclusion of the Joint Declaration, HK entered into the second phase of its decolonization process: the transitional period for the transfer of sovereignty and administration from the UK to the PRC, which lasted from 1985 to 1997.[138] The PRC announced a series of basic policies in the Joint Declaration for HK after the resumption of its sovereignty in 1997, including one country, two systems; a high degree of autonomy; and HK people rule HK.[139] As stipulated in the Joint Declaration, these policies were to be incorporated into a constitutional document for HK, known as the Basic Law, and remain unchanged for 50 years.[140] Both countries agreed to establish a Sino–British Joint Liaison Group to implement the Joint Declaration.[141]

The most important implementation of the Joint Declaration is to draft a new constitutional document for HK, the Basic Law, to incorporate those Chinese policies. During the drafting process, there were 23 representatives from HK among 59 members of the drafting committee.[142] Although these representatives

[137] The trial of Lai Chee-ying is one example. He was charged with allegedly conspiring and colluding with foreign forces to endanger national security. See, Jimmy Lai Trial, at: https://www.scmp.com/topics/jimmy-lai-trial, accessed on March 15, 2025.

[138] Yash Ghai, Hong Kong's New Constitutional Order (2nd ed, Hong Kong University Press, 1999) chapter 2.

[139] See Article 3, Joint Declaration of the Government of the United Kingdom of Great Britain and Northern Ireland and the Government of the People's Republic of China on the Question of Hong Kong.

[140] See Article 2, Paragraph 12, ibid.

[141] See Article 5, ibid.

[142] See Drafting and Promulgation of the Basic Law and Hong Kong's Reunification with the Motherland, p. 3, at: https://www.basiclaw.gov.hk/filemanager/content/en/files/anniversary-reunification15/anniversary-reunification15-ch1-3.pdf, accessed on March 15, 2025.

were selected from various sectors of HK society by the PRC, they arguably represented, to a certain extent, the voices of HK people.[143] They played crucial roles in ensuring that the Basic Law would reflect HK's unique characteristics and aspirations. Here are a few examples of positive contributions made by HK representatives in the drafting process. First, they were instrumental in advocating for provisions that ensured a high degree of autonomy for HK under the 'one country, two systems' framework. They worked to incorporate language that would protect HK's independent legal, economic, and administrative systems, ensuring that HK could maintain its distinct identity and governance structure post-1997.[144] Second, HK representatives were pivotal in securing the continuation of the common law legal system and the independence of the judiciary. They ensured that the Basic Law included provisions for the establishment of the Court of Final Appeal, which would have the authority to interpret the Basic Law and uphold legal principles independently from mainland China.[145] Third, HK representatives played a key role in embedding protections for fundamental rights and freedoms within the Basic Law. They emphasized the importance of safeguarding freedoms of speech, assembly, and the press, as well as ensuring the protection of private property rights. These efforts were crucial in maintaining HK's status as a free and open society.[146] Fourth, they contributed to the drafting of economic provisions that would allow the region to continue thriving as a global financial center. They advocated for maintaining HK's separate customs territory, its ability to enter into international trade agreements, and the preservation of its capitalist system, ensuring that the region could continue to attract international business and investment.[147]

These are just a few examples of positive contributions made by HK representatives during the drafting process. They were essential in shaping a Basic Law that aimed to preserve HK's autonomy and freedoms while facilitating a smooth transition of sovereignty from the UK to the PRC. Their efforts were crucial in addressing the concerns and aspirations of HK people and ensuring that the Basic Law would serve as a foundation for HK's governance and development in the years following the handover.

143 Ibid.

144 See "Compilation of Documents of the Drafting Committee of the Basic Law of the HK Special Administrative Region of the PRC, HK and Macao Affairs Office, 1988 (《中华人民共和国香港特别行政区基本法起草委员会文件汇编》 (国务院港澳办, 1988)).

145 See Xiao Weiyun, The Birth of Hong Kong Basic Law (Peking University Press, 1990) 112–115 (肖蔚云著 《香港基本法的诞生》 ，北京大学出版社, 1990年, 第112–115页。)

146 See "The Report of the Special Committee on Rights and Obligations of Residents by the Drafting Committee of the HK Basic Law, 1988 (《香港基本法起草委员会居民权利与义务专题小组报告》 (1988年)).

147 See "Minutes of the Special Committee on the Topic of Economy of the Drafting Committee of HK Basic Law" (《香港基本法起草委员会经济专题小组会议纪要》(1987年, 第四次会议)) 。

20.4.3 The Basic Law, High Degree of Autonomy (Internal Self-determination), and Its Exercise

20.4.3.1 Incorporation of High Degree of Autonomy in the Basic Law

The Basic Law was enacted by the National People's Congress, the PRC's national legislature, in 1990 and became effective on July 1, 1997.[148] It fully incorporated those basic policies declared by the PRC in the Joint Declaration. It asserts that HK has been part of China's territory since ancient times and emphasizes the necessity to uphold national unity and territorial integrity. The Basic Law explicitly states that the PRC will not implement a socialist system and policies in HK.[149] Second, the Basic Law focuses on the economic stability and prosperity of HK, the primary goal of the Joint Declaration. Given HK's economic importance to the PRC in the 1990s, the latter had a strong incentive to keep the status quo, aligning with the pragmatic tradition established during British rule.[150] Third, under the Basic Law, HK enjoys autonomy over all matters except for foreign affairs and defence. Even in these areas, HK also has a voice when its interests are affected.[151] Fourth, HK's common law system continues, therefore reinforcing its high degree of autonomy.[152] Fifth, with the two international human rights covenants remaining part of HK law and with the enactment of a Bill of Rights Ordinance, the PRC's policies concerning HK are subject to international scrutiny and local judicial oversight.[153] This overview indicates that HK has been granted a high degree of autonomy, or internal self-determination, under the Basic Law.

20.4.3.2 Implementation of High Degree of Autonomy

From 1997 to 2025, HK's high degree of autonomy under the "one country, two systems" framework has manifested in various ways. Here are a few examples illustrating how this high degree of autonomy has operated in practice. The first relates to its independent legal system. HK has maintained its common law legal system, distinct from the mainland's Chinese legal framework with characteristics of a continental legal system. HK's judiciary has operated independently, with the power to interpret the Basic Law, which serves as HK's mini-constitution. Though the Standing Committee of the National People's Congress has interpreted the Basic Law five times since 1997, of which four caused controversy in HK, it has basically not interfered with the independent exercise of judicial authority since the change of sovereignty.[154] Such judicial independence has been crucial

[148] The Basic Law of the Hong Kong Special Administrative Region of the People's Republic of China.
[149] See Preamble, ibid.
[150] See Yash Ghai, "The Past and the Future of Hong Kong's Constitution" (1991) 38 University of Hong Kong Supplement to Gazette 21, 27.
[151] See ibid 28.
[152] See ibid.
[153] See Article 39 of the Basic Law.
[154] See Johannes Chan etc, Law of the Hong Kong Constitution (3rd ed., Sweet & Maxwell 2021) chapter 11, 347–383.

in maintaining both international and public confidence in HK's legal system. Second, HK has retained control over its economic and financial policies, enabling it to operate as a separate customs territory and maintain its own currency, the HK dollar. HK has continued to be a major international financial center, with its own monetary authority (the Hong Kong Monetary Authority) regulating banking and financial activities. This autonomy has allowed HK to establish free trade agreements and participate in international economic organizations independently.[155] Third, HK has maintained its own immigration policies, allowing it to control the entry and exit of people from HK. This autonomy has enabled HK to manage its population and labor market according to its specific needs, separate from the policies of mainland China.[156] Fourth, HK has preserved its educational system, which is distinct from that of mainland China. HK has had the autonomy to develop its own curriculum, educational standards, and language of instruction. This independence has allowed the region to emphasize bilingual education in English and Chinese and to maintain international educational standards, attracting students from around the world.[157] Fifth, HK has been able to participate in various international organizations and forums, such as the World Trade Organization and the Asia-Pacific Economic Cooperation, as a separate entity from the PRC. This participation has allowed HK to engage with the global community and negotiate international agreements that benefit HK's economic and social interests.[158]

20.4.3.3 Challenges to High Degree of Autonomy

While the above examples highlight the high degree of autonomy that HK has enjoyed, it is important to note that its high degree of autonomy has faced challenges and scrutiny, particularly in recent years, as tensions between local and Chinese central authorities have emerged over issues such as political freedoms and the application of national laws.

Critics argue that Beijing's increasing influence over HK's political landscape, particularly through interventions in local elections and legislative processes, has undermined HK's autonomy.[159] The introduction of the National Security Law in 2020 is often cited as a significant turning point, as it grants mainland authorities broad powers to curb dissent, which many see as a direct challenge to the freedoms guaranteed under the Basic Law.[160]

155 Ibid., chapter 12, pp. 387–430.

156 See JMM Chan and BA Rwezaura, Immigration Law in Hong Kong: An Interdisciplinary Study (Sweet & Maxwell 2004).

157 See Johannes Chan (n 154), chapter 14.

158 R Mushkat, One Country, Two International Legal Personalities: The Case of Hong Kong (Hong Kong University Press 1997), chapter 1, pp. 1–42.

159 See Jackson Neagli, Hong Kong's Election Overhaul in Context, at: https://www.lawfaremedia.org/article/hong-kongs-election-overhaul-context, accessed on March 15, 2025.

160 See LIN Feng and FEI Mengtian, The Hong Kong National Security Law—A Paradigm Shift for Its National Security Constitution, Vienna Journal of International Constitutional Law, 2023, at pp. 178–193.

Proponents of Beijing's policies argue that such measures are necessary to maintain national security and stability, asserting that they fall within the sovereign rights of the PRC. They claim that the overall framework of "one country, two systems" remains intact and that economic and administrative autonomy continues to be upheld.[161]

While HK's high degree of autonomy was effectively implemented in many areas, such as its legal and economic systems, increasing political influence from Beijing has raised questions about its future, particularly autonomy in political reform. The balance between maintaining HK's distinct identity and integrating it within the PRC's national framework remains a contentious issue, reflecting broader tensions between local aspirations for a high degree of autonomy (or internal self-determination) and national sovereignty.

20.5 Conclusion

Although the PRC officially considers the three unequal treaties invalid under its revolutionary theory of unequal treaty exception, it has pragmatically honored these unequal treaties in practice. Despite the validity of the three unequal treaties under international law at their conclusion, the UK initiated HK's decolonization process primarily because HK was a unique colony, with China retaining sovereignty over the New Territories even during its colonial period. At a jurisprudential level, the right to self-determination and the principle of territorial integrity are equally important and well-recognized principles of international law, with the prevailing principle in any given case depending on circumstances. HK's decolonization did not follow the conventional path, through HK people's exercise of the right to self-determination. Instead, the PRC's claim of territorial integrity over HK garnered international support and was also accepted by Britain. China's more recent historical territorial link, its continuing sovereignty over the New Territories, the historical territorial claim over Hong Kong island and Kowloon Peninsula, geographical contiguity, and the mutual desire of Britain and China to maintain HK's economic prosperity all contributed to China's territorial integrity prevailing over HK people's right to self-determination. This outcome is consistent with some precedents. Furthermore, the fact that China never lost sovereignty over the New Territories gives HK a sui generis legal status distinct from all other colonies in international law. Such unique legal status justifies a different decolonization path from the traditional one.

Although the HK people's right to external self-determination was denied, the discussion above shows that during the second phase of HK's decolonization

[161] See S Lau, "The National Security Law: Political and Social Effects on the Governance of the Hong Kong Special Administration" [2021] Public Administration and Policy 234–240.

process, representatives of HK people were granted some degree of internal self-determination through involvement in drafting the Basic Law. The Basic Law guarantees HK people a high degree of autonomy, equivalent to internal self-determination. This practice aligns with some precedents discussed in this chapter. Even though HK was removed from the list of colonies in 1972, its decolonization process appears to have drawn on experiences from these precedents. While the PRC's claim of territorial integrity prevailed, HK people's right to internal self-determination has been acknowledged and guaranteed by the Basic Law.

Discussion of the implementation of the Basic Law from 1997 to 2025 reveals that HK people's high degree of autonomy (right to international self-determination) has been respected in most aspects. The challenge to their exercise of high degree of autonomy lies primarily in several political rights when their exercise might be in conflict with the National Security Law. The equal legal status of the National Security Law and the Basic Law within Chinese legal system determines that the National Security Law's restrictions on several political rights have been made constitutional and shall remain in the foreseeable future.

21

China's Evolving (Re-)Engagement with International Law

From the 'Reform and Opening to the Outside World' to Building 'Foreign-Related Rule of Law'

Jacques deLisle

21.1 From Accession to Participation to Influence

Since "reform and opening to the outside world" (*gaige kaifang*) began in the late 1970s, the People's Republic of China has undertaken an unprecedentedly deep and wide-ranging engagement with international law and the international legal order. During this period of nearly half a century, China's approach has evolved from accession, to full-fledged participation, to the pursuit and exercise of influence. Especially during the early years of the Reform Era, China's agenda was primarily obtaining entry into the Western-created international legal order and its principal institutions. During this first phase, China's approach largely accepted status quo norms and rules, including when doing so required committing to substantial changes in China's international behavior and domestic order.

Once China secured membership in the major international legal institutions and multilateral treaties, and explicitly accepted many mainstream international legal norms, the defining features of its engagement shifted to participation and practice. China's approach included a mix of implementing (or not fully implementing) legal obligations, using the instruments of international law to serve its interests and preferences, and framing arguably status quo-challenging positions as consistent with existing rules.

Especially after Xi Jinping came to power, China began to seek, and wield, more influence over international law and in international legal institutions. This change in orientation is reflected in a major policy directive to enhance China's "discourse power" (*huayu quan*) and influence in international legal affairs, and the Xi-era drive to develop "foreign-related rule of law" (*shewai fazhi*). China now exercises varied modes of influence: supporting, reinterpreting, or challenging existing international legal norms and rules; adopting laws that serve Chinese interests and support Chinese actions abroad; actively and ambitiously participating in

Jacques deLisle, *China's Evolving (Re-)Engagement with International Law* In: *Histories of International Law in China*. Edited by: Ignacio de la Rasilla, Jiangyu Wang, and Congyan Cai, Oxford University Press.
DOI: 10.1093/oso/9780198888345.003.0021

established institutions; and taking a leading role in establishing new institutions and arrangements with potential to (re)shape international law.

The three phases are not fully distinct. Features that characterize one period do not disappear in later times, nor do they lack foundations in earlier periods. This chapter's discussion of China's post-1978 engagement with international law addresses broad features that characterize China's participation across many fields of international law. The discussion of multiple substantive areas yields a complex and untidy account—and a necessarily superficial one for any area of law. But this approach reflects how the story of China and international law has unfolded: from the dawn of the Reform Era onward, China's engagement and participation have been primarily the sum of what has occurred in particular areas of law. In this respect, this long era differs from earlier periods, and increasingly so, over nearly five decades.

The arc of China's approach to international law since the late 1970s is also consistent with what theories of international relations would lead us to expect. Seeing China's aims and actions through the lenses of those theories can bring into focus recent past and possible future trajectories.

21.2 Early Reengagement and Accession

During the early Reform Era, China launched a sustained effort to reengage with the existing international legal order and its principal institutions. The process had begun prior to this period, during Mao's final years. Most significantly, the PRC had secured the "Chinese seat" in the United Nations.[1] In addition to advancing its position on the "core" (to Beijing) international law question of sovereignty over Taiwan, the PRC thus gained entry into the foremost international governmental organization and a major institutional locus for shaping international law. The significance of the UN seat for the PRC's place in the international legal system was greater still because it came with the powers (including a veto) of a "permanent five" (P5) member of the Security Council, and the prospect of a PRC jurist on the International Court of Justice (a potential not realized—despite the norm of having judges from all P5 members—until 1985).[2]

In the early to mid-1980s, China began a push to join most major international legal regimes. In keeping with the early Reform Era's focus on rapid economic development with heavy reliance on foreign trade and investment, international

[1] Restoration of the Lawful Rights of the People's Republic of China in the United Nations, UN General Assembly Resolution 2758 (26th Session 1971); Samuel S. Kim, "The People's Republic of China and the Charter-Based International Legal Order" (1978) 72 *AJIL* 317.

[2] 'International Court of Justice—China' <https://www.icj-cij.org/index.php/taxonomy/term/31> accessed July 11, 2025.

economic law and related organizations were a priority.[3] The PRC joined the International Monetary Fund and the World Bank in 1980 and quickly became a major client of the latter. The PRC began to seek accession to the General Agreement on Tariffs and Trade (GATT) in 1986. These moves required China to incur, and comply with, new or impending international legal obligations.

China's goal of joining the international legal regime for trade became more imperative with the advent of the World Trade Organization (WTO) in 1995, which reflected and accelerated economic globalization, and which provided more robust institutional mechanisms for lawmaking (including a court-like dispute resolution process with law-interpreting powers) and a more expansive substantive scope (reaching trade in services, trade-related investment measures, and intellectual property). When China finally gained WTO entry in 2001, it did so on terms that obligated China to accept status quo international legal norms and rules. As a matter of general WTO obligations, China agreed to come into line with the generally liberal or neo-liberal market principles of "most-favored-nation" or "normal trading relations" (treating all similar foreign goods equally, regardless of origin), national treatment (not discriminating against imported goods once they enter domestic markets), foregoing a range of protectionist tools, eschewing dumping (selling exports at unfairly low prices) and many forms of state subsidies (to exporting or import-substituting industries), and undertaking international standard-conforming legal protections for intellectual property, as well as providing for transparency of trade-related regulations and judicial or judicial-like review of trade decisions. In addition, China forwent some of the exceptions to general WTO rules that were available to other developing countries and economies transitioning from socialist planning. China even agreed to allow trading partners to use special measures to protect industries from surges in Chinese exports.[4]

These commitments required reversal of China's prior rejection of—or exclusion from—much of the international economic legal order during the first decades of the People's Republic. They also necessitated significant departures from China's socialist-era legal framework for foreign trade, which had entailed tight restrictions on trading rights, state monopoly trading companies, and the like. WTO membership also demanded sweeping reforms to many domestic laws, which had begun years earlier, in anticipation and in support of WTO entry.[5]

[3] See generally, Margaret M. Pearson, "China's Integration into the International Trade and Investment Regime" in Elizabeth Economy and Michel Oksenberg (eds), *China Joins the World: Progress and Prospects* (Council on Foreign Relations 1999).

[4] Julia Ya Qin, "'WTO-Plus' Obligations and Their Implications for the World Trade Organization Legal System: An Appraisal of the China Accession Protocol" (2003) 37 *J World Trade* 483; Qingjiang Kong, "China's WTO Accession: Commitments and Implications" (2000) 3 *J Intl Economic L* 655.

[5] See generally, Zhang Naigen, "On the Changes in the Chinese Legal System for Implementing WTO Laws" (2013) 1 *Renmin Chinese L Rev* 72; Yeling Tan, "How the WTO Changed China" (2021) *Foreign Affairs* 90.

A similar story unfolded with foreign investment, where there was no legal institution akin to the WTO or GATT. During the first decades of the Reform Era, China adopted laws that came increasingly into line with international norms favoring freer flows of capital (while also retaining significant formal and informal mechanisms of state control). Laws on the forms of foreign investment expanded, during this initial period and into the next, from term-limited and majority Chinese-owned joint ventures to more flexible joint-venture structures; wholly foreign-owned enterprises; inbound mergers and acquisitions; and proliferating modes for indirect foreign investment. Laws regulating sectors open to foreign investment evolved from a narrow focus on foreign exchange-generation and technology transfer to, in much later years, largely a "negative list" approach that excluded only relatively few specified sectors, many (at least ostensibly) implicating national security. Special foreign investment-friendly zones, offering more liberal legal environments, spread from four early coastal enclaves to encompass large swathes of the country. While such developments exemplified early Reform Era engagement with international law, their expansion, deepening, and consequences have extended, and in some respects accelerated, into later periods.[6]

China's (re)engagement with international law extended well beyond economic matters. Beijing acceded to multilateral, often UN-centered treaties that were tentpoles of the international legal order, and it did so on generally regime-accepting terms. For example, the PRC became an early adherent to the UN Convention on the Law of the Sea (UNCLOS) in 1982 and in the 1990s began to adopt laws to implement China's rights as a coastal state under UNCLOS. China's decision to join was significant in the context of fraught, recurring disputes with maritime neighbors.[7]

China joined the major UN human rights conventions, beginning in the 1980s with the Convention on the Elimination of Discrimination Against Women, soon followed by the Convention Against Genocide, the Convention Against Torture, and major accords on refugees. This trend expanded in the 1990s, with the PRC signing the two cornerstone UN human rights treaties: the International Covenant on Civil and Political Rights and the International Covenant on Economic, Social, and Cultural Rights.[8] A pivotal development in this aspect of China's international

[6] See generally, Pitman B. Potter, "Foreign Investment Law in the People's Republic of China: Dilemmas of State Control" (1995) 141 *China Q* 155; Hui Huang, "The Regulation of Foreign Investment in Post-WTO China: A Political Economy Analysis" (2009) 23 *Columbia J Asian L* 185; Yuwen Li and Cheng Bian, *China's Foreign Investment Legal Regime: Progress and Limitations* (Routledge 2022).

[7] Guifang Xue, 'China and the Law of the Sea: An Update', (2008) 84 *Intl L Studes* 98; Zou Keyuan, China's Marine Legal System and the Law of the Sea (Brill 2008).

[8] China ratified the ICESCR in 2001 and has not yet ratified the ICCCPR. "Ratification of International Human Rights Treaties—China" <http://hrlibrary.umn.edu/research/ratification-china.html> accessed July 11, 2025; Chen Dingding, "China's Participation in the International Human Rights Regime: A State Identity Perspective" (2009) 2 *Chinese J Intl Politics* 399; Ann Kent, *China, the United Nations and Human Rights* (U Penn 1999).

legal reengagement was the official acceptance of universal human rights near the beginning of the 1990s, following intense international criticism of China's human rights record in the aftermath of the 1989 Tiananmen Incident.[9] Although the endorsement of universal human rights in government white papers and a growing body of scholarly commentary remained limited by an official relativism (asserting that the specific features of human rights vary by national context) and sovereigntism (claiming a central role, and attendant discretion, for states in securing citizens' human rights) that would persist and resurge in later years, the approach China adopted by the early 1990s departed markedly from earlier rejectionist positions and converged toward international legal norms.

Other aspects of early Reform Era re-engagement with international law had more continuity with earlier periods. Much of China's expanding involvement in, and acceptance of, the existing international legal order took the form of entering treaties. Scholarly commentaries and official statements framed treaties as the preferred source (but a decreasingly preeminent one) of international legal rights and obligations, and a key means for implementing China's agenda of reintegrating with the outside world.[10] For a still-wary China, treaties (or a demanding standard for customary law) reduced the risk of unwitting or unwilling entrapment into new or unwanted obligations. The doctrine of "unequal treaties"—which has pre-PRC origins and persisted after the establishment of the People's Republic—remained in place and was framed as an important Chinese contribution to international law.

Reform-Era PRC sources continued to characterize many nineteenth-century treaties as internationally unlawful (primarily because they impermissibly encroached on Chinese sovereignty) and void *ab initio*.[11] Principal among these were agreements purportedly ceding Hong Kong and Taiwan to foreign powers. In the shadow of this principle, early Reform-Era practice was relatively flexible. Beijing continued earlier patterns of acquiescing in some agreements—and making new ones—concerning contested boundaries.[12] In 1984, the PRC forged a Joint Declaration with the United Kingdom to secure Hong Kong's return (with a similar follow-on agreement for Macau). China did not acknowledge the legitimacy of the nineteenth-century treaties that ceded or leased the territories to the

[9] State Council Information Office, "People's Republic of China, Human Rights in China" (November 1991).

[10] Hungdah Chiu, "Chinese Views on the Sources of International Law" (1987) 28 *Harvard Intl L J* 289; Samuel S. Kim, "The Development of International Law in Post-Mao China: Change and Continuity" (1987) 1 *J Chinese L* 117.

[11] See generally Dong Wang, "The Discourse of Unequal Treaties in Modern China" (2003) 76 *Pacific Affairs* 399; Chen Tiqiang, "The People's Republic of China and Public International Law" (1984) 8 *Dalhousie w J* 3. See also the section on "Unequal Treaties" in Wang Tieya's Hague Lectures, discussed later in this section.

[12] See generally M. Taylor Fravel, "Regime Insecurity and International Cooperation: Explaining China's Compromises in Territorial Disputes" (2005) 30 *Intl Security* 48–63; Allen Carlson, "Constructing the Dragon's Scales: China's Approach to Territorial Sovereignty and Border Relations in the 1980s and 1990s" (2003) 12 *J Contemporary China* 677.

UK. Beijing insisted that it had merely decided to "resume the exercise" of sovereignty that it had never lost. But the PRC's characterizing the Joint Declaration as a treaty-like agreement—and its acceptance of a provision stating the UK's framing of the arrangement as a return of sovereignty in exchange for PRC pledges about Hong Kong's governance—signaled China's at least partial acceptance of a relatively conventional international agreement to address issues arising from an "unequal treaty."[13]

As the foregoing reflects, sovereignty loomed large in early Reform Era engagement with international law. China was one of a dwindling handful of states to retain the absolute theory of sovereign immunity although it mitigated the adverse effects the doctrine would have had for Beijing's trade and foreign investment strategy by providing that immunity did not apply to state-owned enterprises. More broadly, the PRC maintained its long-standing robust conception of sovereignty at international law—one that claimed nearly plenary discretion of states to exercise authority domestically, relatively free from lawful interference by other states or foreign actors, including when such efforts invoked norms of customary international law.

Early Reform Era strong sovereigntism had roots in much earlier PRC concerns about Soviet claims of a right to intervene to quash communist apostasy and in the Bandung Line's pursuit of solidarity with newly independent states created by post-World War II decolonization.[14] China's position was most clearly embodied in the Five Principles of Peaceful Coexistence, which date to the PRC's earliest years and remain vital today. Throughout the Reform Era, official and scholarly commentaries have declared them to be Chinese-influenced principles of international law.[15]

The early years of the Reform Era also brought Chinese international lawyers and legal scholars to new prominence. In high-profile examples, Ni Zhengyu became the first PRC judge on the International Court of Justice in 1985, and Professor Wang Tieya delivered the Hague Academy of International Law Lectures

[13] Jacques deLisle, "Sovereignty Resumed: China's Conception of Law for Hong Kong, and Its Implications for the SAR and US-PRC Relations" (1998) *Harvard Asia Q* 21; Peter Wesley-Smith, "Settlement of the Question of Hong Kong" (1987) 17 *California Western Intl L J* 116.

[14] For accounts of China's approach to sovereignty during the early Reform Era and its background in preceding periods, see Maria Adele Carrai, *Sovereignty in China: A Genealogy of a Concept Since 1840* (CUP 2019), ch 5–6; Jacques deLisle, 'China and Sovereignty in International Law: Across Time and Issue Areas' (2024) 9 *UC Irvine J Intl, Transnational, and Comparative L* 4; Suzanne Ogden, "Sovereignty and International Law: The Perspective of the People's Republic of China" (1974) 7 *New York U J Intl L and Politics* 1.

[15] "Peaceful Coexistence and Contemporary International Law" <https://legal.un.org/avl/pdf/ls/McWhinney_outline_PS.pdf> accessed July 11, 2025; Huikang Huang and Xiaohang Bai, "The Five Principles of Peaceful Coexistence: Connotations in International Law and Contemporary Relevance" (2024) 107 *China Intl Studies* 42; "Five Principles of Peaceful Coexistence Not Outdated: President" *People's Daily*, June 29, 2014, <http://en.people.cn/n/2014/0629/c90785-8748174.html> accessed July 11, 2025.

on "International Law in China" in 1990.[16] Wang's lectures focused on: the relatively recent reception of Western international law in China; China's doctrine of unequal (and therefore void) treaties (especially concerning Hong Kong); the Five Principles of Peaceful Coexistence as a major Chinese contribution to international law; the importance of respect for sovereignty (and, especially, sovereign equality and China's territorial sovereignty); and the centrality of the principle of obeying legitimate treaty commitments (not those in unequal treaties) that create international legal obligations (*pacta sunt servanda*).

Early Reform Era China's quest to (re)join the international legal system on largely status quo-accepting terms—including ones that required significant change by China—is consistent with several theories of international relations. Fitting with a "realist" account, China's relatively limited power in the early Reform Era meant that it had little prospect of negotiating more favorable terms or changes to rules, and had reason to be wary of open-ended and intrusive commitments. As China's wealth and power grew over the first decade and more of the Reform Era, such concerns diminished.

The priority China attached to international economic law and the related commitments it was willing to make were consistent with "interdependence" theories, which see transnational economic ties as beneficial and relatively non-threatening to national interests in times of low security threats, and which predict relatively elaborate legal frameworks. Interdependence-supporting conditions were largely in place during the early Reform Era, and especially with the end of the Cold War. China faced no serious security threats from the Soviet Union or the West. The US and other capitalist states encouraged economic openness toward, and market-conforming integration of, China.

China's engagement with international law during this period also aligned with "ideational" views of international relations. Joining an international order in which China had been marginalized (or self-marginalized) depended in part on its establishing that it was a "normal" state (compared to Cultural Revolution baselines), including in terms of "domestic system type." China needed to adopt behaviors that conformed to international norms and institutional rules (including legal ones).

These are also the types of change that "constructivist" (or "state socialization") and some "institutionalist" theories of international relations emphasize. Indeed, both Chinese leaders (such as Premier Zhu Rongji) and US leaders (such as President Bill Clinton) saw (albeit in different ways) China's deepening international economic and legal engagement—especially through WTO

[16] Tieya Wang, "International Law in China: Historical and Contemporary Perspectives" (1990) 221 *Collected Courses of the Hague Academy Intl L [Receuil des cours]* 195; International Court of Justice, "Judge Zhengyu Ni" <https://www.icj-cij.org/index.php/node/4209> accessed July 11, 2025; Ling Yan, "In Memoriam: Ni Zhengyu" (2004) 3 *Chinese J Intl L* 693.

membership—as something that would "change China," at least in its international actions and perhaps also in its domestic policies and even politics.[17]

21.3 Active Participation in the International Legal Order

China's protracted entry (or re-entry) into the international legal order extended beyond the early years of the Reform Era—not surprisingly, given the magnitude and complexity of the agenda and the multifaceted nature and evolving structures of international legal regimes and institutions. To take two prominent examples, China acceded to the WTO in 2001, just shy of 7 years after the WTO's creation and 15 years after it sought to join GATT, and it became an inaugural member of the UN Human Rights Council in 2006, when the UNHRC superseded the longstanding Commission on Human Rights (of which China had been a member).

On the other hand, the origins of what would become distinctive patterns in China's later engagement with international law emerged early in the Reform Era. As China joined major international legal and law-related institutions and treaties, incurred the international legal obligations (some phased in over multi-year periods) of such memberships, and became more adept at working with the rules and processes of international law and institutions, China's focus shifted from accession to participation. Across areas of international law, this second major phase presented a complex mix of: commitments and changes that brought convergence with established international legal norms and rules; growing use of legal mechanisms—institutional, normative, and doctrinal—to serve China's interests and preferences; behavior that triggered charges that China was violating international legal obligations; and arguments by China that its positions, some of which drew criticism as revisionist, were *infra legem*. At least some of these features—and often most or all of them— can be found in many subfields of international law.

China undertook sweeping reforms of laws and practices relating to foreign trade and investment both in the run-up to and in the wake of WTO entry. China's regulatory structure and enterprises' legal environments thus converged toward the largely market-based and liberal (in the sense of reducing barriers to the flow of goods and services) principles of the established international economic legal order. Implementing commitments and achieving greater conformity to international law-related norms meant substantial marketization, deregulation,

[17] See generally Tan, n 1; Jacques deLisle, "China and the WTO" in Tun-jen Cheng, Jacques deLisle, and Deborah Brown (eds), *China under Hu Jintao* (World Scientific 2006); Susan L. Shirk, *How China Opened Its Door* (Brookings 1994); "Full Text of Clinton's Speech on China Trade Bill" March 9, 2000, <https://www.iatp.org/sites/default/files/Full_Text_of_Clintons_Speech_on_China_Trade_Bi.htm> accessed July 11, 2025.

privatization, and expanded opportunities to bring legal challenges to government actions.[18]

At the same time, criticism from abroad that China was shirking obligations or posing difficult challenges for international economic legal regimes emerged and grew. The complaints, which shifted over time, focused on such matters as inadequate protection of intellectual property, dumping, subsidies, unlevel playing fields that favored domestic and state-linked actors, exchange rate manipulation, crabbed or slow implementation of promises to open service sectors, and more. China became one of the most frequent targets of complaints in the WTO's dispute resolution mechanism.[19] More broadly and fundamentally, foreign commentators argued, China's economic model—including features such as the state's still-expansive role in guiding the economy (including the capacity and will to steer firms' behavior to serve party-state policy goals), the state's material and legal support for and control over state-owned and state-linked enterprises (including those in sectors favored by ambitious industrial policy), the absence of a robust rule of law (especially for government accountability), and so on—precluded effective compliance and, given China's huge role in the global economy, posed challenges to the WTO-centered international economic legal order, which lacked effective means to address issues posed by China's distinctive economic model and policies.[20]

During this period, China also became much more skilled at using the mechanisms provided by the WTO—and other international economic legal regimes—to defend and pursue its interests.[21] China became a frequent—and often successful—complainant or complainant-aligned third-party in the WTO dispute resolution process. When facing complaints from other WTO members, China provided relatively conventional arguments that its actions were lawful. Like other WTO members, China invoked the trade-restricting measures that the WTO permitted

[18] See generally, Nicholas R. Lardy, *Integrating China into the Global Economy* (Brookings 2004); Karen Halverson, 'China's WTO Accession: Economic, Legal, and Political Implications' (2004) 27 *Boston College Intl and Comparative L Rev* 319; see also Jiangyu Wang, "The Rule of Law in China: A Realistic View of the Jurisprudence, the Impact of the WTO, and the Prospects for Future Development" (2004) *Singapore J L Studies*347.

[19] See World Trade Organization, "China: Dispute Settlement Archive" <https://www.wto.org/english/news_e/archive_e/country_subj_arc_e.htm?country1=CHN&subject1=DISP> accessed July 11, 2025; Henry S. Gao, "China's Participation in the WTO: A Lawyer's Perspective" (2007) 11 *Singapore YB Intl L* 41; and Wenhua Ji, "China's Experience in Dealing with WTO Dispute Settlement: A Chinese Perspective" (2011) 45 *J World Trade* 1.

[20] See Pitman B. Potter, "The Legal Implications of China's Accession to the WTO" (2001) 167 *China Q* 592; Mark Wu, "The China, Inc. Challenge to Global Trade Governance" (2016) 57 *Harvard Intl L J* 261. See also Timothy Webster, "Paper Compliance: How China Implements WTO Decisions" (2014) 45 *Michigan J Intl L* 525–578; but see Weihuan Zhou, Henry Gao, and Xue Bai, "Building a Market Economy through WTO-Inspired Reform of State-Owned Enterprises in China" (2019) 68 *ICLQ* 977 (offering a more positive assessment).

[21] Gregory Shaffer and Henry Gao, "China's Rise: How It Took on the U.S. at the WTO" (2018) *U Illinois L Rev* 115; Pasha L. Hsieh, "China's Development of International Economic Law and WTO Legal Capacity Building" (2010) 13 *J Intl Economic L*997.

(such as public health and resource conservation). China did not press for major changes in the legal rules in directions that would have been more accommodating of its economic system. Despite growing interest from the Global South in the PRC's template for sustained and rapid economic progress, official and mainstream Chinese commentators (as well as outside analysts) remained skeptical about the feasibility and wisdom of promoting emulation of China's development model (including its legal elements).[22]

A similar pattern characterized China's engagement with the international law of human rights during this period. Once China had joined major human rights treaties and accepted the principle of universal human rights, its participation in the related international legal regime and discourse expanded. The State Council issued numerous white papers on China's human rights performance—more than 20 between 1991 and 2025—both generally (with a cluster of reports on China's overall human rights progress between 1996 and 2014 and a report on the implementation of a 2012–2015 national action plan) and concerning particular issues and regions, largely affirming China's commitments and touting its accomplishments. China's submission of national reports in the United Nations universal periodic review process had much the same character.[23] Where shortcomings were acknowledged, they were often explained as the products of challenges inherited from an earlier period or the consequences of a still relatively low level of economic development.

At the same time, China embraced arguments favoring forms of pluralism and relativism, and, in turn, accommodation of China's preferences and practices. China was a participant—a prominent one—in the conference that produced the 1993 Bangkok Declaration on Human Rights, which affirmed the importance of sovereignty and non-interference and the economic development preconditions for securing human rights, and which was a signal moment in the emergence of "Asian values" perspectives that emphasize less individualistic and more collectivist interpretations of human rights. China became an ardent proponent of a human right to development. Beijing also assigned priority—and asserted the discretion of individual states in assigning priority—to economic, social, and cultural rights.[24]

China insisted that sovereignty and the sovereign state are indispensable—and principal—mechanisms for the realization of human rights. When a provision

[22] Jacques deLisle, "Law and the China Development Model" in Philip S. Hsu, Yu-Shan Wu and Suisheng Zhao (eds), *In Search of China's Development Model* (Routledge 2011) pp. 148–149, 163; Weitseng Chen, "Introduction: Debating the Consensus" in *The Beijing Consensus?* (CUP 2017) pp. 8–12.

[23] Björn Ahl, "'The Rise of China and International Human Rights Law" (2015) 37 *Human Rights Q* 637.

[24] See generally Jiangyu Wang, "China and the Universal Human Rights Standards" (2001) 29 *Syracuse J Intl L and Commerce* 135; Michael C. Davis, "Human Rights in Asia: China and the Bangkok Declaration" (1995–96) 2 *Buffalo J Intl L* 215.

addressing human rights was added to China's constitution in 2004, its framing was notably state-centric: "The state respects and preserves/safeguards human rights."[25] China's pro-sovereignty gloss dovetailed with its emphasis on the human right to the self-determination of peoples (primarily in the post-decolonization context), rejection of the legitimacy of "humanitarian intervention," and skepticism toward the "responsibility [of states] to protect" against human rights violations in the territories they govern.[26] As China became an increasingly powerful and active member of the UN Human Rights Council, it helped to blunt international human rights law-based criticism of itself and other states, primarily in the Global South.[27] China did not sign on to efforts, gathering force in the early post-Cold War years, to promote a right to (liberal) democratic governance. China eschewed openly challenging universalism or pressing an agenda of reforming human rights law, instead favoring interpreting or advocating for the permissibility of multiple interpretations of it.

After the end of the Cold War, China's participation in the international legal system had to grapple anew with questions of the use of force across borders—notwithstanding the emphasis in Hu Jintao-era foreign policy on building a 'harmonious world' (*hexie shijie*). China's traditional strong defense of the rights of states to be free from encroachment on their sovereignty broadly persisted, but Beijing's anti-interventionism became more complex and nuanced and, thus, more in line with existing UN Charter-based law.[28] China supported the idea that lawful international uses of force should go through the Security Council, where the PRC wielded veto power. China accepted (or acquiesced in) UNSC resolutions authorizing intervention in Kuwait/Iraq (1990–1991), an international security presence in Kosovo (1999, following a withdrawal of Serbian forces), and the early phase of intervention in Libya (2011). China also became a major participant in UN peacekeeping operations and joined in UN-authorized anti-piracy efforts in the Gulf of Aden (beginning in 2008), both of which entailed its involvement in activities that were intervention-adjacent. Beijing did reject "humanitarian intervention," but in

[25] Constitution of the People's Republic of China, art. 33 (2004) (terms are *zunzhong* and *baozhang*.)

[26] Michael C. Davis, "The Reluctant Intervenor: The UN Security Council, China's Worldview, and Humanitarian Intervention" in Michael C. Davis, Wolfgang Dietrich, Bettina Scholden, and Dieter Sepp (eds), *International Intervention in the Post-Cold War World* (M.E. Sharpe, 2004); Andrew Garwood-Gowers, "China's 'Responsible Protection' Concept: Reinterpreting the Responsibility to Protect (R2P) and Military Intervention for Humanitarian Purposes" (2016) 6 *Asian J Intl L* 89.

[27] See generally Xinyuan Dai and Lucie Lu, "Beyond Liberal Narratives: China and the International Human Rights Order" (2025) 101 *Intl Affairs* 459; Katrin Kinzelbach, "An Analysis of China's Statements on Human Rights at the United Nations" (2017) 30 *Netherlands Q Human Rights* 299.

[28] Allen Carlson, "Helping to Keep the Peace (Albeit Reluctantly): China's Recent Stance on Sovereignty and Multilateral Intervention" (2004) 77 *Pacific Affairs* 9; Zhongying Pang, "China's Non-Intervention Question" (2009) 1 *Global Responsibility to Protect* 237; Yitzak Shichor, "Fundamentally Unacceptable yet Occasionally Unavoidable: China's Options on External Interference in the Middle East" (2013) 49 *China Rep* 25. See also Courtney J. Fung, *China and Intervention at the UN Security Council: Reconciling Status* (OUP 2019).

significant part because of its role as a perceived pretext for US and other powers' agendas of regime change.

Questions of sovereignty over territory claimed by China elicited international legal and law-related answers from China that were broadly consistent with the patterns found in other areas of law. After Hong Kong returned to Chinese rule in 1997 and during the run-up to reversion, Beijing took steps that drew criticism in Hong Kong, the UK, and elsewhere as violations of the commitments made in the Joint Declaration, including reversing incipient moves toward democratization in the terminal colonial period, using the national legislature's interpretive powers to reject calls for more rapid progress toward democratization, and backing or mandating measures that restricted civil liberties and local judicial powers.[29] But here, too, the PRC insisted that the criticized moves were consistent with the treaty-like Joint Declaration and the Hong Kong Basic Law that implemented the Joint Declaration, or were required by those framework documents, or were within China's interpretive powers under those instruments, or were (at minimum) within China's sovereign powers to govern Hong Kong.[30]

On the issue of Taiwan, Beijing continued to proffer a version of the Hong Kong "one country, two systems" model which it framed as an international law-consistent means to address the legacy of what it dubbed an invalid unequal treaty.[31] During this period, cross-Strait relations at times descended into crisis (particularly in the run-up to Taiwan's first democratic presidential election in 1995–1996 and when the first non-KMT president in Taiwan edged unacceptably close—in Beijing's eyes—to formal independence in the mid-2000s). China asserted a right to resort to military or other coercive means that would have raised questions about China's commitment to, or interpretation of, core international legal principles on the use of force in international affairs.

But those prospects did not come to pass, and the predominant themes in Beijing's approach were mostly comparatively restrained and framed as consistent with international law. China's policy was one of "peaceful development" of cross-Strait relations, which meant tolerating the status quo for an extended period and postponing a push for unification.[32] China did adopt an Anti-Secession Law, but

[29] Michael C. Davis, "The Basic Law and Democratization in Hong Kong" (2005-06) 3 *Loyola U Chicago Intl L Rev*165; Johannes Chan, "Hong Kong's Constitutional Journey: 1997–2011", <https://hub.hku.hk/bitstream/10722/208344/1/Content.pdf?accept=1> accessed July 11, 2025; Han Zhu, "Beijing's 'Rule of Law' Strategy for Governing Hong Kong: Legalisation without Democratisation?" (2019) *China Perspectives* 23.

[30] State Council Information Office, People's Republic of China, "The Practice of the 'One Country, Two Systems' Policy in the Hong Kong Special Administrative Region" (June 2014) <https://english.www.gov.cn/archive/white_paper/2014/08/23/content_281474982986578.htm> accessed July 11, 2025.

[31] See generally, State Council, People's Republic of China, "The One-China Principle and the Taiwan Issue" (February 2000).

[32] See Chu Shulong, "Mainland China's Peaceful Development Strategy and Cross-Strait Relations," in Jean-Pierre Cabestan and Jacques deLisle (eds), *Political Changes in China Under Ma Ying-jeou* (Routledge 2014); Xin Qiang, *Mainland China's Taiwan Policy* (Routledge 2022) ch 2.

it was tellingly assertive conceptually (claiming that Taiwan was already part of China's sovereign territory) but operationally patient (threatening to use force or other coercive measures that would surely bring charges of violating international law only if Taiwan, or others, changed the status quo).[33]

As China's maritime and territorial disputes with South China Sea and East China Sea neighbors grew more fraught again beginning during the 2000s, the UNCLOS-centered regime became a more salient aspect of the PRC's engagement with international law. China more earnestly pressed legal arguments that were geographically and conceptually expansive: territorial sovereignty over all landforms in the disputed areas (partly on the grounds that purported cessions were the result of unequal treaties) and broad, sovereignty-like jurisdictional rights over the water enclosed by the nine-dash line in the South China Sea; maritime zones anchored by small landforms or lesser marine formations or straight baselines drawn around scattered islands, and extending to points equidistant from large landforms belonging to other states; rights to regulate the passage of foreign warships in claimed territorial seas; rights to restrict other states' vessels' presence on the basis of security interests and regulatory rights in Exclusive Economic Zones; obligations of other states to exercise their legal rights, even on the high seas, with "due regard" for China's state interests; and broad "historic rights" in contested waters.[34]

Although rival claimant states, the United States, and others rejected these assertions as inconsistent with the international law of the sea, China insisted that its positions were correct, or at least permissible, interpretations of relevant law, and generally called for informal resolution of the disputes or "setting aside" questions of territorial sovereignty (on which the authoritative legal resolution of maritime rights depended) in favor of pragmatic arrangements for cooperative development.[35] China's actions and claims sometimes were difficult to reconcile with prevalent understandings of law, but they did not openly challenge existing law or call for its revision.

China's interaction with international law on the environment had a somewhat different dynamic—almost necessarily so, given the field's then-recent emergence

[33] Jacques deLisle, "Legislating the Cross-Strait Status Quo? China's Anti-Secession Law, Taiwan's Constitutional Reform and Referenda, and the United States' Taiwan Relations Act" in Peter C.Y. Chow (ed), *Economic Integration, Democratization and National Security in East Asia* (Edward Elgar 2007); Chunjuan Nancy Wei, "China's Anti-Secession Law and Hu Jintao's Taiwan Policy" (2010) 5 *Yale J Intl Affairs* 112.

[34] See Jacques deLisle, "China's Territorial and Maritime Dispute in the South and East China Seas: What Role for International Law?" in Jacques deLisle and Avery Goldstein (eds), *China's Global Engagement* (Brookings 2017); Zhiguo Gao and Bing Bing Jia, "The Nine-Dash Line in the South China Sea: History, Status, and Implications" (2013) 107 *AJIL* 98.

[35] See, e.g., State Council Information Office, People's Republic of China, 'China Adheres to the Position of Settling through Negotiation the Relevant Disputes Between China and the Philippines in the South China Sea' (July 2016); U.S. Department of State Office of Ocean and Polar Affairs, "People's Republic of China: Maritime Claims in the South China Sea", 150 *Limits in the Seas* (January 2022).

and inchoate character—but one that was broadly consistent with China's overall approach to international law during this period. For example, China signed on to the UN Framework Convention on Climate Change (UNFCCC) and was an active and high-profile participant in the UNFCCC's Conference of Parties (following on earlier participation in Rio, Kyoto, and other seminal moments in international environmental law).[36]

China was also a leading proponent of the obligation-limiting principle of "common but differentiated responsibilities" (CBDR), which provides that more developed countries, which historically had generated the largest share of emissions that drive climate change (and were best able to afford the costs of adjustment), should bear more of the burden of future prevention and mitigation than should China and other developing countries.[37] In addition to being a normatively plausible argument, CBDR was another gloss on international law that served China's interests and preferences without squarely challenging general norms, and it also resonated with the long-standing PRC aim of solidarity with the Global South on international legal issues. China's approach to climate change law also tracked its somewhat diminished but enduring commitment to state sovereignty, most visibly in its recalcitrance toward the effort at the 2009 Copenhagen Conference of Parties to elicit more ambitious, semi-binding emissions pledges from the US, China, and other major emerging economies.

An indicator of the contrast, and also the continuity, between this second phase of the Reform Era and the first is the contributions of an expanding cohort of Chinese international lawyers and legal scholars. International law faculties became increasingly stocked with professors who had studied both under the older generation of Chinese scholars who reemerged to shape the field in the 1980s and in foreign law schools, especially in the West. In 2011, ICJ Judge Xue Hanqin delivered Hague Lectures. She reprised themes that were core to Wang's lectures two decades earlier, including the centrality of state sovereignty and non-interference, the Five Principles of Peaceful Coexistence, and the importance of international obligations—which loomed larger, given China's burgeoning treaty accessions.

But her lectures were much more expansive in scope and reflected themes and perspectives that had gained prominence in the 1990s and 2000s. The tone was one of China's greater confidence and full-fledged engagement in an international legal order with which China had become more aligned, partly due to legal change inside China. With the reversions of Hong Kong and Macau settled, discussion

[36] See, for example, Fuzuo Wu, "Shaping China's Climate Diplomacy: Wealth, Status, and Asymmetric Interdependence" (2016) 21 *J Chinese Political Science* 199; Björn Conrad, "China in Copenhagen: Reconciling the 'Beijing Climate Revolution' and the 'Copenhagen Climate Obstinacy'" (2012) 210 *China Q* 435.

[37] See Hongyi Lai, "The Evolution of China's Climate Change Policy: International and Domestic Political Economy and a Strategy for Working with China" (2021) 9 *J British Academy* 69; Chaoyi Jiang, "Revisiting Leadership in Global Climate Governance: China's Normative Engagement with the CBDRs Principle" (2022) 15 *Chinese J Intl Politics* 183.

of China's territorial disputes emphasized Taiwan and included maritime and inland borders. A clear recognition that transnational challenges, non-state actors, and developments in human rights required a more porous notion of sovereignty was juxtaposed with skepticism toward expansive or pretextual invocations of resurgent natural law, humanitarian concerns, human rights, democracy promotion, and other values-based grounds for intervention, and a critical view of robust state responsibilities to protect and capacious mechanisms for international law's reception into domestic law. Favorable discussion of China's embrace of international human rights law came bundled with an emphasis on the right to development; the salience of cultural, economic, social, and historical conditions and contexts in defining human rights; the limited validity of liberal Western interpretations (and double standards); and the centrality of states' domestic law in achieving human rights. Similar caveats accompanied praise for commitments to sustainable development, including a CBDR-resonant argument for the Global North's greater obligations. A positive account of China's increased engagement in multilateral cooperation in a more interdependent world primarily focused on legally informal, relatively non-binding arrangements.[38]

China's more full-fledged and complex participation in the international legal order during this period is in line with what several theories of international relations would lead one to expect. Consistent with a "realist" account, China could engage more deeply with international legal rules and institutions and accept limitations or encroachments they imposed because China was less vulnerable after a long period of rapid development had made China a more formidable power, the rise of a non-antagonistic relationship with the United States had further reduced security threats, and China had gained leverage over other states and international regimes through its growing wealth, power, and engagement.

With serious security concerns in abeyance and with economic openness having yielded vast benefits, "interdependence" theories seemed still more apt than they had in the 1980s or much of the 1990s. Greatly expanded and deepened economic ties offered—in the favored PRC phrase—"win–win" outcomes and, in turn, generated constituencies that favored, and benefited from, more elaborate international legal frameworks, especially for economic relations.

As "institutionalist" models would predict, China's deepening participation in international regimes offered greater benefits for China (especially as Chinese lawyers and officials gained familiarity, competence, and confidence operating in the UNSC and UNHRC, the WTO dispute resolution process, and more) and imposed potentially greater costs (in the form of reputational harm, collateral sanctions, and more) if China flouted international legal rules and obligations or appeared to have done so.

[38] Xue Hanqin, *Chinese Contemporary Perspectives on International Law* (Hague Academy of International Law 2012).

Perspectives that stress "system type" or "ideational" factors are also in keeping with China's approaches and trajectory. Developments during this second period diminished expectations that China's re-engagement with international law and the international legal order would lead to China's thoroughgoing convergence with existing or Western-favored norms or models of law (both international and domestic).

To expect that China would do so assumed an overly expansive version of "constructivist" international relations theory or greatly underestimated the durability and distinctiveness of China's political order and law-related worldview. Instead, this phase of the Reform Era was—as more restrained versions of such theories would predict—characterized by signs of the limits to assimilation to liberal visions of international law and by China's embrace of a pluralist approach to international legal norms.

21.4 Seeking and Exerting Influence in a Changing Context

Especially since the early 2010s (but with some earlier roots), new trends have emerged in China's engagement with international law and related norms and institutions. To be sure, many of the patterns of the preceding period have persisted. China has continued to participate, proactively and effectively, in international legal regimes and discourse, and has done so in ways largely familiar from the 1990s and 2000s. But this third phase, roughly coinciding with Xi Jinping's tenure as China's top leader, has seen the PRC seeking, and attaining, greater influence in international law. This agenda is manifest in high-level policy framings, including: the 4th Plenum of the 18th Central Committee's call (in 2014) for China to "strengthen foreign-related legal work," "vigorously participate in the formulation of international norms," strengthen "discourse power and influence in international legal affairs," and "use legal methods to safeguard our country's sovereignty, security and development interests";[39] a high-profile and multifaceted commitment (originating just before 2020—and gaining momentum thereafter) to develop "foreign-related rule of law" (*shewai fazhi*) to protect and advance Chinese economic and security interests;[40] and the framing (beginning

[39] Chinese Communist Party Central Committee, "Decision Concerning Several Major Issues in Comprehensively Advancing Governance According to Law" (18th Central Committee, 4th Plenum, October 2014). These calls were echoed in Chinese Communist Party Central Committee, "Plan for Construction of a Rule-of-Law China, 2020–2025" (January 21, 2021) para 25.

[40] "Xi Stresses Development of Foreign-Related Legal System" (Xinhua, November 29, 2023) <https://perma.cc/EV3V-ARMU> accessed July 11, 2025; Moritz Rudolf, "Politburo Whisperer on Advancing 'Foreign-Related Rule of Law'" (NPC Observer, December 2023) <https://npcobserver.com/2023/12/china-politburo-foreign-related-rule-of-law/> accessed July 11, 2025; Matthew S. Erie, "Foreign Policy Implications for China's 'Foreign-Related Rule of Law'" (2023) 67 *Orbis* 565. See also Chinese Communist Party Central Committee, "Plan for Construction of a Rule-of-Law China" n 39, para 25.

in the mid-2010s) of China's development experience (including law-related elements)—and "Chinese-style modernization"—as offering lessons for other countries and new solutions to challenges facing all humankind.[41]

Both China's rising influence and its prospective influence have taken varied forms. In some respects, China has presented itself as a vital supporter of the status quo, but it also has been seen as an increasingly potent force for change in international legal ideas and doctrines, primarily in directions that align with China's preferences and lessons derived from China's experience. China's posture has been partly defensive (law as a shield) and partly offensive (law as a sword). Distinctions between the halves of this pair of patterns are murky, partly due to China's casting of some arguably status quo-challenging positions as *infra legem* and partly because of a lack of settled doctrine, especially in some still emerging areas of international law. In international legal and law-related institutions, China has become a more powerful and assertive actor within established organizations and also has taken a leading role in creating new arrangements that give it options to affect key areas of international law.

In international economic law, China has become a vocal proponent of sustaining a broadly liberal trading order and relative economic openness. This role emerged in the wake of the Global Financial Crisis of 2007–2008, as illustrated by Premier Wen Jiabao's 2009 speech to the World Economic Forum touting China's contributions to global economic recovery and opposing protectionism.[42] While China's position—as reflected in World Economic Forum speeches by Premiers Li Keqiang in 2014 and Li Qiang in 2024[43]—did not change, its significance increased in the 2010s and 2020s as China's role in international trade and as a source of outbound investment grew, and as US support for the existing order waned. China also sharpened its challenge to its long-standing designation by other WTO members as a non-market economy. In the early 2020s, China

[41] Xi Jinping, "Secure a Decisive Victory in Building a Moderately Prosperous Society in All Respects and Strive for the Great Success of Socialism with Chinese Characteristics for a New Era" (Report to the 19th National Congress of the Chinese Communist Party, October 18, 2017); State Council, People's Republic of China, "Xi Stresses Grasping, Advancing Chinese Modernization" (February 8, 2023) <https://english.www.gov.cn/2022special/20thcpccongress/202302/08/content_WS63e3116ac6d0a757729e682c.html> accessed July 11, 2025; Jacques deLisle, "The Chinese Model of Law, China's Agenda in International Law, and Implications for Democracy in Asia and Beyond" in Gilbert Rozman (ed), *Democratization, National Identity, and Foreign Policy in Asia* (Routledge, 2021).

[42] "Full Text of Chinese Premier Wen Jiabao's Speech at 2009 Summer Davos in Dalian" (Ministry of Foreign Affairs, People's Republic of China September 11, 2009) <https://www.mfa.gov.cn/eng/xw/zyjh/202405/t20240530_11340107.html> accessed July 11, 2025.

[43] "Chinese Premier Li Keqiang's Speech at Davos 2015" (World Economic Forum, January 23, 2015)<https://www.weforum.org/stories/2015/01/chinese-premier-li-keqiangs-speech-at-davos-2015/> accessed July 11, 2025; 'Address by China Premier Li Qiang to the Annual Meeting of New Champions' (World Economic Forum, 26 June 2024) <https://www.weforum.org/stories/2024/06/address-by-china-premier-li-qiang-to-the-annual-meeting-of-new-champions/> accessed July 11, 2025.

became the principal champion of a draft WTO Investment Facilitation for Development Agreement.

China's posture on international openness and accompanying pledges to deepen domestic reform did not mean radically liberalizing China's economic laws, or abandoning insistence that a relatively statist and avowedly socialist model was compatible with international law. Indeed, the role of the party-state in directing the economy and actions of individual firms resurged in the later 2010s and 2020s. At the same time, developments in China's foreign economic-related laws reflected, and contributed to, a shift toward illiberalism in the international order, including the "securitization" of transnational economic issues.[44]

Like the US, China began to tighten restrictions on inbound investment and exports of technology or sensitive materials, on the stated basis of protecting national security, and, more broadly, adopted laws and policies promoting self-sufficiency—especially in key technology sectors—to mitigate the risks of trade and investment restrictions imposed by the US and others. By the later 2010s and 2020s, such changes in China and elsewhere had created genuine compliance and conflict of laws problems for companies operating transnationally. This situation was exacerbated (especially in the case of China and the US) by anti-suit injunctions and laws against complying with other states' sanctions, and by the expanding reach of Chinese law to regulate behavior—by Chinese firms and others—outside China's territory.[45]

Another trend limited the salience of general international economic law for China: its apparent preference for enclavist or informal arrangements to govern its growing external economic ties, especially in the Global South. For example, China forged many regional trade agreements (RTAs) and bilateral trade agreements that were only loosely nested in and constrained by WTO law. China forged numerous increasingly investor-protecting, bilateral investment treaties. The legal face of the Belt and Road Initiative (BRI) was often informal MOUs or the "law of the contract" for specific projects or other mechanisms that insulated Chinese investments from local legal risks and thus reduced China's interest in seeking international legal norms with which host states would be pressed to conform. China—and Chinese parties—often favored informal or China-based

[44] See Foreign Investment Law of the People's Republic of China, art. 35 (2019) and Foreign Relations Law of the People's Republic of China, art. 33 (2023).

[45] See generally Mark Wu, "Export Policies, Technology Transfer Policies, and Investment Reviews: How States Compete in the Era of Global High-Tech Value Chains" in Shin-yi Peng, Han-Wei Liu, and Ching-Fu Lin (eds), *Governing Science and Technology under the International Economic Order* (Edward Elgar, 2018); Ji Li, "Superpower Legal Rivalry and the Global Compliance Dilemma" (2023-24) 45 *U Pennsylvania J Intl L* 891; Mathieu Duchâtel and Georgina Wright, "China's Extraterritoriality: A New Stage of Lawfare" (Institut Montaigne, December 2024) <https://www.institutmontaigne.org/en/publications/chinas-extraterritoriality-new-stage-lawfare> accessed July 11, 2025.

resolution of investment disputes, whether through negotiation or one-off arbitration or Chinese or China-influence dispute resolution bodies (such as the China International Commercial Court or the China Africa Joint Arbitration Centre).[46]

In the mid-2010s, another dimension of China's engagement with international economic law indicated greater Chinese impact. China took a leading role in calling for reforms to give it and emerging economies more power in the IMF and World Bank and in establishing new institutions and frameworks, such as the Asian Infrastructure Investment Bank (AIIB), the New Development Bank (formerly the BRICS Bank), and the Regional Comprehensive Economic Partnership (RCEP). In these new organizations, China's power was comparatively great and that of Global North states (and especially the absent US) was much less than in older institutions or other new regional arrangements (such as the Trans-Pacific Partnership). While China has framed such arrangements as consistent with and supportive of existing international legal norms, they create mechanisms with potential to promote change.

Initiated in the early 2020s, China's Global Development Initiative (GDI) went a step further, adopting a vision for a "new model of international development" stressing poverty alleviation, sustainability, and international cooperation. While the GDI lacked specific legal content, it moved beyond the BRI agenda toward China's potentially greater normative influence through its emphasis on multilateral channels, including the UN and its Sustainable Development Goals, and its declared focus on global governance and provision of international public goods.[47]

An additional emerging avenue for China's influence on economic-related international law is oblique and runs through other states' domestic law. During Xi's tenure, China has become much less reticent in asserting that China offers a model of development for other states, primarily in the Global South. Indeed, official party statements have called for "promoting the rule of law abroad" and "telling [to foreign audiences] China's rule of law story well."[48] There has been, sometimes only implicitly, a legal component to the notion of a Chinese alternative to Western-style modernization. Although often bilateral, legally informal, or project-specific, China's engagement—frequently through BRI projects—created a channel for influence on the legal orders in host countries and, especially when coupled with China's diplomatic initiatives and material incentives, their positions on questions of international law.

[46] On this cluster of issues, see generally, Gregory Shaffer and Henry Gao, "A New Chinese Economic Order?" (2020) 23 *Intl Economic L* 607; Michael Sampson, "The Evolution of China's Regional Trade Agreements: Power Dynamics and the Future of the Asia-Pacific" (2019) 34 *Pacific Rev* 259.

[47] See Foreign Ministry of the People's Republic of China, "The Practical Achievements and Global Contributions of the Global Development Initiative" (June 2024) <https://www.mfa.gov.cn/eng/zy/jj/GDI_140002/wj/202406/P020240606606199927074.pdf> accessed July 11, 2025; Marina Rudyak, "China and the Global South: Many Initiatives, One Narrative" (Instituto Affari Internazionali 2023) <http://www.jstor.org/stable/resrep52632> accessed July 11, 2025.

[48] Chinese Communist Party Central Committee, "Plan for Construction of a Rule-of-Law China" n 39 para 25.

More broadly, China's increased importance as a source of exports and investment (especially in the Global South through BRI arrangements) gave Beijing greater leverage to affect other states' legal and policy responses to Chinese trade and investment—a phenomenon that became the focus of analysts' debates about the motives, character, and consequences of China's actions in Global South states.[49] Although still modest in scale and ambition and eschewing robust promotion of a Chinese legal model, China's legal assistance, training, and education projects for the Global South are another, parallel pathway for affecting, albeit indirectly, international law.[50]

China's engagement with international human rights law has broadly paralleled, and in some ways been intertwined with, these patterns in economic law. The BRI and GDI aligned with China's long-standing emphasis on development as a human right, and helped give governments in the Global South economic and diplomatic resources to resist international human rights law-driven sanctions and pressure. China's Xi-era participation in international human rights law has included a muscular version of familiar themes of sovereigntism and non-interference. As a repeatedly serving and especially powerful member of the UN Human Rights Council, China became more assertive in blocking NGO participation, reports, and votes critical of the human rights performance—including conformity with treaty obligations—of China, as well as other states supported by China.[51]

Beyond the UN system, China took a firm line in rejecting the legitimacy of international law-based criticisms of China's human rights record, even as the severity of charges mounted concerning human rights issues such as the mass internment of Uyghurs in Xinjiang, and the imposition of a National Security Law in Hong Kong that limited prior civil liberties and courts' ability to constrain government action. China framed its defense of such measures partly as permissible means to address terrorism, separatism, and threats to public order consistent with international law—Beijing's interpretations of which were highly contested abroad.[52]

[49] See Lutz-Christian Wolff, "Legal Responses to China's 'Belt and Road' Initiative: Necessary, Possible or Pointless Exercise?" (2020) 29 *Transnational L and Contemporary Problems* 249; Tom Ginsburg, "The BRI, Non-Interference, and Democracy" (2021) 62 *Harvard Intl L J* 40.

[50] On these issues, see Matthew Erie and Jacques deLisle, "Chinese Developmentalism as Law" in Jacques deLisle, Matthew S. Erie, and Jaclyn Neo (eds), *Chinese Developmentalism in the Global Legal and Economic Order* (CUP, forthcoming 2026); Samuli Seppänen, "Chinese Legal Development Assistance: Which Rule of Law? Whose Pragmatism?" (2021) 51 *Vanderbilt L Rev* 101.

[51] See Ted Piccone, "China's Long Game on Human Rights at the United Nations" (Brookings Institution, September 2019) <https://www.brookings.edu/wp-content/uploads/2018/09/FP_20181009_china_human_rights.pdf> accessed July 11, 2025.

[52] See Yongjin Zhang and Barry Buzan. 'China and the Global Reach of Human Rights' (2020) 241 *China Q* 169–190; United Nations Office of the High Commissioner of Human Rights, "OHCHR Assessment of Human Rights Concerns in the Xinjiang Uyghur Autonomous Region, PRC" (August 31, 2022) <https://www.ohchr.org/en/documents/country-reports/ohchr-assessment-human-rights-concerns-xinjiang-uyghur-autonomous-region> accessed July 11, 2025; Foreign Ministry of the People's Republic of China, "Six Things You Need to Know About the National Security Legislation

China's embrace of human rights relativism tightened, as pointedly reflected in an early 2010s CCP General Office Document, which condemned as "false ideological trends" several law-related concepts—including ones that resonated with the ICCPR—that were rejected as purportedly universal, but actually Western, values unsuited to China.[53] Such relativism aligned with the ongoing sovereigntist defense against criticism of China's human rights performance, the broader Xi-era discourse on China's traditional culture and values, and the more outward-facing Global Civilization Initiative (GCI, launched in 2023) which proclaimed the equality and diversity of civilizations (and, in turn, their approaches to issues relating to human rights).[54]

At the same time, the Xi-era discourse on the greatness of Chinese civilization and the lessons China's wisdom might provide for the world, as well as the GCI's call for expanding inter-civilizational exchanges, suggested that China might seek to influence other states on matters relevant to human rights and other, related international law issues. Foreign analysts saw in Beijing's foreign policy, including its support for fellow authoritarian states, an agenda to promote "authoritarian international law" (which emphasizes sovereignty and rejects liberal democracy as a universal norm) or, at least, to "make the world safe for autocracy."[55]

China's approach to sovereignty-related issues has evolved in similar—and similarly complex—directions. Support for robust sovereignty and opposition to interference in internal affairs have been evident in Beijing's engagement with the international human rights regime and the aspects of China's "foreign-related rule of law" that have been part of the securitization of transnational economic legal issues. China's wariness toward forcible intervention has been reflected in, among other cases, its critical view of expansive readings of UNSC-sanctioned intervention in Libya, and its veto of UNSC measures concerning the civil conflict in Syria, beginning in the early 2010s.[56]

for Hong Kong SAR" (June 10, 2002) <https://www.fmprc.gov.cn/eng/wjb/zzjg_663340/xws_665282/xgxw_665284/202406/t20240606_11405703.html> accessed July 11, 2025; Dominic Raab, "National Security Legislation in Hong Kong: Foreign Secretary's Statement in Parliament" (July 1, 2020) <https://www.gov.uk/government/speeches/foreign-secretary-statement-on-national-security-legislation-in-hong-kong> accessed July 11, 2025.

[53] Chinese Communist Party Central Committee General Office, "Communique on the Current State of the Ideological Sphere" (April 22, 2013) <https://www.chinafile.com/document-9-chinafile-translation> accessed July 11, 2025 (generally referred to as "Document Number 9").

[54] See Barry Buzan and Feng Zhang, "Multiple Modernities in Civilizational Perspective: An Assessment of the Global Civilization(s) Initiative" (2024) 17 *Chinese J Intl Politics* 104; State Council Information Office, People's Republic of China, "Full Text of Xi Jinping's Keynote Address at the CPC Parties High-Level Meeting" (March 16, 2023) <http://english.scio.gov.cn/topnews/2023-03/16/content_85171478.htm> accessed July 11, 2025 (announcing the GCI).

[55] On these issues, see Pitman B. Potter, *Exporting Virtue? China's International Human Rights Activism in the Age of Xi Jinping* (UBC Press, 2021); Tom Ginsburg, "Authoritarian International Law?" (2020) 114 *AJIL* 221; Jessica Chen Weiss, "A World Safe for Autocracy? China's Rise and the Future of Global Politics" (July/August 2019) *Foreign Affairs* 92.

[56] Mu Ren, *Beyond Rigidity: China's Non-Intervention Policy in the Post-Cold War Period* (Springer 2021) ch 6; Courtney J. Fung, "Separating Intervention from Regime Change: China's Diplomatic Innovations at the UN Security Council Regarding the Syria Crisis" (2018) 235 *China Q* 693.

Long-standing positions on China's sovereignty over territory governed or claimed by China became sharper and more salient amid changing conditions in the 2010s and 2020s. Insistence on broad sovereign discretion of the Chinese state to govern domestically became more pointed, and arguably more expansive and assertive, as China faced stronger criticism of its government's new actions and laws that targeted Xinjiang, Tibet, Hong Kong, and dissidents and critics in the core Chinese mainland, and that responded to perceived threats to security and order more generally.[57]

Concerning Hong Kong, China rebuffed criticisms that its tough National Security Law and kindred local ordinances and its rejection of calls for more rapid democratization were inconsistent with the promises in the Joint Declaration and the Basic Law—a stance in line with China's assertion that the Joint Declaration no longer imposed international legal obligations on China.[58]

In the early 2020s China became more assertive, and relied more heavily on international legal arguments, in maintaining that UN General Assembly Resolution 2758 had settled, as a matter of international law, that Taiwan was part of China's sovereign territory. China also reinforced its 2005 Anti-Secession Law's position concerning Taiwan's status with interpretations criminalizing a range of activities identified as "secessionist."[59] More broadly, China has kept in place institutional arrangements and doctrinal principles that allow only limited entry of international law into Chinese law, with the main mechanisms being legislation that specifically provides for application of treaty provisions or that substantively parallels international legal obligations.

China's engagement with international law relating to state sovereignty diverged more from Beijing's past views in other respects, including where the sovereignty of other states is at issue. Such a pattern is hardly surprising, given the

[57] See Congyan Cai, "Enforcing a New National Security? China's National Security Law and International Law" (2017) 10 *J East Asia and Intl L* 65; Katja Dinhausen and Helena Legarda, "Xi's 'Comprehensive National Security' Framework Shapes China's Behavior at Home and Abroad" (Merics China Montor, September 15, 2022) <https://merics.org/en/report/comprehensive-national-security-unleashed-how-xis-approach-shapes-chinas-policies-home-and> accessed July 11, 2025; Foreign Ministry of the People's Republic of China, 'China is Firmly Committed to a Path of Human Rights Development That Suits Its National Conditions' (September 26, 2021,<https://www.mfa.gov.cn/eng/wjb/zygy/hd/202406/t20240603_11374881.html> accessed July 11, 2025.

[58] 'Ministry of Foreign Affairs: The Sino-British Joint Declaration is a Historical Document and Has No Practical Significance' (Huanqiuwang, June 30, 2017) <https://world.huanqiu.com/article/9CaKrnK3P6v> accessed July 11, 2025.

[59] State Council Taiwan Affairs Office and Information Office, "The Taiwan Question and China's Reunification in the New Era" (August 2022); Jacques deLisle and Bonnie S. Glaser, "Why UN General Assembly Resolution 2758 Does Not Establish Beijing's 'One China' Principle: A Legal Perspective" (German Marshall Fund of the United States, April 2024) <https://www.gmfus.org/sites/default/files/2024-04/GMF_UNGA%20Res.%202758_April%202024%20Report.pdf> accessed July 11, 2025; Bonny Lin and I-Chung Lai (eds), "Employing 'Non-Peaceful' Means Against Taiwan" (Center for Strategic and International Studies, October 2024) <https://csis-website-prod.s3.amazonaws.com/s3fs-public/2024-10/241015_Lin_Means_Taiwan.pdf?VersionId=4PU_wYq.V6AFbR22H8QsRyQFgV2c6X7q> accessed July 11, 2025.

sharp expansion of China's international economic and security interests and its economic, social, and diplomatic presence in other states. One instance was dramatic in practice if murky in principle: China did not condemn Russia's invasion of Ukraine and blocked action in the Security Council while (contrary to Russia's position) purporting to recognize Ukraine's status as a sovereign state and characterizing the Taiwan situation as completely disanalogous.[60]

Other instances of this shift have been less dramatic. For example, China's greatly increased economic presence and political–diplomatic clout with, and within, other states—particularly BRI partners in the Global South—has brought greater capacity to affect how other states exercise their sovereign powers. While such influence often does not raise issues of international unlawfulness, it does extend to behaviors that China once might have condemned as improper interference in other states' internal affairs. For another example, China has extended the extraterritorial reach of its laws, especially criminal and regulatory laws, to govern Chinese and foreign nationals acting in the sovereign territory of other states, near, up to, or arguably beyond standard interpretations of the international law of prescriptive jurisdiction. China also abandoned the absolute theory of sovereign immunity, opening the door to seeking legal redress against foreign states for actions harming Chinese interests.[61]

China's handling of law of the sea and related maritime and territorial disputes is in some respects akin to the mixed developments in other issue areas. Here, too, sustaining prior positions has become more fraught and appeared (especially to rival claimants and the United States) to be more challenging to preexisting norms and rules than was the case in earlier periods. Although China took a step back from long-ambiguous suggestions that the dashed line entailed a claim of sovereignty-like rights over the enclosed area in the South China Sea, it retained its long-standing expansive notions of sovereignty and jurisdiction in disputed maritime issues generally. China rejected the jurisdiction—and the highly adverse decision on the merits (which it dubbed a "piece of wastepaper")—of an arbitral panel in a case brought by the Philippines under UNCLOS provisions for mandatory dispute resolution. The incident sharpened the clash between China's and other interested states' (and the panel's) reading of major law of the sea rules. China also continued to enact domestic laws (for example, baselines for maritime claims and laws empowering coast guard and maritime services) that assert—and provide

[60] Jacques deLisle, "China's Russia/Ukraine Problem, and Why It's Bad for Almost Everyone Else Too" (2022) 66 *Orbis* 402; Sheena Chestnut Greitens, "China's Response to War in Ukraine" (2022) 62 *Asian Survey* 751.

[61] See generally deLisle n 14; Matthew S. Erie, "Legal Systems Inside Out: American Legal Exceptionalism and China's Dream of Legal Cosmopolitanism" (2023) 44 *U Pennsylvania J Intl L* 731; Zhengxin Huo and Man Yip, "Extraterritoriality of Chinese Law: Myths, Realities and the Future" (2021) 9 *Chinese J Comparative L* 328; Foreign Sovereign Immunity Law of the People's Republic of China (2023).

domestic legal bases for acts to impose—more secure and expansive dominion over contested areas.[62]

China's increased global importance and expanded footprint also correlated with changes in its interaction with international law on the environment and climate change. With China having become the leading emitter of greenhouse gases in 2006–2007 and reaching upper-middle income status in 2010, its prior insistence on CBDR came under pressure. China took a leading role in the soft obligation-generating 2015 Paris Accords. But China's support for expanding the reach of international environmental law remained limited in ways consistent with broader patterns in China's engagement with international law. For example, China opposed treaty arrangements that would link international environmental law to human rights and supported leaving much to sovereign choice and national policy. China's turn to law to address environmental issues and to promote green energy transition was extensive, but it focused on domestic measures—which, given the scale of China's role in climate change and green technology industries, would have significant practical, if limited legal, effect internationally.[63]

China's mix of strongly sovereigntist and international norm-shaping approaches extended to another, newly emerging area of international law: cyberspace. China became a leading proponent of the positions that international law should, or does, give sovereign states authority to regulate cyberspace much as they govern physical territory and that international rules should be multilateral, pluralistic, and often take the form of soft law. These views, substantially at odds with the more liberal and commercial perspective favored by the US and Global North democracies, drew support from Russia, Iran, and much of the Global South.[64]

In this period, as before, a prominent assessment by a Chinese international legal scholar, offering a comprehensive account primarily for a foreign audience,

[62] On these issues, see "Chinese Foreign Minister Criticized 'Flawed South China Sea Ruling'" *China Daily* (12 July 2025) https://www.chinadailyasia.com/hk/article/615755 accessed July 11, 2025; Foreign Ministry of the People's Republic of China, 'Position Paper of the Government of the People's Republic of China on the Matter of Jurisdiction in the South China Sea Arbitration Initiated by the Republic of the Philippines' (December 7, 2014) <https://www.mfa.gov.cn/eng/zy/gb/202405/t20240531_11367291.html> accessed July 11, 2025; Ministry of Foreign Affairs People's Republic of China, "Vice Foreign Minister Liu Zhenmin at the Press Conference on the White Paper Titled China Adheres to the Position of Settling Through Negotiation the Relevant Disputes Between China and the Philippines in the South China Sea" (July 13, 2016) <https://www.fmprc.gov.cn/nanhai/eng/wjbxw_1/201607/t20160715_8523355.htm> accessed July 11, 2025; Jacques deLisle, "Political Implications of the July 2016 Arbitration Decision in the Philippines-PRC Case Concerning the South China Sea" (2016) 21 *Asian YB Intl L* 49.

[63] See Anthony H.F. Li, "Hopes of Limiting Global Warming? China and the Paris Agreement on Climate Change" (2016) *China Perspectives* 49; Peter Lawrence and Daryl Wong, "Soft Law in the Paris Climate Agreement: Strength or Weakness?" (2017) 26 *RECIEL* 276.

[64] See Zhixiang Huang and Yaohui Ying, "Chinese Approaches to Cyberspace Governance and International Law in Cyberspace" in Nicholas Tsagourias and Russell Buchan (eds), *Research Handbook on International Law in Cyberspace* (Edward Elgar 2021); Rogier Creemers, "China Conception of Cyber Sovereignty," in Dennis Broeders and Bibi van den Berg (eds), *Governing Cyberspace* (Rowman & Littlefield 2020).

resonates with themes of China's contemporary engagement with international law. Professor Cai Congyan's *The Rise of China and International Law* (2019)[65] covers many of the doctrinal issues addressed in Wang's and Xue's Hague Lectures, but the focus and tone of analysis of the recent period are notably different. As the title implies, it emphasizes China's emergence as a great power. It examines how engagement with international law has facilitated China's rise in ways that range from generating opportunities for economic development facilitated by WTO membership and international law-driven changes in China's laws and institutions, to providing legitimation for China's actions in territorial disputes and accommodation of the 'particularities' of China's domestic political order, approach to human rights, and socialist-statist economic model.

More than his predecessors, Cai addresses China's potential to influence international law, which has risen along with China's economic, hard, and soft power, and international legal capabilities. China is portrayed as: a "norm entrepreneur" pressing international legal ideas and ideals, such as relativism, the extent of obligations, economic rights, and skepticism toward foreign intervention in human rights law, or investment facilitation and infrastructure promotion in international economic law, or sovereignty and multilateralism in cyberspace law, or norms rooted in resurgent socialist identity under Xi; a driving force behind new, potentially law-shaping and global governance-providing institutions, such as the AIIB, and newly emerging areas of law, such as cyberspace; an incipient shaper of international law through influencing other states' internal orders and external policies; and a protector of Chinese interests abroad (including through "foreign-related rule of law"). Cai's account, like others,[66] finds a vital symbiotic relationship between domestic rule-of-law or rule-by-law reform and China's acceptance of international law. Cai's extensive analysis of China's internal laws and institutions also reflects an assertion that Chinese domestic behavior is important state practice shaping (customary) international law, and an assumption that understanding Chinese law is essential in a world where China affects international law and where boundaries between international and internal law have become porous.

Cai also recounts ambivalence (partly based on bitter experience) and limitations in China's "international legal policy." The phrases "on the other hand" and "however" occur frequently. International law—from WTO rules to human rights norms to dispute settlement mechanisms—appears both empowering and threatening, both legitimating (including with states wary of China's rising power) and

[65] Congyan Cai, *The Rise of China and International Law* (OUP 2019). The 2026 Hague Lectures will be given by another leading Chinese international law scholar, Jia Bing Bing. In contrast to Wang and Xue, Jia will not be addressing Chinese perspectives on international law but rather "the Contemporary International Legal Order"). This change may reflect—and is consistent with—a view that China is now so fully and influentially a part of the international legal order that it is no longer appropriate (or, perhaps, feasible) to have a general course at the Academy that addresses (only) the Chinese perspective.

[66] Bing Bing Jia, "A Synthesis of the Notion of Sovereignty and the Ideal of the Rule of Law: Reflections on the Contemporary Chinese Approach to International Law" (2010) 53 *German YB Intl L* 11.

constraining (particularly of the latitude great powers otherwise enjoy). Cai points to potent imperatives to receive, and to rebuff, international law's reach into China's domestic order and influence on China's international behavior. China's impact on international law is presented as still-emerging and unsettled. Lawfare—seen as a vital tool in international dispute resolution processes that increasingly involve China—blurs distinctions between invocation or interpretation of existing law and political manipulation or sub rosa revision of such law.

Principles that China endorses—including harmony in diversity (*he'er butong*) (from the Hu Jintao years), a common future for humankind (written into the constitution under Xi), every state's discretion to interpret human rights and choose its own development path, and a continued (albeit more flexible) emphasis on sovereignty—are (variously) so general or pluralist or consistent with the status quo that they show how China's role as a norm entrepreneur remains nascent or inchoate. "Exceptionalism"—the Chinese version of which Cai urges be taken "seriously"—is, perhaps inescapably, ambiguous. It is compatible with both insisting on China's inimitable uniqueness and its proffering a model for others to follow. It is also an axis of rivalry with another "exceptionalist" power, the United States.[67]

As in earlier phases of the Reform Era, China's approach to international law during this period of increased power and growing quest for influence in a changing world can be understood through the prisms of international relations theories. As 'realists' would predict, a more powerful China is seeking international legal rules that protect and advance its interests, which (especially in the "offensive realist" or "power transition" versions of realism) entails friction and potential conflict with the previously dominant and now relatively declining power (the United States) that had molded the system to serve its interests. China's growing and now-formidable power (across many dimensions) has given it greater wherewithal to incentivize other states to support its interpretations of international law and its agendas for international lawmaking. Amid rising tensions between the US and China and the securitization of economic issues in China's and other states' laws and policies, assessments of transnational economic ties have shifted from the benign visions of 'interdependence' theories to the dangers of asymmetric economic dependence and the resulting vulnerability to adversaries using economic leverage to political ends.

China's approach and actions are also in line with major versions of 'institutionalist' or regime-focused international relations thinking. As the US's relative power and wealth have waned while China's have waxed, the US has become less willing to support the international legal and law-related institutions that Washington did much to forge in the post-World War II era and again in the post-Cold War years. Such institutions, once in place, can survive the fading

[67] Compare Walter MacDougall, *Promised Land, Crusader State: America's Encounter with the World since 1776* (Harper 1998).

of hegemonic support and thus give other states, including rising powers, good reasons to continue to work within them and support them (and reform them)—as China in some respects has done in the 2010s and 2020s. Yet, such institutions also become vulnerable to decline internally and to challenges from new institutions backed by powerful states with their own agendas—a pattern arguably immanent in the China-supported RCEP, AIIB, or Shanghai Cooperation Organization.

By the 2010s and 2020s, 'constructivist' expectations that China would fully assimilate to longstanding, largely liberal readings of international law, and even transform its domestic legal and political order in complementary ways, had long faded. On the rise were notions that China instead would 'socialize' other states, especially in the Global South, to support Beijing's views on international law and, perhaps, models of domestic law and governance.

At the same time, as reflected in talk of a "new Cold War," international relations theories that assert the importance of 'ideational' elements or 'system type' resonated with tightening links on both the PRC and the US side between domestic political-legal orders and great-powerideological competition at the international level, including over legal rules, norms, and institutions. This dynamic has risen across Xi's tenure, accelerated during Joe Biden's presidency in the US, and changed trajectory as Donald Trump's second term brought both a turn away from liberal-democratic values at home and abroad and a persisting, if fluctuating, hostility toward China.

21.5 Pivotal Moments and Uncertain Trajectories

China's engagement with international law in the current period shows the complexities of a transitional phase and the attendant uncertainties of the path ahead. As the account in this chapter indicates, various elements of China's approach appear to point in different directions. In keeping with China's increased power and confidence internationally, Beijing has adopted broad, avowedly change-seeking language about taking an active role in making international law, building foreign-related rule of law, and offering lessons (including lessons about law) that will advance a "common future for mankind." Observers, including from China, increasingly speak of a Chinese model—primarily for economic development with political stability but including, at least implicitly, legal elements.

Yet China has not—or at least not yet—proffered a robust agenda, or become a potent force, for transformative change in international law. China still often frames its legal arguments and practices as *infra legem*—as at least consistent with, and sometimes supportive of, the existing legal order. New PRC-influenced institutions, which have focused primarily on international economic law, have, so far, not departed fundamentally from their senior peers. They have committed to follow established rules and norms or offer supplementary resources to address unmet needs for investment in development.

China's positions on international legal issues and domestic legal orders in other states have not abandoned a long-standing preference for pluralism—one rooted partly in China's continuing embrace of strong sovereignty and relativism, and reinforced by a newer discourse on Chinese international legal exceptionalism and Xi-era initiatives to shape normative and institutional elements of an increasingly fragmented international legal order, especially in the Global South. China's pattern of legally diffuse, eclectic, informal, or project-specific transnational engagement with the legal systems of other states—primarily in the Global South and through the BRI—has not resembled the legal assistance and legal model-exporting efforts of the US and others in the 1960s and 1990s.

China's power and influence, and new China-backed international law-related institutions, may give Beijing tools and options to advance a full-fledged and distinctive vision of international law, analogous to the US-led one that held sway in much of the world after the World War II and after the Cold War. But, at least in the relatively near term, an international legal order in which China actively and influentially engages is likely to be one of complexity and variation across issue areas, institutions, regions, and time. The old order is fraying. Any successor will reflect China's influence. But it is not yet born.

PART V

CHINESE HISTORICAL PORTRAITS IN INTERNATIONAL LAW

22

Wang Chung-hui (1881–1958)

Yang Liu

22.1 Early Years

Born into a Christian family in Hong Kong in 1882, Wang Chung-hui attended St. Paul's School and later Queen's College. Both were highly reputable schools in Hong Kong that offered Western-style education in English. Wang Chung-hui remained steadfast in his Chinese identity, having been well acquainted with Chinese classics through private tutoring at home. In 1895 he gained admission to Peiyang University, the predecessor of today's Tianjin University and arguably the first modern university in China, following the latter's defeat in the Sino–Japanese War. Among the limited subjects offered, Wang Chung-hui opted to study law. After four years of study, he graduated at the top of his class and was awarded the first university degree in China.

After a brief stint at the Nan Yang Public School in Shanghai, Wang Chung-hui commenced his long journey overseas. His first stop was apparently Japan, where he continued his studies in law and began to engage in politics.[1] He co-established Guo Min Bao (国民报) in Tokyo, a newspaper dedicated to promoting revolutionary ideas.[2] In 1902, Wang landed in the United States, initially attending the University of California, Berkeley but later transferring to Yale University, where he received an LLM *summa cum laude* in 1903 and graduated top of the class, with a 107-page thesis entitled *China and the United States, Being a History of the Development of the Commercial and Political Relations Between the Two Countries*.[3] Wang Chung-hui was formally announced by the Dean of the Yale Law School as having the best academic results in the year.[4] Wang's exceptional performance at Yale also earned him the honour of being a speaker at the commencement, as noted and documented by Liang Qichao during a trip to New Haven.[5]

[1] While a number of sources suggest that Wang Chung-hui studied in Japan, Professor Chen Li of Fudan University points out that there exists no evidence to support such a claim. See Li Chen, 'Early Graduate Legal Studies in America and Legal Transplantation: The Case of China's First International and Comparative Legal Scholar', (2019) 68 Journal of Legal Education 716, 716.

[2] Liu Baodong, 王宠惠与孙中山 (Wang Chong-hui and Sun Yat-sen), (2002) 7史学月刊 (Journal of Historical Science) 59, 59.

[3] Li Chen (n 1) 733.

[4] Ibid 737.

[5] This was recorded in Liang Qichao, 新大陆游记 (Travel Notes in New Continent) (Zhonghua Book Co. 1936) 47.

Yang Liu, *Wang Chung-hui (1881–1958)* In: *Histories of International Law in China*. Edited by: Ignacio de la Rasilla, Jiangyu Wang, and Congyan Cai, Oxford University Press. © Yang Liu 2026.
DOI: 10.1093/oso/9780198888345.003.0022

Wang Chung-hui thus became the first Chinese person ever to obtain an LLM degree from the United States, but he advanced still further. Wang Chung-hui went on to spend another two years at Yale and received the degree of Doctor of Civil Law, again *summa cum laude*. His thesis, entitled *Domicil: A Study in Comparative Law*, proposed a new definition of domicil after a robust comparative study across jurisdictions and over materials of multiple languages.[6]

Wang Chung-hui's study in the US was sponsored by the Chinese government under a special scheme for training Chinese talents overseas. The scheme was initiated by the celebrity merchant Sheng Xuanhuai, who also founded the Peiyang University. Sheng's plan was to send a selected number of elite Beiyang graduates to pursue advanced studies in the West.[7] Importantly, during his sejour in the United States, Wang Chung-hui met with Sun Yat-sen in 1904 and assisted the latter in drafting 'The True Solution of Chinese Question' (中国问题的真解决), a well-known English piece advocating revolution against the Qing Government and soliciting sympathy and support from the world.[8] As Sun Yat-sen himself admitted, all but the last five pages of the article were jointly drafted by Sun and Wang.[9] That was not the first encounter between the two. Sun Yat-sen had actually been a long-term friend of Wang Chung-hui's father. As Wang himself recalled, as early as 1895, Sun Yat-sen had braved the risk of arrest by the Qing Government to attend the wedding of Wang Chung-hui's elder brother in Guangzhou.[10] Despite being only 14 years old, Wang Chung-hui intuitively sensed that Sun was not a favoured figure of the Qing Government.[11] Wang Chung-hui officially became a member of the Sun Yat-sen-led alliance Tongmenghui (同盟会) after its founding in 1905. Sun Yat-sen was said to have given generous financial support to Wang Chung-hui during Wang's period of study in the United States.[12] Sun was alleged to have justified this by saying that 'nurturing an internationally renowned jurist is important and worth more than a hundred soldiers'.[13] One can readily perceive the high regard that Sun Yat-sen held for Wang Chung-hui.

As Wang Chung-hui himself admitted, his principal purpose for studying law in the US was to reform and improve the law in China.[14] He was particularly interested in saving China from the shackles of the extraterritoriality system then practised by Western powers in Chinese territory.[15] Throughout his career, he

6 Li Chen (n 1), 742–43.
7 Ibid 719.
8 The full text of the article at Sun Yat-sen Studies Database <https://sunology.culture.tw/detail/7c1695aef9ee30e2eb989a0a488c06a8/> accessed 13 July 2025.
9 Liu Baodong, '法学家王宠惠：生平、著述、思想' (The Jurist Wang Chonghui: Life, Works and Thoughts) (2005) 1 比较法研究 (Journal of Comparative Law) 127, 129.
10 See Liu Baodong (n 2) 59.
11 Ibid.
12 <https://www.bdcconline.net/zh-hans/stories/wang-chonghui> accessed 13 July 2025.
13 Ibid. The original language is '培植一个国际知名的法学家，其重要且过于十万雄师'.
14 Li Chen (n 1) 724.
15 Ibid 733.

incessantly fought for the abolition of such a system, most notably as one of China's representatives to the Washington Disarmament Conference in 1921.[16]

After leaving the US, Wang Chung-hui travelled to Europe and studied public international law and jurisprudence. During this period, he was called to the English bar at the Inner Temple. In 1907, Wang Chung-hui officially published an English translation of the German Civil Code,[17] a major contribution that won him prestige in the US.[18] In the same year, Wang Chung-hui was part of the Chinese delegation to the second Hague Peace Conference.[19] From 1907 to 1911, Wang Chung-hui studied comparative law in Germany and France.[20] In 1910, he served as a member of the Chinese delegation to the first Hague Conference on the Unification of the Law on the Bill of Exchanges.[21] In 1912, Wang Chung-hui was a principal founding member of the short-lived International Law Association (国际法会) in Beijing, a research-oriented society dedicated to international law and sponsored by Lou Tseng-Tsiang.[22] The association was intended as a preparation for the Third Hague Peace Conference,[23] which did not however actually take place due to the outbreak of the First World War. Wang Chung-hui was also a member of the International Academy of Comparative Law, based in Berlin.

22.2 Professional Life

When Sun Yat-sen was inaugurated as the interim president of the provisional government of the Republic of China on 1 January1912, Wang Chung-hui was appointed foreign minister, which was remarkable considering Wang's relatively young age of 31. The appointment also stirred some controversy among the public, as Wu Tingfang, a far more sophisticated veteran diplomat, was bypassed for the post.[24] Shortly thereafter, Yuan Shikai took over power as the interim president, and Wang Chung-hui was elected Minister of Justice under the Premiership of Tang

[16] Ole Spiermann, 'Judge Wang Chung-hui at the Permanent Court of International Justice' (2006) 5 Chinese Journal of International Law 115, 118–19; Liu Baodong (n 9) 131–32.

[17] Wang Chung Hui, *The German Civil Code, Translated and Annotated, with an Historical Introduction and Appendices* (Stevens and Sons, Ltd 1907).

[18] John Bassett Moore, 'The Organization of the Permanent Court of International Justice' (1922) 22 Columbia LR 497, 504.

[19] Ryan Martínez Mitchell, 'China's Participation in the Second Hague Conference and the Concept of Equal Sovereignty in International Law' (2021) 11 Asian JIL 351, 355.

[20] Rapport Annuel de la Cour Permanente de Justice International (1er janvier 1922–15 juin 1925), PCIJ Series E, no 1, 23.

[21] Ibid.

[22] Hsien-Hsiang Feng, '国际法会及其历史之初探 *(1912-1916)*' (A Preliminary Study of the International Law Association and Its History (1912–1916) (2019) 5 国立政治大学历史学报 (Journal of History of National Chengchi University) 55, 60, 62, 66.

[23] Chi-hua Tang, '清末明初中国对《海牙保和会》之参与' (A Study on China's Participation of the Hague Peace Conferences) (2005) 5 国立政治大学历史学报 (Journal of History of National Chengchi University) 45, 73.

[24] Liu Baodong (n 2) 60.

Shaoyi. However, Wang Chung-hui soon resigned in protest against Yuan's violation of the Provisional Constitution.[25] In 1913, he relocated to Shanghai to work as an English editor for Zhonghua Books Co. A separate source suggests that Wang Chung-hui acted as a consultant to a railway company founded by Sun Yat-sen in Shanghai.[26] Wang Chung-hui shortly took the position of the vice-chancellor of Fudan University.[27] During this post, Wang Chung-hui published extensively on constitutional law and improved the quality of legal research in Fudan, a legacy still felt in this renowned university today. From 1917 to 1920, Wang Chung-hui was the president of the Commission on the Codification of Law. In 1920, Wang Chung-hui became the chief justice of the *Da Li Yuan* (大理院), the Chinese supreme court. In 1922, Wang Chung-hui served as Minister of Justice of the Beiyang Government under Li Yuanhong, and briefly as acting Premier from September to November 1922.

In June 1927, Wang Chung-hui was appointed Minister of Justice by the Nanjing Nationalist Government. On 10 October 1928 Wang Chung-hui officially commenced his post as the head of the Judicial Yuan (司法院). Wang Chung-hui was part of a group of Western-educated jurists in the government who collaboratively advanced certain judicial reforms, including initiatives to promote judicial independence. In the same year, Wang Chung-hui was nominated as member of the Permanent Court of Arbitration.[28]

Wang Chung-hui was one of the seventeen members constituting the League of Nations Committee of Experts for the Progressive Codification of International Law, convened pursuant to a resolution adopted by the Assembly on 22 September 1924.[29] Wang Chung-hui was invited by Chairman Hammarskjöld to sit in the Drafting Sub-Committee along with Wickersham and de Visscher.[30] Wang Chung-hui participated in all five sessions of the committee except for the second one in 1924. He later became a member of the sub-committees on two important topics on public international law—state responsibility and piracy, respectively[31]—and two others in private international law (legal situation of non-profit-making international associations and private international foundations, and conflicts of laws concerning contracts for the sale of goods).[32] These sub-committees were entrusted with the task of producing study reports on the assigned topics for consideration by the plenary committee. Wang Chung-hui favoured a broad conception

[25] Liu Baodong (n 9) 130.

[26] Wang Chung-hui, in Biographical Dictionary of Chinese Christianity <https://www.bdcconline.net/zh-hans/stories/wang-chonghui> accessed 13 July 2025.

[27] Liu Baodong (n 9) 130.

[28] Annual Report of the Permanent Court of International Justice (June 15th, 1930–June 15th, 1931), PCIJ Series E no 7, 37.

[29] Shabtai Rosenne, *League of Nations Committee of Experts for the Progressive Codification of International Law [1925–1928]*, vol I (Oceana Publications Inc. 1972) vii.

[30] Ibid 27.

[31] Ibid 45.

[32] Ibid 195–96.

of codification which focused on 'proposals for the alteration of existing rules', as opposed to merely 'a restatement of existing law'.[33]

In 1921, Wang Chung-hui was elected a deputy judge (*juge suppléant*) of the Permanent Court of International Justice ('PCIJ').[34] The PCIJ Statute explicitly provided for the division of its members into eleven ordinary judges (*juge titulaire*) and four deputy judges. Deputy judges were supposed to substitute for ordinary judges in case the latter were unavailable.[35] Deputy judges were generally subject to less strict rules than ordinary judges. For example, a deputy judge was exempt from the duty to refrain from 'exercis[ing] any political or administrative function' that would otherwise apply to judges, except when the deputy judge was performing his duties on the PCIJ.[36] A deputy judge is also prohibited from acting as agent, counsel, or advocate before the PCIJ only in relation to cases where he was called upon to exercise his functions.[37] Wang Chung-hui was unable to attend the very first meeting of the PCIJ in 1922.[38]

During his tenure at the PCIJ, Wang Chung-hui sat in more than thirty cases.[39] However, he did not author any individual opinions of his own, making it difficult to glance into his personal views on the cases. Wang's first case was the well-known *S.S. Wimbledon*, where he joined the majority opinion. In the judgment on merits, the Court, adopting a literal reading of Article 380 of the Treaty of Versailles, held that Germany was wrongful in denying the *S.S. Wimbledon* access to the Kiel Canal.[40] The case was also novel in that the institution of third-party intervention was invoked for the first time and accepted by the Court in a separate judgment.[41] In the third session of the PCIJ, Wang also participated in the decisions of three other cases. In *Eastern Carelia*, the Court was asked to opine on the legal bindingness of the Treaty of Peace between Finland and Russia and the annexed Russian declaration regarding the autonomy of Eastern Carelia,[42] which is essentially related to the dispute between the Soviet Union and Finland. The prominence of this advisory opinion is well manifested in the continuing debate about the appropriateness of touching upon bilateral disputes in advisory proceedings, which has been frequently addressed by the International Court of Justice (ICJ) on various occasions.[43] The case was significant also because the Council of the League of Nations,

[33] Ibid li, 21.
[34] James Brown Scott, 'The Election of Judges for the Permanent Court of International Justice' (1921) 15 American Journal of International Law 556, 557.
[35] Article 25, Statute of the Permanent Court of International Justice, PCIJ Series D no 2, 14.
[36] Article 16, ibid 11–12.
[37] Article 17, ibid 12.
[38] Moore (n 18) 506.
[39] As counted by the number in the General List of the PCIJ.
[40] *S. S. 'Wimbledon'* (1923) PCIJ Series A no 1, 33.
[41] *S. S. 'Wimbledon' (Question of Intervention by Poland)* (1923) PCIJ Series A no 1, 11.
[42] *Status of Eastern Carelia* (1923) PCIJ Series B no 5, 7.
[43] See. e.g. *Legal Consequences Arising from the Policies and Practices of Israel in the Occupied Palestinian Territory, Including East Jerusalem*, Advisory Opinion of 19 July 2024, paras 33-35.

which requested the advisory opinion, could not settle the dispute, as the Soviet government would not consent to submitting it to the Council.[44] Wang Chung-hui formed a majority with Judges Anzilotti, Finlay, Huber, and Moore, who jointly decided to decline the request for advisory opinion.[45] The aforesaid five judges were prepared to dissent should the Court decide to give an advisory opinion, notwithstanding the risk of displeasing the Council.[46] In *German Settlers in Poland*, Wang Chung-hui sat in the drafting committee, together with Judges Huber and Moore.[47] The case concerned the expulsion by Poland of German settlers from the land that the latter had leased.[48] The prior question was whether the Council of the League of Nations possesses the competence to deal with the matter. A negative answer would deprive the Court of its entitlement to render the advisory opinion.[49] The majority opinion was careful to affirm the Council's competence and conclude that Poland's position cannot be justified under international law.[50] A related case is the *Acquisition of Polish Nationality* advisory opinion,[51] which arose out of Poland's non-recognition of certain former German nationals residing in its territory as not having acquired Polish nationality.[52] In a unanimous opinion, the Court concluded that the issue of acquisition of nationality for the relevant persons falls within the competence of the Council and clarified that the relevant factor was the habitual residence of the parents on the date when the person concerned was born.[53]

In the following sessions of the PCIJ, Wang further participated in a number of decisions as a deputy judge. In the fourth session, Wang sat in the *Question of Jaworzina*, in which the Court upheld a commission-decided delimitation between Poland and Czechoslovakia as final.[54] In the seventh session of the PCIJ, Wang was again elected into the drafting committee in *Polish Postal Service in Danzig*, along with Huber and Anzilotti.[55] The questions formulated to the Court in this case seem relatively technical, that is, whether the Polish postal service at Danzig is restricted to its premises or can be extended by such premises and whether the use of such postal service is available to the Polish authorities or to the general public.[56] The Court treated the applicable treaty provisions at its face value

[44] *Status of Eastern Carelia* (n 42) 24.
[45] Ibid 29.
[46] Ole Spiermann, *International Legal Argument in the Permanent Court of International Justice: The Rise of the International Judiciary* (CUP 2005) 162.
[47] Ibid 186.
[48] *German Settlers in Poland* (1923) PCIJ Series B no 6, 6–7.
[49] Ibid 19.
[50] Ibid 43.
[51] *Acquisition of Polish Nationality* (1923) PCIJ Series B no 7, 6.
[52] Ibid.
[53] Ibid 21.
[54] *Question of Jaworzina (Polish–Czechoslovakian Frontier)* (1923) PCIJ Series B no 8, 57.
[55] Spiermann (n 16) 120 and fn 22.
[56] *Polish Postal Service in Danzig* (1925) PCIJ Series B no 11, 8.

and concluded that there was nothing to restrict the operation of the postal service to the premises or to the Polish authorities only.[57] In the eighth session, Wang had its first contentious case in the PCIJ, triggered by Poland's taking over of German interests in Upper Silesia.[58]

In the thirteenth session of the PCIJ, Wang had the opportunity to work on a case involving China. Belgium instituted proceedings against China for the latter's unilateral denunciation of the Treaty of 2 November 1865 between the two States, and President Huber issued an order adopting provisional measures.[59] It was claimed that the denunciation was largely motivated by China's desire to abolish unequal treaties.[60] Records suggest that President Huber was eager to call Wang to sit on this case, but communication between the PCIJ and Judge Wang proved difficult in practical terms at that time.[61] Accordingly, Wang was only able to participate in one of the multiple phases of the proceedings, where the Court made an order fixing the time limit on the submission of written pleadings.[62] Such an order is essentially of a procedural nature and does not involve much legal analysis. China did not formally make any move throughout the proceedings, but the case was ultimately resolved through the conclusion of a preliminary treaty between the parties and Belgium withdrew the case accordingly.[63] Judge Wang further sat in *Jurisdiction of the Courts in Danzig*[64] and *Rights of Minorities in Upper Silesia*[65] in the thirteen session, and in *Upper Savoy*[66] and *River Oder*[67] in the thirteenth session, before the expiry of his term as deputy judge.

In 1930, Wang Chung-hui was elected an ordinary judge of the PCIJ.[68] He was soon to face a politically sensitive case, *Customs Regime between Germany and Austria*, for which the Court rendered its advisory opinion in 1931.[69] The case concerned whether the customs union established by Germany and Austria was compatible with the treaty of Saint-Germain and Protocol No. 1 of 4 October 1922, both of which serve to ensure the independence of Austria.[70] The former treaty

[57] Ibid 37–38.
[58] *Case concerning Certain German Interests in Polish Upper Silesia (Preliminary Objections)* (1925) PCIJ Series A no 6, 5.
[59] *Denunciation of the Treaty of November 2nd, 1865, between China and Belgium, Order of 8 January 1927*, PCIJ Series A, No.8, 4.
[60] Spiermann (n 16) 121.
[61] Ibid 122.
[62] *Denunciation of the Treaty of November 2nd, 1865, between China and Belgium* (1928) PCIJ Series A no 14, 4.
[63] *Denunciation of the Treaty of November 2nd, 1865, between China and Belgium* (1929) PCIJ Series A no 18, 5.
[64] *Jurisdiction of the Courts in Danzig* (1928) PCIJ Series B no 15, 4.
[65] *Rights of Minorities in Upper Silesia (Minority Schools)* (1928) PCIJ Series A, no 15, 4.
[66] *Free Zones of Upper Savoy and the District of Gex* (1929) PCIJ Series A no 22, 5.
[67] *Case Relating to the Territorial Jurisdiction of the International Commission of the River Oder* (1929) PCIJ Series A no 23, 5.
[68] Manley O. Hudson, 'The Election of Members of the Permanent Court of International Justice' (1930) 24 American Journal of International Law 718, 726.
[69] *Customs Regime between Germany and Austria* (1931) PCIJ Series A/B no 41, 37.
[70] Ibid 42.

provides, in Article 88, that 'Austria undertakes in the absence of the consent of the said Council to abstain from any act which might directly or indirectly or by any means whatever compromise her independence',[71] while the latter bestows Austria with certain freedom in tariffs under the condition that Austria 'shall not violate her economic independence by granting to any State a special regime or exclusive advantages calculated to threaten this independence'.[72] The majority, by eight votes against seven with President Anzilotti casting a vote,[73] decided that the conclusion of a customs union, taken as a whole, involved danger to the independence of Austria.[74] Judge Wang and six other judges dissented, questioning how the customs regime would threaten the independence of Austria. The dissenting judges raised a fundamental point that bears on the approach to the issue, as exemplified in the following lines:

> Restrictions on its liberty of action which a State may agree to do not affect its independence, provided that the State does not thereby deprive itself of its organic powers. Still less do restrictions imposed by international law deprive it of its independence.[75]

Based on such an assumption, no threat to Austria's independence can be lightly inferred absent any evidence to that effect.[76] Such an assumption also resonates with the lasting and live debate on the relationship between international law and sovereignty.[77] This case is said to constitute a 'watershed in the history of the Permanent Court', with the reputation of the PCIJ tarnished for treating a legal question as a political one.[78] Meanwhile, the Court also rendered some less controversial decisions, with Judge Wang's participation and with a clear majority, including, for example, *Railway Traffic between Lithuania and Poland*,[79] *Access to, or Anchorage in, the Port of Danzig, of Polish War Vessels*,[80] *Interpretation of the Greco-Bulgarian Agreement of December 9th, 1927*,[81] *Treatment of Polish Nationals and*

[71] Ibid.
[72] Ibid 43.
[73] Austria applied to appoint a judge ad hoc, but the application was the rejected by the Court on the ground that Austria and Germany are in the same interest in this case. See ibid 90. Judge Wang and four other judges dissented to the Court's order. See *Dissenting Opinion of M. Adatci, M. Rostworowski, M. Altamira, M. Anzilotti and M. Wang*, PCIJ Series A/B no 41, 91.
[74] *Customs Regime between Germany and Austria* (n 69), 52.
[75] *Dissenting Opinion of M. Adatci, M. Kellogg, Baron Rolin-Jaequemyns, Sir Cecil Hurst, M. Schücking, Jonkheer van Eysinga and M. Wang* (n 73), 77.
[76] Ibid 82.
[77] James Crawford, *Change, Order, Change: The Course of International Law, General Course of International Law* (Brill 2014), Chapter III.
[78] Spiermann (n 16) 124.
[79] *Railway Traffic between Lithuania and Poland* (1931) PCIJ Series A/B no 42, 108.
[80] *Access to, or Anchorage in, the Port of Danzig, of Polish War Vessels* (1931) PCIJ Series A/B no 43, 128.
[81] *Interpretation of the Greco-Bulgarian Agreement of December 9th, 1927* (1932) PCIJ Series A/B no 45, 68.

Other Persons of Polish Origin or Speech in the Danzig Territory,[82] *Interpretation of the Statute of the Memel Territory*,[83] *Prince von Pless Administration*,[84] *Polish Agrarian Reform and German Minority*,[85] *Lighthouses Case*,[86] and *Consistency of Certain Danzig Legislative Decrees with the Constitution of the Free City*,[87] the final case in which Judge Wang participated in the PCIJ.

Two cases during Judge Wang's second term deserve particular attention. First, in *Appeal from a Judgment of the Hungaro-Czechoslovak Mixed Arbitral Tribunal*,[88] Judge Wang was nominated to the drafting committee for a third time and allegedly played a significant role in the phrasing of the *dispositif* of the judgment.[89] This judgment, which was lauded by President Adatci of the Court as 'one of the best that the Court had pronounced since its creation',[90] is a standard-setting precedent for future decisions.[91] The second is the well-known *Legal Status of Eastern Greenland* case.[92] It arose out of the dispute between Norway and Denmark over the sovereignty of Eastern Greenland, and the PCIJ ultimately sided with Denmark based on the doctrine of effective occupation.[93] Judge Wang and his German colleague Judge Schücking appended certain of their own observations to the judgment, while concurring with the majority.[94] Their observations merely addressed a point of disagreement on interpreting Denmark's documents, which were alleged to showcase its intention to claim sovereignty over the disputed territory. The two judges observed that the record was insufficient to establish such an intention on the part of Denmark to extend its sovereignty to Eastern Greenland.[95] However, it may be suggested that the differences between the two judges and the majority are far more significant than they appear to be, as the former essentially challenged Denmark's sovereignty over Eastern Greenland.[96]

[82] *Treatment of Polish Nationals and Other Persons of Polish Origin or Speech in the Danzig Territory* (1932) PCIJ Series A/B no 44, 4.

[83] *Treatment of Polish Nationals and Other Persons of Polish Origin or Speech in the Danzig Territory* (1932), PCIJ Series A/B no 47, 243; no 49, 294.

[84] *Case concerning the Administration of the Prince von Pless* (1933) PCIJ Series A/B no 52, 11; PCIJ Series A/B no 54, 150; no 59, 194.

[85] *Case concerning the Polish Agrarian Reform and the German Minority* (1933) PCIJ Series A/B no 60, 201.

[86] *Lighthouses Case between France and Greece* (1934) PCIJ Series A/B no 62, 4.

[87] *Consistency of Certain Danzig Legislative Decrees with the Constitution of the Free City* (1935) PCIJ Series A/B no 65, 41.

[88] *Appeal from a Judgment of the Hungaro-Czechoslovak Mixed Arbitral Tribuna*l (1933) PCIJ Series A/B no 61, 208.

[89] Ole Spiermann (n 46) 354.

[90] The quote was recorded in Spiermann, ibid 354. The original language in French by President Adatci was 'un des meilleurs que la cour ait prononcés depuis sa création'.

[91] Spiermann (n 16) 126.

[92] *Legal Status of Eastern Greenland* (1933) PCIJ Series A/B no 53, 22.

[93] Ibid 64.

[94] *Observations by M. Schücking and M. Wang*, ibid 96.

[95] Ibid.

[96] Spiermann (n 16) 125–26.

On 15 January 1936, Wang Chung-hui submitted his letter of resignation to the President of the PCIJ for 'personal and other reasons which compelled him to return to China'.[97] The sentiment of regret was well felt in the PCIJ, as Judge Moore spoke on Wang's departure: '[t]he loss to the Court probably is irreparable.'[98] Åke Hammarskjöld, registrar of the Court, wrote to Wang upon the latter's resignation that 'I need hardly say what a blow this was'.[99] For Hammarskjöld, Wang's resignation was very much anticipated, as the former continued to state that 'sooner or later your country would appeal to your unparalleled experience, learning and skill'.[100] Indeed, upon his return to China, Wang served an important position as minister of foreign affairs starting from 1937 to 1941, an arduous period for China during the Second World War. As foreign minister, Wang signed the Sino–Soviet Non-Aggression Pact on behalf of China on 21 August 1937,[101] at the critical moment at which Japan launched a full-scale invasion against China. After leaving his post, Wang Chung-hui became secretary-general of the Supreme National Defense Council, the highest wartime authority within the Nationalist Government, until 1948. In this role, Wang Chung-hui maintained his service to Chinese diplomacy. In 1943, Wang Chung-hui attended the Cairo Conference with Chiang Kai-shek. Wang Chung-hui was present in a historical photo of the major participants in the conference before the Mena House Hotel in Cairo, including Roosevelt, Churchill, Chiang, and the principal officers of the respective states.[102]

In 1945, Wang Chung-hui was a member of the Chinese Delegation to San Francisco Conference. Immediately prior to the conference, Wang Chung-hui was nominated to the United Nations Committee of Jurists, which was tasked to propose a new world court—the International Court of Justice ('ICJ')—in lieu of the PCIJ. The meeting minutes record some of Wang's learned interventions. First, on whether national judges should be allowed to sit in the cases before the ICJ, Wang Chung-hui observed that 'if the Court were called upon to interpret a multilateral treaty and national judges were not allowed to sit, it might be impossible to get a quorum'.[103] Second, on the jurisdiction of the ICJ, Wang Chung-hui fervently advocated for compulsory jurisdiction, because 'the exercise of compulsory jurisdiction by the Court would promote the rule of law in international society'.[104] In particular, he mentioned that public opinion in China 'strongly

[97] Twelfth Annual Report of the Permanent Court of International Justice, PCIJ Series E no 12, 16.
[98] Quoted in Spiermann (n 46) 369.
[99] Spiermann (n 16) 127.
[100] Ibid.
[101] For the full text of the treaty, see Bruce A. Elleman, *International Rivalry and Secret Diplomacy in East Asia, 1896–1950* (Routledge 2019) 202–03.
[102] 'The Cairo Conference and Taiwan's Liberation' (ThinkChina, 4 February 2022) <https://www.thinkchina.sg/history/photo-story-cairo-conference-and-taiwans-liberation> accessed 13 July 2025.
[103] Documents of the United Nations Conference on International Organizations (1945), vol XIV, 46.
[104] Ibid 147–48.

favored' compulsory jurisdiction for the ICJ.[105] The sub-committee on Article 36, chaired by Wang Chung-hui, unanimously adopted a revision of Article 36 which provided for compulsory jurisdiction of the future ICJ,[106] though it was not ultimately accepted by the plenary committee. Third, Wang Chung-hui played a substantial role in the debate on the method of nominating ICJ judges. It is interesting that a significant divergence occurred in the United Nations Committee of Jurists on whether to reform the existing methods of nomination to the effect that candidates are nominated directly by governments, rather than by the national groups in the PCA. According to the meeting minutes, among the committee members who spoke on this issue there was a strong preference to maintain the existing method, principally out of fear for political influence if governments were able to make the nominations.[107] In contrast, Wang Chung-hui possessed an unambiguous and strong view in favour of the proposal for reform. According to Wang Chung-hui, 'judges should be nominated by governments and ... the governments should consult the highest courts and certain other institutions with respect to the nominations'.[108] This also reflects the position of the then Chinese government. Ultimately, the motion to change failed due to a 16–16 split in the committee,[109] but Wang Chung-hui's strong advocacy on this important issue was well recorded. Fourth, during the discussion, there was a proposal to amend Article 36 of Statute by inserting 'of a legal character' after 'cases', so as to clarify the legal nature of the disputes that the ICJ is capable of resolving. Wang Chung-hui opposed such an amendment for two reasons:

> One was that he could see no reason why a dispute which the·parties were willing to submit to the Court should not be decided by it; the other was that the Court had exercised jurisdiction under Article 36 of the present Statute without any difficulty. He pointed out that all international disputes had at least some political implications and the insertion of the phrase 'of a legal character' might seem restrictive.[110]

The motion for amendment failed,[111] but one necessarily feels Wang Chung-hui's firm belief on the all-inclusive potential of judicial settlement of international disputes.

105 Ibid.
106 Ibid 286–87.
107 Ibid 191–93.
108 Ibid (a corrigendum appeared at 203).
109 Ibid 194–95.
110 Ibid 228.
111 Ibid 229.

Fifth, Wang Chung-hui proposed to limit the use of individual opinions by judges in the majority, as there was no need to for them to express opinions separately other than through the judgment. The weakness of individual opinions of majority judges, as Wang Chung-hui pointed out, was that they 'might differ slightly in various respects and that such differences might affect the authority of the judgment'.[112] In this regard, there is no doubt that Wang Chung-hui's previous experience on the PCIJ bench underscores such a subtle and nuanced observation.

In 1948, Wang Chung-hui was elected a member of the Academia Sinica, and in the next year served again as the president of Judicial Yuan. Wang Chung-hui relocated to Taiwan in 1950 and passed away in 1958. Wang Chun-hui's tomb was located in the campus of Soochow University in Taipei, to whose re-opening Wang contributed significantly, and where Wang served as chairman of the board.[113]

22.3 Wang Chung-hui's Legacy

Wang Chung-hui, while foremost remembered as the first Chinese judge to an international judiciary, has actually worn multiple hats. In addition to being a judge, he was also a diplomat, a scholar and a politician. His distinguished career has significantly impacted international law, especially concerning China.

22.3.1 On International Law

Wang Chung-hui's contribution to international law, in particular international dispute settlement, admits of no doubt. The decisions and the joint separate or dissenting opinions that he participated in during his terms at the PCIJ are living records of his legacy. The collective nature of the judgments rendered in the name of the court makes it difficult to assess Judge Wang's specific contributions, but it would not be difficult to speculate as to the level of legal knowledge and the art of amassing consensus and persuasion that may be indispensable in this process. The high praise sung by Judge Wang's colleagues in the PCIJ acts as powerful testimony in this respect. To quote again Hammarskjöld's sympathy for Judge Wang: 'I can never thank you enough for what you have been and done the past years; and now that chapter seems to be closed, I feel sorely tempted to leave the Hague too.'[114] Judge Wang provides a prime example of a non-Western international lawyer making an impact on a presumably Western-dominated context area.

[112] Ibid 173.

[113] See 'Tomb-Sweeping on Soochow Campus: In Commemoration of Our Late Chairman, and Presidents' (*Soochow University*, 25 April 2018) <https://www-en.scu.edu.tw/news/1764> accessed 13 July 2025.

[114] Spiermann (n 16) 127.

Wang Chung-hui's experience with the PCIJ proved highly valuable for the ICJ. Wang Chung-hui placed substantial emphasis on the continuity between the PCIJ and the ICJ. He famously stated before the United Nations Committee of Jurists that '[i]n endeavoring to organize an International Court, we are not treading on new ground; we are rather to improve upon a system that has been in existence for almost a quarter of a century'.[115] Accordingly, he was cautious of any institutional set-up that would contradict continuity. For example, he expressed reservations about having all or the majority of judges replaced upon the expiry of their first term.[116] The idea of continuity is fully embraced by the ICJ, as is evidenced by the fact that the ICJ Statute is scarcely modified from the PCIJ Statute. The practice and jurisprudence of the PCIJ still offer great insights for the ICJ. Of course, all of Wang Chung-hui's aspirations for the ICJ were not accepted; for example, the promotion of compulsory jurisdiction. In 1945, Wang Chung-hui thought the time was ripe to switch from optional to compulsory jurisdiction, as '45 out of 51 nations had now accepted the optional clause, though with many reservations', which was 'a logical step in the cause of world security'.[117] This did not happen. Nor did we witness an expansion of states favouring ICJ's jurisdiction. Currently only seventy-four states have deposited declarations accepting the compulsory jurisdiction of the ICJ.[118] Such a point does not, however, detract from the significant role of Wang Chung-hui's idea in shaping the ICJ as it is today.

22.3.2 On International Law Profession in China

With solid training on legal studies and excellent mastering of multiple foreign languages, Wang Chung-hui could have made a successful academic career. But he remained always at the disposal of the call of his times and his motherland. Despite taking various political positions, Wang Chung-hui may be better viewed as essentially a technocrat, or scholar-bureaucrat. Back in the 1910s, foreign affairs were not the first priority for the Beiyang government, which haphazardly left significant room for the professionalization of diplomacy.[119] The engagement of western-trained international lawyers, including Wang Chung-hui, in high diplomatic positions contributes a legalist approach to diplomacy in China.[120] Wang Chung-hui was a real patriot who dedicated his expertise in international law to safeguarding the vital interests of China. The extraterritoriality system in

115 Documents of the United Nations Conference on International Organizations (n 103) 38.

116 Ibid 94.

117 Ibid 147–48.

118 See 'Declarations Recognizing the Jurisdiction of the Court as Compulsory' (*International Court of Justice*) <https://www.icj-cij.org/declarations> accessed 13 July 2025.

119 Pasha L. Hsieh, 'The Discipline of International Law in Republican China and Contemporary Taiwan' (2015) 14 Washington University Global Studies Law Review 87, 98.

120 Ibid 99.

Chinese territories caused Wang Chung-hui everlasting pain, and he strived his best to abolish it, albeit not without setbacks. The Cairo Conference may be considered a peak in Wang Chung-hui's diplomatic career, where Wang assisted his country in successfully restoring sovereignty over all territories occupied by Japan, including Manchuria, Formosa (Taiwan), and the Pescadores (Penghu).[121] The Cairo Declaration constitutes a fundamental basis for China's addressing of the so-called Taiwan Issue today.

One aspect that may be illuminating for future Chinese international lawyers is the proper combination by Wang Chung-hui of international lawyer and national lawyer. Wang Chung-hui did not quite start out as an international lawyer. His original expertise was civil law, on which area he wrote his doctoral thesis at Yale. In various governmental positions, however, he dealt with different areas of law, including constitutional law, civil law, and even criminal law. To take the example of constitutional law, as recorded in Wang Chung-hui's biography at the PCIJ, Wang's views on constitutional law exerted a significant influence on the making of the Chinese Constitution.[122] As early as 1913, Wang Chung-hui published an important article entitled 'A Discussion of the Constitution of the Republic of China' (中华民国宪法刍议), where he elaborated his proposal for a future constitution.[123] Wang Chung-hui participated in the 1946 National Constituent Assembly in Nanjing, which adopted the Constitution of the Republic of China, a text that Wang was involved in drafting. Based on his strong comparative law background, Wang Chung-hui introduced fresh, eye-opening perspectives into the Chinese legal system.

One cannot thus fail to note that Wang Chung-hui was an international lawyer grown from a national lawyer. This echoes the observation of the late ICJ Judge James Crawford, that if one wants to be a good international lawyer, one should be a good lawyer first.[124] In Wang Chung-hui's time, the revolving door between the two was more readily available. He lived a life that connected national law and international law, something that current generations of Chinese international lawyers would be eager to engage with. It isimportant that international lawyers do not lose sight of the situation in their national state.

Gradually Wang Chung-hui's expertise in other fields has been overshadowed by his reputation in international law. Students of civil law today are more familiar with the works of Wang Chung-hui's peers, such as Shi Shangkuan. Due to Wang

[121] 'Cairo Conference 1943' (*The Avalon Project*) <https://avalon.law.yale.edu/wwii/cairo.asp> accessed 13 July 2025.

[122] Rapport Annuel de la Cour Permanente de Justice International (n 20) 23.

[123] Liu Baodong (n 9) 130.

[124] Thomas D. Grant, 'James Crawford, International Law Academic, Practitioner, and Judge, 1948-2021' (*Kluwer Arbitration Blog*, 15 July 2021 <https://arbitrationblog.kluwerarbitration.com/2021/07/15/james-crawford-international-law-academic-practitioner-and-judge-1948-2021/> accessed 13 July 2025.

Chung-hui's preoccupation with politics, it is regrettable that even in the field of international law, Wang did not leave any significant treatise or monograph for future generations. Fortunately, Wang Chung-hui's major writings have been compiled into a published anthology in Chinese,[125] allowing future generations to experience this pioneering Chinese international lawyer.

[125] Zhang Renshan (ed), 王宠惠法学文集 (An Anthology of Wang Chonghui's Legal Writings) (Law Press 2008).

23

Wellington Koo (1888–1985)

Maria Adele Carrai

23.1 Early and Formative Years

Wellington Koo (1888–1985), known as Gu Weijun (顾维钧) in Chinese, was born in 1888 in the bustling city of Shanghai. He was the fourth child of the household, born to Mr Gu Rong 顾溶 and Mrs Jiang Fu'an 蒋福安.[1] His birth was surrounded by family financial constraints, but the financial situation took a turn for the better due to his father's new appointment as a bookkeeper at the Shen Yu Foreign Bank 慎裕洋行, owned by the influential entrepreneur Zhu Baosan 朱葆三, leader in modern Shanghai industrial and commercial circles and president of the Shanghai General Chamber of Commerce.[2] From Koo's early years, his life was one of transition and change, mirroring China's own metamorphosis during the twentieth century. His father's career trajectory changed dramatically, moving from an accounting expert to an influential official businessman in 1892. This evolution was in no small part due to Zhu Baosan's patronage and Gu Rong's interactions with pivotal figures of the late Qing Dynasty such as Sheng Xuanhuai and Yuan Shuxun. When, years later, Koo departed for Columbia University in 1905, he still associated with his Shanghai roots, listing his address as 13 Fuzhou Road, the location of Shen Yu Foreign Bank. Raised amid sudden affluence, young Koo's educational journey began in a private Confucian school at the age of three. The foundation of his education was steeped in Chinese culture: reading characters, delving into scriptures, and committing poems to memory. This strong grounding in his native culture, juxtaposed with later exposure to Western education, rendered him uniquely equipped to bridge the cultural chasm in his later diplomatic career. A significant transition in his educational path was his enrolment into the Anglo-Chinese College when he was eleven years old.[3] Here, Western culture and the

[1] Jonathan Clements, *The Makers of the Modern World: Wellington Koo* (Haus Publishing 2008); Jonathan Clements, *Wellington Koo: China* (Chicago University Press 2008). Stephen Craft, *G. V.K. Wellington Koo and the Emergence of Modern China* (UPK 2015); 沈潜,《顾维钧家族》(新星出版社 2018) 29页, 50页 (Shen Qian, *The Gu Weijun Family* (Nova Publishing House 2018) 29, 50).

[2] Located at No. 13 Fuzhou Road, adjacent to the iconic Bund, this bank, placed strategically in the heart of the public concession area, was a bustling hub where many of Shanghai's influential figures gathered. 王溪，鲍蔓华，'"宁波帮"，从老外滩走出',《人民政协报》2021年12月16日 第11版 (Wang Xi and Bao Manhua, '"Ningbo Gang", Out of the Old Bund' *People's Political Consultative Conference Daily* (Beijing, vol 11, 16 December 2021).

[3] Clements (n 1) 20.

Maria Adele Carrai, *Wellington Koo (1888–1985)* In: *Histories of International Law in China*. Edited by: Ignacio de la Rasilla, Jiangyu Wang, and Congyan Cai, Oxford University Press.
DOI: 10.1093/oso/9780198888345.003.0023

English language became central to his curriculum. Despite being younger than his peers, his acumen, especially in English, made him stand out. It was during this phase that he first encountered the principles of international law, a subject that would later define his career. According to the 'Rules and Regulations of the Curriculum of the Anglo-Chinese College' written by Lin Lechi林乐知,[4] the seventh year required the study of international law and nautical surveying.[5]

In 1901 Koo joined St. John's College, an institution founded in 1879 by the American Episcopal Church. This school was pivotal in introducing him to American culture and the broader Western world. The curriculum under the leadership of Francis Lister Hawks Pott 卜舫济 focused on imparting a Western-style education, promoting English-language proficiency and introducing students to Western scientific and cultural advancements.[6] From the time he entered St. John's, the new teaching content and methods opened Koo's mind and strengthened his concern for current events and his desire for new knowledge and new learning. As Koo later recalled, 'I think it was mainly because of the new teachers' ideas that my classmates and I felt more and more the need for change … At the same time, there was a growing interest in Western education among some students, and one by one, they went to foreign countries to study.'[7] His decision to leave the confines of St. John's a year before graduation was emblematic of the broader societal shift at the time, reflecting a growing eagerness among Chinese youth to study overseas and embrace Western education. In August 1904, a year short of graduation from St. John's, Koo went to the United States to study at his father's expense. The years he spent studying at the Shanghai church schools not only gave Koo excellent English reading and writing skills, but also sparked his interest in studying diplomacy, which laid the foundation for his law studies at Columbia University.

During his first year in the United States, Koo, aged seventeen years old, studied at Cook College in Ithaca, a preparatory school.[8] In September 1905 he was admitted to Columbia University, majoring in political science and diplomacy.[9] While at Columbia, Koo participated in speeches and debates sponsored

[4] 林乐知,《中西书院课程规条》,《万国公报》,(66)6, 818页 (Lin Lezhi, 'Zhongxi shuyuan curriculum rules' *Bulletin of Nations* (66) 6, 818); 李楚材,《帝国主义侵华教育史资料—教会教育》(教育科学出版社 1987) 103-104 页. (Li Chucai, *Imperialist Invasion of China Education History Data—Church Education* (Educational Science Publishing House 1987) 103–04).

[5] The actual study period may have been earlier than the seventh year.

[6] 顾维钧,《顾维钧回忆录》第一分册 (中华书局 1983) 21–22 页 (Gu Weijun, *Gu Weijun's Memoirs*, first fascicle (Zhonghua Book Company 1983) 21–22).

[7] ibid 22.

[8] 顾维钧,《顾维钧回忆录》第一分册, (中华书局 2013) 20–21 页 (Gu Wei Jun, *Gu Weijun's Memoirs*, first fascicle (Zhonghua Book Company 2013) 20–21).

[9] Aside from his involvement in clubs, another significant influence on his decision to pursue a career in diplomacy was the visit of a Qing government mission to the United States in late 1905, aimed at studying constitutional politics. This visit had a dual impact on Koo. First, it allowed him to witness the late Qing government's earnest efforts to embrace constitutional reform. Second, it illuminated the potential for a new government to emerge, fostering his interest in diplomatic service. ibid 29.

by the Law Society, winning the Columbia-Cornell Debating Medal; served as an editor for *The Columbia Daily Spectator*, Columbia's school newspaper; and participated in many organizations and clubs, such as the Philolexian Society.[10] He pursued a wide array of courses in liberal arts and sciences, delving into the principles of international law under the tutelage of Professor John Bassett Moore (1860–1947), author of the *Digest of International Law* and renowned for his extensive service within the US government.[11] Furthermore, he expanded his linguistic repertoire, forged enduring friendships with outstanding Chinese students, and encountered future diplomats. His participation in extracurricular activities and newspaper editorial work exposed him to the mechanics of American politics and provided him with fundamental insights into foreign affairs. In the summer of 1908, Koo returned to China via Europe and got married, as ordered by his father. In the autumn, he returned to Columbia. At the end of the year, the school notified him of graduation, but Koo was unwilling to leave Columbia. In 1909 he pursued a MA in Political Science from Columbia University and he then continued to study for a doctorate in international law and diplomacy under the supervision of Moore. In February 1912, at the invitation of the Chinese statement Tang Shaoyi, Koo returned to China to serve as the English Secretary and Foreign Secretary of Yuan Shikai, President of the Republic of China; later in that year he successfully received his PhD from Columbia University.[12]

[10] What motivated Koo to eventually choose politics, was first, his eagerness to do something beneficial to the country, to serve it, and to work on reform, especially in dealing with diplomacy. China had a great need for young officials who could implement reform. Second, Koo said that entering politics was also his father's expectation of him; in fact, Koo's father had already paid for him to reserve an official position, and his father wanted him to be higher in rank than others as soon as he entered. Third, entering politics would bring honour to the family. After a period of uncertainty, Koo made the decision to temporarily attend Cornell University alongside Sun Jialu. His primary objectives were to enhance his proficiency in German and to contemplate the possibility of enrolling at Columbia University. However, it was Professor Jeremiah Whipple Jenks (1856–1929) at Cornell who played a pivotal role in solidifying Koo's determination to pursue his studies at Columbia. Professor Jenks assured Koo that the first two years of Koo's undergraduate education would undoubtedly remove any lingering doubts about his academic path: ibid 25, 27.

[11] '研究宪法的伯吉斯 (John William Burgess), 研究行政法的古德诺 (Frank Johnson Goodnow), 研究经济学的塞利格曼 (Edwin Robert Anderson Seligman), 研究历史的比尔德 (Charles A. Beard), 研究欧洲史的罗宾逊 (James Harvey Robinson), 研究社会学的吉丁斯 (Franklin Henry Giddings), 研究近东和西亚的杰克逊', 33-4; 金光耀, 《顾维钧传》(河北人民出版社 1999) 8页 (Jin Guangyao, *Biography of Gu Weijun* (Hebei People's Publishing House 1999) 8); 'John Bassett Moore', *Encyclopaedia Britannica* <https://www.britannica.com/biography/John-Bassett-Moore> accessed 18 June 2025; 'John Bassett Moore (1860–1947)', *Office of the Historian* <https://history.state.gov/departmenthistory/people/moore-john-bassett> accessed 18 June 2025.

[12] 唐德刚, 《顾维钧回忆录》(中华书局 2013) (Tang De Gang, *Memoirs of Gu Weijun* (Zhonghua Book Company 2013); 'V.K. Wellington Koo', *Columbia 250* <https://c250.columbia.edu/c250_celebrates/remarkable_columbians/v_k_wellington_koo.html> accessed 18 June 2025.

23.2 Professional and Academic Career

In 1915, Koo was made Republic of China's Minister to the United States and Cuba. But his early significant contributions to international law came later, as a member of the Chinese delegation to the Paris Peace Conference of 1919, led by Foreign Minister Lu Zhengxiang. Koo rejected the Japanese 'Twenty-One Demands', a set of demands presented by the Empire of Japan to the Republic of China during in the form of an ultimatum on 18 January 1915, intended to expand Japanese influence and control over China. In 1914, as Japan landed troops in Shandong during the First World War, Koo condemned this action as a clear violation of international law, given that China had declared its neutrality in the European conflict.[13] Koo argued that both belligerents should respect China's neutrality, and thus China had the right to defend its territory against Japanese aggression. At the Paris Conference, the Japanese government demanded that it take over all rights and interests of the defeated Germany in Shandong as the victorious country. To oppose Japanese claims, Koo prepared a speech in which he argued that Shandong was 'the cradle of Chinese civilization' and 'a Holy Land for the Chinese' and that China could not give up Shandong, the birthplace of Confucius, just as Christians could not give up the holy land of Jerusalem. This shocked the European and American representatives, reversed public opinion and won the sympathy of the great powers.[14] Later, as the Kingdom of Italy withdrew from the peace conference due to the Dalmatian issue, Britain, France, and the United States were afraid that Japan's withdrawal threat would take effect and lead to the abortion of the peace conference, so they ceded Germany's original rights and interests in Shandong to Japan.[15] At this time, Lu Zhengxiang, the head of the delegation of the Republic of China, left Paris. Therefore, Koo temporarily assumed the authority of the delegation leader. Under his auspices, the delegation of the Republic of China refused to sign the Treaty of Versailles. Koo did not back down during the meeting and he and Japanese representative Makino Nobuaki engaged in a verbal exchange for dozens of rounds, eventually leaving Makino Nobuaki at a loss and unable to parry. It shocked the attendees and won the praise of US President Woodrow Wilson, one of the Big Three. French Prime Minister Georges Clemenceau and British Prime Minister Lloyd George also expressed admiration.[16] Koo gained the reputation of

[13] 'The landing of Japanese troops at Longkou is a blatant violation of international law, because China has declared its neutrality in the European war. According to international law, both belligerents should respect China's neutrality. Accordingly, in order to demonstrate China's responsibility as a neutral country, it is obliged to defend its territory in order to preserve its position. The reason for resisting Japanese aggression is therefore as obvious as it can be'. Gu (n 8) 113.

[14] Bruce A Elleman, *Wilson and China: A Revised History of the Shandong Question* (M.E. Sharpe 2002) 42.

[15] Gu (n 8) 118.

[16] Margaret MacMillan, *Paris 1919: Six Months That Changed the World* (Random House 2001) 334; Naoko Shimazu, 'A Cultural History of Diplomacy: Reassessing the Japanese "Performance" at the Paris

'the first diplomat of the Republic of China' and received high praise among international public opinion.

In 1921, Koo was briefly appointed as minister to the United Kingdom, but soon after he was appointed as one of the plenipotentiary representatives of the government of the Republic of China to participate in the Washington Conference. Under the leadership of Koo, the Chinese delegation achieved a significant milestone by signing the Treaty of Settlement of the Outstanding Case in Shandong between China and Japan and its Annexed Treaty on February 4, 1922. These agreements facilitated Japan's return of the Jiao'ao Lend-Lease to China, placed all customs under Chinese jurisdiction, and saw Japan waive its German priority in Shandong.[17] The Nine Powers Convention, concluded during the Washington Conference, further underscored the sovereignty and territorial integrity of the Republic of China. Koo's tireless efforts in Western countries were instrumental in achieving this outcome, ultimately resulting in the recognition of China's sovereignty and territorial integrity through the convention.[18]

Koo skilfully employed the tenets of international law to safeguard China's interests. This was not only the case in relation to the Shandong issue; he also played a pivotal role in managing the Sino–Japanese dispute through the League of Nations in the realm of diplomacy, as facilitated by the League of Nations' Lytton Commission following the Mukden Incident of 1931.[19] After the September 18th Incident in 1931, Koo was appointed by the Chinese National Government to participate in the Lytton Investigation Team of the League of Nations. Koo was not afraid of Japanese obstruction or even threats to life. He insisted on going to Northeast China for on-the-spot inspections and conducted a lot of work independently. He submitted a long memorandum to the investigation team exposing Japan's aggression, exerting influence on the investigation team and fighting for China's interests. Koo remained steadfast in his belief that disputes could be resolved through the principles of international law, genuine negotiations, and the support of the global community.[20]

Peace Conference', in Urs Matthias Zachmann (ed), *Asia After Versailles* (Edinburgh University Press 2017) 110.

[17] 青岛海关,'《解决山东悬案条约》及附则'(2017年4月27日) (Qingdao Customs District PRC, 'Treaty for the Settlement of the Outstanding Case of Shantung and by-laws' (27 April 2017) <http://qingdao.customs.gov.cn/qingdao_customs/406496/ztlm/qdhgbwg83/zpjs/1744930/index.html> accessed 18 June 2025).

[18] 孙武，中国出席九国公约签字国布鲁塞尔会议代表与外交部等来往文电(1937.10-11)(二), 民国档案2008 (Sun Wu, *Chinese delegates to the Brussels Conference of the Signatories of the Nine-Power Pact and correspondence with the Ministry of Foreign Affairs* (1937.10-11) (II), R.O.C. Archives 2008).

[19] The Lytton Mission, formally known as the Lytton Commission, was entrusted in 1931 by the League of Nations to evaluate the Mukden Incident, which led to the Empire of Japan's seizure of Manchuria.

[20] The report of 1932 in the end declared Japan as the aggressor in Manchuria, advocating for the region's return to Chinese control. It further asserted that the establishment of the Japanese-controlled puppet state, Manchukuo, was illegitimate, proposing that Manchuria should enjoy a degree of

In March 1936, Koo, together with Li Linsi, Wang Zhengting, and others, was elected director of the Chinese branch of the League of Nations—the China League of Nations Comrades Association.[21] Here he had the chance to appeal to the League of Nations to recognize Japan's aggression in the turbulent summer of 1937 when Japan escalated its aggression against China, launching a full-scale invasion following the Marco Polo Bridge Incident on 7 July. Despite attempts to negotiate with Japanese diplomats in Paris, where Koo served as ambassador from 1932 to 1941, and successfully facilitating the flow of arms to China through a railway link from French Indochina, the response to his appeals for support left him deeply disappointed. He hoped that, at least, public sympathy in the West could have been garnered. However, conversations with French Foreign Minister Yvon Delbos revealed a cynical view of the League's efficacy, further dampening Koo's efforts. His proposal for sanctions was ultimately vetoed by Britain and France, due in part to their belief that without American participation, sanctions would be ineffective. The dire situation was exacerbated by the fall of Nanjing and the subsequent massacre of Chinese civilians between December 1937 and January 1938, along with the Japanese bombing and consequent sinking of the American gunboat *USS Panay* patrolling the Yangzi River in December 1937. Koo's hope that these events might catalyse American action against Japan was once agaian met with disappointment as the US accepted Japan's apology for the *Panay* incident. Despite the fraught international landscape and the precarious position of French Indochina, Koo maintained that assisting China was in the broader interest of regional stability, and managed to keep the vital Indochinese supply route open.

Koo's contributions also extended to preparation for the establishement of the United Nations: he was the first in line to sign the United Nations Charter. His efforts at the UN Preparatory Conference in San Francisco in 1945, where he served as Chinese Delegate to the Conference, helped to secure China's status as a permanent member of the UN Security Council and influenced the inclusion of several Chinese ideas in the UN Charter.[22] He emphasized the importance of codifying international law and establishing the International Court of Justice.[23]

self-governance while remaining under the sovereignty of China. Following the adoption of this report by the General Assembly of the League of Nations, Japan withdrew from the organization. The directives of the report were eventually implemented subsequent to Japan's capitulation in 1945. 顾维钧, 《顾维钧回忆录》 第二分册 (中华书局 2013) 163 页 (Gu Wei Jun, *Gu Weijun's Memoirs*, second fascicle (Zhonghua Book Company 2013) 163).

21 杭州鲜为人知的外交传统, 《人民论坛》, 2016-09-05 ('Hangzhou's little-known diplomatic tradition', *People's Forum* (Beijing, 5 September 2016)).

22 共青团中央, '风卷红旗过大关！50年前的联合国大会，中国终于迎来震耳欲聋的掌声', 2021-10-24 (Central Committee of the Communist Youth League, 'The wind rolls the red flag across the Great Pass! 50 years ago at the United Nations General Assembly, China finally received deafening applause!' (24 October 2021) <https://mp.weixin.qq.com/s/ToARajnT8Vf-LnvVkdMwmA> accessed 18 June 2025).

23 顾维钧, 《顾维钧回忆录》第五分册 (中华书局 2013) 593 页 (Gu Wei Jun, *Gu Weijun's Memoirs*, fifth fascicle (Zhonghua Book Company 2013) 593).

Moreover, he was instrumental in preserving the Republic of China's seat in the Security Council also when its territory became limited to Taiwan after 1949. In June 1946, Koo served as China's ambassador to the United States and Mexico and made great contributions to lobbying of the United States to support the government of the Republic of China. In 1947, in a speech to the World Issues Association, Koo criticized the Yalta Agreement for allowing the Soviet Union to re-enter Northeast China and Northeast Asia.[24] Koo engaged in various discussions with US officials, including Deputy Secretary of State Acheson, to negotiate Japan's compensation to China, among other issues.[25] He advocated for the implementation of Japan's compensation and proposed steps for US aid to China in light of the financial crisis. Koo also spoke at the China–US Business Conference, calling for increased American aid. He suggested extending the Marshall Economic Assistance Plan for Europe to Asia and discussed sharing Japan's domestic industrial assets as part of China's compensation plan. Despite his efforts, including meetings with US Assistant Secretary of State Thorpe and General Marshall to request additional loans, these proposals were not successful. In the midst of the Chinese Civil War, Koo sided with the Kuomintang and sought to secure more US assistance, which he believed was the only hope to save the regime.[26] Koo was willing to involve the US in the Chinese Civil War at the expense of China's sovereignty, arguing that comprehensive assistance should not be limited to monetary forms. He cited the US withdrawal from the Philippines as evidence that American involvement did not necessarily entail imperial ambitions.[27] Yet, in his memoirs, Koo confessed that despite his privileged access to information and his firsthand experience of events, he could not fully grasp how the Nationalist government collapsed so quickly after the Anti-Japanese War or how the Communists secured their decisive victory.[28]

Koo continued to serve the Republic of China and entered the Communist Party's list of war criminals. After the Republic of China government moved to Taipei, Koo and Foreign Minister Ye Gongchao negotiated the Sino–US Mutual Defense Treaty on behalf of the Republic of China in 1954. Koo retired from the post of Ambassador of the Republic of China to the United States in 1956 and was hired by Chiang Kai-shek as Counselor of the Presidential Office. He later served as a judge and vice-president of the International Court of Justice in The Hague from 1957 to 1967, where he actively participated in numerous cases, including high-profile disputes over *West Africa* and the *Temple of Preah Vihear*, supporting the decolonization movement by advocating for the independence of colonies.[29]

[24] 李新,《中华民国史大事记》(中华书局 2011) 8261 页 (Li Xin, *The History of the Republic of China: A Chronology of Events* (Zhonghua Book Company 2011) 8261).

[25] ibid 8267.

[26] ibid 8372.

[27] ibid 8394–95.

[28] Tang (n 12).

[29] International Court of Justice, 'Judge Vi Kuiyuin Wellington Koo' <https://www.icj-cij.org/index.php/node/4199> accessed 18 June 2025.

He brought the idea of decolonization into international tribunal proceedings, particularly in cases involving Portugal and India. He argued that India's aspiration for 'the re-establishment of her geographical and historical unity' should be recognized when considering its relations with Portuguese dominions on the Indian subcontinent.[30] One of his legacies in the ICJ is his contribution to reinforcing the universality of international law, validating the legitimacy of international jurisprudence as the normative basis of post-war global governance.[31] He retired from the Hague in 1967 and settled in New York. In his later years, tormented by the loss of the seat in the UN Security Council of the Republic of China, he dictated the 'Memoirs of Wellington Koo' in 13 volumes and more than 6 million words, which later became important material for the study of China's modern diplomacy. Koo and his family entrusted Columbia University to keep their private letters and documents, which have not been published. Koo died at the age of 97 on 14 November 1985, in New York City.

23.3 Legacy

Koo navigated a turbulent era marked by the shift from an international landscape dominated by Western imperialism to a more institutionalized and global international order. This transitional period was characterized by a world in flux, moving from colonial dominance to the emergence of post-colonial nations. China itself saw its transformation from a multiethnic and multi-normative empire to a sovereign nation.[32] Despite historical constraints and China's relative weakness on the global stage, Koo's unwavering determination and proactive diplomatic endeavours laid the foundation for China's eventual permanent membership in the United Nations. His role in international law and diplomacy was significant, but it must be understood within the broader context of the tumultuous times in which he lived and worked. His defence of Chinese sovereignty at the 1919 Paris Peace Conference is historically significant, not only for his personal advocacy but also for the nationalistic fervour it helped to incite, culminating in the May Fourth Movement. However, it is also a reflection of the geopolitical dynamics of the time, where international decisions often hinged on the interplay of dominant powers rather than the impassioned pleas of smaller, weaker, or allegedly "uncivilized" nations.[33]

[30] International Court of Justice, 'Separate Opinion of Judge V. K. Koo Right of Passage over Indian Territory (Portugal v. India)' <https://www.icj-cij.org/en/case/32> accessed 18 June 2025.

[31] Pasha L. Hsieh, 'Wellington Koo, International Law and Modern China' (2016) 56(3–4) IJIL 307, 311.

[32] Maria Adele Carrai, *Sovereignty in China: A Genealogy of a Concept* (CUP 2019).

[33] 顾维钧,《顾维钧回忆录》第十三分册 (中华书局 2013) 29 页 (Gu Wei Jun, *Gu Weijun's Memoirs*, thirteenth fascicle (Zhonghua Book Company 2013) 29).

Koo's educational background in international law and his role in introducing Western legal concepts to China offered steps towards modernizing China's legal system. The sustained effects of his contributions to the evolution of China's legal system are complex and multifaceted, rooted in the groundwork he laid and further sculpted by historical developments that followed. This is especially highlighted by the advent of the People's Republic of China, a period when his past actions were criminalized and the legal system veered into a new trajectory, distinct from the foundations he had influenced. His involvement in global governance structures such as the League of Nations and the United Nations was a forward-looking endeavour, aiming to raise China's international standing. Today, China's participation in international institutions echoes Koo's early efforts, thought it also aligns with China's evolving strategic interests and its broader foreign policy objectives. Koo's contriution to legal education and scholarship undoubtedly helped nurture China's academic growth in international law,. His diplomatic strategies, marked by a steadfast commitment to legal principles and peaceful negotiation, have set an enduring model for Chinese diplomacy.

In essence, while Koo's work established important milestones on China's path toward modernization and global integration, the course of China's development in international law, diplomacy, and education has been shaped by a far more complex constellation of historical forces. Koo was a significant contributor to this trajectory, but he was not its sole architect.

24

Zhou Gengsheng (1889–1971)

Chao Wang and Guoqiang Luo

24.1 Biography

Initially named Zhou Lan (周览), Zhou Gengsheng (周鲠生, 1889–1971) was born in Changsha, Hunan Province.[1] His tremendous contribution to international law scholarship in contemporary China ranked him among the most renowned international lawyers. In 1942, the Ministry of Education of the Republic of China (ROC) for the first time appointed thirty 'Ministry Professors', and Zhou was the only law scholar to gain this great honour.[2] All Chinese international law scholars benefit either directly or indirectly from Zhou's scholarship of international law.[3]

Zhou was a prodigy. At the age of 13 he passed the Qing government imperial examination and was awarded the title Xiucai (秀才), which was granted to those who passed the county-level imperial examination in the Ming and Qing dynasties. Four years later, supported by a Qing government scholarship, he began to study politics and economics at Waseda University in Japan. On the eve of the 1911 revolution (Xinhai revolution), which led to the founding of the Republic of China (ROC)—the first republican state in Asia—Zhou joined the Tongmenghui (同盟会), an organization founded in 1905 with the aim of overthrowing the Qing government. The Tongmenghui was the predecessor of the Kuomintang (KMT), the ruling party of the ROC. In the same year, Zhou returned to China and worked for the *Republic Daily* as an editor.[4] In July 1913 he went to study in the United Kingdom. He first studied at the University of Edinburgh, and earned a Doctor of Juridical Science (JSD) degree in 1918. He then moved to the University of Paris in France to study French law and obtained a second doctorate in 1921.[5] He then

[1] Liu Meng, 'Iron Shoulders Bear the Moral Responsibility, Skilled Hands Craft Articles—Political Scientist Zhou Gengsheng (Part 1) [铁肩担道义，妙手著文章——记政治学家周鲠生（上）]' (2018) 2 Biographical Literature [传记文学] 111.

[2] He was included in the appointments as a representative of political science. Shen Wei-wei, 'Professors Appointed by the Ministry of Education of the Republic of China and their Remuneration [民国部聘教授及其待遇]', (2019) 4 Journal of Sun Yat-sen University (Social Science Edition) [中山大学学报（社会科学版）] 75.

[3] Chen Tiqiang, 'Zhou Gengsheng's International Law [周鲠生：《国际法》]' (1982) Chinese Yearbook of International Law [中国国际法年刊] 375.

[4] Liu (n 1) 111–112.

[5] Hu Shih, 'Foreword', in S. R. Chow (eds), *Winning the Peace in the Pacific: a Chinese View of Far Eastern Postwar Plans and Requirements for a Stable Security System in the Pacific Area* (Macmillan

Chao Wang and Guoqiang Luo, *Zhou Gengsheng (1889–1971)* In: *Histories of International Law in China*. Edited by: Ignacio de la Rasilla, Jiangyu Wang, and Congyan Cai, Oxford University Press.
DOI: 10.1093/oso/9780198888345.003.0024

went back to China and worked for the Commercial Press, based in Shanghai, as director of the Department of Law and Economics.[6]

A year later, the president of Peking University, Cai Yuanpei, invited Zhou to teach political science.[7] In 1926, after five years at Peking University, Zhou went to Guangzhou to help reorganize Guangdong University into the Sun Yat-sen University. In 1927 he moved to Najnjing and served as a professor and director of Southeast University Department of Politics. There he participated in drafting the ROC Constitution, but he later withdrew because he was unhappy with the authoritarian KMT government.[8] In 1928, as a member of the preparatory committee, he participated in setting up Wuhan University, where he worked until 1949. In January 1935 he was appointed head of the Legal Research Institute at Wuhan University and in October was appointed dean of the Department of Law.[9]

From 1939 to 1945, Zhou was a visiting scholar in the United States. During this period, as the Chinese representative at the Institute of Pacific Relations (IPR), he was invited three times to give speeches before the IPR to discuss China's policy on the Far East region, and in particular Japan's ongoing aggression against China. By doing this he supported the Chinese government's efforts to garner American support for China's fight against Japan's aggression.[10] In 1944, Zhou published a book in English entitled *Winning the Peace in the Pacific*, in which he set out his view of the international security system in the Pacific region after the end of the Second World War. This book attracted much attention in the United States.[11] Zhou was appointed as advisor to the Chinese delegation in the negotiations on the establishment of the United Nations. At a 1944 Dumbarton Oaks Conference, Zhou helped the Chinese delegation submit revisions of the draft UN Charter. Several of these revisions were accepted and incorporated in the final text of the UN Charter.[12] These included 'the settlement of international disputes should emphasise justice and the principles of international law', 'international law should be modified and developed through research and recommendations prompted by the General Assembly', and 'the Economic and Social Council should advance educational and cultural cooperation.' When the United Nations Conference on International Organization was held in 1945, China submitted a proposal for an International

1944); See Chen Yizhou, 'Zhou Gengsheng's Academic Chronology [周鲠生先生学术年表]', in Zhou Gengsheng, *Outline of International Law [国际法大纲]* (Commercial Press 2013).

[6] Liu (n 1) 112.
[7] Liu (n 1) 112.
[8] Liu (n 1) 114.
[9] Liu (n 1) 115.
[10] Zhang Jing, '*Study of the China Institute of Pacific Relations (1925–1945) [中国太平洋国际学会研究 (1925–1945)]*' (Social Sciences Academic Press 2012).
[11] Chen (n 5), p. 257.
[12] Huang Huikang, 'On the Integration of International Law Theory and Diplomatic Practice [论国际法理论与外交实践的融合之道]', (2019) Journal of International Law [中国国际法年刊] 1.

Union Organization for consideration by the Conference. Zhou participated in drafting this Proposal.

In 1945 Zhou returned to China and assumed the presidency of Wuhan University. Civil war soon broke out between the Chinese Communist Party (CCP) and the KMT government, and in this difficult time Zhou demonstrated exceptional leadership. He invited several leading jurists—such as Yan Shutang, Han Depei, and Mei Ru'ao—to join Wuhan University. The international prestige of the university steadily grew.

After the founding of the People's Republic of China (PRC) in 1949, Zhou left Wuhan and started a new career in Beijing. In 1950 he was appointed legal advisor to the Ministry of Foreign Affairs (MFA) and was frequently consulted by the central government on international legal issues.[13] It is said that Premier Zhou Enlai would not sign any significant diplomatic document without the approval of Zhou.[14] Zhou also participated in drafting the Constitution of the PRC (1954).[15] As an international lawyer, Zhou found that Article 36(1) of the proposed draft of the constitution (1954) erred in defining the power of the National People's Congress Standing Committee (NPCSC) in treaty-making by stipulating that the NPCSC had the power to 'ratify and abrogate treaties concluded with foreign states'. In line with internationally recognized practice, Zhou suggested that the power to decide on the ratification and abrogation of treaties should be vested solely in the Standing Committee of the National People's Congress (SCNPC).[16] His suggestion was accepted.

Besides his government service, Zhou was also involved in some non-government activities. For instance, he served as vice president of the Foreign Trade Arbitration Committee affiliated with the China Council for the Promotion of International Trade (1956–1971).[17] He was also a member of the executive committee of the Chinese Red Cross Society (1950–1971).[18]

[13] Liu (n 1) 131.

[14] Liu Zhongmeng, 'A Brief Account of Mr. Zhou Gengsheng [周鲠生先生述略]', (2011) 28 Lantai World [兰台世界] 71.

[15] Li Mousheng, 'A Brief Biography of Professor Zhou Gengsheng [周鲠生教授传略]', (2010) 2 Wuhan University International Law Review [武汉大学国际法评论] 358.

[16] Luo Yaopei, 'The Formulation and Implementation of The 1954 Constitution, along with its Empirical Lessons and Historical Experiences [一九五四年宪法的制定和实施及其经验教训]', *iolaw.cssn.cn [中国法学网]* (27 September 2004) <http://iolaw.cssn.cn/wsxf/200409/t20040927_4593042.shtml> accessed 17 July 2025.

[17] 'Chronicle of Major Events of the China International Economic and Trade Arbitration Commission [中国国际经济贸易仲裁委员会大事记]', *CiEtac Shanghai Sub-Commission [中国国际经济贸易仲裁委员会上海分会]* <http://www.cietacshanghai.org/articles/4201> accessed 17 July 2025.

[18] 'The Red Cross Society of China Convened a National Representative Conference, During Which Future Work Plans were Determined, The Charter was Amended and a New Leadership Body Was Elected (Anon.) [中国红十字会举行全国代表会议，确定了今后工作，修改了会章，选举了新的领导机构]', [1961-10-30] People's Daily [人民日报] 1.

24.2 Scholarship

Zhou published 15 books and more than 300 journal articles. These publications span a wide range of international law, from theory to practice, from history to contemporary practice, and from general international law to Chinese international law practice.

24.2.1 International Law Textbooks

International law scholarship was introduced in China in the mid-nineteenth century.[19] For decades, no international law textbooks were written by Chinese international lawyers. In this regard, Zhou was a pioneer.

24.2.1.1 *An Outline of International Law* (1929)

In 1929 Zhou published *An Outline of International Law*.[20] This was the first international law textbook written by a Chinese international lawyer. Besides the Introduction, which discusses the general issues of the definition, nature, effect, history, and source of international law, the book has 22 chapters divided into two parts: substantive and procedural law.

The significance of the *Outline* cannot be overestimated. It was widely adopted by major law schools in China and it was also used by some law schools in Japan. It had a tremendous impact on international law teaching and research in China.[21] However, generally speaking it introduced Western international law theory.[22] Zhou admitted that it was mainly based on Western international law literature.[23] For instance, referring to Oppenheim's *International Law*,[24] Zhou defined international law as the legal system governing the relations between 'civilized nations'.[25] Like their governments, Western international lawyers generally relied on the theory of 'civilized nations' to humiliate non-Western nations by denying them the capacity to have rights and interests under international law.[26]

[19] See for instance Henry Wheaton, *Elements of International Law [万国公法]* trans. W. A. P. Martin (Tongwenguan [同文馆] 1864).

[20] Zhou Gengsheng, *An Outline of International Law [国际法大纲]* (Commercial Press [商务出版社] 1929).

[21] For example, Zhou Huan, *Public International Law [国际公法]* (World Book Publishing Company [世界图书出版公司] 1932); Zhou Ziya, *New Treatise on International Law [国际法新论]* (New Review Press [新评论出版社] 1944); Cui Shuqin, International Law [国际法] (Commercial Press [商务出版社] 1947); Zhao Lihai, *Public International Law (国际公法]* (Commercial Press [商务出版社] 1947).

[22] See also Chapter 12.

[23] Zhou (n 20) Preface.

[24] Oppenheim, *International Law (Vol.1)* (Longmans, Green, and Co. 1932) 1.

[25] Zhou (n 20) 1–2.

[26] Gerrit W. Gong, *The Standard of 'Civilization' in International Society* (Clarendon Press 1984); Wilhelm G. Grewe, *The Epochs of International Law*, translated and revised by Michael Byers (Walter de Gruyter 2000) 445–496.

24.2.1.2 *International Law* (1976)

In 1964, Zhou wrote a textbook entitled *International Law* (hereafter '1976 textbook'). This was the first Chinese textbook on international law in the PRC era. Unfortunately, it was firstly published in 1976, five years after Zhou passed away. It has about 700 pages and 12 chapters. It has been reprinted several times.[27]

In contrast with the 1929 textbook, the 1976 textbook has two salient features.[28] First, it largely deviates from Western international law theory and instead is based on Marxist and third world approaches to international law. For instance, in contrast with the 1929 book, in which Zhou agreed with Oppenheim's definition of international law, the 1976 textbook criticized Oppenheim's definition, stating that international law 'represents the perspective of the Western bourgeoisie on international law and disguises its class nature'.[29] The 1976 textbook defines international law as 'the totality of behavioural norms, including principles, rules and institutions, which arise in the course of international interactions and are recognised by all states and express the will of the ruling classes of those countries and have legal binding force on states in international relations'.[30] Second, the 1976 textbook pays more attention to Chinese international legal practice, including China's Five Principles of Peaceful Co-existence: nationality, state succession, state responsibility, territory, and international organizations.

The 1976 textbook has acquired great prestige since its publication. It is widely acknowledged to be a classic of international law. This is not only because this volume, far larger than the *Outline* of 1929, contains thorough examinations of international legal theories, regimes, institutions, and practices, but also because it investigates Chinese international legal practice. Therefore, it is a 'must read' for international law students and scholars in China.[31] Nevertheless, it has been subject to criticism for misunderstanding Marxism by heavily referring to Soviet international law theory. For instance, Wang Tieya contended that Zhou's definition of international law, especially his reference to the will of the ruling classes of states, was obviously influenced by Soviet scholars.[32]

24.2.2 Zhou's Scholarship on Unequal Treaties

For all Chinese international lawyers in the twentieth century, 'unequal treaties', which tremendously harmed China in terms of tariffs, leased territories,

27 See for example Zhou Gengsheng, *International Law [国际法]* (Wuhan University Press [武汉大学出版社] 2007).

28 See also Chapter 12.

29 Ibid, pp. 1–8.

30 Zhou (n 27) 3.

31 Chen (n 3) 377.

32 Wang Tieya, *Introduction to International Law [国际法]* (Peking University Press [北京大学出版社] 1998) 24; See also Chen (n 3) 378.

concessions, extraterritoriality, and non-reciprocal most-favoured-nation treatment,[33] were a major bitter concern. In 1928, Zhou published *Ten Lectures on Unequal Treaties*,[34] the first systematic study of this topic.

Zhou defined unequal treaties as agreements that contain provisions establishing diverse legal relationships extending beyond the scope of conventional international law and that unilaterally infringe or limit the sovereignty of at least one contracting party.[35] He acknowledged that states in the international community are not inherently equal either naturally or politically but are only considered equal in legal terms.[36] Consequently, political coercion must be distinguished from legal coercion—the latter refers to pressure exerted on the signatory of a treaty rather than on the state as a whole.[37] This distinction means that in the absence of other legal defects an unequal treaty remains *de jure* valid.

In the view of Zhou, unilateral most-favoured-nation (UMFN) clauses in unequal treaties were the most harmful to China.[38] Unlike most-favoured-nation (MFN) clauses which apply to all contracting parties, UMFN clauses in Chinese unequal treaties were designed to favour contracting states other than China.[39]

Leased territories that some Western powers acquired through unequal treaties were another major concern for Zhou. He contended that these territories required a distinct analytical framework—one that drew on leasing theory in private law—to define their unique nature. According to Zhou, during lease terms Western powers enjoyed extraterritoriality while China's government refrained from exercising sovereignty in leased territories, despite the fact that they still belonged to China.[40] This perspective later provided the theoretical foundation for China's proposal to reclaim its leased territories and maintain its territorial integrity.

Zhou argued that all Chinese unequal treaties should be finally abolished. In his view, there were three approaches. In the first, China would issue a unilateral declaration abolishing an unequal treaty according to the *rebus sic stantibus* doctrine. In the second, China would seek negotiations with all the Western powers. And in

[33] See, for example, Wang Dong, *China's Unequal Treaties: Narrating National History* (Lexington Books 1984) 9–18. For recent Chinese literature on Chinese unequal treaties, see, for example, Li Yumin, *A Study of Sion-Foreign Treaty Relations in the Late Qing Dynasty [晚清中外条约关系研究]* (Law Press [法律出版社] 2018); Cao Ying, *The Collapse of the Traditional System and the Establishment of Treaty Relations, 1689–1860* [传统体制的打破与条约关系的建立 (1689-1860)](Zhonghua Book Company [中华书局] 2022).

[34] Zhou Gengsheng, *Ten Lectures on Unequal Treaties [不平等条约十讲]* (Shanghai Taipin Book Company [上海太平洋书店] 1928), reprinted in Wang Tieya and Zhou Zhonghai (eds), *Zhou Gengsheng's Selected Articles on International Law* [周鲠生国际法论文选] (Haitian Press [海天出版社] 1999).

[35] Ibid, p. 10.

[36] Ibid, p. 3.

[37] Ibid, pp. 4–6.

[38] Ibid, pp. 16–17.

[39] Ibid, pp. 151–152.

[40] Zhou Gengsheng, 'The Legal Nature of Leased Territories [租借地之法律性质]' in Wang and Zhou Zhonghai (n 34) 270–281.

the third, China would seek a bilateral negotiation. Zhou preferred the third approach because it would be expected to reduce pressure from Western powers.[41]

24.2.3 Five Principles of Peaceful Coexistence

The Five Principles of Peaceful Coexistence (Five Principles) represent the cornerstone of Chinese international legal policy. The Five Principles are: (a) mutual respect for each other's territorial integrity and sovereignty; (b) mutual non-aggression; (c) mutual non-interference in each other's internal affairs; (d) equality and mutual benefit; and (e) peaceful coexistence. The Five Principles initially appeared in the Preamble to the Agreement on Trade and Intercourse between the Tibet Region of China and India, which was concluded between China and India in April 1954, and they were soon accepted by Burma in a Joint Statement with China on 29 June 1954. In accordance with the Five Principles, all states 'should undertake intercourses equally, regardless of their social systems, power and positions, and should not impose their will on others. No states should politically force others to do things and neither should they economically exploit others or do what benefits themselves while harming others.'[42]

Zhou made a great contribution to formulating the Five Principles. China's government initially formulated them as follows: mutual respect for territorial sovereignty, mutual non- aggression, mutual non-interference in internal affairs, equality and reciprocity, and peaceful coexistence. However, the fourth principle of 'equality and reciprocity' was revised to 'equality and mutual benefit', which was finally included in the 1954 China–India Agreement. This revision was made due to Zhou's wisdom. In his view, the concept of 'reciprocity' between states requires mutual consent through negotiation and cannot be regarded as a universally applicable principle. The term 'mutual benefit' was deemed more precise from a legal standpoint. Subsequently, the five principles were formally enshrined in joint statements issued by China and India and by China and Myanmar in June 1954. Afterwards, Zhou continued to deliberate and concluded that the initial formulation of the first principle, 'mutual respect for territorial sovereignty', was not entirely appropriate. The sole mention of 'territory' could be misinterpreted as only referring to territories under actual control at the time. In addition, combining 'territory' and 'sovereignty' in a single term risked being misunderstood as implying that 'territory' served as an adjective modifying 'sovereignty', which was also

[41] Zhou Gengsheng, 'The Conference of Extraterritoriality and the Termination of Extraterritoriality [法权会议与收回法权]' in Wuhan International Law Institute (eds), *The Selection of Zhou Gengsheng* (周鲠生文集) (Wuhan University Press [武汉大学出版社] 1993) 49.

[42] Zhou (n 27) 183–185.

problematic. Consequently, Zhou proposed revising the first principle to 'mutual respect for sovereignty and territorial integrity'.

24.3 Legacy

24.3.1 A Critique of West-centric International Law

Zhou argued that since the nineteenth century, countries outside Europe had played increasingly significant roles in the development of international law, leading to a fundamental transformation of the discipline. He identified four key trends driving this shift. First, in the early nineteenth century former European colonies in Central and South America gained independence and became subjects of international law. Second, the Peace Treaty of Paris (1856) concluded after the Crimean War saw Western powers formally recognize the Ottoman Empire—a non-Christian state—as part of the 'concert of public law and Europe'. Third, Asian and African countries were incorporated in the framework of international law either through their colonial status or as a result of unequal treaties imposed by Western powers. Fourth, two world wars led to the emergence of numerous independent states in Eastern Europe, Africa, and Asia, allowing them to actively participate in shaping international law through major diplomatic platforms such as the League of Nations and the United Nations. These developments, Zhou contended, demonstrated that modern international law had evolved into a truly universal legal system applicable to all states.[43]

With his critical reflection on Western legal doctrines, Zhou made significant theoretical contributions to fundamental issues in international law. He was against the definition of international law in Oppenheim's *International Law*, suggesting that it obscured the class character of the discipline by focusing solely on its formal legal aspects. He further argued that Oppenheim's conception of international law based on 'civilized nations' reflected colonialism. Zhou also refuted the concepts of 'special international law' and 'regional international law', arguing that international law only refers to universally recognized rules among the majority of sovereign states. On the other hand, he considered that 'special international law' referred to treaties only binding a limited number of states, while 'regional international law' applied to specific geographical areas. He further criticized the notion of 'Asian-African international law', suggesting that it was infused with colonialist undertones.[44]

Regarding the sources of international law, Zhou maintained that international law only consisted of treaties and international customs. He suggested that the

[43] Zhou (n 27) 50–56.
[44] Ibid, pp. 6–7.

'general principles of law' referenced in Article 38 of the Statute of the International Court of Justice should not be considered an independent source of international law. According to Zhou, these principles could only be recognized as sources if they were incorporated in treaties or customary law. He contended that Article 38 merely allowed the ICJ to apply general legal principles as a supplementary measure in the absence of established legal sources. Some Western scholars have interpreted the reference to general legal principles as a departure from positivist international law, suggesting that the ICJ acknowledges the existence and applicability of international law as natural law. Zhou, however, dismissed this interpretation as an over-extension of subjective analysis by scholars.[45]

24.3.2 The Marxist Approach to International Law

After the founding of the PRC, Zhou embraced Marxism. He was of the view that international law reflects the coordinated will of the ruling classes of various nations rather than a common will shared by all nations—a view he dismissed as the rhetoric of bourgeois scholars.[46] Sharing Marx's historical materialist perspective, Zhou posited that imperialism is an inevitable stage in the evolution of capitalism and that international law transforms in response to historical developments. For example, he observed that the principle of non-intervention was curtailed when it conflicted with imperialist interests.[47] He further suggested that contemporary international law embodies a struggle between imperialism and socialism.[48] He contended that in socialist states, in which the state owns the land, the argument that territorial sovereignty does not encompass the ownership of territory—based on the premise of private land ownership—is inapplicable.[49] In his *International Law* textbook (1976) he frequently classified different schools of international law as bourgeois, imperialist, or socialist, thereby applying a class-based analysis of the evolution of international law. He characterized the international law theories he critiqued as predominantly bourgeois, capitalist, or even imperialist.

24.3.3 The Third World Approach to International Law

China's socialist state identity did not prevent the Chinese government and international lawyers, including Zhou, from adopting the third world approach to international law (TWAIL). Despite his critique of Western colonialism, Zhou's

45 Ibid, pp. 13–14.
46 Ibid, pp. 10–11.
47 Ibid, pp. 51–52.
48 Ibid, pp. 55–56.
49 Ibid, p. 320.

early publications refrained from portraying international law solely as a product of imperialism. In fact, he even expressed admiration for the British tradition of international law and advocated the use of traditional international law theories to help China overcome its semi-colonial status.[50] However, in the PRC era, Zhou's critique of imperialism became increasingly intertwined with reflections on the traditions of international law, which emerged as a central theme in his research. In addition to his discussions on anti-Western-centrism and his support for Marxism, Zhou had a profound awareness of the colonialist and imperialist undertones present in various aspects of international law, and critiqued them.

For instance, Zhou argued that imperialism sometimes conducts interventions in the guise of 'resisting interference' or 'maintaining collective security', yet such actions are mechanically deemed not to violate the principle of non-intervention.[51] He also criticized the monist view that prioritizes the supremacy of international law over domestic law, contending that this perspective serves as a policy of imperialism aimed at world domination, effectively equating international law with the functions of a world government or global constitution.[52] Furthermore, Zhou condemned the unequal treaty system as an integral component of imperialist international law.[53] As for the League of Nations, he viewed it as merely a tool employed by the victorious imperialists of the First World War to consolidate their gains and maintain the status quo.[54]

[50] Chen Yifeng, 'Reconstructing Law and Politics: The British Tradition of International Law and Moving Beyond It [重构法律与政治：国际法的英国传统及其超越]', (2024) 5 China Law Review [中国法律评论] 155.

[51] Zhou Gengsheng, 'The Principle of Peaceful Coexistence from the Viewpoint of International Law [从国际法论和平共处的原则]', (1955) 6 Chinese Journal of Law [中国法学] 38.

[52] Zhou (n 27) 19.

[53] Ibid, p. 51.

[54] Ibid, p. 53.

25
Hsiang Che-chun (1892–1987)

Zenghua Zhuo

25.1 Introduction

In comparison with other well-known international legal scholars from China, Hsiang Che-chun (向哲濬) is less widely recognized both nationally and internationally. Unlike some of his contemporaries, Hsiang neither served as a diplomatic representative of China on the international stage nor produced a large body of academic publications or substantial theoretical contributions to the field of international law. Nevertheless, his work as a prosecutor at the International Military Tribunal for the Far East (IMTFE) represents an indelible contribution, leaving a unique legacy in the histories of both China's and the world's legal systems.

25.2 Hsiang Che-chun's Personal Life: An Overview

25.2.1 Early Years and Education (1892–1925)

Hsiang Che-chun was born in January 1892 into a peasant family in Hunan Province that placed great value on education. At that time, if financially feasible, even rural families sought to provide educational opportunities for their children. Hsiang's family adopted a progressive approach by transforming the village's traditional private school into a modern primary school. This enabled him to benefit from more advanced teaching methods at an early age. His diligence and strong academic performance quickly drew the attention of his elders, who sent him to Changsha, the provincial capital, to continue his education. After completing primary school in Changsha, Hsiang was admitted to Xiuye Middle School (修业中学), one of the most prestigious private schools of the period.[1]

[1] 周芳 (Zhou Fang), 良师爱侣忆明思——向哲濬夫人周芳回忆录 (Liang Shi Ai Lv Yi Ming Si—Xiang Zhejun Fu Ren Zhou Fang Hui Yi Lu) [Memoirs of Zhou Fang, the Wife of Xiang Zhejun] in 向隆万 (Xiang Longwan) (eds), 东京审判·中国检察官向哲濬 *(Dong Jing Shen Pan Zhong Guo Jian Cha Guan Xiang Zhejun) [The Tokyo Trial Chinese Prosecutor Hsiang che-chun(Xiang Zhejun)]* (Shanghai Jiaotong University Press, 2010)

Zenghua Zhuo, *Hsiang Che-chun (1892–1987)* In: *Histories of International Law in China*. Edited by: Ignacio de la Rasilla, Jiangyu Wang, and Congyan Cai, Oxford University Press.
DOI: 10.1093/oso/9780198888345.003.0025

During Hsiang's middle school years, China stood on the eve of the 1911 Revolution. The revolutionary and patriotic fervor of the period left a profound mark on young students such as Hsiang. The seeds of patriotism sown during this formative time would remain with him throughout his life. In 1910, the United States allocated part of the Boxer Indemnities to establish Tsinghua College (then also called the American Indemnity College, later to become today's Tsinghua University), with the aim of preparing promising Chinese students to pursue higher education abroad. That same year, the College recruited students nationwide, attracting many gifted candidates. Hsiang excelled in the entrance examination and gained admission. At Tsinghua, he received one of the most advanced educations available in China at the time, laying a solid foundation for his later studies in the United States.[2]

In 1917, Hsiang graduated from Tsinghua College and continued his studies at Yale University, where he earned a Bachelor of Arts degree in 1919.[3] He then pursued legal studies at Yale Law School and George Washington University Law School, completing his law degrees in 1925.[4] During his years in the United States, Hsiang received a world-class education, particularly in common law and international law, which laid the foundation for his future legal career.

Like most Chinese students studying abroad at the time, Hsiang was deeply concerned about the future of the Chinese nation. The aftermath of World War I—and especially the decisions of the Paris Peace Conference, at which China, despite being among the victors, was forced to transfer Germany's former privileges in Shandong to Japan—provoked widespread indignation among the Chinese people. Hsiang was no exception. Along with other Chinese students in the United States, he organized protests against the Beiyang government (1912–1928) for its acquiescence in upholding unequal treaties.

25.2.2 Early Career (1925–1946)

In the autumn of 1925, Hsiang Che-chun returned to China and immediately began his career in education, committed to sharing the knowledge he had acquired in

[2] 周芳 (Zhou Fang), 良师爱侣忆明思——向哲浚夫人周芳回忆录 (Liang Shi Ai Lv Yi Ming Si — Xiang Zhejun Fu Ren Zhou Fang Hui Yi Lu) [Memoirs of Zhou Fang, the Wife of Xiang Zhejun] in 向隆万 (Xiang Longwan) (eds), 东京审判·中国检察官向哲浚 *(Dong Jing Shen Pan Zhong Guo Jian Cha Guan Xiang Zhejun)[The Tokyo Trial Chinese Prosecutor Hsiang che-chun (Xiang Zhejun)]* (Shanghai Jiaotong University Press, 2010).

[3] Richard C. Levin, 'Tribute to Xiang Zhejun' in 向隆万 (Xiang Longwan) (eds), 东京审判·中国检察官向哲浚 *(Dong Jing Shen Pan Zhong Guo Jian Cha Guan Xiang Zhejun) [The Tokyo Trial Chinese Prosecutor Hsiang che-chun(Xiang Zhejun)]* (Shanghai Jiaotong University Press, 2010)

[4] Frederick M. Lawrence, 'Letter from Frederick M. Lawrence, Dean of the George Washington University Law School' in 向隆万 (Xiang Longwan) (ed/), 东京审判·中国检察官向哲浚 *(Dong Jing Shen Pan Zhong Guo Jian Cha Guan Xiang Zhejun)[The Tokyo Trial Chinese Prosecutor Hsiang che-chun(Xiang Zhejun)]* (Shanghai Jiaotong University Press, 2010).

the United States with Chinese students. He held teaching positions at several universities in Beijing, including Peking University, where he taught English; Beijing Jiaotong University, where he lectured on public international law; and the Beijing School of Political Science and Law, among others. His command of foreign languages and his legal scholarship quickly attracted the attention of the Chinese legal community.

In 1927, following the establishment of the Nanjing National Government, the prominent legal scholar Wang Chonghui, then serving as Minister of Justice, invited Hsiang to act as his secretary. Among the Ministry's key priorities was the abolition of the unequal treaties, in particular the withdrawal of consular jurisdiction. To that end, a special committee was created, with Hsiang appointed as a member owing to his legal expertise and fluency in English. When Wang was succeeded by Luo Wengan, who concurrently held the post of Minister of Foreign Affairs, Hsiang continued in office. Luo, who likewise held him in high esteem, appointed Hsiang as secretary to the Ministry of Foreign Affairs. This position drew him more deeply into the sphere of diplomatic affairs.

As a result of the sustained efforts of the Nanjing National Government, consular jurisdiction in the Shanghai International Settlement was abolished in 1933, enabling China to exercise independent judicial sovereignty there. Special courts were established in the process, which the government regarded as highly significant. The appointment of judges and prosecutors was therefore considered a matter of great importance, and those selected were leading figures in the Chinese legal community. In recognition of his legal reputation, Hsiang was appointed Chief Prosecutor. His professional competence and integrity in this role were widely acknowledged, further consolidating his legal and political standing.

In 1937, with Japan's full-scale invasion of China and the outbreak of nationwide resistance, Shanghai was plunged into protracted warfare. Despite the grave dangers posed by Japanese aggression, Hsiang remained steadfast in his duties. He continued his prosecutorial work in Shanghai until the end of 1942, when the Japanese army occupied the city's concessions—zones where Western powers had long enjoyed extraterritorial rights and consular jurisdiction under the unequal treaties—thereby bringing judicial operations to a halt. Hsiang then relocated to Chongqing, the wartime capital, where he resumed service in the Ministry of Justice before once again being appointed as a prosecutor, playing an essential role in sustaining the Chinese judicial system during the war.[5]

[5] 周芳 (Zhou Fang), 良师爱侣忆明思——向哲浚夫人周芳回忆录 (Liang Shi Ai Lv Yi Ming Si—Xiang Zhejun Fu Ren Zhou Fang Hui Yi Lu) [Memoirs of Zhou Fang, the Wife of Xiang Zhejun] in 向隆万 (Xiang Longwan) (eds), 东京审判·中国检察官向哲浚 *(Dong Jing Shen Pan Zhong Guo Jian Cha Guan Xiang Zhejun) [The Tokyo Trial Chinese Prosecutor Hsiang che-chun (Xiang Zhejun)]* (Shanghai Jiaotong University Press, 2010).

25.2.3 Post-war Career (1946–1987)

After World War II, the Nanjing National Government reestablished its authority across China, and Hsiang was appointed Chief Prosecutor of the Shanghai High Court. Apart from a brief period teaching at universities, Hsiang's career was primarily rooted in the judiciary, particularly in prosecutorial work. This extensive experience laid the groundwork for his 1946 appointment as a prosecutor at the International Military Tribunal for the Far East (IMTFE), where he served for three years. Upon the conclusion of the Tokyo Trial, the Nanjing National Government offered Hsiang several high-ranking positions, including Chief Prosecutor of the Supreme Court Prosecutors Office, in recognition of his contributions. However, having witnessed government corruption, Hsiang declined all these appointments.

Following the collapse of the Nanjing National Government, Hsiang chose not to flee abroad but instead devoted himself to the construction of New China. In February 1949, he accepted teaching positions at several universities, including Daxia University (now East China Normal University) and Soochow University, where he focused on public international law, private international law, and international legal procedure. During the 1950s, following institutional adjustments, Hsiang continued teaching at Fudan University, the Shanghai Academy of Social Sciences, and Shanghai University of Finance and Economics, making significant contributions to legal education and the development of China's legal system in the early years of the People's Republic.

25.3 Contributions at the IMTFE

One week after Japan's surrender on September 2, 1945, General Douglas MacArthur, Supreme Commander of the Allied Powers, ordered the arrest of Japanese war crime suspects.[6] Bringing Japanese war criminals to justice became an immediate priority. Eleven Allied Powers—Australia, Canada, China, France, India, the Netherlands, New Zealand, the Philippines, the Soviet Union, the United Kingdom, and the United States—joined forces to establish the International Military Tribunal for the Far East (IMTFE) to try Japan's leaders for their roles in planning and waging aggressive war.[7]

[6] 杨一心 (Yang yixin), 东京审判中国团队*(Dong Jing Shen Pan Zhong GuoTuan Dui),[Chinese Team at the Tokyo Trial]*(Shanghai Jiaotong University Press, 2020)3.

[7] Special Proclamation by the Supreme Commander for the Allied Powers on Tokyo January 19, 1946<https://digital-commons.usnwc.edu/cgi/viewcontent.cgi?article=2132&context=ils> accessed 10 July 2025

Under the IMTFE Charter, the Chief Prosecutor, appointed by the Supreme Commander, was responsible for investigating and prosecuting war criminals within the tribunal's jurisdiction.[8] US President Harry S. Truman designated Joseph B. Keenan as Chief Prosecutor to lead these efforts.[9] In addition, each Allied Power was entitled to appoint an Associate Prosecutor to assist with the tribunal's proceedings.

To ensure the proper prosecution of Japanese war criminals at the IMTFE, the Nanjing National Government placed great emphasis on selecting qualified judges and prosecutors.[10] At the time, the United States held a dominant role in the tribunal, and the proceedings largely followed American legal procedures. According to the IMTFE Charter, trials and related processes were to be conducted in both English and the language of the accused—primarily English and Japanese.[11] Consequently, the Chinese government needed to appoint professionals proficient in English and familiar with common law.

Hsiang Che-chun, owing to his educational background and expertise in English, was recommended by Wang Chonghui to Chiang Kai-shek, leader of the Kuomintang, for a position in the tribunal. Initially, Hsiang was offered a choice between serving as a judge or as a prosecutor, with the former generally considered the more prestigious role. Hsiang, however, chose to serve as a prosecutor, believing that this position would allow him to more effectively expose to the world the atrocities committed by Japan in China.[12]

Hsiang's significant contributions to the IMTFE can be categorized into three main areas: drafting the Indictment; gathering evidence, including securing the testimony of key witnesses; and participating in trial debates. The extensive work undertaken by Hsiang and his team in each of these areas was instrumental in exposing Japan's wartime atrocities.

[8] Charter of the International Military Tribunal for the Far East, dated January 19, 1946; amended charter dated April 26, 1946,<https://www.un.org/en/genocideprevention/documents/atrocity-crimes/Doc.3_1946%20Tokyo%20Charter.pdf> accessed 10 July 2025

[9] 梅汝璈 (Mei Ru ao), 东京审判亲历记 *(Dong Jing Shen Pan Qin Li Ji) [My Personal Experience At the Tokyo Trial]* (Shanghai Jiaotong University Press, 2016) 82.

[10] 向隆万 (Xiang Longwan), 东京审判征战记 中国检察官向哲濬团队 *(Dong Jing Shen Pan Zheng Zhan Ji-Zhong Guo Jian Cha Guan Xiang ZhejunTuan Dui) [Journey to Justice Inside story of the Chinese Prosecutor Hsiang Che-chun and his team in the Tokyo Trial]* (Shanghai Jiaotong University Press, 2013) 15–20.

[11] Charter of the International Military Tribunal for the Far East, dated January 19, 1946; amended charter dated April 26, 1946,<https://www.un.org/en/genocideprevention/documents/atrocity-crimes/Doc.3_1946%20Tokyo%20Charter.pdf> accessed 10 July 2025.

[12] 周芳 (Zhou Fang), 良师爱侣忆明思——向哲濬夫人周芳回忆录 (Liang Shi Ai Lv Yi Ming Si—Xiang Zhejun Fu Ren Zhou Fang Hui Yi Lu) [Memoirs of Zhou Fang, the Wife of Xiang Zhejun] in 向隆万 (Xiang Longwan) (eds), 东京审判·中国检察官向哲濬 *(Dong Jing Shen Pan Zhong Guo Jian Cha Guan Xiang Zhejun) [The Tokyo Trial Chinese Prosecutor Hsiang che-chun(Xiang Zhejun)]* (Shanghai Jiaotong University Press, 2010)

25.3.1 Drafting the Indictment

According to the IMTFE Charter, the investigation and prosecution of war crimes fell under the responsibility of the International Prosecution Section. One of its primary tasks in the early stages was the preparation of the Indictment. Because Japan's invasion of China spanned many years and involved numerous atrocities, much of the Indictment focused on crimes committed in China. Hsiang was specifically tasked with drafting sections related to the September 18 Incident, also known as the Mukden Incident, when the occupying Japanese army blew up a section of railway in northeastern China in 1931—an event that marked the beginning of the Chinese People's War of Resistance against Japanese Aggression. He also participated in discussions on other parts of the Indictment, undertaking significant responsibilities in this critical phase.

One major point of contention among the Allied prosecutors was determining the start date for Japan's war crimes. Hsiang proposed that it should be the Huanggutun Incident in 1928, when the Japanese Kwantung Army assassinated Zhang Zuolin, a powerful Chinese warlord dominating northeastern China.[13] The issue was complicated because the start dates of Japan's invasions—and the corresponding war crimes in each affected country—varied. Some prosecutors suggested December 7, 1941, the date of Japan's attack on Pearl Harbor, as the beginning of hostilities for the Allied Powers.[14] While Japan had committed numerous military actions and atrocities in China before 1941, the absence of a formal declaration of war between China and Japan made it difficult for some to classify these acts as war crimes.[15]

Hsiang, however, argued that this perspective was deeply unfair to China, as it ignored Japan's more than decade-long aggression. He emphasized that after the Marco Polo Bridge Incident on July 7, 1937, Japan escalated its invasion into a full-scale war, and that the assassination of Zhang Zuolin in 1928 constituted a critical precursor to this broader conflict. These events were interconnected components of Japan's invasion of China. Given the scale and severity of the crimes committed during this period, Hsiang insisted that the prosecution timeline should begin in 1928. Despite strong opposition from Japanese defendants and their lawyers,

13 Hsiang Che-Chun, 'Speeches at IMTFE (14 May 1946, Saturday)' in 向隆万 (Xiang Longwan) (ed.), 东京审判·中国检察官向哲浚 *(Dong Jing Shen Pan Zhong Guo Jian Cha Guan Xiang Zhejun) [The Tokyo Trial Chinese Prosecutor Hsiang che-chun(Xiang Zhejun)]* (Shanghai Jiaotong University Press, 2010).

14 向隆万 (Xiang Longwan), 东京审判征战记 中国检察官向哲浚团队 *(Dong Jing Shen Pan Zheng Zhan Ji-Zhong Guo Jian Cha Guan Xiang ZhejunTuan Dui)[Journey to JusticeInside story of the Chinese Prosecutor Hsiang Che-chun and his team in the Tokyo Trial]* (Shanghai Jiaotong University Press, 2013) 35–36.

15 程兆奇 (Cheng Zhaoqi)、向隆万 (Xiang Longwan), 远东国际军事法庭庭审记录 *(Yuan Dong Guo Ji Jun Shi Fa Ting Ting Shen Ji Lu) [Proceedings of the International Military Tribunal for the Far East]* (Shanghai Jiaotong University Press,2017) 100–101.

Hsiang presented clear arguments supported by substantial evidence, ultimately persuading the Chief Prosecutor and Associate Prosecutors from the other Allied Powers. As a result, the International Prosecution Section agreed to count the timeline for prosecuting Japanese war crimes from 1928.[16]

In addition, responsibilities related to the Indictment included identifying individual perpetrators and specifying their charges. For Hsiang, ensuring that the aggressors were held accountable and not exempt from prosecution was a central mission. Thanks to his efforts, half of the 32 Japanese individuals charged by the Chinese government were included on the list of Class-A war criminals and received a fair trial. For example, Kenji Doihara was initially excluded from the Class-A list due to his comparatively lower rank among other key figures. However, Doihara had conspired in and orchestrated numerous criminal activities in China.[17] To secure his indictment, Hsiang and his team compiled substantial evidence demonstrating the severity of his crimes, ultimately ensuring that Doihara was added to the list.

25.3.2 Investigating and Gathering Evidence

Another critical task undertaken by Hsiang was investigating crimes, gathering evidence, and securing the testimony of key witnesses before the Tribunal. Although the atrocities committed by Japanese war criminals in China were undeniable, sufficient evidence was required to substantiate the charges at the IMTFE in accordance with judicial procedures. Much evidence had been destroyed by Japan, particularly toward the end of the war, and the Chinese government and population had not systematically preserved relevant materials. As a result, Hsiang and his team faced the formidable challenge of investigating these crimes and gathering adequate evidence within a limited timeframe.

Hsiang pursued every available avenue, both domestically and internationally, seeking assistance from national institutions and overseas Chinese communities to collect evidence in various forms. He and his team also made multiple trips back to China to investigate crime sites and obtained materials from Japanese archival agencies, media outlets, and other relevant institutions. Through these efforts, Hsiang uncovered a substantial body of valuable firsthand materials, archival documents, and confidential telegrams documenting Japanese atrocities in

[16] Hsiang Che-Chun, 'Speeches at IMTFE' in 向隆万 (Xiang Longwan) (eds), 东京审判·中国检察官向哲浚 *(Dong Jing Shen Pan Zhong Guo Jian Cha Guan Xiang Zhejun)[The Tokyo Trial Chinese Prosecutor Hsiang che-chun(Xiang Zhejun)],* (Shanghai Jiaotong University Press, 2010).

[17] 向隆万 (Xiang Longwan), 东京审判征战记 中国检察官向哲浚团队 *(Dong Jing Shen Pan Zheng Zhan Ji-Zhong Guo Jian Cha Guan Xiang ZhejunTuan Dui)[Journey to Justice Inside story of the Chinese Prosecutor Hsiang Che-chun and his team in the Tokyo Trial]* (Shanghai Jiaotong University Press, 2013) 88–90.

China.[18] His investigation ultimately yielded irrefutable evidence confirming the extensive crimes committed by Japanese war criminals on Chinese soil.

In addition to collecting evidence, identifying and securing the testimony of key witnesses at the IMTFE was a crucial task. Thanks to Hsiang's efforts, a significant number of key witnesses were able to testify, providing crucial support for establishing that Japanese war criminals had committed numerous atrocities in China. For example, most Japanese defendants denied the Nanjing Massacre, the notorious six-week massacre in 1937 that claimed approximately 300,000 lives in Nanjing, the then Chinese capital. Hsiang and his team successfully located and brought eight witnesses from China to Tokyo, including three Americans, whose testimonies documented a wide range of atrocities, rendering the defendants' denials ineffective.

Notably, Hsiang also persuaded Aisin-Gioro Puyi, the last emperor of the Qing Dynasty (1644–1911) and puppet emperor of Manchukuo (the Japanese-controlled state in northeastern China from 1932 to 1945), to testify at the IMTFE. Initially, Puyi was highly reluctant, fearing that his own testimony might lead to charges against him. However, after persistent efforts by Hsiang, Puyi agreed to testify. He appeared at the Tribunal for eight consecutive days, playing a pivotal role in corroborating the crimes committed by Japanese war criminals.

Despite the considerable challenges, Hsiang and his team worked diligently to gather substantial evidence in a short period, ensuring that every accusation against Japanese war criminals was supported by solid proof.

25.3.3 Participation in Tribunal Debates

In addition to conducting investigations and preparing the Indictment, the International Prosecution Section was responsible for engaging in tribunal debates against accused war criminals. The trial proceedings allowed both the prosecution and the defendants to make opening statements, present evidence, examine witnesses, and address the Tribunal. Most Japanese defendants refused to admit the crimes outlined in the Indictment and denied the accusations.

To ensure the fairness and justice of the trial, each accused, in accordance with the IMTFE Charter, had the right to be represented either by counsel of their own choosing or by counsel appointed by the Tribunal. The active involvement of defense counsel frequently led to heated debates and arguments on a range of issues. As a member of the International Prosecution Section and a representative of

[18] 向隆万 (Xiang Longwan), 东京审判征战记 中国检察官向哲濬团队 *(Dong Jing Shen Pan Zheng Zhan Ji-Zhong Guo Jian Cha Guan Xiang ZhejunTuan Dui)[Journey to Justice Inside story of the Chinese Prosecutor Hsiang Che-chun and his team in the Tokyo Trial]* (Shanghai Jiaotong University Press, 2013) 59–67.

China, Hsiang delivered multiple addresses at the Tribunal, directly responding to the defense arguments of Japanese war criminals. He countered their sophistry by presenting clear facts and solid evidence.[19]

One common strategy employed by the Japanese defendants was to deny that war had occurred between China and Japan, arguing that no formal declaration of war had been made prior to 1941. To support this claim, they contended that Japan had engaged with China diplomatically rather than militarily, managing "Chinese affairs" through negotiations and communications with the duly constituted Chinese government rather than committing acts of war. Hsiang forcefully refuted these arguments before the Tribunal, demonstrating the undeniable reality of Japan's sustained aggression in China.

Hsiang emphasized that, beginning in 1931, Japan deployed troops into Chinese territory without any provocation, initiating acts of war that resulted in the deaths of millions of Chinese civilians. Although China had not formally declared war against Japan prior to 1941, the conflict nonetheless constituted an undeniable state of war. Regarding the Japanese defendants' reference to a so-called duly constituted government of China, Hsiang further argued:

> Our learned counsel for the defense claim that Japan has consistently dealt with the "duly constituted Government of China." I fail to understand what they mean by this term. Japan established puppet regimes in various regions—Manchuria, Eastern Hopeh, Nanking, and elsewhere—each controlled and directed by Japanese authorities. In making this claim, the defense overlooks the legitimate government of China, dismissing the Central Government under Generalissimo Chiang Kai-shek, which has been recognized worldwide both then and now.[20]

Hsiang emphasized that the Chinese Central Government, recognized internationally, had always existed, and that the so-called duly constituted government cited by the Japanese defense was merely a puppet regime established by Japanese invaders to control northeastern China. Consequently, Japan's interactions with these puppet authorities could not obscure the reality of the war between China and Japan.

Another defense strategy employed by some Japanese war criminals was to claim that they were merely low-ranking officials without decision-making authority and thus not involved in planning the war. Kenji Doihara provides a typical

[19] Hsiang Che-Chun, 'Speeches at IMTFE' in 向隆万 (Xiang Longwan) (ed.), 东京审判·中国检察官向哲浚 *(Dong Jing Shen Pan Zhong Guo Jian Cha Guan Xiang Zhejun) [The Tokyo Trial Chinese Prosecutor Hsiang che-chun(Xiang Zhejun)]*(Shanghai Jiaotong University Press, 2010).

[20] Hsiang Che-Chun, 'Speeches at IMTFE' in 向隆万 (Xiang Longwan) (eds), 东京审判·中国检察官向哲浚 *(Dong Jing Shen Pan Zhong Guo Jian Cha Guan Xiang Zhejun)[The Tokyo Trial Chinese Prosecutor Hsiang che-chun (Xiang Zhejun)]* (Shanghai Jiaotong University Press, 2010)

example.[21] He asserted that he was simply a subordinate officer, acting under the orders of his superiors, with no role in formulating policy. He argued that, lacking political power and involvement in Japan's wartime decision-making, he could not be held accountable as a war criminal. In reality, however, Doihara was not a mere low-level executor; he was a principal architect of many criminal operations in China. To rebut this defense, Hsiang stated:

> We shall not repeat the facts and arguments set out in the prosecution's summation, which we respectfully submit demonstrated that Doihara was one of the original conspirators, frequently executing his audacious plans without authorization from the Central Government, which belatedly—and sometimes begrudgingly—accepted them as a fait accompli.[22]

Hsiang exposed Doihara's crimes before the Tribunal by presenting compelling evidence, including his role in the kidnapping of Puyi and the orchestration of the opium trade. It was evident that Japanese war criminals consistently sought to evade responsibility through various defense strategies. Thanks to Hsiang's persistent efforts, these defenses were systematically refuted, ensuring that justice was ultimately served.

25.4 The Legacy of Hsiang

From 1946 to the end of 1948, Hsiang Che-chun served as an Associate Prosecutor at the IMTFE, playing a critical role in ensuring that Japanese war criminals were held accountable. From the outset, the Tokyo Trial faced skepticism, with some critics labeling it as "Victors' Justice,"[23] suggesting that the proceedings were politically motivated and the charges imposed by the Allied Powers.

To counter these claims, Hsiang took on the challenge of demonstrating the heinous crimes committed by Japanese war criminals through the presentation of irrefutable evidence, thereby upholding justice. Despite Japan's defeat and surrender, Hsiang confronted numerous obstacles. The Nanjing National Government, preoccupied with the ongoing civil war, provided limited support in terms of staff and resources. Additionally, both the Chinese government and populace lacked awareness of the importance of preserving evidence, creating further

[21] 倪征㬇 (Ni ZhengAo), '东京审判的回忆 (Dong Jing Shen Pan De Hui Yi)' in上海交通大学东京审判研究中心 (Shang Hai Jiao Tong Da Xue Dong Jing Shen Pan Zhong Xin) (eds), 东京审判文集 (*Dong Jing Shen Pan Wen Ji*) *[Collected Works of the Tokyo Trial]* (Shanghai Jiaotong University Press, 2013)

[22] Hsiang Che-Chun, 'Speeches at IMTFE' in 向隆万 (Xiang Longwan) (eds), 东京审判·中国检察官向哲浚 *(Dong Jing Shen Pan Zhong Guo Jian Cha Guan Xiang Zhejun) [The Tokyo Trial Chinese Prosecutor Hsiang che-chun (Xiang Zhejun)]* (Shanghai Jiaotong University Press, 2010)

[23] Richard H Minear, *Victors' Justice: Tokyo War Crimes Trial* (Princeton University Press, 1971).

difficulties. Nevertheless, Hsiang and his team overcame these challenges, successfully compiling extensive witness testimonies and documentary materials that corroborated Japanese atrocities, providing a strong foundation for convictions at the IMTFE.

Hsiang Che-chun's contributions to the Tokyo Trial carry great significance for both China and the wider world. The trial represented China's equal participation in the international community and symbolized its commitment to justice. By adhering to strict procedural standards, the IMTFE demanded the highest professional rigor from its judges and prosecutors. Through his legal expertise and conscientious work ethic, Hsiang fulfilled his duties as prosecutor with distinction. His efforts, together with those of other prosecutors, ensured that Japanese war criminals were convicted in an international tribunal, with their crimes firmly recorded in history—a lasting legacy of the trial.

Hsiang's work also contributed to the development of international law concerning war crimes. Before World War II, war crimes were largely understood as violations of the laws of war, such as targeting civilians or using prohibited weapons such as poison gas.[24] The Tokyo Trial, alongside the Nuremberg Trials, marked a significant shift by recognizing the initiation and waging of aggressive war as a punishable crime. Importantly, these trials did not exempt low-ranking individuals who acted under orders from prosecution. Hsiang demonstrated a profound understanding of these emerging principles and applied them effectively in his accusations.[25] Most of his arguments aligned with the new legal norms, earning the support of the majority of judges and reinforcing the authority of these international standards, thereby promoting the advancement of international criminal law.

In recent decades there has been a resurgence of Japanese militarism, with some denying the war crimes committed by their country. Such denials not only deepen the suffering of victims but also pose risks to world peace. The legacy of Hsiang and his colleagues, however, preserves invaluable historical evidence, reminding the world of the atrocities committed by Japanese war criminals and the horrors of warfare. Their work serves as a lasting caution, urging the global community to uphold peace while remembering the lessons of history.

[24] Yuki Takatori, 'The Forgotten Judge at the Tokyo War Crimes Trial' 10 (2008), Massachusetts Historical Review 115.

[25] Article 6 of Charter of the International Military Tribunal for the Far East, <https://www.un.org/en/genocideprevention/documents/atrocity-crimes/Doc.3_1946%20Tokyo%20Charter.pdf> accessed 10 July 2025.

26

Li Haopei (1906–1997)

Guoyong Zou and Jue Li

26.1 Life, Education, and Career

26.1.1 Life and Education

Li Haopei (1906–1997) is widely recognized as a distinguished twentieth-century Chinese international lawyer. He was born in 1906 in the Tongde Rice Shop (同德米号) in Shanghai. In 1913 he started his education at an old-fashioned private school (私塾), where he became well versed in the Confucian classics. In 1925, he was admitted to Soochow University (东吴大学) Law School.[1] Soochow Law School was founded by Charles Rankin, an American lawyer, in 1915 and was the first law school in China to provide education in common law with teaching in English. Before the founding of the People's Republic of China (PRC) in 1949, it was recognized as one of the two best law schools in China. Many eminent Chinese international lawyers, including Wang Chonghui and Ni Zhengyu, graduated from Soochow Law School. In 1928 Li graduated with honours, ranking second in his class, and he was awarded a bachelor's degree in law.

In 1936, Li enrolled at the London School of Economics and Political Science (LSE) with financial support from a Boxer Indemnity Scholarship (中英庚款). At the LSE he studied public international law under the supervision of Professor Lauterpacht and private international law and comparative civil law under the supervision of Professor Kahn Freund.[2]

Li passed away in 1997 in The Hague, where he had worked as a judge for the International Criminal Tribunal for Rwanda (ICTR). In memory of Li's international law scholarship and professional contributions, more than two dozen

[1] Soochow University, 'Kenneth Wang School of Law' (1 July 2017) <https://eng.suda.edu.cn/Academics/Schools/201712/a0f07e81-1f00-4f4f-8075-4293b8550a6c.html> accessed 12 July 2025.

[2] Ling Yan, 'International Justice Li Haopei: Active in the Legal Arena for 60 Years' [国际大法官李浩培：活跃法坛六十载] (2007) 2 China Trial News Monthly 21; Hao Tiechuan, 'The Main Force of Chinese Modern Jurists–International Students of Law' [中国近代法学家的主力军——法学留学生] *the People's Court Daily* (China, 27 May 2016) 6.

Guoyong Zou and Jue Li, *Li Haopei (1906–1997)* In: *Histories of International Law in China*. Edited by: Ignacio de la Rasilla, Jiangyu Wang, and Congyan Cai, Oxford University Press.
DOI: 10.1093/oso/9780198888345.003.0026

international lawyers and judges co-authored a book entitled *International Law in the Post-Cold War*.[3]

26.1.2 Career

Li went back to China in 1939. He first served as professor and Dean of the Department of Law at Wuhan University. In 1946 this was followed by a professorship and the position of Dean of the Law School at Zhejiang University.[4] After the founding of the PRC, Li did not leave mainland China. While many other pre-PRC Chinese lawyers whose legal careers came to an end, Li was one of the few fortunate ones. Besides continuing his teaching in China Foreign Affairs University, in December 1949 he was nominated a full-time member of the Foreign-Related Legal Affairs Committee of the Legislative Affairs Commission of the Central People's Government (中央人民政府法制委员会外事法规委员会专职委员), and he participated in drafting the first batch of foreign-related regulations in the People's Republic of China.[5] Li also served as one of the three legal advisers to the Ministry of Foreign Affairs (MFA) from 1963 to 1993.[6]

In the 1950s, Li helped the Chinese government deal with several very challenging international disputes. For instance, among many other possible examples, in an arbitration case involving the collision of an American shipping company vessel and a Chinese fishing boat, after a thorough legal analysis, he held that a Chinese court had jurisdiction over the case.[7]

Li's scholarship was internationally recognized. In 1985 he was elected a member of the Institut de Droit International in Switzerland. He was one of the first citizens of the PRC to lecture at the Hague Academy. In 1990, at the invitation of the Hague Academy of International Law, he gave a series of lectures entitled *Some Recent Developments in the Conflict of Laws of Succession*.[8]

China had been increasing its engagement with the international order, and Li was well positioned to work for his country while defending the international

[3] Sienho Yee and Wang Tieya (eds), *International Law in the Post-Cold War: Essays in Memory of Li Haopei* (Routledge 2001).

[4] Sun Kang, 'A Slice of the History of the Law School of Zhejiang University in the Period of The Republic of China' [浙江大学法学院民国办学史片记] (2018) Zhejiang University Law Review 35.

[5] Liu Liang, 'He went to a foreign country to study and missed his motherland, resulting in long gray hair, until he returned to his homeland and saw the intimate green hills—Interview with Professor Li Haopei, a famous jurist' [岸遥生白发，波尽露青山——访著名法学家李浩培教授] (1984) 5 Law Science Magazine 26, 27.

[6] Deng Lie, 'A Review of Chinese Public International Law Research on the 40th Anniversary of Reform and Opening Up' [改革开放40周年中国国际公法学研究述评] (2018) 3 Law Review 2.

[7] Li Haopei, 'The Legal Issues of the Sinking of U.S. Ship Collided with Chinese Merchant Ship Xin'an' [美轮撞沉新安轮案的法律问题], in Li Haopei, *Selected Works of Li Haopei* [李培浩文选] (Law Press China 2000) 265, 274.

[8] Li, Haopei, *Some Recent Developments in the Conflict of Laws of Succession* [国际私法在遗产继承问题上的新发展] (Brill Nijhoff 1990).

rule of law at international forums. In 1993, the Chinese government nominated him to be an arbitrator at the Permanent Court of Arbitration (PCA). In 1993 Li was elected to be the judge in the United Nations International Criminal Tribunal for the former Yugoslavia (ICTY), and in 1995 to be an appellate judge in the International Criminal Tribunal for Rwanda (ICTR).

26.2 Judge in the ICTY

During his service in the ICTY and the ICTR, Li participated in handling several significant cases. His professional capacity and personal quality highly impressed his colleagues. Judge Antonio Cassese warmly commented:

> I admired his intellectual vigour, his impassioned attachment to the principle of respect for human dignity, as well as his tenacious insisting on treasured legal conceptions while at the same time being prepared to change those conceptions to take into account those of other Judges. One further merit of Judge Li, for which all the other Judges so much appreciated him, was his conciseness. His statements, interventions in plenary meetings and when deliberating, as well as his dissenting or separate Opinions, were always brief, forceful and to the point.[9]

26.2.1 The *Duško Tadić* case

The *Duško Tadić* case was the first trial conducted by the International Criminal Tribunal for the Former Yugoslavia. Duško Tadić was accused of committing war crimes and crimes against humanity during the Bosnian War (1992–1995) in the Prijedor region. Tadić was charged with multiple counts, including breaches of the Geneva Conventions, violations of the laws and customs of war, and crimes against humanity. These charges concerned his involvement in acts of persecution, inhumane treatment, and violence committed in the Omarska, Trnopolje, and Keraterm detention camps. On 7 May 1997 the ICTY's Trial Chamber found him guilty of nine counts and partially guilty of two counts. Both the prosecution and the defence appealed the decision. On 15 July 1999 the ICTY Appeals Chamber modified the judgment, convicting Tadić of additional crimes. Li Haopei agreed with the decision of the Appeals Chamber to dismiss the appellant's appeal, but

[9] Antonio Cassese, 'The Contribution of the International Criminal Tribunal for the Former Yugoslavia to the Ascertainment of General Principles of Law Recognised by the Community of Nations' in Sienho Yee and Wang Tieya (eds), *International Law in the Post-Cold War: Essays in Memory of Li Haopei* (Routledge 2001) 43.

dissented on three legal issues and submitted an *amicus curiae* brief.[10] The three legal issues were: (1) the ruling on the legality of the establishment of the Tribunal; (2) the Tribunal's jurisdiction under Article 3 of the ICTY Statute; and (3) the nature of the conflict in the former Yugoslavia.

Regarding the legality of the establishment of the ICTY, Li held that the ICTY had the power to decide its own jurisdiction. However, the ruling improperly extended this authority to question the Security Council's competence in establishing the Tribunal and whether the decision was appropriate. Furthermore, since the UN Charter did not grant the Tribunal the power to review the legality of Security Council resolutions, it was clear that the Tribunal lacked this authority. Therefore, Li concluded that the review was an overreach and illegal, and the appeal regarding the legality of the Tribunal's establishment should be dismissed without further examination.

Second, the ICTY exceeded its jurisdiction in this case. The ruling asserted that customary international law had developed to the extent that violations of the laws and customs of war, as listed in Articles 3(a) to 3(e) of the Tribunal's Statute, should be prosecuted and punished even if they were committed during non-international armed conflicts. Li disagreed with this interpretation. He concurred with interpretative statements made by the representatives of France, the United States, and the United Kingdom when voting on the Security Council resolution adopting the Tribunal's Statute. He did not agree with Paragraph 91 of the judgment that Article 3 of the Tribunal's Statute granted it jurisdiction over serious crimes that violated international humanitarian law but were not covered by Articles 2, 4 or 5. He viewed the ruling as an unauthorised exercise of legislative power, as no authority had been granted to the Tribunal to exercise such jurisdiction.

Third, the characterization of the conflict in the former Yugoslavia was controversial. There were two possible approaches. The first of these, which was adopted by the appellant, viewed the conflict in isolation and argued that there was no armed conflict in the relevant time and place. The second argued that the conflict in the former Yugoslavia should be regarded as a whole and considered to have an international character. Li disagreed with the first view and supported the second approach, which was the prosecution's position.[11] In conclusion, Li pointed out a flaw in the ruling. Since the judgment did not determine the armed conflict in question to be international in nature, it failed to address a critical factor in establishing the jurisdiction of the Tribunal under Article 2 of its Statute.

[10] Prosecutor v Dusko Tadic, 'Separate and Dissenting Opinion of Judge McDonald Regarding the Applicability of Article 2 of the Statute' <https://www.icty.org/x/cases/tadic/tjug/en/tad-tsojmcd970507e.htm> accessed 12 July 2025.

[11] Li Haopei, 'Separate Opinion on the Appeal in the Tadić Jurisdiction Motion Case' [对塔迪奇关于国际法庭管辖权动议的上诉案的个别意见], in Li Haopei, *Selected Works of Li Haopei* [李浩培文选] (Law Press China 2000) 796.

26.2.2 The *Dražen Erdemović* case

Dražen Erdemović was a significant case heard by the International Criminal Tribunal for the former Yugoslavia (ICTY). Dražen Erdemović, a Bosnian Croat soldier, was involved in the killing of more than 1,000 Bosnian Muslims during the Srebrenica massacre in July 1995. Erdemović was part of a unit that executed the victims after the fall of the Srebrenica enclave, a designated 'safe area' under the protection of the United Nations. Erdemović was therefore arrested and charged with crimes against humanity. He confessed to the crimes but claimed that he had acted under duress and been forced by his superiors to participate in the executions. In 1996 Erdemović pleaded guilty to one count of crimes against humanity (murder) before the ICTY. His defence argued that he had been coerced into committing the murders—a defence of duress. The Trial Chamber found that although he had been under significant pressure, a defence of duress was not sufficient to absolve him of responsibility for the crimes. Erdemović was sentenced to ten years in prison. This sentence was later upheld on appeal, and the Appeals Chamber emphasized that, while his duress claim was considered, it did not fully exonerate him from responsibility for the killings.

On this case, Li differed from the other judges on two major points.[12] The first was that being coerced or obeying superior orders under threat of death could serve as a complete defence for the slaughter of innocent civilians. On this matter, there were no applicable treaties or customary international law to guide the resolution. The domestic laws and practices of different countries on this issue were inconsistent, making it impossible to derive a general principle of law recognized by civilized nations. While Li acknowledged the reasonableness and correctness of such rules and exceptions, he emphasized that since the appeal was concerned with whether such an exception should apply, he would add the following observations: (1) The primary objective of international humanitarian law should be to protect innocent civilians, prisoners of war, and other non-combatants. The life of innocent persons should be essential, and international humanitarian law must strive to safeguard their protection and prevent their destruction. The international community must never tolerate such inhuman policies. (2) As indicated above, domestic laws regarding whether exceptions to this rule are justifiable or necessary differ among nations. Based on these two considerations, Li concluded that coercion could only serve as a mitigating factor and not as a defence for the slaughter of innocent civilians. This view aligned with the separate individual opinion of Judges McDonald and Vohrah and supported their stance.

The second point was related to whether the case should be sent back to the Trial Chamber. Li argued that it would be erroneous to refer the case back to the

12 Prosecutor v Drazen Erdemovic, 'Separate and Dissenting Opinion of Judge Cassese', <https://www.icty.org/x/cases/erdemovic/acjug/en/erd-adojcas971007e.pdf> accessed 12 July 2025.

Trial Chamber, as it was clear that the appellant, in raising the issue of coercion, was merely doing so as a reason to receive a reduced sentence rather than as a complete defence or justification for his actions. Therefore, his plea of guilty was unambiguous. This position was supported by several facts. (1) The severity of a criminal act and the corresponding punishment depend on the nature of the act itself, rather than it being classified in one category or another. (2) There was no reason to assert that crimes against humanity were necessarily more severe than war crimes. (3) The concept of crimes against humanity originated and was formalized on 8 August 1945, when the governments of the United States, France, the United Kingdom, and the Soviet Union concluded the Charter of the International Military Tribunal at Nuremberg to prosecute and punish the major war criminals of the European Axis powers. This Charter was annexed to the London Agreement. It was inaccurate to claim that crimes against humanity constituted a crime against all humankind.[13]

Li concluded that the appellant's guilty plea was clear and valid, as coercion was consistently presented as a request for a lesser sentence not as a justification for actions. Since the Trial Chamber had acknowledged the mitigating circumstances in its sentencing, the Appeals Chamber should allow the appellant's request and reconsider his case to determine whether the sentence imposed by the Trial Chamber was fair and just. Therefore, referring the case back to the Trial Chamber was a mistake, as it would not serve any purpose and would only delay the proceedings.

26.3 Scholarship

As a scholar, Li Haopei had great academic achievements, and the level of his theoretical research was far beyond that of his time. He achieved great success in his research on a series of private and public international law topics.

26.3.1 Private International Law

Li Haopei was a master scholar in the field of private international law. His research focused mainly on conflict of laws and international civil procedure law. From the 1940s, he published a series of works on private international law which not only covered general issues, such as remission and transmission,[14] public order,[15] the

[13] Li Haopei, 'Separate and Dissenting Opinion on the Appeal in Prosecutor v. Erdemović' [对检察官诉埃尔戴莫维奇上诉案的个别和异议意见], in Li Haopei, *Selected Works of Li Haopei* [李浩培文选] (Law Press China 2000) 803.

[14] Li Haopei, 'The Issues of Remission and Transmission in Private International Law' (1944) 3 Chinese Legal Science 6.

[15] Li Haopei, 'The Issues of Public Order in Private International Law' (1945) 1 Chinese Legal Science 4.

lex patriae of parties,[16] private international law theories in the nineteenth century,[17] the new Swiss private international law[18] and the revolution of private international law in the USA,[19] but also the laws applicable to the substantive elements of contract formation and its effectiveness,[20] legal capacity,[21] the right *in rem*,[22] formal elements of marriage formation,[23] jurisdictional conflict and conflict of laws concerning the declaration of death,[24] and specific issues related to tort,[25] divorce and separation,[26] and the formation of marriage.[27] It is particularly worth mentioning that his *General Theories on Private International Law*[28] published in 1945 refers to several important works in English, French, and German. It not only clarifies the basic concepts of private international law, but also examines China's relevant legislation at that time and discusses Chinese scholars' own academic thoughts on the subject.[29] In addition, Li was editor-in-chief for the subject of private international law in the *Chinese Encyclopedia of Law* and wrote twenty-four entries on various related subjects.[30] He believed that private international law, including on conflict of laws, international jurisdiction in civil and commercial matters, and recognition and enforcement of foreign civil and commercial judgments, was domestic law in nature rather than international law, choice-of-law rather than substantive law.[31] He argued that the extraterritorial effect of the domestic law of a foreign country entirely depended on whether the court hearing the case applied

[16] Li Haopei, 'The Lex Patriae of the Parties in Private International Law' (1948) 1 New Legal Science 25.

[17] Li Haopei, 'The Theories on Private International Law in the 19th Century' (1948) 3 New Legal Science 36.

[18] Li Haopei, 'The Swiss New Private International Law' (1989) 4 Law Science 70.

[19] Li Haopei, 'The Revolution of Private International Law in the USA' (1992) 1 Chinese Yearbook of International Law 83.

[20] Li Haopei, 'The Applicable Law for the Substantive Elements of Contract Formation and Its Effectiveness' (1943) 1 National Wuhan University Social Sciences Quarterly 8.

[21] Li Haopei, 'The Applicable Law for Legal Capacity' (1945) 5 Chinese Legal Science 4.

[22] Li Haopei, 'The Applicable Law for Right In Rem' (1947) 2 Zhejiang Journal 1.

[23] Li Haopei, 'The Applicable Law for Formal Elements of Marriage Formation' (1948) 1 Chinese Legal Science 7.

[24] Li Haopei, 'Issues Related to the Jurisdictional Conflict and the Conflict of Laws Concerning the Death Declaration' (1945) 4 Chinese Legal Science 14.

[25] Li Haopei, 'Issues in Private International Law Related to Tort' (1945) 3 Chinese Legal Science 4.

[26] Li Haopei, 'Issues in Private International Law Related to Divorce and Separation' (1948) 5 New Legal Science 74.

[27] Li Haopei, 'Issues in Private International Law Related to the Formation of Marriage' (1948) 1 Zhejiang Journal 104.

[28] Li Haopei, *General Theories on Private International Law* [国际私法总论] (Wuhan University Press 1945).

[29] Zeng Tao, 'Li Haopei and the Development of China's Private International Law in One Hundred Years' (2007) 25 Tribune of Political Science and Law 163, 164.

[30] Editorial Board of the Encyclopedia of China, *Chinese Encyclopedia: Law* (China Encyclopedia Publishing House 1984).

[31] Li Haopei, 'Introduction to International Civil Procedural Law' [国际民事程序法概论], in Li Haopei, *Jurisprudence Collection of LI Haopei* [李浩培法学文集] (Law Press China 2006) 302, 303.

the foreign law according to its choice-of-law rules. If so, the foreign law had extraterritorial effect. Otherwise, it did not.[32]

Li Haopei was an early researcher engaged in international civil procedure law in China. He published *An Introduction to International Civil Procedure Law* in 1996,[33] which dealt in depth with aspects of international civil procedure law, such as immunity, jurisdiction, the status of aliens in civil and commercial litigation, recognition and enforcement of foreign civil and commercial judgments, international judicial assistance in civil and commercial cases, international commercial arbitration, and the like.[34] He also contributed several important papers, such as *the Provisions of the New Swiss Private International Law on International Jurisdiction*,[35] *Multilateral Treaties Regulating International Civil Jurisdiction*,[36] and *The 1968 European Economic Community Convention on Jurisdiction and the Enforcement of Judgments in Civil and Commercial Matters*.[37] In his opinion, the main rules in international civil procedural law were actually domestic laws rather than international law, and even some international treaties had not yet been developed into a system of international law which was universally binding on the signatory states.[38]

Li Haopei attached great importance to the use of comparative methods in his research on private international law. He stated that the study, application, and formulation of private international law could not achieve satisfactory results without comparative methodology.[39] He applied this method in his *The Law of Nationality: A Comparative Study*,[40] focused on problems in cross-border judicial practices. In this book, Li explored in detail the relationship between nationality and international law concerning several issues, including the acquisition, loss, restoration, and conflicts of nationality, citing the nationality laws of ninety-nine countries and dozens of English and French books.

Further contributions on private international law were his translations of several leading books on it. Li read English, French, German, Latin, and Russian very

[32] Lin Hai, 'Li Haopei: I implore God to give me ten more years to fulfil my wish in this life' *Procuratorial Daily* (China, 1 March 2014) 3.

[33] Li Haopei, *An Introduction to International Civil Procedure Law* (Law Press China 1996).

[34] Li Haopei, 'Introduction to International Civil Procedural Law' in Li Haopei, *Jurisprudence Collection of Li Haopei* (Law Press China 2006) 399, 316.

[35] Li Haopei, 'The Provisions of New Swiss Private International Law on International Jurisdiction' (1991) 1 Chinese Yearbook of International Law 19.

[36] Li Haopei, 'Multilateral Treaties Regulating International Civil Jurisdiction' (1993) 3 Chinese Yearbook of International Law 34.

[37] Li Haopei, 'The 1968 European Economic Community Convention on Jurisdiction and the Enforcement of Judgments in Civil and Commercial Matters' (1994) 4 Chinese Yearbook of International Law 76.

[38] Zhang Hui, 'A Review of Li Haopei and His International Law Thoughts' [李浩培及其国际法思想评述] (2009) 9 Wuhan University International Law Review 333.

[39] Li Haopei, *Jurisprudence Collection of Li Haopei* (BLaw Press China 2006) 513, 514.

[40] Li Haopei, *The Law of Nationality: A Comparative Study* [国籍问题的比较研究] (Commercial Press 1979).

well. With his multi-language proficiency, Li translated the *Napoleonic Code (Code Civil Français)*[41] and Martin Wolff's *Private International Law*[42] into Chinese. This helped make Chinese lawyers familiar with the theory and practice of private international law in many countries.

26.3.2 Public International Law

In the field of public international law, although Li Haopei's academic writings are not numerous, he had profound expertise. His book *Introduction to the Law of Treaties*[43] was the first comprehensive and systematic review of the law of treaties after the founding of the People's Republic of China. This classic work traced many principles and rules of treaty law back to their origins.[44] Quoting and citing extensively in order to corroborate his findings, the book was well provided with supporting material on the doctrines of various schools, relevant international treaties, international customs, the doctrines of authoritative scholars, and the jurisprudence of the International Court of Justice. The book profoundly and systematically clarified what were seen as thorny issues of the law of treaties in China and provided the Chinese international legal profession with important information on the theory of treaty law.

Li Haopei also made significant contributions to the study of the origins of international law. In his book *The Concepts and Sources of International Law* he predicted that, theoretically, the sources of international law would develop along with the development of international society and therefore could not be said to be exhaustive. However, regarding the stage of development of contemporary international law, Article 38 of the Statute of the International Court of Justice seemed to meet the needs of international society. This was because the primary sources—international treaties, international customs, and general legal principles— were complemented with include unilateral legal acts and resolutions of international organizations, among others.[45] In his article on *Jus Cogens and International Law*, he argued that international organizations were fundamentally different to countries as such organizations derived their power

[41] Li Haopei, Wu Chuanyi, and Sun Minggang, *Code Civil Français* (Translation) (Commercial Press 1979).

[42] Li Haopei and Martin Wolff, *Private International Law* (Translation) (Law Press China 1988).

[43] Li Haopei, *The Law of Treaties* [条约法概论] (Law Press China 1988).

[44] Liu Liang, 'He went to a foreign country to study and missed his motherland, resulting in long gray hair, until he returned to his homeland and saw the intimate green hills, Interview with Professor Li Haopei, a famous jurist' [岸遥生白发，波尽露青山——访著名法学家李浩培教授] (1984) 5 Law Science Magazine 26, 27.

[45] Li Haopei, *The Concept and Sources of International Law* (Guizhou People's Publishing House 1994) 53.

from limited cessions by sovereign countries which could be revoked at any time, making them more like consultative forums between countries.[46] In contrast, Li Haopei asserted that in some cases, individuals could be the subject of rights and obligations under international law.[47]

Li Haopei's writings on international law were based on and precisely tailored to specific judicial practice since he had long careers in both the Ministry of Foreign Affairs and international courts.[48] He devoted himself to China's diplomatic legal practices and published a series of articles connected with specific diplomatic affairs, which well met the needs of China's diplomatic struggle at that time. For example, a US ship collided with the Chinese merchant ship Xin'an on 20 April 1950, resulting in the death of seventy persons.[49] Li immediately published *Legal Aspects of the Collision Between Sinan and an American Ship*, in which he clearly pointed out that China's courts had indisputable jurisdiction over the case from both civil and criminal perspectives, and he analysed the legal issues involved in applying the law and compensation for damages.[50]

26.4 Legacy

Professor Li Haopei remains a towering figure in the history of international law who provided valuable lessons for future generations. His academic and professional journey exemplifies the integration of multiple cultural perspectives, a dedication to empirical research, and a synthesis of academic scholarship with practical legal service.

First, Li Haopei's education in both China and the West, and particularly his studies at the London School of Economics, equipped him with a unique ability to understand and interpret international law from a cross-cultural perspective. His fluency in multiple languages, including English, French, German, and Latin, allowed him to navigate and synthesize the legal traditions of different cultures. This 'mastery of both Chinese and Western knowledge' (学贯中西) empowered him to appreciate the complexities of international law in its global context and

[46] Li Haopei, 'Jus Cogens and International Law' in Li Haopei, *Selected Works of Li Haopei* (Law Press China 2000) 513.

[47] Li Haopei, *The Concept and Sources of International Law* [国际法的概念和渊源] (Guizhou People's Publishing House 1994) 21, 22.

[48] Deng Lie, 'Review of Chinese Public International Law Research on the 40th Anniversary of Reform and Opening Up' [改革开放40周年中国国际公法学研究述评] (2018) 3 Law Review 12.

[49] Bo Xu and Wu Xiaofang, 'China's Three Musketeers of International Law' [中国国际法"三剑客"] (2011) 2 World Knowledge 52.

[50] Li Haopei, 'Legal Aspects of the Sinking of U.S. Ship Collided with Chinese Merchant Ship Xin'an' [美轮撞沉新安轮案的法律问题], in Li Haopei, *Selected Works of Li Haopei* (Law Press China 2000) 265.

positioned him to significantly contribute to legal discussions that spanned cultural divides.

Second, Li Haopei was a staunch advocate of the empirical approach to international law. His research methodology, which is evident in his work *The Law of Treaties*, relied heavily on state practice and the resolution of international disputes. Rather than relying solely on abstract theory, Li grounded his analyses in the practical realities of international relations. His emphasis on case law, treaties, and historical documents led to groundbreaking insights into treaty law and the practice of diplomacy. His approach serves as a reminder that law is not just a set of theoretical rules but is rooted in how states and actors engage with one another in the international arena.

Finally, Li Haopei's career blended academic excellence with practical legal service. He not only contributed to the intellectual development of international law but also played an active role in its application. His involvement in high-profile international cases, including disputes between China and other nations, and his service as a judge at international tribunals, allowed him to directly influence the resolution of global legal issues. Li's work at the United Nations International Criminal Tribunal for the former Yugoslavia and the International Criminal Tribunal for Rwanda illustrates his deep commitment to ensuring that legal principles were applied in real-world contexts, especially in the pursuit of justice for war crimes and human rights violations. His life shows that the role of the scholar is not isolated from the role of the practitioner, but instead these two spheres are interconnected, each enriching the other.

The legacy of Professor Li Haopei offers profound lessons for today's legal professionals. His ability to bridge cultural divides with language and education, his empirical and grounded approach to legal research, and his steadfast belief in the importance of combining scholarship with practice make him a model for aspiring international lawyers. Future generations can learn from him the value of a comprehensive pragmatic approach to law, and the importance of contributing both to the development of legal theory and to its application in the real world.

27
Ni Zhengyu (1906–2003)

Yayezi Hao and Hong Yu

27.1 Introduction

Ni Zhengyu (倪征燠) was a prominent Chinese international jurist. He served as the first Chinese member of the International Law Commission from 1982 to 1984, and then as the first judge of the People's Republic of China at the International Court of Justice (ICJ) from 1985 to 1994. In 1991 he became a member of the Institut de droit international, and in 1995 he was elected the first President of the newly established Chinese Society for the Law of the Sea. Ni was a graduate of Stanford Law School and had previously served as a District Judge in Shanghai in the 1930s; Chief Advisor of the International Prosecution Section of the International Military Tribunal for the Far East after World War II; professor of international law in the late 1940s and early 1950s; and principal legal counsel of the Ministry of Foreign Affairs of the PRC from the early 1950s to the early 1980s. This chapter revisits Ni's legacy and influence on international law in 20th-century China.

27.2 Background and Legal Education (1906–1930)

Ni was born in 1906 in Wujiang (吴江), a small town on the border of Jiangsu and Zhejiang provinces in China, as one of nine siblings. When he began school, China was still governed by the Qing dynasty, so he attended a traditional private school. After the Xinhai Revolution (1911–1912), which ended the Qing dynasty, the new Republic of China (1912–1949) established a Ministry of Education to modernize the system. Consequently, Ni was able to receive a modern education, including instruction in English.

At the age of 18, Ni undertook study at the University of Shanghai (沪江大学), where he started pursuing a liberal arts degree (1924–1925), before transferring to Soochow University Law School (东吴法学院), located in the nearby ancient city of Suzhou, in 1925. Several factors influenced Ni's decision to pursue a career in law. Ni admired upright and incorruptible officials such as Bao Zheng (包拯) and Hai Rui (海瑞), and yearned for a fair and just social order.[1] However,

[1] Ni Zhengyu, *Memoirs of Ni Zhengyu: Approaching the Hague with Calmness and Composure* (淡泊从容莅海牙) (Beijing: Peking University Press, 2015), pp. 18–22.

Yayezi Hao and Hong Yu, *Ni Zhengyu (1906–2003)* In: *Histories of International Law in China*. Edited by: Ignacio de la Rasilla, Jiangyu Wang, and Congyan Cai, Oxford University Press.
DOI: 10.1093/oso/9780198888345.003.0027

during his adolescence, the status of Westerners and Chinese citizens was unequal in China. Western countries exercised extraterritoriality through consular courts, which compromised the integrity of China's jurisdiction. Ni grew up listening to his family's accounts of the unequal status between Chinese and foreign judges and lawyers in the consular courts. In 1921, during the Conference on the Limitation of Armament in Washington, the Nine-Power Treaty was signed. The treaty indicated the willingness of its States Parties (United States, Imperial Japan, France, Great Britain, Italy, Belgium, Netherlands, and Portugal) to end extraterritoriality in China with the proviso of the establishment of a satisfactory legal system by China. This news provided Ni with fresh inspiration to study law, enhance the Chinese judicial system through studying both Chinese and foreign law, and negotiate with foreign countries, with the ultimate goal of eliminating extraterritoriality in China.

Established in 1915, Soochow University School of Law, known as the "Comparative Law School of China" (中华比较法律学院), is one of China's oldest and most esteemed law schools. It played a crucial role in the development of modern legal education in the country. Soochow School of Law significantly influenced China's approach to international law by integrating Western legal principles with traditional Chinese legal thought. Many of its graduates went on to play significant roles in shaping China's legal landscape and influence its approach to international law. Another well-known Chinese jurist, Li Haopei,[2] also became Ni's classmate at this time. During his three years of study at Soochow Law School, Ni studied courses such as private international law, maritime law, and public international law.[3] Recognizing that the poor litigation procedures were a major hindrance for China to abolish the extraterritorial powers that Western powers had seized since the mid-19th century, Ni devoted himself to the study of procedural law. In 1925, the Floating University "Ryndam," sponsored by the University Travel Association of New York City, made a brief stop in Shanghai. Ni had the opportunity to converse with American students on board the Ryndam, which sparked his desire to attend Stanford Law School to further his studies.[4] He aimed to broaden his career prospects and gain familiarity with foreign laws that were pertinent to his pursuit of an early removal of extraterritoriality in China.[5] Since admission to Stanford required two bachelor's degrees, Ni earned both a Bachelor of Laws from Soochow University Law School and a Bachelor of Arts from Chita

[2] See Chapter 26 in this volume, Zou Guoyong and Li Jue, 'Li Haopei (1906–1997)'.

[3] Zhang Nongji, 'Ni Zhengyu (倪征燠) (1906–2003) International Law and the Law of the Sea' in *Legal Scholars and Scholarship in the People's Republic of China* (Leiden, The Netherlands: Harvard University Asia Center, 2022), pp. 27–32.

[4] Zhang Nongji, 'Ni Zhengyu (倪征燠) (1906–2003) International Law and the Law of the Sea' in *Legal Scholars and Scholarship in the People's Republic of China* (Leiden, The Netherlands: Harvard University Asia Center, 2022), pp. 32–35.

[5] For an introduction to the Floating University, see Henry William Lester, 'A High School on the High Seas,' The School Review 35 (1927): p. 599.

University. In 1928, after graduating from Soochow University Law School, he was awarded a scholarship to attend Stanford Law School.

During his time at Stanford, Ni took classes in Equity and Court Organization, Private International Law, Constitutional Law, and Public International Law. Next to school, he worked part-time as a gardener to earn a living; his employer was Herbert Clark Hoover, who later became the 31st President of the United States. In 1929, Ni was granted a Juris Doctor (JD) degree after completing one year of study. His thesis, "The Progress of Law from Chance to Choice," followed in the footsteps of Ni's early concern with procedural law. Ni first examined the Western legal system's evolution from contingency to choice from the perspective of legal philosophy.[6] In his thesis, Ni reviews the evolution of the means of torture in ancient China and the Western Middle Ages, and argues that while, due to historical reasons, the legal systems of the East and the West each have their own historical backgrounds and evolutionary processes, they are all developing in the direction of civilization and justice. Based on the theory of legal evolution, Ni suggested that traditional Chinese law required a period of reform before it could become modern civil law. In his memoirs, Ni explained that the objective of his thesis was to establish a connection between legal evolution and the termination of extraterritoriality in China as per the Nine-Power Treaty, while also challenging the legal bias based on Western-centrism.[7] After graduating from Stanford, Ni worked as a fellow at Johns Hopkins University Law School for one year.

27.3 Judicial and Prosecutorial Career (1930–1948)

In 1930, Ni returned to Shanghai. He taught courses on international law and Anglo-American law at four schools: Soochow University Law School, the Chitz University, the Great China University, and the China Public Institute. At Soochow University Law School, he also taught two courses in Jurisprudence and Philosophy of Law. On September 18, 1931, as Japan waged a military operation in Shanghai, Ni had to suspend his teaching job in Shanghai and went on to work at the Ministry of Judicial Administration of the Nationalist government in Nanjing, from 1931 to 1933, where he participated in the drafting of the Code of Civil Procedure of the Republic of China. However, in 1933, Ni was reassigned to Shanghai, where he served as a judge at the Shanghai District Court. He worked on foreign-related civil cases at the first, second, and final instance at the Second Branch of the Jiangsu High Court and the Shanghai District Court from 1933 to 1941.

[6] Tsung Yuh Nyi, *The Progress of Law from Chance to Choice* (California: Stanford University, 1929).

[7] Ni Zhengyu, *Memoirs of Ni Zhengyu: Approaching the Hague with Calmness and Composure* (淡泊从容莅海牙) (Beijing: Peking University Press, 2015), at p. 40.

After the Japanese occupation of Shanghai, the personal safety of judges was seriously threatened, so Ni escaped to Chongqing, the wartime capital of China, where he was appointed chief district attorney and president of the Chongqing District Court in 1941. There, Ni tried the first civil case involving an American defendant in the Chongqing area. In 1944, Ni voluntarily applied for a transfer to the Ministry of Judicial Administration and was sent abroadto investigate the litigation and trial systems and legislation on commerce and industry in the United States, Britain, and France. After completing his investigation, he wrote *The Judicial Systems of the United States and the United Kingdom* (美国和英国的司法制度.).[8]

In 1946, in accordance with the Cairo Declaration, the Potsdam Declaration, the Japanese Instrument of Surrender, and the Moscow Conference, the Supreme Commander of the Allied Powers, United States General Douglas MacArthur, issued a special proclamation establishing the International Military Tribunal for the Far East (IMTFE). The IMTFE operated under a common law trial system, which was very different from the trial system in China. The Nationalist government was not well prepared for this trial, had collected insufficient evidence, and had a serious shortage of prosecution staff to be sent to Tokyo to participate in the trial. Therefore, it was in a very disadvantageous position during the prosecution phase. In order to prevent Japanese war criminals escaping justice, Ni, who was familiar with Anglo-American law, was appointed Chief Advisor of the International Prosecution Section, and went to support the Chinese prosecutors' work. In the course of his work, he spent much time reading the existing trial records, and also visited Beijing to collect witness testimonies on site and went to places such as the former Japanese Army Ministry archive to collect evidence. Since Ni joined this work when the prosecution's direct examination phase had ended, he used a litigation strategy in court to present new evidence in the cross-examination phase under the Anglo-American trial system, and finally ensured that Kenji Doihara and Seishirō Itagaki, two Japanese war criminals, were sentenced to death by hanging.

27.4 Academic and Legal Advisor Career (1948–1980)

After the IMTFE ended, Ni returned to China, resigned from his official position, and became a professor and director of the law department at Soochow University Law School. With the founding of New China, he stayed in Shanghai. This period was the low point of Ni's career. Due to the 1952 reorganization of Chinese higher education, Soochow University Law School was closed. He was eventually assigned to work as the director of Tongji University Library and taught Russian classes. It was not until 1956 that he was transferred by Premier Zhou Enlai to work at the

[8] Ni Zhengyu, 'The Judicial Machinery in United States and the United Kingdom', in *Ni Zhengyu Collection Law* (Beijing: Law Press, 2006), pp. 99–122.

Ministry of Foreign Affairs in Beijing. During his work at the Ministry of Foreign Affairs, he participated in editing the *International Treaty Collection (1917–1957)*,[9] translated J.A.C. Thomas's *Private International Law*[10] in 1963, and also participated in translating a series of foreign international law works. In 1964, he completed his monograph *Jurisdictional Issues in International Law*.[11] These books provided a good basis for the training of international law talents in the PRC. In addition, among other legal advising tasks, he and Zhou Gengsheng[12] provided the Central Committee with advisory opinions on the width of the national territorial sea, which became the legal basis for The Statement of the Government of the People's Republic of China on the Territorial Sea.[13]

With United Nations General Assembly Resolution 2758 recognizing the People's Republic of China (PRC) as "the only legitimate representative of China to the United Nations" in 1971, the Chinese government began to participate in various international conferences of the United Nations. Ni was appointed Legal Counsel of the Chinese Delegation to the Twenty-seventh Session of the United Nations General Assembly and Legal Counsel of the Chinese Delegation to the United Nations Sea-bed Committee in 1972, and went to New York twice with the delegation to attend the meetings. At the UN General Assembly, Ni mainly attended the meetings of the Sixth Committee, where there were discussions about the Third United Nations Conference on the Law of the Sea (UNCLOS III) that began in 1973. UNCLOS III held 11 sessions from 1973 to 1982, and Ni also participated in several sessions as Legal Counsel of the Chinese Delegation. Although China was not a member of the drafting committee, the drafting committee established six "language groups" to ensure that the six official authentic texts had in fact been negotiated by the Conference from the point of view of linguistic equivalence.[14] Ni served as the leader of the Chinese "language group" and participated in the relevant meetings of the drafting committee with his assistant Li Shengjiao, where they discussed and finalized the official language versions of the Convention on the Law of the Sea. Ni not only guided the content of the Chinese text of the Convention on the Law of the Sea but also discussed other language versions with

[9] Li Qihan, ed., *International Treaty Collection*, 11 vols (Beijing: World Affairs Press Co. Ltd., 1959–1962).

[10] J.A.C. Thomas, *Private International Law* (London: Hutchinsons University, 1955).

[11] Ni Zhengyu, *Jurisdictional Issues in International Law* (Beijing: World Affairs Press Co. Ltd., 1964).

[12] See Chapter 26 in this volume, Luo Guoqiang and Wang Chao, 'Zhou Gengshen (1889–1971)'.

[13] '中华人民共和国政府关于领海的声明', Ministry of Foreign Affairs of The People's Republic of China, December 19, 2024, https://www.mfa.gov.cn/web//wjb_673085/zzjg_673183/bjhysws_674671/bhsmgb/202405/t20240510_11302691.shtml. accessed August 12, 2024.

[14] See Alan Beesley, 'The Negotiating Strategy of UNCLOS III: Developing and Developed Countries as Partners: A Pattern for Future Multilateral International Conferences?' Law and Contemporary Problems 46 (1983): p. 183, and Treves, Tullio, 'United Nations Convention on the Law of the Sea', United Nations Audiovisual Library of International Law, 2008, http://untreay.un.org/cod/avl/pdf/ha/uncls/uncls_e.pdf. accessed August 12, 2024.

the delegates present, and carefully communicated about every word used in the Convention text, making a great contribution to the final text of the Convention on the Law of the Sea.[15]

In 1979, some American citizens holding "Hukuang Railway Bonds" sued the People's Republic of China in the US District Court for the Northern District of Alabama, demanding payment for a financial debt that had arisen decades earlier from a large international loan concluded in 1911 between the Qing Empire and a consortium of foreign banks to finance the construction of the Hukuang Railway system.

The court accepted the case based on the Foreign Sovereign Immunities Act of 1976 (FSIA) and issued a subpoena to Huang Hua, Minister of Foreign Affairs of China, requiring him to appear in court in what became the famous *Jackson v People's Republic of China* case.[16] After the case was accepted by the court, Ni, as Legal Counsel to the Ministry of Foreign Affairs of the People's Republic of China, participated in the research work on countermeasures for this case. In 1983, Ni published an article entitled "Theory and Practice Concerning the Jurisdictional Immunities of States" in the *Chinese Yearbook of International Law*,[17] which took state immunity theory as its research object; it explained the difference between absolute immunity and restrictive immunity theories, and, combined with then internationally available data on 31 countries' claims and practices on sovereign immunity issues, discussed substantial exceptions to the rule of the damage of immunity to developing countries' interests. In addition to writing articles to provide a theoretical basis for China's position, Ni followed China's diplomats to the United States to discuss with lawyers how to draft a motion to dismiss. Eventually, the US Court found that the FSIA could not be retroactively applied, thus dismissing the lawsuit and safeguarding China's national interests.

27.5 Career at the United Nations: International Law Commission and International Court of Justice (1982–1996)

In 1981, Ni was nominated as the Chinese candidate for the United Nations International Law Commission (ILC) and was successfully elected a member for a term of five years. However, he was also nominated and elected a judge of the

[15] Li Shengjiao, 'Li Shengjiao: Memory of Ni Zhengyu, Prosecutor of Tokyo Trial', China Daily, September 3, 2015, https://column.chinadaily.com.cn/a/201509/03/WS5bf2088aa3101a87ca93e628.html. accessed August 12, 2024.

[16] Jackson v. People's Republic of China, 596 F. Supp. 386 (N.D. Ala. 1984), Justia US Law, https://law.justia.com/cases/federal/district-courts/FSupp/596/386/1676454/ accessed August 12, 2024.

[17] Ni Zhengyu, 'Theory and Practice Concerning Jurisdictional Immunities of States', Chinese Yearbook of International Law (1983).

International Court of Justice in 1984, thus ending his term as a member of the ILC two years before the expiration of his appointment. In the three sessions of the ILC in which Ni participated, the number of topics for each session was around seven or eight, including: "States Responsibility"; "International Liability for Injurious Consequences Arising Out of Acts Not Prohibited by International Law"; "Law of the Non-Navigational Uses of International Watercourses"; "Jurisdictional Immunities of States and Their Property"; "Status of the Diplomatic Courier and the Diplomatic Bag Not Accompanied by Diplomatic Courier"; "Draft Code of Offenses Against the Peace and Security of Mankind."[18] While the content of the topics did not change much over the length of his appointment, it remained difficult to participate in the work of progressive development and codification of international law for a man who was over 75 years old at the time.

However, Ni was still just as dedicated to studying the relevant topics, sometimes working late into the night. He suffered a car accident and was injured for some time, but he insisted on attending the meetings even before he had fully recovered. Throughout the three ILC sessions, Ni made many contributions to the work of the ILC based on China's national interests and attitudes on the relevant topics, combined with his own academic experience and international judicial experience. During the first session of his tenure at the ILC, on the topic "Question of Treaties Concluded Between States and International Organizations or Between Two or More International Organizations," he argued that international organizations and States should be accorded equal status as far as possible, but necessary distinctions should be made between the two, and that rules should be formulated in such a way as to facilitate the work of the international organizations and safeguard the sovereignty and fundamental interests of their member States. In addition, he proposed amendments to the articles regarding how treaties concluded by international organizations should be binding on their member States, which were supported by a dozen member States, including Brazil and Venezuela. In the end, some of Ni's opinions were incorporated by the Drafting Committee into the draft conclusions.[19] On the topic of "Jurisdictional Immunities of States and Their Property," since Ni had done plenty of research and study in preparing for the *Jackson v People's Republic of China* case, he made well-founded contributions. Especially on the legal disputes involving state-owned enterprises, his opinions were aligned with China's domestic enterprise development and its consistent position in international forums at that time, and also in line with the interests of many

[18] United Nations, 'Summary Records of the Thirty-Fifth Session', Yearbook of the International Law Commission 1983, Vol. I, United Nations, 1983, pp. 1–331, https://www.un-ilibrary.org/content/books/9789213620366c011. accessed August 12, 2024.

[19] Ni Zhengyu, *Memoirs of Ni Zhengyu: Approaching the Hague with Calmness and Composure* (淡泊从容莅海牙) (Beijing: Peking University Press, 2015), at p. 262.

developing countries, so he also received support from ILC's members of many developing countries.[20]

As mentioned earlier, Ni was nominated and elected a judge of the International Court of Justice in 1984. Before Ni's election there had been two Chinese judges on the International Court of Justice, both recommended by the Kuomintang government before and after the founding of the People's Republic of China when China's UN seat was not restored. The first was Judge Hsu Mo, who took office in 1946, and the second was Judge Koo Wellington, who took office in 1957 and also served as Vice-President of the International Court of Justice from 1964 to 1967. The terms of these two judges were connected; however, since Koo's retirement in 1967 there had been no Chinese judge on the bench of the ICJ. Ni's election filled the 18-year gap, so it attracted great attention both at home and abroad.[21] Ni took office in 1985 and worked for nine years until retiring and returning to China in 1994, when he was 88 years old. During his tenure as an ICJ judge, Ni participated in seven cases concluded with judgments (expressing separate opinions in two of them); four cases concerning provisional measures (making statements in two of them); and three cases where he issued separate opinions on the merits.[22] The Application for Revision and Interpretation of the Judgment of 24 February 1982 in the Case concerning the Continental Shelf (Tunisia/Libyan Arab Jamahiriya) was the first case in which Ni participated and it was also the first time that the ICJ accepted an application for revision. In response to Tunisia's application for revision, Ni argued that revision was an extraordinary remedy that could only be used under strictly limited conditions; otherwise, the relationship of rights and obligations between States could not be stabilized in the long term, which was not in line with the original intent of article 61 of the Statute of the Court. According to Ni's own account, in his opinion he emphasized the importance of the *res judicata* of

[20] Nations, United. 'Summary Records of the Thirty-Fourth Session', Yearbook of the International Law Commission 1982, Vol. I, United Nations, 1982, pp. 1–343, https://www.un-ilibrary.org/content/books/9789213620373c011. accessed August 12, 2024.

[21] 'Around the World: Peking Judge Chosen For World Court', The New York Times,Nov. 8, 1984, https://www.nytimes.com/1984/11/08/world/around-the-world-peking-judge-chosen-for-world-court.html. accessed August 12, 2024.

[22] Ni has been involved in the following cases: 1. Application for Revision and Interpretation of the Judgment of 24 February 1982 in the Case concerning the Continental Shelf (Tunisia/Libyan Arab Jamahiriya); 2. Military and Paramilitary Activities in and Against Nicaragua; 3. Application for Review of Judgement No. 333 of the United Nations Administrative Tribunal; 4. Applicability of the Obligation to Arbitrate under Section 21 of the United Nations Headquarters Agreement of 26 June 1947; 5. Border and Transborder Armed Actions (Nicaragua v. Honduras); 6. Applicability of Article VI, Section 22, of the Convention on the Privileges and Immunities of the United Nations; 7. Arbitral Award of 31 July 1989; 8. Certain Phosphate Lands in Nauru; 9. Maritime Delimitation in the Area Between Greenland and Jan Mayen. 10. Territorial Dispute (Libyan Arab Jamahiriya/Chad).Cases concerning provisional measures are as follows: 1. Questions of Interpretation and Application of the 1971 Montreal Convention arising from the Aerial Incident at Lockerbie (Libyan Arab Jamahiriya v. United Kingdom); 2. Questions of Interpretation and Application of the 1971 Montreal Convention arising from the Aerial Incident at Lockerbie (Libyan Arab Jamahiriya v. United States of America); 3. Application of the Convention on the Prevention and Punishment of the Crime of Genocide (Bosnia and Herzegovina v. Federal Republic of Yugoslavia); 4. Arbitral Award of 31 July 1989.

the Court's judgments, arguing that revision should not be granted lightly and that the application for revision submitted by Tunisia did not meet the requirements under article 61 of the Statute. In this case, Ni's grassroots court work experience helped other judges understand the practical application of retrial in judicial trials and he was selected to be one of the drafters of the judgment.[23]

27.6 Legacy

Ni Zhengyu passed away in Beijing in 2003 at the age of 93. Looking back at his life, he played an important role in the international law practice of the 20th century and had a great impact on the development of international law in China.. In terms of legal practice before international courts, Ni performed brilliantly in court as a prosecutor at the IMTFE not only bringing several Japanese war criminals to justice for their war crimes but also allowing China to further integrate into the international legal order. After the founding of the People's Republic of China, Ni provided guidance for the new regime to carry out diplomatic work from the perspective of international law. Moreover, especially after China regained its seat in the United Nations. Ni's performance in New York and Geneva meetings enabled China to return to the international legal system established after World War II more quickly and effectively. Ni's work experience in the International Law Commission and the International Court of Justice was in his personal capacity; however, he still devoted himself to safeguarding China's interests and representing China's legal opinions on those occasions. At the same time, his deeds also made the Chinese people aware of the rigor and justice of international law and inspired a generation of Chinese people to study international law with enthusiasm and determination.

Ni made a huge contribution to the cultivation of international law talents in China. Ni's first full-time job was as a lecturer at Suzhou (also known historically as Soochow) University Law School, He had many years of university teaching experience, teaching courses such as Public International Law, Private International Law, Comparative Law, Civil Law, Civil Procedure, Judicial Organization, and so on. He served as a lecturer at Suzhou University Law School, Great China University, China Public Institute, Chita University, Chao Yong Law College, and Suzhou-Shanghai Union College of Law and Commerce, with Suzhou University School of Law and Chao Yong Law College being two of the most famous law schools in China before the 1950s. In addition to teaching at universities, Ni also participated in the training of young diplomats during his tenure as a legal advisor to the Ministry of Foreign Affairs, explaining the judicial system and legal knowledge

[23] Ni Zhengyu, *Memoirs of Ni Zhengyu: Approaching the Hague with Calmness and Composure* (淡泊从容莅海牙) (Beijing: Peking University Press, 2015), at p. 316.

related to Anglo-American countries. When he entered the International Law Commission and the International Court of Justice, he often taught short-term courses for Chinese judges, officials, and legal workers based on his own work experience. He wrote many works and translated many international law works. His main research areas focused on three fields: the Anglo-American judicial system, international maritime law and state jurisdiction theory. These works played a foundational role in the Chinese legal research system. Moreover, the most famous English–Chinese dictionary of Anglo-American law in China was guided by him as an academic consultant during the compilation process.

Ni was also the founder of China's law of the sea field, to which half of his published legal research works were related.[24] These works had an enlightening influence on China's maritime law research from the 1960s to the 1980s. The official Chinese text of the International Maritime Law Convention, which he was involved in proofreading, was described by Shi Jiuyong as "the most accurate expression in Chinese among all conventions established within the scope of the United Nations and the most consistent with other language texts."[25] He initiated the establishment of China Ocean International Issues Research Association, which later served as the foundation for the establishment of the Chinese Society for the Law of the Sea and was elected its inaugural president in 1995. The main purpose of this society remains to provide legislative advisory opinions and suggestions to the government on formulating and improving domestic legal system related to maritime law, to carry out academic research and academic exchange activities on maritime law issues, and safeguard China's maritime interests.

Ni wrote his memoir in 1998, "淡泊从容莅海牙" (*Approaching the Hague with Calmness and Composure*), which was titled after a poem by his good friend James T.C. Liu praising him for not pursuing fame and fortune and coming to The Hague with calmness and composure to serve as a judge of the International Court of Justice[26] aged 79. Despite the fact that during his term, he was almost always the oldest judge sitting on the ICJ , in addition, he participated in many academic activities after his 80th birthday, such as insisting on taking part in person at the meetings of the *Institut de droit international* until he was 91 years old. His spirit of diligent learning and hard work lives on in new generations of Chinese international law students and scholars.

[24] Ni Zhengyu, 'Legal Issues in Ship Collisions', in Ni Zhengyu *Collection Law* (Beijing: Law Press, 2006), pp. 299–337.

[25] Shi Jiuyong, Judge at the International Court of Justice (1994–2010). See Ni Zhengyu, *Memoirs of Ni Zhengyu: Approaching the Hague with Calmness and Composure* (淡泊从容莅海牙) (Beijing: Peking University Press, 2015), at preface 2.

[26] Former Chinese Foreign Minister Qian Qichen commented that the publication of this memoir was a major event in China's diplomatic and international law circles, with important historical value for the formation and development of international law in China and positive practical significance for the further promotion of the study and research of international law.

28
Han Depei (1911–2009)

Yongping Xiao and Jue Li

28.1 Introduction

Han Depei, who was a distinguished professor of humanities and social sciences at Wuhan University, is regarded as one of the founding fathers of private international law and a pioneer of environmental law in China. He served as the first President of the Chinese Society of Private International Law and the first President of the Chinese Society for the Study of Environmental and Resources Law, as well as honorary president of the Chinese Society of International Law.

28.2 Internationalized Education Experience (1925–1945)

Han Depei was born on 6 February 1911, in Rugao (如皋) County, Jiangsu Province. Exceptionally bright from a young age, he entered a private school at six years old and extensively studied the Four Books and Five Classics. In 1925, at the age of fourteen, he was admitted to the second generation of Rugao Normal School (如皋师范), where he was influenced by the intellectual reform movement known as the 'New Culture Movement' (1916–1919)—which became the sociopolitically oriented 'May Fourth Movement' in 1919 (五四新文化)—Western democratic ideas, and Marxist thought. These intellectual influences shaped his lifelong beliefs and pursuits. After graduating in 1928, Han continued his studies at Jiangsu Nantong High School and, in 1930, was admitted to the History and Political Science Department of Zhejiang University. However, six months later, due to a departmental merger with Central University, he transferred to Nanjing, where he decided to study law under the influence of Xie Guanhua, then head of Central University's Law Department and later Minister of the Ministry of Judicial Administration of the National Government.

During his time at Central University, Han extensively read numerous legal works, laying a solid foundation in law while improving his proficiency in foreign languages. He studied works such as Oppenheim's *International Law*, Dicey's *Introduction to the Study of the Law of the Constitution*, Roscoe Pound's *Introduction to the Philosophy of Law*, and Duguit's *The Transformation of Public Law and the Transformation of Private Law*. His foreign language skills significantly

Yongping Xiao and Jue Li, *Han Depei (1911–2009)* In: *Histories of International Law in China*. Edited by: Ignacio de la Rasilla, Jiangyu Wang, and Congyan Cai, Oxford University Press. © Yongping Xiao and Jue Li 2026.
DOI: 10.1093/oso/9780198888345.003.0028

contributed to his later research in law, especially in international law. He also became involved with Marxist thought and participated in patriotic democratic and anti-Japanese resistance movements. In 1934, he graduated with a Bachelor of Laws degree and remained at Central University as an editor and lecturer.

In 1939, Han was awarded a British Boxer Indemnity public scholarship (中英庚款留英公费生) for study in the UK, where he planned to attend the University of Cambridge. However, the onset of the Second World War meant he redirected to the University of Toronto in Canada in August 1940. There, under the guidance of renowned private international law scholar Moffatt Hancock, he conducted research in private international law and Anglo-American common law, completing his master's thesis, *Substantive and Procedural Issues in Private International Law*, and earning his Master of Laws degree in 1942. That same year, he moved to Harvard Law School in the United States as a special research student, focusing on international public law, private international law, and jurisprudence. While at Harvard, he focused primarily on international public law, private international law, and jurisprudence, writing and publishing papers such as *Review of the Five Works of Pound in the United States* and *Review of Hans Kelsen's the Pure Theory of Law*.[1]

28.3 Han and International Law Study at Wuhan University (1945–2009)

After the Second World War, Han accepted an invitation from Wuhan University President Zhou Gengsheng[2] to join the faculty. He taught courses in public international law, private international law, and the history of foreign legal thought. Following the establishment of the People's Republic of China in 1949, he remained at Wuhan University as a professor and chair of the Law Department. He later also served as the Deputy Secretary-General of the University Affairs Committee (at that time the university did not have a president, only a director, deputy director, and secretary-general to manage the university's affairs), assisting in the management of the university's daily operations. After the presidential system was implemented in 1951, he was appointed as the Deputy Academic Dean while continuing as the head of the Law Department, overseeing academic affairs.

From 1945 to 1957, Han focused his main efforts on teaching, university administration, and departmental management, making significant contributions to the development of Wuhan University, particularly the Law Department. On the

[1] Xiao Yongping, 'Academic Spirit and Legal Thoughts of Han Depei' (Wuhan University Institute of International Law, 26 August 2009) <https://translaw.whu.edu.cn/info/1371/11251.htm>, accessed 10 July 2025.

[2] Luo Guoqiang and Chao Wang, 'Zhou Gengsheng (1889-1971)' in Ignacio de la Rasilla and Congyan Cai (eds), *History of International Law in China. All Under Heaven?* (OUP forthcoming 2025).

other hand, he also made new progress in legal research. For instance, in 1947, he published a series of articles in the renowned magazine *Observation*, including *Comments on Immigration Provisions in the Sino-American Commercial Treaty*, which exposed the unequal provisions regarding immigration in the treaty and suggested that the Chinese side should demand that the United States eliminate or amend unreasonable restrictions on Chinese immigration, strengthening the protection of the rights and interests of Chinese nationals in the US. In 1948 he published a lengthy article titled *The Problem of Rebuttal in International Private Law* in Volume 9, Issue 1 of the *Journal of National Wuhan University (Social Sciences Quarterly)*, which remains the most authoritative discussion on this issue in China's international private law community. In 1956, he translated the Russian book *Courts of the Soviet Union and Courts of Capitalist Countries* into Chinese, which was published by Hubei People's Publishing House.

However, he was labelled a 'rightist' (右派分子) during the Anti-Rightist Campaign (反右斗争) in 1957, which led to the loss of all his academic positions and subsequent exile to a labour farm in Shayang, a county of west-central Hubei province. The Anti-Rightist Campaign of 1957 was a political movement initiated by the Chinese Communist Party aimed at targeting intellectuals and social elites labelled as 'rightists'. The context for this movement was the government's desire to promote widespread criticism and self-criticism to improve governance; however, when some intellectuals voiced criticisms of government policies, they were accused of being 'rightists'. This campaign led to the persecution of thousands of intellectuals, many of whom lost their jobs and were subjected to imprisonment or forced labour. The Anti-Rightist Campaign had profound social implications, deepening public distrust in the government and severely undermining the status of intellectuals in the years that followed.

Han's stay at Shayang's Farm for labour re-education was an unexpectedly difficult and painful period in his life. In 1960 he was relieved of his 'rightist' status at Shayang Farm, ending his labour re-education. In 1961 he returned to Wuhan University, but by then the Law Department had been closed, and he was assigned to teach English in the Foreign Languages Department. With the beginning of the Cultural Revolution in 1966, he was again baselessly labelled a 'rightist' and was sent back to the Shayang farm set up by Wuhan University for labour reform. It was only in the later stages of the Cultural Revolution—after the 'Lin Biao Incident' in 1971, a pivotal event during China's Cultural Revolution involving the death in a plane crash of Lin Biao, a prominent military leader and Mao Zedong's designated successor who had allegedly attempted a coup against Mao to consolidate power—that Han's 'rightist' label was removed, although he remained at the farm. Following the downfall of the 'Gang of Four' in 1976, the Cultural Revolution came to an end. In 1978, Han was finally transferred back to Wuhan University, and shortly thereafter he received redress for the 'rightist' accusations of 1957 and the Cultural Revolution, allowing him to regain his professorship and salary. From

1957 to 1978, during the tumultuous years of the Anti-Rightist Campaign and the Cultural Revolution, Han faced political persecution and setbacks, enduring twenty years of unjust grievance. This was not only a personal tragedy for Han but also a tragedy in the history of Chinese legal education.

In 1979, China embarked on the Reform and Opening-up Policy, which, among others, sought to restore the rule of law in China and engagement with international order. As a result, Wuhan University decided to re-establish its law faculty in 1979. As the long-term Dean of Wuhan Law School, Han always advocated that teaching and research must go hand in hand, attaching great importance not only to study of legal theory, but also to the establishment of research institutions. Therefore, he established the Wuhan University Institute of International Law (1980) and Wuhan University Institute of Environmental Law (1981), which over the years trained multiple students, including many who went on to serve in ambassadorial positions across the world. Han also made much of the combination of legal theory and judicial practice, and he presided over a large number of scientific research projects and provided numerous consulting reports to the relevant official departments. Han also devoted much time to academic cooperation and culture exchange between China and foreign countries, travelling extensively abroad—including to the United States and Canada—to promote the cooperation of Chinese and foreign legal academic communities. Moreover, as Dean of Wuhan Law School, he was engaged in a great deal of teaching and research management, which led to the rapid development of legal education and research at Wuhan University and made indelible contributions to the socialist legal system. As the inaugural president of the Chinese Society of Private International Law, and university professor at Wuhan University, he not only influenced his peers with his broad and profound legal knowledge, but also personally supervised more than 200 masters and doctoral students in private international law. His rigorous academic attitude and generous and benevolent care enabled his academic ideas to spread far and wide. However, perhaps most remarkable of all was that, as a scholar in his old age—in his seventies, eighties, and even nineties—Han's body of research continued to grow significantly, with the publication of more than ten books and numerous articles on public international law, private international law, and environmental law.

28.4 Han's Scholarship in Private International Law

Han's academic achievement on private international law mainly includes the following five central aspects. First, Han constructed a theoretical system of Chinese private international law. He advocated that the scope of private international law should not be limited to conflict of laws, but should be extended to the substantive law of foreign-related civil and commercial legal relations. He likened private international law to an aircraft, the connotation of which was the fuselage of the aircraft, including conflict law and uniform substantive law, as well as the *loi d'application immediate* of the states; its extension was the two wings of the aircraft, the first being the nationality and the legal status of foreigners and the second international civil litigation and arbitration procedures.[3] He divided the study of private international law into five parts: basic issues of private international law, conflict law, uniform substantive law, international civil litigation, and international commercial arbitration, through which he scientifically and systematically built a new system of modern Chinese private international law.

Second, he correctly evaluated the role and future of conflict of laws. In response to the neglect of the study of conflict of laws in China's jurisprudence in the early 1980s, Han, in cooperation with Li Shuangyuan, published '*The Study of Conflict of Laws Should Be Given Due Attention*' which clarified some basic theoretical issues of the conflict of laws, answered the question why the domestic courts should recognize foreign judgments and apply foreign laws under certain conditions, and argued that the application of foreign laws would neither undermine China's sovereignty nor necessarily harm the interests of Chinese parties.[4] The complexity of foreign-related civil legal relations required the state to both firmly defend its legitimate rights and interests and develop equal and mutually beneficial foreign relations without compromising its own rights and interests. Conflict of laws, as a more subtle and flexible legal system, was capable of achieving both of these tasks simultaneously as the objective situation changes. Therefore, conflict of laws was an indispensable legal system as long as nation states existed and civil laws of all countries were not completely unified. Third, he analysed modern trends in private international law. In 1988 and 2000, Han published *Recent Trends in Private International Law* and *Recent Developments in Private International Law Legislation*, in which he rationally discussed the current situation and the trend of private international law after the Second World War.[5] The traditional choice of law and application of law approach had been fiercely criticized and attacked by American jurisprudence, leading to significant reforms and developments in private international law theory. First, the flexible connecting factors were overused; second, the resulting oriented principle attracted increasing attention in the procedure of choice of law; third, the principle of party autonomy expanded while

[3] Han Depei, *Private International Law* [国际私法] (3rd edn, Higher Education Press, Peking University Press 2014) 7.

[4] Han Depei and Li Shuangyuan, 'The Study of Conflict of Laws Should be Given Due Attention' ' [应该重视对冲突法的研究] (1983) 6 Wuhan University Journal (Philosophy & Social Science) [武汉大学学报(哲学社会科学版)] 52.

[5] Han Depei, 'Recent Trends in Private International Law' in Han Depei, *Collected Works of Han Depei* [韩德培文集] (Wuhan University Press 2012) 41; Han Depei and Du Tao, ' 'Recent Developments in Private International Law Legislation' [晚近国际私法立法的新发展] (2000) 1 Chinese Yearbook of Private International Law and Comparative Law [中国国际私法与比较法年刊] 3.

being limited; and fourth, the law of *loid application immediate* had been newly developed. Han summarized the legislative trends of private international law in the following aspects: the first was that the legislative form shifted from decentralization to centralization; the second was the convergence of common law and civil law systems; the third was the combination of clarity and flexibility in the procedure of application of the law.

Fourth, Han was the first to offer a solution to China's inter-regional conflict of laws. The problems of inter-regional private law in China arose from the special situation of 'one country, two systems and four jurisdictions', and therefore the conflict of laws would inevitably arise between Hong Kong, Macau, Taiwan, and the mainland. There were three principles to be upheld to resolve the inter-regional legal issues in China, which were national unity, one country-two systems, and equality and mutual benefit. There were two specific methods: first, the National People's Congress should enact a unified inter-regional conflict of laws which was applicable to the whole country, that is, inter-regional private law; second, instead of unified inter-regional private law, Hong Kong, Macau, and Taiwan should apply their own choice of law rules in judicial practice and formulate interregional substantive law and conflict of law when the occasion was ripe. Fifth, he advocated the establishment of a legislative system of private international law with Chinese characteristics. Han believed that the scientization of the concept of legislation, the democratization of the legislative process, the codification of the legislative body, and the modernization of the legislative content should be achieved. In August 2000, the Model Law of the People's Republic of China on Private International Law, drafted by Han's team, was finalized after seven years and published in Chinese by the Law Press, as well as in English and Japanese in the Netherlands and Japan respectively, with a tremendous response in domestic and international jurisprudence.

From the analysis of the abovementioned five aspects it can be seen that, as the master of Chinese private international law, Han not only built a complete theoretical and legislative system of Chinese private international law from a global perspective with his profound theoretical background, but also enriched the theoretical content of Chinese private international law with his professional knowledge on many specific issues, and made great contributions to the development of the Chinese legal system of private international law.

28.5 Han and Environmental Law in China

Han was the pioneer of environmental law theory in China, as well as the advocate and founder of Chinese environmental law education and research. He published numerous works in the field of environmental law. He edited *The Theory and Practice of Chinese Environmental Law*, which systematically discussed Chinese environmental law and was hailed as the 'pioneering theoretical monograph' by the National Social Science Foundation. He edited a textbook on Environmental Law which was the earliest and comprehensive textbook on environmental law in China, and is the only common textbook on environmental law for the national universities to date.[6] Han argued that environmental issues, that is, the relationship between human and nature, are not only domestic but also international issues. To meet the challenge of the rapid deterioration of the global environment, cooperation and coordination among countries is necessary, as is cooperation and coordination among environmental law experts from all countries.

Han was one of the first people in China to take an interest in the emerging discipline of environmental law. In June 1981, Wuhan University Institute of Environmental Law of the Chinese Academy of Environmental Sciences was founded jointly by the Chinese Academy of Environmental Sciences and Wuhan University, with the support of Han and the approval of the State Science and Technology Commission, the former Office of the State Council Leading Group for Environmental Protection, and the former Ministry of Education. The Institute became the largest research institute specialized in environmental law research and teaching in China and Asia, and was among the first key research bases in the humanities and social sciences in China. Soon after the establishment of the Environmental Law Research Institute, Han decided to introduce a course on environmental protection law for undergraduate law students and pushed the Ministry of Education to establish environmental law as a sub-discipline of law. As a result of his efforts, Wuhan University Institute of Environmental Law was awarded the master's and doctoral degrees in Environmental Law in 1984 and 1998 respectively, making it the earliest master's and doctoral degree programme in Environmental Law approved by the Academic Degrees Committee of the State Council in China.

28.6 Han's Contributions to Public International Law

Han, who in 1980 founded the first research institute solely devoted to the study of international law in China—widely and affectionately known as 'the cradle of talents of international law talents in China'—also personally conducted considerable research in the field of public international law. From an overview of his writings on public international law, his insightful discussions had remarkable implication for China's relationship with the General Agreement on Tariffs and Trade (GATT). In 1986, the People's Republic of China made a formal request to GATT for restoration of the country's contracting party status. As an international jurist,

[6] Han Depei, *Textbook on Environmental Protection Law* [环境保护法教程] (8th edn, Law Press 2012).

Han introduced the history, organization, basic principles, and rules of GATT on the one hand, and discussed the reform of GATT and China's restoration of contracting party status of GATT on the other. Han focused on the opportunities and challenges for China in returning to GATT, and offered valuable suggestions for China to meet the challenges. To be more specific, Han made six suggestions: first, to speed up the process of reforming the economic system to create a favourable environment for national industries; second, to effectively use a flexible tariff or differential tariff system to protect national industries; third, to promote the enterprises to cultivate the ability of survival and development in the new competitive environment; fourth, to establish and improve a regulatory system to protect the development of domestic industries; fifth, to cultivate relevant talents vigorously; and sixth, to study and publicize the system and rules of GATT.[7] Han's discussion of GATT was profound and insightful, and supported Chinese jurisprudence's proper understanding of GATT. Although GATT has since been replaced by the World Trade Organization, Han's ideas are very insightful and informative for the implementation of the international agreements in China today.

28.7 Conclusion

Han Depei was the youngest professor at Wuhan University upon his return in 1946 and the oldest professor before his passing, aged almost 100 years, in 2009. His life was marked by resilience, intellectual rigour, and a commitment to legal education and reform. As a scholar, educator, and social activist and institution-builder he made indelible contributions to China's legal system, leaving behind a legacy that continues to influence both Chinese law today and countless Chinese international law scholars, practitioners, and policy-makers.

[7] Han Depei and Zhang Kewen, 'Reforming and Strengthening the Multilateral Trading System of the General Agreement on Tariffs and Trade' [论改革与加强关税及贸易总协定多边贸易体系] (1991) 2 Wuhan University Journal (Philosophy & Social Science) [武汉大学学报(哲学社会科学版)] 54.

29

Wang Tieya (1913–2003)

Ken Yang

29.1 Wang Tieya: The Last 'Worldly Gentleman'

This chapter tells the story of Wang Tieya 王铁崖,[1] the central character behind the efforts to rebuild the international law discipline in the 1980s. Building on the momentum of the Reform and Opening-up policy, Wang Tieya—in partnership with colleagues, most notably Chen Tiqiang 陈体强, and also Wei Min 魏敏 and Zhao Lihai 赵理海—oversaw the creation of the PRC's first international law-focused bachelor programme (1979), first learned society and academic journal devoted to international law (the Chinese Society of International Law was incepted in 1980; the *Chinese Yearbook of International Law*, of which Wang Tieya and Chen Tiqiang served as co-chief editors, came out in 1982), first national textbook (1981), and an university-based research institute in the field of international law (1983) which was second in time only to the one established by Han Depei at Wuhan University in 1980.- Wang was simultaneously at the forefront of Sino–Western academic exchange and had emerged as the leading voice in presenting Chinese perspectives. In 1981, he became the first PRC international lawyer elected as member associate to the *Institut de Droit International* and in 1990, one of the first two PRC lecturers (together with Li Haopei 李浩培) invited to the Hague Academy of International Law. His lectures entitled *International Law in China: Historical and Contemporary Perspectives* remains a canonical text for grasping Chinese attitudes towards international law.

Today, these developments are widely conceptualized as the typical markers of the professionalization and institutionalization of international law within a specific national environment. How did Wang Tieya become the keystone individual

[1] I am grateful to my professors at Peking University who studied under Wang Tieya during the 1980s and 1990s and shared their stories about their mentor over the past four years: Professor Rao Geping, Professor Yuan Ming, Professor Bai Guimei, Professor Li Ming, Professor Li Hongyun, and Professor Song Ying. Professor Chen Yifeng of Peking University, Professor He Chi of Tongji University, and my EUI supervisor, Professor Neha Jain, also offered a series of helpful comments. I am also indebted to Professor Jerome A. Cohen, Professor R. Randle Edwards, and Professor William P. Alford, who recounted their collaborations with Wang during the early 1980s in facilitating Sino–American legal education exchange. I very much appreciate the encouragement from the daughters of Wang Tieya, Wang Yi, Wang Li, and Wang Ting. The biographical details about Wang Tieya are mainly extracted from records retrieved from the University Archives, Dalhousie University.

Ken Yang, *Wang Tieya (1913–2003)* In: *Histories of International Law in China*. Edited by: Ignacio de la Rasilla, Jiangyu Wang, and Congyan Cai, Oxford University Press. © Ken Yang 2026.
DOI: 10.1093/oso/9780198888345.003.0029

behind these crucial advances? What must first be taken into account is Wang Tieya's good fortune and individual qualities. Already as a young man Wang Tieya had ticked all the right boxes in terms of upbringing and educational experience. He later survived the Cultural Revolution with relatively sound health and was able to devote the remaining two decades of his life to teaching and research—a period of time sufficient for him to rebuild the intellectual foundations that would sustain the growth of the international law discipline in the PRC for the next four decades.[2] His integrity, charisma, and amiable personality also rendered him a particularly effective campaigner-interlocutor who could coordinate and mobilize precious personnel and resources for his projects, both within the Chinese discipline and beyond, and between Chinese and non-Chinese international law communities.[3] On top of that, Wang truly cherished his role as a teacher, and had accordingly prioritized nurturing new generations of international law experts over his own research during the last stretch of his career.[4]

However, this study wishes to examine another—perhaps the most important—factor that underpinned his accomplishments during the PRC period: the cultural and social capital he had accumulated during the preceding Republican period (1912–1949), which was carried over to the PRC period (1949–present). This cultural and social capital not only armed Wang with authority, it also contributed to the resilience that helped him weather the turbulent periods of the twentieth century. This chapter thus attempts to connect Wang Tieya's stories before and after 1949 (a watershed moment in modern Chinese history),[5] introducing new archival sources and oral histories.

Wang Tieya exemplifies what I term the 'worldly gentlemen' of Republican China,[6] embodying the last vestiges of this era during the People's Republic of

[2] For some of Wang's contemporaries with comparable qualifications, traumatic experiences during the Cultural Revolution had either led to their premature demise—such was the case for many of his Tsinghua University peers, including Tian Baosheng 田保生 (1966), Shao Xunke 邵循恪 (1975), and Chen Tiqiang (1983)—or significantly impaired their ability to continue their intellectual work, as in the case of Chen Fangzhi 陈芳芝, who in the mid-1980s gave up her academic post to tend to her heart disease; her story is recounted in Chapter 33 on Chinese women in the histories of international law.

[3] Accordingly, in many Chinese biographical entries, Wang's 'international law scholar' (*guoji fa xuejia*) label is always followed by 'educationalist' (*jiaoyu jia*) and 'social campaigner' (*shehui huodong jia*).

[4] Owing to this personal preference, it was only in the early 1990s that Wang Tieya began working on his own international law treatise, by which time the most intensive stage of disciplinary reconstruction had concluded, the discipline itself at a low ebb. It was finally published in 1998, titled 'Introduction to International Law' (*Guoji fa yinlun*; Peking University Press). The vast number of international law scholars who would self-identify as Wang's mentees—which extended beyond students at Peking University—had its own historiographical (or perhaps hagiographical) consequence: making Wang Tieya the most lionized PRC international lawyer.

[5] On treating 1949 as a 'watershed, not an unbridgeable chasm' and the imperative of highlighting the continuities between Kuomingtang and Communist political orientations and policies, see Joseph W. Esherick, 'Ten Theses on the Chinese Revolution', Modern China (1995) vol. 21 no. 1, Symposium: Rethinking the Chinese Revolution, Paradigmatic Issues in Chinese Studies, IV, 45–76.

[6] The image of the 'gentleman' (*shi*) was inspired by my conversations with Professor Randall R. Edwards about his interactions with Wang Tieya. Touched by Wang's character, Edwards described him as 'a true gentleman if there ever was one'.

China. By 'worldly gentlemen', I allude to a small league of Chinese intellectuals born between the late Qing and early Republican periods, who became key actors in shaping Chinese foreign policies and international thought. Owing to the 'internationalization' of China through the dominance and influence of Western powers between the late nineteenth and early twentieth century, 'worldliness'—a competence then typically associated with education at prestigious Western universities which these men possessed[7]—became a valued quality for Chinese statecraft. While rapidly changing social conditions had displaced the intellectual class from China's political centre—which became dominated by new social groups such as modern soldiers, businessmen, and professional revolutionaries[8]—these classically educated men still harboured the sensibilities of the Confucian scholar-officials (*shidafu*) in asserting cultural and ethical leadership.[9] Accordingly, following this gentlemanly sensibility, they pursued leadership roles within Republican China's vibrant public sphere. Finally, invoking the image of the 'gentleman' also highlights the group's gender exclusivity and class identity, which helps us better grasp the inclusion–exclusion dynamics that defined the membership of this small and exclusive league.[10]

While many prominent international law specialists of this period displayed a distinct 'statist' orientation both in their career choices (i.e., entering foreign service) and their approach to international law (i.e., shaping Republican China in accordance with the 'civilized nation' standard),[11] others, such as Zhou Gengsheng 周鲠生 (aka 'S. R. Chow', 1888–1971), deliberately ventured outside government and academia to engage with the wider public and to educate the masses on foreign affairs.[12] Such was also the path chosen by Wang Tieya. Following in the footsteps of his two mentors, Zhou Gengsheng and Qian Duansheng 钱端升 (aka 'Ch'ien Tuan-sheng', 1900–1990), Wang Tieya began to embody the dual persona

[7] A small caveat must be added here about the dominance of 'Western' (read 'American') university-trained students: After the conclusion of the Sino–Japanese War in 1895, Japan and its higher education institutions became the primary destinations for reform-minded Chinese intellectuals. However, Imperial Japan's aggressive policies towards a weakened China drove Chinese society and its elites to become anti-Japanese. This turn also coincided with the return of American-trained students such as V. K. Wellington Koo, which began to shift power from Japanese-trained scholars to American-trained scholars.

[8] Luo Zhitian, 'Original Preface' in Shifts of Power: Modern Chinese Thought and Society, translated by Lane J. Harris and Mei Chun (Boston: Brill, 2017), XXIII.

[9] On the scholar-official tradition, see Timothy Cheek, The Intellectual in Modern Chinese History (Cambridge: Cambridge University Press, 2015), 1–3.

[10] On the inclusion–exclusion dynamic innate to the professionalization of international law, and the systematic exclusion of women participants from the Republican era Chinese international law discipline, see Chapter 33, Introduction.

[11] On the 'statism' characteristic of Republican China's international law discipline, see Pasha L. Hsieh, 'The Discipline of International Law in Republican China and Contemporary Taiwan', Washington University Global Studies Law Review (2015) vol. 14 no. 1, 81–127.

[12] These interventions were the natural outcome of increasing public interaction between the Chinese public and Republican China's foreign policies, a process then conceptualized as 'people's diplomacy' (*renmin waijiao*) and one that was linked with the global trend of democratizing foreign relations after the Great War.

of a professor and public intellectual during the final decade of Republican China. Against the backdrop of the Anti-Japanese War and the Chinese Civil War, Wang published many writings that sought to shape public opinion on China's foreign relations. His public stature and his critical stance against foreign and domestic policies of the Nationalist Government had eased his transition into the incoming PRC era, granting him a place on the outer circles of the PRC's new foreign policy establishment.

However, with the inauguration of the Leninist political order during the PRC, the umbilical cord that once linked intellectuals and society—a crucial social condition that had previously allowed intellectuals (international law specialists included) to maintain limited autonomy from the state—was severed. It was only until the 1980s, a brief window of liberalization in PRC history, that Wang Tieya could masterfully leverage his image as the world-of-yesterday 'scholar-official' as well as his remaining social and cultural capital for the international law field. With these contexts in mind, rather than attempting to exhaust Wang Tieya's rich legacies, this research seeks to treat Wang Tieya's unparalleled life as a unique thread—one that can aid us in highlighting the ruptures and continuations of the international law field during its evolution through Republican and PRC periods.[13] Finally, addressing the stark parallels between the Chinese gentleman's multi-positionality, and the international lawyer ideal type that makes up the 'invisible college' (i.e., the scholar-diplomat),[14] could also help explain Wang's outsized role in revitalizing the Chinese discipline of international law.

29.2 Odyssey in the World of Yesterday

Wang Tieya's connection to international law predated his own lifetime. He was born in 1913 in the southeastern coastal city Fuzhou—one of the original five treaty ports stipulated in the 1842 Treaty of Nanjing—as the youngest child of ten siblings. His father, Wang Shouchang 王寿昌 (1864–1926) was a cadet at the Fuzhou Naval School (*chuanzheng xuetang*), a proto-modern government school established during the Self-Strengthening Movement (1866). In the early 1870s, around the time that American missionary W. A. P. Martin added international law to the curriculum of *Tongwenguan* (School of Combined Learnings) in Beijing, the Naval College also began sending cadets to Europe to study law and international

[13] To a lesser extent through connections of his family members, mainly his father Wang Shouchang 王寿昌 and his first cousin Wang Jingqi 王景岐 (whose father Wang Fuchang was also a Naval College cadet who was sent to France), Wang's life was also tethered to the histories of international law in late-Qing China.

[14] The historical role assumed by scholar-diplomats in the history of international law was most prominently illustrated by Martti Koskenniemi in his sketch of 'the men of 1873'. See Martti Koskenniemi, The Gentle Civilizer of Nations: The Rise and Fall of International Law, 1870–1960 (New York: Cambridge University Press, 2001).

law.[15] As one of these students, Wang Shouchang accordingly studied both French and international law during his six-year sojourn (1885–1891), taking courses at l'Ecole de droit de Paris and l'École libre des sciences politiques.[16] Unfortunately, Wang's return coincided with the decline of the Self-Strengthening Movement, which limited his prospects in government service. It was only during the 1897–1898 Sino–Belgian negotiations concerning Belgium's financing of the planned Beijing–Hankou railway that Wang was given the chance to serve as a translator, a position that finally allowed him to apply his Western learnings. When the Republic of China came into being in 1912, Wang Shouchang was appointed by the Beijing government as the 'Special Commissioner of Foreign Affairs' responsible for handling foreign affairs matters pertaining to Fujian Province on behalf of the central government. His sons and nephews would later follow suit, undertaking study in French-speaking universities and joining the diplomatic service.[17] The most prominent among them was Wang Shouchang's nephew Wang Jingqi 王景岐 ('Wang King-ky', 1884–1941), who served in the newly modernized Ministry of Foreign Affairs.[18] Wang Jingqi later emerged as a crucial actor during the 1926 Sino–Belgian treaty dispute in his capacity as Chinese Minister to Belgium (1921–1929),[19] while serving as senior Chinese delegate at the League of Nations (1926–1928) and a member of the Opium Advisory Committee (1929).

Wang Tieya's interest in international law was thus rooted in his upbringing in a diplomatic family. His early memories included foreign news coverage of the

[15] The Naval School's study-abroad programme was subdivided into the French and British divisions. Some cadets belonging to the British division were assigned to take up criminal law, admiralty, and prize law, while those part of the French division took up public international law (*wanguo gongfa*). Zhang Demei, Tansuo yu xuanze—Wanqing falü yizhi yanjiu [Explorations and Decisions: A Study on Late Qing Legal Transplant] (Beijing: Tsinghua University Press, 2003), 186.

[16] According to Zhu Mingzhe, an expert on the histories of French legal education institutions and the stories of pioneering Chinese students therein, the few Chinese students who studied law in Paris during the late nineteenth century commonly spent time at both institutions. Message from Zhu Mingzhe to author (14 June 2020). The l'Ecole de droit de Paris and l'École libre des sciences politiques both ceased to exist, succeeded respectively by Université Paris-Panthéon-Assas and Sciences Po Paris.

[17] Having witnessed the escalating violence against Chinese immigrants in the late nineteenth and early-twentieth-century United States, Wang Shouchang developed a strong distaste for the US. Taking advantage of the drastic drop in value of the French franc after the Great War, Wang managed to send three of his oldest boys to study in France.

[18] Wang Jingqi's contemporary *Who's Who in China* profile stated that he had 'graduated from the courses in Political Science at l'École des Sciences Politiques in Paris, taking special courses in international law, 1910–11, Oxford.' Who's Who in China: Biographies of Chinese Leaders, 5th edition (Shanghai: The China Weekly Review, 1936), 245. Owing to his long-term stationing in Europe, all four of his children—one son and three daughters—obtained their doctoral degrees at the *Université libre de Bruxelles*. Two of them wrote their theses on topics pertaining to international affairs (Wang Aiding, 王亚徵, La Chine et le probleme de l'opium, 1932; Wang Kiding, 王季徵, La Society des Nations et la paix du monde, 1936), with Wang Aiding later joining the diplomatic service of the Taiwan government.

[19] In 1926, the Beijing government sought to unilaterally abrogate the 1865 Sino–Belgian treaty following its expiration. As Chinese Minister to Belgium, Wang Jingqi lent his support to Chinese diaspora protesting in Brussels to strengthen the hand of the Beijing government in its negotiations. John Patrick Martin, 'Politics of Delay: Belgium's Treaty Negotiations with China, 1926–29' (PhD thesis, St. John's University 1980), 66.

Great War and witnessing his diplomat father engaging in heated arguments with his Japanese counterpart. Intriguingly, Wang Shouchang had initially subjected his sons to private home tutoring where they were taught only Confucian classics. It was only following his dismissal from government service that Wang Tieya was finally sent to modern-style school to ease the family's financial burden.[20]

Wang Tieya began his university studies in 1929at Fudan University in Shanghai but, seeking a better academic environment, transferred to the National Tsinghua University in Beijing in 1931.Tsinghua University was at the time one of the few government universities whose qualified faculty and financial resources allowed Chinese academics to carry out international law research and pedagogy on par with Western 'scientific standards'.[21] Wang Tieya later fondly recalled how Tsinghua's generous budget allowed librarians to purchase expensive Western treatises at his request. The university's ensemble of freshly minted American PhDs also brought to China their scholarly networks, providing ambitious students with valuable information on career opportunities and resources beyond China. Wang Tieya had accordingly become one of the few Chinese students who competed for the Carnegie Endowment for International Peace's student fellowship.[22]

In 1936, after having spent one year at the Tsinghua University Graduate School, Wang Tieya won one of the rare American Boxer Indemnity Scholarship spots reserved for social sciences.[23] With the support of his future lifelong mentor Zhou Gengsheng, Wang Tieya chose the London School of Economics ('LSE') as his destination, hoping to be supervised by Hersch Lauterpacht. Wang admired Lauterpacht for both his scholarship (Wang had already read *The Function of Law* and *Private Law Sources and Analogies*) and his sympathetic stance towards

[20] Like many figures surveyed in the biographical chapters, Wang Tieya too was once a student at missionary schools. He was an alumnus of the prestigious Anglo-Chinese College (*Yinghua Shuyuan*) of Fuzhou, where he first received English education. Owing to his father's influence, French rather than English was the first foreign language to which he was exposed.

[21] For instance, in 1929, Tsinghua University invited American political scientist and international law specialist Quincy Wright to lecture at Tsinghua for a total of six months, for which he was compensated with about 1,600 US dollars (a monthly salary of 500 Mexican pesos). The invitation was tendered by Wright's former doctoral student, then professor of international law and future mentor of Wang Tieya Wang Huacheng 王化成 (1905–1965). To facilitate Wright's teaching of advanced courses, Tsinghua even allocated a special budget of 1,000 US dollars for purchasing the latest publications on international law, international relations, and constitutional law. This was likely the only instance in which a prominent Western international law scholar had a prolonged stay at a Republican Chinese university, which testified to Tsinghua University's favourable conditions. Contract sent to Quincy Wright from Tsinghua University, and H.C. Wang to Quincy Wright, dated 10 June 1929, in Quincy Wright Papers, Box 41, Folder 1 'International Law-T', University of Chicago Library, Special Collections Research Center.

[22] As one of the most junior, and rare, non-Western applicants, Wang Tieya's 1935 application was unsuccessful. See Folder 'Fellowships, 1923, 1926, 1935–1937', Box 202, Carnegie Endowment for International Peace, New York and Washington Offices records, 1910–1954, Columbia University Rare Books and Manuscript Library. Wang Tieya's name was spelled as 'Wang Tiee Yai' in the document.

[23] Following the Manchuria Crisis, the Nationalist Government further pivoted towards supporting students pursuing overseas degrees in engineering, industry, agriculture, and medicine, in the hope of meeting China's growing demands in national defence.

China during legal debates over the Manchuria Crisis. Wang was welcomed by Lauterpacht in London, October 1937, but little did he know that Lauterpacht was set to succeed McNair's Whewell Chair at Cambridge in the forthcoming year. Wang Tieya therefore had to work with Herbert A. Smith at LSE, a 'British Empire man' who did not care for China's plight. His intellectual odyssey was ultimately cut short by Japan's invasion and occupation of China's coastal regions which deprived the government of essential customs revenues, the financial backbone of Wang's scholarship programme. Wang Tieya initially planned to visit his cousin Wang Jingqi (then Chinese Minister to Poland) in August 1939, a trip which he cancelled at the last minute due to the prospect of war breaking out in Europe. This fateful decision spared him from being trapped in Warsaw by Germany's imminent *blitzkrieg*, a fate that soon befell Wang Jingqi.[24] Wang Tieya departed Europe from Marseille by sea and landed in Saigon.

Unfortunately, by the time Wang Tieya reached Kunming—China's wartime capital for higher education—the universities that had retreated there were stretched too thin to offer him a job. Wang Tieya was only able to begin teaching in 1940, when Zhou Gengsheng recommended him to take over his international law chair at National Wuhan University. He taught at Wuhan University for two years before moving on to National Central University. Zhou Gengsheng spent most of the Second World War in New York (1939-1945), embedded in American intellectual circles, advocating for the Chinese war effort and contemplating the post-war order. This position enabled him to convey Wang Tieya's research proposals and funding requests to his American acquaintances.[25] In 1945, Wang Tieya was chosen by the Institute of Pacific Affairs' Chinese branch (to which his mentors Zhou Gengsheng and Qian Duansheng were senior members) for its research programme, designed to improve Western understanding of China and provide financial relief to selected promising young scholars.[26] As Chinese intellectuals

[24] Wang Jingqi, his family, and more than100 Chinese nationals in Poland sheltered inside the Chinese Embassy in Warsaw for nearly a month before they were granted safe passage to leave Poland.

[25] Zhou Gengsheng had on multiple occasions recommended Wang Tieya and his work to his American contacts. In 1943, Zhou referred Wang to the Research Secretary of the Institute of Pacific Relations, William L. Holland, on the latter's plan to compile an up-to-date collection of treaties and international agreements 'to which China is a party and those concluded between third parties but directly concerning China'. This plan finally came to fruition during the 1950s. Letter from S.R. Chow (Zhou Gengsheng) to W.L. Holland, 11 May 1943, in Institute of Pacific Relations records, 1927–1962, Columbia University Rare Books and Manuscript Library, Box 67, Folder 'Chow, S.R.', and Wang Tieya's proposal titled 'Treaties and Agreements with and concerning China, 1919–43'. Again in 1945 Zhou Gengsheng introduced Wang and his work to Manley O. Hudson of Harvard Law School, asking 'whether you could help him in getting a research fellowship such as Carnegie Fellowship in International Law' so that Wang could come to the U.S. to use its research facilities. Letter from S. R. Chow (Zhou Gengsheng) to Manley O. Hudson, dated 7 February 1945, Manley Ottmer Hudson papers, Harvard Law School Library, Historical & Special Collections, Box 15, Folder 38, 'C—Miscellany, 1944–1948'.

[26] The relief programme relied on the generous gift from the New York-based Chinese American businessman Li Guoqin 李国钦 (aka 'Li Kuo-ching' or 'K. C. Li'), a long-time patron of the Institute. 'Memorandum on the use of K. C. Li's gift', Institute of Pacific Relations records, 1927–1962, Columbia University Rare Books and Manuscript Library, Box 69, Folder 'W.L. Holland'. The programme led

were severely squeezed by gruelling wartime inflation, this programme provided Wang's family with a crucial lifeline.[27]

In 1946, on the eve of the Chinese Civil War, Wang Tieya transferred from National Central University in Nanjing to Peking University in Beijing. The move allowed him to succeed his mentor Qian Duansheng as the head of the Department of Political Science at Peking University and to escape from life in the capital, where politics was omnipresent. Like many liberal intellectuals whose coming-of-age overlapped with the Nationalists' ('KMT') rise to power and escalating Japanese aggression, Wang Tieya appeared to have accepted the necessity of an illiberal party-state exercising 'political tutelage' during the national struggle against imperial domination.[28] But the Anti-Japanese War—which saw 'the relative decline ... in the influence and prestige of the more Westernized and liberal groups ... and the relative increase of power of the new class of bureaucrats and military men who are more impressed with the efficiency of the totalitarian methods'—contributed to Wang Tieya's disillusionment with the Nationalist government.[29] Accordingly, he had turned down an offer at the Ministry of Foreign Affairs during wartime, preferring life in academia. Wang's discontent with the KMT further intensified when the latter failed to push back against the American Cold War policy of remilitarizing Japan in 1947, which both Wang and Zhou Gengsheng saw as a betrayal of China's post-war security.[30] Wang subsequently

to the publication of a small pamphlet by Wang titled 'The Status of Aliens and Foreign Enterprise in China' (Chungking, China: China Institute of Pacific Relations, 1945), China Council Series Number Four. The study was produced against the backdrop of the conclusion of the 1943 Sino-American and Sino-British treaties through which both powers renounced their extraterritorial privileges in China. This radical change thus demanded the application of both Chinese laws to aliens and international law principles that 'impose some limitations upon the power of the territorial State in regard to aliens' to 'avoid conflicts between sovereignties', ibid 1.

[27] Wang Tieya had just welcomed the birth of his first daughter and was hence grateful for the opportunity and the additional income of 500 US dollars, at the time a hefty sum.

[28] After having taken national power in 1928, the KMT began incorporating 'Nationalist Party Principles' (*dang yi*) courses into secondary and higher education in 1929. In 1936, Wang Tieya had published an article titled 'Conceptions of International Law from the Standpoint of the Principle of Nationalism' (minzu zhuyi de guoji fa guan). The article was likely inspired by Lawrence Preuss' article 'The National Socialistic Conception of International Law' (The American Political Science Review, 1935), which Wang Tieya's brother Wang Feiya had translated into Chinese and published in the same publication. In his article, Wang Tieya embraced the imperative of grasping 'party principles in control of the will of the state', which included the KMT and Sun Yat-sen's principle of nationalism, and its implications in shaping international legal norms. He rightfully distinguished the worldviews articulated by Sun Yat-sen and by Germany's National Socialist Party, emphasizing that Nationalist China did not place 'absolute moral value' on itself and its interests.

[29] Letter from W. L. Holland to S. R. Chow, dated 28 May 1943, emphasizing the imperative of preserving 'existing democratic tendencies and pro-democratic groups' in Nationalist-controlled China. In Institute of Pacific Relations records, 1927–1962 (n 25).

[30] The policy was known as 'the Reverse Course', during which the American occupation policy for Japan shifted from democratization and demilitarization to economic reconstruction and remilitarization. Zhou Gengsheng pessimistically forecasted that this policy would lead to the 'repeat of history', mirroring Germany's post-Great War rearmament, and would be the root of the next major conflict in East Asia. Wang Tieya saw the new Truman Doctrine as the new 'Monroe Doctrine' in Asia, where the US was then superimposing its own security interests over other nations. Wang Tieya, 'Dulumen

supported left-leaning student protests at Peking University, for he believed that the situation called for a May Fourth Movement redux—'eliminating traitors from within and resistance to foreign powers from without'.[31] Marxist theories and other non-conventional political science curricula were also encouraged under his tenure as the department head.[32] In January 1949, Wang was truly inspired after personally witnessing the People's Liberation Army and its disciplined takeover of Beijing. In a June 1949 letter to his former American colleague Dorothy Borg, Wang Tieya wrote optimistically: 'We began to reconstruct the university [Peking] on a practical basis. The work is hard but were [*sic*] doing it with high spirit. The aims of reconstruction is [*sic*] simply this: to train young people for a new China.'[33]

29.3 Persevering at Times of Radical Transformation

Before diving into Wang Tieya's illustrious achievements during the 1980s, one must treat seriously his experience during the first decade of the PRC. Such was a period of radical change, designed to swiftly induce a 'socialist modernity' modelled after the Soviet experience. Westernized liberal (read 'bourgeois') intellectuals, including Wang, were soon subjected to ideological reforms (1951–1952) reprogramming them for a socialist China.[34] Moreover, their familiar habitats—universities, scholarly societies, newspapers and magazines—had lost their relative autonomy vis-à-vis the new party-state, thus reducing the feasibility of dissenting against or maintaining critical distance from newly established orthodoxies. Preconditions for the growth of the Chinese international law discipline during the previous era—the free flow of international news, scholarly publications, personnel (both students and scholars), and funding between China and the outside world—also came to an abrupt end. The predominant Western international law

zhuyi yu Menluo zhuyi' [The Truman Doctrine and the Monroe Doctrine], Minzhu Luntan, no. 9 (1947), 3–6.

[31] Wang Tieya, 'Zaitan xin wusi yundong' [Again on 'May Fourth Movement redux'], Beijing daxue banyue kan [Peking University Biweekly, vol. 5 (1948), 16 May 1948, 3.

[32] Zhao Baoxu, 'Wang Tieya and the Chinese Discipline of Political Science', in Rao Geping (ed), Shangao shuichang: Wang Tieya xiansheng jinian wenji [As towering as peaks, as lasting as rivers: collected essays in memory of Wang Tieya] (Beijing: Peking University Press, 2004), p. 332. As department head, Wang was well appreciated by the Communist students at Peking University. Some of these earlier students, such as Duanmu Zheng 端木正, Zhao Baoxu 赵宝煦, and Ma Jun 马骏 (surveyed in Chapter 33 on Chinese women), would emerge as important figures within the PRC legal and political studies fields. They would become supporters and collaborators of Wang's projects in the 1980s.

[33] 'Extract of the Letter from Professor Wang Tia-yia, 1949 June 21, to D. Borg', in John K. Fairbank Papers, Box 8, Folder 1949–1950, 'A-Chiu', Harvard University Archive.

[34] The process was referred to as the Thought Reform Movement. Chinese author Yang Jiang wittily dubbed this campaign 'Baptism' in her 1988 novel of the same title. Qian Duansheng recorded in his diary that Wang Tieya had made his 'self-examination' on 8 August 1952. Qian Duansheng Riji (1937–1956) [Qian Duansheng's Diaries], Vol. II (Beijing: China University of Political Science and Law, 2022), 374.

tradition on which the Chinese discipline had modelled itself would soon be politicized, delegitimized, and replaced by the Soviet tradition. Facing these radical transformations, international law scholars such as Wang Tieya could only adapt and try to preserve, as much as possible, their professional identity. Understanding both these seismic shifts and Wang Tieya's resilience is not only essential for grasping his later comeback and legacies, but also the metamorphosis of the Chinese discipline post-1949.

As a 'progressive professor' (*jinbu jiaoshou*) and an ideal candidate for the CCP-led 'united front', Wang Tieya underwent a comparatively smooth transition into New China. While he was not immediately accommodated into the PRC's political processes—a privilege reserved for more seasoned figures such as Zhou Gengsheng and Qian Duansheng[35]—Wang Tieya was nevertheless admitted into the PRC's new foreign policy establishment, albeit arguably placed on its outer orbits. In early 1950, Wang was appointed to the PRC's Permanent Mission to the UN as the group's sole legal expert. The Mission never made it to New York due to the unresolved issue of Chinese representation.[36] Wang's foreign affairs work outside of the university campus was mainly through the Chinese People's Institute of Foreign Affairs (*renmin waijiao xuehui*), an appendage to the PRC Ministry of Foreign Affairs ('MFA'). One of its functions was to spearhead the PRC's 'people-to-people' initiatives, a form of popular diplomacy.[37] Wang was thus made privy to the rare opportunity of international exchange, either through journeys abroad or the reception of visiting foreign guests in China.[38] The Institute also engaged in certain knowledge work pertaining to international law. Between 1951 and 1954, Wang Tieya and colleagues translated *Oppenheim's International Law* (the seventh edition edited by Lauterpacht) into Chinese. While the translation was published and circulated only within state apparatus, it was believed to have been frequently referenced by the MFA. Wang believed that the text represented the only Western international law treatise published prior to 1979.[39]

35 For instance, both Qian Duansheng and Zhou Gengsheng were included as 'legal advisors' to the drafting committee that prepared the text of the PRC's first constitution adopted in 1954. In fact, Zhou Gengsheng was likely the only Chinese international law scholar who—owing to his towering stature—was granted the opportunity to publish international treatises (Modern Trends in British and American International Law, 1963; International Law, 1976). Zhou Rusong [Zhou Gengsheng's daughter], 'Zhou Gengsheng', in Zhongguo dangdai shehui kexue jia, di wu ji [Contemporary Chinese Social Scientists, Vol.5] (Beijing: National Library of China Publishing House, 1983), 157.

36 The Mission consisted of roughly 50 members, with Wang Tieya as the sole expert with an international law background. It disbanded in early 1951. Kang Daisha, Jiazu yu wangshi [My Family and its Stories] (Beijing: World Affairs Press, 2011), 188–199.

37 Ronald C. Keith, Diplomacy of Zhou Enlai (New York: Palgrave Macmillan, 1989), 35–36.

38 Wang's journeys included a 1951 trip to the UK (stranded in Prague due to last-minute visa issues); a 1955 trip to New Delhi to take part in the 1955 'Asian States Conference'; an official conference that was attached to the 1955 Asian-African Conference in Bandung; and a 1956 trip to Brussels to attend the 5th Congress of the International Association of Democratic Lawyers.

39 Other Western-trained international law scholars, including Li Haopei and Chen Tiqiang, also contributed to the translation. Wang Tieya recalled having to act strategically to get the book approved for publication. In support of this goal, their translated text included critical comments added by Soviet scholars in the 1948 Russian edition (*Mezhdunarodnoe parvo* [International Law], Moscow, 1948), as

Wang Tieya's career soon suffered two heavy blows, first in 1952 and again in 1957. Political science departments, where Wang Tieya had received training and was teaching, were summarily abolished across universities during the 1952 Reorganization of Higher Education campaign. Their demise was due to the perceived incompatibility between their bourgeois theoretical foundation and Marxist historical materialism.[40] Moreover, Soviet international law scholarship displaced its Western predecessor as the new orthodoxy. A new circuit of knowledge transfer was established between the USSR and China, with Soviet experts coming to lecture in China (with the newly incorporated Renmin University as headquarters) and Chinese students dispatched to universities in the USSR and other socialist countries.[41] A younger generation of scholars moulded under this new tradition began to dominate classrooms for the next two decades.[42] Among them was Wei Min, Wang Tieya's future colleague. With the Faculty of Law at Peking University also abolished, Wang sought refuge at the Department of History, where he focused on the history of international relations. This transition was somewhat manageable, since the method of study for international law at political science departments—modelled after their American counterparts[43]—was

well as the Russian preface by Sergei Borisovich Krylov. To be extra safe, reservations about Soviet critiques that did not completely align with Chinese views on modern history were also provided in the Chinese preface.

[40] Following the Soviet model, political science and sociology departments were dismissed, its personnel transferred to law, economics, history, and philosophy departments. On the abolition of Chinese political science departments in 1952, see Zhao Baoxu, 'The Revival of Political Science in China', PS (1984) vol. 17 no. 4, 745–757.

[41] According to one estimate, during the 1950s, roughly 38,000 Chinese went to the USSR for training and study, while 10,000 Soviet citizens served as experts, advisors, and teachers in China, of whom close to 600 taught in Chinese universities. Suzzane Pepper, 'Education for the New Order', in Roderick MacFarquhar and John K. Fairbank (eds), The Cambridge History of China, Vol. 14, The People's Republic, Part I: The Emergence of Revolutionary China 1949–1965 (New York: Cambridge University Press, 1987), 201.

[42] Legal historian You Rong, a member of Renmin University Faculty of Law's first graduating class (1950–54), later recalled that China's legal education was during the 1950s under 'the great unity' (*da yi tong*) of Renmin University, with its graduates filling the rank-and-file positions in law faculties across the country. You Rong, 'Legal History at Peking University Law School' (*China Law Society*, 12 April 2018) <https://www.chinalaw.org.cn/portal/article/index/id/16140/cid/71.html>, accessed 30 June 2025. Liang Xi, another member of that cohort who in 1954 was assigned to Peking University's newly resurrected Faculty of Law, recounted that the faculty leadership had prioritised newer generations of scholars trained under the Soviet tradition when it came to lecturing duties. Earlier scholars such as Wang were *de facto* barred from teaching. Interview with Liang Xi, in Zhongguo faxuejia fangtan lu, diyi juan [Talking with Chinese Jurists, Vol.2], He Qinhua (ed) (Beijing: Peking University Press, 2010), 361–362.

[43] Scholars who specialized in international law's disciplinary histories in the US have long noted the divergence between political scientists and legal scholars (based in law schools) in terms of their approaches to international law. Prior to the Second World War, 'the distinction between international law and international relations was not clearly established both institutionally and intellectually' within American universities. International law was often studied by political scientists as part of their historical investigation into foreign affairs. It was after the Second World War, with the rise of realism and the decline of international law curriculum in political science departments, that international law became primarily taught in law schools, its study more exclusively associated with the legal scholars' legalistic approach. See Hatsue Shinohara, U.S. International Lawyers in the Interwar Years: A Forgotten

predominantly 'historical, narrative, and comparative ... not judicially oriented.'[44] During this downtime, Wang committed himself to the compilation of China's unequal treaties, resulting in a three-volume collection amassing nearly 1,200 documents.[45]

In the early summer of 1957, Chinese intellectuals were invited to present criticism and advice to the party-state, supposedly to realize Chairman Mao Zedong's vision to 'let a hundred flowers bloom, let a hundred schools contend'. International law scholars trained during the Republican era, such as Wang Tieya and Chen Tiqiang, sounded the alarm about the 'crisis' within the Chinese discipline. From their perspective, the imposed hierarchy between younger (Soviet-trained) scholars and older (Westernized) scholars since 1949 had hindered the development of the discipline.[46] The intelligentsia's enthusiastic and forceful response was soon deemed out of control by the Party, and the experiment ended abruptly within six weeks. Both men were soon swept up during the ensuing 'Anti-Rightist Campaign', their comments on their experience of alienation were exaggerated in the countercriticisms as wholesale rejections of socialist reforms on higher education and Communist leadership. Not without irony, this hierarchy would become entirely inverted by the 1980s due to both the Sino–Soviet schism and Sino–US rapprochement.

Wang Tieya displayed true resilience during the next two decades. Banished from teaching and publishing, he strove to preserve his professional identity

Crusade (New York: Cambridge University Press, 2012), 2. Federic L. Kirgis, The American Society of International Law's First Century, 1906–2006 (Leiden: Martinus Nijhoff Publishers, 2006), 60.

44 Ronald St. John Macdonald, 'Wang Tieya: Persevering in Adversity and Shaping the Future of Public International Law in China', in Ronald St. John Macdonald (ed), Essays in Honour of Wang Tieya (Leiden: Martinus Nijhoff Publishers, 1994), 4.

45 The volumes were titled 'A Complete Compilation of Sino–Foreign Treaties and Agreements, 1689–1949' (Zhongwai jiu yuezhang huibian), published respectively in 1957, 1959, and 1959 by Joint Publishing. As discussed in footnote 26, Wang Tieya had begun contemplating such a project as early as the 1940s. The collection's comprehensive scope, which included treaties (to which China is a party or concerning China), agreements (between China and foreign non-state entities), and charters (granted by Chinese authorities to foreign actors), reflected Sun Yat-sen's formulation of 'imperialism': That economic imperialism—undergirded by legal arrangements—was at the heart of China's subjugation under foreign powers, to which China must provide a political response. This understanding was also fundamental to the discourse on unequal treaties. The CCP later presented itself as the proper heir to Sun Yat-sen's revolutionary anti-imperialist vision.

46 Both Wang Tieya and Chen Tiqiang had to various degrees questioned the 'scientific' value of the supposed Soviet school of international law that was being institutionalized within Chinese universities and the foreign policy establishment. Wang Tieya went as far as to claim that 'sectarianism [i.e., marginalising talents based on their educational background] had halted the scientific study of international law for seven years'. Wang Tieya, Zhenfa jiaoyujie de sanhai henyanzhong [Dogmatism, bureaucratism, and sectarianism are severely plaguing the legal and political studies circles], speech given by Wang at the Beijing Legal Studies Circles Symposium, 4 June 1957, in Zhengfajie youpai fenzi miulun huiji [Collected absurd speeches of rightists from the legal and political studies circles] (Beijing: China Law Press, 1957), 30.

through translation work and the collection of research materials.[47] A turning point was marked by 1971, as the beginning of normalization of Sino–American relations and the PRC's return to the UN prompted the party-state to make better use of Wang's talents.[48] In 1978, Wang successfully appealed his 'rightist' conviction. In 1979, Wang Tieya and his Peking colleague Wei Min were designated the important task of authoring an editorial in the Party's flagship newspaper *People's Daily*, one that would justify the revitalization of the Chinese international law discipline.[49] The two prefaced their proposal with a cautiously optimistic outlook on the changing global landscape, one that was characterized by increasing interdependence between states, the growing influence of Third World countries, and the emergence of specialized fields and institutions dealing with specific problems (e.g., the Law of the Sea treaty bodies). These developments warranted China's proactive engagement. The officially condemned Cultural Revolution, with its legal nihilism and anti-foreignism, provided the authors with a convenient answer as to why the discipline was in its decimated state. Having entirely circumvented the developments of the 1950s,[50] the two nevertheless diagnosed that the lack of scholarly liberty posed a severe challenge: the more scholars were restricted from publishing, the more likely any published scholarship would be perceived by outsiders as some form of officially anointed position, causing individual scholars to be paralyzed by the fear of unintentionally 'representing' China. The discipline, therefore, must be liberated from this vicious cycle. This prescription of (limited) 'liberalization' laid the groundwork for the majority of Wang Tieya's projects during the 1980s.

[47] One particularly important contribution by Wang Tieya during this period was his translation of the eighth edition of *Oppenheim's International Law* (edited by Lauterpacht, 1955) in collaboration with Chen Tiqiang and other specialists. Due to their disgraced status as 'rightists', the translation was originally published internally under pseudonyms in 1971. It subsequently became the most important reference book on international law of the Reform era when it was re-released to the public in 1981.

[48] In preparation for US President Richard Nixon's official visit to China in 1972, some senior professors at Peking University with Western educational backgrounds, including Wang, were put together to translate Nixon's *Six Crises* (1962). Wang later received more translation assignments related to UN documents. The PRC's engagement with the Third UN Conference on the Law of the Sea (1973–1982) also inspired Wang to work on a compilation of law of the sea materials, published as 'Haiyang fa ziliao huibian' [Compiled materials on the Law of the Sea] (Beijing: People's Publishing House, 1974).

[49] Wang Tieya and Wei Min, 'Guojifa de yanjiu bixu jiaqiang' [Research on international law must be strengthened] *People's Daily* (Beijing, 30 March 1979) 3. The title of the editorial was a direct reference to Communist leader Deng Xiaoping's 1978 speech 'Emancipate the Mind, Seek Truth from Facts, Unite as One in Looking to the Future'. Deng's vision for China's legal system was concluded with one very specific directive: 'Moreover, we should intensify our study of international law.'

[50] None of these earlier figures ever publicized their frustrations regarding the 1950s. During a private conversation in 1980, Columbia Law School professor Randle Edwards approached Wang Tieya with the question, 'What did you say or do was wrong, what mistakes you made, caused you to be sent down?' Wang replied: 'No, I cannot tell you that, because I never made a mistake!' Interview with R. Randle Edwards, former Chair of Committee for Legal Education Exchange with China (Skype, 19 December 2023).

29.4 The Power of 'the International': Wang Tieya during a Window of Liberalization

Having returned to centre stage at the ripe age of 62, Wang Tieya pursued his projects with an immense sense of urgency.[51] From his perspective, the most expedient way for Chinese academia to compensate for lost time was to invest in the upcoming generations of Chinese scholars, whose training under the newly legitimized Western model would enable them to catch up with the latest developments in global fields. This vision stemmed from Wang's positionality as a university-based international law educator.[52] Among the extremely few contemporaries who were of comparable qualification, many were bound by their duties as MFA legal advisors (e.g., Ni Zhengyu, Li Haopei) and were relatively insulated from research and pedagogical projects at universities. Hence, as a genuinely sociable and well-connected person, Wang Tieya often took the lead in bringing together government experts and university faculty.[53] He also made efforts to connect his promising pupils with surviving elderly intellectuals with international experience to facilitate mentorship across generations.[54]

[51] Good fortune and timing were crucial for Wang's rise as this larger-than-life figure of the Chinese discipline. By the end of the 1970s, the surviving 'worldly gentlemen' who came before Wang had either passed away or were too fragile to take up the heavy lifting. Of Wang's closest mentors, Zhou Gengsheng had already passed away in 1971. His two-volume opus *Guoji Fa* [International Law], written during the late 1960s and published posthumously in 1971, was a mismatch for the 1980s field due to its anti-liberal international order premise. Qian Duansheng was close to his eighties by the conclusion of the Cultural Revolution. As one of the principal targets during the 1957 Anti-Rightist Campaign, Qian Duansheng suffered more attacks than his student Wang Tieya. Despite having been a commanding figure in his prime, he had largely faded away from public life during the 1980s. Chen Tiqiang's premature death in 1983, due to overwork and a weakened heart, greatly saddened Wang. The two men had known each other since their student days at Tsinghua University and had collaborated closely since 1949. Wang Tieya had seen Chen as *the* comrade-in-arms who would shoulder the burden of revitalizing the Chinese discipline.

[52] Wang Tieya prioritized the reconstruction projects over participation in Chinese diplomacy. In 1979, Wang Tieya was invited by the MFA to join its delegation to the Third Convention on the Law of the Sea as legal advisor. Wang attended two sessions in Geneva and New York respectively but declined a formal position.

[53] Wang Tieya valued the collaboration between government experts and the scholarly community, believing such exposure was essential for conceptualizing PRC state practices and for the relevant government institutions to continue integrating international law expertise into their operations. Following the publication of the 1981 textbook, Wang Tieya had, in the summer of 1983, put together a symposium at Peking University, which assembled his MFA legal experts, including Ni Zhengyu, Li Haopei, Shi Jiuyong, and Huang Jiahua; established scholars; and international law teachers from universities across the country.

[54] Yuan Ming, one of Wang Tieya's first master's students post-1979, recalled having been introduced by Wang to senior figures including Qian Duansheng, Wu Qiyu (former head of the Department of Political Science, Yenching University), and Chen Hansheng. These senior figures would later loop Yuan Ming into their networks. Interview with Yuan Ming, Professor at the School of International Studies, Peking University (Beijing, China, 12 January 2024). See also, Yuan Ming, 'Heli tuoju wo de laoshi men' [The teachers who had jointly mentored me], in Institute of Humanities and Social Sciences, Peking University (ed), Chuan cheng: women de Beida xueyuan [Lineage: our academic encounter with Peking University] (Beijing: Peking University Press, 2023), 60–61.

Wang Tieya's unparalleled effectiveness during the 1980s also stemmed from his transnational mobility, which allowed him to mobilize valuable resources beyond China to expedite his reconstruction projects.[55] This mobility could be traced back to Wang's active role in the burgeoning Sino–Western (read 'American') legal education exchanges during the early 1980s. At the time, legal scholars (primarily American) who were themselves interested in the Chinese legal system—backed by law schools, UN agencies, but most importantly, private philanthropic organizations such as the Ford Foundation[56]—sought collaboration with their Chinese counterparts who were anxious to improve Chinese legal education.[57] Wang acted as the frontman representing Chinese law professors during the early discussions, which led to the creation of an ambitious legal exchange programme that would dispatch young Chinese academics to American law schools.[58] But Wang Tieya's most consequential foreign contact during this period was Canadian international law scholar Ronald St. John Macdonald (1928–2006), a former dean of Dalhousie Law School. Their friendship began serendipitously in 1980 when Macdonald visited Peking University, during which time Wang Tieya served as his host. The two bonded almost immediately, and Wang Tieya was soon invited to Dalhousie in 1981; by 1982, Peking and Dalhousie had initiated their international law-focused graduate student exchange programme funded by the Canadian International Development Agency.[59]

Macdonald was himself an esteemed publicist, a veteran government advisor, and a 'quintessential cosmopolitan' whose network spanned beyond Canada to reach the most prominent international lawyers in the US and Western Europe.[60] Yet Macdonald was undoubtedly fascinated by Wang Tieya and his experience. From

[55] For instance, the founding and growth of the Peking University Institute of International Law benefited greatly from the funding of the United Nations Development Programme that Wang Tieya had secured. Throughout the 1980s, Wang would mobilize his foreign contacts to donate reference materials and English-language treatises to the Institute, a rare and valuable resource in 1980s China. See Rao Geping, Wang Tieya yu beida guoji fa suo [Wang Tieya and the Peking University Institute of International Law], in Chinese Yearbook of International Law (2012).

[56] R. Randle Edwards, 'An Overview of Chinese Law and Legal Education', The Annals of the American Academy of Political and Social Science (1984) vol. 476, China in Transition, 58–59. Professor Edwards first met Wang Tieya in 1980 during his Ford Foundation-sponsored trip to Beijing. Ford would later support Wang Tieya's journeys to the US and Europe during the early 1980s.

[57] The ultimate goal of this 'legal assistance' was to shape the future of Chinese legal reforms, which they hoped could eventually lead to the institutionalization of the rule of law.

[58] A Ford Foundation study points out that between 1983 and 1995, 'Ford had spent more than $4 million and sent over 200 Chinese scholars to U.S. law schools' through the Committee on Legal Educational Exchanges with China. Hualing Fu and Maggie Lewis, 'From Reform and Opening to Opening without Reform: Lessons from the Ford Foundation's Law Program in China' (*Ford Foundation*, 22 June 2023). <https://www.fordfoundation.org/work/learning/learning-reflections/from-reform-and-opening-to-opening-without-reform-lessons-from-the-ford-foundation-s-law-program-in-china/> accessed 30 June 2025.

[59] By 1985, five Chinese students had already benefited from the programme.

[60] See Craig Scott, 'Ronald St. John Macdonald and International Legal Education', International Law Forum (2002) vol. 4 no. 4, 215–221. In 1980, Macdonald became the first non-European jurist to be elected to the European Court of Human Rights, representing Liechtenstein (1980–1999), an achievement that testified to his global reach.

Macdonald's point of view, Wang Tieya represented a rare witness-participant in the journey of international law in twentieth-century China. His organic connection to that bygone world—including the distant and mysterious classical China—added to the value of his outlook on what the 'Chinese perspective' on international law would be. But most importantly, Wang Tieya appeared to him as a fellow liberal internationalist, one who would reminisce about his student-days admiration for Lauterpacht, whose faith in the profession and its ideals was tested and steeled in the crucible of Maoist China.[61] In the coming two decades, Macdonald would consistently lend his support to Wang Tieya's projects; in the words of Bai Guimei, a mentee of both men, 'Macdonald opened up all his networks and resources [to Wang]'.[62] Macdonald's assistance ranged from mentoring Chinese students sent to Canadian universities by Wang, to guiding Wang on potential funding opportunities, and finally to plugging Wang into the exclusive network of the 'invisible college' after his thirty-year absence (1949–1979). Endeavours belonging to the third category were crucial to Wang's international and domestic stature. It was in fact through Macdonald's referrals that both Wang Tieya and Chen Tiqiang became the first two PRC scholars (1981 and 1983) to be elected to the *Institut de droit international.* Starting in 1991, Macdonald also committed substantive effort to developing a *festschrift* to celebrate Wang Tieya's 80th birthday. The final product consisted of fifty-eight chapters, featuring an illustrious ensemble of publicists including Abi-Saab, Brownlie, Cassese, Bin Cheng, Jennings, Franck, Henkin, Schachter, and Chinkin, a treatment that no other Chinese international lawyer had since enjoyed.[63]

In the summer of 1990, Wang Tieya became the first PRC scholar to offer a public international law lecture at the Hague Academy. The lecture, titled 'International Law in China: Historical and Contemporary Perspectives', became Wang's opus and a definitive text for the disciplinary history of international law in China. Against the background of Wang Tieya's principal objective during the 1980s—reconstructing the Chinese discipline and legitimizing it vis-à-vis the Chinese party-state and beyond—one could perhaps interpret Wang's lecture as an attempt to set down a broadly acceptable historical narrative that would serve these goals. On the one hand, the main storyline adopted by Wang Tieya echoed long-established discourse on how international law (in the form of the unequal

[61] These impressions are drawn from Macdonald's interview of Wang Tieya conducted between 1990 and 1991 when Wang was having his sabbatical in North America. The information collected through the interview eventually became the most comprehensive biography of Wang, which served as the introductory chapter for Wang's *festschrift*.

[62] Interview with Bai Guimei, former Professor of International Law, Peking University Law School (Beijing, China, 3 September 2024).

[63] The only comparable case was the publication of the English-language memorial collection edited by Wang Tieya and Sienho Yee that honoured Li Haopei in 2001. In 2002, as founder and then editor of the Journal of the History of International Law, Macdonald dedicated over half of volume 4 issue 1 to Wang Tieya, who was then approaching his 90th birthday. Both Wang and Macdonald clearly grasped that the two publications would consolidate Wang's centrality within the Chinese discipline.

treaty system) was humiliatingly imposed upon China in modern times, a dire circumstance that called for revolutionary changes and changes through revolution (i.e., the Chinese Communist Revolution and the inauguration of the PRC).[64] On the other hand, Wang's narration of PRC attitudes towards international law also downplayed early Communist leaders' aspirations for 'world revolution' and antistatism. Overall, Wang's nationally oriented tale appeared much more aligned with that of other non-Western nations' experiences with international law. It was thus a story that would appear more familiar and acceptable to Western international lawyers. In a way, Wang's narration of the past and the present created a space for future Chinese international lawyers to sustain their double loyalty—loyalty to the Chinese party-state, and loyalty to international law as a global field. In Wang Tieya's own words to his friend Macdonald: 'I will never lead my thinking away from patriotism and internationalism.'[65]

[64] Accordingly, Wang's lecture mostly skipped over Chinese experience with international law during the Republican era, implying that the legalistic efforts in overturning the unequal treaty system (such as the diplomatic work carried out by V. K. Wellington Koo) had been insufficient if not futile.

[65] Ronald St. John Macdonald, Tenth Conversation with Professor Wang Tieya, Toronto, 13 March 1992, Ronald St. John Macdonald Papers, University Archives, Dalhousie University.

30
Qiu Shaoheng (1913–2009)

Chao Wang

30.1 The Formative Years of a Prominent Chinese Jurist

Qiu Shaoheng (裘劭恒, 1913–2009), also known as Henry Chiu, was a distinguished Chinese jurist highly regarded both domestically and internationally for his expertise, integrity, credibility, and interpersonal acumen. His remarkable contributions to international legal justice and Chinese legal history from the 1940s to the late twentieth century—setting historic milestones in China and far surpassing the achievements of many of his contemporaries—garnered recognition in prominent publications such as *The China Weekly Review*, Reuters, and *The New York Times*.[1]

Amid the turbulent multicultural environment of Shanghai's international settlement, Qiu spent his formative years deeply immersed in both Eastern and Western culture and philosophy. He studied at the Shanghai Conservatory of Music (formerly the National Training School of Music) and Soochow University (SCU), experiences that profoundly shaped him into a brilliant and passionate intellectual. A courageous 'Renaissance man', Qiu actively participated in shaping the course of history.

Even before beginning his academic journey, Shaoheng was deeply influenced by the example of his father, Qiu Tingliang. A dedicated educator and a pioneer of the Chinese vernacular movement, Qiu Tingliang advocated for replacing Classical Chinese with modern written Mandarin. He also made significant contributions to journalism by founding Wuxi's first newspaper.[2]

While inheriting his father's spirit of intellectual curiosity and dedication to societal advancement, Qiu Shaoheng diverged from Qiu Tingliang's example in one significant way. Unlike his father, who emphasized the importance of science and technology and encouraged his children to study agriculture and engineering in

[1] For example, Qiu Shaoheng was described by the New York Times as one of China's 'leading jurists': see Chinese Jurist Defends Trial of 'Gang of Four', UPI. *New York Times*, Late Edition (East Coast); New York, NY. 30 Jan 1981: A.6.

[2] Qiu Tingliang, also known as Ke Fu, also named Bao Liang. See Wang Gengtang, Zhang Zhen, 'An Initial Exploration of Qiu Tingliang's Thoughts' (裘廷梁思想初探) [J], *Journal of Soochow University*, Issue 1, 1983), pp. 120–124, 128 .DOI:10.19563/j.cnki.sdzs.1983.01.023.

Chao Wang, *Qiu Shaoheng (1913–2009)* In: *Histories of International Law in China*. Edited by:
Ignacio de la Rasilla, Jiangyu Wang, and Congyan Cai, Oxford University Press. © Chao Wang 2026.
DOI: 10.1093/oso/9780198888345.003.0030

the West, Qiu Shaoheng, along with his elder brothers, ultimately chose to pursue a career in international law and international relations.

In making this decision, Qiu Shaoheng was undoubtedly influenced by his two brothers, Chiu Chang-Yueng/Qiu Changyun (C.Y. Chiu) and Qiu Fenling (also known as Franklin Chiu). Born in 1890, C. Y. Chiu, the eldest brother of Qiu Shaoheng, also attended Soochow University, graduating with a Bachelor of Arts degree in 1909. He was among the first Chinese students to study in the United States under the Boxer Indemnity Scholarship, arriving in America in September 1909.[3] C. Y. Chiu pursued studies in Agriculture at the University of Wisconsin (1909–1910) and Purdue University (1911–1913), where he earned his B.S. degree in 1913, before continuing with studies in Commerce at Columbia University (1913–1914). In January 1923 he joined the Foreign Ministry of the Republic of China (ROC), later serving as ROC's Consul General in Hamburg, Germany in 1926.[4] Similar to his two younger brothers, C. Y. Chiu was actively involved in Modern China's early forays into international law. For instance, in November 1924 he was appointed by the ROC President as a member of the Sino–Russia Meeting Affairs Office within the Foreign Ministry, tasked with negotiating with Russia[5]—a role that paralleled similar responsibilities undertaken by Franklin Chiu in the Foreign Ministry. Qiu Fenling (Franklin Chiu), born in 1892, was one of the earliest legal professionals in China to engage with international law. He graduated with a law degree from National Peiyang University in 1914 and joined the ROC Ministry of Foreign Affairs in 1916.[6] His distinguished career included assisting with preparations for and attending the Washington Naval Conference in 1921, participating in the China–Russia Negotiations (1924–1927),[7] and serving as the

[3] Zhou Zheng, 'The Entire Process of Selection and Dispatch of the First Batch of Chinese Students Sent to the United States with Geng Funds' (第一批庚款留美学生的考选与派遣全过程), Tsinghua University History Museum, <https://xsg.tsinghua.edu.cn/info/1003/3486.htm> accessed 7 July 2025 . See also 'Geng Funds and Their Connection to Wuxi' (庚款与无锡的渊源), Wuxi Archives and Historical Records Museum. <http://daj.wuxi.gov.cn/doc/2016/02/01/2425463.shtml> accessed 7 July 2025.

[4] Qiu Changyun, ROC Government Post Database, National Chengchi University, <https://gpost.lib.nccu.edu.tw/view_career.php?name=%E8%A3%98%E6%98%8C%E9%81%8B> accessed 7 July 2025.

[5] 'Temporary Established Special Committee for Sino-Russian Conference Affairs of Ministry of Foreign Affairs', ROC Government Post Database, National Chengchi University, <https://gpost.lib.nccu.edu.tw/view_orgpos.php?orgpos1=%E5%A4%96%E4%BA%A4%E9%83%A8%E6%9A%AB%E8%A8%AD%E4%B8%AD%E4%BF%84%E6%9C%83%E8%AD%B0%E6%9C%83%E5%8B%99%E8%99%95;;%E5%B0%88%E9%96%80%E5%A7%94%E5%93%A1.> accessed 7 July 2025.

[6] Wang Jian, 'The Pioneer of University Law Discipline: Tianjin Beiyang University Law Discipline' (首创大学法科:天津北洋大学法律学门), *China Law Review*, Issue 1 (Total Issue 49), 2023, pp. 137–142. See also Wang Jian, 'A Trailblazer in Legal Education Research' (研究法律教育的开路先锋), *Journal of Soochow University (Law Edition)*, Issue 3, 2015.

[7] Tang Qihua, 'A Study of the Sino-Russian Conferences 1924–1927' (1924—1927年中俄会议研究), *Modern Chinese History Studies*, Issue 4, 2007, pp. 29–54, <https://www.krzzjn.com/show-2308-111151.html> accessed 7 July 2025.

first Consul General of the ROC government in Khabarovsk, Russia.[8] Notably, he introduced Soviet criminal law to China by translating the Criminal Code of the Russian Soviet Federative Socialist Republic.[9] Upon his return to China in 1927, Qiu Fenling established a law firm in Shanghai in 1930, which was later to employ the young legal scholar Qiu Shaoheng.

Although Qiu Shaoheng enjoyed studying and performing music during his youth, he soon realized, after enrolling at the Shanghai Conservatory of Music, that music was not a viable lifelong career. From an employment perspective, law appeared to offer greater practicality and stability. After spending only one year at the Conservatory, Qiu was admitted to Soochow University (東吳大學, SCU), where he first earned a Bachelor of Arts degree in Liberal Arts at the College for Arts and Science in Suzhou—an entry requirement for admission to the SCU Law School. He later completed his Bachelor of Laws degree at the SCU School of Law in Shanghai.

Recognized as 'one of the first and most influential' law schools in Republican China,[10] the SCU School of Law was the alma mater of many of the nation's most prominent jurists in the international law, including Ni Zhengyu, Li Haopei, and Xiang Zhejun. Several alumni of the School of Law later joined the International Military Tribunal for the Far East (IMTFE), following the path paved by Qiu Shaoheng. However, few could match Qiu's significant contributions to some of the most pivotal cases in international and Chinese law in the twentieth century.

Studying at SCU set Qiu Shaoheng on the path to becoming one of China's foremost international jurists—not only through his legal studies, but also through his unwavering dedication to mastering the English language. As one commentator observed, 'When he spoke English, you would think he was an American if you didn't look at him'.[11] This achievement was particularly remarkable given that Qiu never travelled to the United States during his lifetime. Throughout his career, Qiu's exceptional English proficiency, combined with his extensive experience in Anglo-American courts, enabled him to bridge cultural divides between China and the West.

[8] Qiu Fenling, ROC Government Post Database, National Chengchi University, <https://gpost.lib.nccu.edu.tw/view_career.php?name=%E8%A3%98%E6%B1%BE%E9%BD%A1> accessed 7 July 2025.

[9] Chen Yi, 'An Introduction to the Translation of Codes during the Periods of Late Qing Dynasty and Republic of China' (清末民国时期法典翻译序说) [J], *Law Science*, Issue 8, 2013.

[10] Alison W. Conner, 'Anglo-American Law at Soochow University', Chapter 7, in Daniel H. Bays & Ellen Widmer, eds, *China's Christian College: Cross-Cultural Connections 1900–1950*, Stanford University Press, 2009, pp. 147–172.

[11] Foundations of New Chinese Music: Russian Pedagogues and Chinese Students, Chapter 5, in Yang, Hon-Lun Helan, Simo Mikkonen, and John Winzenburg. *Networking the Russian Diaspora: Russian Musicians and Musical Activities in Interwar Shanghai*, University of Hawai'i Press, 2020, pp. 126–147. <https://doi.org/10.2307/j.ctvn1td5w> accessed 7 July 2025.

After graduating from SCU, Qiu began his legal career at a law firm in the Shanghai International Settlement, embarking on a path that would span decades, cross continents, and leave a lasting mark on China's legal history.[12]

30.2 The Tokyo Trials and Beyond: Representing China on the International Stage

On 15 August 1945, Japan announced its surrender in the Second World War. Shortly thereafter, on 19 January 1946, the International Military Tribunal for the Far East (IMTFE), commonly referred to as the Tokyo Trials, was convened in Tokyo, Japan, to prosecute Japanese leaders for war crimes. Mei Ru'ao was appointed as the Chinese judge and Xiang Zhejun (Che-Chun Hsiang) served as the Chinese prosecutor. At the time, Qiu Shaoheng, then 33 years old, had already established an exceptional reputation for his legal expertise. On the recommendation of SCU's Professor Liu Shifang, Qiu was selected to represent China on the international stage alongside Mei and Xiang.

Qiu's extensive experience and legal expertise made him an ideal candidate for what was anticipated to be a highly complex series of trials. He was appointed by Xiang as secretary and assistant prosecutor for the Chinese team, becoming the third member of China's delegation at the IMTFE. On 7 February 1946, Qiu and Xiang travelled from Shanghai to Tokyo on a US military plane (with Mei following later), making them the first members of the IMTFE to arrive in Japan for the Tokyo Trials.[13]

Upon their arrival, Qiu and Xiang submitted to the International Prosecution Section of the IMTFE a list of eleven war criminals identified by the Chinese government. However, a challenge arose when Joseph Keenan, the chief prosecutor of the International Prosecution Section, demanded that China provide evidence to substantiate the allegations. At the time, China's Nanjing-based post-war government was focused on stabilizing its regime and was unwilling to prioritize the Tokyo Trials. This was reflected in the remarkably small Chinese delegation—composed of only three members: Mei, Xiang, and Qiu—dispatched to represent the country at the proceedings. In stark contrast, the US delegation consisted of more than 100 judges, prosecutors, and support staff. Furthermore, the Chinese team could only vaguely outline the charges and was unable to present substantial testimony or concrete evidence. Qiu was deeply puzzled by this stark imbalance

[12] As the author is a family friend of Qiu Shaoheng, much of the key information in this chapter was provided by and based on a written interview with Qiu Shaoheng.

[13] 'Judge Che-Chun Hsiang's Trip to China', David Nelson Sutton Papers, Box 1, Folder 3 [Memoranda re Orders and Directions to Sutton and Information on Individual, 1946], Virginia Historical Society, <https://imtfe.law.virginia.edu/collections/sutton/1/3/judge-che-chun-hsiangs-trip-china> accessed 7 July 2025.

in resources, particularly given that China had suffered the most at the hands of Japan.

Qiu, Mei, and Xiang faced significant challenges as they undertook a substantial amount of investigative work. Qiu dedicated much of his time in Japan to searching for relevant information in Tokyo libraries and the archives of the Japanese Ministry of Foreign Affairs. Confronted with limited resources and an urgent need for translators, Qiu negotiated with the International Inspection Team, proposing that China would recruit several translators to assist in evidence provided the American side would agree to cover their salaries.

With the support of the United States, Qiu's next step was to fly to Nanjing, China, to gather evidence of Japanese war crimes committed during the Nanjing Massacre—a campaign of terror inflicted on Chinese civilians in 1937–1938. This task proved extraordinarily challenging due to the strict secrecy maintained by the Japanese military, which had destroyed a significant amount of incriminating evidence following Japan's surrender. Compounding the difficulty was China's failure to systematically collect and preserve evidence during the war.

Between March and June 1946, Qiu collaborated with two American prosecutors in Nanjing, and the three dedicated their days to interviewing survivors, witnesses, and their relatives.[14] Since the American prosecutors did not speak Chinese, Qiu worked tirelessly, often around the clock, to register tens of thousands of complaints and conduct on-site investigations. Ultimately, he compiled a collection of witness testimonies and other materials exceeding one foot in height. The evidence gathered by Qiu and his colleagues conclusively demonstrated that more than 300,000 civilians and prisoners of war were massacred by the Japanese during the first six weeks of their occupation of Nanjing. This body of evidence was instrumental in the trial and subsequent conviction of General Matsui Iwane at the International Military Tribunal for the Far East (IMTFE).[15]

Qiu was also tasked with collecting critical evidence for the trial of Kenji Doihara, a high-ranking Japanese spymaster who played a pivotal role in orchestrating and supporting the establishment of the puppet state of Manchukuo. This undertaking was particularly challenging, as Doihara operated covertly, and his activities were shrouded in secrecy.

Undeterred by the challenge, Qiu relied on his fluency in English and his decade of experience litigating cases in Anglo-American courts. His extensive interactions with American colleagues during his time in Tokyo had also allowed him

[14] Guillemin, J. (2017). 'The 1925 Geneva Protocol: China's CBW Charges Against Japan at the Tokyo War Crimes Tribunal'. In: B. Friedrich, , D. Hoffmann, J. Renn, F. Schmaltz, and M. Wolf (eds) *One Hundred Years of Chemical Warfare: Research, Deployment, Consequences*. Springer, Cham. <https://doi.org/10.1007/978-3-319-51664-6_15> accessed 7 July 2025.

[15] David Sutton, Yang Xiaming, and Cao Jiali, 'Comprehensive Military Aggression against China and Atrocities Against Civilians: Summary of Evidence and Key Arguments' (對中國全面軍事侵略及對平民的暴行——證據總結和論證要點) [J], *Journal of Research on the Nanjing Massacre during the Japanese Invasion of China*, 2021(01), pp. 39–66, 141, 142. DOI:10.13740/j.cnki.jiiohr.2021.01.005.

to cultivate a broad network of contacts, which proved invaluable in gathering critical information. Upon learning from the American side that the International Prosecution Section had obtained certain archives from the Japanese Ministry of Foreign Affairs, Qiu made frequent visits to the archive room whenever time permitted, determined to uncover evidence of Japanese war crimes. On one such occasion, he discovered a telegram sent to the Ministry that provided crucial, concrete evidence of both Kenji Doihara's culpability and Japan's conspiracy to invade China.

Joseph Keenan, the chief prosecutor of the IMTFE, informed Qiu that the telegram would carry greater weight as evidence if Puyi, China's last emperor, could testify in person. Qiu was appointed as the prosecutor's attorney and tasked with convincing Puyi to appear in court. To this end, Qiu made numerous visits to the Soviet embassy, where Puyi was under the guard of Soviet troops, to interview the former emperor. Initially, Puyi was apprehensive of Chinese visitors and anxious about the prospect of being brought to the IMTFE. However, through persistent efforts, Qiu gradually gained his trust. Ultimately, after significant persuasion, Puyi agreed to testify.

To prepare for the defence's cross-examination strategies, Qiu conducted thorough preparation and training sessions with Puyi prior to the trial. As a result, Puyi appeared composed and self-assured in court, meticulously recounting various humiliating events while expressing both anger and sorrow over the indignities he had endured. Puyi testified for eight days, making the longest and most frequent appearances at the Tokyo Trials. His testimony garnered worldwide attention and became headline news—an achievement made possible by Qiu's efforts.

Even more important to Qiu's legacy was a trial addressing Japan's economic aggression against China, a landmark moment in Chinese legal history. Until then, China had been represented by American prosecutors at the Tokyo Trials. However, during this trial, Qiu served as the prosecutor on behalf of China—marking the first time a Chinese individual represented their homeland at the IMTFE. In fact, Qiu was the only Chinese prosecutor to ever appear in court during the tribunal. He demonstrated rigorous analytical thinking and clear legal reasoning, and spoke fluent English without any regional accent. His performance in the courtroom earned widespread acclaim and instilled a sense of pride among the Chinese people.

In September 1946, Qiu resigned from his roles as secretary and assistant prosecutor for the Chinese delegation at the IMTFE, a decision that Joseph Keenan deeply regretted. His resignation was partly due to the complex dynamics of his relationship with his superior, Xiang Zhejun. With permission to step down, Qiu began preparing to return to China. However, before his departure, he was approached by Major General Lee Li-pai, head of the military division of the ROC government's delegation in Japan, who requested that he serve as the Chinese judge in the trial of the 'Shibuya Incident'.

In July 1946, Japanese police in Shibuya, Tokyo, deliberately opened fire on a group of Taiwanese citizens, killing six and injuring more than twenty. Following the incident, the Japanese police distorted the facts, falsely accusing thirty-seven Taiwanese citizens of disrupting order in the occupied area.[16] Judge Mei had recommended Qiu Shaoheng to preside over the trial of the Taiwanese defendants, emphasizing that Qiu's fluency in English, deep understanding of the Anglo-American legal system, and resolute stance against American pressures made him the most qualified candidate for the role.

Initially reluctant to serve as a judge, Qiu ultimately agreed to participate in the trial with the goal of exposing the truth about the atrocities committed by the Japanese police. He emphasized that, in his capacity as judge, he would represent not the ROC government but the Chinese people. In a gesture of support for Qiu's appointment, Judge Mei lent him his judicial robe for the occasion.

The Shibuya Incident trial spanned six weeks, during which the American side provided more than twenty defence lawyers for the Taiwanese defendants. Despite their vigorous efforts, and Qiu's ultimate refusal to vote in what he deemed an unfair trial, the Taiwanese were found guilty. The following day, Qiu publicly objected in court, declaring, 'The verdict is entirely contrary to the law'.[17] His objection garnered enthusiastic support from Reuters war correspondent David Conde and was prominently reported by the American military newspaper *The Stars and Stripes*.[18] Subsequently, Qiu drafted a legal opinion on his objection in English and submitted it to the higher authority overseeing the court, the Eighth Army Judicial Department in Yokohama. In this opinion, he demonstrated that the court's actions had clearly been improper and violated relevant legal provisions. The Chinese newspaper *Da Gong Bao* published an article commending Qiu's efforts and revealing the full account of the Shibuya Incident,[19] authored by James T. C. Liu—then serving as a historical consultant for the Chinese staff at the International Military Tribunal for the Far East (IMTFE), and later a distinguished historian at Stanford University (1960–1965) and Princeton University (from 1965 onward).[20] Thanks to Qiu's efforts in the initial trial, thirty-seven wrongfully accused Taiwanese were spared imprisonment, and thirty-seven families were

[16] Adam Cathcart, 'Bullets of a Defeated Nation: The 1946 Shibuya Incident', in Barak Kushner and Andrew Levidis eds, *In the Ruins of the Japanese Empire: Imperial Violence, State Destruction, and the Reordering of Modern East Asia*, Hong Kong University Press, 2020, pp. 107, 110.

[17] Bian Xiuyue, 'A Study of the Shibuya Incident in Tokyo in 1946' (1946 年東京澀谷事件研究), *Studies of the War of Resistance against Japanese Aggression*, January 2023, pp. 67–79.

[18] Pvt Edward Jones, 'Formosans Sentenced to Prison by Court', *Pacific Star and Stripes*, December 11, 1946.

[19] James T. C. Liu, 'Six-Month Report on the Shibuya Incident: The Circumstances Surrounding the Violent Killing of Taiwanese Nationals by Japanese Police and Its Recent Developments' (涩谷事件半年来的总报告：日警强杀台侨的前后经过与最近发展) *Da Gong Bao (大公报)*, January 6, 1947.

[20] Peter J. Golas, 'Obituary: JAMES T.C. LIU, 1919–1993' *Journal of Song-Yuan Studies*, no. 25, 1995. *JSTOR*, http://www.jstor.org/stable/23495834. Accessed 21 July 2025.

saved from the suffering brought by wrongful incarceration.[21] The case illustrates the limits of Chinese influence on US military policy in Japan, and reveals how American priorities—stability, control, and the rehabilitation of Japan—prevailed over Allied or Chinese calls for postcolonial justice. The outcome contributed to a deepening mistrust in Sino–American relations and symbolized a turning point in the public perception of the US as a biased power favouring Japanese rehabilitation over accountability.[22]

Following his involvement in the IMTFE and the Shibuya Incident trial, the third significant milestone in Qiu's international legal career occurred in 1980, when he was appointed as a legal advisor to the special court convened to prosecute the 'Gang of Four' (四人帮) for crimes committed during the Cultural Revolution (1966–1976). Given the substantial international attention garnered by the public trial, it was crucial for China's judicial system to demonstrate alignment with international standards. Leveraging his extensive experience in Anglo-American legal systems, Qiu proposed a comprehensive set of courtroom proceedings.[23] He also provided examples of courtroom arrangements for high-profile cases in other countries, which were highly valued by the presiding judge, Jiang Hua.[24]

At the age of 73, Qiu undertook his fourth significant contribution to Chinese and international legal history: assisting in the drafting of the Basic Law of the Hong Kong SAR. In early 1985, shortly after the Chinese New Year and following the signing of the Sino–British Joint Declaration in December 1984, the drafting committee was established under the National People's Congress. Qiu was appointed to the committee in his capacity as Deputy Director of the Legal Affairs Committee of the Standing Committee of the National People's Congress.

The drafting of the Basic Law spanned four years and eight months. During this process, Qiu played a key role in facilitating collaboration between the Hong Kong and mainland Chinese members of the committee, whose views frequently diverged. Renowned for his interpersonal skills, integrity, stellar professional reputation, and high credibility, Qiu fostered an environment of open dialogue. The coffee sessions he organized became a focal point for discussion, creating a lively atmosphere where both sides were willing to engage and listen to one another.

[21] James T. C. Liu, 'Six-Month Report on the Shibuya Incident: The Circumstances Surrounding the Violent Killing of Taiwanese Nationals by Japanese Police and Its Recent Developments' (涩谷事件半年来的总报告：日警强杀台侨的前后经过与最近发展), *Da Gong Bao (大公报)*, January 6, 1947.

[22] Adam Cathcart, 'Bullets of a Defeated Nation: The 1946 Shibuya Incident', in Barak Kushner and Andrew Levidis eds, *In the Ruins of the Japanese Empire: Imperial Violence, State Destruction, and the Reordering of Modern East Asia*, Hong Kong University Press, 2020, pp. 107, 110.

[23] Alexander C. Cook, 'China's Gang of Four Trial: The Law v. The Laws of History', in Jens Meierhenrich and Devin O. Pendas eds, *Political Trials in Theory and History*, Cambridge University Press, 2017, p. 280.

[24] Ma Lingguo. 'Legal Advisor to the Special Court' (特別法庭的法律顧問), *Yan Huang Chun Qiu*. Issue 11, 1999, pp. 68–69.

30.3 Bridging Cultures: Qiu Shaoheng's Legal Legacy

Qiu Shaoheng's illustrious career, spanning half a century, was marked by four major milestones: serving as an assistant prosecutor during the Tokyo Trials, acting as a judge in the Shibuya Incident trial, advising the special court in the Gang of Four trial, and contributing as a member of the drafting committee for the Hong Kong Basic Law.

Qiu made history at the IMTFE despite his brief tenure of only eight months. Among the first to arrive in Tokyo, he was one of the few members of the Chinese team initially involved in investigating and gathering evidence. Before the tribunal commenced its sessions, Qiu worked tirelessly and meticulously to search for, collect, and organize a substantial body of evidence. He identified key eyewitnesses and uncovered critical physical evidence, playing an instrumental role in representing China—the largest nation victimized by Japan—and contributing to the successful prosecution and conviction of key figures responsible for atrocities against Chinese citizens. Notably, Qiu was the only Chinese attorney authorized to contact Puyi on behalf of the prosecution. Even more significantly, he became the first lawyer to represent China in court in the prosecution of Japanese individuals, marking a pivotal moment that ended the reliance on American prosecutors to represent China, as had been the case in prior proceedings.

Although the IMFTE often disregarded the opinions of the Chinese delegation and imposed arbitrary provisions that hindered the proper progression of the trials, Qiu refused to yield to the American side. He boldly argued on the basis of the reason, distinguishing himself from the majority of Nanjing government officials at the time. His proficiency in English, combined with his extensive experience in Anglo-American courts, enabled him to effectively bridge the cultural and legal divide between the Chinese and American teams.[25]

These skills were equally pivotal during Qiu's consultancy for the special court convened for the Gang of Four trial, where he played a crucial role in aligning the trial proceedings with Western practices. Through these efforts, he helped demonstrate to the world that China's judicial system could adhere to established practices, embodying both socialist democracy and the principles of socialist rule of law.[26]

[25] He Qinhua, 'A Brief Discussion on the Theory and Practice of China's Adoption of International Law during the Republic of China Period' (略論民國時期中國移植國際法的理論與實踐) [J], *Studies in Legal and Business (Journal of South Central Institute of Political Science and Law)*, Issue 4, 2001, pp. 136–144. DOI:10.16390/j.cnki.issn1672-0393.2001.04.018. p. 143.

[26] Alexander C. Cook, *The Cultural Revolution on Trial: Mao and the Gang of Four*. Cambridge University Press, 2016, pp. 68–69, 180.

Qiu once again earned international recognition for China during and after the Shibuya Incident trial. His principled refusal to participate in an unjust verdict, coupled with his eloquent legal objection, garnered widespread acclaim both domestically and internationally. At the trial, Reuters war correspondent Conde remarked to Qiu, 'As a war journalist who has travelled the world and met many Chinese people, today I finally see the true image of a Chinese person in you'.

The fourth and final remarkable contribution of Qiu's lifelong legal career, solidifying his impressive legacy, came in the 1980s when he played a pivotal role in drafting the Basic Law of the Hong Kong SAR. This critical document established the framework for Hong Kong's governance following its 1997 handover from British to Chinese sovereignty. Qiu's involvement in the drafting process, along with his unwavering commitment to reconciling the diverse opinions and interests represented on the committee, exemplified his dedication to ensuring a smooth transition for Hong Kong while safeguarding its unique legal and social systems. His efforts laid a strong foundation for Hong Kong's governance and its integration with China, all while preserving its distinct cultural identity and way of life.

Impressive as they were, these four milestones in Qiu's career were far from his only contributions to Chinese and international law. As deputy director of the Legal Affairs Committee of the PRC's National People's Congress,[27] he played a key role in drafting the 1984 General Principles of Civil Law of the People's Republic of China, as well as China's Trademark Law, Patent Law, and Copyright Law. Additionally, he served as the chief editor of the English version of the *Compilation of Laws of the People's Republic of China*. In his dedication to aligning Chinese law with international standards, Qiu made significant efforts to promote English-language education in Chinese law schools. He also authored several influential books on English language teaching, including *English Determiners*, *Modern English Grammar*, and *English Modifiers*.[28]

Qiu's expertise extended beyond public international law to include significant contributions to international trade and commercial law. He was the first to translate the INCOTERMS rules—eleven trade terms issued by the International Chamber of Commerce—into Chinese, making them accessible to Chinese practitioners and scholars. In the aftermath of the Cultural Revolution, Qiu played a pivotal role in restoring China's legal education system by reinstating senior

[27] Xia Lina, 'Legislation in the New Era Starts Here: A Thirty-Year Snapshot of the Legislative Affairs Commission of the Standing Committee of the National People's Congress' (新時期的立法從這里起步——全國人大常委會法制工作委員會三十年剪影), China National People's Congress, Issue 1, 2009, pp. 46-49.

[28] Wang Fufang and Lu Gusun, 'Cultivating Awareness of Dictionary Project Quality Control and External Leverage: A Case Study of Quality Control Management in the English-Chinese Dictionary' (詞典項目質量監控意識的培養及外部抓手——以《英漢大詞典》質量控制管理為例), *Dictionary Studies*, Issue 3, 2009, pp. 13–20. DOI:10.16134/j.cnki.cn31-1997/g2.2009.03.021.

legal experts, who had been persecuted and dispersed during the revolution, as frontline educators of international commercial law. Moreover, he led efforts to establish a research centre for international commercial law at the Shanghai Institute of Foreign Trade (now the Shanghai University of International Business and Economics). This centre became one of China's earliest for research on international commercial law, reflecting Qiu's enduring influence in the field.

31
Zhao Lihai (1916–2000)

Ken Yang

31.1 Introduction

Zhao Lihai 赵理海 (aka 'Li-hai Chao', 1916–2000) was one of the most important Chinese international law scholars of the Reform and Opening-up Era. Zhao embodied a profound devotion to international law research. Owing to such devotion, after having persevered through the disruptive Cultural Revolution (1966–1976), Zhao emerged as a foundational figure in the field of the law of the sea in China and mentor to a cadre of distinguished specialists. In August 1996, Zhao became the first Chinese national elected to the International Tribunal for the Law of the Sea (ITLOS) as one of the initial twenty-one judges of the court.

This chapter attempts to provide an intimate sketch of Zhao's personal and professional trajectories. Together, they form a valuable 'keyhole' through which the institutional environment in which international law research was carried out can be examined.[1] New information from archives, interviews, and Zhao's personal papers, will be introduced.[2] In addition to recounting Zhao's rich legacies, this chapter doubles as a case study of the fate of international law as an academic discipline in twentieth-century China. Zhao's unwavering commitment to research makes clear—in stark fashion—how evolving domestic political conditions can radically reshape knowledge practices relating to international law.

31.2 From Landlocked Shanxi to Harvard University (1916–1945)

Zhao Lihai was born in 1916 in the landlocked province of Shanxi in northern China. His father was a member of the prosperous Shanxi banking industry and

[1] Bardo Fassbender and Anne Peters, 'Introduction: Towards A Global History of International Law', in Bardo Fassbender, Anne Peters, Simone Peter, and Daniel Högger (eds), The Oxford Handbook of the History of International Law (Oxford: Oxford University Press, 2012), 15.

[2] I am deeply grateful to Zhao Lihai's wife, Mrs Chen Lingbao, and his daughter, Mrs Zhao Meixing, for allowing me to examine his private papers, hereinafter referred to as the Zhao Lihai Papers. I am also greatly indebted to Professor Li Hongyun 李红云 of Peking University, one of Zhao Lihai's closest disciples, for aiding me in carrying out this research.

Ken Yang, *Zhao Lihai (1916–2000)* In: *Histories of International Law in China*. Edited by: Ignacio de la Rasilla, Jiangyu Wang, and Congyan Cai, Oxford University Press. © Ken Yang 2026.
DOI: 10.1093/oso/9780198888345.003.0031

a businessman, whose wealth later supported Zhao Lihai's studies in the US.[3] He was the youngest of four brothers, who all shared the family generation name *li* 理, meaning 'make sense of (something's inner essence)' and 'put in order'. Each brother's given name corresponds to a type of water body: *Jiang* 江 (river), *he* 河 (also river, but of smaller scale), *hu* 湖 (lake), and *hai* 海 (sea). Exactly eighty years later in 1996, at a UN luncheon organized in support of Zhao Lihai's candidacy for ITLOS, the future judge—known for his austerity—would crack a rare joke that his given name '*li hai*' stands for 'settlement of marine dispute', leaving the room in laughter.[4]

After having undergone traditional private home tutoring, the youngest two of the Zhao brothers—Zhao Lihu and Zhao Lihai—were sent to Beijing to attend high school.[5] Both were enrolled in American missionary schools in the early 1930s.[6] During this period, the two brothers' lives diverged. The older brother, Zhao Lihu, transformed into an activist, while Zhao Lihai remained committed to his duties as a student. A rift emerged between the brothers, with the younger Zhao Lihai voicing his objections to his elder brother's mistaken priority.[7] The immediate backdrop for such disagreement was the ongoing Japanese aggression in northern China during the aftermath of the 'September 18 Incident' of 1931. New uncertainties unsettled students, driving many out of classrooms: some devoted themselves to political activism, some found comfort in self-indulgence.[8] Some, like Zhao Lihai, continued with their studies. Viewed from an extended timescale, the disagreement between the Zhao brothers encapsulated the dilemma that had haunted China's educated class throughout the first half of the twentieth century: does the latest national crisis call for immediate action, or should one focus on supposed long-term solutions, such as scientific endeavours?[9] To this question,

[3] Interview with Chen Lingbao, wife of Zhao Lihai (voice call, 22 September 2022). One of his father's close friends, a Shanxi industrialist named Duan Liancen, also funded his stay in the US.

[4] Zhao Lihai, 'Cong beida jiaoshou dao guoji fating faguan' [From Peking University Professor to International Court Judge], in Qingchun de beida jingshen de meili xubian [The Youthful Peking University: Sequel to The Enchantment of Spirit], edited by Zhao Weimin (Beijing: Peking University Press, 1998), 64. The English rendition cited here was the judge's own.

[5] According to Zhao Lihai, their eldest brother Zhao Lijiang had studied law at the prestigious private law school at Chaoyang University in Beijing. Zhao Lihai, titled 'chedi suqing wode zichan jieji faxue sixiang er nuli' [Striving to eradicate my bourgeois legal thoughts], Zhao Lihai Papers, date unknown, 1.

[6] Zhao Lihai, confessional material containing Zhao Lihai's biographical information, no title, circa 1968, Zhao Lihai Papers .

[7] Zhao Lihu, 'Yi yu lihaidi xiangchu de suiyue' [Remembering the days with my younger brother Zhao Lihai], Cangsang (2002) vol. 2, 46.

[8] Yang Gongsu, Cangsang jiushi nian: yige waijiao dashi de huiyi [The Ebbs and Flows of Nine Decades: Reminiscences of a Diplomat] (Haikou: Hainan Press, 1999), 88.

[9] Intellectual historian Wang Fansen noted that the May Fourth Movement of 1919 had spurred greater dissatisfaction among intellectuals against the 'individualistic approach toward social and political reformation'. Wang Fan-sen, Fu Ssu-nien: A Life in Chinese History and Politics (New York: Cambridge University Press, 2000), 67. That said, answers to this fundamental question also vacillated in step with China's changing political realities. For instance, it was arguably much easier for early Yenching students such as Fei Xiaotong to take up fundamental studies such as sociology before 1931 (Fei was studying at Yenching between 1929 and 1933), for during that brief window between

the Zhao brothers gave different answers. Following Japan's full-scale invasion in 1937, Zhao Lihu left Beijing for Yan'an to enlist in the Chinese Communist Party's Eighth Route Army.[10]

In 1935 Zhao Lihai was admitted to Yenching University, one of the country's top missionary universities, with deep ties to the United States. At the time Yenching hosted the country's leading social science programmes, which benefited from its 'financially lucrative arrangements' with American philanthropic organizations such as the Rockefeller Foundation.[11] Since its inception in 1923, its Department of Political Science had been headed by a succession of political scientists trained in the US: first Xu Shuxi 徐淑希 (aka 'Hsu Shuhsi', 1892–1982), and later his disciples Wu Qiyu 吴其玉 (1900–1995) and Chen Fangzhi 陈芳芝 (aka 'Agnes Chen Fang-chih', 1914–1995; to be featured in Chapter 33).[12] Xu was another supervisee of PCIJ's judge John Bassett Moore (as was V. K. Wellington Koo) and had written his thesis on the internationalization of Manchuria and its current place in Chinese foreign relations. His interest in China's frontier regions and their treatment under the treaty system was also taken up by his students Wu and Chen. All three department heads had accordingly lectured on international law during their tenure.

Despite its Christian and liberal roots, Yenching emerged as an important base for left-wing student activism owing to its open atmosphere and the extra protection linked to the university's extraterritorial privileges.[13] In the decades ahead, some of Zhao's peers who were Communists during their Yenching days—most notably Huang Hua and the sisters Gong Pusheng and Gong Peng—would rise to prominent positions within the PRC's Ministry of Foreign Affairs. Fast forward to the Cultural Revolution, and Zhao Lihai had to 'repent' for his 'complacency' during his student days. He expressed regret for merely harbouring 'patriotic

the unification of China under the Nationalist Government and Japanese invasion of Manchuria, it appeared that China was about to enter a period of stability and reconstruction.

[10] Zhao Lihu, n 7, 46.

[11] Arthur Lewis Rosenbaum, 'Yenching University and Sino-American Interactions, 1919–1952', Journal of American–East Asian Relations (2007) vol. 14 no. 1–2, 21.

[12] The liquidation of Yenching University and the nationwide abolition of political science departments in 1952, combined with an array of factors including Xu Shuxi's departure from mainland China after 1949 and the condemnation of both Wu Qiyu and Chen Fangzhi as 'rightists' in 1957, contributed to the erasure of the institution from legal historiography. Chapter 33 on Chinese women in international law offers a sketch of the professional career of Chen Fangzhi and the Department of Political Science of Yenching University.

[13] Yenching University's status as a missionary college with deep ties to the United States allowed it to hold more autonomy over its administration and its extracurricular activities vis-à-vis the Nationalist Government in comparison with other government universities (such as Peking and Tsinghua Universities). Intense anti-Japanese sentiment was therefore allowed to ferment into fierce criticism against the appeasement policies of the Nationalist Government. See Jessie G. Lutz, 'December 9, 1935: Student Nationalism and the China Christian Colleges', The Journal of Asian Studies (1967) vol. 26, no. 4, 627–648.

feelings', having failed to devote himself to the revolutionary politics that led to the inception of the People's Republic of China in 1949.[14]

Unlike Peking and Tsinghua Universities, Yenching University did not relocate either before or immediately after Japan's occupation of Beijing following the 'July 7th Incident' of 1937. Unable to return to Beijing from his summer break due to the ongoing fighting, Zhao Lihai temporarily studied at the National Northwest Union University in Xi'an.[15] After returning to Beijing and obtaining his bachelor's degree in 1938, Zhao briefly enrolled in Yenching University's Graduate School during the first half of 1940. That autumn, he began master's studies at the University of Chicago. At Chicago, Zhao mostly took political science and history courses. He was particularly proud of having impressed Quincy Wright, another American international law specialist based in a political science department, who had mentored many Chinese international law students throughout his career.[16] Zhao worked through the holidays and managed to finish his two-year master's programme within one and a half years, with Wright as his final examiner.[17]

In September 1941, Zhao Lihai began his doctoral studies at Harvard University, where he was registered at the Faculty of History, Government, and Economics of the University (not Harvard Law School).[18] In Zhao's own words, he had 'during the past nine years been pursuing studies in political science, with international law as my special field'.[19] It took him two years of meticulous work to complete his doctoral thesis,[20] titled *International Law as Applied to Sino–American Treaties*. It was defended in June 1944 and bore the signatures of Payson S. Wild Jr and Charles B. Hagan, both of whom were political scientists with varying degrees of interest in international affairs. George Grafton Wilson, a founding member of the American Society of International Law, also offered input.[21] Zhao's heavily descriptive thesis

[14] In one piece of self-criticism written during the Cultural Revolution, Zhao acknowledged that his Yenching peers actively took part in the Chinese Communist Revolution when he decided to commit to his studies. He expressed his regret at merely participating in some anti-Japanese student marches in December 1936, but fell short of grasping that the event (i.e., the Communist-led 'December 9th Movement') 'constituted a segment of the liberation struggle of the Chinese people'. Zhao Lihai, confessional materials titled 'Right-leaning comments in 1957', date unknown, 15, ZHLP.

[15] Zhao Lihai's biographical information (n 6).

[16] Zhou Enhui, 'Yiyi yuanding qing, quanquan baoguoxin: Ji zhuming guojifaxuejia zhao lihai jiaoshou' [His Gentle Spirit as a Teacher, His Sincere Patriotism: On the Renowned International Law Professor Zhao Lihai], in Zhou Enhui, Zoujin xinzhongguo faxue dajia [Approaching the Great Jurists of the People's Republic of China] (Beijing: Publishing House of the China People's Public Security University, 2009), 270.

[17] Zhao's master's thesis was titled 'A Study of Commercial Treaties between China and the United States', for which he was conferred the degree of Master of Arts in Political Science. Zhao Lihai's transcript from the University of Chicago was included in his Harvard University student records, Harvard University Archives, on file with the author.

[18] According to Zhao's own English résumé, he had completed both MA and PhD programmes at Harvard. Letter from Zhao Lihai (Li-hai Chao) to William L. Holland, dated 31 July 1944, Box 123, Folder 'Ch', Institute of Pacific Relations Records, 1925–1962, Columbia University Rare Books and Manuscript Library.

[19] ibid.

[20] ibid.

[21] ibid.

chronicled the evolution of Sino–US treaty relations, which he concluded as the move towards 'equality and reciprocity' in accordance with 'principles of international law and practice as reflected in modern international procedures and in the modern treaties'.[22] It chose the 1943 Sino–American Treaty for Relinquishment of Extraterritorial Rights in China as a point of departure. Given that this 'epoch-making' agreement marked the formal end to the unequal treaty system, the thesis was decidedly forward-looking. While Zhao had diligently narrated the origin and development of the US's special rights in China, their voluntary relinquishment in 1943 allowed Zhao to circumvent vast literature by Chinese authors that had in the past contested the unequal nature of said treaty arrangements.[23] It is worth noting that Payson S. Wild, one of Zhao's supervisors, had in his previous monograph on treaty sanctity and enforcement mentioned concerns over 'Chinese agitations against the "unequal treaties"', while expressing doubt over 'whether Japan really was so very much a culprit [of the Manchurian Crisis]'.[24] Such circumstances and the pressure for a Chinese student to appear 'scientific' could explain Zhao's cautious approach to his thesis.

Following the defence, Zhao searched for opportunities to publish the thesis in the US, which led him to contact the Institute of Pacific Relations.[25] During the interwar period, the Institute sought to promote peaceful relations by advancing scientific research and popular understanding. It had emerged as an intellectual hub through which many Chinese and Western scholars with social science backgrounds were connected. After Japan invaded China, the organization took on the additional function of supporting Chinese scholars whose lives and academic work were disrupted by the war.[26] After examining the thesis, while recognizing the thesis to be 'a very competent and useful piece of work', the Institute's Research Secretary William L. Holland regretfully informed Zhao that the thesis was 'too detailed and too technical to be suitable for publication by this Institute', given that the Institute's proclaimed goal was reaching broader audiences.[27] After graduation, Zhao registered at Harvard Law School and spent the following year on research.[28]

[22] Zhao Lihai (Li-hai Chao), 'International Law as Applied to the Sino-American Treaties' (PhD thesis, Harvard University 1944), 133, 350.

[23] According to the thesis bibliography, of the 246 monographs and periodical sources cited only 11 were attributed to Chinese authors, all of which were written in English.

[24] Payson S. Wild Jr, Sanctions and Treaty Enforcement (Cambridge, MA: Harvard University Press, 1934), 17, 216–217.

[25] Zhao mentioned in his letter to Holland that he was also preparing to contact Harvard University Press. Zhao Lihai (n 18).

[26] The Institute of Pacific Relations had in 1940 supported the publication of Dong Lin's (a.k.a. 'Tung Lin') doctoral thesis *China and Some Phases of International Law*, which was supervised by Quincy Wright. Wright was an active member at the Institute. Wang Tieya had also benefited from the Institute's research funding. See Chapter 29, Wang Tieya, by the same author, fn. 25, 26, and 27.

[27] Letter from William L. Holland to Zhao Lihai (Li-hai Chao), dated 18 August 1944, Institute of Pacific Relations Records, 1925–1962, Box 123, Folder 'Ch', Columbia University Rare Books and Manuscript Library.

[28] According to his correspondence with Holland, Zhao appeared to have lived in Hastings Hall during this time. It is indicated in the letter that the official affiliation with Harvard Law School solved

According to his wife, Chen Lingbao, Zhao Lihai was not particularly nostalgic about his life in America. His only praise was reserved for the Harvard Law School Library and its 'voluminous book collection' inside the towering Langdell Hall.[29] He created a personal card system used to catalogue all the books he had consumed, with the total exceeding one thousand (his 400-page thesis included 600 citation entries). He also assembled a considerable private collection of treatises on international law, international relations, and history.

31.3 Teaching and Research at Times of Turbulence (1945–1976)

In 1944, Zhao Lihai met Liu Naicheng 刘迺诚, head of the Department of Political Science at Wuhan University. During his visit to Harvard, Liu developed a favourable impression of Zhao, which allowed Zhao to land his first teaching position upon his return in 1945 at Wuhan University School of Law, Department of Political Science. In 1947 he transferred to the National Central University in Nanjing through the introduction of his former Yenching professor Wu Qiyu,[30] and was promoted to full professor.[31] Zhao made the move to Nanjing partly to escape the increasingly destabilizing campus politics at Wuhan, and partly because National Central University enjoyed higher prestige. But by relocating to the country's capital, Zhao inevitably placed himself within the orbit of the Nationalist Government's political elites. Zhao Lihai, who until this point in his life had remained apolitical, was not particularly discontented over the Nationalist Government's failures in governance, even as dissatisfaction with the political status quo was ever rising among his liberal colleagues in Beijing. Between late 1948 and early 1949, he served as an advisor to the Committee on War Reparations (vis-à-vis Japan) under the Executive Yuan and provided opinions on matters pertaining to international law. These brief and allegedly insubstantial associations would become Zhao's vulnerabilities during the Cultural Revolution.

Zhao remained in mainland China in 1949. During the 1952 Reorganization of Higher Education, National Central University was remade into what is now Nanjing University. Departments of political science, alongside many law faculties, were abolished across the country.[32] Their personnel were scheduled to be

his problem with regards to his visa status. In his later reports, he would refer to his status at Harvard Law School as 'auditing student'. Zhao Lihai (n 18).

[29] Chen Lingbao (n 3).

[30] Zhao Lihai (n 4), 59.

[31] Chen Lingbao (n 3).

[32] Since Western social science disciplines did not accept historical materialism as their theoretical foundation, they were deemed unfit for carrying out analyses of social phenomena during the Maoist era. See Zhao Baoxu, 'The Revival of Political Science in China', PS, vol. 17 no. 4 (Autumn, 1984), 745–757.

incorporated into the newly established politics and law colleges. According to Zhao, his planned transfer to the newly established East China College of Politics and Law in Shanghai never materialized, which for a protracted period trapped him in an administrative limbo.[33] Zhao thus took up teaching at the Faculty of History at Nanjing University. Nanjing alumni recalled that Zhao had practically memorized a Soviet history textbook when he gave a course on world medieval history.[34] However, Zhao did not forfeit his professional identity as an international lawyer and continued his research on international law. Finally, in late 1956, Zhao reached out to Wu Defeng 吴德峰,[35] then President of the China Political Science and Law Society (*zhongguo zhengfa xuehui*) and future Vice President of the Supreme People's Court. Zhao asked to be transferred back to a law faculty so that his years of international law training would not go to waste.[36] His request was met with relatively swift approval. International law remained a legitimate field within the Soviet disciplinary landscape and was taught at Peking University following the resurrection of its Faculty of Law in 1954. In April 1957, Zhao moved to Beijing and was made the head of the 'International Law Teaching and Research Section' at Peking University Faculty of Law. He was received by President Ma Yinchu, who expressed his high expectations for the Harvard graduate.[37]

People close to Zhao Lihai remembered him as genuinely preferring the tranquil and simple life of academia. This personal disposition, however, would soon put Zhao at odds with the radical changes brought forth by the socialist reforms. Both the Intellectual Reform Movement of the early 1950s and the 1952 Reorganization of Higher Education greatly strengthened the party-state's control of higher education institutions and individual intellectuals. All university members were mobilized to take up a variety of public roles that would embody the country's new orientation. One particularly challenging development for Zhao was the 'collectivization' (*jiti hua*) of scholarly activities. Most notably, under each teaching and research section, faculty members were expected to share the burden in designing the curriculum and carrying out teaching. Initially, Zhao Lihai displayed discomfort with these new developments. He nevertheless became more proactive in adapting to the political campaigns. Later in 1952, an official communique from Nanjing University reported on Zhao's new attitude and presented it as a success case.[38] While Zhao had escaped the initial maelstrom of the 1957 Anti-Rightist Movement

[33] Zhao Lihai, draft confessional material titled 'My Crime in Slandering the Party's Reorganization of Higher Education Policy during the May 1957 China Political Science and Law Society Symposium', date unknown, 1, Zhao Lihai Papers .

[34] Li Qingyu, 'Zhushi zayi' [Miscellaneous memories of my professors] (*Nanjing University Newspaper,* no. 1004, Fall 2010) <https://alumni.nju.edu.cn/f2/2b/c3029a61995/pagem.htm> accessed 4 July 2025.

[35] Zhao Lihai (n 5). See also Zhao Lihai (n 6) 5.

[36] Chen Lingbao (n 3).

[37] ibid.

[38] Huadong gaodeng xuexiao sixiang gaizao yundong hou de xinqixiang xuanji [Collection of reports on the new atmosphere following the Thought Reform Movement in East China higher education

that had implicated many of his international law colleagues with Western educational backgrounds,[39] he became the target of a minor criticism campaign in the context of the 1958 'Great Leap Forward in Science' movement.[40] Zhao was criticized for having prioritized his personal research work over his duties in teaching and class struggle. According to the criticism, this was the characteristic of individualism, typical of a 'bourgeoisie professor'. Zhao's other misdeeds included having exaggerated 'UN impartiality' (which contradicted contemporary official depiction of the UN as a vessel of American imperialism) and deviating from facts articulated in officially sanctioned diplomatic histories.[41]

Politics finally caught up with Zhao Lihai in 1968 during a particularly frenzied phase of the Cultural Revolution. Threatened with a possible sentence of ten years' imprisonment, Zhao was coerced into confessing to being a 'sleeper agent' planted by the Nationalists just before they retreated to Taiwan. A 1969 report claimed that Zhao 'confessed' to having been 'personally planted by Deputy Minister Zhang Lisheng of Jiang Jieshi [Chiang Kai-shek]'s Executive Yuan, preparing to collaborate from within when [the Nationalists'] counteroffensive takes place'.[42] Zhao later recalled being forced to fabricate this incriminating story in exchange for lenient treatment. He was again attacked in 1973 for the alleged crime of 'cultivating personal professional capacity', referring to Zhao's insistence on continuing his private research projects on international law.[43] After the conclusion of the Cultural Revolution in 1976, Zhao was among the first group of scholars to be rehabilitated.

institutions], January 1954, from the Database of Chinese Political Campaigns in the 1950s: From Land Reform to State-Private Partnership, 1949–1956, The Chinese University of Hong Kong. The communique reported that 'Zhao Lihai of the Faculty of Political Science used to emphasise his personal research projects. He did not take part in the Land Reform movement, nor had he taken up tasks assigned to him by the leadership. Following the recent thought reform and study programme, he has enthusiastically accepted the role as secretary on the [Teachers'] Union's cultural, entertainment, and sports affairs. He says, "I am no expert on these matters, but I am willing to accept whatever task that is assigned to me by the group. I shall abide by all arrangements!"'

39 The 1957 political campaign was bent on purging alleged 'rightist' intellectuals who appeared to favour capitalism and bourgeois thinking, and/or against state collectivization. Most of the figures explored in the biographical chapters, including Han Depei, Wang Tieya, and Chen Tiqiang, were wrongfully condemned as rightists.

40 In the late 1950s, Chinese scientific communities were also swept up in the 'Great Leap Forward' campaign and sought to channel their expertise to serve the socialist cause, allowing politics and ideology to fully override science. See, Zhang Zhihui, '"Kexue dayuejin' chutan (1958–1961)" [A Preliminary Examination of the 'Great Leap Forward in Science' (1958–1961)] (PhD thesis, University of Science and Technology of China, 2007).

41 Beijing daxue falv xi guoji fa pipan xiaozu [Peking University Faculty of Law International Law Criticism Group], Pipan Zhao Lihai xiansheng de zichan jieji jiaoyu sixiang yu xueshu sixiang lunwen ji [Collected papers critiquing Zhao Lihai's bourgeoisie thoughts on teaching and research], circa 1958, Zhao Lihai Papers, 1, 5.

42 Beijing daxue Mao Zedong sixiang xuanchuandui guanyu qingli he gaizao jieji diren de qingkuang baogao [Report by Peking University Mao Zedong Thought Propaganda Team on the Cleansing and Reforming of Class Enemies], 4 September 1969, cited from The Controversial History of the Cultural Revolution in Peking University (II): With a Chronicle 1964–1983, edited by Hu Zongshi and Zhang Duo (Austin, TX: Remembering Publishing, 2022), 200.

43 Zhao Lihai (n 4), 60.

31.4 Becoming the Doyen on the Law of the Sea (1977–2000)

Three decades later, during the celebration of Peking University's centennial in 1998, Zhao shared the details of his struggles in conducting proper academic research during those turbulent decades. During the 1950s, a succession of political campaigns that transformed the PRC into a proper Leninist state instilled paralyzing anxieties among international lawyers. It was later summarized that 'every article published in newspapers and journals was commonly presumed to have been representing the country's official stance', resulting in the experience that 'articles written were often put on the shelf for we dared not publish them'.[44] Against this dynamic, the splitting of teaching duties between scholars inside the teaching and research section served the function of playing things safe and lowering the risk for all; despite this safeguard, Zhao recounted teaching felt like 'playing a record, repeating the lecture scripts year after year, without much advancement'.[45] It was only in 1979 that international lawyers began pushing back against this totalizing conception about the relations between international lawyers and the state.[46] They were finally given some space for the utterance of professional opinions as a result.

Diligent adaptations were made by Zhao, to the best of his abilities, to cope with some of the structural constraints during the first three decades of the PRC. One of them was the limited availability of foreign scholarships. Until the Sino–Soviet split in the late 1960s, Soviet international law literature remained the main source of foreign academic material accessible and citable for most Chinese scholars. Zhao Lihai was thus in possession of copies of the *Soviet Yearbook of International Law* published by the Academy of Science of the USSR; the yearbooks came with Chinese tables of contents and English summaries on selected articles, the latter of which Zhao had made heavy use of.[47] Another constraint was the scarcity of

[44] ibid, 59.

[45] Zhao Lihai (n 14), 2.

[46] See Wang Tieya and Wei Min, 'Guojifa de yanjiu bixu jiaqiang' [Research on international law must be strengthened] *People's Daily* (Beijing, 30 March 1979) 3. In this opinion piece Wang and Wei made a direct reference to the vicious cycle during the Maoist era where 'scholars worried that writings on international law could potentially be misrepresented internationally as representing the state's official stance ... consequently, fewer and fewer articles were produced, and even in cases where articles were written, there were not necessarily platforms brave enough to publish it. This phenomenon had in the long term created a vicious cycle: the fewer articles you publish, the more scrutiny you receive when you do publish; and just like the rare phoenix feathers and unicorn's horn, foreign observers ended up presuming such publication to be representing some sort of official stance.' Wang and Wei thus called for the separation of individual opinions and official state practice—common sense for the rest of the world's international community, but a not-so-small step for the Chinese community at the time.

[47] Zhao had taken extensive notes on the Soviet Yearbooks that were in his possession. These materials, alongside Zhao's collection of Western treatises from his time in the US, were donated to Peking University Law School Library after his passing. During the author's research trip to Peking University Law School Library, the author discovered notecards produced by Zhao which recorded titles of Western monographs based on citations used in the Soviet materials.

basic information on the latest international affairs.[48] Accordingly, Zhao made scrapbooking news articles (most notably the reports and policies published on the flagship newspaper *People's Daily*) part of his daily routine. Throughout this time, his wife Chen Lingbao had taken up the role of his secretary and research assistant, performing essential functions such as transcription, proofreading, scrapbooking, and management of his library loans.[49]

Zhao Lihai had twice in his career attempted to address the prevalent nihilistic attitudes towards international law in China. The first took place during the immediate aftermath of the Second World War, when the war had severely brutalized China while elevating it to superpower status, thus entrenching the long-running 'might is right' mode of thinking. Zhao observed in a 1946 article that 'ordinary people (*yiban ren*) thought that international law was merely a bunch of lofty rhetoric, with no practical significance ... Based on international events of the past decade, their scepticism towards international law had reached unprecedented intensity.'[50] The article thus unfolded as an intervention against such scepticism, recounting that even during the war, international law was still dutifully observed between neutral states. Zhao concluded his article on a cautionary note, reminding his readers that 'counting out international law constitutes a major mistake'.[51] These lines were reproduced word-for-word in the preface of his 1947 textbook *International Law*.[52] In 1990, he again paraphrased this argument in the first chapter of his monograph *Basic Theories of International Law*. This recurring sentiment, according to Zhao, was almost an antecedent to the legal nihilism characteristic of the Maoist era.[53]

Entering the 1980s, Zhao himself played a role in dispelling such nihilism and carving out an intellectual space that would allow the growth of the international law discipline. In 1980, Wang Tieya, Zhao Lihai, and Zhu Qiwu 朱奇武[54] co-authored the opening theoretical chapter of the first-ever international law textbook produced by PRC international law scholars.[55] The chapter included a

[48] Before the Reform and Opening-up era, Reference News (*Cankao xiaoxi*) was the sole international news-focused publication accessible to general members of universities. See Liu Xiange, 'Maozedong, neibu cankao yu dangdai zhongguo de zhengzhi chuanbo' [Mao Zedong, internal reference news, and political communications in contemporary China], Journalism & Communications (2013) vol. 12, 15–26. Zhao later recounted being stonewalled from accessing this publication during the Cultural Revolution due to his status.

[49] Zhou Enhui (n 15), 277.

[50] Zhao Lihai, 'Guoji gongfa de zhanwang' [Prospect of Public International Law], Dalu pinglun [Continental Review] (1946) vol. 2–3, 11–12.

[51] ibid, 12.

[52] Zhao Lihai, Guoji gongfa [Public International Law] (Shanghai: The Commercial Press, 1947), 1.

[53] Zhao Lihai, Guojifa jiben lilun [Basic Theories of International Law] (Beijing: Peking University Press, 1990), 3.

[54] Prof. Zhu Qiwu taught at China University of Political Science and Law. All three men received training in Anglo-American institutions: Wang at London School of Economics, Zhao at Harvard University, and Zhu at Oxford University.

[55] Wang Tieya, Zhao Lihai, and Zhu Qiwu, Chapter One: Introduction, in Wang Tieya and Wei Min (eds), Guo Jifa [International Law] (Beijing: China Law Press, 1981).

steadfast confirmation of international law's legal characteristics. That said, since this was still the early 1980s, the chapter refrained from jettisoning Marxist jurisprudence wholesale, emphasizing that international law still embodied 'class attributes' since it ultimately derives from the 'will of the ruling class' of each state.[56] The chapter nevertheless argued that international law as a legal system could never be dictated by the will of a single domineering ruling class (since there could never be a singular 'ruling class in international society'); therefore, China's participation in and adherence to the existing international legal order predominantly shaped by Western nations, was not equivalent to China voluntarily submitting herself to bourgeois will.

For the Republican era-trained international lawyers like Zhao, the Reform era brought a reversal of fortune. Their connections to elite Western institutions, their command of Western languages and Western international legal expertise (as opposed to Russian and that of the Soviet school), and their perseverance during the turbulent decades were then being celebrated.[57] In 1982, Zhao became one of the fortunate few Chinese professors who were invited to take part in academic exchange programmes in the US; Zhao served as visiting professor at NYU School of Law, an opportunity that allowed him to lecture at half a dozen American universities, including his *alma mater*, Harvard University.[58] That said, remnants of the previous era could still be found in Zhao's later works, reflecting the professor's prudent nature. Keywords such as 'will of the ruling class' were still integrated into his definition of international law in his later publications,[59] even though some of his colleagues had moved on from such ideological components. Zhao was also straightforward with his view on international law's role in 'servicing our country's need in diplomatic struggles (*waijiao douzheng*)', stating that its value as 'a powerful weapon in advancing the human cause of progress' was precisely why China ought to embrace it.[60] During this period, Zhao occasionally published articles for non-specialist readers in mainstream newspapers such as the *People's Daily*, articulating China's official stance from the perspective of international law.

Zhao referred to the years between 1976 and 1996 as his 'golden decades' at Peking University,[61] a period in which he had produced his principal scholarly works, adding up to around two million Chinese characters.[62] His most important contribution was concentrated in the law of the sea. Zhao's earliest work pertaining

[56] ibid, 12.

[57] The rehabilitation and evolution of the state–international lawyer relationship could be better observed in the experience of Wang Tieya during the 1980s. See Chapter 29, Wang Tieya, by the same author.

[58] Zhou Enhui (n 15), 272.

[59] Zhao Lihai (n 52), 23.

[60] ibid, 33, 42. See also, Zhao Lihai, Dangdai Haiyangfa d lilun yu shijian [Contemporary Theories and Practices concerning the Law of the Sea] (Beijing: China Law Press, 1987), 3.

[61] Zhao Lihai (n 4), 60.

[62] Zhou Enhui (n 15), 273.

to this field was a section in his doctoral dissertation where he briefly dealt with the extent of China's territorial sea in the context of American special rights in inland navigation.[63] In 1959, Zhao published an article elaborating China's stance on the 12-nautical-mile territorial sea and its more restrictive view on rights of innocent passage based on China's 1958 Declaration on Territorial Sea.[64] It is not unreasonable to link Zhao's heightened interest in the law of the sea during the Reform era to the Third UN Conference on the Law of the Sea (1973–1982).[65] The Conference marked the first major international conference China participated in since its return to the UN in 1971. The domestic significance of the Conference could be corroborated by the amount of diligent coverage in the *People's Daily*,[66] which at that time served as Zhao's main window for obtaining international news. Judging from the *People's Daily* headlines, it would be reasonable to assume that a Chinese international lawyer would be heartened by Third World countries' proactive engagement with the international law-making process, going head-to-head against the great powers.[67] Having closely followed these developments, during the latter half of the Cultural Revolution Zhao initiated research projects concerning the United Nations and the law of the sea without sanction from the University.[68] Not surprisingly, at the beginning of the Conference, China's attitude was mainly structured by the existing revolutionary sensibility that prioritized support for the Third World's struggle against superpowers over its own national interests.[69] As China moved on from revolutionary politics in the late 1970s, its delegates at the later sessions of the Conference thus began to demonstrate 'more interest in the substantive and technical aspects of the work of the conference'.[70]

[63] Zhao Lihai (n 21), 113–118, on 'Coastal Navigation'. Zhao recounted that both the late Qing and the Nationalist Government had (until 1944) recognized the three-mile limit.

[64] Zhao Lihai, 'Zhonghua renmin gongheguo weihu linghai zhuquan de zhengyi douzheng' [The People's Republic of China's Righteous Struggle in Defence of its Territorial Sea Sovereignty], Journal of Peking University (1959) vol. 3, 35–44. During this stage, the Chinese approach to law of the sea issues closely followed that of the USSR.

[65] Such is the theory endorsed by Professor Li Hongyun. Message from Professor Li Hongyun (13 May 2024).

[66] According to the author's research, between 1973 and 1979, the *People's Daily* published 72 news reports on the Conference.

[67] Following the Sino–Soviet schism of the late 1960s, China often alleged Soviet policies and attitudes related to the law of the sea to be acts of 'hegemonism' and began aligning itself more closely with the Group of 77.

[68] Zhao Lihai (n 4), 60–61.

[69] Huang Jiahua, Guojifa yu waijiao [International Law and Diplomacy], in Guoji fa jiaocai Jiangxi ban fayan cailiao huiji [Transcripts of the Symposium for the 1981 International Law Textbook], June 1983, material for internal circulation, section 1 page 22, stating that '(When China actively supported Latin American countries' claim of 200 nautical miles of maritime rights) we prioritised rightful claims of smaller nations over our own interests.' Internally printed transcript on file with the author.

[70] Hungdah Chiu, 'China and the Law of the Sea Conference', Occasional Papers/Reprints Series in Contemporary Asian Studies (1984) no. 4, 25. In 1979, Zhao Lihai's colleague at Peking University, the newly rehabilitated Wang Tieya, was invited to join the Chinese delegation as a technical adviser at the Third United Nations Conference on the Law of the Sea, a personnel change that also captured this larger trend.

Zhao Lihai had correctly predicted the rising demand for expertise in the law of the sea as China transitioned toward superpower status. Enabled by his research and preparations that had started in the 1970s, in 1984, just two years after UNCLOS III was opened for signature, Zhao published his monograph *New Developments in the Law of the Sea*.[71] The book was the first comprehensive monograph on the law of the sea produced by a Chinese international lawyer that shed light on Chinese practices, complemented by 'meticulous and extensive annotations',[72] an element that was often considered as lacking in publications from the preceding era. With this book, Zhao became one of the first Chinese scholars that begin legitimizing Chinese claims over the South China Sea under the new UNCLOS framework. As a result, the Ministry of Foreign Affairs was said to have sought out Zhao's input on defending Chinese claims over the Nansha Islands ('Spratly Islands');[73] Zhao, in turn, advocated for mutual collaboration between scholars and state institutions, especially calling on the latter to improve the former group's access to international conferences.[74] Between 1981 and 1989, he also had a role in the Chinese International Maritime Affairs as vice president, before moving on to the Chinese Society of the Law of the Sea in 1989 as vice president.[75] In 1984, Zhao Lihai was selected as one of the very first law doctoral supervisors nationwide who were specially approved by the State Council.[76] At Peking University, he began planning the research topics for his prospective doctoral students before their admissions; the goal was that his students' doctoral research projects would eventually cover each and every law of the sea subfield.[77] In 1998, he proudly cited the commendation of a State Oceanic Administration Legal Affairs Director, who praised that there was indeed 'a legion of students waving Professor Zhao's banner' (*zhao jia jun*) when it comes to law of the sea research.[78]

[71] Zhao Lihai, Haiyang fa de xin fazhan [New Developments in the Law of the Sea] (Beijing: Peking University Press, 1984).

[72] Owing to its timeliness, Zhao's book was reviewed in the American Journal of International Law, where the reviewers had highlighted said feature, which 'reflects the emerging trend in the PRC toward systematic, thorough and serious legal scholarship'. Nicholas V. Chen and Mitchell A. Silk, Book Review, American Journal of International Law (1986) vol. 80, no. 4, 1037.

[73] See Qiao Shitong, 'Zhao Lihai jiqi guojifa sixiang pingshu' [A Survey of Zhao Lihai and His International Legal Thoughts], Wuhan University International Law Review (2007) vol. 1, 348.

[74] Zhao Lihai, 'Relie qingzhu beida bainian huadan' [Warmly Celebrates the Centenary of Peking University: Excerpts of Professor Zhao Lihai's Speech at the Ceremony], Faxue zazhi [Judicial Science Journal] (1998) vol. 4, p. 2.

[75] The exact origin of this organization can no longer be traced. We do know from one of Zhao's forewords that the society came into being in 1981 as a separate entity from the Chinese Society for Oceanography and was likely under the aegis of the State Oceanic Administration. It is possible that in 1994, with the founding of Chinese Society of the Law of the Sea, the two societies were merged. Zhao Lihai, Dangdai haiyang fa de lilun yu shijian [Theories and Practices of Contemporary Law of the Sea] (Beijing: China Law Press, 1987), 3.

[76] Wang Jian, 'Kao woguo zizhu peiyang de faxue boshi' [Admission to China's PhD in Law Programmes], *Legal Daily* (Beijing, 6 June 2021) 10.

[77] Interview with Professor Li Hongyun, Peking University Law School (Beijing, China, 27 November 2023).

[78] Zhao Lihai (n 4), 62.

In 1984, Zhao Lihai had written about ITLOS in a mildly optimistic tone, characterizing the new Tribunal as 'having mirrored the balance of force under the current historical conditions ... an innovation for the peaceful resolution of maritime disputes, and the inevitable outcome from the progression of objective circumstances'.[79] Twelve years later in Hamburg, following his inauguration on 18 October 1996, Zhao personally would contribute to this progression, including formulating the Tribunal's Rules of Procedure and Internal Judicial Practice. In 1997, he was elected to the Seabed Disputes Chamber. By his own count, during the first year of the Tribunal, he had offered more than 150 speeches and interventions.[80] During the 1999 M/V 'SAIGA' (No. 2) judgment, Zhao submitted a separate opinion noting his view on the legality of offshore bunkering (i.e., 'the sale of gas oil to vessels at sea'), an issue that the Tribunal had circumvented.[81] Zhao insisted that the practice of bunkering was not an aspect of freedom of navigation or an internationally lawful use of the sea under Art. 58 (1) of UNCLOS, but a 'commercial activity' that can be regulated if it takes place in another state's EEZ.[82] This view seems to echo Zhao's inclinations towards being more protective of coastal states' maritime rights.

During his judgeship, Zhao Lihai travelled between Beijing and Hamburg. He returned to Beijing on 1 October 2000 and passed away ten days later. He was 84.

[79] Zhao Lihai, 'Guoji haiyang fa fating de chuangli' [On the Founding of the International Tribunal for the Law of the Sea], in Zhao Lihai, Dangdai guojifa wenti [Contemporary International Law Problems] (Beijing: China Law Press), 249.

[80] Zhao Lihai (n 72) 2.

[81] M/V 'Saiga' (No. 2) Case (Saint Vincent and the Grenadines v. Guinea), Judgment, ITLOS, 1999, para. 138.

[82] M/V 'Saiga' (No. 2) Case (Saint Vincent and the Grenadines v. Guinea), Separate Opinion of Judge Zhao, para. 2.

32
Chen Ti-Chiang (1917–1983)

Xiaobing Xu

32.1 A Life of a Patriot across the Old and New China

Professor Chen's life spanned Old China (the Republic of China period until 1949) and New China (the People's Republic of China period since 1949). In December 1948, three years after he left China to pursue his PhD in international law in the United Kingdom, he completed his studies at Oxford and returned to China at a time when Old China was nearing its end. He had the option to follow the Nationalist government and fly to Taiwan, but he chose to stay and spend the rest of his life serving New China.

32.1.1 Education in the Old China

Born in 1917 into a diplomatic family in Fuzhou, Fujian Province, Chen spent his childhood and youth migrating back and forth between Beijing, Shanghai, and Fuzhou due to his father's profession, and later travelled between Northern China and Southern China due to the Japanese war of aggression after the July 7th Incident of 1937.

During the period 1923–1935, he undertook schooling in various primary, middle, and high schools in Beijing, Shanghai and Fuzhou, starting with the Foreign Affairs Ministry Elementary School in Beijing, and ending in Zhicheng Middle School (志成中学) in Beijing, where he graduated..[1] He also studied at St. Stephen's College of Hong Kong (香港圣士提反书院), and Gezhi Shanghai high school (上海格致中学), laying a solid foundation in English and Chinese traditional culture.[2]

In 1935, influenced by his father's profession, Chen entered the Department of Political Science in Tsinghua University, where he soon became a student leader participating actively in the December 9th Movement (1935), a

[1] Yang Yun (杨赟), '中国当代国际法学家陈体强：生平与故事' ('Chen Ti-Chiang, Chinese Contemporary Jurist of International Law: Life and Stories'), (2016) 1法律与外交 (Law and Diplomacy) 301, p. 301.
[2] Xie Zheping (谢喆平), 浮云远志 (*Floating Clouds and Lofty Aspirations*) [商务印书馆 (The Commercial Press) 2014], p. 193.

Xiaobing Xu, *Chen Ti-Chiang (1917–1983)* In: *Histories of International Law in China*. Edited by: Ignacio de la Rasilla, Jiangyu Wang, and Congyan Cai, Oxford University Press.
DOI: 10.1093/oso/9780198888345.003.0032

nationwide anti-Japanese aggression and national salvation movement initiated by the Tsinghua University Student Salvation Council (清华大学学生救国会). However, he was better known in Tsinghua for his outstanding academic talent. In 1937, after China's nationwide War of Resistance against Japanese Aggression broke out, Peking University, Tsinghua University, and Nankai University were forced to relocate south and merged to form the Associated National University in Changsha (长沙临时大学) on 10 September 1937. As Changsha was under threat from Japanese troops, the three universities relocated further southwest to Kunming, Yunnan, and formed the National Southwest Associated University (NSAU, 西南联大) in April 1938, where he graduated in July 1939.[3]

Upon graduation, his outstanding academic performance earned him a position as a research assistant in the Teaching and Research Office of Public Administration (行政教研室) in the Department of Political Science at NSAU, where he demonstrated great potential in academic research. In the three years working in NSAU, he produced two monographs: *China's Diplomatic Administration* ('中国外交行政',[4] completed in 1941 and published in October 1943 by the Commercial Press), and *British Administrative Law* ('英国行政法论',[5] completed in July 1942 and published in August 1947 by the same publisher).[6]

To earn more to support his family in Shanghai and pursue better opportunities to study abroad, he resigned from NSAU in 1942 and went to Chongqing to work for the government. In September 1943 he entered the Foreign Affairs Ministry to work in the Second Division of the Treaty Department, having passed various assessments to join the Foreign Affairs Ministry. At that time China had already signed the Sino–American and Sino–British new treaties[7] and was preparing for similar new treaties with other Western Powers such as France, Belgium, and Canada. His personal and firsthand experience in the Treaty Department made

[3] Yang Yun (杨赟), '中国当代国际法学家陈体强：生平与故事' ('Chen Ti-Chiang, Chinese Contemporary Jurist of International Law: Life and Stories'), (2016) 1法律与外交 (Law and Diplomacy) 301, pp. 302–303.

[4] Chen Ti-Chiang (陈体强), 中国外交行政 (*China's Diplomatic Administration*) [商务印书馆 (the Commercial Press) 1943]. The book is still quoted in academic literature today. See, for example, Dai Haibin (戴海斌), '中国外交近代转型的节点——简论庚子事变前后若干外交问题 (1900—1901)' ('The Turning Point in Modern Chinese Diplomatic Transformation: A Brief Discussion on Several Diplomatic Issues Before and After the Boxer Uprising') (2011) 12 社会科学战线 (Social Science Front) 21, p. 22.

[5] Chen Ti-Chiang (陈体强), 英国行政法论 (*British Administrative Law*) [商务印书馆 (Commercial Press) 1947]. The book is still quoted in academic literature today. See, for example, He Haibo (何海波), '司法判决中的正当程序原则' ('The Due Process Principle in Judicial Practice') (2009) 1 法学研究 (Chinese Journal of Law) 124, p. 125, footnote 7.

[6] Chen Dalong (陈达隆), 怀念陈体强先生 (*In Memory of Mr. Chen Ti-Chiang*) (a privately printed memorial essay-photo book 2024), pp. 11–12. Chen Dalong is the son of Chen Ti-Chiang.

[7] They refer to the Treaty between the United States and the Republic of China for the Relinquishment of Extraterritorial Rights in China and the Regulation of Related Matters (中华民国和美国关于取消美国在华治外法权及处理有关问题之条约) and the Treaty between the United Kingdom and the Republic of China for the Relinquishment of Extraterritorial Rights in China and the Regulation of Related Matters (中华民国和英国关于取消英国在华治外法权及处理有关问题之条约). Both were signed on the same day, 11 January 1943, but separately in Washington and Chongqing.

him realize China's weak position in the world and motivated him to study public international law abroad in order to better serve the nation and help secure greater rights and benefits, and project a stronger influence in international affairs, for China.[8]

32.1.2 Studying International Law at Oxford

In August 1944 Chen sat for the Ministry of Education's Boxer Indemnity Scholarship Examination for Studies in Britain (庚款留英考试) and was accepted to undertake doctoral studies in international law in the United Kingdom. He was enthusiastic about this opportunity, as his research at NSAU and experience in the Foreign Affairs Ministry had equipped him well for successful study of public international law in the UK.

However, Chen's three-year doctoral study journey did not go as smoothly as he hoped it would. To his disappointment, when he arrived in the UK in October 1945 with high expectations to study at the University of Cambridge under the supervision of the renowned international law jurist Professor H. Lauterpacht, he was informed that the British Council had already assigned him to study in the University of Oxford.[9] After he failed to persuade the British Council to change his assignment, he settled to study in Oxford under the supervision of Professor J. L. Brierly, also a renowned international law jurist. Until recently we knew very little about his student life in Oxford except that his research focused on the issue of recognition in international law.[10]

The final stage of his research also suffered a significant setback in 1947 when Hersch Lauterpacht published his book *Recognition in International Law*.[11] That was devastating for Chen since Chen's research covered the same subject and overlapped with P Lauterpacht's new which was quickly hailed as a 'masterly treatise'[12] and 'a valuable addition to the vast literature on recognition'. Lauterpacht's approach to the subject was 'distinguished by a strictly legal approach to the subject,

[8] See Chen Dalong (陈达隆), 怀念陈体强先生 (*In Memory of Mr. Chen Ti-Chiang*) (a privately printed memorial essay-photo book 2024), pp. 13–14.

[9] He Bingdi (何炳棣), 读史阅世六十年 (*Sixty Years of Reading History and Observing the World*) [中华书局 (Zhonghua Book Company) 2014], p. 169.

[10] In 2014, Professor Xie Zeping (谢喆平) of Tsinghua University contacted Oxford University Lincoln College in a hope to find out more information about Chen's student life in Oxford. Unfortunately, according to the email in response from Lincoln, 'there is nothing very much in our files apart from his matriculation details, and in the University, just details of his course'. 'Records from the period are very patchy, and that continued until the early 1950s.' See Susan Harrison's email to Professor Xie on 4 July 2014. See, more recently, Chen Lim 'Tracing Chinese Scholar Chen Tiqiang's Pursuit of International Law Education and His Major Contribution to the Doctrine of Recognition', Asian Journal of International Law, 10(1) (2020) pp. 68–93.

[11] H. Lauterpacht, *Recognition in International Law* (CUP 1947).

[12] Yuen-li Liang, 'Book Review' (1947) 14 Brook. L. Rev. 141, p. 143.

close logical reasoning and constant reliance upon the practice of Great Britain and the United States for the purpose of illustrating and supporting the author's views.'[13]

Unfortunately, this was exactly the same approach and method used by Chen in his own Ph.D, research. For a while, Chen even thought of giving up and starting a new research subject. But after the initial fluster and hesitation, he decided to face the challenge. As pointed out by himself, 'the appearance of Professor Lauterpacht's *Recognition in International Law* at the final stage of this work, while setting the author the problem of the extent to which it had become redundant because of duplication, bears testimony, however, to the importance of the problem, and the possible divergence of points of view that justifies the completion of the work.'[14]

Chen's efforts paid off. Within three years, he not only completed his doctoral studies and earned his D.Phil in Law from the University of Oxford in July 1948, but also completed a remarkable research work on the international law of recognition.

Upon his graduation, Chen received a number of job offers, including, notably, invitations from Professor Chen Daisun, Dean of Tsinghua University Law School and Yu Nengmo, Chief of Personnel of the Foreign Affairs Ministry.[15] Without hesitation, he accepted Tsinghua's invitation, as his original aspiration to teach at his alma mater had remained unchanged over time. He refused to work for the Nationalist Government because he consider it corrupt based on his earlier work experience in Chongqing. Upon receiving Tsinghua's job offer he wasted no time and soon embarked on the road back home, without even arranging for the publication of his dissertation. In September 1948, he returned to China and joined Tsinghua University Law School formally as an associate professor of international law, at the height of China's Civil War.

In the middle of December 1948, the People's Liberation Army besieged the city of Beijing and controlled the Tsinghua University campus that was located outside the old city wall. At that critical moment, the Ministry of Education of the Nationalist Government urged faculties in Beijing to escape to the south of China, which was then still under the control of the Nationalist government, and arranged air transportation for them. However, Chen chose to stay. He later recalled that in the night before he left the besieged city area of Beijing for Tsinghua University campus, Professor of Mathematics Yang Wuzhi (杨武之, original name Yang Ko-Chuen 杨克纯, father of Nobel Laureate Chen-Ning Franklin Yang 杨振宁) and Professor of History Liu Chonghong (刘崇鋐) had an all-night conversation with

[13] 'Book Reviews' (1948) 10 Cambridge L.J. 125, pp. 126–127.

[14] Chen Ti-Chiang, *The International Law of Recognition* (Stevens & Sons 1951), p. xiii (Preface).

[15] See Yang Yun (杨赟), '中国当代国际法学家陈体强：生平与故事' ('Chen Ti-Chiang, Chinese Contemporary Jurist of International Law: Life and Stories') (2016) 1 法律与外交 (Law and Diplomacy) 301, p. 305.

him, trying to persuade him to head south together with them. They failed. After they gave up and left, Chen took a bike, exited the Chaoyang Gate of the city, and rushed under gunfire towards the liberated Tsinghua Campus.[16]

32.1.3 Teaching and Research in the New China

Chen's academic career at Tsinghua and personal life in Beijing in the early years (1948°1956) were fulfilling, affluent and happy. He married Fan Ying, a member of the English Faculty at Beijing Foreign Languages Institute, in September 1950. As a well-educated young scholar, his talent did not go unnoticed. In 1949, he became a member of two institutions: the New Chinese Society of Political Science (新政治学研究会, founded on 18 September 1949) and the Chinese People's Institute of Foreign Affairs (CPIFA, 外交学会, founded on 15 December 1949). In 1950, he was appointed associate director of both the Translation Committee and the Research Department of the CPIFA. For a time he participated weekly in a study group discussing international law issues, led by Ke Bonian (柯柏年), Director of the Department of North American and Oceanian Affairs (美大司), Foreign Affairs Ministry. He started to publish a series of articles concerning China's diplomatic practice and international law issues.

The year 1951 marked a significant milestone in his early years in Beijing, as two important events took place. The first was that the famous British law publisher Stevens & Sons published his PhD dissertation, thanks to valuable editing assistance by Mr L. C. Green,[17] lecturer in international law and relations at University College, London. The other was that at the age of 33, he was appointed as a full professor at Tsinghua University. The two events represented a clear recognition of his academic achievement in international law, both at home and abroad.[18]

The subsequent years were naturally the icing on the cake. Since 1951, he had participated as a member of the Chinese delegation in a number of international conferences, such as the 1956 Session of International Law Association in Yugoslavia. In 1952, due to the National College Department Reorganization, he left Tsinghua University and was appointed as Deputy Secretary-General of the CPIFA. In 1956 he was formally transferred to the China Institute of International

[16] See Chen Dalong (陈达隆), 怀念陈体强先生 (*In Memory of Mr. Chen Ti-Chiang*) (a privately printed memorial essay-photo book 2024), p. 20.

[17] As Mr Green pointed out in Editor's Note, '[a]fter completing the manuscript of this work, Dr. Chen returned to China. It was therefore impossible for him to see it through the Press and bring it up to date by including those cases and incidents which had arisen between the date of writing and the setting of the type.' '[S]ince I was unable to discuss my suggestions with Dr. Chen, wherever I have made any material additions, such as the discussion concerning the recognition of Israel or Korea, I have indicated this fact by the use of square brackets'. See Chen Ti-Chiang, *The International Law of Recognition*, Stevens & Sons, 1951, p. xv.

[18] See Chen Dalong (陈达隆), 怀念陈体强先生 (*In Memory of Mr. Chen Ti-Chiang*) (A privately printed memorial essay-photo book 2024), p. 21.

Studies (CIIS, 中国国际问题研究所) under the Foreign Affairs Ministry. He was both a research fellow at the CIIS and a special member of the Treaty Committee of the Foreign Affairs Ministry. In the meantime, he began to take up more social responsibilities and was appointed Deputy Head of the Legal Affairs Group (法制组副组长) of the People's Political Consultative Conference and Deputy Secretary-General of the Chinese Society of Political Science and Law (中国政治法律学会).[19]

Chen's future looked bright before fate took a turn. In the two decades following the early years of the 1950s, his life and career suffered a devastating blow. In the summer of 1957, the Anti-Rightist Movement started in China. Soon he was branded as a 'rightist' because of some critical remarks he had made on different occasions. In 1958, he was assigned to the Foreign Affairs College. His professional title was downgraded to assistant researcher and all other titles and positions were removed. The unwarranted charges and deprivations against him took a heavy toll both physically and mentally. He was only 40 years old but began to suffer from heart disease and diabetes. He also became quiet in character. Moreover, his research on international law went nowhere as he opposed the prevailing Soviet approaches to international law in China at that time. The sole comfort in this period was perhaps the publication in December 1957 of the translated work '海上国际法' (*International Law of the Sea*, written by Alexander Pearce Higgins and Constantine John Colombos). He translated the book in collaboration with Professor Wang Tieya, using the pseudonym Wang Qiangsheng (王强生).[20] This marked the beginning of their long-time academic cooperation in international law.

The year 1960 brought him new hope for international law scholarship and practice because the Central Communist Party leadership decided to enhance international studies. In 1964, the Foreign Affairs Ministry established the Institute of International Law (IIL, 国际法研究所). He and a group of international law scholars were assigned to IIL, including the late Judges Li Haopei (ICTY, 1993–1997) and Shi Jiuyong (ICJ, 1994–2010). He served as head of the library and travelled all over China to search for and collect international law books scattered around the country. He introduced the *Recueil Des Cours* to China.[21] Nevertheless, still under the yoke of political mistreatment, his role was limited, and he published only one article in 1964.[22]

19 Ibid, pp. 21–22.

20 A. P. Higgins and C. J. Colombos (eds), 王强生 (Wang Qiangsheng) (tr), 海上国际法 (*International Law of the Sea*) (Law Publishing House 1957).

21 See Yang Yun (杨赟), '中国当代国际法学家陈体强：生平与故事' ('Chen Ti-Chiang, Chinese Contemporary Jurist of International Law: Life and Stories') (2016) 1法律与外交 (Law and Diplomacy) 301, p. 307.

22 Chen Ti-Chiang, 国际法论文集 (*A Treatise on International Law*) [法律出版社 (Law Publishing House) 1985], pp. 164–173.

Before long the country was hit hard again by an even more devastating political storm—that is, the Cultural Revolution (1966–1976), which put China's international law studies on hold once more. In 1969, Chen was transferred to the May Seventh Cadre School[23] of Foreign Affairs Ministry established in You County, Hunan Province. While doing labour work like a farmer, his dream of international law study was not extinguished. In 1971, he found the courage to collaborate with Professor Wang Tieya again to translate *Oppenheim's International Law* (8th edn) into Chinese. Using the pseudonyms of Shi Di (石蒂) and Chen Jian (陈健), the Commercial Press published the first volume of 奥本海国际法 (*Oppenheim's International Law* (8th edn)) one year later in December 1972[24] and the second volume in August 1973.[25] It was eight years later, in July 1981, that the Commercial Press finally republished the translated work using the collaborators' real names.[26]

In 1973, Chen returned to Beijing to work in the China Institute of International Studies as a researcher. In 1976, the Cultural Revolution formally came to an end. In late 1978, China initiated its reform and opening-up policy. In January 1979, his 'rightist' political label was formally removed. From 1957 to 1978, he and his family suffered greatly during years of China's political turmoil. He lost more than two decades of his best and most productive years. He was then 62 years old.

When the political mistreatment and pressure finally lifted, Professor Chen threw himself back into international law work with renewed energy and full vigour. In 1979, he resumed teaching in the Foreign Affairs College as a professor of international law and at Peking University as an adjunct professor. He was appointed as legal adviser in the Foreign Affairs Ministry. At the end of 1979, he served as Legal Adviser to the Chinese Delegation at the 34th Session of the United Nations General Assembly.[27]

[23] Established during the Cultural Revolution, these schools (reportedly there were more than 100 all over China) aimed to 're-educate' intellectuals, government officials, and professionals by relocating them to rural areas for manual labour (e.g., farming, construction) and ideological reform. Hundreds of thousands of people were transferred to them. On 17 February 1979, the State Council issued the Notice on Issues Related to the Discontinuation of May Seventh Cadre Schools (关于停办'五七'干校有关问题的通知) and formally ended the schools for ideological re-education through manual labour. The practice has been criticized for suppressing intellectual freedom, wasting human capital and inflicting physical and psychological harm.

[24] 劳特帕特修订 (H. Lauterpacht) (ed), 石蒂、陈健译 (Shi Di and Chen Jian) (trs), 奥本海国际法 (上卷) (*Oppenhaim's International Law*, vol 1) [第八版 (8th edn), 商务印书馆 (The Commercial Press) 1972].

[25] 劳特帕特修订 (H. Lauterpacht) (ed), 石蒂、陈健译 (Shi Di and Chen Jian) (trs), 奥本海国际法 (下卷) (*Oppenhaim's International Law*, vol 2) [第八版 (8th edn), 商务印书馆 (The Commercial Press) 1973].

[26] 劳特帕特修订(H. Lauterpacht) (ed), 王铁崖、陈体强译 (Wang Tieya and Chen Ti-chiang) (trs), 奥本海国际法 (上、下卷) (*Oppenhaim's International Law*, 2 vols) [第八版 (8th edn), 商务印书馆 (The Commercial Press) 1981].

[27] See, for example, his speech at the Sixth Committee of the General Assembly on 23 November 1979, A/C.6/34/SR.50, General Assembly official records, 34th session: 6th Committee, 50th meeting, Friday, 23 November 1979, New York, pp. 3–5.

The influence of Professor Chen's academic work was felt both in China and abroad. In 1981, he took an academic trip to North America and Europe. He was a visiting professor at Harvard University and the University of Geneva and lectured at Dalhousie University and the University of London. In the meantime, he launched together with Professor Wang Tieya the *Chinese Yearbook of International Law* and served as Co-Editors in Chief. The first volume of the yearbook was published in November 1982.[28] They also collaborated as Co-Editors-in-Chief, responsible for the public international law entry in the *Encyclopedia of China: Jurisprudence*, published in September 1984.[29]

In recognition of his professional achievements, Chen was elected as a member of the National Committee of the Chinese People's Political Consultative Conference in 1983. He also held professional honours, including Vice President of the Chinese Society of International Law and Associate Member of the Institute of International Law (Institut De Droit International), being elected in August 1983. He was the initial ICJ judge nominee from the People's Republic of China.[30] In June 1985 he became the first international law scholar in the New China to publish his own international law treatise, a rare honour at the time.[31]

Professor Chen died from heart disease in Beijing on 13 October 1983. It was said that on the day he died, he did some final editing work for the *Encyclopedia of China: Jurisprudence* from his hospital bed.[32] It was a huge loss for the international law community at home and abroad as he died at the age of just 66.

32.2 The Legacy of Professor Chen

Professor Chen's legacy is primarily in the areas of public international law scholarship and practice. Although political turbulence and personal health problems caused him immense harm and greatly limited his academic development for more than two decades, he remains and is indeed widely regarded as a renowned Chinese international law scholar with a global reputation. He was also a international law practitioner for his beloved country.

[28] 中国国际法年刊 (1982) (*Chinese Yearbook of International Law 1982*) [中国对外翻译出版公司 (China Translation Corporation) 1982].

[29] 中国大百科全书: 法学 (*Encyclopedia of China: Jurisprudence*) [法律出版社 (Law Publishing House) 1984].

[30] Xie Zheping (谢喆平), 浮云远志 (*Floating Clouds and Lofty Aspirations*) [商务印书馆 (The Commercial Press) 2014], p. 201.

[31] Deng Fang (邓方), '喜读陈体强遗著"国际法论文集"' ('Appreciating the Posthumous Work of Chen Ti-Chiang: *A Treatise on International Law*') (1986) 1 中国法学 (China Legal Science) 59, p. 59

[32] See Yang Yun (杨赟), '中国当代国际法学家陈体强：生平与故事' ('Chen Ti-Chiang, Chinese Contemporary Jurist of International Law: Life and Stories') (2016) 1 法律与外交 (Law and Diplomacy) 301, p. 310.

32.2.1 A Chinese Scholar with an International Reputation

Over the years, in addition to his early publications, Professor Chen published the following major works on international law:

1. Chen Ti-Chiang, *The International Law of Recognition* (Stevens & Sons 1951)
2. A. P. Higgins and C. J. Colombos (eds), Wang Qiangsheng, (tr), 海上国际法 (*International Law of the Sea*) (Law Publishing House 1957)
3. H. Lauterpacht (ed), Wang Tieya and Chen Ti-Chiang (trs), 奥本海国际法 (*Oppenheim's International Law*), 2 vols (8th edn, The Commercial Press 1981)
4. Chen Ti-Chiang, 国际法论文集 (*A Treatise on International Law*) (Law Publishing House 1985)

It was his PhD dissertation, 'The International Law of Recognition', which earned him an international reputation equal to that of Professor Lauterpacht's *Recognition in International Law*. The two books on the same subject were published four years apart, one by one of the most distinguished international law jurists at the time and the other by a PhD student from China, but both were regarded as significant contributions to knowledge in the field. The success of Chen's book was not an academic spectacle out of nowhere. As Oxford Professor Emeritus of International Law J. L. Brierly, Chen's supervisor, pointed out in his foreword to the book, 'Dr. Chen's book will be useful for the full and scholarly examination which he has made of the abundant materials to be found in the practice of States, in judicial decisions, and in the literature of the subject'.[33] Professor Brierly's comment was largely echoed by reviewers. K. Lipstein, for example, said in the last sentence of his review that '[n]ot the least valuable part of the book is the very extensive array of case-references and references to other authorities. This makes it one of the best books of the first approach to any question of recognition.'[34]

The two books are clearly distinguishable as Professor Lauterpacht argued for the constitutive theory while Professor Chen favoured the declaratory theory. According to Lipstein, the first part of Chen's book 'seems to be the most deeply considered part of the whole work and is an excellent analysis of the rival doctrines of recognition—the constitutive and the declaratory—and a vigorous defence of the second, which is maintained through the rest of the book.'[35] When Professor

[33] See Chen Ti-Chiang, *The International Law of Recognition* (Stevens & Sons 1951), Foreword, p. xi.

[34] K. Lipstein, 'Book Reviews' (1952) 1 Int'l & Comp. L. Q. 584, p. 592. Josef L. Kunz wrote in the beginning of his review that '[a]ll the wealth of literature as well as the rich practice of States and jurisprudence of courts concerning the law of recognition has been used by the author in the preparation of this valuable contribution to the material on the subject'. See Kunz, 'Book Review' (1952) 65 Harvard Law Review 713, p. 713.

[35] Lipstein (n 34), pp. 591–592.

James Crawford discusses the declaratory theory, he quotes mainly Chen's book.[36] In his introduction to the 2013 paperback edition of Professor Lauterpacht's book *Recognition in International Law*, Crawford writes that 'the prevailing modern view is that recognition is a substantially declaratory phenomenon' promoted by Chen's book that 'sets forth an influential declaratory view' and reveals 'certain logical defects within Lauterpacht's view of recognition'. Crawford then quotes the following long passage from Chen's book:

> One question naturally suggests itself: if recognition—in the constitutive sense—is a legal duty, to whom is that duty owed? It cannot be to the new State, since it has not yet begun to exist. To the international community as a whole? The international community cannot be deemed to be *entitled* to the right of having a new member recognized unless each of its members is *entitled to claim* from the recalcitrant State the performance of the duty of recognition. That claim cannot be made unless it can be established, in point of fact and according to the notion prevailing in that society, the conditions of statehood are present. But if this fact can be established, the recognition by any particular State would become tautologous. For, by the very establishment of that fact, the possession of personality by the State would have also been established, and there would consequently be no longer any need for creative recognition by any particular State. In other words, the international community can only claim the duty of recognition of a new State from a member State when in the mind of the international community, the new State-person is already in existence.'[37]

Such academic aptitude was also recognized by Professor Brierly, in saying that between the constitutive and the declaratory, Chen had 'adduced powerful arguments to prove that the balance of authority in State practice and in the jurisprudence of courts is strongly in favor of the latter'.[38] Professor Brierly also agreed with Professor Chen by quoting that 'the question of international recognition is but a reflection of the fundamental cleavage between those who regard the State as the ultimate source of international rights and duties and those who regard it as being under a system of Law which determines its rights and duties under that law'.[39]

It should be noted that because Professor Chen chose to work and teach in the New China, one of the reviewers brought up the issue of objectivity and impartiality, as in 1951 more than half the world maintained that 'the Chinese Nationalist Government is the de jure Government of China'.[40] Sir Eric Beckett wrote that

[36] J. Crawford, *The Creation of States in International Law* (2nd edn, OUP 2006), p. 22, footnote 95.

[37] J. Crawford, 'Recognition in International Law: Introduction to the Paperback Edition 2013', in H. Lauterpacht, *Recognition in International Law* (Cambridge University Press 2013), pp. xlvi–xlvii.

[38] See Chen Ti-Chiang, *The International Law of Recognition* (Stevens & Sons 1951), Foreword, p. xi.

[39] Ibid.

[40] By the end of 1951, only 20 states recognized the PRC government. Among them were 11 'socialist countries', such as the USSR, and 9 non-socialist countries, such as India and Sweden.

'[o]ne might be inclined to expect that an author who was expecting to go to the University of Peking might take up an extreme or biased position on the question of recognition of governments, but this is not so. In fact, in the whole book, on this topic as well as others the author is remarkably objective and impartial.'[41]

Today, classic international law textbooks have consistently listed both books as key references on the subject.[42] Chen was also quoted widely by major literature on the subject.[43] He was no doubt one of the most outstanding Chinese students studying social sciences abroad in his time. Historian He Bingdi asserted that '[r]egarding the doctoral dissertations completed by Chinese scholars at prestigious Western universities in the 20th century, Chen's dissertation undeniably occupies a pinnacle position. To the best of my knowledge, only two doctoral dissertations by Chinese scholars in the 20th century were immediately recognized as international classics upon publication.' One of these is Hsiao Kung-chuan (萧公权)'s Cornell dissertation *Political Pluralism: A Study in Contemporary Political Theory*, published in London in 1927. The other is Chen's Oxford dissertation *The International Law of Recognition*.[44] Naturally, Chen's research will continue to serve as an important source of knowledge and aspiration for international law scholars, Chinese and non-Chinese.

32.2.2 A Patriotic International Law Practitioner in the New China

Professor Chen is not merely an international law scholar, but alsoa patriotic international law practitioner forChina.. As discussed earlier, his life was closely linked with China's foreign affairs. Born into a diplomatic family, he ended up teaching at Foreign Affairs College and serving as legal adviser to the Foreign Affairs Ministry.

In addition to his almost lifelong association with the Foreign Affairs Ministry, his important contribution to China's diplomatic practice is best reflected in the posthumous publication of the collection of his forty international law essays in

[41] E., 'Reviews of Books' (1951) 28 Brit. Y. B. Int'l L. 415, p. 423. According to Professor Crawford, 'E' was a pseudonym used by Sir Eric Beckett. See J. Crawford, 'Recognition in International Law: Introduction to the Paperback Edition 2013', in H. Lauterpacht, *Recognition in International Law* (CUP 2013), p. xlvi, footnote 122.

[42] See, for example, R. Jennings and A. Watts (eds), *Oppenheim's International Law*, vol 1 Peace (9th edn, Longman 1992), p. 126; J. Crawford, *Brownlie's Principles of Public International Law* (9th edn, OUP 2019), p. 134, footnote 1; and M. N. Shaw, *International Law* (9th edn, CUP 2021), p. 377, footnote 1.

[43] See, for example, M. J. Peterson, *Recognition of Governments: Legal Doctrine and State Practice, 1815–1995*, (Macmillan 1997), numerous footnotes; S. Talmon, *Recognition of Governments in International Law* (OUP 1998), footnotes 8 and 35 in Part I Meanings of Recognition of Governments in International Law; J. Crawford, *The Creation of States in International Law* (2nd edn, OUP 2006), footnotes 6, 10, 77, 91, 95, 98, and 109 in Chapter 1 Statehood and Recognition.

[44] He Bingdi (何炳棣), 读史阅世六十年 (*Sixty Years of Reading History and Observing the World*) [中华书局 (Zhonghua Book Company) 2014], pp. 177–178.

1985. The essays were selected from his writings over thirty-three years from 1950 to 1983 and covered a wide range of bilateral and multilateral issues faced by the New China at the time. They may be divided into the following groups. The first group discusses various bilateral issues. For example:

(1) Korea War issues such as the legal and moral basis of the Chinese People's Volunteer Army (1950), the US gas warfare (1951), and the US claim on 'non-forced repatriation' (1952);
(2) boundary issues such as the China–Vietnam Beibu Gulf Delimitation (1980), and legal aspects in the China–India border issue (1982);
(3) miscellaneous issues such as the new Sino–British treaty (1950), distorted history in Japan's textbook revision (1982), and the need for the South Korean authorities to severely punish hijackers (1983).

The second group discusses UN-related issues and international law issues in general. Essays concerning the UN-related issues include universality of the UN membership (1955); upholding the UN Charter (1955); the dangerous road of the UN (1956); and why we should define aggression (1953). Essays discussing international law issues include international law prohibiting the use of nuclear weapons (1955); Afro-Asian people's stance against racism (1955); spy balloons (1956); and sovereign immunity of state and international law (1983).

Last but not least important are the nine essays that focus on the Taiwan question. They discuss the following positions: the UN must sanction the crime of US invasion of Chinese territory Taiwan (1954); the UN has no right to interfere with the liberation of Taiwan by the Chinese people (1955); sovereignty over Taiwan belongs to China (1955); the so-called Taiwan legal status question (1955); US arms sales to Taiwan (1982); the illegal occupation of Asian Development Bank membership by the Taiwanese authority (1983); and several legal issues in China–US relations (1983).

A review of these essays reveals vividly how a patriotic international law practitioner uses his expertise to clarify, elaborate, and defend China's positions in legal battles with other nations. Just as Professor Chen pointed out himself in his preface: '[s]ince the founding of the People's Republic of China, her interactions with other nations have been multifaceted—friendly and unfriendly, peaceful and non-peaceful—all of which may implicate questions of international law … As scholars of international law, it falls upon us to elucidate the norms of international law and on the basis of which assess the legal merits of specific events.'[45]

Today, many of the analyses and arguments made by Professor Chen about half a century ago in these essays are still relevant and have important practical

[45] See Chen Ti-Chiang, 国际法论文集 (*A Treatise on International Law*) [法律出版社 (Law Publishing House) 1985], author's preface, p. 3.

significance, especially the essays about the Taiwan question and the Sino–Indian border disputes. As the Taiwan question is still the most important and dangerous issue China faces today, Professor Chen's writings remain valuable. In the 1950s, he argued that the sovereignty over Taiwan belongs to China;[46] that there was no such thing as the so-called Taiwan's legal status question; that Taiwan, a Chinese territory stolen by Japan, should be restored to China according to the Cairo Declaration and the Potsdam Proclamation; and that the Treaty of Peace with Japan does not apply to China.[47] He asserted that to safeguard state sovereignty, China has the right to and must liberate Taiwan.[48] In the early 1980s he warned against US arms sales to Taiwan, deeming it an interference with China's internal affairs.[49] He also argued that the US may not invoke the Taiwan Relations Act as justification for its failure to perform its treaty obligations[50] and that the Taiwanese authority should not be admitted to international intergovernmental organizations.[51]

With his high academic standards and an array of footnotes, Professor Chen's essay on legal aspects of the Sino–Indian border issue was comprehensive in straightening out complicated legal issues lucidly. He proved with compelling arguments that there was no boundary treaty existing between China and India. The 'boundary treaties' claimed by India were neither binding nor concerning boundary. Therefore, China refused to recognize the illegal McMahon Line, admitting only a traditional customary boundary line. However, the two sides disagree on where this line lies. Professor Chen eventually suggested that the two parties settle their boundary disputes through peaceful negotiations.[52] This is exactly China's consistent position with India or other neighbouring states in settling boundary disputes.

It is indeed a great pity that for more than two decades, from 1957 to 1978, Professor Chen published just one article—in 1964[53]—and that after China adopted its reform and opening-up policy, poor health prevented him from becoming an ICJ judge. Otherwise, we would all benefit more from his wisdom and professional expertise in international law. In his preface to the treatise, written in his hospital bed on 30 September 1983, Professor Chen wrote with sorrow, '[a]fter 1957, constrained by the political climate, I laid down my pen and withdrew into obscurity, watching my prime years slip away with no path to serve the nation'.[54] Despite his personal misfortune, Professor Chen had fulfilled the unwavering

[46] Ibid, pp. 100–105.
[47] Ibid, pp. 125–132.
[48] Ibid, pp. 97–99.
[49] Ibid, pp. 254–258.
[50] Ibid, pp. 276-292.
[51] Ibid, pp. 263–265.
[52] Ibid, pp. 196–253.
[53] Ibid, pp. 164–173.
[54] Ibid, p. 3.

patriotic devotion that drove him to study international law abroad in order to secure greater rights and benefits for China on the global stage and to return to China at the height of the Civil War in order to serve his country. His essays are the best evidence, and an enduring monument, of his genuine patriotism and outstanding achievement in international law practice.

33

Chinese Women in the Histories of International Law

Forgotten Names and Unfamiliar Paths

Ken Yang

33.1 Introduction

This chapter focuses on twentieth-century Chinese women and their place in the histories of international law. It is the first attempt at their comprehensive mapping, drawing on new archival sources and oral histories.[1] Aside from bridging substantive gaps in historical knowledge in this area, this study seeks to highlight the scattered social spaces and enabling forces—against an overall disabling environment—that supported a small number of Chinese women in obtaining the competence we now associate with international law.

Like women elsewhere, Chinese women were, for most of the twentieth century, excluded from the international legal profession. This exclusion was particularly evident during the first half of the twentieth century, a period that mostly fell within the Republican era (1912–1949). One expedient way to illuminate this multi-layered exclusion is to return to the small league of 'worldly gentlemen'.[2]

[1] I wish to extend my sincere thanks to family members and students of some of the Republican-period figures, as well as trailblazing women professors educated during the PRC period, for agreeing to be interviewed. In no particular order: Professor Zheng Bijun of Peking University (former student of Chen Fangzhi); Professor Hao Bin of Peking University (former colleague of Chen Fangzhi); Mr Li Yuguo (son-in-law of Ma Jun); Professor Liang Shuying of China University of Political Science and Law; Professor Ling Yan of China University of Political Science and Law; Professor Bai Guimei of Peking University; and Professor Li Hongyun of Peking University.

[2] I coined the term 'worldly gentlemen' for two specific purposes. First, to allude to the fact that these early twentieth-century Chinese intellectuals still embodied, to some degree, the Confucian model of intellectual life. Under such tradition, the educated elites were expected to perform ethical leadership and to embrace public service in government, that is, to act as the scholar-official (*shi dafu*). Second, to draw parallels between international law's professionalisation process in Western countries and that in early twentieth-century China, which similarly involved educated elites asserting their scientific authority vis-à-vis the society and state. Many Western figures behind the professionalization process also share these 'gentlemanly' characteristics. On the 'Men of 1873' and their 'Victorian conscience', see Martti Koskenniemi, The Gentle Civilizer of Nations: The Rise and Fall of International Law, 1870–1960 (New York: Cambridge University Press, 2001), Chapter 1. See also Henri de Waele, 'A New League of Extraordinary Gentlemen? The Professionalization of International Law Scholarship in the Netherlands, 1919–1940', European Journal of International Law (2020) vol. 31, no. 3. See also in this volume Chapter 29 on Wang Tieya, by the same author.

Ken Yang, *Chinese Women in the Histories of International Law* In: *Histories of International Law in China*.
Edited by: Ignacio de la Rasilla, Jiangyu Wang, and Congyan Cai, Oxford University Press. © Ken Yang 2026.
DOI: 10.1093/oso/9780198888345.003.0033

Since the 1980s, they have come to be perceived as the archetype of Chinese international lawyers, whose stories and treatises were central to the construction of contemporary Chinese disciplinary canons and professional identity. The shared patterns in their personal and professional trajectories could help explain why contemporary women 'failed' to join their ranks and were forgotten.

These men were primarily of Han ethnicity, from affluent or well-to-do families, born and/or raised in treaty ports. Many of them were students at missionary schools, where they were exposed to modern learning and foreign language training.[3] In their early adulthood, they studied law and/or international law at prestigious Western universities, including what Koskenniemi called 'academic centres that the culture of international law has grown around'.[4] Their costly odysseys were often funded by prestigious public scholarship programmes that were highly sought after. Having returned from the West, these worldly gentlemen pursued careers as politicians, diplomats, professors, and public intellectuals, positions that were connected to the halls of power. For a fortunate few, their prominence within the public sphere and government circles led to their nomination to authoritative positions at international courts and tribunals and international organizations, and/or enabled them to take part in 'Grotian Moments' (e.g., the San Francisco Conference, the Tokyo Trials) as China's representatives. This last association secured their rightful place within international legal historiography, with some enshrined in the pantheon of renowned publicists. Domestically, their journeys and achievements are persistently lionized by Chinese institutions with which they were once affiliated. They were remembered partly because of their lasting achievements in scholarship, pedagogy, and institution-building, and partly because of their institutions' needs in constructing intellectual lineage and boosting their standings. Such is the politics of disciplinary memory.

The journeys outlined above also encapsulate the socio-historical process now conceptualized as the professionalization of international law. In its essence, professionalization is a process of inclusion and exclusion: one undergoes specialized training to meet the established criteria of a closed community with an authoritative claim over a specific area of social concern. The absence of Chinese women among the ranks of these worldly gentlemen could then be attributed to barriers

[3] The special role assumed by Christian schools and colleges in educating Chinese women accounts for a key focus of this study. However, this emphasis by no means suggests that these institutions exclusively benefited women. One 1922 report suggested that the boy–girl ratio at missionary secondary schools (high schools) was about 5 to 1 (12,644 boys to 2,569 girls). In Christian colleges, the ratio went up to 10 to 1. The Committee of Reference and Counsel of the Foreign Missions Conference of North America, Christian Education in China (1922), 259. Indeed, most, if not all, of the male figures surveyed in the biographical chapters studied at missionary schools. However, as men, it was more plausible for them to move on to government universities that possessed more resources and higher prestige. Hence, their successful careers were often not associated with missionary institutions—at least not in a near-exclusive manner, as in the case of Chinese women.

[4] Martti Koskenniemi, Foreword, in Anthea Roberts, Is International Law International? (Oxford: Oxford University Press, 2017), xiii.

rooted in patriarchy that had obstructed women at nearly every step. Entrenched gender norms delayed women's entry into government universities, which did not occur until the 1920s. According to one contemporary estimate, by 1931, women comprised only 8.5 per cent of all university students.[5] Within universities, women were chronically channelled into a narrow set of academic fields deemed compatible with femininity, including humanities, pedagogy, medicine, and home economics. Nor were the few institutions that had produced the nation's best international lawyers (namely, a handful of well-funded political science departments) enthusiastic about recruiting female students.[6] Chinese international lawyers were also partly responsible, to say the least,[7] for they too reproduced gender bias already present in Western societies.[8]

Women college graduates also faced slim career opportunities. Most found work in primary and secondary education, clerical work, and social service. Highly competitive scholarship programmes also favoured male over female applicants, forcing female students aspiring to pursue graduate studies overseas to either resort to self-financing or seek alternative sources. The lack of more esteemed professional careers and educational pedigree (a highly relevant factor considering China's culture of credentialism that obsesses over diplomas from elite Western universities) impeded women from excelling in the public sphere. Because women

[5] By comparison, female high school students accounted for 15% of the total student body nationwide. Cheng Zhefan, Zhongguo nüzi jiaoyu shi [History of Modern Women's Education in China] (Shanghai: Zhonghua Book Company, 1936), 168, 178–179.

[6] See the anecdote in the mini-portrait of Chen Fangzhi, especially her experience with her uncle Xu Shuxi, head of the Department of Political Science at Yenching University.

[7] Prominent international lawyer Chen Tiqiang, for instance, opted to naturalize women's absence from foreign service. In his 1944 seminal treatise on diplomatic service management in modern China, 'sex' ('maleness', to be exact) was listed as one of the eight essential criteria for foreign service personnel selection. To justify this criterion, Chen selectively highlighted Western objections against the inclusion of women while omitting the opinions in favour mentioned in the same article he cited, thus emphasizingthat 'the sensitive, attractive type of women who alone may be expected to succeed in passing the oral examinations, often find the atmosphere and *esprit de corps* of this man-dominated service uncongenial so that they tire of prolonging their service and retire.' Chen Tiqiang, Zhongguo waijiao xingzheng [The Administration of Chinese Diplomacy] (Chongqing: The Commercial Press, 1943), 257, quoting Ellery C. Stowell, 'The Appointment of Assistant Secretary of State G. Howland Shaw and Our Foreign Service', The American Journal of International Law (1941) vol. 35, no. 2, 340–341.

[8] In the United States, a 1911 survey conducted by the Carnegie Endowment for International Peace revealed a significant gap between male and female attendance in university courses where international law was taught, with male students outnumbering female students 12 to 1. Report on the Teaching of International Law, Vol. 394, 2, CEIP Records, Columbia University Rare Books & Manuscripts Library. Historian Benjamin Allen Coates attributed the gender disparity within the American international law field during the early twentieth century to its preoccupation with the field's 'masculine' nature. Benjamin Allen Coates, Legalist Empire: International Law and American Foreign Relations in the Early Twentieth Century (Oxford: Oxford University Press, 2016), 61–66. Also see Benjamin Allen Coates, 'Transatlantic Advocates: American International Law and U.S. Foreign Relations, 1898–1919' (PhD thesis, Columbia University, 2010). On associating rationality and emotionality respectively with masculinity and femininity in the early twentieth-century US, see Linda K. Schott, Reconstructing Women's Thoughts: The Women's International League for Peace and Freedom before World War II (Stanford, CA: Stanford University Press, 2022), 168–170.

were rarely empowered and represented domestically, they were far less likely to represent China internationally, to say nothing of representing China on international legal matters. Understandably, within the small group of Republican-era female public figures, only a handful had achieved such status through professional achievements alone. For most established women figures of Republican China, marriage and/or patrimony often played a larger role in their prominence. Accordingly, extremely few women were considered members of the foreign policy establishment.[9] All the above factors hampered this generation of women in creating lasting institutional or intellectual legacies that are deemed relevant or valuable by the international law field today.

However, as this chapter shows, twentieth-century Chinese women had engaged with international law and/or international institutions. The issue lies in the fact that the paths they had traversed now lie outside of international law's disciplinary boundaries. The echoes and traces of their endeavours were not entirely lost to time, but were instead preserved in fields and institutional settings that international lawyers do not regard as their own. In short, as Immi Tallgren has rightly pointed out, women—including Chinese women—were neither absent from nor invisible in the histories of international law.[10] Accordingly, to explore the segmented experience of twentieth-century Chinese women, one must first take seriously the inclusion and exclusion mechanisms of professionalization. Moreover, it is necessary to scrutinize the politics of disciplinary memory, which favoured the already powerful, a huge contributing factor to these women's histories being overlooked.[11] Instead of solely focusing on the paths most travelled (by men), this study

[9] It is not a coincidence that the one woman whose contribution to Republican Chinese diplomacy was most significant and remains the focus of scholarly inquiry is Song Meiling 宋美龄 (1898–2003), wife of the Nationalist leader Chiang Kai-shek. During the Second World War, Song became a world figure in her own right through her efforts in mobilizing American support for the Chinese war effort. According to one review of Chinese literature on modern diplomatic history, Song represented the most researched female figure in works published between 1978 and 2018; scholarship featuring Song outnumbered that on the second most researched female figure, Chen Xiangmei 陈香梅 (aka Anna Chennault, 1923-2018, war correspondent and wife of American aviator General Claire Chennault), by 96 to 3. Huang Renguo, 'Minguo waijiao renwu yanjiu de fansi he chonggou [Reflection and Reconstruction of the Study of the Diplomatic Figures in the Republic of China]', China Social Science Review (2019) vol. 1, 90, chart 2. The tendency to focus on historical women who were members of their respective national political establishment—a status often, though not exclusively, secured through marriage and/or patrimony—is prevalent in international legal historiography. Their access to and influence on diplomatic elites, combined with the abundance and likely survival of primary and secondary materials detailing their lives, were major factors contributing to their relative popularity in scholarly research. In the seminal 2012 *Oxford Handbook of the History of International Law*, for instance, the only woman chosen for its portrait section was Austro-Bohemian noblewoman, pacifist, and Nobel Peace Prize laureate Bertha von Suttner. In the same vein, the Chinese figure chosen for the 2023 *Portraits of Women in International Law: New Names and Forgotten Faces?*, Zheng Yuxiu 郑毓秀 (aka Soumay Tcheng, 1891–1959), was herself a veteran of the Chinese Nationalist Party (Kuomintang).

[10] See Immi Tallgren, 'Absent or Invisible? "Women" Intellectuals and Professionals at the Dawn of a Discipline', in Frédéric Mégret and Immi Tallgren (eds), The Dawn of a Discipline: International Criminal Justice and Its Early Exponents (Cambridge: Cambridge University Press, 2020), 381–413.

[11] Ignacio de la Rasilla, International Law and History: Modern Interfaces (Cambridge: Cambridge University Press, 2021), 219.

will direct our attention to institutions and networks—as well as their underlying sensibilities about modern womanhood and its relations to 'the international'—that were comparatively more sympathetic towards women. It was their at times idiosyncratic and unstructured support that allowed these women to accumulate the necessary cultural and social capital to transform themselves into international actors.

These included the Christian missions and their schools, which had evolved into an important stakeholder in women's education in early twentieth-century China. In summary, the search for female versions of V. K. Wellington Koo and Zhou Gengsheng is bound to be self-defeating, while creative readjustment of the 'criteria of belonging'[12] may be crucial for embracing stories of women in future historiographical pursuits. That said, this chapter also deliberately presents Chinese women *alongside* their male contemporaries, many of whom are of canonical significance and featured in preceding biographical chapters. Such approach is both tailored to highlight the hierarchical dynamics between the two gender groups, and a result of methodological necessity—indeed, women could be found in the shadows of established male international lawyers,[13] labouring alongside them in various capacities such as colleagues, assistants, students, and wives and daughters.[14]

The rest of the chapter will proceed in two sections arranged in chronological order, separated by the inception of the People's Republic of China ('PRC') in 1949, the watershed between the Republican era and the PRC era. The first section consists of four interconnected mini-portraits. They were women who engaged with international law and/or international institutions prior to 1949, under the paradigm of liberal internationalism: Wu Yifang 吴贻芳 (1893–1985), educationist, Chinese Christian leader, and Chinese delegate to the 1945 San Francisco

[12] Immi Tallgren (n 10), 412.

[13] For instance, the photo from the United Nations Archive that proves Gong Pusheng's involvement in the preparatory phase for drafting the Universal Declaration of Human Rights was discovered through searching for her superior at the UN Secretariat, Canadian international lawyer John P. Humphrey.

[14] It is important to highlight that both Judge Wang Tieya (ICTY, 1997–2000) and Judge Zhao Lihai (ITLOS, 1996–2000) relied heavily on their wives—respectively, Wang Cai 王彩 (1919–2010) and Chen Lingbao 陈玲宝 (1926–)—for logistical support as the men worked in The Hague in their eighties. Similarly, Ling Yan 凌岩 (1948–), professor of international law at CUPL, looked after her father, Judge Li Haopei (ICTY, 1993–97), during his tenure at The Hague. The wives were both college graduates and had actively assisted their husbands in their professional, scholarly, and pedagogical work before their nominations. Chen Lingbao was known to have provided Zhao Lihai with much secretarial support, including managing library loans, proofreading, and transcribing drafts. One could plausibly theorize about the connections between the two men's resilience and longevity (Wang lived to 89 and Zhao to 84) and their spouses' unreserved commitment—both wives stuck with their husbands when the latter were politically persecuted and weathered the storms together. It is difficult to imagine that the two men could have achieved as much during the final decades of their lives in the absence of their wives' steadfast support. The author believes it is important to both acknowledge their wives' labour as relevant to the histories of international law, while not equating them with the international lawyers' intellectual and professional work. This approach is demonstrated in the inclusion of Maria van Reigersberch, wife of Hugo Grotius, in the 2023 volume *Portraits of Women in International Law*.

Conference; Chen Fangzhi 陈芳芝 (aka 'Agnes Chen Fang-chih', 1914–1995), a US-trained political scientist who specialized in international law, whose journey most resembled that of well-known male Chinese international lawyers—an exception to the norm; Gong Pusheng 龚普生 (aka 'Kung Pu Sheng', 1913–2007), a Chinese Communist revolutionary once embedded in interwar Christian networks, who had worked for the United Nations Secretariat before returning to the PRC, where she served as one of the few female leaders of its nascent Ministry of Foreign Affairs; and lastly Han Youtong 韩幽桐 (born Han Guiqin 韩桂琴, 1908–1985), a Communist revolutionary, women's rights activist, and jurist, who had once pursued graduate studies in international law in Japan but ultimately abandoned the field.

There were many shared traits among the four: they belonged to a fortunate minority who had secured external resources that supported their educational pursuits, which laid the foundation for their respective careers and/or causes; they either delayed their marriage and childbearing or remained celibate;[15] they endured substantive hardships in both the Republican and PRC periods; they were cherished by their families and communities both as individuals and as trailblazers; and while none were international lawyers 'properly so called', their stories merit inclusion in Chinese international legal history. Not only had they obtained professional competence that was associated with the international legal profession, but the unfamiliar paths these women had travelled also illuminate the specific enabling conditions that—against an overall disabling circumstance—were essential for developing said competence.

The second section will be dedicated to the first- and second-generation professional women international lawyers of the PRC era. They were trained in law faculties and had arrived on the scene in the 1950s and 1980s, respectively. This section will begin with an epochal sketch covering the broad transformations fostered by the inception of the Leninist party-state since 1949, which substantively altered Chinese women's relationship with society and the state, reflected in their improved status in higher education, professions, and government settings. The shift towards a state-run public education system post-1949 introduced gender-neutral education and broke down some of the existing barriers.[16] Most importantly, compared to the Republican era, the modes of professionalization shifted

[15] Of these four women, Wu Yifang and Chen Fangzhi were never married. Gong Pusheng only married on the eve of the PRC's founding at the age of 36. Han Youtong married her Communist comrade Zhang Youyu at the age of 25, yet owing to their revolutionary work, which kept them both constantly moving for two decades, she had her first child only after the founding of the PRC, when she was in her 40s.

[16] In the recollection of Wang Zheng, a historian who had grown up in the Maoist era (1950s–1970s), she and her peers had, because of their education and the prevailing ideology of 'women's emancipation', rejected the identity of housewife, wife, or woman (*funü*) in favour of '(female) youth'. In this context, a career was thus taken as a given. See, Wang Zheng, 'Call Me "Qingnian" But Not "Funü": A Maoist Youth in Retrospect', in Xueping Zhong, Wang Zheng, and Bai Di (eds) Some of Us: Chinese Women Growing Up in the Mao Era (New Brunswick, NJ: Rutgers University Press, 2001), 27–52.

from bottom-up to top-down, from fragmented to planned. In essence, the state—rather than individuals or civil society—got to decide who was to become an international lawyer.[17]

What accompanied this change was the deliberate marginalization of Republican-era specialists, whose expertise in Western international law was flagged as problematic owing to its 'bourgeois' premise. Owing to the need for 'new blood'—a new class of politically reliable cadre-experts—some women born between the late 1920s and early 1940s became the unintended (albeit temporary) winners of this disciplinary reshuffle. However, the tables turned when the new CCP leadership settled on the policy of Reform and Opening-up in 1978. Republican-era scholars were rehabilitated and assumed the essential role of reconnecting the Chinese field with its Western counterparts. Given the country's new orientation, they have since been broadly revered as the authoritative bearers of international law knowledge. Ultimately, compared to their Republican-era male predecessors, PRC women have yet to become the focus of scholarly history, which can be attributed to both the contemporary nature of their journeys and their self-evident secondary status within the professional hierarchy from the present-day perspective. In summary, compared to the protagonists surveyed earlier, these PRC-era women were present yet rendered invisible. To counter this invisibility, in addition to introducing new oral history materials, this section also utilizes the approach of group biography (or 'prosopography')—outlining the common characteristics or experiences of a group where individual details are scarce—to fill in the gaps in existing scholarship.[18]

33.2 The Republican Era

33.2.1 Wu Yifang 吴贻芳 (1893–1985)

The mini-portraits begin with Wu Yifang, whose journey offers a valuable lens for examining the unique role of Christian missionary schools in educating Chinese women. Of the four protagonists, three (all except Han Youtong) were direct beneficiaries of missionary schools. Affiliated missionary enterprises, such as the Young

[17] One other overlooked mechanism behind PRC women's entrance into the international law field was that all university graduates were to be 'assigned' (*fen pei*) to their designated work unit, with one's mobility between careers dictated by the work unit and the state. This system was only phased out in the 1980s.

[18] Using group biography (or 'prosopography') as a way to broaden the scope of legal biographies was endorsed by David Sugarman and exercised in Linda Mulcahy's study of women observers in British courtrooms. See, David Sugarman, 'From Legal Biography to Legal Life Writing: Broadening Conceptions of Legal History and Socio-Legal Scholarship', Journal of Law and Society (2015) vol. 42, no. 1, 23–28; see also Linda Mulcahy, 'Watching Women: What Illustrations of Courtroom Scenes Tell Us about Women and the Public Sphere in the Nineteenth Century,' Journal of Law and Society (2015) vol. 42, no. 1, 53–73.

Women's Christian Association ('YWCA'), and transnational networks forged by the interwar Christian internationalist movement were also crucial to their stories. Missionary schools were integral to the grand project of 'Christianizing China'.[19] In the same vein, Chinese girls were identified as an asset for conversion.[20] However, missionary schools—especially Christian colleges—developed into special social spaces that allowed Chinese girls and young women to explore their agency as the 'new women' of modern China. There, they were enabled to engage with a wide range of issues, ranging from women's emancipation to Chinese nationalism. More pertinent to the histories of this study, missionary school education provided Chinese girls and women with rare opportunities and capabilities in representing China—more specifically, modern Chinese womanhood—on the international stage, 'cutting their teeth' in women's diplomacy in the process.

Wu Yifang's journey perfectly reflected these larger developments. Wu was part of the first graduating class (1915–1919) at Ginling Women's College in Nanjing ('Ginling'), which preceded Chinese public universities in conferring bachelor's degrees to Chinese women.[21] In 1928, she took the reins at Ginling and became the country's second Chinese woman college president. Like most prominent educationists of her time, Wu received an advanced degree from a Western research university. On the recommendation of Mary E. Woolley, president of Mount Holyoke College, Wu was brought to the University of Michigan in 1922 through the 'Barbour Scholarships for Oriental Women'.[22] The programme imagined its recipients as prospective emissaries of peace, who, after having undergone an emancipatory Western education, would 'take back whatever they find good and assimilate the blessings among the peoples from which they come'.[23] This vision, with its emphasis on international understanding and the Christian ideal of 'service', was also premised on white paternalism and underpinned by a hierarchical relationship between the Occidental educators and their Oriental students. In 1928, Wu obtained her PhD in Biology.

[19] The origin of missionary schools in China was directly connected to the unequal treaties concluded between Western powers and late-Qing China, which opened up China for missionary work.

[20] According to one report in 1910, 'not that [Chinese] boys and girls should be educated in the same school or follow the same curriculum ... No phase of China's poverty is more impressive or more pathetic than her poverty of homes ... China will never have homes till her women are trained to make them.' Address by Professor Ernest D. Burton titled, 'Educational Work in China', in Report on Christian Education in China (New York: Commission on Christian Education in China, 1910), 32.

[21] Ginling and North China Union Women's College (which became the Women's College of Yenching University in 1920) were established in 1915 and 1916, respectively. Ginling conferred bachelor's degrees to its first class of women students in 1919. By comparison, the first government higher education institution for women, Peking Female Higher Normal College, had its origin in 1917 when it first recruited academic faculty. National universities, such as Peking University, only began admitting women in 1920. Tsinghua started as an all-male preparatory college and only accepted women when it was reorganized into a national university in 1928.

[22] W. Carl Rufus, 'Twenty-Five Years of the Barbour Scholarships', Michigan Alumnus Quarterly Review (1942) vol. 49, no. 11, 18.

[23] ibid, 15, quoting Levi Lewis Barbour, who endowed the Scholarships in 1917.

Wu Yifang was, at the time, lauded as a success story of these Christian institutions.[24] She converted to Christianity during her time at Ginling, and her religious identity continued to play a significant role in her personal and professional life. However, Wu's journey also encapsulated the autonomous explorations undertaken by Chinese Christian women, who sought to reconcile their Christian identity, nationalistic sensibilities, and aspirations for modern womanhood. One must examine such explorations in the context of missionary schools, which provided a relatively liberal and feminist space.[25] For instance, after the May Fourth student protest—against the treatment of China at the 1919 Paris Peace Conference—broke out in Beijing, Wu mobilized her classmates at Ginling to show solidarity, contributing to the movement's national spread. Later in 1925, she was elected Vice President of the Chinese Students' Alliance of America, a hub for Chinese student activism in the US. Wu was therefore experienced in leadership before her ascension to Ginling's presidency in 1928. Her new station elevated her into a proper public figure with a seat at the table on both national[26] and international platforms. Wu went on to represent China, Chinese women, and Chinese Christians respectively at the 1931 Institute of Pacific Relations Conference (Shanghai and Hangzhou), the 1933 International Congress of Women in Chicago, and the 1933 United Foreign Missionary Conferences in the US. It is worth noting that education represented one of the few widely accepted professional careers that educated women could undertake, and that the role of school administrator often served as a springboard for career women's broader public influence.

In April 1945, as China was assembling its delegation for the upcoming United Nations Conference on International Organisation in San Francisco ('UNCIO'), V. K. Wellington Koo lobbied for the appointment of Wu Yifang. China had spent the Second World War persuading its Western allies that China—in contrast to Imperial Japan—truly embodied Western democratic values, and Koo believed Wu's inclusion would render the delegation 'broadly representative'.[27] The war

[24] Wu's conversion to Christianity at Ginling had a huge impact in helping her recover from the severe trauma of losing multiple family members in quick succession at a young age. Mary Jo Waelchli, 'Abundant Life: Matilda Thurston, Wu Yifang and Jinling College, 1915–1951' (PhD thesis, Ohio State University, 2002), 56.

[25] On missionary schoolgirls' attempts to reconcile their multiple identities, see generally, Jennifer Bond, Dreaming the New Women: An Oral History of Missionary Schoolgirls in Republican China (Oxford: Oxford University Press, 2024).

[26] Wu Yifang developed a good relationship with Song Meiling, wife of the KMT leader Chiang Kai-shek. Perhaps not without contradiction, Wu worked with Song on the latter's pet project, the neo-traditionalist 'New Life Movement', which, according to its critics, reinforced gender roles and gender hierarchies.

[27] Aside from Wu, other possible choices in Koo's mind included Zheng Yuxiu and Song Qingling (Madame Sun Yat-sen). Reminiscences of Wellington Koo, Volume V: Second Mission to London Part E (1944–June 1945), Chinese Oral History Project East Asian Institute of Columbia University Part II (1978), Columbia University Rare Books & Manuscripts Library, 783, 809–810. Koo's initiative was directly inspired by Eleanor Roosevelt and her impact on American public affairs during wartime. Coincidentally, Eleanor Roosevelt was credited with insisting that the State Department place one woman on each American delegation to an international conference. Nancy Woloch, The Insider: A Life of Virginia C. Gildersleeve (New York: Columbia University Press, 2022), 160. Wu allegedly attributed

had driven Wu closer to the Nationalist establishment, with the latter occasionally assigning Wu tasks pertaining to foreign relations. At the wartime capital of Chongqing, Wu was tasked with receiving foreign allies; in 1943, she was dispatched to the US with other Chinese cultural luminaries to mobilize support. In San Francisco, Wu garnered wide attention from the US public and was invited as a speaker by many social groups, especially women's groups.[28] To fulfil her duty as a delegate and to meet these public demands—she received a total of 142 invitations and gave 24 talks, 11 broadcasts, 14 interviews, and 5 press conferences[29]—Wu mobilized Ginling College alumnae based in the US for assistance.[30]

Wu Yifang accounted for one of the eight women delegates (out of 850) present at UNCIO, and one of four women who were appointed full delegates and were therefore signatories to the UN Charter; she was the only Asian woman signatory.[31] Women delegates were mostly assigned by their delegations to meetings concerning economic and social questions, as they were perceived as a 'suitably feminine field'.[32] In the same vein, Wu was assigned to Commission II (General Assembly), Committee 3 (Economic and Social Cooperation). Norwegian delegate Åse Gruda Skard organized an informal network consisting of thirteen women delegates and advisors, which allowed them to coordinate their stance on questions relating to women.[33] These women were split on the question of

her appointment to the US government announcing Virginia Gildersleeve as part of its delegation. Virginia Gildersleeve, Many a Good Crusade (New York: The Macmillan Company, 1954), 351.

[28] During UNCIO, women and women's groups were among the non-governmental organizations that actively interacted with delegates. According to Wu's assistant Zhu Juefang, Wu 'did not turn down invitations [from social groups] as long as she could manage', which was Wu's way of promoting American public understanding of China. Zhu Juefang, 'He xiaozhang zai yiqi de rizi' [Days with the President], in Wu Yifang Jinian Ji [Essays in Honour of Wu Yifang] (Nanjing: Jiangsu Education Publishing House, 1987), 166.

[29] Mary Jo Waelchli (n 24), 251, citing Wu's letter to Ginling alumnae in the US ('Sisters in America'), 22 June 1945.

[30] Besides Wu Yifang, the only other woman out of a total of 84 people officially included in the Chinese Delegation was Zhu Juefang 朱觉方 (1913–2009, listed as 'Mrs. T. S. Ma' in the record). United Nations Archives and Records Management Section (New York), reference number S-1005-0001-10-00001, 'Representatives and Observers—Credentials China'. Zhu, a Ginling alumna who was then completing her PhD studies at the University of Chicago, was recruited by Wu Yifang as her secretary. ibid, 165–166.

[31] The other three signatories were the Dominican feminist and the Chair of Inter-American Commission of Women, Minerva Bernardino; Dean of Barnard College, Virginia Gildersleeve of the US; and Brazilian scientist, suffragist, and parliamentarian Bertha Lutz. In addition, there were Jessie Street, Australia; Åse Gruda Skard, Norway; Cora Taylor Casselman, Canada; and Isabel P. de Vidal, Uruguay. Amalia de Castillo Ledón, Adela Formoso de Obregón Santacilia of Mexico, Lucila L. de Pérez Diaz, Isabel Sánchez de Urdaneta Venezuela, attended in their capacity as advisors. Rebecca Adami, Women and the Universal Declaration of Human Rights (New York: Routledge, 2018), 20–21. By one count, women delegates and support staff consisted of only 3 percent of the total at UNCIO. Nancy Woloch (n 27), 163.

[32] Virginia Gildersleeve (n 27), 331.

[33] Torild Skard, 'Introductory Note: Learning journey for a feminist: Making women visible, recognizing women's achievements and demanding power to women' in Rebecca Adami and Dan Plesch (eds) Women and the UN: A New History of Women's International Human Rights (New York: Routledge, 2021), xv.

whether 'women' should be formalized as a distinct category. Latin American (led by Brazilian delegate Bertha Lutz[34]) and Australia's Jessie Street insisted that the Charter preamble make a special reference to equal rights for women. Anglo-American delegates, who already felt aggrieved that their appointments were dictated by their gender rather than credentials and expertise, feared that any such mention of women would 'segregate' women. They argued that since women's rights were already covered by Article 1(3) stating that '[The UN shall promote] respect for human rights and for fundamental freedoms for all', such separatism would be counterproductive and discriminatory.[35]

Wu Yifang and Åse Gruda Skard, two delegates who supposedly occupied an 'intermediary' position,[36] sided with the former faction; the line 'equal rights of men and women' was included in the first paragraph of the preamble. According to Skard, they 'supported women's rights, but not when they thought it was unreasonable'.[37] Intriguingly, when it came to Lutz's proposal for establishing a Commission on the Status of Women under the Economic and Social Council, Wu switched sides and became the only delegate who joined Gildersleeve in opposition.[38] The proposal, with support from even male delegates, was realized in 1946, with the UN General Assembly's Third Committee creating the Sub-commission on the Status of Women under the Human Rights Commission. Wu's Ginling classmate and friend Xu Yizhen 徐亦蓁 (aka 'Zee Yuh-tsung' or 'Mrs Way-sung New', 1894–1981)—who had been Wu's personal assistant during UNCIO—went on to be the first Chinese woman to serve on the UN Sub-Commission.

According to historian Glenda Sluga, the division over 'equal rights' in 1945 was not the result of clashes between 'feminists' and 'antifeminists'; rather, it reflected the general disagreement among women and feminists of the period as to what 'equality' entailed.[39] There is little doubt about Wu's own identification with women's equal rights. Her seemingly contradictory stances at UNCIO, however, likely reflected her uneasiness over post-war challenges for Chinese women.[40] In a

[34] American delegate Virginia Gildersleeve labelled Lutz as having embodied 'an old militant feminism Virginia Gildersleeve (n 27), 350. Lutz felt equally embarrassed by Gildersleeve, who she thought had expressed 'a very old-fashioned anti-feminism'. Nancy Woloch (n 27), 165.

[35] Nancy Woloch (n 27), 164. This position was advocated by American delegate Virginia Gildersleeve and was supported by British and Canadian delegates.

[36] Torild Skard (n 33), xv, citing her mother Åse Gruda Skard's description of her and Wu's position in relation to the two factions.

[37] ibid.

[38] Gildersleeve argued in retrospect that the creation of such a 'special feminine commission' would give men the convenient justification to 'keep them [women] out of other commissions and groups'. Virginia Gildersleeve (n 27), 352.

[39] Glenda Sluga, '"Spectacular Feminism": The International History of Women, World Citizenship and Human Rights', in Francesca de Haan, Margaret Allen, June Purvis, and Krassimira Daskalova (eds) Women's Activism: Global Perspectives from the 1890s to the Present (New York: Routledge, 2013), 48. See also Glenda Sluga, 'Women, Feminism and Twentieth-Century Internationalism', in Glenda Sluga (ed) (Cambridge: Cambridge University Press, 2017), 61–84.

[40] In a 1971 speech likely prepared for the occasion of the restoration of PRC's seat at the UN, Wu made a callback to her experience in 1945. Wu claimed that the Chinese delegation was merely following the US lead and was slighted by its American counterpart. This claim must be viewed in the

1944 speech discussing the progress made by American women in the workplace, Wu brought up the emerging discourse in the US over potential rollbacks of these advances when the men returned from the war. Accordingly, Wu cautioned that the Chinese women's movement 'must develop an understanding of what is achievable through our own strength'.[41] As China's standard-bearing feminist-nationalist, Wu witnessed firsthand regressions in women's rights—changes that were made in the name of tempering China's deepening crisis.[42] More generally, Wu was gravely concerned about China's future in the post-war international order. Writing to Ginling alumnae on the eve of the signing of the UN Charter, Wu conveyed her high expectations but also her ambivalence about whether China could rise to the challenge as one of the 'Big Five': '[China] must build up herself, develop a strong democracy and industrialize in order to support our moral stand on respecting international law and justice. I see a great future for our country, but it depends upon how our government and people would respond.'[43]

Wu swiftly formulated her own answer with regard to this uphill battle. Having returned from San Francisco, Wu emphasized educated women's special duty in lifting China from the ruins of war: they ought to embrace their femininity, choose careers that best resonated with their sympathetic nature, and foster progressive change in their work as enlightened homemakers who could pass down social and cultural heritage.[44]

Like most progressive intellectuals of her time, Wu Yifang grew critical of the Nationalist Government and had twice turned down the offer to become Education Minister. By November 1948, she had 'decided to stay regardless of what may happen'.[45] Owing to her public stature, she was invited to participate in the Chinese People's Political Consultative Conference. On 1 October 1949,

context of widespread anti-Americanism during the Maoist era; it is also unclear whether Wu saw her agreeing with Gildersleeve as belonging to this pattern. Mary Jo Waelchli (n 24), 279, fn. 332, citing a speech draft titled 'Huiyi lianheguo 26 ju nian shuching' [Remembering the United Nations at 26 Years].

41 Wu YifangZhonghua jidu jiao weili gonghui tongxun [Chinese Methodist Church Communique] (1944) vol. 21–22, 22. Speech at the Women's Advisory Committee [funü zhidao weiyuanhui], 28 February 1944.

42 Official and unofficial discourse on 'women returning home' entered the mainstream the during the War of Resistance against Japan (1937–1945). See Zang Jian, '"Women Returning Home"—A Topic of Chinese Women's Liberation', in Mechthild Leutner and Nicola Spakowski (eds) Women in China: The Republican Period in Historical Perspective (Berlin: LIT Verlag, 2005), 376–395. On controversies surrounding restricting women from government employment and debate over women's roles in society during the War, see Lü Fangshang, 'Kangzhan shiqi de nüquan bianlun' [Debates over women's rights during the War of Resistance], Research on Women in Modern Chinese History (1994) vol. 2, 81–115.

43 Mary Jo Waelchli (n 24), 253, citing Wu's correspondence to Ginling alumnae in the US ('Sisters in America'), 22 June 1945.

44 'Role of College Women in New China Outlined by Dr. Wu', *The China Press* (Shanghai, 18 October 1946), 2.

45 Mary Jo Waelchli (n 24), 279, citing Wu Yifang's letter to Matilda Thurston, 15 November 1948.

she joined other luminaries in witnessing the PRC inaugural ceremony from the Tiananmen Gate Tower. Her public roles in the PRC, however, were mostly limited to her native province, Jiangsu, where she served as Vice Governor. Her last notable involvement with international affairs was her appointment to the All-China Women's Federation (*quanguo fulian*) delegation in 1958, through which she attended the Women's International Democratic Federation's fourth congress in Vienna.[46] Contemporary memory of Wu Yifang remains largely defined by her legacy in education.

33.2.2 Chen Fangzhi 陈芳芝 (1914–1995)

The trajectory of Chen Fangzhi (aka 'Agnes Chen Fang-chih', 1914–1995) most closely resembled that of other well-known Chinese international lawyers. Specifically, she stood as one of the very few, if not the only, women international law teachers who had a relatively uninterrupted career and had eventually become a colleague of the discipline's central male figures. She came from a Cantonese Christian family in Chaozhou and was a niece of the Columbia-trained political scientist Xu Shuxi 徐叔希 (aka 'Hsu Shu-hsi'), the founding dean of the Department of Political Science at Yenching University, Beijing.[47] Like Ginling College, Yenching was committed to providing modern higher education to Chinese women. After becoming a co-educational institution (1926), Yenching introduced the Dean of Women system to look after the welfare of women students and faculty members.[48] That said, the gendered academic divisions that steered women students away from political science and international law persisted at Yenching. During the first semester of the 1931–1932 school year, the Department of Political Science, while one

[46] This involvement was mentioned in Wu Yifang Jinian Ji [Essays in Honour of Wu Yifang] (n 28), 23. Wu was named Vice President to the All-China Women's Federation. Women's International Democratic Federation (1945–1991) was a left-feminist international umbrella organization, which during the initial decades of the Cold War, provided the isolated PRC with an important channel for international cultural exchange. Wang Zheng, 'Creating a Socialist Feminist Cultural Front: "Women of China" (1949–1966)', The China Quarterly (2010) no. 204, 834, fn 21.

[47] In her Bryn Marw College Archive records, Chen Fangzhi listed her mother's name as 'Hsu Shuying' (Xu Shuying). Her mother's name shared the same pattern as that of 'Hsu Shu-hsi' (Xu Shuxi). According to one historical research on the Chaozhou Christian mission, Xu Shuying was the daughter of an early Chinese Christian woman, Lin Saiyu, who as a maidservant learned the craft of European drawn thread work from a missionary and girls' school headmistress Lida Scott Ashmore. See Cai Xiangyu, Christianity and Gender in South-East China: The Chaozhou Missions (1849–1949) (PhD thesis, University of Leiden, 2012), 144.

[48] Chen Fangzhi would in 1942 be appointed to the Dean of the Women's College at Yenching, a position that she did not relate to. Chen's discomfort should be interpreted in the context of the then custom that women faculties were expected to 'entertain', an extra labour to burden aside from their academic duties. She complained to her confidant at BMC in 1943 that 'The deanship, to say the best, is a job of service, of such nature as diametrically opposed to my disposition. Sometimes I have to stand and watch a servant boil water properly.' Letter from Agnes Chen to Roger H. Wells, 1 November 1943, Bryn Marw College Archive records.

of the most popular departments in terms of undergraduate enrolment (65), had among the fewest women students (4); meanwhile, none of its 16 graduate students were women.[49] Its men-to-women student ratio was far above Yenching's average, which between the years of 1928 and 1931 had steadily lowered from 3.29 to 2.48.[50] In Chen Fangzhi's own words, her uncle Xu Shuxi had originally objected to her plan of studying political science, since 'girls don't go there'. 'And the more Shu objected, the more I insisted', Chen recalled.[51] It is worth noting that Yenching's had a short-lived (1931–1932) Department of Jurisprudence that was later merged with the Department of Political Science. Such an arrangement allowed Chen to take up many law courses during her bachelor studies.[52] Additionally, Wang Huacheng, the international law specialist at Tsinghua University (and the mentor to Wang Tieya and Chen Tiqiang), co-taught the international law course at Yenching with Xu, owing to the proximity of the two campuses.[53]

American missionary educator and Dean of the Women's College at Yenching, Margaret Bailey Speer (1900–1997) was very fond of Chen's thoughtful and independent nature, a trait which she associated with Chen's role as the eldest sister of eight siblings. When Chen's family silk business failed in 1934, Speer consoled Chen that 'we would see her through college, as she can easily get a scholarship'.[54] In spring 1936, as Chen was finishing her first year at Yenching's graduate school, Speer wrote a reference letter for Chen to her *alma mater* Bryn Mawr College ('BMC'). BMC was one of the elite women's colleges in the US that strove to provide women with advanced academic training on par with Ivy League schools. BMC happily accepted Chen for its graduate school, as its Chinese Scholarship Committee was eager to admit 'a graduate student straight from China' who could bring to BMC her unique perspective.[55] During the next four years, Chen was supplied with a

[49] 'Yenching University College of Public Affairs, Dean's Report, June 1932'. In folder 'Yenching Admin Annual reports of President + Deans to Board of Managers, 1932–1937', RG011-303-4710, United Board of Christian Higher Education in Asia Archives, Yale Divinity Library.

[50] 'Summary of the Annual Report of The Director of Studies, Yenching University, 1931–1932', 5, ibid.

[51] Lin Mengxi, 'Menqiang yongzai, enyuan nanxiao—huainian enshi chen fangzhi' [Mentorship lasts forever, but so does grievance: Remembering my mentor Chen Fangzhi], Yanda xiaoyou tongxun [Yenching University Alumnus Communique] (1997) vol. 24, 70.

[52] Chen Fangzhi had during her sophomore and junior years studied all main areas of law (civil law, criminal law, constitutional law). Yenching University Transcript of Miss Chen, Fang-chih, issued 19 March 1936, Bryn Marw College Archive records. By comparison, her courses at BMC were not law-oriented.

[53] Beiping sili Yenjing daxue yilan [Overview of Private Yenching University of Beijing] (Yenching University handbook, 1936), 160.

[54] Margaret Bailey Speer and Caroline Smith Rittenhouse (ed), Like Good Steel: The China Letters of Margaret Bailey Speer, North China, 1925–1943 (Berwyn, PA: The Round Table Press, 1994), 154.

[55] Before Chen, BMC had admitted one Chinese-American student, Grace Chin Lee 陈玉平 (aka Grace Lee Boggs), to its graduate programme. Grace Chin Lee was born in the US as the daughter of a Chinese immigrant and had obtained her bachelor's from Barnard College. In one letter, a BMC administrator commented that while Chin Lee's viewpoint might be 'interesting', it was not as valuable as that of someone from China proper. Letter from Eunice M. Schenck to Eleanor Brownell, 26 April 1936, Bryn Marw College Archive records. Chen's Chinese perspective would indeed be put to good use by

stipend through funds raised by the Committee; the stipend roughly matched the salary of a white teacher in 1930s America.[56] BMC administrators also introduced Chen to their interconnected networks of women's colleges, women's associations, and Christian groups. These connections afforded Chen additional resources and support. In the summers, she could use the Harvard-Yenching Library while living in Radcliffe College dorms, or work as a counsellor at YWCA camps for extra income. These accommodations proved essential for Chen to complete her doctoral thesis, as the destructive Japanese military campaign between 1938 and 1939 had greatly strained Chen's spirit.

Chen's thesis, titled 'Certain Problems of International Law with Reference to China', was completed in 1939. Her supervisor was Charles G. Fenwick, a prominent political scientist who had been teaching international law at BMC since 1918. Like many contemporary Chinese international lawyers, Chen adhered to a strictly positivist framework (in her own words, 'from a juridical point of view'), presenting first a body of juridical rights that China as a sovereign state in the community of nations was entitled to, followed by recounting how said rights were curtailed in the practices of the Great Powers. Chen's project followed the intellectual lead of her mentors at Yenching, who, under the direction of Xu Shuxi, gravitated towards China's borderland regions, especially their respective histories since the nineteenth century.[57] She returned to China in 1939 to accept an offer as lecturer at Yenching's Department of Political Science. After having persevered through the hardships of the Second World War—during which Yenching was forced to relocate to the Chinese southwest due to Japanese occupation—Chen Fangzhi emerged as one of the leading women academics of her generation. Soon after Yenching resumed operation in Beijing, Chen succeeded Wu Qiyu and became head of the Department of Political Science (1945–1951). She also assumed editorship of the premier English-language publication *Yenching Journal of Social Sciences* (1948–1950). Some of the last cohorts of Yenching would later share fond

BMC. In 1938, for instance, Chen would be invited through the BMC to attend the luncheon at the annual meeting of the Philadelphia Committee for the Cause and Cure of War, as part of the Business and Professional Women's Club of Philadelphia. Anna L. Wiswell to Eunice M. Schenck, 28 January 1938, Bryn Marw College Archive records.

[56] Letter from Eleanor Brownell to Eunice M. Schenck, 5 May 1936, Bryn Marw College Archive records. In December 1937, BMC administrators corresponded over finding money to support Chen's Christmas holidays, as Chen was 'too worried to ask directly'. Eunice M. Schenck to Marjorie Thompson, 11 December 1937, Bryn Marw College Archive records. On US salary in the 1930s, see David T. Blose and Ambrose Caliver, Statistics of the education of Negroes: a decade of progress (Washington, DC: Federal Security Agency, US Office of Education, 1943), pt. 1, 6, table 7.

[57] Xu Shuxi himself wrote his PhD thesis on the internationalization of Manchuria. See Xu Shuxi (Shuhsi Hsu), China and Her Political Entity: A Study of China's Foreign Relations with Reference to Korea, Manchuria and Mongolia (New York: Oxford University Press, 1926). A notable example was Xu's early student at Yenching, Wu Qiyu, who specialised in the history of Chinese borderlands near Central Asia.

memories of Chen, including her ability to invite the Tokyo Trial Judge Mei Ru'ao (aka 'Mei Ju-ao') as their guest lecturer.

Chen Fangzhi's professional success during the last decade of the Republican era had unfortunately become the source of her miseries during the early PRC years. She wrote to her BMC mentors in late 1948 inquiring about potential openings in American women's colleges. She confided in a letter her fatalistic outlook that 'there will be no place for my service' in China, given her specialization in political science.[58] Her prediction became reality in 1952. Clashes between Chinese and American armies on the Korean Peninsula had put a target on Yenching and its members. As a member of its senior leadership, Chen found herself trapped in a vulnerable position. Following the abolition of political science departments nationwide in 1952, Chen was transferred to Beijing College of Politics and Law (a precursor to the China University of Political Science and Law). In 1953, Chen joined her fellow international lawyer-in-exile Wang Tieya at the Department of History, Peking University, where the two worked on the history of foreign relations. From that point onwards, Chen Fangzhi pivoted entirely to historical research. However, as the Sino–Soviet alliance tightened during the early 1950s, Chen's research that alluded to the encroachment on historical Chinese territories by Tsarist Russia drew her detractors. Her health deteriorated greatly during the Cultural Revolution. Consequently, unlike other international lawyers such as Wang Tieya and Zhao Lihai, Chen Fangzhi could not return to the international law scene in the 1980s and leave a legacy like her Republican peers.

In a testament to her character, Yenching alumni laboured to edit and publish Chen's work. A collected volume came out in 1995, just before Chen passed away that year; the majority of its contents were written before 1949.[59] Pursuant to her will, her Yenching students spread her ashes 'north of the Great Wall', a reference to her work on the Chinese borderlands.[60] Her brother Francis Chen later endowed the Chen Family Fund for East Asian Studies at Haverford College—now part of a college consortium with Bryn Mawr College—'in memory of his sister Dr Agnes Fangzhi Chen, PhD'.

[58] Letter from Agnes Chen to Roger H. Wells, 11 November 1948, Bryn Marw College Archive records.

[59] Chen Fangzhi, Dongbei shi tantao [Historical Studies of Northeast China] (Beijing: China Social Sciences Press, 1995).

[60] See, for instance, Xia Ziqiang and Zheng Bijun, 'Zhisi buyu de ai—Diao Fangzhi shi' [Unfailing Love for Country and Science: Remembering Our Teacher Chen Fangzhi], in Yanda xiaoyou tongxun [Yenching University Alumnus Communique] (1996) vol. 21, 81.

33.2.3 Gong Pusheng 龚普生 (1913–2007)

As mentioned, in spite of its roots in missionary education, Yenching University was an important hub for left-wing student activism. For those Yenching students who were radicalized by Japanese aggression—as well as the Nationalist Government's apparent appeasement—choosing science over immediate political action bordered on indulgence. The Manchuria Crisis of 1931 had greatly accelerated activism within Christian colleges, in part due to the students' deepening identity crisis as alleged products of Western cultural imperialism.[61] Many, like the sisters Gong Pusheng 龚普生 (aka 'Kung Pu Sheng', 1913–2007) and Gong Peng 龚澎 (born Gong Weihang 龚维航, 1914–1970), transformed into professional revolutionaries. Sinologist John K. Fairbank later characterized these missionary school students-turned-revolutionaries as China's 'home missionaries': they were proficient in English, presented themselves capably as liberal democrats (hence relatable to their Western target audiences), and were 'working on us [Western diplomats and journalists stationed in China] all like missionaries'.[62] The Gong sisters represented the archetype of a small cohort of Communist women who pioneered international affairs work. Their contributions to the revolution later propelled them into the PRC's foreign policy establishment (see Part III). The older sister, Gong Pusheng, however, had traversed an exceptional path, which made her experience overlap more with contemporary Western (white) women internationalists than with her Chinese comrades.

The Gong sisters were the daughters of the late-Qing military officer Gong Zhengzhou, an early supporter of Sun Yat-sen and his revolution. Gong Zhengzhou invested heavily in his daughters' education and enrolled them at St. Mary's Hall in Shanghai, whose student body was made up of girls from the city's upper-class families. Both sisters converted to Christianity at St. Mary's.[63] They were both admitted to Yenching University: Gong Pusheng studied at the Department of Economics

[61] On the mental world of Yenching students during the 1930s, see Jessie G. Lutz, 'December 9, 1935: Student Nationalism and the China Christian Colleges', The Journal of Asian Studies (1967) vol. 26, no. 4, 627–648.

[62] John King Fairbank, A Fifty-Year Memoir (New York: Harper & Row Publishers, 1982), 270–271. During his time in the wartime capital of Chongqing during the 1940s, Fairbank had fraternized with both Gong Peng and Yang Gang, two Communist women who would later occupy leadership positions in the PRC MFA.

[63] Gong Peng's daughter recounted that her mother's initial enthusiasm for religion receded due to the deepening national crisis. Gong Peng subsequently transformed into a 'famous heretic' on the St. Mary's campus. Qiao Songdu, Qiao Guanhua yu Gong Peng: wo de fuqin muqin [Qiao Guanhua and Gong Peng: My Father and Mother] (Beijing: Zhonghua Book Company, 2008), 13. A 17-year-old Gong Pusheng also once expressed her affinity for Christianity in a school assignment. Interestingly, Gong Pusheng inserted a proactive response against 'outsiders', who upon learning about her thinking, will 'certainly claim I was influenced by the missionary school'. Identifying herself as a maverick, Gong Pusheng believed she had arrived at this affinity on her own terms. The clarification certainly marked the ambivalence of a young Chinese Christian in the environment of rising nationalism. Gong Pusheng, 'Yu youren lun zongjiao shu' [Letter to a Friend on Religion], Feng Zao [The Phoenix: St. Mary's School Annual] (Shanghai: Thomas Chu & Sons, 1931), 35.

(1932–1936), while Gong Peng attended the Department of History (1933–1937). During the 'December 9th Movement' of 1935, Yenching students joined with other Beijing students in calling on the Nationalist Government to prioritize resisting Japanese aggression over the suppression of the Communists. Aside from organizing the protest, the public-spirited sisters held an English press conference at Yenching where they addressed Western reporters on the movement.[64]

Between 1936 and 1940, the two sisters, while united by the same cause, went their separate ways. Gong Peng relocated to the CCP Yan'an headquarters, while Gong Pusheng embedded herself in Shanghai as a Young Women's Christian Association ('YWCA') student secretary.[65] Over the years, Japanese aggression had pushed the Chinese YWCA towards a nationalistic identity; the invasion of Manchuria in 1931, for instance, prompted its women leaders to appeal to the Lytton Commission in 1932.[66] The YWCA position thus provided Gong with an apt cover, as well as international mobility. On the eve of the Second World War in Europe, Gong attended the 1939 Conference of Christian Youth in Amsterdam and the World Student Conference in Paris, occasions that Gong used to spread awareness about the ongoing war in China.

Having learned about these travels, CCP leader Zhou Enlai counselled Gong to continue her studies in the US and expand her network there.[67] Soon after, Gong obtained a fellowship at Union Theological Seminary of Columbia University,[68] where she received a Master of Arts in Religious Education (1941–1942).[69] From 1942 to 1943, Gong toured US campuses in more than two dozen states as a YWCA field representative to promote international understanding.[70] Her YWCA work

[64] The press conference was made possible with the help of American journalist Edgar Snow. Snow taught part-time at the Department of Journalism at Yenching and was close to the left-wing students there. Lois Wheeler Snow, Edgar Snow's China: A Personal Account of the Chinese Revolution compiled from the Writings of Edgar Snow (New York: Random House, 1981), 103, featuring a group photo of the Gong sisters.

[65] Jennifer Bond, 'Inculcating a Gendered Christian Internationalism: The Chinese Student YWCA', Journal of Women's History (2023) vol. 35, no. 1, 49.

[66] Elizabeth A. Littell-Lamb, The YWCA in China: The Making of a Chinese Christian Women's Institution, 1899–1957 (Chicago: University of Chicago Press, 2023), 99–100, 194.

[67] At the time, it was an established strategy to have overseas CCP members to make contact with Chinese students studying in Western universities. Gong Pusheng was likely given the instruction by the CCP Southern Bureau. Christopher D. Sneller, Let the World Come to Union and Union Go into the World: Union Theological Seminary in the City of New York and the Quest for Indigenous Christianity in Twentieth Century China (PhD thesis, King's College London, 2015), 77, fn 455.

[68] Union Theological Seminary was *alma mater* to many prominent Chinese Christian leaders. One research pointed out that Gong Pusheng's network at Union later allowed her to connect said leaders with Zhou Enlai. The collaboration that ensued proved crucial for projects of 'sinicizing Christianity' in mainland China after 1949. Christopher D. Sneller, 'The Role of Union Theological Seminary (New York) in Sinicizing Christianity', Zheng Yangwen (ed), Sinicizing Christianity (Leiden; Boston: Brill, 2017), 70.

[69] 'Chinese "Y" Field Representative Grants Interview during Visit' The Bennett Banner (1943) vol. XII no.6, 1, 3. Gong Pusheng had written her master's thesis on 'Chinese Christian Student Movement, 1937-1941'.

[70] Ye Zufu, Zishen nü waijiao jia Gong Pusheng [Seasoned Female Diplomat Gong Pusheng], Guoji rencai jiaoliu [International Talent] (1995) vol. 9, 28. During her outreach with American audiences, Gong would at times sneak in subtle rebukes of the Nationalist Government. When asked about how

gradually allowed her to befriend novelist Pearl S. Buck,[71] civil rights activists Paul and Eslanda Goode Robeson,[72] and First Lady Eleanor Roosevelt.[73] Buck's East and West Association—which evolved into a left-leaning network nurturing critical perspectives against racial and colonial dynamics in Allied nations[74]—would provide Gong with crucial logistical assistance during wartime.[75]

After Gong had returned to China in 1943, Zhou Enlai again encouraged her to pursue academic training in the West. Zhou directly cited Wu Yifang as a role model: 'How great it would be if we had a great scholar of the calibre of Wu Yifang inside our Party!'[76] Gong originally planned to pursue doctoral studies in

she viewed Madame Chiang Kai-shek (Song Meiling)—who, through her wartime visits, enchanted both the American political class and the public—Gong politely suggested that 'there are women in China who are just as potent in leadership as Mme. Chiang but they are little known because they do not have high social status of Mme. Chiang.' The Bennet Banner (n 69), 3. In her later writings for the American audience, her rejection of KMT politics became more apparent. Writing for *People through Books* in 1945, Gong asserted that 'the Chinese people had rejected Chiang's and Guomindang [KMT]'s claim to be the superman and superparty of China.' Robert Shaffer, 'Pearl S. Buck and the East and West Association: Trajectory and Fate of "Critical Internationalism", 1940–1950', Peace & Change (2003) vol. 28, no. 1, 9.

[71] Pearl S. Buck (Chinese name '赛珍珠', 1892–1973) was herself a missionary kid born and raised in China. Her novel *The Good Earth* was considered to be one of the earliest works that offered truly sympathetic depictions of the Chinese people. Buck was an ardent anti-imperialist and proponent of racial equality, a close confidant to Eleanor Roosevelt, and a flagbearer of the Chinese cause during the Second World War. She was also critical of Nationalist leader Chiang Kai-shek and the KMT. Gong's relationship with her was likely central for her networking initiatives that put her in touch with many American luminaries.

[72] Robeson took up the Chinese cause during the Second World War. Collaborating with left-wing musician Liu Liangmo, Robeson helped introduce 'March of the Volunteers', the future PRC national anthem, to Western audiences. When Gong returned to the US in 1950 for a United Nations session, she connected the Chinese delegation with Robeson. At that occasion, the Chinese Ambassador Wu Xiuquan reciprocated support for the African American civil rights cause on behalf of the PRC.

[73] Gong Pusheng and Eleanor Roosevelt's meeting was reported in both Chinese biographies of Gong and Western publications. According to one Chinese depiction, Gong met Roosevelt on three occasions in 1943, including one visit to Roosevelt's Hyde Park residence, where Gong briefed the American First Lady on the war situation in Asia. French journalist Roger Faligot, however, painted Gong as having successfully inserted herself as a 'close friend and confidante'; with such status, Gong 'gathered valuable intelligence that she passed onto the Chinese secret service.' Roger Faligot, Chinese Spies: From Chairman Mao to Xi Jinping (Natasha Lehrer trs, London: Hurst & Company, 2015), 52. One ought to treat Faligot's claim with a grain of salt, for his description of the Gong sisters was littered with factual errors, and no citations were given for his main claim. Faligot mentioned that Gong Pusheng's meeting with Roosevelt was picked up by the Federal Bureau of Investigation agents, although she was merely identified as the daughter of a KMT officer. It might be possible to find traces of Gong Pusheng in the voluminous investigative files on Eleanor Roosevelt and Pearl S. Buck produced by the Federal Bureau of Investigation; the author's research on this matter has so far been fruitless.

[74] On the East and West Association's anti-racist and anti-colonial activism, see Robert Shaffer (n 70).

[75] In an official biography, Gong was listed as a 'secretary' at Buck's East and West Association. See, 'Gong Pusheng tongzhi shengping' [Biography of comrade Gong Pusheng] (MFA Bureau for Retired Personnel, August 2007) <http://www.cspfs.com.cn/Longpusheng.html> accessed 20 June 2025. A *New York Times Magazine* profile on the 1950 PRC UN delegation identified Gong as 'Buck's translator'. Walter Sullivan, 'Wu of China: "More General than Diplomat"', *New York Times Magazine* (New York, 17 December 1950), section 6, 12. It was said that Gong only managed to return to the US in 1945 thanks to the invitation extended by Buck's East and West Association. See also Ye Zufu (n 70), 8.

[76] Ye Zufu (n 70), 29.

international affairs at Columbia, but the final stretch of the Second World War had her stranded in Calcutta, India, for six months.[77] By the time she reached the US in August 1945, the networks that had previously supported her were besieged by growing anti-Communist activities. She eventually spent one year attending Columbia University Extension, which offered academic programmes for part-time students and professionals.[78] By 1946, with her visa approaching expiration, Gong obtained a position—through the introduction of an American luminary—at the United Nations Secretariat. She worked first as a staff member to the Division of Human Rights,[79] and later at the Division of Social Activities.[80] Gong was fond of her days at the Lake Success UN Headquarters, surrounded by like-minded colleagues who had stood against fascism and shared the vision for 'a new world truly free and equal'.[81] The Division of Human Rights was then under the directorship of Canadian international lawyer John Humphrey. He was entrusted with producing a preliminary draft of what would become the Universal Declaration of Human Rights, which Humphrey completed—with the support of his staff—by June 1947.[82] Gong could be spotted in a 1947 photo documenting a Commission

[77] Gong's stay in India was likely supported by YWCA China. Jennifer Bond (n 65), 49. Gong spent some of these six months rendering novellas by Ding Ling—Yan'an's foremost left-wing feminist writer—into English, published as *When I Was in Sha Chuan (Cloud Village)* in Bombay (Mumbai) that same year. Gong's translations added many annotations describing and contextualizing life inside CCP-controlled regions. The project was largely understood as an attempt to win Indian sympathy for the Chinese cause, which again fitted Gong's mission of constructing an 'international united front' for the Chinese cause. See Xiong Ying, 'Fan faxisi zhanzheng zhong de "yinbi liliang": yi Ding Ling wo zai xiacun de shihou jiqi fanyi wei li' ['Hidden Forces' during the Anti-Fascism War: A case study of Ding Ling's When I Was in Sha Chuan and its translation], Wenxue pinglun [Literary Review] (2015) vol. 5, 44–52.

[78] 'CUer is Chinese Envoy', *Columbia Daily Spectator* (New York, 28 November 1950), 4. Columbia University Extensions was later restructured as School of General Studies.

[79] Richard Jolly, Interview with Margaret Bruce, former colleague and roommate with Gong Pusheng at the UN Secretariat (Mount Kisco, NY, United States, 25 October 2003), United Nations Intellectual History Project, the Graduate School and University Center, City University of New York, 9.

[80] Both Divisions were under the Department of Social Affairs, one of eight original Secretariat bodies United Nations. 'Social Welfare Advisory Functions—Seminar Far East—India—1949', Reference Code: S-0441-0102-07-00001, United Nations Archives and Records Management Section, New York.

[81] Ruan Hong, 'Waishi shengya liushi nian' [Six Decades of Foreign Affairs Work], in Cheng Xiangjun (ed), Nü Waijiao guan [Women Diplomats] (Beijing: People's Sports Publishing House, 1995), 436. Her office-mate Margaret Bruce recalled that while she was unaware of Gong's CCP membership, she could sense that those who socialized with Gong at the UN held sympathy for leftist politics. Interview with Margaret Bruce (n 79), 32.

[82] Humphrey, himself a scholar of international law, recalled that he had produced the Secretariat draft text from his residence. He did acknowledge having referenced 'a score of drafts' the Secretariat had collected. John P. Humphrey, Human Rights and the United Nations: A Great Adventure (Dobbs Ferry, NY: Transnational Publishers, 1984), 31. Another study specified that 'He [Humphrey] and his multinational staff had been collecting and studying pertinent materials from all over the world'; the final volume of proposals, models, and drafts collected was vast enough to overwhelm members of the Commission. Mary Ann Glendon, A World Made New: Eleanor Roosevelt and the Universal Declaration of Human Rights (New York: Random House, 2001), 49–50. Said preparatory work must be accredited to Humphrey's staff that included Gong Pusheng, which he described as small but capable: 'Intellectually, the members of the Division of Human Rights could have held their own in most

of Human Rights meeting, with Roosevelt and Humphrey chairing the session.[83]

Gong Pusheng returned to China in 1948 and worked on women's affairs inside the CCP before leading the Department of International Organisation and Conference at the PRC MFA.[84] While the PRC's early attitude towards the UN vacillated between favourable and antagonistic,[85] it had attached great significance to its membership in international organizations and participation of international conferences. Its Nationalist rival was, by 1949, well embedded in important international institutions. Support from the US and US allies further consolidated the Nationalist Government's ability to represent 'China' at these international fora. The PRC government had been wary of simultaneous PRC and Nationalist presence in international organizations and international conferences, which contributed to the 'two-China situation'. Gong's mandate was to survey relevant international organizations on behalf of the MFA and coordinate with allies on strategies.[86] During the nineteenth International Conference of the Red Cross in New Delhi, 1957, the US proposal allowing 'all governments invited to attend the conference [were to] be addressed according to their own official titles' prevailed over the PRC's counter-proposal. Such development accordingly allowed the Nationalist Government to attend as 'Republic of China'. As the leader of the PRC government delegation, Gong choreographed a protest: when the Nationalist delegation entered the venue, the Chinese government delegation and the Chinese Red Cross Society exited, followed by a third of the total delegations present, including the host society the Indian Red Cross.[87]

groups of civil servants or academics ... The fact that they were of man races, nationalities and creeds added to their richness as a team.' ibid, John P. Humphrey, 7.

[83] 'Commission of Human Rights of the United Nations Economic and Social Council, 27 January 1947' (UN Photo) <https://media.un.org/photo/en/asset/oun7/oun7742877> accessed 5 July 2025.

[84] In 1950 Gong was also named a council member of the reorganized Red Cross Society of China, and later became its Vice President (likely during the 1980s). [Tushuo 110 nian: xin zhongguo gaizu] '110 years of Red Cross Society of China in Pictures (III): reorganisation in the PRC', Hong [Red] (2015) vol. 1, 58.

[85] While striving to restore its seat at the UN, the PRC also attempted international outreach through other unofficial and semi-official channels, in which Gong took part. For instance, Gong had worked as an intermediary who facilitated communications between the MFA and the Chinese Academy of Science in 1955 when Chinese geologist Li Siguang (Vice President of the Academy) was invited to co-sign the Russell–Einstein Manifesto. Research on this episode indicated that Gong was assigned to a supporting role. See Gordon Barrett, China's Cold War Science Diplomacy (Cambridge: Cambridge University Press, 2022), Chapter 2, citing PRC Ministry of Foreign Affairs Archive sources.

[86] Soviet official K. A. Krutikov had in his 1958 report detailed Gong's explanation of the Chinese position in scenarios when dealing with the representation of China in international organisations. 'From the Journal of K. A. Krutikov, "Record of a Conversation with GONG PUSHENG, Chief of the PRC MFA Department of International Organizations"', 1 March 1958, Gary Goldberg (trs) (*Wilson Center Digital Archive*, Record ID 280698, 17 November 2021) <https://digitalarchive.wilsoncenter.org/document/280698>, accessed 5 July 2025.

[87] François Bugnion, 'The International Conference of the Red Cross and Red Crescent: Challenges, Key Issues and Achievements' Mrs Glynis Thompson (trs), International Review of the Red Cross (2009) vol. 91, no. 876, 681–682. Ruan Hong (n 81), 442–43.

33.2.4 Han Youtong 韩幽桐 (1908–1985)

Han Youtong's contact with international law was primarily the byproduct of her journey as a Communist revolutionary, making her case a unique window for observing a 'Chinese Communist's encounter' with an inherently liberal field. Unlike the other three protagonists, she was born into a poverty-stricken Hui family in rural Jilin Province. Her early education relied on public girls' schools rather than the increasingly expensive missionary schools. After middle school, she came under the tutelage of May Fourth-period women's rights advocate Guo Longzhen through the introduction of her cousin (another early CCP member).[88] Having been inducted into the CCP at age 18, Han edited the Communist magazine *Women's Friend (Funü zhiyou)*. In the aftermath of the magazine's closure following the KMT crackdown in 1927, Han studied law at Beiping University School of Business and Law while continuing her activism. She met her future husband, fellow Communist, journalist, and future jurist Zhang Youyu, when both were arrested in an anti-government protest in 1927. Han relocated to Tokyo in 1932, partly to continue her legal studies, partly to save her and her partner from KMT encirclement.[89] After one year of preparatory work at Waseda University, Han applied for the Graduate School of Tokyo Imperial University Faculty of Law in 1933. Having passed exams required by the Faculty Council,[90] Han became the first female student admitted to the faculty's graduate programme, preceding native Japanese students. She was supervised by Yokota Kisaburō 横田喜三郎 and Kamikawa Hikomatsu 神川彦松, respectively, on international law and diplomatic history. She became a 'selected subsidized student' in Japan's version of the Boxer Indemnity scholarship programme.[91]

Han's graduate work at Tokyo was marked by ambivalence. On the one hand, her graduate writings—which focused on recent Sino–Soviet diplomatic

[88] Han Youtong's cousin was Ma Jun (not to be confused with the PRC international lawyer in 33.4), a comrade of Zhou Enlai and Guo Longzhen in Tianjin during the May Fourth Movement.

[89] Details about Han Youtong's time in Japan mainly referenced her reminiscence, Han Youtong, '東京大學法學部研究室での五年間' [Five Years at the Tokyo University Faculty of Law Graduate School] in わが青春の日本: 中国知識人の日本回想 [The Japan of My Youth: Chinese Intellectuals' Recollections of Japan] (Beijing: People's China, 1982), 113–125.

[90] Tokyo Imperial University only began admitting girls into its undergraduate programmes in 1946, mostly because Japanese women could not access schools that prepare students for imperial university admissions. At the graduate level, however, each faculty council enjoyed a certain discretion. Han Youtong represented the turning point for women at Tokyo Imperial University, and soon more women followed in her footsteps.

[91] According to historian Zhou Yichuan, the Japanese government established its own 'foreign students subsidy system' with its share of the Boxer Indemnity, which it had formulated as a part of its 'China Cultural Project' under the aegis of its Ministry of Foreign Affairs. The program in which Han was selected was administered exclusively by the Japanese government (hence 'selected subsidized student'). Han Youtong had received subsidies under this system between 1934–36 and 1937–38. 周一川 Zhou Yichuan, '帝国大学における中国人女子留学生 (1924-1944年) 一データ解読と事例分析' [Study of Female Chinese Students at Imperial Universities (1927–1944): Data Analysis and Case Studies], Kanagawa University Bulletin of the Institute for Humanities Research (2022) vol. 68, 53–54.

histories—seemed like a natural extension of her Communist identity.[92] Most interestingly, Han invested part of her spare time in socializing with Japanese working-class people and members of a progressive society as an exercise of Marxism-inspired fieldwork. On the other hand, her relationship with supervisor Yokota Kisaburō appeared to have kindled a fleeting yet genuine hope for new international legal scholarship of the interwar period. Yokota, a Japanese liberal and avowed Kelsenian, was 'the only scholar of international law in Japan who openly challenged the position of the military and the government with regard to the Manchurian Incident of 1931'.[93] Han appeared inspired by Yokota's critical stance on Japan's aggression and offered to translate Yokota's 1932 international law textbook (volume I). In Han's translator's preface, which she wrote in 1933, Han displayed a newfound hope in the school of 'Pure Theory of Law'. For Han, Yokota's commitment to 'objectivity' through 'pure theory' and an 'international community-based standpoint'[94] represented a rebuke against 'old school international lawyers, whose state-centric scholarship had only served to legitimise aggression from the strong while discrediting resistance from the weak'.[95] The latter observation was a reference to the Sino–Japanese lawfare over the Manchuria Crisis, over which Japanese scholars had justified Japanese military actions as self-defence against 'illegal' Chinese boycotts of Japanese goods.[96] Writing during the aftermath of the release of the Lytton Report and the similarly fruitless lawfare efforts, Han also registered her displeasure with Chinese international lawyers who 'continued to pander to the scholarship of those [apologist old school international lawyers]'.

Han's hope had evidently dimmed by the time of the translation's publication by the Commercial Press in Shanghai in January 1937, just half a year shy of Japan's full-scale invasion. During this time, Han had witnessed the unfolding of the Abyssinia Crisis and commented on the crisis at the League.[97] She departed from Tokyo immediately after the 'Marco Polo Incident' of 7 July 1937—which marked

[92] ibid, 49.

[93] Shimoda Takeso, 'In Memoriam: Dr. Kisaburo Yokota (1896–1993)', Japanese Annual of International Law (1993) vol. 36, 2. Between 1931 and 1933, Yokota was one of the lonely voices that criticized Japan's aggression, including its framing of its occupation of Manchuria as self-defence, its recognition of the puppet regime Manchukuo, and its subsequent withdrawal from the League of Nations. Ian Nish, Japan's Struggle with Internationalism: Japan, China and the League of Nations, 1931–1933 (London and New York: Routledge, 2009), 159, 239. Han's other supervisor, Kamikawa, by comparison, proposed that Manchuria ought to be made into a neutral territory.

[94] Yokota Kisaburō, 'Author's Preface', in Yokota Kisaburō, Guojifa, shang juan [International Law, Vol. I], Han Guiqin (Han Youtong) (trs) (Shanghai: The Commercial Press, 1937).

[95] Han Youtong, 'Translator's Preface', ibid.

[96] On examples of Sino–Japanese exchange on the legality of Chinese boycotts of Japanese goods, see Kenzo Takayanagi, 'On the Legality of the Chinese Boycott', Pacific Affairs (1932) vol. 5 no. 10, 855–862; and H. C. Wang [Wang Huacheng], 'International Law and Anti-Japanese Boycott', Pacific Affairs (1933) vol. 6 no. 7, 373–378.

[97] Han Guiqin (Han Youtong), 'Yiya zhanzheng jieshu yu guoji lianmeng zhi weiji' [Conclusion of the Italo- Abyssinian War and Crisis for the League of Nations], Liudong xuebao [Journal for Chinese Students in Japan] (1936) vol. 2 no. 3.

the beginning of Japan's invasion—and left her graduate studies behind. To resume her Communist work, Han dropped her given name '*gui qin*' (the characters for 'sweet osmanthus' and 'music instrument') for the slightly more gender-neutral '*you tong*' ('secluded' and 'paulownia tree'). Between 1937 and 1938, Han briefly taught international law at the National Northwest Union University at Xi'an, before she and other left-leaning professors were ousted by the Ministry of Education. After her firing, Han devoted herself fully to writing. Her wartime publication focused on two areas: international affairs, the various aspects of the Second World War, and women's issues in China, often intended as a critique of Nationalist policies. Save for one article where Han introduced and complimented the Soviet Union's instrumental attitude towards international law (i.e., 'seizing and appropriating international law' as an instrument in inter-state struggles),[98] she appeared to have mostly withdrawn from the field. In her 1946 monograph Methodology for Researching International Issues, where she elaborated an anti-formalist approach premised upon historical materialism, international law was mentioned only once, solely within the context that international legal rules counted as one type of research material when cataloguing collected information.[99]

Like other Chinese Communist women of her generation, Han Youtong's career path during the PRC was shaped by Party directives. She went on to split her time between women's affairs and law.[100] However, her expertise in law and women's rights placed her on semi-official international channels, the so-called people-to-people exchanges.[101] In her dual capacity as an executive member of the All-China Women's Federation and a leading PRC jurist, Han Youtong visited the UK, Pakistan, Algeria, the USSR, Japan, and Austria respectively.[102]

33.3 The People's Republic of China Era

To illuminate the place of professional women in the PRC, one must first attempt to curate the complicated relationship between the Chinese Communist revolutionary movement and 'women's emancipation'. During the New Cultural Movement (1916–1920s), future CCP founders Li Dazhao and Chen Duxiu both

[98] Han Youtong, Weide shi dui lixiang de zhuiqiu [For the Pursuit of Ideals] (China Law Press, 1989), 131. This article accounted for the only international law-themed writing included in two essay collections published after Han's passing.

[99] Han Youtong, Guoji wenti yanjiu fa' [Methodology for Researching International Issues] (Beiping: Zhongwai chubanshe, 1946), 63.

[100] During the early years of the PRC, Han acted as a major authority on marriage law, and was particularly vocal on the women's right to divorce.

[101] One should not discount this form of popular diplomacy, which during the 1950s accounted for the main avenue for Republican-era intellectuals Wang Tieya to fraternize with foreign counterparts outside of China. See Chapter 29 by the same author.

[102] 'Zhizhuo di wei gongchan zhuyi shiye fendou—daonian Han Youtong' [Persistently Fighting for the Communist Cause: Remembering Han Youtong], People's Daily, 2 March 1986.

engaged with the 'woman question' and advocated for the liberation of women, an element of their broader project of dismantling Chinese society's 'feudal' elements and fostering transformation.[103] In 1924, as the CCP and KMT formed the First United Front to struggle against conservative warlord regimes (an episode known as the 'National Revolution'), both parties set up feminist programmes to mobilize the mass participation of women. After the KMT–CCP coalition collapsed in 1927, the rival parties both retreated from their prior feminist aspirations while continuing to politicize gender issues to their respective advantage. In the 1930s, the reigning KMT initiated the neotraditional 'New Life Movement', which naturalized conventional gender roles for the sake of national rejuvenation. The CCP, after being forced to relocate to China's rural hinterlands, recalibrated its commitment towards 'women's emancipation' (*funü jiefang*). This decision was based on both retrospection of previous feminist programmes (now judged as having overly catered to 'bourgeois women') and the challenges of governing rural regions where patriarchal control of women was deeply rooted.[104]

During its revolutionary years, gender hierarchy was also apparent in the daily operations of the CCP.[105] Women cadres were predominantly assigned to supportive roles. Those who were proficient in English and comparatively knowledgeable about international affairs—often the fruits of missionary school education—were allocated the duties of translators, interpreters, propagandists, international news editors, intelligence collectors, and united front workers. These types of labour would later be categorized as 'foreign affairs work' (*waishi gongzuo*)[106] by the growing CCP foreign policy apparatus led by Zhou Enlai, the future PRC Premier and Foreign Minister. When the Ministry of Foreign Affairs ('MFA') was established in November 1949, women cadres accounted for less than a third of its initial 285 staff. Of the roughly two dozen leadership positions, three were occupied by women (the Gong sisters accounted for two).[107]

[103] See Li Dazhao, 'The Postwar Woman Question' [Zhanhou zhi furen wenti] (1919); and Chen Duxiu, The Woman Question and Socialism [Funü wenti yu shehui zhuyi] (1921), in Chinese Studies in History (1997) vol. 31, no. 2.

[104] Christina Kelley Gilmartin, Engendering the Chinese Revolution: Radical Women, Communist Politics, and Mass Movements in the 1920s (University of California Press, 1995), 215–216.

[105] Leftist women writer Ding Ling, for one, was shocked by the mistreatment and discrimination against women cadres at the CCP headquarters Yan'an following her relocation there, which she documented in her 1942 essay 'Sanba jie yougan' [Thoughts on March 8].

[106] 'Foreign affairs work' (*waishi gongzuo*) serves as an umbrella term for all forms of work outside of the core diplomatic functions executed by central governmental authorities. Zhang Lili, Waijiao juece [Foreign Policy Analysis] (Beijing: World Affairs Press, 2007), 44.

[107] Ronald C. Keith, Diplomacy of Zhou Enlai (New York: Palgrave Macmillan, 1989), 39. Of these three women, Gong Peng served as Director of the Department of Intelligence (later renamed the Department of Press, Communication and Public Diplomacy); Gong Pusheng served as Deputy Director and later Director of the Department of International Organisations and Conferences; and Yang Gang 杨刚 (1908–1957) served as secretary of the Foreign Policy Committee. Yang Gang was a prominent journalist who once studied at Radcliffe College on a fellowship. More specifically, Gong Peng was also the only female cadre who was directly involved in designing the structure of the new MFA. Yang Fajin, Xin zhongguo chengli chuqi de waijiao duiwu [The Foreign Service in New China's Early Phases], Dangshi bolan [General Review of the Communist Party of China] (2023) vol. 1, 43.

The new MFA was designed to execute Chairman Mao Zedong's vision of 'starting anew' and 'cleaning house before entertaining guests': Republican-era foreign relations shall be disavowed, its diplomatic institutions abandoned. The PRC was to restart its relationship with foreign countries on fresh and equal terms. In contrast to the diplomats of 'Old China' who 'had conducted diplomacy on their knees',[108] the PRC foreign service was to be 'armed' with Marxist-Leninist ideology and military-like discipline. This vision was reflected in the MFA's personnel composition, which can be broken down into four types: high-level party functionaries; senior military officers; cadres with foreign affairs work experience; and students trained in CCP schools. However, the first two groups were given precedence in terms of leadership positions and ambassadorships. Women cadres—which were concentrated in the third and fourth categories, with diplomatic spouses accounting for another contingent source[109]—again performed supportive functions. It was only until 1973 had the MFA saw its first female Deputy Minister in Wang Hairong (王海容, 1938–2017),[110] and 1979 when Ding Xuesong (丁雪松, 1918–2011) and Gong Pusheng were appointed as ambassadors to the Netherlands and Ireland, respectively.

While the CCP retained a handful of seasoned international law specialists from the Republican era—sometimes amiably referred to by MFA insiders as the

During my interviews, the Gong sisters were often cited as proof that the new PRC establishment was more conscientious about gender equality. A former MFA member who studied first-generation women diplomats also placed the Gong sisters as trailblazers in the group. See, Cheng Xiangjun, 'Preface', in Cheng Xiangjun (ed), Nü Waijiao guan [Women Diplomats] (Beijing: People's Sports Publishing House, 1995).

108 Zhou Enlai's speech at the inaugurating ceremony for the Ministry of Foreign Affairs, 8 November 1949, in Zhou Enlai waijiao wenxuan [Selected Papers of Zhou Enlai on Diplomacy] (Beijing: Central Party Literature Publishing House, 2000), 4–5.

109 Within this group, tensions between ideals of women's emancipation and reality had at one point manifested in stark terms. As their husbands were appointed ambassadors and consuls overseas, many of these Communist women found themselves in the uncomfortable situation of forfeiting their established careers and taking up conventional domestic roles performed by diplomatic wives (e.g., entertaining guests). Their discontent was severe enough—with some threatening divorce—that Zhou Enlai was compelled to send in his wife Deng Yingchao to pacify the wives. Liu Xiaohong, Chinese Ambassadors: The Rise of Diplomatic Professionalism since 1949 (Hong Kong: Hong Kong University Press, 2001), 20. See also, Jiang Huajie, Geming waijiao de zhangli: guanyu xin zhongguo furen wijiao de lishi kaocha (1950-1965) [Tension of Revolutionary Diplomacy: A Historical Examination of PRC Lady Diplomacy (1950–1965)], CPC History Studies (2016) vol. 5, 35–46.

110 The rise of Wang Hairong (who was promoted to Deputy Minister at the age of 36) could perhaps be attributed to the openings and mobility wrought by the chaotic Cultural Revolution, which came at the expense of established figures including Gong Pusheng and Gong Peng. During this period, a group of relatively young women—Zhang Hanzhi (1935–2008), Wang Hairong (1938–2017), Tang Wensheng (1943–), Qi Zonghua (1930–), Luo Xu (1934–2001), referred to as the MFA's 'Five Golden Flowers'—obtained influence disproportionate to their seniority and rank. Both their entrance into the MFA and their rise to power were ostensibly linked to their gender and family lineage. All five worked as interpreters. During the period of Sino-American rapprochement, these women worked closely with top CCP leaders, most importantly Chairman Mao Zedong. It is theorized that the combination of unique historical circumstances gave some of these women outsized access to these towering figures, consequently elevating some of them to impactful powerbrokers within MFA.

'veteran experts' (*lao zhuanjia*)—most non-Party intellectuals were treated with various levels of suspicion given their Western educational pedigree. Both Wu Yifang and Chen Fangzhi were given this treatment. In 1950, Renmin University of China (Chinese People's University) was founded in Beijing as the Party-decreed bastion for introducing Soviet scholarship and academic culture. With the introduction of Soviet instructors and textbooks, Russian replaced English as the primary foreign language underpinning higher learning.[111] There, the Soviet school of international law was taught in Renmin's law and diplomacy faculties. Some of its early cadets were young women who had contributed to the revolution. This was the origin story for the leading first-generation women international lawyers, including Ma Jun 马骏 (1925–2006), Cheng Xiaoxia 程晓霞 (1933–2014), and Liu Huishan 刘慧珊 (1932–2020). Ma Jun was a student Party member embedded at Peking University;[112] Cheng Xiaoxia had served as secretary and cultural instructor inside the People's Liberation Army; and Liu Huishan worked as a student messenger and propagandist. After the 1952 National Reorganization of Higher Education—during which important Republican-era international law research and education institutions (Tsinghua, Yenching, Peking, Soochow, Wuhan) were dismantled—Renmin emerged as the *de facto* centre for PRC international law studies. In the coming years, Renmin University International Law Teaching and Research Section played an essential role in reshaping the disciplinary landscape, achieved through the translation of Soviet scholarship and the cultivation of new teachers to be assigned to other institutions. In 1955, Renmin's Faculty of Diplomacy was reorganized into China University of Foreign Affairs ('CUFA'). Ma Jun was promoted to the new leadership at CUFA and its international law section; with this transition, Zhou Enlai allegedly credited Ma Jun as 'the PRC's first woman international lawyer'.[113] A third new institution appeared in 1959 under the aegis of the Chinese Academy of Sciences, which hosted many law students who had returned from their sponsored studies in the USSR and Eastern European socialist countries. It became home to two early PRC women scholars with rare[114]

[111] Many PRC women academics had Russian as their primary foreign language. Liu Huishan, who had studied Russian in the People's Liberation Army Foreign Language College prior to 1949, was not merely a student at the Faculty of Law but had simultaneously served as interpreter to the Soviet instructors. Liu Huishan and Wang Keju would go on to translate many Soviet classics, such as Tunkin's *Theory of International Law*. See Tongjin [Tunkin], Guoji fa lilun wenti [Theory of International Law] (Beijing: World Affairs Press, 1965).

[112] Ma Jun was part of the concerted effort that mobilized the anti-American movement protesting the rape of Peking student Shen Chong in 1946.

[113] Interview with Li Yuguo, Ma Jun's son-in-law and former student at China University of Foreign Affairs (WeChat voice call, 16 September 2024).

[114] Several batches of Chinese law students were sponsored by the USSR and other socialist countries, which added to the difficulties in identifying the gender composition of each cohort. That said, the first cohort of 12 Chinese students who reached the USSR in 1951 included only one woman, 司马念媛Sima Nianyuan.

international experience: the Bulgarian-trained Wang Keju (王可菊) and the USSR-trained Wu Yunqi (吴云琪).[115]

While it remains difficult to ascertain the exact status of early PRC women academics due to the scarcity of historical data, one can still reasonably deduce from published oral histories that women remained underrepresented in academia and study-abroad opportunities.[116] However, the advantage that first-generation women had over their Republican-era predecessors did not grow beyond the 1950s. From the mid-1950s onwards, escalating political campaigns caused stagnation of the careers of early PRC scholars.[117] The general atmosphere of 'legal nihilism' made it difficult to publish legal research,[118] while the collectivist academic culture pushed scholars to co-author research projects without individual credit.[119] Additionally, authority rooted in the new institutions' proximity to Soviet knowledge evaporated as the Sino–Soviet schism grew. There were new graduates between the late 1950s and early 1960s, who should have theoretically made up a second generation of women international lawyers. However, chaos unleashed by the Cultural Revolution robbed this cohort of their careers. Such was the experience of Liang Shuying 梁淑英 (1940–), who had obtained her law degree at Beijing College of Politics and Law (1960–1964; now China University of Political Science and Law), yet whose teaching career froze after 1966. During the early

[115] Wang Keju and Wu Yunqi's time in the USSR and Bulgaria was briefly recounted by their study-abroad cohorts at a 2010 reunion. See, 'Faxue suo, guoji fa suo liusu dong xuezhe zuotanhui zai waibin shi juxing' [Symposium hosted by the CASS Institute of Law and Institute of International Law with Scholars who had studied in the USSR and Eastern European Socialist Countries, held at the Guest Hall] (China Legal Science, 30 September 2010) <http://iolaw.cssn.cn/xshy/201009/t20100930_4608243.shtml> accessed 5 July 2025. Wang and Wu accounted for the only two women contributors in the PRC's first ever international law textbook published in 1981, edited by Wang Tieya and Weimin. The duo (together with Wang Sunhuan) co-authored the chapter on the law of the sea (Chapter 5), a field that Wu was familiar with due to her previous work in translating Soviet materials on the same subject.

[116] In one seminal oral history work whose first volume collected the interviews of 48 surviving PRC jurists born before 1935 (who were educated prior to 1957), only 3 were women. See Zhongguo faxuejia fangtan lu, diyi juan [Talking with Chinese Jurists, Vol. 1], He Qinhua (ed) (Beijing: Peking University Press, 2010).

[117] The 1958 Great Leap Forward was a turning point for university life, during which period many faculty members and students prioritized physical labour as a form of political education, greatly disrupting knowledge research and teaching.

[118] 'Wang Jiafu' [Interview of Wang Jiafu], in He Qinhua (ed) (n 116), 48–49.

[119] For instance, Ma Jun and Chen Tiqiang, colleagues at CUFA, had in 1964 co-written an article that was published under their respective pennames Yang Xin 杨欣 and Chen Jian 陈健. The name Yang Xin likely alluded to Ma Jun's original name, Yang Guixin 杨桂馨, which she had forfeited during the late 1940s as a measure to shield her family from repercussions due to her CCP activities. Yang Xin and Chen Jian, 'Jielu he pipan diguo zhuyi zhe guanyu guojia zhuquan wenti de miulu' [Expose and criticise the imperialist fallacies on the issue of national sovereignty], Zhengfa yanjiu [Political-Legal Research] (1964) vol. 4. This connection was only revealed when a collection of Chen Tiqiang's writings was published posthumously, in which Ma Jun's contribution was credited. This is a quite literal case of an early PRC woman international lawyer and her memory being bound to the shadows of her male seniors. Chen Tiqiang wenji [Collected Essays of Chen Tiqiang] (Beijing: China Law Press, 1985), Introduction.

1980s, she would join younger students in Wang Tieya's classroom to renew her understanding of international law.

However, even as the country was sliding towards radicalism and isolationism, within certain bubbles (such as the MFA and its appendage institutions, such as the CUFA) the culture of pragmatism was preserved. Within these environments, it was still possible to observe the resilience of established professional hierarchies and enduring values of legal expertise. Between 1958 and 1961, Liu Huishan was placed under one-on-one tutelage of the LSE-trained lawyer Li Haopei on the topic of private international law. When Liu was bogged down by assignments due to her lack of fundamentals in Western private law, she received additional guidance from her Oxford-trained neighbour Chen Tiqiang.[120] Similarly, in 1976, Sheng Yu (盛愉, 1925–2006) preceded her Soviet-trained women peers in working in international institutions, in her case, as a deputy of the Chinese Delegation to UNESCO.[121] Sheng Yu represented a more unique case: an alumna of the Republican-era French-Catholic Aurora University in Shanghai (1943–1947), Sheng Yu later obtained her doctorate in law at the University of Paris.[122] Although she did not work exclusively in the field of international law post 1949, she was proficient in Western legal scholarship.[123] Unlike most Republican-era male international lawyers, Sheng had been a CCP member since her student days, leaving her somewhat wedged between the typical old-school intellectuals and early PRC women international lawyers. Thus, as a trusted insider, Sheng was granted priority access to the world of international organizations.

Entering the 1980s, rehabilitated Republican-era scholars—with Wang Tieya and Chen Tiqiang leading the charge—seized the momentum of China's Reform and Opening-up and began reshaping the decimated disciplinary landscape. Their educational background in elite Western institutions became an important source of cultural and social capital within both China and the West, enabling them to procure desperately needed external resources for building up libraries and sending students to Western institutions. Wang Tieya was adamant that the Chinese discipline must swiftly familiarize itself with the latest Western scholarship to make up

[120] Professor Yang Yun of CUFA had interviewed Liu Huishan in 2018 and is now in the process of writing her biography. I am grateful that Prof. Yang has authorized me to use this anecdote on the relationship between Liu Huishan, Li Haopei, and Chen Tiqiang.

[121] In 1971, UNESCO automatically applied UNGA Resolution 2758 and recognised the PRC's representation of China. Sheng Yu's name can be found on lists detailing national delegations since 1976. See, for example, Resolutions and decisions adopted by the Executive Board at its 100th session, Paris and Nairobi, 27 September–14 October, 26 October–30 November 1976, Doc No.: 100 EX/Decisions, UNESCO Digital Library. Sheng Yu later assumed a teaching post at the Chinese Academy of Social Sciences in 1979.

[122] Sheng Chengmao, Shengshi jiazu·Suzhou·liu yuan [The Sheng family, Suzhou, the Lingering Garden] (Shanghai: Wenhui Press, 2016), 109–110, 138–139.

[123] There is little literature detailing Sheng Yu's educational pedigree. However, since the early 1980s she had consistently published on international law topics, covering areas such as anti-hegemonism, nationality law, and international currencies and finance.

for lost time. For this purpose, he arranged for the transfer of reference librarian Tian Ruxuan 田如萱 (1932–2019) from CUFA to Peking University. Tian was part of the last cohorts at Soochow University Law School in Shanghai (Republican China's one-of-a-kind American-style law school), and one of the earlier graduates of Renmin University Faculty of Diplomacy. The duo succeeded in establishing a reference library complete with collections of treaty sources, jurisprudence of international courts and tribunals, UN publications, and scholarly works, attached to the Peking University Institute of International Law.[124] In the coming years, Tian would routinely receive future scholars-in-training who wished to utilize the library's resources.

Wang Tieya's sense of urgency in reconnecting the Chinese discipline with its foreign counterparts also manifested in his pedagogical practices. He prioritized admission of graduate students with better English proficiency: in his reasoning, compared to inadequacy in processing English-language sources, deficiency in legal fundamentals was relatively easy to remedy. Many graduate students who studied at Peking during the 1980s were thus women with prior bachelor's degrees[125] in English,[126] some of whom later emerged as leading members of the second-generation women international lawyers. Such was the case for Bai Guimei 白桂梅 (1954–; Peking University English Department, 1974–1978), Li Hongyun 李红云 (1951–; Beijing International Studies University), Song Ying 宋英 (Beijing International Studies University, 1979–1983), Mei Xiaokan 梅小侃 (1950–; Hohhot Normal Junior College, English major, 1977–1980), and the current ICJ Judge Xue Hanqin 薛捍勤 (1955–; Beijing Foreign Studies University, English Department, 1976–1980).[127] Additionally, the two heavyweights at Peking University, Wang Tieya and Zhao Lihai, were also part of the early groups of senior professors authorized to supervise doctoral candidates (Wang in 1981, Zhao in 1984). These circumstances facilitated their women disciples' future pursuit of doctoral studies. In 1986, Mei Xiaokan, a supervisee

[124] Wang and Tian also co-edited a reference material collection in 1982. See, Wang Tieya and Tian Ruxuan (eds) Guoji fa ziliao xuanbian [Selected Materials of International Law] (Beijing: China Law Press, 1982).

[125] This prerequisite for English-language proficiency privileged students from cities with high-quality public education and those from intellectual families. All of the following individuals were from Beijing or Shanghai (Judge Xue Hanqin).

[126] It is important to point out the almost universal perception that language is a 'female subject', and that women hold some form of advantage in acquiring second and foreign languages (although opinions varied among the interviewees on this matter). Current empirical studies on the question, however, revealed 'inconclusive and inconsistent findings', including whether the source of said advantage is 'nature or nurture'. See Venus Chan, 'Nature or Nurture? A Critical Analysis of Gender Differences in Second and Foreign Language Learning', Social Sciences and Education Research Review (2021) vol. 8 no. 1, 26–41.

[127] Judge Xue Hanqin was likely not a full-time student at Peking, given that she was already working for the MFA Department of Treaty and Law. Judge Xue nevertheless refers to Wang Tieya as her mentor. Her time at Peking is included in her official resume.

of Wang, defended her doctoral thesis 'On Membership in International Organizations' and became the PRC's first PhD in law.[128] Bai, Li, and Song, who assumed teaching international law at Peking, all obtained their doctorates in the 1990s.

Wang Tieya collaborated with first-generation women international lawyers on many occasions.[129] Ma Jun, known for being an effective administrator of university and party affairs, served for extended periods as the Chinese Society of International Law's Secretary-General (1985–1992). Wang Tieya and Chen Tiqiang also worked with Wang Keju in editing the international law section of the Encyclopaedia of China.[130] Ultimately, however, Wang Tieya and his generation's colossal success in remaking the field ensured that the 1980s would displace the 1950s as the Chinese discipline's golden decade. The first-generation women were thus stuck with an awkward intellectual pedigree disconnected from the present.[131] Furthermore, the specific types of labour once taken on by these women—say, Ma Jun's work in running the Chinese Society, or Liu Huishan, Wang Keju, and Wu Yunqi's contributions in rendering Soviet scholarship into Chinese—were not given equal attention compared to the treatises produced by their male seniors, due to the latter's evident intellectual value. The second-generation women, themselves the product of these men's success stories, were naturally more attached to their male mentors.[132] Intriguingly, precisely because these women had grown up in PRC's gender-neutral atmosphere, the absence of female forerunners in their field (who were on par with their male mentors) was often viewed matter-of-factly, not as a phenomenon to be problematized or traced to some larger structural issue.[133] Additionally, the same pattern of male dominance within the international law field reappeared in the 1990s. Male colleagues have since evidently

[128] Hao Tiechuan, 'Kao woguo zizhu peiyang de faxue boshi' [A Study on Doctorates in Law Fostered in the PRC] *Legal Daily* (Beijing, 9 June 2021), 10.

[129] This welcoming and supportive attitude that were embodied by the likes of Wang Tieya, Li Haopei, and Chen Tiqiang should not be taken for granted. Some early figures were certainly less subtle about their sense of superiority over women scholars trained during the PRC.

[130] Wang Tieya and Chen Tiqiang were credited as 'co-editors', while Wang Keju was listed as 'member'. See, Zhongguo da baike quanshu faxue [Encyclopaedia of China Law] (Beijing: Encyclopedia of China Publishing House, 1984).

[131] When recounting her experiences—enduring the chaos of the 1960s and 1970s and reinventing herself as an international lawyer proper in the 1980s—Professor Liang Shuying of China University of Political Science and Law stated that she was at peace with the past, that 'each generation has its duties'. Interview with Liang Shuying (WeChat voicecall, 6 June 2024).

[132] That said, women international lawyers still found inspiration from each other on a micro, interpersonal level. Professor Bai Guimei, for instance, recalled how she was impressed by Ma Jun's social skills and how Cheng Xiaoxia had encouraged her to pursue doctoral studies and career excellence. Interview with Bai Guimei (WeChat voicecall, 9 May 2024).

[133] It also just happened that some first-generation women had by the 1980s entered their fifties, at a time when the retirement age for women was set at 55. As a result, in my conversations with second-generation women scholars, many would bring up impressions of fleeting encounters with first-generation women in the early 1980s, who were beginning to retreat from the scene.

outperformed second-generation women in terms of full professorship,[134] institutional leadership, and access to the foreign policy establishment.[135] These dynamics thus bound the PRC's first- and second-generation women international lawyers in the shadows of the towering Republican-era gentlemen.

[134] Owing to the relatively late introduction of first and second-wave feminist literature into the PRC (which only began in the 1980s), most interviewees did not process their own work experience through the lens of feminism. That said, certain recurring themes during these conversations do hint at gender being a crucial factor. One interviewee brought up the effects of childrearing, how being separated from her young child while studying at academic institutions abroad became too emotionally straining. Juggling between child-rearing duties at home and teaching and research duties at the campus (particularly in the context of pursuing full professorship) was overwhelming.

[135] For instance, when the Advisory Committee on International Law of the Ministry of Foreign Affairs was first founded in 2015, Professor Huang Yao 黃瑶 (Sun Yat-sen University Faculty of Law, 1983–86; disciple of Duanmu Zheng) was its only female member.

Index

For the benefit of digital users, indexed terms that span two pages (e.g., 52–53) may, on occasion, appear on only one of those pages.